One of the best British politics texts on the market: comprehensive but approachable, up-to-date but historically aware, it strikes just the right balance between fine-grained analysis and sheer readability.

—Tim Bale, Queen Mary University London, UK

Exploring British Politics provides an authoritative and up-to-date introduction to the key institutions and processes of British politics. At a time of considerable flux and fragmentation in the UK political system, this book gives students the opportunity to explore key debates – from the role of Parliament to Britain's relationship with the European Union – that look set to shape our politics long into the future.

—Patrick Diamond, Queen Mary University London, UK

This is the premier textbook of British politics available on the market today. It's gauged appropriately for university-level students, well written, and insightful. My US-based students find the book to be interesting reading and I would not wish to teach without this most excellent of texts, which lays the foundation for my lectures brilliantly.

—Heather Mbaye, University of West Georgia, USA

Exploring British Politics is pitched perfectly both to students completely new to the British political system and those who are steeped in its complexities.

—Craig Ortsey, Purdue University Fort Wayne, USA

Once again, Garnett, Dorey and Lynch offer a clear and accessible introduction to some complex political issues, neatly capturing the changing landscape of British politics. This superb book remains a go-to book for all political science students.

—Louise Thompson, University of Manchester, UK

This updated edition of *Exploring British Politics* provides a clear and thought-provoking assessment of recent developments in British politics and is an invaluable resource for both students and teachers. The book provides a comprehensive analysis of a wide range of issues and debates in Britain today.

—Samantha Wolstencroft, Manchester Metropolitan University, UK

Exploring British Politics

Exploring British Politics is a concise, comprehensive, and accessible guide to the subject. Fully updated and revised, the new edition covers developments since 2016 in the role of the executive, Parliament, the civil service, political parties, general elections, party ideology and membership, as well as examines turmoil and leadership battles within the Labour and Conservative parties, the politics of growing inequality, demographic trends and their political consequences, and the future of the UK itself. Stimulating critical analysis and lively debate, it provides new perspectives on two key themes – the health of British democracy and the transition from traditional models of government to more flexible forms of 'governance'.

Key features include:

- a comprehensive analysis of the 2019 general election, Brexit developments since the 2016 referendum to today's ongoing negotiations, and the shadow cast by the COVID-19 global pandemic and its implications;
- topical coverage of the fall of the Corbyn and May leaderships, the new Starmer and Johnson era, the rise and fall of the 'Change UK' party, the economic crisis, the role of special advisers, new social movements such as Extinction Rebellion and Black Lives Matter, and much more;
- extensive guides to further reading at the end of each chapter; and
- rich illustrations visually representing examples and data.

Whilst the book provides an essential historical background, contemporary issues are to the fore throughout, and readers are encouraged to assess critically received wisdoms and develop their own thoughts and ideas. Whether studying the subject for the first time or revisiting it, *Exploring British Politics* is the ideal undergraduate text.

Mark Garnett is senior lecturer, Department of Politics and International Relations, Lancaster University, UK.

Peter Dorey is professor of British politics, School of Law and Politics, Cardiff University, UK.

Philip Lynch is associate professor in politics in the Department of Politics and International Relations, University of Leicester, UK.

Exploring British Politics

Fifth Edition

Mark Garnett, Peter Dorey, and Philip Lynch

Routledge
Taylor & Francis Group

LONDON AND NEW YORK

Fifth edition published 2021
by Routledge
2 Park Square, Milton Park, Abingdon, Oxon OX14 4RN

and by Routledge
52 Vanderbilt Avenue, New York, NY 10017

Routledge is an imprint of the Taylor & Francis Group, an informa business

First edition published by Pearson Education 2007
Fourth edition published by Routledge 2016

British Library Cataloguing-in-Publication Data
A catalogue record for this book is available from the British Library

Library of Congress Cataloging-in-Publication Data
Names: Garnett, Mark, 1963- author. | Dorey, Peter, 1967- author. |
Lynch, Philip, author.
Title: Exploring British politics / Mark Garnett, Peter Dorey and Philip Lynch.
Description: Fifth edition. | Abingdon, Oxon; New York, NY: Routledge,
2021. | Includes bibliographical references and index.
Identifiers: LCCN 2020029428 (print) | LCCN 2020029429 (ebook) |
ISBN 9780367142391 (hardback) | ISBN 9780367142407 (paperback) |
ISBN 9780429030864 (ebook)
Subjects: LCSH: Public administration—Great Britain. | Great Britain—Politics
and government.
Classification: LCC JN318 .G37 2021 (print) | LCC JN318 (ebook) |
DDC 320.441—dc23
LC record available at https://lccn.loc.gov/2020029428
LC ebook record available at https://lccn.loc.gov/2020029429

ISBN: 978-0-367-14239-1 (hbk)
ISBN: 978-0-367-14240-7 (pbk)
ISBN: 978-0-429-03086-4 (ebk)

Typeset in Bembo
by codeMantra

Visit the eResources: www.routledge.com/9780367142407

In memory of John William Allan Garnett (1924–2012), with gratitude and love

Brief contents

Guided tour   xviii
Guide to features   xx
Preface   xxvi

Part 1   Context

Chapter 1   Understanding British politics   3
Chapter 2   Analysing British politics   23
Chapter 3   UK government in historical context   45
Chapter 4   Economy and society   70
Chapter 5   The media and communications   100

Part 2   Constitution and institutions

Chapter 6   The constitution   135
Chapter 7   The core executive   167
Chapter 8   Parliament   202
Chapter 9   The judiciary and the law   247

Part 3   Multilevel governance

Chapter 10 The changing state   275
Chapter 11 Local government to local governance   307
Chapter 12 Devolution   334
Chapter 13 The UK and the European Union   378

Part 4   Political parties

Chapter 14   UK party systems   419

Chapter 15   Party organisation   440

Chapter 16   Ideology and party competition   479

Part 5   Participation

Chapter 17   Elections and electoral systems   519

Chapter 18   Voting behaviour   562

Chapter 19   Participation beyond elections   595

Part 6   Conclusions

Chapter 20   Governance and democracy in the UK   627

Index   647

Contents

Guided tour   xviii

Guide to features   xx

Preface   xxvi

Part 1   Context

Chapter 1   Understanding British politics   **3**

Learning outcomes   3
Introduction   3
Liberal democracy   11
The changing state   17
Conclusion and summary   20
Further reading   21
Websites   22

Chapter 2   Analysing British politics   **23**

Learning outcomes   23
Introduction   23
The Westminster model and the study of British politics   23
Alternative models   28
Approaches to British politics   33
Research methods   38
Conclusion and summary   42
Further reading   43
Websites   44

Chapter 3   UK government in historical context   **45**

Learning outcomes   45
Introduction   45
The post-war 'consensus'   46
The end of consensus, 1970–79   55
Thatcherism, 1979–97   57

New Labour and after 64
Further reading 68
Websites 69

Chapter 4 Economy and society **70**

Learning outcomes 70
Introduction 70
Britain: a divided nation? 71
Sources of cohesion 91
Conclusion and summary 96
Further reading 98
Websites 99

Chapter 5 The media and communications **100**

Learning outcomes 100
Introduction 100
The UK media: not one, but many 101
Theories of media influence 104
New Labour and the media 109
The media and the 2010 general election 118
The media in the elections of 2015, 2017, and 2019 119
The 'phone-hacking' scandal 125
Conclusion and summary 129
Further reading 130
Websites 130

Part 2 Constitution and institutions

Chapter 6 The constitution **135**

Learning outcomes 135
Introduction 135
The uncodified constitution 136
Sources of the UK constitution 136
Statute law 138
Common law 138
Conventions 139
Main principles of the UK constitution 141
The constitution under pressure 148
New Labour and constitutional reform 151
A new constitutional settlement? 155
The 2014 referendum on Scottish independence 160
The 2016 EU Referendum 162
Conclusion and summary 164
Further reading 165
Websites 166

Chapter 7   The core executive   **167**

Learning outcomes   167
Introduction   167
The core executive model   167
The prime minister   169
The cabinet   184
Ministerial responsibility   187
Ministers and departments   192
Conclusion and summary   199
Further reading   200
Websites   201

Chapter 8   Parliament   **202**

Learning outcomes   202
Introduction   202
The House of Lords   238
Reform of the House of Lords   242
Conclusion and summary   244
Further reading   245
Websites   246

Chapter 9   The judiciary and the law   **247**

Learning outcomes   247
Introduction   247
The judicial system in the UK   248
Judicial review   249
The Human Rights Act 1998 and the European
Court of Human Rights   251
Who are the judges?   254
New Labour's constitutional reforms   259
The judiciary, the coalition, and Brexit   262
The police   264
Conclusion and summary   270
Further reading   271
Websites   271

Part 3   Multilevel governance

Chapter 10   The changing state   **275**

Learning outcomes   275
Introduction   275
Government to governance   276
Changing attitudes towards the state   277
New Labour and the state   280
Reform of the civil service   281

Agencification 284
The quango state 289
Privatisation and regulation 295
Globalisation 301
Conclusion and summary 304
Further reading 305
Websites 306

Chapter 11   Local government to local governance 307

Learning outcomes 307
Introduction 307
Government to governance 307
The structure of local government 308
Unitaries but not uniformity 310
Internal organisation 311
Directly elected mayors 312
Functions of local authorities 316
From provider to enabler 319
Localism from Blair to Cameron 321
Local government finance 322
Local taxes 323
Other sources of revenue 326
Local government in a multilevel polity 327
The local quango state 329
Devolution and local government 330
Local democracy 330
Conclusion and summary 332
Further reading 332
Websites 333

Chapter 12   Devolution 334

Learning outcomes 334
Introduction 334
The Union 334
Towards devolution 338
Devolution in Scotland and Wales 341
England 355
Changes to UK government 357
Northern Ireland 362
Devolution, 'Brexit', and Coronavirus 371
The post-devolution polity 373
Conclusion and summary 375
Further reading 376
Websites 377

Chapter 13   The UK and the European Union 378

Learning outcomes 378
Introduction 378

The development of the European Union 379
The UK and the European Union 388
An 'awkward partner' 402
Conclusion and summary 411
Further reading 414
Websites 415
Notes 415

Part 4   Political parties

Chapter 14 UK party systems **419**

Learning outcomes 419
Introduction 419
History of a two-party system 420
The UK party system since 1997 426
Party systems in Scotland and Wales 430
The party system in Northern Ireland 434
Conclusion and summary 437
Further reading 438
Websites 438

Chapter 15 Party organisation **440**

Learning outcomes 440
Introduction 440
From cadre parties to mass parties 440
Conservative party organisation 442
Party members 461
Liberal Democrat organisation 463
Party finance 469
Back to cadre parties? 473
Conclusion and summary 477
Further reading 477
Websites 478

Chapter 16 Ideology and party competition **479**

Learning outcomes 479
Introduction 479
The nature of ideology 480
Conservatism 482
Socialism 486
Ideology and British political parties 490
The Labour Party and socialism 498
Alternative voices 511
Conclusion and summary 514
Further reading 515
Websites 516

Part 5   Participation

Chapter 17   Elections and electoral systems — 519

Learning outcomes — 519
Introduction — 519
Elections in the United Kingdom — 519
Functions of elections — 525
Election campaigns — 540
Electoral systems in the United Kingdom — 543
Electoral reform — 554
Impact of the new electoral systems — 557
Conclusion and summary — 559
Further reading — 560
Websites — 560

Chapter 18   Voting behaviour — 562

Learning outcomes — 562
Introduction — 562
Class voting and partisanship — 562
Dealignment — 565
Other social factors — 575
Rational choice approaches — 579
The press and party support — 589
Realignment or dealignment? — 591
Conclusion and summary — 592
Further reading — 593
Websites — 594

Chapter 19   Participation beyond elections — 595

Learning outcomes — 595
Introduction — 595
Referendums — 596
Pressure groups — 605
Pressure groups and democracy — 620
Conclusion and summary — 622
Further reading — 623
Websites — 623

Part 6   Conclusions

Chapter 20   Governance and democracy in the UK — 627

Learning outcomes — 627
Introduction — 627

The old order changes   627
The more things change…   631
A strong centre   632
The condition of British democracy   634
From Blair/Brown to Cameron/Clegg   640
'Brexit' and after   643
Conclusion and summary   644
Further reading   645
Websites   645

Index   647

Guided tour

Learning outcomes list the topics covered and what you should understand by the end of the chapter

Case studies bring key issues to the fore with real life examples of politics in action

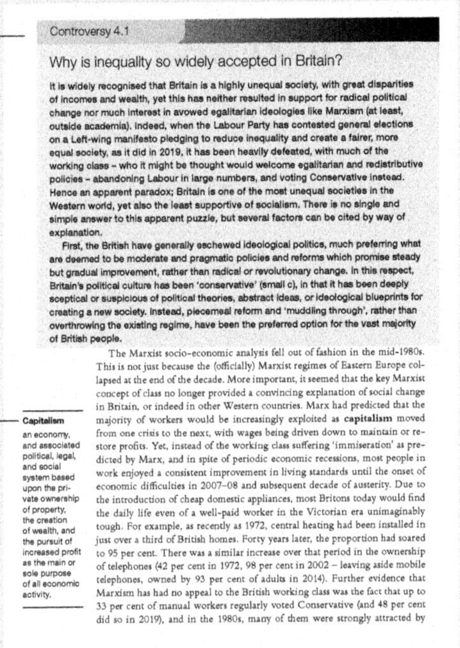

Controversy 4.1

Why is inequality so widely accepted in Britain?

It is widely recognised that Britain is a highly unequal society, with great disparities of incomes and wealth, yet this has neither resulted in support for radical political change nor much interest in avowed egalitarian ideologies like Marxism (at least, outside academia). Indeed, when the Labour Party has contested general elections on a Left-wing manifesto pledging to reduce inequality and create a fairer, more equal society, as it did in 2019, it has been heavily defeated, with much of the working class – who it might be thought would welcome egalitarian and redistributive policies – abandoning Labour in large numbers, and voting Conservative instead. Hence an apparent paradox; Britain is one of the most unequal societies in the Western world, yet also the least supportive of socialism. There is no single and simple answer to this apparent puzzle, but several factors can be cited by way of explanation.

First, the British have generally eschewed ideological politics, much preferring what are deemed to be moderate and pragmatic policies and reforms which promise steady but gradual improvement, rather than radical or revolutionary change. In this respect, Britain's political culture has been 'conservative' (small c), in that it has been deeply sceptical or suspicious of political theories, abstract ideas, or ideological blueprints for creating a new society. Instead, piecemeal reform and 'muddling through', rather than overthrowing the existing regime, have been the preferred option for the vast majority of British people.

The Marxist socio-economic analysis fell out of fashion in the mid-1980s. This is not just because the (officially) Marxist regimes of Eastern Europe collapsed at the end of the decade. More important, it seemed that the key Marxist concept of class no longer provided a convincing explanation of social change in Britain, or indeed in other Western countries. Marx had predicted that the majority of workers would be increasingly exploited as **capitalism** moved from one crisis to the next, with wages being driven down to maintain or restore profits. Yet, instead of the working class suffering 'immiseration' as predicted by Marx, and in spite of periodic economic recessions, most people in work enjoyed a consistent improvement in living standards until the onset of economic difficulties in 2007–08 and subsequent decade of austerity. Due to the introduction of cheap domestic appliances, most Britons today would find the daily life even of a well-paid worker in the Victorian era unimaginably tough. For example, as recently as 1972, central heating had been installed in just over a third of British homes. Forty years later, the proportion had soared to 95 per cent. There was a similar increase over that period in the ownership of telephones (42 per cent in 1972, 98 per cent in 2002 – leaving aside mobile telephones, owned by 93 per cent of adults in 2014). Further evidence that Marxism has had no appeal to the British working class was the fact that up to 33 per cent of manual workers regularly voted Conservative (and 48 per cent did so in 2019), and in the 1980s, many of them were strongly attracted by

Capitalism an economy, and associated political, legal, and social system based upon the private ownership of property, the creation of wealth, and the pursuit of increased profit as the main or sole purpose of all economic activity.

Key terms introduce and define important words and concepts throughout the text

Each chapter contains **Controversy boxes** that discuss issues that have been, and continue to be, sources of debate

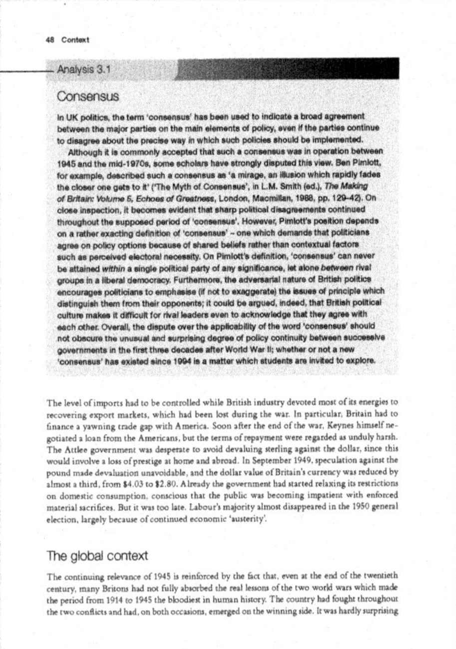

48 Context

Analysis 3.1

Consensus

In UK politics, the term 'consensus' has been used to indicate a broad agreement between the major parties on the main elements of policy, even if the parties continue to disagree about the precise way in which such policies should be implemented.

Although it is commonly accepted that such a consensus was in operation between 1945 and the mid-1970s, some scholars have strongly disputed this view. Ben Pimlott, for example, described such a consensus as 'a mirage, an illusion which rapidly fades the closer one gets to it' ('The Myth of Consensus', in L.M. Smith (ed.), *The Making of Britain: Volume 5, Echoes of Greatness*, London, Macmillan, 1988, pp. 129–42). On close inspection, it becomes evident that sharp political disagreements continued throughout the supposed period of 'consensus'. However, Pimlott's position depends on a rather exacting definition of 'consensus' – one which demands that politicians agree on policy options because of shared beliefs rather than contextual factors such as perceived electoral necessity. On Pimlott's definition, 'consensus' can never be attained *within* a single political party of any significance, let alone *between* rival groups in a liberal democracy. Furthermore, the adversarial nature of British politics encourages politicians to emphasise (if not to exaggerate) the issues of principle which distinguish them from their opponents; it could be argued, indeed, that British political culture makes it difficult for rival leaders even to acknowledge that they agree with each other. Overall, the dispute over the applicability of the word 'consensus' should not obscure the unusual and surprising degree of policy continuity between successive governments in the first three decades after World War II; whether or not a new 'consensus' has existed since 1994 is a matter which students are invited to explore.

The level of imports had to be controlled while British industry devoted most of its energies to recovering export markets, which had been lost during the war. In particular, Britain had to finance a yawning trade gap with America. Soon after the end of the war, Keynes himself negotiated a loan from the Americans, but the terms of repayment were regarded as unduly harsh. The Attlee government was desperate to avoid devaluing sterling against the dollar, since this would involve a loss of prestige at home and abroad. In September 1949, speculation against the pound made devaluation unavoidable, and the dollar value of Britain's currency was reduced by almost a third, from $4.03 to $2.80. Already the government had started relaxing its restrictions on domestic consumption, conscious that the public was becoming impatient with enforced material sacrifices. But it was too late. Labour's majority almost disappeared in the 1950 general election, largely because of continued economic 'austerity'.

The global context

The continuing relevance of 1945 is reinforced by the fact that, even at the end of the twentieth century, many Britons had not fully absorbed the real lessons of the two world wars which made the period from 1914 to 1945 the bloodiest in human history. The country had fought throughout the two conflicts and had, on both occasions, emerged on the winning side. It was hardly surprising

Analysis boxes examine concepts in the study of British politics

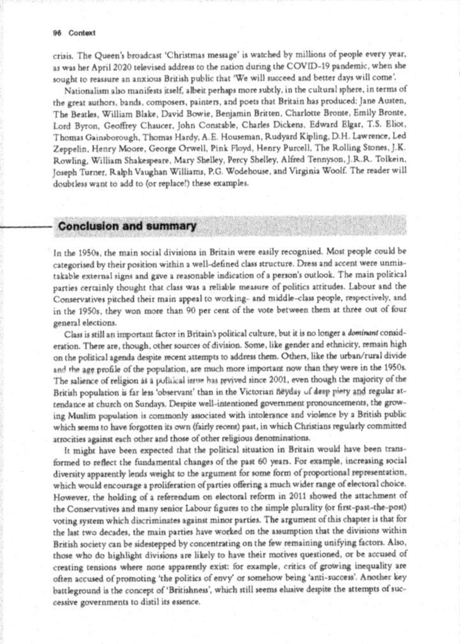

96 Context

crisis. The Queen's broadcast 'Christmas message' is watched by millions of people every year, as was her April 2020 televised address to the nation during the COVID-19 pandemic, when she sought to reassure an anxious British public that 'We will succeed and better days will come'.

Nationalism also manifests itself, albeit perhaps more subtly, in the cultural sphere, in terms of the great authors, bands, composers, painters, and poets that Britain has produced: Jane Austen, The Beatles, William Blake, David Bowie, Benjamin Britten, Charlotte Bronte, Emily Bronte, Lord Byron, Geoffrey Chaucer, John Constable, Charles Dickens, Edward Elgar, T.S. Eliot, Thomas Gainsborough, Thomas Hardy, A.E. Houseman, Rudyard Kipling, D.H. Lawrence, Led Zeppelin, Henry Moore, George Orwell, Pink Floyd, Henry Purcell, The Rolling Stones, J.K. Rowling, William Shakespeare, Mary Shelley, Percy Shelley, Alfred Tennyson, J.R.R. Tolkein, Joseph Turner, Ralph Vaughan Williams, P.G. Wodehouse, and Virginia Woolf. The reader will doubtless want to add to (or replace!) these examples.

Conclusion and summary

In the 1950s, the main social divisions in Britain were easily recognised. Most people could be categorised by their position within a well-defined class structure. Dress and accent were unmistakable external signs and gave a reasonable indication of a person's outlook. The main political parties certainly thought that class was a reliable measure of politics attitudes. Labour and the Conservatives pitched their main appeal to working- and middle-class people, respectively, and in the 1950s, they won more than 90 per cent of the vote between them at three out of four general elections.

Class is still an important factor in Britain's political culture, but it is no longer a *dominant* consideration. There are, though, other sources of division. Some, like gender and ethnicity, remain high on the political agenda despite recent attempts to address them. Others, like the urban/rural divide and the age profile of the population, are much more important now than they were in the 1950s. The salience of religion as a political issue has revived since 2001, even though the majority of the British population is far less 'observant' than in the Victorian heyday of deep piety and regular attendance at church on Sundays. Despite well-intentioned government pronouncements, the growing Muslim population is commonly associated with intolerance and violence by a British public which seems to have forgotten its own (fairly recent) past, in which Christians regularly committed atrocities against each other and those of other religious denominations.

It might have been expected that the political situation in Britain would have been transformed to reflect the fundamental changes of the past 60 years. For example, increasing social diversity apparently lends weight to the argument for some form of proportional representation, which would encourage a proliferation of parties offering a much wider range of electoral choice. However, the holding of a referendum on electoral reform in 2011 showed the attachment of the Conservatives and many senior Labour figures to the simple plurality (or first-past-the-post) voting system which discriminates against minor parties. The argument of this chapter is that for the last two decades, the main parties have worked on the assumption that the divisions within British society can be sidestepped by concentrating on the few remaining unifying factors. Also, those who do highlight divisions are likely to have their motives questioned, or be accused of creating tensions where none apparently exist: for example, critics of growing inequality are often accused of promoting 'the politics of envy' or somehow being 'anti-success'. Another key battleground is the concept of 'Britishness', which still seems elusive despite the attempts of successive governments to distil its essence.

Conclusion and summaries bring together the key issues dealt with in the chapter succinctly and clearly to aid understanding.

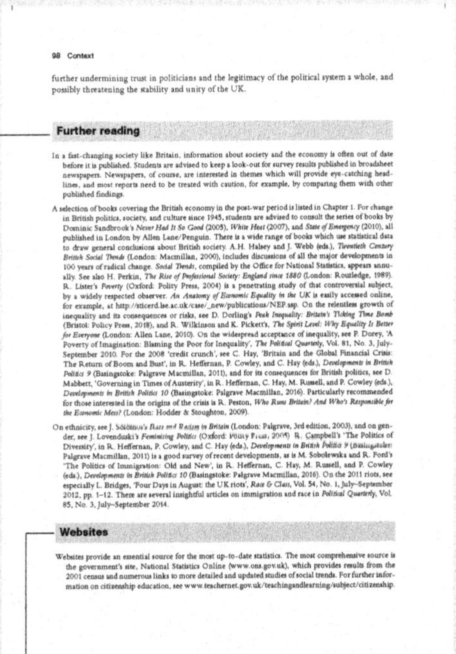

98 Context

further undermining trust in politicians and the legitimacy of the political system a whole, and possibly threatening the stability and unity of the UK.

Further reading

In a fast-changing society like Britain, information about society and the economy is often out of date before it is published. Students are advised to keep a look-out for survey results published in broadsheet newspapers. Newspapers, of course, are interested in themes which will provide eye-catching headlines, and most reports need to be treated with caution, for example, by comparing them with other published findings.

A selection of books covering the British economy in the post-war period is listed in Chapter 1. For change in British politics, society, and culture since 1945, students are advised to consult the series of books by Dominic Sandbrook's *Never Had It So Good* (2005), *White Heat* (2007), and *State of Emergency* (2010), all published in London by Allen Lane/Penguin. There is a wide range of books which use statistical data to draw general conclusions about British society. A.H. Halsey and J. Webb (eds.), *Twentieth Century British Social Trends* (London: Macmillan, 2000), includes discussions of all the major developments in 100 years of radical change. *Social Trends*, compiled by the Office for National Statistics, appears annually. See also H. Perkin, *The Rise of Professional Society: England since 1880* (London: Routledge, 1989). R. Lister's *Poverty* (Oxford: Polity Press, 2004) is a penetrating study of that controversial subject, by a widely respected observer. *An Anatomy of Economic Equality in the UK* is easily accessed online, for example, at http://sticerd.lse.ac.uk/case/_new/publications/NEP.asp. On the relentless growth of inequality and its consequences or risks, see D. Dorling's *Peak Inequality: Britain's Ticking Time Bomb* (Bristol: Policy Press, 2018), and R. Wilkinson and K. Pickett's, *The Spirit Level: Why Equality Is Better for Everyone* (London: Allen Lane, 2010). On the widespread acceptance of inequality, see P. Dorey, 'A Poverty of Imagination: Blaming the Poor for Inequality', *The Political Quarterly*, Vol. 81, No. 3, July-September 2010. For the 2008 'credit crunch', see C. Hay, 'Britain and the Global Financial Crisis: The Return of Boom and Bust', in R. Heffernan, P. Cowley, and C. Hay (eds.), *Developments in British Politics 9* (Basingstoke: Palgrave Macmillan, 2011), and for its consequences for British politics, see D. Mabbett, 'Governing in Times of Austerity', in R. Heffernan, C. Hay, M. Russell, and P. Cowley (eds.), *Developments in British Politics 10* (Basingstoke: Palgrave Macmillan, 2016). Particularly recommended for those interested in the origins of the crisis is R. Peston, *Who Runs Britain? And Who's Responsible for the Economic Mess?* (London: Hodder & Stoughton, 2009).

On ethnicity, see J. Solomos's *Race and Racism in Britain* (London: Palgrave, 3rd edition, 2003), and on gender, see J. Lovenduski's *Feminising Politics* (Oxford: Polity Press, 2005). R. Campbell's 'The Politics of Diversity', in R. Heffernan, P. Cowley, and C. Hay (eds.), *Developments in British Politics 9* (Basingstoke: Palgrave Macmillan, 2011) is a good survey of recent developments, as is M. Sobolewska and R. Ford's 'The Politics of Immigration: Old and New', in R. Heffernan, C. Hay, M. Russell, and P. Cowley (eds.), *Developments in British Politics 10* (Basingstoke: Palgrave Macmillan, 2016). On the 2011 riots, see especially L. Bridges, 'Four Days in August: the UK riots', *Race & Class*, Vol. 54, No. 1, July–September 2012, pp. 1–12. There are several insightful articles on immigration and race in *Political Quarterly*, Vol. 85, No. 3, July–September 2014.

Websites

Websites provide an essential source for the most up-to-date statistics. The most comprehensive source is the government's site, National Statistics Online (www.ons.gov.uk), which provides results from the 2001 census and numerous links to more detailed and updated studies of social trends. For further information on citizenship education, see www.teachernet.gov.uk/teachingandlearning/subject/citizenship.

Websites provide a wealth of valuable resources for further study and interest

Every chapter is supported by a **Further reading** section to help you find more information and continue your study

Guide to features

Analysis boxes

1.1	What is politics?	10
1.2	Elitism and neo-pluralism	14
2.1	Majoritarian democracy	26
2.2	Policy networks	30
2.3	Political biographies	41
3.1	Consensus	48
3.2	The 'special relationship'	49
3.3	Corporatism and neo-corporatism	54
3.4	Government 'overload'	57
3.5	Monetarism	60
6.1	Codified and uncodified constitutions	137
7.1	A British presidency?	183
9.1	Judicial independence	257
9.2	Institutional racism	269
11.1	Policy disasters – the poll tax	324
11.2	Centre-local relations	328
12.1	Unitary and union states	336
12.2	Consociationalism and the Good Friday Agreement	368
13.1	EEC, EC, and EU	380
13.2	Euroscepticism	386
13.3	Sovereignty	404
13.4	Europeanisation	405
14.1	The classification of party systems	421
14.2	'Catch-all' parties and the two-party system	425
14.3	The problems faced by third parties in Britain	432
15.1	The 'iron law of oligarchy'	452
15.2	Beyond the mass party	475
16.1	'Left' and 'right' in UK politics	483
16.2	Neo-conservatism	485
16.3	Ideology and the post-war 'consensus'	497
17.1	Direct democracy and the right of recall	526
17.2	Positive action	528
17.3	Second-order elections	558

18.1   Social class   569
18.2   Valence issues   580
19.1   Insider and outsider groups   608
19.2   Pressure groups and the New Right   611

Case studies

1.1   The Westminster model abroad   6
2.1   Were the Conservatives irrational?   35
3.1   The Commonwealth   51
3.2   The political implications of 'consensus'   53
3.3   Suez   53
3.4   The fuel crisis, 1973–74   58
4.1   The decline of manufacturing industry   75
4.2   Ethnicity in Britain: 2011 census   77
4.3   How Britain has changed   80
4.4   Economic inequality in Britain   86
4.5   The much-contested concept of 'Britishness'   92
5.1   Tabloids and broadsheets   103
5.2   Politics and the Internet   116
5.3   The shifting allegiances of The Sun newspaper   120
6.1   Thatcherism and the monarchy   150
7.1   Post-war Prime Ministers   171
8.1   Parliamentary weapons for the backbencher   207
8.2   Conservative MPs opposing HS2   211
8.3   The passage of a bill   219
8.4   Hunting – the history of a private member's Bill   224
9.1   The Human Rights Act 1998   252
9.2   Crime in England and Wales   265
9.3   The Police Service of Northern Ireland   268
10.1   The Bank of England   279
10.2   'Nudge'   282
10.3   NICE work? Regulating NHS treatments   299
11.1   Recycling   320
12.1   Who voted for Scottish independence?   348
13.1   Differentiated integration in the EU   385
13.2   'Black Wednesday' 1992   392
15.1   New Labour and Cameron's
        Conservatives in comparison   445
15.2   The Conservative Party Board   449
15.3   Parties and multi-level governance   460
15.4   New Labour's organisation   462
15.5   The Political Parties, Elections and
        Referendums Act 2000   469
15.6   The Phillips Report on party funding   473

16.1   'Built to Last' and 'the Big Society':
       the ideology of David Cameron   494
16.2   Ideology and Cameron's coalition   507
17.1   Fixed-term elections   520
17.2   The short and eventful history of Change UK   529
17.3   Young people and voting   536
17.4   Opinion polls   542
17.5   Open primaries in the United Kingdom   548
17.6   The d'Hondt formula   551
18.1   Tactical voting   588
19.1   Referendums in the UK   597
19.2   Pressure group tactics   609
19.3   Pressure groups, the EU, and devolution   612
19.4   Black Lives Matter   616
19.5   Extinction Rebellion   618

Controversy boxes

1.1   Economics and liberal democracy   16
3.1   Thatcherism: for and against   62
4.1   Why is inequality so widely accepted in Britain?   89
5.1   Do the media help or hinder the democratic process?   115
5.2   Brexit and the British media   123
6.1   Terrorism and the rule of law   145
6.2   The traditional constitution   147
6.3   'Brexit' and the constitution   162
8.1   'Sleaze' and the interests of MPs: before
       the expenses scandal   225
9.1   The courts and the Wapping dispute   257
9.2   The Attorney General and the invasion of Iraq   261
10.1   PFI problems – from the Skye Road Bridge to the NHS   287
10.2   Rail privatisation   298
11.1   Congestion charging   318
11.2   Council tax revaluation   327
12.1   Scottish independence   344
12.2   The West Lothian Question   360
13.1   The democratic deficit   387
13.2   The costs and benefits of EU membership   412
15.1   The Militant Tendency and Momentum   454
15.2   'Cash for honours'   471
16.1   Meritocracy and education   492
16.2   Blair and 'the forces of conservatism'   502
17.1   Votes at sixteen   533
17.2   Compulsory voting   537
18.1   Who supported UKIP?   583

Figures

8.1	How does a bill become a law?	219
11.1	Local Authority Districts, Counties, and Unitary Authorities (December 2017) in United Kingdom	315
13.1	The European Union	383

Tables

1.1	The Westminster model	5
3.1	British governments, 1945–2015	47
3.2	Unemployment, 1947–93	59
4.1	Population of UK, mid-2019	72
4.2	The rising UK population, 1951–2019 (millions)	76
4.3	Religious affiliation in England and Wales, 1983–2018	82
4.4	Classification of social categories (used in official statistics since 2001)	85
5.1	Newspaper ownership and circulation, January 2020	102
5.2	Partisan support of daily newspapers in general election years, 2001–19	110
5.3	Party supported by daily newspaper readers, 2019	112
6.1	New Labour's constitutional reforms	152
6.2	The Governance of Britain (2008) – key proposals	157
7.1	Prime ministerial resources and constraints	175
7.2	Boris Johnson's Cabinet, 2020	185
7.3	Cabinet committees, June 2020	187
7.4	Ministerial resignations: collective responsibility (examples)	188
7.5	Ministerial resignations: individual ministerial responsibility (examples)	190
8.1	Occupational backgrounds of Conservative, Labour and Liberal Democrat MPs	215
8.2	Conservative and Labour MPs' occupations, 2017	215
8.3	Educational backgrounds of Conservative, Labour, and Liberal Democrat MPs, 1992–2017	216
8.4	Women candidates and MPs, 1983–2019	217
8.5	Examples of successful private members' bills	223
8.6	Select committees in the House of Commons	229
8.7	Examples of inquiries conducted, or reports published, by Departmental Select Committees, 2017–19	231
8.8	Examples of individuals and organisations which submitted evidence to a Home Affairs Select Committee inquiry into domestic abuse, 2017–18	232
8.9	Examples of Inquiries conducted by the Public Accounts Committee since 2017	234

8.10	Examples of Inquiries conducted by the Public Administration and Constitutional Affairs Committee since 2017	235
8.11	Previous occupations or professions of life peers, 2018	241
9.1	The justices of the Supreme Court, September 2015	255
9.2	Britain's top judges and law officers, 2020	260
10.1	Government to governance	276
10.2	Executive agencies, 2020 (examples)	285
10.3	Non-departmental public bodies, 2020 (examples)	291
10.4	Privatisation and the regulatory state	297
10.5	International organisations (examples of bodies of which the UK is a member: figures as of July 2011)	303
11.1	UK directly elected mayors, 2020	314
12.1	Initial powers of the devolved institutions	343
12.2	Elections to the Welsh Assembly, 2016	352
12.3	Elections to the Scottish Parliament, 2016	352
12.4	Examples of policy divergence	354
12.5	Elections to the Northern Ireland Assembly, 2017	369
12.6	Preferred long-term policy for Northern Ireland, 2018 (%)	370
12.7	Results of the 2016 EU referendum by UK nation	372
12.8	National identity in England, Scotland, and Wales in the aftermath of devolution	375
13.1	Policy competences of the EU (selected)	384
13.2	Result of the 2016 EU Referendum, by UK regions – votes	396
13.3	Social characteristics of Leave and Remain supporters in the 2016 EU referendum	397
14.1	Share of the UK vote for the three main parties, 1922–31	423
14.2	Combined vote share of Conservatives and Labour, 1979–2019	427
14.3	Distribution of seats in the Welsh Assembly and Scottish Parliament, 2011 and 2016	431
14.4	Share of votes for the main parties in Northern Ireland, 1997–2019 (%)	436
15.1	Main party leaders since 1945	443
15.2	Conservative Party leadership election, June-July 2019	447
15.3	Party membership, 1996–2019	450
15.4	Labour leadership election, 2015	458
15.5	Declared party spending in 2017 general election campaign	470
16.1	Typical attitudes of the main ideologies on key issues	491
17.1	Estimated turnout at the 2019 general election	535
17.2	Average number of votes required to win a single seat, 2017 and 2019 general elections	545
17.3	Election of Mayor of London, 2016	550
17.4	Seats won at the 2015 general election under different voting systems	556
17.5	Deviation from proportionality (DV) in recent UK general elections	557
17.6	Elections to the Scottish Parliament, 2016	558
18.1	Social class and party support in 1959, 1964, 1966, and 1970	563

18.2	Party identification in 1964, 1966, and 1970	563
18.3	Conservative and Labour share of the vote in general elections 1945–2019	566
18.4	Class voting since 1974	573
18.5	When voters decided which party to vote for in the 2017 and 2019 general elections	574
18.6	Gender and voting since 1974	577
18.7	Voting by age cohort in the 2019 general election	577
18.8	Ranking of issues, in terms of their importance, by Labour and Conservative voters in the 2017 election	581
18.9	Party leadership ratings in elections since 1992	585
18:10	Newspaper readership and voting in 2017	590
19.1	Number of people who had done, in last 12 months, or would be willing to	606
19.2	Confidence in the following to act in the national interest	606
20.1	The Westminster model under strain	629
20.2	Rating the system of governing Britain	639

Timelines

11.1	The development of local government	309
12.1	Scottish and Welsh devolution	339
12.2	The Northern Ireland peace process, 1988–2014	365
13.1	The UK and European integration	389
15.1	Conservative leadership election rules	444
17.1	The development of the electoral system	532

Preface

In the Preface to the fourth edition of this book (2016), the authors attempted a concise overview of the main developments in British politics since the previous (2012) version. At the time of writing, David Cameron's Conservative Party had recently secured a slender overall majority after five years in coalition with the Liberal Democrats. The main challenge facing him was an in-out referendum on Britain's membership of the European Union (EU), which had been promised early in the Parliament which was supposed to last until 2020. The authors tried to anticipate the Prime Minister's attitude as he prepared to engage with the EU partners in talks which would result in meaningful concessions for the UK: 'Since Cameron clearly wanted Britain to stay within the EU (after a renegotiation of the membership terms), he was hoping to achieve a kind of "conservative" Triple Crown – letting "the people decide" on the three crucial issues of electoral reform, the future of the union, and the UK's membership of the EU, and guiding (or "nudging") them towards decisions which maintained the status quo in every case'.

The authors knew that Cameron's third referendum – following the poll on a change to the voting system (2011) and Scottish independence (2014) – would be his greatest challenge. However, the 2016 edition of *Exploring British Politics* reflected the general assumption that his preference would prevail when the time came. So much has happened since the referendum of 23 June 2016 that it would be impossible to review even the key developments without extending the Preface to chapter-length. Suffice it to say that this new Preface is being written on the fourth anniversary of the referendum; the current Prime Minister is another alumnus of Eton College and Oxford University, and, on paper, Boris Johnson commands the kind of overall Conservative majority which Cameron could only dream of – 80 seats, thanks to the general election of December 2019, following the inconclusive contest of May 2017. However, the spine-chilling economic prognosis offered by Cameron's fellow 'Remain' supporters back in 2016 now seems unduly optimistic compared to predictions of the effects of the coronavirus pandemic which forced Britain into a period of restrictions on personal liberty which were unprecedented even in wartime. These challenges arrived at a time when average living standards had still not recovered from the effects of the global financial crisis which began in 2007, and the ensuing years of 'austerity'. The UK has officially left the EU, but difficult negotiations for a post-severance relationship are incomplete at the time of writing, and the UK itself is subject to greater tensions than it was at the time of the Scottish independence referendum.

It has never been more important to explore British politics with an open mind – not least because this gives serious students an enviable advantage over the many Britons who prefer the self-defeating approach of taking entrenched positions into what passes for 'debate' on social media and elsewhere. However, it has never been more difficult to write books on a subject which is so susceptible to 'events'. We have not compiled this edition in the expectation that a protracted period of turbulence in British politics has come to an end; we cannot even be certain that seismic shocks on a similar scale to the 2016 referendum will not happen before this edition is published. But every reader of the 4th edition of *Exploring British Politics* will now know that Cameron failed in his 'Triple Crown' attempt, and although the ultimate consequences of his gamble are still uncertain, this is likely to remain the case for several years. Writing about British politics at a time when everything seems to be in flux might entail the risk of being overtaken by events; however, accepting this risk is certainly more helpful to students of the subject than holding off in the hope that more tranquil times are just around the corner. While the media headlines have focused on new problems for UK government – leaving the EU, dealing with a pandemic – these issues have merely highlighted underlying dilemmas, such as the proper role of the executive within a parliamentary democracy, with 'the rule of law' as its ultimate guarantor, and the proper relationship between the component parts of a 'union state'.

While we hope that we have incorporated all of the important developments in UK politics since 2016, we have followed the practice of the first four editions of this book in keeping our exposition and analysis as concise as possible, in the belief that this approach is best suited to the needs of undergraduate and A-level students. The overall purpose of books of this kind is not to reach unquestionable conclusions, but to encourage their readers to reach their own considered views on contemporary controversies, based on a thorough understanding of the interplay between individuals, ideas, and institutions which have always characterised British politics – in quiet times as well as in periods of upheaval.

In preparing this new edition, Mark Garnett has once again depended heavily on the expertise of Professor David Denver, who continues to make a mockery of the concept of 'retirement'. He is also very grateful to Richard Johnson, a more recent but equally valuable arrival at Lancaster University, for punctual responses to questions within his area of expertise. Any remaining errors of fact or interpretation remain our responsibility. We would also like to express our thanks for the unfailing patience and skill of the various people who have helped in the production and promotion of the book since the idea was first discussed with Morten Fuglevand of what was then Longman, back in 2003. Special thanks are due to Andrew Taylor and Sophie Iddamalgoda, whose never-failing support for this project is greatly appreciated.

Part 1

Context

Chapter 1

Understanding British politics

Learning outcomes

After reading this chapter, you will:

- appreciate that the subject matter of politics is open to competing interpretations;
- understand that there are various approaches to the study of British politics;
- become familiar with the concept of 'liberal democracy';
- understand the issues involved in a shift from 'government' to 'governance' in the UK.

Introduction

Despite occasional dissenting voices, until the mid-1960s, it was common to present the British political system as a success story – the product of gradual progress over several centuries towards a democratic society in which all citizens could feel represented and involved in the political process. Nowadays, it is much easier to identify fundamental failings, and since the beginning of the present century, there have been three unmistakable symptoms of public dissatisfaction which would have caused incredulity in the context of the 1960s. The first, in the general election of 2001, was a slump in voter turnout to less than 60 per cent. This was comfortably the lowest turnout since 1928, when the UK adopted universal suffrage for people over 21; in 1964, the turnout had been 77 per cent. The second development was the scandal which erupted in May 2009, when the *Daily Telegraph* newspaper began to publish details of expenses claims lodged by the Members of Parliament (MPs). The *Telegraph* – traditionally regarded as a bastion of the British 'establishment' – was able to sustain these revelations over several weeks, raising public doubts about the integrity of numerous elected representatives, and casting a cloud over the reputation of the whole democratic process in the UK. Finally, the 2016 referendum on Britain's membership of the European Union resulted in a rejection of the clear recommendation of a majority of cabinet ministers, after a campaign which was marked by symptoms of antipathy towards the 'metropolitan elite' as well as to the EU itself. This followed the 2014 referendum on Scotland's place within the United Kingdom, in which the supporters of the status quo prevailed, but by a much narrower margin than initially expected.

Executive

the branch of government responsible for putting laws into operation. In the UK, the executive consists of the prime minister, other members of the cabinet, junior ministers, senior civil servants, and special advisers.

Such evidence should be sufficient to cure any interested observer of complacency about the health of British democracy. However, the present book is not designed to form part of the chorus of complaint, or indeed to vindicate the UK system from its critics. Its main purpose is to enable students to explore British politics in an analytical spirit and to draw conclusions of their own. Accordingly, while taking account of common criticisms of the British political system, we attempt to give due weight to contrary arguments. By the end of the book, we hope that readers will have learned something about their own ideas, as well as reaching a deeper understanding of the subject.

The main text of the book is divided into five parts:

1. *Context:* exploring the historical, economic, and social background to contemporary British politics, and the ways in which it can be studied.
2. *Constitution and institutions:* covering the uncodified British constitution, the core executive, Parliament, and the legal system.
3. *Multi-level governance:* explaining recent developments relating to the changing state, devolution within the UK, local government, and the impact of the EU prior to the decision to withdraw.
4. *Political parties:* discussing party systems, ideology, and the structure of the main parties.
5. *Participation:* assessing electoral systems, voting behaviour, referendums, and pressure groups.

This chapter introduces some of the main themes which appear in several parts of the book.

UK politics, representative democracy, and the 'Westminster model'

Broadly speaking, there are two ways in which any country's politics can be understood. The most familiar approach is to focus on specific institutions, practices, and people: for example, Parliament, elections, and party leaders. The advantage of this view of politics, exemplified in the UK by the 'Westminster model', is that the subject matter is clearly delineated. It takes politics to be a specialised activity, undertaken by a relatively small number of 'experts'.

Legislature

the part of government which makes laws. In the UK, the Westminster Parliament is the legislative body and is dominated by the elected House of Commons.

The Westminster model (see Chapter 2) reflects the long-standing UK tradition of strong centralised government, run by strictly disciplined political parties (see Table 1.1). In the Westminster model, the government (the executive) is dominant, backed by a majority in the House of Commons (the main element of the legislature) and advised by a professional civil service as well as unelected special advisers. A crucial feature of the UK system is that the executive and legislative branches of government are *fused*: that is, the effective head of the executive, the prime minister, cannot govern without the ability to command a dependable majority in the legislature. There is no codified constitution, and institutions like the judiciary and local government can be reshaped according to the wishes of the government, so long as the Parliament agrees. This system is

TABLE 1.1 The Westminster model

Aspect of political system	Features of the Westminster model
Constitution	Uncodified constitution; no special procedures required for constitutional amendment
Sovereignty	Parliamentary sovereignty – supreme legislative authority of Westminster; no other body can overturn parliamentary legislation
Core executive	Prime ministerial government – prime minister is the predominant figure in cabinet system
Collective and individual responsibility	Ministers accountable to Parliament
Bureaucracy	Civil service – neutral, permanent, knowledgeable
	Public service ethos, but perception that 'Whitehall knows best'
Executive-legislative relations	Dominant executive – fusion of executive and legislature. Limited parliamentary scrutiny and amendment of legislation; strong party discipline
Electoral system	Simple plurality electoral system – expected to produce 'artificial' parliamentary majorities for winning party; single-party government is the norm; regular, free elections ensure accountability of decision-makers
Party system	Two-party system – clear choice for voters
	Mass parties evolved into 'catch-all' parties with broad appeal
Judiciary	Courts cannot challenge constitutionality of legislation
	Limited powers of judicial review, though ministers and officials are not above the law
Territorial politics	Unitary state – political power concentrated at the centre. Weak local government – no constitutional protection
	No subnational government in Great Britain – Scottish Office and Welsh Office represent interests at the centre

Judiciary

the branch of government which decides disputes about the law, punishes individuals who have been convicted of illegal acts by the courts, and decides whether agents of the state have properly applied laws passed by the legislature.

highly unusual (but see Case study 1.1). In most democratic countries, the executive, legislature, and judiciary are kept separate in accordance with a codified constitution (see Chapter 6). The nature of the UK system reflects the political development of the country since the seventeenth century, when effective political power began to pass from the monarchy to Parliament.

The Westminster model approach to UK politics was accepted by most political scientists until the 1970s. It encouraged students to focus on such questions as the role of the prime minister, the influence of the Parliament, and ministerial responsibility. Outside academia, advocates of the Westminster model claimed that it provided government which combined the virtues of strength and flexibility. In a two-party system (see Chapter 14), the majority party would be able to implement its policy programme because parliamentary discipline would ensure the loyalty of its elected representatives. The parliamentary opposition would point out the government's real (or perceived) failings, in the hope of replacing it at a subsequent election. On any working day, virtually all of the key actors in UK politics could be found either in the Parliament at Westminster or in the surrounding area of Whitehall.

However, there is an inherent tension between this view of UK politics and the long-accepted notion that Britain is a 'representative democracy'. In such systems, when politicians take decisions, they are acting on behalf of the people who elected them. Since 1928, the UK electorate has included all adults (with a few exceptions such as convicted criminals serving prison sentences). In a representative democracy, MPs must submit themselves for re-election at periodic intervals. As the Fixed-term Parliaments Act 2011 demonstrated (see Chapter 17), Parliament has the power to change the arrangements governing elections without asking for its proposals to be endorsed in a referendum. However, despite the superficial radicalism of the Fixed-term Parliaments Act, in one respect it confirmed the existing arrangement under which a new election cannot be delayed to more than five years after the previous one. The Parliament would be most unlikely to *increase* the maximum interlude between elections, except at a time of grave national emergency (thus, for example, there was no general election between 1935 and 1945).

It is characteristic of constitutional change in the UK that fixed-term parliaments, while strongly recommended by some reformers, were far less widely canvassed than other proposed changes which have *not* been implemented. For example, more attention was focused on the argument for a change from the long-established 'simple plurality' (often known as 'first-past-the-post') voting system to a proportional one which would bring electoral outcomes closer to public preferences (see Chapter 17). However, when a referendum was held on electoral reform in May 2011, the proposed new system (the alternative vote [AV]) was comprehensively rejected, despite the fact that, as a non-proportional system, the AV system was regarded by reformers as a first step rather than the truly radical change which

Case study 1.1

The Westminster model abroad

Westminster is often described as the 'mother of parliaments'. This is actually a misquotation from the radical politician John Bright (1811–89), who spoke of *England* as 'the mother of parliaments'. But the confusion is understandable. Although Iceland and the Isle of Man vie for the honour of having the oldest parliamentary system, Westminster has a long history, and the system of parliamentary democracy in a constitutional monarchy has been exported to many countries in the Commonwealth. These include Australia, Canada, Jamaica, and New Zealand. Here, the *head of state* is the British monarch, while the *head of government* is usually the leader of the largest party in the Parliament. The executive branch is made up of members of the legislature and operates a cabinet system in which the prime minister is the key actor. Bicameral legislatures are the norm (except in New Zealand), and parliamentary ceremony often replicates that found in England. Two-party systems and simple plurality electoral systems are found in many Commonwealth states. Another similarity is that civil law is based on English common law (see Chapter 9).

But there are significant differences in the way a Westminster-style system operates in Commonwealth states that adopted the British model of government. Almost all have written constitutions and a codified Bill of Rights (New Zealand does not have a single codified constitutional document), but conventions remain important. Australia and Canada are federal states. The suitability of the Westminster model has also been a subject of political controversy in some Commonwealth states. New Zealand moved to a mixed electoral system in 1996, while the British monarch's position as head of state is a thorny issue in Australia.

The Westminster model was not adopted in continental Europe where codified constitutions, elected second chambers, strong regional government, proportional representation, and multi-party systems are common.

was required. This outcome made it difficult to envisage a further public vote on the subject for many years.

Other proposed changes to British democratic institutions and practices would either widen the franchise further (by reducing the voting age to 16) or make participation easier (e.g. by introducing new voting methods, changing polling day from the traditional Thursday to a weekend). Meanwhile, reformers continue to argue for a House of Lords which is either fully or partially elected, among other possible ways of restraining the executive (see Chapter 6). While fixed-term parliaments went from being a remote possibility to an established fact in the period immediately before and after the 2010 general election, successive governments have promised to reform the House of Lords on democratic lines since 1997, but have lacked either the ability or the will to settle the issue.

Voters and voting behaviour are thus clearly part of the subject matter of politics. And people can vote (or abstain from voting) for a wide variety of reasons, from hard-headed assessments of political programmes to half-remembered parental influences or even an irrational passion for a particular candidate. Thus, in order to understand even the formal political process in any representative democracy like the UK, it seems sensible to look beyond specific institutions and to examine developments within society as a whole. Yet participation in politics by the general public is not restricted to voting. Between elections, people can try to influence decisions by writing to their MPs, signing petitions, or joining demonstrations. They might even take their objections to government policy to the length of breaking the law. The 2016 referendum was a spectacular example of political change resulting from participation between elections. All of these activities must be included in any comprehensive account of the politics of a representative democracy (see Chapter 19).

The decline of the Westminster model

Long before the advent of universal electoral suffrage in the UK, members of the political class developed a theory which promised to reconcile the Westminster model with representative institutions. On this view, the MPs were elected because voters decided that they could trust them to exercise judgement on their behalf. At the next election, they would be assessed on the personal qualities they had shown in discharging their duties. This made them *representatives* in a strict sense, rather than *delegates* who could be subjected to constant instruction by their constituents *between* elections.

Whatever the merits of this theory of representation when it was first expounded, since the eighteenth century it has been undermined by the emergence of tightly disciplined political parties. Instead of being judged on their individual records, candidates tend to win or lose their seats, depending on the popularity of their parties at the national level. But even this departure from the old idea of representation could be squared with the Westminster model. It could be argued that a party which won an overall majority of MPs in the House of Commons had secured a 'mandate' from the voters – that is, the winning party's policy programme had been approved by the electorate as a whole. Even if they had never met (or heard of) their constituency representative, voters had expressed a preference for his or her party, and thanks to the disciplinary procedures exercised at Westminster through the 'whipping' system (see Chapter 8), the MPs could be expected to act in accordance with the popular mandate.

At least in part, the present dissatisfaction with politics in the UK can be attributed to this stubborn attachment to the Westminster model. There is a tendency for any group of 'specialists' to become isolated from the rest of the public, and in some professions this need not be a disaster. But MPs are particularly vulnerable to the charge that they are 'out of touch' with developments in society as a whole. It is not that politicians have no interest in winning public respect; indeed, most of them want to be loved. They also seem keener than ever to find out what the public is thinking between elections, fussing over opinion polls and focus groups. However, when they receive this information, they tend to filter it through the mindset of the 'Westminster Village' – a network of media people and policy advisers, all of whom tend to view politics in the same way and to reinforce each other's responses to political developments.

By seeking out any evidence of party disunity in the hope of exciting audiences, the media have undoubtedly helped to create a context in which the MPs are ordered to stay loyal and 'on message' at all times (see Chapter 5). But the disciplinary impulse has always been present to some extent. In particular, parties which either hold office or believe that they will soon form a government have a tendency to vote *en bloc* against any measure which threatens to diminish the power of the executive. Thus, for example, Labour came to power in 1997, promising to 'modernise' key elements of the constitution, notably the House of Lords. An obvious move in this strategy would have been to introduce elections to the upper house. Yet this would have increased its authority, making it a potential rival to the Commons, and thus a more effective check on the executive. Prime Minister Tony Blair emphasised this point, and although the MPs were theoretically allowed a free vote on the future of the Lords, during his premiership the Labour whips privately intervened in support of his preference for a wholly *appointed* chamber. For example, a vote in February 2003 ended in fiasco, with the Commons rejecting all of the options for reform (see Chapter 8).

Despite the problems over Lords reform, the first two terms of Labour government after 1997 produced important constitutional changes which weakened the Westminster model. Devolution to Scotland, Wales, and Northern Ireland has undermined old ideas about London's dominance (see Chapter 12) as did the UK membership of the European Union (see Chapter 13). There have also been moves to promote a more independent judiciary, particularly in the context of the Human Rights Act 1998 and the introduction of a Supreme Court (see Chapter 9). The UK government has often been reluctant to loosen its grip; for example, in the early days of the devolved institutions, Labour tried unsuccessfully to dictate the choice of the First Secretary in the Welsh administration. But even if Blair and his colleagues were hoping to minimise the impact of devolution on Britain's institutional architecture, they inaugurated a process which has brought the Westminster model, as a basis for governance, under searching scrutiny. Advocates of the traditional British centralism are now challenged to justify practices which previous generations took pretty much for granted.

Beyond the Westminster model

It can thus be argued that the Westminster model is not just inaccurate as a description of politics in a representative democracy like the UK. It also has a more practical impact, helping to explain why people are obviously still interested in political issues, but increasingly disillusioned with a political *process* which seems alien to their daily experiences.

The approach in this book acknowledges the continuing relevance of the Westminster model. However, we move beyond this narrow focus and adopt an approach to politics which gives equal prominence to public participation (see Photo 1.1). The difficulty with a broader definition of politics is placing a limit on its subject matter. Which social phenomena should count as 'political'? In this book, we confine ourselves to the most obvious factors. Social changes, such as the blurring of class divisions, the improved status of women, and questions of culture and ethnicity, clearly have a significant bearing on the political landscape. But changing economic factors are also important. For example, until 1979, the UK governments were keen to preserve a strong manufacturing base, through subsidies or other forms of protection from overseas competitors. But since the election of the first Thatcher government in 1979, the contribution of manufacturing industry to Britain's overall economic activity has declined sharply. The service sector – particularly the financial interests based in the City of London – has been given priority. Despite the economic problems which over-reliance on the financial sector have caused in the UK since 2007, it is unclear that this imbalance will be rectified in the near future, and this has obvious political implications.

One important but little-noticed political by-product of this trend has been the dramatic decline in the balance of payments (the difference between the value of UK imports and exports) as a factor in electoral fortunes. Labour lost the 1970 general election, at least in part, because the balance of payments dipped into a small deficit just before the poll. The trivial and short-lived 'trade gap' of May 1970 would nowadays be regarded as a triumph. In 1992, by contrast, the deficit in trade in goods was a record £46.3 billion, yet the Conservative government was re-elected. Unwanted new records were also established in 2013, but this did not prevent the Conservatives from using the economic record of the coalition government as a key campaigning theme in the 2015 general election. The shift from manufacturing to services has had additional consequences. Manufacturing was more suited to the development of lifelong political allegiances and was associated with a relatively inflexible class structure. Now that most people work in the service sector, class boundaries are regarded as more fluid and people on the whole are far more volatile in their voting behaviour (see Chapter 18).

When Britain's world status was higher, students of politics could relegate consideration of the outside world to cursory discussions of foreign policy. This option is no longer available. In a 'globalised' economy – and in an era of worldwide terrorist networks – an insular understanding of UK politics is inadequate. British politicians are affected on a day-to-day basis by the decisions of other actors on the world stage, and agreement on one subject does not preclude tensions elsewhere. In 2002, for example, while Tony Blair was discussing an invasion of Iraq with US President George W. Bush, the EU was locked in a battle over the protection of the American steel industry against European imports. Blair himself was hopeful that one day, he could persuade the British people to join the European single currency (the euro), which was

PHOTO 1.1 To understand contemporary British politics, we must look beyond Westminster (© pptara/Shutterstock).

Analysis 1.1

What is politics?

'Politics' can be defined in several different ways, which give rise to very different approaches. The orthodox view associates politics with certain institutions and individuals, for example, the UK Parliament, political parties, and government ministers. This definition treats politics as a specialised activity, confined to people who hold particular offices which entitle them to a meaningful role in key decisions. On this 'elitist' view, the general public plays a minimal role in politics.

This approach to the subject matter of politics is still widely accepted, even in democratic states like the UK. However, it conflicts with current ideas about participation and citizenship. Non-specialists can affect political developments through elections, referendums, opinion polls, and pressure group activity. Even on the most cynical view of public participation, it cannot be denied that these devices offer at least a theoretical opportunity to influence important public decisions. Some theorists, particularly feminists, have advocated an even wider definition of politics. In their view, politics is found wherever human beings associate – in the workplace, in clubs and societies, and (especially) within the family.

This definition is particularly useful because it draws attention to the fundamental nature of political activity. In institutions like the UK Parliament, 'politics' is about the resolution of disputes. This understanding of politics can be used more generally. We can speak, for example, of 'office politics', even when the office concerned has nothing to do with any kind of government institutions. In this sense, 'politics' is often used in a negative sense – people say, for example, that one 'shouldn't bring politics' into a discussion. But if we accept that politics is about the resolution of disputes, it is impossible to *exclude* politics from anything other than the most trivial decisions, when more than one individual is involved.

The problem with the wider definition is that it makes it very difficult to provide a comprehensive survey of the 'politics' in a village, let alone in a much larger and more complex society like Britain. However, one can safely conclude that a study of politics which fails to mention wider social developments, will give an inadequate account.

A further question is whether violence should be included within the definition of politics. Some commentators argue that violence is what happens when politics *fails* – that is, politics is about the *peaceful* resolution of disputes. However, this is a naïve view. In many disputes, the threat or reality of violence is a factor in negotiations, even if it is never used except as a final resort. This applies not just to politics at the international level. In order to understand the politics of a country like the UK, one must pay close attention to institutions which symbolise the power of the state, like the police and the judicial system, as well as groups which use violence in order to challenge the state's authority.

To summarise, politics is best understood as a means of resolving disputes which invariably arise from the interactions of individuals and groups. Ideally, such disputes are settled by peaceful discussion. But when talks fail to bring a resolution and the quarrel becomes violent, the parties concerned do not stop thinking 'politically'. On the most plausible definition, politics can only stop with the extinction of human society.

widely regarded as a potential rival to the mighty US dollar. These diverse and sometimes contradictory considerations were not secondary distractions from the business of politics; rather, they formed an integral part of the context in which political decisions were taken in the UK, and even those voters who were unaware of this wider stage would feel their effects. The point was reinforced in 2007, when difficulties in the US banking system precipitated an economic crisis in the UK and in many other countries.

Liberal democracy

State

a political association that has a monopoly of force within a specific territory.

Civil society

the sphere of voluntary activity, where associations can be formed independently of the state.

In studying UK politics, then, we are addressing much more than a set of institutions in London, and the people who operate within them: if there were any doubts about the wisdom of this broader view, the referendums of 2014 and 2016 should have set them at rest. Social, economic, and global factors are all relevant to a proper understanding of the subject. They are discussed in more detail in Chapters 3 and 4. But the study of politics involves more than the identification of relevant subject matter and the accumulation of evidence. Some scholars have argued that politics can and should be studied 'scientifically' – that is, with the kind of objectivity which is associated with the natural sciences. However, such hopes are misplaced. There is some scope for objective study in politics; for example, statistics based on electoral data can be analysed in a way which leaves little room for reasonable doubt. But the question of 'objectivity' is highly problematic even before we start to assemble the raw data. Why do we decide that some statistics are more important than others? For example, the British balance-of-payments figures were regarded as crucial economic indicators in the 1970s, but they were barely reported in the perilous economic context which overshadowed the general election of May 2010, or in the 'Brexit' elections of 2017 and 2019. And while certain figures presented in graphs might give rise to conclusions which no reasonable observer can dispute, invariably we find ourselves trying to explain the data in a wider context, which brings in factors (like ideologies) which are not susceptible to 'scientific' evaluation (see Chapter 16).

No student of British politics today can approach the subject without feeling the influence of liberal democratic ideas. The phrase 'liberal democracy' is liable to create some confusion – particularly since there is a prominent party of a very similar name in the UK – but there is no better shorthand term for the broad framework of ideas within which British politics has been conducted for many decades. Indeed, it can be argued that a strong element of liberal democracy in the UK predates the relatively recent introduction of universal adult suffrage. That is because liberal democracy is not about an individual political

Liberal democracy

a state governed in accordance with long-established liberal principles, such as the right to participate in free and fair elections, freedom of expression, and the impartial administration of justice.

party, or even a specific electoral system, as the phrase might suggest. Rather, the precepts of liberal democracy assert that elections should be free from intimidation or other forms of corruption, and the outcome broadly representative of public opinion. Thus, for example, the result of the 2000 US presidential election was not disputed on the grounds that the successful candidate, George W. Bush, happened to win fewer votes than his rival Al Gore. That was (generally) accepted as a by-product of the electoral system under which the contest took place (a situation which was replicated in Donald Trump's 2016 victory). The system itself was open to criticism, but few people seriously suggested that the contest between Bush and Gore should be rerun using a different method to compile the results. Rather, the argument concerned the way in which the decisive state of Florida had conducted the election, with allegations that some voters were prevented from reaching the polls and serious questions raised about the way in which the votes had been counted. Similar objections were raised in some quarters in relation to alleged Russian involvement in Trump's 2016 'win'.

The idea that political controversies should be settled by broadly accepted 'free and fair' procedures rather than by the use of force is the key principle of liberal democracy. This does not mean that the resort to force lies outside the domain of politics. Ultimately, the authority of the liberal democratic state rests on the recognition by its citizens that it can legitimately resort to force in certain circumstances. However, in liberal democracies, it is assumed that force will be exercised within a framework of laws and accepted procedures. This principle, summed up in the phrase 'the rule of law', means that all citizens should be treated equally; if they are accused of a crime, they should be given a fair and open trial. In the UK, this principle dates back to mediaeval times, and hence the fierce controversy over the treatment of suspected terrorists in the wake of the attacks on the United States on 11 September 2001 (see Chapter 9).

In liberal democracies, the state is supposed to exist for the benefit of its citizens rather than vice versa. Members of the public ought to be treated as rational, autonomous individuals, who should enjoy protection from the state so long as they do not break the laws. This sphere of private activity, and of the associated voluntary organisations (like charities, clubs, trade unions, and political parties themselves), is often denoted by the umbrella term of 'civil society'. Unless people are allowed to associate freely for their own purposes, it is asserted, the political institutions of liberal democracy will be meaningless. These considerations became highly relevant in the UK during the 2020 coronavirus pandemic, when some observers argued that even serious risks to public health provide an insufficient justification for the suspension of basic liberties.

Pluralism

In theory, at least, liberal democracies accept the notion that reasonable people will reach different conclusions about political issues. In their daily lives, they will also have a wide range of interests which often conflict, and they should be free to express their views in association with others who feel the same. Politics, on this view,

Pluralism

the belief that
the existence of
various volun-
tary groups and
the expression
of diverse
opinions within
a society is
healthy.

is about the peaceful adjustment of such interests. The ideal outcome of political debate will be a succession of compromises which leave all sides broadly satisfied. But if this is impossible, at least all the parties to the dispute should be left with the feeling that nothing has prevented them from winning a fair hearing.

These ideas are associated with another key liberal democratic principle – that of pluralism. This underpins the principle of free speech, which can be exercised within the scope of the law even by people who express unpopular views. Originally, pluralist thinkers like the French philosopher Voltaire (1694–1778) and the Briton John Stuart Mill (1806–73) argued that pluralism was the best guarantee of intellectual progress; if unpopular ideas are suppressed, the public will be deprived of useful debates and possibly miss out on some benefi-cial proposals for change. Other pluralists argue that the dissemination of ideas should be as free as possible as a matter of principle, regardless of the conse-quences. In particular, there must be minimal state interference in the activities of the media. During the Cold War (usually seen as prevailing between 1946 and 1991), in which liberal democracies ranged against 'totalitarian' Commu-nist regimes, Western scholars and propagandists tended to argue that whether or not society actively benefitted from free speech, at least it was permitted in their countries – unlike the Soviet Union and its allies, where the state con-trolled the flow of information to the public. The key figure associated with post-war pluralism is the American academic Robert Dahl (1915–2014), who envisaged (among other things) that the state should act as a neutral 'umpire' in disputes between various groups competing for influence.

More generally, pluralist ideas can be contrasted with the elitist position (see Analysis 1.2). While elitists want to keep the impact of public opinion on decision-making down to a minimum – or accept, reluctantly, that meaningful participation will always be restricted to a few – pluralists argue that it should be maximised. For pluralists, the existence of political 'specialists' is problem-atic in itself. Although such people might be more knowledgeable on political matters, the key point for pluralists is that they should always be open to chal-lenge, and that in debate they should have no other advantage than the respect they have earned from their previous record. For pluralists, the unthinking assumption that 'the government always knows best' is the death-knell of a free society. There were clear echoes of this view among leading 'Leave' campaign-ers in the 2016 EU referendum, although in that instance it is not impossible that the hostility towards 'experts' might have been more muted if the experts in question had been more supportive of the case for withdrawal.

The limits of liberal democracy

While liberal democratic ideas have been widely accepted for many years in Western Europe and North America, they have received an additional impetus since the late 1980s with the virtual disappearance of old-style Communist regimes like the Soviet Union. Other countries which remain formally Com-munist, like China, seem gradually to be moving towards liberal democratic practices in some respects, even if free and open elections are still absent. It has been argued, most famously by the US writer Francis Fukuyama (born 1952),

Analysis 1.2

Elitism and neo-pluralism

Elitists argue that politics is a specialised activity, and that the most important decisions should be left to people with the relevant qualifications. In its purest form, elitism is anti-democratic; according to some elitists, allowing the general public to influence important decisions is a recipe for disaster. Thus, while pluralists think that things are going well when political leaders are representative of society, elitists take this as a sign that things have gone wrong. On the elitist view, leaders should be 'better' than the people they govern.

However, some elitists (like the economist Joseph Schumpeter (1883–1950)) accept democracy on the grounds that the parties which compete for votes are themselves elites. 'Democratic elitists' argue that politicians who rise to the top of their parties are likely to have acquired the skills necessary for good government. On this view, free competition between organised parties is unlikely to be damaging to a state, since the rulers at any time will still constitute an elite, even if the competition between them is adjudicated by voters who have limited knowledge of politics.

The main strength of the elitist argument is that it seems to reflect the practices of successful political parties – even those which profess support for mass participation. In his 1911 book *Political Parties*, the German-born sociologist Robert Michels argued that even the German Social Democratic Party was subject to an 'iron law of oligarchy', which resulted in the dominance of an elite.

In response to such arguments, some pluralists have shifted towards a revised position generally characterised as 'neo-pluralism'. This approach retains the pluralist ideal of free competition for influence among a wide range of organised groups. However, it recognises that some groups have an advantage in this competition, often due to their economic resources rather than the quality of their arguments. For some neo-pluralists, this insight suggests that the state should move beyond the role of a neutral 'umpire' which is prescribed by 'classical' pluralist theory. Instead, it should ensure that all groups gain a proper hearing, for example, by actively inviting less-advantaged groups into official consultations. It could be argued, though, that elitist theories like the 'iron law of oligarchy' still apply, and that any institution of significant size will continue to be dominated by a relatively small group, leaving ordinary members with a largely passive role. Equally, policymakers who consult 'networks' of relevant individuals and organisations will always include powerful economic interests, even if they try to balance this by seeking out alternative voices.

that the worldwide triumph of liberal democracy is inevitable. Among other reasons, it is claimed that liberal democracies are associated with free economies, which are far more efficient than totalitarian states. Thus, liberal democracy is not just morally superior to any alternative; it also works better and leads to greater prosperity. For some, these arguments lend support to the view that liberal democracies are justified in interfering in the internal affairs of the so-called 'failing' (or 'rogue') states, like Iraq or Libya. On this view, even the imposition of liberal democracy by armed force will improve the lives of people who currently lack its benefits.

However, even those who accept the superiority of liberal democratic ideas may continue to question the extent to which they are actually reflected in the institutions and practices of a particular state at a specific time. In the case of the UK, we have already referred to concerns about the impact of the Westminster model, the party system, and the media. A more general question is how readily liberal democracy can accommodate significant inequalities of wealth. Pluralists might accept that key business interests have a special right to be heard by governments, since their fortunes can affect a nation's general prosperity. But when questions seem to be settled by the size of a bank balance rather than by the weight of an argument, many liberal democratic assumptions begin to ring hollow (hence the acceptance by many pluralists of a revised, 'neo-pluralist approach; see Analysis 1.2). In the UK, this difficulty has been recognised by restrictions on party funding through legislation enacted in 2000, 2006, and 2009. Unlike the USA, the UK has strict guidelines on the nature and extent of party-political coverage on radio and television. However, since the 1990s concerns have been raised that money could win privileged access to decision-makers, regardless of the conduct of elections (see Chapter 15).

A second question is the appropriate response of liberal democracies to new terrorist threats. In the UK, this problem had been debated long before 11 September 2001 attack, because of the campaign of violence by Irish terrorists which began in the early 1970s. Among other things, this had already prompted the erection of iron gates at the entrance to Downing Street (in 1989, when Margaret Thatcher was the prime minister). However justified for security reasons, this was still a regrettable symbol of an enforced distance between politicians and the people. It even prevented demonstrations of spontaneous enthusiasm, so that when Tony Blair approached Number 10 after Labour's landslide victory in May 1997, the television footage of rejoicing citizens in Downing Street was actually a stage-managed display from selected party supporters.

The threat from global terrorist groups, understandably, has prompted the extension of tight security to many other public buildings and to restrictions on the right to demonstrate in sensitive areas. MPs are still accessible to the public in other ways. But when they take decisions which affect the civil rights of even a small minority of people – or vote to take the country into war – it is legitimate to ask whether they are truly accountable to their real employers, who elect them and pay their salaries. Despite a rapidly changing context, this remains one of the key principles of liberal democracy. The weakness of *accountability* was a serious flaw in the old Westminster model. If, as the evidence suggests, true accountability has been weakening in recent years, there is a danger that decision-makers could lose sight of the necessary balance between liberty and security, thus fulfilling a major objective of the enemies of Western liberal democracy.

The Iraq War produced new allegations that liberal democracies are too susceptible to the influence of money. The role of the USA was particularly vulnerable to this charge. Critics suspected that the ideal of a 'liberated' Iraq was merely introduced as a smokescreen for the real motive, which was to gain control of the country's extensive oil reserves. The fact that the US President George W. Bush had close links with oil companies – and had previously been governor of the oil-dominated state of Texas – did nothing to allay these fears. Bush had also resisted attempts to tackle the problem of global pollution, allegedly under the impulsion of the same profit motive. Few believed that Tony Blair had committed the UK forces to the assault on Iraq because he was under the direct influence of the oil industry. But since his position was clearly influenced by the US determination to depose the regime of Saddam Hussein, critics argued that it amounted to the same thing. There had been instances when the Blair government was accused of granting privileged access to business people who had contributed to its election coffers. Similar allegations had beset the previous Conservative governments led by Margaret Thatcher and John Major (1979–97).

Although opinions continue to be divided about the Iraq War, it seems reasonable to suggest that the course of events lent support to the ideas of democratic elitists (see Analysis 1.2), rather than their pluralist opponents. The position of democratic elitists implies that most people – that

Economics and liberal democracy

During the 1970s and 1980s, a key element of the case for a free-market economy was the notion that it had a mutually supportive relationship with liberal democracy. On this view, excessive state intervention was a threat to political as well as economic freedom. Supporters of the free market used the example of the Soviet Union – where the ruling party controlled the media, the economy, and the political process – to argue that freedom was indivisible. They also borrowed an older argument: that countries which traded freely with each other were most unlikely to resort to force to settle their disagreements. Thus, the free market was the best guarantor of international peace as well as domestic prosperity.

Conservative electoral success between 1979 and 1997 – and the gradual Labour acceptance of most key Conservative arguments – suggested that the free-marketers had won the debate. The circumstances in which the Soviet Union collapsed pointed to the same conclusion. Under Mikhail Gorbachev in the mid-1980s, economic reforms were introduced before meaningful democratic institutions had been established. The result was a growing demand for political freedom which could not be contained within the old Soviet system.

However, subsequent events suggest a more complex relationship between the economy and politics. Although Russia is no longer communist, its blood-soaked intervention in Chechnya during the first decade of the twenty-first century, and its more recent conflicts with Georgia and Ukraine, are distinct echoes of the old days. Meanwhile, social inequalities in Russia have widened to an extent which is unthinkable even in the Western democracies. A tiny handful of people have become wildly rich through a flawed privatisation process, and something like a 'mafia' threatens to fill the vacuum left by the all-powerful Communist Party. President Vladimir Putin exercised an iron grip over the electronic media, and although he received almost two-thirds of the votes in the 2012 presidential election, international observers criticised the conduct of the poll.

The Russian and Chinese examples suggest that a liberal economy can coexist with a political culture in which democratic values are either absent or ineffectual. The same lesson can be derived from Far Eastern states, like Malaysia, where most traditional media are under government control. In the 1990s, while Western intellectuals were hailing the inevitable triumph of liberal democracy, such states were experiencing dramatic rates of economic growth while curtailing personal liberty.

Recent experience suggests that while a (relatively) free economy may help to underpin political freedoms, it is by no means a guarantee that citizens will enjoy real influence over their leaders. In fact, the ideal business context may be one in which investors can feel confident of complete political stability, so that they can plan ahead. It is not necessary for a government to keep a majority of its citizens happy in order to enjoy prolonged tenure of office. So long as the government serves the interests of the most influential sections of society, along with most of the media and the armed forces, it can expect to stay in power. From this perspective, critics argue that in consumerist societies like the UK (or the USA), democratic practices can be permitted in the reasonable expectation that they will never produce unprofitable outcomes. In a variant of this argument, commentators have perceived a rise in 'populism' in the USA and elsewhere, which is intended to give voters the feeling that they are rising up against the governing elite, when, in reality, they are being tricked into serving the interests of dominant economic interests.

is, those who take only a sporadic interest in political issues – are actually relieved when 'experts' take decisions out of their hands. In the UK, it was noteworthy that public opinion suddenly became more favourable to the war once the government had committed troops, even though the quality of the arguments on either side had not significantly changed (indeed, the fact that the Iraqi regime did not instantly use weapons of mass destruction, despite the overwhelming force deployed against it, reinforced the views of those who had doubted the formal justification for war). However, we also argued earlier that there is likely to be a connection between an elitist view of politics and a decline in electoral turnout. This implies that democratic elitists are mistaken in their pessimistic view of human nature, and that many people do want to live in a society which truly reflects pluralist ideas. On present trends, the danger is that, ironically, the people most likely to participate in elections are the ones who would be happy to leave decisions to others, while those who are eager to make a meaningful contribution stay at home in the belief that their vote will change nothing. In such circumstances, active citizens are more likely to participate in politics through pressure groups (see Chapter 19). These have a valuable place in a liberal democracy, but it is doubtful whether the system would survive if large numbers of people regarded them, rather than political parties, as the only realistic vehicle to effect change.

The changing state

The emergence of a more demanding (and fickle) electorate is one important explanatory factor behind the recent changes in the UK state. It was commonly argued during the mid-1970s that the British state had become 'overloaded' by an excessive burden of duties, reducing government effectiveness and stretching democratic accountability beyond reasonable limits. For example, ministers were supposed to be accountable to Parliament for the performance of nationalised industries, the detailed operations of which they lacked either the time or the expertise to master. More controversially, it could also be argued that 'micromanagement' of the economy – particularly through direct government intervention designed to control inflation – had proved counterproductive in practice (see Chapter 3).

The Conservative Party won the 1979 general election under a leader who was determined to reverse Britain's relative decline in global status, and Margaret Thatcher believed that a radical change in the role of the state was a crucial part of this process. In theory, Thatcher was a staunch supporter of the Westminster model: she had a profound respect for the idea of parliamentary sovereignty, for example. Yet the ultimate and cumulative effect of her reforms was to undermine traditional understandings of British government and politics.

The most spectacular change during the 1980s was the government's programme of 'privatisation' (or denationalisation), under which the state sold off its holdings in several major industries (see Chapter 10). In many cases – particularly where the privatised firms still enjoyed a dominant market position – direct political control was replaced by a regime of appointed regulators. In addition, many of the more traditional functions of the central state were 'hived-off' to semi-autonomous agencies, and a distinction was drawn between 'policy' and 'operational' matters (see Chapter 10). Ministers could still be held responsible for policy guidelines, but not for day-to-day operations. The prisons, for example, had been regarded as the direct responsibility of the Home Secretary. Once the Prison Service had been given agency status, however, embarrassing escapes could be blamed on the chief executive and subordinate officials – even if the escapes took place against a background of prison overcrowding and low staff morale, attributable to government policies and ministerial decisions.

Before 1979, the Conservatives promised to abolish many of the semi-official bodies known as 'quangos' (quasi-autonomous non-governmental organisations), which were not directly accountable to the public despite the fact that they distributed billions of pounds of government revenue. However, the emergence of a 'regulatory state' under Thatcher triggered the creation of new quangos. Before it came into office in 1997, Labour was also committed to a cull of quangos, but, in practice, its efforts were equally ineffectual. In 2005, it was estimated that there were more than 500 of these bodies, including such obscure organisations as the British Potato Council and the Milk Development Council. Opposition parties promised radical reform, and the coalition government, which took office in 2010, quickly drew up plans to scrap almost 200 quangos. But based on the experience of the previous quarter-century, such targets could be treated with scepticism; governments of all parties find quangos too useful to effect a dramatic reduction of their functions or spending power, even if their numbers are whittled down.

The relationship between local authorities and central government also underwent a considerable change in this period. Thatcher and her allies believed that the services offered by local government, such as council housing, created a large body of dependent 'clients' who were likely to vote for the party which offered the most generous provision, regardless of efficiency. The government also objected to the tendency of Labour-controlled councils to spend ratepayers' money on political campaigns, often on behalf of minority groups (a policy which, incidentally, could easily be squared with neo-pluralist theory: see Analysis 1.2). The overall effect of successive measures imposed by central government was to force local councils to base their services on value for money and radically to reduce their scope for independent political initiative. As a result, by the end of the twentieth century, most councils were acting more like businesses than as embodiments of distinctive local opinions.

In 1990, Conservative policy towards local government rebounded against Thatcher, when the new community charge (or poll tax) caused widespread resentment. However, this controversy ended by increasing the scope of central government interference, because the Treasury was forced to provide more generous subsidies in order to cushion the impact of the new tax (and that of its successor, the council tax). While Labour was less antagonistic towards local authorities, after it returned to office in 1997 councils tended to persevere in their new role rather than reverting to their old one. In particular, there was little sign that councils would recover their former prominence in housing provision. Rather, even a Labour government preferred to work through unelected housing associations. Other, more ambitious, building projects were conducted in partnership with private companies – an approach which New Labour greatly extended after inheriting the idea from the Conservatives. The coalition government, which took office in 2010, displayed an enthusiasm for 'localism', but it was debatable whether its initiatives were intended to inspire a genuine revival of democratic local government, or rather to offload unpopular decisions in areas such as Health onto councilors or appointed local officials, and/or to encourage unelected voluntary organisations to take on many of their traditional functions.

From 'government' to 'governance'

Government

decision-making through formal institutions and rules.

Governance

decision-making by multiple actors in networks.

A positive way of interpreting these developments is to say that the UK has moved from the old Westminster model of government to a new style of 'governance' (see Chapters 2 and 10). Even in the Thatcher years, the central state issued orders and expected compliance. However, some governmental decisions of that time actually made it more difficult to ensure compliance – for example, ministers no longer exercised direct control over nationalised industries, and although, at first, ministers continued to treat agencies as subordinates, ultimately such bodies were always likely to widen their spheres of independent action.

It would be going too far to say that the Thatcher years saw a general relaxation of central control – if anything, the experience of local authorities suggested that Westminster was increasing its power. However, from a wider perspective, many developments of the 1979–97 period can be seen as complementary to some important New Labour reforms. In particular, the introduction of devolved institutions in Scotland, Wales, and Northern Ireland meant that ministers had to start thinking in terms of negotiation and bargaining rather than relying on the old system of centralised command (Photo 1.2). Not only did they have to take into account more powerful subnational bodies, but they also dealt on a regular basis with supranational organisations like the European Union (EU) and the United Nations (UN). From this perspective, another notable move from government to governance was Labour's immediate decision to give control over interest rates to a committee of the Bank of England. Previously, this key economic lever had been under the control of the Chancellor of the Exchequer. Similarly, the 2010–15 coalition government established an Office for Budget Responsibility (OBR) with a remit to publish economic forecasts and data, which were previously provided from within the Treasury.

However one assesses the real significance of recent changes, it is clearly unhelpful to study UK politics in the traditional fashion, focusing on the Westminster

PHOTO 1.2 The Scottish Parliament: the new face of the multilevel UK polity (© Tudoran Andrei/Shuttersttock).

model and the dominance of central government. Yet it is misleadingly simplistic to talk of a completed transition from government to governance in the UK. Three obvious problems remain. First, the notion of 'governance' suggests that central dictation has given way across the board to a process of bargaining with a variety of institutions. But even after the establishment of devolved institutions, central government tried to interfere with important business, like Tony Blair's attempt to hand-pick the First Minister in Wales. While incidents such as these are extremely unlikely in the fore-seeable future – particularly after the coronavirus pandemic cemented the autonomy of devolved authorities – this is not to say that the central UK government will not explore other, more subtle possible means of interference; through the Barnett funding formula, it still enjoys considerable economic leverage (see Chapter 12). Other legislation that has been passed since 1997, for example, the Human Rights Act 1998 (see Chapter 9) and the Freedom of Information Act 2000, have obvious potential to reduce the power of central government over British citizens. But both measures have caused considerable disquiet in government circles, and the Conservatives have a long-standing intention to replace the Human Rights Act with a British Bill of Rights.

Second, in specific areas – notably in matters of national security, but also in their attempts to reform public services – Westminster politicians have actually become more determined to push through their proposals, even in the face of concerted opposition. Far from 'rolling back' the frontiers of the state since 1979, the central government has tried to compensate for its loss of influence in certain areas by extending it in others (i.e. greater interference in matters which were previously governed by personal choice, such as hunting with dogs and smoking in public places). Third, the transition to governance has been accompanied by a definite reduction in the extent to which ministers can be held responsible for decisions of a political nature. For example, in 2005, Blair openly criticised the operations of the Child Support Agency (which had been set up by the Major administration), without any fear that a member of his government would have to resign as a result of its alleged institutional failures. He was able to do so despite the fact that his party had enjoyed eight years in which to sort out the problems in this policy area. Other Labour ministers were prepared to state publicly that their departments were 'unfit for purpose', long after the party's landslide victory in the 1997 general election.

Thus, while it is certainly possible to detect a shift from a system of 'government' to one of 'governance', it is worth questioning whether this is more apparent than real, and, furthermore, to ask whether the trend is beneficial in a liberal democracy. The key to such a system is that the individuals who make important decisions should be held accountable by members of the general public. With its low electoral turnouts, the UK is hardly unique in facing a 'crisis of accountability', but students should be aware that future changes in the UK state might merely add complications to this problem rather than generating tangible improvements. In particular, the 'Leave' campaign in the 2016 referendum rehearsed the argument that withdrawal from the EU would make it easier for British voters to hold policymakers to account for their decisions. However, the Johnson government, which oversaw Britain's official departure on 31 January 2020, had already shown a tendency to defend ministers from allegations of incompetence (and worse), regardless of whether or not such claims were well founded. In doing so, arguably, the government was merely following a trend set by its predecessors since 1979.

Conclusion and summary

The UK is usually counted among the world's most successful representative democracies. Although it has not been free from violent outbreaks – the summer of 2011, for example, saw widespread disorder in many English cities – since the seventeenth century, it has avoided the kind of revolutionary upheavals which have affected so much of the European mainland. It has a strong tradition of free and fair elections and upholds other key liberal democratic principles such as the right to free speech.

However, in the circumstances of the early twenty-first century, it would be a mistake to embark on the study of UK politics in a spirit of complacency. We have identified several potent threats to pluralism and liberal democracy, if those terms are to retain much of their original (highly laudable) meaning. The most obvious danger remains the impact of global terrorism. But this relatively new threat materialised at a time when an increasingly diverse and demanding electorate already had good reasons for unease. It is impossible to deny that rich business interests enjoy privileged access to decision-makers, whichever party is in office, and at one time or another, serious doubts have been cast on the integrity of all UK governments since 1979. In addition, strict party discipline at Westminster encourages ambitious MPs to support certain policies in public, regardless of strong personal reservations. It seems increasingly difficult to hold ministers to account for their actions through the traditional mechanisms of parliamentary debate. The result has been to reinforce an 'accountability gap' which, in any case, is widening under the influence of global developments.

All of these factors help to explain the recent decline in electoral turnout in the UK, and a growing feeling of disillusion with the political process which undoubtedly underpinned the 'Leave' vote in the 2016 referendum. This is the most worrying development of all, since the concept of representative democracy obviously depends on a high level of participation from citizens who, even if not particularly well-informed, are at least not easily susceptible to misinformation. There are signs that the increasing availability of political opinions (and purported 'facts'), thanks to 24-hour news and social media, has not coincided with a significant improvement in public understanding of the numerous problems affecting the political process in the UK. Thus, a critical study of UK politics is more important today than at any time since the institution of universal suffrage back in 1928.

Further reading

Introductory texts on liberal democracy include A. Arblaster's *Democracy* (Milton Keynes: Open University Press, 2002), and D. Held's *Models of Democracy* (Cambridge: Polity Press, 3rd edition, 2006). On theories of the state, see C. Hay, M. Lister, and D. Marsh (eds.), *The State: Theories and Issues* (London: Palgrave, 2005), and P. Dunleavy, *Theories of the State. The Politics of Liberal Democracy* (London: Palgrave, 1987).

W.H. Greenleaf's *The British Political Tradition* (London: Methuen, 3 volumes, 1983 and 1987) is a lengthy, but rewarding, account which identifies different traditions in the study of British politics. L. Tivey's *Interpretations of British Politics* (London: Harvester Wheatsheaf, 1988) is a shorter study of interpretations of British politics. A. Gamble, 'Theories of British Politics', *Political Studies*, Vol. 38, No. 3 (1990), pp. 404–20, M. Bevir and R. Rhodes, 'Studying British Government: Reconstructing the Research Agenda', *British Journal of Politics and International Relations*, Vol. 1, No. 2 (1999), pp. 215–39, and J. Dearlove, 'The Political Science of British Politics', *Parliamentary Affairs*, Vol. 35 (1982), pp. 436–55, are very useful overviews of developments in the study of British politics.

W. Bagehot's *The English Constitution* (Oxford: Oxford Paperbacks, 2001, original 1867), and A.V. Dicey's *Introduction to the Study of the Law and the Constitution* (Indianapolis: Liberty Fund, 1982, original 1885) are classic texts. A.H. Birch's *Representative and Responsible Government* (London: George Allen & Unwin, 1964) sets out some of the key attributes of the Westminster model in a fashion which invites fruitful comparisons to the present situation. D. Marsh, J. Buller, C. Hay, J. Johnstone, P. Kerr, S. McAnulla, and M. Watson's *Postwar British Politics in Perspective* (Oxford: Polity Press, 1999) challenges the orthodox Westminster model perspective. R. Rhodes's *Understanding Governance: Policy Networks, Governance,*

Reflexivity and Accountability (Buckingham: Open University Press, 1997) provides a sample of Rhodes's influential work on the move from government to governance.

Websites

Two 'gateways' providing links to a series of useful websites on politics in the UK are highly recommended: the Political Studies Association (www.psa.ac.uk) and Richard Kimber's Political Science Resources site (www.politicsresources.net).

Chapter 2

Analysing British politics

Learning outcomes

After reading this chapter, you will:

- be able to evaluate competing explanatory models of British politics;
- appreciate the main elements of contrasting theoretical approaches to the study of British politics;
- be aware of key methods employed in research into British politics.

Introduction

The shift from top-down 'government' to looser forms of 'governance', and the health of liberal democracy in Britain, are the two main themes explored in this book. They pose significant challenges to the traditional perspective on the British political system – the Westminster model – and to the approach to understanding British politics which is associated with that model. This chapter reviews the key features of the Westminster model as an 'organising perspective', before examining two alternative models – the 'differentiated polity' model and the 'asymmetric power' model – that seek to explain British politics in the new era of governance. Having explored these explanatory frameworks, it moves on to examine three of the main theoretical approaches used in the study of British politics – rational choice theory, institutionalism, and interpretive approaches – and some of the most important research methods employed.

Organising perspective

a framework for understanding a political system; a set of assumptions about how a political system operates.

The Westminster model and the study of British politics

The Westminster model was the dominant overarching theory or **organising perspective** of British politics for much of the twentieth century (see Chapter 1). In the last 30 years or so, however, it has come under severe strain, and, although it is still used by many academics and media commentators, its

Empirical

based on observable data; verifiable by observation.

Normative

relating to norms, ideals, or standards, for example, what is right or just.

utility as an explanatory framework has been questioned. The methods of study associated with the Westminster model are legal, philosophical, and historical, the focus being on constitutional principles and institutional design. The **empirical** and **normative** elements within this organising perspective are often fused. That is, the Westminster model not only provides a description of the workings of the British polity (see Table 1.1) but also claims explicitly (or assumes implicitly) that this is how a political system *ought* to operate. Defenders of the Westminster model see a close fit between constitutional ideals and political practice, but an important reformist critique has argued that significant reforms are required to enhance liberal democracy in Britain.

The Westminster model is a prime example of a *majoritarian* democracy in which power is concentrated at the political centre (see Analysis 2.1). Parliamentary sovereignty, the guiding principle of the Westminster model, locates supreme political authority at Westminster. Parliament can make any law of its choosing, and no other body can overturn its legislation. The uncodified constitution can be amended through the normal legislative process, instead of requiring a lengthy process of ratification as in countries like the USA. The legislature and executive are *fused:* a government with a parliamentary majority controls the legislative process, with strong party discipline in the House of Commons and government control over the parliamentary timetable ensuring that its policy proposals are put into practice. Parliament has only limited prospects of amending or even delaying government bills. The simple plurality electoral system almost invariably gives one party an overall majority in the Parliament; the 2010 election, which resulted in a 'hung' parliament with no overall majority, was the first of its kind since 1974, and despite a hard-fought election in 2015, 'normal service' was resumed with a majority Conservative government. This pattern repeated itself in 2017 and 2019, with another hung parliament (resulting in the Conservatives forming a 'pact' – but not a coalition – with Northern Ireland's Democratic Unionist Party) followed, in 2019, by a majority Conservative government (this time, an emphatic majority too). Beyond the centre, local government is weak, and subnational government was, except in Northern Ireland, absent for most of the twentieth century. The Westminster model perspective views this centralisation of political power as a desirable feature of the British political system because it usually delivers strong and effective government, which, it turn, enhances the idea of accountability.

The Westminster model is also a hierarchical one: the prime minister is the dominant figure in a cabinet which is bound by collective responsibility; civil servants present their elected political masters with options from which they determine policy; and central government dominates subnational institutions. 'Patrician' attitudes were common among members of the political elite into the second half of the twentieth century. Many MPs entered politics with a desire to serve their country or to improve the lot of the British people, while a public service ethos expected a neutral civil service to work in the national interest. The view within Whitehall and Westminster was, and to some extent remains, that the political elite is uniquely equipped to discern the long-term public interest, while the public itself is often mistaken in its preferences. Of course, this perspective has been a key reason for the rise of 'populism', as symbolised by the support for UKIP in 2015 and the subsequent vote in favour of Brexit in the 2016 referendum, in which the Leave campaign mobilised popular discontent with the so-called arrogant, corrupt, out-of-touch, liberal, Westminster 'elite', which had looked down its noses at, and ignored, the 'left-behind' sections of British society. Of course, it was deeply ironic that some of the leading political figures in favour of the UK leaving the EU, reflecting an anti-elite backlash, were public-school-educated politicians like Nigel Farage, Boris Johnson, and Jacob Rees-Mogg, none of whom could be considered financially hard-up or excluded from 'the Establishment'.

The vision of liberal democracy inherent in the Westminster model is a limited and an elitist one. Britain is a parliamentary democracy in which ministers are supposed to be responsible and accountable to the Parliament. MPs are representatives, free to vote according to their own beliefs (but in practice, they have been required to obey the party whips). The government is ultimately accountable to the people through regular free elections, but citizens have few opportunities for more extensive political participation. Representative democracy is valued for giving the political system *legitimacy*, rather than as a vehicle of popular *participation*. The two-party system gives voters a clear choice between two disciplined bodies – a governing party held to account for its record in office, and an opposition party ready to take the reins of power. The rule of law defends basic civil liberties and ensures that power is not exercised arbitrarily. Ministers and officials are not above the law, and the judiciary is independent (despite the fact that until very recently, the Lord Chancellor was head of the judiciary, a member of the cabinet and of the legislature, and as such embodied the fusion of powers under the uncodified UK constitution).

The study of British politics both deepened and widened during the heyday of the Westminster model. Voting behaviour and public policy became important subfields of study, for example. Yet alternative theories of power in Britain, such as the Marxist analysis of the divide between the capitalist ruling class and the working class, did not seriously challenge the Westminster model's status as the dominant organising perspective. As Andrew Gamble points outs in 'Theories of British Politics' (*Political Studies*, Vol. 38, No. 3, 1990), the main debates often concerned the gap between constitutional theory and political practice, and were framed within the Westminster model perspective rather than challenging it. Thus, for example, in his classic study *The English Constitution* (1867), Walter Bagehot identified the gap between the 'dignified' parts of the constitution (the monarchy) and the 'efficient' parts (the cabinet) where political power actually resided. The debate about whether Britain has prime ministerial government or cabinet government has rumbled on for many years and shows no sign of abating.

The Westminster model under strain

The underlying problems affecting the Westminster model became increasingly apparent amidst the political and economic crises of the 1970s. In that decade, Lord Hailsham warned that executive dominance of Parliament was producing an 'elective dictatorship'. Academics echoed opposition politicians and many journalists by questioning whether Britain had become 'ungovernable' – with government unable to implement its policies in the face of trade union resistance – and whether the government was suffering from 'overload' – unable to meet voters' demands for increased public spending during a global recession. Membership of the European Economic Community (EEC), the decline of the two-party system, minority government, demands for devolution in Scotland and Wales, and the 'Troubles' in Northern Ireland suggested that the Westminster model was no longer delivering strong and responsible government for the UK. In the 1980s, the dominance of the Thatcher government prompted discussion of the

Analysis 2.1

Majoritarian democracy

The Dutch political scientist Arend Lijphart located liberal democracies on a spectrum with majoritarian democracy at one extreme and consensual democracy at the other. In a majoritarian democracy, political power is concentrated at the centre, with few constitutional limits on its exercise. Common features include a flexible constitution, a unitary state, a dominant executive, a simple plurality electoral system, and a two-party system. In a consensual democracy, by contrast, political power is diffuse. Typical features include a rigid constitution, federalism, the separation of powers, proportional representation, and a multiparty system. There are also important differences in political culture: politics is 'adversarial' in a majoritarian democracy, whereas power-sharing and bargaining are the norms in a consensual democracy.

Majoritarian and consensual democracy

Aspect of the political system	Majoritarian democracy	Consensual democracy
Constitution	Flexible constitution which can be amended by a simple legislative majority votes	Rigid constitution which can be amended only by weighted majorities
Executive–legislative relations	Dominant executive controls the legislative branch	Balance of power between the executive and legislative branches
Judiciary	The legislature, not the courts, ultimately determines the constitutionality of its own laws	Laws can be struck down by a constitutional court
Territorial division	Unitary state with power concentrated at the centre	Federal system with power divided between tiers of government
Electoral system	Majoritarian electoral system gives election 'winner' a parliamentary majority	Proportional representation translates votes into legislative seats with greater accuracy
Party system	Adversarial two-party system	Cooperative multiparty system
Interest groups	Neo-pluralism: competition between groups, but business is particularly influential	Corporatism: coordination between government, business, and trade unions

Based on: A. Lijphart, *Patterns of Democracy. Government Forms and Performance in Thirty-Six Countries* (London: Yale University Press, 1999); M. Flinders, 'Majoritarian Democracy in Britain: New Labour and the Constitution', West *European Politics*, Vol. 28, No. 1 (2005), pp. 61–93.

The British Westminster model is the prime example of a majoritarian democracy; Switzerland is a leading example of consensual democracy. The constitutional reforms of the Blair and Brown governments (see Chapter 6) introduced elements of consensual democracy to the UK polity, notably devolution, new electoral systems beyond Westminster, and the Human Rights Act. But the UK is still close to the majoritarian extreme. Parliamentary sovereignty remains the core doctrine of the British constitution (which remains uncodified), the fusion of the executive and legislative branches of government has not been disturbed greatly, and the simple plurality electoral system is still used for Westminster elections. Disputes between successive home secretaries and the courts over counterterrorism and immigration legislation also illustrate the continuing tensions between the majoritarian focus on national security and the rights of the individual. The coalition government formed in 2010 made little difference in this respect, despite the inclusion of the traditionally anti-elitist Liberal Democrats.

However, there was a major clash between Boris Johnson's Conservative government and the judiciary in September 2019, when the Supreme Court ruled that the suspension of Parliament, as pursued by Johnson himself, was unlawful, whereupon Parliament resumed its business immediately. Not for the first time since the Leave vote in the 2016, some pro-Brexit newspapers and other supporters denounced Britain's senior judges as 'enemies of the people' – an insult also hurled at civil servants, pro-Remain MPs (including some Conservatives), the Speaker (of the House of Commons), and even the House of Lords: all were variously accused of trying to sabotage Brexit through a variety of procedural and delaying tactics orchestrated by 'Remainers' who allegedly refused to accept the 'will of the people'.

Unionist hegemony in Northern Ireland during the devolved Stormont regime (1922–72) provides an example of problems associated with majoritarian democracy in a divided society. The minority Roman Catholic population was excluded from power and suffered institutional discrimination (e.g. the gerrymandering of electoral boundaries). The 1998 Good Friday Agreement was designed to foster consensual democracy. The single transferable vote system is used to elect the Northern Ireland Assembly and to distribute ministerial posts in a power-sharing executive. Legislation on sensitive matters must achieve a weighted majority and 'parallel consent' (i.e. the support of both unionist and nationalist parties) in the Assembly. But such arrangements do not automatically change political culture, and it has proved difficult to engender trust between the two communities (see Chapter 12).

perceived erosion of civil liberties, the weakening of local government and intermediate groups, and the questionable legitimacy of the simple plurality electoral system which seriously distorted the political preferences of a sharply divided polity. By the 1990s, European integration and globalisation were also exerting a significant effect on the British political system. Demands for devolution revived in Scotland, trust in Parliament declined as 'sleaze' entered the political lexicon, an array of unelected agencies and networks became involved in policy implementation, judges were increasingly ruling that ministers had overstepped their powers, and there were a number of high-profile policy disasters, notably Mrs Thatcher's community charge (or 'poll tax'), which helped to force her resignation, and Britain's forcible ejection from the European Exchange Rate Mechanism (ERM) in September 1992.

Responses from those studying British politics to these strains on the Westminster model have varied. A reformist perspective emerged which argued for a modernisation of the archaic elements of the traditional constitution, a rebalancing of the relationship between executive and legislature, the devolution of power away from the centre, and greater protection of the rights of citizens. This perspective proved politically influential, its liberal constitutional reform agenda being taken up by the Labour Party after 1992 under John Smith and Tony Blair. As we will see in Chapter 6, the Blair and Brown governments partially enacted a major programme of constitutional reform. But advocates of this reformist position argue that further changes – a codified constitution, an elected House of Lords, electoral reform for Westminster, and further devolution – are still required to enhance British democracy. While the Liberal Democrats are closely associated with such views, their inclusion within a coalition government for the first time since 1945, did not result in significant progress towards a coherent solution to perceived constitutional problems.

Many academics, commentators, and politicians recognise that the Westminster model faces significant challenges and that this raises questions about its utility as an organising perspective. But this is not necessarily to say that the Westminster model is damaged irreparably or that its core elements have undergone such radical transformation that they are no longer recognisable. The label 'two-party system' may not fit the British case comfortably any more (see Chapter 14), but although the simple plurality system failed to produce a clear outcome in 2010 and 2017 – and only just did so in 2015 – it continues to discriminate against minor parties, and the attempt to replace it with the AV system was rejected by a public vote in 2011. Devolution, the Human Rights Act, and the European integration may have challenged the doctrine of parliamentary sovereignty, but the Westminster Parliament still retains the authority to legislate to alter these arrangements as it sees fit. Contemporary prime ministers may appear more 'presidential' than their predecessors, but comparisons between the British core executive and the executive branch in the United States reveal significant differences. Many of these themes are explored in more detail in this book and will be re-examined in the final chapter.

Alternative models

More comprehensive critiques of the Westminster model have been provided by political scientists who contend that it no longer provides an effective understanding of the political system. Two important alternative organising perspectives have emerged in recent years: the 'differentiated polity model' proposed by Rod Rhodes, and the 'asymmetric power model' developed by David Marsh, David Richards, and Martin Smith. Both are critical of the Westminster model, but they draw different conclusions about the extent of change brought about by the move from government to governance and about where power is located within the British political system. These models will be examined in turn.

The hollowing out of the state

Professor Rod Rhodes argues that the autonomy of Britain's central government has been eroded significantly, its functions being dispersed to supranational bodies, subnational institutions, and a large number of specialist agencies (see, for example, his 'The Hollowing Out of the State', *Political Quarterly*, Vol. 63, No. 1, 1994). Rhodes describes the UK state as a 'differentiated polity', the main features of which are as follows:

1. The hierarchical form of government that was a central factor of the Westminster model has been replaced by a looser form of governance in which self-organising networks enjoy significant autonomy from the state. There is no 'sovereign actor' in contemporary British politics: governance is 'governing without government'.

2. The differential polity is fragmented. Even before Scottish and Welsh devolution, Rhodes had identified intergovernmental relations – interactions between interdependent government units such as central government, local authorities, the EU, and specialist agencies – as a defining feature in the era of governance. The centre does not enjoy a monopoly of power but engages in bargaining with other authoritative actors.

Power-dependence

power relations characterised by the interdependence of key political actors and the exchange of resources between them.

3. Centre–local relations are, Rhodes claims, characterised by **power-dependence** rather than command. Different tiers of government have their own resources, and their relationship is an interdependent one in which resources are exchanged.

4. The core executive is segmented, as it consists of various actors and networks which can draw upon their own resources. Central government departments try to protect their own interests and seek increased resources (money and competences). Decision-making is not the exclusive preserve of the prime minister or the cabinet; it is instead characterised by bargaining within and between networks. Power is understood in terms of resource exchange between actors who depend upon each other: the prime minister needs the support of cabinet ministers, ministers rely on advice from civil servants, and civil servants need ministers to act on behalf of their departments in the cabinet and (until 2020) the European Union.

5. Policy networks are a defining feature of the policy-making process (see Analysis 2.2). They take different forms, ranging from loose 'issue networks', whose membership fluctuates, to closed 'policy communities' which consist of small, tightly integrated groups. Policy networks set the agenda and the rules of the game by determining which actors should participate in the policy process, defining their roles and privileging certain actors over others. Power-dependence and resource exchange between public bodies and private interests are key features. With the creation of executive agencies, government departments are no longer dominant members of policy networks.

6. The state is being 'hollowed out', as functions are transferred away from the core executive – upwards to the EU (until the UK formally left in 31 January 2020), downwards to subnational bodies, and outwards to quangos and the private sector. Trends such as globalisation, further European integration, devolution, and privatisation have eroded the capacity of the state.

Rhodes argues that the hollowing out of the state has, in turn, generated a number of problems.

1. *A fragmentation of decision-making*: Services are delivered not by central or local government alone, but by a combination of public bodies, actors from the private and voluntary sectors, and specialist agencies. Effective policymaking and policy implementation requires coordination, but the absence of a single

Analysis 2.2

Policy networks

The concept of policy networks is an influential one in the study of policymaking. The policy networks perspective claims that the nature of the relationship between government and pressure groups varies across policy fields. There is no one simple model that explains policy making across all areas of public policy: power is dispersed across a large number of relatively autonomous networks in the era of governance. At one end of the policy network spectrum are issue networks, which are relatively open and contain a large number of actors (government departments, agencies, and pressure groups) which move in and out of the network as the policy focus shifts. Policy communities are located at the other end of the spectrum. These are much tighter, closed groupings containing a smaller number of actors. Government departments and 'insider' groups enjoy privileged status and have a relationship of mutual dependency (see Chapter 19).

A concern raised about the policy network approach is that it underplays the capacity of central government to steer or even control the policy process. Successive governments since 1979 have, for example, acted to open up some policy communities which were previously closed. The health policy community, for example, was dominated by the Department of Health and professional bodies such as the British Medical Association (BMA, representing general practitioners) and the royal colleges (representing consultants). The Thatcher government sought to reduce the influence of health professionals by creating a new layer of National Health Service (NHS) managers who would make policy decisions, while the Blair governments required Primary Care Trusts to consult with their local communities. The limited success of such measures in undermining the strength of the BMA is indicated by the problems faced by the Conservative–Liberal Democrat coalition when attempting to reform the NHS after 2010.

In agriculture, bodies representing the interests of food producers (farmers) enjoyed a privileged relationship with the Ministry for Agriculture Food and Fisheries (MAFF), while bodies representing consumer interests had only 'outsider' status. Following a series of food safety scares, the Blair government replaced MAFF with a new Department for the Environment, Food and Rural Affairs (DEFRA) in which consumer interests would more readily be heard, and set up a new regulatory body, the Food Standards Agency (FSA). When the coalition government proposed to abolish the Agency in 2010, critics claimed that the decision had been prompted by a powerful combination of retailers and food producers: the FSA duly survived the axe. Other observers argue that the retailers (notably the giant supermarket chains) now have far more power to influence government than the producers.

authoritative body makes this less likely. In short, central government has seen its capacity to *steer* from the centre reduced.

2. *A greater likelihood of policy disasters* (see Analysis 11.1, p. 289): Policy disasters are major failures in public policy that are attributable to serious shortcomings in the policymaking process. The number of policy disasters has increased in recent years. Some, such as the problems in the Child Support Agency, the controversy over the cost of the Millennium Dome, and the

events which led up to the 'credit crunch', are illustrative of the dangers of agencification and insufficient regulation of relationships with the private sector.

3. *A weakening of accountability*: Fragmentation has eroded lines of democratic accountability, notably the principle that ministers are accountable to Parliament for decisions or actions taken within their departments. It is not always clear whether a minister in a central government department, or the chief executive of a Next Steps executive agency, should be held accountable for policy outcomes. A prime example of the blurred lines of responsibility was the 1995 dispute between the Home Secretary Michael Howard, and the chief executive of the Prison Service Derek Lewis, over who was accountable for a series of escapes by prisoners. Lewis was sacked, despite the objections of Howard's own ministerial colleague, Ann Widdecombe. This much-publicised altercation arose at a relatively early stage in the process, while ministers and unelected public servants were still learning to adapt to the new arrangements; however, the underlying problem has not gone away. The government distinguishes between *policy*, for which the minister is accountable, and *operation* (or management), where responsibility has been delegated to agency chief executives. Yet the distinction between accountability and responsibility is ambiguous and challenges Parliament's status as the institution primarily responsible for scrutinising and legitimising policy.

Traditional forms of accountability have been undermined, but new forms have emerged. Centrally determined performance targets, systems of audit and regulation, and the production of league tables are used to hold semi-autonomous agencies accountable for their record in delivering public goods. Here an agency is no longer accountable simply to an institution further up the policymaking hierarchy, but upwards to ministers, outwards to groups within the policy network, and (in theory at least) downwards to consumers of public services.

A reconstituted state

The impact of governance and claims that the state has been 'hollowed out' are disputed. David Marsh, David Richards, and Martin Smith (see, for example, their 'Unequal Plurality: Towards an Asymmetric Power Model of British Politics', *Government and Opposition*, Vol. 38, No. 3, 2003) accept that governance has undermined the utility of the Westminster model, but argue that the state has been reconstituted rather than fundamentally transformed. They dispute Rhodes's estimation of the extent to which new forms of governance have undermined the capacity of the centre. Their 'asymmetric power model' asserts that the relationship between central government and other actors is asymmetric, as the former retains a unique set of resources (for example, the state bureaucracy, authority, and substantial tax-raising powers). Its main features are as follows:

1. Power is 'asymmetric'. Resources have shifted away from the core executive, but governance has not removed 'government' from the process of governing. The core executive may rely on networks of actors (e.g. executive agencies, quangos, regulatory bodies) in the delivery of public policy, but they, in turn, rely on central government, which sets the boundaries of their authority, provides resources, and gives them legitimacy.
2. The core executive is segmented, but it remains the dominant actor within the political system. Actors in the core executive still play a dominant role in policymaking, the resources they possess being much greater than those of other actors. Central government has, for example, been able to restructure local government and curtail its discretionary powers (see Chapter 11). Government departments are also the most significant actors in policy networks because they have the greatest

resources; the most influential interest groups are those with close relationships with government departments. The core executive is not a unified body, but within it the prime minister enjoys significant resource advantages (for example, patronage, authority, party leadership), although no prime minister can possibly exert a monopoly over decision-making.

3. Power involves the exchange of resources, but this is based on patterns of dependence. The strength of the core executive and its control of resources (for example, money, authority, legitimacy) mean that government is well positioned to achieve its objectives in processes of exchange with other actors.

4. Key elements of the British political tradition remain intact, notably a Whitehall culture that 'government knows best'. Ministers and civil servants continue to view British politics in terms of parliamentary sovereignty, and resist attempts to open their world to greater scrutiny even when these are backed by legislation (such as the Freedom of Information Act). Citizens are still subject to considerable state power, as seen, for example, in recent restrictions upon civil liberties.

5. Unequal access to the political process remains a feature of the British political system. Certain groups – the poor people, women, and ethnic minorities – continue to suffer disadvantages and discrimination. They are denied effective access to power and are losers in the free market economy.

Developments under the Blair and Brown governments added weight to claims that central government has sought to reassert its position in response to the dispersal of resources to other actors. In particular, Blair extended Number 10's control over public policy by promoting 'joined-up government' and setting targets for policy implementation and service delivery (see Chapter 7). Special government units and taskforces were established to promote coordination in cross-cutting policy areas populated by an array of networks. When Gordon Brown was chancellor between 1997 and 2007, the Treasury enhanced its coordinating role through the Comprehensive Spending Review process and use of Public Service Agreements. The scope of central influence expanded in some respects, mainly through the extension of regulatory regimes. The coalition government took office at a time of grave economic difficulty, which prompted a drive to curb central bureaucracy. However, initiatives generated by the centre (such as the 'target culture') were still in evidence in 2015, despite a sharp fall in civil service staff numbers (from 484,000 in 2010, to a little over 400,000 five years later) (Photo 2.1).

PHOTO 2.1 Customers withdraw savings from Northern Rock in September 2008, prior to its nationalisation (© Cate Gillon/Getty Images).

Government intervention in the economy increased markedly in response to the 'credit crunch' which began in 2007. However, New Labour had no desire to breathe new life into the concept of public ownership. Although responsibility for railway infrastructure was brought back under government control and the Northern Rock bank was nationalised in 2008, these measures were taken because there seemed to be no viable alternatives. Prior to this, New Labour governments had designed policies with the declared aim of promoting economic competitiveness as well as social justice, but the level of intervention was modest compared to the habitual practice of early post-war governments. There were also some significant government interventions by Boris Johnson's Conservative government in 2019 and 2002, with both Northern Rail and the Probation Service returned to public ownership due to serious failings or problems in private hands. The most obvious and far-reaching intervention in the economy, though, occurred during the spring and summer of 2020, when the Johnson government ordered most shops, pubs, restaurants, leisure centres, garden centres, live music venues, and sports stadiums to close – along with universities and many schools – in order to slow down the spread of the coronavirus (COVID-19). Moreover, with millions of employees affected by these government-enforced closures, and often unable to continue working, the Treasury assumed responsibility for covering 80 per cent of their wages or salaries for several months, which massively increased government borrowing. This degree of state intervention and control, and the sheer scale of government borrowing to fund the 'lost' earnings for so many temporarily laid-off workers, was unprecedented in modern times, and certainly totally at odds with the ideological stance of a Conservative government formally committed to free-market economics (neoliberalism), 'rolling back the State' and minimising public (government) debt – particularly after a decade of austerity to 'balance the books' financially.

Yet the Johnson government, and particularly the Treasury, were compelled to massively intervene in the economy and borrow tens of billions of pounds, due to the sheer scale and urgency of the problems caused by the COVID-19 global pandemic. As with response to the 2007–08 'credit crunch', there was no alternative. Or, rather, the alternative was politically and socially unacceptable, in terms of the disastrous consequences of doing nothing: unprecedented bankruptcies, record redundancies, soaring unemployment, repossessions (of homes) and evictions (for non-payment of rent), and a massive slump in consumer spending – in short, possible total economic collapse. Sheer economic imperative transcended political ideology and short-term crisis management superseded long-term government strategy.

Approaches to British politics

This section explores some of the main approaches to the study of British politics and key theoretical tools employed by political scientists. It highlights three of the most influential approaches in contemporary British political science – rational choice theory, institutionalism, and interpretive approaches – providing a brief overview of each and examples of their application in the British context.

Rational choice theory

The focus of rational choice theory is individuals and their actions, its basic premise being that individuals are 'rational' actors who weigh up the costs and benefits of particular actions and choose the ones which will maximise their own interests – in other words, they are 'utility maximisers'. It assumes that individuals have clear preferences, that they rank these preferences in a consistent way – that is, if they prefer option *a* to option b, and option *b* to option c, then they will choose option *a* over option *c* – and that they possess adequate information and time to make an informed choice. Social phenomena are thus the products of the conscious choices made by individuals.

Applied to the political realm, rational choice theory views voters, politicians, and civil servants as self-interested actors. In *An Economic Theory of Democracy* (New York: Harper and Row, 1957), Anthony Downs expounded his influential rational choice theory of party competition and elections. His 'spatial' theory of party competition states that parties are vote maximisers which seek to occupy the political space inhabited by the 'median' voter, whose political outlook is located at the very centre of the left–right ideological axis. Electors vote 'rationally' for the party closest to them in political space. Downsian theory thus predicts that, in a two-party system, the government and main opposition party will converge on the 'centre ground'. To the rational choice analyst, this explains why Labour suffered a heavy electoral defeat in 1983 when it moved to the left and vacated a political space which was then occupied by the newly formed Social Democratic Party (SDP). Only when New Labour moved back towards the median voter in the centre ground (under Tony Blair after 1994) could it return to office.

Despite this supporting evidence, however, there are a number of problems with the Downsian approach. It assumes, for example, that parties can change their policies and position relatively painlessly, that politicians are motivated by winning elections rather than by ideology, that political space is one-dimensional (that is, only the left–right axis is significant), and, above all, that voters really make 'rational' decisions on the basis of declared party policy. All of these presuppositions are open to dispute (see Case study 2.1, and Chapter 16).

Free-riders

individuals who enjoy the benefits of collective action without contributing to it.

Another important insight provided by rational choice theory concerns collective action and the problem of '**free-riders**'. Mancur Olson's *The Logic of Collective Action* (Cambridge, MA: Harvard University Press, 1965) noted that collective action is sometimes required in order to achieve a common goal, but it may not be in anybody's individual interest to bear the costs involved when the rewards will be available to all. The logical course of action for the individual will be to 'free ride', that is, to avoid contributing to a collective endeavour from which he or she will nonetheless benefit. To overcome this problem, 'sectional' interest groups pursuing a collective good (for example, trade unions) must offer additional incentives to members, or threaten non-members with sanctions such as ostracism in the workplace. Climate change is a more dramatic example: action to cut carbon emissions may be necessary to limit global warming, but for the individual (and for individual states), the costs involved in reducing their carbon footprint may be high, particularly when one considers the minimal impact of a single individual's actions on a global problem. Governments thus encourage recycling and curbs on pollution by offering incentives and/or penalising those individuals and organisations which ignore the rules. However, they find it harder to impose viable sanctions on states which pay no

Were the Conservatives irrational?

Downsian theory suggests that the Conservative Party should have responded to its general election defeat in 1997 by moving to the centre ground, where the 'median voter' was located. But the popular view is that the Conservatives instead positioned themselves significantly to the right of Labour and campaigned on traditional right-wing issues that appealed to their 'core' vote, such as law and order, immigration, opposition to further European integration, and support for tax cuts. This approach failed to dent Labour's huge majority in 2001, and fared little better in 2005. Why, then, did the Conservatives pursue such a flawed electoral strategy?

Pippa Norris and Joni Lovenduski claim that rational politicians seek to implant themselves within a 'zone of acquiescence' where the electorate is in accord with their policies, but at the 2001 general election, the Conservatives positioned themselves to the right of this. This occurred because of 'selective perception' among Conservative politicians, many of whom were to the right of voters on Europe and tax. The strength of their personal convictions encouraged them to mistake the prevailing policy mood, and to believe that the 'core' Conservative supporter (let alone the 'median' voter) was more right-wing than was the case. Thus, they failed to respond to changes in public opinion, which were apparent to observers who were not afflicted by the same 'selective perception'.

An alternative interpretation is offered by Jane Green. Rather than utilising the Downsian model of spatial competition, she employs an 'issue ownership' model, which suggests that parties should concentrate on those issues on which they are seen as competent by the electorate and seek to minimise the impact of those issues on which the rival party is favoured. From this perspective, it was perfectly rational for the Conservatives to try to raise the salience of 'their' issues, and try to depress the salience of those issues on which Labour enjoyed an advantage – not least because party strategists recognised that they were in any case likely to lose the 2001 and 2005 elections. Thus, in 2005, Michael Howard tried to steer the agenda of public debate towards issues such as immigration, on which voters preferred the Conservative position; to quash Labour's advantage on issues like health by focusing on government failings (for example, an increase in hospital-acquired infections); and to depress turnout among Labour voters by repeating the message that Blair could not be trusted.

Green also recognises that the Conservatives began their move towards the centre ground *before* David Cameron became party leader. In both the 2001 and 2005 general elections, they moved leftwards along the left–right economic axis, pledging to match Labour's public spending commitments and promising only limited, targeted tax cuts. This message did not, however, filter through to an electorate which continued to perceive the Conservatives as 'out of touch', and to trust Labour more on the economy and public services. Accordingly, a central feature of Cameron's leadership before the 2010 general election was his effort to 'decontaminate the brand' by changing the image of the Conservative Party, focusing on new issues (for example, the environment) and competing with Labour on its own favoured terrain (such as health). The strategy had to be adapted as the 2010 general election approached and Britain's economic problems dominated the agenda. However, it can be argued that Cameron's attempts to refurbish his party's image ensured that his tough line on spending cuts, though controversial, was not widely equated as a return to the days when the Conservatives were regarded as a 'nasty' party.

See: P. Norris and J. Lovenduski, 'Why Parties Fail to Learn: Electoral Defeat, Selective Perception and British Party Politics', *Party Politics*, Vol. 10, No. 1 (2004), pp. 85–104; J. Green, 'Conservative Party Rationality: Learning the Lessons from the Last Election for the Next', *Journal of Elections, Public Opinion and Parties*, Vol. 15, No. 1 (2005), pp. 111–27; and J. Green, 'When Voters and Parties Agree: Valence Issues and Party Competition', *Political Studies*, Vol. 55, No. 3 (2007), pp. 629–55.

heed to international agreements in the hope that pollution from their home-based industries will somehow be 'offset' by the efforts of more environmentally conscious countries.

A final example concerns the motives of civil servants. Rational choice theory suggests that bureaucrats are not motivated by a 'public service' ethos, as they habitually claim when they justify their practices. Rather, they seek to promote their own interests by securing additional resources (i.e. power and money) for their departments. Accordingly, they will seek to obstruct government proposals that threaten to reduce their influence or funding. In *Democracy, Bureaucracy and Public Choice* (London: Longman, 1991), Patrick Dunleavy reworked this perspective by arguing that civil servants are 'bureau shapers' who try to protect those aspects of their work that they find most rewarding.

Rational choice theory has made an important contribution to the understanding of British politics. But it has a number of significant problems. Its assumption that individuals are motivated by self-interest denies the existence of other plausible motivations for action, notably altruism and/or political principles. Some variants of rational choice theory recognise that the information available to individuals can never be perfect: for example, the 'valence' approach to voting behaviour argues that voters use their perceptions of party leaders as shortcuts when deciding how to vote because obtaining additional information may be unduly time-consuming (see Analysis 18.2, and Chapter 18). Valence voting can even be characterised as a 'rational' way of choosing one party over another, which avoids the necessity of extending one's 'rational' faculties to an 'irrational' extent! This is just a convoluted way of expressing the obvious point that 'rationality', in politics as elsewhere, is in the eye of the beholder rather than something that can be determined objectively. Critics also suggest that rational choice theory is wrong to treat social phenomena as outcomes of choices made by individuals. Alternative perspectives argue that individuals are located within social structures which shape their behaviour – for example, sociological accounts of voting behaviour claim that social class determines how people vote. Institutions, social norms, and ideologies all influence individual behaviour in the political realm.

Institutionalism

Institutions have long been central to the study of politics in Britain. The approach associated with the Westminster model was primarily concerned with formal institutions, particularly the constitution and law, offering detailed descriptions coupled with a normative approach that presented the British system as a paragon of representative and responsible democratic government. This narrow focus on formal institutions is now referred to as the 'old institutionalism'. It contrasts with the 'new institutionalism' which emerged in the 1960s, with efforts to 'bring the state back in' to political analysis by shifting the focus away from the individual to the state and its institutions. The new institutionalism defined institutions more broadly, to encompass not just formal laws and procedures but also informal practices, procedures, and norms. Institutions are not defined by the aggregated interests of the individuals that work within them, but are depicted as developing their own customs and norms over time.

Although new institutionalists share a belief that institutions matter, they are not a unified 'school'. Four variants can be identified. Historical institutionalism asserts that formal rules and procedures, and informal practices and norms ('the way things should be done') developed in the past, continue to be followed within an institution thereafter. Its key concept is **path dependency**: the historical path taken by an institution or state will invariably lead to actions of a similar type being taken in future occasions. Thus, for example, Whitehall norms have persisted despite the twin challenges of EU membership and devolution. In 'The Europeanization of UK Central Government: From Quiet Revolution to Explicit Step-Change?' (*Public Administration*, Vol. 83, No. 4, 2005), Simon Bulmer and Martin Burch argue that the adaptation of UK central government to EU membership occurred gradually and relatively smoothly, with many of Whitehall's traditional ways of operating evolving, rather than being transformed. But the Blair government brought about a 'step change' by introducing new structures and processes in an attempt to forge a more proactive European policy. Similarly, relations between the UK government and the devolved administrations in Scotland and Wales did not initially cause major tensions, in part because the ethos of the civil service and its talent for pragmatic adaptation belied the assumptions of rational choice theory by persisting through these radical changes.

Sociological institutionalism focuses on the culture, values, and shared understandings that institutions develop and which inform the choices made by individuals within them. A government department may thus develop its own enduring ethos or world view. Traditionally, for example, the UK Foreign and Commonwealth Office (FCO) has been more pro-European than the Ministry of Defence; almost invariably, the Treasury seeks to limit public spending, regardless of the party in office. Rational choice institutionalism claims that the choices made by political actors are constrained by institutional rules ('bounded rationality'), and that institutions foster decisions and actions to promote their own interests. Finally, constructivist institutionalism focuses on the dynamic role of ideas, claiming that the other variants of institutionalism are too 'static' to offer convincing explanations of change within institutions.

Path dependency

the tendency of initial decisions and institutional frameworks which then determine subsequent choices.

Interpretive approaches

Interpretive approaches examine the beliefs, ideas, and meanings that shape institutions and actions. They claim that we cannot understand human activity unless we appreciate how people interpret the world in which they operate – for example, we can only understand how ministers and civil servants act when we truly understand how they perceive their world. People act on their beliefs, but we cannot understand such beliefs simply by observing their social status or by making universal assumptions, such as individuals being 'self-interested'. Political actors draw on particular traditions (or narratives) which shape their interpretation of the world. Thus, for example, socialists viewed Tony Blair's New Labour project as a betrayal of the party's social democratic traditions, whereas many neoliberals welcomed it as an acceptance of the realities of globalisation. Ideas matter, and they play an important role in bringing about political change.

The most significant interpretive approach to British politics is that provided by Mark Bevir and Rod Rhodes in *Governance Stories* (London: Routledge, 2005). The authors examine the move from the Westminster model towards governance through an analysis of different British political traditions – Tory, Whig, liberal, and socialist. Each offers a different narrative on the development of the British state. The Tory view of the British political history is one of state authority, the Whig narrative is one of gradual change, the liberal one espouses limited government, and the socialist view welcomes the development of the bureaucratic state. The Tory perspective on governance focuses on the need to restore intermediate institutions, the Whig position promotes evolutionary reform, and the 'socialist' (Labour) view focuses on joined-up government and the enabling state. This interpretive approach underpins Rhodes's differentiated polity model outlined earlier in the chapter.

Synthesis or antithesis?

Adherents of each of these three approaches are often highly critical of rival interpretations, denying their usefulness as explanatory theories. The core tenets of the approaches differ sharply: individuals are the focal point for rational choice theories, institutionalism focuses on structures, and the interpretive approach emphasises ideas. These, in turn, lead to alternative explanations of political phenomena. Rational choice theories stress the significance of *agency* (that is, the important role played by individuals, such as the prime minister), institutionalism focuses on the significance of *structures* (the formal rules and informal practices shaping decision-making within the core executive), and interpretive approaches emphasise the significance of *beliefs* (how actors within the core executive view their world).

Despite the obvious contrasts in these approaches, there have been notable attempts to synthesise their key elements. For rational choice institutionalism, for example, institutions cannot make decisions themselves, and, although institutional rules are important, it is up to individuals whether or not to follow them. In his work on Thatcherism (see 'Explaining "Thatcherite" Policies: Beyond Unidimensional Explanation', *Political Studies*, Vol. 43, No. 4, 1995), David Marsh rejected partial explanations – Thatcherism as nothing more than Thatcher's conviction politics, New Right ideology, or a response to the economic crisis of the 1970s. Instead, an evolutionary approach was required that interprets change as the result of political actors developing strategies in response to changes in the domestic and international environment.

Research methods

the techniques used by researchers to gather and analyse evidence.

Research methods

A range of **research methods** are employed in the study of British politics. The final section of this chapter provides a brief overview of documentary analysis, interviews, and questionnaires which are used most frequently by academics, and which undergraduate students may also use when undertaking their own research projects and dissertations. Research methods in the social sciences fall into two main categories: *quantitative* and *qualitative*. Quantitative research involves the gathering and analysis of numerical data. By studying variables in a large number of cases, researchers look for relationships from which they can draw inferences about political behaviour. Data-gathering techniques include large-scale surveys in which respondents answer standardised questions. Once the raw information has been obtained, it should be coded and examined, using statistical packages and techniques that look for the influence of a number of factors on the phenomenon being studied.

Surveys of the whole population of the subject group being researched may be possible in some cases (for example, the voting records of all MPs). In most cases, such as in the study of voting behaviour, a representative sample of the population being studied is identified, allowing wider conclusions to be drawn. Polling organisations seek responses to standardised questions through face-to-face interviews, telephone interviews, or online surveys. Questionnaires are frequently used in academic research on British politics, for example, in surveys of party members, candidates, and MPs. The quality of the results will depend crucially on the nature of the questions. These should be unambiguous and follow a logical sequence; a mixture of closed questions (inviting the respondent to select only from a given list of options) and open-ended questions (allowing the respondent to choose anything they wish) may be used. Loaded questions will produce distorted data – the questions 'Do you support joining the euro at some point?' and 'Are you willing to give up the pound?' may produce very different responses. The response rate is also crucial: a low response rate may mean that a representative sample has not been obtained. Postal questionnaires have a lower response rate than face-to-face interviews, and usually require follow-up reminders. Even then, some politicians routinely refuse to take part, and it is not unknown for party officials to advise MPs to ignore surveys conducted by social scientists. Data from commercial polling bodies may be available on their websites, but the most detailed data on voting behaviour are available from the British Election Study (www.essex.ac.bes/), a long-running academic study on voting in British general elections.

Qualitative research seeks a deeper understanding of the nature and meaning of the subject matter, through techniques such as documentary analysis and interviewing. There are two kinds of documentary evidence: primary sources and secondary sources (although the boundaries between the two are increasingly blurred). Secondary sources are interpretations of evidence produced by others, including academic texts, journal articles, and the like. Primary sources are those produced by authoritative sources, often at the time of the event that is being studied. They include official publications from government, political parties, and others; speeches; memoirs, and diaries produced by politicians; official election results; party political broadcasts; and the work of well-informed journalists. A large number of official publications should readily be available to students of contemporary British politics in university libraries and online. A study of recent reforms of the House of Lords might, for example, look at current legislation, government White Papers and Green Papers, the report of the Wakeham Commission (published in 2000), ministerial statements, parliamentary debates and votes (reported in *Hansard*), the reports and evidence presented to parliamentary committees, and the memoirs or diaries of former ministers (e.g. Tony Blair and Robin Cook). These can be supplemented by reports from independent researchers (e.g. the Constitution Unit based in University College London), the proposals of other political parties, and newspaper reports and commentaries (Photo 2.2).

Primary source material from the UK government, including cabinet minutes and papers, is deposited in the UK National Archives and is normally subject to the standard 30-year closure period, introduced in 1958. The Freedom of Information Act (2000) has, however, brought some

PHOTO 2.2 Government documents at the National Archives in Kew are normally closed for 30 years (© Scott Barbour/Getty Images).

government documents to light far earlier than this, and the rules are being gradually relaxed. In 2005, the Treasury released its internal assessments of sterling's enforced exit from the ERM in 1992. Other archives, such as that of the Labour Party in Manchester's People's History Museum, operate a ten-year closure period. Archival research requires careful planning, such as catalogue searches and requests for access to documents of interest in advance of a visit. The National Archives catalogue is available online, but in most cases, the documents can only be read (and appreciated) in full at Kew.

Political memoirs and diaries provide information about major events that may be known only to privileged insiders, such as government ministers, long before the archives are opened to the public. The diaries of the late Labour Cabinet Minister (and former politics academic) Richard Crossman caused a publishing sensation in the 1970s when they were serialised in the *Sunday Times* without receiving clearance from the Cabinet Secretary. The diaries provided extensive first-hand accounts of cabinet discussions and Crossman's personal reflections. Diaries and auto-biographical memoirs also give us a sense of the prevailing mood of the time and insights into the personalities of key individuals, in sharp contrast to the carefully edited (if not distorted) cabinet minutes. Diaries, in particular, have a sense of immediacy: they are written at or near the time that the events took place, and the opinions contained within them are not shaped by hindsight. However, there are also pitfalls. There may be doubts about their reliability – politicians may use their memoirs as a vehicle for self-justification, presenting an inflated account of their importance and achievements. They may not fully recall events that occurred years before. Edward Heath's memoirs were published some 25 years after he left Downing Street, and the author was assisted by a team of researchers who found it difficult to challenge Heath's own recollections even when they confronted him with documentary evidence. The memoirs of John Major and Norman Lamont offer valuable insights of the events of 'Black Wednesday', but they also differ in their recollection of key facts. Alastair Campbell's first volume of diaries (*The Blair Years*, 2007) was heavily edited prior to publication, removing passages dealing with disputes between Tony Blair and Gordon Brown. The full diaries appeared in four volumes between 2010 and 2012 (when New Labour was no longer in office).

Elite interviews are widely used by political researchers looking for insights into the roles, actions, beliefs, and perceptions of ministers, MPs, civil servants, party officials, and others. They often have a semi-structured format in which the interviewer works from a prepared list of questions covering the major topics they wish to discuss, but still allows scope for supplementary

Analysis 2.3

Political biographies

Political scientists tend to be rather dismissive of biographies of political figures, viewing them as light entertainment rather than an important scholarly resource. There may be some good reasons for this. Biographies are secondary rather than primary sources. They focus on individuals rather than processes: an account of one individual's role in a major policy decision may be of interest, but for reasons of space, even scrupulous biographers are unlikely to provide much detail about the policymaking process. The role of biographers may also be open to question. Were they intent on producing a favourable or unduly critical account? The level of access granted to the biographer is also relevant. The author of an unauthorised biography may be denied access to crucial documents and key players. If colleagues are willing to cooperate, this may be because they want to tell a one-sided story. A rash of premature biographies, published when the politician in question has reached high office but before the most significant aspects of their political life can be assessed, has also tended to devalue the genre.

We should not, however, dismiss political biographies entirely because of the failings of the weakest examples. The best biographies shed new light on individuals and events. This is particularly true of authorised biographies of politicians who have left the political limelight or died, and which draw upon private sources of information (for example, political papers, correspondence, diaries) and an array of cooperative interviewees. Biographies of contemporary figures need not be superficial affairs. Charles Moore's authorised biography of Margaret Thatcher, which benefitted from access to her private papers, began to be published after her death in 2013. While the first volume was very well received, Moore was a well-known admirer of Mrs Thatcher, and his study is best read alongside existing 'unofficial' portraits, such as John Campbell's *Margaret Thatcher: The Grocer's Daughter* (London: Pimlico, 2001) and *Margaret Thatcher: The Iron Lady* (London: Vintage, 2007), which provide valuable insights into her character and leadership, and E.H.H. Green's *Thatcher* (London: Hodder Arnold, 2006), which eschews traditional biography in favour of a rigorous study of her core values based on material from the Thatcher Archive at Churchill College, Cambridge.

In 2015, the former Conservative Treasurer Lord Ashcroft published an unauthorised biography of Prime Minister David Cameron (co-written by the experienced journalist Isabel Oakeshott). It was well known that Ashcroft had no great affection for Cameron, and the value of the book to students of British politics seemed to be reduced by salacious allegations about the latter's exploits at Oxford University. However, apart from his own considerable personal observation of Cameron, Ashcroft was able to interview many of his close acquaintances, and his book was clearly much more than an attempt to settle old scores. Students of politics should always consult such sources, even if only to satisfy themselves that they do not contain much of value.

See: M. Garnett, 'Banality in Politics: Margaret Thatcher and the Biographers', *Political Studies Review*, Vol. 5, No. 2 (2007), pp. 172–81.

questions and for the interviewee to introduce other relevant material. The dynamics of inter-views can vary greatly: some interviewees who possess privileged information prove reluctant to divulge much of interest, whereas others may provide unexpected revelations which are difficult to verify. A researcher may have to conduct some 20 or more interviews to achieve a rounded picture, but gaining access to senior political figures can be close to impossible.

Focus groups are now commonly used by polling organisations and political parties. A small group of individuals is carefully selected to take part in a planned discussion about an area of in-terest. Interaction between members of the group is a core feature, and topics can be explored in greater depth. But representativeness is not possible in small groups, so reputable research projects that use focus groups tend also to conduct larger surveys.

Sharp distinctions are often drawn between quantitative and qualitative methods. Research-ers using quantitative methods aim to find *causal* explanations (for example, the effect of social class on voting behaviour) and adopt a *deductive* approach – that is, using a theory (e.g. class voting) to generate a hypothesis (such as 'working class voters will support the Labour Party'), which can then be tested empirically. Large amounts of data are gathered and examined using statistical techniques. Those employing qualitative methods often adopt an *inductive* approach, using observations gleaned through documentary analysis or interviews to generate inter-pretations of the political world. In practice, political research may utilise a mix of qualita-tive and quantitative methods, for example, by using interviews or focus groups to generate questions for a large-scale survey. Material produced from documentary analysis and inter-views may also be coded to allow for statistical analysis. The Comparative Manifestos Project (https://manifestoproject.wzb.eu/), for example, codes statements found in party manifestos in order to determine the location of parties on the political spectrum. Discourse analysis traces continuities and change in the use of language, and may employ computer software packages to study, for example, thousands of words from speeches made by politicians.

Conclusion and summary

For much of the twentieth century, most people who studied the British political system did so within the confines of the organising perspective known as the Westminster model. But the model has come under serious strain in recent years, and it no longer offers the optimal explanatory framework for understanding British politics. However, claims that the British state has been 'hollowed out', and the autonomy of central government all but ended, are ex-aggerated. The centre has sought both to defend its policymaking autonomy and to enhance its capacity to coordinate the delivery of public goods.

The reforms of the Blair and Brown governments altered some of the British constitution's defining features, and the shift from a hierarchical model of government to looser networks of governance poses a significant challenge to the Westminster model's explanatory power. By its very nature, the coalition government established in 2010 increased the pressure on traditional views of British politics. Yet the Westminster model remains an influential one. The building blocks of the Westminster model, such as parliamentary sovereignty, the simple plurality system, and the two-party system, have come under strain but have not collapsed completely or been abandoned entirely by political elites at Westminster and Whitehall, who continue to view their world through the prism of the Westminster model. Meanwhile, political scientists will continue to adopt a variety of approaches, offering students a range of valuable insights, which can inform their own explorations of the changing British scene.

Further reading

For material on the Westminster model, see the Further reading section of Chapter 1. P. Dunleavy, 'The Westminster Model and the Distinctiveness of British Politics', in P. Dunleavy, R. Heffernan, P. Cowley, and C. Hay (eds.), *Developments in British Politics 8* (London: Palgrave, 2006), examines different perspectives on its utility. D. Richards, 'Challenges to the Westminster Model', *Politics Review*, Vol. 17, No. 3 (2008), pp. 14–17, provides a brief introduction to the three organising perspectives discussed in this chapter.

For more recent critiques, see M. Bull, 'Whatever Happened to the Westminster Model? The 'Italianisation' of British Politics', *Democratic Audit UK*, 9 October 2019 (available at https://www.democraticaudit.com/2019/10/09/whatever-happened-to-the-westminster-model-the-italianisation-of-british-politics/), and J. Garland, 'Brexit Has Shown the Limits of Britain's Broken "Westminster Model" of Politics', *Democratic Audit UK*, 31 May 2019 (available at https://www.democraticaudit.com/2019/05/31/brexit-has-shown-the-limits-of-britains-broken-westminster-model-of-politics/).

The differentiated polity model is developed in R. Rhodes, *Understanding Governance: Policy Networks, Governance, Reflexivity and Accountability* (Buckingham: Open University Press, 1997), and R. Rhodes, 'The New Governance: Governing without Government', *Political Studies*, Vol. 44, No. 4 (1996), pp. 652–67. R. Rhodes, 'The Hollowing Out of the State', *Political Quarterly*, Vol. 65, No. 2 (1994), pp. 138–51, is a key article, and I. Holliday, 'Is the British State Hollowing Out?', *Political Quarterly*, Vol. 71, No. 2 (2000), pp. 167–76, an important response. D. Marsh, D. Richards, and M. Smith, 'Unequal Plurality: Towards an Asymmetric Power Model of British Politics', *Government and Opposition*, Vol. 38, No. 3 (2003), pp. 306–32, challenges Rhodes's approach. Their major works include D. Marsh, D. Richards, and M. Smith, *Changing Patterns of Governance in the United Kingdom: Reinventing Whitehall* (London: Palgrave, 2001).

Good introductions to political science theories are D. Marsh and G. Stoker, *Theory and Methods in Political Science* (London: Palgrave, 2nd edition, 2002), and its successor C. Hay, M. Lister, and D. Marsh, *The State: Theories and Issues* (London: Palgrave, 2006). On rational choice theory, see A. Hindmoor, *Rational Choice* (London: Palgrave, 2006), and I. McLean, *British Politics and Rational Choice* (Oxford: Oxford University Press, 2001). The new institutionalism is examined in P. Hall and R. Taylor, 'Political Science and the Three New Institutionalisms', *Political Studies*, Vol. 44, No. 4 (1996), pp. 936–57, and V. Lowndes, 'Varieties of New Institutionalism: A Critical Appraisal', *Public Administration*, Vol. 74, No. 2 (1996), pp. 181–97. S. Bulmer, M. Burch, C. Carter, P. Hogwood, and A. Scott, *British Devolution and European Policy-Making: Transforming Britain into Multi-Level Governance* (London: Palgrave, 2002), applies an institutional approach to major developments in the UK. On synthesising rational choice theory and institutionalism, see K. Dowding, 'The Compatibility of Behaviouralism, Rational Choice and "New Institutionalism"', *Journal of Theoretical Politics*, Vol. 6, No. 1 (1994), pp. 105–17.

The interpretive approach to British politics is set out in two books by M. Bevir and R. Rhodes, *Interpreting British Governance* (London: Routledge, 2003) and *Governance Stories* (London: Routledge, 2005). A shorter account is by M. Bevir and R. Rhodes, 'Searching for Civil Society: Changing Patterns of Governance in Britain', *Public Administration*, Vol. 81, No. 1 (2003), pp. 41–62. It is critiqued in a series of articles in *British Journal of Politics and International Relations*, Vol. 6, No. 2 (2004), and in D. Marsh, 'Competing Models of British Politics', *British Journal of Politics and International Relations*, Vol. 10, No. 2 (2008), pp. 251–68.

The best introduction to research methods is P. Burnham, K. Gilland Lutz, W. Grant, and Z. Layton-Henry, *Research Methods in Politics* (London: Palgrave, 2nd edition, 2008). L. Harrison, *Political Research: An Introduction* (London: Routledge, 2001) is also recommended. R. Pierce, *Research Methods in Politics* (London: SAGE, 2008), is more advanced but rewarding.

On memoirs, see A. Gamble 'Political Memoirs', *British Journal of Politics and International Relations*, Vol. 4, No. 1 (2002), pp. 141–51, and two reports by the House of Commons Public Administration Select Committee, *Whitehall Confidential? The Publication of Political Memoirs*, Fifth Report, 2005–06, HC 689-I, and *Mandarins Unpeeled: Memoirs and Commentary by Former Ministers and Civil Servants*, HC 664,

2008. For advice on elite interviewing, see D. Lilleker, 'Interviewing the Political Elite: Navigating a Potential Minefield', *Politics*, Vol. 23, No. 2 (2003), pp. 207–14, and D. Richards, 'Elite Interviewing: Approaches and Pitfalls', *Politics*, Vol. 16, No. 3 (1996), pp. 199–204.

Websites

Academic papers presented to the annual conferences of associations of political scientists discuss theories and methods in the study of British politics. They can often be accessed through the websites of the Political Studies Association and its Elections, Public Opinion and Parties specialist group (www.psa.ac.uk/spgrp/epop/epop.asp). For a range of data on UK general elections (including 2015), see www.britishelectionstudy.com. The National Archives website is www.nationalarchives.gov.uk. The Archives Hub (www.archiveshub.ac.uk/index.html) is a gateway to archival collections in UK universities. The UK Data Archive (www.data-archive.ac.uk/Introduction.asp) includes data sets from research projects funded by the Economic and Social Research Council.

Chapter 3

UK government in historical context

From Attlee to 'austerity'

Learning outcomes

After reading this chapter, you will:

- have an understanding of the main political developments in Britain since 1945, judging the relative impact of changes and continuity;
- be able to identify the most important developments in the UK's economic and foreign policy since 1945;
- appreciate the leading themes from the past which are relevant to an understanding of contemporary British politics.

Introduction

Despite the far-reaching changes in British politics since the mid-1970s, it is impossible to understand contemporary developments without some knowledge of earlier events. Even the most radical British politician still has to work through long-established institutions, which have developed distinctive practices and attitudes over the years. Also, memories of the past have been crucial factors in shaping the most important political projects of recent years. Thus, for example, 'Thatcherism' was a conscious reaction against the trend of previous post-war policies. In turn, the legacy of the Thatcher government (1979–90) is still warmly debated within and between the main UK parties.

Britain is very different from the country that emerged, badly bruised though unbeaten, from World War II. However, the economic and social reforms of the 1945–51 Labour government established a general policy framework which was accepted by most politicians until the mid-1970s, and remains clearly discernable in a variety of policy areas. For this reason, the present chapter will use the traditional timeframe in order to explain the elements of change and continuity in British politics, beginning with the 1945 election and ending with the return of a majority Conservative government in 2015. Developments since that time are covered in detail elsewhere in the book.

The post-war 'consensus'

The 1945 general election resulted in a landslide victory for the Labour Party, led by Clement Attlee. The result was seen as a judgement on the record of inter-war governments, most of which had been dominated by the Conservatives. There had been two Labour governments between the wars, but in neither case did the party enjoy an overall majority in the House of Commons, and between them, the stints in office lasted little more than three years. With a majority of almost 150 after the 1945 election, and backed by a widespread feeling that previous governments had failed the country, Labour finally had the chance to put its ideals into practice.

Nationalisation
the transfer of private assets into public ownership, often as public corporations.

The Attlee government is associated above all with **nationalisation** and the welfare state. Under the first policy, several key industries were brought under public ownership: coal (1946), electricity (1947), gas, railways and canals (1948), and iron and steel (1949). The Bank of England was also nationalised in 1946. Many supporters – and critics – regarded these measures as early steps towards the implementation of a fully fledged socialist programme. However, although the *scale* of Labour's programme was a radical break from the past, nationalisation itself was not new. The BBC and the London Passenger Transport Board had been set up as public corporations between the wars, and the distribution (rather than generation) of electricity was entrusted to a government board in 1926. Also, coal and the railways had been struggling badly in private hands before World War II; despite this, the previous owners were generously compensated when these industries were taken over by the state. Generally speaking, the nationalised concerns were seen either as natural monopolies, 'public utilities' whose survival was essential to the country, or both. Iron and steel nationalisation was by far the most controversial measure, and this sector was returned to private hands by the Churchill government in 1953.

The Attlee government also pursued a radical programme of social reform. It introduced Family Allowances (1945), compulsory National Insurance (1946), and the National Health Service (NHS, 1948). These policies represented a concentrated attack on the economic insecurity which had afflicted many workers between the wars. Britons were now offered assistance, when in need, and at all stages of life – literally from 'the cradle to the grave', since family allowances were payable for every child after the first one, and the National Insurance Act provided state subsidies for funerals. These measures followed the 1942 Beveridge Report on social policy, which had been accepted (with varying degrees of enthusiasm) by all three main parties. As with nationalisation, although they represented a comprehensive and ambitious package in combination, the individual policies built on previous reforms, notably those of the Liberal governments led by H.H. Asquith (1908–16). Significantly, Labour did not abolish private education or healthcare, thus ensuring that the rich still enjoyed access to a wider range of service provision in these fields. The wartime coalition led by Winston Churchill had passed another crucial piece of social legislation, the Education Act (1944), which proposed the raising of the school leaving age to 16 (though this change was delayed for nearly 30 years). It also reorganised secondary schools into a tripartite system (grammar, modern, and technical schools) whose pupils were selected via examination after passing grade 11 (Table 3.1).

TABLE 3.1 British governments, 1945–2015

Period	Party	Overall majority	Share of the vote (%)
1945–50	Labour	146	47.8
1950–51	Labour	5	46.1
1951–55	Conservative	17	48.0
1955–59	Conservative	58	49.7
1959–63	Conservative	100	49.4
1963–64	Labour	4	44.1
1966–70	Labour	96	48.7
1970–74	Conservative	30	46.5
1974	Labour	−17	38.0
1974–79	Labour	3	40.2
1979–83	Conservative	43	44.9
1983–87	Conservative	144	42.5
1987–92	Conservative	102	43.4
1992–97	Conservative	21	41.9
1997–2001	Labour	179	43.2
2001–05	Labour	167	42.0
2005–10	Labour	67	35.2
2010–15	Conservative–Liberal Democrat coalition	34 (combined seats)	59.1 (combined vote)
2015–17	Conservative	12	36.9
2017–19	Conservative	−8	42.4
2019–	Conservative	80	43.6

Note: The Labour government formed after the February 1974 general election relied on support from minority parties.

Apart from the Beveridge Report, the other key wartime development in domestic policy was the 1944 White Paper on unemployment. This document, inspired by the great liberal economist John Maynard Keynes (1883–1946), committed post-war governments to policies which promised to ensure a 'high and stable level of employment'. This was always going to be a priority for a post-war government of any colour, so long as a majority of voters retained vivid memories of the 1930s, tainted by economic depression and an official unemployment tally which had rarely dipped below two million. But the 1944 White Paper added an official imprint to a political necessity. Keynes's followers assumed that it would be possible to manage the economy in such a way that unemployment could be kept under control without causing excessive inflation. The key economic lever of **Keynesianism** was 'demand management'; taxes and interest rates could be manipulated to increase or reduce demand, depending on whether the economy was stagnant or overheating. Careful management by the state could keep unemployment and inflation relatively constant, avoiding the 'boom and bust' associated with pre-war capitalism. Confidence among the Keynesian economists was increased by the knowledge that civil service expertise had been a key factor in the organisation of Britain's successful resistance to the Nazis. This mood was summed up by the Labour MP (and subsequent cabinet minister) Douglas Jay, who wrote, in 1947, that 'the gentleman in Whitehall really does know better what is good for people than the people know themselves'.

The 'gentleman in Whitehall' would have been kept busy enough in normal times by Labour's industrial and social policies. But the Attlee government was faced with the additional task of revitalising an economy which had been ravaged by the war effort. Wartime rationing was retained (and even extended in 1946 to bread) in order to reduce domestic consumption.

Keynesianism

an economic doctrine based on the work of John Maynard Keynes, which advocates that government should intervene in the economy to manage demand.

Analysis 3.1

Consensus

In UK politics, the term 'consensus' has been used to indicate a broad agreement between the major parties on the main elements of policy, even if the parties continue to disagree about the precise way in which such policies should be implemented.

Although it is commonly accepted that such a consensus was in operation between 1945 and the mid-1970s, some scholars have strongly disputed this view. Ben Pimlott, for example, described such a consensus as 'a mirage, an illusion which rapidly fades the closer one gets to it' ('The Myth of Consensus', in L.M. Smith (ed.), *The Making of Britain: Volume 5, Echoes of Greatness*, London, Macmillan, 1988, pp. 129–42). On close inspection, it becomes evident that sharp political disagreements continued throughout the supposed period of 'consensus'. However, Pimlott's position depends on a rather exacting definition of 'consensus' – one which demands that politicians agree on policy options because of shared beliefs rather than contextual factors such as perceived electoral necessity. On Pimlott's definition, 'consensus' can never be attained *within* a single political party of any significance, let alone *between* rival groups in a liberal democracy. Furthermore, the adversarial nature of British politics encourages politicians to emphasise (if not to exaggerate) the issues of principle which distinguish them from their opponents; it could be argued, indeed, that British political culture makes it difficult for rival leaders ever to acknowledge that they agree with each other. Overall, the dispute over the applicability of the word 'consensus' should not obscure the unusual and surprising degree of policy continuity between successive governments in the first three decades after World War II.

The level of imports had to be controlled while British industry devoted most of its energies to recovering export markets, which had been lost during the war. In particular, Britain had to finance a yawning trade gap with America. Soon after the end of the war, Keynes himself negotiated a loan from the Americans, but the terms of repayment were regarded as unduly harsh. The Attlee government was desperate to avoid devaluing sterling against the dollar, since this would involve a loss of prestige at home and abroad. In September 1949, speculation against the pound made devaluation unavoidable, and the dollar value of Britain's currency was reduced by almost a third, from $4.03 to $2.80. Already the government had started relaxing its restrictions on domestic consumption, conscious that the public was becoming impatient with enforced material sacrifices. But it was too late. Labour's majority almost disappeared in the 1950 general election, largely because of continued economic 'austerity'.

The global context

The continuing relevance of 1945 is reinforced by the fact that, even almost eighty years later, many Britons had not fully absorbed the real lessons of the two world wars which made the period from 1914 to 1945 the bloodiest in human history. The country had fought throughout the two conflicts and had, on both occasions, emerged on the winning side. It was hardly surprising that many members of the public found it hard to accept that Britain had actually been one of the chief *losers* in terms of its relative global status before and after the war.

Realities were obscured by the fact that Britain still enjoyed some of the external trappings of great power status; in a phrase used rather too easily and too often in this context, it was allowed to punch above its newly reduced weight. It was made a permanent member of the United Nations Security Council, along with the United States of America (USA), the Union of Soviet Socialist Republics (USSR, also known as the Soviet Union), China, and France. It helped to found the North Atlantic Treaty Organization (NATO) in 1949, thus ensuring a continuing US military presence in Europe. In 1952, it successfully tested an atomic device, the new badge of 'great power' status; only America and the USSR had preceded it in joining the nuclear club. Optimists like Churchill could argue that Britain was uniquely placed to influence world affairs, since its geographical situation made it a part of Europe, its monarch was head of the far-flung Commonwealth, and ties of language and culture were assumed to give it a 'special relationship' with the USA (see Analysis 3.2).

However, in the post-war period none of these links was a source of unmixed satisfaction to the British. As we have seen, the Americans provided a loan, but on hard-headed terms – in keeping with the country's attitude between 1939 and December 1941 when, contrary to the notion of a 'special relationship' between the two countries, it entered World War II because of a Japanese attack (and a German declaration of hostilities) rather than out of affection for the embattled British. In 1948, Britain benefitted under the more generous Marshall Plan, designed by the Americans to promote economic reconstruction in Europe as a whole. NATO seemed

Analysis 3.2

The 'special relationship'

Since World War II, it has generally been assumed by the British political establishment, the media, and the public that the country enjoys a unique place in the affections of the American people, reflected in an unshakable diplomatic and military alliance.

However, there have always been dissenters from this positive view. During the 1960s and 1970s there were divisions over America's intervention in the Vietnam War, and in the following decade, the siting of American-controlled cruise missiles in Britain encountered widespread resistance. Since the terrorist actions of September 2001, and the subsequent 'war on terror', the nature of the 'special relationship' has become more controversial than ever.

There are many ways of interpreting the history of UK–US relations, and the following summaries represent only a small sample:

1. There is indeed a 'special relationship'. Although Britain is not America's equal in economic muscle and spends far less on defence, its armed forces are highly skilled and (relatively) well equipped. Above all, the Americans know that the British are their most reliable allies. This was proved during the course of the Cold War, and the legacy continues in a new age of terrorism. The Americans will listen to British advice because they have an identical interest in ensuring a peaceful, democratic world.

2. There is indeed a 'special relationship', but it is a friendship between thieves. Throughout the Cold War, Britain was no more than a willing stooge for the USA. Both countries had an interest in the economic exploitation of the Third World and in resisting

popular liberation movements which were unfriendly towards capitalism. Once the British Empire was wound down, America began to exploit Britain itself, using it as a glorified 'aircraft carrier' during the 1980s, when the installation of cruise missiles on British soil actually made an attack from the Soviet Union more likely. Despite the ending of the Cold War, Britain has once again become a valued partner in crime, seeking economic self-interest in places like Iraq and Libya (with distinctly mixed results).

3. Britain does have a natural affinity for America, based on culture and language. However, the relationship on both sides has been dictated by necessity rather than sentiment. During the Cold War, British dependence on America brought many unfortunate results, but the alternative scenario would have been infinitely worse. Now that the Cold War is over, the British can afford to be more selective in their support for their ally, adopting the unsentimental approach which the Americans have consistently followed – and to take a more sober look at the reality of the relationship over the years. To base one's foreign policy on unthinking support for America in all things is a (potentially very damaging) mistake.

The first attitude is associated with the Conservative Party, but was followed by Tony Blair between 1997 and 2007; the second is fairly common within 'Old Labour', but is more typical of Marxists who may or may not support Labour. The third would probably be endorsed by a majority of academic observers, and may be growing more common in Britain since the 2003 Iraq War. The 'Brexit' vote of 2016, followed within months by the election of the controversial Donald Trump as US president, has increased the complexity of the relationship, even if British governments since 2016 have tried to pretend otherwise.

an essential bulwark against the military power of the USSR, which blockaded West Berlin in 1948, having previously inspired a Communist coup in Czechoslovakia. But American friendship continued to come at a price. Britain was expected to maintain a large peacetime army: even three years after the end of war in Europe, its strength was still one million, and a system of compulsory peacetime national service was introduced. Britain contributed to the US-led Korean War of 1950–53, involving expenditure which forced the Attlee government to impose charges on false teeth and spectacles previously supplied free by the NHS. This move provoked the resignation from the government of Aneurin Bevan (1897–1960), the founder of the NHS.

In this crucial respect, the post-war 'consensus' was shaped not by 'socialism' (see Chapter 16), but by the anti-socialist America. The Attlee government was a committed participant in the Cold War against the USSR, but it was very much a junior partner. The message conveyed by America's economic dealings with Britain was echoed in the passage by the US Congress of the McMahon Act (1946) which prevented any cooperation on nuclear technology with other countries. Britain was not exempted from these terms until 1958, despite the fact that it had shared its own knowledge freely with America during the war.

The most important reason for American ambivalence about Britain was its empire. After all, the USA was at one time a British colony and celebrates its victorious War of Independence on 4 July every year (although it is unlikely that many Britons realise that these festivities are directed against them). If Churchill had remained prime minister, there could have been a serious divergence on this subject immediately after the war, because he had a strong romantic attachment to the British Empire and had declared his intention to preserve it. But Labour was far more willing to accelerate the dismantling of the Empire, particularly in countries which showed unmistakable symptoms of resistance or which were of limited economic or strategic value. Thus, India and Pakistan were granted independence in 1947, followed by Burma (now Myanmar) and Ceylon (later Sri Lanka) in 1948. In the same year, British troops left Palestine, which Britain had administered under an international mandate since 1922.

The Empire was gradually being transformed into a loose association of self-governing states known as the Commonwealth (see Case study 3.1). But it still left Britain with obligations and perceived interests which made it difficult to contemplate a serious move towards close cooperation with other European states. For the same reason, the USA persistently urged Britain to focus on Europe rather than clinging to its imperial past. But in 1950, the Labour government gave a negative response to the Schuman Plan, the first step towards the later EEC and the European Union (EU: see Chapter 13). However, Britain did join the intergovernmental Council of Europe (established by the Treaty of London in 1949) and was an active promoter of its Convention on Human Rights – a document which would come back to haunt UK politicians. The experience of total war had convinced both Labour and the Conservatives that they should get involved in any European initiative that seemed likely to help avoid a future conflict – but only if there was no question of a loss of 'sovereignty'. This was an ironic attitude, since the force of events had already required Britain to surrender much of its capacity for independent action to the Americans (and in 1940, the Churchill coalition had proposed that Britain and France should be merged into a single nation).

Interlude: Conservative government, 1951–59

In hindsight, the 1950s looks like a decade of relative calm in British politics. The Conservatives won three consecutive general elections (1951, 1955, and 1959) under three different leaders (Churchill 1951–55, Sir Anthony Eden 1955–57, and Harold Macmillan 1957–63). Domestically, there was little policy change of significance. Most of the industries nationalised by Labour remained in state hands. There was some disquiet among Conservative MPs about the

---

Case study 3.1

The Commonwealth

The Commonwealth of Nations (until 1949, the *British* Commonwealth of Nations) today includes 54 states, most of which were formerly incorporated within the British Empire but which now enjoy self-government. Representing around 2.4 billion citizens (approximately a third of the global population), in theory it could be a potent force in world politics. Until the 1970s, most senior British politicians spoke fondly of the country's historic ties with its former colonies. However, UK membership of the EEC helped to loosen the bond, and positive sentiments were also undermined by public unease at the extent of immigration from certain Commonwealth countries, initially under the terms of the 1948 British Nationality Act which gave all subjects within the Empire the right to settle in Britain. For some people – like the controversial Conservative Enoch Powell (1912–98) – the Commonwealth was at best a meaningless monument to nostalgia for an imperial era which was now over. For her part, Margaret Thatcher resented the tendency of Commonwealth leaders to attack UK policy on issues like sanctions against the racist regime in South Africa – and with some justification, since the moral lectures were often delivered by ruthless dictators. The

Commonwealth has caused less embarrassment to Thatcher's successors, partly because the main sources of division have been resolved. Indeed, many supporters of 'Brexit' regard Britain's departure from the EU as an opportunity to deepen political and economic ties with Commonwealth countries (Photo 3.1).

PHOTO 3.1 For Britons, the lowering of the union flag was a poignant symbol of the end of the Empire (© Pictures Ltd./Corbis via Getty Images).

likely cost and implications of the welfare state, but the Guillebaud Report (1956) into the NHS indicated that it would be sustainable. While most people voted according to their social class (see Chapter 18), this left the 'core' support for both main parties closely matched. Thus, the parties tried to extend their appeal to less committed voters in the 'middle ground', promising to deliver the increased and painless prosperity, which, for the first time in history, most voters were now learning to expect as a key government responsibility.

The main developments were in Britain's relationship with the outside world. The Suez misadventure of 1956 underlined the fact that the UK was now subservient to the USA (see Case study 3.3). It destroyed the premiership of Anthony Eden, but not his government. The fact that the Conservative Party was able to recover quickly enough to win the 1959 general election illustrates the new predominance of domestic issues in British politics.

The other key development in international affairs was Britain's refusal to join the emerging EEC. It sent only a junior representative to the talks which led to the signature of the Treaty of Rome (1957), and at first was disinclined to take the new initiative seriously. However, towards the end of the decade the Conservative government, headed by Harold Macmillan, had second thoughts. It was impressed by the rising living standards in the EEC countries, and concluded that future prosperity would best be secured by membership of an alternative trading bloc. In November 1959, it helped to establish the European Free Trade Association (EFTA), with Austria, Denmark, Norway, Portugal, Sweden, and Switzerland. For Eurosceptics, the brief career of this organisation was a lost opportunity for Britain because it lacked the political dimension which made them suspicious of the EEC. However, it soon became clear that EFTA's members lacked the collective industrial and economic muscle of the rival organisation.

Case study 3.2

The political implications of 'consensus'

Whatever the precise nature of the post-war political framework (see Analysis 3.1), it certainly increased the responsibilities facing British governments:

- *Keynesian demand management*: government was held responsible if inflation or unemployment rose too steeply.
- *Nationalisation*: government was held accountable for poor performance of state-run industries. Ministers had a direct role in pay talks and could be blamed for strikes.
- *Social services*: spending on welfare had to be maintained at a high (and preferably rising) level.

Once governments had taken on these responsibilities, it was very difficult to back away from them, whatever the misgivings of the party in power. There were implications for international politics, too. The Attlee government set the post-war precedent of acting as if Britain retained 'great power' status, even though its capacity for independent action was much reduced. Subsequent governments had to keep up this act, for fear of alienating large sections of the media and electorate.

Case study 3.3

Suez

In July 1956, the Egyptian President, Colonel Nasser, nationalised the Suez Canal Company, in which the British and French governments were major shareholders. This was in retaliation for the refusal of Britain and America to finance the construction of the Aswan Dam on the River Nile. The new British Prime Minister Sir Anthony Eden was outraged by Nasser's decision, and a secret plan was hatched to seize the canal. Israel was to attack Egypt, and Britain and France would send troops under the pretence of restoring order. Although the British captured Port Said in early November 1956, the action was condemned by the United Nations. The US President Eisenhower was incensed – not least because the Soviet Union took advantage of the crisis to suppress a revolt in its client state of Hungary – and the Americans withheld support from sterling on the international exchanges. With their currency on the verge of collapse, the British backed down. Eden resigned early the next year.

Suez divided opinion in the UK itself. Within the Conservative Party, some MPs remained convinced that Britain would have secured its objectives in Egypt if it had pressed on. But to have done so would have risked conflict with the Soviet Union (which had replaced the Western powers as Nasser's ally as a result of the row over the Aswan Dam), as well as causing outrage in Washington. The real reason for the unhappiness of the dissident backbench Conservative 'Suez Group' was that the incident had exposed Britain's reduced status in the world. Even after the humiliating climb-down, the reality of Suez was obscured by the revelation that Eden's judgement had been affected by a chronic illness. Eden's successor Harold Macmillan dealt with the situation so skilfully that Suez had little effect on Conservative fortunes in the next general election (1959).

The age of corporatism, 1959–70

In July 1957, Harold Macmillan coined one of the best-known, post-war political phrases when he told a party rally that 'most of our people have never had it so good'. Two years later, his government fought an election with the slogan 'Life's better with the Conservatives. Don't let Labour ruin it'. Macmillan's 1957 speech is usually taken as a sign of complacency, but, in fact, he was warning that prosperity was far from secure. One major problem was that Britain was still not producing enough consumer goods to satisfy domestic demand, so that when governments tried to stimulate economic activity along broadly 'Keynesian' lines, the main result was a significant increase in the country's import bill. In turn, this put pressure on sterling, so governments had to act to curb demand as soon as trouble seemed to be brewing. The result was a policy pattern which became known as 'stop–go' – although 'go–stop' would be more accurate – with the government pressing the economic accelerator (usually before elections, to make voters feel more prosperous), then slamming on the brakes (normally very soon after the election) by increasing interest rates, raising taxes, and/or cutting public spending.

One serious obstacle to consistent and stable economic growth was Britain's poor industrial relations. Disruptive strike action made Britain an unreliable trading partner for overseas customers and also weakened the ability of domestic firms to compete with foreign producers in

Analysis 3.3

Corporatism and neo-corporatism

The corporatist approach to economic management rests on the view that the interests of employers and workers can be reconciled if their chief representatives meet regularly to discuss current problems under the benign guidance of the government. It is an *elitist* theory, assuming that the leaders of trade unions and employers' organisations can exercise a decisive effect on the behaviour of their members and that 'The Man in Whitehall' is fully conversant with the needs and interests of ordinary people. Its reputation was tarnished by the fact that it was first practised in a systematic way by the fascist dictator Mussolini in interwar Italy.

The term 'neo-corporatism' is used to designate a more democratic version of the process, exemplified by the British system between the early 1960s and 1979. But even this was criticised by pluralists, mainly on the grounds that the arrangement provided inadequate representation for *consumer* interests (see Chapter 1).

the home market. The solution was to bring harmony to the workplace by devising corporatist, or more precisely neo-corporatist, institutions, which would allow constructive talks between both sides of industry (see Analysis 3.3). The elected government would mediate between unions and employers as an 'honest broker', just as it hoped to do on the international stage whenever tensions increased between the USA and the Soviet Union.

Despite mixed results, this approach lasted until Margaret Thatcher came to power in 1979. One predictable effect was a further addition to the political implications of 'consensus' (see Case study 3.2). Now almost any strike or wage settlement was seen as a government responsibility. In response, politicians were tempted into further intervention, thinking, for example, of ways to punish firms which gave their workers substantial pay increases that threatened to destabilise the British economy through excessive inflation.

Macmillan was also impressed by the apparent success of French governments, which took an active role in economic planning. This process promised to reduce even further the uncertainty of life in a capitalist society. If the government had prior warning about the intentions of individual firms, it could try to manage the economy in order to help fulfil plans for overall economic growth in future. The Labour government of Harold Wilson (1964–70) built on Macmillan's strategy, producing in 1965 a national economic plan. However, this was derailed by further international speculation against the pound. There was a serious sterling crisis in 1966, and the currency was devalued again (from $2.80 to $2.40) in 1967. As before, the attempt to stave off devaluation was based on cuts in government expenditure, resulting in a dramatic economic 'stop' when the national plan had been all about 'go'.

In August 1961, the Macmillan government had finally applied to join the EEC. Key factors behind this dramatic policy change included pressure from the US President John F. Kennedy, the prosperity of the EEC, and hopes that Britain might have real influence over the EEC's development from within. But French President Charles de Gaulle vetoed the application in 1963, citing Britain's subservience to the USA. In 1967, Harold Wilson made a fresh bid for membership of the EEC, but again de Gaulle exercised his veto, noting both Britain's continued closeness to the USA and its weak economy. There was plenty of evidence to support de Gaulle's claim about Britain being a client state of the USA. Britain might have its own nuclear capability, but this 'deterrent' depended on US missile technology and maintenance. In the dramatic 1962 crisis caused by the Soviet construction of missile sites on Cuba, Britain was barely consulted by its ally. The coolness in the 'special relationship' persisted even though Britain was rapidly divesting itself of its empire. During the 1960s independence was granted to numerous countries, including Uganda (1962), Kenya (1963), and Singapore (1965). Macmillan had spoken of a 'wind of change' blowing through Africa, and the prospect of majority (black) rule in the British colony of Southern Rhodesia provoked a unilateral declaration of independence by its white-dominated government. Britain lacked the power to resolve this situation, either by economic sanctions or by force. Civil war forced the illegal government to back down in 1980 (after which Rhodesia won legal independence as Zimbabwe, with the British acting as mediators).

The end of consensus, 1970–79

The Labour government of 1964–70 was a major disappointment to its original supporters. But after the 1967 devaluation of sterling the economic outlook improved, and at least Wilson managed to keep Britain out of America's war in Vietnam. It was a major surprise when he was defeated by Edward Heath's Conservatives in the 1970 general election. Heath was a sign that a 'wind of change' had blown through his party; he was a grammar school boy of relatively humble origins, and in 1965 he had become the first Conservative leader to be elected by his parliamentary colleagues. He also had no illusions about the 'special relationship' and was fully conscious of Britain's reduced role in the world.

Heath's 1970 election pitch was based on the argument that Wilson had mismanaged the economy. His own hopes of an economic resurgence arose from his confidence that he could persuade the French to allow Britain to join the EEC. He was helped in this task by the fact that he was known as a genuine enthusiast for European cooperation, but more importantly by de Gaulle's resignation from the French presidency in 1969. Britain became a member on 1 January 1973 and, after Heath's departure from office, the decision was confirmed by the first ever nationwide referendum, held in 1975 (see Chapter 13).

Heath hoped that the membership of the EEC would cement Britain's post-war economic strategy. UK firms would be forced to compete for markets on equal terms with efficient European counterparts. Among other things, this would give them a clear incentive to work harmoniously with their employees, as the corporate approach indicated. But Heath's economic message was ignored by both sides of industry. Far from embracing the new challenges and opportunities at home, British capitalists preferred to seek easier profits by investing abroad. Meanwhile, workers continued to demand higher wages unrelated to productivity. Heath's attempt to reform the unions, following a half-hearted effort by Wilson in the late 1960s, further increased the militant mood. Industrial action by the National Union of Mineworkers (NUM) forced him to call a general election in February 1974, and the Conservatives were narrowly beaten.

In opposition, the Labour Party had developed radical policies as a response to what many grass-roots activists regarded as Wilson's 'betrayal' of socialism. Wilson himself seemed shaken when his party won in February 1974; he had expected (and probably half hoped) to lose. The main problem he inherited was price inflation, which had been rising for some time but was given an additional spur by the increased cost of oil (see Case study 3.4). Having disappointed his supporters in the 1960s, Wilson knew in advance that his record could be no better this time round. His situation might have improved slightly if he had secured a comfortable parliamentary position. But when he called a new election, in October 1974, Labour won only 18 additional seats. Wilson kept a low profile throughout this precarious premiership, which ended with his surprise resignation in April 1976. In a clear symptom of underlying malaise in British politics, conspiracy theorists quickly assumed that Wilson's departure could not have been voluntary. Some thought that he was hiding a secret which left him open to blackmail by a foreign power. In fact, he had decided to step down some time earlier.

In September 1976, at the Labour Party conference, Wilson's successor James Callaghan effectively announced the end of the post-war consensus when he argued that the British had been 'living on borrowed time'. Instead of facing up to its underlying problems, the country had run up crippling debts in an attempt to maintain living standards. He continued: 'We used to think that you could spend your way out of a recession and increase employment by cutting taxes and boosting government spending. I tell you in all candour that that option no longer exists'.

Callaghan's speech indicated that the government would no longer be guided by Keynesian ideas. In fact, as we have seen, successive administrations since 1951 had *misapplied* Keynes's basic approach, trying to manipulate the economy for electoral purposes. However, now there would not even be a pretence of following Keynes; rather than prioritising the fight against unemployment, control of inflation would be the government's main goal. Callaghan hoped that his

Analysis 3.4

Government 'overload'

In their classic comparative study *The Civic Culture* (1963), the American political scientists Gabriel Almond and Sidney Verba hailed Britain as a successful polity whose citizens were well-informed and motivated while recognising the need for stable government. However, by the mid-1970s, commentators identified a systemic crisis in the British state. The various governmental responsibilities discussed in this chapter might have been manageable in good times. But they were interconnected, and trouble in one quarter could easily have a knock-on effect elsewhere. In particular, satisfactory government performance hinged on economic growth, which would promote feelings of prosperity, fund better public services, and so forth. By contrast, sluggish growth (or a recession) would lead to discontent among an increasingly demanding electorate and confront the government with some tough policy decisions.

To make matters worse, governments had invested so heavily in the successful operation of their strategies that, in times of trouble, they felt compelled to intervene still further. Thus, Wilson and Heath both responded to rising inflation by trying to control prices and incomes by legislation. In the short term, these measures were reasonably successful; but after a while, both sides of industry lost patience with them. In trying to do too much, it seemed to many commentators that the British state was unable to perform *any* of its functions satisfactorily. Although warnings about 'overload' came from a variety of sources (including academic observers), in the circumstances of the mid-1970s, their effect was to lend support to the Thatcherite (or 'New Right') critique of the post-war consensus as a whole.

remarks would impress international financiers, who were speculating against sterling once again. The government had already applied for emergency relief from the International Monetary Fund (IMF), an organisation established in 1945 to foster worldwide economic stability. Callaghan and his Chancellor Denis Healey knew that the price of assistance from the IMF would be savage cuts in public expenditure. The government was struggling to survive in Parliament, where its slender overall majority was further depleted through by-election defeats. In 1977, it negotiated a pact with the Liberals, which shored up its position for a while. But unemployment was rising, and although Callaghan persuaded union leaders to restrain their pay demands, contrary to 'corporatist' assumptions, they were unable to control their rank-and-file members. In the winter of 1978–79 (dubbed 'the winter of discontent' by *The Sun* newspaper), there were numerous strikes, notably in the public services. Britain was beginning to look ungovernable. Callaghan hung on, in the hope that he could call an election in circumstances which would allow Labour to win a workable parliamentary majority. But he ran out of time, losing a vote of confidence in the House of Commons on 28 March 1979.

Thatcherism, 1979–97

In hindsight, Conservatives (and New Labour 'modernisers') often claim that the country was ready for a radical change of direction in the spring of 1979. The old consensus politics

Case study 3.4

The fuel crisis, 1973–74

The growing strains within Britain's post-war 'consensus' were exposed by the repercussions of the Yom Kippur War which broke out between Israeli and Arab forces in October 1973. After their decisive defeat, Arab states punished Western nations for having supplied Israel with its superior weaponry. Their own weapon was an economic asset – oil. Restrictions on supply caused a more than fourfold increase in the cost of this vital fuel. All Western nations were badly affected, but although Heath had tried to adopt a neutral stance towards the conflict in the Middle East, Britain suffered more than most because its underlying economic position was already weak. British-based oil companies snubbed the prime minister when he asked them for special help.

In the short term, there were power cuts and limits on the British working week. The crisis strengthened the bargaining position of the National Union of Mineworkers (NUM), triggering Heath's departure from office. But the most lasting legacy was a considerable boost to domestic inflation, which had been rising anyway because of a general increase in commodity prices on world markets. As the effect of the oil price filtered through the economy, in August 1975, Britain's annual inflation rate reached a record 27 per cent. Ironically, the country was only a few years away from self-sufficiency in oil, thanks to the exploitation of North Sea reserves.

had palpably failed in almost every relevant respect, and voters eagerly grasped the Thatcherite alternative. This account is understandable, given the affection that Thatcher still commands within her party. But it is a myth. First, the Conservative Party concealed its true intentions from the electorate. In 1978, it had attacked the government's record with a poster portraying a lengthy dole queue with the slogan, 'Labour isn't working'. Yet Conservative policies were bound to cause a significant rise in unemployment, at least in the short term (see Table 3.2 and Photo 3.2). Second, the relatively modest Conservative share of the vote in 1979 indicated a distinct lack of enthusiasm for radical change. Indeed, Thatcher benefitted from divided opposition forces as much as any 'sea-change' in public attitudes. Under her leadership, the level of electoral support for the Conservatives never matched the 46.5 per cent secured in 1970, when the party was led by Edward Heath who is normally regarded as having been a lamentable electoral performer.

From one perspective, Thatcherism can be seen as an attempt to solve the problem of government 'overload' (see Analysis 3.4). The strategy involved four core elements:

- *Monetarism:* bearing down on inflation by controlling the money supply, rather than trying directly to control wages and prices (see Analysis 3.5).
- *Privatisation:* selling off state-owned industries rather than subsidising their losses (or developing a serious long-term strategy for running them more efficiently).
- *Trade union reform:* gradually restricting trade union rights in a series of measures (seven important Acts between 1979 and 1990), while refusing to become openly involved in the settlement of disputes.
- *Hiving off:* entrusting many functions of central government to semi-autonomous agencies, thus blurring the conventional lines of departmental responsibility (see Chapter 10).

TABLE 3.2 Unemployment, 1947–93

Year	Maximum figure (month)
1947	1,900,000 (February)
1950	404,000 (January)
1960	461,000 (January)
1970	628,000 (January)
1978	1,608,000 (August)
1980	2,244,000 (December)
1983	3,225,000 (January)
1986	3,408,000 (January)
1987	3,297,000 (January)
1990	1,850,000 (December)
1991	2,552,000 (December)
1993	3,062,000 (January)

Note: During the Thatcher years, there were numerous changes to the way in which unemployment statistics were compiled, almost invariably resulting in a reduction of the official figure. It is therefore more than likely that the maximum tally (in January 1986) was an underestimate, and possible that the number of people out of work in January 1993 exceeded the previous record.

PHOTO 3.2 Conservative propaganda highlights Labour's economic record, 1978 (Saatchi and Saatchi advertising poster) (Image courtesy of The Advertising Archives).
Source: Adapted from D. Butler and G. Butler, *Twentieth Century British Political Facts*, 2000.

The overall purpose was to ensure that although government would do much less, whenever it did choose to act it would be much more effective, thus restoring its authority. The implementation of the strategy required a quality which Thatcher possessed in abundance – determination. Even when the official unemployment figures exceeded three million (in September 1982), she refused to back down. But the other essential ingredient was luck. The possession of North Sea oil cushioned the government from the full effects of the severe economic recession of 1979–81, and provided a springboard for a subsequent recovery. More importantly, the Conservatives benefitted from a feeling of national revival after the Falklands War of April–June 1982. This was ironic, since the government's diplomacy leading up to the Argentine invasion had demonstrated a flexible attitude on the question of sovereignty over the Falkland Islands, while its policy of naval spending cuts had encouraged the regime of General Galtieri to assume that the islands

Analysis 3.5

Monetarism

Monetarism is an economic theory based on the notion that economic stability (particularly the rate of inflation) depends on control over the supply of money. Although there are many varieties of monetarism, its supporters share the general view that if the stock of money in circulation remains broadly stable, prices and incomes have to follow a similar trend unless businesses want to risk bankruptcy and workers to price themselves out of jobs. Direct attempts to control prices and incomes by law, as practised by successive Labour and Conservative governments, were thus either irrelevant or (more likely) damaging to the economy.

The monetarist theory lay at the heart of Thatcherism, since economic mismanagement was held to be the underlying cause of all Britain's post-war woes. Its importance to the Thatcher government is reflected in the tendency of critics to denounce *all* Conservative policy as a product of 'monetarist' thinking and to demonise leading monetarist theorists, like the American Milton Friedman (1912–2006). The Thatcher government certainly brought inflation under control. However, critics claim that monetarism had little or nothing to do with this achievement. In practice, monetarism is far more complicated than the basic theory suggests. It proved very difficult to define 'money', let alone to control the quantity in circulation at any given time (or the speed of its circulation). The Thatcher government regularly set targets for the money supply, but most commentators agree that these were usually missed. Instead, high unemployment sharply reduced the level of demand in the economy and thus suppressed inflationary forces. This could have been predicted under the supposedly discredited Keynesian approach – except that Keynes himself would not have condoned the resulting waste of human resources, which arguably had the long-term effect of fostering a 'dependency culture' among families who had to grow accustomed to the prospect of life on welfare benefits rather than in productive activity.

could be seized (after 150 years of unbroken British rule) without any retaliation. As it turned out, there could have been no better opportunity for Thatcher to show that her tough rhetoric on foreign affairs was matched by an appetite for action. In her second term, she showed equal determination in refusing to settle a year-long miners' strike (1984–85), but here, too, fortune favoured her because the controversial NUM President Arthur Scargill made several disastrous tactical errors during the dispute allowing Thatcher to avenge her party's defeat in 1974.

Of course, Thatcherism was about much more than government retreat from the 'overloaded' responsibilities of the 1970s: indeed, this was one reason why Thatcher was such a divisive figure. After 1976, Labour had itself talked in monetarist terms, but only to appease the financial markets. While it was obvious that the Callaghan government hated the necessity of focusing on inflation and cutting government expenditure, Thatcher clearly relished this new order of priorities. She believed that excessive taxation had been holding back an entrepreneurial spirit among the British people, and was happy to apply much of the revenue from North Sea oil and the privatisation of state-run industries to reducing the burden on the well-to-do. The government's first budget (1979) set the tone, reducing the basic rate of income tax from 33 to 30 per cent and almost doubling value-added tax (VAT) which was levied on everyone regardless of income. At the same time, the top rate of income tax on earned income was slashed from 83 to 60 per cent (in 1988, this was cut further, to 40 per cent).

Ultimately, it was Thatcher's crusading zeal that precipitated her downfall. The community charge, popularly known as the 'poll tax', was brought in to replace the existing system of local government taxation (based on the rateable value of properties) after her third election win in 1987. Always impatient with any symptoms of opposition, the government had already legislated to 'cap' the rates levied by high-spending authorities (1984) and, in 1985, abolished the Greater London Council (GLC). The poll tax had initially been rejected by ministers as an alternative to the rates. But by 1987, the government tended to assume that any of its policies would eventually be accepted, however strong the initial outcry. With the poll tax, it miscalculated badly. At the end of March 1990, a demonstration in central London turned into a riot. In October 1990, the Conservatives lost the Eastbourne parliamentary seat to the Liberal Democrats, even though the vacancy had arisen because of the IRA's assassination of Thatcher's personal friend Ian Gow, and a sympathetic vote for the government might have been anticipated in those circumstances. Michael Heseltine, a known opponent of the poll tax who had resigned from the cabinet in January 1986 after disagreeing with the prime minister over policy and the conduct of cabinet meetings, challenged for the party leadership a few weeks after Eastbourne. Heseltine also took a positive view of the UK's engagement with Europe, whereas Thatcher could not conceal her growing hostility, partly fuelled by the prospect of German reunification. Even parliamentary colleagues who shared her misgivings grew alarmed by a combative approach which was unlikely to serve the interests either of their party or of the country. Thatcher won the first ballot of Conservative MPs, but by an insufficient margin to prevent a second contest. Recognising, very reluctantly, that she would probably lose this further ballot, she resigned on 22 November 1990.

Although Thatcher's successor, John Major, was far less confrontational and quickly replaced the poll tax with the council tax (based, in part, on the value of a property), his election was not the prelude to a change of direction. Privatisation continued, reaching into areas where even Thatcher would have hesitated (notably the railways and, in 1994, the coal industry). Although the Conservatives won the 1992 general election against expectations, within a few months, they had plunged into an economic crisis from which they took more than a decade to recover. 'Black Wednesday' (16 September 1992) actually improved Britain's economic outlook. But the political damage arose not just because it left the government looking helpless. The crisis also brought to a head divisions within the Conservative Party over Europe (see Chapter 13).

Thatcherism abroad, 1979–97

Prior to her election as prime minister, Thatcher had appeared to be a lukewarm pro-European. She had campaigned for a 'yes' vote in the 1975 referendum, although her contribution was trivial compared to that of her predecessor Edward Heath. But at the Dublin Summit in 1979, she bluntly demanded a rebate from Britain's budgetary contribution. Although a satisfactory compromise was eventually negotiated, it was already obvious that, under Thatcher, Britain would tend to be an 'awkward partner' in Europe (see Chapter 13).

Thatcher agreed to the Single European Act (1986) which reduced the scope of Britain's right to veto decisions in the Council of Ministers and foreshadowed the introduction of a European

Controversy 3.1

Thatcherism: for and against

Characteristic arguments of supporters and opponents of the changes of the Thatcher years:

For	Against
Monetarism might have proved difficult to implement, but it revolutionised the economic climate in Britain, proving that the government would never take the soft inflationary option	Monetarism proved unworkable, as expected, and caused years of unnecessary suffering. Even well-run businesses went bankrupt as a result of high interest rates in 1979–81
Thatcher had the courage to take on, and to tame, the trade unions which were wrecking Britain's economic prospects	Even if one accepts that it was necessary to curb the power of trade unions, Thatcher swung the balance too far in favour of employers
Thatcher attacked local government because many councils were irresponsible and some were corrupt	In attacking local government Thatcher showed her contempt for opposition and her preference for centralised power
Privatisation was a runaway success, producing a 'shareholding democracy' and proving that the state cannot run major enterprises	Privatisation was a barefaced swindle, in which public assets were sold well below their real market value. Most of the companies have been poorly run since they were sold off. Many small shareholders realised a quick profit, leaving important utilities in the hands of giant, unaccountable institutional investors
Thatcher stood up for British interests in Europe, and enhanced the country's standing in the world	Thatcher proved to Britain's European partners that the country would never be cooperative, and damaged Britain's reputation abroad because she was too subservient to the USA

single currency. But her true opinion was revealed in her Bruges speech of September 1988. She attacked the idea of an interfering European 'superstate', referring with more pride than precision to her success in reducing the role of the British state. Her opposition to membership of the European ERM cost her the services of her Chancellor Nigel Lawson, who thought that the ERM would provide a more reliable guarantee of financial discipline than monetarist theory (which he had tacitly abandoned). Nevertheless, John Major, Lawson's successor as Chancellor, persuaded Thatcher at a moment of extreme political weakness (October 1990) to commit Britain to the ERM after all. The mechanism fixed the value of the pound in relation to other European currencies, though some commentators warned that sterling was over-valued at the time of joining.

In the following month, Thatcher's continued antagonism towards European integration provoked another resignation, that of her long-serving (and suffering) colleague Sir Geoffrey Howe (Chancellor 1979–83, Foreign Secretary 1983–89, Lord President of the Council 1989–90).

Howe's resignation speech crystallised opposition to Thatcher within her own party, thus proving that in certain circumstances the House of Commons can still have a significant effect on events, and providing the context for Heseltine's leadership challenge.

The fact that after the 1990 leadership election Thatcher was succeeded by Major, who had cajoled her into signing up to the ERM, suggested a more cooperative stance towards the EC. But Major's hope of keeping Britain at 'the very heart of Europe' turned sour after 'Black Wednesday' (16 September 1992). Ministers felt that their European partners had not been very active in resisting speculation against sterling, which led to Britain's enforced and expensive decision to leave the ERM just a few months after Major had led the Conservatives to a fourth consecutive election win.

Before the election, Major had accepted further European integration at the Maastricht Summit of December 1991, albeit with opt-outs for Britain on the proposed single currency and social policy. He now had the task of winning parliamentary approval for the Maastricht Treaty, against a background of growing Conservative discontent and unhelpful utterances from Thatcher, now in the House of Lords. In July 1993, Conservative Eurosceptics voted tactically with Labour on a motion deploring Major's hard-won Maastricht opt-out on social policy, resulting in a narrow government defeat. Although the government won a vote of confidence on the following day, its slender parliamentary majority (down to 17, on paper, by July 1993) gave the Eurosceptics power well out of proportion to their numbers. In November 1994, eight Tory MPs had the party whip withdrawn as a result of their repeated disobedience. Another Eurosceptic refused to accept the whip in protest at this decision. Less than a year later, the 'whipless wonders' were asked to return to the fold, so desperate was the government's parliamentary plight.

Ironically, Major's Conservatives had received in 1992 more votes than any previous British political party. The Thatcherite project of restoring government authority was being undermined by the first-past-the-post electoral system, which had left the government with an inadequate parliamentary majority (see Table 3.1). Major was urged to improve his position by taking a more Eurosceptic stance, but this would not have been credible given his earlier pronouncements. Instead, in June 1995, he took the unprecedented step of resigning as party leader (though not as prime minister), challenging his critics to put up a candidate. Although he survived the ensuing contest (against the former Secretary of State for Wales, John Redwood), his authority was only damaged further. In 1996, he became more antagonistic towards Europe as a result of a ban on imports of British beef provoked by an outbreak of the fatal BSE cattle disease. But by this time, his European counterparts were confident that he would lose the next election, which could not be delayed for more than a year. During the 1997 election campaign, Major was unable to take a convincing line on Europe, trapped between his powerful pro-European Chancellor Kenneth Clarke and the majority of his parliamentary colleagues who were by this time overwhelmingly 'sceptical'. A belated promise that Britain would not join the European single currency without a referendum was matched by a similar pledge from Labour.

Critics on both sides of the argument make much of Major's inability to heal divisions over Europe. But it must be remembered that he had inherited a poisonous situation from Thatcher, in whose downfall Europe had played a crucial part, and his premiership coincided with an unprecedented drive for deeper European integration. Unfortunately for Major, he lacked Thatcher's compensation of warm relations with the USA. Although Britain was an active partner during the first Gulf War (1991) and Major established good relations with George H.W. Bush (1989–93), he could not hope to emulate the emotional bond which had developed between Mrs Thatcher and Bush's predecessor Ronald Reagan (1981–89). Thatcher and Reagan agreed on economic theory (if not practice) and on the proper role of the state. They also shared a profound hostility to the USSR. In opposition, Thatcher had been dubbed the 'Iron Lady' by the Soviet media for her uncompromising rhetoric, and as prime minister she gladly allowed America to install nuclear missiles on British territory. By the time that Major became the prime minister, the Communist bloc had collapsed and Germany had been reunified (October 1990). The reality of the 'special relationship' was suddenly exposed when President Bush made no attempt to hide his view that, in the new circumstances, Germany was as good (or as useful) a friend as Britain.

Even when Thatcher was prime minister, the limitations of the 'special relationship' were apparent. During the Falklands conflict, the Reagan administration was bitterly divided, with some key officials preferring to maintain good relations with Argentina. In October 1983, US forces invaded the Commonwealth island of Grenada without proper consultation with Britain – a Suez in reverse, with a very different outcome reflecting America's ability to override any objections from a third party. Even loyal Thatcherites like Norman Tebbit were dismayed in April 1986 when US planes took off from British bases in a futile raid on Libya (other European countries had refused to let the planes fly over their territory). In other circumstances, under a prime minister who enjoyed less support from the media, these incidents would have caused grave and lasting embarrassment.

Already damaged by Europe, the Major government finally sank under allegations of ministerial misdeeds (whether financial or sexual). A new election was delayed as long as possible, but the reckoning finally came on 1 May 1997. Labour supporters, starved of success for so long, hailed a new dawn under a charismatic leader who won an overwhelming parliamentary majority (even if his party's share of the vote was considerably less than it had been in 1950, when it had won a majority of only five seats).

After his victory, Blair promised that his party would 'govern as New Labour', sticking to its (limited) campaign pledges. This was actually a signal that the government would adhere to the general approach followed by the Conservatives, even though Blair had promised to give a new priority to 'welfare' issues like health and education. The notion of a new, post-Thatcherite consensus was complicated by the fact that, back in opposition, the Conservatives gradually adopted a more abrasive outlook as they searched for ideological clarity ('clear blue water') which would distinguish them from New Labour. It is, at least, reasonable to argue that Blair's aspirations were similar to those of his predecessor, Major. The question remained whether, with a much larger parliamentary majority and a greater emphasis on public relations, Blair could realise John Major's hope of building 'a country at ease with itself'.

New Labour and after

Many key developments in the years between 1997 and the new era of 'austerity' under the Conservative–Liberal Democrat coalition (2010–15) are covered in detail elsewhere in this book. As a result, this section provides only a brief overview.

We have seen that during the 1970s it became clear to most observers that the British state had over-reached itself, taking on responsibilities which it could not fulfil. This situation was transformed during the Thatcher–Major years, mainly because these Conservative governments were successful in disengaging themselves from the oversight of major industrial concerns. Under 'New' Labour, the record was mixed. From the point of view of reducing the burdens on ministers, there were three steps forward and three back:

1. The most obvious change was devolution to Scotland, Wales, and Northern Ireland. With important governmental functions transferred to the constituent nations of the UK, ministers based in London have fewer factors to take into account (despite the wide variety of conditions within

England itself; see Chapter 4). Arguably the impact of devolution on the responsibilities of central government was greater than that of the EU between 1997 and the 2016 referendum, despite several treaty changes (see Chapter 13). If anything, the greatest problems for governments arose from areas like migration from within the EU, over which they had relinquished control.

2. In addition to further privatisations and the 'hiving off of functions to semi-independent agencies, the New Labour government gave the Bank of England operational independence. This decision, which was not foreshadowed in Labour's 1997 manifesto, deprived Chancellors of the Exchequer of a key economic instrument (the control of interest rates) which arguably had provided more headaches than benefits in the earlier post-war period. The Bank could now be blamed if inflation got out of control; but it was also likely to share responsibility if Britain suffered an economic recession, or if the value of the pound fluctuated too wildly. The Conservative–Liberal Democrat coalition also established an independent Office for Budget Responsibility (OBR) which provided alternative economic forecasts to those of the Treasury.

3. Ministers can now rely on far more support from special advisers (or 'spin-doctors'). This gives them an important second line of defence against adverse publicity. Sometimes the advisers can themselves become a problem, but the advantages of a skilful public relations team are obvious (for example, bad news can be disguised in a way which was never contemplated in the 1970s).

However, there are at least three ways in which the role of government has been made more complicated:

1. State spending on certain public services (notably education and health) increased sharply after 2001. Although New Labour did not make significant changes from the institutional and policy framework established by the Conservatives, the level of public expectation was encouraged to rise, and in spite of their concerted efforts, ministers arguably made themselves more vulnerable than ever before to criticisms relating to the performance of the public services.

2. The Thatcher government claimed that it reduced the level of interference in the economy, but passed new laws on trade unions, local government, and criminal justice with far more regularity than any of its predecessors. Similarly, New Labour showed a much greater willingness than previous governments to create new criminal offences and to interfere with personal habits and pastimes. Hunting, smoking, the disposal of waste, the treatment of children, and even eating habits are now under parliamentary scrutiny as never before, leading to accusations of a 'nanny state'. The Blair government's response to the terrorist threat – even before '9/11' – was highly reminiscent of the Thatcherite 'authoritarianism' which Labour had denounced when it was in opposition; allegations that the state has become a menace to civil liberty rather than a protector of freedom have persisted since 2010, especially in respect of data protection in the age of the Internet.

3. The incorporation into British law of the European Convention on Human Rights (by means of the Human Rights Act 1998 (HRA)) has increased the complexity of policymaking. Even before 1998, governmental decisions were being challenged more frequently in the British courts (see Chapter 9). Now legislation must be checked before passage to ensure that it complies with the terms of the HRA, and if the courts rule that it fails this test, there is an expectation that it will have to be revised. This proved particularly difficult when ministers tried to introduce measures in response to terrorist attacks in America (September 2001) and London itself (July 2005).

Overall, despite dramatic state intervention to tackle the 'credit crunch' which began in 2007 and the coronavirus pandemic of 2020 which created unprecedented challenges, it would be reasonable to conclude that the British state is not in imminent danger of 'overloading' as it was in the 1970s. There is, for example, little prospect that fully fledged corporatism will be revived – that trade unions, employers, and government representatives will be meeting in the near future to discuss the prospects of individual industries. However, concerns about the level of state interference in the personal choices of citizens are not confined to dogmatic 'libertarians'. In many other areas, in contrast, there are grounds for unease at the extent to which the post-war central state has been 'hollowed out', leaving ministers unable to respond effectively even to issues that would have seemed fairly routine for governments during the 'consensus' years.

The role of the prime minister

During the course of our survey, there has been a tendency for the names of individual prime ministers to appear with increasing frequency. This is no accident. Although his government introduced many radical measures, Clement Attlee (1888–1967) acted as something like a low-profile 'chairman of the board' in cabinet. Blair, by contrast, dominated the public image of his government (although behind the scenes, Gordon Brown exercised a comparable influence). The impact of the electronic media is important here (see Chapter 5), making the prime minister seem more 'presidential'. In this respect – if not others – Blair imitated Thatcher. During the 1980s, for example, Thatcher's official spokesman, Bernard Ingham, often announced that the prime minister would be taking a special interest in a subject when the relevant departmental minister seemed to be struggling. This practice continued under Blair (though in both cases, the announcements were rarely followed by any concrete evidence of government action). When Gordon Brown took over from Blair in 2007, he proposed a series of reforms to curb the political role of the prime minister, but nothing of importance was achieved before he lost office in 2010, and his successors have shown less interest in the question.

We saw that the House of Commons can still have a crucial influence over events, in cases like the resignation speech of Geoffrey Howe and the Maastricht debates of 1993. Under the coalition, the government was defeated for the first time since the conflict with the American colonies in a vote concerning military action (the Syria vote of August 2013). In the aftermath of the 2016 'Brexit' referendum, conflict between Parliament and the prime minister – the executive and the legislature – reached unprecedented levels in the democratic era. However, there was no sign that prime ministers since 2016 have treated the House of Commons with greater respect – rather the reverse, in fact. They are rarely seen at Westminster apart from their very brief visits for Prime Minister's Question Time. The television studio is now reckoned to be more important than Parliament. While the Commons has been declining for many decades, the eclipse of the cabinet is strictly a post-war phenomenon. Nowadays, prime ministers tend to transact business directly with their relevant colleagues (and with their unelected special advisers) rather than asking the cabinet to give a collective opinion.

Economics and democracy

An implicit theme of the survey up to the mid-1970s was the tendency of governments to use Keynesian techniques of demand management to manipulate the British economy so that elections coincided with times of maximum prosperity. This practice would not have appealed to Keynes himself. Even so, no one can deny that it had serious consequences for the economy, leading in particular to the process of 'stop–go'.

In this respect, at least, the end of the post-war consensus could have been a welcome development. But ingrained habits die very hard, and politicians have continued to try to generate a 'feel-good factor' at election time. Difficult decisions can still be put off, and populist measures brought forward, depending on the electoral timetable. New Labour was not very different from its immediate predecessors in this respect, and despite the context of economic 'austerity', the coalition's Chancellor, George Osborne, was unashamedly political. Whoever was originally to blame for this development – and whether or not it is an inevitable feature of liberal democracy – it has certainly contributed to a deepening cynicism among British politicians and voters alike.

The international scene

Throughout this chapter we have encountered strong evidence to suggest that the so-called 'special relationship' with America is largely a product of wishful thinking on the British side. It would be far more accurate to say that since 1945, the relationship has been generally warm, with occasional 'hot-spots' like the Reagan/Thatcher years when the political leaders of Britain and America admired each other personally and agreed on ideological questions.

But over time, an illusion can take on some of the trappings of reality. In particular, the expectation that Britain should be the most trusted partner of the United States has become ingrained among many media commentators and voters on this side of the Atlantic. Blair took this facet of post-war policy further than any of his predecessors. For most of her premiership, Thatcher dealt with presidents who represented the Republican Party, which has traditionally been linked with the Tories, and in this respect, the intimacy of the relationship in the 1980s was understandable. Furthermore, cooperation with America could always be justified by the Cold War alliance against the USSR. Neither of these factors could explain Blair's relationship with George W. Bush. An alliance against terrorism after the events of 11 September 2001 was fully in line with post-war British policy, but it was always questionable that this more general cause would be helped by a war on Iraq. The Republican Bush sympathised with many policy positions which were anathema to New Labour, on subjects such as welfare, capital punishment, and abortion. But this did not prevent Blair from treating Bush with even more respect than he had given to his White House predecessor, the Democrat Bill Clinton.

Iraq exposed the old divisions between Britain and its major European partners, reminding observers of the reasons why de Gaulle rebuffed British membership of the EEC back in the 1960s. Nevertheless, Blair had echoed John Major's desire to be 'at the very heart of Europe'. He persisted with this rhetoric, although he abandoned his attempt to take Britain into the European single currency, despite his personal popularity after the 1997 general election and his party's crushing majority in the Commons.

With hindsight, it is now clear that Blair missed an opportunity to trigger a much-needed debate over Britain's place in the world, at a time when rational considerations were unlikely to be outweighed by emotive issues. In effect, he chose not to jeopardise his own position, and the future of his New Labour project, by forcing the British public to face up to a dilemma which it had been doing its best to avoid since 1945: was it primarily a European power, or was it still sufficiently strong to harbour global ambitions? After deciding against a referendum on Europe, Blair was increasingly attracted to the role of subservient partner to the USA, even though it was difficult to see how this could serve the long-term national interest; after Iraq, it was impossible for him to rebuild his bridges with Europe, and he ended up sabotaging New Labour and his own reputation without coming close to leaving a more constructive legacy.

Institutional developments (particularly the relative decline of the Foreign and Common-wealth Office [FCO] since the 1970s) suggest that prime ministers will continue to play a dominant role in Britain's foreign policy, rather than taking a sustained interest in domestic affairs where decisive interventions are far more difficult. Gordon Brown was preoccupied by the economic problems which began almost as soon as he succeeded Blair; arguably his role in coordinating the international response to the global financial crisis made him a more formidable presence on the world stage than Blair had ever been, but this did little to improve his electoral fortunes. David Cameron reverted to the Blair model, particularly in his attitude to intervention in Libya. But while Blair could have held a referendum on Britain's place in Europe from a position of strength, Cameron was forced to promise a poll at a time of weakness. Whatever the real merits of the arguments on both sides of the 2016 referendum question, the debate amongst politicians was influenced by half-remembered images of the country's past rather than by sober-minded considerations of the future.

Further reading

For an excellent survey of politics from the end of World War II to the fall of Thatcher, see A. Sked and C. Cook's *Post-War Britain: A Political History* (London: Penguin, 4th edition, 1993). For contrasting viewpoints on Britain's economic performance, see A. Gamble's *Britain in Decline: Economic Policy, Political Strategy and the British State* (London: Macmillan, 4th edition, 1994), W. Hutton's *The State We're In* (London: Vintage, 1996, and G. Bernstein's *The Myth of Decline: The Rise of Britain since 1945* (London: Pimlico, 2004).

On the debate about the post-war 'consensus', see D. Kavanagh and P. Morris's *Consensus Politics: From Attlee to Major* (Oxford: Blackwell, 2nd edition, 1994), and H. Jones and M. Kandiah's (eds.), *The Myth of Consensus. New Views on British History, 1945–64* (London: Macmillan, 1996). Invaluable and accessible statistical information can be found in D. Butler and G. Butler's *Twentieth Century British Political Facts 1900–2000* (London: Palgrave, 2000), and R. Mortimer and A. Blick's *Butler's British Political Facts* (London: Palgrave, 2018).

While there are many good books covering post-war developments as a whole, some studies of specific periods are well worth reading. P. Hennessy's *Never Again* (London: Jonathan Cape, 1992), *Having It So Good* (London: Allen Lane, 2006), and *Winds of Change: Britain in the Early Sixties* (London: Allen Lane, 2019) build a detailed and highly readable account of the period from 1945 to 1964. For an important article on the crucial years of the post-war period, see A. King, 'Overload: Problems of Governing in the 1970s', *Political Studies*, Vol. 33 (1975), pp. 284–96. On the Thatcher years, see I. Gilmour, *Dancing with Dogma: Britain under Thatcherism* (London: Simon & Schuster, 1992) for a highly critical account; on the other side of the debate is S.R. Letwin's *The Anatomy of Thatcherism* (London: Fontana, 1992). A special issue of *British Politics* (Vol. 10, No. 1, April 2015) is devoted to an analysis of Thatcher's legacy. On Blair's first government, see A. Seldon (ed.), *The Blair Effect* (London: Little, Brown, 2001), and on the second, A. Seldon and D. Kavanagh (eds.), *The Blair Effect, 2001–05* (Cambridge: Cambridge University Press, 2005). An interesting collection of articles on the New Labour period can be found in *Political Studies Review*, Vol. 9, No. 2 (May 2011).

On the history of Britain's relations with the wider world, see A. Gamble's *Beyond Europe and America: The Future of British Politics* (London: Palgrave, 2003), S. George's *An Awkward Partner: Britain in the European Community* (Oxford: Oxford University Press, 3rd edition, 1998), M. Garnett, S. Mabon, and R. Smith's *British Foreign Policy since 1945* (London: Routledge, 2017), D. Sanders's *Losing an Empire, Finding a Role* (London: Macmillan, 1990), and R. Self's *British Foreign and Defence Policy since 1945* (Houndmills: Palgrave, 2010).

Changes in the role of the British prime minister since 1945 are traced in P. Hennessy's *The Prime Minister. The Office and Its Holders since 1945* (London: Penguin, 2001), and M. Foley's *The Rise of the British Presidency* (Manchester: Manchester University Press, 1993).

Websites

The National Archives at Kew maintain documents from central government departments. A small selection of their material is available online at www.nationalarchives.gov.uk. A useful 'gateway' providing links to primary documents on British history is http://eudocs.lib.byu.edu/ index.php/History_of_the_United_Kingdom:_Primary_Documents. The Thatcher Foundation (www.margaretthatcher.org) has an extensive collection of material available online.

Chapter 4

Economy and society

Learning outcomes

After reading this chapter, you will:

* understand some of the key social and economic features of contemporary Britain;
* be able to assess the main causes of division and cohesion in British society; and
* appreciate the relevance of social and economic factors to an understanding of British politics, particularly in the context of recent economic difficulties.

Introduction

No political system can be understood in any depth without at least a basic awareness of the social and economic context in the relevant territory. This is particularly true of liberal democracies, whose politicians are expected at least to take note of public demands, and whose institutions can lose credibility if they prove incapable of adaptation to social and economic change. Samuel Johnson once wrote, 'How small of all that human hearts endure/ That part which laws or kings can cause or cure!' Nevertheless, government decisions affect social and economic life, for example, by legalising or outlawing some activities or practices, by subsidising industries, or by changing the tax and benefit systems.

No serious observer can dispute that British society has been transformed since World War II: it is only when the debate turns to the question of whether or not the changes have been for the better that profound differences of opinion often arise. While many people welcome Britain's transformation into a multiracial, multicultural society, which has adopted more liberal – 'live and let live' – attitudes on sexual identity and personal preferences, relationships which are not confined to heterosexual marriage, and where the emphasis is on 'consent' not conformity in sexual activity, other (often older) people disapprove of what they view as loss of national identity and culture, 'permissiveness', and lack of morality or discipline, which, in turn, they blame for many social problems such as crime, juvenile delinquency, drugs, gangs, sexually transmitted diseases, and single-parent families (especially unmarried teenage mums). Some commentators believe that Britain is experiencing something of a 'culture war' between (social) conservatives and liberals, and between traditionalists and progressives.

Britain: a divided nation?

Most developed nations are subject to internal tensions, and many have been less successful than Britain in containing potential friction. Some countries are characterised by divisions arising either from religion, language, ethnicity, competing national identities, or urban–rural tensions. Compared to most other countries, and with the notable and tragic exception of Northern Ireland (which has experienced violent conflict between two communities divided both by religion and national identity), Britain has mostly been relatively free of such divisions. Certainly, until recently, the British political system was widely admired for its cohesion, moderation, and stability, qualities which were attributed to the strong degree of 'homogeneity' – shared values among its people, whereby broadly similar attitudes and views fostered a sense of national identity and unity which transcended distinctions based on class or other forms of inequality. Such differences and disagreements which did exist were usually capable of being resolved within the existing parliamentary system, and, as such, there was very little support for 'direct action' or 'anti-system' political parties. Certainly, there has been no discernible support for revolutionary politics and ideologies, such as Marxism. Indeed, to the constant frustration of Left-wing intellectuals, the British working class has shown no interest in Marxism – an ideology which promotes the overthrow of Capitalism in order to 'liberate' workers from exploitation by the 'bourgeoisie' and wage slavery. On the contrary, up to one-third of the British working class has regularly voted Conservative, and whenever the Labour Party adopted a Left-wing or avowedly 'socialist' stance, as in the 1983 and 2019 general elections, it lost even more working-class support to the Conservatives.

However, the degree of national unity and homogeneity should not be overstated, for *some* differences and divisions have always existed in modern Britain, and some of these have actually become wider or deeper in recent decades, to the extent that, by 2019, Britain's political and parliamentary system was viewed by some commentators to be in crisis. After all, the more extensive the cultural, economic, and social divisions in society, the more difficult it becomes for governments and parties to satisfy large numbers of people; it is harder to achieve compromises and build a consensus in a polarised society, particularly when mainstream politicians themselves are viewed with suspicion or contempt and as a major part of the problem in the first place.

National and regional divisions

Although the economic history of the UK since 1945 has often been described as a process of gradual or genteel decline (punctuated by a crisis roughly once a decade), the country as a whole remains very prosperous by global standards. In 2014, the IMF placed it in the fifth position in terms of gross domestic product (GDP), while the World Bank ranked it sixth. Adjusting for cost of living factors and population (resulting in calculations of purchasing power parity (PPP) per capita), the UK fares less well but is still placed within the top 30 nations by most organisations. However, those figures are averages and conceal a diversity of socio-economic conditions at various levels within the UK. After all, if one person is paid £100,000 and another receives £20,000, their *average* income is £60,000!

The United Kingdom consists of four territories: England, Scotland, Wales (collectively known as Great Britain), and Northern Ireland. England has the largest population by far (see Table 4.1); its greater size, economic strength, and military power have always been reflected in its relations with its UK partners. Wales was the first of the smaller countries to come under English rule, having been conquered in the Middle Ages. After centuries of sporadic conflict, Scotland was peacefully united with England under the terms of the 1707 Act of Union, although it retained many of its distinctive institutions in, for example, the legal and religious spheres. Ireland followed suit in 1800–01. In 1921, after a bloody civil war, the island of Ireland was partitioned, with six northern counties staying within the United Kingdom of Great Britain and Northern Ireland.

Political tensions between the component parts of the UK are discussed in the context of devolution in Chapter 12. It is important to stress that although commentators usually focus on differences between the four nations, they have significant internal contrasts of their own in terms of culture, religion, and economic prosperity. For example, Scotland contains both the rural Highlands and the central belt dominated by the large cities of Glasgow and Edinburgh, and Wales is characterised by a rural west and northwest and industrial south and southeast, where the Welsh coal mines, steel works, and main ports were mostly located. It is also in northwest Wales that the Welsh language is most widely spoken, and where the Welsh nationalist party *Plaid Cymru* has often been strongest electorally, but the eastern area adjacent to the English border is heavily anglicised, while Pembrokeshire, in the far southwest, has variously been referred to as 'Little England beyond Wales'. Northern Ireland is itself a product of bitter religious, cultural, and nationalist conflict, which has continued with varying degrees of intensity since 1922.

The demand for devolution to Scotland and Wales led to referendums in both countries in 1979. In Wales, the proposition was defeated, while in Scotland, the majority in favour was not high enough to meet the threshold stipulated in the relevant legislation. However, during the 1980s, nationalist feeling remained strong, especially as it was believed that Margaret Thatcher's Conservative governments at Westminster gave excessive priority to England's economic interests, and particularly those of southeast England or the Home Counties. While many parts of Wales and Scotland suffered economic decline in those years, so too did some regions in England, where 'deindustrialisation' meant that heavy industries like coal mining, ship-building and steel-making were all affected by closures, contraction, and cutbacks. In the UK, as a whole, two million manufacturing jobs disappeared between 1979 and 1987, most of them in the North and in South Wales (see Case study 4.1). Most of the new jobs which have been created since the 1980s have been in the 'service sector' – banking, IT, leisure, retail, and so forth.

Regional inequalities within England are summed up by the often-used expression 'the north–south divide'. Yet this is an inexact, shorthand phrase for a complex phenomenon. Economic decline left some parts of the north almost unaffected, while some areas in the south were far from prosperous. London included affluent boroughs like Kensington and Chelsea, as well as areas of serious deprivation like Lambeth and Tower Hamlets. Yet even within prosperous districts, there are often extremes of wealth and poverty – it was in Kensington that the Grenfell Tower fire tragedy occurred in June 2017, drawing attention to the socio-economic deprivation which existed just a few streets away from beautiful houses whose average price was over £2 million. Yet more prosperous areas, particularly in parts of London and southeast England, with high house prices,

TABLE 4.1 Population of UK, mid-2019

United Kingdom (total)	66,796,807
England	56,286,961
Scotland	5,463,300
Wales	3,152,879
Northern Ireland	1,893,667

Source: Office for National Statistics, www.ons.gov.uk.

have experienced a very different problem, namely, that many public servants, like teachers and nurses, have found it difficult to afford either to rent or to buy accommodation in these areas; as property prices increased in some areas, so too did the number of unfilled vacancies for staff in local schools and hospitals.

More recently, in the twenty-first century, a new problem has emerged because of escalating house prices, namely that a growing number of young people who cannot afford to buy a flat or a house are compelled either to pay exorbitant rent – sometimes more than half their earnings in London – to a landlord in the private rented sector, or live at home with their parents, even when they are in their 30s. This, in turn, makes it difficult for young people who would like to 'settle down' –get married and have a family – but simply cannot afford to do so. The problem is made even worse by the relative lack of secure, long-term, well-paid jobs available to young people in an era of short-term or zero-hours contracts – what many politicians defend as 'labour market flexibility' – and stagnant pay after a decade of austerity and low rates of economic growth. Of course, for many, 'graduate debt' compounds the problems.

The country versus the cities

Until fairly recently, it has been easy to overlook another tension which cuts across regions of the UK. In the early stages of the (1780–1850) Industrial Revolution, the rural/urban split was a key domestic political issue. In an early manifestation of 'globalisation', the parliamentary allies of the agricultural interest fought to keep out cheap imports of wheat in order to maintain relatively high prices for their own produce, while industrialists campaigned for the removal of import controls, arguing that cheaper bread would improve the living standards of their workers without the need to increase wages. In short, urban manufacturers tended to favour free trade in food, while rural agriculturalists were normally 'protectionists'. The manufacturers won this battle, and agricultural workers continued to flock into the towns and cities which offered more lucrative (if not more healthy) work opportunities.

By the end of the twentieth century, only about 2 per cent of Britain's workforce was employed in agriculture, forestry, or fishing. Farming formerly enjoyed a political influence out of proportion to numbers, through the close relationship between the old Ministry of Agriculture, and the National Farmers' Union (NFU), which were part of a tight 'policy community' (see Chapter 19). The system of subsidies channelled through the European Union's Common Agricultural Policy (CAP) was inappropriate for British conditions, since it was devised for the benefit of relatively inefficient farmers in other EU member states. Among other results, it offered payments to British farmers in return for removing a proportion of their land from productive use, an arrangement which revived some of the old public resentment towards the (much reduced) agricultural interest, especially when British industrialists were being told that they must compete in a global free market or face bankruptcy, rather than receive government subsidies as they had previously. The antagonism increased on both sides during the 1990s and in the first decade of the twenty-first century, in the wake of outbreaks of the animal diseases BSE and foot-and-mouth, when farmers were accused of risking human health by cutting corners and costs in their procedures. For their part, farmers resented the heavy-handed political response to their problems. Meanwhile, the system of subsidies helped vast supermarket chains to dictate low prices for agricultural produce, making farming an increasingly unattractive career option even for those who had been raised on the land, and providing an additional incentive for cost-cutting practices.

After 1997, Labour's determination to ban hunting with dogs was seen by many rural dwellers as an attempt to interfere with their leisure activities by a government which also seemed antagonistic to their economic interests. The attack on fox-hunting was also portrayed by many countryside citizens and Conservatives as a form of 'class war', with Labour accused of supporting the ban, not on the grounds of genuine animal welfare and love of foxes but because of a belief that fox-hunters tended to be 'toffs' – wealthy landowners and rural aristocrats. In this context, many rural residents claimed that this was part of attack by the Left on their culture, lifestyles, and traditions. The issue led to the 1997 formation of the Countryside Alliance pressure group, whose relationship with government was a far cry from the days of cosy post-war cooperation between farmers and politicians.

Rural hostility towards the Labour government was reinforced by the high tax on fuel, which hit isolated rural dwellers particularly hard (and which prompted the 2001 'fuel blockades' by disgruntled tractor drivers and lorry drivers); by the poor state of rural transport; by the disappearance of many village amenities like post offices; by the shortage of affordable housing due to 'outsiders' buying holiday homes, which meant that younger people had to move away – and thus the original community slowly died out. Most of these problems predated Labour's election in 1997 and could have been blamed on the free-market policies pursued previously by the Conservatives, where unprofitable services were permitted to go out of business rather than be kept afloat through subsidies, and where 'the market' determined the supply and cots of housing, not local authorities or central government. Yet despite the vociferous rural support for the Alliance, it soon became clear that the countryside was divided against itself on the subject of hunting. In part, this was because of a large influx of people who had prospered in the cities, but subsequently migrated or retired to the countryside, in the hope of enjoying a more relaxed lifestyle without adopting any of the traditional rural pastimes.

Ethnicity

Until the second half of the twentieth century, Britain suffered from relatively few ethnic tensions. Ill-feeling against Jews who had fled from persecution in Eastern Europe led to the passage of restrictive Aliens Acts in 1905 and 1919. But in the 1930s, Oswald Mosley (1896–1980), leader of the British Union of Fascists, was unable to attract significant support for antisemitic policies.

Anti-Irish sentiment was strong in some areas, and the arrival of black and Asian immigrants in the second half of the twentieth century created new social tensions, while more recent years have seen some hostility directed towards migrant workers from Poland and Romania, who moved to Britain to work under the auspices of the European Union's 'free movement of labour'. The resentment this caused in some communities was a major factor in the vote to Leave the EU, in the June 2016 referendum (see Chapter 13). Until blatant racial discrimination was outlawed in the 1960s, it was not uncommon for landlords to advertise rooms-to-rent by placing a poster or piece of paper in their window, stipulating 'No Blacks, No Irish, No dogs'.

It was natural for newly arrived immigrants to congregate in specific areas (just as the British do themselves when they settle abroad, creating self-contained communities of 'ex-pats' in parts of southern Spain and southwest France especially), and this option became a means of self-preservation when immigrants encountered the hostility of some local white people. As many immigrants were disproportionately employed in low-paid jobs, this also meant that they were confined to cheaper accommodation located in the most run-down districts of towns and cities. However, they then sometimes found themselves being blamed for the socio-economic deprivation and poor-quality housing in particular neighbourhoods, such as statements like 'that part of town has gone downhill since the immigrants moved in', whereas, in fact, the area was often run-down before immigration. In other words, the concentration of immigrants

The decline of manufacturing industry

In the eighteenth century, Britain was the first country to experience an industrial revolution. Its initial competitive advantage was based on the exploitation of key raw materials, notably coal, but this was reinforced by British inventions, like the steam engine. In the second half of the nineteenth century, Britain's economic pre-eminence was eroded by competition from overseas, as new sources of raw materials were opened up by improvements in transport, and other countries adopted industrial techniques. But the number of workers employed in manufacturing industry continued to increase; between 1921 and 1951, it rose by 1.5 million, to 8.3 million (38 per cent of workers). Traditional industries like coal mining and iron and steel were now supplemented by the domestic manufacture of consumer goods like household appliances and motor cars. A strong manufacturing base was held to be vital, not least because Britain's industrial strength had helped it to survive two global conflicts. Also, it was felt that the country's prosperity depended on its ability to sell its goods in world markets.

However, since the early 1970s, Britain's manufacturing industry has declined sharply; its share of economic output fell from 30 per cent to 10 per cent. In part, this is the result of improved wages and living standards, which means that Britain has found it more difficult to compete with overseas producers in an increasingly 'globalised' economy. Successive governments tried to prop up manufacturing industry through subsidies; even the Conservative governments of 1979–97 resorted to this method to some extent, although Thatcherites objected to the practice in principle. A more relaxed attitude to manufacturing evolved not least because it was improbable that the nation would ever face 'total war' on the previous models of 1914–18 and 1939–45; if the UK ever became embroiled in a global conflict, it was likely to be decided by a rapid exchange of nuclear weapons rather than a concerted and prolonged productive effort from industry.

By 2014, manufacturing accounted for less than 8 per cent of employment in the UK. Some industries saw a truly spectacular decline; textiles, which had employed over a million people in the 1970s, fell to below 200,000. Meanwhile, the service sector had rapidly increased; around three-quarters of the working population was employed in concerns like retail, tourism, and banking. This change in occupational patterns had profound political consequences, not least because the service industries did not lend themselves so easily to trade union activity as did the old techniques of mass production. Another consequence was that the UK's import bill no longer matched the value of its 'visible' exports. This chronic trade deficit was partly offset by the 'invisible' earnings of the financial sector, so that companies based in the City of London, which had always been powerful, now commanded the automatic respect of any political party with realistic prospects of holding office. Between its defeat in the 1992 general election and its landslide 1997 victory, Labour made a priority of proving that it could run the economy without injuring the interests of the City. It had come to share the Conservative view that the global market should decide whether or not the country continued to manufacture goods on a significant scale. As a result, when it returned to office, Labour allowed the City considerable scope to regulate its own activities, allowing it to plunge the UK economy into crisis in 2007–08.

TABLE 4.2 The rising UK
population, 1951–2019 (millions)

Date	Total
1951	50.2
1961	52.7
1971	55.5
1981	56.4
1991	57.6
2001	59.5
2011	63.1
2019	66.7

Source: Office for National Statistics,
www.ons.gov.uk.

in districts of poverty and cheap housing was a case of correlation, not causation. Moreover, because of the tendency, due to cultural, familial, and economic reasons, for immigrants and ethnic minorities to live in close proximity to each other, they were often accused simultaneously of 'taking over' particular neighbourhoods – Margaret Thatcher once used the term 'swamped' – and of refusing to 'integrate' with the local indigenous white population, even though the latter might have displayed hostility in the first place and made the immigrants feel unwelcome (Table 4.2).

It is often implied in the popular press that UK politicians have been inactive in the face of mass immigration. In fact, restrictions have been imposed by legislation, notably in 1962, 1968, 1971, and 1981. The automatic right for would-be immigrants from outside Europe to settle in Britain is now virtually restricted to people with at least one British grandparent. However, in the 1990s, public attention switched to the asylum system, which allows the right of residence to people who have a well-founded fear of persecution in their home countries. Politicians of both main parties spoke freely of 'bogus' asylum seekers who, allegedly, are really 'economic migrants' in search of better living standards. Despite legislation of 1965, 1968, and 1976 aimed at improving race relations, 'playing the race card' continued to be regarded as a rewarding electoral tactic in some quarters. When Margaret Thatcher, in 1978, expressed her understanding of people who thought they were being 'swamped' by immigrants, the previously increasing support for the far-Right, anti-immigrant political party, the National Front, collapsed, as many of those citizens who feared or disliked immigrants switched to the Conservative Party in the 1979 general election.

At the start of this century, ethnic tensions (mainly in northern towns with high unemployment, like Blackburn, Burnley, and Oldham) were exploited by the British National Party (BNP), which campaigns for an end to all immigration, and, even more recently, the English Defence League (EDL), formed in 2009, which is hostile towards Muslims in particular. The 1999 Macpherson Report (see Chapter 9) exposed the problem of 'institutional racism' within the Metropolitan Police Force (which was well known among black people at the time of the 1981 inner-city riots). Prejudice was sometime unconscious, but this merely underlined its prevalence within society as a whole.

There is evidence to suggest that attitudes towards ethnicity have improved overall since the Macpherson Report. For example, in July 2005, when a black teenager, Anthony Walker, was brutally murdered in Liverpool, there was a national outcry which suggested a new level of public sensitivity towards racially motivated crime. However, following the 2016 vote to leave the EU, in which concern about immigration played a significant part, publicly expressed racist

Case study 4.2

Ethnicity in Britain: 2011 census

- In the 2011 census, 80.5 per cent of people living in England and Wales described themselves as 'White British'. The figure in Wales was 96 per cent.
- When questioned about their sense of national identity, more than nine in ten UK residents mentioned at least one UK identity (British, English, Scottish, Welsh, or Northern Irish).
- In Redcar and Cleveland in the northeast of England, the proportion of people describing themselves as 'White British' was 97.6 per cent. In the London borough of Newham, the corresponding figure was 16.7 per cent.
- In Leicester, 28.3 per cent of residents were 'Indian' in ethnic origin. In Redcar and Cleveland, the corresponding figure was 0.1 per cent.
- In the London borough of Kensington and Chelsea, 28.9 per cent of residents were categorised as 'Any other White' (i.e. 'White' but not British).
- In London, overall, the proportion of 'White British' was just 44.9 per cent.
- Outside London, the lowest proportion of white British was 34.5 per cent, recorded in Slough, Berkshire.
- Between the censuses of 1991 and 2011, the proportion of 'White' residents in England and Wales fell from 94.1 per cent to 86 per cent.
- In all, 13 per cent of the population of England and Wales had been born overseas.

Source: 2011 census, Office for National Statistics, www.ons.gov.uk.

abuse and vile insults towards various black public figures, such as MPs (Labour's David Lammy and Diane Abbott especially have been targeted), sportspeople, and journalists, have increased alarmingly, aided by social media: Twitter in particular.

Although discrimination against Commonwealth immigrants (and their descendants) has remained a serious problem, the successive enlargements of the European Union after 2002 complicated the issue for those who based their opposition to immigration on grounds of 'colour'. The right of free movement within the EU inspired many people from countries like Poland to seek work within the UK. In 2012, it was estimated that the number of Polish-born people in Britain had risen from about 60,000 in 2001 to over 640,000. Immigration from Eastern Europe was a major reason for an increase in the non-British-born population, from an estimated 9.1 per cent in 2005 to more than 13 per cent in 2011. Such figures suggested that the UK was emulating the archetypal 'melting pot' society of the USA, where the overseas-born proportion was similar. One symbol of (generally) improving race relations is the fact that the number of people described as 'mixed race' on census forms almost doubled between 2001 and 2011, to 1.2 million. Around 2.3 million people in England and Wales were either married to, or living with, someone from a different ethnic background. In previous decades, there was often widespread disapproval of 'mixed race' relationships, as if being romantically or sexually involved with someone from a different ethnic background was a 'betrayal' of one's own 'race'. Fortunately, such narrow-minded views and intolerance appear to be declining.

Although the official line was that immigration – mainly by young and more vigorous people who would do jobs which might otherwise remain unfilled by British workers – was good for the country, many members of the public felt less sanguine. Some British workers thought that they were being 'priced out' of work, since the newcomers were often willing to accept lower wages for their labour, quite possibly because they would still be paid more than what they would earn in their country of origin. Public services such as health and education also came under serious pressure in some areas, along with housing and transport. Resentment towards migrant workers for 'causing' unemployment, low wages, and shortages of (affordable) housing, and placing a strain on overstretched public services increased after the 2008 financial crash and the subsequent post-2010 decade of austerity. A major political consequence of this resentment and blaming of migrant workers was the rapidly growing popularity of the United Kingdom Independence Party (UKIP), which argued that Britain could only regain control of its borders – and thus halt immigration – if it left the EU completely. In the 2015 general election campaign, the main parties focused on ways of restricting the rights of immigrants to claim benefits, but this approach was unlikely to either affect the overall numbers or the British budget deficit or to assuage the concerns of those who held migrant workers responsible for the problems we have just cited. In 2010, David Cameron had pledged to cut the net number of immigrants to less than 100,000 per year, yet in the month of the 2015 general election, it was revealed that in the previous year, 641,000 people had arrived in the UK, while 323,000 left – a net immigration figure of 318,000. The trend persisted after the election, at a time when the desperate plight of refugees from the civil conflict in Syria was also attracting considerable publicity and giving rise to conflicting emotions within the British public.

The new focus on immigration from within the EU added complexity to an ongoing debate on the concept of 'multiculturalism'. At one time, this notion was taken to mean that immigrants should be encouraged to retain, in full, their former identities and cultures, regardless of their origin. This was contrasted to the ideal of 'integration', in which the immigrants would be expected to conform to British identity and values and become fluent in speaking the English language. The former Conservative Cabinet Minister and Party Chairman, Norman Tebbit, referred to a 'cricket test', implying that the allegiance or loyalty of ethnic minorities should be judged by their sporting loyalties during international cricket matches – who would they support when England played India, Pakistan, or the West Indies? However, this argument merely raised serious questions about the nature of 'Britishness' and exposed the extent to which English people had previously confused that concept with their own specific sense of nationhood: it could hardly be taken for granted, for example, that Scottish-born citizens would be enthusiastic supporters of the England cricket team. The most plausible conclusion from the debate envisaged Britishness as an elastic concept, which could embrace people of varying cultures so long as they accepted the basic values of liberal democracy (see Case study 4.5).

Gender

Traditionally, the major source of conflict in the area of gender has been discrimination against women. In this sphere, there has been a remarkable change since the Victorian age, when women could not vote, 'surrendered' their property to their husband upon marriage, and could be subjected to violence (including sexual assault) by their husbands: when getting married, a woman, in the eyes of the law, was her husband's possession, to do with as he pleased, and it was not until the early 1990s that rape-in-marriage was made a criminal offence. Yet, despite considerable improvements in these spheres, gender remains a serious source of social division in the UK. A particular grievance is the fact that women (including both full- and part-time employees) receive, on average, around 80 per cent of the earnings of their male counterparts, despite legislation on equal pay (1970) and to outlaw sexual discrimination (1975), consolidated and augmented by the Equality Act of 2010.

If Britain was a genuine meritocracy, women could be expected marginally to outnumber men in all powerful positions. After all, due to differential life expectancy between the sexes, there are marginally more women than men (33.6 million to 32.7 million in 2018), while girls now consistently perform better than boys in school examinations. But despite spectacular exceptions, like the career of Margaret Thatcher, most women are still prevented from putting their talents to full use and are under-represented in many professions, with the most senior (and well-paid) posts still mostly occupied by men. The number of women attaining more powerful or senior posts in the workplace is increasing, but the pace and scale of change have often been slow, as sexist attitudes have sometimes proved hard to eradicate (and actually prove in court or an employment tribunal). Some men have resented women challenging their seniority and associated privileges, or sneered at the promotion of gender equality in the workplace as 'political correctness gone mad'. The good news, though, is that as history has shown, dinosaurs do eventually die out.

The usual rationale for not appointing or promoting more women is that many women will, at some point, want to stop work to raise children. While some old-fashioned employers might view this as a reason for not appointing young women in the first place, such discrimination is unlawful, and so other reasons will be cited to 'justify' the failure to appoint or promote more women: they do not have the same experience or qualifications as the appointed or promoted man, or that they do not have the same continuity of employment (because they have taken career breaks to raise children). In some instances or professions, men might indirectly increase their promotion prospects by 'bonding' or socialising with their colleagues after work, and thus 'proving' that they are a key team player, or establishing their popularity as 'one of the lads', whereas women who still have prime responsibility of looking after children (or maybe an elderly family member) will find it much more difficult to partake in evening or weekend social events with their work colleagues. In such circumstances, it is often difficult for women to *prove* that they have been discriminated against when overlooked for promotion by one of their male colleagues. Furthermore, women still face the risk that if they do take legal action against an employer for sexual discrimination, they might then be labelled 'one of those feminists' or 'a troublemaker' by other employers, and thus continue to encounter difficulties in securing employment or promotion subsequently. In other words, in tackling sexism, they will often be met with even more sexism from the perpetrators, as well as encountering the syndrome of 'blaming the victim'. Yet if women do not challenge such sexism and campaign for genuine equality in the workplace (and beyond), then discrimination and under-representation will not be eradicated.

In spite of residual sexism in the workplace (and beyond), women now find it much easier to escape from the previous socially ascribed role of subservient housewife and mother, and they exercise this right in increasing numbers. The 2011 census found that the population now included more than five million divorced or separated people; among the marriages contracted in 1972, around a fifth had ended in divorce within 15 years, whereas the corresponding figure for 1997 marriages was almost a third. In 2011, less than half of the UK's adults were married (or remarried). Cohabitation outside marriage was increasing significantly, but compared to 12.3 million households occupied by a married couple with or without children, in 2013, there were 1.9 million houses in which a lone parent was bringing up at least one dependent child.

Lone-parent households – usually, though by no means always, headed by a woman – suffer from obvious economic disadvantages and present an acute problem for policymakers who recognise that childhood poverty, and associated emotional or psychological problems, can have a detrimental effect on children's future life chances, thereby perpetuating a 'cycle of deprivation'

Case study 4.3

How Britain has changed

- In 1981, men in paid employment outnumbered women by more than three million. By 2019, the difference was less than two million (17.2.3 million to 15.5 million). However, 40 per cent of women worked part-time, compared to just 13 per cent of men.
- In 1970, the proportion of live births to unmarried women was less than 10 per cent. By 1993, this had risen to 32.2 per cent, and by2018, 48.3 per cent of children were born to women who were not married or in a civil partnership. Clearly, the former stigma (for women) of having children 'out of wedlock' has steadily declined.
- In 1911, the proportion of manual workers in Britain was around three-quarters. This had fallen to less than a half by 1981, and by 2018, it was only a quarter. By contrast, the largest occupational category in 2018 was 'professionals', including account-ants, bankers, engineers, IT managers/designers, lawyers, medics, management/business consultants, police, scientists, social workers, teachers, and so forth. Britain continued to move away from blue-collar manufacturing industry to a white-collar service-based economy.
- In 1971, just under half of UK households were owner-occupiers. By 2007, the pro-portion had risen to 73.3 per cent, but had declined to 63.4 per cent in 2016, as stag-nant earnings, insecure employment, graduate debt, and general unaffordability of many houses prevented younger people from buying a home of their own, and thus forced many of them to privately rent (either alone, or as part of a house-share) or move back home and live with their parents. Meanwhile, the number of households in the private rented sector increased from 2.8 million in 2007 to 4.5 million in 2017, by which time, people in the 25–34 age group constituted the largest cohort, ac-counting for just over a third of all private renters in the UK. In 1971, around a third of households lived in council accommodation, but by 2016, this figure had fallen to just 8 per cent, due both the 'Right to Buy' policy imposed on councils by the first (1979–83) Thatcher government, and the failure to replace the council houses sold in the 1980s (a deliberate decision intended to eradicate most public housing alto-gether in favour of owner-occupation and private renting), meaning that there is a dearth of such housing today.

over generations. The Child Support Act 1991 was an attempt to ensure that both parents con-tributed to the maintenance of their children, but the difficulty of applying the rules with sensi-tivity to a wide variety of circumstances often caused additional friction between many divorced and separated couples, and was often particularly traumatic for women who had fled an abusive, alcoholic, or a violent partner. Moreover, while the Child Support Agency (established in 1993) could be portrayed by its supporters as a means of helping lone parents secure financial support and justice, critics suspected that it was really motivated by a political drive to demonise and denigrate 'feckless' single parents, particularly young, unmarried mothers, who were sometimes made scapegoats for many of Britain's growing social problems in the late 1980s and 1990s, and the emerging 'underclass'. The existing system of child support was denounced in 2006 by the Secretary of State for Work and Pensions and by a subsequent report. After a brief period when the issue was dealt with by a non-departmental Child Maintenance and Enforcement Commission, in 2012, a Child Maintenance Group was established within the Department for Work and Pensions.

An increasingly asked question today is how British people can achieve a suitable 'work/life balance'. Although this is a serious difficulty for people of both sexes, it is particularly pressing for women, some of whom have decided to abandon the idea of raising a family in order to advance their careers. In some high-profile cases, however, talented women have taken the opposite course. Such dilemmas are a by-product of successful campaigns which have given women the freedom to choose on issues like abortion. Many of these changes were won by the (liberal) feminist movement of the 1960s and 1970s. Ironically, one of the chief victims of these successful battles has been the feminist movement itself, which has lost some of its cohesion, as the most glaring abuses have been addressed, at least in part. But this is not to say that the battle for real equality has been won – far from it, and a new generation of feminists has emerged in recent years to tackle not only ongoing sexism but also new forms of misogyny (or forms of misogyny which were not previously recognised as such): campaigns against pornography (often entailing the sexual abuse of women who are coerced into, or trapped in, the porn industry due to debt or drug addiction) and the #MeToo movement are examples of this 'new wave' of twenty-first century feminism.

While most discussions of gender focus on the need for policies which will improve the life chances of women (e.g. better childcare facilities allowing them to work full-time), there are also clear signs that some men are experiencing difficulties in the wake of the 'sexual revolution'. Spectacular stunts by the Fathers4Justice pressure group in the 2000s were a reminder to policymakers that measures which help one section of society can cause resentment, derived from a sense of injustice or discrimination, among another (see Chapter 19). Meanwhile, surveys have revealed that many men would like to spend more time with their children or/and partners, but fear that requests to reduce or rearrange their working hours will be viewed unsympathetically by their employers; management might suspect that such men are not fully committed to the company or their career, or are not 'macho' enough, certainly when compared to previous generations.

Religion

The terrorist attacks of 11 September 2001 in New York and Washington, perpetrated in the name of Islam, brought the issue of religion back onto the agenda of British politics, after a period in which it had been widely assumed that Britain was becoming a secular society in which religious identity was of declining importance. Like the rural/urban clash, this is an unwelcome echo of the past. Conflict between Protestants and Catholics was endemic between the sixteenth-century Reformation and the removal of (most) anti-Catholic discrimination in 1829. Another intolerant law, which prevented Jews from sitting in the House of Commons, was repealed in 1858.

The more liberal climate of the Victorian period was a sign of genuine tolerance, because many policymakers cared deeply about religion, but agreed nevertheless to extend civil rights to people whose beliefs they vehemently rejected. By contrast, the relaxed attitude of the twentieth century was fostered by the general indifference towards religious faith, and for a growing number of British people, religious beliefs (or their absence) were viewed as a private matter. Some religious tensions persisted in cities like Glasgow and Liverpool, partly as an overspill from the conflict between Protestants and Catholics in Northern Ireland, but overall, the civil unrest which erupted there in the late 1960s was a spectacular exception which proved the general rule. By that time, few Britons on the mainland appreciated that religious discrimination could still

TABLE 4.3 Religious affiliation in England and
Wales, 1983–2018

% self-defining as	1983	2018
Church of England/Anglican	40	12
Roman Catholic	10	7
Methodist	4	1
Christian – no denomination	3	13
Jewish	1	a
Muslim	1	6
Other	1	3
No religion	31	52

[a]Less than 0.5% of respondents defined themselves as Jewish
in 2018.
Source: Office for National Statistics, www.ons.gov.uk.

create genuine outrage anywhere in the UK, and hostility towards Irish Republican terrorism in Britain was all the greater because its roots were so little understood (see Chapter 12).

Popular misconceptions threatened to increase the inevitable tensions after the events of 11 September 2001. Islam is the fastest-growing faith in Britain, its adherents increasing, from just 1 per cent of the population in 1983 to 6 per cent in 2018, and causing concern among those who – post 9/11 – equate Islam with violence and strongly anti-Western views and values. The issue inevitably became entangled with concurrent controversies over race relations, asylum, and new modes or sources of terrorism, especially after the terrorist attack on the London transport system in July 2005, when explosives were detonated by four young Muslim suicide bombers from Leeds and Luton. The explosions killed 52 people and seriously injured more than 100. In 2009, the English Defence League (EDL) was formed, a far-Right group motivated by hatred of 'radical' Islam and its Muslim followers, and engaged in 'street politics' to protest against Islam and its alleged threat to British values. In many respects, the EDL has superseded the National Front and the British National Party for far-Right activists who like to see themselves as ultra-patriotic, and defenders of a white working class which has apparently been abandoned by mainstream politicians and scorned by 'politically correct' liberals. Some of those involved with the EDL are ex-football hooligans, seeking a new outlet for their visceral hatred of 'the Other', and an opportunity to engage in 'direct action' or physical violence, rather than mainstream electoral politics.

Apart from the increase in citizens defining themselves as Muslims, the other main trend evident in Table 4.3 is the decline in the number of people defining themselves as Church of England or Anglican, for having constituted 40 per cent of respondents in 1983, they now represent just 12 per cent of the population. However, it should be recognised that the 40 per cent in 1983 might have exaggerated the genuine number of this religious denomination, because, previously, many people who did not want publicly to admit to being 'non-believers' declared themselves to be Church of England by default. The corollary of this decline is the number of British citizens who now declare themselves to be non-religious, their numbers having increased from 31 per cent in 1983 to 52 per cent in 2018 – from less than a third to over half. However, this might belie a demographic trend, whereby older people retain a religious identity, but many younger people are non-identifiers or non-believers. As with various other social trends and values, the headline figures conceal generational differences.

Age

A major dilemma for British policymakers today is the increasing proportion of elderly people in the population. For many years, there have been predictions of a 'pensions crisis', as advances in medical science and a declining birth rate have transformed the balance of numbers between people in work and those over the retirement age. In 1971, the proportion of over-65s was 13 per cent; by 2016, this had risen to 18 per cent, meaning that there were 300 pensioners for every 1,000 people working. More than one million people were aged over 85. In 2007, the Office for National Statistics (ONS) revealed that for the first time ever, the number of people aged over 65 had exceeded those who were 16 or younger. It is now anticipated that a male baby born in Britain today can (global warming and pandemics notwithstanding) expect to live for 79 years and a girl to 83 years, with 22 per cent of newborn boys and 28 per cent of newborn girls likely to live to 100 years. This ageing population – due to factors such as the post-war 'baby boom' reaching retirement, better medical cures and treatments, improving diets, healthier lifestyles, and (for many, but not all) improved housing and living conditions – has caused concern for policymakers, because of the pensions' costs, and also the fact that older people tend to suffer from more health problems, and are thus increasingly likely to spend time in hospital. At the same time, cutbacks in social services funding, facilities, and staff mean that there is often a lack of (affordable) social care for frail or infirm elderly people, be it nursing homes providing permanent residential care or 'home helps' who visit an elderly person in their home on a daily or weekly basis. The main policy response of recent governments has been to warn that the retirement age needs to be increased, to 66 in 2020, and then to 67 by 2028. However, in the summer of 2019, the Centre for Social Justice, a Right-wing think tank originally created by Iain Duncan Smith, a former Work and Pensions Secretary (and 'architect' of Universal Credit), suggested that the retirement age should be raised to 70 by 2028 and to 75 by 2035, in order to make substantial savings from the £92billion annual cost of providing old age pensions.

In addition to this economic problem, there are also growing cultural tensions between members of different generations. As people live longer, they are more likely to be baffled and alienated by the leisure activities and attitudes of young people, and new modes or definitions of social or sexual identity and behaviour. Accelerating technological change has also increased the cultural contrasts in recent decades, with relatively new innovations like the home computer and the mobile telephone creating suspicion and unease among many of the elderly people. Older people were strong supporters of the 2016 vote to Leave the EU, many of them doubtless nostalgic for the days of the British Empire or Commonwealth, and reminiscing about Britain liberating Europe in 1945 (and therefore resentful of Europe apparently telling Britain what it can and cannot do). Meanwhile, pressure from older people, who feel most vulnerable to crime or hanker after a return to social discipline (including the restoration of national service or military conscription for young people, and the return of the death penalty for the most serious crimes), also helps to keep law and order high on the political agenda (usually to the advantage of the Conservatives), even when official statistics indicate that crime is diminishing.

Interestingly, 'both' generations will often admonish each other for different things, but each claims the moral high ground. Older people will often condemn younger people's widespread or frequent use of (obscene) four-letter words and their willingness to engage in casual sex (rather than wait until they are married) or have same-sex relationships, citing all of these as evidence of young people's lack of morality. In response, young people are likely to consider (many) older people to be homophobic, racist, and sexist, and ask what sort of morality allows, or even encourages, such intolerant and offensive views.

Economic divisions

For some commentators, the aforementioned discussion pays inadequate attention to the true cause of all the friction in British society. Influenced by the work of Karl Marx, they believe that the fundamental cause of all social division is economic. In their view, Britain is marked by significant economic inequalities; and until these are removed, certain groups will continue to suffer discrimination and feel aggrieved. From this perspective, for example, hostility towards immigrants is really an expression of economic insecurity. A mass influx of foreigners, anxious to escape poverty at home and willing to take on any available work, is alleged to present a threat to the livelihood of members of the existing population. Thus, by an unpleasant irony, foreigners who take low-paid jobs will be resented the most by their poor competitors, deflecting attention from the fact that all of them are being exploited by their common enemy – the employers. The same view of society would interpret the 'liberation' of women as a free gift to the capitalist system, since many female workers are part-timers who provide employers and companies with cheap labour, even if they think that their wages provide a useful supplement to the family income.

The Marxist socio-economic analysis fell out of fashion in the mid-1980s. This is not just because the (officially) Marxist regimes of Eastern Europe collapsed at the end of the decade. More important, it seemed that the key Marxist concept of class no longer provided a convincing explanation of social change in Britain, or indeed in other Western countries. Marx had predicted that the majority of workers would be increasingly exploited as **capitalism** moved from one crisis to the next, with wages being driven down to maintain or restore profits. Yet, instead of the working class suffering 'immiseration' as predicted by Marx, and in spite of periodic economic recessions, most people in work enjoyed a consistent improvement in living standards until the onset of economic difficulties in 2007–08 and subsequent decade of austerity. Due to the introduction of cheap domestic appliances, most Britons today would find the daily life even of a well-paid worker in the Victorian era unimaginably tough. For example, as recently as 1972, central heating had been installed in just over a third of British homes. Forty years later, the proportion had soared to 95 per cent. There was a similar increase over that period in the ownership of telephones (42 per cent in 1972, 98 per cent in 2002 – leaving aside mobile telephones, owned by 93 per cent of adults in 2014). Further evidence that Marxism has had no appeal to the British working class was the fact that up to 33 per cent of manual workers regularly voted Conservative (and 48 per cent did so in 2019), and in the 1980s, many of them were strongly attracted by Margaret Thatcher's pledges on selling council house to their tenants, curbing immigration, tackling strikes by trade unions, and strengthening law and order. When the Labour Party offered a 'socialist' manifesto in the 1983 general election, it haemorrhaged support and slumped to its worst post-war result, attracting just 27 per cent of votes cast. Labour offered another Left-wing programme in the 2019 election, and again saw many workers turn their backs on the Party, this time voting for a Conservative Party led by Boris Johnson.

As we discuss in Chapter 18, social class still provides part of the explanation for voting behaviour and political commitment in general, but the situation has become much more complicated than it was in the earlier post-war period. Orthodox Marxism, though, insists that in advanced capitalist societies, there are only two classes – those who own and control the 'means of production' (the bourgeoisie), and those who have to sell their labour in order to survive

Capitalism

an economy, and associated political, legal, and social system based upon the private ownership of property, the creation of wealth, and the pursuit of increased profit as the main or sole purpose of all economic activity.

(the proletariat). In Britain, the official classification of occupational groups is linked to status within the overall workforce (see Table 4.4). This reflects the country's self-image as a **meritocracy**. In general, the higher the social ranking, the greater the formal educational qualifications. It is now widely assumed, for example, that a university education is essential to anyone hoping to build a successful career in the managerial and higher professional occupations. But the list does not necessarily tally with public respect for the various activities; highly educated journalists (in the second group in Table 4.4) invariably feature near the bottom of any league table of popular esteem, alongside politicians.

Other classifications rest on divisions between manual and non-manual labour (sometimes called 'white-collar' and 'blue-collar', respectively) and subdivide the manual category into 'skilled' or 'semi-skilled'. This reflects the old assumption that people who work with their hands earn less than 'brain workers'. But this no longer holds true; plumbers, for example, can earn considerably more than clerks in offices. Until 1961, when a limit on their wages was removed, professional footballers would have ranked fairly low in any classification. Their current earning power and lavish lifestyles show how difficult it is to fit particular individuals into any list.

Soon after becoming prime minister in 1990, John Major promised that over the next decade, the division between blue- and white-collar workers would be eroded further, so that Britain would become 'a genuinely classless society'. His remark is often misquoted as a promise to reduce *economic inequality*, rather than to help undermine the traditional stereotypes associated with particular occupations and to promote more social mobility, whereby people from poorer backgrounds can rise to higher social positions. After all, Major himself had emanated from a relatively humble family background, and unlike most of his predecessors, had not gone to university; he himself seemed to symbolise the classless, meritocratic, Britain, which he claimed to want to establish. Major's successor, Prime Minister Tony Blair, similarly portrayed a more 'socially mobile' Britain, with greater opportunities for citizens from poorer or disadvantaged backgrounds and communities to rise to more affluent, middle-class jobs and lifestyles: this was a major reason why Blair placed so much emphasis on education and training, for in an era when white-collar jobs have replaced many blue-collar or manual occupations, qualifications have become more important than ever before. As such, Blair was convinced that expanding and improving education – most notably increasing the number of university students – was a major way of ensuring that more people obtained (or had the chance to obtain) the qualifications and skills which would enable

Meritocracy

a society in which the most powerful positions in all important spheres are allocated according to the ability, experience, qualifications, skills, or talent of the candidates, rather than other factors such as birth (inheritance), age, race, or sex/gender. Inequalities and higher earnings derived from merit are generally considered to be 'legitimate' and deserved.

TABLE 4.4 Classification of social categories (used in official statistics since 2001)

1. Higher managerial and professional occupations (e.g. company directors, doctors, and lawyers)
2. Lower managerial and professional occupations (e.g. nurses, journalists, and junior police officers)
3. Intermediate occupations (e.g. secretaries)
4. Small employers (e.g. farmers)
5. Lower supervisory occupations (e.g. train drivers)
6. Semi-routine occupations (e.g. shop assistants)
7. Routine occupations (e.g. waiters and refuse collectors)
8. Long-term unemployed

them to obtain employment in the globalised 'knowledge economy'. Much more recently, Boris Johnson has similarly spoken of his desire to create a Britain characterised by 'levelling-up' in order to tackle socio-economic deprivation, particularly among the 'left behind', many of whom were the keenest supporters of Brexit (see Chapter 13).

It should be emphasised, though, that advocacy of greater equality of opportunities and social mobility allows Conservatives, 'social democratic' Labour politicians, liberals, and 'progressives' to express concern about inequality and poverty without actually introducing measures to narrow the gap between the rich and the poor. Rather than directly tackle (curb) boardroom greed and corporate excesses – whereby many city bankers and company CEOs are paid millions of pounds – in order to create fairer, more equal society, and thus eradicate poverty, the focus of Conservatives, New Labour, and Liberal Democrats alike has been to concentrate on measures to create pathways out of poverty and deprivation for poorer citizens and communities, and thereby promote 'social mobility', which, in turn, is equated with

Case study 4.4

Economic inequality in Britain

To the non-specialist, statistics on this subject can often seem bewildering since some refer to *income* (the amount earned regularly, for example, in the form of salaries, benefits, or interest on savings), while others focus on *wealth* (overall assets, usually including the value of any property owned, as well as accumulated savings).

On any measure, British society is marked by significant inequalities. The poorest 20 per cent of households receive 8 per cent of total national income, whereas the top 20 per cent earn 40 per cent of the total. In 2017–18, the average disposable income for a non-retired household without children, in the lowest 20 per cent, was £14,095, while for the top 20 per cent, the figure was £78,383. There is also considerable inequality among the richest households, with the top 0.1 per cent earning an average of £941,582 in 2012, compared to an average of £259,917 for the top 1.0 per cent (while the median household income was around £24,000). Household income in London and the Southeast was considerably higher than in other areas, although so too was the cost of accommodation, either to buy or to rent. Without taxation and benefits, inequality would be even more marked; in 2013–14, the average income of the top 20 per cent would have been 15 times greater than that of the poorest 20 per cent.

In terms of wealth, in 2016, the richest 1 per cent owned 13 per cent of wealth and the top 10 per cent of households owned 44 per cent, whereas the poorest 50 per cent owned just 9 per cent. Wealth inequality also has a regional dimension, with London and the Southeast enjoying far higher levels of wealth than the rest of the UK: the northeast of England and Wales have the lowest levels of wealth. Internationally, according to 2017 OECD data, Britain is the eighth most unequal country in the world in terms of income distribution.

Sources: Office for National Statistics (ONS) (https://www.ons.gov.uk/peoplepopulation andcommunity/personalandhouseholdfinances/incomeandwealth), Organisation for Economic Cooperation and Development (OECD) (http://www.oecd.org/unitedkingdom/OECD-Income-Inequality-UK.pdf), Equality Trust (https://www.equalitytrust.org.uk/scale-economic-inequality-uk).

classlessness and 'meritocracy'. However, this does not actually reduce enormous inequalities of earnings or wealth, but instead seeks to ensure that more poorer citizens are promised opportunities to become better-off themselves; tackling the deeper-rooted structural or systemic causes of inequality and poverty is thereby sidestepped. Furthermore, it places the onus for escaping poverty on the individuals affected; governments can say 'we gave you more opportunities, but you have failed to take them or make enough effort, so it is your own fault that you are still struggling'. This reflects and reinforces the widespread 'common sense' view (see Controversy 4.1) that much, if not most, poverty and socio-economic deprivation are due to the alleged failings, laziness, or irresponsibility of the poor themselves, rather than being inherent and intrinsic to free-market capitalism and neoliberalism; poverty and hardship are thus blamed on the affected individuals, not the economic system itself or the employers who pay low wages (often while paying themselves huge salaries and bonuses for their apparent hard work).

While there can be no dispute about the existence of substantial economic inequality in Britain, its effect on society as a whole is still controversial, reflecting continuing ideological divisions (see Chapter 16). For economic liberals like Margaret Thatcher, individuals are primarily motivated by the desire to improve the living standards of themselves and their families. The free market will decide who deserves the greatest rewards, and this acts as a spur to make ambitious people more productive. An 'incentivised' society benefits everyone within it; more jobs will be created, and even those who cannot find work of any kind will be guaranteed a subsistence income out of the proceeds. In keeping with these ideas, after Thatcher became party leader in 1975, the Conservatives explicitly singled out 'aspiring' members of the working class as potential supporters. By contrast, socialists believe that inequality is intrinsically wrong (outside modest limits), inherent in Capitalism, and cruelly denies anything like equal life chances to those who are born into poor households. Thus, from the perspective of socialists, the competition which is prized by economic liberals is rigged from the start – against those who are born into impoverished households. In 2015, the prestigious Organisation for Economic Co-operation and Development (OECD) added a more practical argument against inequality, arguing that economic growth is hampered when the gap between rich and poor is too wide, while academics like Danny Dorling have written extensively about the political risks posed by growing inequality in Britain; a 'ticking time bomb' (see 'Further reading' at the end of this chapter). A further condemnation of 'excessive' inequality was provided in R. Wilkinson's and K. Pickett's *The Spirit Level*, where they highlight the damaging social and psychological consequences; it is literally bad for people's health, and for the health of society in general. Yet as Controversy 4.1 explains, inequality is widely accepted in Britain and has certainly not undermined or 'delegitimised' the economic or political system; indeed, much of the working class regularly votes Conservative, a party which, ideologically, believes in the importance, inevitability, and necessity of inequality.

Poverty

To many commentators, particularly on the Right, poverty hardly exists in the UK today, certainly in comparison to the nineteenth century. Statistics relating to life expectancy illustrate this argument. Men born in 1901 could not expect to survive beyond the age of 45, while average life expectancy for women was 49. In 2011, the respective figures had risen to almost 78 and 82, and continue to rise. These data obviously reflect improvements in healthcare and discoveries like antibiotics; however, it is also a reasonable indication that the benefits of economic growth and higher earnings have been widely shared, otherwise high mortality rates among the poor would have had a greater effect in holding down the average. Nevertheless, the overall UK figures conceal remarkable disparities. For example, a female born in the London borough of Kensington and Chelsea in 2010 could expect to live almost to the age of 90, while her counterpart born in Glasgow would die 12 years earlier. On average, men born in Glasgow would die seven years before the male national average.

Clearly, *absolute* poverty has been greatly reduced since 1901. Few Britons totally lack access to the basic amenities of life, like adequate food and shelter (although the recent increases in food banks and homelessness suggest that even this claim can be challenged). But when commentators emphasise the continued existence of *relative* poverty, they are pointing to a real dilemma for policymakers. The general improvement over the last century or so has also led to a rise in demands among a more comfortable population, and those whose lifestyles would have aroused uncomprehending envy among the poor of 1901 can still be numbered among the ranks of the 'socially excluded' today, because they enjoy much less than a full share of the technological and other advances over the period. For example, by 2001, more households (seven million) were in possession of two cars than those (6.7 million) who lacked a single vehicle; in 2011, there were 12 cars for every 10 households in the UK. This indicator of economic inequality (in a society which often regards a car as a necessity, not a luxury) was not a serious consideration back in 1901! In 1995, only 20 per cent of people regarded a home computer as a necessity for a child; within just four years, this proportion had more than doubled, to 42 per cent.

Relative poverty is officially defined as occurring when a household's income falls below 60 per cent of the national median (as opposed to the average) income. On this criterion, the Blair government estimated that child poverty doubled under Conservative rule between 1979 and 1997, to about 4.4 million. It claimed that its own policies had reduced the level by half a million by 2001. This was regarded as a reasonable start, but campaigning organisations like the Child Poverty Action Group (CPAG) pointed out that the government itself had embarked on its programme with the goal of reducing the figure by over a million during this period. According to the 2001 census, there were around 12 million young people under 15 in the UK; if more than a quarter of these were suffering from relative economic deprivation, the country was clearly a long way from the meritocratic goal of liberal democracy. The impression was confirmed in 2007, when it was estimated that 3.8 million children were living in poverty – an increase, after six years of slow decline in the figures. In 2011, Save the Children estimated that 1.6 million children were living in *severe* poverty – that is, they were living in households with less than *half* the national average income. In Manchester, the proportion of children in this plight was estimated at 27 per cent. This was before the impact of changes in welfare payments introduced by the coalition government had been felt. In 2015, CPAG anticipated that, if current 'austerity' policies continued, there would be 4.7 million children living in poverty by 2020 – more than when New Labour came to office in 1997. However, like unemployment and the more general issue of inequality, poverty was not a major issue in the 2015 general election, reflecting perhaps not a general insensitivity to the problem so much as a feeling that there was little that government could do about it, beyond fostering an economic context which favoured economic growth and job creation. To that extent, debate (or absence of) on these socio-economic issues, even well into the twenty-first century, could plausibly be regarded as part of the legacy of Thatcherism, which effectively 'delegitimized' advocacy of equality via curbs on bosses' pay, higher taxes on the rich, and direct wealth redistribution.

Controversy 4.1

Why is inequality so widely accepted in Britain?

It is widely recognised that Britain is a highly unequal society, with great disparities of incomes and wealth, yet this has neither resulted in support for radical political change nor much interest in avowed egalitarian ideologies like Marxism (at least, outside academia). Indeed, when the Labour Party has contested general elections on a Left-wing manifesto pledging to reduce inequality and create a fairer, more equal society, as it did in 2019, it has been heavily defeated, with much of the working class – who it might be thought would welcome egalitarian and redistributive policies – abandoning Labour in large numbers, and voting Conservative instead. Hence an apparent paradox; Britain is one of the most unequal societies in the Western world, yet also the least supportive of socialism. There is no single and simple answer to this apparent puzzle, but several factors can be cited by way of explanation.

First, the British have generally eschewed ideological politics, much preferring what are deemed to be moderate and pragmatic policies and reforms which promise steady but gradual improvement, rather than radical or revolutionary change. In this respect, Britain's political culture has been 'conservative' (small c), in that it has been deeply sceptical or suspicious of political theories, abstract ideas, or ideological blueprints for creating a new society. Instead, piecemeal reform and 'muddling through', rather than overthrowing the existing regime, have been the preferred option for the vast majority of British people.

Second, those who advocate radical political change and greater equality find it difficult to point to attractive examples of an existing 'socialist' society. Hitherto, those societies which have called (or still call) themselves 'socialist', 'Communist', or a 'people's democracy' – the former Soviet Union, Albania, China, Cuba, North Korea, Venezuela, and so forth – have been renowned for their lack of individual freedom or democracy, their appalling record on human rights, and their disastrous economic performance, with most of their citizens experiencing appalling hardship and hunger. This reinforces British people's preference for non-ideological, pragmatic reform and changes which do not mean jeopardising the economy or destroying freedom and democracy. Ultimately, the vast majority of British citizens believe that whatever problems or hardships some people experience here in Britain, they are not even remotely as bad as they are in these supposedly socialist or communist countries. Moreover, it is widely assumed that any economic or social problems that exist in Britain stand a much greater chance of being solved than the problems which exist in these other countries.

Third, there is considerable deference and respect in Britain towards wealthy business people and entrepreneurs, for not only are people like Richard Branson, James Dyson, Jacqueline Gold, Martha Lane Fox, and Alan Sugar widely admired for their hard work, success, and thoroughly deserved riches (particularly if they started out with nothing), they are also viewed as 'wealth creators' who generate growth and employment for thousands of other people, which ultimately benefits the whole of British society, via the 'trickle down' effect. Nor is it only wealthy businesspeople who are often widely admired and revered: many authors, musicians, and sportspeople are also highly respected or viewed as role models for others to emulate, such as Adele, Steph Houghton, Anthony Joshua, Harry Kane, J.K. Rowling, Ed Sheeran, Ben Stokes, and Stormzy. For many British citizens, the success and concomitant wealth of such people are admired, not resented, the dominant sentiment usually being 'good for them, they deserve it'.

Fourth, it has traditionally been widely assumed that many people who are poor or in poverty are ultimately to be blamed for their situation; their lack of money or job has often been attributed to their own alleged personal failings, bad lifestyle choices, laziness, or lack of ambition, or because life is 'too comfortable' for those on welfare benefits. While it is also widely accepted that those born into wealth have many more chances and opportunities than the poor, there is still a common belief that being born into a low-income household or impoverished community, while certainly an obstacle to be overcome, is not an insurmountable barrier to self-improvement and success (however defined), as long as the people concerned have enough drive and determination to succeed. Such assumptions are reinforced by governments claiming to be committed to increasingly equality of opportunity and promoting social mobility, because when poverty and socio-economic deprivation continue to exist, it becomes even easier to blame it on individuals who have failed to seize the chances and opportunities apparently offered to them.

Fifth, the poor themselves in Britain have been remarkably acquiescent or passive in accepting their low incomes or lack of wealth. Many of them seem to have adopted a fatalistic attitude, accepting that 'this is simply how it is', and that nothing is likely to change; 'it's always been this way'. It is also the case that some of the poor have what the sociologist Walter Runciman termed a 'narrow frame of reference', whereby they compare themselves to the people around them, who are obviously most visible. Ironically, if they see lots of other poor people in their neighbourhood or town, instead of fuelling anger or resentment at the scale of poverty or inequality, and just how many people are experiencing it, this is likely to reaffirm the assumption that this is 'natural'. In effect, the poor compare themselves to people in a similar situation, instead of comparing themselves to the rich: they will not normally see the latter or have any contact with them. Politically, the poor are more likely than better-off people to become politically apathetic or otherwise disengaged, to the extent of not voting in elections. This might be because their mental energy is focused wholly and solely on getting through each day and surviving financially, scraping the money together to pay for food, rent, and domestic fuel bills, or their political disengagement might derive from acceptance – born of bitter experience – that whichever party has been in government, they have been neglected, ignored, or even, perhaps, blamed by politicians, and so it is deemed pointless voting. A few of the poor, however, might be persuaded that their low incomes or poverty are the fault of others, such as immigrants 'taking our jobs' or driving-down wages, in which case, political support might be offered to far-Right groups or parties.

Sources of cohesion

As we noted earlier, the convenience of examining British society by means of its divisions should not blind us to the many sources of social cohesion. Not least of these is the persisting general confidence in the UK political system itself. The liberal democratic idea that power can change hands peacefully as a result of free and fair elections seems to be as strong as ever, even if the electoral turnout is poor by historical standards. There is also a consistent level of support for such associated values as the right to freedom of expression. Overall, an optimistic observer could claim that Britain has become a more pluralistic nation (see Chapter 1). On this view, the presence of diverse groups, and the absence of serious friction between them, signifies a healthy democracy in operation. Opinion poll evidence also reveals increasing tolerance for 'minority groups' like the lesbian, gay, bisexual, and transgender (LGBT) 'communities' that have suffered in the past from serious discrimination in a variety of fields, as well as greater (if not universal) acceptance of ethnic minorities. It appears that these trends have been fostered by the growth of higher education, among other factors.

Citizenship

Citizenship

a status that bestows rights and imposes obligations on a person as a full member of a state.

The values of liberal democracy are associated with the notion of a common **citizenship**, in which the inhabitants of a country and their government are bound together by a widely accepted framework of rights and responsibilities. Traditionally, in Britain, individuals have been regarded as subjects of the Crown, and the institution of monarchy has been deployed as an evocative emblem of national unity (especially at times of crisis like the two world wars of the twentieth century). But, even before the well-publicised problems which affected the royal family in the 1990s, critics were arguing that the monarchy was out of touch with the lives of modern Britons, harking back to the pre-democratic age of Empire. The idea of 'subjecthood' implied a passive, pseudo-religious obedience to monarchy and its symbols. By contrast, citizenship has always carried connotations of active independence, much more characteristic of a liberal democratic order.

The introduction by the Blair government of Citizenship as part of the national schools' curriculum implied a decisive move away from subjecthood. However, the break with the past has not been complete. When new applicants are accepted for citizenship, they still swear allegiance to the British monarch; in a characteristic British 'fudge', they claim the status of citizens of a state in a form of words which implies that they owe allegiance to an individual ('and her heirs and successors according to law'). More importantly, citizenship is normally associated with a codified constitution, laying down specific rights for individuals. Despite the passage of the Human Rights Act 1998, Britain still lacks a document of this kind (see Chapter 6).

The much-contested concept of 'Britishness'

Long before he became prime minister in 2007, Gordon Brown showed that he was interested in defining and defending the concept of 'Britishness' as a unifying force within the UK. In July 2004, for example, he delivered a lengthy speech on the subject in the annual lecture of the British Council. In a text which showed a remarkable range of reading for a busy politician, Brown claimed that

> just about every central question about our national future – from the constitution to our role in Europe, from citizenship to the challenges of multiculturalism – even the question of how and why we deliver public services in the manner we do – can only be fully answered if we are clear about what we value about being British.

Brown went on to define Britishness in terms of 'core' values – 'a passion for liberty anchored in a sense of duty and an intrinsic commitment to tolerance and fair play'.

Well-meaning and well-informed as they were, Brown's efforts were open to at least two objections. First, his interventions drew attention to strains within the union, the apparently weakening attraction of the 'British' identity, and his own position as a Scottish MP in the context of new devolved institutions in the component parts of the UK. If Brown had produced a definition of 'Britishness' which satisfied everyone, these problems would have been resolved; however, it was unlikely that his contribution would put an end to the discussion, because 'Britishness' is an elusive concept. Second, it was one thing for private individuals to speculate about what a 'British' identity might mean in the twenty-first century; but when senior politicians start to offer their own definitions and claim that this issue has serious policy implications, advocates of a pluralist democracy should feel concerned. The clear implication is that those people who fail the test of Britishness somehow do (or should) not *belong* to the nation. This is particularly hazardous when politicians base their definitions on character traits like 'tolerance' and a sense of 'fair play'. These ideas are by no means confined to the British; indeed, it might be said that many British-born people exhibit them rather weakly.

In March 2008, a report commissioned by Gordon Brown recommended that there should be a public holiday called 'Britishness Day', and that schoolchildren should pledge allegiance to the Queen. The government did not adopt the proposal, and public debate on the subject soon subsided. However, this did not deter politicians from gnawing at the Britishness bone. In 2014, David Cameron argued that British values should be emphasised more strongly in schools, citing the 1215 Magna Carta as the foundation of the country's liberties. Presumably Cameron was unaware that the venerated document in question can plausibly be interpreted as an attempt by the aristocracy to assert its privileges against monarchical interference, rather than a demand to extend civil rights to ordinary people; if so, some critics of his own affluent background would regard this as a very instructive mistake!

One difficulty with applying the idea of citizenship to modern Britain is that in its fullest sense, the concept seems best suited to relatively small-scale, pre-industrial societies. In a state like ancient Athens, for example, it was easy to accept that citizenship entailed duties to others as well as rights for oneself, since many citizens knew each other (by contrast, a recent study has suggested that the average Briton will have fewer than 400 friends in their whole lives, and no more than 33 at any one time). In 'face-to-face' societies like Athens, participation in a democratic system meant far more than the periodic casting of votes for candidates seeking public office. Citizens attended decision-making assemblies and could make their voices heard (equally, of course, women and slaves were denied the status of citizens in Athens).

Another problem identified by critics is that the idea of citizenship is undermined by significant economic inequalities. For example, individuals who can afford to work fewer hours will be able to inform themselves about current affairs, and to take a personal part in community activities, in a way which is barely possible for low-paid workers who struggle to make ends meet, or the long-term unemployed who often lack a sense of 'belonging'. It was from this perspective that some commentators criticised David Cameron's vision of a 'Big Society', which encouraged citizens to undertake voluntary activities to help the wider community. Notoriously, the middle classes have also been able to gain considerable benefits from the welfare state, while many of the less well-off have been unaware of their full entitlements. The idea of 'social exclusion' implies that some individuals can be denied meaningful citizenship simply because they were born to the 'wrong' parents or in the 'wrong' neighbourhood.

Citizens or consumers?

Many of these considerations were used to criticise John Major's initiative of a 'Citizen's Charter'. First launched in 1991, the idea was intended to promote improvements in public service delivery, notably by making providers more accountable to the public. But critics could not fail to notice that it had been deliberately called the *Citizen's* Charter (that is, the charter of the individual citizen, thus conforming to the ideology of the Conservative government), rather than the *Citizens'* Charter (i.e. a charter for people in a collective capacity). The poor, who are most dependent on public services, would still be less likely to complain than well-off individuals who, in the last resort, can 'opt out' and look for alternative provision in the private sector. To these critics, in short, the Citizen's Charter merely underlined the existence of a two-tier citizenship in Britain, reflecting the difference between the 'haves' and 'have-nots'. It also threatened to deflect critical attention away from politicians who set public service guidelines and budgets, to the individuals 'on the front line' who operate under constraints imposed from above. Thus, while ordinary public service employees were being made more accountable, their political masters would be more likely to escape any blame. In this respect, the Citizen's Charter could be seen as another symptom of a shift from traditional notions of 'government' to a more ambiguous one of 'governance'.

In 1998, the Blair government relaunched the Charter programme under the less question-begging name 'Service First'. However, this was the only terminological revision of any significance. Users of public services were still referred to as 'clients' or 'customers'. In part, this reflected an assumption that public services would become more efficient if they adopted the free-market outlook. Yet it also suggested that both of the main parties now agreed to accept an intimate link

Consumerism

a belief that the ever-increasing consumption of goods and services is inherently a good thing, as well as being beneficial to a country's economy.

between the exercise of 'citizenship' and economic activity. One might even suggest that they have come to see **consumerism** as the unifying principle which transcends the various divisions in British society. As if to confirm this suspicion, before the 2005 general election, several senior Labour ministers urged that the consumerist leanings of most voters should be granted increasing recognition by policymakers.

The results of the 2000–01 'Citizen's Audit', a detailed survey funded by the Economic and Social Research Council (ESRC), underlined the complex relationship between consumerism and citizenship. The survey found quite strong support for the basic propositions of citizenship in a liberal democracy (that is, willingness to obey the law and to pay taxes). However, when respondents were asked about their political participation, the most significant changes since the last similar survey in 1984 were in categories which are characteristic of a consumerist society. The proportion of people who had boycotted a product had soared from just 4 per cent to almost a third. In 1984, a total of 30 per cent claimed to have contacted a politician, but the figure in 2000 was just 13 per cent. Over the same period, the proportion of respondents who had contacted the media more than doubled (from 4 to 9 per cent). Subsequent surveys by a range of organisations have found similar levels and patterns of engagement.

On this view, individuals might seem to have different interests arising from issues of gender, age, ethnicity, religion, and so forth, but their ultimate interest lies in securing or preserving a comfortable lifestyle; additionally, they are increasingly likely to express their views by acting as consumers; contentment, even happiness, is achieved or pursued by acquiring more 'stuff' – new clothes (and often particular 'brands' or 'designer labels'), a new car, the latest smartphone, a bigger flatscreen TV, more household gadgets, and so forth. This would hardly make Britain unique among liberal democracies. In the USA – a society which is even more diverse and consumerist than Britain – the idea of the 'American Dream' is a vital unifying principle. It is assumed that every American has the chance to rise to riches through individual effort, whatever the circumstances of his or her birth. But in the USA, electoral turnout is usually low, at least in part because large numbers of citizens fail to register to vote, in the belief that the two main political parties do not come close to addressing their needs or reflecting their views. We will return to this subject in later chapters (see, in particular, Chapters 16 and 19), but in the meantime, it can be argued that the confusion between consumerism and citizenship helps to explain why so many people, who are either disillusioned with the affluent society or unable to share its fruits, are increasingly disinclined to vote. It certainly helps to explain why the main political parties sound so similar, at a time when British society is actually more diverse than ever. By directing their appeal to economic self-interest, they have been targeting the one feature of life which voters seem to have in common. The prevalence of consumerism among most sectors of society was underlined during the English urban disturbances of summer 2011, when a riot against police in Tottenham, London, triggered widespread looting elsewhere. The shops targeted by the looters – who came from a wide range of backgrounds – tended to be the ones that sold highly desirable consumer items rather than life's necessities. The riots, however, were complex events which attracted widespread commentary, often reflecting pre-existing assumptions about the nature of British society as a whole.

Nationalism

Nationalism is both a source of cohesion and a cause of social division, but, in the latter case, this to can be exploited by politicians to rally the majority of the population to the flag and foster national unity against an 'enemy' or 'threat'. As noted earlier (Controversy 4.1), one of the reasons why inequality in Britain is so widely and passively tolerated is that a strong sense of national identity and unity transcends socio-economic divisions. Indeed, as George Orwell (author of the classic dystopian 'political novels' *Animal Farm*, and *1984*) noted in his incisive collection of essays entitled *The Lion and the Unicorn* (London: Secker and Warburg, 1941), it is often among the working class that patriotism is most noticeable, although this often manifests itself as dislike or distrust of 'foreigners', and this proletarian patriotism is invariably stronger, and politically more important, than class identity, which partly explains why the British working class has never shown any interest in Marxism or other forms of radical socialism. On the contrary, it is among the working class that support for far-Right anti-immigrant parties has often been strongest, as was support for Brexit, with (stopping) immigration most commonly cited as the main motive for voting to leave the EU. It is also notable that when the England team is playing in a major international football competition, such as the four-yearly World Cup, some sections of society are much more inclined than others to drape their windows and cars with the flag of St George, in order to display, very publicly, their support for, and allegiance to, England. Much of the British (English) working class is very aware of its socio-economic status, and the material hardships this often entails, but generally, 'class consciousness' is often less important politically than national identity and pride in being British, or English. In this crucial regard, nationalism is a source of unity which binds all classes together with a shared sense of history and values, and this means that the working class generally dislikes 'foreigners' more than it resents the rich, or what Marxists refer to as 'the Ruling Class'. This, of course, is a trait which has often been skilfully and successfully exploited by the Conservative Party for electoral gain, while also portraying Labour as unpatriotic and even accusing the Left of 'hating Britain'.

In times of economic crisis or recession, when unemployment rises and cuts to government spending have a damaging impact on public services (overcrowded school classrooms, longer NHS waiting lists, lack of social housing, etc.), unscrupulous politicians will often use nationalism and supposedly patriotic flag-waving to divert blame onto immigrants and ethnic minorities. The British people are then encouraged to blame job losses, low wages, poverty, and under-funded, overstretched, public services on 'foreigners' living and working in Britain. It is no coincidence that racist views (and publicly expressing them) and racially motivated assaults increase in times of recession and austerity, as does support for anti-immigrant or overtly nationalist parties of the Right, who persuade some sections of society that the country's economic and social problems are caused by immigrants and ethnic minorities, rather than a consequence of consciously chosen or ideologically motivated government policies.

Yet nationalism in Britain manifests itself in other ways too, and thus fosters a sense of national unity and shared culture or history which transcends other divisions and inequalities. Love of the Royal Family is a good example. Far from being viewed as a symbol of privilege, wealth, and inheritance, the Royal Family is very widely revered and expected, the Queen especially. To many people, the Royal Family is 'the family of the nation' and itself a symbol of British history, greatness, and national unity, and thus a source of reassurance and stability in times of national crisis. The Queen's broadcast 'Christmas message' is watched by millions of people every year, as was her April 2020 televised address to the nation during the COVID-19 pandemic, when she sought to reassure an anxious British public that 'We will succeed and better days will come'.

Nationalism also manifests itself, albeit perhaps more subtly, in the cultural sphere, in terms of the great authors, bands, composers, painters, and poets that Britain has produced: Jane Austen, The Beatles, William Blake, David Bowie, Benjamin Britten, Charlotte Bronte, Emily Bronte, Lord Byron, Geoffrey Chaucer, John Constable, Charles Dickens, Edward Elgar, T.S. Eliot, Thomas Gainsborough, Thomas Hardy, A.E. Houseman, Rudyard Kipling, D.H. Lawrence, Led Zeppelin, Henry Moore, George Orwell, Pink Floyd, Henry Purcell, The Rolling Stones, J.K. Rowling, William Shakespeare, Mary Shelley, Percy Shelley, Alfred Tennyson, J.R.R. Tolkein, Joseph Turner, Ralph Vaughan Williams, P.G. Wodehouse, and Virginia Woolf. The reader will doubtless want to add to (or replace!) these examples.

Conclusion and summary

In the 1950s, the main social divisions in Britain were easily recognised. Most people could be categorised by their position within a well-defined class structure. Dress and accent were unmistakable external signs and gave a reasonable indication of a person's outlook. The main political parties certainly thought that class was a reliable measure of politics attitudes. Labour and the Conservatives pitched their main appeal to working- and middle-class people, respectively, and in the 1950s, they won more than 90 per cent of the vote between them at three out of four general elections.

Class is still an important factor in Britain's political culture, but it is no longer a *dominant* consideration. There are, though, other sources of division. Some, like gender and ethnicity, remain high on the political agenda despite recent attempts to address them. Others, like the urban/rural divide and the age profile of the population, are much more important now than they were in the 1950s. The salience of religion as a political issue has revived since 2001, even though the majority of the British population is far less 'observant' than in the Victorian heyday of deep piety and regular attendance at church on Sundays. Despite well-intentioned government pronouncements, the growing Muslim population is commonly associated with intolerance and violence by a British public which seems to have forgotten its own (fairly recent) past, in which Christians regularly committed atrocities against each other and those of other religious denominations.

It might have been expected that the political situation in Britain would have been transformed to reflect the fundamental changes of the past 60 years. For example, increasing social diversity apparently lends weight to the argument for some form of proportional representation, which would encourage a proliferation of parties offering a much wider range of electoral choice. However, the holding of a referendum on electoral reform in 2011 showed the attachment of the Conservatives and many senior Labour figures to the simple plurality (or first-past-the-post) voting system which discriminates against minor parties. The argument of this chapter is that for the last two decades, the main parties have worked on the assumption that the divisions within British society can be sidestepped by concentrating on the few remaining unifying factors. Also, those who do highlight divisions are likely to have their motives questioned, or be accused of creating tensions where none apparently exist: for example, critics of growing inequality are often accused of promoting 'the politics of envy' or somehow being 'anti-success'. Another key battleground is the concept of 'Britishness', which still seems elusive despite the attempts of successive governments to distil its essence.

Significantly, at the general elections of 1983 and 1987, Labour pitched its appeal to a variety of dissatisfied minority groups – the economically disadvantaged, ethnic minorities, and so forth – hoping to assemble a winning 'rainbow' coalition. This strategy failed comprehensively, so the party leadership embarked on the course which led to New Labour. At least until the election of Jeremy Corbyn as Labour leader in 2015, the major parties seemed unwilling or unable to imagine (let alone adopt) electoral strategies which challenge the perceived interests of the 'contented majority', or the growing power of big business and 'the City'. This, though, allowed the rise of the UKIP, which was well-placed to attract the discontented and 'left behind', whatever their previous allegiances, and target frustration and resentment against the EU and immigrants (another way of promoting Britishness, or even Englishness), as well as the 'liberal elite' which had apparently betrayed the British people. Meanwhile, in Scotland, the Scottish National Party (SNP) had recently enjoyed remarkable success by rejecting the politics and polices of New Labour, the Conservatives, and 'austerity'.

Yet until 2015, the major parties did not seem particularly perturbed by evidence of shrinking support; low electoral turnout did not matter much, provided that Labour and the Conservatives continued to attract a majority of those who actually did bother to vote, and their declining number of votes still usually enabled them to win majorities in the House of Commons (2010 was assumed to be a one-off). However, after the 2015 election, it was clear that Labour was faced with a considerable challenge if it was to continue winning support across an increasingly fragmented UK, while the Conservatives, despite their dominance of English seats, also had cause for concern; they had not won a large parliamentary majority since 1987, and much of its former middle-class base was now feeling increasingly anxious about its own economic future and job security, while also seeing its offspring struggling with zero-hours contracts, graduate debt, and unaffordable housing; the formerly Conservative middle class had itself fallen victim to the downsides of neoliberalism, rampant competition, and 'labour market flexibility'. Having won only a narrow parliamentary majority in 2015, the Conservatives lost it in 2017, while Labour surprised virtually everyone (including itself) by increasing its share of the vote from 30 per cent in 2015 to 40 per cent in 2017, in spite of a notably Left-wing manifesto and leader (Jeremy Corbyn) and unrelentingly hostile coverage in most of the press. However, Labour's hope that 'one last heave' would deliver victory in the 2019 election proved disastrously naïve, for, by this time, Corbyn had become an electoral liability, and the charisma-free zone, commonly known as Theresa May, had been replaced by the charismatic and rambunctious Boris Johnson. The latter attracted electoral support from many former Labour voters in the north of England – who disliked Corbyn anyway – by promising to 'get Brexit done'. Meanwhile, some of Labour's former middle-class supporters, unhappy and frustrated at Corbyn's continuous equivocation over Brexit, switched to the Liberal Democrats or the Greens.

Yet while the 2019 election was dominated by Brexit (and to some extent Corbyn's leadership – or lack of), many of the socio-economic problems which underpinned support for Brexit in the first place remain: job insecurity, low wages, lack of affordable housing and homelessness, increasing reliance on food banks, student debt, overcrowded classrooms, an underfunded and overstretched NHS, congested roads and unreliable public transport, fuel poverty, widening inequality, and so forth. Many hope that Brexit will somehow result in a New Dawn for the UK, whereby many of these problems will dissipate, and a more prosperous Britain emerges. This assumes, though, that these problems were actually caused or greatly exacerbated by EU membership and European migrants. If, however, these problems remain, or even get worse, after Brexit, the sense of anger and betrayal among many British citizens is quite likely to increase much more, possibly creating new divisions, or by widening or deepening existing ones, thus further undermining trust in politicians and the legitimacy of the political system a whole, and possibly threatening the stability and unity of the UK.

Further reading

In a fast-changing society like Britain, information about society and the economy is often out of date before it is published. Students are advised to keep a look-out for survey results published in broadsheet newspapers. Newspapers, of course, are interested in themes which will provide eye-catching headlines, and most reports need to be treated with caution, for example, by comparing them with other published findings.

A selection of books covering the British economy in the post-war period is listed in Chapter 1. For change in British politics, society, and culture since 1945, students are advised to consult the series of books by Dominic Sandbrook's *Never Had It So Good* (2005), *White Heat* (2007), and *State of Emergency* (2010), all published in London by Allen Lane/Penguin. There is a wide range of books which use statistical data to draw general conclusions about British society. A.H. Halsey and J. Webb (eds.), *Twentieth Century British Social Trends* (London: Macmillan, 2000), includes discussions of all the major developments in 100 years of radical change. *Social Trends*, compiled by the Office for National Statistics, appears annually. See also H. Perkin, *The Rise of Professional Society: England since 1880* (London: Routledge, 1989). R. Lister's *Poverty* (Oxford: Polity Press, 2004) is a penetrating study of that controversial subject, by a widely respected observer. *An Anatomy of Economic Equality in the UK* is easily accessed online, for example, at http://sticerd.lse.ac.uk/case/_new/publications/NEP.asp. On the relentless growth of inequality and its consequences or risks, see D. Dorling's *Peak Inequality: Britain's Ticking Time Bomb* (Bristol: Policy Press, 2018), and R. Wilkinson and K. Pickett's, *The Spirit Level: Why Equality Is Better for Everyone* (London: Allen Lane, 2010). On the widespread acceptance of inequality, see P. Dorey, 'A Poverty of Imagination: Blaming the Poor for Inequality', *The Political Quarterly*, Vol. 81, No. 3, July–September 2010. For the 2008 'credit crunch', see C. Hay, 'Britain and the Global Financial Crisis: The Return of Boom and Bust', in R. Heffernan, P. Cowley, and C. Hay (eds.), *Developments in British Politics 9* (Basingstoke: Palgrave Macmillan, 2011), and for its consequences for British politics, see D. Mabbett, 'Governing in Times of Austerity', in R. Heffernan, C. Hay, M. Russell, and P. Cowley (eds.), *Developments in British Politics 10* (Basingstoke: Palgrave Macmillan, 2016). Particularly recommended for those interested in the origins of the crisis is R. Peston, *Who Runs Britain? And Who's Responsible for the Economic Mess?* (London: Hodder & Stoughton, 2009).

On ethnicity, see J. Solomos's *Race and Racism in Britain* (London: Palgrave, 3rd edition, 2003), and on gender, see J. Lovenduski's *Feminising Politics* (Oxford: Polity Press, 2005). R. Campbell's 'The Politics of Diversity', in R. Heffernan, P. Cowley, and C. Hay (eds.), *Developments in British Politics 9* (Basingstoke: Palgrave Macmillan, 2011) is a good survey of recent developments, as is M. Sobolewska and R. Ford's 'The Politics of Immigration: Old and New', in R. Heffernan, C. Hay, M. Russell, and P. Cowley (eds.), *Developments in British Politics 10* (Basingstoke: Palgrave Macmillan, 2016). On the 2011 riots, see especially L. Bridges, 'Four Days in August: the UK riots', *Race & Class*, Vol. 54, No. 1, July–September 2012, pp. 1–12. There are several insightful articles on immigration and race in *Political Quarterly*, Vol. 85, No. 3, July–September 2014.

A fascinating contribution to the debate about age, by a senior politician, is D. Willetts's *The Pinch: How the Baby Boomers Took Their Children's Future – and Why They Should Give It Back* (London: Atlantic Books, 2010). Another widely read (and provocative) book on recent social changes is Owen Jones's *Chavs: The Demonization of the Working Class* (London: Verson, 2nd revised edition, 2012). See also C. Ainsley's *The New Working Class: How to Win Hearts, Minds and Votes* (Bristol: Policy Press, 2018).

K. Faulks, *Citizenship in Modern Britain* (Edinburgh: Edinburgh University Press, 1998), presents a strong argument against the economic understanding of citizenship. Some findings from the 2000–01 'Citizen Audit' are summarised in C. Pattie, P. Seyd, and P. Whiteley, 'Civic Attitudes and Engagement in Modern Britain', *Parliamentary Affairs*, Vol. 56, No. 4 (2003), pp. 616–33. A fuller analysis of the findings is in C. Pattie, P. Seyd, and P. Whiteley, *Citizenship in Britain. Values, Participation and Democracy* (Cambridge:

Cambridge University Press, 2004). The classic text on this subject, R.D. Putnam's *Bowling Alone. The Collapse and Revival of American Community* (London: Simon & Schuster, 2000), is worth reading, although its findings relate to the USA.

Websites

Websites provide an essential source for the most up-to-date statistics. The most comprehensive source is the government's site, National Statistics Online (www.ons.gov.uk), which provides results from the 2001 census and numerous links to more detailed and updated studies of social trends. For further information on citizenship education, see www.teachernet.gov.uk/teachingandlearning/subject/citizenship.

Chapter 5

The media and communications

Learning outcomes

After reading this chapter, you will:

- be able to develop a critical analysis of different approaches to the question of media influence on voting behaviour and more general attitudes to political questions;
- appreciate the impact of recent technological developments, such as social media;
- understand the role of political 'spin doctors'; and
- see that the relationship between the media and politicians has had important implications for liberal democracy in the UK.

Introduction

The relationship between politicians and the media is crucial to understanding British politics today. Almost all voters are dependent on newspapers, television, and the Internet for information about current political developments. Coverage is exhaustive, particularly in the electronic media where special television channels are devoted to 24-hour news, Internet sites dealing with political issues have proliferated, and many politicians either publish their own online blogs or share their daily musings on platforms like Twitter.

Since the media provide the prism through which almost everyone experiences UK politics, their performance is widely debated. Most people have a view about the quality of the media, and opinions tend to be polarised. Some attribute increasing public cynicism and apathy to the powerful influence of media organisations, which show insufficient respect towards politicians. Others claim that, despite some irresponsible or frivolous exceptions, the British media as a whole fulfil the invaluable function of holding politicians to account. On this view, politicians have brought themselves into disrepute and continue to make matters worse for themselves by trying to evade public-spirited journalistic scrutiny. Alternatively, it is possible to argue that responsibility for recent negative publicity is shared in roughly equal measure. Opinion polls suggest that both politicians and journalists are deeply unpopular compared to people like doctors and teachers. As we shall see later in the chapter, scandals involving politicians and the media have been among the biggest news stories of recent years, and this has done nothing to make the public more positive towards the subjects of these stories or the people who publish them.

The debate over the nature and extent of media influence on democratic politics is complicated by the difficulty of measuring 'influence', whether for ill or for good. We will return to this tricky question later. However, almost everyone agrees that whether or not the media as a whole enable voters to take well-informed views on public issues, their freedom (within certain well-defined limits) is an essential component of a liberal democracy.

The UK media: not one, but many

The media

newspapers, magazines, radio, television, and online outlets considered in a collective capacity.

The press

the news media, including newspapers and magazines (radio and television news are sometimes included).

When we talk of **the media** and British politics, there is a danger of thinking that 'the media' signifies a uniform body. Critics of particular media outlets are particularly liable to speak in this way. However, there are now numerous means of communication. In specific relation to politics, people can receive information from a wide variety of sources: newspapers, radio, television, the Internet, and so forth. The obvious distinction is between printed sources, normally given the collective name of **the press**, and the ever-diversifying electronic media which established a mass audience during the second half of the twentieth century.

All of these various media compete for public attention, and only the outlets provided by the British Broadcasting Corporation (BBC) are publicly owned (the BBC began as a private company in 1922, but became a chartered corporation four years later). Furthermore, although the BBC's chairperson and 12 appointed board members have to pay close attention to the wishes of the government of the day, the Corporation has a long history of independence, particularly in its treatment of current affairs.

Superficially, this seems a promising scenario for pluralism (see Chapter 1), in which individuals can easily access relevant information and a wide range of opinions on issues of public concern. However, this judgement is subject to important qualifications. First, although the press seems to be at a serious disadvantage compared to the situation before the advent of electronic media – and sales of newspapers have fallen sharply in recent years – it still commands a disproportionate influence over the terms of public debate. Apart from its direct input, most television and radio news programmes take their cues from the press when deciding which issues to address. Internet commentators pay very close attention to 'the dead-tree press'. Furthermore, newspaper journalists are frequently invited to elaborate their views on discussion programmes, and indeed many television and radio presenters also write for newspapers and magazines. Arguably, then, the press still has the capacity to *set the agenda* for the media as a whole, and if not exactly dominant, it can, at the very least, be regarded as 'first among equals' within the media (see later in the chapter).

Second, the press is dominated by relatively few corporations, some of which have major shareholders with strong personalities and clear political agendas of their own. For example, the Australian-born Rupert Murdoch (now an American citizen) controls *The Sun, The Times, The Sunday Times,* and *The Sun on Sunday* (known as *The News of the World* until 2011). As well as accounting for more than a quarter of the UK's national daily newspaper circulation, Murdoch's News UK (formerly News International, until a reorganisation in 2013) was part of a network of worldwide media interests, including a major stake in the satellite broadcaster Sky plc., the *Wall Street Journal*, the Fox Corporation, as well as various global Internet ventures.

Murdoch certainly does not impose a uniform editorial line on his various media outlets, but his opinions on specific subjects are well known and senior staff are unlikely to oppose them. In particular, trade unions rarely receive a favourable mention from Murdoch's stable of newspapers. In 1985, he broke the power of the printers' unions in the UK, with the wholehearted support of Margaret Thatcher, after workers attempted to stop him moving the production of his newspapers to Wapping, East London. Murdoch is also a strong Eurosceptic, and this position is reflected to varying degrees by his UK newspapers.

Despite its global operations, not even News Corp can afford to be wholly complacent. Robert Maxwell, Murdoch's rival, built a similar multinational media empire, but this collapsed as a result of dubious and overambitious business dealings after Maxwell's death in November 1991. Even so, the massive resources of the media giants are a significant deterrent to would-be competitors. For example, the richest media outfits can engage in prolonged price-cutting wars against market rivals and offer the highest salaries to poach the best-known journalists.

With 20 British national daily and Sunday newspapers controlled by just six individuals or organisations (see Table 5.1), it would be unrealistic to expect a wide range of opinions in their pages. But regardless of ownership, there is a tendency for media outlets of any significance to approach public issues from a broadly similar perspective. Competition in the 'mainstream' media focuses on two targets. Bare circulation statistics for the press and audience figures for television and radio constitute one obvious reference point (as 'likes' and subscribers do for Internet outlets). But a great deal also depends on the *nature* of the audience. Most of the media are dependent on advertising revenue. Above all, advertisers want to reach free-spending individuals rather than the poor or the thrifty. Hence, for example, a specialist magazine whose subscribers

TABLE 5.1 Newspaper ownership and circulation, January 2020

Title	Proprietor	Circulation
Times	News Corporation (Rupert Murdoch)	359,960
Telegraph	Press Holdings (Sir David and Sir Frederick Barclay)	317,817
Guardian	Scott Trust Ltd	126,879
I	Daily Mail & General Trust	215,934
Financial Times	Nikkei Inc.	155,009
Sun	News Corporation (Rupert Murdoch)	1,206,505
Mirror	Reach PLC	441,934
Star	Reach PLC	274,808
Mail	Daily Mail & General Trust (Lord Rothermere)	1,134,184
Express	Reach PLC	289,679
Sunday Times	News Corporation (Rupert Murdoch)	633,567
Observer	Scott Trust	155,021
Sunday Telegraph	Press Holdings (Sir David and Sir Frederick Barclay)	248,288
Mail on Sunday	Daily Mail & General Trust (Lord Rothermere)	962,084
Sunday Express	Reach PLC	245,629
Sun on Sunday	News Corporation (Rupert Murdoch)	1,022,485
Sunday Mirror	Reach PLC	356,621
Sunday People	Reach PLC	137,275
Daily Star Sunday	Reach PLC	158,101

Source: Data on circulation is from the Audit Bureau of Circulations Ltd, www.abc.org.uk. Figures omit free newspapers (such as the *Metro* and the *Evening Standard*).

Case study 5.1

Tabloids and broadsheets

Until quite recently, media commentators had a convenient way of distinguishing between Britain's national newspapers according to the size of their pages. The large-format 'broadsheets' included papers like *The Times*, the *Daily Telegraph*, and *The Guardian*. They were marked by extensive, detailed political coverage; commentary was provided by recognised experts who, while not exactly 'impartial', at least tended to do justice to the complexity of key issues rather than presenting them as straightforward choices between good and evil. By contrast, tabloids like *The Sun*, the *Mirror*, and the *Daily Mail* aimed at the heart rather than the head. Assuming that their readers had little time to spare for the nuances of political debate – and knowing that they would have to adorn their stories with 'sensational' headlines in order to win attention from potential purchasers who would otherwise have relied on electronic media – they spelled out their messages in vivid language. The headline alone would usually be enough to inform the reader of the 'correct' position to take on any issue.

For some broadsheet readers, the very inconvenience of the larger format was reassuring; the difficulty of turning the pages on crowded commuter trains symbolised the pains they were prepared to take in order to be well informed. However, in 2003, the broadsheet newspaper *The Independent* began to print a tabloid edition, and in the following year *The Times* adopted the format in all but name. As a result, the old tabloids are often given the collective name of 'Red Tops' to denote their more sensational style of journalism, since some (but not all) of them emblazon their names against a red background on their front pages.

Critics have linked the 'tabloidisation' of the more serious newspapers to a general trend towards 'dumbing down' in the media as a whole. Even the remaining broadsheets now report the 'celebrity' gossip which has always characterised the tabloids; the *Daily Telegraph*, once the house journal of sober-minded country squires and retired army officers, loses no opportunity to print pictures of attractive individuals. Coverage of political and economic issues is still extensive. But it can be argued that politics itself has been transformed by the tabloid effect, and that this has led Britain into an era of simplistic sound bites and spin doctors which would have caused consternation even among the most 'populist' politicians of 1945. The same old question can still be raised: have the politicians succumbed to the influence of the tabloids, or have they simply become more responsive to a public demand which was always present, but is now more readily satisfied?

The classic example of this phenomenon is the fate of the left-wing *Daily Herald*, which went out of business in 1964 despite a substantial readership. It was relaunched as *The Sun*, which was bought by Murdoch in 1969. Within a decade, a popular, Labour-supporting paper had been turned into socialism's most vociferous press opponent. Ironically, Murdoch himself had been attracted by socialist ideas in his youth. Now he was a champion of the free market and could claim that *The Sun*'s success as a vehicle for anti-socialist opinions merely underlined the popularity of his own views. His critics, however, argued that the operations of the free market in news and comment prevented alternative viewpoints from securing a proper hearing.

are affluent but not numerous is likely to be in a healthier financial state than a mass-circulation newspaper that appeals primarily to the low-paid and unemployed.

Theories of media influence

While the effect of market forces on the British press undoubtedly tends to restrict rather than expand the range of opinions covered, it is still possible to argue that the present situation satisfies the basic requirements of liberal pluralism. Debates on this subject are very difficult to resolve because there is no agreement on the extent to which the media shape public opinion, as opposed to merely reflecting existing views. Opinion polls, indeed, usually suggest that influence is slight. But the accuracy of such polls depends on the honesty (and self-knowledge) of respondents. Even people who are conscious of being influenced are often reluctant to admit that their choices have been swayed; others will genuinely be unaware that their thinking has been affected. Thus, people commonly claim to form their opinions on the basis of 'factual' reports on television rather than taking their ideas from the 'biased' press. However, there is a danger that these respondents will have exaggerated the influence of television because moving pictures have a more vivid, immediate impact than the printed word, which might nevertheless exert a more subtle and lasting influence. And in any case, as we have noted, television (and radio) discussion programmes have their agendas shaped to a considerable extent by the content of newspapers.

Most academic analysis on this subject is informed by three broad theories:

1. *Reinforcement theory:* On this view, the media merely respond to existing demand. Far from moulding opinions, the most that a media outlet can do is to give people additional reasons for what they believe already, as a result of other, more profound influences such as the views of parents, work colleagues, and friends. When they encounter information or arguments which challenge their existing views, media consumers 'screen it out' by ignoring or reinterpreting such messages to suit their previous predilections. In an ultra-competitive market, a newspaper which persistently advocates unpopular causes will win very few converts; rather, it will quickly lose readers and revenue. The changing allegiances of *The Sun* newspaper are often explained from this perspective (see Controversy 5.2).

2. *Agenda-setting:* This approach accepts that the media cannot change the way that people think on particular issues. But it argues that media sources can affect the political agenda by concentrating on specific subjects and refusing to publicise others. Thus, for example, the general public might be hostile to corruption in all walks of life, but newspaper owners can direct their editors to focus attention on the misdeeds of hostile politicians rather than exposing dubious business practices which could lead to awkward questions about their own activities. At election time, the media can help to shape an agenda of salient issues which favour one party over another (see Chapter 18).

3. *Direct effects:* The most critical approach to media influence argues that it can directly affect the way people think about politics as well as setting the agenda. Gullible readers can be directed towards certain conclusions by means of selective or distorted reporting, which determines their views and their voting behaviour while flattering them into thinking that they have exercised 'impartial' judgement. But the same effect can be achieved in more subtle ways, freighting apparently 'objective' reports with value-laden terminology when addressing certain issues, parties, or individuals.

The obvious problem with all such theories is that individual voters differ. Some people are never content with a single viewpoint; if their preferred newspaper supports a particular policy, they will actively seek out a media source which provides an opposing view. Not many individuals will take this approach of their own volition, but many BBC programmes (such as *Question Time*) offer it to their viewers and listeners by choosing panelists who endorse sharply contrasting positions. At the other extreme, some individuals accept blatantly one-sided arguments without question. The overwhelming majority of people fall somewhere between these poles of painstaking objectivity and unhesitating bias.

Thus, our response to the rival theories outlined earlier will depend, to a considerable extent, on our assessment of the level of public knowledge of political issues. In turn, this has implications for the relative health of liberal democracy in the UK. Reinforcement theory tallies reasonably well with the pluralist approach, which argues that most people are rational enough to make political decisions after considering a range of proposals. To varying degrees, the agenda-setting and direct effects models suggest a largely passive electorate, and are thus more compatible with elitist interpretations of the democratic process (see Chapter 1).

As we have seen, empirical evidence on this subject is open to question and evades objective interpretation. For example, it was not until the time of the 1983 general election that a majority of *Sun* readers was able correctly to identify the political allegiance of that newspaper, despite its vehement backing of the Conservatives since the mid-1970s. On one level, this evidence could suggest that newspapers have a limited effect on partisan loyalties. But a different interpretation is possible. If millions of *Sun* readers were unable to detect the glaring pro-Tory bias of the newspaper's news coverage and editorial content, it is hardly likely that they would be fully conscious of any change in their own voting preferences which might have resulted from their reading of the paper. And even if *The Sun* did not persuade many people to switch directly from Labour to the Conservatives after Murdoch took it over, this does not rule out the possibility that many Labour supporters at the time had their loyalties *loosened* through daily exposure to the paper's polemics, making them more likely to abstain from voting or to plump for a third party – unless the Labour Party was prepared to elect a leader who was ready to adopt policy priorities which were more compatible with *The Sun's* editorial line, in which case the newspaper would be prepared to swing behind Labour again if it looked likely to return to office.

While the bias of *The Sun* should have been obvious to anyone with rudimentary political knowledge, some students of the subject concentrate on the more subtle manipulations of the media. In the mid-1970s, the Glasgow Media Group (Glasgow University Mass Media Unit) began to study the language used in television news reports. Their most interesting finding was the extent to which even supposedly 'neutral' reports (e.g. those on BBC news programmes) featured value-laden terms. Thus, for example, if trade union leaders were repeatedly described as 'making demands' (rather than a more neutral phrase, like 'offering proposals'), it was likely that they would forfeit public sympathy. The Group argued that there was an endemic bias against the Left in the UK media. But their analysis actually revealed a deeper problem. Even if existing coverage could be proved to be biased, it was difficult to see how a completely 'neutral' form of words could be substituted, given the essentially emotive nature of all meaningful political language.

Although political influence is a highly complex phenomenon, there are at least three reasons for supposing that the 'direct effects' approach has more value than most political scientists have been prepared to allow. First, most forms of media are intimately related to the advertising industry, which depends on the assumption that attitudes can be shaped by words and images. In most cases, advertisers try to manipulate potential customers into switching from one brand to another. These techniques have been borrowed by political parties in recent decades. It would be strange if media moguls with strong political agendas of their own had not been tempted to emulate the advertisers. In recent years, promotion of certain products has been subjected to controls on the assumption that such techniques do indeed affect behaviour. New Labour, for example, was particularly keen to impose such restrictions on products like tobacco. This is perfectly consistent with the party's belief in the power of words and images to manipulate political opinion, either through its own propaganda or through articles published in friendly media outlets.

Second, elements of the privately owned press certainly behave as if they have a strong influence. Some of them make no secret of their party preferences, and in the run-up to general elections, most newspapers publish leading articles advising readers on the best way to use their votes. After the 1992 general election, which resulted in an unexpected fourth successive victory for the Conservatives, *The Sun* crowed that its intervention had proved decisive. It had launched furious attacks on Labour, rather than offering readers positive reasons for staying loyal to John Major's government. Although its boast ('It's The Sun Wot Won It') was a cheerful exaggeration, it would be a mistake to suppose that its coverage of that election had left voters entirely unmoved, either through a 'direct effect' or, more subtly, the ability of this widely read newspaper to set the agenda for the British media as a whole. Newspapers also freely boast of their influence on subjects which lack a direct party political element; for example, *The News of the World* (now *The Sun on Sunday*) campaigned strongly on the issue of paedophilia in the early 2000s. It would be odd if the press can make a difference on such issues while having no effect on the political views of their readers. The impact of media coverage is also recognised when (as in the case of the Ethiopian famine of the mid-1980s) its coverage evokes positive human emotions. While some well-informed voters are clearly too astute to be brainwashed by blatant propaganda, people who do not follow public affairs very closely are bound to feel, to an extent which can in some circumstances prove decisive, the effect of vivid and oft-repeated messages in the headlines even of newspapers which they do not buy and merely glimpse on the shelves of newsagents and supermarkets.

Third, the argument that biased reporting has minimal effects on voters depends crucially on the assumption that most citizens already have fixed loyalties. In order to reinforce a preference for one party over another, that preference has to exist already, for reasons unconnected with the arguments of the newspapers. Until the 1970s, when strong attachment to the two main parties was common, this was a fairly safe assumption to make; but in the era of partisan *dealignment* (see Chapter 18), the situation is very different. Far fewer people nowadays feel a strong attachment to a party, and only a minority express views which could meaningfully be interpreted as 'loyal'. There is, in short, much more scope for the press to exercise direct influence, compared to the situation when the first 'scientific' studies of British voting behaviour were conducted.

An additional consideration is that although analysis of voting behaviour can provide some insights into media influence, it is important not to overlook the extent to which the media try to shape the overall *context* in which party competition takes place. While elements of the press enjoy praising one party and abusing the others, for some media operatives the ideal situation would be a contest between parties which broadly agreed with each other in advocating policies that suited the interests of big business. It can be argued that, largely thanks to the influence of News Corp, this scenario had come about in the UK by the time of the 1997 general election. Murdoch's papers swung behind Labour after more than two decades of raucous support for the Conservatives. Reinforcement theory invites the conclusion that *The Sun* and *The News of the World* merely recognised a shift in public preferences, and they supported Labour because they wanted to be on the winning side. However, it is debatable whether they would have done so had Labour not made an exhaustive effort to woo Rupert Murdoch in the period between 1992 and 1997. Certainly, the Murdoch press would not have endorsed Labour with such enthusiasm if the party had stuck to its 1992 policy of increasing income tax for high earners, even if public opinion polls had indicated that the Conservatives were bound to lose the 1997 election. After all, the message of the polls before the 1992 contest hardly suggested that the Conservatives would be runaway winners, yet this did not deter *The Sun* from suggesting that a change of government would be a disaster. It might not have been '*The Sun* Wot Won It' in 1992, but the newspaper certainly helped Labour lose.

This consideration seems to provide a decisive riposte to the view that biased reporting can do no more than *reinforce* existing attitudes. While academics continue to debate the nature and extent of press influence, political leaders have been acting as if the influence is real and significant. As long ago as 1931, the Conservative Prime Minister Stanley Baldwin attacked the press for exercising 'power without responsibility'. If Baldwin was guilty of exaggerating the influence of the press, he was certainly not the last prime minister to do so. However, unlike almost all of his successors, he was not prepared to allow that perceived influence to go unchallenged. By stark contrast, Tony Blair, in particular, was prepared to risk antagonising Labour loyalists in his attempts to keep the Murdoch press happy, while successive Labour Home Secretaries were noticeably anxious not to offend the *Daily Mail*, which consistently upholds a hard line on law and order. Labour's fear of the *Daily Mail's* influence over the news agenda as a whole is particularly telling, since that newspaper had defied reinforcement theory by continuing to support the Conservative Party even when its electoral fortunes were at their bleakest.

Thus, the question of influence ends up looking like a hall of mirrors: whatever the extent of its direct impact on ordinary voters, the press enjoys considerable influence over political debate because politicians *believe* that it is influential, to the extent that they are sometimes willing to propitiate their media opponents even if this annoys their most passionate supporters. It can hardly be denied that, when politicians consider the likely reaction of particular newspapers to their proposals, the press is exercising a direct effect on the political process. Hence, even if voters can 'filter out' the biased message of many media outlets, their efforts are thwarted because they will be choosing from a relatively narrow field of politicians, most of whom present policy programmes which have been profoundly affected by the media.

Leaving aside the endlessly contestable subject of media influence over voters and the policy proposals of politicians, there can be no room for reasonable doubt that the media have exercised a direct effect on the *conduct* of politics in the UK and other liberal democracies. Two examples will suffice to illustrate the extent of this influence.

First, the major political parties now clearly regard a pleasing media image as a crucial characteristic when selecting their leaders. This explains, at least in part, why Labour opted for Tony Blair in 1994, and Gordon Brown chose not to stand against him. Similar considerations influenced the Conservatives' choice of David Cameron in 2005, when his main opponent, David Davis, was more appealing to the party in ideological terms but much less polished in his public performances. A more spectacular example was the fate of Sir Menzies Campbell, Liberal Democrat leader from March 2006 to October 2007. Campbell had limitations as a leader, but most of these related to 'presentational' factors; although he had excelled on television as an expert commentator on foreign affairs while Charles Kennedy was leader, he was less sure-footed after he had succeeded Kennedy and interviewers became more aggressive towards him. Most important, he looked old on television, and when Gordon Brown ruled out an election in either 2007 or 2008, Liberal Democrat MPs saw their chance to replace Campbell with a younger champion in good time before the next national contest. Campbell's eventual successor, Nick Clegg, was clearly much more in tune with the age of the electronic media.

The second example is part of a more general story about the decline of the UK's Parliament (see Chapter 8). Under New Labour, in particular, major policy initiatives tended to be announced on the radio or in the television studios, rather than the traditional venue of the House of Commons. While the 2010–15 coalition seemed keen to revert to former practice, even ministerial statements delivered to the Commons still tended to be heavily 'trailed' in the media in advance: and after the 2015 general election, the first legislative programme of the incoming Conservative government was known before the Queen began to announce it. On this evidence, it looks unlikely that the old constitutional convention of addressing the nation's elected representatives at the first opportunity could ever be restored – except on those rare occasions when the executive deems it advantageous to spring a genuine surprise on MPs. Media influence can also help to explain the diminished importance and democratic vitality of the main parties' annual conferences. Rather than being meaningful forums for debate on policy, these events are now carefully stage-managed by the parties, so that media coverage will show their leaders in the best possible light.

The post-war media

Even those who continue to deny the reality (or even the potential) of media influence have to accept that there has been a change in the attitude of journalists over recent years. They are far more inclined to be combative in their approach to politicians, whether in television interviews or in newspaper commentary. This development is significant in itself, suggesting that, whatever they might say about their role in public, when this comes under scrutiny, journalists work on the confident assumption that they enjoy more influence than ever before.

In 'Will a Crisis in Journalism Provoke a Crisis in Democracy?' (*Political Quarterly*, Vol. 73, No. 4 (2002), pp. 400–08), Steven Barnett identified four phases of British journalism since 1945. They are:

1. An *age of deference*, from the 1940s to the early 1960s. This period was marked by exaggerated respect among journalists, who acted as if politicians were bestowing great favours on themselves and their audience by agreeing to say a few anodyne words.
2. An *age of equal engagement*, between 1964 and 1979. The early 1960s were marked by increasing friction between the press and a political class which was discredited by a succession of scandals. These events were exploited by young satirists who heaped ridicule on 'the establishment' in general. This context was sure to affect news journalists in turn, but at first they exercised restraint. In part, this was because senior reporters had learned their trade during the age of deference; the change could only be registered when they had been replaced by a new generation which had grown up laughing along with the satirists.
3. An *age of journalistic disdain*, emerging in the late 1970s. During this time, the politicians themselves became more reliant on techniques derived from journalism and advertising. When people agree to market themselves like soap powder, they can hardly expect to be treated like heroic figures. Equally, one can argue that this period reflected the new dominance of the electronic media, with the printed press taking its tone from more aggressive television interviewers.
4. Barnett argues that we are living in an *age of contempt*, in which journalists spend most of their time trying to trap politicians into damaging admissions (either about policy or their private lives), while politicians avoid giving straight answers. The result has been an increase in public cynicism about public life in general. This has created a vicious circle; sensing that the public

Soundbite

a short phrase
that is easy to
remember.

attaches a low priority to politics, the media give it less thorough coverage and tend to focus on **soundbites** and frivolities – the very things which helped to generate public contempt in the first place.

Significantly, on Barnett's chronology the 'age of contempt' began shortly after the then Conservative government had fired warning shots over press intrusion into the private lives of public figures. In January 1991, the Minister of State at the Home Office (and later Secretary of State for National Heritage), David Mellor, warned the press that it was 'drinking in the last chance saloon', and that its existing system of self-regulation under the Press Council would be replaced by a more rigorous regime. Earlier that year, a Home Office committee had been set up to inquire into the behaviour of the press. But these threats merely resulted in a revamped regulatory body, the Press Complaints Commission (PCC), which included representatives of the worst-offending newspapers and held no legal powers to punish editors. Mellor himself was forced to resign from the cabinet in September 1992 after the tabloids revealed details of his own private life, which presumably would not have been publicised if he had shown less pugnacity towards the press (ironically, after the end of his political career Mellor became a radio presenter).

One can argue that Barnett's time frame creates a misleading impression of unbroken decline in relations between the press and politicians, because it omits the period between the wars when the 'press barons', Lord Beaverbrook and Lord Rothermere, tried to bully Stanley Baldwin into adopting their preferred policies on trade and the Empire. However, among other useful features it illustrates the complex relationship between the media and politicians and the broader context in which they operate (what one might call 'the climate of opinion'). If journalists and politicians are now treated with contempt by the public, the history of their relationship suggests that they are almost equally to blame – a position tacitly accepted by David Cameron during the 2011 'phone hacking' scandal (described later). The media might have taken the initiative by adopting a more hostile stance, but politicians have done themselves no favours in their response to this challenge. Indeed, Baldwin's successor as prime minister, Neville Chamberlain (1937–40), can be seen as the real instigator of this lamentable process, since he encouraged the press to inflate his own merits and to denigrate his political opponents, notably Winston Churchill. After World War II, of course, Chamberlain's name was used by the press as a synonym for political and personal cowardice – a sign that, even at that early stage in the relationship, those who try to manipulate the media will usually come off worse in the long run.

New Labour and the media

It is no coincidence that Barnett's 'age of contempt' also embraces New Labour's period of political ascendancy. Although the Conservative governments led by Margaret Thatcher and John Major gave a high priority to dealings with the media, for Blair's Labour Party the relationship turned into an obsession.

In the general elections of 1979, 1983, and 1987, Labour faced a hostile press, and on each occasion it lost heavily. Even before 1987, there were signs that the party was willing to adapt to the media environment rather than struggling to change it. During the election campaign of that year, a special party political broadcast was devoted to improving the image of the then leader, Neil Kinnock. This was judged to be so successful that it was broadcast twice, denying the party a crucial opportunity to explain its policies in more detail in an era when many voters watched such broadcasts. There had also been a concerted effort to rebrand the Labour Party as a whole, with the adoption of a red rose as its symbol in order to distance it from the traditional socialist emblem of the red flag. When these symbolic gestures proved futile and Labour lost the 1987 election, it embarked on more substantive policy changes, driven through on the assumption that the electorate had become more 'Thatcherite' since 1979. Opinion poll findings did not bear out this view, suggesting that the New Labour high command had mistaken the undoubted popularity of Thatcherite newspapers like *The Sun* for a significant shift in public attitudes on key political issues (on this point, see in particular Ivor Crewe, 'Has the Electorate Become Thatcherite?', in Robert Skidelsky (ed.), *Thatcherism* (Oxford: Basil Blackwell, 1998), pp. 25–49) (Table 5.2).

A further electoral defeat in 1992 presented Labour with an acute dilemma. It could conclude either that it had lost credibility with voters through its drive to secure more sympathetic media coverage, or that it should go even further to win approval from the Conservative-supporting press. Kinnock's successor John Smith accepted that presentational changes had been necessary, but took the view that the party would win power next time round if it merely avoided factional disputes and waited for the Conservatives to inflict damage on themselves. Thus, despite his lasting popularity among ordinary party members, Smith satisfied neither Labour's 'traditionalists' nor the media-focused 'modernisers'.

When Smith died suddenly in 1994, the choice of his successor lay between two modernisers, Tony Blair and Gordon Brown. They were equally ambitious, and given the popularity of both men they were unlikely to split the modernising vote in a way which would allow a more traditional figure to win the leadership election. However, Brown was persuaded to leave the way clear for Blair.

TABLE 5.2 Partisan support of daily newspapers in general election years, 2001–19

Newspaper	2001	2005	2010	2015	2017	2019
Sun	Labour	Labour	Conservative	Conservative	Conservative	Conservative
Mirror/Record	Labour	Labour	Labour	Labour	Labour	Labour
Star	Conservative	Not interested	Not interested	Not interested	Not interested	Not interested
Mail	Anti-Labour	Conservative	Conservative	Conservative	Conservative	Conservative
Express	Labour	Labour	Conservative	UKIP	Conservative	Conservative
Telegraph	Conservative	Conservative	Conservative	Conservative	Conservative	Conservative
Guardian	Labour	Labour (with misgivings)	Liberal Democrats	Labour	Anti-Conservative	Labour
Times	Labour (with misgivings)	Labour (with misgivings)	Conservative	Conservative	Conservative	Conservative
Independent	Anti-Conservative	Liberal Democrats	Liberal Democrats	Liberal Democrats	Liberal Democrats	Anti-Conservative
Financial Times	Labour (with misgivings)	Labour	Conservative (with misgivings)	Conservative	Conservative	No preference

Note: This table is designed to give a general impression of trends within the press. While some newspapers' (e.g. the *Daily Mirror* and the *Daily Mail*) loyalties tend to be all-or-nothing affairs, with editorial lines suggesting that anyone who opposes the chosen party must be deluded or corrupt, other papers are more open-minded and print opinion pieces which go against the prevailing message found on other pages. Thus, for example, *The Guardian*, which Conservative newspapers tend to depict as an unflagging mouthpiece for Labour, has never been an uncritical friend of that party.

An important player in the manoeuvres leading up to this decision was Peter Mandelson, a former TV producer who had helped in Labour's rebranding after 1987. Mandelson was regarded as the archetype of a **spin doctor** – a term which had been imported from America to identify political operators who tried to ensure favourable media coverage for their paymasters. Whatever Mandelson's precise role, his preference for Blair as leader was a typical spin doctor's decision. Brown's assets (his longer service to his party, and his experience of front-bench politics) were outweighed by the knowledge that Blair would look better on television.

New Labour strategists had considerable success in courting the press. At the 1992 election, only the *Daily Mirror* and *The Guardian* had been firm Labour supporters – most other daily newspapers backed the Conservatives. By polling day in 1997, the *Daily Star, The Independent*, and, most significantly, *The Sun* had all moved into the Labour camp. The remaining 'Tory press' was highly critical of John Major's record and offered the Conservatives only lukewarm endorsements. Twice as many people read a Labour-supporting paper in 1997 than had been the case in 1992. Only three daily newspapers endorsed the Conservatives in 2005, when *The Times, Financial Times*, and *The Sun* (all firm Tory supporters in the 1980s) once again backed Labour. A majority of *Sun* readers voted for Labour for the third election in a row (see Table 5.3). Coverage of the party's record and proposals on health and education was largely positive in the Labour-supporting press, but it was fiercely criticised in some papers (particularly the *Daily Mirror*) on the conduct of the war in Iraq and the issue of trust.

The Blair governments and the media

Labour's crushing victory in 1997 should have given the party an ideal opportunity to take stock of its relationship with the media. Although the leadership had refused to make ambitious promises, the overwhelming scale of the win and symptoms of strong public enthusiasm offered extensive room for manoeuvre. In particular, newspapers like *The Sun*, which had been very influential during the Thatcher years, had reason to expect that their voices would now carry less weight in Downing Street, compared to the *Daily Mirror* which had been faithful to Labour through the bad times (Photo 5.1).

However, Blair had promised that his party would govern in the way that it had campaigned, and this proved to be especially true of its attitude towards the media. From their headquarters in the Millbank Tower near the Houses of Parliament, New Labour spin doctors continued to 'rebut' potentially damaging stories at the first opportunity and to push out more positive publicity at the most favourable moment, through either deliberate 'leaks' or formal announcements. As in opposition, this approach was informed by the twin beliefs that the media were highly influential and instinctively hostile to the Labour movement and its aims.

If anything, the years after 1992 had cemented these views. The harsh treatment of Major and his ministers – by newspapers which had so recently advised their readers to vote Conservative – suggested that New Labour could expect no mercy from its fair-weather media friends if it encountered turbulence in office. The main lesson, according to the modernisers, was to avoid any concessions to 'Old' Labour views. Unless the party stuck rigidly to its new course, it would

Spin doctor

someone who is employed to promote the image of a specific politician and party, hoping to generate positive publicity and to prevent the appearance of negative media stories.

PHOTO 5.1 *The Sun* abandons Labour, 30 August 2009 (© Dan Kitwood/Getty Images).

TABLE 5.3 Party supported by daily newspaper readers, 2019 (2017 in brackets)

Newspaper	Party supported by readers (%)		
	Con	*Lab*	*Lib Dem*
Sun	65 (59)	20 (30)	6 (3)
Daily Mirror	22 (19)	57 (69)	7 (6)
Daily Mail	76 (74)	12 (17)	6 (3)
Daily Express	79 (77)	9 (15)	4 (1)
Daily Telegraph	78 (79)	7 (12)	8 (6)
The Times	49 (58)	18 (24)	24 (14)
Guardian	6 (8)	64 (73)	19 (12)
Independent	18 (15)	50 (66)	22 (12)

Source: Figures for 2017 from YouGov, https://yougov.co.uk; those for 2019 are taken from the British Electoral Study data (https://www.britishelectionstudy.com/).

allow elements within the media to combine both of their favourite habits – attacking a government and left-wing policies at the same time.

A key influence on Labour's strategy was Alastair Campbell, Blair's official spokesperson and later Director of Communications (Photo 5.2). Campbell was so close to Blair that, after 1997, some people regarded him as the real 'Deputy Prime Minister'. Unusually, although he was not a civil servant himself, he was given authority over officials. A former tabloid journalist, Campbell had no illusions about the real motivations of his old colleagues. For all their talk of serving the public by holding governments to account, many journalists merely wanted to advance their personal interests by publishing sensational stories – whether true or not. Although Campbell often accused journalists of focusing on 'froth' and 'process' rather than issues of substance, an important part of his job was to ensure that the media had nothing of real substance to report. Thus, MPs and even senior ministers were warned to 'stay on message'; only the most reliable loyalists were allowed to address the media on behalf of the government.

Spinning into trouble

One problem with Campbell's approach was that, over time, he became a subject of media interest in his own right, inadvertently breaking his own rule that spin doctors should never become

PHOTO 5.2 Alastair Campbell, New Labour's communications supremo, with Tony Blair (© Tom Stoddart Archive/Getty Images).

part of a story. In a sense, his prominence was an important service to the government, since it often deflected hostile attention away from Blair. But his iron grip on official information led to allegations that Britain was governed by 'control freaks'. Ulterior motives began to be detected behind every official announcement. Whatever their personal feelings about New Labour, many journalists felt that their profession was being undermined. It was thus a matter of professional pride to cause the government as much trouble as possible, particularly at a time when the elected opposition parties were numerically weak in parliament.

The new emphasis on presentation was illustrated in the early days of the government, when several departmental information officers were removed, apparently for harbouring doubts about the New Labour project. A small army of 'special advisers' was brought into Whitehall; their number more than doubled, from 38 in 1997 to 87 by 2004 (with 29 attached to Downing Street). One of the special advisers, Jo Moore, sent an email suggesting that the terrorist attacks of 11 September 2001 presented an opportunity to 'bury' government announcements which would otherwise have attracted adverse publicity. When the email was leaked, Moore's immediate boss, the Transport Secretary Stephen Byers, refused to sack her. Eventually both resigned, but only after serious damage had been done to the image of the government as a whole.

It can be argued, indeed, that far from helping the government to fulfil a constructive mission, the obsession with 'spin' presented the greatest threat to its popularity. It provided a unifying target for people who had become alienated from Labour for a variety of reasons. Byers was not the only minister to fall as a result of a press campaign. Mandelson himself was forced out twice – over allegations concerning his personal finances (December 1998) and his alleged role in trying to secure passports for controversial businessmen (January 2001). When the Home Secretary David Blunkett stepped down in December 2004 because of complications in his private life and alleged misuse of ministerial powers, commentators were strongly reminded of the Major era. Despite the prime minister's public declarations of support, Blunkett was compelled to resign because elements of the press persisted in publishing damaging stories. Blunkett's restoration to the cabinet after the 2005 general election was thus a clear indication of Blair's true feelings towards the media. Equally, when Blunkett ran into new trouble over his financial dealings within a few months of his reappointment, few media commentators were sad to see him emulating Mandelson with a second resignation (see Chapter 7).

Of these examples, the Mandelson case was the most instructive. Even after his second resignation he continued to enjoy Blair's personal support, and in 2004 he was nominated to the EU Commission, which made him far more powerful than he had been as a minister. Gordon Brown, who had good reasons for mixed feelings about Mandelson, brought him back into the Cabinet in 2008. The newly dubbed Lord Mandelson finally proved that his administrative skills were on a par (at least) with his aptitude for manipulation; however, his new status as de facto deputy prime minister was unlikely to reassure voters who had become tired of New Labour's obsession with media presentation, and not even a Merlin of the spin doctor's art could have made Brown seem like a vote-winner.

Iraq, the BBC, and the Hutton inquiry

The Blair government always anticipated trouble from the newspapers, which have no duty to be impartial (or consistent). But the BBC was a different matter. The Corporation is dependent on public funding through the licence fee, and the government appoints the board members as well as the BBC chairperson (formerly the director general). As a public service broadcaster, it is supposed to be impartial in its political coverage. In practice, though, it has been criticised by Conservative and Labour governments, particularly at times of crisis such as the Falklands War (1982) and the American-led intervention in Iraq (2003); more recently, it was slated by both sides during the EU referendum campaign (2016). Even at the best of times, there is an underlying tension in what appears to be an unequal relationship; and for the BBC, 'the best of times' is a very distant memory. Since the government can starve the BBC of funds by reducing the real value of the licence fee – or take the ultimate options of refusing to renew its Charter or privatising it – the Corporation is acutely vulnerable to political pressure, and arguably even more dependent on public approval than independent companies which are funded by advertising revenue or subscribers who pay to view.

This context explains why the BBC, rather than more openly critical newspapers like the *Daily Mirror*, bore the brunt of government anger after the Iraq War of 2003. Radio 4's *Today* programme carried a report by a BBC defence correspondent, Andrew Gilligan, in which it was claimed that the government had distorted the threat from Iraq in the build-up to the conflict. In particular, Gilligan said that on the basis of an interview with a well-placed official source, it seemed probable that the government had known in advance that the regime of Saddam Hussein was in no position to threaten any British troops within 45 minutes of an order being given. Even so, the government had reported this threat in a dossier based on intelligence findings, which made the case for war to Parliament and the public. Much was made of the '45-minute claim' by newspapers which were well disposed towards the government.

Gilligan's report was broadcast very early in the morning, and was not repeated. Even so, it caused an uproar in Downing Street. Alastair Campbell demanded an apology for what he regarded as a slur on his integrity. After all, he had been involved in the process of compiling the published dossier. Meanwhile, a search began for the source of Gilligan's story. Dr David Kelly revealed that he had spoken to Gilligan, although he felt that these conversations had not been accurately reported. Kelly was not a senior official in the Ministry of Defence, but he knew the situation in Iraq very well as a former UN weapons inspector. When it became clear that Kelly was indeed the source of Gilligan's remarks on the 45-minute claim, the government paraded him before a parliamentary select committee without the usual high-level support. It was clear that Kelly felt painfully isolated, and once he had been exposed as Gilligan's source it was only a matter of time before the media started to intrude on his family's privacy. Dr Kelly was still in the media spotlight when he was found dead near his home in July 2003.

The government immediately set up an inquiry under Lord Hutton, a senior Law Lord (see Chapter 9). It was open to members of the public, and, although the proceedings were not televised, the inquiry received intensive media coverage. Initially, the government's critics were hopeful that Hutton would produce a damning report. However, Hutton had been given restricted terms of reference; and even within these limits, he excluded many potentially awkward questions. This meant that his report, published in January 2004, was a surprise even to many of the government's supporters. Gilligan and the BBC were roundly criticised; by contrast, on the basis of Hutton's report, an outside observer would have concluded that the government had behaved impeccably.

The immediate public response to the report was overwhelmingly hostile. Early polls suggested that nine voters out of ten regarded Hutton's investigation as a 'whitewash'. But no minister ever resigned as a result of actions taken in support of the Iraq War; the only cabinet casualties, Robin Cook and Clare Short, left the government because of their *opposition* to the conflict. Campbell himself left his post shortly after the Hutton Report, but it was clear that he would be brought back in some informal capacity whenever his old boss needed him. There were, though,

Controversy 5.1

Do the media help or hinder the democratic process?

For	Against
The media ensure that the electorate is well informed on key issues	The media distort and oversimplify key issues
The media provide important insights into the character of political leaders	The media are obsessed with personalities, usually focusing on irrelevant characteristics
The media provide citizens with a vital means of participation between elections	With their endless opinion polls and phone-in shows, the media distract the electorate from more direct and effectual forms of participation
The media are the voice of the people, and can keep politicians informed about changes in the public mood	The media are unrepresentative of real public opinion and pressurise politicians to take decisions which are contrary to the national interest
The media hold governments to account when the parliamentary opposition is weak	Unlike an elected opposition, the media can ask awkward questions without facing the prospect of holding office and having to take tough decisions. Their irresponsible tactics encourage voters to dismiss quiet, constructive opposition as 'weak'
Owners of newspapers and other media organs are successful business people who can offer useful advice to elected politicians	Media moguls enjoy too much influence as it is. They might pose as champions of the national interest, but their only concern is to make money. They should never be invited to Downing Street

Case study 5.2

Politics and the Internet

The Internet has become the main tool for government services. The Blair government had a strategy for e-government under which government departments and related agencies were required to publish material online. These sites, which have been developed further under Blair's successors, are excellent resources for students of politics. Some government services can also be accessed online: in 2018–19, for example, more than 88 per cent of the income tax returns received by Her Majesty's Revenue and Customs (HMRC) were submitted electronically.

In terms of partisan activity, the Internet is now almost equally well established and prominent. New technology, of which the Internet is a key part, poses a challenge for the 'old' media, as citizens can now easily access a phenomenal quantity of information online rather than having to rely on the press. Most 'old' media outlets have responded to this by developing their own news websites; the BBC's output attracted 600 million worldwide 'visitors' in May 2020, and some newspapers (such as the Murdoch press) require online users to pay a subscription fee. Some politicians quickly realised the potential of this new electronic medium. In 2006, the Conservative leader David Cameron started up a site, which included a video diary ('WebCameron') that the party deleted from its YouTube site in 2013. During the expenses scandal of 2009, Gordon Brown was also induced to venture into the field, posting a video on YouTube in an attempt to show voters a warmer side to his character. The result was a fiasco (see www.youtube.com/watch?v=sBXj5l6ShpA).

The attractions of the Internet for political parties and activists are obvious. The voluntary services of party members can make it a very cost-effective medium of communication; it also allows parties to send messages, direct and undiluted, to citizens rather than having to disseminate them through unreliable intermediaries in the traditional media. It also provides a mechanism for political participation by ordinary citizens. This is evidenced by the growth of political 'blog' sites produced by independent commentators – albeit many of them written by people connected to the 'Westminster village'. Recent general elections have also seen the emergence of sites offering 'guidance' on how to vote (e.g. www.whoshouldyouvotefor.com). Pressure groups and new social movements also use the Internet to publicise their causes and mobilise citizens (see Chapter 19). Meanwhile, online political discussion between interested citizens thrives on sites such as Facebook and Twitter; in the ten weeks before the 2015 general election, it was estimated that there were about 21 million interactions on Facebook and seven million Tweets directly related to the contest.

By 2019, a total of 93 per cent of UK households had Internet access, and a slightly higher proportion of adults had used it at some time. The ubiquity of the Internet encouraged some commentators to dub the 2015 contest 'the first social media election', and the major parties (particularly the Conservatives) devoted considerable resources to online campaigning. In 2017, the Conservatives spent £2.1 million on advertisements for a single social media outlet – Facebook – while Labour spent £577,000 and the Liberal Democrats £412,000. In 2018, Facebook was implicated in a scandal concerning the political consulting company Cambridge Analytica, which was accused of 'harvesting' personal information relating to Facebook users and selling these data to political organisations. Despite this adverse publicity, Labour and the Liberal Democrats increased their spending on Facebook advertisements in 2019.

Despite the Cambridge Analytica scandal, there is little evidence to suggest that the impact of this relatively new technology is as profound in the UK as it has been in the USA, where it has undoubtedly made a difference in fund-raising activities. In other respects, the mind-numbing range of subjects covered by the Internet – and the diversity of perspectives offered on each of these subjects by professional and 'freelance' pundits – makes it unlikely that many users will endeavour to access sites whose message conflicts with their own views, or to stumble across challenging arguments by accident. As such, the Internet can be regarded as almost the perfect example of a medium which *reinforces* opinions. Even highly misleading adverts, carefully targeted and personalised by the parties on the basis of information culled from Facebook profiles, can be seen as means of *motivating* existing sympathisers to vote, rather than brainwashing techniques. Even before they realised the potential of online campaigning, parties had become adept at posting printed propaganda to likely supporters. Furthermore, while Facebook and Twitter can generate political stories, in the UK these usually revolve around unguarded comments made by politicians on those sites (like the remarks made by Eleanor Thornberry during the Rochester and Strood by-election of November 2014, which led to her resignation from Labour's front bench). Given the fragmented nature of social media, these *causes célèbres* tend to become topics for general discussion only if and when 'traditional' media outlets deem them to be newsworthy; Britain still awaits its first 'mis-Tweeting' prime minister to match Donald Trump, whose late-night ruminations make Thornberry's gaffe seem like a model of restraint.

more lasting departures from the BBC – Andrew Gilligan resigned, followed by the Director General, Greg Dyke. Changes followed in the management structure of the Corporation, to tighten up the way it monitored its own output; the old Board of Governors was disbanded in 2006, and its functions divided.

In the medium term, the Hutton Report did the government few favours. It was still difficult to say who was most to blame for the death of Dr Kelly – the media or the politicians. People who had consistently opposed the intervention in Iraq tended to harden their views rather than change them. Fears that the BBC would tone down its criticisms of government decisions on a range of issues seemed to be exaggerated. Before long, it had screened a documentary series which claimed that the British and the US governments habitually exaggerated security threats for their own ends.

Even on the worst interpretation of the government's actions over the Iraq War, it could be argued that something valuable had been gained over the course of the twentieth century. In 1914, millions of Britons had enlisted in what turned out to be a world war, anxious to participate in a quarrel which few of them understood. In 2003, by contrast, a government with a crushing parliamentary majority felt unable to commit a few thousand of its citizens into battle without making the most of the intelligence reports at its disposal. There were no official inquiries into the causes of World War I. From this perspective, it might be concluded that in one important respect, the media 'age of contempt' is preferable to a time of excessive deference.

The media and the 2010 general election

Even academics who remained sceptical about the extent of media influence in British politics had to admit that the contours of the 2010 contest were shaped to an unusual degree by the various forms of media. A significant background factor was the expenses scandal of the previous year, which had arisen from media inquiries and full-scale exposure of parliamentary misdeeds in the pages of the *Daily Telegraph* (see Chapter 8). However, that agenda-setting episode was only the beginning of the media's effect in 2010.

On 15 April 2010, the leaders of the three main UK parties took part in the county's first ever televised leadership debate. Obviously, Gordon Brown, David Cameron, and Nick Clegg participated in televised encounters in every week that Parliament was sitting, at Prime Minister's Questions (PMQs). But the set piece electoral format was completely different from those ritual clashes, in which other MPs had the chance of affecting the contest by cheering or jeering. This time the verbal showdown would be umpired by a (supposedly) neutral journalist, and the audience was warned against audible expressions of approval or dissent.

The first debate, aired by ITV1, was watched by an average of 9.4 million viewers. A week later, Sky News hosted its own event (watched by four million), and the BBC took its turn on 29 April, just a week before the election. The average viewing figure for this third debate was 8.4 million. Although the audiences were not as large as some optimists had forecast, they did suggest a satisfactory level of interest among voters, apparently ensuring that such debates would become permanent features of general election campaigns.

The obvious reaction to the screening of these events was that they confirmed an existing tendency of UK politics to become more 'presidential', inviting voters to regard general elections as referendums on the qualities of party leaders rather than as judgements on policy performance or platforms set out in manifestos. A more nuanced view was that voters did indeed take more account of leaders in an era of 'valence' voting, when governing competence, rather than ideological differences or deep-rooted party allegiances based on social class, had become key influences on electoral outcomes (see Chapter 18); voters wanting a competent government, but lacking the free time to conduct rigorous research, could take a 'short-cut' to judgement by evaluating the rival candidates for the post of prime minister. But whether one regarded the debates as an alien innovation, imported from the very different US political context, or as an additional aid to voters who would make their choices on the basis of numerous factors, no one could seriously deny that they dominated the 2010 campaign and made this the most media-driven election in British history.

Before the first debate, it was obvious to expert analysts that the Liberal Democrat leader Nick Clegg had the most to gain from debates which gave him equal billing with his two main rivals, unlike the usual televised election coverage in which the third party was given less exposure, in line with a formula based on relative performance at the previous election. However, Clegg's display in the first debate overturned all expectations. According to the opinion polls, he was judged to have 'won' the debate by a wide margin; an ITN poll found that 43 per cent thought he had won, compared to 26 per cent for David Cameron and 20 per cent for Gordon Brown. In part, this judgement was probably influenced by the fact that, unlike his rivals, he spoke directly to the camera rather than addressing the studio audience. Whatever the reason for Clegg's success, the Liberal Democrats subsequently surged in the opinion polls, even taking the lead in some surveys. If there had only been one televised leadership debate, just a few days before the poll, the Clegg sensation might have carried his party to an election result way beyond its rational expectations. As it was, the second (Sky) debate saw Cameron recovering from an uncertain initial performance, so that most observers assessed it as a draw between Cameron and Clegg, with Brown winning plaudits for the substance of his answers but failing to connect with most voters. On balance, the third debate was seen as a narrow 'victory' for Cameron.

Judged against the eventual electoral outcome, the initial leaders' debates can be seen as a sensational non-event. After all the speculation about an amazing Liberal Democrat breakthrough to something over 100 seats, the party actually found itself with a reduced parliamentary representation. It is possible that the debates had merely made the average voter think a bit more carefully about Clegg and his colleagues before reverting to the familiar pattern, and deciding that a vote for the Liberal Democrats could never be more than a waste. However, the eruption of 'Cleggmania' after the first debate produced an equally volcanic response from Conservative-supporting newspapers. Screaming headlines from the *Daily Mail*, the *Daily Express*, the *Daily Telegraph,* and (predictably) *The Sun* testified to various reasons why Clegg was unsuitable as an aspirant to Britain's top political job.

Whether or not the coordinated attack on Clegg had the desired effect of depressing the Liberal Democrat vote, it certainly underlined the extent to which the national press felt compelled to fight for attention in a campaign whose agenda had been captured from the outset by electronic media. Apart from the leader debates, the most notable incident from the media perspective was another television 'scoop'. During an electioneering visit to the marginal seat of Rochdale, Lancashire, Gordon Brown was interrogated at some length by a female voter who held strong views on immigration. During the confrontation, Brown responded with tactful words; but once he thought he was out of earshot of the voters he characterised his verbal assailant as 'bigoted'. Even those who thought that Brown's assessment might be justified could only admit that the encounter and its aftermath had been a public relations disaster; if the questioner had indeed shown signs of prejudice against immigrants, Brown had undoubtedly given the appearance of treating her remarks with respect before denouncing her when he thought it was safe to express his real opinion. Whichever way one looked, Britain's prime minister had been made to appear two-faced; and rather than being exposed by representatives of the press, Brown's unguarded comment had been picked up by a Sky microphone which he had failed to remove before climbing into his car. In a subsequent BBC interview, Brown realised the enormity of his error, and the footage bore witness to his misery as he held his head in his hands (see, for example, www.youtube.com/watch?v=C3F_ly9xSqQ).

The media in the elections of 2015, 2017, and 2019

The 2010 televised leader debates were so popular with the public that it was natural to assume that they would become a permanent fixture of British general elections, as they have become in US presidential campaigns. However, this assumption overlooked the fact that the circumstances of 2010 had been very unusual. For various reasons, the leaders of all three main

The shifting allegiances of *The Sun* newspaper

As we noted earlier, the pro-Conservative leanings of *The Sun* – Britain's best-selling newspaper since 1978 – were apparently too subtle to be detected by the majority of readers until 1983 (by which time the paper had been in the Tory camp for the best part of a decade). This can be regarded as a tribute to the entrepreneurial acumen of Rupert Murdoch, who had realised that a newspaper could secure loyal readers by focusing mainly on popular culture and the deeds of transient celebrities. On this basis, *The Sun* claimed to articulate the sentiments of 'ordinary' Britons, who wanted to enjoy life without troubling themselves too much with political nuances. Thus, when *The Sun* advised its readers to vote Conservative after 1974, it did so under the pretence that its preference was merely a reflection of good old British common sense rather than the product of a pronounced ideological commitment.

Despite the skill of Murdoch and his editorial staff, reinforcement theory suggests that their efforts would have been fruitless if their political project had conflicted with the long-standing political allegiances of their readers. However, Murdoch's greatest achievement was to detect that, by the mid-1970s, such fixed allegiances, based mainly on social class, were crumbling. Thus, while the majority of *Sun* readers came from social backgrounds which in (say) 1945 would have indicated a loyalty to Labour, such ties had weakened considerably over the subsequent decades. In addition, while Margaret Thatcher was in some ways an unlikely heroine for *Sun* readers, she was at least a passionate patriot, while many leading Labour politicians (such as Tony Benn) who came from relatively affluent backgrounds seemed anxious to befriend Britain's enemies (such as the Soviet Union and the IRA).

It would be fanciful to claim that *The Sun's* unaided efforts 'converted' a significant section of the working class into Tory supporters in the late 1970s – and even if it did achieve this unlikely feat, there could never be conclusive evidence to *prove* it. Even so, it seems reasonable to argue that the newspaper did play some role in changing allegiances during an unusual period in which 'tribal' political identities were softening into more volatile gestures of partisan support. Thatcher and Murdoch were duly grateful to each other. This did not mean that *The Sun* was tied to the Conservative Party as an institution, but it would not abandon its allegiance lightly, even if its readers showed a clear preference for another party. In 1992, as we have seen, the newspaper threw its weight against Neil Kinnock and the Labour Party, even though it was unenthusiastic about Thatcher's successor, John Major. But in 1997, it abandoned Major and gave a positive endorsement to Tony Blair and New Labour.

Advocates of reinforcement theory have interpreted this as concrete evidence that, in the final analysis, newspapers have no alternative but to follow their readers. However, almost from the moment that he was elected as Labour leader, Tony Blair set out to woo *The Sun*, so that long before 1997 Murdoch could be confident that, as prime minister, the Labour leader would defend Thatcher's free market legacy at least as well as John Major would ever do. From this perspective, it is more telling that *The Sun's* endorsement of Blair was delayed until the beginning of the 1997 election campaign – by which time it was obvious that a majority of *The Sun* readers were more than ready to vote Labour rather than Conservative. Indeed, the day after the death of Blair's predecessor John Smith in 1994, *The Sun* had acknowledged that, if he had lived, Smith would have been Britain's next prime minister.

On the face of it, reinforcement theory provides a better explanation for *The Sun's* switch *back* to the Tories, after 12 years in the New Labour camp. By 2009, after all, the Conservatives were leading in the opinion polls, and Gordon Brown's government looked unlikely to recover its initial popularity. However, far from jumping aboard an unstoppable bandwagon, *The Sun* deserted New Labour when it was clear that the public remained unconvinced by David Cameron and his party – indeed, it turned out that the Conservatives were not popular enough to secure an overall parliamentary majority even with *The Sun's* backing. From this perspective, it is instructive that *The Sun* made its move several months *before* the 2010 general election – at the time of Labour's 2009 party conference, when its abandonment of Brown was sure to damage the government's morale as well as giving a significant boost to the Conservatives. In horse-racing terms, this was not a case of backing an obvious winner: rather, *The Sun's* tipsters were laying a wager on the favourite for the race, and then giving him a dose of steroids while slipping his main rival a powerful sedative.

Thus, the best rationale for *The Sun's* behaviour under Murdoch's ownership is that as soon as it felt confident of its ability to influence opinion, it showed its owner's true colours, by backing the Conservatives. When they seemed unelectable, the newspaper gave belated backing to a Labour Party which presented no serious ideological threat; but as soon as the Conservatives showed clear signs of reviving, it was happy to endorse them – and to return to its old practice of giving its readers a sharp nudge in the hope of helping to bring about the result its proprietor wanted.

In 2015, *The Sun* stayed true to the Conservatives – except in its Scottish edition, which strongly favoured the SNP (having previously denounced the party). This, at last, *does* look like an example of reinforcement theory in action, since the SNP was obviously going to be the biggest party in Scotland after the election. However, Rupert Murdoch has no love for the British 'establishment', and, as such, he may have been happy to support the SNP (with whose leaders he had apparently established very cordial relations) north of the border, to the extent that the Scottish version of *The Sun* stayed neutral in the 2014 independence referendum. Needless to say, in 2017 and 2019, the London version of the paper was raucously supportive of the pro-Brexit Conservatives.

parties were keen to take part – or, at least, were not so strongly opposed that they searched for excuses *not* to take part. David Cameron – initially, at least – thought he could perform better than Gordon Brown and thus help his party to a decisive election victory. Brown, for his part, saw the debates as an opportunity to overturn, or at least to reduce, the lead which Cameron enjoyed over him in opinion polls about the 'Best Person for PM'. As we have seen, Nick Clegg was eager to grasp this opportunity to fight on roughly equal terms against the Labour and Conservative leaders.

The considerable public interest aroused by the 2010 leader debates ensured that media companies would be eager for a repetition in 2015. As in 2010, the leaders of the Labour Party (Ed Miliband) and the Liberal Democrats (Nick Clegg) were very keen to take part, though for different reasons. Miliband's ratings as a leader had always lagged far behind David Cameron's, and hostile media outlets had highlighted trivial incidents such as a difficult encounter with a bacon sandwich as evidence of his unsuitability. A direct televised debate with his rivals looked like an opportunity to appeal directly to voters. Miliband would have nothing to lose in such a contest, while Clegg could hope for another successful performance to lift his party's flagging fortunes.

While the enthusiasm of Miliband and Clegg came as no surprise, David Cameron had changed his mind about televised debates. His uncomfortable experience in 2010 had under-lined the wisdom of his supposed role model, Tony Blair, in refusing to take part in such debates throughout his time as Labour leader. Even a leader who is already popular can gain an additional boost from a brilliant televised performance; but there is a much greater chance that one rival or other will land an effective blow, and that this will dominate subsequent media commentary. In short, there had been little for Cameron to gain even in 2010, when he led the main party of opposition; and as the incumbent prime minister in 2015, there was even less reason to risk his considerable opinion-poll lead over his rivals.

Accordingly, Cameron did his best to ensure that, even if televised debates took place, they would only do so on his favoured terms. He could afford to drive a hard bargain with the broad-casters because it was unlikely that a refusal to cooperate would cost him many votes. After all, when Tony Blair had refused to take part in debates in 1997, the Conservatives had hired some-one to dress up as a chicken and harass the Labour leader during the campaign. This had made no impact except for providing light-hearted interludes in media coverage, especially when Labour recruited a 'pantomime fox' to attack the bothersome bird.

After a protracted trail of strength between Cameron and the broadcasters, a series of media events was agreed; but although Cameron would participate, he would only debate directly with his main rivals if all seven significant parties – Conservative, Labour, Liberal Democrat, UKIP, Greens, SNP, and Plaid Cymru – were represented. His other appearances would be in less confrontational formats, like BBC's *Question Time*. The audience figures showed that the British public (unlike the prime minister) retained some appetite for these events, but they were signif-icantly lower than in 2010. On 16 April, a million more people tuned into ITV's interminable soap-opera *Emmerdale* than the BBC debate among the leaders of opposition parties – a sombre testament to the rival attractions of the 'real world' compared to highly improbable fiction.

Overall, the media's impact in 2015 was probably less than it had been in 2010, partly re-flecting (and vindicating) Cameron's refusal to back down under pressure from the broadcasters. While the politicians had learned from the inaugural debates, it looked as if the audience had also reflected over the intervening period; the instant survey responses certainly suggested that more people this time round evaluated the participants on their prime ministerial potential rather than deciding the 'winner' on each occasion in isolation from other factors. The real 'winner' was the SNP's Nicola Sturgeon, whose ratings easily exceeded anything that could have been expected for the leader of a party which was running candidates in only one of the four nations of the UK. Sturgeon herself was not even a candidate in the 2015 general elec-tion. Her performance in the debates was widely acclaimed in Scotland, but it is difficult to say whether or not it made much difference to the election result in that country, since the SNP was heading for an unprecedented result anyway in the wake of its effective campaign in the 2014 independence referendum.

In the elections of 2017 and 2019, the Conservative Party conducted campaigns around the personalities of its respective leaders, Theresa May and Boris Johnson. However, this 'presidential' approach did not include a full-hearted endorsement of the leader debates. Rather, on both oc-casions, the party protected them from unnecessary exposure. In 2017, there was no repetition

Controversy 5.2

Brexit and the British media

In this chapter, the question of media influence has been examined in the context of voting behaviour in general elections. The case is different in respect of referendums, especially those which are presented as binary ('Yes'/'No') choices. When voters decide on their voting preferences in general elections, they have a variety of factors to consider, however much media outlets try to simplify the decision. Amongst other things, invariably there are more than two parties to choose between.

In a referendum, the considerations might be highly complex, but the final decision is a simple one: 'Do I want this or that outcome?' compared to 'Which of these parties do I prefer?' As such, it is reasonable to suppose that media outlets have greater potential to exercise influence over individual votes, especially if the referendum is held on an issue where public knowledge is limited.

In the 2016 EU referendum, more than half of Britain's newspapers (by circulation) favoured 'Leave'. Roughly a third backed 'Remain', while the rest did not campaign strongly either way. This contrasted very sharply with the media battle over EC membership in 1975, when only the small-circulation *Morning Star* campaigned to withdraw. It was also very different from the media's approach to the 2014 referendum on Scottish independence, where only one newspaper (the Scottish *Sunday Herald*) advocated separation from the UK.

One obvious conclusion is that in 1975 and 2014, a considerable number of voters ignored the message of their favourite newspapers, since almost a third voted against EEC membership in 1975, and in 2014 the argument for Scottish independence almost prevailed. This evidence would suggest that voters are not as susceptible to media influence as some theories would suggest, even on binary questions (incidentally, it also reflects rather badly on the ability of the 'free press' to cater for the opinions of its readers even on crucial matters).

There is, though, another way to interpret the 1975 and 2014 results. In both instances, the 'establishment' view prevailed, but many voters chose the 'radical' option. We will never know what would have happened in either instance if the overall media coverage had been balanced, but it is not fanciful to suppose that the relatively narrow (55 per cent to 45 per cent) verdict in Scotland could have been overturned, while the 1975 outcome might not have been as comfortable as the advocates of EC membership were able to claim.

Although the electorate had changed dramatically between 1975 and 2016, the result of the EU referendum in the latter year could be seen as a vindication for those who had always claimed that the 1975 result had been secured by an establishment 'plot', in which the media were active participants. On this view, the case for withdrawal prevailed in 2016 because, on this occasion, significant elements of the free press refused to play along with the establishment plot, ensuring that 'Leave' gained a fair hearing.

Opinions on this subject are likely to be as polarised as they were (and continue to be) on the referendum question itself. However, a couple of additional complications are worth raising. First, bare statistics cannot provide a full picture of the media's role in elections. A newspaper which recommends a vote on the basis of careful arguments is very different from one which purveys highly contentious (if not fabricated) stories under lurid headlines. In the 2016 referendum, the 'Remain'-supporting newspapers tended to fall into the first category, while the 'Leavers' enjoyed considerable support from the old sensationalist 'red tops' (e.g. *The Sun, The Daily Express, The Daily Mail,* and their Sunday stablemates).

Second, the 'Leave'-supporting press had been 'preparing the battlefield' long before 2016 – indeed, negative stories about the EU had been a regular feature of its coverage since the 1980s. For readers of such newspapers, the option to leave the EU was likely to appear as a long-delayed opportunity to free Britain from an institution which had only ever harmed its interests. By contrast, 'Remainers' and their media allies only started to talk up the EU in the months before the poll – and even then they tended to argue that leaving would be a mistake, rather than presenting the EU in a positive light. Their only chance of matching the style of pro-Leave coverage was to maximise the risks of withdrawal. In the Scottish referendum campaign, such tactics had been dubbed 'Project Fear'; but their effectiveness was enhanced by the endorsement of an overwhelming majority of newspapers. In 2016, the notion that the 'establishment' was trying to scare voters with unfounded predictions of doom carried far more credibility, because this version of 'Project Fear' was ridiculed by a very significant proportion of the press.

While Leave-supporting journalists joined battle in 2016 with considerable relish, BBC journalists could only anticipate the campaign with trepidation. The duty to present the rival campaigns 'impartially' only made sense if the contesting forces had agreed to present different interpretations of accepted facts. Instead, the BBC was forced to give equal coverage to arguments which were highly dubious or grossly distorted, in a context where the leading 'Leaver', Michael Gove, had invited voters to ignore the views of 'experts'. Since it was criticised from both sides, it could be argued that the BBC emerged from this nightmare with considerable credit. Equally, and ironically, the toxic campaign lent weight to the argument that the Corporation should be privatised for the sake of its journalists, who would never again have to keep a straight face while reporting brazen lies if they were free from the duty to be impartial.

of the 2010 format; on one occasion Home Secretary Amber Rudd stood in for May against Jeremy Corbyn, even though she had suffered a family bereavement. In 2019, there was one head-to-head encounter between Johnson and Corbyn; but this took place in mid-November, almost a month before the election itself. While preparations for the 2010 debates had been very time-consuming, the governing party now had to devote similar resources to thinking up ways of *avoiding* these potential pit-falls.

The campaigns of 2017 and 2019 were highly unusual since they took place in the aftermath of the 2016 'Brexit' referendum, in which the media had played a highly controversial role (see Controversy 5.3). Although Mrs May hoped to discuss other issues apart from Britain's withdrawal from the EU, Conservative-supporting newspapers concentrated on this subject. For example, the *Daily Mail* – fresh from its attempt to brand senior judges as 'Enemies of the People' for ruling that Parliament should be allowed a say over the terms of withdrawal (see Chapter 9) – began its electoral coverage with a front-page photograph of May and the headline

'Crush the Saboteurs'. Expecting a comfortable victory for the Conservatives, the Right-wing press tended to treat the Labour leader Jeremy Corbyn as a joke rather than a serious threat. When the attacks came – *The Sun*, for example, warned Britons not to 'chuck' the country into the 'Cor-bin' – they were far less effective than similar tactics had proved against Neil Kinnock in 1987 and 1992.

The course of the 2019 campaign was equally surprising to the Conservative press. Since Boris Johnson had been chosen as party leader for his presumed vote-winning prowess, newspapers like *The Sun* (and *The Daily Telegraph*, Johnson's favourite media outlet) expected to report on a series of events which would be more like a Royal progress than an electoral campaign. However, Johnson proved no more inspiring than Theresa May had been in 2017; he shirked an interview with the BBC's Andrew Neil, and on one occasion he even took refuge from reporters in an industrial fridge. In its election-day edition, *The Sun* tacitly recognised that it was having to plagiarise its own Kinnock-knocking exploits of yesteryear, superimposing a flattering picture of Johnson on a gleaming light bulb, while Corbyn was presented as the man who would turn the lights out forever. This was *The Sun's* own version of 'Project Fear'; the contrasting message – 'If Boris wins today a bright future begins tomorrow' – was probably not taken very seriously even by its own headline-writers.

The 'phone-hacking' scandal

A glimpse of the newspaper headlines during election campaigns since 1987 might give the impression that nothing had changed: whether or not many voters paid attention to their endorsements, the press as a whole remained confident that it was a credible source of political advice to public-spirited Britons. The threat from the Internet had made no difference to the self-image of 'the dead-tree press', and nothing had happened over the years to dent its reputation among voters.

However, in 2011 the media had proved that it was quite capable of generating negative stories through its own activities. Revelations of illegal information-gathering by employees of Rupert Murdoch's News International (part of News Corp: owner of *The Sun*, *The News of the World*, *The Times,* and *The Sunday Times*) caused a feeling of revulsion at least as deep and widespread as the expenses scandal, and went to the heart of long-running debates about the proper role of the media in liberal democratic societies.

In November 2005, *The News of the World* published a story about a knee injury suffered by Prince William. It seemed likely that the newspaper had obtained this information by intercepting voicemail messages exchanged within the royal entourage. After a police investigation, in January 2007 *The News of the World's* royal editor, Clive Goodman, was jailed for four months; a private investigator, Glenn Mulcaire, was sent to prison for six months. During the court proceedings, it became clear that royals were not the only targets for these techniques, with attention initially focusing on the likelihood that the newspaper had 'eavesdropped' on the private conversations of the celebrities who provide the tabloids with so much of their content. The editor of *The News of the World*, Andy Coulson, resigned once the 'guilty' verdicts had been delivered, taking responsibility for the affair although he denied any knowledge of malpractice. In July, Coulson was appointed director of communications by the Conservative Party, having apparently offered assurances about his role in the affair.

In July 2009, *The Guardian* newspaper claimed that as many as 3,000 celebrities had been targeted. Investigations at this stage by the House of Commons Culture, Media and Sport select committee, the PCC and the police themselves were producing little evidence to suggest that the affair involved more than one or two 'bad apples'. However, in September 2010, *The New York Times* published a report which alleged that phone hacking was a common practice at *The News of the World*, and Andy Coulson (now working for David Cameron's coalition government) was alleged to be implicated directly.

In January 2011 actress Sienna Miller started a civil action against *The News of the World* and subsequently won £100,000 in damages and the profound apologies of News International. By this time, Coulson had left government employment, and the Metropolitan Police had started a new investigation after receiving fresh information. Other public figures (including the former Deputy Prime Minister John (now Lord) Prescott) revealed that police had warned them that their private communications had probably been intercepted. New arrests of individuals associated with *The News of the World* began in April, and the paper announced that it would set up a special fund to compensate victims. Characteristically, the paper published an apology on page 2 of its 10 April issue rather than giving it front-page prominence.

Even at this stage, the story had not really caught fire in the 'mainstream' print and broadcast media – a telling contrast to the feeding frenzy which accompanied the *Telegraph's* revelations about politicians' expenses. This all changed at the beginning of July 2011, when it emerged that the mobile telephone of Milly Dowler, a schoolgirl murdered in 2002, had allegedly been 'hacked into' by *The News of the World's* 'investigators' while it remained possible that she was alive. The public mood, which had not been seriously affected by the earlier allegations about intrusion on celebrities, now became sulphurous, and the print media in general found that it had lost control of the news agenda. The ill-feeling was sustained over the next week by revelations concerning the families of schoolgirls who had been murdered in Cambridgeshire (also in 2002), and relatives of servicepeople killed in Iraq and Afghanistan. Faced with this volume of evidence, News International announced that the next issue of *The News of the World* would be the last, bringing a close to a chapter in British journalism which had begun in 1843, and had sometimes been honourable.

This, though, was not the end of the affair. While private individuals could have given celebrity mobile telephone numbers to the *The News of the World*, there was a strong suspicion that members of the police had been involved in the Milly Dowler case. Since the early police investigations into phone-hacking allegations had been so ineffectual – despite the enormous body of evidence made available after *The Guardian* became involved – it was natural to assume that there had been an attempted cover-up. It emerged that senior serving police officers had close links with News International, accepting hospitality and, in one case, even a job after retirement.

The House of Commons Culture, Media and Sport Committee demanded that the chairman and chief executive of News International's parent company, News Corp, should appear before it. Once Murdoch himself became directly involved, it was likely that questions would be raised about the activities of his worldwide network of companies (in which *The News of the World* was not very significant). Meanwhile, both Andy Coulson and Rebekah Brooks (another former *News of the World* editors who had become Chief Executive of News International) were arrested and questioned by police. On 19 July, the Commissioner of the Metropolitan Police, Sir Paul Stephenson, resigned after it was revealed that a former *News of the World* employee had worked for the force as a media consultant. Two days later, Murdoch and his son James appeared before the Commons' committee; Murdoch was attacked by a protestor armed with a shaving-foam pie, and spoke freely about the numerous occasions – under successive prime ministers – when he had been smuggled secretly into Number 10 (ironically, to avoid attracting attention from the beastly media!).

One effect of the phone-hacking scandal was to turn the spotlight onto the issue of media ownership. As we have seen (see Table 5.1), national newspapers in Britain are controlled by a relatively small number of individuals and organisations. As a controversial figure who had never been a British citizen, Rupert Murdoch was seen in some quarters as an inappropriate person to own newspapers with such a considerable share of the UK market. News Corp's worldwide interest in the broadcast media and the Internet did nothing to allay fears for the future of a 'pluralistic' British media when Murdoch launched a bid to take full control of the satellite broadcaster BSkyB in June 2010. Whatever the merits of his case from a purely business point of view, Murdoch was such an emotive figure that the BSkyB bid had become a subject of widespread speculation long before the hacking scandal began to dominate the headlines. In this case, too, a story about the media was given a sensational 'twist' by dubious media methods. Under the impression that he was gossiping with constituents, the coalition's (Liberal Democrat) Business Secretary Vince Cable had told undercover *Daily Telegraph* reporters in December 2010 that he was 'at war' with Murdoch and wanted to throw obstacles in the way of the BSkyB takeover. The resulting media storm meant that Cable was deprived of all responsibility for Murdoch's bid. But in July 2011, against a background of near-universal public and political condemnation thanks to the hacking scandal, News Corp announced that it was withdrawing its bid for BSkyB. What had seemed a serious misjudgement by Cable back in December 2010, now looked like an example of foresight, though his ministerial responsibilities in this area were not restored.

The Leveson Enquiry

In the wake of the Millie Dowler allegations, the government could no longer leave investigation of the media to the appropriate parliamentary committee. In July 2011, a judicial public inquiry was established, under Lord Justice Leveson, with a broad remit to examine 'the culture, practices and ethics of the press'. The inquiry was conducted in three stages – relations between the press and the public, dealings between the press and the police, and the links between the press and politicians. After protracted hearings, the 2,000-page Leveson Report was published in November 2012.

Leveson's main finding was that self-regulation by the press was ineffective. He recommended the replacement of the PCC by a new independent body which would be able to impose fines and demand that apologies were given appropriate prominence by offending publications. It would not be compulsory to recognise the authority of this new body, but press outlets which refused to do so would be liable for punitive damages if found guilty of malpractice by the courts.

These findings presented David Cameron with an unpleasant dilemma. He had set up the inquiry, and had pledged to honour its proposals in full unless these proved to be 'bonkers'. Unfortunately for Cameron, Leveson had come up with a package which was seriously displeasing to the press while bearing all the hallmarks of rational thought. Even so, while welcoming much of the report, Cameron was unwilling to accept Leveson's proposal that the new body would be established by legislation. By contrast, the Labour opposition and Cameron's Liberal Democrat coalition partners argued that the report should be implemented in full. This view was also given eloquent support by the pressure group 'Hacked Off', which included many high-profile figures whose privacy had been invaded by newspapers (see Chapter 19).

The result was a compromise. The new Independent Press Standards Organisation (IPSO) was established not by parliamentary statute but rather by means of a Royal Charter authorised by the archaic Privy Council. The obvious problem with this constitutional ruse was that if the Charter enjoyed full legal backing, it would be unacceptable to the press; and, if it did not, it would leave press regulation much as it had been before Leveson – unduly influenced by the press itself and incapable of taking effective action even when it chose to stir itself. Either the press was still regulating itself – in which case many of its representatives would continue to interpret 'liberty' in a way which most observers would regard as a 'licence' to flout common decency – or it was being regulated by outsiders, in which case the press could fall back on the well-rehearsed cry that freedom of speech should be sacrosanct in a liberal democracy.

Supporters of IPSO could argue that its membership was configured in a way which made it less likely to err on the side of leniency; its 12-member strong board, chaired by a retired judge, has a majority of members with no direct connections to the press (and even those who do have close media links are highly respected and independent-minded). Furthermore, the establishment of IPSO in September 2014 was quickly followed by the appearance of a related body, the Press Recognition Panel (PRP), to oversee the regulatory process.

Although even the most salacious media outlet will now think twice before hacking into mobile phones, there is no evidence that the new complaints procedures have changed the *culture* of the British press. Certainly, its tendency to 'hype-up' up 'celebrities' in the hope of being able to report on their fall from grace has not diminished. The death of the television presenter Caroline Flack in February 2020 provoked a new outcry over media intrusion.

Overall, the phone-hacking scandal gives rise to various reflections on the role of the media in British society and politics:

- Despite its damaging implications for the British press, the episode actually illustrated both the considerable strength and the ultimate limitations of its 'agenda-setting' role. Until the tide of revelations became irresistible, the 'mainstream' media refused to give much publicity to *The News of the World's* problems, either because it was afraid of Murdoch's influence or because some of its own operatives had themselves indulged in phone hacking. Fear of provoking Murdoch – who was already highly antagonistic to the BBC (his greatest UK media rival) – presumably explained why the Corporation tended to play down the early stages of the scandal.

- Once it became clear that News Corp was in serious trouble, politicians who had been anxious to cultivate Murdoch's support in happier days suddenly decided that his influence had been malevolent all along (at the same time, it was revealed that Tony Blair had agreed to act as godfather to one of Murdoch's children – a shocking testament to the intimacy between senior politicians and the media). This reinforces the point made earlier that, regardless of its effect on voters, the media is influential in UK politics insofar as senior politicians *believe* it to be influential. Once that belief is undermined, they seem willing to echo public criticism of newspapers and their owners – at least until the initial expressions of outrage have died away. In this respect, the repercussions of the 'phone-hacking' scandal reflect very badly on the courage and integrity of many (though by no means all) British politicians, as David Cameron freely admitted.

- In several respects, the episode indicated that money and power have an undue influence over the (supposedly impartial) legal process. Even if the police acted in good faith throughout – and the extent of linkage between News International and senior officers leaves ample room for speculation in this respect – well-resourced celebrities were quick to seek redress through the courts. If *The News of the World* had been wiser in its choice of 'non-celebrity' victims – that is, going after criminals rather than the *victims* of notorious crimes – it would almost certainly have avoided closure.

Announcing the Leveson Inquiry, David Cameron tried to deflect attention from his own ill-judged dealings with Andy Coulson (and the fact that he had met News International operatives on 26 recorded occasions since taking office). He was right to imply that New Labour had been equally (if not more) guilty. However, the rot had really set in during the years of Conservative rule under Margaret Thatcher (on Steven Barnett's terms, the age in which media 'disdain' turned into 'contempt'). In particular, the overt support offered to News International's strike-breaking efforts during the 1980s had formed an umbilical link between politicians and the media. Indeed, the whole New Labour project could be seen as an attempt to neutralise the perceived success of the Murdoch empire in persuading the British public between 1979 and 1992 that there was 'no alternative' to governments which followed the broad tendency of Margaret Thatcher's policies, regardless of their party label.

Conclusion and summary

A free media is a necessary, but not a sufficient, component of a democratic society (see Controversy 5.1). That is, when the media are under the control of the state, there can be no free expression in a meaningful sense. Equally, though, there is no guarantee that a media which is entirely (or mainly) in private hands will allow (let alone actively encourage) the free expression of the full range of public opinions. The familiar argument that the public gets the media it deserves can only reflect a naïve faith in the operations of the free market. Despite the availability of new media forms like the Internet (see Case study 5.2), false opinions backed by money have a far better chance of reaching a significant audience than any view – however logical or insightful – which is given to the world unaided. Ironically, far from being a danger to democracy, the state-funded BBC, for all of its frailties, is still probably the most reliable defender of minority viewpoints in Britain today.

Although scholars dispute the extent of direct media effect on voting behaviour, that an important influence exists is indisputable – even if the only people who are directly influenced are the politicians themselves. Awareness (one might say 'fear') of the media's power has helped to shape the range of policy options offered to the public at election time. According to pluralist theory, a free media ought to widen the choice for voters; however, this promise has not been borne out in practice. At the time of the phone-hacking scandal, some politicians (including the Prime Minister David Cameron) expressed the hope that the media would be more responsible in future. However, despite the cogent arguments expressed in the Leveson Report, this seems to be one market in which quality products will always be outsold by superficial and sensationalist rivals, regardless of whether or not they use illegal methods to obtain their stories.

The relationship between politicians and journalists has changed considerably in recent years. The media were quite deferential until the 1970s, but are now openly combative. In part, this is a result of the emergence of television, which encouraged interviewers to act like public inquisitors. The balance of power has shifted so dramatically that people who would formerly have sought eminence in politics now tend to plump (at least initially) for careers within the media, even though journalists are among the least popular members of society. If the media have begun to drain talent away from public service in this fashion, that alone would be enough to raise questions about their real value to the democratic process in the present 'age of contempt'. The fact that some journalists (like Michael Gove and Boris Johnson) have used their celebrity in order to pursue political careers is not necessarily a reassuring development.

Further reading

The best scholarly introductions to this subject are C. Seymour-Ure's *The British Press and Broadcasting since 1945* (Oxford: Blackwell, 2nd edition, 1996), R. Negrine's *Politics and the Mass Media in Britain* (London: Routledge, 2nd edition, 1994), and R. Kuhn's *Politics and the Media in Britain* (London: Palgrave, 2007). J. Curran and J. Seaton's *Power without Responsibility: The Press, Broadcasting and the Internet in Britain* (London: Routledge, 8th edition, 2018) is a critical account. M. Cockerell's *Live from Number 10: The Inside Story of Prime Ministers and Television* (London: Faber and Faber, 1988) includes a wealth of anecdotes and insights about the developing relationship between the media and politicians. Invaluable articles include A. Chadwick and J. Stanyer's 'The Changing News Media Environment', in R. Heffernan, P. Cowley, and C. Hay (eds.), *Developments in British Politics 9* (Houndmills: Palgrave, 2011), pp. 215–33, and J. Stanyer, 'Politics and the Media: A Breakdown in Relations for New Labour', *Parliamentary Affairs*, Vol. 56, No. 2 (2003), pp. 309–21. S. Barnett, 'Will a Crisis in Journalism Provoke a Crisis in Democracy?', *Political Quarterly*, Vol. 73, No. 4 (2002), pp. 400–08, is a forcefully argued contribution to the debate. On the Hutton Inquiry, see W.G. Runciman's (ed.) *Hutton and Butler: Lifting the Lid on the Workings of Power* (Oxford: Oxford University Press, 2004), and S. Rodgers's (ed.) *The Hutton Inquiry and its Impact* (London: Politico's, 2004). On Leveson, see S. Barnett, 'Leveson Past, Present and Future: The Politics of Press Regulation', *Political Quarterly*, Vol. 84, No. 3 (October 2013), pp. 353–61.

Published studies of recent general elections invariably offer useful studies, for example, D. Wring and S. Ward, 'Exit Velocity: The Media Election', in A. Geddes and J. Tonge (eds.), *Britain Votes 2015* (Oxford: Oxford University Press). For the 2010 campaign, see D. Wring, R. Mortimore, and S. Atkinson's (eds.) *Political Communication in Britain: The Leader Debates, the Campaign and the Media in the 2010 General Election* (Houndmills: Palgrave Macmillan, 2011). C. Pattie and R. Johnson subject the most prominent events of the 2010 election to rigorous analysis in 'A Tale of Sound and Fury, Signifying Something? The Impact of the Leaders' Debates in the 2010 UK General Election', *Journal of Elections, Public Opinion and Parties*, Vol. 21, No. 2 (May 2011), pp. 147–77.

For media coverage of the 2016 referendum, see the studies published by King's College, London (Michael Moore and Gordon Ramsay, *UK Media Coverage of the 2016 EU Referendum Campaign*, https://www.kcl.ac.uk/policy-institute/assets/cmcp/uk-media-coverage-of-the-2016-eu-referendum-campaign.pdf), Reuters (in association with the University of Oxford: D. Levy, B. Aslan and D. Bironzo, *UK Press Coverage of the EU Referendum*, https://reutersinstitute.politics.ox.ac.uk/sites/default/files/2018-11/UK_Press_Coverage_of_the_%20EU_Referendum.pdf, and various reports from Loughborough's Centre for Research in Communication and Culture (https://blog.lboro.ac.uk/crcc/eu-referendum/media-voters-campaign/). For an expose of Cambridge Analytica's activities, see C. Wylie, *Mindf*ck: Inside Cambridge Analytica's Plot to Break the World* (London: Profile Books, 2019). On the BBC, see R. Aitken, *The Noble Liar: How and Why the BBC Distorts the News to Promote a Liberal Agenda* (London: Biteback, 2018).

Memoirs by political journalists may also be consulted: see, for example, J. Cole, *As It Seemed to Me: Political Memoirs* (London: Weidenfeld & Nicolson, 1995) and A. Marr, *My Trade. A Short History of British Journalism* (London: Pan, 2005). From the other side of the battle lines between media and politicians, A. Campbell's voluminous diaries, conveniently condensed in *The Blair Years* (London: Hutchinson, 2007), and L. Price, *The Spin Doctor's Diary* (London: Hodder & Stoughton, 2005) provide entertainment and insights.

Websites

Most national daily and Sunday newspapers have websites that contain full electronic versions of their print editions. The best coverage of the media and politics is found in the media section of *The Guardian* (http://media.guardian.co.uk). Circulation figures are published by the Audit Bureau of Circulations (www.abc.org.uk). Details of the organisation of the BBC are at www.bbc.co.uk/info.

The Department for Culture, Media and Sport (www.culture.gov.uk) is the responsible government department and Ofcom (www.ofcom.org.uk), the independent regulator for the communications industry. The Independent Press Standards Organisation (IPSO) (www.ipso.co.uk) includes details of a code of practice for the press. The Hutton Inquiry site (www.the-hutton-inquiry.org.uk) sets new standards for government transparency by releasing hundreds of documents; the proceedings and report of the Leveson Inquiry are available in full on a site hosted by the National Archives (https://webarchive.nationalarchives.gov.uk/20140122144906/http://www.levesoninquiry.org.uk/).

Part 2

Constitution and institutions

Chapter 6

The constitution

Learning outcomes

After reading this chapter, you will:

- understand the traditional features and sources of the UK constitution;
- have an insight into the factors which have placed the traditional constitution under strain in recent decades; and
- be able to evaluate the various constitutional reforms which have been proposed or implemented since 1997.

Introduction

The UK constitution is often regarded as an arid subject, suitable for discussion only among academics or political obsessives. Constitutional experts rarely intrude upon everyday life unless they are invited to speculate on television about the latest crisis to affect the monarchy. In itself, this attitude tells us something important about British political culture. It reflects a feeling given eloquent expression by the eighteenth-century poet Alexander Pope: 'For forms of government let fools contest/Whate'er is best administered is best'. Other countries have made a considerable fuss about constitutional arrangements. The ancient Greeks venerated the makers of constitutions, and the philosopher Aristotle conducted an intensive study of the various systems of his time. Eighteenth-century revolutionaries in America and France conducted lengthy and passionate debates about constitutional arrangements. But this has not been the British way. The UK constitution has *evolved*, thanks to countless practical decisions which, according to its supporters, have served the public interest rather than following abstract ideas of one kind or another.

This benign view of the UK constitution has never won universal acceptance. For many years, critics have claimed that unplanned evolution has left the country with outdated institutions, fit for a living museum rather than a nation which hopes to combine freedom and prosperity in a fast-changing modern world. The 1997 general election gave these critical voices new prominence, and the nature of the constitution has been a key feature of political debates ever since (although characteristic British attitudes persist, and many voters are probably unaware that recent political controversies are about much more than Britain's relationship with the EU). This chapter includes many themes which are also mentioned elsewhere, but this only underlines the relevance of constitutional questions throughout the subject matter of UK politics.

The uncodified constitution

Aristotle believed that a constitution was integral to the way of life of any political society. A more precise definition would characterise it as an authoritative set of laws, rules, and practices which specifies how a state is to be governed and the relationship between the state and the individual. It provides a framework for the political system and establishes the main institutions of government, outlining their powers and the relationship between them. It also determines where 'sovereignty' – traditionally defined as the ultimate decision-making power – resides within the state.

A distinction is frequently drawn between written and unwritten constitutions. In a written constitution, the main rules and principles governing the state are enshrined in constitutional texts with special status. In an unwritten constitution, such rules are found in conventions or tradition. The British constitution is usually classed as unwritten, because the UK has no single constitutional document. This makes the country unusual among liberal democracies; only Israel, New Zealand, and (arguably) Canada are in the same position. By contrast, the written US constitution dates back to 1787 (though it has been subject to various partial revisions). Many of the constitutions of Western Europe were rewritten after World War II; for example, the present French constitution was introduced in 1958.

The British constitution is certainly flexible. In 1940, for example, the British War Cabinet decided, after only the briefest of discussions, to propose a union of the UK state with France, which was then on the brink of surrender to Nazi Germany. Only the refusal of the French government thwarted this dramatic deal. Yet it is too simplistic to describe the UK constitution as 'unwritten'. A more accurate word is *uncodified*. This is because, in practice, all constitutions contain a mixture of written and unwritten rules. A written constitution is not a detailed instruction manual, but rather a reference point for a political system which is subject to change. Thus, the US constitution includes judicial decisions and conventions, as well as the written constitutional text; an interventionist presidency, for example, is alien to the original spirit of the constitution. By the same token, some of the most important rules governing political activity in the UK are written in the form of Acts of Parliament or judicial rulings; some distinction, however, must still be made because the UK lacks a single, formal constitutional document (see Analysis 6.1).

Sources of the UK constitution

In the absence of a single codified document, there are four principal sources of the UK constitution:

1. statute law
2. common law
3. conventions
4. authoritative works

Before the 'Brexit' referendum of 2016, EU law was considered to be a fifth constitutional source. Once Britain has formalised its future relationship with the EU, it might continue to

Analysis 6.1

Codified and uncodified constitutions

Advocates of a codified constitution for the UK claim that it would be an essential guarantee of liberal democracy, recognising that British people are active citizens rather than passive 'subjects'. However, this is not to say that uncodified constitutions are invariably flawless. It is worth remembering that the Weimar Republic, introduced in Germany after World War I, had a codified liberal constitution. While the Nazi regime of Adolf Hitler was not exactly a *product* of the Weimar Republic, the latter's liberal democratic processes did little to prevent the Nazi rise to power.

In codified constitutions, the powers of the branches of government – executive, legislature, and judiciary – may be clearly laid down in a single authoritative document. There will usually be provisions for amending the constitution, depending on circumstances, but changes will require much more than a simple vote of the legislature. The basic rights of citizens are identified in a way which allows them to claim protection against the state. Political disputes may arise within the state, but unless a fundamental issue of principle is at stake, the parties to the quarrel will at least have to abide by mutually recognised rules of engagement.

Supporters of uncodified constitutions, like the UK, argue that they are flexible enough to meet sudden emergencies (whereas constitutional changes in a country like the USA can only take place after a cumbersome and time-consuming process). Because emergencies do arise, countries with codified constitutions can find themselves having to bend the rules, thus undermining the main justification for a formal constitutional document. It is also argued that the accumulated wisdom of the past is the best guide to present dilemmas. The founders of the US constitution might have been extremely wise, but it is against all probability that more wisdom was contained in that generation than in the combined brain-power of all their successors. Finally, codified constitutions place considerable influence in the hands of unelected judges, like the US Supreme Court, which can overrule politicians if their laws do not accord with constitutional principles. Elected politicians might make mistakes, but at least they can be held to account by the public in the UK. If their decisions are wrong, they can be rectified at a general election rather than being nullified by a group of legally trained individuals who are also capable of making mistakes, and who might be utterly unrepresentative of public opinion.

accept EU law in some respects, but it will do so because its own Parliament has endorsed such laws. Before the referendum (and the Cameron government's voluntary decision to accept that narrow verdict as binding), the EU enjoyed a significant constitutional role because its laws were considered to override any British legislation on the same subjects.

It should be noted here – because even serious students of the subject so often get this wrong – that Britain's withdrawal from the EU had no bearing on its relationship with the European Court of Human Rights (ECHR), which was established by the Council of Europe before the EEC came into existence.

Statute law

Statute law

law derived
from Acts of
Parliament and
subordinate
legislation.

Statute law is created by Parliament. Legislative proposals (bills) become Acts of Parliament and enter into law once they have been passed by both Houses of Parliament and have received the Royal Assent (which they do automatically, since the UK is a constitutional monarchy). They are implemented by the executive and enforced by the courts.

Under the doctrine of parliamentary sovereignty (see later in the chapter), Parliament is the supreme law-making body in the UK. It can repeal or amend any existing statute. But some Acts of Parliament have greater constitutional significance than others. For example, a succession of statutes (1832, 1867, 1884, 1885, 1918, 1928, 1948, and 1969) gave the vote to all Britons over 18. The Parliament Act of 1911 formally established the superiority of the House of Commons. The UK joined the EEC under the terms of the European Communities Act 1972, and reversed that decision through the European Union (Withdrawal Agreement) Act 2020. Under the first Blair government (1997–2001), several key constitutional statutes were passed, such as the Scotland Act 1998, which created a Scottish Parliament; the Human Rights Act 1998, which incorporated the European Convention on Human Rights into UK law; and the House of Lords Act 1999, which removed most hereditary peers from the upper chamber. In 2011, the Conservative–Liberal Democrat coalition government passed legislation giving the UK fixed-term Parliaments for the first time. There was no serious suggestion that the government would have to call a referendum before passing this statute, despite its considerable constitutional significance.

Common law

Common law

law derived
from decisions
in court cases
and from
general legal
custom.

**Prerogative
powers**

discretionary
powers of the
Crown that are
exercised by
ministers.

In legal cases where there is no clear statute law, the courts interpret and clarify the legal position. Such rulings become part of the **common law**, and take precedence over previous judicial rulings. However, Parliament retains the right to supersede common law through further Acts of Parliament.

The common law also includes customs and precedents that have been accepted over time. The most important of these are the Crown's **prerogative powers**, including the right to declare war and negotiate treaties, to dissolve Parliament, and to appoint government ministers and judges. These powers remained in the hands of the monarchy despite two revolutions in the seventeenth century. Since then, they have passed to government ministers, who exercise them in the name of the Crown. Thus, the prime minister secured the right to declare war, to decide the timing of general elections, and to appoint ministers. The monarch was normally consulted, but this was purely formal. There has been a long-running debate about whether a monarch could refuse the dissolution of Parliament if a viable government could be constituted from the existing House of Commons. The passage of the

Fixed-Term Parliaments Act 2011 seemed to eliminate this problem, since the legislation placed any decision about an early dissolution in the hands of Parliament. Boris Johnson's plan to circumvent the 2011 Act included a request to the Queen to prevent Parliament from sitting (through the device known as 'prorogation'); the monarch's compliance with a move which the courts subsequently nullified was another sign that the 'Head of State' was merely a figurehead (see Controversy 6.2). Even the Queen's Birthday Honours list is not under her control. Ultimately, the prime minister is more powerful than any British monarch since the seventeenth century, because his or her control over Parliament is direct, whereas the monarch could never be totally confident of its support.

Conventions

Convention

an established norm of political behaviour that is considered binding, but which lacks a firm basis in law.

Conventions are rules or norms that are considered to be binding. The flexibility of the UK constitution is enhanced because some of its key elements are based on conventional practices which are open to change without a protracted decision-making process (indeed, often without a conscious 'decision' of any kind).

One important convention is that the prime minister should be a member of the House of Commons. In 1940, when Neville Chamberlain resigned as prime minister, an influential body of opinion believed that his successor should be the Foreign Secretary, Lord Halifax. If Halifax had pressed his case with energy, he might have been chosen. But he hesitated, partly because he felt that the national leader during wartime should be a member of the elected House. Winston Churchill took the position instead. In 1963, another peer, the Earl of Home, became prime minister only because he was able to renounce his title under the terms of the newly passed Peerage Act. As Sir Alec Douglas-Home, he quickly gained a seat in the Commons through a by-election.

The flexible nature of the UK constitution is tested when a general election does not produce a clear winner, as in 2010 and 2017. Such an outcome is called a 'hung parliament'. The prospect of a very close result in 2010 encouraged experts to examine this subject closely, and the precedents (as usual) were not entirely clear. However, Lord (Peter) Hennessy, a seasoned observer of the constitution, argued that the incumbent Prime Minister (Gordon Brown) would remain in office until his attempts to negotiate with other parties had failed. If (as turned out to be the case) Brown proved unable to put together a viable coalition, the monarch would invite the leader of the largest opposition party to form an administration. The fact that in 2010 the Conservatives had won 49 seats more than Labour was relevant, but not decisive (contrary to the claims of both David Cameron and Nick Clegg); the Conservatives had not secured an overall majority and had no automatic right to take the initiative in coalition-building. If Cameron and Clegg had not been able to strike a deal, a new general election almost certainly would have been called. It was not surprising that Cameron and Clegg were able to act as if precedents did not matter, since, until 2010, the British electoral system had usually managed to perform its expected function of delivering overall parliamentary majorities to parties even if their candidates had been opposed by more than half of the electorate. Before 2010, the last hung parliament had been elected in February 1974, when Labour's Harold Wilson eventually formed a government even though his party won fewer votes than the Conservatives. A new general election was duly called in October of the same year.

In 2017, when Theresa May's Conservative government failed to secure an overall parliamentary majority, the kind of impromptu (or opportunistic) thinking which had informed the creation of the 2010 coalition indicated that she should have submitted her government's resignation. In 2010, Cameron and Clegg were able to present the election result as a repudiation of Gordon Brown's legitimacy, since he had lost his parliamentary majority. However, exactly the same fate befell Mrs May in 2017; unlike Brown, she had called the general election in order to transform a slender parliamentary majority into a decisive one. If anything, the blow to Mrs May's authority as prime minister was greater than the one suffered by Brown in 2010. The difference was that (unlike Labour in 2010) her party had won enough seats to scrape through its electoral disaster by striking a deal with just one other party – the Democratic Unionists (DUP) of Northern Ireland. For Mrs May (if not her party), the deal struck with the DUP served only to delay the inevitable departure from office.

Convention also governs the circumstances in which governments or ministers should resign. The convention of *collective* responsibility means that ministers ought to retire from the government if they do not accept a policy position agreed by the cabinet. In 2003, Robin Cook and Clare Short both resigned because they disagreed with the Blair government's position on war in Iraq. The convention of *individual* ministerial responsibility means that a minister should resign if serious mistakes are made within their departments – even if they played no part in the mistaken decision.

In reality, though, these conventions are more often disregarded than followed. In 1982, the Foreign Secretary, Lord Carrington, and two of his junior ministers resigned because they were held to be partly responsible for the Argentine invasion of the Falklands Islands. Carrington and his colleagues took responsibility on themselves to appease the mood in Parliament and the country; their own role in precipitating the invasion was arguably less than that of the Prime Minister, Margaret Thatcher, who had authorised cuts in defence spending which left the islands vulnerable to attack. In recent years, many ministers have refused to stand down even when they have clearly made serious mistakes. If they subsequently resign, it will be because the prime minister has decided they must go; there are numerous recent examples of ministers submitting their resignations but being persuaded to stay in post by the prime minister. Whatever her record in other respects, Theresa May tried to uphold the principle of individual responsibility by sacking Priti Patel (Overseas Development) and Gavin Williamson (Defence) for serious misdemeanours, although the post-Thatcher pattern continued with the resignations of Michael Fallon (Williamson's predecessor at Defence) and Damian Green (First Secretary of State) in the face of personal, rather than professional, allegations.

The convention of collective ministerial responsibility was stretched in the 1990s, when John Major struggled to keep order within a cabinet which was profoundly split over Europe. Several ministers made it clear that they disagreed with the prime minister's approach, either by leaking their private thoughts to journalists or by making 'coded' speeches of dissent. They were not sacked, because the prime minister's position was weak. The 2010–15 coalition government presented an interesting challenge to the doctrine of collective responsibility, which was relaxed in crucial policy areas such as electoral reform and student finance. The end of the coalition in 2015 confronted David Cameron with a different dilemma, as members of his Conservative cabinet were sure to take different sides in the pending referendum on EU membership. Cameron's attempt to stipulate that his colleagues should take a common approach once negotiations were completed aroused predictable opposition, and eventually he decided to follow Harold Wilson's precedent of 1975, suspending collective responsibility for the duration of the campaign.

Authoritative works

There are a number of established legal and political texts which are accepted as works of authority on the UK constitution. Such texts have no *formal* legal status but are regularly consulted as reliable guides to the workings of institutions and of the political system in general. The best known of these is Erskine May's *Treatise on the Law, Privileges, Proceedings and Usage of Parliament* (first published in 1844 but regularly updated). It is regarded as the 'Bible' of parliamentary practice and is used by the Speaker of the House of Commons and other senior officials. The ghost of Erskine May would have smiled in March 2019 when Speaker John Bercow cited his work as the basis for a controversial ruling that Theresa May (no relation) could not persist in her repeated attempts to persuade the Commons to support her EU withdrawal proposals. The precedent (dating back to 1604) was that 'It is a rule, in both houses, not to permit any question or bill to be offered, which is substantially the same as one on which their judgement has already been expressed, in the same session'.

European Union law

When the UK Parliament passed the European Communities Act 1972, it accepted that EEC (now EU) law would take precedence over UK statute law if there was a conflict between the two. There was a general recognition that this development would have a radical effect on the British constitution. However, Parliament retained the power to repeal the legislation, and used this power in 2020.

Main principles of the UK constitution

There are four main building blocks of the traditional UK constitution:

1. parliamentary sovereignty
2. the rule of law
3. a unitary state
4. representative government

Once again, until the 2016, there were five 'blocks', but since the referendum in that year, the fifth (membership of the European Union) has been removed.

Parliamentary sovereignty

Parliamentary Sovereignty

the doctrine that Parliament is the supreme law-making authority in the UK

The doctrine of **Parliamentary sovereignty** is the key element of the UK constitution. It means that the Westminster Parliament is regarded as the supreme law-making institution. The doctrine has three main elements:

- Parliament can legislate on any subject it chooses;
- acts of Parliament cannot be overturned by any other authority;
- no Parliament can bind its successors, meaning that any piece of current legislation may be repealed by a future Parliament.

In practice, though, Parliament is not in control. The legislative and executive branches of the UK government are *fused*. The executive, or government, is composed of members of the two Houses of Parliament. By contrast, in countries like the USA, which have a constitutional separation of powers, the executive is excluded from the legislature (or has only token representation) and has to bargain with members of the legislature in order to secure the passage of laws. The UK government is normally in a dominant position in the House of Commons, through the 'whipping' system of party discipline and its control over the legislative timetable. In turn, the Commons has far more power than the House of Lords, unlike the situation in the USA where the Upper House, the Senate, is more prestigious than the House of Representatives and has greater influence in areas like executive appointments and the making of treaties.

In most other liberal democracies, laws which have significant constitutional implications cannot be passed simply by securing a majority in the legislature; such laws are said to be 'entrenched'. There are no such safeguards in the UK. The executive-dominated House of Commons does not even need to secure the consent of the House of Lords under the terms of the Parliament Acts of 1911 and 1949, which confined the power of the Lords to a period of delay. The executive can also take decisions, like authorising armed intervention by British forces, without consulting Parliament. This is because the executive in Parliament has inherited many of the powers which were once 'royal prerogatives' under the control of the monarch. Before wars are declared, the government will normally ask for the consent of Parliament; but this is not automatic, and as in the USA, the involvement of the legislature can be evaded by claiming that military intervention (even on a significant scale) is not a 'war'. In 2013, the Commons voted against the coalition's motion on possible military action in Syria, but this did not prevent the government from authorising specific actions (including drone strikes) in the area, and in 2018 Theresa May reasserted the familiar position that, in some situations, it was not in the national interest to consult MPs in advance. Parliament is also able to establish or abolish subsidiary authorities, like local government, since these do not enjoy special constitutionally protected status as they do in most liberal democracies, even those which are not formally 'federal' in nature.

There are, though, significant *external* constraints on Parliament and the executive. British power and prestige declined steeply during the course of the twentieth century, greatly reducing the scope and reach of parliamentary decisions. Withdrawal from the EU will make no difference in this respect; Parliament can still pass any legislation it approves, but this will only be *effective* if global circumstances (and the capacity of the British state) allow. In practice, laws can also be made inoperative if the courts hold them to breach the terms of the Human Rights Act 1998, which incorporated the European Convention on Human Rights into the UK law (see Chapter 9).

However, the main restrictions on the executive are informal conventions and traditions of behaviour. Governments regularly claim a mandate for certain policies which have featured in their election manifestos. These may or may not have been important issues during the campaign, but normally questions of constitutional significance will give rise to considerable discussion. It is recognised that some issues are so important that they cannot be implemented without a referendum, and that a government will abide by the result even though this technically infringes the sovereignty of Parliament. While no Parliament can bind its successors, it would be very difficult, for example, for a future government to abolish the Scottish Parliament without obtaining popular consent through a new referendum (see Chapter 19).

The Rule of Law

a system of rule where the relationship between the state and its citizens is governed by the law, rather than being subject to arbitrary decisions.

The rule of law

The rule of law is a crucial principle in all liberal democracies – the ultimate guarantee against the arbitrary exercise of power. It ensures that all citizens of a state are to be treated equally and impartially. When they

PHOTO 6.1 'I don't know who writes these terrible scripts': The Queen reads out the government's legislative programme (© Tim Graham/Getty Images).

are charged with offences against the law, they can expect a fair trial from an independent judiciary – a principle which dates back to Magna Carta, signed in 1215. Although errors can be made in the judicial process, there are procedures for overturning wrongful verdicts. Citizens can also seek redress from the state if any of its servants have acted unlawfully. On the other hand, numerous laws are designed to protect individuals from unlawful activity by their fellow citizens. The state is expected to maintain an adequate police force to uphold these laws; the police should also be impartial in their work, disregarding irrelevant factors like ethnicity, gender, or social status (see Chapter 9).

The principle of impartial law enforcement highlights a characteristic constitutional anomaly in the UK, which Labour attempted to redress after its re-election in 2001. The head of the judiciary, responsible for all key appointments, was the Lord Chancellor; yet this cabinet minister was not strictly independent at all, being appointed by the prime minister. Furthermore, the Lord Chancellor was also Speaker of the House of Lords, making him an important member of the legislature. Thus, the Chancellor belonged to all three branches of government –the judiciary, the executive, and the legislature – making it likely that he would be subject to conflicts of interest. From the perspective of constitutional theory, this situation was bizarre (or dangerous, depending on the observer's outlook). Yet it could be argued that in a perverse way the system actually promoted a degree of independence, because it was presumed that the legal profession would never tolerate a government appointee who tried to interfere with its traditional practices. However, the second Blair government decided to address the anomaly, with distinctly mixed results. Its attempts to abolish the office of Lord Chancellor were thwarted by the resistance of the House of Lords, and the post was reprieved. However, the Lord Chancellor's constitutional powers were significantly reduced by the Constitutional Reform Act 2005 (see Chapter 9). Since 2007, Justice Secretaries have also held the title of Lord Chancellor, even though they have not been members of the House of Lords – a good example of the tendency of the UK constitutional reform to replace one anomaly with another.

Critics have argued that the rule of law is vulnerable in the UK for other reasons. Historic rights, like trial by jury, have been overturned at times of crisis: 'Diplock courts', where a judge sat without a jury, were introduced to deal with terrorist cases in Northern Ireland in 1973 (they were abolished in 2007; since that year, trials without juries have been allowed in specific cases, e.g. when there is reason to suppose that attempts will be made to tamper with or intimidate jury members). The terrorist attack on New York in September 2001 was also cited as a reason for new restrictions on civil rights, even though this took place on foreign soil. Detention without trial, which was also used in Northern Ireland during 'the Troubles', and in the rest of the UK during World War II, is a clear breach of traditional liberties. However, after '9/11', the UK government argued that the terrorist threat made detention without trial necessary in specific instances, provoking a debate which goes to the heart of liberal democratic principles.

A unitary state

The UK is composed of four constituent nations: England, Scotland, Wales, and Northern Ireland. It is far from being united, in respect of culture, language, or tradition (see Chapters 3 and 12). Yet the UK is commonly regarded as a **unitary state**, not least by the law-makers at Westminster. A unitary state is highly centralised, with the dominant power located in national institutions. Certain powers might be delegated to subnational or local levels, but they are not protected by constitutional safeguards. Thus, in 1985, the Thatcher government was able to abolish

Controversy 6.1

Terrorism and the rule of law

Activities by terrorists with a political motivation constitute a formidable challenge to liberal democracies. Such states uphold the idea that all political disputes must be resolved by dialogue rather than violence. At most, people with a grievance may resort to peaceful civil disobedience if the democratic process cannot satisfy their demands. Yet if their actions infringe the law, they can expect to be punished by the courts under their usual procedures.

However, the potential threat from terrorism today has changed the terms of debate. On the one hand, it can be argued that people who kill and maim have put themselves outside the protection of liberal procedures, so traditional understandings of the rule of law should be set aside to deal with them. An alternative view is that many terrorists have the explicit aim of undermining liberal democracy. If their actions can provoke arbitrary acts, like imprisonment without trial, they will have won a kind of victory. A more practical objection, with particular relevance to the UK, is that several miscarriages of justice occurred in the 1970s, when the country was faced with a terrorist campaign by Irish Republicans. Although trial by jury was maintained on the mainland, several suspects were convicted on fabricated evidence because of a prevailing atmosphere of panic and a thirst for vengeance. This precedent could hardly inspire public confidence in any future government which declared that certain people had to be detained on the basis of evidence which was kept secret because of alleged (but undisclosed) security considerations. More radical critics argued that governments have a vested interest in suspending traditional liberties, and that it was quite possible for ministers to create a lasting sense of panic which would transform a temporary suspension of the rule of law into a permanent arrangement.

Unitary State

a homogeneous state in which power is concentrated at the centre.

the Greater London Council (which had been created by another Conservative administration in 1963) and six metropolitan county councils. By contrast, in federal systems, power is shared between national and regional governments. Federal constitutions grant specific powers to the different tiers of government. In the UK, the word 'federal' is now widely regarded in a negative light, and Eurosceptics associate federalism with the construction of a European polity. Yet, when ministers devised constitutions for other countries within the old British Empire, the federal principle was often followed, for the good reason that it maximised the sense of self-government for people who would have resented centralised power.

The component nations of the UK came together in different ways. Wales was conquered by England, while both Scotland and Ireland joined the Union through negotiated agreement. England and Wales became closely integrated for most administrative purposes; however, the Welsh language has survived, and the strong tradition of Welsh religious dissent was recognised when the Church of England was disestablished in that country in 1920. Scotland retained its own legal and judicial systems. The Irish Free State formally seceded from the Union in 1922, after further bloodshed. Northern Ireland, which remained within the Union, retained separate institutions and a highly distinctive style of politics.

A classic unitary state exhibits a high degree of both centralisation and standardisation, with all parts of the state being governed in the same way. The UK never fitted this model. It is more accurate to describe it as a **Union state**, reflecting the political and cultural variations which remained after the different countries came together. Defenders of this arrangement claimed that it was far more flexible than a formal federation, allowing 'asymmetrical' institutional development to reflect local circumstances. Thus, there has been a Secretary of State for Scotland since 1885, but a similar post for Wales was not created until 1964, in response to an upsurge in Welsh nationalism. The devolved institutions established in Scotland, Wales, and Northern Ireland differ from each other (see Chapter 12). While critics argued that **devolution** on this scale signalled the end of the United Kingdom, supporters of the move could claim that it vindicated the flexible nature of the Union state.

Union State

a state in which the component parts are culturally distinct and, despite a strong centre, are governed in different ways.

Devolution

the transfer of decision-making authority from central to subnational government.

Representative government

Although universal adult suffrage is a relatively recent development in the UK (dating back only to 1928), the principle of representation is as old as the House of Commons (which originated in 1265). Over the centuries, the importance of the representative principle has strengthened with the development of political parties and the supremacy of the Commons over the unelected Lords. From the constitutional monarchy of the late seventeenth century, the UK system evolved into a more recognisable, if still somewhat eccentric, form of liberal democracy. The legislative and executive branches are still fused rather than separate. Government takes place through Parliament under a constitutional monarchy. Ministers are politically accountable to Parliament, and legally accountable to the Crown through the courts.

By the mid-nineteenth century, as the great constitutional writer Walter Bagehot affirmed, the British political system was one of cabinet government. Cabinet was the key policymaking body, but even if certain ministers sat in the House of Lords, it was understood that a government could not survive without a workable majority in the Commons. A century later, considerable powers had been accumulated by the prime minister, who was now much more than 'first among equals'. But even in the era of prime ministerial government, no one could hold that office without enjoying the support of a majority of the people's representatives or being able to win a parliamentary seat. The government is still regarded as being accountable for its actions, although tight party discipline makes it very unlikely that a government with a sizeable parliamentary majority will lose a vote of confidence in the Commons. It will be judged on its record at a general election, which cannot be called more than five years after the previous contest. The Fixed-Term Parliaments Act 2011 removed the conventional right of prime ministers to call general elections at a time of their choosing within the five-year term, entrusting this decision to Parliament. The five-year term splits the difference between previous laws: an act of 1694 specified a maximum of three years between elections, but was replaced in 1716 by the Septennial Act, which remained in force until 1911.

In Britain, a clear distinction has been drawn between a 'representative' (someone chosen to act on behalf of others) and a 'delegate' (a person who acts/votes in accordance with *instructions* given by others). British MPs claim to be representatives of their constituents, so that they can exercise their own judgement until the voters have a chance to deliver a verdict at the end of the allotted term. At the same time, governments often claim that electoral victory gives their party a *mandate* to carry out the policy programmes included in their manifestos. This is a complex and oft-debated subject; for the present purpose, it is sufficient to say that a plausible interpretation of the situation in the UK is one of a representative system based on political parties – unlike the USA, where the system is much more 'candidate-centred' at every level of government.

Joining – and leaving – the EU

While membership of the EU raised serious questions in itself, this episode in British constitutional history inspired more than one departure from traditional British practice. The first UK-wide referendum was held on the issue in 1975. The coalition government passed the European Union Act 2011, which introduced a referendum 'lock' – preventing the British ratification of any further EU treaty without a public vote. This conflicted with the doctrine of parliamentary

Controversy 6.2

The traditional constitution

Defenders of the traditional UK constitution claim that:

- It is flexible enough to accommodate social and political change.
- It provides government which is strong but accountable to the public at regular intervals.
- The rule of law guarantees the rights of the individual against the state.
- The constitution has evolved in response to genuine needs and has stood the test of time.

Key arguments raised by critics included the following:

- There are inadequate constitutional controls over the executive.
- The system is over-centralised, leaving subsidiary government institutions at the mercy of the centre.
- Non-democratic institutions, such as the monarchy and the House of Lords, have survived and still enjoy influence over political decisions.
- Individuals are still treated as subjects, rather than citizens, and their rights can easily be overridden. In the absence of a codified constitution, it is far too easy to restrict liberty on the pretext of the 'national interest'.

sovereignty in two respects: first, by implying that the people, rather than their representatives, ought to have the decisive say on questions concerning EU integration; and second, by challenging the idea that no Parliament can bind its successors. The European Union Act could, of course, be repealed like any other statute; those who sponsored the legislation obviously believed that, once passed, it would be regarded as a permanent fixture. Thus, ironically, the constitutional 'traditionalists' who disliked Britain's involvement in 'Europe' found themselves advocating 'non-traditional' constitutional practices in the hope of arresting or reversing a constitutional development which they detested. Once they had achieved the desired outcome – and Britain had 'taken back control' – many of these innovators clearly hoped that constitutional 'normality' would be restored. However, they had no plausible argument of principle to offer against 'Remainers' (now, effectively, 'Rejoiners') who advocated a further referendum. This question was only settled (for the time being) by the 2019 general election, in which the first-past-the-post electoral system provided a comfortable majority for the pro-Leave Conservatives.

The constitution under pressure

The Establishment

the most influential people in a country, especially those with a similar social background who support the status quo.

Although there were many important changes to the UK constitution in the first half of the twentieth century, these were rarely accompanied by sustained and searching debate about the nature of the constitution itself. This only became a regular feature of political discourse in the 1960s, as part of a more general inquest into the reasons for the decline of the UK, which was now too obvious to ignore. Unease was expressed by commentators outside Parliament, but senior politicians from both main parties (e.g. Richard Crossman from the Labour Party and Lord Hailsham from the Conservative Party) added their voices, while the Liberals (now the Liberal Democrats) have always taken a serious interest in constitutional matters.

Elective Dictatorship

a situation in which an elected government, particularly the prime minister, is able to act without fear of constraint by other institutions.

The constitution was coming under pressure for a variety of reasons. The central state was forced to recognise the growing strength of nationalism in Scotland and Wales; unrest in Northern Ireland threatened to provoke a full-scale civil war. A decline in social deference from the 1960s onwards produced a new, more critical approach to the British **Establishment**, including the monarchy. But the main focus of attention was the state. Critics argued that, since World War II, central government had taken on too many functions and had become 'overloaded' (see Chapter 3). In the process, too much power had accumulated in the hands of a single person – the prime minister. The Conservative Lord Hailsham – who had served as Lord Chancellor from 1970 to 1974 – warned in 1976 that the UK was in the process of becoming an **elective dictatorship**.

The impact of Thatcherism

Ironically, Hailsham went on to serve a second term as Lord Chancellor in a government which brought many of these fears to a head. Margaret Thatcher herself was far from radical in her view of the constitution; for example, in 1975, she opposed the use of a referendum to settle the question of UK membership of the EEC on the grounds that it would infringe parliamentary sovereignty (a view which she later modified). But her determined opposition to the ideas of the post-war 'consensus' led her to attack many established institutions (see Chapter 3). Her most startling innovation was to abolish the Greater London Council (GLC) and six other metropolitan authorities. The surviving local authorities were subjected to regular reforms, progressively reducing them to the status of service deliverers rather than hubs of political activity. Many of their functions were allotted to unelected 'quangos' and other agencies, leading to a loss of political accountability (see Chapter 11).

At the centre, Thatcher was accused of politicising the civil service. Whitehall bureaucrats had been regarded as a key element of the constitution, acting as impartial servants of the public, regardless of which party happened to be in power. But since the 1960s, they had been undermined along with other members of the 'Establishment'. Mrs Thatcher saw them as a drain on the public purse, who only stirred themselves into action when their own interests were under threat. Her direct impact can be exaggerated – while she was prime minister, it was still possible for old-style 'mandarins' to win promotion. But the ethos of the civil service was transformed. Instead of advising ministers from the perspective of Britain's long-term interests, senior civil servants became much more willing to see things from the point of view of their political masters, who lived from one election to the next in the constant expectation of being shuffled to another post and thus had little incentive to focus on long-term considerations.

Thatcher's appetite for conflict and change extended beyond Whitehall and local government. The trade unions, which had been drawn into an uneasy partnership with post-war governments, were no longer consulted and were subjected to a series of reforms. Their opposition to Thatcher's aims was predictable. But the prime minister also clashed with venerable elements within the establishment, notably the Church of England, which criticised the social effect of her economic policies. Teachers, academics, doctors, lawyers, and even the police were antagonised by attempts to make them more 'businesslike'.

In the 1980s, there were also growing concerns about civil liberties. In part, this was due to technological advances which made it much easier for the state to keep its own citizens under surveillance. But Mrs Thatcher's rhetoric increased fears that these instruments would be put to extensive use as a matter of routine. She was preoccupied by 'the enemies within', regarding socialists as little better than traitors; even moderates who did not share her views were dismissed as appeasers. The battle with 'the enemies within' came to a head during the year-long miners' strike (1984–85), for which the government had made extensive preparations. At that time, freedom of movement was restricted in mining areas, and the traditional independence of Britain's police forces was overridden by central coordination.

Thatcher's battle against established institutions had several ironic consequences. In some respects, she fulfilled her promise to reduce the scope of central state activity; for example, her governments returned many nationalised industries to the private sector. However, in other respects, state responsibilities increased (and even the privatised utilities were still subject to state regulation). The inescapable problem for Thatcher was that her ability to effect change derived from her position within the very central state which she had promised to 'roll back'. Judging by her attendance records, she had limited respect for Parliament, but she could not achieve her aims without it.

The main (though unintended) effect of Thatcher's premiership was to expose the lack of accountability in the UK constitution. Her own electoral successes raised questions about the first-past-the-post system, since she implemented divisive reforms without coming near to securing a majority of the votes cast (unlike the Attlee government which had established the 'consensus' after the 1945

Case study 6.1

Thatcherism and the monarchy

The emergence of Britain's first female prime minister when a woman, Elizabeth II, also occupied the throne turned out to be something less than a happy coincidence. The real source of friction was ideology rather than gender, but when it became clear that Buckingham Palace and Downing Street were not in full accord, it was natural for the media to adopt their familiar tactic of focusing on personalities rather than principles. The Thatcherite ethos, with its heavy emphasis on individual ambition, hard work, and thrift, was directly antipathetic to the concept of monarchy, whose undemocratic hereditary basis was now held to be justified by the ideal of public service. Thatcher also offended the Queen with her attitude to the Commonwealth, which she regarded as (at best) an irritating forum for gesture-politics. The battle for the Falklands (1982) was very much Thatcher's war, and no one could have drawn any other conclusion from the victory celebrations despite the fact that the Queen was Commander-in-Chief of the armed forces.

The imperfect sympathy between the prime minister and the Queen provided an opportunity for Republicans within the media, notably the Australia-born Rupert Murdoch, to chip away at the traditional ties between Conservative voters and the throne (see Chapter 5). A potent source of grievance was the cost of the extended royal family, although the Right-wing press kept silent about more spectacular examples of government profligacy and condoned the privatisation of public utilities at a fraction of their true market value. Thus, the monarchy had been softened up by negative media 'spin' even before the domestic problems of the Prince of Wales and his siblings hit the headlines in the 1990s. The legacy of the Thatcher years could be seen in 2019, when Boris Johnson used the Queen's authority to prorogue Parliament and seemed completely unabashed by the resulting furore (see Controversy 6.3).

election in which its candidates won an average of more than 50 per cent of the vote in every seat they contested). Elsewhere, the 'hiving off' of state functions eroded the chain of responsibility which formerly ended with supposedly accountable departmental ministers. Quangos still disbursed taxpayers' money, but if abuses were exposed, their leaders, rather than the ministers who appointed them, would lose their jobs (see Chapter 10). The resignations of Lord Carrington and his Foreign Office colleagues in 1982 proved to be honourable exceptions. By the end of the Thatcher years, it was much more likely that a minister would resign because of a personal indiscretion than through some professional failing (for example, the prime minister's close ally, Nicholas Ridley, was forced to leave the cabinet in 1989 after claiming in a magazine interview that the European Community was 'a German racket' dedicated to succeeding where Hitler had narrowly failed).

In turn, after Thatcher's own resignation, the tendency for ministers to survive avoidable policy blunders led to a new media interest in the private lives of senior politicians. During the 1990s, the Major government came to be regarded as the epitome of financial and moral iniquity: the embodiment of 'sleaze'. Having served Thatcher's purposes – and, almost uniquely, escaped her reforming impulses – Parliament now suffered the consequences. Although most long-established institutions were damaged in the 1980s and 1990s, Parliament's reputation probably fell further than the others. The full extent of the problem only became apparent in 2009, when changes to the system of MPs' expenses, which had begun during the Thatcher years, led directly to the most serious scandal in the long history of the Westminster Parliament (see Chapter 8).

New Labour and constitutional reform

For most of its history, the Labour Party has tended to regard constitutional reform as a distraction from important business. The experience of Thatcherism changed its outlook. Eighteen years of unavailing struggle against policies which enjoyed only minority public support was a sharp reminder of the importance and vulnerability of institutions – like local government – which mediated between the individual and the central state. Tactical considerations also played a part in Labour's new focus on the constitution, which allowed the party to pick up support from pressure groups (like Unlock Democracy, formerly known as Charter 88) which were springing up to defend civil liberties and to agitate for radical constitutional reforms. Before the 1997 general election, Tony Blair and Liberal Democrat leader Paddy Ashdown developed a joint approach on major constitutional issues such as devolution. By this time, New Labour was advocating a liberal constitutional reform agenda of devolution, a strengthening of civil liberties, reform of the House of Lords, and greater freedom of information. This was in marked contrast to the socialist perspective Labour had embraced in the early 1980s, which proposed the abolition of the House of Lords and withdrawal from the European Community while leaving the power of the executive unchecked.

At the 1997 general election, Labour's manifesto commitments covered four main constitutional themes:

1. rights
2. modernisation
3. democratisation
4. decentralisation.

The election result apparently gave New Labour an impressive mandate for change, especially since the Conservatives made much of their opposition to devolution during the campaign. But Labour's landslide victory was also a source of temptation. Between 1979 and 1997, for understandable reasons, the party had developed an 'oppositionist' mentality. Now that power had fallen into its hands in such a dramatic fashion, the party leadership suddenly woke up to the possibility of using the governmental weapons they had inherited from the Conservatives, rather than decommissioning them as they had promised.

The detail of Labour's constitutional reforms is discussed in the relevant chapters (see also Table 6.1). The reform of the House of Lords is assessed in Chapter 8, the Human Rights Act 1998 in Chapter 9, devolution in Chapter 12, and electoral reform in Chapter 17. For the present purpose, it is most convenient to provide an overview, under the headings of 'core' and 'optional' reforms. The core reforms are the ones in which Labour had invested the greatest political capital prior to the 1997 general election; the optional agenda consists of changes which the government could have postponed without serious loss of credibility.

Core reforms

In 1997, Labour won 56 out of 72 Scottish seats at Westminster, and 34 of the 40 constituencies in Wales – the best results the party had ever achieved outside England. Scotland and Wales had suffered badly during the Thatcher–Major years, losing much of their traditional manufacturing industry. Scotland had also been used as a guinea pig for the poll tax, and under John Major, the lack of Conservative legitimacy in Wales had been underlined by the choice of two (very) English MPs (John Redwood and William Hague), with English seats, to serve as Secretaries of State for Wales. It was natural for the government's opponents in those countries to hope for reform from Labour, despite the unsuccessful devolution experiment of the late 1970s. At the same time, Labour strategists knew that a second failure to establish devolved institutions would fuel an upsurge of support for the Scottish Nationalists and Plaid Cymru.

Devolution was thus an immediate priority for the new government, and referendums were held in both Scotland and Wales as soon as it was practical after the 1997 general election. The resulting Scottish Parliament and Welsh Assembly reinforced the idea of the UK as a 'union', rather than a 'unitary', state (see Chapter 12). The Westminster Parliament retained the right to repeal the relevant legislation, and certain powers remained at the centre. The Scottish Parliament could set a rate of income tax which differed from that which applied to the UK as a whole. Both Scotland and Wales kept their Secretaries of State in London, although in a cabinet reshuffle in June 2003 these were combined with other posts to signify a fall in their ministerial status at UK level. The government's heavy-handed attempts to influence the choice of leader of the Welsh Labour Party betrayed its hope that the new institutions would be more obedient than autonomous. Ultimately, though, it had to accept meaningful devolution as a necessary price for retaining control at Westminster, with the backing of many members elected from Wales and Scotland.

Another core reform was the establishment of the Greater London Authority (GLA) and an elected mayor of London. Although the party had fared badly since 1979 in the southeast of England, Labour had retained its enclaves in the capital itself; also, the proposals would reverse the 1986 abolition of the Greater London Council (GLC), a Conservative decision which Labour activists regarded as purely vindictive. For Labour, there was a most unwelcome reminder of the GLC in the election of its last leader, Ken Livingstone, as London's first mayor – as an independent candidate in 2000 and as the official Labour candidate in 2004. As in Wales, the Labour Party had fought hard before accepting this predictable consequence of its own reforms.

TABLE 6.1 New Labour's constitutional reforms

Area	First Blair government (1997–2001)	Second Blair government (2001–05)	Third Blair government (2005–07)	Brown government (2007–10)
Devolution	Creation of: • Scottish Parliament with legislative and tax-raising powers • Welsh Assembly with secondary legislative powers • Northern Ireland Assembly and powersharing executive • Regional Development Agencies in English regions	2002 White Paper on elected regional assemblies in England; but 'no' vote in referendum in North East (2004) Northern Ireland Assembly suspended (2002–07) Changes to role of Scotland Office and Wales Office	Government of Wales Act 2006 proposed a strengthening of the powers of the Welsh Assembly Devolution restored in Northern Ireland (2007)	Calman Commission examines further devolution for Scotland as SNP government proposes an independence referendum

Area	First Blair government (1997–2001)	Second Blair government (2001–05)	Third Blair government (2005–07)	Brown government (2007–10)
Parliament	House of Lords Act 1999 removes all but 92 hereditary peers	Parliament fails to approve any of seven options for House of Lords reform (2003)	No further progress on Lords reform	Predominantly elected upper chamber supported by MPs, but legislation is delayed
Rights and judiciary	Human Rights Act 1998 incorporates European Convention on Human Rights into UK law. Freedom of Information Act 2000	Derogation from Article 5 of Human Rights Act (2001–05). Freedom of Information Act comes into force fully (2005). Constitutional Reform Act 2005 reforms the office of Lord Chancellor, sets up Judicial Appointments Commission and paves the way for a Supreme Court. Creation of Department for Constitutional Affairs (2003)		Powers of the Attorney General to be reduced. Governance of Britain proposes new Bill of Rights and Duties
Electoral reform	New electoral systems for devolved administrations, European Parliament and elected mayors. Jenkins Report on electoral reform for Westminster (1998)		Government of Wales Act 2006 bans dual candidacy. Single Transferable Vote introduced for Scottish local elections (2007)	Government's review of voting system supportive of status quo at Westminster elections
Participation	Referendums on devolution in Scotland, Wales (1997) and Northern Ireland (1998) Referendum on elected mayor of London (1998) Political Parties, Elections and Referendums Act 2000 regulates conduct of parties, elections and regulations	Trials of alternative voting methods (e.g. at 2004 European Parliament elections). Referendum on assembly for North East England (2004)	Proposed referendum on EU Constitution postponed after 'no' votes in France and the Netherlands (2005)	No referendum on Treaty of Lisbon. Governance of Britain White Paper proposes national debate on a British statement of values and greater use of citizens' juries

Labour's 1997 election manifesto also included commitments to incorporate the (non-EU) European Convention on Human Rights into UK law, to introduce a Freedom of Information Act (FOIA), and to reform the House of Lords. The first of these promises was fulfilled by the Human Rights Act 1998 (see Chapter 9). In opposition, Labour had promised that the incorporated Convention would represent a minimum guarantee of human rights and indicated that it would build further on that framework. However, in the wake of the September 2001 terrorist attacks in the USA, the UK government used its right to derogate from the provisions in the Convention relating to detention without either trial or deportation procedures. The UK was the only European country to respond to 9/11 in this way, raising the question of whether Labour had truly accepted a culture of rights, rather than exploiting the issue to discredit John Major's administration. Critics have argued that the government ought to have devised its own Bill of Rights, specifically applicable to the British context, rather than importing a document whose meaning was often necessarily vague.

The government did introduce a Freedom of Information Bill, which passed in 2000 (to Tony Blair's subsequent regret). Among other things, it gave individuals a greater right of access to personal information held on them by a range of public bodies. However, the Act disappointed radical reformers and marked a retreat from principles set out in a 1997 White Paper. The full provisions of the Act came into force at the beginning of 2005. In 2008, a request under the Freedom of Information Act for publication of MPs' expenses was accepted, despite dogged resistance from MPs. By the time that the data were published (in expurgated form), the details had been 'leaked' to the *Daily Telegraph*. However, there is no doubt that the FOIA played a key role in the process. In 2015, despite determined governmental opposition, the terms of the Act also secured the public release of letters written to ministers by the Prince of Wales.

If New Labour had not taken some action over the Human Rights Convention or freedom of information, its credibility with the civil rights lobby would have been destroyed. Even more pressing was the need to carry out a reform of the House of Lords, which was a long-standing target for party activists. However, as recounted in Chapter 8, the reform of the Lords turned into a long-running farce. Ostensibly, the reason was that no parliamentary consensus could be formed behind any of the proposed reforms. But it was difficult to avoid the conclusion that the government simply lacked the political will to satisfy demands even for a partly elected upper chamber.

Optional reforms

The Labour government of 1997–2001 got off to a dramatic start, with the announcement that interest rates would, in future, be set by the Monetary Policy Committee of the Bank of England (see Case study 10.1). Far from being a manifesto commitment, this move was a surprise even to some ministers. While it was welcomed by many economists, the decision was best seen in the context of the existing shift from 'government' to 'governance' (see Chapter 10). It was unlikely that future Chancellors of the Exchequer would refuse to take the credit to themselves if the Bank of England set interest rates which helped to secure the twin goals of sustainable economic growth and low inflation. However, there would now be someone else to blame if these targets were not met.

The government also promised a referendum on the electoral system, and after the election it set up a Commission under former cabinet minister Roy Jenkins to investigate alternatives. However, the result of the 1997 general election made a referendum (let alone a completed reform) into an option rather than a necessity. Blair had conducted lengthy negotiations with Paddy Ashdown about the introduction of a proportional voting system. However, Labour had always been divided on the attractions of proportional representation, and reform lost its appeal when first-past-the-post spoke so decisively in favour of the party. Despite a well-argued report by the Jenkins Commission, the government ditched any plan for a referendum.

In its 1997 manifesto, Labour committed itself to referendums on regional government in England. This was the English equivalent of devolution for Scotland and Wales, and it looked like a 'win-win' scenario for Labour. The manifesto recognised that demand for elected regional assemblies varied in different parts of England; and the areas of highest demand tended to be those, like the North East, where voters had stayed loyal to Labour through the Thatcher and Major years. It came as a shock to the central party when, in November 2004, a referendum in the North East rejected the proposal. But the seven-year gap between the original promise and the calling of a referendum suggested a lack of political will on the government's part; from the outset it had been stressed that the regional assemblies would have very limited powers.

To the general public, the most baffling of Labour's reforms was the proposed abolition of the office of Lord Chancellor. This was the oldest position in government, dating back to 605 AD. Yet, as we have seen, it had come to symbolise the eccentricity of the UK constitution, since the holder of the post was simultaneously a member of the executive (as a cabinet minister) and the legislature (as Speaker of the House of Lords), as well as being head of the judiciary. A decision by the European Court of Human Rights in 1999 suggested that the existence of such a multifaceted figure was in itself an infringement of the Convention on Human Rights; since this had just been incorporated into UK law through the Human Rights Act 1998, the continued existence of the Lord Chancellor was a potential source of grave embarrassment. There were also growing demands for reform among the judiciary and legal commentators.

Whatever the motives behind it, the attempt to abolish the office of Lord Chancellor turned into another constitutional fiasco (see Chapter 9 for details). The plans were obviously drawn up in haste, as a by-product of a cabinet reshuffle. It was not even realised that legislation would be required to abolish the ancient post. A year later, the House of Lords agreed that the present Lord Chancellor, Lord Falconer, would no longer appoint judges or sit in a judicial capacity himself. But although Falconer headed a new Department of Constitutional Affairs, replacing the old Lord Chancellor's Department, he was still lumbered with the old title. His successor Jack Straw (appointed in 2007) headed a renamed Ministry for Justice and also retained the title of Lord Chancellor even though he was not a member of the House of Lords and had not been given a peerage.

For many Conservative supporters, the affair of the Lord Chancellor finally exposed the government as a group of constitutional vandals. On the other flank, radical reformers approved the measure but lamented the lack of any coherent agenda for modernisation. It seemed that the government only took effective action in response to tactical necessities. Even then, in cases like devolution and the Human Rights Act, it seemed uneasy with the practical effects of its own handiwork. But when it acted on its own initiative, it tended to botch the job. According to these critics, everything would have been different if Labour had set out with a planned programme of change, culminating in a properly codified constitution.

A new constitutional settlement?

Even if questions can be raised about the coherence of New Labour's constitutional thinking, the changes introduced by the Blair government added up to the most significant programme of reform in modern British history. Commentators talked of a new settlement replacing the traditional constitution. Many of the institutions and processes associated with the traditional constitution have been affected by New Labour's reforms. Acts creating the Scottish Parliament and Welsh Assembly and incorporating the European Convention on Human Rights into British law can be regarded as marking a further codification of the UK constitution, as they set out in statute law important principles concerning the relationship between institutions and between the state and its citizens. Some experts argue that this legislation is of such constitutional significance that it should be regarded as de facto 'higher law'. In *Thoburn v Sunderland City Council* (2002), the Law Lords argued that there was now a hierarchy of Acts of Parliament, headed by 'ordinary' statutes and 'constitutional' statutes (e.g. the European Communities Act 1972 and Human Rights Act 1998) that should only be repealed if and when Parliament did so by express provision, rather than as an unintended consequence of a new law (see Chapter 9).

However, New Labour's reforms can also be seen as evolutionary rather than revolutionary. The Blair government never developed an overarching vision of its new constitutional settlement as a means of bringing Britain noticeably closer to more orthodox liberal democratic states. As a result, reform was more piecemeal than purposeful. Proposals for a second stage of reform of the House of Lords stalled during Blair's second term, and plans for elected regional assemblies were put on ice after the 'no' vote in a referendum in the North East. The Blair government consciously steered away from direct challenges to the traditional principles of the UK constitution, outlined earlier. Devolution and the Human Rights Act 1998 have important implications for the sovereignty of the Westminster Parliament. But the relevant legislation sought to safeguard the doctrine of parliamentary sovereignty within the existing constitutional settlement. The Scotland Act 1998, for example, made it clear that the Westminster Parliament remains sovereign and retains the power to legislate for Scotland. In practice, however, Westminster accepted that it should not legislate on matters devolved to the Scottish Parliament, so parliamentary sovereignty no longer means that Westminster has real power to make law across the UK. Devolution has also clarified the UK's status as a Union state in which the component nations of the Union are governed in different ways.

The Human Rights Act 1998 also preserved parliamentary sovereignty by dictating that if the courts find legislation to be incompatible with the European Convention on Human Rights, that legislation is not automatically struck down; it is left to Parliament to decide on amendments. The Human Rights Act strengthened the rule of law by clarifying and expanding the rights of citizens in statute law. But parliamentary sovereignty allowed the government to restrict the rights granted by these Acts, for example, by obtaining a temporary derogation from Article 5 on the right to liberty and security after the 9/11 terrorist attacks. As we have seen, the government's response to the terrorist threat was to restrict civil liberties. The Constitutional Reform Act 2005 paved the way for a new Supreme Court, which (after some delay) began work on 1 October 2009. However, this grandly named body is unable to quash Acts of Parliament like its US counterpart (see Chapter 9).

Gordon Brown's reform agenda

In his first Commons speech after becoming Labour leader and prime minister in June 2007, Gordon Brown gave new heart to liberal theorists by signalling that constitutional reform would play a central role in his administration. He proposed changes in numerous areas, which, if implemented, would result in an important check to executive power in Britain (see Table 6.2). Brown's reform agenda seemed to be the sincere product of serious reflection on constitutional issues – a level of intellectual engagement that Blair had not shown. Apparently, the new prime minister favoured a codified constitution (complete with a Bill of Rights and Duties to offer further protection to the citizen against the state), and his ideas represented a significant first step in that direction.

TABLE 6.2 *The Governance of Britain* (2008) – key proposals

Theme	Detailed proposals
Making the executive more accountable	Parliamentary approval required for deployment of armed forces abroad
	Arrangements for parliamentary scrutiny of treaties to be placed on a statutory footing
	Proposals for a dissolution of Parliament to be subject to a vote in the House of Commons
	Speaker of House of Commons to have the power to recall Parliament
	Civil service to be placed on a statutory footing, reinforcing its impartiality
	Role of the Attorney General to be streamlined – s/he will lose power to take decisions on individual cases, except in exceptional circumstances
	Prime minister's active role in judicial appointments and those in the Church of England has ended
	Parliamentary Committees to hold pre-appointment hearings for some public appointments
	Prime minister will not add or remove names from final list of people recommended for honours
	Intelligence and Security Committee to operate in a similar way to other select committees
	Government publishes a National Security Strategy
	Appointment of ministers for each of the nine English regions
	Government publishes Draft Legislative Proposals at early stage
	More parliamentary time for departmental debates
	Creation of independent UK Statistics Authority
	Revised Ministerial Code published
Reinvigorating our democracy	Further consultation on House of Lords reform
	Extend time period for all-women shortlists
	Consultation on moving election day to weekend
	Review of voting systems completed – however, there were no recommendations for changes for Westminster elections
	Make it easier for public to petition Parliament
	Right for people to protest in vicinity of Parliament
	Local authorities have a duty to involve local people in their decisions
The citizen and the state	Review of citizenship
	Greater use of Union flag
	Public consultation leading to a British Statement of Values
	Bill of Rights and Duties to build on the Human Rights Act 1998

Two main themes were discernible, both of which were welcome to constitutional observers. Some of the proposals promised at least a partial remedy to a key problem with executive power in Britain – namely, the fact that elected governments enjoyed the old prerogative powers of the monarchy and had progressively extended these by virtue of their supposed democratic legitimacy. In promising to lay down or share many of these powers, particularly those relating to appointments, foreign policy, and the dissolution of Parliament, Brown was attacking some of the key pillars of Britain's alleged 'elective dictatorship'.

The second theme almost certainly was a product of Brown's desire to present his government as a refreshing change from that of his predecessor and rival, Tony Blair. Under political pressure,

Blair had consulted Parliament before declaring war, but his theoretical ability to commit troops without a formal vote had increased the anger of his opponents. Blair's critics were also to be assuaged by increased parliamentary scrutiny of the security services and a tightening of procedure in relation to civil service appointments (an implicit pledge that there would never be another Alastair Campbell: see Chapter 5). The reduction of the executive's power over individual prosecutions was a reference to the power of the Attorney General, whose role in the Iraq War had been highly controversial (see Chapter 9).

Brown's proposals were duly included in a consultative Green Paper, *The Governance of Britain* (Cm 7170), followed in March 2008 by a White Paper (Cm 7342-I) and a draft bill (Cm 7342-II) (see Table 6.2). But by that time, the initial impetus had dissipated, mainly because the government was grappling with an economic crisis but also because the government's declarations in the general field of constitutional reform seemed to be contradicted by its concrete decisions in other fields. Of particular concern was the government's attitude towards individual liberties, including a new drive to introduce identity cards. In May 2008, Brown was alleged to have cut a series of parliamentary deals in order to win a Commons vote to allow the detention of terrorist suspects for 42 days – a decision which provoked the Conservative Home Affairs spokesman David Davis to resign his parliamentary seat and fight a by-election as a protest against what he saw as 'the insidious, surreptitious and relentless erosion of fundamental British freedoms'. Brown showed no desire to repeal recent legislation which had modified long-held legal rights such as trial by jury, the right to silence, and the rule of double jeopardy (which had prevented suspects from being tried twice for the same offence). In terms of the rights of Parliament to hold the executive to account, Blair's government had passed the innocuously named Legislative and Regulatory Reform Act 2006, which actually increased the power of ministers to amend laws without parliamentary scrutiny, and the Civil Contingencies Act 2004, which gave dictatorial powers to government whenever it considered the country to be faced with an 'emergency'. A similar power – the right to decide what constituted the 'national interest' – served to obstruct a truly radical reduction in the power of the Attorney General over individual prosecutions.

It would be tempting to cite Brown's record on constitutional issues as a classic example of prime ministerial behaviour – a beginning full of good intentions, followed by a growing reluctance to relinquish powers which made life much easier for the executive (see Chapter 7). But since 'events' so quickly diverted Brown from his original approach, it would be charitable to offer him the benefit of the doubt for his failure to introduce any meaningful reforms.

The constitution and the coalition

As we have seen, the events between the inconclusive 2010 general election and the formation of a Conservative–Liberal Democrat coalition were themselves of unusual constitutional interest. The notion that winning most seats entitles a party to take the initiative in coalition-building in a hung parliament was not universally accepted, but is likely to become a constitutional convention in an era when closely fought elections could become the rule rather than the exception. It might not be true that the Liberal Democrat leader Nick Clegg had begun to favour an alliance with the Conservatives because his relationship with Gordon Brown was poor, but it would not have been the first time that personal considerations have shaped the UK constitution; for example, the marital problems of Henry VIII triggered a series of dramatic constitutional changes in the sixteenth century.

The inclusion within the coalition of Liberal Democrats, with their long-standing interest in constitutional reform, promised a renewed burst of activity on this front. Their main concern, understandably, was to secure reform of the electoral system. Before the election, Labour had shown much more interest in this topic than the Conservatives; however, in the ensuing negotiations, David Cameron agreed to support legislation to pave the way for a referendum on the Alternative Vote (AV). This was also the system which Labour had been flirting with, and since it was not proportional, it represented something less than an optimal choice for the Liberal Democrats. As it was, the agreement with Cameron came to nothing since the referendum held in May 2011 resulted in a heavy defeat for the reformers (see Chapter 17).

One electoral reform which the coalition did manage to implement affected the timetable of elections rather than the voting system – a move to fixed-term parliaments. The Liberal Democrats had been pressing for this change before the election, but in the circumstances of 2010, it looked as though the coalition partners had chosen to embrace it for their own short-term convenience. Although the legislation which finally emerged included provisions to dissolve Parliament before the five-year term had been exhausted, the Fixed-Term Parliaments Act was explicitly designed to offer short-term reassurance to both coalition partners. It would place considerable obstacles in the path of either party if, at some point between 2010 and May 2015, one of them decided that an early election would give them a tactical advantage. So, for example, if the Conservatives slumped in the opinion polls because of their economic measures, the Liberal Democrats would not be able to cash in on their unpopularity by joining with the opposition parties and voting to force an election; by the same token, the Conservatives had no chance of exploiting any downturn in Liberal Democrat poll ratings by calling a 'snap' election. The latter scenario was always the more likely, and materialised straight after the formation of the coalition, because in matters relating to the economy and education policy the Liberal Democrats were widely held to have betrayed pre-election pledges. The Fixed-Term Parliaments Bill received the royal assent in September 2011; after strong opposition from members of the Lords, it contained a provision to review the Act before the end of 2020. At the time of writing (June 2020), this process has yet to start, but its deliberations will be interesting. In 2017 and 2019, Theresa May and Boris Johnson were both able to secure Commons' majorities for early elections, despite the fact that on both occasions a majority of MPs were privately opposed.

The most striking example of self-interest at work in constitutional matters was the coalition government's attitude to the right of voters to 'recall' MPs who had been proven guilty of abusing their offices. All three main parties had embraced this idea in the immediate aftermath of the expenses scandal (see Chapter 8), but once in office, the Conservatives and (especially) the Liberal Democrats became apprised of the practical difficulties. Unless the legislation was carefully crafted, the right of recall could be misused by voters who chose to target MPs because they were unpopular rather than guilty of serious misdemeanours. Even in the coalition agreement, forged in the immediate aftermath of the election, there were signs that the parties were beginning to regret their original enthusiasm for the idea; Nick Clegg himself might have run the risk of being unscated from the Sheffield Hallam constituency because of his volte-face on tuition fees. There is no reason to doubt the sincerity of coalition ministers who spoke about the urgent need to clean up politics and bring coherent principles to bear on the ramshackle constitutional situation bequeathed by New Labour; however, like their predecessors, they were very reluctant to take decisions which could make life more difficult for themselves. A draft Recall Bill was published in December 2012, but the legislation only reached the statute book in the last weeks of the 2010–15 Parliament, and in a form which left most campaigners gravely dissatisfied.

Thus, the emergence of Britain's first coalition government since 1945 could be seen as a new way of delivering 'business as usual' so far as the constitution was concerned; there was much talk of civil liberties and the need to decentralise power, but it was apparent that this agenda would not be followed with excessive enthusiasm unless it was likely to work to the advantage of one or both of the coalition partners. For example, although the parties agreed in principle on a predominantly elected House of Lords, this marked improvement from the Blair years was not exploited in the form of early legislation. Even if it had wanted to do so, the coalition could not realistically have prevented the Welsh people from holding a referendum on the devolution of additional powers to their Assembly, and this duly occurred in March 2011. In Scotland, the coalition accepted the proposals of the Calman Report (see Chapter 12), but the election of a majority SNP government in 2011 raised the prospect of a referendum on full independence. While the initiative towards further reform in Wales and Scotland now lay in the hands of their voters and politicians – and in Northern Ireland, continuing internal divisions made it difficult to envisage any radical changes in the immediate future – in England itself devolution seemed to be a dead letter. The coalition wanted to dismantle existing regional institutions rather than establishing new ones, and although the 'West Lothian Question' was to be examined by a new commission, there was no sign of an early solution.

On the EU, despite Cameron's hard-line rhetoric in opposition, once in office he adopted the pragmatic outlook which was clearly his default position. Significant new powers would not be transferred without a referendum, but this position seemed to be based on a calculation that the EU's own constitutional development had stalled since the troubled saga of the Lisbon Treaty. This compromise was not enough to satisfy Conservative Eurosceptics, and Cameron came under additional pressure, thanks to the rise of UKIP. In January 2013, he announced that, if his party won the next election, there would be an in-out referendum on EU membership.

Meanwhile, Cameron took a typically 'Blairite' attitude to foreign policy developments; his decision to intervene in Libya was ratified by a parliamentary vote, but Britain's role was soon expanded beyond the advertised purpose of protecting civilians to include a barely concealed desire for 'regime-change'. MPs clearly had this precedent (as well as the ill-starred parliamentary endorsement of Blair's Iraq strategy) in mind when, in August 2013, they voted against a government motion which would have paved the way for intervention in the Syrian civil war (see Chapter 8). Another echo of New Labour came with the coalition's establishment of a new OBR, to scrutinise the government's own financial statistics and to provide independent forecasts. Like Blair's decision to give the Bank of England authority over interest rates, there was always a risk that the OBR would serve to provide presentational 'cover' to ministers facing adverse economic conditions. Before the end of the coalition's five-year term, the Chancellor George Osborne had criticised the OBR for its 'unhelpful' analysis of the likely scale of spending cuts after the 2015 election.

Probably the most promising constitutional decision taken by the coalition was to accept proposals giving greater autonomy to House of Commons' select committees (see Chapter 8). By reducing the power of party managers to influence the composition of such committees, the government greatly increased their potential as a check on executive power. However, this was essentially an enforced decision; the House of Commons had spoken clearly before the election in favour of the proposals (which had been drawn up by the Labour MP Tony Wright). Cameron's immediate predecessors would probably have tried to amend them in some way which protected the power of the executive, but unlike them, David Cameron could not command a House of Commons majority without help from the Liberal Democrats, who would have found it impossible to vote against the proposals en bloc.

The 2014 referendum on Scottish independence

For the coalition, the legacy of New Labour loomed hideously large over developments in Scotland, where the SDP's promised referendum on the country's future within the UK was held on 18 September 2014. The tortuous process leading up to the referendum laid bare the oddities of the UK constitution which the SNP was proposing to leave behind, as well as its flexibility. Thus, there was considerable debate about the right of the Scottish Parliament to call a referendum on this issue; in January 2012, the Advocate General for Scotland, Lord Wallace, ruled that this lay beyond its authority, so a special agreement between the coalition and the Scottish government had to be negotiated in order to transfer the necessary powers from Westminster to Holyrood. The Edinburgh Agreement specified that the wording of the referendum question would have to be accepted by the UK-wide Electoral Commission, which rejected the first version ('Do you agree that Scotland should be an independent country?') on the grounds that it unduly favoured a positive answer. The accepted alternative was 'Should Scotland be an independent country?'.

Another headache for those overseeing the campaign was the question of expenditure. While the 'official' campaigns – which both began work more than two years before the vote itself – could be subjected to rigorous spending limits, it was more difficult to deal with 'unofficial' bodies which might raise and spend money on one side or another. Finally (and contrary to common assumptions), the principle of parliamentary sovereignty, strictly interpreted, means that referendum results in the UK are not necessarily binding. In this instance, the Westminster government affirmed that, even if the referendum resulted in a virtual dead-heat between the 'yes' and 'no' campaigns, the verdict of the Scottish electorate would be decisive. However, in this respect (as opposed to the wording of the referendum question), the dice were loaded in favour of the 'No' camp. If there was a very clear vote *against* independence, the matter would be closed unless and until the SNP managed to reopen it. But a 'yes' vote, which seemed equally unequivocal, would only serve as the prelude to negotiations for a separation which would make the proceedings in normal divorce cases look like child's play, covering the physical defence of the former United Kingdom as well as complicated economic entanglements. It is hardly surprising that, as the opinion polls moved strongly towards 'yes' in the closing weeks of the campaign, the UK government began to emphasise (if not exaggerate) the extent of these difficulties, particularly in respect of the ability of an independent Scotland to use the pound sterling.

To even the balance, whereas a fairly close vote (around the range of 53 to 47 per cent) in favour of independence would have provided the 'yes' campaign with the 'mandate' it needed, the opponents of independence knew that anything less than 55 to 45 would keep this divisive question very much alive, particularly if there was a high turnout of qualified voters. The latter consideration was all the more important since the Scottish Parliament had decided to reduce the minimum age of voting eligibility from 18 to 16, and in most UK contests younger people are notoriously difficult to motivate. From this perspective the most arresting aspect of the 2014 referendum was the overall turnout. The Scottish electorate, both young and old, was clearly invigorated by the issue and the campaign, resulting in an astonishing turnout of 84.6 per cent. By contrast, when UK voters as a whole had rejected the Alternative Vote in the 2011 referendum on a franchise restricted to the over-18s, the turnout had been a miserable 42.2 per cent.

In the last days of the campaign, the opponents of Scottish independence had mobilised all of their human resources; Gordon Brown was particularly prominent in urging his fellow Scots to stay within the UK, and, having kept relatively aloof in the earlier stages, David Cameron joined the pleas for a continuation of the Union. The promises extended to wavering voters, if subsequently enacted, would make Scotland all but autonomous in such matters as taxation and public spending. The final outcome – 47.7 per cent 'no', compared to 53.3 per cent 'yes' – fell just within the range of acceptability for those who wanted the UK to remain as a 'Union state'. However, the SNP could argue that the relatively narrow verdict had only been secured as a result of last-minute concessions which would now have to be delivered – and, whether true or not, this argument was irresistible. One thing was clear: to outward appearances, in constitutional terms, the UK had seemed like a region of extinct volcanoes before the 1997 general election, but by 2014, it had become the point of convergence for tectonic plates, and its residents were just awaiting the next seismic event.

The 2016 EU Referendum

The earthquake duly arrived in June 2016.

Cameron's promised in-out referendum on EU membership was authorised by the European Referendum Act, which passed its second reading in the Commons within weeks of the narrow Conservative victory in the 2015 general election. Only MPs from the SNP voted against it.

The prelude to the referendum bore some resemblance to the 2014 experience. There was considerable debate about the most suitable question, which was settled by the Electoral Commission during the passage of the European Referendum Act: 'Should the United Kingdom remain a member of the European Union or leave the European Union?'. As in the Scottish example, 'official' campaigning groups ('Britain Stronger in Europe' and 'Vote Leave', respectively) were endorsed and subjected to spending limits. Another similarity was the absence of any stipulation in the legislation concerning the necessary level of support for change, unlike the 'threshold' provisions which were applied to the 1979 referendums on devolution. The status of a vote to 'Leave' would be the same, whether it prevailed by a single vote on a dismal turnout or won unanimous support from the UK electorate.

Controversy 6.3

'Brexit' and the constitution

The political and economic repercussions of 'Brexit' – including the composition of the UK itself (see Chapter 12) – will not be fully registered for many years. However, the campaign itself and its immediate aftermath had very significant constitutional implications.

The 'Leave' campaign argued that membership of the EU had cost Britain control of its laws, including (not least) its ability to introduce legislation restricting inward migration. For many leavers, the idea that Britain's institutions could be over-ruled by a supra-national body based in Brussels was a sufficient reason for withdrawal. However, it was also argued that the EU lacked democratic credibility, and infringed the crucial idea that decision-makers should be held to account. Some claimed that Britain's departure would create a new climate of accountability; instead of being able to hide behind the EU as a 'scapegoat' for decisions which they had fully accepted, UK ministers would now have to answer for their mistakes.

On the face of it, this argument was both plausible and laudable. However, as we have seen, the tendency since the Thatcher years has been for ministers to avoid accountability for a variety of reasons, among which EU membership was not particularly prominent. After the Brexit vote, Theresa May dismissed two ministers (Priti Patel [Overseas Development] and Gavin Williamson [Defence]); however, in neither case did their alleged offences have any connection with the EU. May's successor, Boris Johnson, was happy to remove the party whip from Conservative MPs who disagreed with him, but offered effusive support (in advance of proper inquiries) for ministers who were accused of misconduct. This approach did not seem to cause much disquiet amongst 'Brexiteers' who had emphasised the accountability issue during the referendum. Equally, Johnson retained the services of his unelected special adviser, Dominic Cummings, despite widespread criticism of his activities during the coronavirus crisis. Former 'Remainers' found it all too easy to point out the inconsistency in the prime minister's attitude to unelected individuals when they worked for him rather than for the EU. However, the charge of inconsistency could be levelled against Remainers who had been relaxed about the role of the EU Commission but were quick to find fault with Cummings.

Whatever the merits of these arguments, there were unequivocal signs that in practice 'Taking back control' would entail at least a temporary constitutional shift in favour of the executive, which, arguably, already enjoyed too much influence within the British system. Thus, Theresa May claimed that she could trigger the process of withdrawal from the EU (under the terms of Article 50 of the Lisbon Treaty) without parliamentary consent. In August 2019, Boris Johnson asked the Queen to prorogue Parliament for five weeks, with the ill-concealed intention of preventing the passage of legislation which would rule out Britain leaving the EU without a formal withdrawal agreement.

In both of these instances, executive 'power grabs' were thwarted by the courts (see Chapter 9), to the furious consternation of Brexit supporters. While the reaction (which included the *Daily Mail*'s accusation that High Court judges were 'Enemies of the People') was troubling enough, it was at least equally alarming that the courts had been forced to step in to reassert constitutional probity. In other words, relief that the executive had been thwarted could only be mingled with concern that it had tried to by-pass Parliament in the first place.

The reason for this behaviour was that the referendum result was a serious blow to the executive – forcing the immediate resignation of Prime Minister Cameron – and its instant response had been to 'take control' of the process as if it had always been in favour of withdrawal. Thus, even before she had replaced Cameron, Theresa May (who had been a lukewarm 'Remainer') ignored the obvious divisions in the country and spoke as if there had been an overwhelming 'Leave' vote whose fulfilment she regarded as a patriotic duty. At least this attitude came naturally to Boris Johnson, who had been the most prominent of all 'Leave' campaigners. However, by drawing the Queen into his tactical manoeuvres, Johnson crossed a constitutional line which May would not have approached.

The fact that the courts were induced to ride to the defence of parliamentary sovereignty is testimony to the weakness of Parliament, which proved unable to take advantage of the legal rulings on its behalf. Already seriously weakened in public estimation by the 2009 expenses scandal, during the Brexit process MPs tacitly relinquished the idea that they were representatives who should be trusted to take decisions on behalf of voters. Despite their attempts to block a 'no deal' Brexit, by voting to authorise a general election at a time when a Conservative victory was overwhelmingly likely, MPs were effectively acting as delegates on behalf of a 'Leave' argument which (if the opinion polls were to be believed) now enjoyed the support of less than half the electorate.

Ultimately, the success of any constitutional arrangements in a liberal democracy rests upon widespread consent. Once the rules underpinning the political process are subject to vehement dispute from a significant proportion of citizens, orderly government is gravely endangered. Arguably (and ironically), Britain was able to avoid a breakdown of this kind in the wake of the referendum, because interest in the constitution is still a minority pastime. However, nobody in Britain could escape an awareness of serious problems in something even more fundamental than its uncodified constitution, namely, its *political culture*. This is now far removed from the satisfactory condition depicted by Gabriel Almond and Sidney Verba in their classic 1964 study *The Civic Culture*. During the referendum campaign, the Labour MP Jo Cox was assassinated. Families and friends were divided, not by the usual 'tribal' party considerations but by sharply contrasting views about their country and its place in the world. At times (and especially for those who observed exchanges on social media), Britain seemed to resemble Matthew Arnold's vision in his poem 'Dover Beach' – a 'darkling plain/Where ignorant armies clash by night'. To say the least, it was an unpropitious background for the coronavirus pandemic which began to affect Britain just six weeks after the 2019 general election.

But what, exactly, would be the status of a vote to leave? Here, there was a significant divergence from the Scottish example, where the relevant legislation had included a government promise to honour the result. In the case of the EU referendum, David Cameron offered verbal assurances that he would accept the result either way. To do otherwise would have contradicted his own insistence that this was a momentous 'once in a generation' vote. There was no constitutional basis for this remark – any more than there had been after the 1975 referendum on the same question, when Harold Wilson declared that the issue had been settled forever. Rather, it was a vital element of Cameron's strategy to encourage 'Remainers' to vote or face the consequences. As so often in Britain's constitutional story, the rules were being made up for tactical convenience.

Another important contrast with the Scottish referendum was that 16–18-year-olds were not allowed to vote; an attempt in the House of Lords to amend the legislation to this effect was rejected. Once again, the supporters of a lower voting age could be accused of doing so for tactical reasons. However, in agreeing to enfranchise 16–18-year-olds before the 2014 independence referendum, the UK government had tacitly accepted the rationale behind such a move, that is, that the status of Scotland was of significant interest to young adults (certainly more so than to very elderly people). The real reason for rejecting the reform in 2016 was that it would pave the way for a similar change in voting rights for UK general elections, a prospect which most Conservatives regarded with horror.

Finally, while the Scottish referendum had been promoted with considerable enthusiasm by the incumbent SNP government, the UK prime minister called the 2016 poll because of divisions within his party. Whatever their 2015 manifestos might have said, and despite their overwhelming support for the legislation, a majority of ministers and MPs did not want to place Britain's EU membership in jeopardy. Arguably and ironically it was this contextual feature which did the most to ensure that the 'Remain' campaign was (narrowly) defeated.

Conclusion and summary

The UK constitution has undergone radical changes since 1979. This could be seen as a tribute to its boasted flexibility, since society has also been transformed and it would have been absurd if uncodified conventions and traditions had obstructed a degree of modernisation. However, there is plenty of scope for arguing that instead of keeping pace with social change, the UK constitution has been altered primarily to suit the interests of the governing parties. Significantly, while other institutions have been forced to adapt to the wishes of successive governments, the House of Commons has barely been touched. Almost the only change which threatened to curb the already overmighty executive came at the beginning of the Thatcher years, when the select committees were strengthened – significantly enough, by a minister, Norman St John-Stevas, who was dismissed before his reforms had bedded down. These reforms have now been augmented, and the select committees enjoy much greater autonomy and prestige (see Chapter 8); however, this has not been achieved without a protracted and bitter struggle with the executive.

Labour's 1997 manifesto claimed that UK government was 'centralised, inefficient, and bureaucratic'. Despite devolution and other reforms, few would claim that things were very different by the middle of its third term. After the eventful but ultimately disappointing coalition interlude, the Conservatives returned to office armed with constitutional proposals (e.g. on EU membership and human rights), which reflected partisan concerns rather than the overall coherence of the system they inherited. The party's manifesto only came close to an impassioned display of constitutional principle when it discussed the urgent need for more equal electorates in parliamentary constituencies – an important point, no doubt, but one which the Conservatives would have been willing to overlook if it had not served their immediate purposes. It was in keeping with traditional British practice that the measure was thwarted by the Liberal Democrat members of the coalition, for purely tactical reasons.

Since the narrow victory of the Conservatives in the 2015 general election, the days of even half-baked constitutional reforms have seemed very distant. Boris Johnson's 'oven-ready' Brexit deal emerged after a process which would not have found favour with the judges on *The Great British Bake-off*. The general chaos was epitomised by the fact that the government which called the 2016 referendum made no serious preparations for the situation it would face if the voters opted for withdrawal. Despite the stated aspirations of the Leave campaign, there is as yet little reason to expect any augmentation of democratic accountability in post-Brexit Britain, and the case for a proper national debate on the constitution is more pressing than ever – more than two decades since New Labour thought it had addressed the most serious issues.

Further reading

The best recent book on the constitution is V. Bogdanor's *The New British Constitution* (Oxford: Hart Publishing, 2009), which he has followed up with *Beyond Brexit: Towards a British Constitution* (London: I.B Tauris, 2019). See also M. Flinders, 'Bagehot Smiling: Gordon Brown's "New Constitution" and the Revolution that did not Happen', *Political Quarterly*, Vol. 81, No. 1 (2010), pp. 57–73, and M. Russell, 'Constitutional Politics', in R. Heffernan, P. Cowley and C. Hay (eds.), *Developments in British Politics 9* (Houndmills: Palgrave Macmillan, 2011), pp. 7–28.

Detailed texts on the traditional UK constitution include V. Bogdanor (ed.), *The British Constitution in the Twentieth Century* (Oxford: Oxford University Press, 2004) and R. Brazier's *Constitutional Practice. The Foundations of British Government* (Oxford: Oxford University Press, 3rd edition, 1999). P. Hennessy's *The Hidden Wiring: Unearthing Britain's Constitution* (London: Orion, 1996) is a shorter introduction. On the reforms introduced by the Blair governments, see R. Brazier, *Constitutional Reform: Reshaping the British Political System* (Oxford: Oxford University Press, 3rd edition, 2008) and P. Norton, 'The Constitution', in A. Seldon (ed.), *Blair's Britain 1997–2007* (Cambridge: Cambridge University Press, 2007), pp. 104–22. Studies of Blair's early reforms include D. Oliver, *Constitutional Reform in the UK* (Oxford: Oxford University Press, 2003), and V. Bogdanor, 'Constitutional Reform', in A. Seldon (ed.), *The Blair Effect* (London: Little, Brown, 2001), pp. 139–58. N. Johnson, *Reshaping the British Constitution* (London: Palgrave, 2004), is a full and critical assessment, and A. King, *Does the United Kingdom still Have a Constitution?* (London: Sweet and Maxwell, 2001), is a thought-provoking survey. M. Flinders and D. Curry, 'Bi-Constitutionality: Unravelling New Labour's Constitutional Orientations', *Parliamentary Affairs*, Vol. 61, No. 1 (2008), pp. 99–121, examines the tensions inherent in Labour's reform programme.

On Gordon Brown and the constitution, see P. Norton, 'The Constitution under Gordon Brown', *Politics Review*, Vol. 17, No. 3 (2008), pp. 26–29. The coalition's record is examined in P. Norton and L. Thompson, 'Parliament and the Constitution: The Coalition in Conflict', in M. Beech and S. Lee (eds.), *The Conservative-Liberal Coalition* (Houndmills: Palgrave, 2015), pp. 129–44.

Authoritative studies of specific aspects of the constitution include V. Bogdanor's *The Monarchy and the Constitution* (Oxford: Clarendon Press, 1997), and V. Bogdanor's *Devolution in the United Kingdom* (Oxford: Oxford Paperbacks, 2001) (for further reading on devolution, see Chapter 12).

Websites

The Ministry of Justice (www.justice.gov.uk) has responsibility for rights, the legal system, reform of the House of Lords, and electoral administration. The monarchy has also gone online: www.royal.gov.uk contains information about the current role of the monarchy and offers the chance to email the Queen.

There are authoritative discussions of recent developments on the site of the Constitution Unit, based in University College, London (www.ucl.ac.uk/constitution-unit). Particularly useful are the 'Monitor' newsletters and the summary assessments of constitutional reform under the Blair and Brown governments. The Democratic Audit (www.democraticaudit.com) is an independent research unit that has produced audits of democracy in Britain, including constitutional reform. Unlock Democracy (formerly Charter 88) has been the most influential pro-constitutional reform pressure group. Its website (www.unlockdemocracy.org.uk) includes updates on recent developments and campaign material. Other groups with an interest in constitutional reform include the Electoral Reform Society (www.electoral-reform.org.uk) and the civil liberties group Liberty (www.liberty-human-rights.org.uk).

Chapter 7

The core executive

Learning outcomes

After reading this chapter, you will:

- understand the main explanatory approaches relating to the UK executive;
- identify the key individuals and institutions which together constitute the core executive;
- appreciate the resources that are available to the prime minister;
- understand the role played by the cabinet and government ministers;
- be able to assess the relationship between ministers and civil servants; and
- understand the role played by supporting bodies like the Cabinet Office.

Introduction

The core executive is the dominant branch of British government, taking major decisions on issues of public policy and exercising significant control over the legislative process. The core executive includes the prime minister, the cabinet and its committees, the prime minister's office, and the Cabinet Office. The prime minister is acknowledged to be the most important figure in British politics, but his or her power is not fixed, and is subject to important constraints. The cabinet takes relatively few decisions, because the details of most policies are decided within its committees. This chapter explores where power lies within the core executive, and assesses developments in the role of prime minister over recent decades, particularly since 1997.

Cabinet Government
executive power is vested in the cabinet whose members (senior ministers) exercise collective responsibility.

The core executive model

For much of the twentieth century, an enduring question in the study of British politics was whether the UK had a system of **cabinet government** or **prime**

Prime Ministerial Government

executive power is vested in the prime minister who is the dominant figure in the cabinet system.

ministerial government, and where did political power ultimately reside? Those who emphasised the continuing importance of the cabinet note that the British constitution provides for collective government exercised by senior ministers. In *The English Constitution* (1867), the highly respected political observer Walter Bagehot described a system of cabinet government in which the prime minister was certainly 'first among equals', but far from an all-powerful figure. Virtually 100 years later, G.W. Jones (1965/1985) argued that the prime minister was only as strong as his/her colleagues allowed them to be: the support of the prime minister's fellow ministers or backbench MPs could, in certain circumstances, be withdrawn, possibly to the extent that s/he would resign, as happened to Margaret Thatcher in November 1990, Tony Blair in 2007, and Theresa May in May 2019. Against this view, advocates of the 'prime ministerial government' perspective point to the growth in the powers of the prime minister and the corresponding diminution of the cabinet in the twentieth century. This alleged establishment of prime ministerial government was apparently reinforced by the rise of career politicians who were willing to show obedience to their party leader in order to increase their chances of promotion to ministerial office when in government. In an essay introducing a 1963 edition of Bagehot's classic text, the Labour MP and future minister Richard Crossman argued that the prime minister was the most powerful actor, and determined policy with limited reference to the full cabinet. He claimed that the twentieth century had seen Britain move from a system of cabinet government to prime ministerial government. More recently, academics like Michael Foley (1993, 2000) have referred to the emergence of a British presidency, due to the strong and charismatic premierships of Margaret Thatcher (1979–1990) and Tony Blair (1997–2007).

Core Executive

those organisations and actors which coordinate the activities of central government.

An alternative approach to the cabinet government *versus* prime ministerial government debate has emerged since the 1990s. This is the 'core executive model', developed by political scientists such as Martin J. Smith (*The Core Executive in Britain*, London: Palgrave, 1999). The **core executive** is defined as those organisations and actors that coordinate the activities of central government. It includes the prime minister and his/her advisers, the cabinet and its committees, the prime minister's office and Cabinet Office, government departments (Education, Home Office, the Treasury, Work and Pensions, etc.), and the senior civil servants who work in them. The core executive approach argues that the long-running debate on whether Britain has either prime ministerial government or cabinet government is based on a fundamental misconception. Power is not inevitably located in one or the other; it is not either/or, neither is it 'zero-sum', whereby more power for one must mean less power for the other. Instead, power is shared between political (and administrative) actors who are mutually dependent: they must work together in order to achieve their political and policy goals. This will entail forming alliances, exchanging or sharing resources, communicating and working with their colleagues, and so forth. The core executive is partly fragmented, as it consists of a range of institutions and individuals forming overlapping networks and alliances. Power is thus based on mutual cooperation and dependence, not command and diktat.

However, the core executive approach does not deny that prime ministers have considerable resources at their disposal. They have extensive powers of patronage (most notably the power to appoint – and sack – ministers), chair the cabinet, lead the governing political party, and have a high profile in the life of the nation. But the resources available to the prime minister are not fixed; how they are utilised depends on a number of variables. These include external factors (e.g. policy success, parliamentary majority, government popularity, party unity) and the strategies of resource exchange (e.g. the leadership style) adopted by the prime minister. Cabinet ministers also have resources. Most of them head a government department, giving them authority and policy knowledge. They may also enjoy strong support within their party (possibly to the extent of being widely viewed as potential rivals to the prime minister) and enhance their reputations through policy successes. Departmental civil servants are also significant actors, possessing detailed knowledge and experience as well as links across the Whitehall network.

Prime ministers need the support of cabinet colleagues and officials to achieve their objectives. Martin J. Smith contends that Margaret Thatcher's downfall (1990) became inevitable when she failed to recognise her dependence on the support of cabinet ministers at a time when her government ran into difficulties. By contrast, John Major navigated the turbulent waters of his premiership as he recognised that the prime minister needs the support of other actors within the core executive. Huge parliamentary majorities and a concentration of resources in 10 Downing Street strengthened Tony Blair's position, but his uneasy relationship with Chancellor Gordon Brown was a key feature of his premiership. In turn, when Brown became prime minister in 2007, he inherited the divisions which he had helped to create, and faction-fighting between 'Brownites' and 'Blairites' within ministerial ranks blighted his tenure of Number 10. Brown's successor, David Cameron, found himself in a very different position as head of a Conservative–Liberal Democrat coalition government, before leading his party to a narrow overall victory in the 2015 general election. His experiences provide fascinating insights into the prime minister's role, showing that apparent constraints can be turned into opportunities – and vice versa.

Having succeeded Cameron in June 2016, Theresa May was soon viewed as a weak prime minister, due in large part to the deep divisions in the Conservative Party over Brexit, which dominated and destabilised her premiership. Her authority was further weakened by the result of the 2017 general election, which saw the Conservatives lose their narrow parliamentary majority (most opinion polls had predicted a landslide victory), in spite of winning more votes than in 2015, due to the surprising advances made by Labour under Jeremy Corbyn's controversial leadership. A further reason why May struggled to establish her authority was her poor communication skills: her rather stilted, wooden speaking style led *The Guardian* journalist Jim Crace to label her 'The Maybot'. Her successor, Boris Johnson, was initially in a much stronger position, buoyed by the degree of support he received in the leadership contest, his avowed determination to 'get Brexit done', the Conservatives' emphatic victory in the 2019 election, and the UK's formal departure from the EU on 31 January 2020. He was also a much more charismatic and ebullient leader, at least initially. However, by the spring and summer of 2020, Johnson was facing mounting criticism over his government's allegedly slow and inadequate response to the COVID-19 pandemic. By this time, Johnson was also facing a very much more effective Leader of the Opposition, Sir Keir Starmer, who used his ex-barrister's skills to subject Johnson to rigorous scrutiny at Prime Minister's Question Time, and sometimes leave the Conservative leader visibly struggling to provide a coherent answer.

The prime minister

The title of 'prime minister' has been bestowed on the holder of the office of First Lord of the Treasury since 1730, with Sir Robert Walpole (1721–42) generally recognised as its first recipient. Enjoying the support of the House of Commons and Cabinet, he was a commanding political figure even by modern standards; his critics, even more than his supporters, saw him as the personification of his government. However, Walpole's dominance did not set an unvarying precedent; some of his eighteenth-century successors rivaled his power, but others were relatively weak and are now almost forgotten. The role of the prime minister expanded from the mid-nineteenth century; the operation of central government was formalised, the extension of the franchise (right to vote) led to the rise of large, centrally organised and tightly disciplined political parties, government activity mushroomed, and the prime minister took over many of the prerogative powers of the monarch. However, the powers of the prime minister have never been set out in statute law. Tony Blair believed that 'it is not possible to precisely define them', while Herbert Asquith (prime minister from 1908 to 1916) felt that 'the office of Prime Minister is what the holder chooses and is able to make of it'.

A basic job description for the office might run along the following lines:

> The Prime Minister is head of the government, providing political leadership within the core executive, and the country at large. Specific tasks include the appointment and dismissal of government ministers (patronage); presiding over the Cabinet and its committees; advising the monarch on many key appointments; and representing the United Kingdom in the international arena.

Of the 15 (including Boris Johnson) post-war premiers, Tony Blair and David Cameron are the only two who lacked previous ministerial experience. Both men were in their 44th year when they took office; Cameron, who was a few months younger in May 2010 than Blair had been in May 1997, thus overtook his supposed role model as the youngest prime minister since Lord Liverpool began his 15-year stint in 1812. Sir Winston Churchill was the oldest post-war premier, beginning his second term in office a few days short of his 77th birthday. Churchill, James Callaghan, and John Major were the only ones not to attend university.

The prime minister is formally appointed by the monarch, but the appointment is usually straightforward, a formality, as constitutional convention (as well as common sense) determines that the leader whose party has won a majority of seats/MPs in the House of Commons should be invited to form a government. However, sometimes general elections are inconclusive, producing a 'hung parliament' where no party enjoys an overall majority. When this happened in February 1974, the Conservative leader Edward Heath was given time to discuss a coalition with the Liberals, but when no agreement could be reached, Harold Wilson was invited to form a minority Labour government instead. There was another hung parliament in the May 2010 election, whereupon the Liberal Democrats entered into a coalition government with the Conservatives, the latter having emerged as the largest party. The most likely alternative would have been a minority Conservative government, which, some feared, would not provide the country with sufficient stability at a time of economic crisis. Britain was again faced with the prospect of a minority Conservative government after the inconclusive 2017 general election, but the party was able to establish a narrow parliamentary majority by striking a 'confidence-and-supply' deal with Northern Ireland's DUP. This, though, was a parliamentary pact, not a coalition government, because the DUP was not allocated any ministerial posts or seats in the cabinet.

A minority government is likely to be unstable because the prime minister requires the continued support of Parliament – or, in practice, another party, to stay in office. Indeed, the prime minister is officially accountable to Parliament, the most obvious symbol of which is Prime Minister's Questions, a key event in the House of Commons' schedule, this being held every Wednesday for 30 minutes, except when Parliament is 'in recess' (closed for holidays or other breaks). The prime minister is also obliged to make statements to the House on major developments, or in the event of a national crisis. However, research conducted by Patrick Dunleavy and others shows

Post-war Prime Ministers

Clement Attlee, Labour (1945–51)

Attlee was the first Labour prime minister to lead a majority government – one that created the modern welfare state and greatly extended the state ownership of industry. He was a low-key but astute leader of a cabinet of political heavyweights. He died in 1967.

Sir Winston Churchill, Conservative (1951–55)

Voted the greatest Briton in a BBC poll of 2002, Churchill's reputation as leader was forged in his first spell as prime minister (1940–45) during World War II. Back in Downing Street after six years of Labour government, Churchill concentrated on international affairs and allowed cabinet ministers to shape important aspects of domestic policy. Dogged by ill health, he resigned in 1955. He died in 1965.

Sir Anthony Eden, Conservative (1955–57)

Eden earned a great reputation at the Foreign Office, but as prime minister, he led his country to national humiliation at Suez (1956), having kept the cabinet in the dark on much of the planning of the Anglo–French invasion (see Chapter 3). He resigned the following year on the grounds of ill health. He died in 1977.

Harold Macmillan, Conservative (1957–63)

Dubbed 'Supermac' during a period of economic growth, Macmillan's aristocratic demeanour belied a ruthless streak apparent when he sacked six cabinet ministers in the 1962 'Night of the Long Knives'. His government also presided over an acceleration of British retreat from Empire, and made an unsuccessful bid to join the EEC. He died in 1986.

Sir Alec Douglas-Home, Conservative (1963–64)

A surprise choice as Macmillan's successor, the Earl of Home renounced his peerage on becoming prime minister and won a parliamentary by-election. He became the only post-war prime minister to return to a cabinet position when taking the post of Foreign Secretary in 1970. He died in 1995.

Harold Wilson, Labour (1964–70 and 1974–76)

A technocrat rather than a deep political thinker, Wilson had a reputation for putting party unity before principle. In his second spell as prime minister, he suspended the doctrine of collective responsibility to allow cabinet ministers to campaign on opposing sides in the 1975 referendum on EEC membership. His sudden resignation in 1976 still inspires conspiracy theories. He died in 1995.

Edward Heath, Conservative (1970–74)

Heath achieved his main political goal by securing British entry into the EEC. However, although the cabinet was united behind him, he suffered numerous setbacks on the domestic front, mainly as a result of trade union hostility, and various policy 'u-turns'. He died in 2005.

James Callaghan, Labour (1976–79)

Callaghan was the only person to hold all four major offices of state in the twentieth century, but his spell as premier was overshadowed by economic problems and divisions within his party. The 'Lib–Lab pact' sustained his government in office until defeated in a vote of confidence in 1979. He died in 2005.

Margaret Thatcher, Conservative (1979–90)

The most controversial of post-war prime ministers, Thatcher was a conviction politician who gave her name to a New Right ideology. In her first term in office, she set the agenda despite having only a few ideological allies in the cabinet. But her increasingly ideological approach alienated some key cabinet ministers, who withdrew their support when she failed to secure outright victory in the first ballot of the 1990 Conservative leadership election. She died in 2013.

John Major, Conservative (1990–97)

Castigated by his critics as a grey man lacking a 'big idea', but admired by supporters as a calming figure after Thatcher, Major survived as leader of a deeply divided party for six and a half years, largely because he recognised his dependence on the support of senior cabinet colleagues.

Tony Blair, Labour (1997–2007)

The architect of New Labour, Blair saw effective political communications as essential. He centralised power in Downing Street, while allowing Chancellor Gordon Brown significant autonomy in economic and social policy. Blair enjoyed high opinion poll ratings in his first term, but his popularity waned after he took Britain to war in Iraq in 2003.

Gordon Brown, Labour (2007–10)

He finally became prime minister after a decade as a powerful chancellor. However, having rejected the chance to capitalise on his initial popularity with a 'snap' general election, he saw his poll ratings damaged by the 2008 global financial crisis and consequent recession. He proved ineffective as a public communicator, and was dogged by rumours of 'psychological flaws' – notably an inability to tolerate the perceived shortcomings of close colleagues.

David Cameron, Conservative (2010–16)

Cameron initially portrayed himself as a Conservative 'moderniser' who wanted to steer the Conservative Party away from Thatcherism and its recent (but divisive) obsession with Europe, and broaden its electoral appeal in the way that Blair had done with New Labour. He led a coalition with the Liberal Democrats (2010–15), but ultimately fell victim to the European issue he had wanted to avoid. He resigned in June 2016 after Leave won the Referendum that Cameron had called; he had been confident that he would secure a vote for the UK to Remain in the EU.

Theresa May (2016–19)

She succeeded Cameron, and pledged her commitment to prioritising ordinary people who were 'just about managing' (the 'jams') financially, after six years of austerity. However, her premiership was dominated by divisions in the Conservative Party over the type of 'Brexit' the UK should pursue, and further undermined by her 'wooden' public persona and poor communication skills.

Boris Johnson (2019–)

He replaced May in July 2019, but remained a colourful/controversial character. Critics condemned his showmanship and cavalier attitude (comparing him unfavourably to the US President, Donald Trump), whereas his admirers applauded his willingness to ignore 'political correctness' and easily offended 'liberal snowflakes'. He led the Conservatives to an emphatic victory in the 2019 general election, and attracted much support by pledging that he would finally 'get Brexit done' after three years of wrangling and delay since the vote to 'Leave' in the 2016 referendum.

a decline in prime ministerial engagement with Parliament. Prime ministers nowadays make far fewer speeches than they used to do, and tend to be present only for major set-piece events. This could be interpreted as evasiveness and an avoidance of accountability, but it might also reflect the fact that prime ministers are generally much busier than in the past, not least because, in an era of globalisation, greater terrorist threats, and pandemics (like COVID-19), they have to devote more time to foreign affairs, international summits, and security issues. Consequently, prime ministers are often overseas, meeting other national leaders to discuss global problems and how national governments can work together to tackle them.

The distribution of power within the core executive creates the *potential* for prime ministerial predominance, but the position is far from being free from institutional constraints (see Table 7.1). As such, some political scientists have argued that the core executive is characterised by 'exchange relationships' and 'resource dependency', because ministers, including the prime minister, are often reliant on the acquiescence and cooperation of their ministerial colleagues and senior officials to achieve their policy goals; they are, to a considerable degree, dependent on each other. The power of prime ministers also depends on factors such as effective leadership and a favourable political climate. The main resources (formal and informal) available to the prime minister are:

- powers of patronage
- the authority of the office

- party leadership
- public standing
- policymaking input
- the Prime Minister's Office
- the Cabinet Office.

Patronage

The prime minister was previously charged with making a range of Crown and public appointments, including senior positions within the civil service, military, intelligence and security services, judiciary, and Church of England, plus various positions in the public sector, and chairs of key committees of inquiry (e.g. the Hutton and Leveson Inquiries (see Chapter 5)). Although the prime minister no longer enjoys a free choice among candidates for these important positions – which nowadays tend to fall under the remit of independent selection committees – it is almost inevitable that political considerations will be taken into account; either the prime minister has a direct influence over appointments or the decisions are influenced to some extent by cabinet ministers who are appointed by the PM.

Recommendations for most of the honours officially bestowed by the Crown emanate from Downing Street. In recent years, the system has been reformed so that more honours are given to members of the general public, and individuals can nominate people via the Cabinet Office website, but the results of this populist experiment have been limited. Prime ministers have long used the honours system to reward the support of loyal MPs, and this practice has survived despite demands for greater transparency in the system. In the political domain, the most significant awards are peerages, since hereditary peerages (until the 1999 reforms) and life peerages have entailed membership of the House of Lords. Prime ministers have used these patronage powers to alter the party balance within the upper house in their favour, although no party enjoys an overall majority in the Lords, not even the government. An independent Appointments Commission now makes recommendations on non-party appointments to the Lords, but the PM retains the power to make party nominations. Of twenty-eight individuals appointed between January 2019 and April 2020, thirteen were Conservatives (almost half of the appointees during this period), seven were Crossbenchers, three were Labour, two were non-affiliated, two were Bishops ('Lords Spiritual', and who are politically neutral), and one was a Green.

The prime minister's most significant patronage powers cover the appointment and dismissal of government ministers. They give the PM a clear advantage over their ministerial colleagues, for s/he or she can have a significant impact on their careers, for good or for ill. In theory, prime ministers can create a cabinet in their own image, promoting allies and excluding MPs whose views do not tally with theirs. In practice, the PM's choice is always constrained to some extent. A prime minister should be wary of overlooking senior party figures – including those who have in the past been, or could in future become, rivals for their job. In such cases, US President Lyndon Johnson noted that 'it is probably better to have him inside the tent pissing out, than outside the tent pissing in'. John Major included both of his opponents in the 1990 Conservative Party leadership election, Michael Heseltine and Douglas Hurd, in his cabinet. Similarly, Blair gave senior posts to his 1994 leadership rivals, John Prescott and Margaret Beckett. When Gordon Brown appointed Lord (Peter) Mandelson as business secretary in 2008, it was widely interpreted as a sign of weakness, since Mandelson was so closely associated with Tony Blair. However, in practice, Mandelson proved loyal to Brown and worked to prevent plots against the prime minister. After the 2010 general election, David Cameron had no option but to appoint senior Liberal

TABLE 7.1 Prime ministerial resources and constraints

Resources	Constraints

1. Patronage
Appoints ministers
Reshuffles cabinet
Dismisses ministers
	Senior colleagues have claims for inclusion
	Need to ensure ideological balance
	Danger of overlooked or dismissed ministers
	    cultivating a loyal following on the backbenches,
	    and emerging as rivals for the leadership
	Backbench MPs consistently overlooked for
	    promotion might become resentful and less loyal,
	    and thus weaken party unity

2. Authority in the cabinet system Chairs cabinet meetings Determines outcome of cabinet discussions Holds bilateral meetings with ministers Appoints members of cabinet committees Restructures central government	Requires cabinet support on major issues Senior ministers have authority and may challenge PM's preferred policy Ministers have departmental resources Not involved in detailed policymaking in many Cabinet committees

3. Party leadership
Leader of largest party in House of Commons
Elected by MPs and party members
	Support of party is not unconditional: government
	    MPs might move motion of 'no confidence' to
	    force a leadership contest
	Possibility of backbench rebellions on parliamentary
	    votes

4. Public profile
High public profile
Communicator-in-chief for the government
Speaks for nation in times of crisis
Represents UK on world stage
	Poor response to crisis undermines authority
	May become focus of media criticism
	Unpopularity weakens loyalty of MPs/ministers,
	    who fear electoral defeat, and loss of their own
	    seats

5. Policymaking input Directs government policy and sets agenda Has authority to get involved in any policy area Political rewards of policy success	Lacks time and detailed knowledge Lacks resources provided by a specific government department May be personally associated with failure of a key policy
6. Prime Minister's Office Provides independent advice and support Helps PM to direct policy	Prime Minister's Office has limited resources Other departments have own interests Appointing more advisers also means more staff to manage, and more scope for conflicting advice

Source: Adapted from M. Garnett and P. Lynch, *AS UK Government and Politics* (Deddington: Philip Allan Updates, 2nd edition, 2005), pp. 271–73; P. Dorey, *Policy Making in Britain* (London: Sage, 2nd edition, 2014), p. 76; M.J. Smith, *The Core Executive in Britain* (Basingstoke: Palgrave Macmillan, 1999), p. 32.

Democrats to his coalition government, although this actually gave him an excuse for excluding members of his own party who might have used ministerial positions to oppose his policies. His successor, Theresa May, suffered a grievous loss of political authority when her government lost its narrow parliamentary majority in the June 2017 election, which she had called in response to opinion polls, suggesting a landslide Conservative victory. This reduced her scope for changing her cabinet because her room for manoeuvre, and her practical choices, were severely limited.

Boris Johnson inherited May's lack of a Conservative majority, but his 'mandate' in winning the 2019 party leadership contest, and his willingness to defy constitutional convention, meant that he was willing to create a cabinet with much less ideological 'balance'. As such, several ministers associated with the Right and/or a Hard Brexit, were appointed to key posts, such as Dominic Raab as foreign secretary and Priti Patel as home secretary. Johnson's position as prime minister was greatly strengthened when he led the Conservatives to a decisive victory in the December 2019 general election; he was now 'his own man', and could expect loyalty from many Conservative MPs who, Johnson could claim, partly owed their own election to him. However, from March 2020 onwards, Johnson found himself grappling with the COVID-19 pandemic, with even some pro-Conservative newspapers criticising his slow or indecisive responses and poor communication. By this time, Johnson was also faced with a much more effective Opposition leader in Sir Keir Starmer, the latter earning immediate plaudits for his detailed probing (he was, after all, a former barrister; indeed an ex-Director of Public Prosecutions) of Johnson in his first few Prime Minister's Question Time appearances, at which the Conservative leader clearly struggled against a much more formidable parliamentary opponent than he had faced hitherto. The pandemic cruelly illustrated just how quickly a prime minister can be engulfed – and their authority weakened – by an unforeseen crisis, one which, in this instance, literally started on the other side of the world. Suddenly, the confidence they previously exuded, or inspired, can evaporate; certainly, Johnson's notoriously cavalier, jocular, and sometimes flippant response to questioning suddenly seemed totally inadequate and inappropriate.

When appointing their cabinet, it is not just *who* a prime minister appoints which is important, but *which* post or department ministers are allocated. Margaret Thatcher was renowned for appointing her key supporters – those who shared her strong free-market views – to the all-important economic ministries, namely, the Treasury, Trade and Industry, and (after 1981) Employment, from which her political priorities could be pursued: cuts in tax and public spending, curbing the money supply in order to squeeze inflation out of the economy, privatisation, cutting regulations and red-tape on business, and weakening the trade unions in order both to reduce strikes and strengthen the authority of employers and management over workers. Much more recently, as just noted, Boris Johnson chose Right-wing or/and pro-Hard Brexit ministers to fill key cabinet posts, with Dominic Raab appointed foreign secretary and Priti Patel as home secretary, thereby signalling his intention to pursue more radical policies in key areas than his predecessor.

Finally, the prime minister's choice when appointing ministers depends on the pool of talent within their party. Some MPs may be considered too old or too inexperienced, while others may simply not be talented enough or lack the requisite communication skills (especially important in the age of 24/7 media and 'rolling' news updates) to serve as ministers. Of course, a prime minister's ministerial choices will also be affected by the number of MPs their party has: a landslide general election victory will mean more MPs to choose from, while a narrow majority or even a minority government will reduce the number of MPs from whom the prime minister can choose. On the other hand, a large parliamentary majority might make it harder to keep the government's MPs happy, as there are more backbenchers who might feel upset or resentful at being overlooked when ministerial appointments were made. This might create problems for party management, in terms of weakening loyalty and unity due to simmering discontent and frustration on the backbenches; thwarted ambition can breed resentment.

Cabinet reshuffles are often used to demote underachievers and dissenters, promote allies and successful junior ministers, and freshen-up both the government's ranks and its public image; new faces imply a revamp and renewed energy or focus. The ability to dismiss ministers is a powerful weapon in the prime minister's arsenal, but it can backfire. A botched reshuffle can raise questions about the prime minister's judgement, expose intra-party or intra-cabinet divisions, and draw attention to policy failures. Macmillan's infamous sacking of a third of his cabinet in 1962 (the 'Night of the Long Knives'), instead of making him appear tough and decisive, seriously damaged his political authority and fuelled resentment: not only did it look like panic and blame-shifting, it also begged the question as to why Macmillan had appointed these ministers in the first place. Meanwhile, rather than reducing or removing intra-cabinet divisions, Blair's reshuffles often provoked further disputes between the rival Blairite and Brownite camps. More recently, Theresa May's political authority – already damaged by failing to lead the Conservatives to victory in the 2017 general election – was continually weakened by successive ministerial resignations, during 2018 and early 2019, over her policy on Brexit. Eventually, she felt compelled to announce her own resignation as Conservative leader and prime minister; her position had become untenable.

Sacked or demoted ministers might also make damaging public criticisms, as Geoffrey Howe did in November 1990, when he used his resignation speech, in a packed House of Commons, to make a scathing attack on Margaret Thatcher's increasingly anti-European views and autocratic style of leadership; Howe effectively called upon someone in the Conservative Party to put themselves forward as a leadership contender, in order to give the party an opportunity to replace Thatcher. She was then replaced by John Major, who was himself strongly criticised by his ex-Chancellor Norman Lamont, who claimed in his 1993 resignation speech that the Major government was 'in office but not in power'. Yet, failure to act decisively and swiftly in sacking a minister can be perceived as weakness or misplaced loyalty. Major was accused of not being ruthless enough in dismissing ministers such as Secretary of State for National Heritage, David Mellor, who became embroiled in scandals over aspects of his private life, and Tony Blair was reluctant to sack close allies such as Peter Mandelson and David Blunkett when they were subject to allegations of financial impropriety.

Theresa May's weakness as prime minister after losing her narrow parliamentary majority in the 2017 election was further highlighted by her seeming inability to sack Chancellor Philip Hammond, who many commentators had predicted would be replaced if – as was widely expected – the Conservatives were re-elected with a large majority. Instead, the result simultaneously weakened May's political authority, while reducing the number of MPs from whom she could recruit new ministers in order to replace (sack) existing ones.

Authority in the cabinet system

The Prime Minister's office gives its holder considerable authority within the cabinet system. As chair of the cabinet, the prime minister can steer discussions in the direction of his/her preferred option prevails. The prime minister determines the agenda of cabinet meetings. Potentially difficult issues can be excluded from the agenda and dealt with instead in committee or bilateral discussions. The prime minister can also control the information presented to ministers by determining the issues and papers brought before cabinet. For example, the 2004 Butler inquiry found that crucial papers on alleged weapons of mass destruction in Iraq were not placed before the cabinet. It is the prime minister who determines which ministers speak in cabinet, in what order, at what length, and also how much (if any) discussion occurs on various issues. Some prime ministers will allow (or even encourage) discussion among ministers, either on specific policies or about the government's overall priorities and strategy, while other premiers (such as Thatcher and Blair) view three-hour cabinet meetings as a waste of everyone's time, and will thus seek to curtail lengthy or detailed discussions and instead treat cabinet as an arena for officially authorising decisions and policy proposals on which the relevant minister(s) will then act.

Items on the cabinet agenda are only rarely subject to formal votes. Usually, the prime minister determines the course of action, often by weighing up the overall 'mood' or balance of opinion in the cabinet in support of (or opposition to) a particular proposal, although they might also ascribe more weight to the views of senior ministers rather than simply 'count heads', but this does not give the prime minister licence to do as s/he wishes against the advice of, or strength of feeling among, cabinet colleagues. Again, it is important to recogise that a prime minister who is perceived to be too dominant (or indecisive) in the cabinet will, sooner or later, weaken their own position. Ministers also have resources within the core executive, which is why power should not be viewed as simply 'zero-sum', as if more power for one individual can only mean less power for another. A prime minister's wishes might be thwarted if senior ministers collectively say 'No' or/and threaten to resign. However, prime ministers are expected to provide a sense of direction and purpose, strategic leadership, and establish the government's overall framework or key policy goals. They also decide the membership, chairs, and remit of cabinet committees, where much detailed work occurs on policy issues which are administratively or technically complex and require the involvement of several departments and their ministers (see farther in the text).

The prime minister can restructure central government by creating or merging government departments. Blair created the Department for Environment, Food and Rural Affairs, and the Department for Work and Pensions; Gordon Brown created the Department of Energy and Climate Change; and Theresa May established the Department for Exiting the European Union, which her successor, Boris Johnson abolished when the UK formally left the EU in January 2020. Blair also boosted the role and resources of the Prime Minister's Office considerably, most notably by the appointment of more special advisers to the Downing Street Policy Unit. Cameron also created the National Security Council (NSC) to coordinate policy in an era of security risks. The prime minister also holds the title of Minister for the Civil Service and is formally responsible for its organisation and management. Thatcher, Major, and Blair all carried out extensive reforms of the civil service (see Chapter 10).

Party leadership

The prime minister is usually (though not always) the leader of the largest party in the House of Commons, and this is an obvious source of authority. Those whose parties command a working parliamentary majority are well placed to enact their legislative programmes and manifesto pledges. However, rebellions by backbench MPs have become more frequent in the last 40 years and can derail government policy (see Chapter 8). Blair suffered sizeable rebellions on the war in Iraq, university tuition fees, and 'foundation' hospitals in his second term. In his first year in office, Brown had to make concessions to rebel Labour MPs on the abolition of the 10 pence tax band. Cameron lost a crucial vote intended to pave the way for military action against the Assad regime in Syria, and decided not to ask for parliamentary approval of several other policies (e.g. House of Lords reform) when it looked likely that he would lose. Cameron also saw about half of his Conservative MPs vote *against* the legislation to allow same-sex marriage, although the Bill was enacted due to support from MPs from most other parties. His successor, Theresa May, suffered repeated parliamentary defeats over her plan ('Withdrawal Agreement') for leaving the EU, in accordance with the 'Leave' victory in the 2016 referendum. Conservative 'hard Eurosceptics' did not consider her proposals to go far enough in making a clean break with the EU, and so they kept voting against her proposals in the House of Commons. Because she had lost her majority in the 2017 election, the Conservatives' hardline anti-Europeans effectively enjoyed considerable power – had she won in 2017 with a 100+ majority, she would have been in a much stronger position to withstand these backbench rebellions by hard Eurosceptics, most notably the 50–60 Conservative MPs who belonged to the European Research Group, led by Jacob Rees-Mogg.

Labour and Conservative Party leaders are normally elected by a combination of MPs and party members, and, in theory, this ought to enhance the legitimacy of a newly chosen leader. However, as already alluded to, party support is generally conditional, and beyond the initial 'honeymoon' period, leaders and prime ministers often face either intermittent, or increasing, criticism from their own colleagues. This can sometimes result in their resignation and replacement. Despite having led her party to three consecutive general election victories, Margaret Thatcher was forced to resign when she failed to muster sufficient support from Conservative MPs in the 1990 leadership contest. John Major resigned as Conservative leader (but not as prime minister) in 1995, calling a leadership contest that he hoped would strengthen his position against Eurosceptic critics. He secured a 218 to 89 votes victory over John Redwood, but with several Conservative MPs abstaining, it meant that one-third of the parliamentary party had failed to support him, thus leaving his authority further weakened. Few prime ministers enjoyed a more dominant position within their party than Blair. He propelled Labour from what seemed to be perpetual opposition and possible terminal decline, and continued the reform of the party organization in a way that enhanced the leader's power. However, the war in Iraq damaged his standing in the party, as did some of his social policies, such as the 2006 introduction of fees for university students; in his third term, Blair faced a concerted attempt by some Labour MPs to force him out of office. The political legitimacy of his successor Gordon Brown was seriously weakened by the fact that he took over the party leadership and the premiership without facing a ballot of Labour MPs, let alone the British public as a whole via a general election, and then, the following year, the global financial crash occurred. David Cameron felt obliged to resign just hours after the Leave result of the June 2016 EU referendum was announced; he had campaigned for the UK to Remain in the EU. A year later, Theresa May's political authority was seriously weakened when she failed to lead the Conservatives to victory in the 2017 general election, in spite of starting the campaign with an enormous lead in the opinion polls.

Public standing

The media spotlight on prime ministers has intensified so that they have become communicators-in-chief for the government, articulating official policy and speaking on behalf of the nation during times of crisis. Blair excelled in this role, initiating monthly media sessions and regular prime ministerial appearances before the House of Commons Liaison Committee (comprised of the chairs of the select committees). High opinion poll ratings further strengthen the prime minister's hand, whereas poor ratings may persuade MPs that a change of leader is required, especially if a general election is due within the next year or two. Though a divisive figure, Thatcher was widely regarded as a determined leader with a clear agenda. This was a profitable image early in her premiership, but thereafter she was increasingly regarded as dogmatic and unbending, to the extent that even some of her closest, most senior, colleagues eventually turned against her. Blair enjoyed high poll ratings during his first term, but excessive reliance on manipulation of the news agenda ('spin') and the war in Iraq cost him the trust of many voters. In the first weeks after taking over from Blair, Gordon Brown was highly popular, but he refused to cash in on an opinion poll lead by calling an early election, and was ridiculed for his alleged lack of courage. Afterwards, his public standing was further undermined by the 2008 financial crash which, it was argued, he had failed to foresee or plan for ('fix the roof while the sun shines') while he was Chancellor of the Exchequer during the previous ten years. It was also alleged, by his Conservative critics, that the financial crash was greatly exacerbated by his 'excessive' public expenditure while he was the chancellor; he had 'maxed-out' on the nation's credit card and was thus blamed for the austerity which followed.

By contrast, his successor in 10 Downing Street, David Cameron, was widely viewed as an 'heir to Blair', generally giving confident performances before domestic and international audiences, in spite of having failed to lead the Conservatives to outright victory in the 2010 general election, and thus obliged to enter into coalition with the Liberal Democrats. Like Blair, Cameron was particularly adept at Prime Minister's Question Time, where he routinely performed authoritatively and effectively – critics would say arrogantly – against Labour's 2010–15 leader, Ed Miliband. Good performances in such parliamentary events can greatly enhance a prime minister's reputation and inspire confidence both among their colleagues and the party's supporters, although it is unclear how much influence this has on the wider electorate. The initial goodwill and political capital that Theresa May enjoyed when she succeeded Cameron in July 2016 evaporated when she called a constitutionally unnecessary election in 2017. She had hoped to increase the Conservatives' narrow parliamentary majority – which most opinion polls suggested would easily be achieved – but the party actually lost it, after a disastrous campaign in which May herself proved to be a poor communicator and campaigner, thereby living up to the cruel caricature of The Maybot. This seriously weakened her credibility and authority, and left her vulnerable to constant speculation about leadership challenges. Her premiership was further damaged by the deep divisions in the Conservative Party over Brexit and her handling of the negotiations with EU officials: pro-European and anti-European Conservatives alike were critical of her stance, convinced that she was yielding too much to the other 'side'. When Boris Johnson replaced May in July 2019, and then led the party to a clear victory in a general election five months later, he attracted considerable support from Conservatives who welcomed his pledge to 'get Brexit done', even if it meant leaving the EU without a deal. By this time, even some people who had voted Remain in the 2016 referendum just wanted Brexit to be over with, or had at least resigned themselves to its inevitability, and wanted British politics to 'move on' to address other political issues. However, Johnson soon found his premiership engulfed in the crisis, entailing 10,000s of deaths, caused by the COVID-19 pandemic in the spring and summer of 2020. Overnight, Johnson's ultra-laid-back ebullience and devil-may-care insouciance became wholly inappropriate and ill-suited to the unfolding tragedy affecting Britain. He also struggled to display mastery over details when answering parliamentary questions or being questioned at press conferences. Critics suggested that Johnson was 'out of his depth', and his previously high opinion poll (approval) ratings plummeted.

Policy-making input

Unlike other ministers who work within departments, a prime minister's authority is not confined to specific fields of government policy. Rather, s/he has overall charge of government objectives and political priorities (strategic leadership) and establishes the general tenor of domestic and foreign policy. Thatcher and Blair set out broad goals which they expected departmental ministers to act upon, and Johnson made clear his expectation that ministers would prioritise 'getting Brexit done', although from March 2020, his government was forced to divert its attention to tackling the global coronavirus (COVID-19) pandemic and minimisng the loss of lives while scientists across the world frantically worked to create a vaccine. Economic and foreign affairs are areas in which prime ministers are especially likely to take an active interest, whether or not they have had previous relevant ministerial experience. The Chancellor of the Exchequer and Foreign Secretary are important actors in their own right, but the prime minister tends to be proactive in setting objectives and coordinating policy, given the importance of these areas. The prime minister also takes the lead role in times of crisis. Blair took direct charge of the government response to the 2000 fuel blockade, the 2001 foot-and-mouth outbreak, the 9/11 terrorist attacks on New York and Washington, and the 7/7 attacks in London, while Brown coordinated an international response to the 2008 global financial crash. A few years later, May, and then Johnson (initially), focused on negotiating the UK's departure from the EU.

The prime minister can also choose to play an active role in issues of particular interest to them. Prime ministerial involvement can make a significant difference, pushing a policy up, or even onto, the agenda or forcing a department to change trajectory. Thatcher was a hands-on politician who intervened in a wide range of domestic policy – sometimes to the annoyance of the minister formally in charge of the department – including, education, health, local government, privatisation, and trade union reform. With the last of these policy areas, Thatcher repeatedly clashed with her first Employment Secretary, James Prior, due to her impatience with his 'softly, softly' approach: it was no surprise when Prior was replaced, in Thatcher's first cabinet reshuffle in September 1981, by Norman Tebbit, who was ideologically aligned with Thatcher. Policy successes, such as victory in the Falklands War, council house sales, and privatisation, strengthened her position, but the dramatic failure of the Poll Tax – which she championed as a 'flagship policy' – undermined her; indeed, it was a factor in her downfall in November 1990. Major's key initiatives were the Northern Ireland peace process and the Citizen's Charter. The latter brought some improvement in public services but failed to enthuse voters. Blair's personal initiatives came largely in foreign affairs (e.g. Kosovo and Iraq – the latter subsequently grievously damaging his popularity and legacy), and Northern Ireland, where the 1998 Good Friday Agreement could be classed as Blair's greatest success. Blair also took a keen interest in education, both in terms of improving choice and standards in schools and expanding higher education (universities) to ensure that many more young people obtained degrees. He showed less enthusiasm for constitutional reform, allowing cabinet committees to fill in the details. While Brown came to office with a range of policy ideas, he was soon immersed in economic problems and dogged by accusations that, as prime minister, he was hardly the right person to deal with problems which had accumulated while he was Chancellor of the Exchequer. David Cameron adopted a prominent profile in foreign policy questions, particularly in relation to intervention in Libya and Syria; in sharp contrast to Brown, he was content to leave economic policy to his Chancellor, George Osborne. Having become prime minister when Cameron resigned following the 'Leave' win in the 2016 EU referendum, Theresa May's premiership was dominated – and ultimately destroyed – by the complex, often convoluted, negotiations over Britain's withdrawal from the European Union, which were conducted against the backdrop of bitter in-fighting inside the Conservative Party. As a consequence, May was unable to devote much time to her domestic policy agenda, having initially pledged to focus on the JAMs ('just about managing' to survive financially) and pursue a more compassionate or one-nation mode of conservatism. Boris Johnson was actually enthusiastic about focusing on Brexit and keen to secure his place in history as the PM who finally 'liberated' the UK from the European Union, but he then found his attention diverted by the Spring 2020 COVID-19 crisis. In other words, whereas May had wanted to focus on a particular domestic policy issue but was required to concentrate instead on Brexit, Johnson had wanted to focus on Brexit but was then compelled to concentrate on an entirely different, and more urgent, issue. This also illustrates how prime ministers, regardless of their constitutional powers, are sometimes constrained, or have their attention diverted, by issues and events beyond their control.

The Prime Minister's Office

Although there is no official prime minister's department in British government, there is a Prime Minister's Office, and this has grown in importance in the last 25 years. Partly based in 10

Downing Street and partly in the Cabinet Office (discussed later), and with a staff of approximately 180–90 (it varies from one prime minister to the next), the Prime Minister's Office provides support across the range of prime ministerial responsibilities. Since a 2001 reorganisation, it has comprised three main directorates:

Policy and government directorate – It provides policy advice and coordinates the development and implementation of policies across government departments. It provided the prime minister with an alternative source of policy advice and included chief advisers on key issues such as foreign affairs and, pre-2020, the European Union. Indeed, the modern prime minister has a wide range of special advisers (SPADS), often a couple on each aspect of domestic policy, and three or four on broader areas, such as economic affairs and foreign policy. For example, at the end of 2018, Theresa May had 37 SPADs, while a year later, Boris Johnson had 44.

Communications and strategy directorate – It is responsible for policy presentation and relations with the media. This, of course, reflects the growing importance of media management in an era of 24/7 news and reportage. It also includes a Research and Information Unit which provides factual information to No. 10.

Government and political relations directorate – It addresses relations with the governing party, both in Parliament and in the constituencies.

Overall, the bolstering of the Prime Minister's Office in recent decades has strengthened the PM's position within the core executive.

The Cabinet Office

The Cabinet Office was created in 1916, and plays a major role in coordinating the work of ministers and their departments, and monitoring the progress of policy development. It regulates core executive business by circulating papers between ministers and maintaining a flow of information, preparing the agenda for cabinet meetings, and then writing-up the minutes to provide an official record of what was agreed. The Head of the Home Civil Service (Sir Mark Sedwill 2018-2020, Simon Case, current) is head of the Cabinet Secretariat and attends cabinet meetings as Secretary of the Cabinet. The current (2020) minister for the Cabinet Office is Michael Gove, who is also is a full member of the cabinet, whereas some of his predecessors only attended meetings when specifically invited. This, of course, illustrates how some roles are at least partly defined or determined by the prime minister.

The Cabinet Office is physically connected to Number 10, and its proximity has sometimes tempted prime ministers to treat it as if its main purpose was to serve them exclusively, rather than all senior ministers, their department, and the cabinet as a whole. In effect, the Cabinet Office serves as a conduit or connecting thread between the key actors, individual and institutional, in the core executive, and, as such, is itself a major component at the heart of British government. Due to the breadth and importance of its communication and coordinating roles, the Cabinet Office is divided into several secretariats, units, or groups, each focusing on a specific function of government or sphere of policy, namely:

- Civil Contingencies Secretariat
- Economic and Domestic Affairs Secretariat
- EU Exit Implementation Group
- European Unit
- Government Communications
- Government Digital Service
- Government in Parliament

- Implementation Unit
- Infrastructure Projects
- National Security Secretariat
- Prime Minister's Office

The range of functions which the Cabinet Office performs and coordinates in serving and supporting the work of British governments (regardless of the party in Office) reflects the growing complexity of governing society in the twenty-first century, and the range of domestic, European, and global issues which the core executive has to grapple with.

Analysis 7.1

A British presidency?

Michael Foley argues in *The British Presidency* (Manchester: Manchester University Press, 2000) that the office of the British prime minister has become more 'presidential'. He claims that the 'presidentialisation' of the post of prime minister has created not a pale imitation of the US presidency, but a 'de facto British Presidency'. Two concepts are identified as central to this development: 'leadership stretch' and 'spatial leadership'. The former refers to the greater emphasis placed on personalised leadership and communications; the latter points to the creation of a sense of distance between the prime minister and his or her government and party. The political and media spotlight falls on the prime minister to a far greater extent than any other minister – the prime minister has thus become communicator-in-chief for the government and spokesperson for the nation. British election campaigns have become more akin to their American counterparts in their focus on the leader. Leadership is also of greater importance in public policy. The prime minister is personally associated with policy initiatives, claiming to represent the public interest and making populist criticisms of the failure of government organisations (e.g. Blair's claim that public sector and civil service lethargy in policy delivery left 'scars on my back'). Foley recognises that presidentialism can create problems for the prime minister: Blair's position became exposed after the invasion of Iraq when trust in his leadership declined and the legitimacy of his leadership style was questioned.

Foley's is an important contribution to debates on prime ministerial power, but his thesis has been criticised by adherents to the core executive model. For Richard Heffernan, prime ministers are predominant figures within the core executive and have the potential to exercise leadership when they utilise institutional power resources effectively and make judicious use of their own personal skills. But they cannot have a monopoly of power. Heffernan notes in 'Why the Prime Minister cannot be a President: Comparing Institutional Imperatives in Britain and America' (*Parliamentary Affairs*, Vol. 58, No. 1, 2005, pp. 53–70) that institutional factors prevent a prime minister becoming a president. So, the prime minister is indirectly elected, is accountable to the legislature, and is head of a collegial executive. But a British prime minister also has greater resources than a US president, given the former is leader of a political party and the British constitution allows for executive dominance of the legislature (Parliament), whereas the separation of powers is a guiding principle of the US constitution.

The cabinet

The cabinet consists of the most senior government ministers, most of whom are the political heads of government departments. Below it is a network of committees that report to the cabinet. There are also regular *ad hoc* meetings of ministers, as well as bilateral discussions between the PM and ministers. The 'Cabinet government' model suggests that executive power is vested in a cabinet whose members, as the most senior ministers, exercise 'collective responsibility'; they must all publicly support and defend government policies, even if they harbour private reservations or disagreement or were not present at the meeting which endorsed them. However, the doctrine of 'collective responsibility' has increasingly been applied more widely, so that it now applies to all ministers, and not only those in the cabinet. Indeed, the steady increase in the number of junior ministers during the last century means that there are many more ministers outside the cabinet than in it. Although it would be wrong to write off the cabinet as merely a 'dignified institution' with little influence, its practical political importance has declined somewhat in recent decades, to the extent that it now has only a limited role in actual decision-taking and policymaking, because many decisions are taken, and policies drafted, elsewhere in the core executive. Hence, the concept of 'Cabinet government' is of limited explanatory value today.

For most of the twentieth century, the cabinet averaged some 20 members, but in the twenty-first century, this has generally increased slightly, to 22 or even 23. A few other ministers attend occasionally – usually when there is a particular item or policy issue on the agenda which they are best qualified to address - but they are not formal members. As most of them are the political heads of government departments, cabinet ministers usually have the title Secretary of State (for Education, Health, Transport, Work and Pensions, etc.). Those heading the most prestigious departments – the Treasury, Foreign Office, and Home Office – plus major spending departments such as health and education have long been full members of the cabinet, whereas other posts and their ministers are relatively recent creations:

Post	Date post created
Secretary of State for International Development	1997
Secretary of State for Digital, Culture, Media and Sport	1997
Secretary of State for Environment, Food & Rural Affairs	2001
Secretary of State for Work and Pensions	2001
Secretary of State for Justice	2007
Secretary of State for Energy and Climate Change	2008 (until 2016)
Secretary of State for Business, Innovation, and Skills	2009 (until 2016)
Secretary of State for Business, Energy, and Industrial Strategy	2016
Secretary of State for Exiting the European Union	2016 (until 2020)
Secretary of State for Housing, Communities, and Local Government	2018
Secretary of State for Health and Social Care	2018

Ministers tend to remain in post for longer in the more senior cabinet positions, and for most, this will mark the pinnacle of their careers – unless they subsequently become prime minister. Cabinet ministers must be Members of Parliament (either MPs in the House of Commons or peers in the House of Lords), to which they are politically accountable. This accountability is ensured through such forums as Ministers' Question Time (generally every four weeks for a maximum of one hour) and giving evidence to Departmental Select Committees as and when summoned (see Chapter 8). Most cabinet ministers are drawn from the House of Commons, whereas peers tend to be appointed as junior ministers – generally one per department. The last member of the Lords to hold one of the main offices of state was Lord Carrington, foreign secretary from 1979 to 1982.

TABLE 7.2 Boris Johnson's Cabinet, 2020

Prime minister, First Lord of the Treasury and Minister for the Civil Service	Boris Johnson
Chancellor of the Duchy of Lancaster, and Minister for the Cabinet Office	Michael Gove
Chancellor of the Exchequer	Rishi Sunak
Foreign Secretary and First Secretary of State	Dominic Raab
Home Secretary	Priti Patel
Secretary of State for Defence	Ben Wallace
Lord Chancellor and Secretary of State for Justice	Robert Buckland
Secretary of State for Health and Social Care	Matt Hancock
Secretary of State for Business, Energy and Industrial Strategy	Alok Sharma
Secretary of State for Housing, Communities and Local Government	Robert Jenrick
Secretary of State for International Trade and President of the Board of Trade	Elizabeth Truss
Secretary of State for Education	Gavin Williamson
Secretary of State for Environment, Food and Rural Affairs	George Eustice
Secretary of State for Transport	Grant Shapps
Secretary of State for Work and Pensions	Thérèse Coffey
Leader of the House of Lords and Lord Privy Seal	Baroness Evans
Secretary of State for Scotland	Alister Jack
Secretary of State for Wales	Simon Hart
Secretary of State for Northern Ireland	Brandon Lewis
Secretary of State for International Development	Anne-Maria Trevelyan
Secretary of State for Digital, Culture, Media and Sport	Oliver Dowden
Minister without Portfolio (Cabinet Office)	Amanda Milling

The work of the cabinet is governed by convention rather than statute law, although authoritative guidance for ministers is contained in the *Ministerial Code*. This was made public in 1992 (when it was known as *Questions of Procedure for Ministers*) and can be viewed on the Cabinet Office website (https://www.gov.uk/government/publications/ministerial-code). It includes guidance on ministers' relationships with Parliament, the civil service, and their constituencies (as most ministers are MPs, they still have constituency responsibilities to perform). The *Ministerial Code* specifies that legislative proposals must receive prior approval from the Treasury (in case they have financial implications) and government law officers (Table 7.2).

The cabinet's main functions are:

- recording and ratifying decisions taken elsewhere within the core executive, but which require formal cabinet approval;
- reaching or endorsing final decisions on major issues;
- settling disputes between government departments; and
- determining forthcoming government business and priorities in Parliament.

The *Ministerial Code* states that the main business of the cabinet system is discussion of major issues that engage the collective responsibility of ministers and the final resolution of disputes between government departments. The cabinet itself takes relatively few detailed decisions, though some major issues might be discussed by it, but most are reported to the cabinet mainly as a formality. Cabinet approval of decisions taken elsewhere in the core executive is usually automatic, because the relevant ministers, special advisers, and senior civil servants will already have worked on the policy in detail, and, as such, other ministers are unlikely to challenge it when it is finally presented to the cabinet for final approval, particularly if the policy does not impinge upon their own departmental remit or policy goals. Indeed, ministers are usually strongly discouraged from challenging or reopening issues on which a decision has already been reached. The cabinet's ability to decide policy is constrained by its size, the detailed nature of much policy, and the infrequency of meetings. It is impractical for more than 20 ministers to engage in detailed discussion of complex issues. Ministers are primarily concerned with their specific departmental remits and usually have little time or desire to involve themselves with other complex issues beyond their own department.

The agenda for cabinet meetings is determined in advance by the prime minister and cabinet secretary, although most sessions include reports from the relevant ministers on forthcoming parliamentary business and current developments in domestic and foreign affairs, although, as just noted, there is usually little detailed discussion. Prime ministers generally do not want lengthy debate on their favoured course of action, but neither is it in their interest to curtail discussion in a way which could encourage ministerial discontent to fester or for grievances to grow. When proposals emanating from a particular department are on the agenda, the appropriate secretary of state will introduce the item, after which the prime minister sums up any discussion or views expressed, and announces the outcome. Cabinet normally met twice per week in the 1950s, but since the 1980s, it has usually met once a week (on a Thursday, having met on a Tuesday under Gordon Brown) when Parliament is in session. When Blair was prime minister, the diminished number of cabinet meetings was matched by a reduction in their length, from about three hours to just one hour on many occasions. Like Thatcher, Blair was not interested in encouraging discussions and contributions from around the cabinet table: instead, he wanted decisions taken and the relevant minister to go away and act upon, or implement ('deliver') what had been formally approved or agreed. Other prime ministers, like John Major, David Cameron, and Theresa May, were more collegial in how they chaired cabinet meetings, such that they became longer-lasting again. Although this largely reflected the style and personality of these leaders, it is important to emphasise that Cameron was head of a coalition government, and therefore would almost certainly have felt obliged to permit fuller or wider discussion between senior ministers from two different parties. At the time of writing this edition of *Exploring British Politics*, details had not emerged of Boris Johnson's style of chairing and managing his cabinet, but as he initially instructed senior ministers to focus on 'delivering' the pledges in the Conservative Party's 2019 manifesto, it seems highly unlikely that he would want to continue with the more discursive format and longer meetings of his three predecessors. Instead, a return to the shorter meetings redolent of the Thatcher and Blair premierships seemed likely; these succinct, more decisive, cabinet meetings grant ministers with more time to 'deliver' their policies, rather than discussing them.

Cabinet committees

As very little detailed discussion normally occurs in the full cabinet, much of the really in-depth policy work of governments takes place in cabinet committees. The prime minister formally decides their membership and terms of reference (remit), but many of the ministers who serve on a cabinet committee are appointed 'automatically', in the sense that their department is directly involved in, or affected by, a policy proposal; as such, most of the membership is effectively self-selecting. For much of the twentieth century, there was a combination of 'standing' and *ad hoc* cabinet committees: the former was permanent and dealt with ongoing or permanent issues, while the latter was established on a temporary basis, to address a particular issue or problem, before being disbanded when its work was complete. However, in the last 20 years, there has been a shift to fewer, but often, larger or broad-ranging, standing cabinet committees, with some of these then establishing subcommittees to deal with really complex or detailed issues. As such, there are now far fewer *ad hoc* committees, for whereas prime ministers previously would often create them in response to a particular issue, they now tend to allocate issues or problems to an existing cabinet committee or subcommittee. This allows for more continuity in the cabinet committee system, and therefore the development of greater expertise among the ministers serving on each committee

TABLE 7.3 Cabinet committees, June 2020

Title/Subject	Chair
EU Exit Strategy (XS)	Boris Johnson
EU Exit, Economy and Trade (XET)	Boris Johnson
EU Exit Operations (XO)	Michael Gove
Domestic Affairs & the Union (DAU)	Boris Johnson
Climate change	Boris Johnson
Parliamentary Business and Legislation	Jacob Rees-Mogg
National Security Council	Boris Johnson

or subcommittee. Once a cabinet committee or subcommittee has addressed an issue, and perhaps developed a policy to be sent to the full cabinet for ratification, instead of being disbanded, it simply turns its attention to the next issue or problem delegated to it (Table 7.3).

Ministerial responsibility

In theory, the cabinet is a united body as it is usually made up of senior members of the same party who stood on an agreed manifesto at the general election. However, the sense of unity is variously undermined by departmental, ideological, and personal rivalries. Ministers usually fight for the interests of the government department they represent. Departments provide ministers with authority and expertise (which they hope to strengthen by winning additional resources) and influence over policy. In negotiations with the Treasury on spending, ministers may act primarily as departmental chiefs rather than members of a collegiate body.

Collective responsibility

Collective Responsibility

the convention that ministers are responsible collectively for government policy and should resign their posts if they cannot support a key element of it.

The necessity of unity for the smooth functioning of the executive is made apparent by a key convention of cabinet government, that of **collective responsibility**. All government ministers assume collective responsibility for decisions made in the cabinet and its committees, regardless of whether they had opposed the policy or even been consulted about it. Ministers can express their views, confidentially, in cabinet during any discussions, but once a decision has been taken and a policy formally confirmed, ministers should support it or tender their resignations. During Tony Blair's premiership, two cabinet ministers (Robin Cook and Clare Short) resigned in 2003 because they strongly disagreed with policy on Iraq (see Table 7.4). Rather more recently, in 2018 and early 2019, several senior ministers resigned from Theresa May's cabinet because they disagreed with her proposed version of Brexit. Ministers must also keep details of discussions in the cabinet system secret, ostensibly to ensure that sensitive information does not enter the public domain, but also to conceal disagreements and divisions between ministers, which might well be embarrassing or even politically damaging if they became publicly known. Finally, collective responsibility requires the

TABLE 7.4 Ministerial resignations: collective responsibility (examples)

Date	Minister	Post	Reason for resignation
1985	Ian Gow	Minister of State, Treasury	Opposed Anglo-Irish Agreement
1986	Michael Heseltine	Secretary of State for Defence	Opposed defence procurement decision ('Westland affair')
1989	Nigel Lawson	Chancellor of the Exchequer	Clashes with Thatcher over aspects of economic policy conduct
1990	Sir Geoffrey Howe	Leader of the House of Commons	Opposed Thatcher's growing hostility towards Europe
1995	John Redwood	Secretary of State for Wales	Launched leadership challenge
2003	Robin Cook	President of the Council and Leader of the House of Commons	Opposed Blair government's policy on war with Iraq
2003	Clare Short	Secretary of State for Overseas Development	Opposed policy on Iraq
2009	James Purnell	Secretary of State for Work and Pensions	Loss of confidence in prime minister
2016	Iain Duncan Smith	Secretary of State for Work and Pensions	Opposition to cuts in Disability Benefit in the Budget
2018	David Davis	Secretary of State for Exiting the European Union	Opposition to Theresa May's policy on Brexit
2018	Boris Johnson	Foreign Secretary	Opposition to Theresa May's policy on Brexit
2018	Dominic Raab	Secretary of State for Exiting the European Union	Opposition to Theresa May's policy on Brexit
2018	Esther McVey	Secretary of State for Work and Pensions	Opposition to Theresa May's policy on Brexit
2019	Andrea Leadsom	Leader of the House of Commons Lord President of the Council	Opposition to Theresa May's policy on Brexit
2020	Sajid Javid	Chancellor of the Exchequer	Clashes with Boris Johnson and Dominic Cummings over economic policy/austerity

government as a whole to resign if it is defeated in a vote of confidence in the House of Commons. The last time this happened was in 1979 when James Callaghan's Labour government was forced to resign following defeat in a parliamentary vote of 'no confidence'. Callaghan's government then lost the consequent general election, paving the way for 18 years of Conservative rule.

Despite being the first principle of conduct set out in the *Ministerial Code*, collective responsibility has been eroded over recent decades. It was suspended temporarily during the 1975 referendum on the EEC, when Wilson allowed ministers to campaign on either side of a debate that divided the Labour Party. More recently, in the 2011 referendum on electoral reform, cabinet colleagues from the Conservative and Liberal Democrat parties were in open (and sometimes strong) disagreement. Liberal Democrat ministers were also given the option of abstention in parliamentary votes on the sensitive issue of student tuition fees. In preparation for an 'in-out' referendum on the EU to be held before the end of 2017 (it was actually held in June 2016), David Cameron was faced with a considerable dilemma about whether or not to maintain the principle of collective responsibility, and provoked anger within his party when he suggested that his colleagues might be expected to support his own position, which was that the UK should remain a member of the EU.

In spite of the convention of collective ministerial responsibility, relatively recent political history has seen ministers who disagree with government policy often stay in post while making their dissatisfaction public, often through 'coded' speeches in which the criticisms were partly hidden 'between the lines'. This was the certainly case with 'wets', such as Ian Gilmour and Francis Pym, in Thatcher's first administration, although the Eurosceptics in Major's cabinet were often less subtle in their public criticism of official policy towards the EU. Clare Short remained in the cabinet for two months after publicly criticising the war with Iraq, while Vince Cable remained in his cabinet post in the 2010–15 coalition in spite of making publicly clear his frustration over the government's failure to tackle 'excessive' boardroom pay in an era of austerity. Finally, the requirement for cabinet secrecy has been rather undermined by ministers revealing details of discussions and disagreements in their published diaries and memoirs. Such publications really began with former Labour cabinet ministers, Richard Crossman, Barbara Castle, and Tony Benn in the 1970s, but since then, at least one or two ministers from all subsequent governments have published personal records and recollections, or revealing autobiographies. Indeed, most prime ministers themselves have published their memoirs – Harold Wilson, James Callaghan, Margaret Thatcher, John Major, Tony Blair, David Cameron – thereby further revealing arguments and clashes between ministers in their respective governments.

Individual ministerial responsibility

Individual ministerial responsibility

the convention that ministers are responsible to Parliament for the policy of their department, the actions of officials working within it, and for their own personal conduct.

According to the convention of **individual ministerial responsibility**, ministers are accountable to Parliament for the policies they pursue, for their own conduct, and for the conduct of civil servants within their departments. They must answer questions about the policy and activities of their departments on the floor of the House and in select committees. The *Ministerial Code* states that ministers have a duty to give Parliament 'as full information as possible' and 'not to deceive or mislead parliament and the public'. Ministers are also expected to follow the seven principles of public life set out by the Committee on Standards in Public Life in 1995: selflessness, integrity, objectivity, accountability, openness, honesty, and leadership. But the convention of individual ministerial responsibility is imprecise, resulting in a lack of constitutional clarity about the circumstances when ministers should resign. Ministerial resignations may result from a range of circumstances including health worries, a desire for a less stressful lifestyle, or the chance of a more lucrative career (though these may conceal political reasons for leaving). Resignations on the grounds of individual ministerial responsibility fall into four main categories, although, in practice, these often overlap (see Table 7.5):

- mistakes made within the department;
- policy failure;
- political and media pressure; and
- personal misconduct.

TABLE 7.5 Ministerial resignations: individual ministerial responsibility (examples)

Date	Minister	Post	Reason for resignation
1963	John Profumo	Minister of War	Misled Parliament about sexual relationship with 'call-girl'
1972	Reginald Maudling	Home Secretary	Financial misconduct
1982	Lord Carrington (and two others)	Foreign Secretary	Misjudgements made before the Argentine invasion of the Falkland Islands
1983	Cecil Parkinson	Secretary of State for Trade and Industry	Extra-marital affair/mistress pregnant
1986	Leon Brittan	Secretary of State for Trade and Industry	Authorised leak of confidential letter about Westland affair
1992	David Mellor	Secretary of State for National Heritage	Financial dealings and extra-marital affair
1998	Ron Davies	Secretary of State for Wales	Allegations about personal conduct
1998	Peter Mandelson	Secretary of State for Trade and Industry	Failed to disclose loan
2001	Peter Mandelson	Secretary of State for Northern Ireland	Allegations of abuse of office
2002	Stephen Byers	Secretary of State for Transport	Policy problems and misled Parliament on departmental management
2002	Estelle Morris	Secretary of State for Education and Skills	Policy problems and self-criticism
2004	David Blunkett	Home Secretary	Allegations of abuse of office
2005	David Blunkett	Secretary of State for Work and Pensions	Failed to consult committee on private sector job
2008	Peter Hain	Secretary of State for Work and Pensions, Secretary of State for Wales	Police investigation into donations to his Labour Party deputy leadership campaign
2010	David Laws	Chief Secretary to the Treasury	Expenses scandal
2011	Liam Fox	Secretary of State for Defence	Activities of special advisor
2012	Chris Huhne	Secretary of State for Energy and Climate Change	Criminal charges
2014	Maria Miller	Secretary of State for Culture, Media and Sport	Expenses scandal, compounded by inadequate apology to Parliament
2017	Michael Fallon	Secretary of State for Defence	Allegations of historically inappropriate sexual conduct
2017	Priti Patel	Secretary of State for International Development	Unauthorised secret meetings with Israeli politicians and senior officials
2017	Damian Green	Minister for the Cabinet Office	Pornography on office computer
2018	Amber Rudd	Home Secretary	Misled Parliament over deportation of immigrants
2019	Gavin Williamson	Secretary of State for Defence	Leaked highly sensitive classified information

The textbook example of a minister resigning because of mistakes made by civil servants is more than 60 years old. Agriculture minister Sir Thomas Dugdale resigned in 1954 ostensibly over mistakes made by civil servants regarding the compulsory purchase of land in the Crichel Down case. But he did not fall on his sword without political pressure being applied. One might say Sir Thomas resigned in accordance with a convention which is conventionally disregarded. The norm is that ministers are not obliged to resign if misjudgements can be traced to the actions (or inaction) of civil servants rather than to ministers directly. In cases such as the sale of arms to Sierra Leone (1998–99), official inquiries pointed to errors by officials and thus allowed ministers to deny direct responsibility. The BSE inquiry was critical of ministers and civil servants, but those ministers accused of misleading the public had left office long before the official verdict was disclosed in the Phillips Report of 2000.

Confusion over the respective responsibility of ministers and civil servants was apparent in the controversy provoked by the 1996 Scott Report on the sale of arms to Iraq by British companies in the late 1980s. It found that ministers (assisted by civil servants) had misled Parliament by concealing a change in government policy on arms sales. Despite the criticism, no minister resigned. Instead, the government took refuge in the verbal formula that ministers were only culpable if they 'knowingly' misled Parliament. They could not be held accountable for operational decisions taken by officials without ministerial knowledge.

The 1988 creation of Next Steps agencies which deliver public services, but have an arms-length relationship with their Whitehall departments, has further muddied the waters of responsibility (see Chapter 10). Following a series of prison escapes, Home Secretary Michael Howard sacked Derek Lewis, the Chief Executive of the Prison Service in 1995. Howard was ultimately responsible for policy but pinned the blame on Lewis, who was in charge of the day-to-day operational management of prisons. Apart from the question of whether or not Howard had issued direct instructions to Lewis, it was also difficult to say that a Director of Prisons could really be held 'responsible' for decisions taken within a context (e.g. of financial resources made available to the Prison Service) established by ministers. It is worth noting that the distinction between operational and policy issues is not new: in the days before Next Steps agencies, Northern Ireland Secretary James Prior did not resign after a mass escape from the Maze prison in 1983.

A classic example of ministerial resignation in response to policy failure occurred when Foreign Secretary Lord Carrington and two junior ministers resigned following the Argentine invasion of the Falkland Islands in 1982. Yet Defence Secretary John Nott remained in office, and Mrs Thatcher herself had played a key role in the events which led to war because of her insistence on defence cuts which affected the security of the Falklands. Inconsistency is also apparent in the cases of two Chancellors, James Callaghan and Norman Lamont. Callaghan resigned after the devaluation of sterling in 1967, but Lamont initially survived sterling's exit from the ERM in 1992 (allegedly because Prime Minister John Major was at least equally responsible for the policy failure). Resignations on these grounds are actually the exception rather than the norm. Home Secretary Charles Clarke refused to resign in April 2006 when it became clear that the Home Office had failed to deport – or record the location of – foreign nationals who had been released after serving prison sentences. Clarke accepted responsibility but, contrary to the convention of individual ministerial responsibility, argued that he should remain in post so that he could rectify mistakes. Blair initially supported Clarke's reasoning but subsequently sacked him in a cabinet reshuffle a few weeks later.

Ministerial resignations often arise from cumulative pressure rather than a single incidence of failure. The prime minister, House of Commons, political party, or media can all apply pressure on ministers they perceive to be underperforming. The resignations of Stephen Byers and Estelle Morris in 2002 fall into this category. Byers endured failures in the transport system, disputes between advisers and civil servants in the Department for Transport, Local Government and the Regions (DTLR) – on which matter he gave an 'incorrect understanding' to the Commons – and a hostile press. Morris claimed that she resigned because she felt she was not up to the job of Secretary of State for Education (she later took a post in higher education but returned to government as a junior minister in 2005). Many commentators praised her honesty, but Morris had earlier made a public pledge to resign if government targets on literacy and numeracy were not met.

Personal misconduct has triggered the downfall of numerous ministers since the 1990s, and is now the most common reason for resignations, rather than responsibility for policy failures. Allegations of financial 'sleaze' or abuse of office often end with a resignation. Neil Hamilton and Tim Smith resigned in 1994 when the 'cash for questions' (in Parliament) scandal erupted. Peter Mandelson was twice obliged to leave the Blair cabinet: first when details of an undisclosed loan emerged (1998), and then when it was suggested that he misused his position by speaking to the immigration minister about obtaining British citizenship for an Indian businessman (2001). A subsequent inquiry on the latter affair exonerated Mandelson, but the case illustrated that a minister is normally doomed from the moment that the prime minister considers media publicity to have become too damaging. David Blunkett also resigned from the cabinet twice, in 2004 and 2006, having fallen foul of the *Ministerial Code*. In the 2010–15 coalition government, the Liberal Democrats' David Laws resigned as Chief Secretary to the Treasury, just a couple of weeks after his appointment, when it was revealed that he had claimed expenses to pay rent to his partner, while his party colleague, Christopher Huhne, resigned as Secretary of State for Energy and Climate Change, in 2012, when he was alleged to have avoided a speeding fine (and possible driving ban due to accumulated points) by allowing his (then) wife to claim that it was she who had been driving and broken the speed limit; in effect, they were both accused of perverting the course of justice and subsequently received short prison sentences. Incidentally, the Director of Public Prosecutions at the time was a barrister called Keir Starmer.

In today's more liberal and tolerant social climate, sex scandals do not automatically trigger resignation. During Blair's premiership, Robin Cook and John Prescott remained in the cabinet when their extra-marital affairs were exposed, although their political standing was undoubtedly reduced. In the case of David Laws mentioned earlier, the scandal was his inappropriate claim for expenses to cover rent, not the fact that the money was actually paid to his (up until then) secret boyfriend. A minister's chances of surviving a personal scandal depend upon three factors: the actual nature or seriousness of their misdemeanour; the prime minister's view of whether the minister made serious errors of judgement, although support from the top is rarely enough to save ministers if media interest is prolonged; and the degree of support (or hostility) among their backbench colleagues.

Ministers and departments

The British government contains more than 100 ministers. Senior ministers hold the rank of Secretary of State, sit in the cabinet and head government departments, while below them in the hierarchy come ministers of state, then parliamentary undersecretaries, who cover specific areas of their departmental remits. The last two categories are also referred to as junior ministers. Secretaries of State generally perform a number of roles, the most significant of which is strategic leadership and policy supervision in their department, but some ministers (e.g. Michael Howard and David Blunkett at the Home Office, somewhat more recently Michael Gove at Education, and Iain Duncan Smith at Work and Pensions) have clear agendas and push through major reform programmes. However, few ministers have the time or specialist knowledge to play a hands-on role across their policy brief, so tend to concentrate on policy initiation and selection, and strategic direction, but often delegate to their junior ministers to deal with the nitty-gritty and administrative or technical details. Ministers also act as departmental representatives in the cabinet,

Parliament, and in international meetings. Prior to January 2020, they would also regularly have attended meetings with their counterparts in the Council of the European Union (formerly known as the Council of Ministers).

Government departments are the primary administrative units of central government. They are chiefly located in the Whitehall area of London – hence the usage of the term 'Whitehall' as a shorthand to describe the core executive – but in the last decade or so, a few departments have created 'satellite' offices and 'hubs' in other parts of Britain, with some of their civil servants relocating too. In March 2020, the government announced that it intended to move 22,000 civil servants out of London by 2030. Departments are organised according to function (i.e. the policy area they are responsible for, such as health or transport) or the sections of society they serve (e.g. those receiving social security benefits). The work of some departments (e.g. the Ministry of Defence) covers the whole of the UK, but some (e.g. the Department for Work and Pensions) cover England, Scotland, and Wales, but not Northern Ireland, and as the process of devolution progresses, the scope of Whitehall departments will shrink. On matters already devolved to the Scottish Parliament, central government departments are responsible for England and Wales only. The functions of government departments include providing policy advice to ministers, policy implementation – which is often delegated to the sundry 'agencies' acting under the auspices of the department – managing public spending, and fostering relations with interested parties such as pressure groups, for example, DEFRA and the National Farmers Union. Whitehall departments also oversee the provision of public services, although again, responsibility for much day-to-day policy delivery has been transferred to semi-autonomous executive agencies (see Chapter 10).

Governments often restructure departments and reallocate responsibilities to reflect their priorities or the preferences of senior ministers. Responsibility for transport was subsumed within the Department for the Environment, Transport and the Regions in 1997 to reflect the policy interests of John Prescott. It was then shifted to a Department of Transport, Local Government and the Regions in 2001, before becoming a separate department in 2002 (see Table 7.2). The reorganisation of the Home Office in 2007 was particularly significant: responsibility for civil law, criminal law, and prisons was transferred to a new Ministry of Justice, leaving the Home Office to focus on national security and counterterrorism. The following year saw the creation of Department of Energy and Climate Change, in response to growing recognition of the scale of global warming. This then became the Department for Business, Energy & Industrial Strategy in 2016 (perhaps reflecting the lower priority ascribed to, or scepticism about, climate change among some Conservatives). Also established in 2016, following the referendum vote to leave the EU, was the Department for Exiting the European Union, which was then dissolved on 31 January 2020, the day that the UK formally left the EU. Meanwhile, in 2018, the Department of Health was expanded to become the Department of Health and Social Care.

The Treasury is undoubtedly the most important department in Whitehall. It controls public spending, and other departments need its approval to undertake major new financial commitments. Under the Comprehensive Spending Review, the Treasury sets firm spending limits for each government department over a cycle of several years. As Chancellor, Gordon Brown used this power to mould policy development in high-spending policy areas such as education, health, and welfare reform. In the 2010–15 coalition government, Chancellor George Osborne was the key driver of austerity, using his annual budgets to impose repeated cuts in public spending and welfare provision. Not surprisingly, therefore, the rapport and trust between the chancellor and the prime minister is usually the most important relationship in a government; if they fall-out or disagree, the whole government can be destabilised.

The civil service

Civil Servant

an official employed in a civil capacity by the Crown, usually to advise on, or/ and administer or implement ('deliver') government policies and public services.

Government departments are staffed by **civil servants**, career administrators who are responsible to the Crown. The number of full-time civil servants was reduced from 732,000 in 1979 to below half a million in the mid-1990s, before rising to 554,000 in 2004. Following the Gershon Report on civil service efficiency, the Blair government announced plans to cut some 80,000 jobs and redeploy others outside London. By 2011, the number of civil servants had reportedly fallen to 471,000, and by 2014, under the coalition government's Civil Service Reform Plan, the tally was down to little more than 400,000. By the end of 2019, though, the total had crept back up to 421,000. The civil service is structured along hierarchical lines in which posts range from junior positions (e.g. clerks) to those in the senior civil service, which employed about 4,800 in 2014, ironically, an increase since the advent of the cost-cutting coalition.

The civil service has traditionally operated according to four principles: impartiality, anonymity, permanence, and meritocracy. As civil servants serve the Crown, rather than the government of the day, they are expected to be politically impartial. Anonymity means that individual civil servants should not be identified as the authors of advice to ministers. All civil servants must sign the Official Secrets Act and keep government information secret, although civil servants may be called before parliamentary select committees where, under the 'Osmotherly rules' drawn up by a civil servant in 1980 and subsequently updated, they give evidence 'on behalf of ministers and under their directions'. Permanence means that civil servants stay in their posts when there is a change of government, in contrast to the politicised system in the USA.

The British civil service is unusual in that senior officials are not political appointments, but are recruited on merit. Government departments have traditionally been staffed not by experts (in, say, law or economics) but by 'generalists'. Recruitment through competitive examinations and interviews was established by the 1854 Northcote–Trevelyan Report, and it remained virtually constant for almost 150 years. Two important changes have occurred in the last three decades. First, more outsiders have been recruited from the private sector: many chief executives of Next Steps agencies were brought in from private companies rather than promoted from within. A drive to recruit people with specialist skills and experience in finance, IT, communications, and policy has been launched. Second, efforts have been made to increase diversity in the senior civil service. Into the 1980s, senior ranks were largely made up of white, middle-class men who had a public school and Oxbridge education. By 2014, women made up about two-fifths of the senior civil service and ethnic minorities 7 per cent, which represented significant improvements even if there was obvious scope for further change.

The traditional principles of the civil service have come under strain in recent years as concern has grown that it is being politicised and its neutrality undermined – particularly when the same government is repeatedly re-elected in accordance with a dominant party system (see Chapter 14). There are sometimes suggestions that senior civil servants who are viewed as out-of-sympathy with government policy or specific ministers have fared less well in promotions than those perceived to be more amenable or enthusiastic. Given the greater emphasis on policy presentation, ministers expect civil servants to publicise policy achievements. The boundary between legitimate civil service work and party political activity is not always clear, but such actions could be deemed as *justifying* rather than simply *reporting* policies which are often highly controversial. Civil service impartiality is more obviously threatened when civil servants are asked to undertake research on the opposition parties' policy proposals, to help ministers discredit them and thereby score partisan points.

Civil service anonymity has also been eroded. Sensitive information has, on occasion, been leaked by civil servants. In 1983, Foreign Office clerk Sarah Tisdall was jailed for six months for leaking information about the deployment of cruise missiles. A year later, however, a jury cleared Clive Ponting, a senior civil servant in the Ministry of Defence, of breaking the Official Secrets Act 1911 by revealing details of the 1982 sinking of the Argentine cruiser, the *General Belgrano*. David Shayler revealed information about MI5's covert activities in the late 1990s. He claimed to be acting in the public interest but was jailed for six months in 2002 for breaking the Official Secrets Act. Of greater significance is the willingness of ministers to allow civil servants to be named and identified as being responsible for mistakes or misjudgements. Chief executives of Next Steps agencies have faced tough questioning from parliamentary committees. The 2003 suicide of Dr David Kelly, an expert on Iraq's weapons of mass destruction at the Ministry of Defence, served as a tragic warning about the costs of apportioning blame. The Freedom of Information Act (2000) has also allowed the public release of confidential policy advice produced by civil servants. In 2008, a junior Home Office civil servant, Christopher Galley, was sacked for leaking documents relating to immigration to the Conservative spokesperson, Damian Green (who was arrested but released without charge).

The permanence of the civil service has been undermined by the hiving off of policy implementation responsibilities to executive agencies, with their own management and pay structures. As we will see in Chapter 10, new methods of management, market-testing, contracting-out, and recruitment from the private sector have eroded the traditional model of a unified, hierarchical civil service, in which officials have a guaranteed 'job for life' and a generous (gold-plated) pension in retirement.

Under the 2010 Constitutional Reform and Governance Act, the core values of the civil service – impartiality, integrity, honesty, and objectivity – were enshrined in law. The Civil Service Commission was also placed on a statutory footing, its role being to ensure that appointments to the civil service are made on merit following open competition. When originally devised, this legislation was intended to reinforce the distinction between the permanent machinery of the state and the party political government of the day. However, this key distinction has been eroded so much since 1979 that it was unlikely to be restored by the passage of a single law.

Special Adviser
a temporary political appointment made by a minister.

Special advisers

The prominence of **special advisers** has also impacted upon the role and status of civil servants. Their number increased from 38 under Major to 87 under Blair in 2004, of whom 29 worked for the prime minister compared to just three under Major. Brown reduced their numbers: a total of 68 worked across Whitehall, 18 of them at Number 10. According to figures released in October 2010, a similar number were employed by the coalition government; 18 worked in the Prime Minister's Office, and four assisted his Deputy (Nick Clegg). However, by 2014, the number had increased to a record 103, with some earning more than an MP's salary. There had been a further slight increase by the end of 2019, when there were 109 SPADs altogether, 44 of them directly working for Boris Johnson.

Special advisers are not career civil servants but are political appointments made by ministers. They fall into two main categories, policy advisers and media advisers (spin doctors). Special advisers are permitted to convey instructions and commission work from civil servants on behalf of their minister. Two special advisers in Blair's Number 10 – Chief of Staff Jonathan Powell and press officer (then Director of Communications) Alastair Campbell – were allowed to exercise managerial control over civil servants, although this understandably created tensions The Committee on Standards in Public Life (2000) conveniently concluded that the increased influence of special advisers was not endangering civil service impartiality, although it did recommend a new Code of Conduct, and a limit on numbers. Similarly, a 2001 investigation by the House of Commons' Public Administration Select Committee argued that special advisers need not threaten the civil service, but did recommend improved accountability and clarity over funding. Both committees pressed for a Civil Service Act to set out the constitutional framework within which the civil service operates. A Civil Service Code setting out the duties of civil servants had been enacted in 1996, but critics believed that it did not spell out fully the relationship between ministers and civil servants (including SPADS). Eventually, in 2010, the Constitutional Reform and Governance Act provided clarification of the role of special advisers, confirming that they are political appointees and not subject to the requirements of impartiality and objectivity. However, SPADs continued to arouse controversy, and so, also in 2010, the Cabinet Office issued its own guidance about the precise roles of SPADs. These included:

- Reviewing papers going to the minister, and giving advice to him/her when s/he is taking part in party political activities.
- Checking facts and research findings from a party political viewpoint.
- Preparing speculative or 'blue skies thinking' policy papers which can generate long-term policy thinking within the department.
- Contributing to policy planning within the department, including ideas which extend the existing range of options available to the minister with a political viewpoint in mind.
- Liaising with the minister's party, both to explain the department's own approach to the governing party's MPs, but also to elicit the views of the government's backbenchers.
- Liaising with outside interest groups to elicit their advice or expertise.
- Speechwriting and related research, including adding party political content to non-political material prepared by permanent civil servants.
- Representing the views of their minister to the media, when they had been authorised by the minister to do so.
- Providing expert advice as a specialist in a particular field.
- Attending party functions and maintaining contact with party members.
- Taking part in policy reviews organised by the party or their minister.

In spite of such attempts at clarifying and codifying the role of SPADs, they have remained sometimes controversial figures, particularly those serving the prime minister. In 1989, Margaret Thatcher's refusal to sack her Economic Adviser, Sir Alan Walters, led to the resignation of her Chancellor Nigel Lawson (who claimed that Walters' comments and views were causing confusion about aspects of the government's economic policy, and undermining

PHOTO 7.1 Britain's Prime Minister Boris Johnson and Number 10 special adviser Dominic Cummings (© Tolga Akmen/AFP/Getty Images).

Lawson's own credibility). Meanwhile, the Conservatives' disastrous 2017 election campaign was partly attributed to the role of two of Theresa May's Special Advisers, Nick Timothy and Fiona Hill, who, some other Conservatives complained, had been granted too much influence, both over policy development in general and in drafting parts of the party's election manifesto in particular.

May's successor, Boris Johnson, also appointed a controversial figure as his most senior Special Advisers, Dominic Cummings. Having been viewed as the mastermind behind the Leave Campaign in the 2016 EU Referendum, and apparently coining the slogan 'Take Back Control', Cummings has attracted critical comments as Johnson's chief SPAD, both for the radicalism of some of his political views and policy proposals, and because of his alleged interference in the appointment and dismissal of other Ministers' SPADS (Photo 7.1).

In short, even some other senior Conservatives feared that Cummings had been granted too much influence and power and should be reined-in by Johnson: several years ago, David Cameron reportedly referred to Cummings as a 'career psychopath'. For his part, Cummings made no secret of his disdain for 'the Establishment' and the 'political class' in general, and 'conservative' civil servants in particular.

Civil servants and ministers

The civil service is active throughout the policymaking process, consulting with interested 'parties' (such as organised interests, professional bodies, other experts), formulating options, providing advice to ministers, drafting legislation, and overseeing policy implementation, or what is now called 'delivery'. Government departments often cultivate networks of contacts with interest groups within their policy field (see Chapter 19). The Department of Transport, for example, has lines of communication with producer, consumer, and promotional groups including the motor industry, multinational oil companies, road users' groups, local authorities, and the environmental movement. However, since the 1980s, some former 'policy communities' have been weakened or dismantled, because ministers considered the organised groups to be 'too conservative' or acting as self-serving 'producer interests', and thus an obstacle to the type of radical reforms the government wanted to enact, often in the name of boosting the interests of consumers and service users. For example, many of the NHS reforms of the last three decades have been imposed in spite of opposition from the medical profession. Indeed, the BMA has often found itself ignored and excluded from discussions over health policies, both because ministers already know what they want to achieve, and because they sometimes view the 'conservative' medical profession itself as part of the problem. Much the same can be said of successive education reforms since the late 1980s, with the teaching unions often deemed to be part of the problem, and so bypassed and denigrated, rather than treated as partners with governments and education ministers – as they were in the 1960s and 1970s, when there was much more active pursuit of consensus and dialogue in policymaking. Certainly, in the 2010–15 coalition government, the Education Secretary, Michael Gove, seemed to derive great pleasure and kudos from upsetting the teaching profession, and contemptuously referred to the so-called education establishment as 'the blob [bloated bureaucracy]'.

Civil servants in Whitehall provide ministers with policy advice – although, as we will see in Chapter 10, the vast majority of civil servants are involved in the delivery of services and now work in executive agencies. Only a few 100 or of the most senior civil servants are actually based in Whitehall and involved, on a daily basis, in policy advice and formulation. However, the 'Westminster model' perspective is that while civil servants advise, it is the ministers who decide and are accountable to Parliament for those decisions – individual ministerial responsibility. In practice, though, the relationship is less clear-cut, because ministers and civil servants all have resources. For example, their contacts with particular interest groups can imbue senior civil servants with greater expertise or specialist knowledge on a particular issue, and this might then be deployed to persuade an uncertain or newly appointed minister to choose a specific option, this being the preference of the civil servants themselves, even though the minister will formally have made the decision or policy choice – and will be constitutionally responsible for it.

Concerns that civil servants had too great an influence in the policy process were aired by critics from the Left and the Right in the 1970s and 1980s. On the Left, Tony Benn's diaries revealed his fears that his socialist agenda was obstructed by the institutional 'conservatism' of the civil service. The Right complained that civil servants were maximising their own resources rather than promoting efficiency and enterprise, and were too 'conservative', favouring a cosy consensus which avoided tough decisions or challenging 'vested interests'. The BBC comedy *Yes Minister* – which Thatcher apparently watched avidly – memorably depicted the power struggle between Whitehall mandarin Sir Humphrey Appleby and the minister James Hacker, whose proposals the former sought to frustrate (unless they happened to coincide with civil service interests). Since the mid-1990, the balance has shifted in favour of ministers, as demonstrated by another BBC comedy series, *The Thick of It*, which shows how special advisers, appointed by ministers, provide an alternative source of policy advice to departmental civil servants. The civil service has also been fragmented by the creation of executive agencies, and its culture has been changed by the introduction of new managerial techniques. Senior civil servants now spend somewhat less time on frontline policymaking and more on departmental management and policy delivery.

Some government departments develop a strong ethos that informs the policy advice presented to ministers. The FCO has traditionally displayed a pro-European outlook that Thatcher in particular disparaged. By contrast, the Treasury appeared institutionally sceptical about British membership of the European single currency. It had supported ERM membership in the late 1980s, but Treasury documents released in 2005, assessing sterling's exit on Black Wednesday in September 1992, revealed doubts about fixed exchange rates and criticism of the actions of politicians. Ministers may find it difficult to force through changes in policy that run against the grain of thinking in their departments, but successive Conservative ministers managed to overturn the interventionist ethos of the old Department of Trade and Industry and instil a *laissez-faire* outlook reflected in the name of its successor – Business, Innovation and Skills. The Department of Transport, meanwhile, has long been suspected of having an institutional bias in favour of private transport and car drivers, at the expense of public transport users and rail commuters.

The role of the civil service in the implementation stage of the policymaking process has also changed. Since the mid-1980s, much of its policy implementation role has been transferred from Whitehall to semi-autonomous Next Steps agencies, often operating in accordance with a 'business model' to promote efficiency, cost-effectiveness, and value-for-money. Government departments oversee the policy delivery records of these bodies, but usually leave the day-to-day administration to them. However, this can create further problems of accountability, because if a policy fails, there are likely to be arguments between ministers and agency chiefs over who is to blame: ministers are likely to argue that the policy was clear and coherent, and was therefore implemented ('delivered') incompetently by the relevant agency, whereas the agency chiefs are likely to insist that they acted properly and in good faith, but were compelled to implement a policy which was doomed to fail, either due to its poor design or because the agency (or the policy itself) had not been given adequate resources by the minister(s).

Conclusion and summary

Two countervailing trends are apparent in the contemporary core executive: centralisation and fragmentation. Resources have been further concentrated at Number 10, thereby increasing the potential for prime ministerial predominance. Blair's quest for a 'strong centre' saw the Prime Minister's Office strengthened and Number 10's role in policymaking and delivery extended, through bilateral meetings with ministers and the creation of new units within the Cabinet Office concerned with strategy and delivery. Cabinet plays only a limited role in detailed decision-making; many decisions are reached in informal meetings of an inner circle of ministers and advisers.

The strengthening of the centre has bolstered the support available to the prime minister despite the absence of a formal prime minister's department. But the neglect of formal mechanisms for decision-making, the influence of special advisers, and an excessive focus on government communications under Blair, raised concerns about the health of British democracy. Brown promised a more collegiate approach, but soon reinforced the Prime Minister's Office. As the Butler Report implied, one need not hold an idealised view of collective government to have concerns about the absence of checks and balances at the centre. A culture in which a coterie of advisers and ministers tell a prime minister what they think he or she wants to hear is not conducive to good government. These lessons cannot have been lost on Brown's successor David Cameron, and he seems to have been conscious of them since becoming prime minister in 2010. After an initial period where his 'Big Society' idea seemed to be winning undue attention from institutions which are supposed to work on behalf of the government as a whole, a more judicious balance was struck. Nevertheless, underlying questions about civil service impartiality are as pertinent as ever – indeed, possibly even more so, since the days of the fictional Sir Humphrey Appleby of *Yes, Minister* seem increasingly distant (tellingly, in 2013, an attempt to update the show proved unsuccessful).

The second trend evident in the core executive is fragmentation. Blair may have appeared a more dominant prime minister than many of his predecessors, but (often to his chagrin) he allowed Chancellor Gordon Brown to set the agenda in economic and social policy, as well as extending Treasury control of departmental spending. Policy competences have been transferred away from the core executive to bodies such as the Scottish Parliament, Welsh Assembly, and (prior to 2020) the European Union. Interest rates were a prominent concern of Thatcher and her chancellors, but these are now determined by the Bank of England's Monetary Policy Committee. The Cameron coalition established an OBR to provide key economic statistics and forecasts. As Chapter 10 will examine, the fragmentation of the civil service and the emergence of new forms of governance weakened the centre's capacity to dictate policy. The Cabinet Office's remit on 'joined-up government' only partially addressed this. The same chapter will also explore the impact of globalisation. A prime minister in the early twenty-first century enjoys greater resources within the core executive; but his/her predecessor 100 years before took decisions that impacted upon the lives of hundreds of millions of people living within the global boundaries of the British Empire. Definitive verdicts on where power lies within the core executive are thus elusive.

The resources available to the prime minister are undoubtedly extensive, but they vary over time, according to the institutional practices prevalent within the core executive, the leadership style of the prime minister, and the wider political environment.

Further reading

The prime minister has attracted a huge volume of scholarly literature in recent years. D. Richards, 'Changing Patterns of Executive Governance', in R. Heffernan, P. Cowley, and C. Hay (eds.), *Developments in British Politics* 9 (Basingstoke: Palgrave Macmillan, 2011), pp. 29–50, is a very convenient summary of recent developments. M. Smith, *The Core Executive* (Basingstoke: Palgrave, 1999); M. Smith, 'Prime Minister and Cabinet', in J. Fisher, D. Denver, and J. Benyon (eds.), *Central Debates in British Politics* (Harlow: Longman, 2003), and R. Rhodes and P. Dunleavy (eds.), *Prime Minister, Cabinet & Core Executive* (Basingstoke: Palgrave, 1995), introduce the core executive model. R. Heffernan's 'Prime Ministerial Predominance? Core Executive Politics in the UK', *British Journal of Politics and International Relations*, Vol. 5, No. 3 (2003), pp. 347–72, is also worth consulting. For more recent publications, see P. Dorey, 'The Core Executive', in M. Garnett (ed.), *The Routledge Handbook of British Politics and Society* (London: Routledge, 2020). The 'British Presidency' thesis is developed in M. Foley, *The British Presidency* (Manchester: Manchester University Press, 2000), and M. Foley, 'The Presidential Dynamics of Leadership Decline in Contemporary British Politics: The Illustrative Case of Tony Blair', *Contemporary Politics*, Vol. 14, No. 1 (2008), pp. 53–69. R. Heffernan, 'Why the Prime Minister cannot be a President: Comparing Institutional Imperatives in Britain and America', *Parliamentary Affairs*, Vol. 58, No. 1 (2005), pp. 53–70, offers a critique. D. Kavanagh and A. Seldon's *The Powers Behind the Prime Minister* (London: Harper Collins, 2001) and M. Burch and I. Holliday's 'The Prime Minister's and Cabinet Offices: An Executive Office in all but Name', *Parliamentary Affairs*, Vol. 52, No. 1 (1999), pp. 32–45, examine the Downing Street support network.

On Blair as prime minister, see D. Kavanagh, 'The Blair Premiership' and P. Fawcett and R. Rhodes, 'Central Government', both in A. Seldon (ed.), *The Blair Years, 1997–2007* (Cambridge: Cambridge University Press, 2007), M. Burch and I. Holliday, 'The Blair Government and the Core Executive', *Government and Opposition*, Vol. 39, No. 1 (2004), pp. 1–21, and P. Hennessy, 'Rulers and Servants of the State: The Blair Style of Government 1997–2004', *Parliamentary Affairs*, Vol. 58, No. 1 (2005), pp. 6–16. A. Seldon's, *Blair* (London: Free Press, 2005) and *Blair Unbound* (Pocket Books, 2007), are the most detailed biographies. Alastair Campbell's diaries, starting with the heavily edited *The Blair Years* (London: Arrow Books, 2008), provide an insider account of life at Number 10 by a key Blair ally. R. Cook, *The Point of Departure* (London: Pocket Books, 2004), is the best of the memoirs produced by cabinet ministers who served under Blair. On David Cameron's premiership, see A. Selden and P. Snowdon (eds.), *Cameron at 10: The Verdict* (London: William Collins, 2016), and on Theresa May's premiership, see A. Seldon, *May at 10* (London: Biteback, 2019).

The coalition's record is examined in P. Dorey and M. Garnett, *The British Coalition Government, 2010– 2015: A Marriage of Inconvenience* (Basingstoke: Palgrave Macmillan, 2016),

A. Seldon, 'David Cameron as Prime Minister, 2010–2015: The Verdict of History', and P. Riddell, 'The Coalition and the Executive', both in A. Seldon and M. Finn (eds.), *The Coalition Effect 2010–2015* (Cambridge: Cambridge University Press, 2015), pp. 1–30 and 113–35.

Introductory texts on the Cabinet include S. James, *British Cabinet Government* (Abingdon: Routledge, 1999), and M. Burch and I. Holliday, *The British Cabinet System* (London: Harvester Wheatsheaf, 1995). The role of ministers is explored in D. Marsh et al., 'Reassessing the Role of Departmental Cabinet Ministers', *Public Administration*, Vol. 78, No. 2 (2000), pp. 305–26, and V. Bogdanor, 'Ministerial Accountability', *Parliamentary Affairs*, Vol. 50, No. 1 (1997), pp. 71–83. On government departments, see D. Kavanagh and D. Richards, 'Departmentalism and Joined-up Government', *Parliamentary Affairs*, Vol. 54, No. 1 (2001), pp. 1–18. P. Hennessy, *Whitehall* (London: Pimlico, 2001) is still the best study of the civil service. M. Stanley, *How to Be a Civil Servant* (London: Methuen, 2004), provides an insider guide to the role. On civil service reform, see R. Rhodes, 'New Labour's Civil Service: Summing-up Joining-up', *Political Quarterly*, Vol. 71, No. 2 (2000), pp. 151–66, V. Bogdanor, 'Civil Service Reform: A Critique', *Political Quarterly*, Vol. 72, No. 3 (2001), pp. 291–99, and R. Pyper and J. Burnham, 'The British Civil Service: Perspectives on "Decline" and "Modernisation"', *British Journal of Politics and International Relations*, Vol. 13, No. 2 (2011), pp. 189–205.

Websites

The 10 Downing Street website (www.number-10.gov.uk) provides transcripts of the prime minister's speeches and of daily press briefings but includes little on the Prime Minister's Office. The Cabinet Office website (www.cabinet-office.gov.uk) has detailed information on the *Ministerial Code*, cabinet committees, and the civil service. The www.direct.gov.uk site was set up as part of the e-government strategy and includes an A–Z of central government with links. On the civil service, the Cabinet Office site (www.civil service.gov.uk) and the companion site to Martin Stanley's book *How to be a Civil Servant* (www.civilservant.org.uk) cover the organisation and its reform.

Chapter 8

Parliament

Learning outcomes

After reading this chapter, you will:

- be able to summarise the main functions of the House of Commons and the House of Lords;
- understand the effect of the 'fusion' between executive and legislature in the UK;
- understand some of the reasons for public dissatisfaction with Westminster politics; and
- be able to evaluate some recent changes to parliamentary procedures, and understand why reform has been so sporadic or hesitant.

Introduction

For most democratic theorists, the nature and status of the legislative body in any political system is a primary consideration. While the executive and judicial branches of government play crucial roles in their respective spheres, the legislature is the *creative* element of any constitution. It is essential in a representative democracy that the law-making body should broadly reflect public opinion, and that its members should be directly accountable to voters in case they fail to discharge this function in a satisfactory manner.

The British Houses of Parliament, based in the Palace of Westminster, are among the best-known symbols of democratic government in the world. However, this familiarity reflects the relative longevity of representative British institutions, and the nation's former position at the centre of a worldwide empire, rather than the success of today's Parliament as a legislature. It can be argued, indeed, that the prominence of Westminster as a political icon has become an *obstacle* to a realistic understanding of the legislature within the uncodified British constitution. From the viewpoint of liberal democracy, the House of Commons is at best a curious anomaly; at worst, critics portray it as a travesty of constitutional principle, a mere rubber stamp for decisions taken by the executive. The so-called 'upper chamber', the House of Lords, is even more of an oddity in a liberal or representative democracy, because despite relatively recent reforms, its members are still not accountable to the British people through elections.

Few observers today would argue that the UK Parliament is working well, when judged against the expected functions of a healthy legislature. Complaints about Parliament are nothing new (they have been heard since at least the late nineteenth century), and this leads some commentators to take refuge in the thought that the problem lies in unrealistic expectations among pundits or the public, rather than in the institution itself. However, the long series of complaints can also be taken at face value – that is, that Parliament has been undergoing a continuous decline since the mid-nineteenth century, and that each generation of parliamentarians *is* less satisfactory than its predecessor. Certainly, we have reached a point when many critics speak of a crisis of democratic institutions, exemplified in the 2009 expenses scandal, the downward trend in electoral turnout (59 per cent in 2001), and culminating in the problems faced by Parliament in achieving agreement on the details and terms of the UK's departure from the EU – although these difficulties could also be interpreted as evidence of Parliament seeking to 'take back control' from the Executive. Nonetheless, while almost every aspect of public life in Britain has been subjected to radical change in recent years, the House of Commons has been subject to only relatively minor procedural reforms, while the House of Lords still remains unelected, and thus unaccountable to the British public.

Before we discuss the six main functions of Parliament, it is necessary to outline its structure, in terms of the key 'actors': the government, the Opposition, the frontbenches, the backbenches, the party whips, and the Speaker.

The government

The party which wins a majority of the 650 seats in the House of Commons in a general election becomes the government. However, on a few occasions, no party wins such a majority, namely 326 seats, in which case, there are usually three options:

a) The party with the largest number of seats forms a minority government, although the viability of doing so depends very much on how many seats short of an overall majority it is; two seats short makes this option viable, whereas 20 seats short renders it highly unlikely. When a party decides to form a minority government, it will be expecting to attract support from one (or more) of the other parties on key votes, in order to ensure a majority on that occasion. Of course, this might mean a need to engage in almost constant bargaining with a small party (or parties) before each important vote in the House of Commons, and an obligation to offer concessions as the price of obtaining such support. The inconclusive general election in February 1974 led to a minority Labour government, but this called another election in October that year, in order to obtain an overall parliamentary majority, albeit a very narrow one on this occasion.

b) The party with the largest number of seats enters into a formal agreement or 'parliamentary pact' with one the smaller parties, whereby the other party will be consulted over policy proposals and legislation and be granted opportunities to suggest policies of its own, in return for supporting (voting with) the largest party in key votes in the House of Commons. Such support will ensure that – provided all of the largest party's own MPs also support it – in each parliamentary vote, a majority will be obtained to enact the 'government's' policies and legislation. This arrangement is often referred to as 'confidence and supply'. After failing to win an overall majority in the 2017 general election, Theresa May's Conservative Party entered into such a pact with Northern Ireland's DUP: the Conservatives' 318 MPs and the DUP's 10 MPs meant that, combined, they would have 328 MPs, sufficient to deliver a very small parliamentary majority in key votes – assuming, of course, that every MP in the two parties actually voted in support of a policy or legislation. Prior to this, the last 'parliamentary pact' had been formed back in March 1977, between the Labour government (which had lost its wafer-thin parliamentary majority due to by-election defeats, and also a few of its MPs 'defecting' to other parties) and the Liberal

Party, the latter having 13 MPs. A 'parliamentary pact' or 'confidence and supply' agreement is not a coalition government, because the minor party is not allocated any ministerial posts; the partnership is solely at parliamentary, not executive, level.

c) The largest party forms a coalition government with one (or more) of the small parties. This means that the small party is offered ministerial posts, including seats in the cabinet, and directly shares power with the largest party at executive level; they govern Britain together and jointly develop laws and policies. However, this does not mean the two (or more) parties in the coalition are equal in strength; the largest party will invariably have a majority of cabinet and other ministerial posts, which also means that more of its manifesto pledges and other policy proposals are likely to be enacted, albeit with the approval or acquiescence of the other party/parties. The latter will also be entitled to enact some of their own policies. Britain had a coalition government from 2010 to 2015, after the inconclusive 2010 general election led to the Conservative Party and the Liberal Democrats agreeing to govern together, although the Liberal Democrats, as the smaller party, were allocated just five cabinet posts. Moreover, Conservatives occupied the most senior departmental portfolios and cabinet seats, such as Defence, Education, Foreign Office, Health, Home Office, and the Treasury. The Liberal Democrats were clearly the junior partner in the coalition government, but understandably reasoned that half a loaf was much better than no loaf.

As the government usually occupies a majority of the seats in the House of Commons, it is constitutionally in a very strong position. Provided that its MPs remain loyal in parliamentary votes (known as 'Divisions'), it can normally enact almost any policy or legislation it wishes, although it cannot pass a law which would directly 'bind' (restrict) its successor – the next government. A wise government will also recognise that if it abuses the power granted by its parliamentary majority, by attempting to enact extreme laws or other deeply unpopular policies, then, in the short-term, it will provoke clashes with the House of Lords (discussed later) and, in the longer-term, alienate swathes of voters, and thus risk losing the next general election. This risk, of course, is greatly increased by the existence of a credible and united Opposition, one which is widely viewed as a government-in-waiting. In the absence of such an Opposition, the government might become arrogant or complacent, and more inclined to enact reckless legislation. In such circumstances, there is the risk that a government might become more authoritarian and contemptuous of all criticism, of its political opponents, and maybe of the rights or liberties of social minorities.

The other main way in which the government enjoys considerable power in the House of Commons is its control of most of the parliamentary timetable. The government can also shape the news agenda to its own advantage by choosing the best moment to publicise its concrete achievements, and by the same token, it can, and often does, 'bury bad news' by releasing politically damaging or embarrassing information when the media's attention is focused elsewhere.

The Opposition

The second largest party in the House of Commons is known as the official, or Her Majesty's, 'Opposition'. Its leader is paid an additional salary from public funds in recognition of the fact that democracy can only thrive when there is a potential alternative government in existence. The very architecture of the House of Commons is 'adversarial', with the government and the Opposition directly facing each other, and often adopting different stances on key policy issues.

Indeed, one of the most familiar clichés in British politics is that the Opposition has 'a duty to oppose', although, in normal circumstances, this opposition is certain to end in failure, because the government's parliamentary majority means that it can ignore, and outvote, alternative views and counterproposals from the Opposition. Consequently, when the government enjoys a secure majority, the Opposition tends to endure several years of frustration, because its criticisms of the government, and suggestions for different policies, will largely be ignored. Yet, hope springs eternal, because of the prospect either of damaging splits within the government ranks, a major scandal or sudden crisis, and/or plummeting opinion poll ratings which imply the likelihood of the government's defeat at the next general election. There will also be the occasional by-election victory to provide concrete evidence of an upsurge in support for the Opposition party.

The frontbenches

In both main parties, the frontbench refers to the most senior figures in the party, who sit directly facing each other, on the benches in the House of Commons nearest to the 'Despatch Box' (see Photo 8.1). During major debates and at Prime Minister's Question Time, the government frontbench is occupied by cabinet ministers, and is intended to provide a formidable public display of party unity and political strength, as well as signifying their support for, and solidarity with, their leader and prime minister. On other occasions, such as Ministers' Question Time (see later), or when speaking in support of a bill, the main occupants of the frontbench are the relevant cabinet minister and his/her junior ministers in their department (see Chapter 7). The Opposition frontbench is comprised of the 'shadow' ministers, so called because they 'shadow' the relevant minister(s), and act as the Opposition's spokespersons for that area of policy. When the Opposition party wins a general election, most of its 'shadow' ministers will almost automatically become the government's frontbench.

The backbenches

Behind the frontbenchers (government *and* Opposition), logically enough, sit the 'backbenchers', who occupy several rows of green seats on both sides of the House of Commons chamber. When the chamber is full, it reinforces the common image of the House comprising the massed ranks of two 'armies' facing each other ready to do battle. It is the government's backbenchers who are

PHOTO 8.1 House of Commons main chamber (©UK Parliament/Jessica Taylor. creativecommons.org/licenses/by/3.0/).

crucial to its ability to secure the passage of its legislation in the House of Commons, because if they all vote for their government and its bills, then each bill will be approved and become law (assuming that it also proceeds successfully through the House of Lords, which we discuss later). However, if enough of a government's backbench MPs vote against it (or abstain – simply do not vote), then the government will be defeated, because the number of its own MPs *not* supporting it, added to the number of Opposition MPs voting against the government, will mean that the bill fails to secure an overall majority, and can proceed no further. In effect, when the media report that a government has suffered a parliamentary defeat, what has really happened is that enough of the government's own backbench MPs have voted against it, or abstained in large enough numbers to deprive it of its overall majority. Normally, governments do not experience defeats on major bills or other key votes – only on three occasions in the twentieth century did governments suffer parliamentary defeats at the crucial second reading stage (see later) – especially if they have a reasonably large parliamentary majority, and a three-line whip has been imposed (see later); the larger its majority, the more of its backbench MPs will need to abstain or vote against it in order to inflict a defeat.

However, as extensive research by academics like Lord (Professor Philip) Norton and Professor Philip Cowley has shown, government backbenchers have become less loyal, by being more willing to vote against their own leader and prime minister on legislation or other issues which those MPs feel strongly about: prime ministers can no longer take the support of their backbenchers for granted, but must – usually via the government whips, but occasionally in person – talk to them, listen to them, persuade them, and sometimes offer concessions. Yet even this might not be enough to win over unhappy government backbenchers if they strongly oppose a bill or policy for ideological or personal reasons, or because of its likely (negative) impact on their constituencies (see Case study 8.2). When the 2010–15 coalition introduced the bill which legalised same-sex marriage, about half of Conservative MPs voted against it (due to their belief that a true marriage could only be between a man and a woman; a heterosexual couple). More recently, Theresa May's 2016–19 premiership was increasingly undermined by the repeated defeats inflicted by Conservative backbenchers who were opposed to her 'Withdrawal Agreement', which laid out the details of Britain's exit from, and future relationship with, the EU. Many Conservative MPs wanted a more hardline 'Brexit', and a much clearer and stronger separation from the EU, rather than one whereby the UK would still retain close trade links with Europe; as such, they did not consider May's Withdrawal Agreement to go far enough in establishing the UK's complete independence from the EU. By repeatedly voting against May's proposals in the House of Commons, they steadily weakened her authority as leader – which had already been damaged by her failure to lead the Conservatives to an emphatic victory in the 2017 election – to the extent that she resigned in the summer of 2019, to be replaced by Boris Johnson (which is exactly the scenario that many of the Conservatives' backbench 'rebels' seemed to have envisaged when they started voting against May).

Party whips

Whips are MPs (in the Commons) or peers (in the Lords) who are appointed to facilitate obedient voting from their party's parliamentary supporters, using a judicious blend of principled arguments, flattery, promises, or threats, as the situation is deemed to warrant. The whips might carefully and calmly explain to an MP or peer why they should support their party leadership on a certain issue or in a vote, relying on reason and persuasion to secure support. Sometimes, though, the whips(s) might resort to threats, perhaps telling a 'rebel' MP that their chances of promotion will be seriously weakened if they do not vote in accordance with the wishes of their party's leadership on a particular issue. There have also been occasional claims that some whips

Case study 8.1

Parliamentary weapons for the backbencher

In addition to private member's bills, there are several other ways in which backbenchers can hope to win publicity for a cause:

Questions to ministers: Apart from Prime Minister's Question Time (which now lasts for 30 minutes on Wednesdays, having been split into two quarter-hour sessions, on Tuesdays and Thursdays, until 1997), there are other regular sessions during which MPs can question departmental ministers. As well as oral questions on the floor of the House, backbenchers expect answers to written questions; ministerial responses are published in the official parliamentary record, Hansard.

Early day motions (EDMs): Backbench MPs can make a point by putting down a state-ment in the form of a motion (not exceeding 250 words), which is supposed to be for discussion on 'an early day'. In practice, the subjects are very rarely discussed, let alone voted on; indeed, EDMs are usually advanced by MPs who feel that they have no chance of gaining a hearing through more orthodox channels. On these occasions, they are attempts to gauge parliamentary opinion; if the motion attracts any support, it will be available until the end of the session to MPs who want to sign it. Some MPs use EDMs to express support for constituency matters (or perhaps to give public backing to their local football team), and get an issue onto the political (or media) agenda.

Adjournment debates: At the end of a day's official business, MPs (chosen by ballot) have half an hour to raise an issue of interest to them, often concerning constituency matters. A minister from the relevant department will reply to the debate, after other interested MPs have contributed. Debates are now also held in Westminster Hall, outside the Commons chamber.

Ten-minute rule bills: MPs who lose out in the ballot for the right to introduce a private member's bill can plead for their cause for ten minutes before the beginning of official business on specific days. These bills have even less chance of success, but they give another fleeting chance of winning publicity.

Backbench business committee: Established in 2010, this committee, currently com-prising eight MPs (five Conservatives, two Labour and one SNP), provides a forum through which all backbenchers can choose topics for parliamentary debate on up to 35 days each year. On any of these days, the committee might choose to debate one topic all day, or devote half a day each to two topics. As such, the number of topics chosen for debate by backbench MPs will often total more than 35.

Backbench subject groups: Each of the main parties in the House of Commons contains subject groups for backbench MPs who have a particular interest in a policy issue: the Conservative backbench defence committee, the Labour backbench education com-mittee, and so forth. These are *not* select committees, but instead provide an arena in which the party's backbenchers can meet, in private, to discuss a particular issue or problem, and perhaps their party's policy (or lack of). Although these committees have no power, they can invite their party's (relevant) minister or spokesperson to give a talk and/or answer questions. On these occasions, the party's backbench MPs might express their dissatisfaction with, or opposition to, the leadership's stance on an issue, and demand a change of policy.

The 'hidden face' of power: Government backbenchers can sometimes indirectly influence their leadership's policies by making it clear, either to the whips or, perhaps, through briefings to the media, that they will oppose their government if it pursues a proposed or rumoured policy. On such occasions, the government might decide not to proceed with the policy, rather than risk suffering an embarrassing defeat when it is voted upon in the House of Commons. This would represent a victory for the backbench opponents of the policy, because the government would have quietly abandoned a proposed policy due to likely – rather than actual, formal, and publicly visible – defeat. The backbenchers would have exercised 'hidden power' behind the scenes.

have blackmailed MPs into supporting their party leadership in a key vote, by threatening to reveal to the media or the public something embarrassing about the MP's private life: a drink or drug problem, gambling addiction or debts, or perhaps their extra-marital (or other inappropriate) sexual activities while away from home, in London, during the week.

However, this popular image of manipulative whips, so loved by much of the media and producers of TV political dramas (such as the UK version of *House of Cards* in the early 1990s), overlooks the second vital role that they fulfil, namely, acting as an important two-way channel of communication between their party leadership and backbenchers. Not only do the whips explain to their backbenchers what the party's leadership is doing or planning, and why the MPs/peers should be publicly supportive, they also keep the leadership informed of the views and 'the mood' on the backbenches. This helps each party's frontbench (government ministers or Opposition 'shadow' ministers) to gauge what issues or policies are supported by their backbench colleagues, and which issues or policies are causing them particular anxiety or annoyance. The latter is often especially important in helping to avoid embarrassing (to the leadership) backbench 'rebellions' or defeats in key parliamentary votes. For example, MPs from the governing party might report, to the whips, that their constituents are very unhappy or alarmed about a proposed (or rumoured) new policy, in which case, if enough MPs are 'picking up' this public concern, the chief whip – who attends the cabinet partly for this very purpose – will inform ministers of this deep unease, and the damage it might cause (maybe a fatal loss of marginal seats in the next general election), in the hope that the leadership will abandon or delay the contentious policy; this would be an instance of the 'hidden face of power' discussed earlier. At the very least, ministers might be persuaded that it needs to work much harder at explaining the policy, hopeful allaying the concerns that currently exist, or perhaps offer concessions.

The term 'whip' also has another meaning in Parliament, referring to the written instruction to MPs about how they are expected to vote in any division. All MPs receive a written programme or 'agenda' of parliamentary business for the week ahead, detailing times and topics of debates and where these are being held (The Main Chamber or Westminster Hall), Ministers' and Prime Minister's Questions, and committee meetings. This weekly bulletin will also indicate to each party's MPs how they are expected to vote in scheduled divisions, with relevant divisions underlined once, twice of three times. A one-line or two-line whip means that MPs are expected to vote accordingly if available. However, it is the three-line whip which is most well known, because it means that MPs' attendance and support (for the party leadership's stance for or against a policy) is deemed essential; the relevant item is underlined three times to signify its utmost importance. As a consequence, it is usually a very serious matter if a government suffers a large backbench 'rebellion', and possible parliamentary defeat, on a three-line whip, because this would imply deliberate defiance of their leadership and whips by several, or perhaps many, of the party's backbench MPs. In such circumstances, the authority of the party leader/prime minister might also be undermined, because it would be apparent that on the particular issue or policy, at least some of their own MPs do not agree with or support the leadership. At the very least, it would draw attention to divisions inside the party, and possibly damage morale – or fuel resentment – among those MPs who did adhere to the three-line whip and display loyalty to their leadership.

The Speaker

The Speaker plays a vital role in seeking to maintain order in the House of Commons, especially during debates and question time. Indeed, the sight and sound of the Speaker shouting 'Order! Order!' to boisterous MPs is probably one of the most notable images of the House of Commons for many people. In addition, the Speaker has the responsibility of ensuring that MPs from different parties have an opportunity to speak in debates or ask questions, with broad parity maintained between government and Opposition MPs. For example, if a government backbencher has just asked a question or spoken in a debate, the Speaker will usually ensure that the next MP to ask a question or speak is from an Opposition party. The Speaker is also responsible for ensuring that rules concerning parliamentary etiquette and procedure are adhered to, for, in spite of the rowdiness and barracking often heard emanating from the House of Commons' main chamber, MPs must abide by certain rules and conduct: if they are referring to a minister, they must refer to him/her by their title (the Secretary of State for Health, the Minister of State for Universities, for example), while if they are referring to another backbench MP, they should refer to them by their constituency (such as the Honourable Member for Sheffield Hallam), not their name. The Speaker must also ensure that MPs do not use 'unparliamentary language' in attacking their political opponents: it is not permissible to call another MP or a minister 'a liar', for example. If an MP does use such language or name-calling, then the Speaker will insist that the offensive word is withdrawn, or else the MP will be ordered to leave the chamber for the rest of the day's business, and possibly longer – a political 'red card'. For example, in April 2016, the veteran Left-wing Labour MP, Dennis Skinner, was ordered to leave the House of Commons by the Speaker, after referring to David Cameron as 'Dodgy Dave' and then refusing to withdraw the word 'Dodgy' when ordered to do so.

PHOTO 8.2 'Mr Speaker' (2009–19) John Bercow (©UK Parliament/Jessica Taylor. creativecommons.org/licenses/by/3.0/).

Other roles performed by the Speaker are selecting amendments to bills and some other debates (such as that which is held on the Queen's Speech, which usually opens each parliamentary session), and interpreting the application of parliamentary rules, particularly when a point of order or other procedural query is raised by an MP. In this role, the Speaker might seek the advice of one of the parliamentary clerks who sit directly in front of his/her chair.

As the Speaker is effectively acting as an umpire or referee in the House of Commons, s/he must become politically neutral, and therefore cease to be the MP for a particular party. For example, John Bercow, who was elected the Speaker in 2009 (and resigned in 2019), was previously a Conservative. In the 2010, 2015, and 2017 general elections, he still sought re-election in his Buckingham constituency, but on the ballot paper, he was simply listed as John Bercow, the Speaker. The same will now apply to his successor, Lindsay Hoyle, the erstwhile Labour MP for Chorley (Lancashire). It is also a constitutional convention (custom or tradition) that the main Opposition parties do not put up candidates against the Speaker in their constituency, partly as a courtesy and mark of respect, but also to avoid embroiling him/her in political controversies that would compromise their formal neutrality in the House of Commons.

In assessing the role of the elected House of Commons in the British political system, six main activities or functions need to be considered:

1. Representation
2. Passing legislation
3. Debating
4. Scrutiny
5. Recruitment of ministers
6. Accountability

Although analytically separate, these six functions are, in practice, inextricably linked and mutually reinforcing, For example, the passing of legislation entails scrutiny of the government, and ensures that the ministers responsible for a new law are accountable to Parliament in being required to explain and defend it.

Representation

The House of Commons consists of 650 MPs, elected from single-member constituencies via the first-past-the-post electoral system, and on the basis of universal suffrage among adults over 18. The geographical nature of representation is supposed to ensure that individual MPs can be identified as the exclusive representatives of their constituents, as opposed to the multi-member arrangements produced by proportional representation systems (see Chapter 17). In this regard, an MP is expected to represent all of the people in their constituency, not just those who actually voted for them or who support the MP's party.

MPs represent their constituents in two distinct ways. First, they are expected to act as advisers and advocates for individual people living in their constituency – known as constituents – and seek 'redress of grievances' on their behalf, often involving problems with another public body: for example, a constituent (or several of them) might be having problems waiting to be housed/re-housed by their local council, or their claim for Universal Credit might have been delayed or rejected, thus leaving them penniless and facing eviction for rent arrears. Or a local resident might have had an application for asylum or British citizenship rejected by the Home Office, with deportation likely or imminent. In such instances, the aggrieved or anxious constituent might contact their local MP in the hope that s/he will be take up their case with the relevant authority, department, or minister, and have the problem resolved or an unfavourable decision reconsidered, and ultimately reversed. Occasionally, particularly if a problem is affecting many constituents, a local MP might raise the issue at Ministers' Question in the House of Commons, in the hope that such a public (and possibly politically embarrassing) airing of the issue will spur the relevant minister to look into the problem as a matter of urgency; it might even, in exceptional circumstances, lead to a policy being modified. In dealing with their constituents' problems, many MPs view themselves as political 'social workers', but in so doing, their local reputation can be greatly enhanced, thus increasing the respect they enjoy as a good and effective representative of their constituents. This, in turn, can slightly increase their chances of being re-elected at the next election – a notable consideration in an era of voter dealignment and increasing electoral volatility (see Chapter 18).

The second way in which MPs represents their constituents is by defending or promoting the interests of the constituency itself, in terms of campaigning for new investment, and thus jobs, or fighting against the closure of a local company or industry, which would result in hundreds or thousands of local people losing their livelihoods. This would also having damaging knock-on effects for other local businesses, in terms of reduced spending power and lower sales. An MP might also serve their constituency as a whole by seeking to prevent the closure of a local maternity unit, for example, or by opposing the building of a motorway – or new rail network – too close to their town or city (see Case study 8.2).

Case study 8.2

Conservative MPs opposing HS2

The planned high-speed rail network (HS2) provides a contemporary example of several backbench MPs defying their government's official policy, often because of serious concerns over the impact on their constituencies. The HS2 scheme entails the two-phase construction of a high-speed rail service, initially between London and Birmingham, scheduled to be operational by 2026. Then, two further routes will be built, one from Birmingham to Leeds, and the other from Birmingham to Manchester, due to be completed by 2033. With the trains intended to reach speeds of 250 mph, the government envisages that journey time from/to London will be greatly reduced. However, quite apart from growing opposition based on the increasing costs of construction – £56 billion (in 2019) compared to the initial (2010) planned cost of £33 billion – there has also been considerable hostility because HS2 will eventually pass through about 70 parliamentary constituencies.

Initially, it was mainly Conservative MPs in parts of Buckinghamshire, Northamptonshire, Oxfordshire, and Warwickshire who called for the HS2 rail link to be either abandoned, or slightly diverted so that it does not pass too close to their constituencies. They had several concerns such as noise and disruption both during and after construction, quality of life for local residents and constituents, possible negative impact on property price, and likely harm to the natural environment and wildlife. For example, in January 2019, the Conservative MP for Chesham & Amersham, Cheryl Gillan (a consistent and prominent of HS2), used Prime Minister's Question Time to urge Theresa May to cancel the HS2 project altogether. Gillan also directed several critical questions to the Transport Secretary during Ministers' Question Time in February and March 2019. Other Conservative MPs who expressed opposition either to HS2 itself, or at least the planned 'phase one' route, include Steve Baker (Wycombe), Sir Tony Baldry (North Oxfordshire), Chris Heaton-Harris (Daventry), David Lidington (Aylesbury), Chris White (Warwick & Leamington, until 2017), and Jeremy Wright (Kenilworth and Southam).

Their opposition was subsequently echoed by other several other Conservative MPs following the announcement of the route for 'phase two' between Birmingham and Leeds/Manchester. These 'north of Birmingham' Conservative opponents of HS2 include Andrew Bridgen (North West Leicestershire), Bill Cash (Stone), Michael Fabricant (Lichfield), Jeremy Lefroy (Stafford), and Christopher Pincher (Tamworth). A further tranche of Conservative MPs publicly opposed HS2 following the party's victory in the 2019 general election, when it won several former Labour seats in northern England. For some of these new Conservative MPs, opposition to HS2 was not solely because of the possible physical impact on their constituencies, but also because the new railway would not really benefit their constituents anyway. This new objection was crisply expressed by the new Conservative MP for Warrington North, Andy Carter, who argued that 'Getting from Manchester to Leeds, getting from Warrington to Liverpool, is a priority for people that live in the north of England. I suspect that priority is well ahead of getting down to London'. By early 2020, it was suggested that nearly 60 Conservative MPs supported the HS2 Review Group, while the cabinet was reportedly divided over whether or not to proceed with HS2, particularly as the original costs were already increasing, and likely to increase further during the course of the project. https://inews.co.uk/news/politics/hs2-latest-conservative-mps-boris-johnson-upgrades-public-transport-1370832

Delegate

representative who is under instruction to vote in a particular way.

Representative

someone who is chosen to take part in decision-making and to make up his or her own mind after hearing the evidence.

MPs may also represent the opinions and interests of their constituents in parliamentary votes. Strictly speaking, those who allow their votes to be dictated by constituency opinion rather than following their personal judgement are acting as **delegates** rather than **representatives**. This delegate view of MPs has rarely been advocated in British politics – at least, not outside the left of the 'Old' Labour Party. MPs are far more likely to cite the eighteenth-century politician Edmund Burke, who argued that representatives should be chosen because of their personal qualities and ability to exercise their judgement and discretion in making decisions, rather than their obedience to anyone else's opinion, and that if voters dislike their decisions, they can always choose another representative at the ensuing election. In practice, though, a prudent MP will strike a judicious balance when taking decisions, weighing up constituency interests, personal convictions, allegiance to their party, and the perceived national interest. For example, some Labour MPs who voted Remain in the 2016 Referendum on the UK's membership of the EU found themselves facing the dilemma that a majority of their constituents voted Leave. Some of these MPs were also convinced that it was not in their constituents' economic interests for the UK to leave the EU (due to potential or likely job losses as firms relocated to Europe), yet to have told then they were wrong or misguided would have sounded arrogant and insulting, and have confirmed Brexiter allegations that many 'Remainers' were out-of-touch, elitist, and contemptuous of ordinary people who held different views.

However, it can be argued that the vast majority of MPs today are indeed delegates – but the opinions they habitually follow are those of their party leaders rather than the majority of their constituents. Although significant rebellions against the party line happen more frequently than some critics suppose, they rarely result in a defeat for the governing party. Thus, even on controversial policies like the war on Iraq and the introduction of university tuition fees, the Blair government was able to secure majority support. For example, in the division on the crucial second reading of the bill to introduce tuition fees, 72 Labour MPs voted against, but the government still won, albeit by just five votes. Concerted appeals by Tony Blair and Gordon Brown persuaded a few MPs to swallow their misgivings, in the knowledge that a full-scale rebellion could bring down the government and trigger an election, while exposing damaging divisions within the party ranks. In March 2007 – when the government's majority had been reduced to 67 seats – 94 Labour MPs rebelled against the decision to renew Britain's Trident nuclear weapons system. The government won on that occasion because of support from the Conservatives. In June 2008, Gordon Brown's government won a vote on 42-day detention of terrorist suspects, thanks to last-minute support from the Democratic Unionists (DUP), which outweighed the rebellion of 36 Labour MPs. Far from interpreting the rebellion on this subject as a symptom of parliamentary revival, the Shadow Home Secretary David Davis resigned his seat in order to force a by-election which, he hoped, would be the most effective way of alerting the British public to this breach of traditional liberties.

In April 2009, the Brown government was defeated on a motion giving retired Gurkha soldiers the right to settle in Britain. This would have been a serious embarrassment for any government, because the campaign on behalf of the Gurkhas was led by the popular actress and TV presenter, Joanna Lumley, who attracted enormous media publicity. However, the damage was accentuated by the fact that, since 1997, Labour had tasted defeat so rarely, and Gordon Brown's authority was being challenged in other respects. As such, the vote formed part of a media narrative about a once mighty government beginning to unravel – a relative common occurrence in British politics.

Philip Cowley and Mark Stuart have demonstrated that members of the 2005–10 Parliament were the most rebellious since World War II, exceeding a record set in the previous (2001–05) Parliament. The Blair government lost an important House of Commons vote, in November 2005, on proposals to allow the detention of terrorist subjects for up to 90 days. The vote, which saw a government defeat by 322 to 291, was a considerable blow to the prime minister since he had invested some of his personal authority in the outcome. In February 2006, the government also had to make important concessions before introducing an education bill. Despite the concessions, 52 Labour MPs persisted in their opposition. On the crucial second reading, the government only secured a majority thanks to Conservative support or abstentions. After the formation of a coalition government in 2010, the habit of rebellion showed no sign of abating, especially among Conservative MPs who had never been reconciled to Cameron's leadership, let alone the new alliance with the Liberal Democrats. It was particularly noteworthy that many newly elected Conservative MPs were quick to contract the virus of rebellion (almost half had rebelled by January 2012). In May 2013, 133 Conservative MPs voted against the Marriage (same-sex couples) Bill; this was a 'free vote' on an issue of conscience, but it enjoyed public support from the prime minister, and it was apparent that the rebels (who included two cabinet ministers) knew they would be incurring the displeasure of their leadership. By the time of the 2015 general election, the 'coalition parliament' had surpassed the previous record for rebellions; it was particularly notable that, of the Conservative MPs who were first elected in 2010 and remained on the backbenches, 85 per cent rebelled against their party on at least one occasion.

While the evidence of backbench mutiny is impressive, it has to be seen in context. Most governments gradually accumulate a phalanx of dissidents who are prepared to rebel because of a mixture of frustrated ambition and genuine ideological disagreements. Yet there were times after 1997 when it appeared that Tony Blair was actively seeking to *maximise* discontent by introducing policies which were directly antagonistic towards long-established Labour positions on key questions like civil liberties and the public sector. If the same proposals had been introduced by a Conservative government, it is likely that the overwhelming majority of Labour MPs would have opposed them without any need for prompting from the whips. On the tuition fees bill, even the ultra-loyal Deputy Prime Minister, John Prescott, openly voiced his concern. Significantly, despite notable exceptions like Robin Cook, the government's so-called 'payroll vote' of cabinet and junior ministers usually stayed loyal, although many of them undoubtedly harboured strong reservations about the direction of policy on a wide range of issues after 1997.

Under the coalition, party discipline came under increasing strain. However, despite its precarious position on paper, the government continued to enjoy comfortable majorities on most key issues because only a few Conservatives broke ranks on each specific occasion, and when Liberal Democrats rebelled, the Conservatives tended to stay loyal (or vice versa). In short, open parliamentary rebellions that really matter, that is, effectively challenge the power of the executive, are still rare. Under the coalition, the most notable example came in August 2013, when a government motion paving the way for military action against the Assad regime in Syria was defeated by 285 to 272. Thirty Conservatives and nine Liberal Democrats voted against the coalition's policy. More important, and more difficult to show in statistical form, are the *potential* rebellions that are *so* effective that the government backs down before submitting its proposals to a vote – the 'hidden face of power' referred to earlier. This happened frequently under the coalition – for understandable reasons – including the damaging decision to abandon House of Lords reform in August 2012, which Liberal Democrat MPs avenged in January 2013 by voting to ensure that changes in parliamentary constituency boundaries were delayed until 2018 (they have still not been enacted, mainly because Parliament has been so focused on Brexit).

Meanwhile, as noted earlier, Theresa May's 2017–19 premiership was increasingly undermined by repeated defeats in parliamentary votes over her proposals – the Withdrawal Agreement – for the UK's departure from the EU, following the 2016 referendum. Many Conservative MPs, and some ministers, wanted her to pursue a more hard-line approach than she was prepared to do, and so her policy was constantly voted down by Right-wing Conservatives, while several ministers resigned during early 2019, in accordance with the principle of 'collective ministerial responsibility'. Unable to secure parliamentary support (in effect, enough Conservative support) for her preferred version of Brexit, May resigned in the summer of June 2019; the only surprise was that she had managed to survive for this long.

Are MPs socially representative?

Apart from the ways in which MPs represent their constituents, they can also be judged by the extent to which they are socially 'representative' as individuals. In seeking to explain the recent unpopularity of politicians, some critics have focused on their apparent remoteness from the 'real world'. In this respect, there have been three particular criticisms about how 'unrepresentative' MPs are, namely, their occupations prior to entering the House of Commons, their educational backgrounds, and the under-representation of women, although the latter has increased from 60 after the 1992 general election to 145 in 2010 and 191 in 2015 (see Table 8.1 for occupational background, and Chapter 17). In terms of prior occupations, Table 8.1 clearly illustrates not only the extent to which the MPs of the largest parties in the House of Commons emanate from a

TABLE 8.1 Occupational backgrounds of Conservative, Labour, and Liberal Democrat MPs

(combined) 1997–2017, plus SNP MPs since 2015.	1997	2001	2005	2010	2015	2017
Agriculture/Farming	7	6	8	10	7	6
Business	113	107	118	156	192	155
Civil service/Local Government	37	35	28	18	16	9
Health	9	8	6	9	10	9
Law (barristers/solicitors)	64	68	72	86	89	66
Manual	56	53	38	25	19	7
Media	47	50	43	38	34	18
Political	60	66	87	90	107	92
School teachers	65	64	47	24	16	31[a]
University lecturers	61	53	44	25	16	
White collar	72	76	78	84	71	N/A

Source: Lukas Audickas and Richard Cracknell, *Social Background of MPs 1979–2019*, House of Commons Library, Briefing Paper, Number CBP 7483, 27 March 2020, Accessible at: https://researchbriefings.files.parliament.uk/documents/CBP-7483/CBP-7483.pdf.

[a] In 2017, some of the categories were modified, with school teachers and university lectures both categorised as 'Education', rather than listed separately.

TABLE 8.2 Conservative and Labour MPs' occupations, 2017

	Conservative	Labour
Agriculture/Farming	6	0
Business	130	15
Education (teachers/lecturers)	6	20
Health	9	10
Law (barristers/solicitors)	38	25
Lobbyists	19	5
Local government	28	47
Manual	2	4
Media	10	6
Political	44	41
Trade Union official	0	30
Voluntary sector (charities, etc.)	5	32

Source: Rosie Campbell and Jennifer Hudson, 'Political Recruitment Under Pressure: MPs and Candidates', in Philip Cowley and Dennis Kavanagh (eds.), *The British General Election of 2017* (Basingstoke: Palgrave Macmillan), p. 401, Table 15.6.

relatively small range of careers and professions, but also how these have changed since the late 1980s, arguably making Parliament even less socially representative of the British electorate. For example, one of the most notable changes is the marked decline in MPs from manual (working class) backgrounds, down from 73 in 1987 to just 7 in 2017. On the other hand, the same period has witnessed a significant increase in the number of MPs from 'white collar' (clerical, administrative, and managerial) jobs, and also from 'political' careers, for example, working for a think tank or political party (behind-the-scenes or at grass-roots level), or as a researcher or a policy adviser, prior to becoming an MP. The number of MPs with prior 'political' careers increased from 34 in 1987 to 107 in 2015, and this trend is one of the main reasons why some people complain that MPs have little or no experience of the 'real world', having been involved in politics full-time since graduating. However, as Table 8.2 illustrates, there are some key differences between the pre-parliamentary careers of Conservative and Labour MPs. For example, the vast majority of MPs from backgrounds in business are Conservatives (which has always been widely viewed, indeed proudly portrayed itself, as 'the Party of business'): indeed, in terms of occupational background, this is now the single largest category of Conservative MP, followed by 'political' workers, and lawyers. For the Labour Party, local government provided 47 of its

MPs, while 41 emanated from 'political' careers, 32 previously worked in the voluntary sector (which does not mean that they themselves were doing voluntary work), and 30 had been trade union officials. Only four Labour MPs had been manual workers, thus clearly illustrating the extent to which the party has ceased to be a 'working class party' in terms of its parliamentary membership. Of course, much of this decline reflects wider changes in Britain's socio-economic structure, as deindustrialisation, globalisation, automation, and simple cost-cutting (to boost profits and shareholders' dividends) have led to the loss of millions of jobs in such sectors as car manufacturing, coal-mining, ship-building, and steel-making (see Chapter 4).

That the overwhelming majority of MPs emanate from a relatively small range of occupations and professions has led some writers to claim that Britain is now governed by a wholly unrepresentative 'political class' (for example, see Peter Oborne's *The Triumph of the Political Class*, London: Simon and Schuster, 2007). Indeed, it can be argued that one of the (many) reasons why 'Leave' defeated 'Remain' in the 2016 EU referendum was that some voters with a minimal education, who were unemployed or in unsatisfying jobs paying low wages, and who lived in deprived, run-down towns with overstretched, underfunded public services, wanted to vent their anger and frustration at seemingly overeducated, out-of-touch politicians in Westminster.

The socially 'unrepresentative' character of Britain's MPs is also reflected in their educational backgrounds, as illustrated in Table 8.3. In all three of the main (English) parties, there has been a notable increase in the proportion of MPs going to university, but it is in the Labour Party that this trend has been most significant – 56 per cent of Labour MPs had been graduates in 1987, whereas 84 per cent of Labour's 2017 MPs had attended university. In the same period, the proportion of university-educated Conservative MPs rose from 70 per cent to 83 per cent, while for the Liberal Democrats, the figures were 73 per cent and 92 per cent, respectively (having hit 100 per cent in 2015, albeit it only had 8 MPs in this election). However, what is also striking about the data in Table 8.3 is that the majority of these university-educated MPs have been to universities other than Oxford or Cambridge (Oxbridge). Indeed, among Conservative MPs, the proportion of Oxbridge graduates fell from 44 per cent in 1987 to 34 per cent in 2017. The same period also saw a ten-point decline in Oxbridge-educated Liberal Democrat MPs, down from 27 per cent to 17 per cent. Only Labour has actually increased its proportion of Oxbridge MPs, up from 15 per cent in 1987 to 20 per cent in 2017, but this still means that 80 per cent of Labour MPs who are university graduates were educated at universities other than Oxford or Cambridge.

TABLE 8.3 Educational backgrounds of Conservative, Labour, and Liberal Democrat MPs, 1992–2017[a] (% who attended)

		1992	1997	2001	2005	2010	2015	2017
Cons	Public	62	66	64	60	54	50	44
	University	73	81	83	81	80	81	83
	Oxbridge	45	51	48	43	34	30	34
Labour	Public	15	16	17	18	14	16	13
	University	61	66	67	64	72	77	84
	Oxbridge	16	15	16	16	17	21	20
Lib Dem	Public	50	41	35	39	39	13	30
	University	75	70	69	79	81	100	92
	Oxbridge	30	33	27	31	28	13	17

Source: Lukas Audickas and Richard Cracknell, *Social Background of MPs 1979–2019*, House of Commons Library, Briefing Paper, Number CBP 7483, 27 March 2020, Accessible at: https://researchbriefings.files.parliament.uk/documents/CBP-7483/CBP-7483.pdf.

[a] Data for 2019 election not available at time of writing.

TABLE 8.4 Women candidates and MPs, 1983–2019

Year	Conservative		Labour		Lib Dem		Total women
	Candidates	MPs	Candidates	MPs	Candidates	MPs	MPs
1987	46	17	92	21	105	2	41
1992	59	20	138	37	144	2	60
1997	66	13	155	101	139	3	120
2001	93	14	148	95	140	5	118
2005	123	17	166	98	145	10	128
2010	151	49	190	81	134	7	143
2015	169	68	215	99	166	0	191
2017	184	67	256	119	184	4	208
2019	194	87	335	104	186	7	220

Source: Data from various House of Commons research papers, and the British General Election of…. Series, usually co-authored by Dennis Kavanagh and one other senior academic electoral expert (in 2017, it was Philip Cowley). Note: 'Total women MPs' include MPs from other parties; for example, in 2015 there were 20 women MPs elected for the SNP.

Of course, there is a correlation between the educational and occupational backgrounds of many MPs, because most of the careers and professions from which many of them have been recruited are 'graduate jobs', for which a degree is a formal requirement. In other words, a university education tends to lead to a particular range of prestigious or high-status occupations. The other way in which Parliament is socially unrepresentative of the British public is in terms of the relatively low number of women MPs, although this has improved overall in recent general election, not least because the main parties have made a conscious effort to adopt more female candidates, and in winnable seats too. As Table 8.4 shows, only 41 women were elected in 1987, even though the three main parties fielded 140 female candidates. Many of these, though, seemed to have been picked in seats which their party was unlikely to win, while more men were adopted as candidates in 'safe' seats for their party. As such, a party's commitment to sexual equality in Parliament cannot be measured simply by counting how many women it adopts as candidates, but by examining how many women are chosen as candidates in 'safe' or 'winnable' seats. Since 1987, most general elections have seen a steady increase in the number of women candidates adopted *and* female MPs elected. The largest increase has been in the Labour Party, in which the number of women candidates has increased from 92 in 1987 to 335 in 2019, while the number of female Labour MPs elected during this time rose from 21 to 119 in 2017, before falling back to 104 in the 2019 election, when Labour lost 59 seats overall. The Conservatives have also made a concerted effort to attract and adopt more women to stand in elections, such that the party's female candidates increased from 46 in 1987 to 194 in 2019, during which time its number of female MPs rose from 17 to 87. Overall, the number of female MPs has risen from 41 in 1987 to 220 in 2019. While this is impressive in itself, it means that women are still under-represented in the House of Commons. As the House of Commons has 650 MPs, the 208 female MPs elected in 2017 constituted 32 per cent of its elected membership, even though women are actually 51 per cent of the British adult population. Considerable progress has been made since the 1980s, but clearly, there is still some way to go before women are fully represented in the House of Commons.

Passing legislation

In theory, the UK Parliament has a free hand in passing legislation. No decision made by Parliament can be binding on its successors, so that (for example) MPs could, if they really wanted to, bring an end to devolution, get rid of student fees, or even abolish the Monarchy. In this sense, one can claim that Parliament is still the sovereign body in the UK, and argue that this is entirely proper, since the House of Commons is directly elected by the British people.

In practice, the situation is very different, because it is the government (or executive), rather than Parliament itself, which is responsible for almost all the laws which are passed in the UK, although the devolved legislative bodies in Scotland, Wales, and Northern Ireland also have legislative powers in specified spheres of policy pertaining to their nation. Instead of being a *law-making* body in any meaningful sense, the UK legislature is expected to *legitimise* government decisions: at most, it is a 'policy-influencing' legislature, sometimes modifying policies but rarely actually making them. Even this role is heavily dependent on a range of factors, most notably the willingness of the executive to respond positively to Parliament's concerns or criticisms about a particular policy, the willingness of the government's own backbench MPs to defy their cabinet colleagues on a specific issue, and the size of the government's parliamentary majority – the narrower its majority in the House of Commons, the more vulnerable it will be to 'rebellions' if and when its own backbench MPs are strongly opposed to what their ministers are proposing or pursuing. Such 'rebellions' have become more numerous or frequent in recent decades, partly reflecting a decline in deference among backbench MPs, particularly in the Conservative Party, for whom obedience and loyalty to the leadership were once a major reason for its political success, resulting in public displays of unity, competence in government, and an increased chance or re-election – features which political scientists sometimes refer to as 'statecraft'.

The legislative process

On paper, proposals laid before Parliament are faced with a formidable obstacle course before they become law. The government announces its programme at the beginning of the annual parliamentary session in the Queen's Speech, although this is actually written by ministers; another indication that the Monarch's role in British politics is now mostly ceremonial and symbolic. A lengthy parliamentary debate then follows, usually over five days, which gives the government some idea of which particular policies are likely to prove most controversial and thus provoke opposition, particularly among its own backbench MPs, whose lack of support could prove fatal to a planned policy or law.

There are three types of legislation, although only the second and third need to concern us: private bills, public (government) bills, and private members' bills.

A **private bill** is that introduced on behalf of a private body or public institution, usually to seek specific powers for a particular purpose. This type of legislation represents only a very small number of all the laws introduced each year; in the 2017–19 parliamentary sessions, only five such private bills were introduced.

Public (government) bills

These are by far the most common type of legislation, for, as their name clearly indicates, these are laws enacted by the government (executive). In the first year or two after a general election, most of the bills introduced by the government will be based on policies pledged in its manifesto. A government might claim that its election victory constituted **a mandate** by the voters to enact the policies in its manifesto, but this is controversial for three reasons: (a) very few voters actually read election manifestoes; (b) even if they did (or have), it does not mean that they agree with, and support every, policy in the manifesto of the party they voted for; (c) Britain's first-past-the-post electoral system (see Chapter 17) usually produces governments supported by just 36–44 per cent (so rather less than half) of voters, which undermines any government's claim that its manifesto pledges have been endorsed by 'the electorate'.

How does a bill become a low?

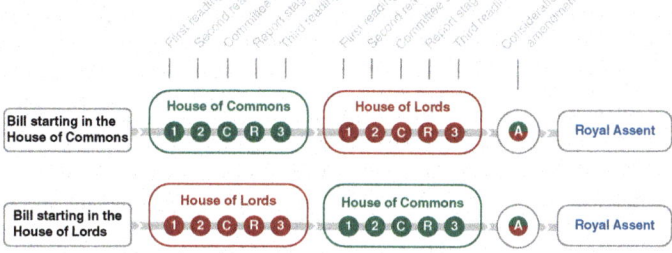

FIGURE 8.1 How does a bill become a law?

Source: Parliament UK: https://www.parliament.uk/about/how/laws/passage-bill/ Parliamentary information licensed under the Open Parliament Licence v3.0.

In addition to introducing laws based on its manifesto pledges, governments will also introduce bills on other issues, often in response to a new issue or crisis which arises during its term in Office, or perhaps in response to strong public pressure to tackle a problem. In the latter instance, prominent media coverage of an issue might create a 'moral panic' and a demand that the government 'does something' to deal with the issue. If the government fails to legislate, it might be viewed as arrogant, complacent, uncaring, or out-of-touch, and so lose public support.

The stages which a public (government) bill passes through before becoming law – an Act of Parliament – is illustrated in Figure 8.1, and then outlined in Case study 8.3. Although the majority of these bills start in the House of Commons, some will begin in the House of Lords, but the stages through which each bill goes are exactly the same.

Case study 8.3

The passage of a bill

Whether a bill is first introduced in the House of Commons or the House of Lords, it will go through the following stages in the legislative process:

First reading: Usually a simple announcement of a Bill's title and the date for the second reading. At this stage, the bill is not even printed in full; the proposer lays a printed 'dummy bill' before the House.

Second reading: The general principles of the bill are debated by the whole House, followed by a vote. The minister responsible for the bill outlines its main contents (clauses) and its purpose; the relevant opposition spokesperson replies. After contributions from backbenchers on all sides, the debate is wound up by frontbenchers, with the government having the last word. Governments are rarely defeated at this stage, because even if some of their own backbenchers have particular doubts or reservations about specific aspects of the bill, they will usually be willing to support the overall principle and purpose of the bill, perhaps with promises that the relevant minister will accept amendments at the next stage, to make the bill more acceptable to these sceptical backbenchers. Only three bills have been defeated in a vote at second reading in the last 100 years.

Committee stage: Most bills are then scrutinised by a Public Bill Committee (formerly a 'standing committee'), which invariably reflects the overall composition of the House. The amount of time taken varies, sometimes stretching over a few weeks (though the members only meet at specific times). At any one time, several Public Bill Committees will be at work in different committee rooms at Westminster. Normally consisting 16–50 (but usually at the lower end of this range) MPs, since 2007, the Public Bill Committees have enjoyed the right to consider both oral and written evidence before beginning the scrutiny process. Then they debate each clause of the bill and consider amendments to clarify or improve it. Often, these will be introduced by the government itself, to close loopholes in the original bill which have either been highlighted in the second reading debates, or have been signalled privately to ministers by concerned government backbenchers. Some amendments might also be tabled by the government, in response to concerns raised about specific aspects of a bill during the second reading. However, because the second reading has given formal parliamentary approval to the principles and purpose of a bill, no amendments 'tabled' at Committee Stage can change these broad objectives, only particular details. As such, many of the amendments and debates in these committees are administrative or technical.

Report stage: When the Committee has completed its deliberations, its decisions are reported back to the full House. More amendments can be considered at this stage, most likely by MPs who did not serve on the Public Bill Committee.

Third reading: This takes place immediately after the report stage. Normally, by this time, the opponents of the bill will have accepted that further resistance is futile, although on particularly contentious matters, dissenting MPs will want to put their objections on record once again. The relevant minister will usually restate the government's case in support of the bill, doubtless arguing that the amendments have made it even better, while the Opposition will almost certainly maintain that the bill is still inadequate or irrelevant, in spite of the amendments.

To the House of Lords: If a bill has started in the House of Commons, and passes its third reading (usually a formality), it is then sent to the House of Lords where these stages are repeated (if the bill started in the House of Lords, then it is sent to the House of Commons to go through the same stages). This means that a bill has been considered by both Houses of Parliament, which ensures (in principle) that legislation has received rigorous parliamentary debate and scrutiny, and potential problems or pitfalls addressed.

The only difference between the legislative stages is that, unlike the House of Commons, the committee stage in the House of Lords is open to all members of the Upper House, rather than a 'representative' sample as in the Commons. In other words, the Lords' Committee Stage is a committee of the whole House, and is conducted in the main chamber ('on the Floor of the House'), rather than in an actual committee room. If a bill is amended in the House of Lords, it returns to the Commons where the proposed amendments are considered. A compromise is usually reached to iron out any differences between the two Houses and prevent further delay to the bill, so that the bill can be presented for the *Royal Assent.* This final formality – it has not been refused since 1707 – makes the bill into law. On very rare occasions, though, the two Houses find it impossible to compromise, as in the case of the 2004 Hunting Bill. In these situations, governments can invoke the provisions of the 1949 Parliament Act, which ensures that in almost all circumstances, the will of the Commons (in effect, the will of the government) ultimately prevails.

Even before the Queen's Speech, the government will sometimes have consulted with relevant 'stakeholders' who might have a particular interest in, or be affected by, planned legislation. At an early stage in its deliberations, it may issue a **Green Paper**, setting out the various arguments and options, and inviting further comment from 'interested parties'. A **White Paper** indicates that the government has made up its mind, and the document usually forms the basis of a subsequent **bill**.

Green Paper

a document published by the government setting out various optiowns and inviting comment.

Extensive consultation before a bill is introduced ought to satisfy most critics of representative democracy. Under Gordon Brown, New Labour even began to announce its programme before the end of the previous Parliament, theoretically giving every interested party the chance to have a say. However, in the UK, the process is likely to be inadequate for a variety of reasons. Sometimes, there is a real need for action in a particular area, and the government genuinely has limited time for talking. More often, the government will only consult favoured organisations ('insider groups' – see Chapter 19). This is because it will have promised action to its supporters, both inside and outside Parliament, and is simply not prepared to listen even to constructive objections from other quarters. This explains the fate of the community charge (or poll tax), which seemed watertight to many Conservative supporters before it was fully implemented in 1990, but soon proved to be unworkable. Inadequate consultation can also occur because most ministers are keen to make a mark in their present (but temporary) posts. As such, they will tend to exaggerate the level of support for their ideas, and to discount any criticisms as the product of 'prejudice' or 'obstructive' tactics. On the other hand, governments in vulnerable parliamentary positions can run the risk of looking indecisive by continuing to consult relevant groups *after* they have made up their own minds. In the summer of 2011, for example, the Conservative–Liberal Democrat coalition government was accused of chronic weakness because it had modified a series of proposals, ranging from the privatisation of forests to criminal justice reform and the role of private companies in the NHS. Yet, if governments fail to modify policies in the face of strong or widespread criticism, they are liable to be accused of being arrogant or dictatorial, and lose popularity.

White Paper

a government document setting out detailed proposals for legislation.

Bill

A proposed piece of legislation that is yet to complete the legislative process.

Private members' bills

The discussion so far has been based on the assumption that a successful bill will normally be sponsored by the government of the day. This is slightly misleading – but only slightly. Early in each session (parliamentary year), MPs wishing to introduce a bill of their own take part in a ballot. Twenty names are chosen at random. Some of those selected will be hoping at the very least to win publicity for a cherished cause; others may have entered the ballot under instruction from the party whips, having no bright ideas of their own to suggest. They will soon be bombarded with proposals from pressure groups and lobbyists of all kinds. Often, such groups will provide ready-drafted or 'dummy' bills, to save the MP the trouble of asking a parliamentary clerk to compose the text.

A shrewd MP might try to curry favour with ministers by sponsoring a proposal which the government would like to see on the statute book but lacks the time (or the political courage) to offer open support. In the 1960s, several controversial 'permissive' measures of social and sexual reform became law because the Labour Home Secretary, Roy Jenkins, supported private member's bills even though he knew that members of his own party had mixed feelings. Alternatively, the government might decide that a particular private member's bill is so popular with Parliament and the public that it should lend it full-hearted support. Either way, private member's bills have virtually no chance of success unless they enjoy at least the benevolent neutrality of the government; in most years, only four or five (out of twenty) private members' bills are successfully enacted (become law). Constraint of time means that most bills are 'talked out' by determined opponents. Their chances are equally poor if they are uncontentious, because bills will fail unless enough MPs feel sufficiently motivated to turn up for the debate. Case study 8.4 presents an atypical saga, but it illustrates the difficulties faced even by a private member's bill that enjoys substantial cross-party support. The ban on tobacco advertising, passed into law in 2002, also began as a private member's bill. In 2013, a proposal for a referendum on British membership of the EU was taken up by a backbench MP James Wharton. The bill, which passed its Commons' stages but was predictably less fortunate in the Lords, had begun life as a draft bill, with support from Conservative leaders who were anxious to appease anti-EU sentiment among backbenchers and the media. It featured as a prominent party pledge in the 2015 general election campaign. Table 8.5 shows some of the most notable private members' bills since the 1960s. Occasionally, a private members' bill might achieve its objective without completing its passage through Parliament. This is most likely when ministers acknowledge the merit in the bill's objective(s) and incorporate the proposed reform into the government's own legislation or statutory regulations. For example, in 2018, a private members' bill was introduced to protect existing live music venues from closure when new residential properties were built near or next to them. For example, The Fleece, a small but popular live music venue in Bristol, had opened in 2010, in a commercial district, surrounded by several large office blocks which were empty at night. Several years later, though, these office were sold and turned into city-centre apartments, which led to concerns about the future of The Fleece, because in such circumstances, new residents or tenants who moved into property near, or next, to an existing live music venue could complain about the noise, and have the venue's licence revoked (often resulting in the venue closing), even though the venue had been there long before the new residents. After several similar live music venues had been closed, or prevented from hosting bands, because of such complaints, the Planning (Agent of Change) Bill was introduced, by Labour MP John Spellar, which would place a legal onus on property companies to pay for, or provide, soundproofing when building residential properties in the immediate vicinity of a live music venue. However, Spellar withdrew his bill when the Conservative government acknowledged the problem he was seeking to solve, and enshrined his proposed remedy into planning guidelines (https://www.gov.uk/government/news/strengthened-planning-rules-to-protect-music-venues-and-their-neighbours).

Debating

It is usually argued that, whatever its other limitations, Parliament provides the nation with a grand forum for debate on important occasions. The parliamentary debates on the Falklands War in 1982, the Westland Affair (1986), and the Maastricht Treaty (1993) are remembered as dramatic occasions, although only the last-named took place after the television cameras had been

TABLE 8.5 Examples of successful private members' bills

Year enacted	Name of Bill/Act	Change in public policy
1965	Murder (Abolition of the Death Penalty)	Death penalty abolished for those found guilty of murder; life imprisonment to be imposed instead.
1967	Abortion	Legalised abortion up until the 28th week of pregnancy.
1967	Sexual Offences	Legalised homosexuality.
1967	The National Health Service (Family Planning)	Permitted Local Health Authorities to give contraceptive advice, regardless of marital status, and on social as well as medical grounds.
1968	Theatres	Abolished censorship of plays and other public performances in theatres.
1969	Divorce Reform	Permitted divorce on the grounds of 'irretrievable breakdown of marriage'.
1972	Sunday Cinemas	Permitted cinemas to open on Sundays.
1972	Sunday Theatre	Allowed theatres to open on Sundays.
1973	Employment of Children	Imposed limits on the employment of children below the school-leaving age.
1975	Guard Dogs	Regulate the circumstances and conditions in which, and by who, guard dogs can be kept and used.
1978	Protection of Children	Outlawed the taking, distribution, or display of indecent photos of children.
1984	Cycle Tracks	Enable a local or highway authority to designate a footpath (or part of it) as a cycle track, shared with pedestrians.
1985	Prohibition of Female Circumcision	Outlawed surgery on the female genitalia (or female circumcision) unless performed solely for essential medical – as opposed to cultural/religious – reasons.
1985	Sexual Offences	Outlawed 'kerb crawling' (driving slowly, or sitting, in a vehicle, in order to proposition women for the purpose of prostitution).
1986	Protection of Children (Tobacco)	Made it an offence to sell tobacco to anyone under 16 years of age.
1987	Access to Personal Files	Gave individuals the right to see files (or other information) on them, held and used by various public authorities.
1987	Motorcycle Noise	Made it an offence to sell or supply motorcycle exhaust systems which were likely to produce excessive noise.
1988	Access to Medical Records	Gave individuals the right to see their medical record before their GP supplied a copy in response to a request by an employer or insurance company.
1990	Computer Misuse	Outlawed unauthorised access to another person's computer and the files or date contained on it ('computer hacking').
1991	Football (Offences)	Prohibited both the throwing of objects and the chanting of indecent or racist language.
1991	Smoke Detectors	All new residential properties to have smoke detectors installed, with at least one on each level or storey.
1994	Marriage	Allowed marriages to be conducted in 'approved premises', other than churches and registry offices.
1996	Dogs (Fouling of Land)	Obliged dog owners to clear up and dispose of their dog's faeces from 'designated land'.

(continued)

Year enacted	Name of Bill/Act	Change in public policy
1999	Protection of Children	Established an official list of people deemed unsuitable to work with children, and require 'child care organisations' to check the list prior to appointing staff. Other bodies working with children expected to check as part of their recruitment procedure.
2003	Female Genital Mutilation	Made it illegal to take or send a girl abroad to undergo female circumcision or any other form of genital 'surgery'.
2004	Christmas Day (Trading)	Prohibited large shops (supermarkets and chain stores) from opening on Christmas day.
2006	Emergency Workers (Obstruction)	Made it unlawful to obstruct or hinder an emergency worker while they were dealing with an emergency situation.
2007	Forced Marriage (Civil Protection)	Provided legal protection and redress for individuals threatened or coerced into a marriage without their free and full consent.
2010	Sunbeds (Regulation)	Sunbed use prohibited for individuals under 18 years of age.
2014	International Development (Gender Equality)	Ensure that overseas aid is conditional on the recipient country guaranteeing sexual/gender equality.
2018	Assaults on Emergency Workers (Offences) Act	To create a new criminal offence of assaulting emergency workers when exercising their public duties.

Source: https://commonslibrary.parliament.uk/research-briefings/sn04568/.

Case study 8.4

Hunting – the history of a private member's bill

Between 1992 and 1995, three private member's bills were introduced by Labour MPs hoping to outlaw hunting. All ended in failure, following previous attempts (dating back to the 1960s) to ban hare coursing. However, in its 1997 manifesto, Labour offered hope to campaigners by promising a free vote on hunting. Any anti-hunting MP who was successful in the private members' ballot could, therefore, be certain of 'benevolent neutrality' from the incoming government.

In March 1998, a bill sponsored by Labour's Michael Foster gained its second reading in the Commons. However, the hunting lobby had already reacted to the new political climate, organising a mass protest rally in Hyde Park in July 1997. Foster's bill was 'talked out' by its parliamentary opponents on third reading. In the summer of 1999, Tony Blair revealed on television that he would like to see a ban introduced before the next election. Evidently, the government still wanted to secure this result by means of a private member's bill, which might reduce any direct political damage. However, Blair's remark made it difficult to avoid a more direct commitment. In 2000, a new bill was duly introduced by the Home Office minister Mike O'Brien. The major difference from the previous proposal was that MPs could opt for a compromise, allowing hunting with hounds to continue under licence. When this formula was rejected by the Commons, the bill as a whole was thrown out by the Lords. Under the provisions of the Parliament Act of 1949, the bill lapsed when Blair called a general election for June 2001. The new bill had been introduced too late in the Parliament to ensure its success.

After Labour had been re-elected, Blair clearly still hoped for a compromise. But by this time, it was clear that the Commons would settle for nothing less than an outright ban. A game of 'ping-pong' ensued, with the Commons passing a new bill, and the Lords rejecting it. At length, in November 2004, the Commons Speaker Michael Martin declared that the terms of the Parliament Act had been satisfied, and the bill was given the Royal Assent. The ban came into force in February 2005. For the opponents of hunting, however, the saga had only completed its first phase. The Countryside Alliance launched an unsuccessful legal challenge to the Parliament Act itself, and also tried to overturn the legislation by appealing to the Human Rights Act 1998 (see Chapter 9). In the 2005 general election, the Countryside Alliance campaigned against several anti-hunting MPs, and claimed to have played a decisive role in several seats. Ironically, after all the parliamentary time spent on this issue, in his memoirs, Tony Blair revealed that he had been convinced by a member of the hunting lobby that the legislation had been misguided, and hinted that he had no desire to see this particular law enforced very rigorously (Tony Blair, *A Journey*, London: Hutchinson, 2010, p. 306; see Chapter 19).

The story did not end there, however. The 2015 Conservative manifesto included the promise of a free vote on the repeal of the Hunting Act, and the matter was duly brought forward within weeks of the party's narrow victory in the general election. This was not an ideal issue for a new government which had flaunted its 'One Nation' credentials in the aftermath of the election, but was led by highly privileged individuals of the kind who (rightly or wrongly) are identified with hunting. Just before the vote, the SNP leader Nicola Sturgeon announced that her newly augmented party in the Westminster Parliament would vote against repeal, even if this would not affect the situation in Scotland. This made a likely Commons defeat for repeal into a certainty, so the government postponed the vote, clearly hoping that voters would regard this as an unwarranted intrusion by Scottish MPs into an issue which affected England and Wales, and thus an egregious example of the 'West Lothian Question' (see Chapter 6).

Controversy 8.1

'Sleaze' and the interests of MPs: before the expenses scandal

When most MPs enjoyed private means and regarded politics as something of a hobby, it was taken as a matter of course that they would have extensive financial interests outside the House. One reason for the eccentric business hours of Parliament was the assumption that busy people would have to attend to other matters during 'normal' working hours. The new dominance of 'professional' politicians, with fewer outside interests, is thus one reason why reform of the parliamentary timetable could be contemplated after 1997. But it also coincided with a rise in media attention to the business interests of politicians.

In 1975, a Register of Interests was introduced, in which all members of the Lords and Commons declared their financial dealings. Nevertheless, during the 1990s, a series of scandals was exposed, including several instances where MPs were accused of having asked questions in Parliament in return for cash. Under pressure, in October 1994, Prime Minister John Major set up a Committee on Standards in Public Life under a judge, Lord Nolan. In the following year, the Committee recommended that MPs should make full disclosures of their business interests, including the sums involved. The government accepted most of the proposals, despite some furious opposition from its own backbenchers, who resented the imputation that all MPs were potentially corrupt and required special monitoring to make sure that they were behaving well. Nolan's seven principles of public life – selflessness, integrity, objectivity, accountability, openness, honesty, and leadership – were indeed open to the criticism that they were more relevant to the qualities expected of a saint than of a legislator in tune with the modern world.

A Commissioner for Parliamentary Standards was appointed, who would work with a new parliamentary select committee on Standards and Privileges. But the second holder of the post, Elizabeth Filkin (1999–2002), was effectively sacked because she took the job too seriously, issuing several critical reports which embarrassed the Blair government. Thus, MPs ended up with the worst of both worlds; if they lost the support of the executive for one reason or another, they could be punished under regulations which were excessively intrusive, but they also stood accused by the public of trying their best to evade them. So much for 'selflessness, integrity' and all the rest!

There was a revival of interest in MPs' integrity in 2008, after it was revealed that a Tory MP, Derek Conway, had paid his son more than £40,000 for research work, even though the son had been a full-time student in Newcastle at the time. This led to the establishment of a register in which MPs had to make a full declaration of any relatives in their employment. The Secretary of State for Work and Pensions, Peter Hain, resigned from the government after the Electoral Commission, which had been investigating donations to his 2007 campaign for the Labour Party's Deputy Leadership, passed the case on to the police. No prosecution resulted.

In 2004, the money claimed by MPs in expenses was published for the first time; the annual average was £118,000 – twice the official parliamentary salary. In March 2008, a detailed breakdown of the expenses on offer was published after a request under the Freedom of Information Act. In a foretaste of the expenses scandal which broke the following year, it revealed that, among other things, MPs could claim up to £12,000 for a new kitchen. The Conservative MPs Ann and Sir Nicholas Winterton were subjected to press criticism because they claimed expenses for rent on a London flat, when they owned the property and had already paid off the mortgage. During the controversy, even the Speaker of the House of Commons, Michael Martin, was called upon to defend the expenses he claimed. Martin's stubborn defence of the existing system made him the first and, in some ways, most notable victim of the full-blown expenses scandal; despite making a public apology, he was forced to resign in June 2009, the first speaker to leave involuntarily for more than three centuries.

allowed into the Commons (in November 1989; continuous radio broadcasts began in 1978). It is interesting that the momentous debates before the 2003 Iraq War have not lingered in the public memory, despite extensive television coverage; certainly, the reputation of the Commons has not been improved by public exposure.

Nowadays, aficionados can observe parliamentary proceedings all day long on a special digital TV channel. However, most people will only ever catch a glimpse of the Commons chamber when snippets from Prime Minister's Question Time are included in the evening news bulletins. In part, the lack of interest in parliamentary activities can be attributed to the media, which prefers to secure its own 'scoops' through set-piece studio interviews with the leading players. However, it does seem that the sense of drama has been leaking away from the chamber for other reasons. One indication of the decline can be registered in the virtual disappearance of MPs who were widely regarded as great 'House of Commons men', that is, people who were steeped in respect for the procedures of the House, even when (like Enoch Powell, 1912–98) they were also prepared to use venues outside Westminster to express iconoclastic views on a range of issues. Nowadays, 'elder statesmen' who could command an audience by virtue of their prolonged experience and eloquence of debate tend to accept a seat in the House of Lords at the first general election after the end of their ministerial careers. In this respect, perhaps the most significant moment was the retirement of Tony Benn (first elected in 1945) at the 2001 general election. Although still vigorous and determined to influence public debate, Benn believed that his membership of the Commons was a drawback rather than an asset; he wryly declared that he was leaving Parliament 'to go into politics'.

Scrutiny

In addition to the scrutiny provided when examining bills, particularly in Public Bill Committees, and via debates, the two main modes of explicit scrutiny in the House of Commons are Question Time, and select committees. Both entail the questioning of ministers by backbench MPs, although the format of the two is very different, and the actual impact on policy is generally perceived to be limited.

Question Time

There are actually two types of Question Time in the House of Commons, Prime Ministers' Questions (PMQs), and Ministers' Questions. Of course, it is PMQs which are most well known, due to the high-profile and widely reported weekly clashes between the prime minister and the leader of the Opposition in a usually full Commons' chamber. However, the cheering, jeering, and political point-scoring which PMQs often entail is also a reason why many people have less faith in Parliament, and lower respect for politicians, than in earlier decades, not least because Parliament was not televised until 1989. The passions aroused inside the House are matched by the disgust and dismay which PMQs often generate among outside observers, the shouting of MPs more akin to rowdy supporters at a football match. It is often an unedifying spectacle, and hardly conducive to restoring public confidence in Parliament and politicians – a point which John Bercow often sought to remind MPs of when he was Speaker.

PMQs are held on Wednesdays at 12.00, for 30 minutes, invariably in a crowded House of Commons' main chamber. Indeed, it is usually the best attended event of the parliamentary week, although it usually generates much more heat than light, and does much to reinforce the 'Punch and Judy' image of British politics, whereby the main political leaders often trade insults and score partisan points against each other. After the leader of the Opposition has opened proceedings with a few questions, other backbenchers (from all parties, including the government) are permitted to participate. However, questions to the prime minister are usually about overall government policies or objectives, or perhaps a crisis, because more detailed questions about specific policies will usually be directed to the relevant minister(s) when they appear to answer departmental questions, generally once every four weeks. In many respects, the conduct of PMQs depends on the participants, particularly the leaders. Boris Johnson could not conceal his contempt for Jeremy Corbyn when the latter was asking questions as leader of the (Labour) Opposition, but Johnson found it much more difficult to adopt a cavalier attitude or mocking stance when he was confronted by Corbyn's successor as Labour leader, Sir Keir Starmer, a former barrister and Director of Public Prosecutions, whose calm, almost forensic, questioning of Johnson – particularly over his government's handling of the COVID-19 pandemic, in the spring of 2020 – cruelly exposed Johnson's inadequate grasp of detail and facts when he could not resort to bluster, flippancy, and insults.

By contrast, all other ministers face Questions every four weeks or so, in accordance with a published rota. This is because ordinary Ministers' Question Time is concerned with the policies of departments, and there are over 20 departments, each of which answers questions for between 30 and 60 minutes, depending on the size of the department or the breadth of its policy remit. At Ministers' Question Time, all of the department's ministers will be present, because junior ministers tend to focus on a specific aspect of departmental policy, and so are better suited or equipped to answer many of the more detailed questions than the Secretary of State who heads the department, but who is usually more concerned with overall strategy and leadership.

There are actually two types of Questions to Ministers, oral and written. **Oral Questions** are asked by backbench MPs (including the government's own backbenchers) during the allotted time in the main chamber. Having asked their question – for which the Department's ministers will have received advance notification so that they (or their civil servants) can prepare an answer, which might necessitate researching data or other factual evidence – the MP can ask a 'supplementary' or follow-up question, and it is this which is often the most probing or awkward question, and thus intended to put the minister(s) under pressure or politically embarrass them. After the 'supplementary' question has been answered, the Speaker will usually allow a few other MPs to ask further follow-up questions before moving on to the next question on that day's list. In so doing, the Speaker will ensure that a balance is struck between government backbenchers and MPs from the Opposition parties. This process is repeated until the end of the allotted time.

There are various reasons why MPs ask oral questions. They might genuinely seek information or clarification about a policy, or to find out how the government intends to tackle a problem

PHOTO 8.3 The prototype of Prime Minister's Question Time? (© Richard Gardner/Shutterstock).

or new issue. MPs might also, of course, hope to embarrass a minister, in an attempt at portraying him/her, or even the government of which they are part, as incompetent, uncaring, or out-of-touch. Some MPs will occasionally ask an **oral question** in relation to a matter involving their constituency (perhaps concerning jobs losses due to a firm closing or relocating, or the planned HS2 rail link threatening to damage the local countryside or harm wildlife), or even individual constituents (maybe pertaining to delays in the payment of Universal Credit, for example, or someone about to be deported because their application for political asylum has been rejected). Of course, in cases involving problems or apparent injustices experienced by individual constituents, the local MP is also likely to contact the relevant authority or department directly, but hope that an **oral question** will expedite a solution or prompt the relevant minister to intervene personally. An additional motive for asking an **oral question** on a constituency matter is that it is likely to gain the MP publicity in the local media, and thereby maintain or raise their profile. This will serve to remind constituents what a good, diligent MP they have, fighting for their interests in the corridors of power, and so worthy of being re-elected – a particularly pertinent factor in an era of **dealignment** and declining loyalty to a specific political party.

The other type of question asked by MPs (of all parties) is **written questions**, which receive a written answer published in Hansard. These questions often seek detailed information, perhaps entailing statistical evidence, which would be difficult to provide in a clear or succinct oral answer.

However, the most effective mechanism of parliamentary scrutiny is the system of select committees which operate in the House of Commons, and which provide much more in-depth and rigorous examination of the effectiveness or impact of policies and legislation than Ministers' Question Time. As Table 8.6 shows, there are two types of select committee, those which 'shadow' a Department and those which are more thematic or 'functional'.

The Departmental Select Committees were established in 1979, primarily to provide more thorough parliamentary scrutiny of the executive (government) via its departments and their ministers, but also because many backbench MPs were becoming more assertive and wanted to play a more active role in the policy process; they were no longer content to be treated as passive

TABLE 8.6 Select committees in the House of Commons

Departmental	Thematic
Business, Energy and Industrial Strategy	Backbench Business
Defence	Environmental Audit
Digital, Culture, Media and Sport	European Scrutiny
Education	Liaison
Environment, Food and Rural Affairs	Petitions
Foreign Affairs	Privileges
Health and Social Care	Procedure
Home Affairs	Public Accounts
Housing, Communities and Local Government	Public Administration and Constitutional Affairs
International Development.	Science and Technology
International Trade	
Justice	
Northern Ireland Affairs	
Scottish Affairs	
Transport	
Treasury	
Welsh Affairs	
Women and Equalities	
Work and Pensions	

and obedient 'lobby fodder'. Each department is 'shadowed' by a select committee, whose role has always been to examine the administration, expenditure, and policies of 'its' department and, in so doing, hold the ministers to account (to Parliament) for their decisions and policies. When a new department is created, a new select committee will similarly be established to monitor its activities. These select committees are completely independent of the department which they monitor and scrutinise; if they were not, their ability to pursue effective and rigorous scrutiny would be seriously compromised, and concerns raised about conflicts of interests or divided loyalties.

The vast majority of Departmental Select Committees comprise eleven MPs, six from the government backbenches and five from the Opposition parties (most from Labour, as the largest Opposition party, but the other parties will also be allocated a seat on many select committees), although a few have thirteen MPs, in which case seven will be government backbenchers and six from the Opposition parties. Crucially, the government's backbenches generally act 'independently' when engaging in select committee inquiries – they are there to scrutinise the department and its ministers, not act as party allies. Prior to 2010, there was concern that the party whips sometimes exercised too much influence over which MPs served on select committees, or who would be chosen to chair one, and this fuelled suspicions that membership from the government's backbenchers was sometimes allocated as a reward for loyalty to the leadership, or given to MPs who were trusted not to pursue lines of inquiry or questioning which would embarrass their ministerial colleagues, perhaps by exposing incompetence. This would rather defeat the purpose of the Departmental Select Committees, which is to provide in-depth and 'independent' scrutiny of the work of government departments, and of their ministers, senior civil servants, and special advisers. As a consequence of such concerns, 2010 heralded the 'Wright reforms' (named after the modernising Labour MP, Tony Wright, who was chair of the prestigious Public Administration Select Committee), strongly supported by the then Speaker, John Bercow (who adopted the role of 'champion of backbenchers' in relation to the executive), which meant that membership of select committees would now be determined by a secret ballot of MPs. This would finally ensure the complete independence of Departmental Select Committees and their members – particularly the backbench MPs drawn from the governing party – from actual or potential influence by the party whips. The MPs and chairs of the select committees were now chosen solely by their parliamentary colleagues and acted on their behalf in providing regular, in-depth scrutiny of government departments and their policies.

In fulfilling this vital role, and thereby ensuring more systematic parliamentary scrutiny of the executive, the select committees can choose what issues or topics to investigate: they might choose a general topic about the overall or long-term effectiveness of a policy, or conduct an investigation into a specific aspect of a policy. Although these inquiries will often examine recent or current policy developments or results, they will sometimes opt to examine (expected) future developments or trends, in order to evaluate how prepared the relevant department is – or perhaps make suggestions about how it ought to prepare. Select committees will also return to previous inquiries and reports, to consider how far – if at all – a department has acted upon the suggestions of the select committee when it last investigated an issue or problem. Table 8.7 gives examples of inquiries conducted by each of the Departmental Select Committees since 2017.

One other role acquired by Departmental Select Committees, in the twenty-first century, is that of pre-legislative scrutiny, whereby they can conduct inquiries into 'Draft Bills', the intention being that the actual bills will have been improved and refined before being formally introduced to the House of Commons, thus producing legislation of higher quality. However, pre-legislative scrutiny is rather haphazard or *ad hoc*, not regular or systematic, and governments can still disregard recommendations which they disagree with on partisan grounds.

TABLE 8.7 Examples of inquiries conducted, or reports published, by Departmental Select Committees, 2017–19

Select Committee	Topic of Inquiry
Business, Energy and Industrial Strategy	Automation and the future of work. Gender pay gap reporting.
Defence	US, NATO, and UK Defence relations. North Korea and the threat it poses.
Digital, Culture, Media & Sport	Live music. Disinformation and 'fake news'.
Education	Value for money in higher education. Tackling disadvantage in the early years.
Environment, Food and Rural Affairs	Britain's fishing industry beyond Brexit Coastal flooding and adaptation to climate change.
Foreign Affairs	Russian corruption in the UK. The future of UK diplomacy in Europe.
Health and Social Care	Drugs policy: medicinal cannabis. Improving air quality.
Home Affairs	Immigration policy. Domestic abuse.
Housing, Communities and Local Government	The private rented sector. Modern methods of construction.
International Development	UK aid for combating climate change. UK arms exports during 2016.
International Trade	UK–US trade relations. UK trade options beyond 2019.
Justice	Young adults in the criminal justice system. Criminal legal aid.
Northern Ireland Affairs	The land border between Northern Ireland and Ireland. Brexit and agriculture in Northern Ireland.
Scottish Affairs	The future of Scottish agriculture post-Brexit. The relationship between the UK and Scottish governments.
Transport	Road safety: driving while using a mobile phone. Bus services in England outside London
Treasury	Student loans. Household finances: income, saving, and debt.
Welsh Affairs	The cancellation of rail electrification in South Wales. Prison provision in Wales.
Women and Equalities	High heels and workplace dress codes. Sexual harassment of women and girls in public places.
Work & Pensions	Employment opportunities for young people. Benefit sanctions.

Source: https://www.parliament.uk/business/publications/committees/select-committee-publications/.

Select committees – conducted in a series of rooms located on the first floor of the House of Commons – have wide powers to summon witnesses and to examine official documents and papers relevant to the adoption or development of a policy The most prominent 'witnesses' are government ministers themselves, who are often summoned to answer detailed questions in 'oral evidence' sessions, often lasting for two hours. If a committee's MPs are not satisfied with a minister's answers, or want further information, s/he can be summoned to return for another oral evidence session and be questioned until the committee is satisfied that it has obtained all the 'evidence' it needs from the minister. This means that select committee scrutiny of minsters is much more thorough than that provided by Ministers' Question Time once every four weeks or so. Moreover, a minister appearing before a select committee cannot give glib answers or engage in the kind of partisan point-scoring so often heard in the main chamber. As such, most ministers would probably confess that they are usually much more nervous about answering questions in front of 11 or 13 MPs than they are in front of dozens, or maybe even 100s, of MPs on the floor of the House of Commons at Ministers' Question Time.

However, it is not just ministers who are summoned to provide oral evidence to Departmental Select Committee inquiries. Other senior colleagues from their departments are sometimes 'invited' (they are not expected to decline a request to appear), such as junior ministers, senior civil servants, and special advisers – any or all of whom might have played a significant role in developing or implementing a departmental policy, and can therefore be expected to answer questions themselves.

Yet, Departmental Select Committees can invite almost anyone to submit oral evidence, depending on the topic or policy being investigated. For example, many inquiries will elicit evidence from the leaders of representative bodies, professional associations, or relevant charities: an inquiry into an aspect of education policy might entail leaders of the main teaching unions being questioned about the impact on the profession, while an educational psychologist or professor of education might be asked about the impact of a policy on pupils themselves. Similarly, a select committee inquiry into juvenile crime is likely to hold oral evidence sessions with representatives from the police, the probation service, social workers, and/or academics who teach or research criminology. Occasionally, a select committee will seek evidence from relevant members of the public to gauge how a policy or issue has affected them.

For example, when the Home Affairs Select Committee conducted, in 2017–18, an inquiry into domestic abuse, some of the 'witnesses' who submitted written evidence were women who had themselves suffered from abuse and violence in their homes, usually at the hands of an aggressive or violent boyfriend or husband. In this instance, the women were allowed to submit their evidence anonymously, rather than being named or asked to provide additional oral evidence, which might have placed them in further danger from their abusive (ex-)partners. Other examples of individuals and organisations who submitted written or/and oral evidence is provided in Table 8.8.

TABLE 8.8 Examples of individuals and organisations which submitted evidence to a Home Affairs Select Committee inquiry into domestic abuse, 2017–18

Action for Children	Liberty
Amnesty International	Local Government Association
Barnardo's	Rape Crisis England and Wales
British Association of Social Workers	Rights of Women
British Pregnancy Advisory Service	Rochdale Connections Trust
Children and Family Court Advisory and Support Service	Southall Black Sisters
Centre for Gender and Violence Research, University of Bristol	Suzy Lamplugh Trust
Crown Prosecution Service	Shazia Choudhry (Professor of Law)
Elizabeth A. Bates (Senior Lecturer in Applied Psychology)	Victim Support
End Violence Against Women Coalition	Welsh Women's Aid
Family Planning Association	Women Against Rape & Black Women's Rape Action Project
Institute of Alcohol Studies	Women's Aid Federation of England

Source: https://publications.parliament.uk/pa/cm201719/cmselect/cmhaff/1015/101512.htm#_idTextAnchor102.

When a select committee has finished taking written and oral evidence, usually over several weeks, or even months, it will usually publish a report in which it will summarise the main findings and conclusions from its inquiry, and make a series of recommendations about how the policy or problem investigated could or should be tackled by the Minister or Department. Sometimes, a report might include over 100 recommendations. Although ministers are not obliged to accept or act upon any of the recommendations, they are required to publish a response, within 60 days of a committee report's publication, in which each and every one of the recommendations is individually addressed. For each of them, the Minister or Department must either state what change will be made to the current policy or explain why no change will be made – in effect, why the government rejects the recommendation or the argument(s) on which it is based. As such, even when no changes are to be made, the minister will have been compelled to defend, in writing, their policy or stance (even if it is one of inaction). This further facilitates ministerial accountability to Parliament, via the backbench MPs on a select committee.

Although Departmental Select Committees cannot compel a minister or department, and ultimately the government, to implement its recommendations, research by Meg Russell and Meghan Benton (of the Constitution Unit at University College London) has revealed that about 40 per cent of select committee recommendations are accepted by governments, which result in policy amendment or change. Given that the committees lack any power of compulsion in enforcing their recommendations, the fact that 40 per cent of them are voluntarily accepted by British governments is actually highly impressive, and testimony to the importance – and influence – of Departmental Select Committees. Moreover, because they are comprised of backbench MPs from government and Opposition alike, these committees can be said to offer (in most instances) bipartisan, evidence-based, rather than party-political or ideological, recommendations, which might be a further reason why ministers and governments are often willing to accept some of their recommendations; they can do so without losing face. The bipartisan character of Departmental Select Committees is reinforced by their physical layout, for as the picture below shows, the MPs sit around a horseshoe- or semicircular-shaped table, rather than directly opposite each other, and this generally removes the adversarial us-versus-them atmosphere and conduct found in the main chamber ('on the floor') of the House of Commons. Moreover, the MPs on a select committee are deliberately 'mingled', so that they sit next to an MP from a different party.

Also, because MPs usually serve for a five-year term (which can be renewed – subject to re-election by other MPs – after the next general election), they steadily acquire considerable expertise in the sphere of policy covered by their select committee, be that education, health, pensions, or transport, for example. This, in turn, means that they can ask more rigorous or

PHOTO 8.4 Select Committee (© Catherine Bebbington/Parliamentary Copyright creativecommons.org/licenses/by/3.0/).

robust questions of minsters in oral evidence sessions and more readily recognise if and when they are not receiving a candid answer.

These oral evidence sessions are also, in most cases, open to members of the public, with seating provided at the back of the committee rooms for those who wish to observe. However, those observing are not permitted to speak or ask questions; they must watch and listen in respectful silence.

In addition to the Departmental Select Committees, there are a few 'thematic' select committees, such as the science and technology committee. Two of the most renowned are the Public Accounts Committee and the Public Administration and Constitutional Affairs Committee. The Public Accounts Committee, established in 1867, mostly examines the expenditure of government departments and their agencies, as well as the 'value for money' of major projects commissioned by the governments or its departments. Examples of recent (since 2017) inquiries by the Public Accounts Committee are illustrated in Table 8.9.

The Public Accounts Committee will sometimes attract headlines for the strength of its criticisms of financial mismanagement, or other forms of economic incompetence, by government departments or those commissioned to provide services on their behalf. Since 2018, the Committee's reports have:

- accused the government of failing to sell off enough land to build affordable and social housing, thereby exacerbating the UK housing crisis.
- criticised 'Universal Credit' for causing 'unacceptable hardship'.
- condemned the underfunding of public services, especially education, and health/social care.
- criticised the secrecy over Brexit consultancy spending.
- condemned the selling-off of the Student Loans system, which was sold 'too cheaply'.
- criticised 'exorbitantly expensive' private finance initiative (PFI) contracts.
- condemned NHS managers over waiting lists, accusing them of not understanding the impact on patients – physically, mentally, and emotionally – of delays to operations and surgery.
- criticised the delays, 'overspend', and serious mismanagement of 'Crossrail' (the across-London rail project).

Back in 2012, the Public Accounts Committee had made the headlines when it bitterly attacked major companies like Amazon, Google, and Starbucks over (corporation) tax avoidance. The Committee also condemned HM Revenue & Customs (part of the Treasury) for being 'way too lenient' in dealing with large companies which avoided paying taxes. The then Chancellor, George Osborne, immediately responded by announcing new measures, and more Inland Revenue staff, to tackle corporate tax evasion.

TABLE 8.9 Examples of inquiries conducted by the Public Accounts Committee since 2017

Defence Equipment Plan 2018–28
Department of Health and Social Care accounts
Financial sustainability of police forces in England and Wales
BBC commercial activities
Exiting the EU: The financial settlement
The Higher Education market
Rail franchising in the UK
The growing threat of online fraud
Academy schools' finances
Private Finance Initiatives
Universal Credit

TABLE 8.10 Examples of inquiries conducted by the Public Administration and Constitutional Affairs Committee since 2017

The work of the Cabinet Office

The Fixed-term Parliaments Act 2011

The work of the Office for National Statistics

Strategic Leadership in the Civil Service

A smaller House of Lords

After Carillion: Public sector outsourcing and contracting

The Minister and the Official: The Fulcrum of Whitehall Effectiveness

Parliamentary Boundary Reviews

The Government's management of major projects

Source: https://committees.parliament.uk/committee/327/public-administration-and-constitutional-affairs-committee.

Meanwhile, the Public Administration and Constitutional Affairs Committee scrutinises aspects of governance, such as the administration and operation of governments bodies and agencies – what might be called 'the machinery of government'. It also, as the name clearly suggests, examines constitutional issues. Examples of recent (since 2017) inquiries by the Public Administration and Constitutional Affairs Committee are illustrated in Table 8.10.

One other important select committee is the Backbench Business Committee, which was established as part of the aforementioned Wright Reforms in 2010. However, rather than operating through the sifting of evidence, and summonsing of witnesses, prior to publishing a report containing recommendations, this Committee pursues backbench scrutiny by choosing the topics for debate in the House of Commons' main chamber on up to 35 days per year. It should be noted that the Committee can either choose to devote a whole day to debating a single topic, or opt to have two shorter debates on different topics. As such, the total number of topics chosen for debate by the Backbench Business Committee might well be greater than the maximum of 35 days allocated each year. Examples of topics chosen for debate in 2019 included:

- Assisted dying
- Whistleblowing
- Social housing
- Grenfell Tower fire
- Medical cannabis
- Beer taxation and pubs
- International Women's Day
- Antisocial behaviour
- Rough sleeping
- Children's social care in England

As governments have always controlled the vast majority of the parliamentary timetable, conceding so many days to an all-party backbench committee was a significant reform and represented a further shift in power away from the executive back towards Parliament. Furthermore, by permitting the creation of a Backbench Business Committee, and granting it the right to choose what was debated on up to 35 days per year, the government was effectively enabling backbench MPs to debate topics which ministers might otherwise have preferred to avoid, or discuss less publicly.

Recruitment of ministers

It is a 'convention' of British politics that all ministers must be members of either the House of Commons or the House of Lords, in order to ensure that they can be held to account for their decisions and policies by Parliament, via MPs and peers. Indeed, during the twentieth century, as political power shifted decisively from the House of Lords to the House of Commons, the vast majority of ministers were recruited from the latter. In this respect, Parliament is the arena in which backbench MPs can make a name for themselves and advance their political careers, perhaps by their loyalty to their leader, their communication skills in debates, their impressive grasp of detail when asking questions (notwithstanding that few ministers are experts in their sphere of policy), or their diligent service on a parliamentary committee. Through such skill or talent, some backbench MPs get noticed by their party leader or the whips, and find themselves being given a ministerial (or shadow ministerial) post in the next reshuffle, or in the wake of a minister resigning.

What has also increased the importance of Parliament as an arena for the recruitment of ministers is that the number of ministerial posts has increased over time, so that many more of them are appointed compared to 50 or 100 years ago (see Chapter 7). Furthermore, recent decades have witnessed the emergence of the 'career politician', for whom parliamentary politics is a long-term career (subject, of course, to regular re-election), with the aspiration, in many instances, of being promoted to a ministerial post. Of course, the expansion in the number of ministers makes such promotion much more likely, which, in turn, makes becoming an MP a more attractive career option for those individuals with either a strong sense of public service (although, of course, this might lead to other careers) or firm ideological convictions.

Another reason why Parliament, although primarily the House of Commons, is an important source of ministerial recruitment is that through their membership, MPs learn the 'rules of the game' in terms of parliamentary customs and conventions, along with procedural rules and requirements. This is the 'socialisation' aspect of being an MP. As new MPs do not receive formal training in how to be a good parliamentarian, they rely very much on learning by observing and doing; they learn 'on the job'. Given how strongly many veteran MPs believe in the customs and traditions of 'the House', it is important for younger or newer MPs to show some deference to these long-established and revered parliamentary practices if they wish to enhance their political career prospects.

Occasionally, a prime minister might want to appoint an 'outsider' to a ministerial post, due to their valuable and relevant 'real-world' experience and expertise. In such instances, the person concerned will need to become a parliamentarian, which means the prime minister has two options: either use a by-election to enable the favoured individual to become an MP, or recommend them for a peerage so that they can then sit in the House of Lords. However, relying on a by-election can be risky, because if such an election is prompted by sending the current MP to the House of Lords, in order to create a vacancy in the constituency as the pre-text for a by-election, then local voters might resent such manouvering (especially if the local MP was very popular), and thus decline to vote for the new candidate who has suddenly been imposed upon them. As such, the much safer option for a prime minister is to arrange for their favoured individual to be awarded a peerage, so that they can then sit in the House of Lords, whereupon they will be eligible to become a minister.

Accountability

The roles of debate and scrutiny are themselves vital to ensuring that the government in general, and ministers in particular, are **accountable** to Parliament, in terms of defending and explaining their decisions and policies, and accepting responsibility in instances of major misjudgement or misconduct.

This, in turn, is a major reason why ministers must be members of Parliament, either as MPs (in the vast majority of instances) or peers. Only by being such members can they be accountable and answerable to their fellow parliamentarians and, indirectly at last, the electorate beyond Parliament. Governments and ministers must constantly, through the mechanisms outlined, explain and justify their decisions and policies. In theory – if not always in practice – such accountability is supposed to ensure that governments and ministers behave with a reasonable degree of moderation and integrity, aware that that if they behave rashly and recklessly, they will be challenged by other MPs, and their arrogance or incompetence publicly highlighted. In extreme cases, they might be obliged to resign, their political career brought to a premature end.

Verdict

Does the House of Commons do its job?

There is an obvious danger of appraising the performance of the House of Commons against standards which could not be met by any elected legislature. However, given the central role of representative institutions within any liberal democracy, they ought to be judged against high standards. Taking in turn the categories we have discussed, it seems reasonable to argue that:

- Due to the fusion of powers between legislature and executive, the House of Commons cannot realistically hope to hold the government to account on a consistent basis. However, even within these limits, it is surely reasonable to expect (for example) that ministerial resignations should occur after the Commons has debated policy errors, rather than because of media revelations about private indiscretions. Between 1990 and 2015, the majority of resignations have followed media 'witch-hunts' against specific individuals. The public appetite for such scandals might reflect, at least in part, the difficulty of removing ministers for failings which are more relevant to their jobs.
- As we have seen, Parliament as a whole is not 'representative' of the British public, in a variety of respects. Attempts to redress the imbalance have tended to focus on gender and ethnicity. On this front, there have been notable and laudable advances; but these would only enhance Parliament's reputation if they were part of a more general drive to give Britain's voters a Parliament which contained people more like themselves in terms of outlook and upbringing. The proportion of 'ordinary people', with experience of life outside politics and the media, has declined to a noticeable extent since 2001, when electoral turnout fell below 60 per cent for the first time since the very 'atypical' contest of 1918. The current 'political class' in the UK is not just different in terms of life experience, its members also tend to *think* in a way which is alien to most voters, for example, by giving undue attention to short-term partisan considerations rather than focusing on the long-term national interest.
- Parliamentary debates can be viewed more easily than ever before, due to a television channel specifically devoted to Westminster. Nor is it just debates: the increasingly effective and prestigious select committees provide a genuine reason for optimism, since their proceedings can make 'good television', while highlighting the ability of MPs to hold powerful public

figures to account, and sometimes prompt a change of policy by the government. However, in the Commons chamber itself, MPs have little incentive to shine in debate because, except for the often unedifying ritual of Prime Minister's Question Time, it can be safely assumed that only a handful of people will be paying attention. In this respect, it can be argued that the introduction of cameras into the Commons was a retrograde step; confining coverage to radio broadcasts on set piece occasions would have preserved some of the mystique which had been stripped away long before the 2009 expenses scandal.

- No one denies that Parliament is good at *passing* legislation, but it is easy to argue that too much legislation is inadequate. For much of the period between 1979 and 2010, governments enjoyed overwhelming majorities and had little incentive to listen to constructive suggestions from opposition MPs or non-parliamentary observers. The Conservative–Liberal Democrat coalition seemed more anxious than its predecessors to listen to the public; but, as the 2012 Health and Social Care Act showed, this did not necessarily lead to more constructive or sensitive law-making. It would be preferable if the Commons was a more truly 'representative' body, which could frame workable legislation without having to bring in the real 'experts' on a range of policy issues *after* a proposal has been debated.

- Parliament continues to be good at recruiting political leaders; however, since ministers have to be serving members of one of the two Houses, it would be difficult for Westminster *not* to perform this function. Talented (and even mildly eccentric) people continue to serve in government after an apprenticeship in one of the two houses, but the orthodox political process definitely favours individuals who conform to a particular profile. To recruit ministers who offer something different, recent prime ministers have elevated people to the House of Lords with the specific purpose of giving them jobs in government. So, although Parliament can hardly *fail* to recruit ministers, in recent years, it could have done the job much better and in a fashion which is more compatible with the liberal–democratic precepts which legislatures are specifically charged with upholding.

The House of Lords

Also known as the Upper House or second chamber, the House of Lords performs the same roles and activities as the House of Commons, but with a few important variations in *how* these are conducted. It also has a wholly different basis of membership, and limited power: due to the 1949 Parliament Act, it can only delay a bill by a year. The latter reflects and reinforces the fact that the House of Lords is, ultimately, subordinate to the House of Commons, not least because the latter enjoys legitimacy by virtue of being directly elected, whereas the members of the House of Lords, known as peers, are appointed (see later in the chapter). The supremacy of the House of Commons was reaffirmed by the White Paper titled *Modernising Parliament: Reforming the House of Lords*, which preceded the 1999 reform of the House of Lords (see below): this emphasised 'the need to maintain the position of the House of Commons as the pre-eminent chamber of Parliament', which served as a warning that whatever reform of the House of Lords was introduced, it must not strengthen the second chamber in a way which would make it equal alongside the House of Commons.

It must immediately be emphasised that the relationship between the House of Lords and House of Commons is not normally adversarial or confrontational. Although there are occasionally clashes and stand-offs which are given prominent coverage by the sensation-seeking media, such instances are the exception to what is normally a cooperative and complementary relationship. The House of Lords generally accepts its subordinate or 'junior partner' relationship to the elected House of Commons, while the latter recognises that, without the House of Lords, it would struggle to cope with its legislative and scrutiny functions: the second chamber shares some of the workload of the Lower House, and thereby alleviates some of the pressure which MPs would otherwise face. In other words, if the House of Lords did not already exist, a second chamber of some kind would almost certainly need to be created. This is one of the reasons why the Labour Left's demands for abolition of the House of Lords have not been more widely supported in the party.

The House of Lords therefore plays a vital role both in the parliamentary legislative process and in the scrutiny of government. As noted earlier, Bills proceed through exactly the same sequence or stages in the House of Lords as they do in the Commons – first reading, second reading, and so forth. This is the case regardless of whether a bill starts its parliamentary journey in the Lords or the Commons. The only difference occurs at committee stage, for in the House of Lords, this is held on the floor of the House, meaning that all peers are entitled to take part, whereas in the Commons, a bill is usually (but not always) 'sent upstairs' to be considered by a committee comprised of a relatively small number of MPs. The 'committee stage' in the House of Lords can see further amendments 'tabled' to a bill, although whether these remain in the final version of the bill will depend on how far the government is willing to accept them. If it is unhappy with any amendment, the government is likely to seek its removal, and hope that the Lords will accept this by backing down. However, occasionally, a government might reluctantly accept a Lords' amendment in order to avoid a bill being sent back and forth between the two Houses – literally known as ping-pong – and thereby risk a delay in it receiving the Royal Assent.

There are also some subtle but still significant differences between the House of Lords and the House of Commons in terms of the scrutiny function, whereby government policies and ministers are held to account. The first concerns Question Time in the House of Lords, which is usually a less adversarial event than in the Commons. The team of ministers in each government department will usually include a peer, and one of his/her responsibilities will be to answer questions in the Lords on a regular basis, although because there are fewer ministers in the Lords than in the Commons – and many of them are junior ministers – they are expected to answer on a somewhat broader range of policy issues. A second difference is that debates in the House of Lords tend to be conducted in a calmer, more courteous, manner, with much lower levels of partisanship and political point-scoring, even though most peers sit and vote with 'their' party (see later). Debates are mostly free of barracking from the 'other side', and even when disagreements are expressed between peers from different parties, they are usually much less likely to entail the cheering or jeering so often heard in the Commons. Part of this more civilised conduct reflects the greater maturity of many peers: many are in their 60s or 70s (with a few in their 80s), and are likely to have mellowed or calmed-down, at least in their public behaviour, if not in their political views. It is also the case that many peers have expertise on particular issues, due to their former careers, and hence often speak with authority or direct experience when speaking about a policy or problem. This too means that debates and scrutiny in the House of Lords are often better 'informed' and conducted in a more dignified and respectful manner: peers from one party often respect the first-hand knowledge and professional experience of a peer from another party, and concede that 'he/she really knows what they are talking about', even when they still disagree politically.

The third main difference between the House of Lords and the House of Commons in terms of scrutiny concerns the select committees in the second chamber. Whereas the House of Commons' select committees directly 'shadow' government departments, the House of Lords' committees are 'thematic', meaning that they examine particular aspects of policy or issues, rather than the work of a specific department. For example, instead of having a Treasury select committee, the House of Lords has a select committee on Economic Affairs, and instead of a Foreign Affairs Select Committee shadowing the Foreign Office, the Upper House has select committee on International Relations and Defence.

Composition

There are three main types of peer in the House of Lords: Lords Spiritual, hereditary peers, and life peers. The 'Lords Spiritual' is the collective term for the 26 peers who represent the Church of England: archbishops and bishops. Hereditary peers are those who have inherited their titles, and, in turn, previously had a right to sit in the House of Lords if they wished. Many of these peers are descendants of the old aristocracy, whereby family titles (and wealth and property) were passed down to the eldest son when his father died. However, in 1999, the vast majority of hereditary peers were removed from the House of Lords, although 92 were permitted to remain, as a compromise, on a temporary basis, although they are still there. This did not mean that hereditary peerages were actually abolished, but that someone inheriting a title (such as Lord X, Viscount Y or Baron Z) no longer enjoyed an automatic right to sit in the House of Lords. The overwhelming majority of peers are life peers, who are awarded a title and a place in the second chamber until they retire or die: their title is not passed on to their offspring, but effectively dies with them. Life peers were first created in 1958 in order to rejuvenate and modernise the membership of the House of Lords – pouring new wine into an old bottle – and reduce the dominance of the hereditary peers without actually abolishing them: for the Conservative government at that time, abolition would have been too radical. Over time, life peers increased in number as new ones were created each year, meaning that even without actually cutting the number of hereditary peers, the latter declined as a proportion of the Lords' membership. Life peerages are usually awarded to individuals who have made a significant contribution to professional or public life; for example, via academia, the arts, business, charity, finance, industry, politics, science, and voluntary work. In this regard, life peerages are recognition of major achievement or success in a particular field of activity, and thus a reward.

The introduction of life peers had three important long-term consequences, beyond reducing the hitherto dominance of hereditary peers. First, it slowly reduced the overwhelming preponderance of men in the House of Lords, as women were increasingly awarded life peerages, whereas they could not (usually) inherit a title due to the (patriarchal) male lineage in aristocratic families. Since 1958, therefore, the number of women in the House of Lords has increased, although there is still a long way to go before they achieve parity with men: in May 2020, out of a total of 784 peers, 215 were women, so still only just over a quarter.

Second, the expansion of life peers has reduced the former Conservative preponderance in the House of Lords. As hereditary peers often emanated from aristocratic backgrounds and families, with the associated land, property, and wealth, the vast majority of them were Conservatives. This meant that a Conservative-dominated second chamber could obstruct the laws and policies approved by an elected Liberal or Labour government in the House of Commons, notwithstanding the one-year veto. Eventually, more enlightened or forward-thinking Conservatives recognised that this could undermine the legitimacy of the House of Lords and lead to demands for its abolition, which is largely why the 1955–59 Conservative government passed the 1958 Life Peerage Act, to allow the creation of non-hereditary peers. One consequence was that the House of Lords slowly acquired relatively greater political balance, as some life peers sat on the Labour or Liberal benches, or became politically 'independent' cross benchers. Some of the latter were peers who chose not to be associated with a particular political party, while others were appointees whose recent careers required them to be politically neutral, such as former senior civil servants and judges. For many years now, no party has enjoyed a majority in the House of Lords – in May 2020, the total number of number of peers per party (hereditary peers in brackets) was:

Conservatives – 245 (46)
Labour – 178 (4)

Liberal Democrat – 90 (3)
Crossbenchers – 182 (29)
Non-affiliated – 47 (6)
Lords Spiritual – 26 (0)
Democratic Unionist Party – 4 (0)
Ulster Unionist Party – 2 (0)
Green Party – 2 (0)
Plaid Cymru – 1 (0)

In effect, on some issues, the balance of power on decisive votes is held by the cross benchers. This might also be another reason why debates in the House of Lords are often calmer and more 'rational' than those held in the House of Commons. If a Conservative or Labour peer is seeking to secure the support of the cross benchers for a policy or bill, then they are highly unlikely to achieve this by engaging in partisan point-scoring or political hyperbole. Instead, cross bench (and other non-affiliated) peers will usually need to be convinced by the clarity and logic of the arguments and evidence put forward, and the calmness with which these are presented. The third long-term consequence of introducing life peerages has been to infuse the House of Lords with considerable expertise – certainly more than usually exists in the House of Commons. This is because, as noted earlier, life peerages are usually awarded in recognition of a lifetime's achievement in a prominent career or professional role. True, this reinforces the middle-class over-representation in Parliament – someone is unlikely to be awarded a life peerage as a reward for being a successful bus-driver or superb supermarket check-out operator for 30 years – but it does mean that the House of Lords is *relatively* more 'representative' of British society than when it was dominated by hereditary peers whose only 'qualification' was having been born into a wealthy or high-ranking family! Based on data published by the Electoral Reform Society in 2018 (the latest year for which detailed information was available at the time of writing), Table 8.11 shows the previous occupations or professions of life peers.

TABLE 8.11 Previous occupations or professions of life peers, 2018

Former occupation or profession	Number of peers	% of peers
Agriculture	19	2
Architecture, engineering, and construction	8	1
Armed forces	15	2
Banking and finance	49	6
Business and commerce	70	9
Civil service (UK)	13	2
Culture, arts, and sport	18	2
Education and training (not HE)	5	1
Higher education	43	5
International affairs and diplomacy	10	1
Journalism, media, and publishing	32	4
Law	55	7
Medical and healthcare	17	2
MPs & ministers	235	29
Police	8	1
Political staff and activists	68	8
Trade Unions	22	3
Voluntary sector, NGOs, and think tanks	32	4

Source: Electoral Reform Society, *New Figures Reveal Lords Is Dominated by Ex-Politicians and South East*, Press Release 18 June 2018, https://www.electoral-reform.org.uk/latest-news-and-research/media-centre/press-releases/new-figures-reveal-lords-is-dominated-by-ex-politicians-and-south-east/.

As just suggested, this expertise often means that debates in the House of Lords are rather calmer and more courteous than those in the House of Commons, with much less overt partisanship too. Very often, peers will be speaking on the basis of experience or expertise, and, as such, even peers from other parties will usually listen in respectful silence, perhaps reinforced by having mellowed with age and maturity. This expertise is particularly notable in the membership of the House of Lords' select committees. For example, the 13 members of the Economic Affairs (select) Committee include:

- a former chairman of Santander UK
- a former Director of the Bank of England, and of Sainsbury's
- a chairman of Dixons Carphone, having previously held senior posts with British Telecom.
- a Professor of Political Economy
- a former chairman of Blue Circle, and then Santander
- a former Director of GKN (Aerospace & Engineering)
- a former senior adviser to the Bank of Scotland, and previous holder of various directorships
- a former Professor of Economics, senior official in the Treasury, and Chief Economist of the World Bank
- a former Deputy Chairman of JP Morgan (investment bank).

No House of Commons select committee could boast such breadth, depth, and relevance of expertise.

Reform of the House of Lords

For more than a century, the second chamber has been regarded very much as subordinate to the House of Commons, primarily because only the latter is elected by 'the people'. For example, the last prime minister to retain a seat in the House of Lords while occupying 10 Downing Street was the third Marquess of Salisbury, who left office in 1902. The steady decline of the House of Lords in the following decades was marked by the passage of two Parliament Acts (1911 and 1949), which removed its power of veto. After 1949, the Lords could merely delay the passage of most legislation for a maximum of 13 months. Another crucial landmark was the Life Peerages Act of 1958, a measure which promised to enhance the quality of the House of Lords, since the new life peers owed their membership to their own achievements (real or reputed) rather than the circumstances of their birth. However, there was a danger that the Act would make the Lords less *distinctive* compared to the Commons, because many of the most prominent life peers had previously been MPs and ministers rather than achieving eminence in other fields. In 1963, the Conservative government of Harold Macmillan also passed the Peerage Act, allowing ambitious politicians to renounce inherited titles which would otherwise make them ineligible for a seat in the Commons. This legislation was quickly utilised by the 14th Earl of Home, who reverted to Sir Alec Douglas-Home in order to succeed Macmillan as prime minister (1963–64). After a further stint as Foreign Secretary (1970–74), Home rejoined the Lords, but this time as a life peer.

In combination, these measures made the House of Lords into a 'revising' chamber. Leaders of the House of Lords, like Viscount Whitelaw (1983–88), believed that peers should only persist in their opposition to a bill when some crucial principle was at stake. The role of the Lords, in Whitelaw's view, was to give the Commons a chance to reconsider legislation which had not been thought through properly. Superficially, this was a modest ambition, but it clearly implied that the Commons could not be relied upon to give adequate scrutiny to Bills. One effect of the 1958 Life Peerages Act had been to make the Lords into something like a retirement home for former ministers, who could bring their accumulated wisdom and experience to bear when the Commons had been overly hasty.

Supporters of the House of Lords argue that it has performed a valuable role in a liberal democracy, even though few people would have designed it in its existing form. A second chamber provides an additional mechanism of 'checks-and-balances' – alongside the formal separation of powers between the legislature, executive, and the judiciary – by making it more difficult for governments to push through radical or reckless legislation too rapidly. Conservatives could also point approvingly to the 'accumulated wisdom' which was enshrined in the House of Lords, by virtue of its supposedly illustrious and experienced membership.

However, the Labour Party has traditionally been more critical of the House of Lords, deeming it undemocratic that a political institution packed with (mostly Conservative) hereditary peers could veto legislation passed by an elected Labour government in the House of Commons. That the House of Lords very rarely invoked this veto did not assuage Labour's hostility – the potential was always there if a Labour government introduced a law which the hereditary peers strongly objected to. Yet Labour has never been agreed about what to do about the House of Lords, partly because Labour has never developed a coherent theory of 'the state' or constitutional reform, and partly because there have been various potential options for reform. Having passed the 1949 Parliament Act, to reduce the House of Lords' veto from two years to one, the Labour Party subsequently struggled to agree on what to do next. Some of its MPs wanted to further reduce the veto, perhaps to six months, but others argued that the Lords would be more likely to invoke a shorter veto more often; it mostly refrained from using the one-year veto because this a 'nuclear option', but a shorter veto might be used more freely and frequently, and thereby cause chaos to the government's legislative programme and timetable. It was also argued that the veto itself was not really the problem, but who was liable to invoke it – the Conservative hereditary peers. As such, rather than worry about the one-year veto, it was argued that a Labour government should reform the 'composition' of the Upper House by removing the hereditaries.

Yet this then raised a series of further questions which the Labour Party has never been able to answer, at least not unanimously: how would a non-hereditary membership be determined – appointment or election? Appointment might increase prime ministerial patronage, while an elected House of Lords might acquire so much 'legitimacy' that it would rival the House of Commons, and be much more likely to challenge it than at present. Also, if the House of Lords was to be elected, what method of election would be adopted (first-past-the-post, or some form of PR), and when would the elections be held – the same time as general elections, or perhaps at the mid-point between them? If the former, the House of Lords, might simply mirror the party composition of the House of Commons, whereas if the latter, then a government suffering the 'mid-term blues' might lose support to the Opposition after two to three years, meaning that a Labour government in the Commons could be confronted with an elected Conservative majority in the Lords. This could be a recipe for constitutional chaos, with the House of Lords claiming to more accurately reflect current public opinion than the government in the House of Commons elected two to three years ago. For all these reason, Labour's long-standing criticisms of the House of Lords have never been matched by a clear, coherent, and consistent or agreed policy of reform.

In 1998, Tony Blair's New Labour government published a White Paper, *Modernising Parliament: Reforming the House of Lords* (Cm 4183), which envisaged the removal of all hereditary peers after a transitional period – a two-stage programme of reform. In future, new members of the House would be appointed by an independent commission, rather than the prime minister. However, when the relevant legislation was passed in 1999, this proposal had been watered down, after a deal negotiated with the astute leader of the Conservative peers, Viscount Cranborne. Ninety-two hereditaries – elected by their fellow peers – were allowed to remain, pending the report of a Royal

Commission (see Table 8.4). Headed by the former Conservative minister Lord Wakeham, the members of the Commission were carefully selected in the expectation that they would opt for a wholly appointed Lords. However, the Commission decided that the best long-term solution was an Upper House with a mixed composition, including an elected element which might be chosen through proportional representation on a regional basis, and the House would retain its existing power. The changes had not been implemented by the time of the 2001 general election, but Labour promised that, if re-elected, it would broadly follow the Commission's guidelines. A White Paper published in 2001, based on the findings of the Royal Commission, was optimistically entitled *The House of Lords: Completing the Reform* (Cm 5291), but to this day, what was supposed to be 'stage two' of House of Lords reform has still not been enacted. As was widely envisaged, once all but 92 of the (Conservative) hereditary peers had been removed, Blair, and many of his New Labour colleagues, lost interest in further reform of the House of Lords; they were content with the 'new' Upper House in which the Conservative no longer enjoyed an in-built majority. Meanwhile, those Labour MPs who did want to pursue 'stage two' could not agree on the various options – a fully elected second chamber, 80 per cent elected and 20 per cent appointed, 60 per cent elected and 40 per cent appointed, 50/50, 40 per cent elected and 60 per cent appointed, and so forth. When MPs were given the opportunity to vote on these options, none of them secured majority support, and the voting record showed just how deeply divided the Labour Party remained.

When it came to office after the 2010 general election, the Conservative–Liberal Democrat coalition took its turn to pick up the hot (and now somewhat battered) potato. The key question now seemed to be whether the upper chamber would be wholly or predominantly elected, and on what basis. The joint policy document published when the coalition was formed leaned towards the latter solution, with elected members serving long, unrenewable terms. In May 2011, more detailed proposals were announced along those lines, in a draft bill. The House would contain 300 members, with 20 per cent appointed and 12 places reserved for bishops. Members would be chosen by single transferable vote (STV), in elections which would be staggered so that a third would be elected at any one time. The parallels with the US Senate were obvious, and the plan satisfied the requirement that the two chambers of Parliament should be elected by contrasting systems rather than by duplicating each other. However, this carefully prepared proposal foundered in the face of Conservative opposition in the Commons, enraging the Liberal Democrats. The coalition's only notable reform concerning the Upper House was the 2014 House of Lords Reform Act, which allowed peers the opportunity to relinquish their legislative role by retiring from the second chamber, an initiative which could be presented in populist terms as reducing (albeit voluntarily) the number of politicians in general, and elderly peers in particular. Beyond this was little appetite among Conservatives for further House of Lords reform, so the second chamber today, in 2020, remains almost entirely appointed, but with about 90 hereditary peers still enjoying membership.

Conclusion and summary

For all its democratic symbolism, the British Parliament is clearly in need of reform. It might have acted as a powerful constraint on the executive during the nineteenth century, but increasingly that period looks like a freakish exception to the general trend of growing executive dominance. In the early modern period, the unelected monarch was the obvious target for opposition from politicians hoping to restrain the overly mighty executive. The fact that the source of power has changed – and that many MPs dream of one day taking the premiership, while they never contemplate seizing the throne – does not mean that Parliament should abandon the executive-checking role it once discharged with reasonable success. It should merely switch its target, from the hereditary monarch to the prime minister who would otherwise be an 'elected dictator'.

As this chapter has shown, the main obstacle to change is the fact that the legislature and executive in the UK is fused, and the executive power of the prime minister depends on his or her ability to command a majority in the House of Commons. In turn, this power arises from the still relatively strong party discipline among MPs, whose ranks include an increasing proportion of 'career politicians'. Even when Opposition parties have criticised executive arrogance towards Parliament and pledged to introduce reforms to reset the balance when they are next in power, their ministers have invariably lost interest when they are next in government; they discover they really rather relish the power that being in office gives them, even though that power will once again, sooner or later, be wielded by their political opponents. After all, strengthening either House would almost certainly mean more effective scrutiny of the government itself, and quite probably a slower passage of legislation as MPs and/or peers examined it more carefully and closely. Indeed, when governments do (occasionally) pursue parliamentary reform, they are usually motivated by a desire to increase the 'efficiency' of Parliament, meaning that they want to streamline procedures or structures in order to get more legislation enacted more quickly. The alternative rationale for reform, namely, to improve the 'effectiveness' of Parliament, by increasing its capacity to conduct more thorough scrutiny and improve ministerial accountability, is not the objective that governments usually wish to pursue. As such, to the extent that parliamentary reform does occasionally move up the political agenda, there is usually a divergence between the type of reform(s) favoured by governments and the type of reform(s) favoured by backbenchers and/or Opposition parties. So it continues – periodic acknowledgement that Parliament needs to be reformed and modernised, but a perennial failure to agree on precisely how, and to what exact purpose.

Further reading

R. Rogers and R. Walters, *How Parliament Works* (Harlow: Longman, 6th edition, 2006), is an invaluable guide for students and practitioners alike. M. Rush's *Parliament Today* (Manchester: Manchester University Press, 2005) is a very sound introduction. Lord (Philip)) Norton has produced several insightful and accessible articles and books on this subject, notably *Parliament in British Politics,* second edition (Basingstoke: Palgrave, 2014). C. Leston-Bandeira and L. Thompson (eds.), *Exploring Parliament* (Oxford: Oxford University Press, 2018), is a comprehensive collection of essays about Parliament, with chapters written by academics and parliamentary clerks who teach on a specially designed 'Parliamentary Studies' module at 25 UK universities. See also Thompson's chapter 'UK Parliament', in M. Garnett (ed.), *The Routledge Handbook of British Politics and Society* (London: Routledge, 2020), and M. Russell, 'Parliament: A Significant Constraint on Government', in R. Heffernan, C. Hay, M. Russell, and P. Cowley (eds.), *Developments in British Politics 10* (Basingstoke: Palgrave Macmillan, 2016). On the House of Lords specifically, D. Shell's, *The House of Lords* (Manchester: Manchester University Press, 2007) remains a clear and concise account of the second chamber's activities and membership.

On parliamentary reform and other recent developments, see A. Kelso's *Parliamentary Reform at Westminster* (Manchester: Manchester University Press, 2009), P. Dorey and A. Kelso's *Must the Lords Go? House of Lords Reform since 2011* (Basingstoke: Palgrave Macmillan, 2011), P. Norton's *Reform of the House of Lords* (Manchester: Manchester University Press, 2017), A. Kelso's 'Changing Parliamentary Landscapes', in R. Heffernan, P. Cowley, and C. Hay (eds.), *Developments in British Politics 9* (Basingstoke: Palgrave Macmillan, 2011), pp. 51–69; and L. Fisher's 'The Growing Power and Autonomy of House of Commons Select Committees: Causes and Effects', *Political Quarterly*, Vol. 86, No. 3 (July–September

2015), pp. 419–26. It is difficult to publish academic commentaries fast enough to keep pace with the meandering course of Lords reform. C. Farrington, 'Lords Reform: Some Inconvenient Truths', *Political Quarterly*, Vol. 86, No. 3 (July September 2015), pp. 297–306, discusses the coalition's record and offers some new perspectives. On Labour's ambivalence and hesitancy over Lords reform, see P. Dorey, '1949, 1969, 1999: The Labour Party and House of Lords Reform', *Parliamentary Affairs*, Vol. 59.4 (2006), and P. Dorey's 'Stumbling Through "Stage Two": New Labour and House of Lords Reform', *British Politics*, Vol. 3, No. 1 (2008), pp. 22–44. M. Russell, *Reforming the House of Lords: Lessons from Overseas* (Oxford: Oxford University Press, 2000), is a comparative study. Most aspects of Parliament, and the reform process in particular, are covered in a special issue of *Parliamentary Affairs*, Vol. 57, No. 4 (2004).

An invigorating account of backbench disobedience is P. Cowley, *The Rebels: How Blair Mislaid His Majority* (London: Methuen, 2005). On women in the Commons, see S. Childs, *New Labour's MPs: Women Representing Women* (London: Routledge, 2004), and J. Lovenduski and P. Norris, 'Westminster Women: The Politics of Presence', *Political Studies*, Vol. 51, No. 1 (2003), pp. 84–102. R. Campbell and S. Childs updated this theme in '"Wags", "Wives" and "Mothers"… But What About Women Politicians?', in A. Geddes and J. Tonge (eds.), *Britain Votes 2010* (Oxford: Oxford University Press, 2010). G. Brandreth's *Breaking the Code: Westminster Diaries, 1992–97* (London: Weidenfeld & Nicolson, 1999) provides an insider view of the work of the whips at a particularly difficult historical juncture; C. Mullins' diaries (A *View from the Foothills* (2009) and *Decline and Fall* (2010), both published in London by Profile Books), also chronicle the life of a backbencher and junior minister.

A lively, affectionate study of the parliamentary mindset is provided by P. Riddell, *Honest Opportunism: How We Get the Politicians We Deserve* (London: Indigo, 1996). A reconsideration of the role of MPs in the wake of the expenses scandal, from one of the greatest recent servants of the House of Commons, is T. Wright, 'What are MPs For?', *Political Quarterly*, Vol. 81, No. 3 (July–September 2010), pp. 298–308. Those with a more jaundiced view of our legislators will find plenty of support for their pessimism in D. Leigh and E. Vulliamy's *Sleaze: The Corruption of Parliament* (London: Fourth Estate, 1997), and P. Oborne's *The Triumph of the Political Class* (London: Simon & Schuster, 2007). Some fascinating insights into New Labour's true commitment to modernisation can be gleaned from the late Robin Cook's memoir, *The Point of Departure* (London: Simon & Schuster, 2003).

Websites

By far the best resource for students of Parliament is the official website: www.parliament.the-stationery-office.co.uk. This provides links to sites for the House of Commons and the House of Lords, giving concise introductions to parliamentary procedure and recent reforms. It also provides access to the official record of debates (Hansard) and even contact addresses for MPs and peers. A specialist politics news website (www.politics.co.uk) features many useful links to articles with more critical content. The Ministry of Justice is responsible for reform of the Lords and includes full details of recent reform proposals at www.justice.gov.uk.

Three sites on the activities and behaviour of MPs can be recommended. Philip Cowley and Mark Stuart's website (www.revolts.co.uk) provides a comprehensive analysis of backbench rebellions, complete with spirited commentary; the Public Whip (www.publicwhip.org.uk/index.php) provides details of the voting records of MPs since 1997, and They Work for You (www.theyworkforyou.com) has a search facility for everything each MP and peer has said in Parliament since 2001.

The judiciary and the law

Introduction

In most courses on British politics, law and order and the judiciary have been treated as something of an 'optional extra'. In itself, this tells us something important about traditional understandings of the British system of government. In many liberal democracies, notably the United States, the judiciary is a fully separate branch of government, whose role is specified within a written constitution. In the UK, it has a more ambiguous status. Both the judiciary and the police have tended to be regarded as 'above' (or at least 'outside') politics.

This approach was always highly misleading and is no longer tenable. Law and order was a central political issue long before February 1993 when, as Shadow Home Secretary, Tony Blair promised that Labour would be 'tough on crime and tough on the causes of crime'. In recent elections, topics like the level of recorded crime and police numbers have been widely discussed. Meanwhile, the attitudes of the police on sensitive issues like race have come under unprecedented scrutiny, and the 'phone-hacking' scandal has raised serious concerns about the relationship between senior police officers and the media (see Chapter 5).

In recent decades, the relationship between the (appointed) judiciary and elected politicians has become increasingly strained, at least in part because of the British constitution's failure to establish a clear separation of powers (see Chapter 6). Senior judges have frequently complained about undue interference from politicians. But in their turn, they have found themselves under regular attack, from politicians and, more vociferously, from sections of the media. Relations reached new depths in the aftermath of the 2016 referendum, when judges were accused of taking nakedly 'political' decisions. Friction between government and the police has been less severe, but several Home Secretaries have been given rough receptions by police conferences in recent years, and the police have shown a willingness to contemplate taking some form of industrial action in support of pay claims – something which would have been unthinkable until quite recently. In this chapter, we examine the reasons for these tensions in the context of constitutional change, and discuss other issues involving the British judiciary and police forces.

The judicial system in the UK

Justice in Britain is administered through a complex network of courts which have evolved over many centuries. There are important variations between the systems in the component parts of the UK, but for convenience, we will follow the usual practice and focus on the system in England and Wales.

Most minor criminal cases – those leading to sentences of six months' imprisonment or less on conviction – are heard in magistrates' courts. There are around 160 of these courts in England and Wales; their numbers have been reduced by half since 2010. They are staffed by around 16,000 magistrates (also known as Justices of the Peace or JPs). This office dates back to the reign of Richard I in the twelfth century. Most magistrates are part-time and unpaid, appointed by advisory panels under the authority of the Lord Chief Justice. The magistrates in some large urban areas are known as 'District Judges' (formerly 'stipendiary' magistrates) and are paid to reflect the fact that they are required to have extensive previous experience as legal practitioners. Magistrates sit without a jury, in panels of between two and seven members. Most of them have no formal legal training, and their judgements are supposed to reflect the 'common sense' of the local community. They can, though, draw on technical advice from legally trained officials. Around 97 per cent of cases in England and Wales are dealt with in this way; in 2018, about 1.5 million cases were received by magistrates' courts.

Magistrates send more serious criminal cases for trial before a judge and jury at the local Crown Court. Currently, the Crown Court sits in around 80 locations in England and Wales, including the Central Criminal Court in London (better known as the Old Bailey). More than half of the defendants plead guilty before the case opens, so that the proceedings only concern the appropriate sentence. Appeals against Crown Court verdicts are heard by senior judges sitting in the Criminal Division of the Court of Appeal. When an important point of law has been raised and requires clarification, the Appeal Court can give leave for a further appeal to the Supreme Court (formerly the judicial committee of the House of Lords). This committee consists of 12 specially appointed justices (formerly Lords of Appeal in Ordinary) chosen for their experience and knowledge (see Table 9.1 on p. 243).

Criminal cases concern offences technically committed against the Crown. *Civil* cases relate to disputes between private parties, and most of these are dealt with by separate institutions. The overwhelming majority of civil cases are heard in the County Courts, of which there are about 160 in England and Wales (reduced from about 260 under the Conservative–Liberal Democrat coalition). More complicated cases go to the High Court (based at the Royal Courts of Justice on the Strand in London), which is divided into three branches (the Queen's Bench, Chancery, and Family Divisions), depending on the nature of the case. Appeals from these courts are heard in the Civil Division of the Court of Appeal; also, as in criminal cases, further appeals may be heard in the Supreme Court.

The Queen's Bench contains an administrative subdivision which hears cases brought by individuals or organisations against ministers and other public officials who are alleged to have exceeded their statutory powers. There is obvious potential here for clashes between politicians and judges. More mundane cases of alleged maladministration by public authorities are heard by a wide variety of tribunals. These hearings, usually held in public, tend to be quicker (and cheaper) than more formal court cases. The tribunal system (which became part of HM Courts and Tribunals Service as a result of a 2011 merger) deals with cases concerning the highly sensitive areas of social security, child support, immigration, and asylum. Reforms introduced in 2007 were intended to address criticisms that tribunals were insufficiently independent; they were reorganised into 'First-Tier' and 'Upper' Tribunals, overseen by a senior president of Tribunals.

Citizens seeking redress against official decisions on a range of issues can also write to their MPs requesting a ruling from the Parliamentary and Health Service **Ombudsman**. The Ombudsman – a position which originated in Sweden and was established in Britain in 1967 – does not have the power to enforce decisions, but normally public bodies will accept it. There are a range of Ombudsman services relating to various government activities, connected to the devolved institutions as well as Westminster government proposals that are likely to prove controversial, such as the siting of new roads and power stations, which can be examined by public inquiries.

Ombudsman

an independent official who investigates complaints made against the government by citizens.

Legal aid

Among the many reforms introduced by the post-war Attlee governments was the Legal Aid and Advice Act of 1949, which provided assistance to citizens involved in most criminal (and many civil) cases. This was an essential pillar of the developing welfare state, helping to ensure that individuals without the means to defend themselves in court would not fall victim to miscarriages of justice.

By 2012, the annual cost of the system had exceeded £2 billion in England and Wales, and at a time of 'austerity', the Conservative–Liberal Democrat coalition regarded it as a prime candidate for spending cuts. The Legal Aid, Sentencing and Punishment of Offenders Act of 2012 abolished the Legal Aid Commission which previously administered the system, replacing it with a Legal Aid Agency with much closer links to the Ministry of Justice. The legislation encountered furious opposition in the House of Lords, where the government was defeated in 14 separate votes. It removed legal aid from most cases on a range of issues, including housing, welfare, debt, and immigration, in the hope of saving more than £200 million. The government argued that the reform would concentrate financial assistance where it was most needed, but it caused dismay within the legal profession, and many lawyers protested by boycotting court cases – another sign of a more fraught relationship between governments and the legal profession.

Judicial review

In the USA, the nine justices of the Supreme Court are able to rule that legislative acts are unconstitutional, and thus null and void. Since Britain lacks a codified constitution, not even the most senior judges can strike down Acts of

Judiciary

the branch of government responsible for the interpretation and enforcement of laws though the courts.

Parliament in this way. However, they do have the power of **judicial review**, which can force ministers to change the way in which they implement legislation. Rulings can be made against the decisions of public authorities on several grounds. For example, the procedure leading up to a decision could be judged 'improper' if the relevant authority did not give reasonable consideration to the arguments on both sides of the dispute. Judges can also rule that authorities have exceeded their legal powers in making a particular decision. This involves detailed scrutiny of the relevant legislation. If the wording is unclear, judges are required to interpret the intentions of Parliament at the time that it was passed. To this end, they can consult the written record (*Hansard*) to see what was said by the proposers of the measure. However, in practice, they will often be using their own judgement, deciding what Parliament *ought* to have meant when it passed the legislation.

In recent years, judicial review has been exercised more widely and, it seems, more willingly. There are several contributory factors:

- The importance of judicial review was underlined in the 1980s when the courts were asked to pronounce on controversial new legislation, notably concerning industrial relations.
- Also beginning in the 1980s, successive governments have proposed reforms which members of the **judiciary** have interpreted as attempts to undermine their independence. This made them less likely to give ministers the benefit of the doubt in any dispute.

Judicial Review

the review of the legality of ministerial decisions by the courts.

- Legislation has become increasingly complicated in recent decades, allowing ministers wider scope for discretion which, in turn, might be open to legal challenge.
- Some judges have come to see themselves as custodians of civil liberties, in the face of perceived encroachments by successive governments; this ethos seems to have been reinforced by the passage of the 1998 Human Rights Act (see later), which in itself has increased the scope and grounds for judicial review.
- The new willingness of judges to side against governments has encouraged would-be applicants for judicial review to come forward when other sources of redress have been exhausted.

Thus, to a considerable extent, judicial activism is self-reinforcing; the more active the judges, the more likely it is that they will be called upon to take part in political controversies. The effect has been remarkable. In the early 1970s, there were fewer than 200 judicial reviews every year. By 1985, there were more than 1,000 applications for permission to apply for judicial review; in 1998 the figure exceeded 4,500, and by 2013, it was more than 15,600. In 2003, nearly two-thirds of applications for judicial review were related to official decisions on immigration; in that year, 829 attempts to trigger a judicial review in immigration cases were successful, while more than 2,500 were dismissed. However, judicial review can apply across the full range of government decision-making, from instances where only specific individuals are affected to major political controversies. In one of the best-publicised cases, the former editor of *The Times* newspaper, Lord Rees-Mogg, challenged the right of Parliament to ratify the Maastricht Treaty. His case was rejected by the High Court in July 1993, but Lord Justice Lloyd confirmed that it had been a proper subject for review. In 2007, the Law Lords turned down a request from the Countryside Alliance pressure group (see Chapter 19) for a judicial review of the 2004 Hunting Act (see Chapter 8). In December 2010, the former Labour Minister Phil Woolas admitted defeat in his attempt to persuade the High Court to allow a judicial review of the Election Court's decision to strip him of his Oldham East and Saddleworth seat, because of unfounded allegations his campaign team had levelled against his Liberal Democrat opponent in the 2010 general election (see Chapter 17). The Criminal Justice and Courts Act of 2015 was an attempt by the coalition government to reduce the number of judicial reviews by tightening the conditions which allow such cases to proceed. Thanks in part to this reform, the number of claims for judicial review fell to 3,600 in 2018, but at a cost of arousing further opposition within the legal profession.

The Human Rights Act 1998 and the European Court of Human Rights

The judiciary fought many bruising battles against Conservative governments during the 1990s, and relations with New Labour proved to be little better. This was in spite of an amicable start, when the Blair government passed the HRA in 1998 (see Case study 9.1). This legislation incorporated into British law the European Convention on Human Rights. The UK had been a co-signatory of the Convention in 1951, but until 1998 British citizens seeking protection under its terms had to apply for a ruling from the European Court of Human Rights (ECHR) at Strasbourg when all other avenues had been exhausted. By the time of the 1997 general election, the legal profession in general, including many senior judges, favoured the passage of a HRA which would allow such cases to be heard in the UK.

The HRA was a radical change, which was always likely to provide additional impetus to judicial activism. All new legislation has to be tested against the HRA before it receives the Royal Assent. But any UK law judged to be incompatible with the terms of the HRA would become impossible to enforce. Ministers either have to appeal against the judgement to the Supreme Court, or revise the legislation to make it compatible. Early rulings of incompatibility were the Crime (Sentences) Act 1997, and the Anti-Terrorism, Crime and Security Act 2001.

The latter legislation had been rushed through Parliament in the wake of the terrorist attacks on New York in September 2001. Among several controversial new powers, the Act gave the government the right to imprison foreign nationals suspected of terrorist offences without trial. Although this was a clear breach of the HRA, ministers had persuaded Parliament that a national emergency existed, which meant that Article 5 of the HRA could be suspended. However, the Law Lords subsequently ruled that the specific application of the new powers to foreign nationals was discriminatory, and therefore in breach of Article 14 which had not been suspended. In response, the government had to bring forward new legislation which became the Prevention of Terrorism Act 2005.

The HRA has also been used to overrule individual ministerial decisions. In November 2006, it was decided that, under the terms of the HRA, the Home Office was wrong to prevent addicts from receiving drugs while in prison; 200 prisoners won compensation of £3,500 each. This followed a High Court ruling that nine Afghans who hijacked a plane in order to claim asylum in the UK should be allowed to proceed with their claim. In 2007, the Asylum and Immigration Tribunal ruled that the Italian-born murderer of a school headmaster, Philip Lawrence, could not be deported after his release from prison. Whatever the real reasons for such judicial rulings,

Case study 9.1

The Human Rights Act 1998

The HRA 1998 incorporated the rights set out in Articles 2 to 12 and Article 14 of the European Convention on Human Rights. It did not incorporate Article 13 – providing the right of effective redress to people whose rights under the Convention had been breached – because the government believed the HRA itself met this requirement.

The Convention rights incorporated in the HRA 1998 are:

- Article 2. Right to life
- Article 3. Freedom from torture
- Article 4. Freedom from slavery and forced labour
- Article 5. Right to liberty and security
- Article 6. Right to a fair trial
- Article 7. No punishment without legal process
- Article 8. Right to respect for private and family life
- Article 9. Freedom of thought, conscience, and religion
- Article 10. Right to freedom of expression
- Article 11. Freedom of assembly and association
- Article 12. Right to marry and found a family
- Article 14. Freedom from discrimination

The Act also includes the three articles of the First Protocol to the Convention:

- Protection of property
- Right to education
- Right to free elections

they increased public disquiet about the effect of the HRA. Critics were able to claim that parts of the Act were vague and even contradictory. Thus, for example, the press was deeply concerned about the right to privacy, which seemed to endanger its lucrative practice of celebrity-hounding. Any restrictions on such reporting would seem to conflict with the right to freedom of expression which is also enshrined in the Convention. In practice, judges seemed willing to side with privacy rather than the press. The HRA has helped several celebrities to win substantial damages from intrusive publications (see Chapter 5). In July 2008, Max Mosley, the president of the body which governs motor sport worldwide, was awarded damages after a newspaper published allegations about his colourful private life. Critics argued that judges were now using the HRA to create a new law on privacy, even though specific legislation of this kind had never been passed by Parliament. This raised obvious questions about the role of judges within a system of representative democracy, not least because it seemed that only rich victims of press 'intrusion' would be in a position to take legal action.

Although government ministers initially claimed that the media were exaggerating the impact of the HRA, by the summer of 2008 it had become clear that senior figures were ready to look again at the protection afforded to the rights of citizens. *The Governance of Britain* Green Paper (Cm 7170) suggested that a new Bill of Rights and Duties should build upon the HRA. This envisaged

PHOTO 9.1 Human rights or national security? A dilemma for policymakers after the attack in London on 7 July 2005 (© Oli Scarff/AFP/Getty Images).

the provision of additional rights (e.g. economic and social rights) and, significantly, would have given explicit recognition that citizens in a democratic society have obligations as well as rights. The Conservative leader David Cameron took a different approach. In opposition, he promised to repeal the HRA, and to replace it with a British Bill of Rights which, in his view, would be more relevant to realities in Britain. Cameron was concerned that the HRA had prevented ministers from strengthening counterterrorism legislation and deporting foreign nationals convicted of crimes. (Photo 9.1) This issue is often treated as a by-product of the UK's membership of the EU. However, this is a serious mistake; as we have seen, the HRA represents the incorporation into UK law of the Convention on Human Rights, a document which was composed before the EEC came into existence (and which was heavily influenced by British juridical thinking). As a signatory to the European Convention, Britain would still be subject to the ECHR even if the HRA was repealed or (what seemed more unlikely before 2016) it withdrew from the European Union.

As it was, opposition from his coalition partners, the Liberal Democrats, forced Cameron to set up a commission to examine the subject rather than taking legislative action straight after becoming prime minister. Much to Cameron's discomfort, in November 2010 his government was forced to signal its compliance with an ECHR ruling on the voting rights of prisoners. The ruling had been made in 2005 (the case itself had first been lodged with the ECHR as far back as 2001). The House of Commons subsequently voted to defy the ECHR, and it was not entirely clear whether the ruling would apply to all prisoners or only to those serving relatively short sentences. The case inspired a torrent of anti-EU abuse from newspapers like the *Daily Express*, which either did not understand that the ECHR was unconnected to the EU or calculated that its readers would fail to spot the mistake. In the summer of 2011, two rulings, within a few days of each other, underlined Cameron's dilemma. At the end of June, the UK's Supreme Court overturned a previous High Court ruling that British soldiers fighting abroad should be protected in full by the terms of the HRA. In early July, however, the ECHR decided that, contrary to a 2007 ruling by the House of Lords, British soldiers allegedly responsible for ill-treatment of detainees during the 2003 Iraq War *were* subject to the terms of the Convention on Human Rights. The obvious implication was that British judges were less willing than the ECHR justices to develop a broad interpretation of the Convention's terms. This was little comfort to the government, since UK citizens can appeal to the ECHR against Supreme Court rulings; in matters relating to human rights, all European roads still lead to Strasbourg.

In any case, despite its relative restraint, the Supreme Court was perfectly capable of interpreting the HRA in a way which infuriated ministers. In 2010, for example, it ruled that convicted sex offenders, who were required to register with the police for the rest of their lives, should have the right to appeal against this provision. The Home Secretary, Theresa May, changed the rules but only granted the right to appeal 15 years after the offenders had been released from prison. The incident reinforced Cameron's personal determination to replace the HRA with a British Bill of Rights, and this pledge duly featured in the 2015 Conservative manifesto. However, although the party won an overall majority, it was still difficult to see how it could effect significant change without withdrawing Britain from the European Convention, which would damage the country's international reputation. Failing this drastic step, a British Bill of Rights, which differed significantly from the Convention, would result in an increase in the number of cases which ended up before the ECHR at Strasbourg – and, almost certainly, a greater number of embarrassing judgements for the government. On the other hand, if the British Bill of Rights turned out to be virtually identical to the terms of the Convention, critics would be entitled to ask what all the fuss had been about. Understandably, after winning the 2015 election, the government postponed action pending further consultations; at the time of writing (June 2020), the British Bill of Rights still awaited implementation.

Leaving aside the inadvertent or deliberate media misreporting of the ECHR and its original British inspiration, the impact of the EEC (now the EU) on UK legal practices has certainly been significant enough to outlast 'Brexit'. When the UK joined the EEC in 1973, its laws became invalid if they conflicted with European legislation. Ideally, this arrangement would not concern the courts; UK governments would simply ensure that they never passed legislation which conflicted with EEC law. However, in 1988, the UK Parliament passed the Merchant Shipping Act, part of which banned foreign companies from registering their vessels as British for the purpose of fishing. As the European Court of Justice (ECJ) ruled in June 1990, this was contrary to European law. Later, the House of Lords confirmed the verdict. Superficially, this *Factortame* case suggests that the highest courts in the UK have the right to strike down unambiguous laws passed by Parliament. However, the situation is more complicated; the case really hinged on the intervention of the ECJ, whose jurisdiction in this matter had been established under the UK legislation which brought the country into the EEC. Even so, it is reasonable to cite the *Factortame* case as part of the trend towards greater judicial activism in the UK (as well as being a favourite piece of evidence advanced by those who campaigned for Britain to leave the EU).

Who are the judges?

Whatever its other merits, the British judiciary could not be rated as the most democratic of the country's institutions. It epitomises the traditional 'Establishment' – male, white, affluent, and well-furnished with friends in high places. Until recently, Britain's judges were appointed by politicians, and the decisive power of patronage rested with the Lord Chancellor, an unelected member of the House of Lords who was chosen by the prime minister.

As the list of current Supreme Court justices suggests (see Table 9.1), the senior ranks of the judiciary are dominated by Oxbridge-educated men who are either near or over the legal retirement age for other professions (in fact, judges now have to retire at 70 unless they were first appointed to a judicial office before the end of March 1995). In 2004, Baroness Hale of Richmond became the first woman 'Law Lord' (later becoming a notable president of the Supreme Court), and the same year saw the appointment of Linda Dobbs as the only representative of the ethnic minorities among more than 100 High Court judges. In August 2011, the Bristol-born Cambridge graduate Rabinder Singh became the first Sikh to be appointed as a High Court judge, and confirmed that he would wear a turban rather than the traditional wig when presiding over cases. These are exceptions that only underline the nature of the previous practices. Despite a concerted recruitment drive, there also remains a significant gender disparity; in 2019, less than a quarter of the judges in the Court of Appeal, and 27 per cent of those in the High Court, were women. But even these serious discrepancies are less glaring than the inadequate representation of members of the ethnic minorities, regardless of gender, although efforts are being made to ensure that new recruits bear a reasonable relationship to the ethnic balance of the population as a whole.

It might be thought that the social background of senior judges is of limited importance for most people, since if they infringe the law they are much more likely to come into contact with magistrates, who are fairly representative of the local community. But the law is a hierarchical profession, which takes its tone from the top. If the senior judiciary became more socially representative, it might be less easy to criticise its judgements in future; whenever the tabloid press finds fault with a court decision, it almost invariably tries to back its argument by giving reasons for thinking that the legal profession must be 'out of touch' with ordinary people, complete with a picture of an elderly, bewigged gentleman (as in the infamous *Daily Mail* 'Enemies of the People' diatribe: see Controversy 9.3). In November 2004, it was proposed that some High Court cases would be televised on an experimental basis, but this initiative was abandoned. In September 2011, Justice Secretary Kenneth Clarke announced that legislation would be introduced to allow the closing remarks of appeal court judges to be televised, with the possibility that this would be extended to Crown Court cases. Limited coverage of a case in the Court of Appeal was broadcast in October 2013, and legislative proposals to allow the televising of judges' sentencing comments

TABLE 9.1 The justices of the Supreme Court, September 2015

Name	Year of birth	University
Lord Reed (President)	1956	Edinburgh and Oxford
Lord Hodge (Deputy President)	1953	Cambridge and Edinburgh
Lord Kerr of Tonaghmore	1948	Queen's University Belfast
Lady Black	1954	Durham
Lord Lloyd-Jones	1952	Cambridge
Lord Briggs of Westbourne	1954	Oxford
Lady Arden of Heswall	1947	Cambridge and Harvard
Lord Kitchin	1955	Cambridge
Lord Sales	1962	Cambridge and Oxford
Lord Hamblen of Kersay	1957	Oxford and Harvard
Lord Leggatt	1957	Cambridge and Harvard
Lord Carnwath of Notting Hill	1957	Oxford

Source: Judiciary of England and Wales, www.judiciary.gov.uk.

in serious criminal cases were announced early in 2020. The proceedings of the Supreme Court have been available to view since 2015 (https://www.supremecourt.uk/live/court-01.html).

There have been other efforts to make the judiciary seem more accessible (if not more accountable), including press conferences given by senior members of the judiciary. Yet the status of judges within a democratic society is likely to remain problematic, since the prospect of elected judges is as foreign to traditional British practice as the idea that they could be subject to removal by politicians.

Are judges biased?

Worries about the social composition of the senior judiciary are not new. In the first edition of his classic book, *The Politics of the Judiciary* (London: Fontana, 1977), John Griffiths argued that although judges drawn predominantly from the upper classes were not necessarily biased in a party political sense, their rulings were characterised by an unconscious 'conservatism' (in the sense of favouring the status quo). At around the time that Griffiths was writing, there were two widely publicised cases involving local authorities which strongly suggested a distaste for political radicalism. In 1976, the newly elected Conservative Tameside Council reversed a decision by its Labour predecessor to convert local grammar schools into comprehensives. The Labour Secretary of State for Education, Fred Mulley, ordered the council to press ahead with the comprehensive scheme, taking his authority from the Education Act 1944, which allowed him to overrule the local authority if he were satisfied that its actions were 'unreasonable'. Mulley's intervention was challenged by the council, whose defiance was backed by the Court of Appeal and the House of Lords.

In the Tameside case, it could be argued that Mulley had indeed overstretched the terms of the 1944 Act, and that in electing a Conservative council the local voters had registered their opposition to comprehensive education. As such, the higher courts could claim that they were fighting on the side of local democracy against the power of the central state. In 1981, they had the chance to strike again in the same general cause. Labour had won the previous GLC elections, partly because of a promise to reduce fares on London public transport. One Conservative-controlled borough objected to the policy. The High Court upheld the GLC's position, but this verdict was subsequently reversed by the Court of Appeal and the Lords. The flimsy justification for these rulings was the statutory requirement that the GLC should provide transport on an 'economic' basis. Comparing this decision with the Tameside case, critics were entitled to draw the conclusion that senior judges only chose to fight for the rights of local voters during periods when the central government was controlled by Labour.

During the 1980s, there were several examples of 'conservative' decisions by the judiciary, particularly on trade union matters (see Controversy 9.1). In 1985, one important case went against the Thatcher government. Clive Ponting, a senior civil servant, was acquitted on a charge of breaking the Official Secrets Act, having leaked details relating to the sinking of the Argentine vessel *General Belgrano* during the Falklands War. However, this blow against the power of the state was landed by the *jury*, which had defied the judge's firm direction that they should equate the 'public interest' with the political imperatives of the Conservative government. The general mood within the judiciary at the time was apparent in the case of another civil servant, Sarah Tisdall, who, in 1983, had given *The Guardian* newspaper copies of documents concerning the siting of American cruise missiles. After an intervention by the Attorney General on grounds of national security had been backed by the courts, the newspaper handed the documents over to the authorities, enabling them to identify Tisdall as the source of the leak. She was later sentenced to six months in prison.

Controversy 9.1

The courts and the Wapping dispute

During the 1980s, the courts found no serious fault with any of the Thatcher government's repeated measures to constrain trade union power. In one celebrated case, they actually showed an inclination to *extend* the terms of Conservative legislation. In 1986, SOGAT 82, a print-workers' union, was fined after its members had picketed a newspaper distribution company owned by the media magnate Rupert Murdoch (see Chapter 5). The dispute with Murdoch had been triggered by his decision to move the printing of *The Times, The Sun,* and other newspapers to modern premises in Wapping, East London, allowing him to sack many of the printers. The Court of Appeal ruled that the distribution plant was an entirely separate company from Murdoch's News International, and that SOGAT's actions were thus instances of illegal 'secondary picketing'. The ruling helped Murdoch to win the dispute, which was seen as a final blow to old-style union action following the defeat of the miners' strike in the previous year.

However, discussions of conservative judicial bias had begun to look ironic by 1998, when an Appeal Court judgement was set aside because one of the judges was accused of being too *radical*. The former Chilean dictator Augusto Pinochet had been arrested in London on the application of the Spanish government, which wanted him extradited to face charges relating to his period in office. The High Court ruled in Pinochet's favour, but this judgement was overturned by 3–2 in the Court of Appeal. It transpired that one of the majority, Lord Hoffman, had an indirect interest in the work of the pressure group Amnesty International. This was held to invalidate the verdict, and the case was heard again. This time, the Appeal Court ruled that the final decision should lie with the Home Secretary, who eventually allowed Pinochet to return to Chile.

Analysis 9.1

Judicial independence

From the perspective of democracy and governance in contemporary Britain, the story of relations between politicians and the judiciary in recent years is salutary. The increasing prominence of law and order (a key 'valence' issue: see Chapter 18) on the electoral agenda has encouraged politicians to make ambitious promises about cracking down on crime. In doing so, they have forgotten the need for cooperation from a legal profession which prides itself on its independence. Even if they were generally in favour of harsher punishments and stern ministerial decisions on issues like asylum, senior judges would feel inclined to think twice if they perceived that they were being bullied by politicians who were stretching their powers. The idea that tougher measures were needed implied that previous judicial decisions had been too soft. It was little wonder that judges began to dig in their heels after 1993, when Labour Home Affairs spokesperson Tony Blair adopted the slogan 'Tough on crime, tough on the causes of crime'. Prior to this, while questions relating to crime and punishment had always been highly political, the partisan battle had been so one-sided that this had been regarded as virtually uncontested Tory territory. Blair's challenge was taken up enthusiastically by the Conservative Home Secretary, Michael Howard, and in the ensuing verbal jousts, eminent members of the judiciary were unlikely to accept the role of passive onlookers.

Although some observers (especially politicians) have been taken aback by the assertion of judicial independence, it should be remembered that the founders of the US constitution admired British principles (if not the practice) in this respect. They tried to institutionalise the ideal of independence by separating the three branches of executive, legislature, and judiciary. But British judges have traditionally felt that they could assert their independence without codified constitutional provisions of that kind. On this argument, whenever British judges have sided with governments, they have done so without feeling constrained by the fact that the Lord Chancellor who appointed them was also a member of the executive and the legislature. In their own minds, they were merely upholding the impartial rule of law.

One member of the Appeal Court who thought that Hoffman's views made him an unsuitable judge in this matter was Lord Hutton, who, in 2003–4, became famous for presiding over the inquiry into the circumstances surrounding the death of the weapons inspector Dr David Kelly. At the time of his appointment, Hutton was hailed as a fearless judge who would seek the truth no matter where it led. But during the inquiry, he stuck rigidly to an interpretation of his brief which would allow him to avoid any criticism of the government's conduct. By contrast, he was merciless in his treatment of the BBC (see Chapter 5). Hutton (born 1931, educated at public school and Oxford) thus exemplified a type which had seemed on the verge of extinction – the 'safe' lawyer brought in to make sure that a public inquiry could be held without undue embarrassment to the existing government. Previous appointees (like Sir Richard Scott, who reported in 1996 on the sale of arms to Iraq, and Sir William Macpherson [see later in the chapter]) had proved to be far less sensitive to the needs of central government. It is not the fault of judges that they are invariably chosen to perform such duties, but the publicity surrounding public inquiries does add urgency to the task of making the senior ranks of the judiciary more representative of British society as a whole. With senior judges now playing a key role in resolving disputes arising from devolution, national origins have become key considerations as well as socio-economic background.

The judges in rebellion

The idea that a Law Lord could be accused of Left-wing bias was not as startling in 1998 as it might have been ten years before. The Thatcher government was rarely challenged by the judiciary, but the situation under Thatcher's successor John Major was very different. Ministerial decisions were often overturned in the courts. Major's last Home Secretary, Michael Howard (1993–97), was particularly unfortunate in this respect. Although he was an experienced barrister, he fell foul of several high-profile rulings on his use of the powers of deportation and exclusion. The courts also ruled against his attempts to increase the sentences imposed on the child-murderers of the toddler James Bulger, a decision confirmed subsequently by the European Court of Human Rights (ECHR).

A cynical observer could trace the new restive mood to the attempt by the Thatcher government in 1989–90 to push through a radical reform of the legal profession. The main proposal was to abolish the distinction between barristers (who argue cases in court) and solicitors (who prepare cases for the barristers). If implemented, this might have reduced the costs of litigation and speeded up the judicial process. However, it was fiercely resisted by the barristers; judges, who are mainly recruited from the ranks of the barristers, were equally determined to defend their privileged position. Although they succeeded in watering down the proposals, members of the legal profession understood that this skirmish was likely to be the first of many. If they had expected Thatcher (who herself had a legal background) to spare them out of gratitude for their previous help in her battles with other vested interests, they had been sadly mistaken.

Under Major, the new conflict between judges and politicians was diverted into different fields. If the government could not reform the traditional career structure of the legal profession, it could try to undermine the ability of judges to exercise their own discretion in sentencing convicted criminals. In 1994, Michael Howard introduced mandatory sentences for certain categories of repeat offenders. Spurred on by the Law Lords, the House of Lords amended this legislation. With Labour now promising to be 'tough on crime, tough on the causes of crime', it seemed as if the supposedly conservative judges were now fighting a lonely battle on the liberal side of the argument about penal policy.

After the fall of the Conservative government in 1997, senior judges found themselves in the unusual position of attacking Labour ministers from the Left. The then Lord Chief Justice, Lord Woolf, had been a feisty critic of Howard, and continued his campaign against the Labour Home Secretary, David Blunkett. In March 2004, Woolf attacked Labour for its plans to streamline the appeals procedure for failed asylum seekers. This came after the High Court had ruled against Blunkett's policy of denying benefits to asylum seekers who failed to apply on arrival. Woolf also lambasted the government for allowing the prison population to rise to nearly 75,000 in England and Wales (a record at that time, although the figure now rarely dips below 80,000). This reflected the view of many judges that, contrary to Howard's favourite slogan, prison does *not* work as an effective means of protecting the community in the long term, not least because of the overcrowded conditions and the low morale of poorly paid prison officers. But in voicing this opinion, Lord Woolf aroused serious displeasure in the Home Office (and the tabloid press).

Woolf retired as Lord Chief Justice in 2005, and was succeeded by Lord Phillips of Worth Matravers. Reforms to the office gave Lord Phillips a wider role, hearing the most important appeals in civil and family as well as criminal law, and continuing to set sentencing guidelines. The Constitutional Reform Act 2005 states that the Lord Chief Justice represents the views of the judiciary in England and Wales to Parliament and to ministers, and can make written representations to Parliament on matters relating to the judiciary. This arrangement promised to reduce the potential for conflict between the executive and the judiciary. The Lord Chief Justice (currently Lord Burnett of Maldon) also took over the judicial functions of the Lord Chancellor, becoming president of the Courts in England and Wales (see below, and Table 9.2).

New Labour's constitutional reforms

While the judges were at loggerheads with the Blair government over specific policies and ministerial decisions, a new controversy erupted on the subject of constitutional reform. The government accepted that the position of Lord Chancellor had become increasingly anomalous. He sat in the cabinet, presided over the House of Lords, and as head of the judiciary was responsible for the key judicial appointments. As such, he was at once a member of the executive, the legislature, and the judiciary, making a mockery of the liberal constitutional principle that these branches

TABLE 9.2 Britain's top judges and law officers, 2020

Appointed

Judges	Title	Duty
Lord Chief Justice of England and Wales	Lord Burnett of Maldon (born 1958, appointed 2017)	Head of the judiciary in England and Wales and the criminal branch of Court of Appeal; key role in judicial appointments
Master of the Rolls	Sir Terence Etherton (born 1951, appointed 2016)	Heads civil branch of Court of Appeal;
President of the Queen's Bench Division	Dame Victoria Sharp (born 1956, appointed 2019)	Head of Criminal Justice
President of the Family Division	Sir Andrew McFarlane (born 1954, appointed 2018)	Heads Family Division of High Court
Chancellor of the High Court	Sir Geoffrey Vos (born 1955, appointed 2016)	Heads Chancery Division of High Court
Government law officers		
Title	Appointed	Duty
Lord Chancellor and Secretary of State for Justice	Robert Buckland (born 1968, appointed 2019)	Responsible for independence of court system
Attorney General	Suella Braverman (born 1980, appointed 2020)	Chief legal adviser to the government; oversees work of the Crown Prosecution Service and Serious Fraud Office
Solicitor General	Michael Ellis (born 1967, appointed 2019)	Acts as deputy to the Attorney General
In Scotland, the relevant officials advising the Scottish government are the Lord Advocate (James Wolffe) and the Solicitor General (Alison di Rollo).		

Source: Judiciary of England and Wales, www.judiciary.gov.uk.

of government should be divided. The office could even be held to contravene the terms of the HRA, which decrees that trials should be conducted by an 'independent and impartial tribunal'.

In June 2003, it was announced that the then Lord Chancellor, Lord Irvine of Lairg, would be standing down as part of a wider government reshuffle. He was replaced by Lord Falconer of Thoroton who was, like Irvine himself, a close friend of the prime minister. But the proposed changes went further. It was envisaged that Falconer would be the last Lord Chancellor, and hold that title only for a transitional period. He would no longer sit as a judge, and his powers of judicial patronage would be handed to an independent appointments commission. A Department for Constitutional Affairs (later renamed the Ministry of Justice) was to take over many of the functions of the Lord Chancellor's department. Last, but by no means least, the judicial committee of the House of Lords would be replaced by a Supreme Court, sitting outside Parliament. The existing Law Lords would staff this court, and would no longer be entitled to vote in the House of Lords itself. The overall effect would be to reaffirm the principle of a separation of powers, and was regarded in some quarters as an early and important step towards a codified constitution for the UK.

Reform along these lines had long been advocated by expert observers of the judicial scene. However, the announcement provoked a furore. It seemed that ministers had only realised at the last minute that the post of Lord Chancellor, which dated back to the seventh century, could not be abolished without legislation. The impression of another botched job – at a time when the government had changed the composition of the old House of Lords without a clear idea what to do next (see Chapter 8) – lent weight to the argument that traditional institutions were being reformed on the hoof in order to appease Labour's radical supporters.

After protracted manoeuvres, the Constitutional Reform Act was passed in 2005. The government had retreated from its plan to abolish the post of Lord Chancellor. Falconer kept that title, but the office was reformed, with its judicial functions transferred to the Lord Chief Justice, who became president of the Courts in England and Wales. For the first time, the Act enshrined in law a duty on ministers to respect the independence of the judiciary (see Analysis 9.1). It barred them from seeking special access to judges. An independent Judicial Appointments Commission would recommend candidates for judicial positions to the Lord Chancellor.

The Act also established a Supreme Court, which would take over the judicial role of the House of Lords, and whose members would be appointed by an independent body when vacancies arose among the existing Law Lords. Despite initial hopes, the establishment of a UK Supreme Court looked like a typical 'New' Labour gambit – giving the impression of a major constitutional change while minimising the practical impact on existing arrangements. The failure to find an appropriate building for the Supreme Court delayed its launch, which was rescheduled for October 2009 in the Middlesex Guildhall, near Parliament. To the consternation of constitutional purists, it had been accepted that the members of the Supreme Court would retain their membership of the House of Lords, thus being members of the legislature as well as the judiciary. The problem was that if they were debarred from the Lords, the House would have to consider important legislation without the direct input of the country's finest legal minds. Ultimately, a compromise was found on this issue, and the Supreme Court justices do not now sit in the House of Lords until they have retired from their judicial duties. In practice, the new Court has acted along the lines established during the last years of the Law Lords – it is certainly not a creature of the government, but in the absence of a codified constitution, its powers pale in comparison to those of the US Supreme Court.

Controversy 9.2

The Attorney General and the invasion of Iraq

The difficult relationship between the law and politics was illustrated by the controversy surrounding the treatment of advice given to the government by the then Attorney General, Lord Goldsmith, about the legality of the invasion of Iraq under international law. The Attorney General is the chief legal adviser to the government; by convention, he or she is not normally a full cabinet member, but often attends meetings and obviously has a close relationship with ministerial colleagues.

During the 2005 general election campaign, it emerged that the attorney general had amended his advice on the legality of the intervention in Iraq in the days leading up to the invasion by American and British forces. In a lengthy written answer to Parliament on 7 March 2003, Goldsmith had stated unequivocally that the invasion of Iraq was legal under international law, citing the combined effect of United Nations resolutions

678, 687, and 1441 as grounds for military action. The latter was particularly important as it stated that the Iraqi regime would face 'serious consequences' if it failed to 'comply with its disarmament obligations'.

However, in an unpublished document sent to the prime minister ten days before his submission to Parliament, the attorney general had stated that the 'language of resolution 1441 leaves the position unclear'. He outlined a number of difficulties of interpretation and stated that 'the safest legal course would be to secure the adoption of a further [UN] resolution to authorise the use of force'. This earlier document only came to light because of a leak to the media.

The main points of controversy included: (i) Blair's perceived failure to inform the cabinet and Parliament of the reservations expressed in the attorney general's initial assessment, and (ii) whether the attorney general had been put under political pressure to amend his legal advice. Downing Street responded by noting that technically the attorney general had not changed his advice on the legality of the invasion because he had not reached a firm conclusion in his first, unpublished memo. However, if the initial assessment had been released at the time, it would have been much more difficult for the government to secure the support of Parliament for the war. This brought the constitutional role of the attorney general under the spotlight; if he were not a government appointee, his motives in apparently changing his advice would not have been so controversial.

Meanwhile, the role of the attorney general – the chief legal adviser to the government – came under scrutiny because of the dispute over Lord Goldsmith's advice on the legality of the invasion of Iraq (see Controversy 9.2). The attorney general's role was highlighted again in December 2006 when Lord Goldsmith, on the advice of the Serious Fraud Office (SFO), ordered that an investigation into a lucrative arms deal with Saudi Arabia should be halted in the national interest. That decision was subsequently overruled by the High Court, but, in turn, this was quashed by the Law Lords on the grounds that Saudi Arabia might withhold cooperation in the war on terror if the SFO investigation went ahead. In the aftermath of this incident, the Select Committee on Constitutional Affairs recommended changes to the attorney general's role. The government subsequently curtailed the influence of the attorney general over prosecutions, but critics complained that the retention of a 'national interest' provision (as in the aforementioned Tisdall case) meant that the attorney could still intervene in the legal process as well as giving advice to ministers.

The judiciary, the coalition, and Brexit

With the advent of 'austerity' and the creation in 2010 of a Conservative–Liberal Democrat coalition government, the emphasis turned from reform to retrenchment. Cuts in legal aid aroused fears that the poor would be denied equal access to justice, as did the reduction in the number of magistrates' courts which meant that many individuals would have to travel further to have their day in court.

At least for the first two years of the coalition, the Minister for Justice was Kenneth Clarke (QC), who was sympathetic to the judiciary and, in particular, held liberal views on sentencing policy. However, in 2012, he was replaced by Chris Grayling, whose background was in the media and public relations rather than the law. After the 2015 general election, this trend continued, with the appointment of the journalist Michael Gove. Indeed, the position (which still included the title of Lord Chancellor) seemed not to be taken very seriously by successive Conservative prime ministers; between 2015 and 2020, there were six different Ministers for Justice.

At least the Home Office was led throughout the coalition years by a single individual, Theresa May. By 2015, however, many judges probably had mixed feelings about ministerial continuity. May was acutely aware of the potential for negative media headlines, particularly in relation to terrorism and immigration. Her hard-line approach was typified in her stated desire to create 'a really hostile environment for illegal immigrants', and led to the deportation of more than 80 members of the so-called 'Windrush generation' (people who had arrived in Britain before 1973 and who, in many cases, had been born as British subjects). Mrs May's hostility was also felt by judges who took a liberal approach to human rights; in 2013 she claimed that their generous interpretation of Article 8 of the HRA – establishing the right to a family life – was threatening to 'subvert democracy'. Article 8 had been used to prevent the deportation of several convicted criminals to their countries of origin after serving their sentences.

Thus, while May's elevation to the premiership in the aftermath of the 2016 referendum was welcomed by many Britons as an important step towards national reconciliation, members of the judiciary had good reasons for trepidation. May regarded the successful implementation of 'Brexit' as her over-riding duty, but was faced by a House of Commons with a majority of members who (like herself) had supported 'Remain'. Fearing obstruction at every stage, she proposed to begin the process of withdrawal (by triggering Article 50 of the EU's Lisbon Treaty) without consulting Parliament. This decision was subject to a legal challenge by Gina Miller, a highly successful entrepreneur and philanthropist. In November 2016, the High Court ruled in Miller's favour, and the government's subsequent appeal was rejected by the Supreme Court, by a majority of eight to three.

After the initial High Court ruling, the pro-Brexit press launched strident attacks on the judges. The *Daily Mail* dubbed them as 'Enemies of the People', which suggested that the British 'people' now consisted exclusively of Brexit supporters but also that the ruling had been politically motivated. In fact, the High Court judges had *resisted* the kind of pressures which, in the past, would have prompted them to side with the government. In the absence of such pressures there could be no reasonable doubt about their judgement; the process of joining the (then) EEC had been conducted in accordance with parliamentary sovereignty, and there was no reason why the same approach should not be followed on the road to withdrawal (unless, of course, the government wanted to assert that parliamentary sovereignty no longer applied in Britain, which would have been an ironic by-product of a successful campaign to 'take back control'). Indeed, far from being constitutional innovators, the judges rejected plausible applications by the devolved institutions in Scotland, Wales, and Northern Ireland to have a say over the withdrawal process.

In her response to the Miller case, Mrs May followed her previous practice of paying lip service to the principle of judicial independence while failing to criticise the Right-wing press. Her failure to capitalise on her early popularity in the snap 2017 general election left her in no better position to secure parliamentary consent for her proposed withdrawal settlement with the EU. After her repeated failures in this respect, she was replaced by Boris Johnson, who inherited the same dilemma. A key component of his tactical approach was to threaten the EU that, unless a satisfactory compromise could be reached, Britain would leave without a negotiated settlement. However, this was never likely to win parliamentary approval; indeed, far from acquiescing, the House of Commons held a series of votes which raised the possibility that it might formulate its own approach to withdrawal. To forestall this parliamentary insurgency, at the end of August

2019 Johnson asked the Queen to authorise the prorogation of Parliament for six weeks – reducing the chances that the Commons could find its own solution, with the deadline for withdrawal (then 31 October) looming.

Legal action against Johnson's ploy began immediately. The SNP's justice spokesperson, Joanna Cherry, supported by Gina Miller and others, took the case to the Scottish courts. On 11 September 2019, the Inner House of the Court of Session – Scotland's highest court – ruled that the prorogation had been unlawful. As in the previous Miller case, it was widely anticipated that the Supreme Court would find reasons to qualify or even quash a judgement which would be acutely embarrassing to the government – effectively, dismissing the government's appeal would mean that the British courts had accused the prime minister of misleading the Queen when he stated his reasons for requesting the prorogation. To enhance the political sensitivity for the prime minister, among those supporting the case against the government was the former Conservative Prime Minister, Sir John Major. Yet this time, the Supreme Court was unanimous in its findings, which were announced before a live television audience by the Court's charismatic President, Baroness Hale. Parliament duly reassembled, as if the prorogation had never happened. Remarkably, the government had felt it necessary to promise that, if defeated, it would comply with the ruling of Britain's highest court.

For constitution-watchers, this was a dramatic development – easily the most important judicial intervention of modern times. However, the *political* consequences were highly equivocal. It was easy for the government's supporters to present Miller and her allies as representatives of a 'liberal elite' which were 'out of touch' with public opinion; and, as in the previous Miller case, the judges stood accused of aiding and abetting those who were seeking to overturn the *democratic* verdict of 2016. As such, it is possible that the government's defeat actually helped it to resolve its fundamental problem, forming part of a 'people *versus* elite' narrative which was extremely helpful to Johnson and the Conservatives in the 2019 general election.

The longer-term consequences, though, are less clear-cut. Before 'Brexit', the courts were understandably reluctant to interfere in cases which had an obvious bearing on party-political matters. Arguably, in the two Miller cases, the government had acted in ways which made it impossible for the courts *not* to intervene, unless they were prepared to acknowledge that neither they, nor Parliament itself, enjoyed sufficient constitutional status to act as a check on the executive. Also, the fact that the successful action against prorogation had begun in the Scottish courts served as a reminder of the Supreme Court's role in questions relating to devolution. There was every chance that this was one intensely political area which would keep the courts very busy in future. The Johnson government's predictable response was to issue threats against judicial independence, even raising the possibility that senior appointments could return to the control of politicians who would be less inclined to exercise the discretion of the Lord Chancellors of old. Not even the unbridled populism of the *Daily Mail* could guarantee that a Conservative government would succeed in that battle.

The police

Respect for the police force is an essential ingredient of any democratic society, which depends upon the voluntary consent of its citizens. In popularity polls, the British police always rank highly among public servants. However, they have aroused suspicion, and even hatred, in some sections of the community who feel that they do not enforce the law impartially.

The key role of the police as defenders of a free society has led critics to demand that they be subject to democratic controls. But a workable system has proved elusive. Currently, there are 43 police forces in England and Wales: until 1964, there were more than 200. (For the situation in Northern Ireland, see Case study 9.3.) Until 2012, police forces were supervised by police authorities, composed of magistrates, local councillors, and other prominent local figures. Councillors had a majority on the authorities, despite determined and repeated attempts by Westminster governments to tilt the balance towards non-elected nominees. But, in practice, the authorities had little control over the conduct of the forces. This lay with the chief constables, who were responsible to the Home Secretary. The reality of the situation was brought home in 2004 when the Home Secretary, David Blunkett, ordered the suspension of the chief constable of Humberside in the wake of adverse findings in a report into a notorious murder case at Soham, Cambridgeshire. The police authority in Humberside wanted to keep their chief constable, and as local people their opinion should have carried weight. But Blunkett was bound to get a compromise on his own terms, because the power of the Home Secretary to suspend chief constables had been verified by the Police Reform Act 2002.

New Labour introduced a series of measures in an attempt to mollify public fears about crime. In November 2004, the Blair government issued a White Paper, *Building Communities, Beating Crime* (Cm 6360), including several proposals to improve links between the police and local people. The police would be made more accessible, and their numbers increased by 12,000 from the existing 140,000. The government also aimed to recruit 20,000 additional Community Support Officers, who lack many of the powers of ordinary police officers but are presumed to have a reassuring effect on local people. At the same time, the government was encouraging the use

Case study 9.2

Crime in England and Wales

The importance of law and order as an electoral issue means that official crime statistics are subjected to close scrutiny. In 2018–19, there were 6.3 million reported crimes in the UK as a whole. The British Crime Survey (BCS) is often cited as a more reliable measure since it focuses on the experience of people rather than on police activity; however, it excludes certain categories of crime, including shoplifting and crime against young people. At least it was beyond dispute that the level of police detection was low; on the most optimistic estimate, less than 8 per cent of crimes were 'cleared up' in 2019, despite the ubiquity of aides to detection such as surveillance cameras.

Crime played a more muted role in the 2015 general election than usual. The Conservatives, who lost their advantage as the most trusted party on this issue during the 1990s, recovered it before the end of Tony Blair's first term and, according to the polling organisation Ipsos MORI, led Labour by a comfortable margin in 2015. After the election, they pressed ahead with cuts in the Home Office budget, despite fears that the overall fall in recorded crime had bred a dangerous complacency and that some parts of the UK (especially rural areas) were now virtually unpoliced. In 2019, despite the overwhelming focus on 'Brexit' and previous spending cuts affecting the police and the criminal justice system in general, the Conservatives tried to exploit their hard-line reputation by promising tougher sentences and an expansion of prisons.

Source: Home Office (www.homeoffice.gov.uk).

of Anti-Social Behaviour Orders (ASBOs), introduced by the Crime and Disorder Act 1998, to address the problem of persistent 'low-level' crime.

In 2006, the government announced proposals for the merger of police forces which would reduce the number to 24. A unified national police force was ruled out, but some critics claimed that this was already happening by stealth. A National Policing Plan had already been introduced by the 2002 Police Reform Act. There are good operational reasons for closer coordination between forces on complex operations against terrorism and organised crime, and for the establishment of national databases to track down criminals who do not restrict their operations to a single area. Yet the lingering suspicion of a national force is not just based on respect for traditional demarcations. During the miners' strike of 1984–85, when local forces were closely coordinated through the National Reporting Centre (NRC), critics alleged that the police were being used to impose the will of a particular government rather than upholding the rule of law. There is also a danger that a nationwide force would blur the lines of political responsibility. In reality, police shortcomings can be caused by inadequate resources supplied by central government – and, ironically, officers complain that the paperwork demanded by Whitehall initiatives absorbs much of the time that could be spent on detection or deterring crime through a more visible police presence. These considerations, and funding problems, ensured that the government's planned mergers had been scrapped before the end of 2006. Meanwhile, police were becoming increasingly dissatisfied with their lot. In January 2008, thousands of officers took to the streets of London to protest against a below-inflation pay increase.

The Conservative–Liberal Democrat coalition formed after the 2010 general election took a different tack, abolishing the existing police authorities in England and Wales (which were heavily influenced by local government) and replacing them with directly elected Police and Crime Commissioners. This radical innovation followed the traditional practice of the USA rather than Britain, and was criticised in the House of Lords, on the grounds that it could politicise local policing and confuse the existing responsibilities for firing and hiring chief constables.

The first elections were held in November 2012. Labour and the Conservatives contested each of the 41 positions – the two London forces retained separate arrangements – and the Liberal Democrats and UKIP fielded 24 and 23 candidates, respectively. The system used was the Supplementary Vote (SV), as in the election of the London Mayor. Turnout was a derisory 15 per cent, apparently defeating the object of the whole exercise which was to give the public more meaningful democratic influence over local police operations. Independent candidates polled strongly, winning 11 of the positions (in addition, the elected Commissioner for Surrey was a candidate running on the 'Zero Tolerance Policing' ticket). There were 16 successful Conservative candidates and 11 Labour; the Liberal Democrats and UKIP were left empty-handed. In 2016, the turnout rose to over 27 per cent, and the results showed increasing 'politicisation' of the positions: in what were now just 36 contests, 20 were won by Conservative candidates, 13 by Labour, and only 3 by independents. The increased turnout suggested that this was one central government initiative which might overcome initial cynicism and prove to be a useful element of local accountability.

In another notable development, in 2013 a National Crime Agency (NCA) was established by Home Secretary Theresa May to take over the functions of several existing bodies tackling serious crime, particularly involving organised gangs either based in Britain or operating across borders, and the growing problem of 'cybercrime'. The Agency is headed by a director general who is responsible to the Home Secretary; in turn, he or she can direct the activities of regional police forces. This situation invited comparisons with the American Federal Bureau of Investigation (FBI). In various ways, and by faltering steps, a national police service was taking shape.

Policing controversies

The police themselves have often been criticised for the irresponsible exercise of power. During the 1970s, for example, there were several high-profile prosecutions (such as the cases of the Birmingham Six and the Bridgewater Four) which were subsequently exposed as **miscarriages of justice**, with police misconduct a recurring theme in the evidence which cleared the convicted individuals. In 1986, the responsibility for deciding whether or not to prosecute was taken away from the police and given to a **Crown Prosecution Service (CPS)**, staffed by solicitors under an independent Director of Public Prosecutions. The CPS – headed between 2008 and 2013 by the future Labour leader Sir Keir Starmer – is responsible for bringing most prosecutions, though it is 'supervised' by the attorney general (as described earlier), whose role in this respect is still a constitutional anomaly, since the holder of the office normally has connections to the political party in office. The police were also vulnerable to criticism because (like the media, see Chapter 5) they investigated alleged abuses within their own ranks. The Police Complaints Authority (PCA) established as a result of the Police and Criminal Evidence Act (1984) was not independent enough for the liking of some observers, particularly when it investigated deaths in police custody. It was replaced by an Independent Police Complaints Commission (IPCC) which began work in April 2004. Despite its official independence of the police and the Home Office, the IPCC has not been free from controversy; it was accused, for example, of an inadequate investigation into the death of Ian Tomlison after a confrontation with police at a London demonstration in April 2009. In March 2015, it issued a report into the fatal shooting of Mark Duggan in Tottenham four years previously – an incident which helped to precipitate an outbreak of rioting and looting in London and other cities. Critics described the report as a 'whitewash' and called for the IPCC itself to be disbanded. The need for a truly independent and rigorous body to judge police conduct was emphasised by revelations about the handling of the Hillsborough disaster of 1989, which claimed the lives of 96 football fans, and its aftermath; only in 2012 did an independent panel clear Liverpool supporters of any blame, identifying grave police failures, and the first criminal charges were laid in 2017 – 28 years after the incident. Despite fresh evidence of police misconduct during the 1984–85 miner's strike, in June 2015 the IPCC announced that it would not be conducting a formal investigation.

Miscarriage of Justice

a situation in which someone is punished by the courts for a crime when the evidence is insufficient to secure a conviction.

Crown Prosecution Service (CPS)

an independent body which advises the police on possible prosecutions, reviews cases submitted by them, determines what charges are to be faced, and prosecutes cases in court.

The police and society

After the widespread rioting in English cities in 1981, a senior judge, Lord Scarman, compiled a wide-ranging report into the underlying problems of Britain's inner cities. Although the riots had numerous causes, some of the worst outbreaks took place in areas marked by long-standing tension between ethnic minorities and the police.

Scarman recommended a new emphasis on more sensitive 'community policing'. He also urged a recruitment drive among minority ethnic groups, along with an attempt to root out existing discrimination in police ranks. But

Case study 9.3

The Police Service of Northern Ireland

The importance of consent to the effective operation of a police force was illustrated by the findings of the Patten Commission which examined policing in Northern Ireland after the 1998 Good Friday Agreement. In a society almost evenly divided by religion, the existing Royal Ulster Constabulary (RUC) was predominantly Protestant. Its very name implied that members were staunch defenders of the union between Britain and Northern Ireland. If this were not enough to deter Republicans from joining, would-be Catholic recruits were often intimidated (and sometimes killed) by paramilitaries.

The Patten Commission recommended the replacement of the RUC with a Police Service of Northern Ireland (PSNI), which was duly established in November 2001. The new force was committed to equal recruitment from both communities, and although this aspiration was not fulfilled, it soon became clear that the PSNI enjoyed much wider backing from the population as a whole. The leading Republican Party Sinn Fein initially withheld its support, but announced its full acceptance in 2007. In 2010, responsibility for policing was devolved from Westminster to the Northern Ireland Assembly. Officers continue to be targeted by militants, with an annual average of 3,000 recorded assaults of varying kinds in the decade after 2009. Two officers were murdered in that period, reflecting the continuing difficulties which any organisation must face when policing a divided society.

although the government acted on many of Scarman's findings, concrete progress was painfully slow. By 2004, less than 3 per cent of police came from the ethnic minorities. The government set a target of 7 per cent by 2009, while in multicultural London the Metropolitan Police were aiming at no less than 26 per cent by the same date. In fact, by March 2009, the proportion of Metropolitan Police officers from ethnic minority groups was still less than 10 per cent; in 2019, the proportion for England and Wales as a whole was still below the 2009 target of 7 per cent.

The Metropolitan Police had reason to be particularly sensitive on this issue in 2004, since five years earlier they had been the subject of one of the most critical official reports in British history. The Macpherson Report of 1999 identified 'institutional racism' within the force (see Analysis 9.2). It seemed that the Metropolitan Police, at least, were all too representative of one unpalatable element of society. Previous research had highlighted sexism within the ranks. In 2004, women accounted for 20 per cent of police officers. The government aimed to raise the proportion to 35 per cent, and by 2018 it had increased to almost 30 per cent. The question remained whether such moves would be sufficient to overcome the so-called 'canteen culture' which had shaped attitudes among so many generations of police.

Murderous attacks on London's transport network by suicide bombers on 7 July 2005 presented a serious test of attitudes within the Metropolitan Police. They were strongly criticised in some quarters after the fatal shooting of the Brazilian-born electrician Jean Charles de Menezes on a London tube train two weeks after the terrorist attack. In a trial which ended in November 2006, the police were found guilty by a jury of endangering the public under Health and Safety rules, but no individual officer was held to be responsible for the mistaken identification of de Menezes as a would-be terrorist. If this dramatic episode were not enough, in September 2008, an assistant commissioner of the Metropolitan Police started tribunal proceedings against

Analysis 9.2

Institutional racism

In April 1993, a black teenager, Stephen Lawrence, was murdered in Eltham, South London. When no charges were brought in the case, the victim's family began to campaign for an official inquiry into the police investigation. The calls were resisted until 1998, when the Labour Home Secretary Jack Straw appointed a former High Court judge, Sir William Macpherson, to examine the conduct of the Metropolitan Police. When he reported in the following year Macpherson found that the investigation into Lawrence's death had been highly incompetent. More seriously, he also found that the force was tainted with 'institutional racism'. In other words, Macpherson had identified a pervasive culture within the Metropolitan Police, which meant that officers discriminated against members of the ethnic minorities, whether they were suspected criminals or victims of criminal activity. The collective attitude of the police might reflect unconscious bias rather than malevolent prejudice. But this implied that the police were not alone in their unacceptable attitudes. Rather, and more worryingly, it could be argued that they merely reflected prevailing views in society as a whole.

Macpherson listed 70 recommendations, most of which were accepted. Among other things, future recruits were to be screened to see if they betrayed signs of racism. But progress would have to be monitored closely, since Macpherson was revisiting much of the territory which had been examined by Lord Scarman nearly two decades earlier, apparently to limited effect. The police shooting of Mark Duggan in August 2011 led to allegations of police misconduct and to riots in London and elsewhere. Persistent allegation that the police were still misusing 'stop and search powers' helped to fuel numerous demonstrations in June 2020, although their proximate cause was an appalling incident of police brutality in the USA.

See: *The Stephen Lawrence Inquiry. Report of an Inquiry by Sir William Macpherson of Cluny* (Cm 462-I) February 1999.

his employer on the grounds of racial discrimination, increasing the pressure on his boss, Sir Ian Blair. Blair resigned the following month, while the official inquest into de Menezes's death was still in progress. London's elected Mayor, the Conservative Boris Johnson, played a key role in Blair's departure, underlining the complex relationship between Britain's top police and its elected politicians (the London mayor acts as the capital's 'Police and Crime Commissioner', even though he or she is not elected for that specific purpose).

Controversy continued to dog 'the Met', not least because of its tactic of 'kettling' – the practice of confining people within a relatively small area during demonstrations. Such an operation was taking place when Ian Tomlinson died during a London demonstration against a meeting of the G20 group of major economic powers. In April 2011, the High Court ruled that one 'kettling' procedure carried out by the Met that day was 'not lawful', indicating that the police had resorted to this drastic tactic without good reason. In July 2011, the Met again came under the spotlight during the 'phone-hacking' scandal (see Chapter 5), when it was alleged that police officers had provided information which helped the illegal activities of *News of the World* investigators. The cooperation between police and the media could be helpful to the public, especially in publicising appeals for witnesses. However, at times during the 'phone hacking' scandal, it seemed as if law enforcement officers had become as intertwined as politicians in the milieu (and moral values) of the media. Public support for Britain's police looked more fragile than at any other stage since Sir Robert Peel established the Met in 1829; a survey conducted in 2018 suggested that just over three-quarters of adult respondents had confidence in their local forces, with slightly lower figures from BAME respondents.

Almost certainly, falling confidence in the police was affected by their declining *visibility* over the years. Before the 1980s, officers were familiar figures within local communities, but since then, various operational changes (such as motorised patrols) had eroded this connection between police and people, even before the 'austerity' cuts had reduced police ranks in England and Wales by almost 22,000 officers. Although in the 2019 general election the Conservatives promised to replenish their numbers, this measure had not begun to take effect when the outbreak of the coronavirus pandemic added a new and unexpected element to the tasks faced by Britain's forces of law and order.

Conclusion and summary

It is a key principle of liberal democracy that the police and judiciary should be impartial enforcers of the law, rather than the servants of existing governments. Traditionally, supporters of the British system of government have claimed that it satisfies this requirement even in the absence of a codified constitution.

Relations between government and law enforcers have become more problematic in Britain since the 1970s. During the Thatcher years, police and judges were often accused of pandering to the government's will. But since the beginning of the 1990s there have been frequent clashes between successive Home Secretaries, the police, and the judges. In part, this friction has arisen because politicians have made ambitious electoral promises about law and order. Their attempts to exert greater control have been helped by a widespread sense that neither the judiciary nor the police are democratically accountable, or representative of society as a whole.

Since the 1990s, attempts have been made to change the social composition of the police and the judiciary. It seems fair to say that the police are now less independent of politicians than they were 30 years ago; not only are they coming under closer direction from Westminster and Whitehall, but the 'phone-hacking' scandal of 2011 suggested that they had embraced the penchant for media manipulation which has become characteristic of politicians. The introduction of Police and Crime Commissioners, though initially greeted with public indifference, has some potential to arrest these developments. Ultimately, however, the effectiveness of police forces throughout the UK is dependent on funding. In this respect, the coalition government's generosity towards bankers presented a stark contrast to its refusal to shield police forces from the impact of 'austerity'. Among other things, this marked a profound change from the policy priorities of the Thatcher years, when senior Conservatives felt that they should not take the loyal support of the police for granted.

By contrast, the judiciary has become more conscious of its boasted role as the independent guardian of traditional British liberties. Senior judges continue to resist developments which they find unpalatable, and the establishment of a Supreme Court has strengthened their position, despite the limits of its real authority within an uncodified constitution and unresolved issues about the social background of senior legal figures within an increasingly diverse society. Recent rulings in cases relating to 'Brexit' show that judges are unafraid to trespass into 'party-political' territory when they feel that the balance of the constitution is under threat. Even before the 2016 referendum, it was clear that the traditional 'conservatism' of the judiciary had been overturned, and that the executive branch (regardless of the party in office) could no longer take for granted that judges would give it the benefit of the doubt.

Further reading

Although his central thesis is more than 30 years old, J.A.G. Griffith's *The Politics of the Judiciary* (London: Fontana, 5th edition, 1997) is still well worth consulting for its incisive commentary. Similar issues are covered in S. Shetreet and S. Turenne's *Judges on Trial: The Independence and Accountability of the English Judiciary* (Cambridge: Cambridge University Press, 2nd edition, 2013). On recent reforms, see S. Prince, 'The Law and Politics: Rumours of the Demise of the Lord Chancellor have been Exaggerated', *Parliamentary Affairs*, Vol. 58, No. 2 (2005), pp. 248–57, and S. Prince, 'The Law and Politics: Upsetting the Judicial Apple-Cart', *Parliamentary Affairs*, Vol. 57, No. 2 (2004), pp. 288–300. M. Garnett, 'Supreme Justice? The US and UK Supreme Courts', *Political Insight*, Vol. 2, No. 1 (April 2011), pp. 26–28, discusses early developments in the UK's Supreme Court. Judicial review is explored in A. Le Sueur, 'The Judicial Review Debate: From Partnership to Friction', *Government and Opposition*, Vol. 36, No. 1 (1996), pp. 190–210. A lively account of the judiciary, based on interviews with leading legal figures, is C. Banner and A. Deane's *Off with Their Wigs! Judicial Revolution in Modern Britain* (London: Imprint Academic, 2003).

On the Human Rights Act 1998, see the article by the former Lord Chancellor, Lord Irvine – D. Irvine, 'The Human Rights Act: Principle and Practice', *Parliamentary Affairs*, Vol. 57, No. 4 (2004), pp. 744–53. For academic assessments, see I. Loveland, 'Incorporating the European Convention on Human Rights into UK Law', *Parliamentary Affairs*, Vol. 52, No. 1 (1999), pp. 113–27, and the special issue of *Political Quarterly*, Vol. 68, No. 2 (1997). On further reform, see F. Klug, 'A Bill of Rights: Do We Need One or Do We Already Have One?', *Public Law* (Winter 2007), pp. 701–19, and H. Wildbore, 'Does Britain Need a Bill of Rights', *Politics Review*, Vol. 17, No. 4 (2008), pp. 17–19. C. Gearty's *Civil Liberties* (Oxford: Oxford University Press, 2007) is an excellent survey of the subject.

Developments under the Blair government are examined in M. Beloff, 'Law and the Judiciary', in A. Seldon (ed.), *Blair's Britain 1997–2007* (Cambridge: Cambridge University Press, 2007), pp. 291–317. Students should also consult D. Beetham, I. Byrne, P. Nogan, and S. Weir (eds.), *Democracy under Blair: A Democratic Audit of the United Kingdom* (London: Politico's, 2002), for an appraisal of the judicial system and the police against exacting criteria of democracy and human rights. See V. Bogdanor, *The New British Constitution* (Oxford: Hart Publishing 2009), for an excellent analysis of change in this sphere in the overall constitutional context. On early developments relating to the courts and the 2016 referendum, see D. Feldman, 'Pulling a Trigger or Starting a Journey? Brexit in the Supreme Court', *Cambridge Law Journal*, Vol. 76, No. 2 (2017), pp. 217–33. J. Sumption's *Trials of the State: Law and the Decline of Politics* (London: Profile Books, 2019) is a lively and thought-provoking tract. See also J. Rozenberg, *Enemies of the People? How Judges Shape Society* (Bristol: Bristol University Press, 2020).

On the police, B. Bowling, R. Reiner, and J. Sheptycki's *The Politics of the Police* (Oxford: Oxford University Press, 5th edition, 2019) is an accessible and comprehensive account. See also B. Loveday, 'Politics and the Police', in M. Garnett (ed) *The Routledge Handbook of British Politics and Society* (London: Routledge, 2020).

Websites

The websites for the Ministry of Justice (www.justice.gov.uk) and the Home Office (www. homeoffice. gov.uk) provide internal and external links for students in search of up-to-date information on judicial and police matters. Latest developments in the field of human rights can be consulted on the website of the pressure group Liberty (www.liberty-human-rights.org.uk). The HRA can be read in full on www.opsi.gov.uk/ACTS/ acts1998/ukpga_19980042_en_1; the Macpherson Report is available at www.archive.official-documents.co.uk/document/cm42/4262/4262.htm.

Part 3

Multilevel governance

Chapter 10

The changing state

Learning outcomes

After reading this chapter, you will:

- be able to identify the main features of the move from 'government' to 'governance';
- appreciate the major issues raised by the development of the quango state; and
- be able to evaluate the significance of new forms of governance for the UK state.

Introduction

For much of the twentieth century, the United Kingdom was one of the most centralised of liberal democratic states. The Westminster model of government was one in which power was concentrated at the centre. The doctrine of parliamentary sovereignty dictated that no other body could challenge Parliament's legislative supremacy. The fusion of the executive and legislative branches, with ministers recruited from within Parliament, meant that a governing party commanding a majority in the House of Commons dominated the policymaking process. Aside from local government, which was relatively weak, there was no tier of government beyond the centre in Great Britain.

A major theme of this book is the decline of the Westminster model, both as a description of the British political system and as an explanatory framework. In Chapter 7, we suggested that the 'core executive' model of resource exchange has greater explanatory value than long-running debates about prime ministerial versus cabinet government. This chapter examines the changing role of the state, focusing on the transition from an era of 'government' in which formal political institutions were the dominant actors, to 'governance' in which a range of public bodies, private organisations, and specialist agencies are involved in policymaking. Particular attention will be paid to the reform of the civil service, the enhanced role of quangos and regulatory agencies, and the impact of globalisation.

Government to governance

Government

decision-
making through
formal institu-
tions and rules,
and political
power generally
centralised.

The changing nature of the UK state is encapsulated by the notion of a shift from **government** to **governance** (see Table 10.1). Government involves decision-making through formal institutions and rules; it is hierarchical, with clear lines of control and accountability. Governance refers to the role of multiple non-state actors and networks in decision-making. It is characterised by fragmentation rather than centralisation, inter-dependence rather than hierarchy, coordination and regulation rather than direct command and control. Governance requires bargaining and cooperation between actors working within the same or linked policy fields, whereas government implies clear lines of authority. The key developments in this transition from government to governance have been:

Governance

decision-
making by mul-
tiple actors in
networks, and
political power
more widely
shared or
decentralised.

- the separation of policymaking and policy implementation functions within central government;
- the emergence of an 'enabling' or 'regulatory' state which *oversees* the provision of public goods by a range of actors rather than providing them *directly*; 'steering, rather than rowing';
- the introduction of market forces and private sector management practices in public administration; and
- the diffusion of decision-making from the centre, both upwards to supranational, and downwards to subnational, bodies.

These trends have been apparent in central government, local government, the welfare state, and the European Union (EU) (which the UK formally left on 31 January 2020). Reform of the civil service has seen the creation of semi-autonomous executive agencies responsible for policy implementation, the

TABLE 10.1 Government to governance

Government – the Westminster model	Governance
The centre	
Parliamentary sovereignty	Intergovernmental relations
Cabinet or prime ministerial government	Resource exchange within the core executive
Ministerial accountability to Parliament	Distinction between accountability and responsibility
Hierarchical civil service	Division between policy advice and policy implementation functions
Significant state role in the provision of public goods	Enabling state and regulatory state
Subnational politics	
Unitary (or 'Union') state	Multilevel governance; devolution
Scottish Office and Welsh Office	Scottish Parliament and Welsh Assembly
Local government	Local governance
External relations	
Sovereign nation-state	Pooling of sovereignty
Intergovernmental cooperation	European integration
World of nation-states	Globalisation

Market-testing

the policy that activities provided by public bodies should be tested to see if they could be provided more efficiently by the private sector.

market-testing of activities, and the rise of a new managerial regime and its associated culture. Elected local authorities have lost functions to private companies (via contracting-out of public services), quangos, and agencies; have been required to put contracts for service delivery out to competitive tender; and are subject to a comprehensive inspection regime. Within the welfare state, schools and hospitals have been given greater responsibility over their day-to-day running, but are also subject to inspection and central intervention. As we will see in Chapter 13, the EU's legislative and regulatory roles have also been extended.

Changing attitudes towards the state

In the period of consensus politics (1945–75), Labour and the Conservatives were broadly agreed that the state should play a leading role in the economy and welfare provision. Nationalised industries such as coal, electricity, and the railways were run as public corporations under state direction. Other forms of state intervention included public subsidies (e.g. regional aid and funding for companies in financial difficulties), the regulation of monopolies, laws on the environment, and so forth. Within the welfare state, the NHS also had a centralised system of management which gave local hospitals and general practices limited scope for independent initiative.

The Thatcher and Major governments 'rolled back' the state's role in economic management and the provision of public goods. They enhanced the role of 'the market' by privatising nationalised industries, contracting-out the 'delivery' of public services to private sector competition, and using private sector funding for public projects, that is, the PFIs. Thatcherism was hostile to bureaucracy, believing that it was monolithic, a bottomless pit into which taxpayer's money was constantly thrown, inefficient, unproductive (did not generate a profit), poorly managed, averse to enterprise and innovation, and prone to expansion as bureaucrats engaged in administrative 'empire-building'. Right-wing Conservatives offered a similar critique of the welfare state, claiming additionally that it had fostered a 'dependency culture' in which individuals came to rely on state benefits, and thus had little incentive to seek employment. More generally, 'bashing bureaucrats' and denigrating welfare claimants had a populist appeal, pitting 'hard-working taxpayers' against allegedly bossy pen-pushers and paper-shufflers, and against apparently work-shy social security scroungers. Politicians would then portray themselves as being 'on the side of the people', promising to curb these two unpopular sections of society and claiming that large sums of tax-payers' money would be saved as a result.

The reforms implemented by the governments of John Major and Margaret Thatcher, though introduced as piecemeal rather than as a single master plan, amounted to a new vision of the UK state. The state lost its monopoly status in the provision of public goods: many services would still be government-funded, but they would be delivered by the private sector, voluntary groups, specialist agencies, or the family unit, rather than by central government or local authorities. American New Right theorists David Osborne and Ted

Gaebler advocated this change in *Reinventing Government* (Harlow: Addison Wesley, 1992), where they wrote that government ought to 'steer' rather than 'row'. Conservative minister Nicholas Ridley used the term 'enabling authority' to describe the role of local councils which no longer provided all aspects of services (such as housing and education) directly, but funded them and set a framework in which private companies, voluntary associations, and quangos delivered local services. Similar trends in the civil service and the welfare state amounted to the development of an **enabling state**.

Enabling state

state that sets the framework for the provision of public goods by a range of bodies rather than providing them itself.

It would be wrong, however, to claim that New Right ideology was the sole or primary factor in the development of policies such as civil service reform, contracting-out, or privatisation. Pragmatic political considerations – for example, raising revenue to finance tax cuts, or attracting enough electoral support to win the next election – were often more significant. Nor did Conservative attempts to roll back the state always succeed. The Thatcher and Major governments were unable to achieve significant reductions in public spending, as cuts in some areas were countered by increases in others. The higher unemployment that resulted from the contraction of manufacturing industry and the neoliberal refusal to save bankrupt companies or industries via subsidies, increased the social security bill. Public spending increases were also evident in defence, and law-and-order. These were prioritised by the 'neo-conservative' branch of Thatcherism which saw a strong state as essential to uphold the authority of the government, and promote or restore traditional social and moral values. The Thatcherite rhetoric about 'rolling back the state' did not mean a weaker state, but a state which focused its energies on a narrower range of activities, and would presumably perform these fewer roles more efficiently and effectively – quality, not quantity. Hence, the political scientist Andrew Gamble summarised Thatcherism as 'the free economy and the strong state'.

As we will see in the following analysis, privatisation and the transfer of functions from authorities to semi-autonomous agencies transformed rather than ended state involvement. State provision of public goods was superseded by a regulatory state of government-created regimes, in which service providers were required to meet specified targets – a regime which continues today.

The Citizen's Charter

The Citizen's Charter introduced by the Major government in 1991 provides a good example of changing conceptions of the role of the state. It also shows that Major was not persuaded by New Right ideologues – while the latter wanted to roll back the state further through an extensive privatisation of the welfare state, Major sought to make the state provision of public services more responsive to those using them. The Citizen's Charter treatment of citizens as consumers or customers did fit the neoliberal emphasis on the individual, but government still set performance targets for services. The Charter aimed to improve public service performance through market-testing and greater competition, the setting of performance targets, and the publication of league tables. The latter was designed to bring greater transparency, allowing people

Case study 10.1

The Bank of England

The Bank of England is the UK's central bank. It is responsible for ensuring monetary and financial stability; its key functions include setting interest rate levels and issuing banknotes. The Bank was nationalised in 1946, but the Blair government granted it operational independence in 1997. Decisions on interest rate levels have been taken by the Bank's Monetary Policy Committee (MPC) since then. This deprived the Chancellor of the Exchequer of a key economic lever, since, prior to 1997, decisions on the level of interest rates could be (and often were) decided by political considerations (e.g. the desirability of a pre-election rates cut) as well as economic ones. The Chancellor does retain a significant role under the new system, since he or she sets an overall target for inflation (originally 2.5 per cent on the Consumer Price Index, and lowered to 2 per cent in 2003). The MPC then has to judge the interest rate level required to meet that target. It the target is missed, the Governor of the Bank of England must write an open letter to the chancellor explaining why. Chancellor George Osborne set out a secondary objective – supporting growth and employment – to the MPC's remit in 2013.

The chancellor also appoints four of the nine members of the MPC; three other members (the Governor of the Bank of England, serving a five-year renewable term, and two deputies) are appointed by the Crown. A Treasury representative is present at MPC meetings and takes part in discussions, but cannot vote. Minutes and voting records of the monthly meetings of the MPC are published, recording disagreements among MPC members as to the appropriate level of interest rates and other key economic matters. The Bank also publishes inflation reports and forecasts.

The extent of true Bank independence is open to question; thus, during the 'credit crunch' of 2007–08 and the ensuing economic downturn, it cooperated closely with successive governments in the practice of 'quantitative easing', which increased the financial resources available to the banking sector as a whole. A new Financial Policy Committee was established in 2011, and is charged with identifying and acting upon risks to the UK financial system.

to compare the performances of providers of public goods (e.g. on hospital waiting times, school exam results, or the punctuality of trains) and encouraging poor performers to explain how they would improve. Good service providers would be rewarded with a 'Charter Mark'. The Citizen's Charter spawned a series of specific charters such as the Patient's Charter and Passenger's Charter.

The Citizen's Charter was much derided at the time as a big idea that failed to take off. The fate of the Cones Hotline seemed symbolic. This was a telephone service which motorists could contact to complain when motorway lanes were cordoned off without good reason. In three years, it received only a few hundred calls at a disproportionate cost and was closed down. In 1998, the Blair government relaunched the Charter as Service First, and in later years, Public Service Guarantees were favoured. However, even if names have changed, in retrospect, the Citizen's Charter can be seen as a significant step in the development of the state, given the endurance of its methodology of consumerism and accountability for public service provision through performance targets and league tables, which continue today, and which, indeed, are widely taken for granted.

New Labour and the state

New Labour accepted the broad thrust of the changes to the civil service, local government, and welfare state introduced by the (1979–97) Thatcher–Major governments under the Conservatives. Few of the reforms in these areas were reversed or repealed, and where policies were reformed (e.g. the move to Service First, or the abolition of the NHS internal market), these were not so comprehensive as to mark a return to the *status quo ante*. In effect, New Labour signified a consolidation of most of the Conservatives' policies with regard to restructuring the state and reforming public services. New Labour's main concern with regard to the role of the state was with constitutional reform (see Chapter 6). Here, the trends of fragmentation and the dispersal of functions away from the core executive were developed. This was most apparent in the case of devolution, with policy competences transferred to devolved administrations in Scotland, Wales, and Northern Ireland (see Chapter 12). This restricted the core executive's authority to make policy with UK-wide application. The decision to grant the Bank of England operational independence to set interest rate levels also reduced the policymaking resources of the core executive (see Case study 10.1).

Fragmentation and centralisation have gone hand-in-hand. Blair believed that the centre would have to strengthen its capacity to coordinate and 'steer' if New Labour's reform of public service delivery was to be effective. Fragmentation in the core executive and the delivery of public goods was to be addressed through 'joined–up government'. This involved centralisation, with Number 10 playing a strategic role in directing and coordinating policymaking and policy delivery across Whitehall. As we saw in Chapter 7, special units charged with coordinating cross-cutting policies and ensuring policy delivery report directly to the prime minister. The Treasury has similarly stepped up its efforts at coordination. Several hundred ad hoc policy review bodies and taskforces also offer policy expertise on specific subjects; they are distinguished from other government-sponsored bodies because of their shorter duration (usually less than two years).

New Labour sought to tackle social and economic problems through a 'third way' that eschewed both the centralised bureaucracy of the post-war welfare state and the neoliberal approach, which relies on the market for solutions (see Chapter 16). It built up the role of markets by extending the PFI, which uses private finance to fund public projects (see later), and promoting managerial change, advocating partnership between public, private, and voluntary actors. The regulatory state was extended, with the centre setting more performance targets, offering rewards for public sector institutions that perform well (in effect, imitating the profit motive of the private sector), but intervening when they fail. Service delivery agencies are expected to pay greater attention to the needs of service users, who are increasingly regarded in the same way that private businesses treat their customers.

The extension of the state under Blair and, in particular, Brown was seen in the increase in public expenditure and the public sector. In real terms, public expenditure increased by a third between 1997 and 2010, the largest rises being in health and education. Government spending reached a modern high of 48 per cent of GDP in 2010, in part because of bank bailouts. The level of public borrowing also rose, with gross UK debt increasing from under 50 per cent of GDP in 1997 to almost 70 per cent in 2010 – and this continued to rise under the Conservative–Liberal Democrat coalition. The number of people employed by the state increased from 5.2 million in 1997 to 6.1 million in 2009.

The financial crisis of 2007–08 also brought about an extension of the role of the state in the economy. Northern Rock, which had given subprime mortgages to high-risk customers, was unable to raise funds to repay its loans, and a run on the bank began in September 2007 as savers withdrew their money. The Brown government stepped in to provide funds and announced that it would guarantee the first £85,000 of a saver's deposits. When private sector bids for the troubled bank failed, the government nationalised Northern Rock in February 2008. The government also nationalised the mortgage accounts of Bradford and Bingley and partially nationalised the Royal Bank of Scotland (RBS), HBOS, and Lloyds TSB (which merged to form Lloyds Banking Group) by acquiring large stakes in them as part of a bank recapitalisation package. However, nationalisation was intended to be temporary, with the Labour government committed to selling its shares in these banks when market conditions improved.

The coalition, the Conservatives, and the state

The Conservatives entered a coalition government with the Liberal Democrats in 2010, determined to cut public spending, reduce the size of the state, and promote David Cameron's personal vision of a 'Big Society'. Local government spending was cut significantly, and the number of public sector jobs fell from 6.1 million in 2010 to 5.4 million in 2015. The coalition encouraged the creation of more than 100 public service mutuals – employee-led organisations which have spun-off from the public sector and deliver public services. The coalition government was also critical of New Labour's top-down regime of targets and inspections, relaxing the performance framework for local authorities. A new wave of privatisation was launched as the coalition began the sale of the government's stake in the rescued banks, and privatised the Royal Mail.

While this evidence suggests a return to a Thatcherite agenda under David Cameron, the Conservatives protected health and secondary education from the most severe public spending cuts – although the teaching grant paid to universities was reduced to almost nothing (especially for arts and humanities degrees), with the shortfall to be covered by the trebling of student fees from £3,000 to £9,000 – embraced decentralisation and adopted an altruistic view of individuals volunteering to provide for their communities. Cameron's 'Big Society' would be one in which responsibility to deliver local services was devolved to individuals, voluntary bodies, and the private sector. Community organisations and voluntary groups can, for example, apply to run a service currently delivered by a local authority (e.g. a library) or set up free schools. Critics of the 'Big Society' claimed that its main objective was to further shrink the state and to invite the private sector to carry out more functions and services that central government no longer wished to fund in an age of austerity. But voluntary bodies are often reliant on grants from the centre or local government, so spending cuts made the 'Big Society' more difficult to establish.

Many Conservatives were also critical of government intervention that limited individual choice, such as legislation prohibiting smoking in public spaces and banning fox hunting. The coalition government established a Behavioural Insights Team in the Cabinet Office, which enjoyed some success in applying 'nudge' theories that argued that governments could change the behaviour of individuals in positive ways, by making small changes to the ways in which choices are presented to them (see Case study 10.2).

Reform of the civil service

The principles under which the civil service operated in the early 1980s were not radically different from those of the 1880s. Previous attempts at reform such as the 1968 Fulton Report, which urged increased professionalism in the service as opposed to the prevailing culture of 'the

Case study 10.2

'Nudge'

The work of American behavioural economists Richard Thaler and Cass Sunstein, notably their 2008 book *Nudge*, influenced modernisers within the Conservative Party who sought alternatives to big government and state intervention that limited individual choice. Thaler and Sunstein noted that individuals do not always act in their own best interests – they might, for example, be tempted by chocolate bars placed near a supermarket checkout even though they are trying to lose weight. Bad choices can harm the individual and cost the state money. Nudge argued that the government (or private companies) can alter people's behaviour by making subtle changes to the way in which choices are presented to them. This 'libertarian paternalism' guides people's choices and makes it more likely that they will act in their best interests, without prohibiting less desirable choices by law.

The Conservative–Liberal Democrat government created a Behavioural Insights Team (also dubbed the 'Nudge Unit') in 2010 to conduct experiments that 'nudged' people towards better choices. It was originally located in the Cabinet Office and headed by David Halpern, before being part-privatised and becoming a 'social purpose company' in 2014. The Behavioural Insights Team claims that its experiments, often involving small changes to the ways in which messages are presented, have successfully changed many individuals' behaviour and benefitted wider society. Successful schemes that have now been implemented more widely since 2013 include the following:

- Her Majesty's Revenue and Customs (HMRC) changed the style of letters informing people that the deadline for submitting their income tax forms was looming and they had not yet paid. Letters which mentioned that most people in the recipient's neighbourhood had already paid produced a 15 per cent increase in the rate of repayment.
- Payment rates among high-earning tax debtors increased by 43 per cent when they were sent letters pointing out that without their tax, some local services would be closed.
- The dropout rate on further education courses was reduced by a third when students were sent encouraging text messages.
- The proportion of people turning up to a job centre increased by 27 per cent when text messages to unemployed people were personalised and wished them good luck in the job interview.
- A 20 per cent reduction in speeding in the six months after including a one-side explanation of why and how speeding limits are set in police correspondence to drivers caught speeding.
- A 34 per cent increase in acceptances by students from under-represented schools to top universities following a letter from a current top-tier university student from a similar background.
- People were twice as likely to choose vegetarian options in cafes and restaurants if food was described as 'field-grown' rather than 'meat-free'.

Source: Behavioural Insights Team Update, annual reports 2013=2019, available from: https://www.bi.team/our-work/publications/

Following the Conservatives' narrow victory in the 2015 general election, David Cameron established a number of 'implementation task forces', addressing:

- Childcare
- Child protection
- Digital infrastructure and inclusion
- Earn or learn
- Health and social care
- Exports
- Housing
- Immigration
- Syrian returners
- Tackling extremism in communities
- Troubled families

However, several of these were relatively short-lived and operational for less than a year. Cameron's successor, Theresa May, established four further implementation taskforces, these seemingly reflecting her professed desire to develop a more compassionate mode of Conservatism:

- Employment skills
- Industrial strategy
- Rough sleeping and homelessness reduction
- Tackling modern slavery and people trafficking.

None of these implementation task forces were retained by Boris Johnson when he replaced Theresa May in July 2019. However, in response to the COVID-19 pandemic of Spring 2020, Johnson's government established (in May) five 'roadmap' taskforces in order to facilitate Britain's phased emergence from two months of semi-lockdown to contain the spread of the virus, and thereby prevent the NHS from being completely overwhelmed. These roadmap taskforces addressed international aviation, non-essential retail, places of worship, pubs and restaurants, and recreation, leisure, and tourism, and each comprised relevant ministers and departmental officials, scientific and medical experts, and 'stakeholders' from the relevant industries and sectors of the economy or society, and also representatives from the devolved administrations (Company News, 13 May 2020, https://www.companynewshq.com/coronavirus-news/government-announces-roadmap-taskforces/).

gentleman amateur', did not produce the scale of change envisaged at the time, largely because of civil service resistance, and the fact that Prime Minister Harold Wilson was distracted by other problems and crises. The reorganisation of the civil service under the Conservative governments of 1979–97 did, however, bring about dramatic changes in the organisation and culture of the civil service. Influenced by New Right ideology, these governments viewed the civil service as inefficient, badly managed, and resistant to change.

The main themes in the subsequent reform of the civil service have been:

- the separation of policymaking and policy-implementation functions;
- the creation of semi-autonomous executive agencies;
- the introduction of market-testing and private finance;
- the introduction of managerial practices imitated from the private sector.

The defining development in the reform process was the publication of the 1988 'Next Steps' report by Sir Robin Ibbs, the head of the Thatcher government's Efficiency Unit. It claimed that the civil service was failing to provide effective policy advice (an allegation which often means not telling ministers what they want to hear) or deliver quality services. The Next Steps report recommended that the civil service should be broken up as it was too large to be managed as a single organisation. The reforms that followed separated its policymaking and policy-implementation roles. Government departments continued to provide policy advice, but responsibility for the implementation of policy and delivery of public services was transferred to newly created executive agencies (sometimes known as 'Next Steps' agencies).

Agencification

Agencification

the creation of specialist agencies with responsibility for determining and/or implementing public policy.

Executive agencies are staffed by civil servants but led by specially appointed chief executives with overall managerial responsibility. The relationship between agencies and their parent government departments is set out in framework documents which specify the division of responsibility and lines of communication. Agencies have to meet performance targets determined in Whitehall. By 1997, a total of 138 executive agencies had been created, although the number then fell to 86 by 2005 as agencies were privatised or merged: by 2017, their number had fallen considerably further, to 38. Before the end of the 1990s, three-quarters of civil servants were working in Next Steps agencies, or in departments such as HMRC that operate along Next Steps lines. Executive agencies vary greatly in their size and scope (see Table 10.2). The largest was the organisation formally known as JobCentre Plus, with around 100,000 staff, which delivered benefits and provided advice to the unemployed, and the National Offender Management Service (44,000), which manages public sector prisons in England and Wales.

Official reviews suggest that executive agencies have been generally successful in achieving efficiency savings and improving service. The Driver and Vehicle Licensing Agency (DVLA) has, for example, reduced the time it takes to issue driving licence. However, there have been high-profile problems, and these have often highlighted issues concerning accountability and responsibility. There was a major dispute in 1995 between Home Secretary Michael Howard and Derek Lewis, chief executive of the Prison Service, over who was responsible for a series of escapes from prison, thus raising the question of whether the minister's policy itself was flawed, or the 'delivery' of it by Agency staff. The Child Support Agency (CSA), established in 1993, proved to be disastrous. Designed to collect payments from absent fathers or mothers

TABLE 10.2 Executive agencies, 2020 (examples)

Parent Department	Agencies
Business, Energy & Industrial Strategy	Companies House
	Met Office
	UK Space Agency
Defence	Defence Electronics and Components Agency
	Defence Science and Technology Laboratory
Education	Education and Skills Funding Agency
	Standards and Testing Agency
	Teaching Regulation Agency
Environment Food & Rural Affairs	Animal and Plant Health Agency
	Rural Payments Agency
	Veterinary Medicines Directorate
Health and Social Care	Medicines and Healthcare products Regulatory Agency
	Public Health England
Justice	Criminal Injuries Compensation Authority
	HM Courts & Tribunals Service
	Her Majesty's Prison and Probation Service
	Legal Aid Agency
Transport	Driver and Vehicle Licensing Agency
	Driver and Vehicle Standards Agency
	Maritime and Coastguard Agency
Treasury	Government Internal Audit Agency
	National Infrastructure Commission
	UK Debt Management Office

Source: Cabinet Office, https://www.gov.uk/government/organisations#cabinet-office.

who refused to contribute to the costs of raising their children, the CSA consistently failed to meet performance targets, built up a huge backlog of cases, and provoked large numbers of complaints, with many MPs being contacted by angry or desperate constituents concerning problems they were experiencing with the CSA; single parents reported chronic delays in payments, and many 'absent fathers' complained that the CSA was demanding more than they could realistically afford (it only looked at a man's salary, not his housing costs, fares to work, or whether he now had another family to provide for). The CSA was also repeatedly condemned by parliamentary select committees when they conducted inquiries into its shambolic performance and interviewed people affected by it. After a restructuring that failed to improve matters, the government scrapped the CSA and replace it with a new body – the Child Maintenance and Enforcement Commission – which was responsible for a new system of child maintenance. In turn, this body was absorbed into the Department of Work and Pensions under the 2010–15 coalition government.

In more recent years, HMRC has attracted serious criticisms for its alleged tendency to take a lenient view of the tax liabilities of multinational corporations, and in 2013, the prestigious parliamentary Public Accounts Committee published a report which was highly critical of HMRC for failing to tackle repeated tax-dodging by several major international companies. In 2013, the UK's Border Agency, which had dealt with matters relating to immigration, was reorganised and lost its agency status in the face of consistent negative publicity. Its various functions are now under the direct control of the Home Office. The status or names of agencies can change for a variety of reasons. In 2015, Highways England was created from part of the previous Highways Agency, and made into a government-owned company.

Marketisation

the extension of market mechanisms into government and the public sector.

Marketisation

The role played by the private sector in central government has been extended beyond recognition since 1979. Market-testing was introduced into the civil service in 1991. It required that the activities of government departments and executive agencies (e.g. IT services) must be examined to ascertain whether the private sector could deliver services more efficiently and economically (cheaply) than 'in-house' providers. By 1995, over £2 billion of activities had been market-tested, purportedly producing savings of £800 million. Some executive agencies, including Her Majesty's Stationery Office, have been privatised, but market-testing has also brought problems. The failure of IT systems provided by the private sector in the CSA caused long delays in processing claims and issuing payments, and cost millions of pounds. The Blair government ended the requirement that activities should be market-tested, but regular reviews of service provision have continued.

The Blair and Brown governments made extensive use of public–private partnerships (PPPs). These are formal agreements between government bodies (e.g. government departments, agencies, and local authorities) and the private sector to deliver or manage public goods. The most controversial form of partnership is the **private finance initiative (PFI)** which allows for private sector funding of large-scale projects providing public goods. In these PPPs, a private company undertakes an infrastructure project (often, building or equipping hospitals, prisons, schools, etc.) and delivers the associated service for a specified period of time, normally 25–30 years. However, the government (or the relevant public body, such as an NHS Trust) pays for the services, along with a premium to cover the financial risks taken by the company. PFI was introduced by the Major government in 1992, but it really accelerated and expanded under New Labour; by May 2010, contracts for 920 PFI projects had been signed. The largest were transport projects such as the redevelopment of the London Underground, the Channel Tunnel rail link, and the M6 Toll. The most common were hospital infrastructure projects. At the time, the government claimed that PFI produced much-needed increased public investment and delivered it more efficiently, while avoiding the tax increases which would otherwise be necessary to spend more on public sector infrastructure and other projects. However, critics have repeatedly argued that the projects do not provide value for money as the borrowing costs are high (see Controversy 10.1). In 2010, it was estimated that the overall cost to the taxpayer of PFI projects would be an astonishing £210 billion over 25 years, with payments rising to around £10 billion per year. It was not surprising that, in a new era of financial stringency, the Cameron coalition showed diminished enthusiasm for the idea, despite its obvious advantages for the Conservatives' preferred private sector. The Chancellor, George Osborne, did authorise new PFI contracts, but on less generous terms. Several parliamentary select inquiries, particularly by the Public Accounts Committee, have been critical of PFI in the last

Private finance initiative (PFI)

a policy promoting the use of private sector funding for the provision of public goods.

10 years, and disputed their professed efficiency and value-for-money. These strong criticisms have been echoed by the National Audit Office. The fortnightly magazine *Private Eye* (whose editor is the *Have I Got News For You* panelist Ian Hislop) – which contains a marvellous blend of investigative journalism, exposés of political corruption and incompetence, and scathing political satire – regularly exposes scandals and disasters accruing from PFIs. One particular problem which became evident during the decade (2010–20) of austerity was that the annual payments to the private consortiums which carried out major work under PFI were contractually fixed, and so still had to be paid by the relevant public sector organisation even when its funding was cut. This meant that in some instances, staff or services had to be cut, as cutting the PFI repayments was not an option. In a few extreme cases, this meant that new hospitals could not run at full capacity, because the local NHS Trust's PFI repayments meant that it could not afford to employ all of the staff needed or open all sections of the hospital – parts of the new state-of-the-art hospital remained closed in order to afford the PFI payments to the company which had built it, even while NHS waiting lists grew. Following the 2018 collapse of Carillion (see later in this chapter), the Conservatives announced a halt to new PFIs, while the Labour Party contested the 2019 election pledging to end contracting-out (except when it was absolutely unavoidable or necessary) and restore 'in-house' provision of public services.

Controversy 10.1

PFI problems – from the Skye Road Bridge to the NHS

The Skye Bridge, which opened in 1995, was one of the most contentious PFI projects. The bridge linking the Isle of Skye with the mainland was built by a commercial group funded by the US investors and run by Skye Bridge Limited. It cost £39 million to construct, £12 million of which came from central government. The money would be recouped through a toll imposed on users of the bridge. Motorists staged a 'can pay, won't pay' campaign from the outset, and more than 100 people were convicted for refusing to pay. The Scottish government signalled its unease in 2000 by freezing the toll at £11.40 for a return trip – the original cost of a journey had been estimated at 40p – then bought back the bridge from its owners in 2005 and abolished the tolls completely. The purchase price was £27 million, but the Scottish government calculated that it would have cost £18 million in subsidies to freeze the toll at £11.40 for the remaining years of the franchise.

Concerns about the costs of PFI schemes have also arisen elsewhere. The Department of Health was deeply concerned about the costs of PFI schemes in the NHS (e.g. a proposed £1 billion refurbishment of St Bartholomew's Hospital in London) given the level of debts already accrued by NHS foundation trusts. By 2015, NHS foundation trusts were spending around £2 billion in annual PFI repayments. A *Daily Telegraph* report (22 September 2011) found that 22 NHS trusts were in deficit solely because of the money they were having to repay each year due to PFI contracts, while a more recent headline in *The Independent* (18 January 2018) declared that 'PFI deals are bleeding the NHS dry'. After it came to office in 2010, the Conservative–Liberal

Democrat coalition heavily criticised New Labour's use of PFI, which was somewhat ironic since the Conservatives had invented the approach under John Major. Yet, despite this criticism, the new Chancellor George Osborne continued to authorise new PFI deals.

By 2018, the National Audit Office noted that there were over 700 PFI deals in operation, and forecast that by the 2040s, the cost of repayments (ultimately funded by the taxpayer) would be about £200 billion. Part of the problem was that the private companies awarded PFI contracts had to generate a surplus (profit) in order to pay dividends to their shareholders – which a public body would not need to do. However, what really exposed the problems of relying so heavily on PFIs was the January 2018 collapse of Carillion, a major construction company, with debts of £7 billion. Carillion had been one of the main beneficiaries of government contracts to build public infrastructure under the PFI. Its bankruptcy did not just affect Carillion and its now redundant employees, but also the various other firms in its supply chain, or from which it commissioned work that it could not pay for, and who themselves now faced financial ruin and job losses.

New public management

The 1988 Next Steps Report aimed to transform the culture of the civil service by instilling a more 'professional' approach to management and performance. Central to this was the introduction of management techniques used in the private sector, including efficiency drives to ensure value for money, clear lines of managerial responsibility, the measurement of staff activities and achievements against specific targets, and responsiveness to consumer demands. This managerial revolution and emphasis on market mechanisms are collectively known as the **new public management**, and although it was initially applied to the civil service, it has long since been extended to the whole of the public sector, so that it applies equally to doctors, librarians, nurses, police officers, probation officers, social workers, teachers, and university lecturers.

New public management

the emphasis on market mechanisms and private sector managerial practices in government organisations.

The new managerial culture has permeated both executive agencies and government departments. Executive agencies have significant discretion in the management of their finances and the pay and working conditions of their employees. Many agency chief executives are recruited from the private sector through open competition rather than promoted from within the civil service. Government departments have also been given greater discretion regarding their internal organisation. The Senior Civil Service, the top echelon of policymakers in Whitehall, was created in 1995 with open competition and written employment contracts the norm. Recruitment from the private sector, fast-track promotions, the recruitment of specialists (e.g. in IT, finance, management, and communications), and efforts to improve diversity within the civil service, all developed further under New Labour and the Conservative–Liberal Democrat coalition.

The Blair governments adopted a pragmatic approach to civil service reform, accepting the majority of the Conservative reforms and promising further improvements. Since the rationale behind the Conservative reforms reflected the ideological view that civil servants are not really 'public spirited', but self-interested like everyone else, the New Labour approach on the matter was eloquent testimony to the extent to which it accepted 'Thatcherite' assumptions about 'selfish' human nature (see Chapter 16). Blair's emphasis in terms of public service delivery was on 'what works'; but this apparent non-ideological, evidence-based pragmatism disguised a clear conviction that the private sector worked best, which was fully shared by Chancellor Gordon Brown. The 1999 White Paper *Modernising Government* (Cm 4310) identified efficient public service delivery, coordination, innovation, and diversity as New Labour's priorities. By 2004, Blair's vision was of a smaller core civil service, with a clearer sense of purpose, greater recruitment from the private sector, and more effective leadership within departments. When the Thatcher government took office in 1979, there were 732,000 (full-time equivalent) civil servants, but by 1997, the figure had fallen to 500,000. Initially, civil service numbers increased again under New Labour, to 554,000 in 2004, but following that year's Gershon Report on efficiency savings, the government announced that 104,000 civil service posts would be cut and another 20,000 relocated to the English regions. By 2008, the number of civil servants had fallen back to about the level which New Labour had inherited. The Conservative–Liberal Democrat coalition government embarked on a wide-ranging programme of expenditure cuts, with civil service jobs (plus pay and pensions) a prime target. By the time of the 2015 general election, the official number of civil service employees was little over 400,000, a reduction of 80,000 since the coalition entered office in 2010, and the lowest number since World War II. By the end of 2019, though, the number had risen again, to 421,000, but historically still relatively low.

Meanwhile, repeated reforms since the 1980s have provoked concerns that the civil service's traditional principles of impartiality, anonymity, and permanence have been undermined, especially as some ideologically driven ministers dislike being told that their plans or proposed policies are not feasible or practicable. The separation of the policy advice and policy implementation functions of the civil service has brought fragmentation and problems of effective control. The creation of Next Steps agencies has also blurred the lines of accountability. It is not clear whether agency chief executives or government ministers should ultimately be held responsible for policy failures. Ministers have used this confusion to avoid being held accountable for problems, while also seeking policy advice from other sources, such as special advisers (see Chapter 7). Critics claim that market forces and private sector management practices have undermined the public service ethos of the civil service, and that relentless cost-cutting and associated reductions in staff numbers have often damaged the efficiency and quality of public service 'delivery'. They also point to 'accountability' problems created by the contracting-out of public services to the private sector, and to the long-term costs associated with PFI schemes, which have often proved to be rather higher than originally envisaged.

The quango state

The creation of executive agencies responsible for the implementation of government policies is an example of a restructuring of the state that has brought about an increase in the number and role of specialist agencies. Executive agencies differ from the other agencies discussed in this section, as they operate within the terms of framework documents drawn up by their 'parent' government department, and their staff are civil servants. The agencies discussed here

Quango

a quasi-autonomous non-governmental organisation which takes decisions on how public money should be spent but which has significant autonomy from government and is not directly accountable to it.

are known as **quangos**, an acronym for 'quasi-autonomous non-governmental organisations'. Quangos are non-departmental bodies (i.e. they have significant autonomy from government departments), are not directly accountable to ministers or local councils, and their staff are neither civil servants nor local government officials. The broad remit and budgets of many of these organisations are, though, set by central government. Quangos are thus funded by the taxpayer but are not democratically accountable to Parliament or the electorate.

The presence of quangos within the UK state is not a new phenomenon. The Arts Council, which distributed around £450 million among projects in music, the theatre, dance, and the visual arts until its budget was cut by the coalition government, was created in 1946. But the last 30 years have seen an expansion in the scope and number of agencies. The Thatcher and Major governments abolished some quangos (e.g. nationalised industries), but created more (e.g. regulatory agencies). Like their Conservative predecessors, the Blair governments did not reduce the number of quangos or make them more democratic despite pledging to do so while in opposition. Instead, New Labour established new bodies with responsibilities in areas such as health, training, housing, and regional development.

The definition and measurement of quangos is disputed. The government prefers to use the term non-departmental public body (NDPB) to describe agencies funded by the state to develop, manage, and provide public goods, but which are neither elected nor controlled directly by central government (see Table 10.3). The Cabinet Office identifies four main types of NDPB:

- *Executive NDPBs* are established by statute and are responsible for administrative, regulatory, or commercial functions. They have their own staff and budget. There were 198 executive NDPBs in 2009, reduced to 154 by 2014.
- *Advisory NDPBs* provide expert advice to ministers, such as the Veterinary Products Committee or the Advisory Council on the Misuse of Drugs. Their staff and budget come from the sponsor government department. There were 405 advisory NDPBs in 2009, reduced to just 149 by 2014.
- *Tribunal NDPBs* have quasi-judicial power in particular fields of law, such as the Competition Appeal Tribunal or the Police Discipline Appeals Tribunal. Their staff and budget come from the sponsor government department. There were 19 of these bodies in 2009, cut to 14 five years later. *Independent monitoring board NDPBs*, formerly known as 'boards of visitors', are responsible for prison inspections. They are funded by the sponsor department and numbered 132 in 2014 (down from 150 in 2009).

This Cabinet Office typology of quangos is based on a minimalist approach that is rejected by other observers. The aforementioned official figures count Clinical Commissioning Groups (formally Primary Care Trusts, of which there were more than 200 in 2014) as elements of a single quango – the NHS Commissioning Board. An array of other bodies are excluded from the figures. So the official definition does not extend to quangos such as city academies, public corporations (e.g. the BBC), or government taskforces. This is because they have different appointment processes and have looser links to government departments.

TABLE 10.3 Non-departmental public bodies, 2020 (examples)

Parent Department	NDPB	Category
Business, Energy & Industrial Strategy	Advisory, Conciliation and Arbitration Service	Executive NDPB
		Executive NDPB
	Committee on Climate Change	Advisory NDPB
	Committee on Fuel Poverty	Advisory NDPB
	Low Pay Commission	
Education	Office for Students	Executive NDPB
	Office of the Children's Commissioner	Executive NDPB
	School Teachers' Review Body	Advisory NDPB
	Social Mobility Commission	Advisory NDPB
Environment Food & Rural Affairs	Joint Nature Conservation Committee	Executive NDPB
	Sea Fish Industry Authority	Executive NDPB
	Advisory Committee on Releases to the Environment	Advisory NDPB
		Advisory NDPB
	Science Advisory Council	
Health and Social Care	Care Quality Commission	Executive NDPB
	Social Work England	Executive NDPB
	Commission on Human Medicines	Advisory NDPB
	NHS Pay Review Body	Advisory NDPB
Home Office	Independent Office for Police Conduct	Executive NDPB
	Security Industry Authority	Executive NDPB
	Advisory Council on the Misuse of Drugs	Advisory NDPB
		Advisory NDPB
	Police Remuneration Review Body	
Housing, Communities & Local Government	Housing Ombudsman	Executive NDPB
	Regulator of Social Housing	Executive NDPB
	Building Regulations Advisory Committee	Advisory NDPB
Justice	Criminal Cases Review Commission.	Executive NDPB
	Parole Board.	Executive NDPB
	Advisory Committees on Justices of the Peace	Advisory NDPB
		Advisory NDPB
	Law Commission	
Transport	Trinity House (General Lighthouse Authority)	Executive NDPB
		Executive NDPB
	British Transport Police Authority	Advisory NDPB
	Independent Commission on Civil Aviation Noise	
Treasury	Office for Budget Responsibility	Executive NDPB
	Royal Mint Advisory Committee	Advisory NDPB
Work and Pensions	Health and Safety Executive	Executive NDPB
	The Pensions Regulator	Executive NDPB
	Industrial Injuries Advisory Council	Advisory NDPB
	Social Security Advisory Committee	Advisory NDPB

Source: Cabinet Office, https://www.gov.uk/government/organisations.

Stuart Weir and Wendy Hall in 1994 provided a more accurate picture of the extent of the quango state in *EGO-TRIP* (Democratic Audit Paper No. 2, 1994), identifying 5,521 quangos, most of which operated at local level and were excluded from the government's tally of NDPBs. The 2001 House of Commons Public Administration Select Committee Report *Mapping the Quango State* also adopted a broad perspective when identifying more than 5,000 state-funded bodies that provided public goods at local level, employing some 60,000 people. In contrast, the

Cabinet Office database of public bodies recorded a fall in the number of NDPBs from 1,128 in 1997 to 742 in 2010, and then fell further, to 245, by 2017. This reflected the abolition of some such bodies, the merger of some others, and, for several others, the transfer of departmental 'sponsorship' from central government to the devolved administrations.

Whatever the real figures, the scope of the quango state is enormous and raises concerns for democrats, notably:

- patronage and the process of appointments to quangos;
- the lack of openness in the way quangos conduct their work;
- the accountability of quangos to elected bodies.

The House of Commons Public Administration Select Committees 2003 Report *Opening up the Patronage State* noted that hundreds of thousands of posts in public bodies such as quangos, the lower courts, and the welfare state were filled by appointment. Until the 1990s, ministers and civil servants were responsible for many of these appointments. Following recommendations from the Nolan Committee on Standards in Public Life, a post of Commissioner for Public Appointments was created. He or she monitors appointments to many quangos and insists that they should be made on merit. Many posts are advertised in the national press. More women and ethnic minorities have been appointed in recent years, though they remain under-represented. Since 2008, parliamentary select committees have been able to hold pre-appointment hearings for some public appointments. But these hearings are only advisory – although, exceptionally, the Treasury Select Committee has a veto over the appointment of the head of the Office of Budget Responsibility (OBR) – and ministers retain the final say on appointments to many national bodies. Only four of 68 candidates had received negative assessments from a select committee by September 2014, of whom one was not appointed by the minister and one withdrew. Ministers are sometimes accused of filling posts with supporters of their political party. According to data released by the Public Appointments Commissioner, in 2006–07, almost 70 per cent of ministerial appointees to public bodies who admitted political activity (which goes beyond merely supporting a political party) were Labour activists, but they amounted to only 10 per cent of all appointees that year. In 2012–13, Conservative activists (36) marginally outnumbered Labour activists (33), but 989 appointees declared 'no political activity'.

Transparency is also lacking: not all quangos issue annual reports and few hold public meetings, although government departments conduct periodic reviews and parliamentary select committees can scrutinise their work. The freedom from direct government control and partisan politics enjoyed by some organisations can be a good thing, the BBC (a public corporation) and the Electoral Commission being cases in point. But the transfer of decision-making power from elected politicians to quangos has exacerbated a 'democratic deficit', particularly at local level.

The Conservative–Liberal Democrat coalition government which took office in 2010 was not unusual in declaring its antipathy to quangos, but it had the additional incentive of seeking a dramatic reduction in public expenditure. It planned to abolish 199 NDPBs (many of which were very small), merge 120, and reform another 179. This followed a formal review of whether each NDPB performed a technical function requiring political impartiality and independence. Among those that were axed were the Audit Commission, the General Teaching Council for England, the Health Protection Agency, and Regional Development Agencies. The total number of public bodies was reduced by more than 280, but those with concerns about the tenacity of the quangocracy could not have been surprised by the inexorable reduction of the planned 'bonfire of the quangos'. While critics argued that lobby groups of one kind or another could always find reasons for the preservation of these bodies, it was more difficult to see why some of them had been lined up for abolition in the first place. For example, the Consumer Council for

Water (which was under review but 'reprieved' in July 2011) worked on behalf of water consumers in England and Wales. Given the perennially problematic relationship between consumers, regulators, and the privatised water industry, it seemed eminently sensible to retain a separate official watchdog in this instance.

Although the coalition boasted success in reducing the UK's 'quangocracy' – claiming savings of £2.6 billion – NDPB functions were often not abolished but instead re-distributed to other public bodies. New quangos such as the Office for Budget Responsibility (OBR), National Crime Agency (NCA), and Public Health England (PHA) were also created by the coalition. But the Cabinet Office's capacity to review and monitor NDPBs was enhanced (e.g. through the introduction of triennial reviews) and transparency was improved (e.g. through the publication of additional data).

The local quango state

The trends identified in this chapter – the hiving-off of functions to specialist agencies, the creation of an elaborate regulatory framework, the introduction of markets and private capital, and a managerial culture – have also changed the character of local government and the welfare state (see Chapter 11). In addition to seeing many of their services contracted-out to private companies, local councils have lost functions to quangos and were subject to a comprehensive inspection regime through the Audit Commission until its closure in 2015. It carried out inspections of local authorities and health service trusts, publishing information on their performance and assessing whether they delivered value for money. The government rewards the best-performing local authorities by granting them greater discretionary powers, while penalising those that fare badly by subjecting them to central intervention.

In education, local authority control over schools has been weakened considerably. Many schools have opted-out of local authority control: they are funded directly by the state with governors and head teachers responsible for the day-to-day running of their schools. The Thatcher and Major governments encouraged 'grant-maintained schools' to opt-out of local authority control. Despite attacking these institutions in opposition, New Labour merely replaced them with very similar 'academy' schools; the coalition government built on this programme and allowed charities, businesses, parents, and others to set up 'free schools'. Schools have not exactly been 'forced to be free', but Jean-Jacques Rousseau would have admired the way in which successive governments have 'nudged' educational establishments away from democratic oversight since 1979. Schools are subject to regular inspection by the Office for Standards in Education, Children's Services and Skills (OFSTED). Special management teams are sent into schools with poor records, and the worst are closed down. Despite the apparent decentralisation of recent years, the real purpose of the changes has been to exclude elected *local* politicians from the education system. Whitehall still pays the bills and exercises ever more detailed control in some respects; national targets for examination passes and class size are set by the centre.

The Thatcher and Major governments separated the purchaser and provider roles within the NHS by creating an internal market. This was a quasi-market, in which district health authorities and general practices purchased healthcare from hospitals. Hospitals and general practices were given greater freedom to run their own affairs, the former as self-governing NHS Trusts and the latter as GP fundholders. The Blair governments abolished the quasi-market but established 'foundation hospitals' (in England) which enjoyed greater budgetary and managerial discretion. Compulsory Competitive Tendering in the NHS saw contracts to provide services such as cleaning and catering awarded to private companies. The PFI was used extensively to fund the building and renovation of hospitals. In turn, the Conservative–Liberal Democrat coalition replaced NHS Trusts with foundation trusts, of which there were 147 by 2015, and transferred responsibility for healthcare funds to clinical commissioning groups which were partly run by GPs. The Health and Social Care Act 2012 brought about further marketisation of the NHS, but claims of large-scale privatisation of the NHS appear exaggerated, since only £10 billion of the £113 billion budget was spent on care commissioned from non-NHS providers. The NHS is overseen by a plethora of regulatory bodies, including Monitor (the economic regulator), the Care Quality Commission, Public Health England, and NICE, and is subject to inspection by national auditors and appraisal through the publication of performance league tables. The government sets national targets for reducing deaths from cancer and heart disease, for example.

Few would argue that greater transparency in public services is undesirable, but the methods for achieving this have been questioned. Setting national performance targets and producing league tables allow for comparisons between different providers of health and education, but the data that are used is often flawed. The first Blair government focused on reducing hospital waiting lists, but hospitals could manipulate the statistics by undertaking simple operations rather than more costly or complex ones. The government then turned its attention to waiting *times*. School heads also complain that league tables do not pay sufficient attention to factors such as the relative deprivation of their catchment area. Moreover, a common complaint by public service professionals is that the accountability exercises and inspections are often extremely bureaucratic and time-consuming, and actually prevent them from fully focusing on their core, front-line roles – the very activities which are supposedly being measured or audited. Also, the way in which public servants perform their roles has often been changed, not because it is better for service users but to make it easier to be 'measured' by those conducting the audits; the bureaucratic tail wags the professional dog! This has certainly become a common complaint in education, where teachers and lecturers have to design and deliver their classes in a manner which can be evaluated or monitored in a tick-box fashion by those carrying out inspections. The result is often demoralised teachers and demotivated pupils.

Anyone but an obsessive observer of state and quasi-state institutions would be hard pressed to keep up with all the changes of recent years. Decentralisation has marched in tandem with increased state intervention; mergers between some institutions have been matched by the splitting of functions in other cases. Even when functions have remained constant, there has often been rebranding for some cosmetic purpose. For the student of UK politics, at least the overall rationale for these changes is relatively simple. Most national politicians nowadays like the idea of decentralisation, which lends itself to rhetoric about 'letting the people choose' or 'returning power to individual citizens'. They also like the idea because it promises to reduce the burdens of direct responsibility on their own shoulders. However, they also relish reeling off statistics, which suggests that things have improved under their stewardship (or deteriorated while their opponents were in charge). In almost every policy field, something is almost always going wrong, and either the government itself or some independent watchdog is always ready to publicise the damning statistical evidence. As a result, ministers still want to feel that they exercise some degree of control. Sometimes, real improvements can be effected, but if not, some relief from political pressure can be gained by announcing reforms, reorganisations, mergers, de-mergers, and so forth. If anything, this process has accelerated in recent years, as economic austerity adds the need to save money to the list of imperatives driving reform. Yet, despite everything, it would still be difficult to identify many areas in which the government is *less* intrusive; even in many privatised industries, the state is still active through regulatory bodies.

The regulatory state

Regulatory agency

an independent organisation created by government to regulate an area of public life.

Central government has played a regulatory role in the British economy and society over many decades. **Regulatory agencies** responsible for working conditions and pollution control first appeared in the nineteenth century. Local authorities have long held regulatory powers, for example, in public health and planning. Quasi-judicial bodies such as employment and immigration tribunals are also well-established features of the British legal system (see Chapter 9). But self-regulation has been the norm in many areas of economic and social life.

The number of regulatory agencies has increased in the last 30 years or so, producing a 'regulatory state'. Rather than acting as owner or sole provider of public goods, the state has transferred these functions to the private sector or to semi-autonomous agencies. The state has transformed its role to that of regulator by creating regulatory regimes in the hope of promoting appropriate levels of performance. The alternative title of 'contract state' is also used to describe the system in which central and local government fund the provision of some services which are delivered by private companies that compete for contracts. The establishment of this regulatory regime means that we should be wary of accepting, at face value, claims about 'rolling back the state' since the 1980s, in spite of the dismantling of the nationalised industries via privatisation (see below) and contracting-out of many public services. Instead, it can be argued that the British state has been restructured, and now intervenes in economic and social affairs in different, more indirect, or behind-the-scene ways.

Privatisation and regulation

Privatisation

the transfer of state-owned bodies to the private sector, often through the sale of shares.

The **privatisation** of public corporations, and the accompanying creation of regulatory agencies in the 1980s and 1990s, are prime examples of the expansion of the state's regulatory role and its restructuring. The nationalisation programme of Clement Attlee's Labour government (1945–51) had given the state responsibility for the provision of public goods such as energy, public transport, utilities, and some manufactured goods (see Chapter 2). Most of the nationalised industries were swept away by the privatisation programme of the Thatcher and Major governments. During the financial crisis of 2007–08, the Brown government nationalised Northern Rock and partially nationalised other major banks by acquiring sizeable shareholdings in them as part of a temporary recapitalisation scheme.

Privatisation changes the balance between the public and private sectors by reducing the size of the public sector through the extension of the free market. Broadly defined, it includes the breaking of monopolies (e.g. the deregulation of bus services) and the private provision of public goods (e.g. through competitive tendering or the PFI). But the most significant form of privatisation was the sale of public corporations to the private sector after 1979. This brought significant sums of money into the Treasury, although there were costs involved such as writing-off or cancelling the debts of some industries (to make them attractive to private investors). It also increased, initially, the number of 'small' shareholders – what some Conservatives enthusiastically promoted as 'popular capitalism' – although as any prescient observer could have predicted, most shares ended up in the hands of City institutions.

The largest privatisations took the form of stock market flotations in which shares in the new companies were offered to individual and corporate buyers, usually at prices below their market value to make them financially affordable and attractive. Among the industries sold in this way were nationalised corporations such as British Petroleum, British Airways, and British Telecom plus publicly owned utilities like water, gas, and electricity. The privatisation of British Rail involved the sale of franchises – a licence to provide a service for a set time period – to private companies, while the rail infrastructure was owned by a new company, Railtrack. Privatising public utilities such as water, gas, and electricity posed particular problems as they are natural monopolies in which it is difficult to introduce or maintain competition. The operational functions of gas and electricity utilities (e.g. ownership of generators and pipelines) were separated from their supply and service activities, which were taken over by regional companies.

The nationalisation of the Northern Rock bank in February 2008 was the first time that a company had been taken into public ownership since the 1970s. It was the first high-profile victim of the credit crunch, having to be rescued by the Bank of England when it was unable to raise money from the financial markets, then being nationalised when a takeover could not be agreed. In the autumn of 2008, a government rescue package injected some £40 billion into the banking system, and the government acquired large stakes in RBS, HBOS, and Lloyds TSB. This dramatic episode shows that the state is still prepared to intervene in the economic life of its citizens on a massive scale when the need arises – but it was emphatically not intended to be a long-term policy. The banking section of Northern Rock was sold to Virgin Money in 2011 under the Conservative–Liberal Democrat coalition, and the sale to institutional investors of shares in Lloyds Banking Group began in 2013. The coalition government also sold 70 per cent of its stake in the Royal Mail through a share issue in 2013. The initial sale raised some £2 billion for the Treasury; criticism from MPs that the government had significantly undervalued the shares was rejected in an official report. Privatisation then accelerated under the Conservative government with the sale of shares in RSB and additional shares in Lloyds and the Royal Mail, plus plans to sell off the government's stake in Eurostar, the mortgage books of Northern Rock and Bradford and Bingley, and the student loan book.

Privatisation transformed the role of the state in the former nationalised industries, but it did not end it completely. The process did not create truly private companies accountable only to their shareholders, but rather 'hybrid' companies over which the state still exercised some control. In some cases, the government retained a 'golden share', giving it the right to block developments (e.g. takeovers) deemed contrary to the public interest. The main development was the change in the role of the state from owner to regulator. Regulatory agencies with statutory powers were created in the hope of ensuring that privatised companies acted in the public interest (see Table 10.4). These bodies have the power to set a pricing formula which may cap price increases or force reductions, and promote competition by breaking up monopolies. Of course, if privatisation worked in the manner which many Conservatives initially envisaged or promised, then there would be little need for a new regulatory regime, because competition for customers between privatised companies would automatically lead to lower prices, higher quality, better service, and improved performance. This was how 'the market' was supposed to work, and why it was deemed to be so much better than state-control and public provision of goods and services. Yet, in practice, many of the privatisations merely resulted in public monopolies and monolithic industries being transferred to the private sector, and although many were, sooner

TABLE 10.4 Privatisation and the regulatory state

Company	Date of privatisation	Regulatory agency
British Telecom	1984	Office of Communications (OFCOM)
British Gas	1986	Office of Gas and Electricity Markets (OFGEM)
Water companies (12 in UK)	1989	Water Services Regulation Authority (OFWAT)
Distribution network operators (14)	1990	Office of Gas and Electricity Markets (OFGEM)
National Power and Power Gen (electricity generators)	1991	Office of Gas and Electricity Markets (OFGEM)
Railtrack (railway infrastructure)	1996	Strategic Rail Authority – until 2005 when many of its functions were transferred to the Department of Transport's Rail Group
Railway operating companies	1995	Office of Rail Regulation (ORR)
Royal Mail	2013	Office of Communications (OFCOM)

or later, broken up into smaller or regional companies, there often remained a relative lack of competition; for example, on most rail routes, only one or two train companies provide a service, because it is not practicable to have ten different train companies racing against each other, on the same length of track, to be the first to arrive at a station. Hence, the privatisation programme was accompanied by the parallel establishment of a regulatory regime, to ensure that (in theory at least) customers were treated fairly in terms of prices charged and quality of service provided, and with the privatised firms subject to large fines (or, ultimately, in some instances, non-renewal of their franchise) if they fail to provide a specified level of service (Photo 10.1).

Although they have no direct role in the provision of services, the regulators manage the rules of the game under which privatised companies operate. The Office of Telecommunications (OFTEL) forced British Telecom to reduce prices, improve the standards of its service to customers, and open up its telecommunications infrastructure to competitors in the telephone, mobile phone, and Internet markets. The energy regulator OFGEM ended regional monopolies in domestic gas and electricity supply by mandating competition between supply companies. But the effectiveness of regulatory agencies is open to question. Regulatory bodies responsible for the railways failed to force real improvements in the rail infrastructure (see Controversy 10.2). OFGEM might have curbed the tendency of energy

PHOTO 10.1 The Ufton Nervet crash 2004: safety on the railways was seriously questioned after privatisation (© Scott Barbour/Getty Images).

Controversy 10.2

Rail privatisation

Although privatisation has always been controversial, the sell-off of Britain's railways provides an unarguable example of policy failure. When British Rail was privatised in 1996, ownership of the rail infrastructure was transferred to Railtrack, a company floated on the stock market, and franchises for 18 passenger services were awarded to private train-operating companies. Responsibility for regulation of the railways was split between two regulators, the Office of the Rail Regulator and the Office of Passenger Rail Franchising. However, train services showed little improvement or actually deteriorated, while chronic underinvestment in the rail network (e.g. tracks and signalling) was a factor in a number of serious train accidents. Leadership and clear lines of responsibility were obviously lacking.

Railtrack made a series of heavy losses and required government funding to stay afloat. In 2001, the Secretary of State for Transport, Stephen Byers, decided to end the subsidy as he believed that Railtrack was incapable of solving the problems of the industry. This forced Railtrack into administration and left its shareholders with limited compensation – enraging many investors who had been encouraged by government propaganda to regard privatisation as a risk-free adventure. Responsibility for the railway system and timetabling was then transferred to a new not-for-profit company, Network Rail. Government involvement was extended when the Strategic Rail Authority was wound up in 2005 and the Department of Transport regained control of national rail strategy. The renamed Office of Rail Regulation (ORR) remained as an independent regulator and took over responsibility for rail safety from the Health and Safety Executive (HSE). The system for issuing franchises for train operators was also changed: the number of franchises was reduced and more account taken of the past record of operators when franchises were awarded. Problems with this system were exposed in 2012 when the government cancelled the award of the West Coast Main Line franchise to FirstGroup after a legal challenge uncovered failings in the Department of Transport's handling of the process.

At the 2015 general election, Labour proposed that public sector operators should be allowed to run rail lines. This stopped short of the full nationalisation supported by some on the Left, including the Greens and Jeremy Corbyn, who was elected Labour leader in September 2015 and immediately established a policy group to work on rail renationalisation. By the 2017 and 2019 general elections, official Labour policy had shifted to an open commitment to renationalisation of the railways, although to avoid having to pay billions of pounds to the current owners and shareholders of train companies, it was proposed that they would only be taken back into public ownership when their current franchises expired. In the meantime, the Conservative government took Northern Rail back into public ownership in January 2020, thus relieving Arriva of its franchise after years of operational problems and complaints from passengers about the poor and unreliable service. The Transport Secretary, Grant Shapps, acknowledged that 'We know change is needed and change is coming … This is a new beginning but it is only a beginning' – comments which cast doubt over the future of the rest of Britain's privatised railways.

companies to respond to world market prices in a way which inflates their profits, but that practice still goes on. A wider concern is that regulatory agencies may grow too close to the bodies they oversee and thus share similar views of what is best for the sector. Studies from the USA speak of 'regulatory capture' in which agencies become complicit with the bodies they are responsible for, and lose sight of their duty to prioritise the interests of citizens and consumers.

Case study 10.3

NICE work? Regulating NHS treatments

The National Institute for Health and Care Excellence (NICE) is an independent body responsible for developing clinical guidelines and for recommending the use of new and existing medicines in the NHS in England and Wales. Guidelines and new technologies are referred to NICE by the Department of Health and Welsh Assembly. In licensing drugs and treatments, NICE takes account of both clinical evidence (how well do they work?) and economic evidence (do they offer value for money?). The House of Commons Health Select Committee and the World Health Organization have been critical of the lack of transparency of NICE's decision-making process.

With NICE appraisals of new medicines taking up to 14 months, there is pressure on Clinical Commissioning Groups and government ministers to make promising new drugs available as quickly as possible to those in need. Fast-track appraisals are expected to be used in less-complex cases. Controversy arose over the availability of the drug Herceptin in 2005. Although it had been licensed for late-stage breast cancer, it had not been approved by NICE for the treatment of early stages of the disease. With Herceptin being provided to relevant patients by some Primary Care Trusts but not others, the Secretary of State for Health, Patricia Hewitt, intervened to fast-track use of the drug and warn Trusts that they should not refuse to provide it on the grounds of cost if the drug had been recommended by a consultant. Critics argued that Hewitt's intervention had undermined NICE's independence.

Decisions made by NICE also have important financial implications for the NHS. NICE estimated that its 2005 decision that statins which reduce levels of cholesterol should be prescribed for people at risk of heart attack or strokes would cost the NHS up to £82 million per year. Five years earlier, NICE ruled that the drug beta interferon should not be given to every NHS patient with multiple sclerosis, as it would not guarantee good value for money.

The coalition government established a Cancer Drugs Fund, worth £200 million a year, to give patients access to drugs that were not routinely available on the NHS, effectively bypassing NICE. But it was criticised for overspending and funding ineffective treatments, and NICE was given managerial responsibility for the Fund in 2015.

Despite its memorable acronym, NICE has not been immune to the renaming game. In 2012, what had been (since a 2005 reorganisation) the National Institute for Health and *Clinical* Excellence was relaunched under its present name, and made an executive non-departmental body under the Department of Health.

Other regulatory bodies

Aside from privatisation, the shortcomings of self-regulation have also prompted the government to establish regulatory agencies. A number of food safety scares arose in the 1990s, notably the spread of bovine spongiform encephalopathy (BSE) in cattle. After a damning report by a public inquiry into BSE, the Food Standards Agency was set up in 2000 to ensure that food production met stricter public health standards. In 2010, the Agency was earmarked for abolition, leading to claims that the coalition government had been unduly influenced by food producers and retailers; the Agency was duly reprieved, though some of its functions were assumed by related government departments.

The expansion in the number of agencies also reflects a belief that some areas of life should be subject to regulation at arm's length from the government. Scientific and medical advances are a case in point, with the Human Fertilisation and Embryology Authority (HFEA) regulating human cloning and the NICE responsible for licensing new medicines (see Case study 10.3). Regulation has also increased in sport, where UK Sport and others promote participation, and the Olympic Delivery Authority was given responsibility for preparations for the 2012 London Olympic Games. The EU also had a significant role in regulating British society, particularly in environmental policy and working conditions, although its tiny bureaucracy meant that it relied on British officials to implement its decisions.

The Financial Services Authority (FSA) was established in 1999 to regulate banking, insurance, and mortgage services. The credibility of self-regulation in the City of London financial markets had been undermined by scandals such as the mis-sale of endowment mortgages, pensions, and payment protection insurance. The FSA tightened procedures and gave customers greater protection, but it also provides a major example of regulatory failure. The FSA admitted that it had paid insufficient attention to Northern Rock's risky operations before the bank sought emergency funding from the Bank of England. The Labour government took belated steps to tighten bank regulation in 2008, and, in 2011, the Conservative–Liberal Democrat coalition embarked on the task of abolishing the FSA and returning its regulatory functions to the Bank of England. The Financial Services Act of 2012 replaced the FSA with a Financial Conduct Authority (FCA), financed by the industry itself but responsible to the Treasury and to Parliament, which worked alongside the Bank's Prudential Regulatory Authority (PRA).

As the coalition government wrestled with the financial regulatory framework, it looked as if it might be presented with an equally acute dilemma in the form of press regulation. The 'phone-hacking' scandal had prompted the establishment of the Leveson Inquiry (2012) which reported in favour of a statutory regulatory body in place of the inadequate, independent PCC. After discussions between party leaders, a new body, the Independent Press Standards Organisation (IPSO), was established by Royal Charter, with enhanced powers and broader-based membership. The conduct of the free press was one minefield where state regulators rightly feared to tread.

Multilevel governance

So far, this chapter has concentrated on the transfer of functions *outwards,* from the core executive to semi-autonomous agencies and the private sector. But functions have also been transferred from the core executive *downwards* to subnational bodies and *upwards* to supranational institutions. Devolution has seen legislative authority on issues such as health, education, and economic development delegated by Westminster to devolved bodies in Scotland, Wales, and Northern Ireland. The powers of the devolved administrations and the implications of devolution for British politics are explored in detail in Chapter 12. The EU has extensive policy competences. It is the lead actor in areas such as agriculture and trade; even in fields where policy competence is shared between the EU and its member states, 'qualified majority voting' often applies, meaning that individual states cannot veto legislative proposals.

The term 'multilevel governance' describes this dispersal of decision-making authority across different tiers of government. The development of multilevel governance has transformed the role of the state. Nation-states remained key actors in EU policymaking prior to the UK's departure in January 2020, but EU membership also limited the policy autonomy of the core executive, and fostered policy networks of subnational, national, and supranational actors. In EU regional policy, the devolved administrations and local authorities engaged directly with the European Commission, thereby limiting central government's ability to act as a 'gatekeeper' between the supranational and subnational tiers of government. The impact of Britain's former EU membership is assessed more fully in Chapter 13.

The multilevel governance perspective captures the transfer of policymaking authority from the centre to subnational and supranational tiers of government. However, it exaggerates the extent to which this has eroded the capacity of both central government and the nation-state. Legislation establishing the devolved administrations safeguards the supremacy of the Westminster Parliament, and the centre is the dominant actor in institutions established to coordinate intergovernmental relations (i.e. relations between the UK government and devolved administrations). Nation-states take the leading role in 'history-making decisions' within the EU (e.g. treaty reform) and the autonomy enjoyed by supranational institutions is limited.

Globalisation

Globalisation is one of the most pervasive buzzwords in contemporary political analysis, but its character and impact are disputed. It refers to a widening and deepening interconnectedness between peoples and societies in many forms of activity. The boundaries between the national or domestic, and the international, have become blurred: politics within the nation-state is increasingly influenced by transnational forces. The following are key trends associated with globalisation:

- the development of a global economy;
- the increased size, scale, and political influence of multinational companies;
- the increased importance of international organisations;
- the development of global communications;
- the permeability of state boundaries;
- the development of a global culture.

The emergence of a global economy is central to the concept of globalisation. This global economy is characterised by the free movement of capital and the dominant position of multinational corporations. The liberalisation of capital movements, banking, and financial markets has allowed billions of pounds worth of financial transactions to occur daily across national boundaries. Currencies, investments, and markets are interconnected: significant movements in the value of the dollar or of shares in Tokyo may have knock-on effects across the developed world. The 2008 global crash originated in the United States' financial system and then spread very quickly across the Atlantic, resulting in a major economic recession in much of Europe, and, in turn, fuelling electoral support for populist parties and leaders of Left and Right. Multinational corporations such as BP, Ford, and Siemens are key players in the global economy, investing in countries beyond their home state and expanding their market share. Their turnovers, even profits, dwarf the gross national product of many newly industrialising countries. However, they are still subject to the laws and regulations of their home state and others, as BP found in 2010 when the US government ensured that it was saddled with responsibility for clearing up a devastating oil spill in the Gulf of Mexico.

The era of globalisation is often traced back to the 1960s, as this was when the political significance of the trends mentioned earlier became apparent, but it is since the 1990s that globalisation has really widened and deepened, facilitated by trade liberalisation, abolition of exchange controls, deregulation of financial services, and technological advances (millions of pounds can be transferred instantly by the mere click of a mouse, for example).

While many embrace globalisation, it has had serious implications for national governments, and arguably democracy itself, because the sheer scale, wealth, and mobility of multinational companies can limit the policy choices of individual countries and their political leaders. Since the 1990s, British governments of all parties have insisted on the need for low taxes, labour market 'flexibility', minimal employment protection (workers' rights), and weak trade unions, because of Britain's reliance on attracting inward investment. The neoliberal argument has been that if wages or taxes are too high, or workers are granted more legal rights or protection, then overseas firms will not want to invest in Britain or relocate here, but will move to countries which have lower taxes and weaker employment laws or trade unions. This is not generally a problem for Conservatives – even though their opposition to the EU was often about loss of sovereignty and a desire to 'take back control' of our own decisions, rather than dictated to by 'foreigners' – but it is a serious problem for parties of the Left. In 2019, several firms threatened to relocate overseas if Labour won the election, and Jeremy Corbyn became prime minister, with John McDonnell as chancellor. Economically, their concerns were understandable, but politically, their warnings raise questions about the strength of British democracy in an era of globalisation: 'we can vote for whoever we want to, provided that we vote for a party approved by big business and millionaires'.

International organisations

The number of international organisations has mushroomed to more than 250 as states look to global or regional cooperation on economic, security, and environmental issues (see Table 10.5). The most significant are those which are able to issue authoritative decisions that are binding on their member states (e.g. the EU). The UK is a permanent member of the Security Council of the United Nations, giving it the right to veto proposed resolutions. It is also a founding member of the North Atlantic Treaty Organization (NATO), the major post-war defence organisation, and the G8 group of leading economic states.

International trade is an area in which the autonomy of the British government is notably curtailed. Trade negotiations are conducted by the EU, while the World Trade Organization (WTO) is responsible for regulating international trade. It requires states to abide by WTO trade agreements and issues binding decisions when resolving disputes about tariffs and other barriers to free trade. It ruled in 2003 that tariffs imposed by the USA on steel imports were unfair and allowed the EU to retaliate by imposing tariffs on some US goods. President George W. Bush removed the steel tariffs to prevent the trade dispute from escalating.

TABLE 10.5 International organisations (examples of bodies of which the UK is a member: figures as of July 2011)

International organisation	Year founded	Functions
United Nations (UN)	1945	Promote peace and security, development, humanitarian aid, etc.
International Monetary Fund (IMF)	1945	Issue loans to states experiencing balance of payments problems
World Bank	1945	Economic assistance to developing states
North Atlantic Treaty Organization (NATO)	1949	Defence alliance (originally against Soviet Union)
European Union (EU)[a]	1957	Economic and political integration; originally named the European Economic Community (EEC)
Organisation for Economic Co-operation and Development (OECD)	1961	Promote economic and social improvement through cooperation and coordination, and tackle shared problems such as climate change and COVD-19
G8	1975	Discuss economic strategies of the leading economies; originally named the G6
World Trade Organization (WTO)	1995	Promote and regulate global free trade; successor to the General Agreement on Trade and Tariffs (GATT) of 1947
G20	1999	Similar to G8 (see above), but wider membership to recognise changed global economy since 1975.

[a]The UK left the EU on 31 January 2020.

The International Monetary Fund (IMF) was formed in 1945, with the task of securing international financial stability, issuing loans to states experiencing economic difficulties, but requiring in return that the recipient states introduce economic reforms. When the Callaghan government received a £2.3 billion loan from the IMF in 1976 following a run on sterling, it was required to cut public spending and tighten monetary policy, arguably bringing an end to Britain's post-war 'consensus' (see Chapter 3). Public sector strikes followed, but the IMF had played an important role in developing an economic framework that would be taken up enthusiastically by the Thatcher governments. The IMF also issues annual reports on the major economies, although these do not mandate national action.

Those sceptical of claims about the significance of globalisation note that the key economic and political developments are occurring at regional rather than global level. Economic and political integration is most advanced in Europe, where the previously 28-member (now 27) EU has supranational authority and extensive policy competences. The EU's 'Lisbon process' of economic reforms and its common immigration policy are intended to address the challenges of globalisation. In world trade, the EU is best viewed as a regional actor in competition with trading blocs in North America and Asia-Pacific, rather than as part of a truly global economy. As we will see in Chapter 13, the EU has also exerted considerable influence over British politics and the UK political system.

The scope of international law expanded in the second half of the twentieth century and now covers human rights and crimes against humanity. The UK (but not the USA) ratified the 1998 treaty establishing the International Criminal Court. The UK is also a signatory to international protocols such as the Kyoto Accord on climate change, which is binding upon its signatories – but not on those like the USA that did not ratify it. One of the most high-profile cases of international law seen in British courts in recent years was that concerning former Chilean military dictator General Augusto Pinochet. The House of Lords ruled in 1999 that Pinochet could be extradited from Britain to face charges under international law prohibiting torture (see Chapter 9). He was subsequently spared extradition from the UK on the grounds of ill health and, despite facing multiple charges in Chile, died in 2006 without standing trial.

International non-governmental organisations (INGOs) have also grown in number and significance, with groups such as Amnesty International operating at a global level. The UK government departments such as the Department for International Development work closely with the Red Cross and Oxfam. The impact of development issues on British politics was also apparent in the Make Poverty History campaign and 2005 Live8 concerts.

International policymaking is generally of two kinds: **supranational** and **intergovernmental**. Supranationalism is when an external body, over, above, and beyond the member states, makes decisions which are applicable to all of them. The individual states jointly create the organisation and contribute to its decisions, but once decisions have been taken, all are expected to abide by them. By contrast, intergovernmentalism is when individual nation-states or their governments come together on an ad hoc informal or voluntary basis, perhaps via an international conference or summit, to tackle a common problem (such as climate change, people trafficking, or sex slavery). Participation, and agreement to accept and act upon decisions reached, are entirely voluntary. The 'alliance' is likely to be dissolved once the problem has been successfully tackled. In general, Britain much prefers the latter mode of international decision-taking, because it is compatible with Britain's version of sovereignty, in contrast to supranationalism. Of course, this was a major reason why Britain was often so uncomfortable with membership of the EU.

Conclusion and summary

In the last three decades, the role of the British state has undergone significant changes. State intervention in the economy and society was commonplace in the post-war period, but by the end of the twentieth century, this aspect of state activity had been reduced significantly or, perhaps, transformed. However, the nationalisation of Northern Rock in 2008, and northern rail in 2020, showed that the state retains its capacity for large-scale intervention, albeit when there is no viable alternative. Government has given way to governance as decision-making functions were transferred from the core executive to supranational bodies, subnational institutions, and a large number of specialist agencies. The major trends in this era of governance were the separation of policymaking and policy-implementation functions, the development of an enabling or regulatory state which oversees the provision of public goods by a range of actors rather than providing them directly itself, and the introduction of market forces and private sector practices into public service delivery. Certainly, in many public services, the lines between the public and the private have become blurred.

New forms of governance present a serious challenge to the traditional view of representative government, in which ministers were held accountable to Parliament for policies that were made and then implemented by their departments. The transfer of functions from government departments to executive agencies has blurred the lines of accountability. The expansion of the quango state has also widened the 'democratic deficit', particularly at local level, raising concerns about accountability, transparency, and patronage. But new forms of accountability have emerged in a regulatory state which measures the performance of bodies responsible for delivering public goods. Finally, the development of multilevel governance has had both negative and positive consequences for British democracy. Devolution has brought decision-making closer to the people of Scotland, Wales, and Northern Ireland, and opened up new avenues for participation, whereas the transfer of policy competences to the EU (prior to January 2020) posed new challenges for effective scrutiny and accountability. Moreover, the power of multinational companies, and the relative ease with which many firms can relocate to countries with lower taxes, more 'flexible' labour markets, weaker trade unions and workers' rights, and explicitly pro-business governments, all raise concerns about the health of British democracy; what if the people vote for a government whose policies are not approved of by big business – or, indeed, the threats from big business deter people from voting for their preferred party in the first place?

Further reading

D. Richards and M. Smith's *Governance and Public Policy in the UK* (Oxford: Oxford University Press, 2002) is the best text on the changing state, although it is now dated. The best introduction to the civil service is J. Burnham and R. Pyper's *Britain's Modernised Civil Service* (London: Palgrave, 2008); a sophisticated analysis is provided by D. Richards in *New Labour and the Civil Service. Reconstituting the Westminster Model* (London: Palgrave, 2007). J. Burnham and S. Horton's *Public Management in the United Kingdom* (Basingstoke: Palgrave Macmillan, 2013) is an excellent introduction to the new public management in Britain's public services.

Rod Rhodes has been particularly influential in the study of governance. R. Rhodes's *Understanding Governance: Policy Networks, Governance, Reflexivity and Accountability* (Buckingham: Open University Press, 1997) brings together some of his most important work. D. Marsh, D. Richards, and M. Smith's *Changing Patterns of Governance in the United Kingdom: Reinventing Whitehall* (London: Palgrave, 2001) is also important. On the Conservative–Liberal Democrat coalition and the state, see M. Smith and R. Jones's 'From Big Society to Small State: Conservatism and the Privatization of Government', *British Politics*, Vol. 10, No. 2 (2015), pp. 226–48.

The most comprehensive study of quangos and delegation in British government is M. Flinders, *Delegated Governance and the British State. Walking without Order* (Oxford: Oxford University Press, 2008). The regulatory state is examined in M. Moran, 'Understanding the Regulatory State', *British Journal of Political Science*, Vol. 32, No. 2 (2002), pp. 391–413, and his excellent full-length study, *The British Regulatory State: High Modernism and Hyper-innovation* (Oxford: Oxford University Press, 2007). K. Dommett, M. Flinders, C. Skelcher, and K. Tonkiss, 'Did they "Read before Burning"? The Coalition and Quangos', *The Political Quarterly*, Vol. 85, No. 2 (2014), pp. 133–142, assesses the coalition government's 'bonfire of the quangos'.

V. Bogdanor (ed.), *Joined-Up Government* (Oxford: Oxford University Press, 2005) assesses the Blair governments' efforts to address fragmentation in central government. On policy disasters, see the special issue of *Parliamentary Affairs*, Vol. 56, No. 3 (2003), and A. King and I. Crewe, *The Blunders of Our Governments* (London: Oneworld Publications, 2013).

I. Bache and M. Flinders (eds.), *Multi-Level Governance* (Oxford: Oxford University Press, 2004), includes essays on the UK and EU. On recent developments in devolution, see C. Jeffery, 'The United Kingdom after the Scottish Referendum' in R. Heffernan, C. Hay, M. Russell, and P. Cowley (eds.), *Developments in British Politics 10* (Basingstoke: Palgrave Macmillan, 2016), and chapters 15–21 in M. Garnett (ed.), *The Routledge Handbook of British Politics and Society* (London: Routledge, 2020).

Introductions to globalisation include J. Baylis, S. Smith, and P. Owens (eds.), *The Globalisation of World Politics* (Oxford: Oxford University Press, 6th edition, 2014), J. Ravenhill's *Global Political Economy* (Oxford: Oxford University Press, 4th edition, 2014), and J. Michie (ed.), *The Handbook of Globalisation* (Cheltenham: Edward Elgar, 3rd edition, 2019).

Websites

The Cabinet Office website (www.gov.uk/government/organisations/cabinet-office) is a valuable source of information on central government and non-departmental public bodies, as is the Institute for Government website (https://www.instituteforgovernment.org.uk/). The civil service website (www.gov.uk/government/organisations/civil-service) includes information on its structure and reform, as does: https://www.civilservant.org.uk/index.html. Information on quangos and public bodies is available from the UK government website (www.gov.uk/government/collections/-public-bodies). Reports from the House of Commons Public Administration and Constitutional Affairs Select Committee are available at http://www.parliament.uk/business/committees/committees-a-z/commons-select/public-administration-and-constitutional-affairs-committee/.

Most executive agencies, quangos, and regulatory bodies have websites but their quality varies greatly. Those mentioned in this chapter include HM Prison Service (www.gov.uk/government/organisations/-hm-prison-service), the National Institute for Health and Clinical Excellence (www.nice.org.uk/), the Office of Rail Regulation (http://orr.gov.uk/), and the Financial Conduct Authority (www.fca.org.uk/). Websites of international organisations referred to in this chapter include the United Nations (www.un.org), the International Monetary Fund (www.imf.org), and the World Trade Organization (www.wto.org).

Chapter 11

Local government to local governance

Learning outcomes

After reading this chapter, you will:

- be aware of the structure and internal organisation of local government;
- be aware of the functions and financing of local government; and
- understand the move from local government to local governance.

Introduction

There are compelling reasons why a liberal democratic state such as the United Kingdom should have a robust system of local government. In a country of more than 65 million people, central government does not have the capacity to handle all the functions associated with the modern state, so the centre delegates some decision-making power to local bodies. There are strong normative arguments for granting local decision-making powers to democratic bodies such as elected local councils. Pluralists argue that power should be dispersed among different tiers of government rather than concentrated at the centre. Decentralisation is beneficial as it brings decision-making closer to the people: local authorities are better able to recognise and meet the needs of local communities. They also provide opportunities for people to participate in local politics.

Government to governance

Local government

a system in which elected local authorities are responsible for the provision of many local services.

The term **local government** refers to the network of local authorities and other organisations in the UK. Elected local councillors within these authorities take decisions on behalf of the citizens and communities they represent. Local government in the UK is weaker than in many other liberal democracies. It is not afforded constitutionally protected status, meaning that central government can – and often does – change the structure and powers of local government with limited consultation. Local councils now have a power of general competence but must still follow instructions from central government. Much of the legislation affecting local government did, historically, give councils extensive discretionary powers that allowed them to set their own priorities and adopt different policies. Councils also have the power to levy local taxes. But the financial and policy discretion afforded to local authorities by the centre has declined significantly.

For much of the twentieth century, local government was the predominant actor in local service delivery, with responsibility for education, housing, social care, policing, and so forth. This position has been eroded over the last 50 years as the autonomy (or discretionary power) afforded to local authorities has been reined in by the centre. Central government has extended its control over local government activity by taking over some of its functions, transferring others to non-elected agencies, and putting in place an inspection regime which penalises councils for failing to meet nationally determined targets. The centre has also tightened its grip on local government finance so that it controls much of the money available to local authorities.

Local governance

a system in which a range of bodies and networks are involved in the provision of local services.

The last two decades have also seen a move away from local government, in which elected local authorities provided most local services directly (e.g. education and housing), to **local governance,** in which a range of bodies are involved in decision-making and service provision at local level. These bodies include specialist agencies or quangos, local partnerships, voluntary bodies, and private companies. The emergence of local governance has necessitated a rethinking of the role of local authorities and the nature of local democracy.

The structure of local government

In 2020, the local government in England was structured as follows:

- 57 unitary authorities
- 25 county councils
- 188 district councils
- 36 metropolitan boroughs
- 33 London boroughs
- City of London Corporation
- Council of the Isles of Scilly
- 10,000 Parish/town councils.

In the rest of the UK, the structure was:

- Wales: 22 unitary authorities
- Scotland: 32 unitary authorities
- Northern Ireland: 11 district councils.

Recent decades have seen several major reorganisations of local government (see Timeline 11.1). The 1974 reorganisation of local government in England

TIMELINE 11.1

The development of local government

1888	Local Government Act establishes two-tier system of county councils and borough councils in rural England and Wales
1894	Local Government Act creates urban and rural district councils
1963	London Government Act creates Greater London Council and 32 London boroughs
1973	Local Government Act creates two-tier system of local government in urban areas and shire counties of England and Wales (comes into effect in 1974)
1980	Local Government Planning and Land Act introduces Compulsory Competitive Tendering (CCT)
1984	Rates Act introduces rate-capping
1985	Local Government Act abolishes Greater London Council and six metropolitan councils (came into effect in 1986)
1988	Local Government Finance Act replaces domestic rates with community charge (poll tax) and business rates with national non-domestic rates. Education Act allows schools to 'opt out' of local authority control
1992	Local Government Finance Act replaces community charge with council tax
1994–98	Forty-six unitary authorities are created in England. Two-tier systems of local government replaced by unitary authorities in Scotland and Wales
2000	Local Government Act requires local authorities to select one of three models of political management First elections to Greater London Authority and for Mayor of London
2002	Directly elected mayors established in some English local authorities following approval in referendums
2009	Creation of nine new unitary authorities in England
2011	Localism Act gives new rights to local people to take over the running of local services and facilities First 'combined authority' established in Greater Manchester
2016	Cities and Local Government Devolution Act extends and expands system of elected city mayors, and devolves further policy roles to them and the relevant local authority.
2017–20	New councils established in Buckinghamshire, Dorset, Northamptonshire, Somerset, and Suffolk.

and Wales introduced a two-tier system in which the functions of local authorities were divided between two levels of local government. In England, different arrangements were put in place for the major urban conurbations and the rural shire counties. Six metropolitan councils were established in the major urban areas of the West Midlands, South Yorkshire, West Yorkshire, Tyne and Wear, Greater Manchester, and Merseyside. These were major strategic bodies with responsibility for transport, policing, and strategic planning. Below the metropolitan council tier were 36 metropolitan districts responsible for big-spending local services such as education, personal social services, housing and leisure.

The names and division of labour between the two tiers were different in rural areas. Here, county councils in England and Wales were responsible for education and social services in addition to the strategic functions such as policing and transport handled by the metropolitan councils. A total of 333 district councils were responsible for housing, leisure, and other services. To further confuse the picture, the English and Welsh shires also have a lower tier of parish councils that run such things as village halls, allotments and cemeteries.

Different arrangements applied in London and Scotland. In London, the GLC had been established in 1965. It had strategic responsibilities similar to those of the metropolitan councils, although the Inner London Education Authority (ILEA) was responsible for education across the capital. Thirty-two London boroughs, plus the City of London Corporation, provided those services delivered by the metropolitan districts in other urban areas. Local government in Scotland was reorganised in 1975, with the creation of nine regional councils and 53 district councils.

The new pattern of local government was more uniform and streamlined than the diverse patchwork of authorities that had been in place for the previous 100 years. The number of local authorities was greatly reduced, with the 333 district councils in England replacing more than 1,000 bodies. But the reorganisation aroused opposition in some areas because it transferred strategic functions to larger authorities and redrew many traditional boundaries.

Unitaries but not uniformity

The 1974 reorganisation did not settle the structure of local government: far from it; since it has been subjected to subsequent alterations by central government, producing a more fragmented pattern.

Local government was one area in which Margaret Thatcher was strongly disinclined to 'roll back' the central state. Labour administrations in the GLC and metropolitan counties frustrated the Thatcher government's efforts to control local authority spending and taxation. Her government hit back by abolishing the GLC and the six metropolitan councils in 1986; the ILEA was abolished in 1990. Some of their responsibilities shifted to the London boroughs and the 36 metropolitan boroughs, but others were transferred to unelected agencies. London became the only major West European capital city without a large strategic authority.

The Major government wanted to create unitary authorities (i.e. a single tier of local government) in Great Britain. But an independent commission recommended fewer changes than the government had envisaged. The resulting picture was an uneven one: 46 unitary authorities were established in England by 1998, leaving a two-tier structure of 34 county councils and 238 district councils elsewhere. Historic names such as Rutland, which had been abolished in 1974, returned to the map but only four county councils – Avon, Berkshire, Cleveland, and Humberside – disappeared. Unitary authorities were, however, established in Scotland (32) and Wales (22).

Under the Blair governments, 44 councils were replaced by nine new unitary authorities in 2009: Bedfordshire (two unitary authorities), Cheshire (2), Cornwall, Durham, Northumberland, Shropshire, and Wiltshire. But the main structural reforms introduced by the Blair government were in the capital where the GLA was created. It has two elements: a 25-member London Assembly elected by the Additional Member System (see Chapter 17) and a directly elected executive mayor. The GLA has strategic responsibility in areas such as transport, economic development, policing and planning. These functions are carried out by agencies (e.g. Transport for London) accountable to the mayor. The mayor sets the budget (£18.5 billion in 2019) and determines policy; the Assembly scrutinises these and makes recommendations. The mayor's powers are limited, evidenced by the failure of Ken Livingstone – who was elected in 2000 as an independent and in 2004 as a Labour candidate – to persuade the government to drop its preference for a public–private partnership to finance redevelopment of the London Underground. His main initiative was a congestion charge for drivers entering Central London (see Controversy 11.1). Conservative Boris Johnson defeated Livingstone in the 2008 mayoral election and was re-elected in 2012. Five parties won seats in the 2016 Assembly election: Labour (12 seats), Conservative (8), Green Party (2), UKIP (2) and Liberal Democrats (1).

The Brown government paved the way for local authorities in major urban areas to work together in 'combined authorities'. These were then formed under David Cameron's Conservative–Liberal Democrat coalition (2010–15) and the subsequent majority Conservative government (2015–). Combined authorities are not local authorities but legal bodies consisting of several adjoining local authorities which remain in place and whose leaders sit in the cabinet of the combined authority. The Greater Manchester combined authority was the first to be created in 2011, followed by Sheffield city region, Liverpool city region, and North East combined authorities in 2014, West Midlands and Tees Valley (2016), West of England and Cambridge and Peterborough (2017), and North of Tyne (2018). Central government has granted the combined authorities greater strategic powers over transport and economic development, while Greater Manchester was given greater power over its health budget in 2015. The Cities and Local Government Devolution Act (2016) proposed the creation of more directly elected mayors, and the devolution to them of additional powers over housing, planning, and policing.

Internal organisation

Some 20,000 local councillors, serving in 339 principal authorities in England, are elected on four-year terms, although they are not all elected at the same time; the elections are 'staggered', perhaps with one-third of councillors elected every year, with one year 'free' of elections. The simple plurality system is used in single-member seats, but where more than one councillor is elected from a ward, a variant known as the 'block vote' is used. In a ward electing three councillors, an elector can vote for three candidates; the top three candidates are elected without any redistribution of votes.

Councillors undertake a number of functions, such as participating in local policymaking or scrutinising council activity, and represent their constituents. Most councillors do not receive a salary for their local authority work; allowances have increased but are not equivalent to the average wage.

In the early post-war period, political party involvement in local politics was limited in non-urban areas. Many councillors stood as independents, concealing any party affinity they may have had. Around half of all councillors were returned to office unopposed. The situation has changed dramatically. Most elections are contested, and more than 90 per cent of councillors represent a national party. A number of party systems exist at local level:

- *Dominant-party system* where one party has held a majority of seats and ran the local authority for many years. Labour has, for example, controlled Manchester City Council since 1974 and held 93 (out of 96) seats on the council in the 2019 elections.
- *Two-party systems* where most seats are held by two parties. These may alternate in power, form minority administrations, or work together in coalition. The Conservatives and Labour controlled more than three-quarters of councils in Great Britain after the 2019 local elections (the scheduled 2020 local elections were deferred to 2021 due to the COVID-19 pandemic and associated lockdown) – 143 and 91, respectively. The Liberal Democrats had been an important presence in local government since the 1990s but lost many of their seats after entering coalition government with the Conservatives in 2010, and in the 2019 local elections, won or retained control of just 23 councils. No single party had overall control of 79 of England's 339 councils after the 2019 elections. In Scotland, where the single transferable vote is used, no one party is in control of 29 of 32 unitary authorities following the 2017 local elections north of the border.
- *Multi-party systems* where council seats are divided between three or more parties, making majority rule unlikely. The largest party may run a minority administration, or a coalition of two or more parties may take control. Five parties briefly shared power on Lancaster council after 2008. The Greens, UKIP, Respect Party, and the British National Party have all won council seats in England in recent years. The Greens ran Brighton and Hove City Council from 2011 to 2015, while UKIP won control of Thanet District Council in 2015.

Party groups meet to discuss policy and agree their positions. Councillors may face sanctions if they do not vote with their party. The influence of party groups reached its apogee in Labour-run metropolitan councils in the 1980s when major decisions were taken by senior party figures away from the council chamber.

Local government officers provide policy advice to councillors and implement council decisions. In many councils, policy work is conducted within service departments (e.g. social services) and central departments (e.g. finance) that are staffed by officials and headed by a chief officer who has professional experience in that area. Most authorities have a chief executive who assumes overall re-sponsibility for the work of the council and its departments. Despite a recent decline associated with economic 'austerity', around two million people are employed in local government in the UK.

Decision-making by committee was the norm in local government in the twentieth century. Committees handled decision-making in areas in which councils provided services. They in-cluded councillors from both the ruling group and other parties, thus allowing discussions on alternative proposals but also lengthening the time it took to make policy. Nor was decision-making as transparent as this implies, since key decisions were often taken by small groups behind closed doors. Committee work did allow councillors to concentrate on those areas in which they had professional experience. But it also produced compartmentalisation, whereby councillors and officials concentrated on their areas of interest rather than focusing on the bigger picture.

Directly elected mayors

Interest in the idea of directly elected mayors grew in the 1990s. Conservative Secretary of State for the Environment Michael Heseltine was a long-standing advocate, while key New Labour politicians such as Tony Blair also saw its attractions. In office, the Blair government proposed a separation of the executive and scrutiny functions of local authorities. Council leaders would take strategic decisions, while the remaining non-executive councillors scrutinised their activities. It was hoped that this would professionalise local government, provide stronger community leadership, and improve accountability. The Local Government Act 2000 duly required councils with a population of over 85,000 to introduce one of three models of political management:

- a directly elected mayor with a cabinet;
- a directly elected mayor with a full-time council manager; and
- a cabinet with an executive leader chosen by councillors.

The cabinet with an executive leader model was chosen by 316 local authorities, that is, 82 per cent of the total number. Here, the council leader is indirectly elected by councillors, which, in practice, means that the leader of the largest political group becomes council leader. He or she shares executive power with a cabinet of up to nine councillors selected from the majority party or the ruling coalition. The cabinet and executive leader model was the preferred option of most councils because it was the closest to the existing pattern of informal inner cabinets consisting of the council leader and the chairs of committees.

The Blair government's preferred model was the directly elected mayor and cabinet. It believed that elected local mayors would become the key political actors in their communities, taking policy initiatives, setting the budget, and taking executive decisions. Direct election would also give the mayor added legitimacy and a higher profile. Councillors who were not members of the cabinet would scrutinise the activities of the council executive, propose policy or budgetary amendments, and act as community representatives. Supporters of the mayoral model pointed to the effective political and economic leadership provided by mayors in American cities, but UK directly elected mayors pale in comparison given the limited powers of their local authorities. It is also worth noting that directly elected mayors are not the same as, and do not replace, civic mayors whose role is largely ceremonial. However, established players in local government were wary of the mayoral option, fearing that their influence would be diminished further.

Only one local authority, Stoke-on-Trent, adopted the mayor with council manager model. The Local Government and Public Involvement in Health Act 2007 removed this option, requiring English local authorities to choose either a directly elected mayor and cabinet or an indirectly elected leader (i.e. chosen by the council) and cabinet with a four-year mandate. But things changed yet again when the Localism Act 2011 allowed councils to operate either a leader and cabinet or a committee system. The latter option was closer to the executive arrangements that existed before the Blair reforms.

The Local Government Act 2000 required councils to hold a referendum if they wished to move to a directly elected mayor. Referendums on directly elected mayors were held in 30 authorities in 2001–2, but only 11 produced votes in favour. Voters in Torbay (2005), Tower Hamlets (2010), and Copeland (2014) later approved a move to directly elected mayors. But the requirement for a referendum before a local authority could adopt the directly elected mayor model was dropped in 2007: a vote of the council will suffice (as happened in Leicester and Liverpool), although local citizens can still petition for a referendum (as in Salford). By 2015, a total of 51 referendums had been held on moving to the directly elected mayor model, with 16 approving the move and 35 rejecting it. In two areas, Hartlepool and Stoke-on-Trent, voters approved the abolition of the post of directly elected mayor.

The Conservative–Liberal Democrat coalition also favoured directly elected mayors for large cities. Using the Localism Act 2011, 10 English cities held referendums in 2012 on whether to switch to directly elected mayors. But only Bristol voted for a mayoral system. However, the government continued to press for the mayoral system, and, as part of its plans to create combined authorities (or city regions) with greater strategic powers, the Greater Manchester combined authority agreed to move to the directly elected mayoral model – despite voters rejecting the mayoral model in a referendum in 2012. An interim mayor was appointed in 2015 and in May 2017 Labour's Andy Burnham was elected. More city mayors have been established following the 2016 Cities and Local Government Devolution Act (Figure 11.1).

The fact that the majority of these mayors are drawn from the Labour Party probably reflects the fact that urban areas tend to vote Labour more than rural districts or small towns, and it is mainly cities which have an elected mayor – or in Liverpool's case, two!

Directly elected mayors are elected by the supplementary vote system in which voters indicate a first and a second preference. If no candidate secures 50 per cent at the first count, all but the top two candidates are eliminated and the second preference votes are redistributed. Independent (i.e. non-aligned) candidates have performed well in mayoral elections (see Table 11.1). Those with a high profile included former police chief Ray Mallon in Middlesbrough (2002–15) and Stuart Drummond – better known as 'H'Angus the Monkey', Hartlepool United's club mascot – in Hartlepool (2002–13). Luftur Rahman, an independent candidate, was elected mayor of Tower Hamlets in 2010, and re-elected in 2014. But the latter result was challenged in court where Rahman was found guilty of electoral fraud, and therefore, the election was declared void and Rahman was disqualified from office.

Academic research suggests that directly elected mayors have generated more effective leadership, delivered improved performance, and have a higher public recognition rating than other local politicians. However, political and structural problems (e.g. resistance to change from local councillors and dysfunctional decision-making) have meant that implementation of the mayoral model has been patchy. During the 'second wave' of the COVID-19 pandemic, elected Mayors like Greater Manchester's Andy Burnham took on new significance as they fought the central government for greater support for local businesses.

TABLE 11.1 UK directly elected mayors, 2020

Local authority	Mayor	Party affiliation	Post created
Bedford	Dave Hodgson	Liberal Democrat	2002
Bristol	Marvin Rees	Labour	2012
Cambridgeshire	James Palmer	Conservative	2017
Copeland	Mike Starkie	Independent	2015
Doncaster	Ros Jones	Labour	2002
Greater Manchester	Andy Burnham	Labour	2017
Hackney	Philip Glanville	Labour	2002
Leicester	Sir Peter Soulsby	Labour	2011
Lewisham	Damien Egan	Labour	2002
Liverpool City	Joe Anderson	Labour	2012
Liverpool Region	Steve Rotheram	Labour	2017
London	Sadiq Khan	Labour	2000
Mansfield	Andy Abrahams	Labour	2002
Middlesbrough	Andy Preston	Independent	2002
Newham	Sir Robin Wales	Labour	2002
North Tyneside	Norma Redfearn	Labour	2002
Northumberland	Jamie Driscoll	Labour	2019
Salford	Paul Dennett	Labour	2012
South Yorkshire	Dan Jarvis	Labour	2018
Tees Valley	Ben Houchen	Conservative	2017
Tower Hamlets	John Biggs	Labour	2010
Watford	Dorothy Thornhill	Liberal Democrat	2002
West of England	Tom Bowles	Conservative	2017
West Midlands	Andy Street	Conservative	2017

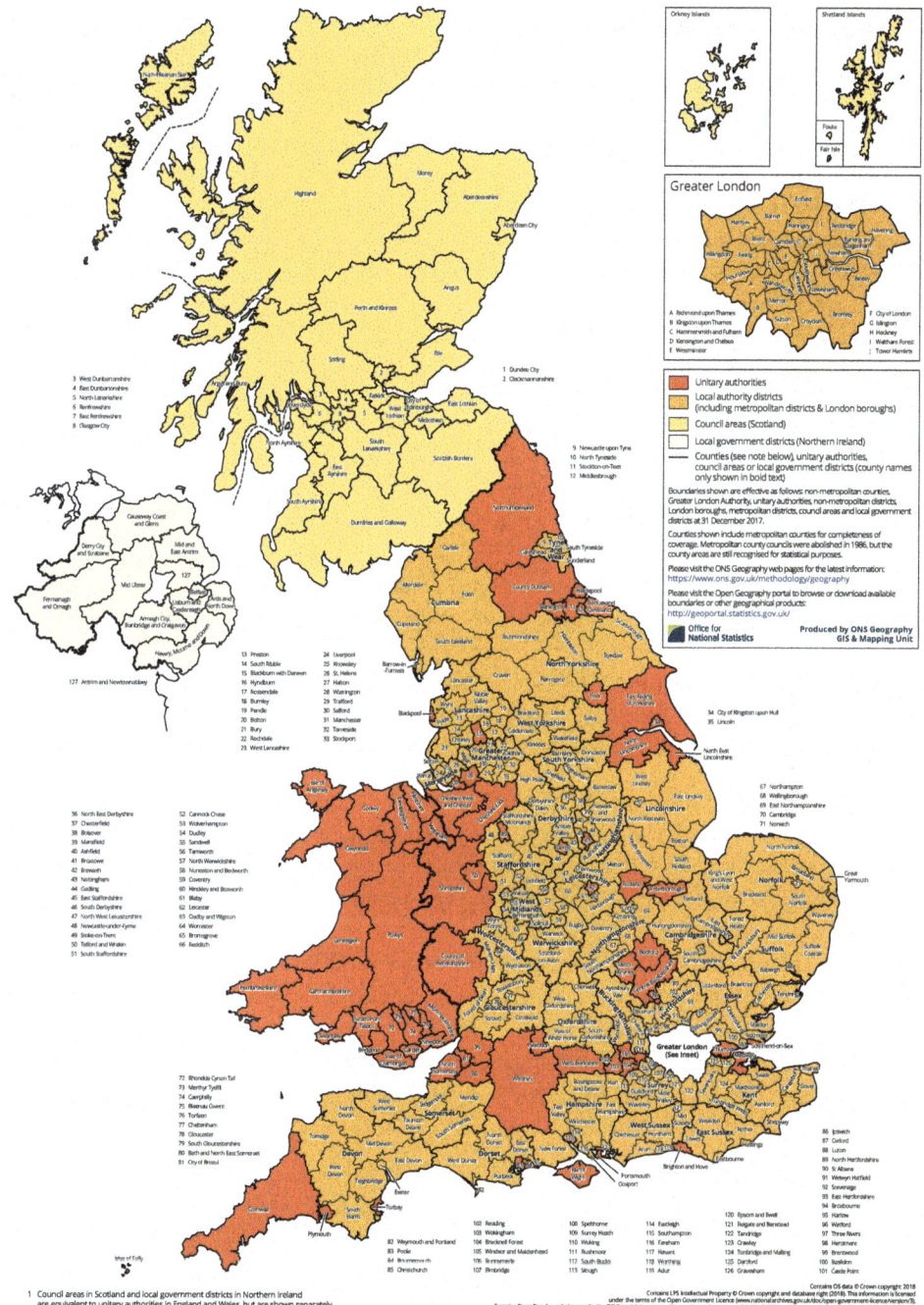

FIGURE 11.1 Local Authority Districts, Counties, and Unitary Authorities (December 2017) in United Kingdom.

Source: Office for National Statistics, contains public sector information licensed under the Open Government Licence v3.0.

Functions of local authorities

Local authorities are responsible for many of the services that citizens utilise on a regular basis. Until recently, local authorities could only perform functions that the law gave them specific permission to carry out – anything else would be viewed by the courts as acting beyond their powers. The Localism Act 2011 then applied a new general power of competence for local authorities: it states that 'a local authority has power to do anything that individuals generally may do'. However, this does not permit local authorities to raise tax or expand their powers to issue by-laws. Local authorities are still required to follow instructions issued by central government and lack the funds to greatly expand their functions.

The main functions performed by local authorities include:

- Education: primary and secondary schools, nurseries, youth services, and adult education;
- Social services: residential care and care in the community;
- Housing: public housing, redevelopment, services for the homeless;
- Highways: road building and maintenance (except motorways and trunk roads), traffic regulation and road safety (e.g. speed limits);
- Public transport: bus services, licensing of taxis, and so forth;
- Planning: decisions on planning applications, strategic planning (in conjunction with regional bodies);
- Environmental health: refuse collection, recycling, pollution control, health and safety inspections of commercial premises;
- Leisure and culture: public libraries, arts, leisure centres, parks.

In its heyday in the late nineteenth and early twentieth centuries, local government provided many of the public services associated with the modern state. These included public housing, primary and secondary education, public health, policing, and the supply of water, gas, and electricity. But local government's service provision role has declined over the last half century, regardless of the party in power at Westminster.

The nationalisation of public utilities in the 1940s saw local authorities lose functional responsibility for the provision of water, electricity, and gas. The creation of the NHS in 1948 ended local authority ownership of most hospitals.

The focus of this section is on the changes to local government's service provision role introduced by successive governments since 1979. A number of trends are evident, mirroring those found in the central state (see Chapter 10):

- the transformation of local authorities into 'enabling authorities' which oversee the provision of services by other bodies, rather than providing them directly themselves;
- the move from local government to local governance, with local services being delivered by a variety of bodies including quangos, voluntary organisations, and private companies;
- the increased role of market forces and the private sector in local service delivery;
- the changing nature of local accountability. Local elections used to be the main way in which councillors were held to account for the quality of local services. Now service providers must meet targets and are subject to inspection by regulatory bodies.

Primary and secondary *education* is the largest area of local authority expenditure (37 per cent of expenditure in 2018–19). Funding for education comes in the form of a ring-fenced specific grant, the Dedicated Schools Grant, which cannot be used for other purposes. The Education Act 1944 stated that local councils would be local education authorities with responsibility for the provision, management, and staffing of primary and secondary schools. Responsibility for polytechnics and higher education colleges was removed from local authorities in the early 1990s and transferred to new agencies. The Education Act 1988 allowed state schools to opt out of local authority control, subject to approval by a ballot of parents, and become 'grant-maintained schools' funded directly by central government. The Blair governments ended grant-maintained status but created academy schools which are state-funded but self-governing and independent of local authority control. While following the national curriculum, academies were initially encouraged to specialise in particular subjects. The Conservative–Liberal Democrat coalition expanded the academies programme and went further by encouraging the establishment of 'free schools', again funded by the state rather than local authorities, by businesses, charities, or groups of teachers or parents. State-funded schools are subject to regular inspection by the Office for Standards in Education (OFSTED), which provides another example of the development of the regulatory state (see Chapter 10). Schools with poor records may be forced to introduce 'special measures' or be closed down.

Public *housing* was a major function of local authorities in the 1950s, when councils were required to build new homes to meet local needs. The Thatcher governments gave council tenants the right to buy their homes at a discounted price. This removed more than two million houses from local authority control; Housing Action Trusts (HATs) were created to manage public-owned housing. Councils also faced restrictions on borrowing money to repair houses or build new ones. The Blair governments encouraged councils to transfer ownership of their housing stock to 'registered social landlords' (e.g. housing associations set up by councils), subject to approval in residents' ballots. Housing associations do not face the same restrictions on borrowing money. By 2010, registered social landlords of various kinds were challenging (if not surpassing) local councils as providers of housing. Local authorities are responsible for administering mandatory housing benefits, reclaiming the money they have paid from the Department for Work and Pensions.

Local authorities have statutory responsibility for decisions on *planning* (e.g. building new homes and developing land) and are required to produce development strategies. The Localism Act 2011 allowed councils to produce neighbourhood plans, which would then have to be taken into account when planning decisions are made. In some cases, such as the construction of the High Speed 2 (HS2) rail link or applications for fracking, central government has intervened to fast-track the planning process.

Social care is the second largest area of local authority expenditure (adult social care constituting 17 per cent of expenditure in 2018–19 and children's social care 9 per cent). Most of the money that local authorities raise from the council tax (as opposed to receipts from central government grants) is spent here. Local authorities are responsible for *personal services* to elderly people, children, young people, and those with mental health problems. They provide services such as residential and day care, help in the home (e.g. meals on wheels), and child protection. This is one of the few areas in which government legislation has extended rather than reduced the role of local authorities. Since the 1990s, social workers employed by local councils have been responsible for assessing requests for residential care and providing care in the community. The Conservative–Liberal Democrat coalition and its Conservative successor have negotiated the devolution of some *healthcare* functions to local authorities and local health commissioning bodies. The Greater Manchester combined authority was granted control of a combined £6 billion budget for health and social care in 2015.

Local authority involvement in *economic development* has also expanded. This has resulted from both central government pressure (e.g. the Local Government Act 2000 required local authorities to promote economic development), the role of the European Union (EU) (which provided funding for regeneration projects directly to local authorities), and local initiatives. Councils have become leading actors in networks – which include businesses, chambers of commerce, training bodies, and voluntary agencies – that seek to promote investment and employment. But vocational training is now controlled by specialised agencies (learning and skills councils) rather than local authorities. Local authority-led regeneration has been particularly evident in areas that suffered from the decline of manufacturing industry, such as South Wales and North East England. Public–private partnerships have also revitalised *public transport* systems, funding new tram networks in cities such as Manchester and Nottingham. Some councils have considered introducing congestion charges (see Controversy 11.1). New combined authorities have been given greater powers over transport and economic development.

Local authority involvement in *policing* has diminished. Councillors once made up a majority of members serving on committees which held chief constables accountable, but no longer do so. The Conservative–Liberal Democrat coalition abolished police authorities and introduced directly elected police and crime commissioners to oversee spending, raise additional funds through precepts to the council tax, and hold chief constables to account. Nonetheless, policing accounted for 12 per cent of English local authority spending in 2018–19.

Controversy 11.1

Congestion charging

Congestion charging is one of the most controversial examples of policy innovation by local government. The most significant scheme is that introduced by the Mayor of London and Greater London Authority in February 2003. Drivers of private vehicles entering a defined 'central zone' between 7.00 am and 6.00 pm on weekdays would be charged an initial £5 per day (which had risen to £15 by 2020). Cameras read the registration number of cars on entering the zone and check it against a database. Non-payers face a standard £160 penalty. Various categories of people and vehicles are entitled to discounts, including people living within the congestion charging zone, disabled drivers, taxis, and motorcycles.

The scheme aimed to tackle the worst city centre congestion and air quality in the UK by encouraging people to use buses, rail, and the tube rather than their cars. Much of the money raised by the charge would be used to improve public transport. Before the charge was introduced, the average speed in London was 11 miles per hour and drivers spent more than half their time in queues. Ten years after the introduction of the congestion charge, traffic had fallen by 10 per cent and more people used public transport. But charging has not been welcomed universally. Only half of Londoners support it, and small businesses claim to have lost trade. The western extension of the charge zone, introduced in 2007, was cancelled in 2011.

The Transport Act 2000 allowed local authorities to introduce congestion charging at their discretion. A number of councils have given it serious consideration, but few have taken the plunge. Durham City Council introduced a £2 charge to enter part of the city in 2002. A congestion charge for central Edinburgh was overwhelmingly rejected in a local referendum in 2005; then voters in Manchester similarly rejected a congestion charge for peak time travel within the M60 ring road in 2008.

In its initial response to the COVID-19 pandemic in 2020, Boris Johnson's government announced an additional £3.2 billion for England's local authorities (separate additional funding was also announced for Scotland, Wales, and Northern Ireland) in order to assist with the additional and unavoidable costs incurred in addressing the immediate impact of the crisis, with most of the additional sums targeted towards social care, children's services, and providing temporary accommodation for the homeless.

From provider to enabler

Enabling authority

a local authority that sets a framework in which a range of bodies provide local services but which does not provide many of these services itself.

The Conservative vision was of local authorities as **enabling authorities** that established the strategic priorities for services and set out a framework for competition between would-be service providers, but would no longer be universal service providers themselves. This mirrored the emphasis on government acting as an enabler or regulator that underpinned changes occurring at the centre, such as the reform of the civil service. This perspective challenged the traditional view of local democracy by focusing not on the interests of local government, but on those of local citizens who, as consumers of local services, wanted more efficient and/or economical services. Service providers would be held accountable through contracts and charters, while councillors remained accountable to the electorate for strategic and budgetary decisions. Rather than providing services directly, local authorities now organise, supervise, regulate, and fund the provision of services by other competing bodies.

The Conservatives argued that this amounted to decentralisation of power to the citizen, but it took interventionist measures to bring this about.

Compulsory Competitive Tendering (CCT)

the policy that public bodies are required to open up contracts for service provision to the private sector.

Compulsory Competitive Tendering (CCT) was introduced in 1980, and extended in 1988 and 1992. It required local authorities to put contracts for service provision out to tender, meaning that council departments had to compete with outside contractors for the right to provide services such as refuse collection and leisure facilities (see Case study 11.1). The contract would be awarded to the lowest bidder. Conservatives supported CCT as it brought about the separation of local authorities' previous roles as both a purchaser and provider of services, tackled the monopoly status of local government services, and (not least) weakened trade union influence. In-house bids were successful in many large contracts, but the CCT process forced local authorities to make efficiency savings so that they could compete with the private sector. It was also expected to improve the efficiency of service provision, but critics argued that savings were made at the expense of quality and working conditions.

The Blair government replaced CCT with 'Best Value' in 2000. Councils were no longer forced to put contracts out to tender, but were required to obtain best value. They had to conduct regular reviews of their services to ensure that 'continuous improvement' was underway. Local authority services were also subject to inspections and faced sanctions if they were deemed to be underperforming. Under the Comprehensive Performance Assessment (CPA) introduced in 2002, key services and the overall performance of councils were

Case study 11.1

Recycling

Recycling is an issue that illustrates the nature of multilevel governance in the UK, the potential for policy innovation in local government, and subsequent intervention by the centre. Local authorities have been at the forefront of efforts to increase recycling in Britain as they are responsible for waste management. In shire counties where two tiers of local government remain, district councils are responsible for the regular collection of household waste, but county councils provide waste disposal sites. Since the introduction of CCT, private companies have won many of the contracts to collect and dispose of domestic refuse.

Local authorities in England are required to meet targets for recycling set by central government. The Blair governments set a series of targets for councils and required them to collect at least two separate recyclable materials (e.g. paper, glass, cans, and plastics) from households by 2010. The Conservative–Liberal Democrat coalition was less favourable towards centrally imposed targets, but the European Commission set a recycling target of 50 per cent of household waste by 2020, which the UK was confident of meeting. Some 45 per cent of household waste was recycled in England in 2013–14 – the latest available statistics – but there were significant differences in local authority performance. South Oxfordshire district council sent 66 per cent of household waste for recycling, reuse, or composting, whereas the worst performer, the London borough of Newham, managed just 18 per cent.

Some of the measures taken by local authorities to meet their recycling targets have proved controversial. More than 80 per cent of local authorities now use alternate weekly collections of household waste – recyclable material is collected one week and non-recyclable material the next. In theory, this would encourage recycling and reduce the costs of waste collection. In response to public disquiet, the coalition government signalled that it favoured a return to weekly collections and introduced a support scheme to help fund switches back to weekly collections. However, the scheme had little impact as only one local authority (Stoke-on-Trent) reinstated weekly bin collections – and subsequently changed its mind. Local authorities complained that, in an era of major spending cuts, government funding did not cover the costs of a return to weekly collections.

The coalition government did, though, curb the power of councils to fine residents who misused 'green bins' and abolished the associated criminal offence. Instead, the government encouraged councils to adopt incentive-based schemes that rewarded people for effective recycling (e.g. through local competitions with vouchers as prizes).

ranked from poor to excellent by the Audit Commission. Councils rated as excellent in priority service areas (e.g. education, social care, and transport) were given 'additional freedoms' such as more discretion in spending, while those rated good or better faced 'lighter touch' inspections in the future. But poor performers faced having special management teams sent in to address their shortcomings. A new framework, the Comprehensive Area Assessment (CAA), based on some 200 national indicators, replaced the CPA from 2009. However, the Conservative–Liberal Democrat coalition announced its abolition (and that of the Audit Commission) as part of its agreed strategy of reducing local government inspection. In 2014, a new company, Public Sector

Audit Appointments, Ltd., was set up by the Local Government Association to oversee the monitoring of local authority performance.

Localism from Blair to Cameron

Localism

the devolution of power or functions from the centre to local institutions and local communities.

Localism refers to the devolution of powers or functions from central government to local institutions and communities. All governments since 1997 have been committed to localism, seeking to give local citizens a greater say in shaping local priorities. New Labour gave community bodies a greater role in setting policies in their neighbourhoods and allowed local citizens to run assets such as community centres. It was a managerial form of localism in which local authorities and community groupings were required to meet targets set by the centre and were subject to inspections. This performance-led localism rewarded local authorities who met their targets, but those that fell short faced intervention from the centre.

Localism was further developed, albeit in a different format, by the coalition government. The Conservative–Liberal Democrat coalition promised to effect 'a fundamental shift of power from Westminster to people'. David Cameron had made 'the Big Society' his main campaigning slogan in 2010, and decentralisation was a key element of this vision (see Chapter 16). The coalition government argued that the previous regime of performance targets and ring-fenced funding was overly bureaucratic and denied citizens a real say in decision-making on local issues. But Cameron's 'Big Society' also departed from Thatcherism by promising to devolve powers to local authorities rather than taking powers from them, and by taking an optimistic view of the role of active citizens and community groups.

The Localism Act 2011 was intended to devolve further decision-making powers to local authorities and to empower individuals and communities. It permitted local authorities to be more independent and creative by giving them a general power of competence and relaxing the performance framework associated with the Audit Commission. Councils are now expected to appoint private auditors and develop their own performance measures and standards, but were required to be more transparent by publishing items of expenditures over £500. Local authorities were also given greater freedom in how they spend funds from central government. Community budgets gave a range of local service providers greater control over funding with the goal of dealing with problems such as 'troubled families'. Finally, local authorities were now permitted to change their internal executive arrangements to a committee system.

The Act sought to enhance local citizens' role in democratic decision-making. Citizens were granted a greater involvement in planning decisions, while large increases in council tax would have to be approved in local referendums. The legislation also paved the way for referendums on directly elected mayors in England's 12 largest cities outside London. Additional legislation created new directly elected police and crime commissioners. Community organisations and voluntary groups were also empowered, being encouraged to play a greater role in delivering local services. They can now apply to run services currently delivered by a local authority, set up free schools, and buy local authority assets that are threatened with closure.

However, there was an uneasy tension between localism and the more general policies of the coalition government. Local authorities were given greater autonomy through their new general power of competence, greater control over their budgets, and the devolution of powers to combined authorities. But central government still dictated much of what local authorities can and cannot do. It led another reorganisation of local and regional government, requiring combined authorities to adopt the directly elected mayor model despite its rejection in referendums in 11 English cities in 2012. More significantly, austerity measures brought large-scale cuts in spending on local government and public services, which further restricted the spending power and financial autonomy of local authorities. Cutting budgets also arguably made it more difficult to mobilise community action. Critics of the 'Big Society' argued that it was designed to bring private providers in to fill the gaps in service provision that local authorities could not fulfil in an age of austerity. Whereas groups from civil society were expected to work in partnership with local and central government in New Labour's version of localism, now these groups were expected to replace the functions carried out by a retreating state.

Local government finance

Local government expenditure accounts for about a quarter of all public spending in England. Overall, local government revenue expenditure in England was £96.2 billion in 2019–20, down from £117 billion in 2009–10. Funding for local authorities comes from a number of sources, notably:

- grants from central government;
- local taxation on domestic properties, that is, the council tax;
- local taxation on business properties, that is, the national non-domestic rate; and
- charges for services, rents, and so forth.

The financial regime for local government in England is one of the most centralised in Western Europe, giving local authorities only limited financial autonomy. Only the council tax is under the direct influence of local authorities, but levels are subject to capping by central government. The percentage of local authority finance controlled by councils themselves has fallen since 1990. In 1989–90, the last year of the old rates system, central government provided 41 per cent of local government income, while councils raised the rest through taxes on domestic and business properties. By 2015–16, central government grants accounted for 60 per cent of local authority revenue expenditure, while the council tax provided 26 per cent of revenue and the business tax 13 per cent. The fall in the ratio of contributions from local taxes was significant as it means that large increases in council tax bills are needed to provide relatively small sums of money. Local authorities thus have less discretion in spending, forcing them to make difficult decisions about how money should be allocated. Thanks to the central government policy of 'austerity', the proportion of local government revenue raised locally had risen to almost 70 per cent in 2018–19. The main areas of local authority expenditure in 2019–20 were education (£34 billion), social care (£26 billion), housing (£19 billion, mainly on housing benefit), and policing (£12 billion).

Changes to the way in which central government provides grants to local authorities have also eroded local authority autonomy. Prior to 1979, funding from the centre came largely in the form of lump sum payments which local authorities could then decide how to distribute. But the Thatcher government moved towards targeted funding, making greater use of specific grants earmarked for particular purposes (e.g. teachers' pay). A system of central targets and penalties for overspending councils was also put in place.

From 1990 to 2013, the level of central government funding was determined by reference to a Standard Spending Assessment (SSA). This was the centre's assessment of how much each individual local authority must spend to reach a 'standard level of service' in major local services. Calculations were made on the basis of indicators ranging from the total population of the area to the numbers of pensioners and primary school children who lived there. The SSA system was heavily criticised within local government for its insensitivity to local differences and for the further erosion of their ability to focus spending on areas which were priorities for themselves and for local residents.

The Conservative–Liberal Democrat coalition allowed local authorities to decide from 2013 how to spend most of the funding they received from the centre (except that earmarked for schools and public health), which now came in the form of a single Local Services Support Grant. The ending of 'ring-fenced' funding marked an important shift away from central control of local government spending. However, funding from central government also declined significantly, with local government being one of the main casualties of cuts in public spending. Local government spending in England fell by some 20 per cent in real terms between 2010 and 2015, with cuts in spending power felt particularly by local authorities in deprived areas, with a lower proportion of council tax payers. The number of people employed by local authorities declined by more than half a million under the coalition's 'austerity' programme. This had effectively ended by the time of the coronavirus pandemic of 2020, which placed significant additional burdens on local government. The long-term consequences of the pandemic on local government finance are unclear at the time of writing (June 2020), but the central government's initial response showed a recognition of the new difficulties that councils were facing.

Local taxes

The domestic rates were the main local tax until 1990. Paid by the head of household, the rates were based upon the value of a property (its 'rateable value') and took no account of the number of people resident within it. As a tax on property rather than on individuals, it produced some glaring anomalies. A single old-age pensioner living in a large house would pay the same amount as a family in a neighbouring property, even though they made less use of local services and could include several wage-earners. Businesses also paid rates based on the value of their properties (e.g. shops or factories). The 1980s and 1990s brought significant change in these arrangements.

The Thatcher governments sought to curb local authority spending and revenue-raising. The Rates Act 1984 gave the government the power to 'rate-cap' individual local authorities (i.e. limit the revenue they could raise through local taxes by setting a ceiling on the level of the rates). This power was then universally applied from 1992 to 1999. Most councils now cap themselves by setting their budgets at the limit imposed by the centre. The Local Government Act 1999 ended universal rate-capping, although the centre reserved the power to place a ceiling on council tax levels. The Blair government did not use these powers until 2004 when five local authorities had their council tax levels capped. The coalition government's encouragement of local referendums on tax rises was meant, at least in part, to prevent the need for rate-capping from the centre.

The major reform of the Thatcher period was the Local Government Finance Act 1988. It had three main elements:

- the replacement of the domestic rates with a personal 'community charge';
- the replacement of the business rates with a centrally set 'national non-domestic rate'; and
- the introduction of a Revenue Support Grant allocated on the basis of a central government SSA.

The community charge, commonly known as the 'poll tax', was supposed to make local authorities more accountable for their spending decisions (see Analysis 11.1). The Conservative case for the poll tax argued that under the rates system, the burden of local taxation fell on too few shoulders. Half of the electorate did not pay the domestic rates and a further one in six was entitled to rebates reducing their rates bills. Only 34 per cent of the adult population paid the full

Analysis 11.1

Policy disasters – the poll tax

A policy disaster is a significant and very costly failure of government policy which has major political repercussions and is widely perceived to be disastrous. Such a policy would clearly fail to meet the objectives set for it and would produce a chain of events that make the situation far worse than would be the case if alternative policies had been pursued.

In the last 30 years, policy failures have appeared to occur more frequently and to be more costly than in the past. Examples include the BSE crisis, Britain's unhappy period as a member of the European Exchange Rate Mechanism, the poll tax, and virtually every government initiative connected with information technology (see Anthony King and Ivor Crewe, *The Blunders of Our Governments* (London: Oneworld Publications, 2013). The prevalence of policy failure is sometimes attributed to an overly centralised system of government that does not allow for sufficient consideration of policy within the core executive or Parliament. In the case of the poll tax, ministers who were convinced of its ideological merits ignored warnings from the Treasury that it would prove costly; once the idea had gained momentum, even ministers who thought it was problematic helped to force it onto the statute book. Conservative MPs who were concerned about the possibility of large bills for their constituents and the perceived unfairness of the poll tax proposed changes (e.g. linking it to the ability to pay), but these were defeated in the House of Commons. Nor were local authorities, who warned of difficulties in collecting the poll tax, consulted properly.

The Thatcher government's objectives when introducing the poll tax included greater local accountability and control of local authority spending. But the situation was made worse rather than better. People blamed the government rather than their local council for large poll tax bills, forcing it to both 'charge cap' authorities proposing sizeable poll tax bills and increase VAT to pay for additional funding for local councils. Ministers had lost control of events. The political damage caused by the poll tax debacle added to the pressure that forced Thatcher's resignation in 1990. All three candidates who stood in the second ballot of that year's Conservative leadership election promised to scrap the poll tax. It was eventually replaced by the council tax in 1993.

PHOTO 11.1 Rioting greeted the introduction of the poll tax in England 1990 (© Howard Davies/Corbis/Getty Images).

rates. The Thatcher government believed that the poll tax would increase local accountability as all citizens would have to pay something. If they deemed that high community charges were not producing efficiency and quality in local services, electors could remove overspending councils through the ballot box. This was not what happened in practice. When they received higher than predicted poll tax bills, voters blamed the Thatcher government rather than their local council. The centre retained its powers to set a ceiling for the levels of local tax bills ('capping'), but this undermined its claim that the new tax made councils more accountable for local taxation (Photo 11.1).

Implementation problems also bedevilled the poll tax. It proved difficult for local authorities to collect, notably because of a campaign of civil disobedience under which people refused to pay the tax or dropped off the electoral register in an attempt to avoid detection. Riots in London preceded the introduction of the tax in England and Wales in April 1990 (it had been introduced a year earlier in Scotland, where a revaluation of the rates was due). The government responded to criticism from Conservative MPs, who feared that middle-class voters would desert the party in protest at the tax, by providing transitional relief to local authorities in order to help them keep poll tax bills low. This negated one of the aims of the tax, namely, a reduction in spending. In 1991, the government also increased VAT to fund a reduction in poll tax bills.

One of John Major's main priorities on winning the 1990 Conservative leadership election was to find an alternative to the poll tax. The council tax was duly introduced under the Local Government Finance Act 1992, and came into effect the following year. It is a hybrid local tax that combines a property element and a personal element. The level of the council tax is determined according to the value of a property, with properties allocated to eight different 'bands'. It is paid by the head of household rather than by all adults living in the property, but there is a 25 per cent reduction for single-member households. Councils can also create discounts or exemptions. Although no tax can be considered popular, the introduction of the council tax did not provoke significant protest from political elites or the electorate. The average bill for a band D property in England with two adult residents was £1,671 in 2018–19 compared to £568 in 1993–94.

In 2004, the Blair government set up an independent inquiry, chaired by Sir Michael Lyons, to examine local government funding. It recommended that new valuation bands be introduced for those in the lowest value properties so as to reduce their bills, with those in the highest bands paying more. But no subsequent government has moved ahead with revaluation (see Controversy 11.2). In 2019, the council tax was therefore levied on the basis of property valuations, which were more than a quarter of a century old. The Localism Act 2011 replaced central government's power to cap council tax with a requirement that proposed rises in council tax above a certain level set by central government must be put to a binding local referendum. Local authorities that freeze council tax levels have been rewarded with (limited) additional grant money from the centre.

Business rates used to be set by local authorities, but their replacement, the national non-domestic rate (often known as the uniform business rate), is set by central government. Councils collect it, but revenues are paid into a central fund and returned to local authorities by the government according to their populations. This removed an established method of raising revenue from local authorities and transferred it to the centre. But in 2013, the coalition government permitted local authorities to keep a proportion of these funds if revenue from businesses in their area increased.

Other sources of revenue

Local authorities supplement their income from grants and local taxes in a number of ways. Councils are permitted to set discretionary charges for many of the services they provide. Most apply charges for services such as leisure facilities, meals on wheels, and car parking, but levels vary. An authority that wants to cut congestion may, for example, impose prohibitive fees for car parking in a city centre and operate a park-and-ride scheme. The Lyons Report recommended that councils should be able to impose extra charges for domestic waste collection, but such ideas remained highly controversial.

Councils also collect rent from tenants living in local authority-owned housing, but the sale of council houses in the 1980s reduced the scope for revenue-raising. Faced by cash shortages and restrictions on borrowing, many councils sold off assets in the 1980s and 1990s. This produced unintended consequences: the sale of playing fields reduced people's opportunities to participate in sport at a time when the government was emphasising the importance of regular exercise to combat child obesity.

The EU was an important source of funding after the late 1980s when the sums available through its structural funds were increased. Poorer regions of the UK (e.g. Merseyside) were eligible for large sums from the European Regional Development Fund; others won grants from the European Social Fund. Roadside signs indicating that a new road has been paid for by EU funding became a familiar sight in parts of the UK, but evidently not sufficiently noticeable to cajole a majority of voters into supporting 'Remain' in the 2016 referendum.

The most controversial form of revenue-raising to emerge in recent years is the PFI. This has been open to local authorities since New Labour came to power, and has been used to fund infrastructure projects such as the building of new schools and transport systems (see Chapter 10). In PFI schemes, the private sector finances large-scale construction projects and provides the associated services for a set period (usually more than 20 years). The local authority pays for the services over this period and also pays a premium to cover the financial risks taken by the company. Supporters of the scheme claim that it has brought much-needed investment, but its critics argue that PFI projects are more expensive and merely put off unpalatable costs until a later date. Under the coalition, the Treasury seemed more responsive to criticism and moved to tighten its grip on the system, but contracts continued to be signed.

Controversy 11.2

Council tax revaluation

When the council tax was introduced in 1993, residential properties were placed into one of eight bands (with 'band A' the lowest, and 'band H' the highest) based on their value in 1991. Since then, property prices have increased dramatically, but successive governments have resisted calls for a council tax revaluation in England.

The increase in property prices does not mean that houses will automatically be placed in a higher council tax band. It is the relative value rather than absolute value that is significant: if the value of all properties had increased by the same rate since 1991, all houses would stay in the same bands. This, of course, has not happened as property hot spots have seen above-average increases, particularly in the southeast of England. A council tax revaluation took place in Wales in 2004. Some 58 per cent of houses stayed in the same band, and 8 per cent moved down. But a third of houses have moved up one or more bands. In property hot spots such as Cardiff (62 per cent) and Wrexham (52 per cent), the proportion was higher. A ninth band was created for the costliest properties.

Ministers were (rightly) concerned about the political costs of big increases in council tax bills for large numbers of householders in England. A year before the council tax revaluation in England was due to begin in 2006, the government announced that this would be postponed and the revaluation issue added to the remit of the review of local government finance being conducted by Sir Michael Lyons. Lyons recommended that new valuation bands should be introduced for the lowest-value properties and that those living in higher-band properties should pay more. But the Labour government did not act on this recommendation, and in 2010, the coalition government decided to subject the revaluation of property to a further period of delay which, at the time of writing (June 2020), had yet to come to an end.

Local government in a multilevel polity

The relationship between central and local government is inevitably unbalanced and has often been strained in recent years (see Analysis 11.2). Central government controls the main part of local authorities' revenue, keeps tight control over local authority spending and taxation, and has put in place an extensive inspection system for local authority performance. Legislation from the centre has also dramatically altered the structure and functions of local government. The discretion of local authorities to determine their own spending priorities and introduce policy initiatives has decreased, but they are still able to make political decisions that affect the daily lives of citizens.

In the early post-war period, the centre adopted a hands-off approach to local government, allowing councils considerable leeway in how they spend general grant funding. Intervention by the centre in the terrain of local government was infrequent and was preceded by consultation. The economic turmoil of the 1970s induced a rethink, and in 1975, the Environment Secretary, Anthony Crosland, famously warned high-spending councils that 'the party's over'. Relations worsened in the 1980s when Conservative governments sought, first, to control public

Analysis 11.2

Centre–local relations

Academics have developed a number of models to explain the relationship between central and local governments. Among the most influential have been:

1. *The partnership model:* This envisaged central and local governments as partners. Central government afforded local authorities significant financial and political discretion, consulting with them on matters of mutual interest. Centralisation in the 1980s made this perspective seem outdated.

2. *The agency model:* This views local authorities as mere agents of central government, implementing policies determined at a national level with little scope for discretion. This model encapsulates the centralising trends of the last two decades but downplays the (admittedly limited) room for manoeuvre that local authorities still have in spending and implementing policy.

3. *The power-dependence model:* This recognises that both central and local governments have resources and engage in a process of bargaining. Central government controls legislation and much local finance, but local councils have influence as elected bodies and key players in local policy networks. This model has been developed by Rod Rhodes, notably in his book *Beyond Westminster and Whitehall* (London: Allen & Unwin, 1988).

expenditure by reining in local authority spending and, second, to redefine the role of local authorities by transferring some of their functions to the centre, to specialist agencies, or to the private sector. Labour-controlled authorities resisted government efforts to control local spending and limit their policy discretion, but the centre responded through legislation and ministerial diktats that abolished the metropolitan counties, restructured and capped local taxation, and required councils to open up contracts for service provision to the private sector.

New Labour's election victory in 1997 brought a limited rapprochement in centre–local relations. Local authorities welcomed the positive tone on localism and a greater willingness to engage in dialogue. The emphasis on a leadership role for councils in their communities and promises of greater autonomy for the best performing councils suggested a brighter future for local government. But the Blair and Brown governments retained control over local authority finances, established a comprehensive inspection regime, intervened when councils failed to meet targets set by the centre, and left the local quango state largely untouched. Subsequent Conservative-led governments have, to some extent, departed from the trend towards centralisation by giving local authorities greater control of their funding and devolving some powers to combined authorities. But these developments have to be understood in the context of 'austerity' and major spending cuts which have further eroded the spending power of local authorities.

Local authorities reacted to increased intervention from the centre by strengthening their lobbying efforts at the national level. The Local Government Association, created in 1997 from an amalgamation of existing bodies, has provided a more professional national voice for the interests of local authorities in their collective dealings with the centre. It also offers valuable advice to councils on implementing new legislation and adopting best practice. Local authorities also developed more effective lobbying strategies at EU level, before the 2016 referendum. Grants from the EU were paid directly to local authorities, enabling recipients to pursue economic re-generation projects that might otherwise be beyond their means. But central government tried to maintain its control over local authority spending by setting conditions for the provision of 'matching funding' from the centre.

Many of the directives implemented by local authorities on issues such as water quality, public procurement, or health and safety in the workplace originated from the EU. Local authorities thus began to lobby the European Commission in order to secure funding and influence leg-islative proposals. When local authorities were concerned about policy emanating from central government (as in the 1980s and 1990s), they looked to the Commission to introduce alternative legislation. But they were far more likely to achieve results when they have the active support of the UK government. Although local authorities competed with each other for funding, engage-ment in EU policy-making encouraged pan-European cooperation on issues of mutual concern. Lobbying by organisations representing subnational governments was, for example, a factor in the creation in 1993 of the EU Committee of the Regions, on which UK local authorities were represented. The results of this constructive relationship between UK local government and the EU included considerable tensions among Conservative councillors, some of whom resigned in protest at their party's hard-line position after the 2016 referendum, while others threatened to defect to UKIP because they thought that Theresa May, in particular, was far too conciliatory!

The local quango state

Elected local authorities are just one element in a complex network of bodies involved in ser-vice provision at local level. Local government, in which decisions are taken by elected local authorities, has been replaced by local *governance* in which a plethora of unelected or indirectly elected agencies also make decisions on the allocation of resources at local level. Whereas local government was characterised by decision-making by a hierarchical authority, local governance involves greater flexibility, fluid boundaries, and interdependent relationships between councils, agencies, and private companies.

Unelected specialist agencies, known as quangos, are a major feature of local governance (see Chapter 10). The House of Commons Public Administration Select Committee's 2001 report *Mapping the Quango State* identified more than 5,000 bodies providing public services operating at local level. This 'local quango state' includes foundation schools, registered social landlords, NHS trusts, and primary care groups. The number of staff employed by these bodies (some 60,000 people) was almost three times higher than the total number of elected councillors.

Many quangos perform important functions in an efficient and non-partisan manner, but the extent of the local quango state has raised concerns about the health of local democracy. The Committee on Standards in Public Life has produced guidelines on appointments, but there is limited scrutiny of ministerial decisions on who should serve on quangos. The lack of lo-cal accountability, transparency, and scrutiny of decisions taken by quangos has aggravated the democratic deficit in local government. Not all quangos issue annual reports, few hold public meetings, and their chief executives are not required to explain their decisions to elected local representatives.

The Blair governments required local authorities to develop partnerships with voluntary bodies and private companies in order to deliver economic, social, and environmental rede-velopment. This was known as the 'new localism'. Key priorities were set out in local area agreements which were drawn up by a range of actors including local authorities, regional government offices, health authorities, police, business and voluntary groups. Partnership is seen as a means of overcoming the problems of fragmentation in policy areas where multiple agencies have overlapping responsibilities. There is considerable variation in the character of these networks and partnerships across local authorities and policy fields. The introduction of elected police and crime commissioners in 2012 might have been welcome from a democratic perspective, but it greatly increased the complexity of local politics and the difficulty of holding the crucial decision-makers to account. In relation to Tony Blair's famous soundbite, councillors continued to be responsible for addressing some of the perceived 'causes of crime', such as inadequate leisure facilities for young local residents, but were no longer accountable for the way in which criminal activity was handled, even though they still funded the local police forces.

Devolution and local government

The creation of devolved institutions in Scotland and Wales in 1999 had important implications for local government in those nations. Local government is among those policy competences devolved from Westminster to the Scottish Parliament and Welsh Senedd. They provide grant funding to local authorities and set targets for service delivery. The devolved bodies can also restructure local government and redefine their responsibilities. The Scottish Parliament, for example, introduced the single transferable vote for local elections in Scotland in 2007 (see Chapter 17). The devolved bodies also have responsibility for policies that are mainstays of local government activity (e.g. education and economic development) and oversee the work of a series of quangos.

In England, devolution to the regions has been controversial and problematic. The Major government created Government Offices for the Regions to handle the implementation at regional level of policy developed by various Whitehall departments. The Blair government further bolstered regional government by setting up unelected Regional Development Agencies (RDAs) in the English regions in 1999 (see Chapter 12). These were charged with promoting economic development but were abolished by the Conservative–Liberal Democrat coalition in 2010. Labour also planned to introduced elected regional assemblies which would have had limited powers over economic development, planning, and housing. The initiative was opposed by local authorities, who feared a further reduction in their powers. The 2004 'no' vote in a referendum on introducing a directly elected assembly for the northeast of England spelled the end of Labour's plans. As we have seen, Conservative-led governments since 2010 have promoted the development of 'city regions', creating combined authorities and devolving some powers over transport, economic development, and health to them. But the logic of this trend suggests greater revenue-raising powers for local authorities in England and Wales, and central government is reluctant to take a step which would imply a drastic change in the balance of authority between Westminster and subnational authorities.

Local democracy

The move from local government to local governance has important implications for notions of local democracy. The predominant view in the twentieth century saw elected local councils as the main expression of local democracy and as bulwarks of a pluralist system. Local councillors were afforded 'principal actor' status since they were elected by and accountable to citizens. There was widespread agreement among political elites that local councils were best placed to provide education, housing, and other local services and should be accorded the necessary autonomy in respect of expenditure and policymaking.

Although attractive to pluralists, this vision of local democracy had its limitations. Participation in local politics was limited, with turnout in local elections lower than for general elections, averaging only 40 per cent at the end of the twentieth century. The party politicisation of local politics since the 1970s, along with the new dominance of national media outlets, lessened the focus on purely local matters. Local service provision was also questioned as both public expenditure and local taxes increased without matching improvements in service efficiency or quality. Scandals in Westminster City Council in the 1980s and Doncaster Council at the start of this century damaged the reputation of local politicians. The Committee on Standards in Public Life found little evidence of corruption in local government but recommended an ethical framework for councillors which New Labour enacted in 2000. Since then, local councils have been accused of negligence, or worse, in relation to scandals involving sexual abuse.

Reforms introduced by successive governments since 1979 have necessitated a new perspective on local democracy. Elected councils are no longer directly responsible for the provision of core local services. They are just one part (albeit a crucial one) of a world of local governance inhabited by a plethora of public and private actors. The spread of the quango state has exacerbated the democratic deficit in local government.

New Labour sought to renew local democracy by promoting community engagement in decision-making and citizen participation through local referendums (e.g. on directly elected mayors) and 'citizens' juries' which discussed policy proposals. The Conservative–Liberal Democrat coalition dismantled the regime of performance targets and inspections put in place by New Labour. It sought to promote community engagement, but this time in place of, rather than in partnership with, local authorities. The coalition maintained New Labour's preference for directly elected mayors, but 11 of 12 local authority areas to hold referendums voted against adopting the mayoral model. Another coalition initiative aimed at improving local representative democracy was the creation of directly elected police and crime commissioners. But turnout in the 41 elections held in England and Wales in 2012 averaged just 15 per cent. The coalition also promoted direct democracy in the local context. A referendum must now be held should a local authority want to increase council tax by more than a rate stipulated by the centre. The first such referendum, held in 2015, rejected a proposed 15.8 per cent rise in council tax in Bedfordshire. Local referendums may also be held on neighbourhood plans which, if approved, then inform future development planning decisions. By 2014, a total of 13 neighbourhood plans had been approved in local referendums, for example, in the Leicestershire village of Broughton Astley where the plan was approved by 89 per cent of voters on a turnout of 38 per cent. In 2019, the referendum on the neighbourhood plan concerning Berrick Salome in South Oxfordshire attracted a turnout which almost exactly matched that for the 2001 UK general election – 59.5 per cent.

Despite such effusions of 'localism', it was not unduly cynical to suggest that, when local autonomy suited the central state, citizens would be encouraged (or even forced) to be 'free', but if their exercise of freedom began to cause serious inconvenience to the incumbent government, they would be given salutary reminders of the imbalance of power between local and national politicians.

Conclusion and summary

In some respects, local government is in a healthier position than it was in the mid-1980s. Local authorities now have a general power of competence, have greater discretion in how they spend funding from central government, and new powers over health and transport have been devolved to combined authorities. However, cuts in central government funding have further eroded the spending power of local authorities. Many of the services once provided directly by local authorities have been entrusted to voluntary bodies, community groups, private companies, and others. Initiatives to enhance local democracy have had mixed results, and UK local authorities cover larger territories than is the case in many European states, meaning that decisions are not taken particularly close to the people they affect. The absence of formal constitutional safeguards for local government also leaves local authorities in the UK in a more parlous position than their counterparts in most other Western liberal democracies.

The regime of economic 'austerity' overseen by Conservative-dominated UK governments between 2010 and 2019 conflicted sharply with the idea of localism, since most local authorities had no choice but to curtail important services in the face of severe budget cuts. Nevertheless, some relics of the coalition government's 'localism' – notably the encouragement of cooperation between local authorities in the north of England – promise to outlast the short-term impact of 'austerity', the coronavirus pandemic, and Brexit. The pandemic underlined the importance of local government but also highlighted its overdependence of central funding and the difficulties of coordinating the delivery of essential services through a complex and often overlapping network of substate institutions and private sector actors. Indeed, the response to the pandemic could be seen as an opportunity to review central government policy towards local government since the late 1970s; and it was difficult to avoid a damning verdict.

Further reading

The most comprehensive textbook is D. Wilson and C. Game's *Local Government in the United Kingdom* (London: Palgrave, 4th edition, 2006). J. Morphet's *Modern Local Government* (London: Sage, 2008) and J. Chandler's *Local Government Today* (Manchester: Manchester University Press, 4th edition, 2009) are also good introductions to the topic. R. Leach and J. Percy-Smith's *Local Governance in Britain* (London: Palgrave, 2001) is dated but reflects the shift from local government to governance.

Changes in local government over 40 years are helpfully examined in J. Stewar's 'An Era of Continuing Change: Reflections on Local Government in England 1974–2014', *Local Government Studies*, Vol. 40, No. 6 (2014), pp. 835–50. G. Stoker and D. Wilson's (eds.) *British Local Government into the 21st Century* (London: Palgrave, 2004) analyses developments in local government under New Labour. T. Travers, 'Local Government', in A. Seldon (ed.), *Blair's Britain, 1997–2007* (Cambridge: Cambridge University Press, 2007), pp. 54–78, provides a brief overview of policy under Blair. New Labour's localism is examined in L. Pratchett's 'Local Autonomy, Local Democracy and the "New Localism"', *Political Studies*, Vol. 52, No. 2 (2004), pp. 358–75, while localism under the Conservative-Liberal Democrat government is assessed in V. Lowndes and L. Pratchett's 'Local Governance under the Coalition: Austerity, Localism and the "Big Society"', *Local Government Studies*, Vol. 38, No. 1 (2012), pp. 21–40. Coalition policy is also examined in T. Travers, 'The Coalition and Society (1): Home Affairs and Local Government', in A. Seldon and M. Finn (eds.), *The Coalition Effect, 2010–15* (Cambridge: Cambridge University Press, 2015), pp. 228–56.

On local government and councils generally, see M. Sandford's *Local Government in England: Structures*, House of Commons Library, Briefing Paper No. 07014, 2020 (available at https://commonslibrary.

parliament.uk/research-briefings/sn07104/), M. Sandford's *Parish and Town Councils: Recent Issues*, House of Commons Library, Briefing Paper No. 04827, 2019 (available at https://commonslibrary.parliament.uk/research-briefings/sn04827/), and M. Sandford's *Devolution to Local Government in England*, House of Commons Library, Briefing Paper No. 07029, 2020 (available at https://commonslibrary.parliament.uk/research-briefings/sn07029/).

On directly elected mayors, see C. Copus's *Leading the Localities: Executive Mayors in English Local Governance* (Manchester: Manchester University Press, 2013), J. Fenwick and H. Elcock's 'Elected Mayors: Leading Locally?', *Local Government Studies*, Vol. 40, No. 4 (2014), pp. 581–99, and M. Sandford's *Directly-Elected Mayors*, House of Commons Library, Briefing Paper No. 05000, 2019 (available at https://commonslibrary.parliament.uk/research-briefings/sn05000/). T. Travers's *The Politics of London* (London: Palgrave, 2003) examines the governance of the capital. On the Northern Powerhouse, see N. Lee's 'Powerhouse of Cards? Understanding the "Northern Powerhouse"', *Regional Studies*, Vol. 51, No. 3, 478–89.

D. Butler, A. Adonis, and T. Travers's, *Failure in British Government: The Politics of the Poll Tax* (Oxford: Oxford University Press, 1994) is the definitive study of the poll tax policy disaster; other recent fiascos involving local government are chronicled in A. King and I. Crewe's *The Blunders of Our Governments* (London: Oneworld, 2013). R. Rhodes's *Beyond Westminster and Whitehall* (London: Allen & Unwin, 1988) and his *Control and Power in Central–Local Government Relations* (London: Ashgate, 2nd edition, 1999) offer sophisticated theoretical approaches.

Websites

The Department for Communities and Local Government (www.gov.uk/government/organisations/-department-for-communities-and-local-government) is responsible for local government in England. The gov.uk website also provides links to local authority websites (www.gov.uk/find-your-local-council).

The Local Government Association (www.local.gov.uk/) represents the interests of English and Welsh local authorities. Its website has information on developments in local government, its structure, and its elections. Two think tanks on local government issues are the New Local Government Network (www.nlgn.org.uk/public) and the Local Government Information Unit (www.lgiu.org.uk). The Lyons Inquiry (www.lyonsinquiry.org.uk) was a major review of local government, but not all its recommendations were accepted. The *Guardian* website (www.theguardian.com/society/localgovernment) has a section devoted to news and commentary on local government.

The Elections Centre website (http://www.electionscentre.co.uk/) conducted by Colin Rallings and Michael Thrasher of Nuffield College, Oxford, provides detailed and up-to-date information on local elections, including data on political party representation and control of local authorities.

Chapter 12

Devolution

Learning outcomes

After reading this chapter, you will:

- appreciate the development of the multinational United Kingdom;
- be aware of powers of the devolved institutions in Scotland, Wales, and Northern Ireland;
- understand the impact of devolution on the UK and its component nations; and
- be able to evaluate the character and the prospects of the post-devolution state.

Introduction

The creation of devolved institutions in Scotland, Wales, and Northern Ireland has added a new tier of government to the UK's multilevel polity. The devolution settlement implemented by the Blair government gave new institutional expression to the distinctive character of the four component parts of the multinational UK state. But devolution has been asymmetrical: each nation is governed in a different way. Devolution has also radically changed the traditional constitution, requiring new procedures to manage relations between the nations of the UK and reform of central government. The new arrangements bedded down without major incident, but the process of devolution is clearly far from its final destination. The 2014 referendum on Scottish independence resulted in a decision to stay within the Union but only after promises had been made of greater devolved powers for the Scottish government; the 2016 EU referendum, which exposed the political differences between the constituent parts of the UK, was an additional complication which also raised very serious questions about the status of Northern Ireland. Although the demand for full independence has far less support in Wales than in Scotland, the former country's devolved institutions have been augmented at regular intervals.

The Union

The integration of the four nations of the UK was uneven: they joined the Union at different times, under different circumstances and with very different degrees of enthusiasm. England completed its conquest of Wales in 1536, imposing rule from London. Despite forcible anglicisation, Wales retained its distinctive identity and culture, particularly in terms of language (though Welsh was in decline by the mid-twentieth century) and religion (with nonconformism a major issue in Welsh politics until the 1920s). The 2001 census found that 20.8 per cent of people in Wales could speak Welsh; ten years later this proportion had declined, to 19 per cent.

Scotland was an independent state until the 1707 Act of Union. This was an international treaty negotiated between the two states by which Scotland would be governed by a sovereign Parliament at Westminster while retaining its separate legal, education, and local government systems plus the Presbyterian Church. A strong Scottish civic identity thus endured. Though key decisions were thereafter made in London, Scottish distinctiveness was recognised through special administrative arrangements at the centre.

Ireland joined the Union in 1800 through an Act of Union after centuries of English and Scottish settlement. The Union was a troubled one as Catholic grievances fuelled a popular Irish nationalism in the south, whereas Protestant settlers in Ulster identified with the British Crown. The 'Irish Question' dominated politics at Westminster in the late nineteenth and early twentieth centuries. By the 1880s, over 80 of Ireland's 101 seats in the House of Commons were held by nationalists. Under Gladstone's leadership, the Liberal Party presented Home Rule as the optimal means of accommodating Irish nationalism while preserving the Union. But three Home Rule Bills (1886, 1893, and 1913) failed in the face of resistance from Conservatives and Liberal Unionists. The onset of World War I averted serious unrest in Great Britain, although the 1916 Easter Rising in Dublin was crushed by British troops.

Negotiations between the British government and Irish republicans led to the 1920 Government of Ireland Act which partitioned Ireland. Twenty-six counties in the south – all with substantial Catholic majorities – were granted self-government and under the 1921 Anglo-Irish Treaty formed the Irish Free State, a dominion within the Commonwealth which in turn became the independent Republic of Ireland in 1949. Six counties in the north of Ireland with a Protestant majority exercised their right under the 1920 Act to remain part of the UK as Northern Ireland. Northern Ireland was governed by a devolved Parliament at Stormont until direct rule from London was imposed in 1972 in response to the deteriorating security situation.

The union state

Unitary state

a culturally and politically homogeneous state in which all parts are governed in the same way from a powerful centre.

Fifty years ago, textbooks on British politics described the United Kingdom as a unitary state; that is, one exhibiting high levels of centralisation, standardisation, and homogeneity. Power was concentrated at the centre, and subnational institutions were weak; policy was implemented in the same way throughout the state, and there were few economic, political, or cultural differences within the UK. This was an accurate characterisation to the untrained eye. Parliamentary sovereignty and executive dominance of the House of Commons concentrated power in London, local government was weak, and substate nationalism had made little impact. But even in 1970 the unitary state concept did not adequately convey the peculiarities of the UK state. Politics was different in the Celtic nations – Northern Ireland had a separate Parliament, Scotland its own legal and local

Analysis 12.1

Unitary and union states

A typology developed by Stein Rokkan and Derek Urwin distinguishes between a *unitary state* and a *union state*:

> The unitary state [is] built up around one unambiguous political centre which enjoys economic dominance and pursues a more or less undeviating policy of administrative standardisation. All areas of the state are treated alike, and all institutions are directly under the control of the centre.
>
> The union state [is] not the result of straightforward dynastic conquest. Incorporation of at least parts of its territory has been achieved through personal dynastic union, for example by treaty, marriage or inheritance. Integration is less than perfect. While administrative standardisation prevails over most of the territory, the consequences of personal union entail the survival in some areas of pre-union rights and institutional infrastructures which preserve some degree of regional autonomy and serve as agencies of indigenous elite recruitment.

An alternative typology, based on the extent of regionalism found in many EU states, distinguishes between three types of unitary states:

- *Regionalised unitary states* have directly elected regional assemblies enjoying legislative powers or significant autonomy from the centre.
- *Decentralised unitary states* have only unelected regional bodies created by central government to carry out administrative functions.
- *Centralised unitary states* have no elected regional assemblies. Subnational government is weak.

From this perspective, the UK is now considered a regionalised unitary state, whereas prior to devolution it was best understood as a centralised unitary state (albeit one with unusual features).

Source: S. Rokkan and D. Urwin, 'Introduction: Centres and Peripheries in Western Europe', in S. Rokkan and D. Urwin (eds.), *The Politics of Territorial Identity: Studies in European Regionalism* (London: SAGE, 1982), p. 11.

government systems, and Scotland and Wales were subject to specific administrative arrangements. British identity provided a common bond between the peoples of the UK. Rather than replacing other identities, it enabled the Welsh and Scottish to retain their own distinctive cultures and identities while also sharing an overarching feeling of 'Britishness'. The latter was constructed around symbols of the UK state such as the monarchy, Parliament, and Empire, but these were in decline by the early 1960s. As they faded as unifying factors, the welfare state became more important, with its principle of uniform, universal provision; but by the mid-1970s, even this was coming under strain. Identity was a particularly contentious issue in Northern Ireland where many Catholics identified with the Republic of Ireland rather than the UK.

The rise of substate nationalisms brought fresh academic thinking on the nature of UK territorial politics. Michael Hechter focused on a core–periphery divide in British politics: political and economic elites in the southeast of England exploited resources in the Celtic fringe. Jim Bulpitt characterised the UK as a 'dual polity' in which local elites were afforded relatively free rein on mundane matters so that the political elite in London could concentrate on issues of 'high politics' such as the economy and foreign affairs. Stein Rokkan and Derek Urwin developed a typology that distinguished between unitary and union states (see Analysis 12.1). Whereas unitary states were highly integrated, union states were multinational states in which political and cultural differences persisted. The UK was best understood as a **union state**: its component nations came together in different ways and retained some distinctive features.

Union state

state in which cultural differences survive the union of different areas, and parts of the state are governed differently, but which has a strong political center.

Two types of devolution have been found in the UK: legislative and administrative. Legislative devolution involves the creation of separate Parliaments with legislative authority and has been the norm since 1999. Legislative devolution also existed in Northern Ireland in the Stormont period (1921–72). Prior to 1999, administrative devolution was the norm for the UK union state. Scottish and Welsh interests were addressed through distinctive procedures at Whitehall and Westminster, but Scotland and Wales were denied their own Parliaments.

The Scottish Office was established as a government department in 1885, the Welsh Office in 1964, and the Northern Ireland Office in 1972. The relevant Secretaries of State normally enjoyed Cabinet status; only the post of Secretary of State for Scotland was consistently awarded to an MP sitting for a constituency in the nation in question. The territorial ministries were responsible for a range of government activities (e.g. agriculture, education, health, local government) in their respective nations but had only limited influence within Whitehall. They represented their nation's interests in central government and implemented government policies in their respective territories. However, opinions differed about the performance of these institutions. By the 1980s, for example, critics depicted the Scottish Office as an agent of a hostile Conservative government rather than an effective lobbyist for Scotland.

Devolution

the transfer of decision-making authority by central government to subnational government.

In the House of Commons, the Scottish Grand Committee and Welsh Grand Committee discussed matters relating to these nations. They contained all MPs representing Scottish and Welsh constituencies, respectively. Special standing committees considered legislation applying to Scotland and Wales. Departmental select committees on Scottish affairs and Welsh affairs were created in 1979 to monitor the work of the territorial ministries. A Northern Ireland Select Committee was established in 1995. Scotland and Wales were over-represented in the Commons, having more MPs per head of population than England. Under the Barnett formula (see later) Scotland, Wales, and Northern Ireland also enjoyed higher levels of public spending per head of population than England, in part because of the greater incidence of social deprivation.

England is easily the largest of the UK's four nations, with an estimated population of 56 million (84.3 per cent of the total UK population). Scotland has a population of 5.44 million, Wales just over 3 million, and Northern Ireland 1.9 million (see Chapter 4). Significant regional disparities exist within the UK. Cities such as Manchester, Birmingham, and Leeds are thriving regional centres, but wealth and influence are concentrated in the southeast of England. Most central government, financial, and media institutions are located in London. Economic and social conditions are better in the prosperous middle-class areas surrounding London than in poorer areas in the north of England, Wales, Scotland, and Northern

Ireland – though some inner-city London boroughs are among the poorest in the UK. After prospering in the nineteenth century, areas such as Glasgow, Lancashire, the Black Country, South Wales, and Belfast suffered economic and social deprivation as manufacturing industry declined dramatically in the second half of the twentieth century. Poverty, unemployment, and poor health are more pronounced in these areas, necessitating higher levels of welfare spending by central government.

Towards devolution

Studies of the road to devolution taken by Scotland and Wales focus on three main factors:

1. the development of substate nationalism in Scotland and Wales;
2. the changing attitudes of elite actors, particularly political parties; and
3. the changing economic and political environment.

Substate nationalism

Popular support for nationalist parties increased in Scotland and Wales in the 1960s and 1970s when the UK state and economy were under unprecedented strain. But Labour and the Conservatives were divided on the issue, and proposals for devolution failed. Popular support for devolution underwent a revival in the 1980s and 1990s, with a changing context (e.g. further European integration) again a factor. This time, devolution also secured strong elite support, particularly in the Labour Party (see Timeline 12.1).

Plaid Cymru and the SNP promoted their respective national cultures and sought greater political autonomy. Political and economic change brought opportunities for the nationalists. They were beneficiaries of voter dissatisfaction with the performance of the main parties and the limited modernisation of the British state. Retreat from Empire and entry into the EEC posed questions about British identity at a time when Scottish and Welsh popular cultures were blossoming. The UK's relative economic decline also fuelled substate nationalism; the SNP argued that the discovery of North Sea oil confirmed the economic viability of an independent Scotland. There were tensions within the nationalist parties, however. The SNP experienced internal disputes over the optimal strategy for achieving independence and its place on the Left–Right political spectrum. Cultural issues were problematic for Plaid Cymru as some members emphasised Welsh language issues, while others urged a broader appeal.

The rise of substate nationalism posed difficult questions for Labour and the Conservatives. Conservative leader Edward Heath signalled in 1968 that his party would create a Scottish Assembly, despite opposition from Scottish Tories. The pledge was not implemented by the Heath government (1970–74), which introduced local government reform instead. Mrs Thatcher steered the Conservatives towards implacable opposition to legislative devolution after her 1975 leadership victory.

Labour had focused historically on class politics; it was committed to a redistribution of resources to produce common minimum standards of welfare provision. In the 1970s, Labour's electoral dominance in Scotland and Wales came under threat from the nationalists. Two broad camps developed in the Labour Party. Opponents of devolution, such as future leader Neil Kinnock, feared that it would undermine the equitable provision of public services and break up the Union. Supporters believed it would bolster support for Labour in its heartlands and reduce the nationalists' appeal.

Harold Wilson took some of the heat out of the issue in 1969 by setting up a Royal Commission on the Constitution. Its 1973 Kilbrandon Report favoured an elected Scottish Assembly. The

TIMELINE 12.1

Scottish and Welsh devolution

1885	Creation of Scottish Office
1925	Plaid Cymru founded
1934	Scottish National Party (SNP) formed following merger of National Party of Scotland (formed 1928) and the Scottish Party (1932)
1944	SNP wins its first Westminster seat at Motherwell by-election
1964	Creation of Welsh Office
1966	Plaid Cymru wins its first Westminster seat in Carmarthen by-election.
1974	October general election: SNP wins 30.4 per cent of vote in Scotland and 11 seats; Plaid Cymru wins 10.8 per cent of the vote in Wales and three seats
1978	Westminster Parliament passes legislation on Scottish and Welsh devolution.
1979	Scottish devolution referendum produces 51.6 per cent 'yes' vote but fails to meet requisite threshold of support of 40 per cent of the Scottish electorate. Only 20 per cent support devolution in Welsh referendum
1989	Conservative government introduces poll tax in Scotland, a year before England and Wales
1995	Scottish Constitutional Convention issues blueprint for a Scottish Parliament with legislative and tax-varying powers
1997	New Labour wins general election and issues devolution White Papers. Devolution approved in referendums in Scotland (74 per cent 'yes' on Scottish Parliament, 64 per cent 'yes' on tax-varying powers) and Wales (50.3 per cent 'yes')
1999	Devolved bodies begin operating after first elections. Labour–Liberal Democrat coalition takes power in Scotland; minority Labour administration in Wales
2000	Alun Michael resigns as Welsh First Secretary and is succeeded by Rhodri Morgan, who subsequently forms a Labour–Liberal Democrat coalition. Death of Scottish First Minister Donald Dewar; Henry McLeish replaces him
2001	McLeish resigns as First Minister and is succeeded by Jack McConnell
2003	Second elections to the Scottish Parliament and Welsh Assembly. Labour–Liberal Democrat coalition formed in Scotland; Labour governs alone in Wales
2006	Government of Wales Act extends the powers of the Welsh Assembly
2007	SNP forms minority government in Scotland, with Alex Salmond as First Minister. Labour–Plaid Cymru coalition takes power in Wales. Calman Commission established to review progress of Scottish devolution
2008	All Wales Convention established to advise the Assembly on a referendum on further devolution

2011	Welsh referendum agrees to increase powers of Welsh Assembly. Elections to Scottish Parliament and Welsh Assembly. SNP forms majority government in Scotland. Labour forms minority administration in Wales
2012	Scotland Act devolves further policies and paves the way for a Scottish rate of income tax David Cameron and Alex Salmond sign Edinburgh Agreement on a Scottish independence referendum
2014	Scottish independence referendum: 55.3 per cent vote against independence. Leaders of main UK parties promise further devolution Alex Salmond resigns as Scottish First Minister and SNP leader; succeeded by Nicola Sturgeon Wales Act devolves further powers to the Welsh Assembly
2015	SNP wins 56 of 59 seats in Scotland in UK general election. Scotland Bill published.
2016	62 per cent of Scottish voters support 'Remain' in EU referendum, leading to renewed calls for a second vote on independence
2020	National Assembly for Wales renamed 'Synedd Cymru'

Callaghan government (1976–79), which was reliant on support from the Liberals in the House of Commons, introduced bills establishing assemblies in Scotland and Wales. But legislation would not come into force unless devolution was approved in referendums in Scotland and Wales. Furthermore, MPs backed a parliamentary amendment stipulating that the Scottish Assembly must win the support of at least 40 per cent of the total Scottish electorate. The Welsh referendum produced a decisive 'no': only 20 per cent of those who voted backed devolution. In Scotland, 51.6 per cent of those who voted supported devolution, but only 32.8 per cent of the whole electorate had voted 'yes'. The proposal was thus defeated, as the 40 per cent threshold was not reached. The Callaghan government soon fell and was replaced by a Conservative administration opposed to devolution.

Elite conversion

Support for devolution regained momentum in the late 1980s, particularly in Scotland. The Conservatives won four general elections between 1979 and 1992, but saw their already low level of support in Scotland and Wales decline still further. Power was concentrated in Whitehall, as the Thatcher governments appeared unsympathetic to Scottish distinctiveness, notably when imposing the poll tax in Scotland a year before England. The free market, individualist ethos of Thatcherism ran counter to a Scottish political culture supportive of state intervention and community politics. The decline of manufacturing industry and restructuring of the public sector had a disproportionate impact, as relatively high numbers of Scots were employed in these sectors or claimed welfare benefits. European integration also boosted the case for devolution: the European Community actively involved subnational bodies in decisions on structural fund spending in poorer regions. Regions in other member states gained more autonomy and became adept at lobbying in Brussels. Local actors in the UK (e.g. councils, businesses, and trade unions) argued that greater autonomy was an essential step towards economic regeneration.

The Major governments (1990–97) sought belatedly to bolster declining support for the Union by granting the Scottish Office limited new powers but were unable to turn the devolutionary tide. The Conservatives supported legislative devolution for Northern Ireland but were the only mainstream party to oppose devolution to Scotland and Wales at the 1997 election, warning that it would create constitutional anomalies and hasten Scottish independence. The Tories were seen as pro-English and were heavily defeated, failing to win a single seat in Scotland or Wales. Following the 1997 referendums called by the Blair government, the Conservatives dropped their opposition to devolution and promised to work constructively within the new institutions while challenging the perceived shortcomings of the devolution settlement.

Labour's conversion to devolution was crucial to the prospects for a Scottish Parliament. Influential figures like John Smith (Labour leader, 1992–94) saw devolution as a key facet of constitutional modernisation and also as a way of shoring up the party's support in face of the nationalist challenge. Support for devolution put Labour at the heart of political debate in Scotland, notably in the Scottish Constitutional Convention. This was a nongovernmental body established in 1989 by leading figures from Scottish politics and civil society to develop a blueprint for a Scottish Parliament. The Liberal Democrats also took part, but the Conservatives and the SNP did not. The Convention's proposals ultimately mirrored Labour's preferred option of a Parliament with legislative and tax-raising powers.

Tony Blair maintained Labour's support for devolution but overruled the Scottish Labour Party by insisting on a two-question referendum that asked electors to endorse both the Parliament and its tax-varying powers. Labour's 1997 election manifesto proposed devolution referendums in Scotland and Wales – a Scottish Parliament with legislative and tax-varying powers and a Welsh Assembly with secondary legislative powers – and elected assemblies in some English regions. The Liberal Democrats also supported a Scottish Parliament. Within the SNP, gradualists who viewed devolution as a stepping stone to independence had achieved ascendancy over fundamentalists who viewed it as an unwelcome distraction. Plaid Cymru supported devolution but sought greater autonomy for the proposed Welsh Assembly.

The Blair government detailed its proposals in two White Papers before calling referendums for September 1997. The Scottish referendum produced large 'yes' votes on both the creation of a Scottish Parliament (74.3 per cent) and on tax-varying powers (63.5 per cent). Support for the Parliament in all 32 local authority areas (two areas opposed the tax-varying powers) on a turnout of 60 per cent gave it added legitimacy. The convincing outcome reflected the development of a cross-party consensus on devolution over the previous decade.

The Welsh devolution referendum produced a wafer-thin majority as 50.3 per cent voted 'yes' and 49.7 per cent 'no'. On a turnout of 50.1 per cent, less than a quarter of people in Wales had voted for devolution. The result revealed a divided principality. Eleven local authority areas voted in favour of devolution and eleven against. Those areas voting 'no' were (with the exception of Pembrokeshire) located in the east of Wales and had closer connections with England than areas voting 'yes', which were located in west Wales and contained a higher proportion of Welsh speakers. There was no popular consensus on the merits of devolution, and the Welsh Labour Party was divided. A low-key referendum campaign, which was overshadowed by the death of Diana, Princess of Wales, did little to boost interest.

Devolution in Scotland and Wales

Labour's devolution settlement was asymmetrical: each of the devolved institutions was given different powers and distinctive features. The Scottish Parliament initially had legislative and tax-varying powers, whereas the Welsh Assembly had only secondary legislative powers. They started life in temporary homes in Edinburgh and Cardiff, before moving to new – and in the case of Scotland, vastly over-budget – buildings at Holyrood and Cardiff Bay.

The Scottish Parliament

The Scottish Parliament has 129 members (MSPs) elected by the Additional Member System (AMS). Seventy-three MSPs (57 per cent of the total) are elected in single-member constituencies using the simple plurality system; the remaining 56 MSPs (43 per cent) are 'additional members' chosen from party lists. They are elected in eight multi-member regional constituencies, each of which elects seven members using the list system of proportional representation. These seats are allocated to parties on a corrective basis so that the distribution of seats is a more accurate reflection of the share of the vote won by the parties (see Chapter 17). Initially, elections were held every four years. But the poll scheduled for 2015 was postponed until 2016 to avoid a clash with the UK general election, and in 2020 the Scottish Parliament accepted a proposal to extend the interval to five years.

The Scottish Parliament was given primary legislative powers over a range of policy areas including law and order, health, education, transport, the environment, and economic development (see Table 12.1). Westminster no longer makes law for Scotland on these matters. However, the Scotland Act of 1998 placed a number of limits on the Scottish Parliament's legislative powers. It specified policy areas in which the Scottish Parliament has no legislative authority. These 'reserved powers' remained the sole responsibility of Westminster. They included the UK constitution, economic policy, foreign policy, and relations with the EU. Additional competences have since been transferred to the Scottish Parliament, notably by the Scotland Acts of 2012 and 2016 (see later).

The 1998 Act also states that Westminster remains sovereign in all matters but has chosen to exercise its sovereignty by devolving legislative responsibility to a Scottish Parliament without diminishing its own powers. Westminster retains the right to override the Scottish Parliament in areas where legislative powers have been devolved. It may even legislate to abolish the Scottish Parliament, though it is difficult to envisage any circumstances in which this might be attempted.

The Scottish Executive, renamed the Scottish government by the SNP after it took power in 2007, draws up policy proposals and implements legislation passed by the Parliament. The First Minister, usually the leader of the largest party at Holyrood, heads the Scottish government and appoints the cabinet. There are currently six executive departments (or directorates-general). Ministers exercise statutory powers, issuing secondary legislation and making public appointments, for example. They are accountable to the Scottish Parliament (Photo 12.1).

The Parliament is funded by a block grant from the UK Treasury, totalling around £28 billion in 2019. The Scottish government and Parliament determine how this money will be allocated. The size of the grant is determined by the 'Barnett formula' – an automatic formula agreed in 1978 by which public spending is allocated to Scotland, Wales, and Northern Ireland based on spending levels in England. The Scottish Parliament was initially given tax-varying powers: it could raise or lower the rate of income tax in Scotland by up to 3 per cent (i.e. three pence in the pound). It also decided the basis of local taxation in Scotland.

The Scotland Act 1998 signalled that the number of MPs sitting for Scottish constituencies at Westminster should be reduced to address Scotland's over-representation. The number of constituencies was reduced from 72 to 59 by the time of the 2005 general election. Constituency boundaries for Westminster and Holyrood are no longer coterminous.

TABLE 12.1 Initial powers of the devolved institutions

Institution	Powers
Scottish Parliament	Law and home affairs
	Economic development (including industry, administration of EU structural funds, inward investment and tourism)
	Agriculture, fisheries, and forestry
	Education and training
	Local government
	Health
	Social work
	Housing
	Environment
	Transport
	Culture and sport
	Research and statistics
	Tax-varying power of plus or minus three pence in the pound
National Assembly for Wales	Economic development (including industry, administration of EU structural funds, inward investment and tourism)
	Agriculture, fisheries, and forestry
	Education and training
	Local government
	Health
	Social work
	Housing
	Environment
	Transport
	Culture, the Welsh language, and sport
Northern Ireland Assembly	Economic development (including industry, administration of EU structural funds, inward investment and tourism)
	Agriculture, fisheries, and forestry
	Education and training
	Local government
	Policing
	Justice
	Health and social services
	Housing
	Environment
	Transport
	Planning
	Sport and the arts tourism
Reserved powers (remain the responsibility of Westminster)	Constitution of the UK
	Defence and national security
	Foreign policy, including relations with the EU
	Fiscal, economic, and monetary systems
	Common market for UK goods and services
	Employment legislation
	Social security
	Transport safety and regulation
	Some areas of health (e.g. abortion)
	Media and culture
	Protection of borders

PHOTO 12.1 Debate on the floor of the Scottish Parliament (© Andrew Cowan/Scottish Parliament).

Scottish independence

The SNP government in Scotland set out its vision for an independent Scotland in the 2013 White Paper, *Scotland's Future*. It envisaged Scotland becoming an independent country in a 'personal union' with the UK. Scotland would have a written constitution drawn up by a constitutional convention. It would be a constitutional monarchy with the Queen as head of state. British citizens living in Scotland on Independence Day, British citizens born in Scotland but normally living elsewhere, and people born to a Scottish parent would all automatically qualify for Scottish citizenship.

The SNP claimed that an independent Scotland would retain the pound sterling in a currency union with the remainder of the UK. The Bank of England would remain lender of last resort. The 'personal union' proposed by the SNP thus fell short of full independence, as a customs union would require a ceding of sovereignty. Scotland's currency became one of the most contentious issues of the ensuing referendum campaign. The UK Treasury insisted that England, Wales, and Northern Ireland would not enter a currency union with Scotland as it would not be in their economic interests and that there was no legal reason why the pound would be shared. The size of the Scottish financial sector and the risks of an economic downturn as oil revenue declined also made the UK government unwilling to enter a currency union that would require it to bail out Scotland in times of trouble.

The economic impact of independence also featured prominently in the referendum. 'Yes Scotland' claimed that an independent Scotland would be in a healthier financial position than the remainder of the UK, arguing that Scotland's public finances were stronger and that the country would benefit from oil and gas revenue. However, the UK government countered by arguing that independence would damage Scotland's economy, with Scottish firms moving south to avoid the economic uncertainty. It argued that an independent Scotland would not be able to sustain current levels of public spending, particularly as revenue from North Sea oil and gas declined, so taxes would have to rise.

Much of the SNP's case for independence focused not on constitutional issues but on the policies that an SNP government would pursue when armed with the additional powers independence would bring. On Independence Day, the Scottish government and Parliament would assume full responsibility for all currently reserved competences, ending the UK Parliament's authority to legislate for Scotland and the UK government's right to take executive action in the country. *Scotland's Future* pledged that a future SNP government would abolish the coalition's controversial 'bedroom tax' and Universal Credit, increase the state pension, provide additional free childcare, and increase the minimum wage in line with inflation. The White Paper also stated that Royal Mail would be renationalised, and BBC Scotland would be replaced by a Scottish Broadcasting Service, but would retain close ties with the BBC and show its most popular programmes.

An independent Scotland would take responsibility for foreign and defence policy. An SNP government would remove Trident nuclear weapons from Scotland, but the SNP envisaged an independent Scotland being a member of the North Atlantic Treaty Organisation (NATO). A Scottish Defence Force and intelligence agency would be created. *Scotland's Future* also envisaged an independent Scotland becoming a member of the EU on Independence Day. But the president of the European Commission, Jose Manuel Barroso, warned that an independent Scotland could not automatically join the EU. Instead, it would have to follow the established procedures for aspiring new members. This route could take many years, and, with existing member states retaining a veto over applicants, it could be blocked by a state that wanted to dampen substate nationalism within its own borders (e.g. Spain).

The SNP suggested that, if there was a 'yes' vote in the referendum, Scotland could be independent by 2016. But complex issues – such as Scotland's share of the UK national debt, social security benefits, and UK assets such as energy reserves – would have had to be settled in negotiations during the transition period. These would remain among the thorny issues to be resolved if a future referendum overturns the verdict of the 2014 poll.

Further devolution or independence?

The election of an SNP minority government in 2007 triggered further change. The SNP launched a 'national conversation' to discuss three main options for Scotland's constitutional future: the status quo, further devolution, and independence. The latter was the SNP's preferred option, but without a majority in the Scottish Parliament, the party was unable to achieve its objective of holding a referendum on opening negotiations on independence with the UK government. The main UK parties opposed independence and jointly agreed to establish the Calman Commission to examine the case for further devolution – but not independence.

The 2009 Calman Report claimed that devolution had been successful but recommended that the Scottish Parliament should be given greater income tax-varying powers, responsibility for some other taxes and duties and for policy on issues such as drink-driving and speed limits. The main parties at Westminster accepted most of these recommendations and the Conservative–Liberal Democrat coalition government enacted them in the Scotland Act 2012. The Act gave the Scottish Parliament, from 2016, the power to set a Scottish rate of income tax, varying from the corresponding UK rates by up to 10 per cent. Responsibility for land fill tax and stamp duty were devolved by the Scotland Act of 2012, which also gave the Scottish government limited borrowing rights. Policy on air guns, misuse of drugs, drink-driving limits, speed limits on roads, and the administration of Scottish Parliament elections were also devolved.

The SNP won a majority of seats in the 2011 Scottish Parliament elections and pledged to hold a referendum on independence. With the constitution a reserved matter (i.e. the responsibility of Westminster), this raised the prospect of a serious dispute between the Scottish and UK governments. But in October 2012, David Cameron and Alex Salmond signed the Edinburgh Agreement which gave legal status to an independence referendum and established key principles for its conduct. The UK government granted temporary powers to the Scottish Parliament, under Section 30 of the Scotland Act 1998, to hold a referendum in 2014. The referendum would have a single question. The SNP had initially proposed that voters could choose between the status quo, further devolution, and independence; but the UK government rejected this. The Scottish government subsequently accepted the Electoral Commission's recommendation of a single referendum question: 'Should Scotland be an independent country?' The SNP did, however, win its argument that the voting age should be lowered from 18 to 16 for the referendum. The franchise included UK citizens living in Scotland, but not the 800,000 Scots living in other parts of the UK.

The referendum campaign was protracted, with the rival 'Yes Scotland' and 'Better Together' campaign groups launched in 2012. The SNP were the dominant force within Yes Scotland, while the Scottish Labour, Conservative, and Liberal Democrat parties cooperated in Better Together. The Scottish government detailed its case for independence in the 2013 *Scotland's Future* White Paper (see Controversy 12.1). Scotland would become an independent state within two years of a 'yes' vote in the referendum but would keep the pound, and the Queen would remain head of state. The UK government responded with a series of assessments of the benefits of the Union and the costs of independence.

For much of the campaign, opinion polls showed that voters were likely to reject independence by a wide margin. But the preferred constitutional option of a plurality of voters was further devolution – an option that would not be available in the single question independence referendum. Better Together thus had to argue that a vote against independence was not a vote for the status quo but one for further devolution. However, Better Together (and the UK government) were criticised for the negative tone of their campaign, which focused more on the costs of independence than on the benefits of remaining within the Union. The main parties also differed in their views on further devolution, with the Conservatives (notwithstanding their Unionist credentials) offering the most far-reaching changes. Late in the campaign, spooked by opinion polls suggesting that the 'yes' camp might win, former Prime Minister Gordon Brown signalled that additional powers would be devolved soon after a 'no' vote. The leaders of the three main parties at Westminster then issued a 'vow' pledging speedily to bring forward proposals for further devolution.

The referendum of 18 September 2014 on whether Scotland should be an independent country delivered a 55.3 per cent 'no' vote. More than 1.6 million voters (44.7 per cent) had, however, supported independence (see Case study 12.1). Turnout was 84.5 per cent, a very high figure that confirmed the success of the referendum in terms of democratic participation. Salmond resigned immediately and was succeeded as First Minister and SNP leader by Nicola Sturgeon. But the referendum did not settle Scotland's constitutional future even for the short term. The morning after the referendum, David Cameron announced that while he would devolve additional powers to Scotland, this would be done in tandem with the introduction of 'English votes for English laws' at Westminster (see later). The Smith Commission was established to consider the next steps on Scottish devolution, recommending that the Scottish Parliament should:

- be given complete power to set income tax rates and bands;
- receive a proportion (the first 10 per cent) of VAT revenue raised in Scotland;
- have control over Airport Passenger Duty;
- have greater borrowing powers;
- have control over some benefits, including the Disability Living Allowance, the Personal Independence Payment, the housing element of Universal Credit, and the 'bedroom tax';
- be granted discretionary powers in any areas of welfare;
- have the power to extend the franchise for Scottish Parliament elections to 16- and 17-year-olds;
- have the power to allow public sector operators to bid for rail franchises; and
- control the licensing of onshore oil and gas extraction in Scotland.

The Smith Commission recommended that the block grant should continue to be determined by the Barnett formula.

The main Westminster parties accepted the Smith Commission's recommendations. But the SNP argued that the proposals did not go far enough and warned that, in certain circumstances (e.g. a UK referendum vote to leave the EU), it would seek a second independence referendum. The proposals also fell short of 'devo max', a far-reaching form of devolution which would have seen the Scottish Parliament take responsibility for all taxes, duties, and spending (i.e. 'full fiscal autonomy'), and all laws, except for defence, foreign policy, monetary policy, and the UK currency, which would remain with the UK government. Nonetheless, the Smith Commission's proposals and the resulting 2016 Scotland Act marked a very significant extension of devolution, creating tax and welfare systems in Scotland that differed from those in the rest of the UK.

The new provisions relating to income tax aroused considerable interest, especially since the SNP argued that its approach to such questions was more 'progressive' than that of the Westminster government. The subject was highly complicated, since the Smith Commission had argued that the Barnett formula should continue to apply, suitably adjusted to allow for the proportion of tax revenue which the Scottish government would keep for its own use. Under the resulting Fiscal Framework, the SNP government hoped that around 50 per cent of its revenue would be raised in Scotland. It used its new powers to implement five different income tax bands, in contrast to the UK which, in 2020–21, had just three (20 per cent for taxable income up to £50,000, 40 per cent on income up to £150,000, and an 'additional rate' of 45 per cent above that level). The main differences in Scotland were that there were three 'lower rates' (19, 20, and 21 per cent, depending on income); the next level was 41 per cent, and began at a lower taxable income (£43, 431); and incomes above £150,000 were taxed at 46 per cent. The Scottish government was also given the right to set its own tax on air travel, but its plan to phase out the tax entirely in order to boost the Scottish economy was abandoned in the face of environmental concerns. Some campaigners argued that the Scottish government should be allowed to set its own rate of corporation tax in order to make its economy more competitive, but this power has yet to be devolved.

Although it could only be regarded by nationalists as a limited step on the road to independence, the 2016 Scotland Act had a significant effect on the relationship between the Scottish and Westminster governments. Instances of 'policy divergence' on devolved issues became more striking. Thus, for example, in 2018, the SNP government introduced minimum pricing for alcohol, a step which was followed by its Welsh counterpart (and the Republic of Ireland), attracting considerable support in England. More generally, after the referendum and the 2016 Act, there was a noticeable change in the approach of the Scottish government, which became more insistent on its right to exercise influence over UK-wide policies.This tendency became even more marked in Scotland's response to the 2020 COVID-19 pandemic.

Case study 12.1

Who voted for Scottish independence?

The 2014 referendum on Scottish independence saw 44.7 per cent of voters, more than 1.6 million people, vote 'yes' to the question 'Should Scotland be an independent country?'. Four of the 32 Scottish local authority areas saw a majority vote 'yes': Dundee, West Dunbartonshire, Glasgow, and North Lanarkshire.

Opinion polls conducted on or shortly after polling day revealed some demographic differences between 'yes' and 'no' voters. Men were more likely than women to vote 'yes', as were those aged under 55. Working-class voters were more likely to support independence than middle-class voters. The most-deprived areas of Scotland and those with the highest levels of unemployment produced the largest 'yes' votes.

The implications of independence for the Scottish economy had been a key theme during the campaign. Unsurprisingly, people who were pessimistic about the economic consequences of Scottish independence were more likely to vote 'no'. National identity was also important to how people voted. According to Ipsos MORI, 88 per cent of those who identified themselves as 'Scottish not British' and 65 per cent of those feeling 'more Scottish than British' voted for independence. But only 9 per cent of people identifying themselves as 'more British than Scottish' and 26 per cent of those feeling 'equally Scottish and British' did so. Almost half of those born in Scotland voted 'yes', whereas only about a quarter of voters who were born elsewhere in the UK opted for independence.

Apart from its obvious appeal to SNP voters, the 'Yes Scotland' campaign also attracted significant levels of support from previous Labour loyalists – and many of these then switched allegiance to the SNP for future elections to Westminster as well as Hollyrood.

See: 'So who voted yes and who voted no?', What Scotland Thinks, http://blog. whatscotlandthinks.org/2014/09/ voted-yes-voted/

The Welsh Assembly

The Senedd Cymru (or Welsh Parliament) has 60 assembly members (AMs) elected by the AMS. Forty members are elected in single-member constituencies using the simple plurality system; the remaining 20 are elected in five multi-member constituencies by the list system of proportional representation. Elections were originally held every four years, but this was extended to five years by the Wales Act 2014.

Initially, the Senedd was known as the National Assembly of Wales and was considerably weaker than the Scottish Parliament: until 2011, it had only executive and secondary legislative powers, not primary law-making authority. That is, it determined how legislation passed by Westminster on a range of Welsh issues should be implemented. If Westminster left significant scope for interpretation, the Assembly could play an important role in determining policy in Wales. But if Westminster legislation was tightly drawn, the prospects for Assembly initiative were very limited. Funding comes from a Treasury block grant (about £14 billion in 2018–19) determined by the Barnett formula. The Assembly decided how to allocate this money and could alter the basis of local taxation; but unlike Scotland, it did not have tax-varying powers.

The 1998 Government of Wales Act specified the policy areas in which the Assembly initially enjoyed executive power. They included education, health, transport, environment, and economic development (see Table 12.1). Limited additional competences, for example on higher education, were granted to the Assembly by the UK government in its early years. In 2004, the Richard Commission, an independent inquiry established by the Assembly, proposed that the Assembly should gain primary legislative powers in certain policy areas. It also recommended an increase in the size of the Assembly (to 80) and a move to the single transferable vote (STV) system of proportional representation. Neither the Assembly government nor the UK government accepted these recommendations. Instead the Government of Wales Act 2006 enabled the Assembly to seek further legislative competences from the UK Parliament to allow it to make Assembly Measures. The Assembly government could seek these additional competences through Orders in Council laid before Parliament but required agreement with Whitehall and Westminster. If the new competence was approved, it would have enduring effect. In the first year of this system, eleven formal requests were made, six of them by individual AMs. Further devolution thus occurred on an incremental basis. The Government of Wales Act 2006 also included provisions that promised to give the Assembly primary legislative competence, equivalent to the powers of the Scottish Parliament. For this to happen, two-thirds of Assembly members would have to vote for a referendum on new powers, as would both Houses of the Westminster Parliament, and Welsh voters would have to deliver a 'yes' vote in the referendum. The Labour–Plaid Cymru coalition set up the All Wales Convention to gauge public opinion, and after this body had reported favourably, a unanimous vote in the Assembly agreed that the referendum would be held in 2011 (Photo 12.2).

The 2011 Welsh referendum and after

The referendum duly took place on 3 March 2011. It asked whether voters wanted the Assembly 'to be able to make law on all matters in the 20 subject areas it has powers for'. The main parties campaigned for a 'yes' vote, while the 'no' campaign lacked funds and well-known supporters. The final outcome was a victory for the 'yes' campaign, by 63.5 to 36.5 per cent. Of

PHOTO 12.2 The Senedd Cymru (formerly the Welsh National Assembly) (© Matthew Horwood/Getty Images).

the 22 unitary authorities in Wales, all but one (Monmouthshire) recorded a majority in favour. However, the turnout was low at just 35.2 per cent.

The Assembly passed its first truly independent legislative act in July 2012. But the debate over devolution was moving on as Calman's recommendations for Scottish devolution and the Scottish independence referendum had a knock-on effect on devolution in Wales, despite support for Welsh independence being much lower than in Scotland (just 5 per cent according to a 2014 poll). The Conservative–Liberal Democrat coalition established the Silk Commission to consider the case for the transfer of further powers. Across two reports, it proposed that the Welsh Assembly should gain the power to vary income tax, as well as powers over policing, youth justice, and regulatory powers over water and transport. It also proposed an increase in the size of the Assembly to at least 80 members. The coalition government put many of the first Silk report's recommendations (primarily concerning taxation) into effect through the Wales Act 2014. This permitted the Welsh government to hold a referendum on whether an element of income tax, as well as control of landfill tax and stamp duty, should be devolved. The Act also formally changed the Welsh Assembly government's name to the Welsh government and extended the Assembly's term to five years. Elections scheduled for 2015 had already been postponed until 2016 to avoid a clash with the UK general election.

The UK government's 2015 St David's Day Agreement and 'Powers for a Purpose' command paper accepted most of the recommendations of the second Silk report, but not those on the devolution of policing and criminal justice. Wales would move to a system of reserved powers similar to that in Scotland, with UK legislation making it clear that any power not reserved to Westminster was devolved to the Assembly. The UK government also introduced a floor in the level of relative funding it provided to the Welsh government; it allowed the Welsh government to vary the rate of income tax by up to 10 per cent above or below the UK level. Further powers to be devolved included those relating to Assembly elections (e.g. lowering the voting age). The Assembly would also be able to rename itself the 'Welsh Parliament'. The 2017 Wales Act put these proposals into effect; the new name for the Assembly, Senedd, took effect in May 2020.

Overall, the devolution process in Wales has mirrored that in Scotland quite closely, albeit from a starting position which was a couple of important steps behind. Although there is still an obvious asymmetry in the respective arrangements in Scotland and Wales, the days when Wales had only an Assembly in which to debate legislation passed elsewhere are long gone. It is particularly noteworthy that the Welsh institutions have grown in authority and policy competence despite the absence of powerful pressure from a highly popular national party. Plaid Cymru performs respectably in elections but has come nowhere near the breakthrough achieved by the SNP since 2007.

Scottish and Welsh devolution in action

Devolution has confirmed the distinctive nature of party systems in Scotland and Wales. Both have multi-party systems in which four main parties regularly receive more than 10 per cent of the vote. Support for Labour has historically been higher in Scotland and Wales than in many English regions, the Conservative vote is lower, and nationalist parties are firmly established. Differential voting patterns have also developed as many electors support different parties for Westminster than they do when selecting representatives for devolved institutions.

The Labour, Conservative, and Liberal Democrat parties in Scotland and Wales have been granted more autonomy since devolution. They select candidates, determine their own policy priorities, and conduct election campaigns with relatively little interference from London. This

has afforded greater influence to local Labour activists and trade unionists. They tended to oppose 'New Labour' policies such as foundation hospitals, making policy divergence from the
UK party line more likely. Tensions between the UK and subnational parties quickly emerged,
notably in the 1999 Welsh Labour Party leadership election in which Blair's favoured candidate,
Alun Michael, received heavy-handed backing from London.

The voting system AMS has helped to increase the representation of smaller parties in the
devolved assemblies, particularly in the larger Scottish Parliament where the Scottish Greens and
Scottish Socialists have won 'list' seats. No party won an absolute majority of votes or seats in
Scotland or Wales in the 1999 elections. Labour was the largest party in both bodies, with the
nationalist parties forming the main opposition. The Conservatives were third placed in both
contests but relied heavily on list seats; the Liberal Democrats were fourth. In Scotland, Labour
and the Liberal Democrats quickly agreed a joint programme and formed a coalition government. In Wales, Labour initially formed a minority administration but entered a 'partnership'
with the Liberal Democrats in November 2000.

Labour was returned as the largest party in the 2003 elections in Scotland and Wales. In Scotland, Labour and the Liberal Democrats again formed a coalition government. In Wales, Labour
took 30 of the 60 seats in the Assembly, but had a technical majority because the Presiding
Officer and his deputy were Plaid Cymru and independent members, respectively. This situation
changed in 2005 when Labour AM Peter Law left the party to sit as an independent.

Labour lost four seats in Wales in 2007, but it remained the largest party. For a time, it appeared that a 'rainbow coalition' of Plaid Cymru, Conservatives, and Liberal Democrats might
take power, but Liberal Democrat party members vetoed the All Wales Accord agreed by the
party leaders. Labour leader Rhodri Morgan formed a minority administration but soon reached
agreement on a coalition with Plaid Cymru, offering a referendum on primary legislative powers
as part of a 'One Wales' deal. The deal was a remarkable one considering the history of enmity
between the two parties. Labour gained ground in the 2011 elections and, falling just short of an
overall majority, formed a minority administration. Plaid Cymru suffered its worst results since
devolution in the 2011 elections.

In Scotland, however, the SNP made spectacular gains. It won 47 seats, one more than Labour,
in the 2007 elections, allowing Alex Salmond to form a minority administration. The Scottish
Greens refused an invitation to form a coalition but agreed to back the SNP on key votes. The
SNP then achieved an even more remarkable result in 2011, forming a majority government with
69 seats and 45 per cent of the vote. Despite defeat in the independence referendum, the SNP's
upturn continued into the 2015 UK general election when it polled 50 per cent of the vote in
Scotland and won 56 of 59 seats.

The surge in the SNP's fortunes and the demise of Labour hegemony in Scotland arose from
a number of factors. The SNP benefitted from favourable views of its record in office and of its
leaders. In the recent past, not all SNP voters have supported independence, but an electorate
coming round to the idea of an independence referendum bolstered its support in 2011. The party
then persuaded many of those who had voted 'yes' in the referendum to vote SNP in the 2015
general election by presenting itself as the party best placed to defend Scottish interests at Westminster (with most forecasters predicting a hung parliament) and to resist Conservative 'austerity'
measures. Labour, meanwhile, has suffered from its record in office in both Edinburgh and London. Cooperation with the Conservatives in the 2014 'Better Together' campaign and perceptions that it did not offer a sufficiently distinctive or radical alternative to spending cuts also saw
Labour outflanked by the SNP on both constitutional and economic issues. Longer-term factors,
such as the decline of the trade unions and the end of its dominance in local government, have
also contributed to falling support for the Scottish Labour Party (Tables 12.2 and 12.3).

TABLE 12.2 Elections to the Welsh Assembly, 2016

	Constituency contests		Regional lists		
	Share of vote (%)	Seats won	Share of vote (%)	Seats won	Total seats
Con	21.1 (−3.9)	6 (–)	18.8 (−3.7)	5 (−3)	11 (−3)
Lab	34.6 (−7.6)	27 (−1)	31.5 (−5.4)	2 (–)	29 (−1)
Lib Dem	7.7 (−2.9)	1 (–)	6.5 (−1.5)	0 (−4)	1 (−4)
Plaid Cymru	20.5 (+1.2)	6 (+1)	20.8 (+2.9)	6 (–)	12 (+1)
UKIP	12.5 (N/A)	0 (N/A)	13.0 (+8.4)	7 (+7)	7 (+7)

Note: Figures in brackets refer to change since 2011.
Source: The Electoral Commission, www.electoralcommission.org.uk.

TABLE 12.3 Elections to the Scottish Parliament, 2016

	Constituency contests		Regional lists		
	Share of vote (%)	Seats won	Share of vote (%)	Seats won	Total seats
Con	22.0 (+8.1)	7 (+4)	22.9 (+10.6)	24 (+12)	31 (+16)
Lab	22.6 (−9.2)	3 (−12)	19.1 (−7.2)	21 (−1)	24 (−13)
Lib Dem	7.8 (−0.1)	4 (+2)	5.2 (–)	1 (−2)	5 (–)
SNP	46.5 (+1.1)	59 (+6)	41.7 (−2.3)	16 (−10)	63 (−6)
Green	0.6 (N/A)	0 (–)	6.6 (+2.2)	6 (+4)	6 (+4)

Note: Figures in brackets refer to change since 2011.
Source: The Electoral Commission, www.electoralcommission.org.uk.

The 2016 elections in Scotland showed that the SNP had not been damaged by its failure to secure independence. Although it lost six seats compared to 2011, its vote share barely changed, and Nicola Sturgeon remained First Minister at the head of a minority administration. Labour's slump continued; it mustered a paltry three seats in the constituency contests (compared to 35 in 2007) and only remained a significant presence in the Parliament thanks to the candidates returned through regional lists. The big surprise was the surge in support for the Conservatives, who became the second largest party. This achievement was widely attributed to the charismatic Scottish Conservative leader, Ruth Davidson.

There was also a surprise in the 2016 Welsh contest, where UKIP failed to win any constituency contests but 'won' the regional list race, taking 7 of the 20 available seats. A proportion of Welsh voters, like their English counterparts, clearly saw the party as an attractive alternative to its longer-established rivals. In sharp contrast to the Scottish result, Labour retained most of its seats, although its candidate for Rhondda was defeated by the Plaid Cymru leader, Leanne Wood. It was able to form a minority administration, led since 2018 by Mark Drakeford.

A new politics?

In the early years of devolution, there was much talk of a 'new politics', different in style from Westminster's adversarial ethos. Post-devolution politics in Scotland and Wales has been more consensual, inclusive, and transparent. There is a different atmosphere in the devolved assemblies: they have different procedures and most politicians have no experience of Westminster.

Devolution has enhanced democracy and accountability in the UK by bringing decision-making closer to the people. No longer are Scots ruled by a Westminster governing party which lacked local democratic legitimacy. The devolved administrations represent a wider range of opinion and have more women members, thanks to a 'zipping' system that alternates men and women on candidate lists for regional list seats, and Labour's policy of adopting equal numbers of male and female candidates. Women constituted 50 per cent of the Welsh Assembly and almost 40 per cent of the Scottish Parliament in 2003, although the figures fell to 42 per cent and 35 per cent, respectively, at the 2011 elections, and remained the same in 2016.

The Scottish Parliament has encouraged public participation by opening proposed legislation to wider consultation than is the case at Westminster. But turnout fell at the 2003 elections in Scotland (to 49.4 per cent) and Wales (38.2 per cent), and barely exceeded those levels in 2007 and 2011. In Scotland, there was a significant increase (to 55.8 per cent) in 2016, but this fell far short of participation in the 2014 referendum. The Welsh figure (45.3) was much more encouraging.

AMS has produced more proportional election results, but tensions between constituency and list members over the distribution of constituency work have been apparent. The Government of Wales Act 2006 banned 'dual candidacy' in which candidates for constituency seats can also stand for regional lists seats and be elected there if they fail in the former. But the practice was restored by the Wales Act 2014 and is permitted in Scotland (although it is discouraged by Labour). The 2007 Scottish Parliament elections were marred by the high number (146,000) of spoiled ballot papers. Subsequently, an independent inquiry's recommendations that separate ballot papers are used for the constituency and regional list votes were accepted.

Survey evidence suggests that devolution is the preferred constitutional option for a majority of voters in Scotland and Wales. Support for devolution seemed to have solidified in Wales, but according to a 2020 opinion poll up to a quarter of Welsh voters wanted the Parliament to be abolished. Further power for the Scottish Parliament was the preferred option of a majority of Scots in the run-up to the independence referendum. One in three votes supported independence in 2013, but this figure rose to 45 per cent at the 2014 referendum.

Devolved politics has not been immune from the sort of controversy found at Westminster. Scottish First Minister Henry McLeish resigned in 2001 after allegations emerged about payments he received from the lease of a constituency office while an MP at Westminster. Former Scottish Labour leader Wendy Alexander (in 2008) and Scottish Conservative leader David McLetchie (2005) were both forced from office after campaigns by a media that now focuses on devolved politics. The Welsh First Minister Carwen Jones resigned in 2018 following the suicide of his colleague, Carl Sergeant, who had been removed from his cabinet position amid allegations of improper conduct. In March 2020, the former Scottish First Minister Alex Salmond was cleared of criminal charges, including attempted rape.

The Scottish Executive initially adopted a low-key programme but lost its major figure when the popular First Minister Donald Dewar died in October 2000. Henry McLeish won the ensuing Scottish Labour leadership election and became First Minister. His administration began to carve out an agenda different from that of the UK Labour government, notably on tuition fees and free care for the elderly people. Following McLeish's resignation, Jack McConnell was elected unopposed as Labour leader and became Scotland's third First Minister in three years. The SNP minority government that took office in 2007 had to work with other parties to get its legislative proposals through Parliament. Its first budget, for example, required the support of the Conservatives and Greens. Winning a parliamentary majority in 2011 allowed the SNP to press ahead with its plans for an independence referendum.

In Wales, Alun Michael never enjoyed the full confidence of his party during his spell as leader of a minority Labour administration, and a dispute over funding prompted his resignation in 2000. Rhodri Morgan succeeded him and, promising 'clear red water' between policy in Cardiff and London, rejected New Labour positions on health and education. He agreed to a

Labour–Liberal Democrat partnership in 2000, and then led a minority Labour administration from 2003 to 2007 before forming a coalition with Plaid Cymru after the 2007 elections. Morgan retired in 2009.

Policy divergence

Devolution has enabled administrations in Scotland, Wales, and Northern Ireland to adopt policies which differ from those pursued by the UK government in England (see Table 12.4). The Scottish Executive has, for example, introduced free long-term social care for the elderly and abolished tuition fees for university students (later increasing fees for English students attending Scottish universities to stem the rise in applications from bargain-hunting English students). Scottish legislation to introduce a statutory minimum price for alcohol was challenged in the courts, but implemented in 2018. The Welsh Assembly initially had less scope to alter policy but, nonetheless, took initiatives in education by abolishing school league tables and piloting a Welsh Baccalaureate. Policy divergence in taxation and welfare has already occurred in Scotland, and the Welsh government now has powers to follow suit. Important forces nonetheless promote *convergence* in policy frameworks (e.g. the civil service and UK-wide policy communities in health), while the devolved institutions still have limited budgets.

Differential policy can be seen as a healthy consequence of devolution as the devolved bodies react to the particular concerns of their electorates. They have also been 'policy laboratories', testing policies (e.g. Scotland's ban on smoking in public places and the charge for using plastic shopping bags introduced in Wales) which are then implemented elsewhere. But policy

TABLE 12.4 Examples of policy divergence

Country	Example of political divergence
Scotland	Free long-term personal care for the elderly
	Abolition of upfront tuition fees for university students
	Abolition of fox hunting
	Abolition of ban on 'promoting homosexuality' in schools (i.e. repeal of Scottish equivalent of 'Section 28')
	Abolition of feudal system of land tenure
	Prescription charges reduced from 2008 and then abolished in 2011
	Freedom of Information Act with fewer restrictions than UK equivalent
	STV for local government elections
	Ban on smoking in public places takes effect before ban in rest of UK
	Minimum price for units of alcohol
Wales	Abolition of school league tables
	Abolition of 'SATs' tests for 7-, 11-, and 14-year-olds
	Creation of 22 local health boards
	Introduction of Welsh Baccalaureate
	Abolition of prescription charges
	Free bus travel for pensioners
	Free school milk for children under seven
	Establishment of Children's Commissioner
	Charges for using plastic shopping bags introduced before rest of UK
	Minimum process for units of alcohol
Northern Ireland	Abolition of school league tables
	Abolition of prescription charges from 2010
	Free fares for the elderly
	New package for student finance
	Establishment of Children's Commissioner

divergence may cause concern if it produces significant anomalies or widens disparities in welfare provision, undermining the principle of equal rights for UK citizens. The extent of divergence within the NHS is of particular importance: patients in Scotland enjoy free eye and dental check-ups, free care homes for elderly people, and access to cancer drugs which are denied to patients in England. Only in England do patients pay prescription charges. Foundation trusts exist in England, but not in the rest of the UK. Can the NHS be regarded as a truly 'national' body when pensioners in Scotland are entitled to free long-term personal care that is not available to their counterparts in England or when less strict waiting list targets contribute to longer waits for operations in Wales? But devolution is not the only factor: decentralisation (e.g. greater autonomy for hospitals) has revealed differences in standards and raises questions about the equity of 'postcode lotteries' (Photo 12.3).

England

Traditionally, England has been governed as a single entity from Westminster with local (rather than regional) authorities. Nor do most parts of the country have a strong regional identity. Some that do, notably Cornwall, find themselves subsumed into larger administrative units. The Major government established a new regional infrastructure by setting up ten Integrated Regional Offices in 1994. Two main factors accounted for this: first, a desire to rationalise the regional organisation of government departments, the health service, and regional quangos; and second, the EU's emphasis on regional action as seen in its provision of funding for poorer regions.

Regionalisation

the creation, by the centre of administrative agents, of central government at a regional level.

The Blair governments maintained this functional **regionalisation** (i.e. the creation of regional administration by the centre) by setting up Regional Development Agencies (RDAs) in eight English regions in 1999. Another was created for London. RDAs were unelected agencies of central government, charged with promoting economic development. They had limited budgets (totalling £2 billion), were required to draw up regional economic strategies, and were accountable to ministers. Few people mourned when they were abolished soon after the creation of the 2010–15 Conservative–Liberal Democrat coalition.

Regionalism

demands from within the regions for decision-making powers to be transferred to regional government

New Labour was also committed to a democratic **regionalism**; its 1997 manifesto included a pledge to establish elected regional assemblies in areas wherever support was confirmed in a referendum. The 2002 White Paper, *Your Region, Your Choice: Revitalising the English Regions* (Cm 5511), set out plans for regional assemblies, with 25 to 35 members elected every four years by the AMS. They would be relatively weak bodies, having few executive powers and limited budgets. Assemblies would be established only if two conditions were met: (i) the replacement of the two-tier system of local government by unitary authorities throughout the region, and (ii) approval of the proposed assembly in a regional referendum. The first referendum took place in the North East in November 2004. A government consultation exercise suggested that popular support was highest in the North East, where a campaign for an assembly was supported by local businesses, trade unions, and politicians. But the referendum produced a 78 per cent 'no' vote on a turnout of 48 per cent. Reasons for this decisive outcome included:

- the cost to local taxpayers of an assembly;
- opposition to the creation of another tier of government;
- doubts about the usefulness of the assembly given its limited powers;
- concern from local councillors about the creation of unitary authorities; and
- the 'yes' campaign's inability to translate a strong regional identity into support for an assembly.

The 'no' vote signalled the end of the road for Labour's plans for elected regional assemblies. Referendums planned for the North West and Yorkshire and Humberside were abandoned. Regional assemblies did not feature in the 2005 Labour manifesto or in the 2007 *The Governance of Britain* Green Paper. Instead, attention turned again to reform of local government, while Gordon Brown introduced nine new ministerial posts with responsibility for the English regions, including London. No similar appointments were made by David Cameron when he came to office in 2010. The Conservative–Liberal Democrat coalition abolished the RDAs and preferred 'localism' over 'regionalism'. But the coalition moved ahead with plans for 'city regions' that had been mooted by the Brown government. Combined authorities, consisting of adjoining local authorities in urban areas, were established in major cities in northern England and the Midlands and granted additional strategic powers over transport, economic development, and health (see Chapter 11). The 'flagship' of this new initiative, identified in particular with the coalition's Chancellor George Osborne, was the 'Northern Powerhouse' which would depend heavily on improvements to infrastructure.

The 'English question' also encompasses questions about the representation of English interests at Westminster and Whitehall (see later). In recent years, English identity has undergone an intellectual renaissance – seen in a plethora of books on Englishness – and popular revival, evidenced in the greater public display of the St George Cross. Part of this renaissance concerns cultural aspects of Englishness, but English identity also found political expression in response to concerns about England's status within the post-devolution UK. Surveys show that the number of people in England describing themselves as 'English rather than British' has risen. But the predicted English nationalist backlash against inequities in the post-devolution polity was slow to develop. Surveys, often with loaded questions, show dissatisfaction with the 'West Lothian

PHOTO 12.3 Scottish First Minister Sturgeon's keynote speech in Edinburgh, 18 September 2015 (© Robert Perry/EPA/Shutterstock).

PHOTO 12.4 How will a revival of English identity find political expression? (© Alex Livesey/Getty Images).

Question' and the Barnett formula, but these issues were of low political salience. At least to some extent, campaigners for a separate English Parliament were hampered by the widespread assumption that, in effect, Westminster already played that role (Photo 12.4).

Changes to UK government

Intergovernmental relations

relations between the UK government and the devolved administrations

Devolution necessitated new procedures for handling relations between central and subnational government (i.e. **intergovernmental relations**) and changes to the operation of central government. It is important for central and subnational governments to cooperate, share experiences, and iron out difficulties in policy areas where competences are shared. On social inclusion, for example, the UK government is responsible for social security, but devolved bodies make policy on employment and training. Intergovernmental relations proceeded smoothly at first, in part because Labour held power in London, Edinburgh, and Cardiff and the devolved administrations adopted a cautious approach to policy divergence. However, even if the SNP had not made clear its intention to press for independence once it secured an overall majority, there were issues such as nuclear power and local taxation which were expected to create tensions.

Concordats

formal agreements between the UK government departments and the devolved administrations.

A number of formal mechanisms for intergovernmental relations have been put in place. These have developed pragmatically but have become subject to increasing tension in the wake of the 2016 EU referendum (see later). **Concordats** set out the rules governing the relationship between central government departments and the devolved administrations. Discussions between UK government ministers and their counterparts from the devolved administrations on policy in devolved matters are conducted in the Joint Ministerial Committee (JMC), which can also be used to resolve policy disputes. JMC sessions are not meetings of equals; the UK prime minister chairs the meetings, which are attended by senior UK ministers and the heads of the devolved governments. In 2016, Theresa May unveiled plans for annual meetings in rotation between London, Edinburgh, Cardiff, and Belfast, but in the post-Brexit environment consultations, a new EU Negotiations subcommittee was established whose deliberations overshadowed more mundane matters. Ideas are also exchanged in the British–Irish Council, a more equitable but less powerful body created under the Good Friday Agreement of 1998 (see below). The Judicial Committee of the Privy Council was initially the final arbiter in legal disputes between Westminster and the devolved institutions, but this role has been transferred to the Supreme Court, which might have some difficult decisions to make in the near future (see Chapter 9). Three Acts of the Welsh Assembly were referred to the Supreme Court in the first three years after it gained primary legislative powers, to test whether they exceeded the powers of the Assembly.

Devolution has brought about radical change in UK territorial politics, but the new asymmetric settlement is characterised by flexibility and pragmatism. Intergovernmental relations have sometimes been tense. The decision taken in 2009 by Scottish Justice Minister Kenny MacAskill to release Abdelbaset Ali al-Megrahi, the Libyan agent convicted of the Lockerbie bombing, on compassionate grounds provoked considerable disquiet. Public opinion in the USA was strongly negative, and many observers believed that the UK government had exerted a strong influence over the decision. The SNP's arrival in government in Scotland made intergovernmental relations more challenging, particularly when a Conservative–Liberal Democrat coalition committed to public spending cuts took office in London, but pragmatic adaptation has helped find solutions to the most difficult issues.

Whitehall

The UK civil service remains a unified service. Most civil servants who worked in the old territorial ministries were transferred to the devolved institutions, promoting continuity and informal contacts. But they owe their loyalty to the administration for which they work, so poor relations between governments could cause tensions between civil servants in London and Edinburgh.

Once the devolved administrations began operating, the (renamed) Scotland Office and Wales Office were no longer responsible for formulating or implementing policy. They ceased to exist as separate departments in 2003, and are now located within the Ministry of Justice. The posts of Secretary of State for Scotland and Secretary of State for Wales were obviously much less important, to the extent that Blair and Brown thought they could be combined with other portfolios. Des Browne's dual role as both Secretary of State for Defence and Secretary of State for Scotland at a time of conflict in Iraq and Afghanistan attracted controversy. The Conservative–Liberal Democrat coalition returned to the previous system of separate posts. A proposal for a single cabinet position with responsibility for relations with Scotland, Wales, and Northern Ireland has attracted some support but has yet to be implemented. The Secretary of State for Northern Ireland acts as a broker in negotiations in the Province and has responsibility for security. If the Assembly and Executive are suspended, the Northern Ireland Office resumes responsibility for the execution of policy – a situation which is most unlikely to arise in either Scotland or Wales.

A number of government departments (e.g. the Department of Health) now spend much of their time on policy for England. Responsibility for the English regions rested with the Office of the Deputy Prime Minister, where John Prescott had a strong interest under Blair, then with the Department for Communities and Local Government. The Department for Business, Enterprise and Regulatory Reform (now the Department for Business, Energy and Industrial Strategy) assumed lead responsibility for regional economic performance.

Westminster

MPs at Westminster can no longer raise parliamentary questions with the Secretaries of State for Scotland and Wales on solely devolved matters. The remit of the three select committees for Scottish, Welsh, and Northern Ireland Affairs has also been adapted. The Regional Affairs Committee has been revived as a forum for discussions on the English regions. 'Sewel motions' (now formally known as 'legislative consent motions') enable the Scottish Parliament or Northern Ireland Assembly to delegate responsibility for legislating on devolved matters back to Westminster on a case-by-case basis, or for the UK government to legislate on devolved matters with the consent of the devolved institutions. The use of these devices has been interpreted as a diminution of the role of the devolved institutions, but it is often convenient for them to allow Westminster to ensure uniformity on technical matters, for example, giving gay couples in Scotland the same partnership rights as those in England.

West Lothian Question

why should MPs representing Scottish constituencies be permitted to vote on English matters at Westminster when English MPs cannot vote on matters devolved to the Scottish Parliament?

The most controversial issue is the **West Lothian Question** (see Controversy 12.2). It asks why MPs representing Scottish constituencies at Westminster should be permitted to vote on purely English matters (e.g. local government in England) when English MPs have no say over matters devolved to the Scottish and Welsh Parliaments. The question was first raised by Tam Dalyell, MP for West Lothian, in the 1970s, and has yet to be fully answered. Four main solutions have been attempted or proposed:

1. A ban on MPs representing Scottish and Welsh constituencies from voting on legislation on purely English matters, such as health or education in England. Known as 'English votes for English laws', this has been the solution favoured by the Conservative Party since 1999.
2. The creation of elected assemblies with limited executive functions in the English regions. This was the policy of the Blair government, but was shelved after a 'no' vote in a referendum on a North East regional assembly in 2004.
3. The appointment in 2007 of nine regional ministers, charged with representing their regions at Westminster and Whitehall, and representing the government in their respective regions. These posts were abolished by the Conservative–Liberal Democrat coalition in 2010, along with recently created parliamentary select committees for the regions.
4. The creation of an English Parliament to handle English 'domestic' issues. This is supported by some Conservative MPs – and a BBC survey of 2018 found that more than two-fifths of English voters favoured it – but critics fear that it will break up the Union.

Opinion polls suggest that about two-thirds of English voters believe that Scottish MPs should no longer be allowed to vote on laws that only affect England. It has not, however, been a high salience issue – although warnings about the SNP exerting influence over a minority Labour government featured prominently in the Conservatives' general election campaigns in 2015 and 2019.

Controversy 12.2

The West Lothian Question

The West Lothian Question asks why MPs representing Scottish constituencies at Westminster should be able to vote on English 'domestic' matters when English MPs cannot vote on equivalent matters devolved to the Scottish Parliament. It thus questions: (i) House of Commons procedures for dealing with legislation that applies only to England; (ii) the role of Scottish MPs in the House of Commons; and (iii) the relationship between Scottish MPs and their constituencies, given that MSPs are responsible for handling grievances that arise on matters devolved to the Scottish Parliament.

The votes of MPs representing Scottish constituencies have only proved decisive on English matters in a handful of divisions since the creation of the Scottish Parliament. According to the House of Commons Library, in only 25 of some 3,800 divisions held in the House of Commons between 2001 and 2015 would the result have been different if Scottish MPs had been excluded from voting. However, in 2003–4, they were crucial in securing victories for the Blair government on controversial bills establishing foundation hospitals and providing for differential university tuition fees in England. A majority of MPs representing English constituencies opposed both foundation hospitals and tuition fees; if Scottish MPs had been barred from voting, the government would have been defeated.

Date	Division	Vote (for–against the government)	Result if Scottish MPs had been barred from voting
19 November 2003	Health and Social Care (Community Health and Standards) Bill (Division 381)	302–285	258–268
27 January 2004	Higher Education Bill (Division 38)	316–311	270–290
31 March 2004	Higher Education Bill (Division 123)	316–288	269–270

Scottish MPs who voted (both for and against) on foundation hospitals and tuition fees pointed out that the bills contained clauses relating to Scotland. Even if they had not, they also claimed that English-only legislation on health spending would still have an impact upon public spending in Scotland through the Barnett formula and that the introduction of tuition fees would have a knock-on effect on Scottish universities (e.g. increased applications from English students).

In July 2015, David Cameron dropped plans to hold a vote on relaxing the ban on fox hunting in England and Wales when SNP leader Nicola Sturgeon announced that SNP MPs would vote against the government.

The preferred Conservative solution to the West Lothian Question is 'English votes for English laws' (EVEL). In most variants of this approach, the Speaker of the House of Commons would certify some bills (or certain clauses within them) as 'English-only'. But proposals have varied on whether and when Scottish MPs should be prevented from voting on these bills.

The McKay Commission, an independent body set up by the Conservative–Liberal Democrat coalition, recommended in 2013 that parliamentary procedures should be changed to allow the voices of English MPs to be heard on matters concerning England only. But it did not want any MPs to be prevented from voting on any bill and argued that the Commons as a whole should make the final decisions.

In October 2015, the Commons approved an amendment to its Standing Orders so that bills deemed to cover only England are sent to an England-only committee stage after second reading. Then, after report stage, such bills enter a new stage in which a legislative Grand Committee, consisting only of English MPs, will either approve or veto the bill (or any clauses that apply to England only). If clauses are vetoed, a second report stage will consider possible remedies. All MPs vote on the third reading of bills. The new procedures were used for the first time in January 2016 on parts of the Housing and Planning Bill, and are generally deemed to have worked effectively.

See 'England, Scotland, Wales: MPs & Voting in the House of Commons', *House of Commons Library Briefing Paper*, SN07048, June 2015.

Funding

Barnett formula

a formula used to determine relative levels of public spending in the component nations of the UK.

The devolved administrations are funded by block grants from the UK Treasury, the size of which is settled by the **Barnett formula**. This notoriously complex formula, agreed in 1978, translates changes in public spending in England into equivalent changes in the block grants for Scotland, Wales, and Northern Ireland, calculated on the basis of population. Under the formula Scotland, Wales and Northern Ireland have received more public spending (around 20 per cent) per head of population than England. Critics in both the (English) Labour and Conservative parties claim that this amounts to an English subsidy of the other nations of the UK and takes no account of 'needs'. Despite their favourable allocation, Scotland and Wales have seen their relative share of public spending squeezed by 'austerity'. The Welsh government regards the Barnett formula as unfair, as it receives proportionally less than Scotland.

For their first 15 years, the devolved institutions had little scope to distribute large sums of money between policy areas. The Scottish Parliament did not use its tax-varying powers and, even if it had raised income tax by the permitted maximum of 3 per cent, this would only have raised an extra £650 million. The Scotland Act 2012 gave the Scottish Parliament control over 10 pence of income tax from 2016 – a right now enjoyed by the Welsh Senedd. The Scotland Act of 2016 gave the Scottish Parliament complete power to set income tax rates and bands, and to receive some of the VAT revenue raised in Scotland. These changes allowed a reduction in the block grant from the UK government, making the Scottish and Welsh governments more directly accountable for tax and spending levels. However, this does not amount to 'full fiscal autonomy' in which all tax and spending powers would be devolved. The UK government remains reluctant to undertake major revisions of the way in which the Barnett formula is calculated – a remarkable testament to the potential longevity of an improvised measure within the endlessly adaptable UK system.

Northern Ireland

Northern Ireland has long been treated as a 'place apart' by British politicians. The intercommunal tensions between unionists and nationalists are the primary factor in Northern Irish politics, and management of these is the main goal of the UK government. In general terms, unionists want Northern Ireland to remain part of the UK, whereas nationalists favour a united Ireland or, as a minimum, closer links with the Republic. Unionists identify themselves as British and tend to be Protestant, whereas nationalists see themselves as Irish and tend to be Roman Catholic. Both traditions have extreme fringes that have been prepared to use violence to achieve their goals. Loyalists have engaged in sectarian and paramilitary attacks to defend the Union; until the 1990s, many republicans viewed armed struggle as a legitimate means of forcing British withdrawal, and a small minority still do.

Communal tensions colour everyday life in Northern Ireland: unionists and nationalists tend to live and work in different areas, attend different schools, socialise with people from their own community, and read different newspapers. Each community attaches great importance to its history and traditions: marches by the Protestant Orange Order or the display of the Irish tricolour are steeped in symbolism. According to the 2011 census, in Northern Ireland, people who are Protestant (or brought up as such) constituted 48 per cent of the population, compared to a figure of 45 per cent for Catholics.

Civil rights protests against discrimination faced by Catholics gave way to violence in the late 1960s. The Royal Ulster Constabulary (RUC), a police force made up largely of Protestants and distrusted by many Catholics (see Chapter 9), struggled to contain the violence, and in 1969, the British army was sent to restore order. Terrorist groups such as the Provisional Irish Republican Army (PIRA) and Irish National Liberation Army (INLA), plus loyalist paramilitary groups such as the Ulster Defence Association (UDA) and Ulster Volunteer Force (UVF), carried out attacks, often indiscriminately against ordinary citizens. With the security situation deteriorating, the Heath government introduced direct rule from London, but 'the Troubles' continued. Only in the 1990s did the peace process succeed in reducing the violence, by which time more than 3,500 lives had been lost. The Provisional IRA was on ceasefire from 1994 (save for an interlude in 1996–97) to 2005, when it announced the end of its armed struggle. Some loyalist paramilitaries also renounced violence. But dissident groups have carried out sporadic attacks, the most brutal being the Real IRA's Omagh bombing that killed 29 civilians in 1998 (Photo 12.5).

Communal divisions also underpin representative politics in Northern Ireland. Elections are contested between unionist and nationalist parties; the main electoral issue is the constitutional status of Northern Ireland. But differences exist within the unionist and nationalist blocs. The DUP is the main unionist party. Led by Ian Paisley from its formation in 1971 until 2008, then by Peter Robinson and (from 2016) Arlene Foster, it has a strong Presbyterian ethos. The DUP opposed the 1998 Good Friday Agreement and power-sharing until 2007, when it agreed to go into government with Sinn Fein. The Ulster Unionist Party (UUP), led by Steve Aiken since

PHOTO 12.5 War or peace? A loyalist street mural in Belfast (© Charles McQuillan/Getty Images).

November 2019, supports the Good Friday Agreement and has sought to foster a civic unionist identity. It governed Northern Ireland during the Stormont period (1921 until 1972) and remained the dominant unionist party until 2003. Its support is more middle class than that of the DUP. An alliance between the UUP and the Conservatives at the 2005 general election proved disastrous for the former, as MP Lady Sylvia Harman resigned from the party in protest, leaving it no representation at Westminster. Electoral alliances between the DUP and UUP delivered two gains for the latter in 2015, but the seats were lost in 2017.

The Social Democratic and Labour Party (SDLP), which favours a greater role for the Republic in the affairs of Northern Ireland, was the main representative of the nationalist community until 2001. Formed in 1970 and led by Colum Eastwood since 2015, it is committed to bringing about constitutional change through exclusively peaceful means. It attracts support mainly from middle-class Catholics. Its main rival within the nationalist bloc is Sinn Fein, a republican party whose president is Mary Lou McDonald, who succeeded the long-serving Gerry Adams in February 2018. Sinn Fein was the political wing of the Provisional IRA, whose armed struggle it supported. In the 1990s, the leadership of Sinn Fein embraced the political process ahead of the armed struggle ('the ballot rather than the bullet'), but the party retained links to the PIRA until the latter formally disbanded. Sinn Fein contests UK general elections, winning seven constituencies in 2019, but refuses to take its seats at Westminster.

The Alliance Party of Northern Ireland operates in the non-sectarian centre ground but attracted limited support until quite recently. It has one member of the Northern Ireland Executive (the Justice Minister and Alliance Party leader Noami Long), and one MP at Westminster.

Direct rule and devolution

Northern Ireland has always been governed differently from the rest of the UK. Between 1921 and 1972, it was the only part of the UK to have a devolved Parliament with legislative and executive powers. This period of rule by the Stormont Parliament and executive highlighted the problems of majoritarian democracy in a divided community. Dominated by unionist politicians, Stormont pursued policies that discriminated against the minority Roman Catholic population in representative politics (by gerrymandering constituencies) and social affairs (where Catholics experienced poorer housing and higher unemployment).

With the 'Troubles' escalating, the British government suspended the Stormont Parliament and imposed **direct rule** from London in 1972. The Northern Ireland Office was created to administer the Province; the Secretary of State and junior ministers were drawn from the UK governing party rather than parties from Northern Ireland. The Northern Ireland Constitution Act 1973 stated that the constitutional status of Northern Ireland is conditional on the consent of the people of Northern Ireland. It will remain a part of the UK while that remains the wish of a majority of the people of Northern Ireland. A huge majority supported the constitutional status quo in a referendum largely boycotted by nationalists in 1973. Surveys since then show that a majority want Northern Ireland to remain part of the UK, although there seems to be increasing support for a referendum on the subject in the wake of 'Brexit' (see later).

The lack of input from Northern Ireland politicians, the leeway afforded to civil servants in policymaking, and the limited scrutiny of Northern Irish issues at Westminster – where policy was made through Orders in Council rather than primary legislation – created a democratic deficit under direct rule. The main British political parties have tended not to contest elections in Northern Ireland. The Conservatives had a formal alliance with the Ulster Unionists at Westminster until 1974; all formal ties between the two were revoked after the Anglo-Irish Agreement of 1985. An electoral alliance was revived in 2008 as the Ulster Conservatives and Unionists – New Force (UCUNF). In the 2010 general election, it won just 15.2 per cent of the vote in Northern Ireland, and none of the seats. Labour finally agreed to allow people living in Northern Ireland to become party members in 2003, having been threatened with legal action, but the party rarely contests elections. At Westminster, Labour and the Conservatives have also tried to keep the constitutional status of Northern Ireland out of mainstream British party competition.

Since direct rule, successive British governments have been committed to **power-sharing devolution**. Devolved institutions would be constructed to ensure that representatives of the unionist and nationalist communities shared power: there would be no return to majoritarian rule. A variety of initiatives were tried and failed. One of the most significant was the 1974 Sunningdale Agreement, which proposed a power-sharing executive and Council of Ireland but collapsed when unionists orchestrated a general strike which paralysed the Province.

The search for peace

After another failed initiative in the early 1980s, the British government changed its tactics, if not its underlying strategy. The 1985 Anglo-Irish Agreement gave the Republic of Ireland a formal role in the search for a settlement by establishing a consultative intergovernmental body and recognising that the Republic represented the interests of Catholics in Northern Ireland. Unionists resisted the Agreement, and progress faltered. But the peace process was revived in the late 1980s and early 1990s (see Timeline 12.2). Various factors were significant:

- changes in the strategies pursued by political parties in Northern Ireland;
- changes in the approach of the British government;

Direct rule

the government of Northern Ireland through special arrangements at Whitehall and Westminster.

Power-sharing devolution

a system in which decision-making authority is devolved to institutions that have special arrangements to ensure cross-community representation and support for key policies

- changes in the wider environment, notably a rethinking of Irish identity, the end of the Cold War, and the election of President Bill Clinton in the USA; and
- a growing 'war-weariness' among all sections of the population of Northern Ireland, not least in respect of the economic damage caused by the conflict and the loss of opportunities for young people.

In 1988, John Hume of the SDLP and Gerry Adams began talks that persuaded the Sinn Fein leadership that they could achieve a change in Northern Ireland's constitutional status through the political process. Senior figures in Sinn Fein had already concluded that the armed struggle had produced a stalemate and that representative politics offered the best prospect for advancing their goals. Pressure from the Clinton administration on Irish republicans and the two governments helped open up the space for Sinn Fein's participation in the peace process. Sinn Fein was admitted to multi-party talks in 1997, once the IRA had restored its ceasefire and a commission chaired by US Senator George Mitchell had established principles of non-violence that included the total disarmament of paramilitary organisations.

The public rhetoric of the British government was also changing. Secretary of State for Northern Ireland Peter Brooke announced in 1990 that Britain has 'no selfish strategic or economic interest in Northern Ireland'. With the Cold War over, UK concerns about Irish neutrality and Sinn Fein rhetoric about revolutionary change were in abeyance. The British government now

TIMELINE 12.2

The Northern Ireland peace process, 1988–2014

1988	Talks between SDLP leader John Hume and Sinn Fein leader Gerry Adams begin
1990	Secretary of State for Northern Ireland declares that Britain has 'no selfish strategic or economic interest in Northern Ireland'. Secret backchannel communications between British government and IRA
1991–92	Talks between main constitutional parties
1993	Downing Street Declaration issued by Prime Minister John Major and Taoiseach Albert Reynolds
1994	IRA announces ceasefire; loyalist paramilitaries follow suit
1995	UK and Irish governments issue Framework Documents. David Trimble becomes UUP leader. Bill Clinton's first visit to Belfast
1996	Mitchell Commission issues Principles for Non-Violence, including total decommissioning of paramilitary weapons. Multi-party talks between parties reach stalemate. IRA ceasefire ends
1997	New Labour government elected. IRA ceasefire restored. Sinn Fein enters multi-party talks, DUP withdraws from them
1998	Good Friday Agreement on power-sharing devolution, cross-border bodies, and so forth. Approved in referendums in Northern Ireland and the Republic. David Trimble selected as First Minister, Seamus Mallon as Deputy First Minister (they take office in 1999). First Assembly elections: UUP and SDLP are the main representatives of the unionist and nationalist communities. 'Real IRA' bombs Omagh

1999	Power formally devolved to Northern Ireland Assembly in December. Executive includes two Sinn Fein ministers
2000–1	Assembly and Executive temporarily suspended on three occasions as dispute over decommissioning continues. IRA puts some arms 'beyond use'
2002	Assembly and Executive suspended in October. Reform of Police Service of Northern Ireland
2003	Second Assembly elections see DUP and Sinn Fein emerge as main unionist and nationalist parties
2005	Provisional IRA declares an end to conflict and puts its weapons 'beyond use'
2006	St Andrews Agreement offers basis for restoration of devolved powers
2007	DUP and Sinn Fein are largest parties in Assembly elections and agree to share power; Ian Paisley and Martin McGuinness become First Minister and Deputy First Minister, respectively
2008	Ian Paisley retires; Peter Robinson succeeds him as First Minister and DUP leader
2010	Responsibility for police and justice system devolved to Northern Ireland Assembly
2014	Stormont House Agreement seeks to resolve disputes over welfare reform and parades, and alter the structure of the Assembly and Executive
2017	Resignation of Deputy First Minister Martin McGuinness leads to collapse of institutions and 'snap' Assembly elections.
2020	Reinstatement of institutions

presented itself as a neutral facilitator in the search for a political settlement. It also reopened secretive backchannel communications with the IRA. The British and Irish governments set out parameters for an agreement in the 1993 Downing Street Declaration and the 1995 Framework Document. The latter signalled that an agreement would have three strands: power-sharing devolution in Northern Ireland, the relationship between the north and south of Ireland, and the relationship between the British and Irish governments.

Unionist parties did not change their positions as dramatically as did Sinn Fein. But UUP leader David Trimble was eventually persuaded to accept Sinn Fein participation in a devolved executive and the creation of weak North–South bodies, provided that this formed part of a settlement that bolstered Northern Ireland's place in the Union and brought about the full decommissioning of IRA arms. This entailed the amendment of Articles 2 and 3 of the Irish Constitution (which referred to the 'national territory' as constituting the whole of Ireland) and a Republican commitment to the principle that Northern Ireland's status should not change without the consent of a majority of its people.

The Good Friday Agreement

The year 1997 brought a Labour election victory and Sinn Fein's entry into multi-party talks that culminated in the 1998 Good Friday Agreement (officially titled 'the Belfast Agreement').

Consent was again a key principle: parties to the agreement accepted there would be no change in the constitutional status of Northern Ireland without the consent of the majority of its people. The Republic amended its constitution to remove its territorial claim over Northern Ireland. Parity of esteem was another defining principle: the Agreement recognised the legitimacy of both unionist and nationalist identities and included provisions on equality and human rights.

Consociationalism (i.e. power-sharing) is the key principle underpinning the arrangements for devolution in Northern Ireland (see Analysis 12.2). A 108-member Northern Ireland Assembly was given primary legislative power over a range of policy areas including economic development, agriculture, and education (see Table 12.1). Its responsibilities are similar to those initially granted to the Scottish Parliament, although the Assembly does not have tax-raising powers. Responsibility for the controversial subjects of policing and justice was devolved in 2010. The 2014 Stormont House Agreement reduced the size of the Assembly to 90 members (five rather than six per constituency).

The Assembly is elected by the STV, a system of proportional representation in which electors rank candidates standing in multi-member constituencies (see Chapter 17). This system ensures that a wide range of opinions is represented in the Assembly. Parallel consent (i.e. cross-community support) and weighted majorities are required on controversial issues. The Agreement also ensures that both unionists and nationalists are represented within the Northern Ireland Executive. It is headed by a First Minister and Deputy First Minister elected from the unionist and nationalist blocs in the Assembly. UUP leader David Trimble became First Minister and the SDLP's Seamus Mallon Deputy First Minister in 1999. Since then, the DUP's Ian Paisley (2007–8), Peter Robinson (2008–16), and Arlene Foster (2016–) have served as First Minister; the deputies have been the SDLP's Mark Durkan (2001–02); and Martin McGuiness (2007–17) and Michelle O'Neill (since January 2020) from Sinn Fein. Ministerial posts in the Executive Committee are allocated on a proportional basis, according to party strength in the Assembly. Most ministers head departments dealing with specific policy areas. Five parties have been represented in the Executive Committee: the UUP (four seats in 1999, two in 2007, just one since 2011), the DUP (two in 1999, currently four), SDLP (four in 1999, one since 2007), Sinn Fein (two in 1999, currently three), and the Alliance (one). The 2014 Stormont House Agreement reduced the number of departments (and ministerial portfolios) in the Executive from 12 to 9. It also allowed parties to form an official opposition rather than join a power-sharing government. This option was taken up by the UUP and SDLP after the 2016 Assembly elections.

The Agreement also established north–south, east–west, and intergovernmental bodies. The Northern Ireland administration and Irish government cooperate on cross-border issues in a North–South Ministerial Council which has some executive powers. The British–Irish Council offers an arena for the exchange of ideas and policy cooperation in a number of areas. Its members include sovereign states (the British and Irish governments), devolved administrations (from Scotland, Wales, and Northern Ireland), and Crown Dominions (the Isle of Man and Jersey). A British–Irish Intergovernmental Conference is a forum for formal discussions on Northern Ireland matters between the two governments (Table 12.5).

Finally, the Agreement established an independent commission on policing (the Patten Commission) which recommended major changes to the RUC, now remodelled as the Police Service of Northern Ireland (PSNI: see Chapter 9). Provision was made for the early release of prisoners, and political parties pledged to use their best endeavours to bring about the decommissioning of weapons held by paramilitary groups.

The Agreement won overwhelming approval in referendums in Northern Ireland (71 per cent 'yes') and the Republic (94 per cent). However, only a narrow majority of unionists supported

Analysis 12.2

Consociationalism and the Good Friday Agreement

In the 1970s, the Dutch political scientist Arend Lijphart developed a model of consociational democracy for divided societies. It is most suited to deeply divided societies in transition, for consociationalism requires elite negotiation, accommodation, and compromise. Four main principles underpin consociational agreements:

- *Executive power-sharing*: power in the executive branch of government is shared by representatives of all significant communities;
- *Segmental autonomy:* each community regulates its own internal affairs; the equality and autonomy of communities is protected by law;
- *Proportionality:* elections take place under proportional representation, and government posts are shared in proportion to representation in the legislature. Public spending and posts in the public sector may also be allocated on a proportional basis;
- *Veto rights:* the minority group has the right to veto proposals which they believe violate their basic interests.

The internal arrangements for the government of Northern Ireland set out in the 1998 Good Friday Agreement follow these principles. They are designed to promote consent and accommodation between unionists and nationalists, while protecting their basic interests and identities. First, power in the Northern Ireland Executive is shared between representatives of the main communities in a 'grand coalition'. The main unionist and nationalist parties hold ministerial posts in the Executive, which is headed jointly by a First Minister and Deputy First Minister drawn from the two blocs in the Assembly.

Second, the Agreement legitimises and affords equal respect to British and Irish identities in Northern Ireland. It also calls for a tailor-made Bill of Rights to supplement the European Convention on Human Rights and obliges the UK government to create a Human Rights Commission.

Proportionality is also built into the Agreement. Elections to the Assembly take place under the STV system in 18 multi-member constituencies. STV was believed to encourage cross-community vote transfers (e.g. from the pro-Agreement SDLP to the pro-Agreement UUP), though this remains the exception rather than the norm in Northern Ireland. Ministerial posts in the Executive are allocated to parties in proportion to their strength in the Assembly. The d'Hondt rule is used to determine the order in which posts are allocated (see Chapter 17). Proportionality rules also apply to Assembly committees.

Finally, controversial legislative proposals – ones which provoke the signature of a 'petition of concern' by at least a third of Assembly members – must pass special procedures in the Assembly. They must secure 'parallel consent' (i.e. majority support from both unionists and nationalists) and also a 'weighted majority' (i.e. 60 per cent support from Assembly members present). Assembly members are obliged to designate themselves as 'unionist', 'nationalist', or 'other' for this purpose.

Some critics of the Good Friday Agreement argue that its consociational features have institutionalised and frozen existing ethnic divisions. Rather than encouraging citizens of Northern Ireland to see themselves as members of a single community, it has legitimised the unionist–nationalist divide and done little to address sectarianism. Some academics favour alternative models of conflict resolution that encourage inter-group accommodation by rewarding political parties which win cross-community support or actively promote social change in order to end sectarianism.

TABLE 12.5 Elections to the Northern Ireland Assembly, 2017

	First preference vote (%)	Seats
Unionist		
Democratic Unionist Party	28.1 (−1.2)	28 (−10)
Ulster Unionist Party	12.9 (–)	10 (−6)
Traditional Ulster Voice	2.6 (−0.9)	1 (–)
Nationalist		
Sinn Fein	27.9 (+3.9)	27 (−1)
Social Democratic and Labour Party	11.9 (−0.1)	12 (+1)
Others		
Alliance Party	9.1 (+2.1)	8 (–)
Greens	2.3 (−0.4)	1 (–)
People Before Profit	1.8 (−0.2)	1 (–)

Note: Figures in brackets refer to change since 2016.

it. Pro-Agreement parties won 80 of the 108 seats in the first Assembly elections, where the UUP and SDLP came first and second. Vote transfers turned a majority of first preference votes for 'anti-Agreement' unionists (the DUP and smaller parties) into an overall majority for 'pro-Agreement' unionists (the UUP and Progressive Unionist Party) in the Assembly.

Devolution was dogged in its early years by problems such as Orange Order parades, paramilitary activity, and, most importantly, decommissioning. The IRA did not fully decommission its arms or declare explicitly that its conflict was over until 2005. This ran counter to the letter and spirit of the Agreement – but so did the actions of other parties to the Agreement, albeit less spectacularly. The UK government has suspended the devolved institutions and reimposed direct rule on five occasions. The longest period of suspension lasted from October 2002 to May 2007.

Most of the main actors remained committed to the Good Friday Agreement during this prolonged suspension, but differences between the blocs on its full implementation were deep-rooted. Unionist support for the Agreement fell significantly. Opinion polls at this time showed that a majority of unionists opposed the Agreement, believing that it had given too much ground to nationalists and republicans, while failing to deliver on key unionist demands. The UUP suffered serious divisions: David Trimble faced numerous leadership challenges, three UUP Assembly members defected to the DUP in 2003, and the Orange Order severed its ties with the party. The DUP overtook the UUP as the main representative of the unionist community. It benefitted from discontent with the operation of the Agreement among unionist voters, and a feeling that the UUP had made too many concessions to republicans. Trimble lost his Westminster seat in the 2005 general election and resigned as UUP leader. The hollowing out of the pro-Agreement centre was confirmed by Sinn Fein becoming the main nationalist party. Many nationalist voters now viewed Sinn Fein as the most effective representative of their community, believing that it had extracted concessions from the unionists and UK government even though its MPs never set foot the House of Commons. It also had a more effective party organisation than the SDLP.

The Agreement still offered the best prospect of political stability. Continued direct rule was the likeliest alternative, but all major Northern Ireland parties now favoured some form of devolution. Other scenarios are improbable. A return to devolution minus north–south bodies and some aspects of power-sharing (favoured by the DUP until 2007) lacked cross-community support for understandable reasons. Scottish and Welsh devolution made the full integration of Northern Ireland into the UK (favoured by some on the unionist fringe) unlikely. An independent Northern Ireland was barely viable. A united 32-county Ireland is a possibility in the longer term, but as a decisive majority of Protestants (and many Catholics) support Northern Ireland's place in the Union, it would fail the key test of consent (see Table 12.6).

The IRA's 2005 decision to put its weapons 'beyond use' was a highly significant development, but IRA members were still suspected of involvement in a variety of criminal activities. The depth of mistrust between the DUP and Sinn Fein suggested that the two could not share power. But, in a remarkable turn of events, the 2006 St Andrews Agreement provided a basis for the restoration of the Assembly, with Sinn Fein subsequently agreeing to support the newly reformed PSNI. The 2007 Assembly elections confirmed the DUP and Sinn Fein as the largest parties. Former bitter enemies Ian Paisley, a Protestant firebrand dubbed 'Dr No' for his refusal to work with Sinn Fein, and Martin McGuinness, one-time IRA commander in Derry, became, respectively, First Minister and Deputy First Minister. The two further confounded expectations by establishing an excellent working relationship which saw them dubbed the 'chuckle brothers'.

The prospects for peace and stable power-sharing government appeared brighter than ever. Opposition to the Agreement in both the unionist and nationalist blocs had been marginalised. Few high-profile DUP members opposed power-sharing in 2007 and, although attacks by dissident republicans persisted, a 2008 report by the Independent Monitoring Commission affirmed that the IRA Army Council had ceased to function. Powers over policing and justice were devolved in 2010 – an unimaginable development as recently as 1997. But divisions between the unionist and nationalist blocs remain acute. Very few votes are transferred across the blocs in Assembly elections. The 'peace' walls separating Protestant and Catholic communities in Belfast provide a stark reminder that sectarianism has not been addressed effectively; a political settlement has been superimposed on a fractured society. There were more than 600 shootings, bombings, and other paramilitary attacks between 2010 and 2015. Disputes over parades and flag flying have also re-emerged, with riots in Belfast in 2012 and 2013.

Economic problems in a new era of 'austerity' after 2008 presented a new challenge to the devolution settlement. As the Conservative–Liberal Democrat coalition cut public spending,

TABLE 12.6 Preferred long-term policy for Northern Ireland, 2018 (%)

Long-term policy	Protestant	Catholic	All
Remain part of the United Kingdom with direct rule	28	12	21
Remain part of the United Kingdom with devolved government	57	27	41
Reunify with the rest of Ireland	5	39	19
Independent state	1	4	2
Other/don't know	7	13	12

Source: Northern Ireland Life and Times Survey 2018, https://www.ark.ac.uk/nilt/2018/Political_Attitudes/NIRELND2.html.

parties in the Executive could not agree on how to implement welfare reforms. The 2014 Stormont House Agreement saw the Northern Ireland parties accept benefit changes, while the UK government agreed to provide an emergency loan and devolve powers over corporation tax (with the block grant reduced accordingly). Both unionists and nationalists hoped that the latter would revive an economy in which the private sector is relatively small. New measures to address parading and flag flying also featured. But the Agreement had not been implemented by summer 2015 as Sinn Fein and the SDLP blocked the Executive's welfare bill. This, and the murder of a former IRA informer, prompted the UUP to withdraw from the Executive: Paisley's successor as DUP First Minister Peter Robinson and all but one of his ministers resigned from their positions. They returned to office within weeks after the UK government helped broker a deal.

At least by 2015 there were signs that, far from being 'a place apart', Northern Ireland was beginning to suffer from the kind of political problems which were more characteristic of other parts of the UK. However, in a society which still suffered from profound underlying divisions, the sort of scandal which could be resolved at UK level by a couple of ministerial resignations could lead to the wholesale disruption of the delicate power-sharing arrangements. In November 2016, reports emerged that a scheme to incentivise energy-saving technology had resulted in the misuse of up to £500 million of public funds. Arlene Foster, who had been responsible for overseeing the Renewable Heat Incentive scheme, had subsequently become Northern Ireland's First Minister. When Foster refused to step down from her position while a full inquiry took place, her deputy, Sinn Fein's Martin McGuinness, resigned, precipitating the collapse of the devolved institutions and the resumption of Direct Rule from London (Photo 12.6).

In the rest of the UK (and particularly in England), the scandal tended to be seen as a purely local affair; the suspension of devolution would only become a matter of serious concern if it led to a renewal of the 'Troubles'. However, its relevance to the politics of the UK as a whole became apparent in June 2017, when Theresa May's Conservatives failed to secure an overall majority and the Prime Minister appealed to Foster and the DUP for parliamentary support. By that time, the voters of Northern Ireland had already signalled their dissatisfaction with the DUP; in the 'snap' Assembly elections which followed the collapse of the institutions, the party lost 10 of its 38 seats, retaining its status as the main party in the Assembly over Sinn Fein by just one seat. In the very different context of the Westminster election which May had called in June 2017, moderate parties were 'squeezed' and the DUP's vote share rose significantly. As a result, Foster was able to drive a hard bargain before she agreed to keep the Conservatives in office. Whatever the UK government might say in public, its dependence on DUP votes in the House of Commons undermined any idea that it might act as an 'honest broker' between the DUP and Sinn Fein in talks which might have led to a restoration of the institutions. It was not until January 2020 – when the Conservatives no longer had any need of DUP support – that devolved institutions could be restored. By that time, the UK Parliament had voted to relax the previous severe restrictions on abortions in Northern Ireland – a move which was bitterly contested by the DUP, but which followed a 2018 referendum on the subject in the Republic of Ireland.

Devolution, 'Brexit', and Coronavirus

Although the process of devolution in the UK was not instigated by the country's membership of the EU – nationalist parties, particularly Scotland's SNP, had attracted considerable support before Britain joined the EEC in 1973 – the crucial developments, in the late 1990s, took place when it seemed reasonable to suppose that the country would stay 'in Europe'. Whatever people

PHOTO 12.6 Northern Ireland Power-Sharing Assembly Sits Again at Stormont after Three Years, January 2020 (© Kelvin Boyes – Pool/Getty Images).

in Scotland, Wales, and Northern Ireland might have felt in the early 1970s, by the time that devolved institutions were established, they had enjoyed more tangible benefits from membership (not least through the EU's Regional Development Fund) than most English voters. In the case of Northern Ireland, the EU's role had been especially positive since it had helped to secure the Good Friday Agreement, and was a guarantor of the settlement.

Whatever one thinks of the quality of debate during the 2016 EU referendum campaign, it would be impossible for any serious observer to maintain that full consideration was given by the mainstream media to the likely effects of a 'Leave' vote on the UK's territorial politics. In hindsight (at least), the most obvious problems of withdrawal would affect Northern Ireland, which would be left with a land-border with an EU country (the Irish Republic). In any circumstances, this would mean that Northern Ireland would be in a complicated situation; the fact that the border was such a sensitive issue for Ireland meant the failure of the rival campaigns to highlight this issue was highly culpable (the 'Remain' camp did at least try unavailingly to draw the public's attention to the border problem, but clearly this was considered to be a minor component of the campaign's strategy).

In 1975, EEC membership had commanded majority support across virtually all the regions of the UK. The results in 2016 were very different (see Table 12.7):

The disparity in the results across the UK could easily be explained. The idea of 'sovereignty' – encapsulated in the 'Leave' slogan that a vote in their favour would mean a resumption of 'control', particularly in the area of immigration – was far more important to English voters than in other parts of the UK, where the full status accorded to nationhood was a distant memory (or, in the Scottish case, a recently revived aspiration). Clearly the economic benefits of EU membership were not regarded by Welsh voters as sufficiently helpful as to outweigh other considerations.

TABLE 12.7 Results of the 2016 EU referendum by UK nation

Nation	'Leave' vote (%)	'Remain' vote (%)	Turnout (%)
England	53.4	46.6	73.0
Scotland	38.0	62.0	67.2
Wales	52.5	47.5	71.7
Northern Ireland	44.2	55.8	62.7

When compared to the turnout in previous referendums relating to devolution, it was apparent that the question of EU membership was far more important to Welsh voters (who had given considerable support to UKIP in the 2016 Assembly elections). By contrast, although Scottish opinion was very clearly in favour of 'Remain', voters were less exercised by this question than by the subject of independence. In Northern Ireland, the decisive 'Remain' vote was a sharp rebuke to the DUP, which supported withdrawal. Nevertheless, as we have seen, the party benefitted from the complexities of UK-wide politics in the 2017 general election, allowing Theresa May to cobble together a 'confidence and supply' deal which helped to keep her in office for two more years.

Devolution had been designed by 'New Labour' as the best way to keep the component parts of the UK together, within the EU. From this perspective, the 2016 result was a serious setback, cruelly exposing the difficulties of establishing a fair distribution of policy influence between the four nations of the UK, when one nation (England) was so dominant in terms of economic strength as well as population. All four UK 'capital cities' – London, Edinburgh, Cardiff, and Belfast – voted for 'Remain'; far from illustrating an important element of unity within the UK, this was often used by 'Leavers' to bolster their presentation of the 'Brexit' result as a revolt of the 'masses' against various 'metropolitan elites'. Although subsequent developments showed that 'Brexiteers' had campaigned for withdrawal from the EU without paying much regard to the issue of the Northern Ireland border, they had also taken scant notice of government pledges during the 2014 independence referendum that Scotland could only be sure of remaining a member of the EU if it voted to stay within the UK. The SNP was quick to alight on this issue as a justification for a new independence referendum. Meanwhile, although a large majority in Northern Ireland continued to favour adhesion to the UK, there was evidence after Brexit to suggest that the question of reunification with the Republic of Ireland was being taken more seriously. DUP supporters who had insisted that Northern Ireland should be treated equally with the rest of the UK were no happier with Boris Johnson's withdrawal agreement than they had been with Theresa May's ill-starred proposals.

Within weeks of the UK's official withdrawal from the EU (January 2020), the outbreak of a new coronavirus, COVID-19, posed another unexpected and formidable challenge to relations between London and the devolved institutions. Since health was a devolved matter, Scotland, Northern Ireland, and Wales devised their own strategies for coping with the pandemic, albeit in close consultation with Whitehall. Since the virus affected different regions of the UK with varying severity, it was difficult to make a fair appraisal of relative performance; but it was widely perceived that the Scottish government, in particular, had communicated with the public with far greater clarity than Boris Johnson and his colleagues. On one hand, the episode, which is far from over at the time of writing (June 2020), could be seen as a vindication for devolution, allowing a flexibility of response which would have been difficult to achieve before the process started. Equally, those who believed that the UK was no longer 'fit for purpose' could see it, along with Brexit, as strong confirmatory evidence.

The post-devolution polity

Devolution has created a new relationship between the UK's component nations. It offers further institutional recognition of the distinctiveness of these nations, but also reflects the current desire of a majority of voters to remain part of a multinational UK state. Rather than enforcing a coherent blueprint, devolution has been asymmetric: the nations of the UK are each governed in different ways. The post-devolution UK no longer comfortably fits the centralised, homogeneous norm of a unitary state. But neither has it been transformed into a federal state in which power is constitutionally divided between autonomous institutions.

In *Devolution in the United Kingdom* (Oxford: Opus, 2001), Vernon Bogdanor characterised the post-devolution UK as a 'quasi-federal' UK. It has some characteristics of **federalism**, while retaining some features of a unitary state. The legislation creating devolved institutions thus established a formal division of powers between central government and the devolved bodies, but Westminster remains sovereign as it limits the powers of the devolved institutions and can overrule or abolish them. When Gladstone sought to recognise the multinational character of the UK state by devolving power to a legislative assembly in Ireland in the late nineteenth century, the great constitutional theorist A.V. Dicey argued that there could be no halfway house between parliamentary sovereignty and separatism. More than a century later, Labour's devolution settlement arguably pushed the UK into this 'middle ground', without the dire consequences foreseen by Dicey. Westminster remains sovereign, but, in practice, this now falls far short of supremacy over policy across the UK. Although sovereignty has formally been delegated rather than devolved, Westminster has accepted that it will not impose legislation in devolved policy areas whose tendency to expand shows no sign of abating.

A federal UK is presented as a solution to some of the anomalies of the devolution settlement by commentators from across the political spectrum – notably the Liberal Democrats but also some enthusiasts for an English Parliament. In a federal UK, Westminster would be a federal Parliament handling areas of 'high politics' such as the economy, constitution, and foreign policy, while 'domestic' issues such as health and education would be devolved to legislative assemblies in England, Scotland, Wales, and Northern Ireland. But the dominance of England is a major obstacle to a viable federal model. The 2014 McKay Commission report on the English Question rejected federalism and an English Parliament (Table 12.8).

There has been much debate about the future of 'Britishness' in the post-devolution UK. The number of people describing themselves as 'primarily' Scottish, Welsh, or English rose in the first decade of devolution, before stabilising or falling back (see Table 12.7). But most people continue to see themselves as having dual identities, that is, being British as well as Scottish, Welsh, or English (see, for example, polling evidence from 2020 at https://www.opinium.co.uk/national-identity-in-britain/#:~:text=At%20its%20core%2C%20British%20identity, under%20one%20British%20identity%20harmoniously.). English voters see the West Lothian Question and funding arrangements as unfair, but these are low salience issues in general elections and the demand for an English Parliament is still confined to a (very vocal) minority. Nonetheless, Gordon Brown invested considerable energy promoting Britishness as a unifying identity and warning against separatism. The nations of Britain, he argued, are stronger together than they would be apart, punching above their weight on the international stage and having a stronger economy, for example. Core British values are held to include toleration, fairness, liberty, and social justice, while institutions such as the

Federalism
a form of government in which the constitution divides decision-making authority between national and regional tiers of government.

TABLE 12.8 National identity in England, Scotland, and Wales in the aftermath of devolution

Respondents were asked to choose how they would describe themselves from the options presented below

Identity	1997	2003	2012
England			
English not British	7	17	17
More English than British	17	19	12
Equally English and British	45	31	44
More British than English	14	13	8
British not English	9	10	10
Scotland			
Scottish not British	23	31	23
More Scottish than British	38	34	30
Equally Scottish and British	27	22	30
More British than Scottish	4	4	5
British not Scottish	4	4	6
Wales			
Welsh not British	17	21	21
More Welsh than British	26	27	17
Equally Welsh and British	34	29	35
More British than Welsh	10	8	8
British not Welsh	12	9	17

Sources: British Social Attitudes 30, www.bsa.natcen. ac.uk/latest-report/british-social-attitudes-30/devolution/- trends-in-national-identity.aspx; J. Curtice, 'Future Identi- ties: Changing Identities in the UK– the Next 10 Years', www.gov.uk/government/uploads/system/uploads/ attachment_data/ file/275762/13-510-national identity- and-constitutional-change.pdf.

Monarchy, Parliament, the NHS, and the armed forces are also important elements of British identity. Those who continue to subscribe to this view of the British will have been com- forted by the fact that, despite persisting polarisation over 'Brexit', the overwhelming majority showed a remarkable degree of compliance with government guidelines during the COVID- 19 crisis. However, with economic problems likely to prevail for the foreseeable future, and a trading relationship with the EU yet to be confirmed, the tests for the UK and its people are far from over.

Conclusion and summary

Former Secretary of State for Wales Ron Davies described devolution as a 'process not an event'. More than 20 years after the process began, neither its final destination nor the stages *en route* are easily predicted. The Scottish referendum might have rejected independence, but it was far from being a warm endorsement of the status quo, and 'Brexit' has added a new factor to the debate. The devolution of some tax and welfare competences may not be enough to satisfy Scottish demands for greater autonomy. There is little demand for independence in Wales, but further devolution has taken place since the 2011 referendum, and the Senedd now has far more power than 'New Labour' envisaged back in 1997. In Northern Ireland, the process has been hampered (and almost derailed) by tensions between the parties, and between the Executive and the UK government. Nonetheless, a high level of underlying support among Catholics for a continuing relationship with the UK suggests that the union with Northern Ireland can only be threatened if London-based governments continue to mishandle the situation.

Pragmatic adaptation, or 'muddling through', has seen territorial politics develop in piecemeal rather than coherent fashion and has left important problems unresolved. Questions about the status of England and the operation of the UK government have yet to be addressed effectively. While the 'West Lothian Question' has been given an answer of sorts, the Barnett formula survives in the absence of easy alternatives and policy divergence within the UK is becoming more apparent. The creation of the devolved institutions marked the 'end of the beginning' for the multilevel UK polity; the 2016 referendum marked the beginning of a new phase, with no certainty about the ultimate outcome or the survival of the Union.

Further reading

R. Heffernan, P. Cowley, and C. Hay's (eds.) *Developments in British Politics 9* (London: Palgrave, 2011) contains two useful chapters relevant to this subject: R. Scully and R. Wyn Jones, 'Territorial Politics in Post-Devolution Britain' (pp. 113–29), and C. Gormley–Heenan, 'Power-Sharing in Northern Ireland' (pp. 130–51). A special issue of *Parliamentary Affairs* (Vol. 63, No. 1, January 2010) includes a series of excellent articles on aspects of devolution in its first ten years. M. Beech and S. Lee (eds.), *The Conservative-Liberal Coalition. Examining the Cameron-Clegg Government* (London: Palgrave, 2015) includes chapters on Scotland by M. Arnott (pp. 162–77), Wales by R. Scully (pp. 178–93), and Northern Ireland by C. Gormley-Heenan and A. Aughey (pp. 194–210).

V. Bogdanor's *Devolution in the United Kingdom* (Oxford: Opus, 2001) concentrates on the historical context of devolution, but offers a clear analysis of its anomalies. Bogdanor's *Beyond Brexit: Towards a New Constitution* (London: I.B Tauris, 2019) is the latest contribution by this prolific author. See also J. Mitchell, *Devolution in the United Kingdom* (Manchester: Manchester University Press, 2012). Analytical accounts of pre-1999 territorial politics include M. Hechter's *Internal Colonialism* (London: Routledge, 1975) and J. Bulpitt's classic text, *Territory and Power in the United Kingdom* (Manchester: Manchester University Press, 1983). J. Bradbury, 'The Political Dynamics of Sub-State Regionalisation', *British Journal of Politics and International Relations*, Vol.5, No. 4 (2003), pp. 543–75, provides a theoretical approach to devolution.

On Scotland, P. Caimey and N. McGarvey's *Scottish Politics* (London: Palgrave, 2nd edition, 2013) is an excellent textbook. The implications of the Scottish independence referendum are assessed in a collection of essays in *The Political Quarterly*, Vol.86, No. 2 (2015). J. Mitchell, L. Bennie, and R. Johns's *The Scottish National Party: Transition to Power* (Oxford: Oxford University Press, 2012) is the best academic study of the SNP, while the early stages of Labour's demise is examined in G. Hassan and E. Shaw's *The Strange Death of Labour in Scotland* (Edinburgh: Edinburgh University Press, 2012). Devolved politics in Wales are less well-served, but K. Morgan and G. Mungham's *Redesigning Democracy: The Making of the Welsh Assembly* (Cardiff: Seren, 2000) examines the early years. Useful comparative studies include P. Lynch, 'Governing Devolution: Understanding the Office of First Ministers in Scotland and Wales', *Parliamentary Affairs*, Vol.59, No. 3 (2006), pp. 420–36, and R. Wyn Jones and R. Scully, 'Devolution and Electoral Politics in Scotland and Wales', *Publius: The Journal of Federalism*, Vol.36, No. 1 (2006), pp. 115–34.

The status of England in the post-devolution UK is examined in R. Hazell's(ed.), *The English Question* (Manchester: Manchester University Press, 2006). M. Kenny's *The Politics of English Nationhood* (Oxford: Oxford University Press, 2014) assesses the revival of Englishness and its political consequences.

There is a substantial literature on Northern Ireland. Good introductions include P. Dixon's *Northern Ireland. The Politics of War and Peace* (London: Palgrave, 2nd edition, 2008), and J. Tonge's *The New Northern Irish Politics* (London: Palgrave, 2004). J. McGarry and B. O'Leary's *Explaining Northern Ireland* (Oxford: Oxford University Press, 1995) offers an advanced analysis of the conflict. Tony Blair's former Chief of Staff Jonathan Powell provides an insider account of the peace process in *Great Hatred, Little Room: Making Peace in Northern Ireland* (London: Bodley Head, 2008).

On the consequences of the 2016 referendum, see the report of the House of Commons' Public Administration and Constitutional Affairs Committee, *Devolution and Exiting the EU*, https://www.parliament. uk/business/committees/committees-a-z/commons-select/public-administration-and-constitutional-affairs-committee/inquiries/parliament-2017/devolution-and-exiting-the-eu-17-19/. There are also very useful chapters by D. Wincott, M. Murphy, and M. Keating in P. Diamond, P. Nedergaard, and B. Roasmond's (eds), *The Routledge Handbook of the Politics of Brexit* (London: Routledge, 2018).

Websites

Students of devolution are well served by the Internet. Various sites provide evidence and academic analysis, notably the Centre on Constitutional Change (www.centreonconstitutionalchange.ac.uk), What Scotland Thinks (www.whatscotlandthinks.org), The Constitution Unit (www.ucl.ac.uk/constitution-unit), and the Devolution Matters blog (www.devolutionmatters.wordpress.com).

The devolved institutions all have informative websites: the Scottish Parliament (www. scottish.parliament.uk) and Scottish government (www.gov.scot); the Welsh Senedd (https://senedd.wales/en/bus-home/Pages/bus-home.aspx); the Welsh government (www.gov.wales); the Northern Ireland Assembly (www.niassembly.gov.uk), and the Northern Ireland Executive (www.northernireland.gov.uk).

Chapter 13

The UK and the European Union

Learning outcomes

After reading this chapter, you will:

- understand the historical development of the European Union and Britain's responses to, and often fraught relations with, it;
- be aware of the policies pursued by successive British governments towards the EU;
- be able to evaluate the impact of EU membership on British politics and the political system;
- understand why Brexit occurred.

Introduction

The United Kingdom joined the EEC – later to become the European Union (EU) – in 1973. Since then, the EU has enlarged to 28 members and has extended its policy competences considerably. Member states form a single market of some 500 million people. Within the EU, the UK was often considered to be an 'awkward partner', wary of deeper economic and political integration. Domestically, the UK's relationship with the EU was a major issue that caused divisions both between and within the main political parties. EU membership also required the British state to adapt some of its practices and procedures.

The EU has some of the characteristics of an international organisation and some of a federal state, but fits the classic definition of neither. In international organisations (e.g. the United Nations) and regional trade bodies (e.g. the North American Free Trade Area), nation-states cooperate voluntarily in areas of mutual concern but retain extensive veto rights. The EU, however, has supranational elements such as its own budget, institutions with independent authority (such as the Commission), and a body of law that has primacy over national legislation.

In federal states, the constitution divides power between two autonomous tiers of government, the federal (i.e. national) government and state (i.e. subnational) government. Some features of the EU suggest a federal system, even a nascent federal state. The Treaties set out the powers held by different levels of government, giving the EU sole decision-taking competence in some policy areas and shared power in others. EU citizens have rights under the Charter of Fundamental Rights and are directly represented in the EP. But the powers of the Commission and EP are not equivalent to those of the executive and legislature of a sovereign state. Member states are represented in the European Council and Council of the EU, where interstate bargaining determines the direction taken by the EU. National governments retain substantial decision-making authority on taxation, social security, and foreign policy. Although European integration has brought about change in the political systems of member states, they retain many of their distinctive features. Finally, citizens still identify primarily with their nation-state rather than the EU.

The development of the European Union

Supranational body

an institution or organisation which has decision-making authority independent of its member states.

Intergovernmental body

an institution or organisation based on cooperation between nation-states.

Following World War II (1939–45), West European states engaged in closer political and economic cooperation to aid their reconstruction and prevent future war. France was the driving force, putting forward the 1950 Schuman Plan that proposed the creation of a European Coal and Steel Community (ECSC). France, West Germany, Italy, Belgium, the Netherlands, and Luxembourg ('the Six') duly set this up in 1952. As a **supranational** body with its own policymaking authority, budget, and law, the ECSC differed from **intergovernmental** bodies (e.g. the Council of Europe created in 1948) in which states cooperated voluntarily and could veto proposals. Its authority, though, was limited to matters relating to the coal and steel industries of the Six.

Further integration followed when the Six signed the 1957 Treaties of Rome establishing the EEC and the European Atomic Energy Community (Euratom). The institutions of the EEC were modelled on those of the ECSC and began operating in 1958. The EEC's early achievements included the creation of a CAP in 1962 and a customs union in 1968, the latter involving the removal of internal tariff barriers and establishment of a common external tariff. Integration stalled in 1965 when President de Gaulle precipitated the 'empty chair crisis' by withdrawing French representatives from the Council of Ministers in protest at proposals to strengthen supranationalism. The 1966 'Luxembourg compromise' resolved the conflict by confirming the veto power of member states, placing them, rather than the supranational Commission, in the ascendancy.

Economic and Monetary Union (EMU): a project creating a single currency, central bank, and common monetary policy for its members.

Global economic crisis contributed to a drop in the pace of integration in the 1970s. Ambitious plans for **EMU** made at the 1969 Hague summit were abandoned. But there were also advances. The first direct elections to the European Parliament (EP) were held in 1979, the year in which the European Monetary System (EMS) was established. Its main element was the exchange rate mechanism (ERM), a currency grid in which the values of member currencies were fixed against each other. The EEC also enlarged, with the UK, Ireland, and Denmark joining in 1973, Greece in 1981, and then Spain and Portugal in 1986.

Analysis 13.1

EEC, EC, and EU

The EU has had a bewildering number of official titles since the EEC was founded in 1958. The three main organisations (the EEC, ECSC, and Euratom) were collectively known as 'European Communities'. The 1965 Merger Treaty created one Council, one Commission, one European Court of Justice, and a single Assembly (later renamed the European Parliament) for the three organisations.

The Maastricht Treaty created a new organisation, the European Union, which was built upon three 'pillars'. The first was the EC, as the EEC was now renamed. But Community laws and methods did not apply in the second pillar (the Common Foreign and Security Policy) or the third pillar (Justice and Home Affairs), where intergovernmental procedures were used. The EU was granted a legal personality by the Lisbon Treaty date which also collapsed the pillars, merging the EC and EU and ending the distinction between the two.

In this chapter, the term EU is used except where it is historically inaccurate.

Single market to single currency

Integration moved up a gear in the mid-1980s as member states pressed for further economic integration to improve Europe's competitive position. This initiative, plus Franco–German plans for institutional reform, was supported by an activist commission led by the former French Finance Minister Jacques Delors. The Single European Act (SEA) was agreed in 1985 and came into effect in 1987. Its centrepiece was the creation of a single market by the end of 1992. The single market is an area without internal frontiers in which the free movement of goods, services, persons, and capital is ensured. Three main forms of barrier – physical, technical, and fiscal – were to be removed. The removal of physical barriers required the abolition of customs checks at internal borders. For technical barriers, the principle of 'mutual recognition' meant that goods meeting minimum standards in one member state could be traded freely in another. Professional and academic qualifications would also be accepted across the EC. New VAT procedures were introduced in an attempt to remove fiscal barriers.

The single market proved a major success, contributing to the creation of 2.75 million jobs and boosting EU GDP by some 15 per cent, but progress in some areas (e.g. the service sector) has been slower than anticipated. It also gave new impetus to the integration process as France, Germany, and the Commission pressed for a greater EC role in social policy, freedom of movement for workers, and EMU. Meanwhile, the end of the Cold War, reunification of Germany, and collapse of Communist regimes in Eastern Europe overturned prevailing assumptions about the security of Europe. In twin Intergovernmental Conferences (IGCs) in 1990–91, member states thrashed out proposals for EMU and political union.

The Maastricht Treaty, properly known as the Treaty on European Union, was agreed in 1991 and came into force in 1993. It created an EU comprised of three 'pillars': (i) the existing EC with responsibility for the single market, trade, agriculture, and so forth, (ii) an intergovernmental pillar on Common Foreign and Security Policy (CFSP), and (iii) another intergovernmental pillar, on Justice and Home Affairs (JHA). Decision-making in the second and third pillars was conducted by national governments which retained veto rights, with little input from the commission or European Court of Justice. The Maastricht Treaty also stated that a single European currency was to be established by 1999 at the latest.

The UK won two treaty exemptions. The first, an opt-out from Stage III of EMU, meant that the UK would not have to join the single currency automatically. Instead, the UK Parliament would decide at a future date whether or not to participate. Second, the UK was alone in refusing to sign the Social Agreement (often referred to as the 'Social Chapter') that extended cooperation in social policy, believing that it would increase costs for British companies.

Ratification of the Treaty proved difficult. It was rejected in a Danish referendum in 1992, narrowly approved in France, and subject to a tortuous parliamentary ratification in Britain. A second Danish vote produced a positive answer, and the Treaty came into force in 1993. Since then, the EU has engaged in both 'deepening' (further integration) and 'widening' (enlargement).

Enlargement the admittance of new members into an international organisation.

Deepening and widening

Maastricht set out a three-stage transition to EMU. Stage I, the completion of the single market, was already under way. In Stage II, member states would engage in greater economic coordination. Stage III would see the creation of an independent European Central Bank (ECB), the irrevocable fixing of exchange rates, and the replacement of national currencies with the single currency (the euro). It would begin in 1999 for those states meeting specified 'convergence criteria' – low inflation, low interest rates, sound public finances (sustainable levels of government debt), and ERM membership. The targets appeared tough, but the Treaty allowed for flexibility if states were moving in the right direction.

Turmoil in the ERM with the exit of the UK and Italy (1992) and the widening of the bands of permitted currency fluctuation (1993) raised doubts about the viability of EMU. The ERM subsequently stabilised, but some states had to cut welfare spending or engage in creative accountancy to meet the convergence criteria. Eleven states – Austria, Belgium, Finland, France, Germany, Ireland, Italy, Luxembourg, the Netherlands, Spain, and Portugal – formed the 'first wave' of states joining the euro on 1 January 1999. Only four unambiguously met the criteria. Britain, Denmark, and Sweden opted out; Greece did not meet the criteria but joined in 2001. Euro notes and coins entered circulation on 1 January 2002, and national currencies ceased to be legal tender the following month.

Budgetary discipline was supposed to be ensured by the Stability and Growth Pact, which allowed sanctions to be imposed on eurozone states that failed to reduce excessive deficits. But political pressure saw France and Germany avoiding fines, despite persistent breaches of the 3 per cent ceiling on budget deficits. The strict criteria were officially relaxed in 2005 despite central bank opposition.

The accession of Austria, Finland, and Sweden to the EU in 1995 proceeded smoothly, but the eastward enlargement of the Union was a far more ambitious project. Twelve Central and Eastern European states applied for membership in the early 1990s, having been freed from communist rule and Soviet influence in 1989. The 1993 Copenhagen European Council agreed to three main criteria for their membership: a liberal democratic political system, a functioning market economy, and acceptance of the *acquis communautaire* (the body of existing EU law). Meeting these criteria was sometimes painful, as it necessitated major political, economic, and administrative reforms in the applicant states.

Ten states eventually joined the EU in 2004: Cyprus, the Czech Republic, Estonia, Hungary, Latvia, Lithuania, Malta, Poland, Slovakia, and Slovenia. Bulgaria and Romania joined in 2007, and then Croatia in 2013 (see Figure 13.1). Seven of these states – Slovenia, Cyprus, Malta, Slovakia, Estonia, Latvia, and Lithuania – have since joined the euro, taking eurozone membership to 19.

One of the most visible results of the 2004 enlargement has been the westward migration of workers from new member states, although a number of states imposed short-term restrictions. Concerns about the absorptive capacity of the EU and the particular problems posed by the next batch of applicants mean that further enlargement is a delicate question. Turkey applied to join in 1987, but it was rejected because of concerns about its political system, weak economy, and poor human rights record. The application remains contentious. Despite political and economic advances in Turkey, questions about how the EU could accommodate a Muslim state, albeit a secular one, were raised. The UK has been a strong supporter of Turkish entry, but there is popular opposition in states with large Turkish or Muslim communities, such as Austria, France, and Germany.

Macedonia, Montenegro, Albania, and Serbia are, like Turkey, officially recognised candidates for EU membership but are a long way from joining the EU. Bosnia and Herzegovina and Kosovo are potential future candidates. Iceland applied for membership in 2009 after its financial sector was hit by the global financial crisis, but its centre-right government formally withdrew the application in 2015.

Treaty reform

EU institutions and policies would have to be reformed if a wider Union was to function effectively. The Commission's *Agenda 2000* programme began the overhaul of the CAP and regional policy. Institutional reform required four treaty revisions: Amsterdam, Nice, the Constitutional Treaty, and Lisbon.

The Amsterdam Treaty was agreed in 1997. Many policy areas within the intergovernmental JHA pillar were transferred to an 'area of freedom, security and justice' in which supranational procedures applied. The UK gained opt-outs from many policies in this area. Legislation on border control issues (e.g. police cooperation) that had previously been agreed by the Schengen Group was also incorporated into EU law. The Schengen Group had been set up in 1985 by a small number of states which sought to remove their border controls without using EC law to do so. The UK is not a Schengen member, but could now 'opt in' to certain aspects of the Schengen system. Flexibility clauses, allowing a majority of member states to pursue further integration without the need for all states to participate also featured in the Amsterdam Treaty.

Qualified majority voting (QMV): a weighted voting system used in the Council of the European Union in which decisions need the support of 55 per cent of member states representing at least 65 per cent of the EU population.

Agreement on institutional reform had to wait until an ill-tempered European Council meeting at Nice in 2000. The Nice Treaty set out changes to **qualified majority voting (QMV)** – a procedure in which states are allocated a certain number of votes according to their

FIGURE 13.1 The European Union. Courtesy of the University of Texas Libraries, The University of Texas at Austin (pre-2020).

populations – and the size of the Commission and EP that would come into effect after enlargement. Its main policy innovation was a European Security and Defence Policy (ESDP) under which the EU would develop a common defence policy and have the capacity for autonomous, albeit limited, military action.

The Nice Treaty did not come into force until 2003 after a second referendum in Ireland reversed an initial 'no' vote. By then, preparations for further treaty reform were under way. The treaty establishing a Constitution for Europe – often referred to as the EU Constitutional Treaty or 'EU Constitution' – was signed at the 2004 Dublin European Council. But it was rejected by voters in referendums in France and the Netherlands in 2005. Two years later, EU leaders agreed on the Lisbon Treaty which retained most of the reforms contained in the Constitutional Treaty but dropped the concept and language of a constitution.

The main changes introduced by the Lisbon Treaty, which came into force in 2009, were:

- a president for the European Council, serving a two-and-a-half-year term;
- a High Representative of the Union for Foreign Affairs and Security Policy, who coordinates the EU's Common Foreign and Security Policy and works with a new European External Action Service (which manages the EU's response to crises);
- greater cooperation between states scheduled to hold the rotating presidency of the Council of the EU;
- a 'dual majority' system of QMV under which legislative proposals require the support of 55 per cent of member states representing 65 per cent of the EU's population. This ends the system under which states are allocated votes according to their population;
- member states can agree that decisions currently taken by unanimity can instead be taken by qualified majority voting, except in defence policy. This can occur without further treaty amendment, but all member states and national parliaments would have to approve;
- the merging of the 'pillars' into one legal entity, the EU;
- the extension of QMV to 15 more areas of EU activity;
- a clearer definition of the competences of the EU and its member states (see Table 13.1);
- a clause (Article 50) establishing the procedures for a negotiated withdrawal should a state wish to leave the EU;
- assurances that the Charter of Fundamental Rights does not create new rights in UK law, and that the UK and Ireland have the right to opt-in to police and judicial matters.

The eurozone crisis and Euroscepticism

EMU has a number of benefits, including an end to exchange rate uncertainty and the reduction of transaction costs on cross-border trade. But it also involves a loss of monetary sovereignty, with interest rates for the eurozone set by the independent European Central Bank. The limited economic convergence of eurozone states and the loosening of rules designed to ensure budgetary discipline and prevent excessive deficit and debt levels became a concern when some southern Europe states ran up unsustainable levels of government debt. This prompted the sovereign debt crisis

TABLE 13.1 Policy competences of the EU (selected)

Exclusive EU competence	Shared EU and member state competence	Supporting competence	Special competences (EU coordinates domestic politics of member states)	Exclusive member state competence
Customs union	Single market	Industry	Macroeconomic policy	Many areas of taxation, including income tax
External trade	Social and employment policy	Culture	Common Foreign and Security Policy	Many areas of public spending, including social security
Monetary policy (in the eurozone)	Economic, social, and territorial cohesion	Education		
Competition policy	Area of freedom, security, and justice	Human health		
Marine conservation	Agriculture and fisheries	Tourism		

that followed the global financial crisis of 2007–08. Greece, Ireland, Spain, Portugal, and Cyprus were unable to guarantee repayment of their government debt and received bailouts from new EU funds. In turn, they were required to introduce new austerity measures by the 'troika' of the European Commission, European Central Bank, and IMF. In response to the crisis, member states also agreed to accelerate moves to complete EMU. The 2012 fiscal compact treaty – officially known as the Treaty on Stability, Coordination and Governance – required states to write balanced budget rules into national law and established tougher sanctions on budget deficits. It was signed by all member states except the UK and Czech Republic, and is (initially) an intergovernmental treaty outside the EU legal framework. A European Banking Union also took shape with a single rule book and ECB supervision of the stability of banks in the eurozone. Further integration in the eurozone accelerated the development of differentiated integration in the EU (see Case study 13.1) and raised questions about the future relationship between eurozone and non-euro states.

Case study 13.1

Differentiated integration in the EU

Not all EU member states have integrated to the same extent or at the same speed. Differentiation is becoming an increasingly important characteristic of European integration. New member states are granted transition periods during which they are temporarily exempted from some obligations (e.g. implementing EU environmental standards) while they adapt their national structures. The term 'multi-speed Europe' captures this type of differentiated integration in which states adopt the same policies at different speeds.

However, differentiated integration also results from legally binding special arrangements negotiated by existing member states that do not want to take part in new EU policy areas and seek to protect their national sovereignty. Five states (Denmark, Ireland, Poland, Sweden, and the UK) negotiated opt-outs in the EU treaties which exempted them from participation in particular EU policy areas. The most significant policy area in which differentiated integration is evident is EMU, where 19 member states have adopted the euro and all but two others are expected to join in time. The EU treaties gave UK and Denmark specific opt-outs from EMU membership. Sweden does not have a formal opt-out but has deliberately avoided meeting the criteria for membership. The UK and Czech Republic did not sign the 2013 Treaty on Stability, Coordination and Governance ('the fiscal compact').

The border-free Schengen Area consists of 22 EU member states and four non-EU members. Four EU member states (Bulgaria, Croatia, Cyprus, and Romania) are legally obliged to join but have not yet been deemed ready to, while the UK and Ireland had opt-outs. Denmark also has an opt-out from the EU's Common Security and Defence Policy. The UK and Poland secured assurances in the Treaty of Lisbon about the impact of the Charter of Fundamental Rights of the European Union on their national law.

The enhanced cooperation procedure was introduced by the Amsterdam Treaty. It allows at least nine member states to establish new areas of integration using EU structures without the other member states being involved. To date, it has only been used for measures on divorce law, patents, and a financial transactions tax.

See: D. Leuffen, B. Rittberger and F. Schimmelfennig, *Differentiated Integration: Explaining Variation in the European Union* (London: Palgrave, 2013).

Euroscepticism

scepticism
or hostility
towards key
elements of the
EU and integra-
tion process.

Euroscepticism was now moving from the fringes to the mainstream of politics in many EU member states. Voters in France and the Netherlands had opposed the EU Constitutional Treaty in referendums in 2005, forcing member states to scale down some of its provisions. The eurozone crisis further fuelled the growth of Euroscepticism, both in states required to introduce austerity measures as conditions for receiving bailouts from the EU and in states

Analysis 13.2

Euroscepticism

The term 'Eurosceptic' became widely used in debates on the Maastricht Treaty. But it is problematic as it is imprecise, being used in popular discourse to describe both *principled* opposition and *qualified* opposition to European integration and the EU. The term is sometimes employed in a narrow sense, where a sceptic is a person who *doubts* the truth or value of a generally held idea or belief. Here, a Eurosceptic will doubt the wisdom of certain EU policies and practices but may not oppose EU membership or European integration per se. But the label is more frequently applied to *convinced opponents* of both European integration and the EU. Such people are sometimes described as 'Europhobes', but they would argue that opposition to the EU does not automatically equate with a dislike of Europe or of cooperation between European countries.

Alex Szczerbiak and Paul Taggart developed a distinction between 'hard Euroscepticism' and 'soft Euroscepticism' in their comparative study: A. Szczerbiak and P. Taggart (eds.), *Opposing Europe: The Comparative Politics of Euroscepticism* (Oxford: Oxford University Press, 2 vols., 2008). Hard Euroscepticism refers to parties that oppose the European integration project as embodied in the EU (i.e. in which powers are transferred to supranational institutions). Soft Eurosceptic parties are not opposed to the European integration project in principle but express qualified opposition to current or planned EU policies. This might be because EU policies are felt to be at odds with the national interest or the party's ideology.

In the British case, the UKIP was the main exponent of hard Euroscepticism, as the party proposed withdrawal from the EU, as did the Brexit party, formed by former UKIP leader Nigel Farage in 2019. The Conservative Party adopted a soft Eurosceptic position since 1997, opposing some existing EU policies (e.g. EMU membership) and the trajectory plotted for the EU by the Lisbon Treaty. However, a substantial number of Conservative MPs were hard Eurosceptics, supporting either withdrawal or a fundamental renegotiation of UK membership to restore parliamentary sovereignty and create a relationship with the EU based largely on free trade.

It is worth noting that the term 'pro-European' is also vague and potentially misleading. In the British context, relatively few 'pro-Europeans' favoured a federal EU state – or, since the eurozone sovereign debt crisis, EMU membership. The position held by most pro-European Conservatives was that the long-term political and economic advantages of constructive engagement with the integration process outweighed any short-term costs associated with the transfer of policy competences to the EU. Many Conservative pro-Europeans supported the sort of EU reforms (e.g. completion of the single market reform of the EU budget) favoured by soft Eurosceptics.

Controversy 13.1

The democratic deficit

The democratic deficit refers to the erosion of democratic accountability that occurs when decision-making authority is transferred from institutions that are directly accountable to ones that are not. National parliaments and voters are less able to hold decision-makers accountable when competences are transferred to the EU. The perceived distance between the EU and its citizens is another element of the democratic deficit. Citizens do not identify with or fully understand the EU and have opposed important developments in the integration process.

The EU has taken a number of steps to address the democratic deficit. It has increased the powers of the European Parliament, the EU's only democratically elected body. The *Spitzenkandidaten* process introduced in 2014 links the election of the President of the European Commission with the outcome of elections to the European Parliament. The candidate of the transnational political party that wins most seats in the European Parliament becomes the lead candidate for the post of Commission President, thus providing a closer link between the executive and voters. However, some integrationists advocate that the Commission President should be directly elected (mirroring a presidential system) or that the Commission should be dependent on majority support in the European Parliament (mirroring a parliamentary system).

The Lisbon Treaty also gave national parliaments a greater role in EU decision-making. Under the 'yellow card' system, if one-third of national parliamentary chambers issues a 'reasoned opinion' claiming that proposed EU legislation violates the principle of subsidiarity, the Commission must rethink its proposal and either withdraw, amend, or explain why it wishes to maintain it. A yellow card has been issued twice. The Commission dropped proposed legislation on the right to strike in 2012, but rejected a yellow card issued in 2013 against plans for a European Public Prosecutor.

The Lisbon Treaty also introduced the European Citizens' Initiative (ECI) under which one million citizens, who are nationals of at least a quarter of member states, can ask the Commission to launch a policy proposal in an area of EU competence. A number of ECIs have been proposed since 2012, the first of them on access to clean water leading to the Drinking Water Directive.

Some scholars have argued that the EU's democratic deficit is overstated. Andrew Moravcsik, in 'In Defence of the Democratic Deficit: Reassessing Legitimacy in the European Union' (*Journal of Common Market Studies*, Vol. 40, No. 4 (2002), pp. 603–34), argues that the EU's supranational institutions have greatest autonomy in technical matters (e.g. monetary policy, competition policy). Such issues are often decided by non-elected bodies (e.g. central banks) in nation-states as well as in the EU. Furthermore, the EU does not have great power over key redistributive policies such as taxation and social security. Finally, the EU system exhibits some of the checks and balances found in national democracies, with legislative power shared by the Council of the EU and the European Parliament.

The eurozone sovereign debt crisis, however, raised further questions about the democratic deficit. Technocratic governments were put in place in Italy and Greece when elected governments collapsed in 2011; then the EU insisted that Greece implement austerity measures despite voters signalling their opposition in a general election and a 2015 referendum.

that were contributors to the bailout funds. Eurosceptic parties on the radical Right and radical Left gained ground across the EU.

Integration theory

Neo-functionalism

a theory of integration that highlights the role played by supranational bodies and interest groups.

Two main theories explaining European integration have emerged in the political science literature: **neo-functionalism** and **intergovernmentalism**. Neo-functionalism was prevalent in the 1950s and 1960s. It held that interest groups and supranational bodies were the key actors in the integration process. Integration is dynamic: cooperation in one area (e.g. coal and steel) produces 'spillover' into other fields (e.g. trade). Neo-functionalists assumed that political and economic elites would then transfer their loyalties to supranational bodies. The theory fell out of favour in the 1970s when national governments reasserted their authority, but it was revived in the 1980s by scholars arguing that the Commission and business interests were responsible for pushing for the single market and EMU.

Intergovern-mentalism

a theory of integration that focuses on the dominant role played by national governments.

Intergovernmentalism affords leading actor status to nation-states: they determine the development of the EU by agreeing to cooperate in areas of mutual benefit but defend their sovereignty in other areas. This perspective argues that EMU came on the EC agenda because key member states saw it as being in their national interest, its precise make-up being decided through interstate bargaining. Liberal intergovernmentalism notes that prior to such negotiations, governments form their policy preferences in response to pressures from groups and institutions in the national arena. Critics argue that intergovernmentalism downplays the influence of supranational bodies and is more applicable as an explanation for 'history-making decisions' than routine policy formation. The European Council, and particularly large member states, have been predominant in decision-making on the long-running eurozone crisis, and the problem of mass migration from Syria and other war-torn territories.

Multilevel governance: an approach that highlights the roles played by supranational, national, and subnational institutions in decision-making.

Scholars were tiring of debates between neo-functionalists and intergovernmentalists by the 1990s and looked instead to frameworks that reflected the diversity and complexity of EU decision-making. **Multilevel governance** is one such approach. It recognises that a range of actors are involved in EU decision-making, their relative importance varying according to the policy areas concerned. National governments remain the most important players, for they have authority in major policy areas and are the main players in crucial decisions such as treaty change or defence. But they do not monopolise decision-making. Supranational bodies like the Commission have their own authority and are the most important actors in technical policy areas such as the single market. Subnational governments also play a role in decision-making, particularly in federal states such as Germany.

The UK and the European Union

The UK rejected invitations to become a founder member of both the ECSC and EEC, because first Clement Attlee's Labour government, then Anthony

Eden's Conservative administration, feared the loss of sovereignty it would entail. Policymakers of the time saw Britain operating within 'three circles': the Commonwealth, the 'special relationship' with the USA, and intergovernmental cooperation in Europe. They supported free trade rather than a customs union, with Britain forming the European Free Trade Association (EFTA) in 1960. Pro-European commentators argued that Britain 'missed the bus', losing out on a chance to shape the EEC from within. But it would be dangerous to assume that had it joined at the outset, Britain could have imposed its own agenda on the Six.

Harold Macmillan's Conservative government applied for EEC membership in 1961. The change in policy arose from a number of factors. The Commonwealth was of declining significance for Britain: trade with Commonwealth states had fallen and Britain's leadership within the organisation was being challenged. This mirrored the UK's waning influence in world affairs, as witnessed by the 1956 Suez debacle when American pressure curtailed British military action in Egypt (see Chapter 3). The EEC was developing successfully by the early 1960s, raising fears that Britain would be left behind. Macmillan saw EEC membership as essential to Britain's modernisation. Crucially, he also came under pressure from the Kennedy administration, which made it clear that Britain would only remain America's main ally in Europe if it entered the Community.

TIMELINE 13.1

The UK and European integration

1950	Attlee government rejects invitation to participate in ECSC
1955	British delegate withdraws from the Spaak Committee discussions on the creation of the EEC
1957	Treaty of Rome establishes the EEC
1960	UK and six other states form EFTA
1961	Macmillan government applies for EEC membership
1963	De Gaulle vetoes UK membership application
1967	Wilson government launches second membership application; it is again vetoed by de Gaulle
1970	EEC begins membership talks with UK (now led by Heath government)
1971	EEC membership negotiations concluded and ratified by parliament
1973	UK joins the EEC
1975	67 per cent 'yes' vote in referendum on renegotiated membership terms
1984	Fontainebleau summit settles the British budgetary question
1985	Thatcher government agrees to the Single European Act
1989	Thatcher's 'Bruges speech' rejects EMU and political union
1990	UK joins the exchange rate mechanism
1991	Major government agrees to Maastricht Treaty; UK has 'opt-out' on EMU

1992	UK leaves the exchange rate mechanism
1993	Maastricht Treaty ratified despite Eurosceptic rebellions in the House of Commons
1997	Blair government agrees to Amsterdam Treaty but rules out joining euro until five economic tests are met
2000	Blair government agrees to Treaty of Nice
2003	Blair government announces that five economic tests for euro entry have not been met
2004	Blair government agrees to EU Constitutional Treaty
2007	Blair government agrees to Lisbon Treaty, which is later signed by Prime Minister Gordon Brown
2011	Coalition government refuses to sign up to an EU fiscal compact treaty
2016	Referendum held in June delivers a 52-48 vote (on a 72 per cent turnout) in favour of the UK leaving the EU. David Cameron resigns within hours of the result being announced.
2019	The 'Withdrawal Agreement' presented to Parliament by Theresa May (Cameron's successor), detailing how the UK was to leave the EU, and what its future relationship would be, suffers repeated defeats in the House of Commons, with many Conservative MPs believing that it did not go far enough in heralding a clear or clean break with the EU. A few pro-European Conservatives quit the Party altogether, to sit as Independents. In the summer, Theresa May resigns and is replaced by Boris Johnson, who then leads the Conservatives to an emphatic victory in a general election in December, in which his main campaign pledge is to 'get Brexit done'.
2020	On 31 January, the UK officially ceases to be a member of the EU, although details of future trade relationships are still to be negotiated, as are the rights of EU citizens in the UK, and British citizens in the EU, and how trade will be conducted between Ireland and Northern Ireland ('the backstop').

The 1961 membership application is sometimes presented as a volte-face in British policy. But in reality, the government hoped to secure some of its traditional objectives within the EEC. Britain did not abandon its opposition to supranationalism, but hoped to promote its vision of an intergovernmental EEC more effectively and to defend its sovereignty from within the EEC. The USA would remain the major strategic ally, and special arrangements for Commonwealth trade were negotiated. However, de Gaulle vetoed the application in 1963, citing Britain's Atlantic, rather than European, outlook. Labour Prime Minister Harold Wilson reapplied in 1967 for similar reasons and met the same fate.

Membership negotiations proved successful under Edward Heath's Conservative government in 1970–71, by which time de Gaulle had departed from the scene. Heath was the most pro-European of British prime ministers and had been chief negotiator at the time of the 1961 application. Now the UK secured a number of concessions, but after joining the EEC in 1973, it quickly gained a reputation as an 'awkward partner'. Harold Wilson extracted further concessions in 1974–75, but there remained discontent about the size of the

UK contribution to the EEC budget. Largely to appease a divided cabinet, in 1975, Wilson called a referendum on continued membership, which produced a decisive 'yes' vote (see Chapter 19).

The Thatcher and Major governments

Margaret Thatcher's Conservative government continued efforts to reduce Britain's budget contributions and reform the CAP, her bruising campaign eventually bearing fruit at the 1984 Fontainebleau summit. Attention was by then turning to the single market, with Britain a leading proponent as the removal of barriers to free trade dovetailed with the Thatcherite commitment to the free market and cutting bureaucracy. Thatcher duly signed the SEA despite her hostility to the institutional reforms it entailed. By the late 1980s, Thatcher was a staunch opponent of further integration, opposing the Social Charter and EMU, which she viewed as anathema to the free market and national sovereignty. Thatcher's uncompromising attitude, expressed memorably in a 1988 speech in Bruges which rallied Conservative Eurosceptics, provoked divisions within her cabinet that contributed to her own downfall in 1990.

John Major had been instrumental in taking Britain into the ERM in the final weeks of Thatcher's premiership. On becoming prime minister, he promised a more constructive approach in the EC but was determined to preserve sovereignty in key areas and resist pressure to join a single currency. He presented the Maastricht Treaty as a good deal for Britain: the UK had an EMU opt-out, had not signed up to the Social Agreement, and had ensured intergovernmental cooperation on foreign policy and immigration. Sterling's forced exit from the ERM on 'Black Wednesday' in 1992 undermined Major's position and fuelled Eurosceptic opposition to EMU (see Case study 13.2). Yet Major maintained his non-committal 'wait and see' policy, believing that it was in Britain's interest to decide on EMU entry only when the economic situation at the launch of Stage III was clear (Photo 13.1).

Major found it increasingly difficult to rally his party behind an agreed position on Europe and to influence the direction of European integration at a time when Britain's minimalist approach left it in a minority in the EU. Policy became more Eurosceptic in tone and substance. Major threatened to veto institutional reform and pursued a short-lived policy of non-cooperation (blocking proposed legislation) in 1996, after the EU banned British beef exports during the BSE crisis. His vision of a flexible Europe in which states could opt out of new areas of EU activity won little support.

The Blair and Brown governments

New Labour came to power in 1997, promising to play a positive, leading role in the EU. Within weeks, the Blair government had agreed to the Amsterdam Treaty. Blair accepted greater use of QMV in both the Amsterdam and Nice Treaties but continued to defend unanimity on issues of 'vital national interest' such as taxation, treaty change, and defence. In negotiations on the EU constitution, Britain proposed a greater role for the European Council and national Parliaments. Blair downplayed the significance of the Constitutional Treaty, claiming that it did not 'alter the fundamental constitutional relationship' between Britain and the EU, but he bowed to political pressure and agreed to hold a referendum on it. During the 2005 UK presidency of the EU, Blair accepted a reduction in the size of the British budget rebate in return for a future review of EU spending.

Case study 13.2

'Black Wednesday' 1992

16 September 1992 ('Black Wednesday') was one of the most dramatic and significant days in recent British political history. It was the day on which sterling was forced out of the ERM. For months, sterling had been close to the bottom of the permitted ERM bands of fluctuation. Media reports on the morning of 16 September that Germany wanted sterling to be devalued pushed its value down, forcing the Major government to intervene by buying sterling on the foreign exchange markets (at a cost of £3.7 billion) and twice raising interest rates (from 10 per cent to 12 per cent and then 15 per cent). These measures were unsuccessful, and the government was forced to suspend sterling's membership of the ERM. It would never rejoin.

The events had long-term repercussions. The Conservative Party's reputation for economic competence was shattered and its opinion poll ratings plummeted, remaining low for more than a decade. Britain's position in the EU was also affected: relations with Germany were damaged, and Eurosceptic opposition to the single currency was reinforced. Treasury papers show that, soon after Black Wednesday, civil servants judged the 1990 decision to join the ERM to have been a mistake which was made for political reasons without due consideration to the impact of German unification, moves towards EMU, or the state of the British economy. But such verdicts were made with the benefit of hindsight – in 1990, the main parties, financial institutions, businesses, and trade unions supported ERM entry. John Major and his Chancellor, Norman Lamont, recognised subsequently the political damage and short-term economic pain that ERM membership caused but argued that it was the key factor in squeezing inflation out of the British economy.

PHOTO 13.1 'Yes but no': Mrs Thatcher began her spell as Conservative leader (1975–90) as a pro-European but ended it as a Eurosceptic (© P. Floyd/Daily Express/Hulton Archive/Getty Images).

The Labour government signed up to the Social Agreement (now properly called the Social Chapter) at Amsterdam but opposed the further extension of EU competence in social policy. Britain was a main architect of an EU employment strategy that balanced labour market flexibility with effective social protection, echoing Blair's domestic 'third way' approach. Blair supported the 'Lisbon Agenda' measures which aimed to improve competitiveness and develop a 'knowledge-based' economy. But economic growth in the eurozone was sluggish, unemployment high, and the targets of 20 million extra jobs and annual economic growth of 3 per cent appeared overambitious.

At Amsterdam, the Blair government maintained Britain's traditional opposition to supranational authority in foreign and defence policy, although Europe's relative inaction during the conflict in Kosovo convinced Blair that the EU must develop a more effective defence and security role. The 1998 Anglo-French St Malo initiative signalled Britain's new willingness to support a greater EU defence role. Britain became an agenda-setter, supporting the Nice Treaty provision for a European Security and Defence Policy. This allowed the EU to deploy rapid reaction forces in conflict prevention and crisis management situations where NATO chose not to act. But divisions between member states over the US-led invasion of Iraq in 2003 damaged Britain's international standing and dashed hopes that the EU could develop a common policy.

EMU was one of the most important issues in British politics in the 1990s. Supporters of EMU entry claimed that it would bring economic benefits such as low inflation and low interest rates, and would enhance British influence in the EU. Opponents argued that the British economy differed from those of other member states and that if the UK economy ran into trouble after joining EMU, the government would be left with few policy options given that interest rates would be set by the ECB. In October 1997, Chancellor Gordon Brown announced that Britain would not join the single currency during Labour's first term in office, although the government would later consider British membership of the eurozone if the economic conditions were right. Labour had no constitutional objection to entry, though it would hold a referendum to seek popular approval for any cabinet decision to join. Brown set five 'economic tests' against which entry would be judged:

- sustainable convergence between the British economy and those of the eurozone;
- sufficient economic flexibility;
- the impact on investment in the UK;
- the impact on financial services; and
- the impact on employment.

Detailed targets were not specified, allowing the government also to take account of the bigger political picture. Should the tests be met and a referendum 'yes' vote secured, the changeover to the euro could be achieved within two years. In June 2003, Brown announced that the cabinet had decided against adopting the euro, with only one of the tests having been met. In its detailed reports, the Treasury concluded that the UK economy had not sufficiently converged with those of the eurozone. The comparatively high level of home ownership in the UK meant that high interest rates in the eurozone could destabilise the British housing market. Nor was the UK economy judged flexible enough to withstand economic problems in the eurozone. The employment and foreign investment tests were not met, though they would be once greater convergence had been achieved. The financial services test was met, with the City of London prospering outside the eurozone.

Despite the appearance of rational decision-making, policy on EMU was shaped primarily by political considerations and by the strained relationship between Blair and Brown. Brown was very cautious about EMU, wary of the impact membership would have on a British economy enjoying low inflation and increased public spending. Blair was instinctively more positive, viewing EMU membership as essential to full British engagement in the Union, but recognised that he had lost the battle.

The fallout from the 2003 invasion of Iraq and the Treasury's negative verdict on euro entry were body-blows to Blair's European policy. But a recovery followed. British influence increased as Blair found new allies in Commission President Barroso (from 2004), German Chancellor Angela Merkel (2005), and French President Sarkozy (2007), who backed British positions on climate change, development policy, and energy security. The French and Dutch referendum 'no' votes spared Blair a difficult referendum on the Constitutional Treaty and allowed him to argue for the less ambitious Lisbon Treaty.

Brown was not instinctively as pro-European as Blair, but his period in office saw little discernible change in policy towards the EU. Climate change, competitiveness, and economic reform remained key planks of British policy. Brown followed his predecessor in refusing to hold a referendum on the Lisbon Treaty, arguing that it did not have the constitutional significance of the failed Constitutional Treaty.

Cameron's coalition and Conservative governments

Tensions between the soft Eurosceptic Conservative Party and pro-European Liberal Democrats were only partially resolved in coalition negotiations that saw the former drop manifesto commitments to repatriate policy competences and the latter accept that there would be no further transfers of power to the EU during the parliament. The European Union Act 2011 introduced a 'referendum lock' requiring future treaties transferring powers from the UK to the EU to be put to a binding referendum. A referendum would also be held if, for example, the UK joined the euro or abolished border controls. But, because the coalition refused to take part in further EU integration, no referendum was required during its term in office. The Act also strengthened requirements for parliamentary approval of EU action and restated that EU law only takes effect in the UK through the will of Parliament.

The eurozone sovereign debt crisis emerged as the dominant issue in the EU. The coalition accepted that eurozone states should strengthen EMU in order to resolve the crisis, but the UK would not take part in these measures or contribute significantly towards bailouts. Cameron vetoed an EU fiscal compact treaty at a European Council meeting in December 2011 when his demands for additional safeguards on the single market and financial services were rejected, but he subsequently accepted that 25 member states (not the UK or Czech Republic) could sign an intergovernmental Treaty on Stability, Coordination and Governance. The coalition sought guarantees that further integration in the eurozone would neither undermine the single market nor discriminate against non-euro states. It secured a system of double majority voting in the European Banking Authority under which proposals require support from a majority of both eurozone and non-euro states and launched a series of legal challenges in the ECJ.

The coalition had a mixed record in building alliances and shaping EU policy. It helped bring about the first real-term cut in the EU budget for 2014–20 and exercised a block opt-out from 100 police and criminal justice measures (although it opted back in to 35 measures, including the European Arrest Warrant). The coalition supported EU measures to strengthen the single market, improve competitiveness, and negotiate a Transatlantic Trade and Investment Partnership (TTIP) with the United States. But Cameron's fiscal compact veto and attempt to block Juncker's nomination as Commission president frustrated other member states without delivering great reward. Overall, the UK was less influential in the EU at the end of the coalition's term in office than it had been at the outset.

In 2013, Cameron suddenly announced that if the Conservatives won the 2015 general election, he would seek to negotiate a 'new settlement' for the UK in the EU and would then hold an in-out referendum by the end of 2017, although he made it clear that he would campaign for the UK to remain in the EU. Cameron identified several objectives for EU reform. Some were limited and relatively uncontentious, such as a reduction in red tape, greater free trade, and national Parliaments being able to work together to block EU legislation. But other objectives were more far reaching. The goal of 'powers flowing away from Brussels' might encompass policy repatriation (reclaiming), while exempting the UK from 'ever-closer union' might have required Treaty change. Most controversial was Cameron's desire to restrict the right of EU migrants to claim welfare benefits as, although some states shared British concerns, they would not countenance the undermining of the principle of free movement.

Cameron had pledged a referendum on the UK's continued membership of the EU for five main reasons. First, he hoped that such a promise would contain or manage the growing divisions in the parliamentary Conservative Party over the EU, for its MPs were increasingly divided between those 'hard Eurosceptics' who wanted complete UK withdrawal and independence, and 'soft Eurosceptics' who ultimately preferred the UK to remain a member, but with renegotiation of the terms and conditions of that membership, so that it was looser or more flexible. Some YouGov polls indicated that a majority of the public would also vote in favour of remaining in the EU if a 'better deal' (however defined) could be secured for the UK. Second, but following directly on from this, in the period between making this pledge and the referendum, Cameron undertook a series of meetings with other EU leaders, to seek the changes to the UK's terms of membership which he believed would persuade many Eurosceptics that the UK now had a better deal, and that it should therefore remain a member. Third, Cameron was understandably anxious about the growing electoral threat posed by UKIP, led by the charismatic Nigel Farage. Although UKIP threatened to attract support from both main parties, it was widely acknowledged that it was the Conservatives who were likely to lose most support, and hence Cameron hoped to pre-empt this scenario by pledging both a referendum after the next election (due in 2015), and to renegotiate the terms and conditions of the UK's membership. Fourth, Cameron was confident that he could persuade a majority of people to vote Remain (in the EU), this confidence seemingly derived from his strong self-belief, and perceived charm and rhetorical eloquence; he would convince people to trust him and follow his lead in voting Remain. Fifth, Cameron seemed to expect that the apparent 'conservatism' of the UK's people (their dislike or fear of change and radicalism) would foster support for maintaining the status quo – *remaining* in the EU, rather than the leap into the unknown which voting Leave supposedly represented.

However, Cameron evidently overestimated his own charisma and powers of persuasion, and also discovered that renegotiating the UK's terms and conditions of EU membership was more difficult than he had originally envisaged; other EU leaders were less amenable or willing to granting the concessions that Cameron had hoped for. Furthermore, during the referendum campaign itself in May–June 2016, Cameron and fellow 'Remainers' found that they were advancing somewhat 'dry' economic or abstract arguments in favour of continued UK membership, whereas the 'Leave' campaign was more emotive or visceral in its appeal; it appealed to people's guts or feelings, rather than their intellects or logic. In other words, while the Remain campaign highlighted the apparent benefits, to the UK economy and people's prosperity, of continued EU membership – arguments which were undermined by the fact that the UK had experienced six years of austerity, unemployment, stagnant wages and living conditions, and underfunded public services under Cameron's leadership – the Leave campaign prioritised issues such as curbing immigration via the 'free movement of people' (especially migrant workers from countries like Poland, which had joined the EU in 2004) and restoring parliamentary sovereignty. These enjoyed an emotive appeal, reinforced by the slogan (apparently coined by one Dominic Cummings) 'Take Back Control', which clearly conveyed the message that by leaving the EU, the UK would regain a long-lost status as a free and independent sovereign nation-state, which could henceforth make all of its own decisions, in its own interests, and agree trade deals with whoever it wanted to, on terms that it had freely and voluntarily negotiated.

The 2016 referendum result

On a turnout of 72 per cent, the 23 June 2016 referendum, asking people 'Should the United Kingdom remain a member of the European Union or leave the European Union?', delivered a 52-48 vote in favour of leaving the EU, yielding the commonly used portmanteau term 'Brexit' – **Brit**ain's (or **Brit**ish) **Exit** from the EU. Two particular features of the result were notable: the geographical distribution, and the demographics, of Leave and Remain voters. As Table 13.2 illustrates, while England and Wales voted to Leave, Scotland and Northern Ireland voted to Remain. Within England itself, though, there were also notable variations in the pattern of support. Most of the towns and cities with the highest Leave vote were in the Eastern half of England, with Boston (Lincolnshire) recording 75.6 per cent in favour of the UK's withdrawal from the EU. Other 'Eastern' towns in which over two-thirds of residents voted to Leave the EU included Great Yarmouth (71.5 per cent), Mansfield (70.9 per cent), Hartlepool (69.6 per cent), Doncaster (69.0 per cent), Basildon (68.6 per cent), Barnsley (68.3 per cent), and Harlow (68.1 per cent).

By contrast, the highest levels of 'Remain' support were in parts of London, and a few notably affluent, bohemian, or 'student' cities in southern or southeast England. Lambeth led the Remain vote, with 78.6 per cent of its residents voting for continued UK membership of the EU. Other boroughs and cities where more than two-thirds of residents voted Remain included Hackney (78.5 per cent), Islington (75.2 per cent), Camden 74.9 per cent), Cambridge (73.8 per cent), Oxford (70.3 per cent), Richmond-upon-Thames (69.3 per cent), and Brighton and Hove

TABLE 13.2 Result of the 2016 EU referendum, by UK regions – votes (% in brackets)

	Leave	Remain	Turnout (%)
UK overall	17,410,742 (51.9)	16,141,241 (48.1)	72.2
England	15,188,406 (53.4)	13,266,996 (46.6)	73.0
Scotland	1,018,322 (38.0)	1,661,191 (62.0)	67.2
Wales	854,572 (52.5)	772,347 (47.5)	71.7
Northern Ireland	349,442 (44.2)	440,707 (55.8)	62.7
London	1,513,232 (40.1)	2,263,519 (59.9)	69.7
South East	2,567,965 (51.8)	2,391,718 (48.2)	76.8
Eastern England	1,880,367 (56.5)	1,448,616 (43.5)	75.7
East Midlands	1,475,479 (58.8)	1,033,036 (41.2)	74.2
Yorkshire/Humberside	1,580,937 (57.7)	1,158,298 (42.3)	70.7
North East	778,103 (58.0)	562,595 (42.0)	69.3
North West	1,966,925 (53.7)	1,699,020 (46.3)	70.0
West Midlands	1,755,687 (59.3)	1,207,175 (40.7)	72.0
South West	1,669,711 (52.6)	1,503,019 (47.4)	76.7

Source: Electoral Commission, 'Results and turnout at the EU referendum', https://www.electoralcommission. org.uk/who-we-are-and-what-we-do/elections-and-referendums/past-elections-and-referendums/eu-referendum/results-and-turnout-eu-referendum.

TABLE 13.3 Social characteristics of Leave and Remain supporters in the 2016 EU referendum

Characteristics	Leave	Remain
Party supported in 2015 election		
Conservative	61	39
Labour	35	65
Liberal Democrat	32	68
UKIP	95	5
Green	20	80
Age cohort		
18–24	29	71
25–49	46	54
50–64	60	40
65+	64	36
Educational qualifications		
GSCE or lower	70	30
A-Level	50	50
Higher below degree	52	48
Degree	68	32

Source: YouGov, available at https://yougov.co.uk/topics/politics/articles-reports/2016/06/27/how-britain-voted.

(68.6 per cent). Beyond London and the south/southeast, the highest Remain vote was in Edinburgh (74.4 per cent).

These geographical patterns closely reflected the wider social characteristics of Leave and Remain voters. As Table 13.3 shows, those who voted for the UK to Leave the EU tended to be older, poorer, and have few, if any, educational qualifications. These aspects are often interlinked or mutually reinforcing. Lack of educational qualifications often leads to lower-paid or more insecure employment, and many old people did not have the opportunity or encouragement to go to university when they were young. In the 1950s, only 3 per cent of the British population attended university: the vast majority left school at 14 or 15 (not until 1972–73 was the school-leaving age raised to 16), and thereafter worked and lived in the same town or city they had been born and raised in. Moving away to London or/and travelling for a year or two, before starting a career, was not an option for the vast majority of people, and besides it is only in the last couple of decades or so that cheap travel has become widely available. Furthermore, many of today's pensioners grew-up in an era when women were widely expected to become wives and mothers, rather than pursue careers of their own and thereupon become financially independent of men, and so very few women were encouraged to go to university.

These sections of society tend to constitute the 'left-behind' – citizens who live in towns, often in the north of England and the South Wales' valleys, which have been most affected by the loss of jobs in coal mining, manufacturing, and textiles since the 1980s (what is referred to as 'deindustrialisation' – see Chapter 4). As a Joseph Rowntree report on who voted for Brexit (and why they did so) highlighted, 'support for Brexit was strongest in areas where a large percentage of the population did not have any qualifications, and were ill-equipped to thrive amid a post-industrial and increasingly competitive economy', one which 'favours those with skills and is operating in the broader context of globalisation'.[1]

Others, though, live in parts of Eastern England (as we saw in Table 13.2), where there has long been a lack of secure or well-paid employment, and thus high levels of socio-economic deprivation, and where resentment at 'migrant workers' from EU countries has grown in recent years. When some East European countries joined, the EU expanded in 2004 and 2007, their citizens acquired the right to live and work in other member states (where wages were often higher), in accordance with the EU's 'free movement of labour'. However, this increasingly caused resentment among the local or indigenous population of the 'host' nations, where such workers, often from Poland and Romania, were often blamed for taking jobs from local British workers or driving-down wages. This hostility towards East European migrant workers increased enormously following the 2008 global financial crash, when widespread job losses, wage freezes, or pay cuts often followed. Then, when the coalition government imposed austerity policies from 2010 onwards, these migrant workers were often blamed for causing or exacerbating the strain on underfunded, overstretched, public services: longer NHS waiting lists, overcrowded classrooms, lack of affordable housing, and so forth.

As a consequence, immigration was the factor most commonly cited as the main reason for voting Leave in 2016: that only by leaving the EU could the UK regain control of its borders and no longer have to accept the 'free movement of labour'. Indeed, some studies have shown that it was not necessarily the actual number of immigrants in an area which fuelled support for Leave, but how quickly or recently the influx of migrants had occurred. In other words, it was where the number of immigrants had increased considerably in the previous ten years or so (since Poland and some other East European countries had joined the EU) that resentment towards migrant workers was strongest, and often underpinned support for Leave in the referendum.

For many of these Leave voters, the EU was viewed either an irrelevance, because it had apparently done nothing to stop or reverse the loss of jobs in recent years which had decimated many livelihoods and local communities, or as a significant cause of unemployment and low wages via the 'free movement of labour', as we have just noted. This is a major reason why the Remain campaign's warnings of the economic damage which would result from leaving the EU failed to convince Leave voters, many of whom dismissed such claims as 'Project Fear'; many Leave voters took the view that life outside the EU could hardly be any worse than it already was, but might actually improve if more, or better-paid, jobs became available once the 'free movement of labour' was stopped.

In stark contrast, those who wanted to Remain in the EU were younger, had higher incomes, and had more or –higher – educational qualifications. Again, there is a correlation between qualifications and incomes, because those with university degrees tend to pursue relatively well-paid careers and professions. At the same time, younger people are much more likely to have a degree because of the relatively recent expansion of higher education, and thus more opportunities to attend university than were available to their grandparents. It is also the case that in the modern post-industrial 'knowledge economy', many more jobs stipulate that a degree is essential. Another reason why younger people might have been much more supportive of the UK remaining in the EU is that many of them will have travelled, perhaps on a 'gap year' before going to university, or at least visited more countries and cities than their grandparents had the opportunities to do when they were young. As such, the world beyond the UK and 'foreigners' are not the source of suspicion or fear that they are for some older people, many of whom seem to have nostalgic memories (not necessarily accurate) of 'Great' Britain before it joined the EEC in 1973 and/or of immigration, and who maybe think that 'the country has gone to the dogs' ever since: 'if only we could turn back the clock to the good old days'. Following on from this last point, younger people will have grown up with the UK as an EU member state, and so be unlikely to hark back to a supposedly Golden Age, such as the 1950s, when life was supposedly better or simpler, before the UK joined the EEC. Instead, many young people will have viewed EU membership as 'normal' – indeed, something which was hardly an issue, and certainly not a problem. After all, the problems faced by many younger people, such as graduate debt, zero-hours-contracts, and unaffordable housing, are hardly the fault of the EU.

Post-referendum developments

Although the referendum had been conducted in June 2016, the UK did not actually leave the EU until 31 January 2020. The three-and-a half years in between had been characterised by bitter arguments over the actual options for, and details of, the UK's departure, in terms of its economic ties and trading relationship with the EU once it had ceased to be a formal member – arguments between both Conservatives and Labour, and, perhaps more importantly, within them, particularly the Conservative Party. Indeed, many of the Conservatives strongest opponents of the EU, usually on the Right of the party, suspected that the lengthy delay between the referendum vote and actually leaving the EU was due to deliberate delaying tactics by 'Remainers', who apparently hoped that the longer it took to negotiate the details of Brexit, the less likely it was the UK would actually Leave. In effect, many 'Leavers' were convinced that Remainers (or 'Remoaners' as they were often called, due to their apparent refusal to accept the legitimacy of the referendum result) were sabotaging Brexit in defiance of 'the will of the people', as symbolised by the 52-48 vote in favour of Leave. To those Leave supporters who strongly suspected such subterfuge against Brexit, this was further proof of 'arrogance' and 'elitism' by pro-Europeans, who were accused of treating Leave voters with contempt and allegedly viewing them as ignorant and racist. In this respect, Leave versus Remain became a surrogate 'culture war' between community-focused, small-town conservatives (often small 'c') and patriots on the one hand, and cosmopolitan, urban, liberals, and internationalists on the other, that is, citizens of somewhere versus citizens of nowhere, it was sometimes claimed or, rather more crudely, according to some on the Right, traditionalists versus traitors (Photo 13.2).

With David Cameron resigning on the morning that the referendum result was announced, Theresa May became Conservative leader and prime minister, and thus assumed political responsibility for leading the negotiations over precisely how Brexit was to be achieved – what sort of relationship would the UK establish with the EU after formally leaving. Those MPs, from all parties, who had voted Remain generally wanted the UK to foster a close working relationship

PHOTO 13.2 Brexit party: Celebrations on 31 January 2020 as the UK learns it will leave the EU (© Anthony Devlin/Getty Images).

with the EU after Brexit, with numerous trade deals envisaged; they wanted to retain as many economic and diplomatic ties as were practicably possible as a non-member. However, more hard-line Eurosceptic Conservative MPs feared that this would undermine Brexit – and suspected that this was precisely what their Remain-voting colleagues were intending. Hence, many staunchly pro-Brexit Conservative MPs were much less concerned about maintaining close and cordial links with the EU, and as such, they wanted May and her ministers to adopt a tough stance when negotiating with European leaders over the UK's future relationship. Some of the most trenchant pro-Brexit Conservatives were willing to walk away with 'No Deal' if the EU failed or refused to offer the deals they wanted, or demanded too much in return. Some of this hard-line stance was driven by 'populist' politics, and a desire to impress Leave voters that they would not be betrayed (even though the referendum had not asked about the type of 'Leave' they wanted), but it also reflected a sanguine assumption that, 'free' from ties with the EU, the UK could deploy its new independence and sovereignty to secure new trade deals with countries anywhere in the world; if need be, Britain could 'go it alone'. Indeed, in this particular regard, some of the most hard-line Conservative Brexiters claimed that, instead of being the insular 'Little Englanders' that Remainers accused them of, they were actually the true internationalists, looking enthusiastically and optimistically to the world far beyond Europe.

The Labour Party was also divided over Brexit, although as it was in Opposition, its divisions were less debilitating than those of the Conservatives, although it did mean that Labour's criticisms of the May government's stance were sometimes opaque or ambiguous. Many Labour MPs had voted Remain in the 2016 referendum, and therefore hoped for a 'soft Brexit', whereby the UK retained a close relationship with the EU after formal departure, with numerous economic and diplomatic ties being maintained or re-established. Some Labour Remainers even hoped that as negotiations between the May government and the EU dragged on over the (often highly-complex) details of leaving the EU, support for Brexit would diminish, and that a second referendum might be held which might produce a different outcome, namely, a vote to Remain in the EU. This hope derived from the anticipation that some of those who voted Leave in June 2016 would change their minds if and when the predicted costs (in terms of fewer jobs and lower living standards) materialised, as firms relocated to mainland Europe as a consequence of Brexit, and also the UK's demographics changed: put crudely, each year would see some of the older Leave voters pass away, while young voters would reach voting age, and presumably (mostly) support Remain.

However, there were also many pro-Remain Labour MPs who felt that they should now fully support Brexit, because their constituencies had voted Leave; to continue opposing Leave would be a betrayal of the wishes of a majority of their constituents, the 'will of the local people'. To have defied the views of their local constituents would have been viewed as sheer arrogance and of being out-of-touch, as well as making it more likely that the MP would lose support at the next general election – a particularly pertinent consideration for those Labour MPs in marginal seats where a small swing could see another party secure victory.

To complicate matters, some Labour MPs either supported, or were strongly suspected of supporting, Brexit – including the then leader, Jeremy Corbyn. There had long been a strand on the Labour Left which viewed the EEC/EU as a 'capitalist club', part of a neoliberal 'project' to entrench the principles and practices of competition, deregulation, free trade, and 'flexibility', and, in so doing, serve the interests and increase the power and privileges of big business, while doing little, if anything, for ordinary working people in Europe. Many on the Left also assumed that EU membership, and further integration, would hinder a future Labour government's pursuit of 'socialist' policies, such as nationalisation, industrial subsidies, and import controls, although other member states (even those with conservative governments) have some publicly owned industries and utilities, most notably railways. Corbyn thus equivocated, refusing to state clearly whether he was personally in favour of Remain or Leave, or even a second referendum, but instead argued that Labour would fight to secure 'a jobs Brexit' – whatever that meant. However, his equivocation was partly understandable in terms of Labour's electoral base, because while a majority of Labour voters (in the 2017 general election) had voted to Remain in the 2016 referendum, a sizeable minority of the Party's supporters had voted Leave. To a large extent, this reflected the two distinct sources of Labour Party support: its traditional working class supporters, often in northern towns and the South Wales valleys, who were often economically Left-leaning but socially conservative (and in England) nationalist, and the Party's middle-class voters who were often in graduate jobs in the public sector or creative industries, were socially liberal or 'progressive', and equated (English) nationalism with xenophobia and racism. By 2019, this unholy alliance was torn asunder, as some of Labour's 2017 working-class supporters switched to the Conservatives, while some of its erstwhile younger middle-class graduate voters turned to the Liberal Democrats or Greens instead.

Due to these different attitudes and approaches to Brexit, Theresa May struggled in vain to secure a parliamentary majority to ratify her 599-page Withdrawal Agreement,[2] which had been agreed with other EU leaders in November 2018, after 524 days of negotiations. May's own authority had been damaged by her failure to lead the Conservatives to a clear victory in the 2017 general election. Much of the Withdrawal Agreement comprised of administratively and technically complex – albeit very important – details and legalities, but opposition to it crystallised around three main issues:

- The 'transition period': to operate for one year after the UK's formal exit from the EU, but could be extended by a further year or two, by mutual agreement. The UK would retain most of the current benefits of EU membership in terms of trade, while new deals were being negotiated and businesses adapted, but would no longer play a role in EU decision-taking and rule-making.
- The 'divorce settlement': how much money the UK would have to pay the EU for current or ongoing commitments from which the UK benefits (or has recently benefitted), and how much would have to be paid if the 'transition period' was extended. Citizens' rights: for how long, and on what basis, would EU nationals living and working in the UK, and UK citizens living and working in EU countries, be permitted to continue living and working in their 'host' country. To what extent would 'freedom of movement' continue? If the UK eventually decided to expel all EU citizens as part of 'taking back control' or 'reclaiming our borders' (as some 'hard Brexiters' wanted), other EU states could retaliate by 'sending home' the many Brits who have moved (often retired) to France and Spain.
- The 'Northern Irish backstop': as the Irish Republic and Northern Ireland (as part of the UK) were both EU member states, people and goods could move freely between them, thus effectively making the border much less important than it was prior to the 1998 Good Friday Agreement (see Chapter 12). However, when the UK (and thus Northern Ireland) left the EU, border controls and checkpoints would need to be reintroduced between Ireland and Northern Ireland, unless some special arrangement could be agreed between London, Belfast, Dublin, and Brussels which somehow avoided a 'hard border' between the two Irelands, which, in turn, might renew the hostilities which existed between many Catholics/Nationalists and Protestants/Unionists prior to 1998.

May suffered several serious parliamentary defeats during late 2018 and early 2019, due to opposition from sections of the Conservative Party over her Withdrawal Agreement, with many of her MPs fearing that the UK would remain too closely tied to the EU – a kind of twilight zone in which it is neither an EU member nor a genuinely independent sovereign nation-state. The most trenchant opposition came from the 'hard Brexiters' on the Right of the Conservative Party, often via the European Research Group (ERG) led, at the time, by Jacob Rees-Mogg. As well as suffering several humiliating parliamentary defeats over her Withdrawal Agreement, May also saw several cabinet ministers resign, which obviously further weakened her political authority. It was not really surprising that in the summer of 2019, she finally resigned, and thereby paved the way for Boris Johnson to become Conservative leader and prime minister. Much of his appeal, both during the Conservative leadership context and in the 2019 general election, was that he would 'get Brexit done', even if that meant walking away from the EU without any deal whatsoever. His tough, no-nonsense stance and rhetoric strongly appealed to Eurosceptic MPs (and Party members) and also, in December 2019, to many Leave voters who were frustrated at the repeated delays to securing Brexit – delays which they attributed to a supposedly pro-Remain liberal elite and Establishment which had consistently conspired to deny 'the will of the people' as expressed in the 2016 referendum. Having led the Conservatives to a landslide victory in the 2019 general election, Johnson 'delivered' the UK's formal departure from the EU on 31 January, although this still left the details of the UK's future trading relationship, beyond the one-year transition period, to be negotiated during the rest of 2020. However, shortly after the UK had officially left the EU, Johnson's government found itself almost wholly preoccupied with the COVID-19 global pandemic (with Johnson himself being hospitalised by the virus) which brought much of Britain to a two-month standstill. The urgency of tackling the pandemic left ministers and senior officials with little time to devote to negotiating the UK's post-transition period relationship with (but outside) the EU, and in the early summer of 2020, it looked increasingly likely that the transition period would need to be extended.

An 'awkward partner'

In a key study of British policy in the EU, Stephen George described Britain as *An Awkward Partner* (Oxford: Oxford University Press, 3rd edition, 1998). George was not claiming that Britain was the only country to fight for its national interest within the EU, but that it was less enthusiastic about integration than most member states and more likely to hold a minority position. Successive British governments had been wary of, or hostile to, proposals for further integration. Rather than having a long-term vision, they had often acted pragmatically, reacting to proposals rather than setting the agenda. Britain preferred intergovernmental cooperation to supranational authority, the single market to EMU, and incremental reform of EU procedures to political union.

British influence was less pronounced than that of other large member states, notably France and Germany. The Thatcher and Major governments did not set the agenda on EMU, but reacted to proposals from other states by trying to slow the pace of integration or minimise its impact. This is not to say that the UK was unimportant in big EU decisions. The UK was an influential supporter of the single market, though it proposed a minimalist approach to institutional reform. The Blair government was also an influential player in EU defence, immigration, and social policy. But the UK had not forged durable alliances with like-minded states across a range of issues, developing instead a series of one-off agreements with member states on single issues. The Blair governments established bilateral links as a basis for joint initiatives, for example, with France on defence policy, Germany on social policy, and Italy on tackling illegal immigration. Cameron worked with a 'northern alliance' of states (e.g. Germany, the Netherlands, and Sweden) on issues such as the EU budget and the single market.

A series of domestic factors explain why Britain was an 'awkward partner'. The first concerns the historical development of the UK. As we will see later, key principles of the British constitution such as parliamentary sovereignty are of enduring significance and were often seen as being challenged by European integration. Other European states experienced major upheavals in the twentieth century; for them, EU membership was part of their modernisation and was not perceived as a threat to national identity. Political economy was also important. British elites did not want to be drawn into exclusively regional relationships, looking instead to strategic relationships with the Commonwealth and the United States. They rarely departed from a global economic outlook, favouring free trade and open markets, for much of the last 200 years.

This section explores three further factors in more detail:

1. the debate about British sovereignty;
2. the impact of the EU on the British state; and
3. disputes between and within the main political parties.

Sovereignty

Sovereignty
ultimate decision-making authority.

The **sovereignty** implications of European integration featured prominently in British debates, but sovereignty is a contested concept (see Analysis 13.3). It has an internal and external dimension. Within the UK, the doctrine of parliamentary sovereignty states that Westminster has final legal authority. National sovereignty refers to the right of national governments to make laws that apply within their territory, free from interference from other states. A distinction between *de jure* and *de facto* sovereignty is also helpful. The *de jure* account links sovereignty with authority – the right to make law – whereas the *de facto* account couples it with power and autonomy – the ability to act without undue interference.

Eurosceptics often define sovereignty in zero-sum terms, as ultimate decision-making authority: a state either has absolute authority or it does not, there can be no middle ground. Sovereignty may be voluntarily delegated when a state signs an international treaty (e.g. to join NATO) or creates a new legislature (e.g. the Scottish Parliament) within its boundaries. But European integration was qualitatively different because, Eurosceptics argued, the EU's supranational institutions have authority independent of the member states, whose laws and interests they could override.

Sovereignty is not just a legal concept for Eurosceptics, as they believed that European integration had a detrimental impact on British democracy and nationhood. Critics argued that the bond between political elites and the people had been weakened, as voters were unable to use the ballot box to remove from office decision-makers in Brussels. Eurosceptics also claimed that legitimate authority is vested in the nation-state, as people identify with national institutions, not the EU, particularly in the UK where Parliament is an important symbol of Britishness. They differed on how sovereignty might be restored. The Conservative Party favours opt-outs from some EU policies and

Analysis 13.3

Sovereignty

An institution is generally understood to be sovereign if it has final legislative authority and can act without undue external constraint. There are three interlinked facets of sovereignty: the state dimension, the constitutional dimension, and the popular dimension. Each figures in British debates about the EU and European integration has impacted upon all three.

The state dimension recognises that sovereignty is the bedrock of the modern nation-state, and that sovereignty has both internal and external dimensions. Sovereignty is territorially bounded (i.e. the sovereign has supreme authority within defined physical borders) and concerns the core functions of the modern state (economic management, defence, law and order, etc.). It is also a guiding principle of the international system: states are the main actors in international affairs and engage in cooperation through treaties. But international organisations recognise that the state has exclusive rights of jurisdiction over its own citizens within its territory.

The constitutional dimension concerns the location of sovereign authority within the state. The supremacy of Parliament is a cornerstone of the British constitution, establishing that Parliament has the right to legislate on any subject of its choosing, that legislation made by Parliament cannot be overturned by any higher authority, and that no Parliament can bind its successors. Finally, the popular dimension concerns the relationship between state and society, claiming that the sovereign authority derives its legitimacy from the consent of the political community.

repatriation (reclaiming) of some EU competences to national governments. UKIP, and the Brexit Party, believed that the EU cannot be reformed from within to meet British interests, and that only by leaving could the UK regain its sovereignty.

Pro-Europeans defined sovereignty in terms of effective influence and a practical capacity to act. Britain had 'pooled' or shared sovereignty with other EU member states. EU membership had, they argue, *enhanced* sovereignty by enabling the UK to achieve policy objectives, such as the single market, that it could not have secured independently. As a member of a strong EU, Britain also had greater influence in world affairs, a perspective which rejected a zero-sum definition of sovereignty as supreme authority. In an interdependent world, nation-states are 'porous', their autonomy constrained by developments, such as economic globalisation, migration, and environmental degradation, that do not respect national boundaries, and as such, pro-Europeans argued that even outside the EU, Britain could not dream of regaining full, unfettered control over all aspects of public policy, and to imagine that it could was a naïve, nostalgic, and ultimately dangerous delusion.

The EU and British sovereignty

EU law had primacy over domestic law: in cases of conflict, domestic law had to be amended so that it complied with EU legislation. The European Communities Act 1972 gave future EU law legal force in the UK and denied effectiveness to national legislation which conflicted with it.

This was illustrated in the 1990 *Factortame* case. The 1988 Merchant Shipping Act prevented non-British citizens from registering fishing boats as British in order to qualify for the UK's quota under the Common Fisheries Policy. But the House of Lords, following a ruling from the ECJ, ruled that the Act was incompatible with EU law and should be 'disapplied'. Compensation was later paid to those fishermen affected by the 1988 Act (see Chapter 9).

The supremacy of Community law would appear to have undermined parliamentary sovereignty, as it implied that Parliament could not legislate on any subject of its choosing, and legislation made by Parliament could be overturned by another authority. However, parliamentary sovereignty was not rendered meaningless, because Parliament retained ultimate legislative authority, such that it could withdraw from the EU by exercising Article 50 of the Lisbon Treaty (as it eventually did) and/or repealing the 1972 European Communities Act.

EU membership impinged on sovereignty in other ways. Member states did not have the right of veto in policy areas where QMV applied. One safeguard, the Luxembourg Compromise of 1966, had fallen into disuse. The extension of EU competences impacted upon the capacity of states to pursue independent policies in many areas. Parliament and the electorate had little opportunity to hold EU decision-makers accountable.

British governments often spoken of defending national sovereignty, but, in practice, they proved willing to cede authority to achieve their key objectives. They thus treated sovereignty as executive autonomy (the capacity of governments to achieve policy objectives) which might be enhanced in the EU, rather than destroyed as Eurosceptics habitually claim.

Analysis 13.4

Europeanisation

The term 'Europeanisation' is used by political scientists examining the impact of EU membership on the policies and institutions of its member states. It is generally held to refer to the adaptation of politics in the domestic arena in ways that reflect the policies and procedures of the EU. But Europeanisation is a complex process that takes a variety of forms. 'Top-down' Europeanisation occurs when EU legislation brings about enforced change in national policy. This is most apparent in areas where the EU has extensive policy competences, though governments have some autonomy in deciding how EU directives should be transposed into national law. The various opt-outs negotiated by British governments also placed limits on 'top-down' Europeanisation in the UK.

Yet Europeanisation can also take the form of an interaction between states and the EU, as national governments export or 'upload' their policy preferences to the Union. The Thatcher governments were able to export existing British deregulatory practices to other member states through the EU's single market project, to the benefit of UK companies. The Blair and Brown governments also sought to export their 'third way' social policy agenda through the Union's Lisbon process.

See: I. Bache and A. Jordan (eds.), *The Europeanization of British Politics* (London: Palgrave, 2006).

The EU and the UK polity

**Europeani-
sation**

the impact of
EU policies and
procedures on
government
and politics in
EU member
states.

Membership of the EU brought about changes in British policies and institutions, though this **Europeanisation** of the UK polity was not as uniform or as dramatic as the term suggests. The impact of European integration on UK policy varied from sector to sector according to the extent of EU competence and the distinctiveness of the British approach. In areas such as trade and agriculture, where the EU had exclusive competence, British policy was extensively Europeanised. Since the launch of the single market, much of the legislation on the standards of goods and services emanated from Brussels. Government departments and local authorities implemented these laws, while the British courts enforced them by hearing cases under EU law. However, it must be noted that Britain will still be bound by the legislation on goods and services having withdrawn from the EU, due to the British government continuing to seek new trade deals with remaining member states.

Although procedures were adapted, EU membership did not produce a major reorganisation of central government. The 'Whitehall ethos' of centralised decision-making remained largely intact; emphasis was placed on the effective coordination of policy. The main actors and institutions involved in developing British policy in the EU were the prime minister, the Cabinet Office, and the Foreign Office. The prime minister shaped the key objectives of British policy and attended European Council meetings. In this respect, membership actually strengthened the position of the prime minister; although cabinet and intra-party divisions on European policy undermined Thatcher and Major's positions, Blair ceded significant responsibility for policy on the euro to the Treasury, and in coalition, Cameron had to appease pro-European Liberal Democrats and increasingly Eurosceptic Conservative MPs.

The European and Global Issues Secretariat, based in the Cabinet Office, coordinated policy and ensured that government departments adhered to the agreed negotiating position. The Secretariat became more closely integrated into the policymaking machinery at 10 Downing Street under Blair, particularly after the appointment of Sir Stephen Wall as the prime minister's special adviser on Europe in 2000. Mats Persson, head of the soft Eurosceptic think tank Open Europe, became Cameron's special adviser on Europe in 2015. A cabinet committee on European affairs chaired by the Foreign Secretary developed Britain's policy position in the EU. Another cabinet committee, the Europe Committee, which was chaired by the prime minister, was established in 2015 to consider issues relating to the EU referendum, while the result of the 2016 referendum led to the establishment of various ministerial committees on aspects of Brexit.

The Foreign and Commonwealth Office (FCO) took the lead diplomatic role in negotiations in the EU, with the Foreign Secretary attending European Council meetings and key meetings of the Council of the European Union, as well as taking charge of many ministerial discussions. The FCO also played a strategic role in forging alliances in the EU and a coordinating role in instructing the UK Representation (UKRep). UKRep consisted of staff seconded from relevant government departments to assist in EU negotiations and UK policy formulation. Its head, the Permanent Representative, held regular meetings with FCO officials and the head of the European and Global Issues Secretariat to clarify and coordinate the British position.

The Treasury kept a tight rein on EU-related expenditure, preventing government departments from bypassing domestic spending constraints by using EU funds. This tough approach sometimes caused conflict between the Treasury and other bodies – for example, in a dispute over the payment of EU regional funding that forced the resignation of Welsh First Minister Alun Michael in 2000. The Treasury also staked a lead role in determining policy on EMU, setting the five economic tests and assessing whether they had been met. Most government departments had specific units responsible for EU matters. EU legislation formed a large part of the workload of the former Department for Business, Innovation and Skills, and also the Department for the Environment, Food and Rural Affairs. However, the extension of EU policy competences meant that other departments, such as the Home Office, were increasingly involved in EU policymaking. Meanwhile, interest groups responded to 'Europeanisation' by switching some of their lobbying efforts to Brussels (see Chapter 19), particularly if they found British governments less receptive to them, as was the case with the trade unions during the Thatcher–Major administrations, when many unions established their own offices in Brussels and often received a more sympathetic hearing.

Although Whitehall sought to maintain centralised policymaking, European integration was a factor in the development of multilevel governance in the UK. The devolved bodies and local authorities were responsible for implementing EU legislation in their respective areas of competence, but this was not simply a top-down relationship. Pressure from local and regional elites on the UK to gain maximum benefit from structural funds and promote their interests more effectively within the EU fuelled demands for regionalism and devolution in the 1980s and 1990s. Poorer regions of the UK, such as Northern Ireland, Cornwall, and Merseyside, received EU regional funding. The European Commission actively encouraged the participation of local and regional actors in decision-making, and many local authorities and regions opened offices in Brussels to lobby on their behalf and keep tabs on policy developments. Nonetheless, central government retained a gatekeeper role in the relationship between English regional and local government and the EU, by ensuring that it ultimately controlled policymaking and expenditure.

Devolution brought a closer fit between the UK state and the EU's multilevel system. It also forced a reworking of the centralised process by which Britain's EU policy was settled. While the EU had competence in many policy fields devolved to the Scottish Parliament, Welsh Assembly, and Northern Ireland Assembly, overall responsibility for Britain's relations with the EU was 'reserved' to Westminster. The devolved administrations were consulted on British policy and had some input (e.g. on environmental policy), but once the UK government's single negotiating line had been settled, they were bound by it. The arrangements operated relatively smoothly overall, but the SNP was critical of Cameron's decision to hold an EU referendum and warned that if the UK as a whole voted to leave the EU, but voters in Scotland supported membership, then a second independence referendum might be held.

Finally, Parliament debated major developments in the EU, but found it difficult to maintain effective scrutiny of the huge volume of EU legislative and policy proposals (over 1,000 a year). The latter task fell to the House of Commons European Scrutiny Committee. Ministers were not normally supposed to agree to EU legislation until Parliament had undertaken scrutiny of the proposals. The EU Select Committee in the House of Lords has a deservedly high reputation for the quality of its scrutiny of, and reports on, developments in the EU and how they impacted on the UK.

Political parties and Europe

Britain's relationship with the EU was an issue that the main political parties found difficult to manage. The UK never really developed the strong elite consensus on the benefits of European integration which is apparent in most other member states. Labour and the Conservatives instead often adopted contrary positions, one adopting a 'sceptical' view, critical of the pro-European outlook of the other, and accusing it of surrendering sovereignty and 'selling out' Britain's interests to Brussels. Yet the issue of the UK's relationship with Europe also caused divisions within the two main parties, where integration was viewed as challenging their ideology or self-image, and the ensuing intra-party divisions proved difficult for their leaders to manage.

British politics is adversarial in character, as the simple plurality electoral system and two-party dominance of the House of Commons encourage parties to take opposing positions on key issues. Differences of principle were evident on Europe, notably in the early 1980s, but the gap between Labour and Conservative positions widened again after 1997. Conservative policy became more Eurosceptic, while Labour, particularly under Blair, adopted integrationist positions. For the most part, the Labour and Conservative leaderships shared a vision of British membership of a free-trading, intergovernmental EU, but they highlighted differences of detail or degree for tactical reasons, in the expectation that accusing the other party of failing to serve the national interest would bring political and electoral rewards. So, Labour was largely supportive of the 1992–93 Maastricht Treaty, but found an excuse to vote against it in Major's refusal to sign the Social Chapter. Unable to rely on Labour support, Major was thus forced to confront Eurosceptics in his own party to force the legislation through Parliament.

The main parties' European policies were also shaped by their ideology and strategic interests. Divisions on Europe were not always easy to locate on the Left-Right axis, where the Left favours economic interventionism and the Right the free market. In the 1980s, Nigel Lawson, Sir Geoffrey Howe, and Mrs Thatcher disagreed on the ERM and EMU despite their shared commitment to neoliberal economics. Instead, divisions could usefully be plotted on a sovereignty-interdependence axis, where pro-Europeans were willing to pool sovereignty and Eurosceptics persisted in the traditional view which viewed sovereignty as indivisible.

Labour and the Conservatives also swapped positions on Europe at various junctures. From the early 1960s to the late 1980s, the Conservatives proclaimed themselves the 'party of Europe'. They were the first to apply for EEC membership (1961), and then secured entry (1973) under the leadership of the staunchly pro-European Edward Heath. There was a close fit between the free trade and free market outlook of the Tories and the EC. The signing of the Maastricht Treaty (1992) proved the high-water mark for pro-European Conservatism. Euroscepticism escalated thereafter, as European integration was seen as a threat to national sovereignty and Thatcherite free-market economics. Thatcher's 1988 Bruges speech – when she denounced the advocacy of a 'social Europe', entailing increased workers' rights – signalled the beginning of this shift in the Conservatives' approach, although her own increasing (and increasingly vocal) Euroscepticism was a major factor in her downfall in November 1990, at a time when the Conservative Party still contained several well-known and highly respected pro-European 'big beasts', such as Kenneth Clarke, Michael Heseltine, Chris Patten, and Douglas Hurd.

Labour opposed the 1961 application, but the Wilson government launched its own unsuccessful entry bid six years later. The leadership supported membership in principle but opposed the EEC entry terms agreed by the Tories in 1971–72 before settling for minor concessions when back in office. Labour moved to the left after its 1979 election defeat, calling in its

1983 manifesto for withdrawal from an EEC depicted as a 'capitalist club' that would frustrate the party's socialist 'alternative economic strategy'. This marked the pinnacle of Labour Euroscepticism.

Under the leadership of Neil Kinnock, later to serve as an EU Commissioner, Labour's ideology moved closer to the 'European social model' favoured by other West European social democratic parties. Many in the Labour movement who had viewed the single market with suspicion now looked favourably on EU social and regional policy, not least because they viewed it as a means of opposing Thatcherism and softening the impact of her free-market policies. The shift in the party's European policy also enabled Labour to reposition itself as a modernised and moderate party, neutralising one of the issues which had helped to promote the formation of the SDP in the early 1980s. Since the last years of that decade, the effects of globalisation convinced Labour leaders that making the British economy more competitive, while ensuring social protection for the poorest in society, could only be practicable in the context of EU membership, although intra-party tensions re-emerged under Jeremy Corbyn's post-2015 leadership, as noted in the next section.

Intra-party divisions

The Labour and Conservative Parties were coalitions of opinion on Europe (and, to varying degrees, other issues and polices), containing convinced pro-Europeans and Eurosceptics, as well as pragmatists. MPs opposed to the official line tended to stay in the party, as there were strong disincentives to leave: resigning the whip would deprive them of access to parliamentary resources, while the electoral system usually discouraged them from setting up minor parties that are unlikely to prosper, as exemplified by the Independent Group for Change, formed in 2019 by a handful of pro-European Conservative and Labour MPs who were deeply dissatisfied with their respective party's stance on Brexit. This often created problems of party management, because leaders hoping to develop a clear European policy often met resistance and rebellions from within their own ranks, and had to fall back on a lowest common denominator position upon which most in the party could agree. This was especially true if the governing party had only a slim or even non-existent parliamentary majority, as was the case with John Major after 1992, and David Cameron from 2010: Major's 'wait and see' stance on EMU, and Cameron's pledge of an in-out referendum, were both designed to manage divisions in the Conservative Party by keeping Eurosceptics 'on board'.

Most Conservative MPs supported EEC entry in the 1960s and 1970s, though some on the right (notably Enoch Powell) warned against the loss of sovereignty. Europe re-emerged as the main fault-line in the party in debates on the Maastricht Treaty in 1992–93. Many Tories previously supportive of the SEA felt that its provisions on EMU and political union rendered Maastricht a 'Treaty too far'. Eurosceptic resistance culminated in 46 Tory MPs voting against the bill ratifying the Treaty at third reading, forcing Major to hold a vote of confidence. Conflict on Europe dogged the remainder of his premiership: eight rebel MPs had the whip temporarily removed in 1994 (and one resigned it), and then John Redwood responded to Major's 1995 invitation to his critics to stand against him in a leadership contest by launching a Eurosceptic challenge that garnered 89 votes.

In opposition, the Conservatives adopted a soft Eurosceptic 'in Europe, not run by Europe' position that opposed EMU membership, sought the repatriation of some EU policies, and promised referendums on new EU treaties. Cameron was a pragmatic Eurosceptic who abandoned his commitment to hold a referendum on the Lisbon Treaty after it was ratified by all member states but pleased Eurosceptics in his party by removing Conservative MEPs from the federalist EPP group.

Back in government after 2010, a perfect storm of factors reopened Conservative divisions in government: the eurozone crisis, the dilution of Conservative EU policy in coalition, the growth of hard Euroscepticism on the Conservative benches, ineffectual party management, and the rise of UKIP. October 2011 brought the largest ever Conservative rebellion on European integration when 81 Conservative MPs defied a three-line whip to support a backbench motion on policy repatriation and a referendum. Cameron averted another major rebellion by taking the unprecedented step of granting backbenchers a free vote on an amendment to the 2013 Queen's Speech regretting the absence of a bill on an EU referendum. Two Conservative MPs, Douglas Carswell and Mark Reckless, defected to UKIP in 2014.

The fault line in the Conservative Party was no longer between pro-Europeans – now a small, diminishing, and relatively silent minority – and Eurosceptics, but between soft Eurosceptics who supported membership of a reformed EU and hard Eurosceptics who favoured either fundamental renegotiation of UK membership or withdrawal. Cameron's renegotiation-referendum pledge kept the lid on intra-party divisions in the 2015 general election. But the creation of the 'Conservatives for Britain' group of some 100 MPs, which demanded fundamental renegotiation, illustrated that Conservative divisions would be further exposed during the referendum campaign, with a substantial section of the party likely to support withdrawal.

Serious divisions occurred in the Labour Party in the 1970s and early 1980s. Most of the Labour movement opposed the terms under which Britain joined the EEC, but the leadership supported membership in principle. Yet 69 Labour MPs defied a three-line whip to vote for entry. Many Labour Eurosceptics (e.g. Tony Benn) were on the left of the party. To limit the damage, Wilson called a referendum on continued membership (1975) in which cabinet ministers were allowed to take opposing sides. Hopes that the 67 per cent 'yes' vote would settle the issue were frustrated. A 1980 Labour conference vote, endorsing a policy of withdrawal, prompted some pro-European MPs to quit and establish the Social Democratic Party (SDP).

Labour's subsequent pro-European conversion was relatively smooth. Pro-European John Smith defeated Eurosceptic Bryan Gould in the 1992 leadership contest, though 66 Labour MPs subsequently voted against the Maastricht Treaty. The Blair governments' support for euro membership in principle did not provoke the level of dissent seen in the Conservative Party in the 1990s, and failure to meet the five economic tests (as a precondition of joining 'the euro') hid the scale of Labour anti-euro sentiment. Only 18 Labour MPs defied the whip to vote against the Treaty of Lisbon. 'The Labour for Britain' group set up in 2015 includes backbench Eurosceptic MPs such as Kate Hoey and Gisella Stuart.

Labour's tensions over EU membership became more prominent following Jeremy Corbyn's election as Party leader in 2015 (strongly supported by the extra-parliamentary party, but only by a handful of Labour MPs) and the 2016 referendum. Most Labour MPs were pro-European, but many of them represented constituencies which voted Leave in the 2016 referendum, which clearly placed some of them in an awkward position, especially those representing Brexit-supporting seats in northern England. Moreover, Corbyn himself was strongly suspected of sharing the Old Left's view that the EU was a 'capitalist club', and as such, throughout his leadership of the Labour Party, he effectively sat on the fence over Brexit, to the frustration of many Labour MPs, particularly those who supported Remain and who wanted Corbyn to display stronger and more decisive leadership on this issue (and many others!). For his part, Corbyn seemed to have been fudging the issue in an attempt at bridging the gap between Labour's working-class Leavers and the Party's middle-class Remainers. This was relatively (and surprisingly) successful in the 2017 general election, but was no longer tenable in 2019, when many of Labour's former working-class supporters switched to Boris Johnson's 'get Brexit done' Conservatives – leading to a collapse of Labour's former northern 'red wall'– while disillusioned pro-European middle-class voters switched to the Liberal Democrats or the Greens.

'Europe' as an election issue

The major political parties have found Europe a difficult issue to exploit for electoral advantage. Taking a clear position risks exposing intra-party divisions, so party leaders have often put forward compromise positions and downplayed the issue. But voter concern about European integration increased and the gap between Labour and Conservative positions widened in the 1990s. The Conservatives saw Europe as a potential vote winner at the 1997 and 2001 general elections because their policies on the EU and the euro were more in tune with public opinion than Labour's. However, this did not deliver substantial electoral reward because the issue was not a very important one to most voters (it lacked 'saliency'), who were also wary of Conservative divisions on the EU. Labour and Conservative leaders then sought to reduce the prominence (and this divisiveness) of the EU issue, and it barely featured in either the 2005 or 2010 general election campaigns, Cameron having warned the Conservatives, when he became leader, that it needed to 'stop banging on about Europe'.

The EU issue became more prominent again after 2010, though, with UKIP shaping the agenda by linking the increasingly salient issue of (East European) immigration with that of EU membership. It claimed that only by leaving the EU could the UK control its borders and prevent low-skilled EU migrants, particularly from countries like Poland, which had joined the EU in 2004, from taking jobs from British workers or claiming welfare benefits. UKIP had come second in the national vote in the 2009 European elections, and then took first place in 2014. Voters were now presented with clearer differences between the EU policies of the main parties, with the Conservatives pledging an in-out referendum, Labour and the Liberal Democrats only committing to a referendum in the unlikely event of them transferring more powers to the EU, and UKIP campaigning for total withdrawal from the EU. UKIP won four million votes (a 13 per cent share) in the 2015 general election, but due to the vagaries of the first-past-the-post electoral system, only the ex-Conservative MP Douglas Carswell won a seat.

The EU was a much more prominent and potent issue in the 2019 general election, because many of those who had voted Leave in the 2016 referendum were angry and frustrated that the UK had still not left the EU. Many such voters were convinced that a 'Remain Establishment' in London had done everything possible to obstruct Brexit, with the ultimate goal of preventing it altogether, and thereby showing total contempt towards 'the will of the people' as expressed in 2016. Thus did Boris Johnson's pledge to 'get Brexit done' prove highly attractive to many voters in December 2019, including some of those who traditionally voted Labour. That said, although Brexit was clearly the key issue for many voters in the 2019 election, Jeremy Corbyn himself was also an issue, with various polls and Labour canvassers suggesting that his leadership (or lack of) and some of his Left-wing views were deterring many people from voting Labour, as were allegations of widespread antisemitism in the party.

Conclusion and summary

It is clear that Britain was never fully or wholeheartedly politically committed to the EEC/EU, and that when it did apply to join, the applications were motivated primarily by calculations and expectations of the economic advantages and benefits of membership. Britain was certainly never in favour of pursuing ever closer political union, particularly because the British conception of indivisible parliamentary sovereignty was at odds with the willingness of most other

Controversy 13.2

The costs and benefits of EU membership

The UK is a net contributor to the EU, paying £11.2 billion net into the EU budget in 2015–16. This equates to 1.5 per cent of public spending, but in the era of austerity, opponents of EU membership argue that the money could be better spent in other areas. The largest proportion of the EU budget (40 per cent) is spent on the CAP, from which the UK receives limited benefits.

The single market has reduced barriers to trade between member states, but requires EU-level regulation to ensure common standards and adherence to the rules. This EU regulation is costly for UK business, particularly for small and medium-sized enterprises that do not trade with the EU. The costs of EU regulation are felt in the financial services sector, a sizeable contributor to the UK economy, with Eurosceptics claiming that UK influence here is diminishing as eurozone states push ahead with an EU banking union. Eurosceptics on the Left and Right make different economic cases against EU membership. While the Left criticises EU support for austerity or the threat the TTIP might pose to the National Health Service, the Right warns of EU hostility towards the City of London and wants to scrap some EU social and employment laws.

Supporters of EU membership argue that it is Britain's main export market (45 per cent in 2014), that 3.5 million jobs are linked to trade with the EU, and that membership makes the UK more attractive to foreign direct investment (FDI). Tariffs could be imposed on British goods if the UK left the EU customs union. But opponents of EU membership counter that British goods would remain attractive to EU markets, the UK imports more than it exports to the EU and so other member states would not want to harm their export prospects, and the World Trade Organisation maintains low tariffs.

With the EU economy still to recover from the sovereign debt crisis, those in favour of withdrawal from the EU argue that the UK should further develop trade links with emerging economies in Asia and elsewhere. Outside the EU, the UK could negotiate bilateral trade details. Switzerland and Iceland have, for example, agreed free trade deals with China, whereas the EU has not. However, EU membership gives states additional clout in trade negotiations, although they have to compromise on some of their objectives.

The overall economic impact of 'Brexit' is difficult to quantify as much would depend on the nature of the UK's future relationship with the EU. The UK government would likely seek access to the single market and a comprehensive free trade agreement if the in-out referendum produced a 'no' vote. Norway and Switzerland offer examples of alternative relationships with the EU. Norway is a member of the European Economic Area, while Switzerland has a looser relationship with the EU based on a series of bilateral treaties. Both enjoy access to the single market and are members of the border-free Schengen Area but do not take part in EU policies such as the customs union, common trade policy, CAP, or foreign and security policy. However, both countries contribute to the EU budget but are not represented in negotiations on EU laws that they must later implement.

See: House of Commons Library, *In Brief: UK-EU Economic Relations*, Briefing Paper 06091, June 2015.

member-states to 'pool sovereignty'. On this crucial point, Britain was always very wary of 'surrendering' political power and national autonomy to a supranational institution, and instead remained wedded to the principle of 'intergovernmentalism' as the most desirable method of international cooperation and joint policymaking, because this ultimately allowed it to retain sovereignty. Thus did every initiative by the EU (as it became in 1993), via new Treaties (Maastricht, Amsterdam, Nice, and Lisbon), to extend its power and expand its policy competences, provoke corresponding resistance from the growing number of Eurosceptic MPs and minsters, mostly (but not solely) in the Conservative Party, who condemned this seemingly relentless erosion of British sovereignty, and the risk that Britain would be subsumed into a European super-state or United States of Europe.

However, although the issue of 'sovereignty' was a potent and highly symbolic one, it was not the sole source of British 'exceptionalism'; other historical and political factors underpinned Britain's resistance to 'ever closer union' and European integration. The legacy of the British Empire in the late nineteenth and early twentieth centuries, when Britain politically governed one-third of the world and thus enjoyed a huge source of cheap goods (and labour) and guaranteed trade, underpinned a sense of British 'greatness', and while the Empire was dismantled a very long time ago, it retains a strong emotional appeal to many (mostly older). Indeed, some of those who supported Brexit can occasionally be heard mooting the idea of voters reviving the British Empire; having resented Britain apparently being 'enslaved' by the EU, some of these people now apparently want to enslave former British colonies in order to ensure Britain's economic survival outside the EU. Also crucial to the sense of British greatness is the nation's victory (albeit in tandem with a few other countries) in the twentieth-century's two world wars. The second world war (1939–45) especially reaffirmed a self-image of British greatness and strength which endures today, and again, some Brexit supporters have been heard declaring that, having survived and won World War II, Britain can survive and prosper outside the EU; people simply need to have more patriotic pride and self-belief, and 'pull together' by reviving the 'Dunkirk spirit'.

Britain's membership of the EEC/EU was a source of both inter- and intra-party division. At various times, Labour and the Conservatives adopted opposing positions – when one party wanted Britain to join the EEC, the other opposed, either on principle or on the grounds that the terms of proposed membership were not right. However, it has been the intra-party divisions which have proved most problematic, for in both main parties, it has been the more 'ideological' MPs and ministers who have been most critical of the EU or opposed to British membership altogether. In the Labour Party, the Left has tended to denounce the EEC/EU as a 'capitalist club' solely serving the interests of corporate capital and big employers, and thus inimical to the interests of ordinary working people. This perception of the EEC/EU also means that the Labour Left viewed it as an obstacle to socialism, and thus an impediment to the implementation of a radical programme of redistribution and reform by a future 'socialist' Labour government, especially policies such as higher public expenditure, nationalisation, and import controls (the latter two especially would apparently have been incompatible with the EEC/EU's commitment to competition, deregulation, and liberalisation).

In the Conservative Party, meanwhile, it was the Right which became increasingly Eurosceptic, although here, there was a division between 'soft' and 'hard' Eurosceptics; the former wanted to modify or loosen Britain's relationship by renegotiating the terms and conditions of membership, while the latter wanted to terminate Britain's membership altogether. The intra-party divisions in the Conservative Party effectively destroyed the premierships of its last four prime ministers – Margaret Thatcher, John Major, David Cameron, and Theresa May – but Boris Johnson can claim to have delivered on his pledge to 'get Brexit done', by ensuring that the UK officially left the EU on 31 January 2020. However, the UK is now in a one-year (renewable) 'transition period', during which many details will need to be negotiated about Britain's post-Brexit relationship and trade links with the EU. These will almost certainly yield further tensions and disagreements in the Conservative Party, and in British politics more widely.

Further reading

The best introductions to Britain's relationship with the EU are A. Geddes's *Britain and the European Union* (London: Palgrave, 2013) and D. Gowland, A. Turner, and A. Wright's *Britain and European Integration since 1945: On the Sidelines* (London: Routledge, 2009). Three good historical perspectives are: J. Young's *Britain and European Unity* (London: Palgrave, 2nd edition, 1999); S. George's *An Awkward Partner: Britain in the European Union* (Oxford: Oxford University Press, 3rd edition, 1998); and H. Young's *This Blessed Plot: Britain in Europe from Churchill to Blair* (London: Papermac, 1999). A. Gamble's *Between Europe and America: The Future of British Politics* (London: Palgrave, 2003) is a compelling analysis of the strategic choices facing the UK.

Textbooks on the EU include M. Cini and N. Perez-Solorzano Borragon (eds.), *European Union Politics* (Oxford: Oxford University Press, 4th edition, 2013), and I. Bache, S. George, and S. Bulmer's *Politics in the European Union* (Oxford: Oxford University Press, 4th edition, 2014). S. Hix and B. Hoyland's *The Political System of the European Union* (London: Palgrave, 3rd edition, 2011) is more advanced but rewarding. The *Journal of Common Market Studies* publishes an *Annual Review of the European Union*.

The Europeanisation of the UK polity is examined in I. Bache (ed.), *The Europeanization of British Politics* (London: Palgrave, 2008), and S. Bulmer and M. Burch's *The Europeanisation of Whitehall: UK Central Government and the European Union* (Manchester: Manchester University Press, 2009). On sovereignty, see C. Gifford, 'The UK and the European Union: Dimensions of Sovereignty and the Problem of Eurosceptic Britishness', *Parliamentary Affairs*, Vol. 63, No. 2 (2010), pp. 321–38.

Conservative Party policy and divisions on European integration are examined in P. Dorey, 'Towards Exit from the EU: The Conservative Party's Increasing Euroscepticism since the 1980s', *Politics and Governance*, Vol.5 No. 2 (2017), pp. 27–40, P. Lynch and R. Whitaker, 'Where There Is Discord, Can They Bring Harmony? Managing Intra-Party Dissent on European Integration in the Conservative Party', *British Journal of Politics and International Relations*, Vol. 15, No. 3 (2013), pp. 317–39, and D. Baker, A. Gamble, and S. Ludlam, 'Sovereign Nations and Global Markets: Modern British Conservatism and Hyperglobalism', *British Journal of Politics and International Relations*, Vol. 4, No. 3 (2002), pp. 399–428. On Labour and the EU, see P. Schnapper, 'The Labour Party and Europe from Brown to Miliband: Back to the Future?', *Journal of Common Market Studies*, Vol. 53, No. 1 (2015), pp. 157–73, and A. Gamble and G. Kelly, 'The British Labour Party and Monetary Union', *West European Politics*, Vol. 32, No. 1 (2000), pp. 1–25. The key book on the rise of UKIP is R. Ford and M. Goodwin's *Revolt on the Right: Explaining Support for the Radical Right in Britain* (London: Routledge, 2014).

The case for and against EU membership is explored by *The Times* journalist David Charter in *Europe: In or Out? Everything You Need to Know* (London: Biteback, 2014). The House of Commons Library has produced a number of research briefings on the impact of leaving the EU, including 'EU Exit: Impact in Key Policy Areas', Number 07213, June 2015. The best introductory text on Euroscepticism in the EU is C. Leconte's *Understanding Euroscepticism* (London: Palgrave, 2010), while British Euroscepticism is examined in K. Tournier-Sol and C. Gifford (eds.), *The UK Challenge to Europeanization: The Persistence of British Euroscepticism* (London: Palgrave, 2014).

British public opinion on the EU is examined in B. Clements, 'The Sociological and Psychological Influences on Public Support for the European Union in Britain, 1983–2005', *British Politics*, Vol. 4, No. 1 (2009), pp. 47–82, and S. Hobolt and P. Riseborough, 'How to Win the UK Referendum on the European Constitution', *The Political Quarterly*, Vol. 76, No. 2 (2005), pp. 241–52. On Cameron's decision to hold an EU referendum, see T. Oliver, 'To Be or Not To Be in Europe: Is That the Question? Britain's

European Question and an in/out Referendum', *International Affairs*, Vol. 91, No. 1 (2015), pp. 77–91, and A. Glencross, 'Why a British Referendum on EU Membership will not Solve the Europe Question', *International Affairs*, Vol. 91, No. 2 (2015), pp. 303–17.

For details and analysis of the 2016 Referendum result, see YouGov, *How Britain Voted at the EU Referendum*, June 2016 (available at https://yougov.co.uk/topics/politics/articles-reports/2016/06/27/how-britain-voted), and Mathew Goodwin and Oliver Heath/Joseph Rowntree Foundation, *Brexit Vote Explained: Poverty, Low Skills and Lack of Opportunities*, August 2016 (available at https://www.jrf.org.uk/report/brexit-vote-explained-poverty-low-skills-and-lack-opportunities?gclid=CjwKCAjw5cL2BRASEiwAENqAPj8MNIgdlWSeob5OI8DK04llqEqCatYf6y8MA9x0oj TfdsAgCoOujRoCxGgQAvD_BwE). The Institute for Government has a large series of downloadable (for free) reports and analysis on Brexit, including several on 'what happens next'; available at https://www.instituteforgovernment.org.uk/our-work/brexit.

Websites

The European Union's official website contains a wealth of information on EU policies, institutions, and current developments. Its homepage (www.europa.eu/index_en.htm) provides an introduction to the work of the EU plus links to the sites of the EU institutions, information on the EU's policy activities, and current legislation. The websites of the main EU institutions have further information on their structure and work:

- The Council of the European Union (www.consilium.europa.eu/en/council-eu).
- The European Commission (www.ec.europa.eu/index_en.htm).
- The European Parliament (www.europarl.europa.eu/portal/en).
- The European Court of Justice (www.curia.europa.eu/jcms/jcms/j_6).

Eurobarometer surveys of opinion can be found at www.ec.europa.eu/public_opinion/index_en.htm. The EU's official website includes a newsroom (www.europa.eu/newsroom/index_en.htm) with information on the recent activities of the EU and its institutions. EU Observer (www.euobserver.com) is an independent site covering developments in the EU.

On UK policy, the Foreign and Commonwealth Office site (www.gov.uk/government/organisations/-foreign-commonwealth-office) has policy information, government documents, and ministerial speeches. The UK in a Changing Europe website (www.ukandeu.ac.uk/) has academic analysis of the UK's relationship with the EU.

Notes

1   Available at: https://www.jrf.org.uk/report/brexit-vote-explained-poverty-low skills-and-lack-opportunities?gclid=CjwKCAjw5cL2BRASEiwAENqAPj8MNIgdlWSeob5OI8DK04llqEq CatYf6y8MA9x0ojTfdsAgCoOujRoCxGgQAvD_BwE.
2   Accessible at https://assets.publishing.service.gov.uk/government/uploads/system/uploads/attachment_data/file/759019/25_November_Agreement_on_the_withdrawal_of_the_United_Kingdom_of_Great_Britain_and_Northern_Ireland_from_the_European_Union_and_the_European_Atomic_Energy_Community.pdf.

Part 4

Political parties

Chapter 14

UK party systems

Learning outcomes

After reading this chapter, you will:

*   be able to explain the development of the Westminster party system;
*   recognise the impact of different voting systems; and
*   understand how the classification of party systems in the UK has become more complicated since the creation of devolved institutions in Scotland, Wales, and Northern Ireland since the late 1990s.

Introduction

In an ideal world of pluralist liberal democracy, every state would include a wide range of political parties, all of which had a realistic chance of gaining at least token representation in the legislature. Such a situation would reflect the fact that people enjoying freedom of thought and expression are likely to hold divergent opinions on key issues and to associate with others of like mind. Indeed, if everyone did think alike on the most important issues, some people would still feel inspired to compete for the right to represent their fellow citizens, and find some grounds for arguing among themselves. In such circumstances, it is inevitable that political parties will develop (see Chapter 15).

Students hoping to gain an insight into the political culture of any society will be rewarded by a close study of the patterns of party competition. But they are well advised to do more than simply count the number of parties which contest elections with a chance of forming a government – which is the usual way of classifying a party system (see Analysis 14.1). For example, the UK and the US have traditionally been regarded as having two-party systems. Since they are both diverse societies, it would be easy to assume that a large proportion of their citizens have been (and continue to be) deprived of a meaningful choice. But this is not necessarily the case: it could be that the main parties are coalitions in themselves, flexible enough to encompass and articulate the opinions of a majority of voters.

However, whether or not this was true at some point in the fairly recent past, there are good reasons for doubting whether two parties – however versatile – could still provide satisfactory choice for voters in the UK (or, indeed, the US). Apart from the ever-increasing diversity of these countries, their citizens seem to be far more selective and difficult to please than in (say) 1950.

In the case of the UK, the long-established idea of two-party competition has come under additional scrutiny since the introduction of devolved institutions in Scotland, Wales, and Northern Ireland, elected by different varieties of proportional representation (PR). It is possible to argue that, at national level, the UK ceased to be a two-party system long before the end of the twentieth century so that the emergence of a coalition government in 2010 was merely a belated confirmation of something which had already happened. Furthermore, because of very different patterns of competition at sub-national level, it is now more appropriate to speak of a number of distinct party *systems* in the UK.

History of a two-party system

Party

an organisation of people with common political beliefs and shared policy goals which competes in elections in an attempt to win power or influence.

Institutionalised **party** conflict in Britain dates back to the seventeenth century and the division between 'Tories' (who supported the full exercise of the Royal prerogative) and 'Whigs' (who favoured a limited or 'constitutional' monarchy). These labels survived through the eighteenth century, but continuing competition was only marginally related to principle after the 'Glorious Revolution' of 1688–89. That settlement was a clear victory for Whig principles, since it established that the monarch could not rule without parliament. Although 'High Tories' continued to hanker after the restoration of the old order, for practical purposes the clash between the parties soon subsided into little more than a faction-fight between retinues of 'ins' and 'outs'. Since the material fruits of office were monopolised by the winning side in this zero-sum game, members of the losing team rarely had difficulty in convincing their supporters (and even themselves) that they were crusaders against corruption who would always put the public good above their own interests.

Meaningful party conflict resumed towards the end of the eighteenth century, in the wake of the French Revolution. Few Whigs advocated a similar upheaval in Britain, but many of them did favour a rationalisation of the electoral franchise and a redistribution of seats to reflect the rising population of cities like Manchester and Birmingham. The Tories, by contrast, preferred to leave things as they were. This battle closed with the passage of the Great Reform Act (1832), which satisfied the demands of most Whigs. In response, the Tories became even more self-conscious in their resistance to change in 'Church and State', and adopted the new name of 'Conservatives' (see Chapter 16). Yet the Whigs were scarcely radical; many of them believed that the Reform Act had 'perfected' the constitution. Thus, in the years after 1832, a rising young Tory, William Gladstone, was able to join the Whigs (who formally adopted the 'Liberal' label in 1859) without feeling that his views had changed very much.

Party system

the set of political parties in a political system and their interactions.

Thus Britain entered the era of mass parties after a second extension of the franchise in 1867 (see Chapter 15) with a recognisable **two-party system.** That is, although party identification was still fairly loose and informal – and defections from one camp to the other were not unusual – parliament was dominated by a governing party and a main opposition which had a realistic expectation of forming an administration in the near future (see Analysis 14.1). The oratorical combat between the Liberal Gladstone and the Conservative

Analysis 14.1

The classification of party systems

The most familiar way of defining party systems is to look at the number of parties which have a realistic chance of participating in a government rather than the number of organisations that nominate candidates at elections. In *one-party* states, like China or North Korea, any elections which may be held are meaningless because either organised opposition is banned or provisions are made to ensure that only members of a specified party are eligible to hold office. But it is also possible to identify *dominant-party* systems, where there are no such restrictions but one party almost always wins. Thus in Sweden the Social Democratic Labour Party was in office for all but two of the years between 1951 and 1993, while the Congress Party governed India without a break for 30 years after the country's independence in 1947. In Northern Ireland, the Ulster Unionist Party won every election for 50 years, from 1922 to 1972.

In *two-party* systems only the government and the main opposition party have a realistic chance of winning power, although there can be any number of minor parties taking part in elections, and perhaps having a few candidates elected. Britain was a classic two-party system from 1945 to 1974, with Labour and the Conservatives constituting the only two serious contenders for political power at Westminster, and other parties, such as the Liberals, only winning a few seats during this time. The United States has also long been a classic example of a two-party system, where elections both to Congress and the Presidency are dominated by the Republicans and the Democrats, and independent candidates for the presidency rarely win a single vote in the electoral college. A variant of this situation is a *two-and-a-half-party* system, in which third parties regularly win sufficient representation to have a potential effect on the overall outcome, without coming close to securing an independent majority. For example, in the 2010 general election in the UK, the Liberal Democrats won 57 seats, while neither Labour nor the Conservatives won an overall parliamentary majority. As a consequence, both parties approached the Lib Dems to invite them to create a coalition, with the negotiations resulting in a Conservative-Lib Dem government. These two parties working together had a majority of parliamentary seats, whereas a Labour-Lib Dem coalition would still have lacked an overall majority, and would therefore have repeatedly needed to do deals with other 'minor' parties before every major parliamentary vote; this would have meant constant bargaining, offering concessions, and general political instability.

In *multi-party* systems, there are several parties with substantial support, meaning that no single party usually wins enough support (and seats) to govern alone. As such, the outcome of elections in multi-party systems is almost invariably a coalition government.

Party systems are closely related to the electoral system in operation. Thus the simple plurality (or first-past-the-post) electoral system, as used in Britain, is associated with two-party systems, while more proportional systems like the Additional Member System (AMS) and the Single Transferable Vote (STV) foster multi-party systems and coalition governments (see Chapter 17).

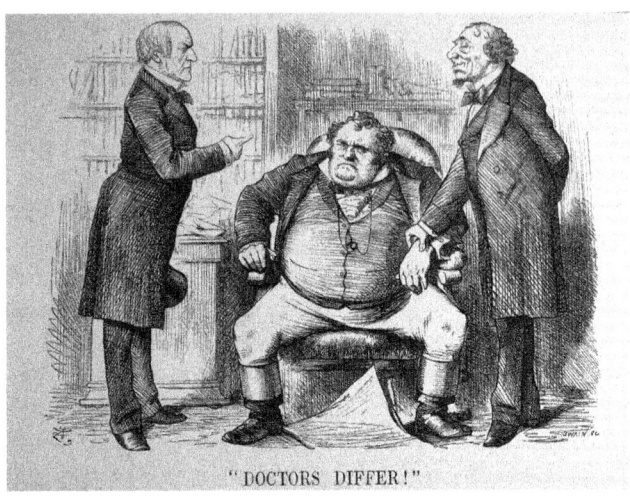

"DOCTORS DIFFER!"

CARTOON 14.1 Gladstone and Disraeli, gladiators in a two-party battle (© Universal History Archive/Universal Images Group via Getty Images).

Benjamin Disraeli dominated exchanges in the House of Commons for many years. Gladstone formed four governments, only retiring in 1894 at the age of 84; Disraeli was Prime Minister on two occasions. In an era of mass production, as well as mass parties, the idolisation of these parliamentary giants was exploited in a wide range of memorabilia, ranging from portraits to dinner-plates. The railways ensured the rapid distribution of party publicity and took leaders like Gladstone on nationwide campaigns to address large crowds of partisan supporters who were mobilised by increasingly sophisticated constituency organisations.

However, the dominance of the Conservatives and the Liberals did not mean that they were the only parties which mattered. From the 1880s until 1918, Irish Nationalists, demanding home rule for their country, could depend on a parliamentary strength of more than 80 MPs. For both main parties, the support of this phalanx was well worth having; the trick, though, was to woo the Nationalists without having to adopt policies which might split their own supporters. Gladstone's decision to embrace home rule in 1885 alienated senior Liberals, including Joseph Chamberlain who had been one of the first politicians to understand the importance of professional organisation in the new political environment. Chamberlain joined the Conservatives, who promptly added 'Unionist' to their title in order to emphasise their opposition to home rule.

The situation became even more complicated when the Labour Representation Committee, the forerunner to the Labour Party, was established in 1900. Initially Labour cooperated closely with the Liberals. But it was always likely that an organisation dedicated to securing parliamentary representation for working people would at some stage establish its independence – and equally probable that this development would create serious complications for its longer-established rivals. The Representation of the People Act 1918, which finally abolished property qualifications and extended the franchise to all males aged 21 and over (and to women over 30), opened the prospect that Labour might become the single dominant force in British politics. The payment of MPs, which began in 1912, made parliamentary service into a potential career rather than a part-time hobby for the rich. Without undue reliance on hindsight, it can be argued that the emergence of Labour in this context forced the Conservatives and the Liberals into a life-and-death struggle to see which would survive as the main challenger to an emerging political force which made up in numbers for the relative poverty of its grassroots activists.

On the face of it, the odds were stacked against the Conservatives, who relied heavily on a declining aristocracy. Yet, as Disraeli had understood, many members of the working class were deferential towards aristocrats, while they regarded the Liberal Party as the representative of directly antagonistic business interests. Also, the Conservatives since 1832 had learned to adapt to an unpromising context; Disraeli's acceptance of electoral reform in 1867 was only the most spectacular example of his party's ability to take pragmatic decisions when survival was at stake. However, after 1918 the most important reason for Conservative success was a disastrous feud between the two leading Liberals, Herbert Henry Asquith (Prime Minister, 1908–16) and David Lloyd George (Prime Minister, 1916–22). The schism was not healed until Asquith's death in 1928, by which time the Liberals had been reduced to just 40 MPs.

Despite the precipitate decline in Liberal parliamentary representation, the period between 1922 and 1931 was a genuine respite from the familiar two-party pattern. The classic three-party split came in 1923, when the main parties were divided by little more than 1.2 million votes out of an electorate of 21.2 million (see Table 14.1). Although the Conservatives won more seats than either of their rivals, Labour formed its first (minority) government with support from the Liberals. This apparent symbol of new friendship between 'progressives' across party lines might have formed the basis for a dominant and lasting anti-Conservative coalition, but the Liberals had no intention of surrendering their historic identity in return for a junior partnership with Labour. Besides, some Liberals have always insisted that because they are anti-socialist, their party should avoid becoming too close to Labour. The main consequence of the short-lived 1924 Labour government was to bring the Liberals into further discredit among opponents of socialism for having made the party of the working class look like a respectable organisation capable of running a government without triggering a social revolution. Further defections from the Liberal ranks led to a dismal performance by the party in the 1924 general election. Asquith's death removed the main obstacle to unity among the remaining Liberal Party members, and Lloyd George's inspired leadership ensured a revival in 1929. But a second minority Labour government, elected in that year, collapsed in the face of an economic crisis in 1931. Despite the apparent need for national unity the Liberals split again, and both factions were dwarfed by the other parties. Between 1931 and 1974, their percentage vote only crept into double figures on one occasion (1964).

During the 1950s the two-party system seemed impregnable in an era of class and partisan alignment (see Chapter 18). In 1951, the two largest parties received almost 97 per cent of the UK vote between them, and in the next two elections (1955 and 1959), their combined share again exceeded 90 per cent. In 1964, when the Liberals achieved a double-figure vote share, the party won only nine out of 630 seats; all of the remainder (excluding Northern Ireland) divided between Labour and the Conservatives. Two years later, the Liberals won three more seats, but their share of the vote fell back to 8.5 per cent, and in 1970, the party's 7.5 per cent of the UK vote saw their number of seats fall back to just six, as it had been throughout the 1950s.

TABLE 14.1 Share of the UK vote for the three main parties, 1922–31 (%)

	1922	1923	1924	1929	1931
Conservative	38	38	48	38	55
Labour	29.5	30.5	33	37	32
Liberal	29	29.6	17.6	23.4	11.7

Note: For 1931, figures for Labour and Liberal are collated from supporters and opponents of the National Government.

The decline of the two-party system

Things began to change with the two general elections of 1974 for two reasons of comparable importance (see Analysis 14.2). The first was that the electorate was growing disillusioned with both main parties, and dissatisfied with their performance in government. Labour's Harold Wilson had come to office in 1964 promising a radical, modern approach to the economy, but these hopes were quickly dashed as his government was beset by economic problems which compelled it to abandon some of its promised policies and reforms. By 1970, Britain was afflicted by a double curse: rising inflation and (relatively) high unemployment. The Conservatives led by Edward Heath returned to office in 1970, but their ambitious programme of reform was largely nullified by trade union resistance. Despite their tarnished images, Wilson and Heath led their respective parties into the two elections of 1974 (held in February and October) offering little change from the policies which had apparently failed. It is little wonder that many voters were beginning to look around for a third option. For more than a decade, the two main parties had both been vulnerable to a Liberal revival at by-elections, which provided ideal opportunities for the public to register its dissatisfaction (outside Scotland and Wales, where nationalist parties offered alternative options).

The second reason for the decline of the two-party system was the phenomenon known as 'class dealignment' – the erosion of the stable link between socio-economic factors (most notably occupation) and voting behaviour which had been so important in underpinning the UK's 'catch-all' parties during the 1950s (see Chapter 18). In particular, this development troubled Labour strategists who could no longer depend on instinctive loyalty from the traditional working class. It was not merely a question of giving this social constituency reasons for continuing to vote Labour; social mobility was diminishing the size of the working class itself. Moreover, social mobility – whereby someone from a working-class background attains a middle-class job and lifestyle – often meant that such individuals no longer identified with the working class, and therefore felt less loyalty to the Labour Party. Concern about Labour's shrinking, and less loyal, working-class base intensified during the 1980s and early 1990s, and was an important factor in the emergence of New Labour and its explicit appeal to 'Middle England', along with its rhetorical emphasis on 'community' rather than 'class'.

The victory of Margaret Thatcher's Conservatives had several important additional effects on the party system. The first of these became obvious in 1981, which saw a conscious attempt to 'break the two-party mould' by a group of Labour defectors led by the former Cabinet ministers Roy Jenkins, David Owen, Shirley Williams, and Bill Rodgers. The so-called 'Gang of Four' had become increasingly disillusioned with Labour's adoption of Left-wing policies on a range of issues, such as withdrawal from Europe, extensive nationalisation, abolition of the House of Lords, and unilateral nuclear disarmament. They founded the Social Democratic Party (SDP) and fought the 1983 election in alliance with the Liberals. The combined SDP/Liberal Alliance vote in 1983 was 7.78 million – only 700,000 behind Labour, and in terms of vote share, the Alliance won 25 per cent, compared to Labour's 27 per cent. However, the impact of the first-past-the-post electoral system meant that the Alliance was under-represented in terms of parliamentary seats won, for it only returned 23 MPs, compared to 209 for Labour. Their main problem had been that they came second in very many constituencies, and thus won a large number of votes in total, but under the first-past-the-post system, it is winner-takes-all, with nothing for the runner-up. After another disappointing result in 1987, the two Alliance parties merged and in 1989 adopted the name 'Liberal Democrats'.

The 1983 and 1987 results also highlighted another serious problem which has traditionally faced 'third parties', the 'wasted vote' syndrome. Many voters might want to support a third

Analysis 14.2

'Catch-all' parties and the two-party system

Some commentators argue that a two-party system is a major influence in support of moderate policies. On this account, if a party wants to keep its place in government, or as the main opposition, it will be forced to seek 'the middle ground' of political opinion in the country. It will devise policies which appeal to a significant number of people, while trying not to alienate important groups (and even trying to detach a few 'converts' from what might be regarded as the opposite camp).

An excellent example of a 'catch-all' party in this mould was the Conservative Party between 1945 and 1975. The 'One Nation' politics espoused by leaders like Harold Macmillan and Edward Heath were based on the view that the nation's internal differences could be reconciled, provided that the elected government was prepared to act as an 'honest broker'. This approach was remarkably successful for two decades, and since this inclusive Conservative Party was competing against Labour, which tried to reach out beyond its own working-class 'core constituency', it is reasonable to argue that during these years the overwhelming majority of British voters could feel satisfied with a choice between just two parties. However, the Heath government (1970–74) was dogged by persistent opposition from increasingly militant trade unions, and when the Prime Minister appealed for support from the electorate in February 1974, he was snubbed. Far from embodying national unity, he was regarded by Labour voters as the stooge of big business and by many of his own party as a weak leader who could not stand up to the unions.

Between the late 1970s and mid-1980s, the UK was still dominated by two parties, but neither could have been described as 'moderate' by post-war standards. Mrs Thatcher made no attempt to conciliate groups which she regarded as 'enemies within'. This strategy proved successful, not least because Labour became for some years a 'sweeping-up party' which tried to stitch together a coalition of voters who had different reasons to dislike Thatcherism. The Social Democratic Party (SDP) tried to exploit the desertion of the 'middle ground' by Labour and the Conservatives, but despite early opinion poll findings which suggested that it had become a successful 'catch-all' party almost overnight, its attempt proved premature.

Labour under Neil Kinnock (1983–92) and the Conservatives under John Major (1990–97) tried unconvincingly to adopt the 'catch-all' role, mainly because both leaders were distracted by powerful party factions hoping to keep them on the path of polarisation. Tony Blair's 'New' Labour was a determined attempt to fulfil the promise of the SDP, and the success of the strategy was marked by election victories deep into 'natural' Conservative territory. But the problem for catch-all parties in the context of a dealigned electorate is that they depend crucially on a reputation for governing competence, which in turn rests heavily on factors like the global economy. Once the coalition of voters assembled by a party like New Labour (or the Conservatives in the 'One Nation' era) begins to doubt its competence, there is little residual loyalty for it to fall back on.

party, but recognise that they cannot win under first-past-the-post, and so decide that if they did support them, their vote would be wasted. For many voters, therefore, the only realistic options were to vote Labour or Conservative, albeit with varying degrees of enthusiasm, or abstain from voting altogether. Third parties have thus been caught in a vicious circle or catch-22 situation; they need some form of *proportional representation* to have a realistic chance of ever winning a general election, but because first-past-the-post prevents them from winning in the first place, they cannot form a government which could then introduce PR. Of course, changing the electoral system in a way which would benefit third parties is not in the interests of the two main parties, Labour and the Conservatives. Whatever else the two main parties disagree upon, they both share a constitutional conservatism, an unwillingness to reform the electoral system in a way which would further weaken their dominance – their duopoly.

Another notable effect of Thatcherism was a continued polarisation of the UK in a geographical sense. The Conservatives owed their four successive victories to a virtual monopoly of electoral support in the south and south east of England outside London – an area which gave them 170 seats in 1987. Labour was equally entrenched in (generally declining) inner-city constituencies, and northern towns and cities, and parts of South Wales. The Conservatives' electoral dominance in southern England and the Home Counties contrasted starkly with its decline in Scotland and Wales. In Scotland, the party won 22 seats in 1979, but none at all in 1997, when it also lost the last of the 14 Welsh constituencies it had held back in 1983. The 2001 Conservative 'recovery' in these countries amounted to the recapture of a single Scottish seat. It fared no better in Scotland in 2005 or 2010, although by the latter year it had recovered sufficiently in Wales to win eight (crucial) seats. By contrast, after the 2001 election, Labour held 55 out of 72 Scottish seats and 34 of 40 in Wales. By 2010, the party's tally in Scotland was down to 41 (out of 59) seats, while in Wales, it now held 26 of 40. So far as Westminster politics was concerned, Scotland was still a dominant-party system, with Labour in the driving seat; in Wales, the situation had become somewhat more complicated, but Labour still held a commanding lead over its rivals.

The UK party system since 1997

These figures underline the danger of over-simplification in assessments of the UK party system. Leaving aside the anomaly of Northern Ireland (see below), when examined in detail, Britain since the 1970s has increasingly been characterised by a series of regional mini-party systems rather than a simple national two-party party system. In fact, even when the national and regional variations are screened out, there is plenty of room for debate about the nature of the UK party system, especially since the 2010 general election. There were four possible arguments:

1. The two-party 'mould' was breaking long before the 2010 election, which provided final confirmation of this trend by resulting in a 'hung' parliament and the formation of a coalition government for the first time since the Second World War. Although the Liberal Democrat vote had only edged upwards by less than 2 per cent in 2001, the party increased its parliamentary representation from 46 to 52 MPs. The trend was reinforced in 2005, when a more significant increase in its vote share (to 22 per cent) delivered the Liberal Democrats 62 MPs, the party's highest ever tally. This implies that many voters no longer believed that a vote for the third party was a wasted vote, but were instead beginning to undermine (though by no means destroy) the impact of the first-past-the-post electoral system through 'tactical voting'. Before the 1997 election, Tony Blair had discussed the prospect of a coalition with the (then) Liberal Democrat

TABLE 14.2 Combined vote share of Conservatives and Labour, 1979–2019 (%)

1979	1983	1987	1992	1997	2001	2005	2010	2015	2017	2019
80.8	70.0	73.1	76.3	73.9	72.4	67.6	65.0	67.3	82.4	75.8

leader, Paddy Ashdown, if New Labour failed to secure an overall majority. It could be predicted (see *Exploring British Politics,* 2nd edition, p. 359) that even if the Liberal Democrats were unable to overtake the Conservatives in the near future, there was every chance that some of its MPs would have to be included in a coalition government of some kind. As it was, in the 2010 election the combined vote share of the Conservative and Labour Parties was marginally less than two-thirds (see Table 14.2), and the Liberal Democrats were the main (but not sole) beneficiaries of this decline in the two-party system. While the formation of the Conservative-Liberal Democrat coalition was the most obvious evidence of a new era of multi-party politics, it was equally telling that Labour could now contemplate, however reluctantly, the possibility of an alternative arrangement, with the Liberal Democrats and other (mainly nationalist) parties.

2. The two-party system remained alive and (reasonably) well, despite the superficial appearances of 2010. In 2001, the Liberal Democrats performed little better in terms of vote share than their Liberal predecessors did in October 1974 when they returned only 13 MPs. Even though the Conservatives ran a poor campaign under an unpopular leader (William Hague) in 2001, the Liberal Democrats did not even come close to challenging them for second place. The Liberal Democrats only edged upwards slightly in 2005, in a general election where they seemed well placed to attract the votes of erstwhile Labour supporters disillusioned by the Iraq War, and the imminent introduction of student fees. Tactical voting is still unusual in a country where people are increasingly disinclined to vote at all, rather than research the likely effects of a tactical switch in seats where the Liberal Democrats are the main challengers to either of their bigger rivals. In the 2010 general election campaign, the Liberal Democrats enjoyed a sudden surge of support after the first televised leadership debate, in which Nick Clegg performed very well, but the electorate soon reverted to type, and the Liberal Democrats actually lost five seats in the 2010 general election, although they still entered a coalition with the Conservatives. However, these were very unusual circumstances, and in any case, they could only be very junior partners; the key Ministerial posts and policy portfolios went to Conservatives, yet in 2015, it was the Liberal Democrats who incurred the wrath of voters for the more unpopular policies enacted by the coalition – they slumped from 57 seats in 2010 to just 8 in 2015.

The Conservatives won a narrow parliamentary majority in 2015, then lost it in 2017, when it felt compelled to enter into a parliamentary pact (not a coalition, because no Ministerial posts were shared) with Northern Ireland's Democratic Unionist Party, in order to muster enough MPs combined to deliver a wafer-thin majority in House of Commons' votes. Not until 2019 did the Conservatives finally win a landslide victory in a general election, the first time it had achieved such a defeat since 1987. Conversely, the 2019 result meant that the Labour Party had failed to win any of the last four general elections, its last victory being back in 2005. By the time of the next general election in 2025 (assuming the Johnson Government serves a full five-year term), Labour will have been in Opposition for 15 years, struggling both to convince the electorate of its economic competence and credibility again, and finding a leader as politically charismatic and popular as Tony Blair was in 1997 and 2001, although Keir Starmer appeared, in the Spring of 2020, to have made a promising start to his leadership, judging by his authoritative performances at Prime Minister's Question Time. Nonetheless, the post-2010 collapse in the Liberal Democrats' support would suggest that Britain or, rather, England has reverted to two-partyism again, with the Conservatives and Labour the only two effective choices for most voters, their combined share of the vote reaching 82.4 per cent in 2017, when the Liberal Democrats slumped to 7.4 per cent of the vote – about a third of its 2010 share.

The claim that Britain has returned to two-partyism is further supported by the experience of the most recent attempt to 'break the mould' of British politics or 'fix Britain's broken politics' (in the words of Anna Soubry MP), namely the formation of The Independent Group. Formed in Spring 2019, the Group – which soon changed its name to Change UK – was created by 11 'moderate' anti-Brexit MPs from the Conservative and Labour Parties, the expectation being that other 'moderates' would soon join them. The leading Labour defectors, such as Chuka Umunna, Luciana Berger, Mike Gapes, Chris Leslie, and Angela Smith, were deeply unhappy with the Left-wing leadership of Jeremy Corbyn and his equivocation over Brexit. Their Conservative counterparts, such as Anna Soubry, Heidi Allen, and Sarah Wollaston, were similarly unhappy with the Rightwards drift of former their Party, and particularly the support of many Tory MPs for a 'hard Brexit', or even a 'No Deal' Brexit. However, following a deeply disappointing performance in the 2019 European Parliament election, when it only attracted 3.4 per cent of votes cast and failed to win any of the UK's seats, the nascent Party split, whereupon a few of its MPs joined the Liberal Democrats (Photo 14.1).

3. The 2010 election showed that the UK had become a *two-and-a-half party system*, at least with regard to Westminster (see Analysis 14.1). With 62 MPs after the 2005 general election, the Liberal Democrats were poised to take a central role in any future contest where the two main parties were relatively evenly matched in terms of support or seats won. After the 2010 contest, the Liberal Democrats were approached by Labour and the Conservatives alike. Despite the plummeting Liberal Democrat opinion poll ratings after entering into a coalition with the Conservatives, and seemingly being held responsible by voters for the more unpopular policies enacted, right up until the 2015 election, it seemed entirely possible that they would retain their place in government as a partner to either of the two main parties. Indeed, it has been claimed that when David Cameron pledged, in 2013, a future referendum on the UK's continued membership of the EU, he was expecting the 2015 general election to be a virtual repeat of 2010, whereupon the Liberal Democrats would oblige him to abandon the promised referendum as the price of renewing the coalition. It proved to be a major tactical blunder by Cameron. Although the Conservatives won an outright (but narrow) parliamentary majority in 2015, the most notable result was that UKIP won four million votes, albeit winning only one seat in the House of Commons, due to

PHOTO 14.1 The Independent Group / Change UK (© Finnbarr Webster/Getty Images).

the vagaries of first-past-the-post. Then, in 2017, the Conservatives lost their narrow majority, and were only able to form a government by entering into a parliamentary 'pact' with Northern Ireland's Democratic Unionist party (DUP), the deal doubtless facilitated by finding an extra £1 billion of funding for Northern Ireland, in spite of the austerity measures being inflicted on the rest of the UK.

4. It is possible to argue that the UK became a *dominant-party system* between 1979 and 2010, even if the life cycle for the dominant parties was relatively short by international standards (see Analysis 14.1). In a genuine two-party system, the leading opposition group should have a reasonable expectation of winning power at the next election. By contrast, the Conservatives were easily re-elected in 1983 and 1987 while the Labour Opposition was in disarray, and despite problems over the poll tax, the Conservative Party still managed to win in 1992, partly because Labour was not trusted on the key issue of economic competence, and because John Major, the Conservative leader, was viewed as a 'safe pair of hands' and a calming influence, both compared to the radicalism of the Thatcher premiership, and in comparison to Labour's leader, Neil Kinnock. After the eventual swing of the political pendulum, Labour's victories in 1997, 2001, and 2005 were regarded as foregone conclusions long before the votes were cast and counted; like the Conservatives in 1992, Labour was able to win in 2005 despite a recent policy disaster (in this case the war on Iraq). Although the party's majority in 2005 was 'only' 66 seats, compared to 167 in 2001, there were no early signs that its performance in office during this third term would mark a significant change from previous trends. It would, in short, behave like a 'dominant' party up until the time when the electorate finally decided to issue the party a P45. That moment came in May 2010, and since neither Labour nor the Conservatives could secure an overall majority in that election, it would seem that the notion of a dominant-party system was disproved by that result. However, 31 years of effective domination by the two main parties amounted to a protracted period in which certain habits were seemingly learned. There was no guarantee in 2010 that the coalition would prove to be anything more than a brief hiatus, after which either a two-party or a dominant-party pattern would reassert itself. Indeed, although the Conservatives did not actually win in 2010 or 2017, and only narrowly won in 2017, it remains the case that the Labour Party has now lost the last four general elections – which hardly seems to suggest a return to two-partyism.

This fourth possibility – that Britain has begun to reflect the characteristics of a dominant-party system – has serious consequences from a democratic perspective. The political culture of the UK – with no codified constitution to curb the ambitions or conduct of a government – encourages winning parties to claim that they have won a clear electoral mandate' to introduce the policies in its manifesto, even though they invariably fall well short of an overall majority (i.e. more than 50 per cent) of votes cast nationally, and in spite of the fact that few voters read the parties' manifestos, or even agree with every policy pledged by 'their' party. Many Labour voters historically have disagreed with the party's formal commitment to nationalisation, and some Conservative supporters have, over time, become less enthusiastic about privatisation. Under the 'Westminster Model', successive governments have exhibited behaviour which the Conservative politician Lord Hailsham (in a celebrated 1976 lecture) called an 'elective dictatorship', even when they have won a relatively small proportion of the popular vote – Labour's 66-seat parliamentary majority in 2005 was secured on just 36 per cent of total votes cast. Governing parties are tempted to treat their parliamentary opponents with contempt, and to make key bureaucratic or political appointments with a view to cementing their power – oblivious to the possibility that the weapons they forge might be used against them when they eventually return to Opposition. In short, governments in a dominant-party system tend to overlook the key distinction between rule in the interest of their party and its supporters (and donors), and governing in the interest of the nation as a whole; governments often conflate their own partisan goals with serving the 'national interest'. This also means that legitimate criticism of a government – essential to holding it to account and subjecting it to scrutiny – might be dismissed, by Ministers, as unpatriotic or 'politically motivated'. Meanwhile, critics also allege that the effects of the 'dominant-party' ethos have been apparent in the conduct of the British civil service since the 1980s, and the nature of appointments (see Chapter 10).

Almost the only crumb of comfort to be derived from the record of dominant parties is that their behaviour usually brings about their own downfall: hubris eventually leads to humiliation. The British people might be slow to anger, but eventually, they will become deeply annoyed by repeated displays of political arrogance and abuse of power by their political leaders; people do not like to feel that they are being taken for granted, or treated as fools, by their elected representatives. Politicians should always heed the warning in the opening lines of G. K Chesterton's 1907 poem 'The Secret People': 'Smile at us, pay us, pass us; but do not quite forget; For we are the people of England, that never have spoken yet'.

During their years of virtually uncontested power, both the Conservatives and Labour have shown a tendency to waste much of their energies on internal faction-fighting, and to become embroiled in allegations of 'sleaze', these usually relating to financial or sexual misconduct and misdemeanours. Maybe, for some senior politicians, political power acts as an aphrodisiac, or can corrupt. These have also been features of dominant parties in other countries: e.g. the Japanese Liberal Democratic Party, which was in power continuously between 1945 and 1993, and the Italian Christian Democrats who enjoyed a similar lease of office. Both eventually collapsed amid allegations of corruption. Maybe Lord Acton was correct when he claimed, in 1887, that 'Power tends to corrupt, and absolute power corrupts absolutely'. Certainly, advocates of electoral reform often claim that the almost inevitable coalition governments which would ensue from a more proportional voting system would make such abuse of power less likely, because the 'third party' holding the balance of power would act as a constraint or moderating influence on the larger party in government. On the other hand, the 'third party' itself might become corrupted as a consequence of sharing political power.

Party systems in Scotland and Wales

As we have seen, the overall pattern of party competition for general (Westminster) elections in recent years would provide a highly misleading impression of the 'regional' contests in Scotland and Wales. The introduction of devolved institutions, elected by the semi-proportional Addition Member System (AMS), has underlined this point, and also illustrated the distorting effect of first-past-the-post in terms of the true levels of party support in these two nations. The effects of different voting systems have been particularly dramatic in Scotland, where Labour initially fared much better in Westminster contests under first-past-the-post than they did in elections to the Scottish Parliament, for which AMS was used. Yet after the 2015 general election, Labour also suffered badly from the operations of a voting system which had previously served them very well in Westminster contests. It seemed that many voters who supported the SNP in Scottish Parliament elections subsequently voted for the party in general elections too, thereby compounding Labour's decline in Scotland.

If the Scottish poet Robert Burns had been alive to witness the electoral consequences of Labour's devolution project in his native land, he would have seen it as evidence for his claim that

'The best laid plans o' mice an' men/Gang aft agley/An' lea'e us nought but grief an' pain'. Tony Blair had not been enthusiastic about devolution in the first place, but calculated that if Scotland was given its own Parliament (while remaining one of the four nations of the UK), then the growing support for the SNP would evaporate – it would have achieved its mission – whereupon Labour would re-establish its former dominance in Scotland. Yet once the Scottish Parliament had been established in 1999, the SNP actually replaced Labour as the main 'progressive' or left-of-centre party in Scotland, particularly as Blair's Party was widely viewed as an English phenomenon which had abandoned many of its socialist principles and policies in order to appeal to conservative 'Middle England'. By the time that Blair had stood down as Labour leader, it was too late: the SNP had won the support of many former Labour supporters in Scotland, and few of them were inclined to abandon their new political allegiance, in spite of the change in Labour's leadership (and the fact that Gordon Brown himself was Scottish).

What compounded Labour's post-devolution decline in Scotland was that AMS had been chosen for elections to the devolved institutions precisely because it was expected to make it much more difficult for the nationalist parties in Scotland and Wales to secure overall majorities, and certainly, after the 1999 and 2003 devolved elections, the prospects of the SNP or Plaid Cymru forming majority governments in their respective countries seemed fairly remote, but the 2007 elections saw major developments. The SNP emerged as the largest party in the Scottish Parliament in 2007, whereupon its leader Alex Salmond was chosen as First Minister – after a parliamentary vote in which the Greens supported him, while the Liberal Democrats and the Conservatives abstained. The SNP increased its support in the 2011 Scottish Parliament election, such that its 69 seats (out of 129) delivered a clear majority, Labour having won 37 seats, the Conservatives 15, and the Liberal Democrats five. Then, in the 2016 Scottish Parliament election, the SNP emerged as the single largest party, but this time two seats short of a majority, having lost six seats. Meanwhile, having won a total of 31 seats, the Conservatives replaced Labour as the second largest Party, as Labour's decline in Scotland continued, losing 13 seats from 2011 and ending up with 24 (Table 14.3).

Meanwhile, in Wales, although Labour has remained the single largest Party in all Welsh Assembly elections since 1999, it has not always won an overall majority of the 60 seats. From 1999 to 2003, Welsh Labour formed a coalition with the Liberal Democrats, while from 2007 to 2011, it governed Wales in a coalition with Plaid Cymru. Meanwhile, in the two most recent Welsh Assembly elections, the Conservatives and Plaid Cymru have been the rivals for second place.

Devolution and a semi-proportional electoral system yielded not only different party systems and permutations in Scotland and Wales, but also 'policy divergence' from England and Westminster, particularly with regard to education, health, and social care policies (see Chapter 12). Both the SNP and Welsh Labour have rejected the Conservatives' and New Labour's policy of

TABLE 14.3 Distribution of seats in the Welsh Assembly and Scottish Parliament, 2011 and 2016

Scotland			Wales		
Party	2011	2016	Party	2011	2016
SNP	69 (+22)	63 (-6)	Labour	30 (+4)	29 (-1)
Labour	37 (-9)	24 (-13)	Conservative	14 (-1)	11 (-3)
Conservative	15 (-2)	31 (+16)	Plaid Cymru	11 (-4)	12 (+1)
Lib Dems	5 (-11)	5 (N/C)	Lib Dems	5 (-1)	1 (-4)
Greens	2 (-)	6 (+4)	UKIP	0 (N/C)	7 (+7)
Independents	1 (-)	0 (-1)			

Note: Figures in brackets refer to change since previous election.

The problems faced by third parties in Britain

Two of the main problems traditionally encountered by third parties in Britain are the first-past-the-post electoral system and class alignment (discussed in Chapters 17 and 18): both of these played a major role in sustaining the dominance of the Conservative and Labour Parties, especially in the House of Commons. Yet vital though these two factors are, third parties have also suffered a range of other problems, although since the 1990s, these have partly or periodically abated. First, these parties have been widely viewed as 'single-issue' parties: the Greens obviously associated with environmental issues, the British National Party within immigration, and both UKIP and the Brexit Party with terminating the UK's membership of the EU. Most of the time, the vast majority of the British electorate has not considered these issues important enough to warrant voting for these parties (quite apart from the 'wasted vote' syndrome caused by the electoral system). In most general elections, most voters either vote on a range of issues – with Labour and the Conservatives viewed as 'catch-all' parties offering a package of policies to address these – or identify which issue(s) they consider to be most important to them, their family or the country. In either scenario, the particular issue most closely associated with a third party is unlikely to be of high importance or 'salience' to many voters, although there are exceptions: UKIP attracted four million votes in the 2015 general election due to either the determination of many voters to secure the UK's departure from the EU or the charismatic/populist appeal of UKIP's leader at that time, Nigel Farage. Usually, though, the issues with which third parties are most closely associated are considered too narrow, unimportant, or niche by most voters. Besides, if the issue does acquire increased importance or 'saliency' among voters, then one (or both) of the two main parties will adopt it, and incorporate it into their own programme or manifesto.

Another problem faced by third parties concerns an absence of credibility due to lack of governing experience. Quite apart from the vagaries of Britain's electoral system, and former class alignment, it has been difficult for third parties to convince many voters of their potential competence as a prospective government. Unlike Labour and the Conservatives, no third party has governed Britain since 1945, notwithstanding the Liberal Democrats' (unhappy) role in the 2010–15 coalition with the Conservatives. As such, third parties are an unknown quantity to most voters, and therefore, voting one of them into government would be deemed a huge risk, due to their lack of experience. This, of course, is a vicious circle or a catch-22; third parties rarely attract much support because they have no recent (if any) track record of governing and thus of having proved their competence, yet they will never be able to illustrate their competence in government until and unless they can attract enough votes to get elected in the first place.

Third parties have also suffered from a relative lack of media coverage and press support. Most of Britain's national daily newspapers are highly partisan, with many of them enthusiastically supporting the Conservatives, while the *Daily Mirror* has always been pro-Labour. Only *The Guardian* has ever been politically sympathetic to the progressive/centrist Liberals, Social Democratic Party, and then the Liberal

Democrats, but the paper has a small readership compared to the 'Tory tabloids' and the *Mirror*. Meanwhile, although broadcasting media (radio and TV) is obliged to be politically neutral (notwithstanding that Left and Right alike both accuse broadcasters – especially the BBC – of being biased in favour of 'the other side'), this neutrality is pursued by simply giving equal airtime to the stance of the Labour and Conservative Parties when reporting on an issue or event: for example, a news item on the future of student finance will usually include a short interview with or quote or soundbite from the Government's education Minister, and a comparable (in length) response from the main Opposition party's education spokesperson or 'shadow Minister'. Rarely will the views or policy preferences of the third parties be sought or conveyed. This is probably not due to deliberate bias by the broadcasters, but because of the editorial practicalities of covering several news items or issues in a limited amount of time; there will not usually be enough time to elicit a range of views beyond those of the two main parties – who, after all, will usually have attracted the vast majority of votes in the most recent general election, and can thus claim to be most representative of most voters. This, though, serves to reinforce a common assumption that on any economic, social, or international issue, there is a Conservative position, and a Labour position – two sides to every story.

Finally, third parties have struggled to compete effectively against the two main parties due to lack of funding, income which can be used to rent well-equipped offices in prime (and thus expensive) locations near Parliament, employ (more) professional full-time staff, and pay for advertising during election campaigns – newspaper adverts, billboard posters, mailshots and leaflets to households, and advertising (both general and targeted) via social media. The Conservatives have always benefitted from donations from companies and wealthy supporters, and Labour has been financially supported by the trade unions. Third parties, however, have usually had to rely on membership fees and fund-raising events, and even when they have attracted additional donations from individual supporters, these have usually been much less than the sums received by the two main parties. For example, in the run-up to the 2019 general election, the Conservatives received donations of £19.4 million, Labour secured £5.4 million, the Liberal Democrats attracted just £1.3 million, and £0.2 million was donated to the Greens (https://commonslibrary.parliament.uk/insights/general-election-2019-which-party-received-the-most-donations/). Britain is a parliamentary democracy with formal political equality, entailing one-person, one-vote, regardless of any individual's wealth or income, but the parties clearly do not compete on a level-playing-field in terms of finance and funding. Once again, the third parties are at a distinct disadvantage compared to the Conservative and Labour Parties, yet their lack of funding is unlikely to change until or unless they are deemed likely to win a general election; only the most committed third party supporter is likely to judge it worthwhile donating a sizeable sum of money to a party which has absolutely no chance of winning an election.

'marketisation' and 'contracting-out' of public services, and instead prioritised keeping services 'in house', while also adopting a co-operative, consultative, style of policy making – thus rejecting 'managerialism' – so that front-line professionals and service-users have a voice in the design and delivery of public services. Also, the Scottish Parliament did not adopt England's student fees regime for Scottish students who studied at a Scottish university – reflecting a cultural difference, whereby higher education in Scotland is viewed as a 'public good' and social investment which benefits society, rather than a 'private economic transaction' by students who are assumed to be investing in their future career and supposedly higher earnings. Meanwhile, since October 2018, trains in Wales have been operated by Transport for Wales, a not-for-profit company (this does not actually mean that it makes no profit – or does not aim to do so – but that any profits are reinvested directly in the firm to maintain and improve services, rather than being extracted by the owners or shareholders).

The experience of Scotland and Wales illustrates how the introduction of electoral systems enshrining 'proportionality' (there are different forms of PR, some more proportional than others – see Chapter 17) can greatly enhance the electoral fortunes of 'third' parties. Whereas such parties often struggle to achieve electoral success under first-past-the-post – an electoral system which tends to underpin two-party or dominant-party systems – when more proportional methods of voting are adopted, other parties often win more seats based on their share of the vote, and in general (Westminster) elections, they are often under-represented, because the number of seats won in the House of Commons does not accurately reflect either the number of votes won or their share of votes cast. Also, when more proportional electoral systems are adopted, voters realise that voting for a 'third' party is much less likely to constitute a 'wasted' vote compared to elections held using first-past-the-post. Furthermore, elections to the devolved institutions have also boosted the electoral fortunes of parties like the SNP and Plaid Cymru because many Scottish and Welsh voters have seen them as more reflective or representative of 'regional' issues or values than the 'national' Labour and Conservative Parties.

The party system in Northern Ireland

In Northern Ireland, the main cleavage between parties has arisen from markedly different cultures, national identities, and religious beliefs, rather than social class, and has therefore resulted in a very different pattern of political competition and representation compared to other parts of Britain, particularly England (see Chapter 12). Elections to the (devolved) Northern Ireland Assembly also deploy a form of PR, namely the Single Transferable Vote (STV), which underpins a multi-party system that reflects the cultural, political, and religious divisions in the Province. However, it must be emphasised that using a form of PR for Northern Ireland Assembly elections has not been the cause of this political fragmentation, but a consequence of it. PR is often adopted in societies which are already characterised by deep or long-standing social cleavages – cultural, ethnic, linguistic, religious, etc. The rationale is that only a high degree of proportionality in elections can ensure that the parties representing different communities will win a sufficient number of seats to ensure that they share governmental power – a coalition government and, in Northern Ireland's case, 'consociational democracy'. In effect, the electoral system is intended to ensure that in a deeply divided society, with a tragically troubled history of bitterness and bloodshed, the parties representing the different communities are virtually compelled to work together, and so gradually establish a degree of trust and willingness to compromise.

The nature of the divisions in Northern Ireland is such that Protestants/Unionists have been represented by the Ulster Unionists (UUP) and Democratic Unionists (DUP), while the Catholics/Nationalists have been represented by Sinn Fein, and the Social Democratic and Labour Party (SDLP). The parties on either side differ in their approaches to the long-running political problems of Northern Ireland. The DUP has been the more hard-line Protestant party, and was initially opposed to the 1998 Good Friday Agreement, which the more moderate or pragmatic UUP accepted. On the Catholic side, the SDLP has always been in favour of a united Ireland achieved peacefully and constitutionally, while Sinn Fein, as the political wing of the Irish Republican Army (IRA), refused to acknowledge the 'legitimacy' of Northern Ireland or the presence of the British Army, and thus pursued a dual approach: the bullet and the ballot box: Sinn Fein took part in elections while the IRA engaged in terrorist or paramilitary activities in pursuit of a 'united Ireland'. As a consequence of the Good Friday Agreement, Sin Fein and the IRA formally abandoned the 'armed struggle', with Sinn Finn committing itself to constitutional and democratic politics. However, 'dissident' Republican terrorist groups – such as 'Continuity IRA' – have occasionally pursued paramilitary violence via bombs and bullets, insisting that the Good Friday Agreement – and Sinn Fein's participation in the Northern Ireland government, in tandem with the IRA surrendering its weapons – was a betrayal of those who had fought (and sometimes been killed) for a united Ireland. Until the implementation of direct rule from Westminster in 1972, Northern Ireland had a dominant-party system. The UUP was genuinely popular among the protestant majority, and it reinforced its position by the creative drawing of electoral boundaries (what is known as 'gerrymandering).

After decades of political conflict and paramilitary violence, the 1998 Good Friday Agreement heralded a new era of relative peace in Northern Ireland, although occasional paramilitary violence still occurs, and the Northern Ireland Assembly has also sometimes been suspended by British governments at Westminster, due to the periodic inability of politicians in the Northern Ireland Assembly to reach agreement on various key issues. When it has operated, and elections to the Assembly held, the electoral fortunes of the UUP and the DUP have been almost exactly reversed; the UUP vote fell from 32.7 per cent in 1997 to a low of 13.2 per cent in 2011, while over the same period the DUP climbed from 13.6 per cent to a high of 33.7 per cent in 2005. The position of the SDLP has deteriorated in a similar fashion vis-à-vis Sinn Fein. Indeed, in the 2010 Westminster elections Sinn Fein actually emerged as the most popular party in terms of vote share – even though its elected representatives would never take up their seats in the old 'Imperial' parliament; they refuse to swear the Oath of Allegiance to the Queen, which is required of new MPs (Table 14.4).

The willingness of voters to defect from the 'respectable' Northern Ireland parties towards politicians who, in some cases, were once dismissed as extremists is an ironic by-product of an initiative which was carefully designed to bolster moderation. The STV system in itself is an effective way to secure representation for a wide range of parties, but the final mix in the Northern Ireland Assembly was supposed to include a strong contingent from smaller moderate groupings (notably the non-sectarian Alliance Party), which had previously lost potential support because they had little chance of winning seats under first-past-the-post. Furthermore, the UK government ensured that the NI executive formed after the 1998 elections was a 'Grand Coalition', containing members of all four main parties. However, this arrangement initially proved unworkable, mainly due to the obstructive attitude of the DUP. Although the 2003 Assembly elections eventually went ahead, the institution had been suspended since October 2002. After the 2007 election, however, the DUP leader Ian Paisley agreed to serve as First Minister alongside Sinn Fein, with the former IRA commander Martin McGuinness as his deputy.

The 2017 elections to the Northern Ireland Assembly were the first to be held following a reduction in the number of seats, from 108 to 90. This seemed to affect the DUP most of all, for although it emerged as the single largest party with 28 seats, this was 10 fewer than it had previously won. Moreover, its 2017 tally was only one more than that attained by Sinn Fein. Indeed, with the two Unionist parties winning a total of 38 seats, and the two Nationalist parties winning a total of 39 seats, it meant that the two Catholic parties had fared marginally better

TABLE 14.4 Share of votes for the main parties in Northern Ireland, 1997–2019 (%)

Party	1997 Westminster	1998 Assembly	2001 Westminster	2003 Assembly	2005 Westminster	2007 Assembly	2010 Westminster	2011 Assembly	2015 Westminster	2016 Assembly	2017 Westminster	2017 Assembly	2019 Westminster
DUP	13.6 (2)	18.1(20)	22.5 (5)	25.6 (30)	33.7 (9)	30.1 (36)	25 (8)	30.0 (8)	25.7 (8)	29.2 (38)	36.0 (10)	28.1 (28)	30.6 (8)
Sinn Fein	16.1 (2)	17.6 (18)	21.7 (4)	23.5 (24)	24.3 (5)	26.2 (28)	25.5 (5)	26.9 (29)	24.5 (4)	24.0 (28)	29.4 (7)	27.9 (27)	29.4 (7)
UUP	32.7 (10)	21.3 (28)	26.8 (6)	22.7 (27)	17.7 (1)	14.9 (18)	15.2 (0)	13.2 (16)	16.0 (2)	12.6 (16)	10.3 (0)	12.9 (10)	14.9 (2)
SDLP	24.1 (3)	22 (24)	21.0 (3)	17 (18)	17.5 (3)	15.2 (16)	16.5 (3)	14.2 (14)	13.9 (3)	12.0 (12)	11.7 (0)	11.9 (12)	11.7 (0)

Note: Figures in brackets refer to seats won.

than the two Protestant parties, the first time this had ever happened in Northern Ireland. This did not mean that the Nationalists actually had an overall majority in the Assembly, because the Alliance Party and the Greens won eight and two seats, respectively, but nonetheless, the advance of the Nationalists – albeit aided by the DUP's loss of seats following the reduction in the size of the NI Assembly – did seem to reflect a change in the demographics of the population. When Northern Ireland was created in 1921, the Protestants constituted 66 per cent of the population, and the Catholics 33 per cent, but in the most recent census (conducted every ten years) in 2011, the balance had changed to 48 per cent and 45 per cent, respectively. Given these demographic and political trends, it is not surprising that many Unionists have been increasingly anxious about their – and Northern Ireland's – future.

Conclusion and summary

When a governing party in the UK fares badly in a contest like a local election, the invariable response is that things will be very different when the nation votes in 'the only contest that really matters' – i.e. the next UK-wide general election. Sometimes this hackneyed claim turns out to be justified, and it is true that many second-order elections are treated by voters as a means of administering a 'painless' warning to a government which retains its underlying popularity.

However, while governments feel that it is relatively harmless to tinker with the electoral systems at sub-national level, it is now valid to ask a question which would have seemed ridiculous in (say) 1955: 'What is the *real* UK party system?'. Although the two-party mould was shaken by the SDP–Liberal alliance in the 1980s, until 1997 the actual results of elections suggested that the old pattern of party competition was fraying at the edges rather than unravelling. After 1997, the revival of the Liberal Democrats as something more than a vehicle for protest votes was significant enough to arouse speculation about genuine multi-party competition. But more importantly, since the introduction of PR for devolved assemblies and the European elections, the underlying diversity of the UK electorate has emerged from the misleading picture of party support created by simple plurality (first-past-the-post). The failure of the 'yes' campaign in the 2011 referendum on electoral reform seems to rule out significant change in the short term, at least, with the likely effect that the disparity between the balance of forces at Westminster and the mood among an increasingly diverse electorate is likely to make itself more before apparent with every election which is held under a proportional system.

The Westminster government still seems to regard rival institutions as strictly subordinated, like a glorified local government. Almost certainly it would have responded in the same way if regional government had been introduced in England and resulted in the predictable multi-party pattern of competition. Until 2014–15, the results of elections to devolved institutions and the European Parliament had made little impact at Westminster, but it was hardly surprising when the underlying patterns of party support revealed by proportional voting systems eventually 'spilled over' in the form of surges of support for UKIP and the SNP. Even the first-past-the-post system, which was reprieved in the 2011 referendum, seemed unlikely to sustain the historic Labour-Conservative duopoly at UK (Westminster) level, although the result of the 2017 election did suggest that reports of its death were premature, and in the 2019 election too, the Conservatives and Labour remained by far the two largest parties in parliament. Unless or until this changes, the distorting and exaggerating effects of the first-past-the-post electoral system are likely to mean that the two major British parties will continue to regard politics as a 'zero sum game' in which the 'winner takes all', and are therefore perfectly entitled to act as if the whole country has awarded them an unequivocal mandate to govern; as if Britain remains an 'elective dictatorship'.

Further reading

The classic work on party systems is G. Sartori, *Parties and Party Systems: A Framework for Analysis* (Cambridge: Cambridge University Press, 1976). P. Webb, *The Modern British Party System* (London: SAGE, 2000) is an excellent advanced text. S. Ingle, *The British Party System: An Introduction* (London: Routledge, 4th edition, 2007) is a highly readable and insightful account, although it also deals at length with party organisation and ideology. L. Robbins, H. Blackmore and R. Pyper (eds.), *Britain's Changing Party System* (Leicester: Leicester University Press, 1994) includes some discussions which are still useful although the system has continued to change since the volume was published. Andrew Heywood's chapter, warning of the emergence of a dominant-party system, is particularly pertinent. Much more recently R. Awan-Scully has published *The End of British Party Politics?* (London: Biteback, 2018). See also P. Webb's 'The Party System: Turbulent Multipartyism or Duoplostic Competition?', and M. Kenny's 'Ideological Politics and the Party System' in R. Heffernan, C. Hay, M. Russell and P. Cowley (eds.), *Developments in British Politics 10* (Basingstoke: Palgrave Macmillan, 2016). P. Cowley, 'Political Parties and the British Party System', in R. Heffernan, P Cowley and C. Hay (eds.), *Developments in British Politics 9* (Basingstoke: Palgrave Macmillan, 2011) is an update in the light of the 2010 general election. R. Garner and P Lynch, 'The Changing Party System', *Parliamentary Affairs*, Vol. 58, No. 3 (2005), pp. 533–54, and A. Russell, 'The Party System: Deep Frozen or Gentle Thawing?', *Parliamentary Affairs*, Vol. 58, No. 2 (2005), pp. 351–65, also include reflections which are still relevant. The significance of electoral systems is assessed in P. Dunleavy, 'Facing up to Multi-Party Politics', *Parliamentary Affairs*, Vol. 58, No. 3 (2005), pp. 503–32. On the situation after the 2015 general election, see A. Geddes and J. Tonge's introductory chapter, 'Single Party Government in a Fragmented System', among other relevant contributions to their edited volume *Britain Votes 2015* (Oxford: Oxford University Press, 2015). For the 2017 election, see J. Tonge, C. Leston-Bandeira, and S. Wilks-Heeg (eds.) *Britain Votes 2017* (Oxford: Oxford University Press, 2018). For the 2019 election, see J. Bartle and N.J. Allen, *Breaking the Deadlock: Britain at the Polls, 2019* (Manchester: Manchester University Press, 2020).

Useful overviews of the various party systems within the UK include a selection of articles that have appeared in *Politics Review*. On the 2005 general election, see D. Denver, 'Four- Party Competition in Scotland', *Politics Review*, Vol. 15, No. 2 (2005), pp. 19–21; J. Bradbury, 'Labour Power under Pressure in Wales', *Politics Review*, Vol. 15, No. 2 (2005), pp. 16–18, and J. Tonge, 'DUP and Sinn Fein Triumph in Northern Ireland', *Politics Review*, Vol. 15, No. 2 (2005), pp. 10–13. On elections to the devolved assemblies, see D. Denver, '2007 Scottish Parliament Elections: a Historic Moment?', *Politics Review*, Vol. 17, No. 1 (2007), pp. 19–21, J. Bradbury, '2007 Welsh Assembly Elections: Electoral Fragmentation and the Politics of Coalition', *Politics Review*, Vol. 17, No. 2 (2007), pp. 13–16, and J. Tonge, 'The Return of Devolved Power-Sharing to Northern Ireland', *Politics* Review, Vol. 17, No. 2 (2007), pp. 8–12. R. Wyn Jones and R. Scully, 'Devolution and Electoral Politics in Scotland and Wales', *Publius: The Journal of Federalism*, Vol. 36, No. 1 (2006), pp. 115–34, is a more detailed study.

Websites

The official websites of British political parties contain details on their election results and policies. Richard Kimber's politics 'gateway' (www.politicsresources.net) provides valuable links. The websites of the main parties in the UK are:

Conservative Party: www.conservatives.com
Labour Party: www.labour.org.uk

Liberal Democrats: www.libdems.org.uk
Plaid Cymru: www.plaidcymru.org
Scottish National Party: www.snp.org
Greens: www.greenparty.org.uk
UK Independence Party: www.ukip.org
Brexit Party: www.thebrexitparty.org/
Democratic Unionist Party: www.dup.org.uk
Ulster Unionist Party: www.uup.org
Sinn Fein: www. sinnfein.ie
Social Democratic and Labour Party: www.sdlp.ie

Chapter 15

Party organisation

Learning outcomes

After reading this chapter, you will:

- be able to explore different perspectives on the role of UK parties;
- understand the organisation of the main political parties in the UK; and
- be able to evaluate the strengths and weaknesses of the rules governing party finance.

Introduction

Most commentators accept that political parties are an inevitable feature of liberal democracy. Yet in the UK today, parties are often accused of bringing democracy into disrepute. Critics claim that they are more interested in 'playing party politics' than in addressing national priorities in a constructive fashion.

It is usually argued that disillusion with political parties is a major factor in the decline in voter turnout in general elections. Certainly this trend, culminating in a figure of below 60 per cent in 2001, coincided with a sharp fall in membership of the parties themselves. In defence of UK parties, it can be argued that their plight merely reflects a more general tendency of people to disengage from traditional forms of voluntary activity. In particular, citizens are more inclined to throw their energies into single-issue pressure groups, which lobby MPs instead of putting themselves to the trouble of securing their own elected representatives (see Chapter 19). However, it is still worth asking whether there are respects in which the main political parties are responsible for their own predicament by mismanaging factors under their own control, like the scope for active participation allowed to their members, and the way in which they raise funds.

From cadre parties to mass parties

It would be an exaggeration to say that politics in the first phase of British party competition was merely a game confined to aristocrats. Some MPs came from relatively humble backgrounds, and people who lacked the vote could exert some influence over decisions by demonstrating in support of their favoured causes. However, even after the franchise was expanded by the 1832 Great Reform Act, non-aristocratic MPs usually owed their seats to aristocratic patronage. The loose political groupings of the eighteenth and early nineteenth centuries – the 'Whigs' and the 'Tories' – are best understood as **cadre parties.** They were associations of affluent individuals who joined together for specific political purposes but retained enough independence to make new alliances (or to retire from public life) if circumstances changed.

An alternative model of political organisation is a **mass party** – one which depends on a large membership to finance the party at national and local levels, publicise its activities, run campaigns, and recruit potential leaders. In the UK, mass parties began to emerge after a further expansion of the franchise in 1867. This second Reform Act was pushed through by the Conservatives, whose position was inspired by the Chancellor of the Exchequer, Benjamin Disraeli. Against critics within his party who feared that reform would lead to revolution, Disraeli argued that the electorate was sure to be expanded soon anyway to include members of the rising middle classes. The Whig Party had benefited from the 1832 Reform Act, cementing the lasting loyalty of many new voters. By persuading the Conservatives to act against their instincts and adopt a relatively radical measure, Disraeli hoped that the rewards this time would go to his own party rather than the Liberals (the new name for the old Whig party).

The 1867 Reform Act did indeed improve Conservative prospects. But the Act had a profound effect on the structure of both parties. More professional organisations were required in order to reach a larger electorate, and local bodies which emerged to work for the election of candidates needed coordination from the centre. A National Union of Conservative and Constitutional Associations was set up in 1867; a National Liberal Federation was established ten years later. While electoral fortunes depended largely on the campaigning energies of unpaid volunteers, the parties also began to appoint paid agents to oversee activities in individual constituencies and regions. Mass parties had arrived in the UK; bureaucracy, and procedures to enforce discipline on what were still voluntary organisations, could not be far behind.

Cadre parties

a political party from an elite in the legislature and whose principal aim is to secure election for its candidates.

Mass party

The functions of mass parties

Those who take a positive view of mass political parties in liberal democracies focus on six main functions:

1. *Representing opinion and building coalitions:* In liberal democracies, political parties try to win power through peaceful persuasion. If they want to be successful at the national level, they must bring together and represent sectional interests whose views are likely to diverge to some extent. Thus, unlike single-issue pressure groups (see Chapter 19), they tend to be broadly based and can be unifying rather than divisive forces.
2. *Ensuring choice for voters:* Parties construct political programmes, featuring a range of alternative policy suggestions which they offer to voters at election time.

3. *Educating the public:* By communicating and explaining their policies to the electorate, parties raise the general level of public knowledge about key issues.
4. *Promoting participation:* Mass political parties are voluntary organisations which welcome new members, allowing them a chance to influence policy, as well as helping to elect congenial representatives from their ranks.
5. *Providing a channel of recruitment:* Through membership of a political party, citizens learn political skills and can maximise their chances of being elected to public office.
6. *Making leaders accountable:* Even if a party has an overwhelming parliamentary majority, its leaders should never forget their ultimate reliance on ordinary members, who can register their views on policies and personnel through recognised channels.

It is important to note that none of these points rest on the assumption that parties are composed of angelic public servants. The six functions could also be fulfilled as benign by-products of a single-minded and self-interested quest for power by party members. However, critics of UK parties deny that they can even produce *accidental* benefits, arguing that:

- Far from enhancing national cohesion, parties exaggerate minimal disagreements and grievances for their own advantage.
- Established parties try to restrict meaningful choice, monopolising media attention at election time and trying to strangle popular new movements at birth.
- Parties hinder public education, by concentrating on their favoured issues, belittling alternative views, and distorting statistical information.
- Parties only welcome the input of members who are prepared to play by the existing rules.
- Ambitious party members will only be selected as candidates for office if they support orthodox views and win the patronage of senior party figures.
- Whether a party is in office or opposition, dissident members will be told to keep quiet in the interests of unity. As a result, action against unsatisfactory leaders will only be taken when the damage is already done.

Opponents and defenders of political parties tend to take polarised positions, arguing that they fulfil either *all* or *none* of their expected roles. But other views are possible – for example, that they carry out some of the roles reasonably well, or most of them in part. Inevitably, assessments will depend to some extent on the expectations of the observer. Expectations of party performance in the UK were arguably higher at the beginning of the twenty-first century than ever before. In their defence, politicians can claim that the public makes unrealistic demands. However, the democratic process in Britain is heavily subsidised by taxpayers, who have a corresponding right to criticise if standards are *perceived* to be slipping. Equally, the most depressing reply to attacks on elected public servants is that 'the public gets the politicians it deserves'. Politicians cannot be immune from wider developments in society, but as elected representatives, they have a responsibility to resist detrimental trends within the electorate as a whole.

Conservative party organisation

Whatever their electoral fortunes at any given time, the Conservatives provide the most convenient starting point for a discussion of UK political parties. The party is regarded as the most successful democratic organisation of modem times, adapting to radical social and constitutional change since the advent of mass parties in the 1860s.

Leadership

Loyalty to the incumbent party leader is a key element of the traditional Conservative ethos. As an aristocratic organisation, the nineteenth-century party had an instinctive preference for hierarchy. The leader was expected to inspire his followers with attractive policies, but it was more important that he should command personal respect.

On paper, the Conservative leader remains an all-powerful figure within the party, whether in government or opposition. There is no formal check on his or her powers over patronage, policy, or party propaganda. In practice, though, the extent of a leader's power is related to popularity and to the party's electoral prospects at any given time. If the Conservatives seem likely to win the next election, and the leader is respected by the general public, he or she will usually be able to muffle (if not silence) any parliamentary dissent.

However, if the electoral prospects are doubtful and the leader's poll rating lags behind the party as a whole, even minor grievances can turn into crises of confidence. This explains the high wastage rate of Conservative leaders between 1992, when the party's poll rating took a decisive downturn, and 2005, when David Cameron was elected as leader at a time when the Labour government was beginning to look vulnerable (see Table 15.1). In 1995, even the incumbent Prime Minister, John Major, only survived as Conservative leader because no convincing alternative candidate could be found when he submitted himself for re-election.

The Conservative leader's freedom of action is heavily circumscribed when the party is divided. Popular figures will usually have to be accommodated within the Cabinet or Shadow Cabinet, whether the leader likes them or not. In recent times, as the party has become increasingly influenced by ideological considerations (see Chapter 16), leaders have been forced to include opponents in their frontbench teams. Thus, for example, Margaret Thatcher had to give posts to leading critics of her economic policy even after she became Prime Minister in 1979. Between 1992 and 1997 John Major's moderate brand of Euroscepticism was drowned out by colleagues who either wanted closer ties with the EU or to withdraw completely (see Chapter 13). David Cameron's choice of Conservative colleagues in the 2010–15 coalition was astute, since for the most part they proved a loyal and united team. His task was undoubtedly made easier by the necessity of sharing cabinet positions with his Liberal Democrat partners, which gave him a pretext for excluding some of the more outspoken dissidents on his own side. As Prime Minister

TABLE 15.1 Main party leaders since 1945

Conservative	Labour	Liberal/Lib Dems
Winston Churchill 1940–55	Clement Attlee 193–555	Clement Davis 1945–56
Sir Anthony Eden 1955–57	Hugh Gaitskell 1955–63[a]	Jo Grimond 1956–67
Harold Macmillan 1957–63	Harold Wilson 1963–76	Jeremy Thorpe 1967–76
Sir Alec Douglas-Home 196–64	James Callaghan 1976–80	David Steel 1976–88
Edward Heath 1965–75	Michael Foot 1980–83	Paddy Ashdown 1988–99
Margaret Thatcher 1975–90	Neil Kinnock 1983–92	Charles Kennedy 1999–2006
John Major 1990–97	John Smith 1992–94[a]	Sir Menzies Campbell 2006–07
William Hague 1997–2001	Tony Blair 1994–2007	Nick Clegg 2007–15
Iain Duncan Smith 2001–03	Gordon Brown 2007–10	Tim Farron 2015–17
		Jo Swinson 2017–19
Michael Howard 2003–05	Ed Miliband 2010–15	Sir Ed Davey 2019–
David Cameron 2005–16	Jeremy Corbyn 2015–20	
Theresa May 2016–19	Sir Keir Starmer 2020–	
Boris Johnson 2019–		

[a]Died in office.

of a single-party government after 2015, his tenure was dominated (and ended) by the divisive European issue. His successor Theresa May looked like an appropriate 'compromise' figure, until her authority was destroyed by her poor performance in the 2017 general election campaign; in December 2018, she survived a confidence vote among her MPs, only to be forced into resignation six months later. Boris Johnson succeeded where May had failed, leading the party to a decisive win in the 2019 election. However, his removal of the party whip from 21 'One Nation' Conservatives in September 2019 caused lasting resentment, and his leadership ran into trouble amid allegations that the government had mishandled the Coronavirus pandemic in the Spring of 2020.

Opinion poll fluctuations and party divisions are not the only factors behind the recent fortunes of Conservative leaders. Changes in society as a whole have also played a part. Sir Alec Douglas-Home succeeded Harold Macmillan in 1963 through what were termed 'the customary processes' of leadership selection. That is, senior party members made informal inquiries among their parliamentary colleagues about the suitability of the various contenders. In a new 'meritocratic' era this was widely regarded as outdated. A system of leadership election was introduced and was used for the first time in 1965.

In itself, the introduction of formal rules for election has destabilised the position of Conservative leaders. Yet the various systems used since 1965 have compounded the problem (see Timeline 15.1). It can be argued that far from improving the original prototype, the subsequent changes have been driven by short-term considerations. Thus, a provision for annual elections was introduced in 1975 to satisfy demands for a vote on Edward Heath's troubled leadership. Later, challenges to the incumbent leader were made more difficult to launch after contests in consecutive years (Sir Anthony Meyer in 1989 and Michael Heseltine in 1990 both challenged Margaret Thatcher). In the 1990 contest, Thatcher beat Heseltine quite comfortably (204–152),

TIMELINE 15.1

Conservative leadership election rules

1965   Vote of MPs to fill leadership vacancy. In order to win on first ballot, candidate requires support of 50 per cent of MPs, and must enjoy a lead of at least 15 per cent over the runner-up. New challengers can emerge for a second ballot, in which the winner requires an overall majority. If this is not forthcoming, the top two candidates proceed to a run-off in a third ballot.

1975   Rules changed to allow annual challenges to incumbent leader. Challengers require only two nominees.

1991   Rules on nomination of challengers tightened; now 10 per cent of MPs must demand an election.

1998   Radical overhaul of rules. Now 15 per cent of MPs must call for a vote of confidence in the incumbent leader. If the leader loses this vote he or she must resign. If more than two candidates contest the vacancy, a series of ballots is held by MPs until the field is reduced to two. The winner is decided by a vote of all party members.

2005   An attempt by the incumbent leader, Michael Howard, to push through a revision of the leadership rules which would return the final choice to MPs was rejected by the party membership.

Case study 15.1

New Labour and Cameron's Conservatives in comparison

During the 2005 Conservative Party conference, where he delivered a speech which brought him strongly into contention for the leadership, David Cameron told journalists that he was the true 'heir to Blair'. Comparisons are often drawn between the two leaders. But were their effects on their respective parties really so similar?

The similarities include:

- Both leaders took over parties which were struggling to come to terms with repeated electoral setbacks;
- They were both young and fluent communicators;
- They both believed that relations with the media were crucial; Blair notoriously flew to Hayman Island, Australia, to address Rupert Murdoch's executives soon after becoming leader, while between his election as Prime Minister and the summer of 2011 David Cameron held 26 meetings with senior figures from Murdoch's News International (see Chapter 5);
- Whatever their private views, they both thought that ideological considerations should be secondary to the quest for office;
- Whatever they thought of their own parties, they were very happy to cooperate with 'outsiders' (particularly Liberal Democrats!); and
- They were prepared to risk losing 'core' supporters in order to appeal to 'middle ground' voters.

However, the contrasts are equally instructive:

- As Blair often remarked, he 'chose' Labour. By contrast, Cameron was born into the Conservative Party. Whatever his critics might claim, Cameron seemed determined to revive the party he led, whereas Blair sought to change Labour into an entirely new movement.
- Blair felt that he had to choose a specific battle in order to take on and beat his critics. There was no such 'Clause IV moment' for Cameron – partly because there was no 'totemic' issue for the Conservatives (although same-sex marriage was equally controversial for many), and also (one strongly suspects) because Cameron was temperamentally more attracted by a gradualist approach to party reform.
- Blair took over a party which had been led by reformers (in the shape of Kinnock and Smith) for over a decade. Cameron was the first Conservative leader to take 'modernisation' seriously. Kinnock and Smith had effectively 'detoxified' the Labour brand; Cameron had to begin that task from scratch.
- Apart from the danger of a *counter-coup* from right-wing members of his own party, Cameron recognised that his fiercest detractors had an alternative party to support in the shape of the UK Independence Party (UKIP). For Blair's critics, there was no such viable alternative.

- Blair made a concerted effort to centralise power in his party – for example, by making the elected Labour chairperson into an appointed official. Cameron made similar efforts (such as his ill-fated 'A' List of candidates) but tended to retreat when they met concerted opposition.

Overall, one might conclude that the task Cameron inherited was more difficult than Blair's, but that the change he promoted was less far-reaching. A 'moderniser' from either of the main parties would probably think that this explains the Conservative failure to win the 2010 general election outright. A more balanced view would stress that the 1997 and 2010 elections took place in very different contexts: the first made it easy for Blair and Labour to promise change for the better, while the economic gloom of 2010 was sure to remind voters of the problems which many Britons had faced during the previous period of Conservative government (1979–97).

but this still left her four votes short of the 15 per cent point lead required for outright victory under the prevailing rules. After consulting Cabinet ministers – many of whom said she would lose – Thatcher resigned. John Major and Douglas Hurd then entered the second ballot against Heseltine, and Major emerged as the winner with 185 votes.

William Hague's *Fresh Future* reforms, introduced in 1998, attempted to assuage grassroots resentment against the parliamentary party which had just been crushed in the 1997 general election. The new rules gave the final decision to party members, after the field had been reduced to two over a series of votes among MPs. The first trial of the system elevated Iain Duncan Smith to the leadership in 2001, although he had trailed his rival, Kenneth Clarke, in the last ballot among MPs. The limited success of the experiment can be measured from Duncan Smith's deposition two years later, without even fighting a general election. His successor, Michael Howard, was chosen without a contest – a process which was not unlike the informal system in place before 1965.

Although there was no significant rise in the Conservative vote under Howard's leadership at the 2005 general election, the party did improve its position at Westminster and it was felt that Howard had kept the party united. When standing down soon after the election, Howard recommended a change to the system for electing the leader, which would take the decisive voice away from the party members. His proposals, however, were rejected. In 2005, David Cameron won the leadership after a contest which was held to have improved the party's image. He came top in the second ballot of Conservative MPs (which Duncan Smith had failed to do in 2001) and beat David Davis by a two to one margin in the vote of party members (see Table 15.2).

Cameron sought to 'modernise' his party and freshen its image by distancing it from (without entirely rejecting) its recent 'Thatcherite' past and by attempting to present the electorate with a more 'representative' slate of candidates. In particular, with only 17 Tory women MPs elected in 2005, Cameron was anxious to redress the gender imbalance. To confirm the impression of a party which was out of touch with modern Britain, there were only two black or Asian Conservative MPs. An 'A-list' of around 160 approved individuals was duly compiled, from which members in the party's target (or 'winnable') seats had to choose their candidates. However, this plan met resistance, and in 2007 a compromise was agreed under which half the candidates on any final constituency shortlist had to be women. Since progress continued to be slow, at the beginning of 2010 the leadership resorted to the idea of all-women shortlists in certain 'winnable' constituencies. In this respect, Cameron's campaign of renewal was assisted by the expenses scandal which

TABLE 15.2 Conservative Party leadership election, June–July 2019

First ballot of Conservative MPs	
Boris Johnson	114
Jeremy Hunt	43
Michael Gove	37
Dominic Raab	27
Sajid Javid	23
Matt Hancock	20
Rory Stewart	19
Andrea Leadsom	11
Mark Harper	10
Esther McVey	9

McVey, Harper, and Leadsom were eliminated; Harper withdrew

Second ballot of Conservative MPs	
Boris Johnson	126
Jeremy Hunt	46
Michael Gove	41
Rory Stewart	37
Sajid Javid	33
Dominic Raab	30

Raab was eliminated.

Third ballot of Conservative MPs	
Boris Johnson	143
Jeremy Hunt	54
Michael Gove	51
Sajid Javid	38
Rory Stewart	27

Stewart was eliminated

Fourth ballot of Conservative MPs	
Boris Johnson	157
Michael Gove	61
Jeremy Hunt	59
Sajid Javid	34

Javid was eliminated

Fifth ballot of Conservative MPs	
Boris Johnson	160
Jeremy Hunt	77
Michael Gove	75
Gove was eliminated	
Ballot of Conservative Party members	
Boris Johnson	92,153 (66.4%)
Jeremy Hunt	46,456 (33.6%)

enveloped Westminster in 2009, helping to ensure that 37 sitting Conservative MPs decided not to fight an election which their party was widely expected to win. In some cases, their decisions to quit were encouraged by a tough 'scrutiny panel' established by Cameron at an early stage in the scandal. While the strategy for modernisation did not go entirely as planned, its overall effect was to change the outward image of Cameron's party so that by the time of the 2010 general election it looked more diverse, youthful, and creative than at any previous time in its long history.

In policy terms, Cameron could not rely on any feeling of deference towards a leader; Iain Duncan Smith had been pushed out without having faced the voters, and there were times in 2006–10 when elements of the media encouraged the view that Cameron might suffer the same fate. A policy review was established, in which Cameron's ideological opponents (like John

Redwood) were included; however, the leader made it clear that he regarded such groups as purely advisory and retained the liberty to pick and choose among their recommendations. Having established a plausible pretext for policy flexibility, Cameron was able to move almost seamlessly in the face of the global 'credit crunch' from an economic policy in which the proceeds of growth would be split between tax cuts and additional public spending to one which was fit for an 'age of austerity', complete with radical *reductions* in spending.

Despite Cameron's relative popularity with the electorate, his party failed to secure an overall majority in the 2010 general election. Although to some extent coalition government suited him, it also acted as a source of grievance to his backbench critics, especially when he persevered with policies like same-sex marriage which were strongly opposed by many party members. His 'modernisation' project had stalled before he became Prime Minister, and he had signally failed in his stated aim of stopping his party from 'banging on about Europe'. Theresa May, who became leader in 2016 without an election (her main opponents having self-destructed in various ways), was associated with the modernisation campaign but was too distracted by 'Brexit' to contemplate party reforms. After Boris Johnson's comfortable victory in the 2019 leadership contest (see Table 15.2), it became clear that Cameron had indeed helped to change the *look* of prominent Conservatives – Johnson was able to appoint four ministers from BAME backgrounds to his first cabinet, and eight women compared to six under Mrs May – but that visual diversity was not reflected in a range of ideological perspectives. Ideological uniformity in the cabinet became even more pronounced after a reshuffle of February 2020.

Despite his embarrassing withdrawal from the contest to succeed David Cameron in 2016, Boris Johnson had been the front-runner from the start of his second stab at the leadership. As a result, his victory with just over two-thirds of the membership vote was presented by the media as a sign that he had established his authority over the party, whereas Cameron, who had come from behind, was seen as a leader with much to prove.

However, close inspection of the voting figures suggests a more complicated picture. First, although Johnson's performance on the first MPs' ballot, in such a crowded field, was highly impressive, in subsequent rounds his support edged upwards very gradually; there was no sign of the 'bandwagon' effect one could have expected if Johnson's parliamentary colleagues had not continued to harbor doubts about his leadership calibre.

In the final ballot among party members – which Johnson was always likely to win, barring mishaps – it was noteworthy that the winning tally fell far below that in the previous contests of 2005 and 2001. The obvious explanation was that party membership had fallen in the interim. As a result, when Cameron was chosen by grassroots members in 2005 he secured more than 134,000 votes – almost equal to the *total* number of votes cast by Conservative members in the 2019 contest. In 2001, the ill-fated Iain Duncan Smith had received almost 156,000 votes; his defeated opponent, Kenneth Clarke, won more votes (100,864) than the victorious Johnson secured in 2019. Yet Duncan Smith, and Cameron, had been chosen to serve as leaders of the Opposition; the winner of the Conservative contest of 2019 was certain to become Prime Minister. Even in 2001, Clarke was at a considerable disadvantage because of his sympathetic approach to the EU. Given the subsequent hardening of the party's official position in the wake of the 2016 referendum, it would be fascinating to know how many of those who voted for Clarke in 2001 were still members of the party in 2019.

The parliamentary Conservative Party

The decline of deference towards Conservative leaders has been particularly evident in the behaviour of the parliamentary party in recent years. Under Margaret Thatcher there were several

Case study 15.2

The Conservative Party Board

Until 1998, the Conservative Party was divided into three sections: the parliamentary party, consisting of MPs and peers; the professional party, consisting of paid officials with their headquarters in London; and the voluntary party, the National Union of Conservative Associations, which represented grassroots constituency members. After reforms proposed by William Hague in 1998, the three branches were united at the top in an overarching management Board which would meet about once a month. This promised to introduce more cohesion into the party. However, it did not make it more democratic. Of the positions on the board (around 20), only five were open to election, by a relatively small number of local officials. Most ordinary members had no say at all in the membership of the Board. Hague's proposals (which included the new system of electing the party leader) were accepted after a ballot of the whole party – but only a third of the members bothered to register their opinions.

rebellions, notably against the community charge or poll tax and plans to charge students for tuition fees. But problems came to a head under John Major. Opponents of the Maastricht Treaty almost brought his government down in July 1993. In the following year, eight persistent rebels were deprived of the party whip, and another Conservative MP resigned the whip in protest. The original eight 'whipless wonders' were wooed back a few months later because of the government's perilous parliamentary position. They were back in the fold in time to vote in the leadership election of July 1995, called by Major in the hope that a resounding victory would force his critics to 'shut up'. The result gave him little respite: 111 MPs (from a full complement of 329) withheld their support; of these, 89 supported the challenger, John Redwood, who had been portrayed as an unruly extremist.

Backbench Conservative MPs have a well-established forum in which they can make their feelings known. The 1922 Committee provides the party leadership with a useful means of detecting unrest; the whips are in attendance to report on the mood. The leader is only allowed to address the Committee by invitation (and when the party is in office, ministers are excluded from membership). Unlike most senior party officials, the 1922 chairperson is elected by MPs, and the result of the contest usually provides an insight into the balance of party factions. Backbench MPs can also influence the leadership through a variety of party committees which cover specific policy subjects. After the 2010 general election, the 1922 Committee demonstrated its independent outlook by resisting an attempt by the leadership to allow ministers to attend its meetings, and electing as its chairperson an MP (Graham Brady) who had become prominent within the party through his opposition to Cameron's policy on grammar schools.

Less formal organised groupings within the parliamentary party are not new, but they have proliferated in recent decades. The One Nation Group (founded in 1950) still exists and is generally seen as a moderating force within the party although its original intellectual impetus seems to have declined. On the right, the 92 Group (founded in 1964) has been joined by the No Turning Back Group (1985), the Cornerstone Group (2005), and, most famously, the European Reform Group (ERG, founded in 1993). Between 2010 and 2019, when the Conservatives were in government but did not have a comfortable parliamentary majority, the strongly eurosceptic ERG exercised very considerable influence, drawing accusations that it was acting like 'a party within a party', being instrumental, for example, in forcing a vote of no confidence in Theresa May's leadership in December 2018.

Party members

The Conservatives are not unusual in having suffered a drastic membership decline. In 1953, a figure of more than 2.8 million was claimed. At that time, the local Young Conservatives were a lively element in the social scene of many constituencies. By contrast, in the mid-1990s it was estimated that the membership had fallen below 400,000, and that more than half of the members were aged 66 or older. The decline has continued since (see Table 15.3).

William Hague's *Fresh Future* reforms of 1998 gave members the appearance of greater influence. But the reality was rather different. There was to be more consultation with members, through a new system of policy forums, but these groups were purely advisory and most of the key decisions were still taken by the leader and his closest allies. Ordinary members had an important say in the choice of their constituency candidates, but this has always been the case in a party where interference from the centre is usually resented. Under David Cameron, efforts to make candidates more 'representative' of society as a whole were stepped up, and the central party enjoyed some success in encouraging selection from a wider basis in terms of ethnicity, gender, and sexual orientation. But the leader's hope that half of party candidates for the 2010 election would be women went unfulfilled; indeed, in 2015 little more than a quarter of Tory candidates were women. In 2019, the proportion was around a third, but many women were selected for 'unwinnable' seats. The use of 'open primaries' to select some candidates is a notable recent innovation which offers ordinary party members an opportunity to exercise influence, although since any registered voter in the constituency can participate it is hardly in itself an incentive for people to join. Party managers retain a powerful role over the choice of shortlisted candidates in such cases. The process was not widely used in either the 2017 or the 2019 general elections, both of which were called at short notice.

For grassroots Conservatives, the annual highlight is the party conference. These gatherings used to be derided by critics as orchestrated rallies rather than serious political meetings. The motions were normally selected to avoid any searching examination of the party's record, and were almost invariably passed by general acclamation. The 'star performers', particularly in the 1990s, were those who could deliver the cheapest jibes against other parties. Until Heath succeeded Douglas-Home in 1965, the leader only bothered to attend the conference on the final day (Photo 15.1).

However, since 1979 Conservative conferences have become more interesting. In part, this is a product of principled public divisions over issues like Europe. But although rousing receptions can still be orchestrated – Duncan Smith received standing ovations a few weeks before he was dumped by his party in 2003 – the audience is much more volatile than it used to be. During the 1990s dissenting speakers on Europe, like the veteran Thatcherite Lord Tebbit, could cause real embarrassment for the party leadership. In 1997, the hostility shown towards former ministers

TABLE 15.3 Party membership, 1996–2019 (approximate figures)

Party	1996	2002	2009	2019
Conservatives	350,000	330,000	250,000	150,000
Labour	400,000	280,000	166,000	485,000
Liberal Democrats	98,000	76,000	60,000	121,000

PHOTO 15.1 Grassroots Conservatives get over-excited at the 2004 party conference (© Scott Barbour/Getty Images).

after Labour's landslide victory gave additional impetus to demands for reform. However, the main influence over policy was exercised in October 1987, after the party had won a third election in a row. The audience at the 1987 conference showed symptoms of impatience that the proposed poll tax was to be introduced in stages, rather than all at once. Grassroots Conservatives got their way, with calamitous results for their heroine, Margaret Thatcher.

The ferocious media spotlight on the leader at Conservative conferences means that when things go wrong the effect is greatly magnified. In 2017, Theresa May's speech would have been difficult enough after her poor performance in the general election earlier that year. During the speech almost *everything* went wrong for Mrs May – the effects of a virus reduced her voice to a semi-audible croak, parts of the stage collapsed, and a prankster rose from the audience to hand her a mock notice of dismissal.

Labour Party organisation

Since the publication of Robert McKenzie's classic study of *British Political Parties* in 1955, the Labour Party has been regarded as an organisation whose democratic pretensions are at odds with its 'oligarchical' practices. That is, although the members have an important role in theory, the decisions that actually matter are taken by a small number of influential people. However, the party's procedures have undergone significant changes since the days of Clement Attlee, and the subject is well worth a fresh examination.

Leadership

Traditionally, Labour supporters have argued that their movement is far more important than any individual. Suspicion of Labour leaders was dramatically reinforced by the economic crisis of 1931, when the Prime Minister, Ramsay MacDonald, allowed King George V to persuade him to stay at the head of a Conservative-dominated coalition, and push through benefit cuts rather than resigning. Although he had played a vital role in making Labour a significant force in British politics, MacDonald had aroused misgivings through his apparent fondness for aristocratic society – hardly the kind of preference one would expect from a devoted servant of working-class interests. Other Labour leaders have found appeals for unity falling on deaf ears; Hugh Gaitskell encountered strong opposition over nuclear weapons and nationalisation, while during the economic crisis of the mid-1970s grassroots critics treated James Callaghan and his Chancellor, Denis Healey, with unconcealed contempt.

However, the contrast with Conservative views of leadership can be exaggerated. As we have seen, despite the party's tradition of deference, Conservative leaders have often been criticised and occasionally deposed. Labour leaders have often felt vulnerable – sometimes for very good reasons – but if anything their party has been less ruthless when the leader has clearly outlived his usefulness (unlike the Conservatives, Labour has not yet had a full-time female leader). Tony Blair was forced to stand down as Labour leader and Prime Minister in 2007, but his 'assassins' had taken a long time to sharpen their daggers. Although many Labour MPs had misgivings about Gordon Brown's suitability as a replacement for Blair, no one stood against him as leader in 2007, and although he began to look like an electoral liability within months of taking the leadership, attempts to unseat him before the 2010 general election ended in dismal, damaging failures. Jeremy Corbyn was challenged for his leadership in 2016, but retained the position quite comfortably (beating Owen Smith by 61.8 to 38.2 per cent).

As traditionally understood, the formal powers of a Labour leader over patronage and policy making are quite limited. But the contrast with the Conservatives was never as sharp as it looked on paper, and recent reforms have chipped away at the remaining differences. In opposition, the frontbench team was elected by the parliamentary party; the party conference was the sovereign policy-making body, and at other times the National Executive Committee (NEC) was responsible for day-to-day management. However, in practice, Labour leaders were usually able to

Analysis 15.1

The 'iron law of oligarchy'

In 1911, the German-born academic Robert Michels (1876–1936) published *Political Parties: A Sociological Study of the Oligarchical Tendencies of Modern Democracy*. Michels argued that any large organisation will be run by a relatively small elite group (an 'oligarchy'). This observation – proclaimed by Michels to be an 'iron law of oligarchy' – is said to apply even to political parties which purport to be open and democratic. Whatever their original intentions, recruits into the leadership group will accumulate special knowledge which sets them apart from the rank-and-file who are incapable of action without direction from the top. This elite will pursue its own interests, presiding over a beguiled and benighted membership.

Michels' work preceded the 1917 Russian revolution, which lent spectacular support to his findings since the Bolshevik Party soon exhibited iron-clad oligarchical tendencies. Michels' book influenced Robert McKenzie's classic study of British political parties in the 1950s. More recent developments might suggest that both Michels and McKenzie were unduly pessimistic in their portrayal of passive grassroots party members. However, their work can still help to explain the behaviour of party leaders, who have been forced to adopt more creative tactics in order to convince supporters that their input really matters, while retaining decisive power over policy making and elite recruitment.

work around these constraints. Although the team members in a Labour Shadow Cabinet were chosen by MPs, the leader decided which positions they should occupy. When the party returned to power, the Shadow team had to be retained at first (though a leader strengthened by electoral victory could take the opportunity to reallocate their jobs). But after a decent interval, he or she could drop any uncongenial colleagues and bring in allies, whether or not they were popular with their Westminster colleagues. In 2011, Labour's leader Ed Miliband persuaded his party to approve a rule change which allowed the leader to choose his or her Shadow Cabinet without a preliminary vote, removing the last significant institutional obstacle which, in theory at least, could make a Labour Opposition leader more vulnerable than his or her counterparts in the other major parties. The party conference and the NEC had already faded as institutional constraints on the Labour leader.

Of course, even a Labour Prime Minister has something less than a free hand when making personnel changes, but that is true of all British party leaders. This point was illustrated vividly in 2004 when a weakened Tony Blair announced that he would only fight one more election as leader. Many observers believed that he had given a licence to would-be parliamentary rebels, but his position was still stronger than that of John Major between 1993 and 1997. David Cameron borrowed a leaf from Tony Blair's political war book when, before the 2015 general election, he let it slip (accidentally on purpose) that whatever the result of the poll he would not serve a third term as Prime Minister. Far from making Cameron a 'lame duck', this sent a signal to his rivals that their chance would come soon enough, giving them a clear incentive to make a show of loyalty for the next few four or five years. Similarly, when Gordon Brown brought the arch-Blairite Peter Mandelson back into his cabinet in 2008, it was easy to conclude that a desperate premier had made his last gamble. However, despite his reservations about Brown's calibre as party leader and Prime Minister, Mandelson seems to have sought to prevent, rather than to promote, subsequent Blairite plotting. Unlike Iain Duncan Smith on the Conservative side, Ed Miliband survived for five years as Labour leader despite a selection process which showed a lack of support among the parliamentary party, and consistently poor opinion poll ratings. The party could hardly have chosen a more divisive figure than Jeremy Corbyn as Miliband's successor, but despite signs of open rebellion in some quarters, there was also a willingness to see if Corbyn could inspire the kind of loyalty which he had denied to his predecessors. This seemed to have been vindicated by a better-than-expected performance in the 2017 general election.

The story is broadly similar where policy making is concerned. Until the late 1950s, Labour leaders could be confident of winning key votes on policy issues in the party conference, thanks to the consistent support of the biggest trade unions. The situation was more volatile for the next two decades, but the trouble usually arose when leaders deliberately challenged trade union interests (for example, when Hugh Gaitskell tried to remove the party's commitment to nationalisation, and when Harold Wilson flirted with reform of the unions themselves). Only in the late 1970s did the relationship between the leadership and the unions come close to breakdown, because the Callaghan government tried to combat an economic crisis through a mixture of spending cuts and pay controls – both of which were regarded by a more radical union movement as direct attacks on working-class interests.

One important result of the restless mood in Labour ranks was the introduction of a new system for electing the leader (and the deputy). Until 1981, the choice of leader had lain with Labour MPs. Afterwards, the decision rested with an electoral college, in which the parliamentary party enjoyed no more influence than the grassroots constituency parties (30 per cent of the vote each), while the greatest share, of 40 per cent, was given to the trade unions. This arrangement reflected the fact that, unlike the Conservative Party, whose members join a unified organisation, Labour is a federal party made up of various affiliated bodies (for example, trade unions and groups like the Fabian Society), and the trade unions were easily the most important element within the 'Labour movement' as a whole. But in the context of 1981,the effect of this 'democratisation' of the party was always likely to reinforce left-wing influence, since the constituency vote was heavily influenced by radical activists, and the old-style union leaders had largely been replaced by more doctrinaire individuals.

The first leader to be chosen by the new electoral college, Neil Kinnock (1983–92), struggled to reassert the authority of his office. Several high-profile activists were expelled from the party in the mid-1980s after a prolonged campaign against the Militant Tendency (see Controversy 15.1). Although the purge failed to convince the public of Kinnock's prime ministerial potential, it did strengthen his position within the party. Labour's campaign for the 1987 general

Controversy 15.1

The Militant Tendency and Momentum

During the 1980s, the battle for Labour's soul focused on the activities of the Militant Tendency, a small revolutionary Trotskyite group within the party which enjoyed the support of several high-profile councillors and MPs, especially in cities like London and Liverpool. The opponents of Militant argued that it contravened the party constitution, as a parasitic 'party within a party' which sought to hijack Labour and redirect it to its own ends. The real controversy concerned Militant's ideas rather than its 'entryist' methods. Militant members rejected the 'orthodox' Labour understanding that socialism could be secured through parliamentary means. In their view, senior Labour politicians had always betrayed the party's constitutional commitment to socialist ideology; thus, if Labour wanted to be true to its original ideas, moderate or 'revisionist' MPs were the 'entryists' who deserved to be purged from the party (see Chapter 16).

The Militant Tendency was never likely to take over the party, as its opponents alleged; only a small handful of MPs sympathised with its aims. But this minority was highly vocal, and capable of providing the Conservatives and their media allies with an easy propaganda target. As a result, Michael Foot and his successor Neil Kinnock both spent much of their energies trying to expel Militant members. In the short term, their campaign merely drew further attention to the problem, exaggerating the extent to which Labour's parliamentarians were divided. But eventual success added greatly to the institutional strength of the Labour leadership so that under Tony Blair the remaining ideological dissidents were almost invisible so far as media coverage was concerned – unlike MPs who were happy to stay 'on message'.

The Militant Tendency presents an interesting contrast with 'Momentum', a radical organisation formed within the Labour Party after Jeremy Corbyn's victory in the 2015 leadership contest. Members of the movement certainly espoused distinctive policies, particularly strong opposition to the 'austerity' economics which had prevailed since the formation of the coalition government in 2010. However, unlike Militant – a pre-existing and highly disciplined organisation whose members had 'infiltrated' Labour – Momentum attracted Labour members and sympathisers. As such, it was little different from other groups within the party such as 'Progress', which supported 'Blairite' policies. The real objections to Momentum arose from dislike of its left-wing stance and its popularity (it had around 40,000 members in 2019).

election was built around Kinnock's forceful personality. When the party lost that contest, and failed again in 1992, Kinnock stepped down. But far from weakening the position of Kinnock's successor, John Smith, the memory of four consecutive defeats strengthened the leadership role within the Labour Party because most ordinary members were now prepared to suppress their differences in the common fight against Conservative rule.

Under Smith, the leadership reversed the previous trend of trying to resist grassroots reform and took the initiative, pushing through radical change from the top. The electoral college was revised, reducing the union vote from 40 to 33 per cent. But the most important change was the introduction of OMOV (one member, one vote). In the past, union leaders had used their votes in leadership elections and conference policy votes without consulting their members. Although this was perfectly satisfactory to the party leadership when the unions were reliable allies, once the relationship soured it was denounced as a serious infringement of democratic principle. From 1993, union votes in Labour's internal elections would only be cast after a ballot of their members.

Despite these reforms, modernisers within the party believed that the process should have gone further, in particular to remove the influence of the union block vote over policy decisions at conference. After taking over as leader, Tony Blair addressed this issue and also led a successful drive to revise Clause IV of the party's constitution. Blair had won the party leadership in 1994, securing a majority in each section of the electoral college, following Smith's sudden death. Although it was already clear that Labour would not reverse the major privatisations of the 1980s and 1990s, the end of the party's historic commitment to the principle of public ownership had far more than symbolic importance. Above all, it allowed Blair's allies to claim that their leader had made Labour 'electable' once again. Losing such a key battle was a crippling blow to the radical wing of the party, which was already being dismissed as 'Old Labour'.

Thus, whatever misgivings some party loyalists may have harboured regarding Blair's policies, by the time he became Prime Minister, the prestige of the Labour leader's office had been restored and looked ripe for further enhancement. In the 1970s and 1980s, dissent and intrigue against senior figures had been integral to the Labour Party ethos. After a second election victory in 2001, Blair seemed invulnerable to any attack from within his own ranks – even from his ambitious Chancellor, Gordon Brown. Like the Conservative leader, the Labour incumbent could be challenged – but only with the backing of 20 per cent of MPs, and after a vote from a special conference. The last challenge to an incumbent leader (under different rules) had come in 1988, when Kinnock defeated Tony Benn. If Labour's rules had allowed just two MPs to trigger a leadership election, as the Conservatives did until 1991, even Blair would have lived in constant expectation of a challenge. As it was, he was able to force through highly controversial policies at home and abroad without the suggestion of a formal attempt to displace him.

There remained a possibility, though, that the stifled dissent of the Blair years might spill over dramatically after his departure. After all, Blair s authority ultimately arose from his party's desperation for an electoral victory. Three successive comfortable wins could breed the strange outlook which undermined the position of Conservative leaders between 1987 and 1997 – superficial complacency, mixed with a readiness to take desperate measures at the first sign that these might be necessary to keep the party in office. Significantly, speculation about Gordon Brown's position began just a few months after he had succeeded Blair. In fact, there had been calls for an election to fill the vacancy created by Blair, but the party rules made it difficult for a challenger to Brown to emerge in the circumstances of 2007. The new rules stipulated that potential candidates needed the backing of 12.5 per cent of the parliamentary party. Given Brown's dominant position within the party, only someone who was prepared to voice serious doubts about his suitability for the top job stood any chance of receiving support on this scale.

PHOTO 15.2 Jeremy Corbyn, Labour's left-field leader (© Anthony Harvey/Shutterstock).

These considerations meant that Brown became party leader, and Prime Minister, without facing any kind of electoral test. In the light of subsequent events, it could be argued that rules which prevent 'frivolous' challenges to a leader – or, in this case, a leader-in-waiting – can also have the effect of leaving the Labour Party with a leader whose position is made weaker by a lack of democratic legitimacy. By September 2008 disgruntled Labour MPs were trying to force a leadership contest, even though there was no obvious successor to Brown in sight. The dramatic reversal in Brown's fortunes showed that the increased focus on the Labour leader was a double-edged sword. When things were going well, the leader could get away with almost anything, but in adverse circumstances, even an individual with a long record of service to the party could suddenly look like a dreadful liability. There is an interesting comparison here between Brown's Labour Party and the Conservatives in 1990. After three successive election victories, the sudden prospect of losing office induced in both cases a concerted move against the leader – even though Brown, like Thatcher before him, had been credited with a pivotal role in his party's previous victories. As it turned out, Labour's tighter rules meant that Brown's critics were able to wound him without inflicting a mortal blow.

After Labour's defeat in the 2010 general election, the party was faced with the prospect of a leadership battle between two brothers. In some circumstances, this might have been helpful to Labour, since the 'Cam and Abel' scenario was likely to appeal to the media. However, the public was more interested in the dynamics of the new coalition government, and while the contenders were well known within the party, they were relative newcomers to public notice. David Miliband (born 1965) had served as Foreign Secretary under Gordon Brown but had not been particularly prominent in the role; members of the public probably knew him best through his failure to challenge Brown for the leadership despite broadcasting his credentials as an alternative leader in a *Guardian* article of July 2008. Ed Miliband (born 1969) was even more obscure to the public, despite having been promoted to the Cabinet when Brown took over from Blair. David Miliband was seen as a Blairite, while Ed was closely connected to Brown; however, the ideological differences between the brothers were vanishingly slender when compared to their distance from the thinking of their late father, the Marxist academic Ralph Miliband (1924–94).

Initially there were five candidates who received the necessary nominations (12.5 per cent of Labour MPs, which amounted to 33 nominations in June 2010). It was clear from the start that MPs wanted a wide-ranging contest, having learned the lesson of Gordon Brown's unopposed elevation in 2007. However, opinion polls among the Labour electorate showed that the Miliband brothers were the only two candidates with a serious chance of winning, and their dominance was not unsettled by four televised leader debates. The contest was conducted under the AV system, which Ed Miliband would later support as a replacement for first-past-the-post in UK general elections. David Miliband was ahead through the first three ballots, and only overhauled by a narrow margin on the final face-off between the brothers. Even in the final ballot, David retained a lead among Labour parliamentarians and full constituency members; the decisive votes were cast by the 'associated members' (i.e. trade unionists). Despite the principle of 'one member, one vote' in such elections, it was easy for Labour's opponents to claim that David Miliband had been robbed of victory by Labour's undemocratic paymasters.

The verdict certainly left the 'victorious' Ed Miliband vulnerable to the same problem which had overshadowed Iain Duncan Smith's leadership of the Conservative Party; had the voting been confined to his parliamentary colleagues, he would never have become leader. In short, he still faced an uphill struggle to establish his credibility. In 2014 – despite the lukewarm public response to his leadership as revealed in opinion polls – Miliband persuaded his party to adopt a rule change which completed the logic of the reforms to leadership elections dating back to John Smith's OMOV. In the future, Labour's leaders would be elected on the simple principle of 'one member, one vote', without the interposition of any kind of electoral college which might give undue influence to a particular section of the Labour movement. At the same time, changes were introduced which made it possible for UK citizens to obtain a vote in this election at minimal cost – a payment of just £3 before a specified deadline would be sufficient to secure a say in the choice of Labour's next leader. This provision caused considerable difficulty for Labour before the September 2015 contest to choose Miliband's successor; in the last days before the deadline, the party received 160,000 applications from new 'members' seeking a vote, some of whom made no secret of their intention to support the candidate who (in their view) was least likely to bring the party electoral success.

Compared to the Conservative procedure, in which MPs hold a series of ballots in order to choose two candidates for a final 'run-off' among party members, Labour's system allows a more restricted 'gatekeeping' role to the parliamentary party. Since the 2014 reforms, candidates must attract nominations from at least 15 per cent of Labour MPs, which meant that in 2015 they needed 35 backers. Two candidates (Andy Burnham (68) and Yvette Cooper (59)) overcame this barrier with relative ease; Liz Kendall, identified with the 'Blairite' wing of the party, trailed the front-runners but eventually received 41 nominations. The fourth contestant, Jeremy Corbyn, scraped through with 36 nominations; almost certainly he would have fallen short if some 'centrist' MPs had not felt that the campaign should give the party a chance to hear a wide range of views, and that Corbyn would be a suitable standard-bearer for the 'left'. The natural expectation among these well-meaning sponsors was that Corbyn would inject some radicalism in the debate without coming close to victory in the election itself (Table 15.4).

As it turned out, such assumptions proved dramatically misleading. Corbyn's campaign took off almost immediately and, long before the ballot itself, his success seemed certain (Photo 15.2). Enthusiasm for his distinctive views and 'unspun' speaking style never wavered, despite a prolonged campaign punctuated by five televised debates (held between June and September) and two similar events on radio (there was also an online event, on 27 August). There was some discussion about the likely role of the 'registered supporters' who paid £3 in order to have their say; supporters (if not full members) of other parties, including the Conservatives, undoubtedly tried to register, and if votes from this ill-assorted constituency had proved decisive, the result almost certainly would have been challenged. However, as Table 15.3 shows, Corbyn topped the poll among full members and 'affiliated supporters' – members of affiliated trade unions who

TABLE 15.4 Labour leadership election, 2015

1st ballot	Full members	Registered supporters	Affiliated supporters	Total	%
Jeremy Corbyn	121,751	88,449	41,217	251,417	59.5
Andy Burnham	55,698	6,160	18,604	80,462	19.0
Yvette Cooper	54,470	8,415	9,043	71,928	17.0
Liz Kendall	13,601	2,574	2,682	18,857	4.5
Totals	245,520	105,598	71,546	422,664	

could sign up for party membership without payment – as well as the £3 franchise-holders. More dramatically and decisively, his support among full members was so strong that his tally from this source alone was more than any of his rivals secured from all three categories; the result might have been caused by an 'insurgency' of sorts, but it certainly was not the product of 1980s-style 'entryism'.

This is not to say, however, that the rule changes made no difference to the outcome in 2015. The fact that non-members could vote for the first time could easily have encouraged other electors to take Corbyn's chances more seriously, and thus help to generate a 'bandwagon' effect in his favour. The effect of Miliband's reforms was certainly seen when Corbyn, unlike all of his predecessors, formed a shadow cabinet without having to await the outcome of a vote among the parliamentary party. His team was balanced in terms of gender, but in all other respects bore a very lop-sided look. Two of his three defeated rivals refused to serve, along with several senior party figures; even some MPs who accepted his offers made no secret of strong misgivings. A subsequent reshuffle deepened party divisions.

The 2014 rule changes certainly gave rise to some awkward moments and can be seen as part of a more general phenomenon in British politics. Various initiatives, including primary elections to select candidates, as well as wider participation in leadership contests, are clearly intended to give ordinary members the feeling that they enjoy real influence. At the same time, however, the ability of such individuals to influence *policy* – whether their preferred party is in government or opposition – has either stayed at the old, minimal level or actually been reduced. Party members were invited to exercise a choice between candidates who, increasingly, were 'career politicians' with limited life-experiences, but this would mark the limit of their influence: once elected, either as MPs or as party leaders, the people they had voted for would be free to follow their own priorities (which would usually mean toeing the party line).

Ironically, then, Corbyn's victory could be seen as an instance of poetic justice being visited on the British political class as a whole. The bright idea of giving party members a *semblance* of influence, rather than a continuous, guaranteed right to be heard, had backfired in spectacular fashion. Having used the rules to his own advantage, Corbyn immediately threatened to contradict their centralising spirit by welcoming policy input from Labour supporters. Before facing his first party conference as Labour leader (September 2015) Corbyn had signaled his determination to defy the 'iron law of oligarchy' by suggesting that the party conference, rather than his frontbench parliamentary team, would have the final say on policy matters, and even asking members of the public for contributions to Prime Minister's Question Time.

However, while Corbyn's policy priorities as Labour leader concerned socio-economic inequalities and public services in an age of 'austerity', media interest focused on the internal battles of the governing Conservative Party. As a veteran campaigner against Britain's involvement in European integration, Corbyn was placed in an awkward position by the prospect of an in-out referendum because a significant proportion of his party favoured 'Remain'. His lacklustre performance in the 2016 campaign crystallised opposition to his leadership within party ranks, leading to a leadership challenge later in the year. Although he won quite comfortably, the unconcealed hostility towards Corbyn amongst Labour MPs made it seem that the party was heading for a disaster when Theresa May called a 'snap' general election for May 2017.

Compared to initial expectations, the 2017 election result was a triumph for Labour. Its share of the vote rose by almost 10 percentage points, and it made a net gain of 30 seats. However, since the Conservative campaign had been little short of a disaster, the outcome could be regarded by Corbyn's internal opponents as a case of 'what might have been'. It certainly made it impossible for them to unseat the leader, whose popularity had risen sharply in the last few weeks despite the predictable vilification of the right-wing press. After the election, Corbyn moved further to consolidate the position of his allies within the party; there were attempts to supplant the elected Deputy Leader, Tom Watson (who resigned from his post in November 2019), and the party's rules were revised yet again, so that candidates for the leadership now required nominations from just 10 per cent of the party's MPs and MEPs. It was clear that Corbyn was hoping to ensure that his successor, when the time came, would come from his wing of the party. However, in the 2019 general election campaign Corbyn was unable to repeat his personal success of 2017; the party's position on 'Brexit' (favouring a second referendum) was too obviously an attempt to straddle the fissures in the party, and Corbyn himself was accused of excessive leniency in the treatment of MPs who were alleged to be anti-semitic.

After Labour's defeat in 2019 Corbyn announced that he would stand down after a short period of reflection. After a campaign running from late February until 4 April – by which time the media were pre-occupied by the COVID-19 pandemic – Sir Keir Starmer was elected with 56.2 per cent of the votes, compared to 27.6 per cent for Corbyn's ally Rebecca Long-Bailey and 16.2 per cent for Lisa Nandy. On 2 April, Angela Rayner, the front-runner throughout the contest for deputy leader, was comfortably elected.

The parliamentary party

Jeremy Corbyn was first elected to parliament in 1983 – a time when Labour MPs were perfecting their reputation for ideological disagreement and factional infighting. However, this image was always misleading to an extent. The most spectacular split, in 1931 when the party was in office, was provoked by the leadership rather than MPs. Internal conflict also surfaced after 1955, when Clement Attlee was succeeded as leader by the social democrat Hugh Gaitskell rather than Aneurin Bevan, the hero of the left. However, despite continuing ideological differences during the 1970s, the parliamentary party remained surprisingly united in its voting. The conduct of Labour MPs between 1974 and 1979, when their governments lacked a secure parliamentary majority, certainly presents a stark contrast with the antics of Conservative backbenchers in the 1992–97 and 2017–19 parliaments. And while the left has usually been associated with troublemaking, the defection of those Labour MPs who formed the Social Democratic Party (SDP) in 1981 came from the other wing of the party. This pattern was repeated in February 2019, when seven Labour MPs who were opposed to the party's direction under Corbyn defected to join an Independent Group (later Change UK; see Chapter 17).

The Parliamentary Labour Party (PLP) holds meetings which allow MPs to air their views, as Conservatives may do in their 1922 Committee. In the 'New Labour' years, the PLP was associated with obedience to the will of the whips and to the party's 'spin doctors' like Peter Mandelson and Alastair Campbell. In particular, the 102 women MPs elected in 1997 included some devoted loyalists; collectively they were given the slighting nicknames 'Blair's Babes' and 'The Stepford Wives', even though the 102 included battle-scarred dissidents like Clare Short

Parties and multi-level governance

Constitutional change has already exercised considerable influence on the main UK parties. Ironically, the greatest impact has fallen on Labour, which pushed through devolution and allowed cities to elect mayors, should they choose to do so. Although Labour was founded with a federal structure, this reflected the various groups which had coalesced under its umbrella rather than distinctive territorial parties. Thus, the Scottish and Welsh parties were not separate organisations, even though devolution was guaranteed to weaken ties with the London-based leadership. There were early problems in Wales, where the Labour leadership failed in its attempts to stop Rhodri Morgan becoming Chief Minister (see Chapter 12). In London, Labour prevented Ken Livingstone from running for mayor as the official party candidate. The result was a humiliating defeat for the party in the 2000 mayoral election. The leadership had no alternative but to endorse Livingstone as its official candidate when he stood for re-election in 2004, 2008, and 2012. On the face of it, these misadventures look like serious blows for the 'control freaks' of the central party. But the most significant thing was not that such interference failed but that it should have been attempted in the first place. In Scotland, long-term dissatisfaction with Labour offered an opportunity to the SNP, especially after the resignation as party leader of the proudly Scottish Gordon Brown in 2010. After the general elections of 2015 and 2019 Labour found itself with just one Scottish MP.

Devolution has also caused serious tension between Conservatives north and south of the English border. Scottish Tories were at a serious disadvantage in the 1999 elections to the Scottish Parliament, having argued against devolution in the referendum less than two years earlier. But their traditional autonomy was strengthened, and they tried to disassociate themselves from the UK leadership as far as good manners allowed. Indeed, between 1912 and a 1965 merger, Scottish Conservatives had been separate from the London-based party (running for election as Unionists). A similar situation arose after 1999, and especially between 2011 and 2019 when the Scottish party was led by Ruth Davidson, a pro-'Remain' and socially liberal Conservative whose views on many subjects were sharply at odds with those of mainstream party members south of the border.

The presence of Liberal Democrats in the Scottish Executive between 1999 and 2007, and (to a lesser extent) the party's inclusion in a coalition in Wales (1999–2003), could only enhance the prestige of leadership positions in the UK party as a whole. Whatever the overall UK electorate might think, MPs and activists were now more inclined to regard the Liberal Democrats as a potential party of government. This may help to explain why Charles Kennedy was forced to resign as party leader in January 2006, when it was felt that he was not living up to the new expectations. In the longer term, it increased the impetus behind tighter party discipline. Since the Liberal Democrats are a truly federal party, their Scottish members enjoy more formal autonomy than their Labour and Conservative counterparts: but that did not protect them from the UK-wide reaction against the party's participation in the 2010–15 coalition, and in the 2015 general election, they lost all but one of their seats in Scotland.

and Gwyneth Dunwoody. But most MPs of both sexes were anxious to remain 'on message' at that time, willingly receiving instructions from party managers on what to say during media interviews. Even after the 2005 general election, despite waning popular appeal and his declared intention of serving less than a full term, Blair received a warm reception from the first meeting of the new PLP. If anything, the level of public support offered to the leader at Prime Minister's Questions has become a more reliable indicator of the state of opinion within the parliamentary party than meetings behind closed doors. After Gordon Brown's initial 'honeymoon' period in 2007, it was noticeable that Labour MPs became less vocal in their backing when he tried to fend off David Cameron's attacks. Although MPs had preferred David Miliband to his brother Ed in the 2010 leadership election, the period of Opposition to Cameron's coalition government was relatively peaceful (if unsuccessful). Miliband's successor, Jeremy Corbyn, would not even have been a candidate in the 2015 leadership election were it not for the tactical support of some MPs who wanted a broad slate of candidates. The reward for this open-mindedness was a period in which the majority of the PLP was desperate to replace the leader but was unable to do so, thanks to his popularity with grassroots members.

Like the Conservatives, Labour has backbench parliamentary party committees covering specific subjects. But while the party is in government, independent-minded MPs have their best chance of making an impact through membership of cross-party select committees – provided, that is, that they do not take their independence so far as to launch damaging attacks on ministers (see Chapter 8). In opposition under the coalition government, select committee chairs like Keith Vaz (Home Affairs) and Margaret Hodge (Public Accounts) commanded more media attention than most Shadow ministers.

Party members

Reflecting the origins of Labour as an amalgamation of several organisations, its members join affiliated bodies rather than signing up to a single organisation. For example, members can enrol in their local constituency parties or join through an affiliated trade union. The link between Labour and the unions was regarded as an important handicap for the party in the 1980s. Since then, the leadership has made a sustained effort to loosen the ties, while union membership has declined. If anything, this tendency increased under the leadership of Ed Miliband (2010–15), who was accused of owing his position to union support. It was sharply reversed (along with many other things) under his successor, Jeremy Corbyn, who had been a union official before becoming an MP.

On the face of it, even prior to the advent of Corbyn grassroots Labour members enjoyed more power than ever before. The introduction of OMOV gave them individual votes in leadership ballots for the first time. Although party members did not get to choose Blair's successor, some excitement (and much media attention) was generated by the 2007 Deputy Leadership contest won by Harriet Harman. The OMOV principle was subsequently extended to votes on policy issues. The 1997 document *Partnership in Power* envisaged a two-year policy-making cycle, with policy commissions actively soliciting the views of the constituency members. Policy forums for ordinary members had been introduced under Neil Kinnock back in 1990.

However, the extent to which these changes have really empowered Labour members can be disputed. Casting a ballot in the leadership election gives members a feeling of participation, and although a single vote might not have affected the overall outcome very much in 1994 (when Blair won easily, with 57 per cent of the vote), in the much closer contest of 2010 it was easier to

Case study 15.4

New Labour's organisation

In the early 1980s, Labour's organisation was regarded as highly inefficient, compared to the smooth-running Conservative election machine. The transformation of Labour's machinery is often credited to Peter Mandelson, appointed Director of Communications by Kinnock in 1985, and Alastair Campbell, a tabloid journalist who had also been close to Kinnock before becoming Tony Blair's press spokesperson in 1994. Their impact was symbolised by a move from Labour's old headquarters, Walworth Road in South London, to modern, well-equipped offices in the Millbank Tower, just a short distance from the House of Commons. While opinions differ about the real quality of Labour's campaigning, the 'Millbank Tendency' certainly helped to ensure that a united party image was conveyed to the media. Even before Labour returned to office in 1997, party strategists were being called 'control freaks'.

An important factor in the rise of 'New' Labour was the taming of the party's NEC. This key body, which among other things was responsible for authorising the party manifesto, used to be the forum for bitter and well-publicised squabbles. Under Smith and Blair, by contrast, it usually hit the headlines only when it took controversial actions to impose the leader's will on other elements within the party. In part this was due to structural changes; in 1997, the membership was increased from 29 to 32. Blair also appointed a party chair for the first time (previously this official had been elected and had a lower media profile). By 2017, the NEC had expanded further, to 38 members.

feel that the principle of 'one person, one vote' really meant something. In 2015, the candidacy of Jeremy Corbyn encouraged even some opponents of the party to stump up £3 (to become 'registered supporters') in the hope of affecting the outcome. But some members clearly feel that they have lost influence on matters closer to home. For example, the left-wing reform movement of the early 1980s had secured mandatory reselection for parliamentary candidates – whether or not they were sitting MPs. Although fear of being deselected in these votes helped to inspire the exodus of MPs into the SDP at this time, in fact the power was used quite sparingly by constituency members.

Under 'New Labour' the power of deselection was more frequently associated with the central party, when it overrode the wishes of local members. Several parliamentary candidates were also selected, thanks to intervention from the NEC (which can veto potential dissidents) rather than any enthusiasm within the constituency. The party's disciplinary machine was particularly ruthless with MPs who had fallen foul of media scrutiny during the expenses scandal of 2009 (see Chapter 8); the MP for Norwich North, Ian Gibson, resigned from the Commons in protest at his treatment, and Labour lost the subsequent by-election. By contrast, defectors from the Conservative Party, like Alan Howarth and Sean Woodward, have been 'parachuted' into selection battles in certain constituencies with heavy NEC backing. Sometimes the existing MP has been rewarded with a peerage for standing down shortly before an election, allowing the NEC to argue that it is too late to go through the usual selection formalities, and ensuring the eventual choice of the candidate favoured by the national leadership. Compulsory all-women shortlists, imposed by the central party in order to change the composition of the parliamentary party, also caused unrest, although they were legalised by the 2002 Sex

Discrimination (Election Candidates) Act. Nevertheless, in the 2005 general election, Labour lost its safe seat of Blaenau Gwent in Wales because of local dissatisfaction with an imposed all-women shortlist.

Furthermore, although changes under New Labour can be dressed up as democratic advances, the input of Labour Party members into policy making can be exaggerated. Before the 2015 general election, the party launched an online initiative, 'Your Britain', inviting supporters to feed their ideas into the work of eight policy commissions. However, under Blair and Brown, the party leadership had seemed more impressed with the findings of non-party focus groups; indeed, it could be accused of paying more heed to the opinions of opponents than those of long-standing members who offer ideas which often conflict with the views of party leaders. In 2003, Blair launched a 'Big Conversation' with Britain as a whole, implying that a dialogue with his own party members was unlikely to generate satisfactory proposals. Significantly, when Gordon Brown's leadership came under serious pressure in May 2008, it was suggested that ordinary members would be given a bigger say in policy making, which implied that Blair's reforms had not satisfied the grassroots desire for influence. It was not unduly cynical to suggest that Brown made this gesture because his image had been tarnished by policy reversals and apparent misjudgements.

For Labour members as for Conservatives, the annual gatherings for the party conference always used to be a highlight. Before the 1980s, key decisions might have been cobbled together in smoke-filled rooms by Labour Party leaders and union bosses who regarded the views of the average members as secondary considerations: but at least the conference in those days had an element of drama. But while Labour was in office between 1997 and 2010 the conference was more like a trade fair, a festival of corporate sponsorship in which many stalls were run by companies which formerly supported the Conservatives. Rule changes have made it very difficult for constituency parties to submit the kind of critical motions which were discussed with considerable alacrity (and procedural complexity) in the days before New Labour. In an astonishing contrast to the mid-1970s, when people who barracked Labour leaders were warmly applauded, in 2005 an 82-year-old activist was forced out of the hall by stewards when he expressed mild dissent during a speech by the Foreign Secretary, Jack Straw. The delegate, Walter Wolfgang, had originally come to Britain as a refugee from Nazi Germany.

Those days suddenly seemed very distant when Jeremy Corbyn won the Labour leadership in 2015. The idea of draconian disciplinary action being used against parliamentarians, let alone those who support the party without material reward, looked absurd when the party's leader was an inveterate dissident. However, whatever Corbyn's own instincts might have dictated, in practice his party was too divided to allow the unbridled expression of dissent in such a public arena. Even Corbyn's critics found it prudent to appeal for unity in their speeches. Key votes tended to go the way the leadership wanted. In 2018, the conference voted to make it easier for local party members to express dissatisfaction in their MPs, raising once again the spectre of wholesale 'deselections' of elected representatives who were insufficiently attuned to leadership thinking.

Liberal Democrat organisation

Between 1950 and 1974, when Liberal representation in the Commons only once reached double figures (in 1966), the party was regarded by many commentators as little more than an eccentric sect whose members only kept the flame alive because of some irrational tribal loyalty. The party conference, in particular, became an object of affectionate fun among media commentators; it was supposed to be the haunt of bearded, sandal-sporting, lentil-guzzling idealists who regularly passed motions on ethical subjects without the slightest hope of affecting policy at Westminster.

Growing disenchantment with the two main parties contradicted this image to some extent, though the personal scandal which engulfed the charismatic Liberal leader Jeremy Thorpe, and induced his resignation in 1976, was a serious setback. Thorpe ended up facing trial for conspiracy to murder, although he was acquitted. Under his successor, David Steel, the Liberals entered a short-lived pact which sustained James Callaghan's Labour government. This was of dubious advantage to the party, and at the 1979 general election it was reduced to just 11 seats.

The party's prospects seemed to be transformed by the emergence in 1981 of the Social Democratic Party as an electoral ally which enjoyed strong media appeal. At that year's Liberal conference, Steel advised delegates to 'Go back to your constituencies and prepare for government'. The opinion polls at the time suggested that the two giants of post-war politics were about to be eclipsed by the Liberal/SDP alliance. But from the beginning, there were reasons for Liberal disquiet. By forming an entirely new party, the SDP's 'Gang of Four' had challenged preconceptions about the political landscape, promising to 'break the mould of British politics'. Yet in taking this course of action, the Labour defectors who founded the SDP implied a criticism of the Liberal Party. After its long years in the wilderness, was it a suitable vehicle for the exercise of power? If ideology alone had been the deciding factor, the SDP leaders would have joined the Liberal Party rather than founding their own organisation (see Chapter 16). The difference, rather, was one of ethos. Liberal activists had good reason to fear that a merger between the two parties would result in an SDP takeover and the imposition of a very different approach to the business of politics and government. There was, in short, a part of the Liberal ethos which recoiled from the sort of compromises which are inseparable from the exercise of power. By contrast, the founders of the SDP were former ministers, accustomed to making their own decisions and not relishing the prospect of eternal opposition.

When the merger finally took place in 1988, after two disappointing general elections, it seemed that Liberal fears had been misplaced. The SDP had run out of steam, and far from being hijacked, it looked as if the older party had performed a salvage operation on its Alliance partner. After a postal ballot of all members (probably little more than 60,000 at that time), the Liberal MP Paddy Ashdown became leader of the merged party, defeating another Liberal, Alan Beith.

However, some elements of the SDP lived on in the new party (which was briefly known as the Social and Liberal Democrats before adopting its present name). Its constitution attempted to strike a balance between the traditional Liberal commitment to grassroots sentiment and the orientation towards strong leadership which was characteristic of the SDP. Thus, the merger was not accepted unanimously, and the SDP leader David Owen was among those who refused to join. But the defectors did not all come from the same camp, and some prominent Liberals also decided to fight on under their old name. Paddy Ashdown, a dynamic character from a military background, was able to edge the Liberal Democrats towards the idea of cooperation with Labour. But he was acutely aware of the need to carry the membership with him at every step, and he was occasionally defeated in conference votes. The party's 1998 conference passed a resolution which stipulated that the leader would have to gain the support of three-quarters of the Liberal Democrat parliamentary party (MPs and peers), as well as similar backing from the Federal Executive, before agreeing to any proposition 'which could affect the party's independence of political action' (i.e. join a coalition government or even agree to support a minority government on crucial votes).

The Liberal Democrat conference remained a meaningful affair for longer than either the Conservative or Labour Party gatherings. Votes on policy took place after intensive debates which were often marked by open dissent. For example, in 2003 a proposal to privatise the

Royal Mail was described by a conference speaker as 'sinister', although it was strongly backed by key frontbenchers. Grassroots members also enjoyed a free hand in selecting parliamentary candidates, after an initial screening by the central party. The relative autonomy of constituency parties reflected the traditional Liberal focus on local issues. Free from central dictation, activists tended to concentrate their fire on their chief local rivals, whether Conservative or Labour. This allowed the main parties to accuse the Liberals of opportunism; instead of enforcing obedience to a specific line of policy, the national party was prepared to tolerate a wide diversity of views in different parts of the UK.

After the Liberal Democrats gained 62 seats in the 2005 general election – the fourth consecutive contest in which their representation had increased – their leader Charles Kennedy announced a far-reaching policy review. The central party clearly hoped to reduce the influence of party activists over policy in the future. Kennedy had argued in 2001 that frontbenchers needed more freedom to suggest ideas in response to fast-developing events. Accordingly, the party leader and his closest allies exercised decisive influence over the content of the 2005 manifesto.

These developments lent support to the 'iron law of oligarchy', in that senior Liberal Democrats demanded more central direction at a time when their party was gaining additional representation at Westminster (see Analysis 15.1). More significant evidence was to follow, as rumours began to circulate that Kennedy was suffering from a drink problem. The party leader was re-elected unopposed after the 2005 general election. But by the beginning of 2006, feeling among Liberal Democrat MPs was sufficiently strong to force Kennedy's resignation. This was a corollary of the view that the Liberal Democrats were now serious rivals to the two main parties, instead of being a potential recipient of protest votes in general elections. Some of the party's MPs thought that they would have won more seats if Kennedy had performed better in the 2005 general election campaign; others were worried that the subsequent election of the young and vigorous David Cameron as Conservative leader meant that Liberal Democrat progress would stall unless they chose a more dynamic leader themselves.

In 1976, the Liberal Party began to elect its leaders through a vote of the entire membership. Since the formation of the Liberal Democrat party, its leaders have been chosen through the Single Transferable Vote (STV) system (see Chapter 17). When Kennedy won the leadership in 1999, candidates required only two sponsors in order to stand. Since then the rules have been tightened, almost in parallel to those of the Conservative Party. Leadership candidates have to be nominated by at least 10 per cent of the parliamentary party, plus 200 party members drawn from a minimum of 20 constituency organisations. In 2006, these provisions led to a three-cornered contest, between Simon Hughes, Chris Huhne, and Sir Menzies Campbell, who emerged as a fairly comfortable victor. Although there were concerns about Campbell's age (64), he made it clear that he would exert strong leadership. Significantly, within a few days of his election, he had persuaded party members to accept the proposal on Royal Mail privatisation, which they had found unacceptable three years earlier.

Yet despite Campbell's ability and long service to the party, initial doubts about his position escalated to the point that, in October 2007, he announced his resignation. Like the short-lived Conservative leader Iain Duncan Smith, he departed shortly after a very warm reception from party members at the annual conference. In his letter of resignation, Campbell complained that speculation about his position was clouding the party's electoral prospects. In the ensuing contest, Chris Huhne ran again, this time against the youthful Nick Clegg, who had only been an MP for two years. Clegg, who won the contest narrowly, was barely known to the public at large. But he was good on television, like his Conservative counterpart David Cameron. He was also on the right wing of the party on most issues, belonging to the faction which agreed with Sir Menzies Campbell's view that additional reform was needed to make the Liberal Democrats more 'professional' – that is, more like its rivals. At the party conference of September 2008, Clegg and his senior colleagues advocated a key policy change, ditching the old emphasis on higher taxes on the rich and promising cuts in tax and public spending. This dramatic shift was endorsed by the conference over the opposition of several MPs and many grassroots members, who felt that the leadership had acted heavy-handedly.

For a brief interlude during the 2010 general election campaign, it looked as if the removal of Kennedy and Campbell would pay off handsomely for the Liberal Democrats. Nick Clegg's performance in the first of three televised leadership debates was so assured that several subsequent opinion polls placed the party ahead of both Labour and the Conservatives. It was a return to the heady days after the formation of the SDP, and it proved equally illusory, since the Liberal Democrats won only 57 seats in 2010, on a vote share which had increased by just 1 percentage point since 2005. Nevertheless, Clegg's performance in the debates had evoked a spirit of euphoria within the party, which was quickly rekindled by the realisation that, although the result was disappointing, the ensuing parliamentary arithmetic had finally created the necessary conditions for a coalition. In this heady atmosphere, the procedural obstacles which had been introduced in 1998 to make the party pause for consideration before giving up its 'independence of political action' were easily surmounted.

The Liberal Democrat intoxication of May 2010 was followed by the inevitable and prolonged hangover. After the formation of the coalition with the Conservatives, the party incurred widespread public hostility because of the policy compromises it had made in order to form a working arrangement in government, particularly with regard to university tuition fees. As their Conservative coalition partners had found back in 1997, the unpopularity of the national leadership can have a devastating effect on a party's performance in local elections. For the first time, instead of seeing the Liberal Democrats as the natural vehicle for protest voters, some erstwhile supporters cast protest votes *against* the party in the local elections of May 2011 – on the same day as a referendum on that long-cherished Liberal Democrat policy, electoral reform (see Chapter 17). The result of the latter poll was clearly affected by dissatisfaction with the Liberal Democrat performance in office. The party continued to lose local councillors throughout the coalition period.

With hindsight, it appeared that Clegg had blundered in exposing his party to the strains of office at what was always going to be a time of difficult decisions for ministers. For his part, Clegg argued that the party's decision proved its aptitude for office, and that any arrangement with the Conservatives short of a fully fledged coalition would have left the country without a stable government at a crucial time. Whatever the merit of these points, it could be argued that, having lost their innocence through the coups against Kennedy and Campbell, the Liberal Democrats could not have reverted to their old, mildly eccentric ways – at least in the short term. Like their counterparts in other parties, Liberal Democrat MPs and grassroots supporters were having to accept that their leader, however unpopular in the country, could not be supplanted unless this would result in an unambiguous improvement in their election prospects.

In May 2015, the party was reduced to just eight MPs, among whom Clegg himself was an unhappy and ironic survivor. He lost no time in stepping down, paving the way for a leadership election in which Tim Farron, who was untainted by service in the coalition, defeated the former junior minister Norman Lamb (who had also served as Clegg's Parliamentary Private Secretary). The turnout in this contest – held after the party had supposedly made a crucial breakthrough by participating in government for the first time since 1945 – was just 33,897, compared to 2007 (41,465) and 2006 (51,325). Remarkably, although the party's membership was said to have 'surged' by more than 10,000 since the May meltdown, Farron received fewer votes in winning the nationwide Liberal Democrat leadership (19,137) than he had attracted as an unsuccessful candidate for the Westmorland and Lonsdale constituency in the 2001 general election (19,339).

Along with the leadership, Farron also inherited a dilemma which Clegg had supposedly solved: were the Liberal Democrats chiefly concerned with the preservation of profound principles, or were they a party of government, flexible enough to negotiate with either of its main rivals if the call should ever come again? Such questions became redundant after the 2016 EU referendum, after which the Liberal Democrats (who had never played partisan games on the subject of 'Europe') were 'squeezed' in terms of electoral support by their bigger, better-funded rivals. In the 2017 general election the Lib Dems recovered slightly in terms of seats (now 12, compared to the derisory 8 of 2015), but their vote share dropped and Farron endured a very unhappy campaign, dogged by questions which exploited the tension between his Christian beliefs and the standard 'liberal' approach to moral questions like same-sex marriage. He stood down as party leader immediately after the election, and was replaced (unopposed) by Sir Vince Cable, who himself gave up the leadership in July 2019.

In the ensuing leadership election, Jo Swinson received 47,997 votes compared to 28,021 for her rival, Sir Ed Davey. Under Swinson's short-lived leadership, the Liberal Democrats campaigned vigorously for the UK to remain an EU member without a second referendum – effectively nullifying the 2016 vote. This certainly gave the Lib Dems a distinctive position in the 2019 general election, but it was not one which consorted well with the party's democratic credentials. Although the party's vote share rose in the election, it suffered a net loss of one parliamentary seat – Swinson herself was defeated in her East Dumbartonshire constituency, making it impossible for her to continue as party leader. Sir Ed Davey, who was elected as Swinson's successor in August 2020 was faced with the all-too familiar task of converting wide, but thinly spread, support within the UK into the kind of parliamentary contingent which can hope to influence government policy. At least Davey had a good idea of what *not* to do in such circumstances, thanks to Nick Clegg.

'Other' Parties

As we saw in Chapter 14, the days of two-party dominance in Westminster politics are over. Seven political parties have been considered to be important enough for their leaders to merit inclusion in televised debates at each election since 2015; a good case could be (and was) made for an even longer cast-list, which (for example) would have included Northern Ireland's Democratic Unionists and even Sinn Fein whose elected representatives always boycotted the 'Imperial' parliament.

Of these increasingly important 'others', three are of particular interest. UKIP topped the poll in the 2014 European Parliamentary election, winning 27.5 per cent of the vote. In the 2015 general election, it failed to build on that performance: far from advancing, it lost one of the two seats it defended. Its leader, Nigel Farage, was beaten in the Thanet South constituency. However, the party was supported by almost four million voters –12.6 per cent of the electorate as a whole. Its membership was reported to be around 47,000 at the time of the 2015 general election – a sharp increase since July 2013, when it was around 30,000.

Founded in 1991, ostensibly UKIP's organisation is based on 12 regions. However, especially during Farage's period as leader authority in the party was centralised. Beginning as a single-issue party – rather like a pressure-group which happened to contest elections – UKIP developed a wide-ranging programme in tandem with its increasing public appeal. At the same time, intense media scrutiny encouraged the party to tighten its disciplinary mechanisms and disown several nominated candidates. UKIP promised to be more than a 'one-man band', but its fortunes declined sharply after Farage's resignation after the 2016 referendum and it could be described as a victim of its own success in helping to achieve 'Brexit'. It underwent a rapid turnover of leaders and was increasingly involved in controversies over the views of individual candidates.

Despite 'Leave's' victory in the 2016 referendum, Nigel Farage himself was keen to maintain the political pressure to ensure that the voters' verdict was implemented. In January 2019 he founded the Brexit Party, which achieved the remarkable feat of topping a national poll (the 2019 EU Parliamentary elections) just four months after its foundation. Officially the party had only three members – to satisfy the Electoral Commission's requirements for political parties – but quickly attracted over 100,000 'registered supporters'. Although the party contested the 2019 general election, it did so on a tactical basis; aware that his party was capable of drawing considerable support away from Labour as well as the Conservatives, Farage initially offered an electoral pact with the latter and, when this was refused, announced that his party would not contest any Conservative-held seats. Although its candidates amassed only 2 per cent of the total UK votes, its influence on the result was undoubtedly significant.

While UKIP was remarkably successful in attracting new members, its performance in this respect had been surpassed by the Scottish National Party (SNP). In September 2018 its membership was estimated at around 125,000, having been only around 10,000 in 2010 and having increased continuously since the 2014 independence referendum campaign. Superficially, the SNP resembles UKIP in that its main goal is separation from a larger political entity, and as such, its *raison d'etre* might disappear once its objective has been secured. However, unlike UKIP the SNP has a long history – it was founded in 1934, as the result of a merger between previous organisations –and after many years of uncertain ideological orientation, it has established a clear centre-left position. This has enabled it to profit from widespread disillusion with 'New' Labour north of the border since 1994, a period which also saw the establishment of devolved institutions which have given the SNP the opportunity to show its ability to govern. While the party's recent leaders, Alex Salmond (1990–2000 and 2004–14), and Nicola Sturgeon (since 2014) are charismatic politicians who have attracted considerable media attention, the party itself has a solid structure based around constituency parties; any assumption that the SNP depended unduly on the popularity of a single individual was dispelled when Sturgeon quickly emerged from Salmond's shadow with polished performances in the televised 2015 leader debates.

From the perspective of party structure, the Greens are probably the most interesting of the 'others'. Tracing its origins back to 1973, the UK Green Party split in 1990 into three organisations: the Green Party of England and Wales, the Green Party of Scotland, and the Green Party of Northern Ireland. Until then, the UK party had seemed unable or unwilling to decide whether it was a political party or a pressure group. Initially, its policies focused almost exclusively on the environment, and despite its excellent performance in the 1999 European Parliamentary election (when it secured more than two million votes), it was not until 2008 that it elected a single leader (Caroline Lucas, who was elected as the party's first MP in 2010) in place of two 'Principal Speakers'. Even so, the party had retained open, democratic procedures; its annual conference is regarded as its 'supreme forum'. Its adoption of wide-ranging policies was emphasised in unfortunate circumstances before the 2015 general election, when Natalie Bennet, leader of the Greens since 2012, was unable to remember specific details relating to her party's housing policy. Despite the party's inability to increase its parliamentary representation at the election, it continued to attract new members, reached an estimated peak of 67,000 in 2015 (having been less than 14,000 in 2013), and has increased its contingent of local councillors to more than 370. Since then numbers seem to have subsided somewhat (to less than 50,000 in 2019). After Bennett's resignation in 2016, the party resumed its dual leadership approach, with contests held every two years. Since September 2018 the co-leaders have been Siân Berry and Jonathan Bartley.

Party finance

For most of the period since 1945, the standard assumptions about British party finance have been that Labour is in the pay of the unions; big business has bought up the Conservatives; and the Liberals are permanently poverty-stricken. These views have been reinforced by the two main parties, who often accuse each other of bowing to their respective paymasters, and by the Liberals and their Liberal Democrat successors, who have regularly denounced the reliance of their rivals on expensive advertising campaigns.

Trade unions and businesses are not the only sources of party funding, of course. Membership subscriptions and voluntary fund-raising events have always played a role. But donations from wealthy organisations and individuals account for a significant proportion of party revenue, and inevitably their importance has grown as membership has declined. Arguing that such payments are rarely given without strings attached, critics have claimed that the influence of large donors over the parties is anti-democratic. The tendency of such party benefactors to receive honours,

---

Case study 15.5

The Political Parties, Elections and Referendums Act 2000

Labour's reforms of electoral practice dealt both with funding and spending. In future, parties had to make a public declaration of any donation worth more than £5,000 (nationally) or £1,000 (to a constituency party), whether the gifts took the form of money or services. Donations from foreign individuals were outlawed, as were 'blind trusts' (which allowed recipients to claim that they knew nothing about the use to which money was put). Parties were required to declare their donations on a regular basis – quarterly in normal times, but every week during a general election campaign. After the 'loans for peerages' scandal of 2006, it became clear that the main parties were exploiting a loophole in the Act, since loans did not need to be declared. Action was taken to remedy this abuse in the 2006 Electoral Administration Act, and tighter controls of donations were introduced in the 2009 Political Parties and Elections Act. Legislation passed in 2014 tightened the restrictions on spending by campaigning organisations, such as lobby groups and charities, which are not contesting the election themselves but whose activities could have the effect of swaying voters one way or another.

In 2001, a cap was imposed for the first time on spending by the parties in their national campaigns. According to the spending formula, the limit for any party which contested all of the 650 UK seats in 2019 was £19.5 million, over the 365 days leading up to the election. These regulations are overseen by the independent Electoral Commission, whose powers were enhanced by the 2009 Political Parties and Elections Act. Since the restrictions on spending applied only to the 12 months before an election, the provisions allowed parties to 'prepare the battleground' in key marginal constituencies in earlier periods, as the Conservatives have done in recent elections thanks in large part to wealthy benefactors like those connected to its secretive 'Leader's Group'.

such as knighthoods and even peerages, is merely a symptom of a practice which suggests a serious (though hardly unique) flaw in British political culture.

During the 1990s, the Conservatives were tainted by several financial scandals. Labour came into office promising a new approach to politics, including a reform of party finance. The Committee on Standards in Public Life produced a report in 1998 which formed the basis of the Political Parties, Elections and Referendums Act (passed in November 2000: see Case study 15.4).

Ironically, Labour's credentials for the task of cleaning up public life had been undermined even before the Committee on Standards compiled its report. Shortly after the 1997 election, it emerged that the motor-racing tycoon Bernie Ecclestone had donated £1 million to the party. It was alleged that this generous gesture played some part in Labour's curious decision to exempt Formula One racing from a ban on tobacco advertising, introduced soon after it returned to government. The incident certainly underlined Labour's success in attracting sponsorship from business-people (although it still depended on the unions for more than a quarter of its funding). After a media furore, Labour repaid the donation. But serious questions remained, particularly since Ecclestone had not previously been known for his sympathy with general Labour party aims. Shortly afterwards, further questions were raised about the lobbying activities of former Labour spin doctors who promised privileged access to their clients. Firms which participated in Labour's Private Finance Initiative (PFI) also developed very close links to the Blair government. Under the PFI, major public sector projects like schools and hospitals were undertaken using private money, which would then be generously repaid by the taxpayer over many years (see Chapter 10). It did not take an over-developed cynical streak to anticipate that a relationship of mutual advantage could develop between certain firms and the governing party which issued such contracts.

Allegations that policy influence could be bought in Britain continued after the passage of the Political Parties, Elections and Referendums Act 2000. Before the 2001 general election, the Conservatives received a pledge of £5 million from a businessman, Stuart Wheeler. Wheeler was not interested in any material favours, but his donation made him an influential figure in subsequent leadership elections and on Conservative policy towards Europe. By 2009, Wheeler had become disillusioned with David Cameron's approach to the EU, and he was expelled from the party after giving £100,000 to UKIP (of which he subsequently became Treasurer).

In its second term, 'New' Labour was accused of changing its policies towards pub opening hours, casinos, and electricity generation under pressure from various donors, including the corrupt US energy firm Enron. After the 2005 general election, Blair gave a junior ministerial post to Lord Drayson, who had contributed £1 million to Labour funds during 2004. Drayson's company, Powderject, had previously won a controversial government contract to supply smallpox vaccine.

TABLE 15.5 Declared party spending in 2017 general election campaign

Party	Spending (£ million)
Conservative	18.6 (15.6)
Labour	11.0 (12.1)
Liberal Democrats	6.8 (3.5)

Note: Figures for 2015 are in brackets.

Source: Electoral Commission, https://www.electoralcommission.org.uk/general-election-spending-returns-larger-parties-published.

Controversy 15.2

'Cash for honours'

In March 2006, the Metropolitan Police began an investigation into charges that the New Labour government had been giving honours in return for donations and loans. The complaint was lodged by a Scottish National Party MP, Angus MacNeil. He claimed that the government's conduct breached the Honours (Abuses) Act 1925.

Initially, MacNeil's allegations were not taken very seriously. Close observers of British politics were well aware that honours were regularly given in return for financial support, and that to some extent, all three major parties were involved in the practice. But Labour stood accused of exploiting a loophole in their own legislation of 2000, which allowed loans which were offered on 'commercial terms'. On the face of it, this meant that the parties would have to repay, with interest, any money advanced by rich benefactors. But it is difficult to establish what exactly is meant by 'commercial terms', and it was theoretically possible that creative accountancy could transform a 'loan' into a donation, for example by delaying indefinitely the repayment period. In any case, the 2000 Act did not supersede the legislation of 1925, which remained on the statute book. Thus, any suggestion that honours were being handed out in return for money in the form of either loans or donations could still give rise to criminal prosecutions.

The 'cash for honours' scandal took a serious turn in April 2006, when a government adviser on education policy was arrested. It was alleged that a headmaster had told potential backers of the government's 'city academies' that financial support for this education policy would be rewarded in due course. No charges were laid in this case. But the arrest showed that the police were taking MacNeil's allegations seriously.

In July 2006, the saga became ominous for the Prime Minister when his chief fundraiser (and tennis partner) Lord Levy was arrested. His role in Tony Blair's entourage made him an obvious target for police interest, but he hotly denied any wrongdoing. Other arrests followed. It emerged that although the government had received £14 million in loans to fund its 2005 general election campaign, the Conservatives had done even better, with £16 million (the Liberal Democrats had only received £850,000, from just three sources). In December 2006, the Prime Minister himself was interviewed by the police (though not under caution). This was the first time that a serving Prime Minister had ever been questioned as part of a criminal investigation. Blair was interviewed again in January 2007.

In July 2007 – a few weeks after Blair left office – the Crown Prosecution Service (CPS) announced that no criminal charges should be brought in relation to the affair. But the honours scandal implied that, despite his early promises, Blair had been no better than his predecessors in his approach to party funding – a matter that was much more under his personal control than the international developments which, for most observers, cast a more lasting and sinister shadow over his time in office.

Whatever its effect on fund-raising, the 2000 Act seemed at least initially to have fostered a more responsible attitude to spending (see Table 15.5). The combined expenditure of the three biggest parties in 2001 (before the legislation came into full force) was *less* than the £28.3 million spent by the Conservatives *alone* in 1997 (a disbursement which left them almost bankrupt). There was a significant increase for all three main parties in 2005, and overall spending totalled £41.7 million, but in 2010 this figure dropped by £10 million, largely due to a much more frugal approach by the cash-strapped Labour Party. This meant that the Conservatives spent more than double the amount which Labour could afford, and almost four times more than the Liberal Democrats. Between the last quarter of 2013 and the spring of 2015, the Conservatives received more than £40 million in donations – more than double the figure for Labour (£19.8 million). The Liberal Democrats lagged as usual, though donations of £7.3 million were respectable given the party's plight in the opinion polls. The gap in spending narrowed in 2015 but was still significant. A notable feature of spending in recent campaigns is the amount spent by the parties on social media advertising; in 2017 the Conservatives spent more than £2.1 million on Facebook alone.

These sums, of course, are chicken-feed compared to the amounts lavished on campaigns in the US. The combined amount spent by the three main parties in 2001 was less than the record transfer fee for a premiership footballer at that time. In this respect, the 2000 Act revealed a party contest which was frighteningly vulnerable to concealed corruption; ironically, if electioneering were far more expensive, it would be more difficult for a single donor to buy influence, and there would be a greater chance that individuals or companies who contributed a significant proportion of a larger total would come under greater public scrutiny.

In the eyes of radical reformers, the 2000 Act could be no more than a staging-post towards the ideal situation in which private funding of any kind is banned and the whole burden falls directly and openly on the taxpayer. Another scandal broke in March 2006, when questions were raised about three Labour benefactors who had been nominated for peerages (see Controversy 15.2). The incident also suggested that the Act needed to be tightened in order to cover loans, as well as 'gifts'; this duly occurred in a hasty addition to the 2006 Electoral Administration Act. After this 'cash for honours' scandal, Tony Blair announced that he had been converted to the idea of state funding, if cross-party agreement could be reached (see Case study 15.5). There were, though, significant obstacles ahead. If parties were funded on the basis of their performance at the previous election – even if calculated on the percentage of votes cast rather than seats won – it might be argued that the majority party would always be at an advantage. However, this is already the case, since governments can use taxpayers' money to publicise their policies between elections, and private companies naturally want to back the winning side when their future prosperity is at stake. The main argument against state funding is that voters are understandably reluctant to subsidise unpopular parties through their taxes. If their election funds were guaranteed in advance, parties would have no incentive to devise popular programmes, or to recruit new members. But against this it can be argued that the current competition for *private* funds is one of the main reasons why parties have become unpopular in the first place.

Fears that the Liberal Democrats would not be able to afford to fight a second general election in 2010 seem to have affected the party's decision to join the Conservatives in coalition and insist on the passage of the Fixed-Term Parliaments Act (2011). Unsurprisingly, the coalition government promised to take action on party funding, and the Committee on Standards in Public Life began to hear evidence on the subject. However, there was never any chance that the government would rush into a decision on a matter fraught with difficulties for would-be reformers, and since July 2013 the issue has resided on the back-burner.

Case study 15.6

The Phillips Report on party funding

After the 'cash for honours' affair hit the headlines in March 2006, Blair announced an inquiry into party funding to be headed by a distinguished former civil servant Sir Hayden Phillips. This was a time-honoured tactic, implying that even if the Prime Minister and/or his associates had acted against the spirit of the law, they could not be blamed because they had been operating within an unviable system. Speculation immediately revolved around the possibility that the taxpayer would be asked to fill the gap left by the desertion of voluntary donors.

In March 2007, Phillips reported conclusions which were broadly similar to those of an earlier House of Commons committee. He argued that parties should receive up to £25 million per year from state funds, depending on performance. Individual donations from other sources should be capped at £50,000 a year. This idea raised obvious problems for New Labour, which still received most of its money from the trade unions despite its attempts to downplay its historic links with these organisations. While the main parties gave a guarded welcome to the recommendations, there was a sense that the Phillips Report was being treated as the first step in a protracted campaign to break public resistance to the idea of state funding.

Just before Phillips produced his proposals, the chairman of the Committee on Standards in Public Life, Sir Alistair Graham, complained that the government attached a 'low priority' to the fight against sleaze. Sir Alistair's three-year term of office had not been renewed, a decision which the government's critics attributed to his candid criticisms of New Labour since his original appointment. In July 2015, the Committee called on the new Conservative government, and the leaders of Opposition parties, to re-open the subject of party funding, but nothing was done. The Committee announced a new consultation on the subject in June 2020.

See: the Phillips Report, www.partyfundingreview.gov.uk; see also https://www.gov. uk/government/organisations/the-committee-on-standards-in-public-life

Back to cadre parties?

As we have seen, the main trends in the respective organisation of the three main parties in the last three decades have been:

1. *Democratisation* or, more accurately, a veneer of democratisation. Party members have been given a number of rights including:
   - a role in the election of the party leader, initially as part of an electoral college in the Labour Party and as the electorate in the second phase of the Conservative leadership election process;
   - the right to a significant (if not decisive) voice in the candidate selection process;
   - the right to participate in the policy-making process by making submissions to policy forums; and

- the occasional opportunity to vote formally on major changes in party policy, such as the abolition of Labour's Clause IV or David Cameron's 2006 statement of beliefs, 'Built to Last' (see Chapter 16).

2. *A strengthening of the position of the leader:* In practice, the rights of ordinary members are limited and real power has been concentrated further in the hands of the party leaders and their advisers. Limits on the role of party members and ways in which the authority of leaders have been enhanced include:

   - Leadership rules make it difficult for the party leader to be removed – unless, as in the case of Iain Duncan Smith in 2003, they have lost the support of much of the parliamentary party, whatever grassroots members might think, or, as in the enforced resignations of Kennedy and Campbell from the Liberal Democrat leadership, they leave without a formal vote of their parties or a negative general election verdict. (By contrast, it was the strength of support for Jeremy Corbyn amongst grassroots members that ensured his survival as leader in 2016.)
   - The central party organisation acts as a 'gatekeeper' over candidate selection (e.g. by drawing up lists of approved candidates, even if the formal choice is thrown open to a wider electorate through devices such as primary elections).
   - Key policy decisions are taken by the leader and his or her advisers; bodies such as policy forums and the party conference have only advisory status.
   - The leader and his or her advisers take the key strategic decisions about the conduct of election campaigns, with the leader acting as a communicator-in-chief for their party.

3. *A decline in party membership:* This means that parties have had to open up new avenues for funding and develop new campaign techniques (e.g. social media advertising) which are less reliant on grassroots activists.

These developments have led some commentators to ask whether the era of mass parties is over (see Analysis 15.2). In recent years, Britain's main parties have certainly been dominated by small groups of people associated with senior figures. In an ideal world, party leaders would love to inspire an endless stream of new members. Apart from anything else, research shows that enthusiastic local members can sway sufficient votes to win closely fought constituency battles. But parties seem to think that they can tolerate a severe decline in membership, mainly because funds can be accumulated from other sources. In the final analysis, it is easier to meet the needs of a handful of rich donors than to formulate a policy programme which satisfies the conflicting hopes of grassroots members and maintains their enthusiasm for campaigning on the doorstep. Indeed, supporters of the new model parties could argue that grassroots morale is best maintained through the provision of ample funds, whatever their source. The introduction of state funding could shield political parties from the appropriate consequences of falling membership, unless the number of party members was made a key factor in deciding the amount of money which each party should receive.

The main development which has undermined the mass party is, arguably, the rise of the media. When Michels put forward his 'iron law of oligarchy', communications technology was in its infancy. Now parties can reach their target audiences through television broadcasts, advertisements, telephone and text messages, and emails.

The same technology which makes a mass constituency membership less important also gives greater prominence to leaders. During election campaigns, leaders travel throughout the UK. But there is still no time to meet many party members, so these tours are conducted mainly for the benefit of the media. Certainly leaders will spend much more time speaking to reporters, who may or may not vote for their party, than listening to the views of their ordinary supporters. It was not surprising that when party leaders like Blair and Brown came into contact with 'real' voters, the results tended to underline the gulf between the political class and the people it

Analysis 15.2

Beyond the mass party

The demise of both the nineteenth-century cadre party and the twentieth-century mass party required a rethinking of the orthodox typology, which had been developed by the French political scientist Maurice Duverger in his classic work *Political Parties* (London: Methuen, 1954). Three alternative models of party organisation in the late twentieth century and beyond are of particular interest:

1. The 'catch-all party'. This model, developed by Otto Kirchheimer, claims that in the 1960s political parties abandoned their efforts to mobilise large social groups and downplayed their ideological convictions. Instead they sought to attract support wherever they could from a 'dealigned' electorate and from interest groups by developing a broad appeal that was light on ideology and focused on factors such as the qualities of their leaders. Although such parties seem to depend on broad support within the electorate, party members have little influence. An exaggerated characterisation of this thesis presents parties as highly opportunistic and prepared to do whatever is required to win votes.

2. The 'electoral-professional party'. This model, developed by Angelo Panebianco, emphasises the role of professionals (e.g. campaign managers, opinion pollsters, and spin doctors) and the leaders they advise within modern political parties. These parties are primarily focused on electoral success and adopt a political marketing approach that emphasises personalities and issues rather than ideology. Again, party members have little influence over policy. The high costs of running an election campaign mean that 'electoral–professional parties' rely heavily on donations from businesses and wealthy individuals.

3. The 'cartel party'. This model, associated with Richard Katz and Peter Mair, concentrates on the symbiosis between the state and political parties. Cartel parties enjoy access to state resources (e.g. state funding for parties and the resources available to MPs) and have a clear advantage over parties that do not have such access. They also have an interest in maintaining this advantage and denying resources to competitor parties. An institutionalised relationship between political parties and the state may undermine the legitimacy of the political system if parties appear to be primarily motivated by the desire to monopolise state resources – or even to collude to ensure a favourable division of the spoils, neglecting their roles as representatives and mobilisers of different interests within civil society.

See: O. Kirchheimer, 'The Transformation of West European Party Systems', in J. LaPalombara and M. Weiner (eds.), *Political Parties and Political Development* (Princeton, NJ: Princeton University Press, 1966), pp. 177–200; A. Panebianco, *Political Parties: Organisation and Power* (Cambridge: Cambridge University Press, 1988); and R. Katz and P. Mair, 'Party Organisation, Party Democracy, and the Emergence of the Cartel Party', *Party Politics*, Vol. 1, No. 1 (1995), pp. 5–28.

purported to serve. Key voters in target seats are now likely to receive personalised letters supposedly written by the leaders themselves, bearing facsimiles of their signatures. This artificial approximation to intimate contact with the voters helps to explain the appeal of politicians – irrespective of their opinions – who either make a genuine effort to talk to ordinary party members (like Jeremy Corbyn) or *act* as if they could hold such conversations if the opportunity arose (e.g. Kenneth Clarke and Nigel Farage).

In place of mass parties, political scientists now refer to *electoral–professional parties* in the UK (see Analysis 15.3). Such organisations lack a genuine mass membership, and channel most of their energies into securing the election of candidates by means of favourable media coverage. As a result, electoral–professional parties are engaged in almost continuous election campaigning – a development which certainly has not been affected by the Fixed-Term Parliament Act of 2011, which has proved ineffective (in 2017 and 2019) against governing parties which were determined to hold 'snap' elections. In a sense, the new situation is rather like a return to the old cadre parties, in a modern context. Personalities, rather than principles, dominate debate, and rival contenders for leadership surround themselves with professional pundits, pollsters, and spin doctors who often generate factional disputes for want of more constructive tasks between elections. Infighting between personal followers was also strongly characteristic of the 'ideology-lite' eighteenth-century conflict between aristocratic Whigs and Tories.

Supporters of the Liberal Democrats consistently argue that their party is an exception to this trend. Overall, their members have enjoyed a more meaningful role in policy formulation, candidate selection, and the choice of leader. This, it can be argued, is at least in part a reflection of liberal individualism; given their beliefs, it is unlikely that grassroots members would remain within a party which denied even the *appearance* of influence in all of its activities.

However, it can be argued that the Liberal Democrats only bucked the trend until the 2005–10 parliament because they were untainted by the realistic prospect of power. It is hardly surprising that their members felt more involved; there were, after all, far fewer of them and the party made a genuine effort to live up to its belief in free speech. The real test was always likely to come when changed circumstances finally presented the Liberal Democrats with a realistic chance of forming part of a UK government (see *Exploring British Politics*, 2nd edition, p. 397). The party had already become more centralised as a result of its encounter with the SDP – an organisation which was consciously devised as a vehicle for winning elections – and after the 2005 general election, there were signs that it was hoping to ditch its more 'eccentric' (i.e. radical) policies for future elections. After the 2005 general election it acted swiftly and ruthlessly to depose not just one but two leaders who seemed unlikely to take it much further. It was criticised for accepting a significant financial donation from a supporter based outside the UK, and subsequently it abandoned its distinctive pledge to increase income tax for high earners. After the 2010 general election, the grassroots of the party were effectively presented with the options of accepting the coalition deal or defecting to other parties (the Greens, or the Labour Party). Many took the latter option.

Taken together, these developments made it more difficult to cite the Liberal Democrats as a contrast to their two main rivals. At the 2015 general election, several parties were considered significant enough to merit inclusion in the televised debates. However, although all these organisations differed in certain respects, the debates themselves reinforced the impression that UK parties could only hope to prosper if they adopted an organisational model which gave predominant influence to the leader and his/her close allies. Despite the important and obvious ways in which Jeremy Corbyn differed from his recent predecessors, in practice he found it impossible to avoid conformity with this trend. The success of the Brexit Party – with a grand total of three full members – might have been a product of unusual circumstances, but it could be seen as a surreal manifestation of an 'iron law of oligarchy' which seems to afflict all successful British parties.

Conclusion and summary

Whatever the future fortunes of the Liberal Democrats and other challengers to two-party supremacy like the SNP and the Greens, there is plenty of evidence to support the view that Britain has entered an era of 'electoral professional' parties. Both Labour and the Conservatives have constitutions which are supposed to encourage participation from their members, and both have tried to win new recruits. However, even post-Corbyn Labour is no longer the truly mass party that it used to be. Despite occasional surges of recruitment in one party or another, membership rolls have been falling sharply in recent decades, and not simply because Britons are becoming more selective when choosing spare-time pursuits. The main parties still have their attractions for individuals with political ambitions, but they are no longer an obvious option for people who want to change the world. If their elected representatives can be accused of being 'out of touch' with ordinary voters, the same is true of party members, who certainly are not typical of the population as a whole. Returning to our six 'ideal' functions listed at the beginning of this chapter, it would be fairest to say that UK parties do carry all of them out to some extent, but that, even on a sober assessment, the conclusion should be 'can do much better'.

Those who accept the accuracy of the 'iron law of oligarchy' will not be surprised by recent developments. Since they believe that all large-scale organisations are inevitably controlled by small cliques, in their view the mass party with real grassroots participation could never have outlived the democratic enthusiasm kindled by the fight for full adult suffrage. Whenever Britons express distaste for 'politics', what they usually mean is that they strongly dislike *party* politics. In recent years this feeling has been fed by the media, whose endless quest for negative stories about politicians can be identified as the most significant factor in the development of post-war political parties. Its chief characteristics – a fixation on personalities, an intolerance of ambiguity, and incessant demands for official statements and 'leaks' – are unlikely to abate any time soon.

Further reading

The classic volume on this subject is R. McKenzie, *British Political Parties* (London: Heinemann, 1955). It is still well worth reading for its analytic framework, even though much has changed since the 1950s. S. Ingle, *The British Party System* (London: Routledge, 4th edition, 2007) is also still well worth consulting. P. Webb, *The Modern British Party System* (London: SAGE, 2000) offers an advanced analysis. Authoritative recent books are A. Clark, *Political Parties in the UK* (London: Palgrave, 2nd edition, 2018), and T. Bale, P. Webb and M. Poletti, *Footsoldiers: Political Party Membership in the Twenty-first Century* (London: Routledge, 2019). On leadership elections, see A. Denham, P. Dorey and A. Crines-Roe, *Choosing Party Leaders: Britain's Conservatives and Labour Compared* (Manchester: Manchester University Press, 2020).

P. Diamond, *The British Labour Party in Opposition and Power 1979–2019: Forward March Halted?* (London: Routledge, forthcoming, 2021) is a balanced and insightful account of the party's eventful recent history. On New Labour, see M. Russell, *Building New Labour. The Politics of Party Organisation* (London: Palgrave, 2005) and S. Fielding, *The Labour Party. Continuity and Change in the Making of New Labour* (London: Palgrave, 2002). Shorter accounts include E. Shaw, 'The Control Freaks? New Labour and the Party', in S. Ludlam and M. Smith (eds.), *Governing as New Labour* (London: Palgrave, 2003), pp. 52–69, and P. Seyd and P. Whiteley, 'New Labour and the Party', in S. Ludlam and M. Smith (eds.), *New Labour in Government* (London: Macmillan, 2001), pp. 73–91. A comprehensive survey of the party was undertaken while Kinnock was beginning the reform process by P. Seyd and P. Whiteley, *Labour's Grass Roots: The Politics of Party Membership* (Oxford: Oxford University Press, 1992). E. Shaw, *Losing Labour's Soul? New Labour and the Blair Government* (London: Routledge, 2007) is a perceptive critique. For the background to 'Corbynism' see L. Panitch and C. Leys, *Searching for Socialism: The Project of the Labour New Left from Benn to Corbyn* (London: Verso, 2020).

A. Seldon and S. Ball (eds.), *Conservative Century: The Conservative Party since 1900* (Oxford: Oxford University Press, 1994) is a massive volume covering almost every aspect of party history up to the mid-1990s. T. Bale, *The Conservative Party: From Thatcher to Cameron* (London: Polity, 2nd edition, 2016) and P. Snowdon, *Back from the Brink: The Inside Story of the Conservative Resurrection* (London: Harper Press, 2010) are both highly readable accounts of the Conservative comeback. The same topic is covered in P. Dorey, M. Garnett and A. Denham, *From Crisis to Coalition: The Conservative Party 1997–2010* (Houndmills: Palgrave Macmillan, 2011). M. Garnett and P. Lynch (eds.), *The Conservatives in Crisis* (Manchester: Manchester University Press, 2003) contains essays on the earlier period of opposition. On the party leadership, see A. Denham and K. O'Hara, *Democratising Conservative Leadership Elections. From Grey Suits to Grassroots* (Manchester: Manchester University Press, 2008) and T. Heppell, *Choosing the Tory Leader. Conservative Party Leadership Elections from Heath to Cameron* (London: I. B. Tauris, 2007). A special issue of *British Politics* (Vol. 10, No. 2, June 2015) was devoted to recent attempts to 'modernise' the party.

The Liberal Democrats have attracted less attention, but A. Russell and E. Fieldhouse, *Neither Left nor Right? The Liberal Democrats and the Electorate* (Manchester: Manchester University Press, 2004), D. Dutton, *A History of the Liberal Party in the Twentieth Century* (London: Palgrave, 2000) and the *Political Quarterly* special edition, Vol. 78, No. 1 (2007) are recommended recent accounts. The party's troubles since 2010 are chronicled by M. Finn, 'The coalition and the Liberal Democrats', in A. Seldon and M. Finn (eds.), *The Coalition Effect* (Cambridge: Cambridge University Press, 2015), and by D. Cutts and A. Russell, 'From Coalition to Catastrophe: The Electoral Meltdown of the Liberal Democrats', in A. Geddes and J. Tonge (eds.), *Britain Votes 2015* (Oxford: Oxford University Press, 2015).

On UKIP, see R. Ford and M. Goodwin, *Revolt on the Right* (London: Routledge, 2014). On the Scottish National Party, see J. Mitchell, L. Bennie and R. Johns, *The Scottish National Party: Transition to Power* (Oxford: Oxford University Press, 2014).

There are excellent chapters on recent developments within all the significant UK parties in J. Tonge, S. Wilks-Heeg and L. Thompson (eds), *Britain Votes: The 2019 General Election* (Oxford: Oxford University Press, 2020).

The Political Parties, Elections and Referendums Act 2000 and the debate on party funding is assessed in J. Fisher, 'Next Step – State Funding for the Parties?', *Political Quarterly*, Vol. 73, No. 4 (2002), pp. 392–99, and J. Fisher, 'Party Funding: Back to Square One (and a Half), or Every Cloud has a Silver Lining', *Political Quarterly*, Vol. 79, No. 1 (2008), pp. 119–25. For updates, see the same author's 'Party Finance', *Parliamentary Affairs*, Vol. 71, No. 1 (2018), pp. 171–88 and 'Party Finance in 2019: Advantage Conservative Party', in J. Tonge, S. Wilks-Heeg and L. Thompson (eds), *Britain Votes: The 2019 General Election* (Oxford: Oxford University Press, 2020), pp. 189–207.

Websites

The main British political parties have websites containing details of their organisation:

Conservative Party: www.conservatives.com
Green Party: www.greenparty.org.uk
Labour Party: www.labour.org.uk
Liberal Democrats: www.libdems.org.uk
Plaid Cymru: www.plaid.cymru
SNP: www.snp.org
UKIP: www.ukip.org

For rules governing party finance and information on donors, see the Electoral Commission (www.electoralcommission.org.uk).

Chapter 16

Ideology and party competition

Learning outcomes

After reading this chapter, you will:

- understand the various definitions of political ideology;
- be able to analyse the relationship between ideology and political practice;
- appreciate recent ideological developments within the main British political parties.

Introduction

Ideology has an ambiguous status in the academic study of British politics. Often it is regarded as a sub-category of political theory rather than having any place within political science. It is difficult enough to present a definition of ideology that will command widespread acceptance, let alone to devise a 'scientific' method of assessing the nature and extent of its influence on party competition and policy formulation.

However, no one can seriously deny that ideas have *some* impact on participation in British politics, at all levels. Despite contemporary cynicism about politics, many people are inspired by their beliefs to vote, join political parties, demonstrate or stand for office. It is generally agreed that ideology is 'action-orientated': it provides a rationale for practical policy ideas, and encourages people either to support or oppose them. Equally, ideas can also help us to understand a *decline* in participation. When parties seem to agree on most of the key issues, and merely exaggerate differences of detail in order to score points, sections of the electorate are likely to feel alienated from the political process.

Ideological conflict was a key element in British politics in the 1970s and 1980s when the major parties were sharply divided. After the downfall of Margaret Thatcher in 1990 – and especially when the Labour Party was led by Tony Blair after 1994 – some commentators spoke of a new ideological 'consensus' in which parties were more concerned with the pursuit of office than principled objectives. However, on the view of ideology outlined in this chapter, it has been present all the time; even if ideological *conflict* diminishes, politicians (and many voters) will continue to hold underlying assumptions which are rightly understood as 'ideological' in nature. Ideological debate sharpened again after 2007, as Britain faced a serious economic downturn caused by a global financial crisis. More recently, 'Brexit' has introduced new divisions in British politics and raised fascinating questions about the role of ideology in the argument between 'Remainers' and 'Leavers'. All this goes to show that students of politics should always take ideology into consideration, along with other factors such as economic, demographic and institutional change.

The nature of ideology

There are several contrasting definitions of ideology. The most familiar of these are:

1. *Ideology as objective thinking:* The word 'ideology' was first used by the French aristocrat Destutt de Tracy (1754–1836) during the French Revolutionary period. The early advances of empirical science persuaded de Tracy that human thinking could be purged of prejudice, superstition and self-interest. For him, ideology was a 'science of ideas' which could show people how to think objectively, trusting only the evidence of their senses.
2. *Ideology as a reflection of class interests:* The concept of ideology was revived by Karl Marx (1818–83) and his followers, notably Antonia Gramsci (1891–1937) but in a very different sense. For them, ideology was *distorted* thinking, the product of social conflict. They argued that the ideas of individuals are shaped by their positions within the class system rather than by any objective 'truth'. In any era the ruling class is the group which holds the dominant economic power. It will generate ideas which justify its position, and will try to enforce this 'ideology' on members of subordinate classes.
3. *Ideology as extremism:* Many commentators use the word 'ideology' as a synonym for rigid or radical thinking. On this view, 'ideologues' are extremists who want the world to conform to their ideas. Their attachment to their favourite theory is so strong that they will continue to work on its behalf regardless of its impact on people. According to this view, Hitler, Stalin and Mao were typical ideologues, and their atrocities prove that ideology is always a very dangerous thing.

These three approaches to ideology are all useful to an extent. The problem is that all of them recommend the removal (or reduction) of political bias, while our purpose as students of politics is to understand its continuing nature and influence.

Ideologies are best understood as belief systems which help us to make sense of the world. They can be compared to moral spectacles, though it is not so easy to put them on and take them off. The ultimate source of our political vision is our personal understanding of human nature. We regard significant political decisions as good or bad depending on whether they coincide with our ideas about the conditions under which human beings can thrive. So, for example, if we think that people are naturally aggressive, we will tend to support strong measures to enforce the law. By contrast, if we believe that human beings are naturally cooperative, we may take the view that harsh laws cause social tension rather than curbing it.

We might think that our own views are 'objective', based on a 'common sense' appraisal of the world as it really is. But although some ideas about human nature obviously make more sense than others, Destutt de Tracy was wrong to think that there could be a 'science of ideas'. One person's 'common sense' can seem dangerously irrational to someone else, and no one has the authority to adjudicate between them.

On this basis we can provide a broad classification of ideologies. Despite the efforts of totalitarian regimes and other would-be agents of mind control, no two individuals think exactly alike. While some commentators have searched for a logic underlying ideological thought, in practice people hold their views with differing degrees of intensity, and they are often inconsistent. But there are sufficient similarities between the ideas of political actors for us to speak of relatively coherent ideological traditions, and to construct fairly cohesive ideological 'families'. We must make sure that the people we are evaluating really have enough in common to make it helpful for us to group them together. Sometimes this can involve a reassessment of common assumptions, and we might even decide that a political figure has been mistaken in claiming membership of a particular ideological family. We might conclude, for example, that a person who thinks of herself as a dedicated socialist really has more in common with one variant of the *liberal* tradition. That is to say, people with strong political commitments are often unreliable judges of their own beliefs.

The role of ideology in British politics

On this view, we can already appreciate that it is a mistake to confine the word 'ideology' to extreme political beliefs. Everyone who engages even in rudimentary thinking about politics is to some extent an 'ideologue'. That is, the judgements we all make about political issues ultimately arise from underlying beliefs about human nature, even if we are sometimes inconsistent, or reach 'illogical' conclusions because of muddled thinking or a lack of information about a particular policy and its likely impact.

If this is right, ideology undoubtedly deserves its place in the study of politics. However, the role of ideology has to be understood in the context of other political factors. After all, where do our ideas about human nature come from? We learn either from our own direct experiences or from the experiences and ideas of others. Whether we realise it or not, our thinking can be affected by watching the television, reading newspapers, following exchanges on social media (see Chapter 5) or even by our day-to-day social interactions. If our experiences do not fit with our existing world view, we might change our minds, either gradually or overnight in a kind of ideological 'conversion'. Some people, for example, start off accepting that the world is imperfect, but end up hoping to change it for the better; others undergo the same process in reverse.

If ordinary voters find that circumstances affect their thinking, politicians face a much wider range of pressures. No successful British politician has been able to go through a whole career without making significant compromises. The process of winning selection for a parliamentary seat can affect their thinking. If they are elected, they come under serious pressure to obey the party whips; if they are promoted to ministerial office, they have to listen to the views of their colleagues or gauge the likely response from the public before they try to implement their most cherished schemes. If they manage to secure the biggest job in British politics, they will either have demonstrated remarkable flexibility in ideological matters – or will rapidly have to learn how to do so.

In short, 'Rab' Butler (1902–82), the former Conservative Chancellor of the Exchequer and Home Secretary, was right to describe British politics as 'the art of the possible'. It is difficult to generalise about the relative impact of ideas, events or institutions on political decisions because they all affect each other. It is often assumed that the influence of ideas varies according to circumstances. Commentators claim, for example, that the premiership of Margaret Thatcher (1979–90) was a period in which ideas were particularly important. But this view is (slightly) misleading. Certainly Thatcher herself was convinced that ideas are crucial in politics, and many voters supported her because she offered a clear alternative to the accepted political wisdom in Britain. But this is not to say that Thatcherism suddenly injected ideology into British politics. Rather, Thatcher and her supporters thought that the ideas which had prevailed before 1979 were based on false and damaging assumptions –indeed, Thatcher herself frequently referred to such ideas as 'socialist' in nature. Equally, as Prime Minister, she often had to compromise, whatever her rhetoric might have suggested.

The best way of explaining the nature of political ideology in Britain is to provide a brief survey of modern British politics from the point of view of ideas. But first we need to provide some account of the competing ideological traditions. Commentators usually focus on three – conservatism, socialism and liberalism.

Conservatism

The Irish-born politician Edmund Burke (1729–97) is usually credited as the intellectual founder of conservative ideology. His *Reflections on the Revolution in France* (1790) argued in favour of gradual reform, rather than violent insurrection. According to Burke, human beings are creatures of passion and prejudice rather than cool calculation. Burke predicted that the French Revolution would prove his point. Instead of being a temporary measure to meet an emergency, violence would become part of the routine business of the new French government.

Burke, then, derived his opposition to revolution from his view of human nature. The denial that human beings are capable of rational conduct – or rather, the assertion that most people are incapable of acting rationally on a consistent basis – is a crucial element in Burkean conservatism. It is best described as a form of *scepticism*. Another aspect of conservatism is **elitism** – the view that power should be entrusted to a minority who, through training or natural ability, are rational enough to rule. Burke believed that aristocrats were best placed to provide such leadership. Their inherited wealth meant that they had no need to prepare for a life of labour, so their education could be devoted to grooming them for political office. Their wealth also gave them a vested interest in defending social stability. Talented people from more humble backgrounds could play some role in government, but their influence had to be kept within limits. Excessive mobility would disrupt a society which Burke compared to a living organism. On this view, individuals are interdependent – they cannot survive in isolation. As in an organism, every part of society is important. But the right balance between the parts has to be maintained; otherwise the organism will sicken and eventually die.

Allied to conservative scepticism about human nature is a support for *prescription*. In most circumstances, it is argued, people should prefer the tried and trusted policies of the past to any radical experiments. Individuals may not be reliably rational, but they are capable of correcting mistakes over time; and this piecemeal process, rather than root and branch reform along the lines of some abstract political theory, is the proper business of politics. Ideological conservatives pride themselves on their **empiricism**; they think that the best kind of government is the one which works best in practice. We have to be pragmatic – to make the best of what we find in an imperfect world. 'If it ain't broke, don't fix it' is a typical conservative maxim.

Burke himself believed in a free market economy. Yet his outlook on this subject should be treated with caution, because he lived in the early stages of

Elitism

the belief that power should be entrusted to a ruling minority.

Empiricism

a belief in facts rather than theories.

Analysis 16.1

'Left' and 'right' in UK politics

Like so many terms in the vocabulary of ideology, the distinction between 'left' and 'right' originated at the time of the French Revolution. The words are a convenient shorthand way of denoting political positions, and are still favoured in media discussions. They can also be used in visual depictions of ideological conflict in Britain, usually in the form of a 'spectrum' with the left wing of the Labour Party at one extreme and right-wing Conservatives at the other. This spectrum is particularly helpful in surveys which ask people to identify their own views on a scale of 1 to 10.

In 1968, the journalist and political economist Samuel Brittan called the division between left and right a 'bogus dilemma'. In reality, he argued, the two main parties stood for very similar policies in office, whatever they might say in opposition. In addition, some people could take 'right-wing' views on topics like immigration while being 'left-wing' on a subject like the welfare state.

The chief difficulty with 'left' and 'right' is that they are *relative* terms, dependent on circumstances. A person's views can be regarded as 'left-wing' at one time and 'right-wing' at another. Thus, for example, the Conservative MP and former Chancellor Kenneth Clarke was undoubtedly a 'centrist' within his party when he became an MP in 1970. But by the time of the 1997 general election, he was widely regarded as being on the left because of his views on European integration. However, on key domestic issues, such as economic management and public sector reform, over the years he had shown himself to be a reliable 'Thatcherite' – i.e. he had become more 'right-wing'. It was ironic that, when the coalition government was formed in 2010, Clarke became Justice Secretary. Whatever had happened to Clarke's thinking since 1970 in other respects, his views on the criminal justice system were much more 'liberal' than those of grass-roots Conservatives, and his proposals for reform were seen by his critics as 'proof' that he had always been a wild left-wing ideologue!

After the 2016 'Brexit' referendum it became common for 'Leavers' to characterise their opponents as 'Lefties'. This vocabulary was influenced by the 'alt-right' in the United States, for whom that term (along with 'liberal') was used as a substitute for any rational debate with ideological opponents. Anyone with a serious interest in politics will find this tactic unsatisfactory and even degrading; hopefully in the United Kingdom it will be short-lived.

Such considerations mean that 'left' and 'right' have only been used in this book if they serve as convenient shorthand terms to indicate *relative* positions. The use made of ideological terms like 'conservative' and 'socialist' could be criticised for the opposite reason – for being *too* absolute and rigid, regardless of circumstances. However, the advantage of this approach is that it provides some yardsticks against which to gauge the changing ideas of political actors and parties, while analyses which continue to use 'left' and 'right' are built on shifting ground.

the Industrial Revolution, before the manufacturing process stimulated the growth of sprawling cities where many workers lived in anonymous poverty, providing a serious challenge to his assumption that the free market was compatible with an 'organic' society. One person who did reflect on industrial Britain was Benjamin Disraeli (1804–81: Prime Minister 1868 and 1874–80). While Burke believed in **paternalism** – the idea that the rich had a duty to help the poor, at least in 'deserving' cases – Disraeli extended that principle to include limited action by the state to improve working conditions. His greatest legacy in domestic politics was the idea that the economic inequality of industrial society had created a Britain of 'Two Nations', whose inhabitants were alien to each other.

Four additional points are worth making here. First, conservatives often deny that their ideas should be classed as 'ideological'. In their view all ideology is programmatic – the politics of the blueprint, usually based on unrealistic expectations about human nature. In other words, they adhere to the view, noted earlier, that ideology is synonymous with *extremism*. But on the present interpretation, it is important not to follow practising politicians in their tendency to use the word 'ideology' as an insult. To be useful to students of politics, it should be taken as referring to underlying political bias of all kinds, whether or not this gives rise to a rigid set of policy ideas. Burkean conservatism is certainly different from other political belief systems but not sufficiently so to make it unsuitable for classification as an ideology. Ironically, the assumptions which Burke regarded as entirely realistic are far removed from the dominant ideas in modern life, and if anyone was serious about restoring a conservative society on traditional 'Burkean' lines, he or she would probably have to resort to the violent methods which Burke deplored.

Second, since the social and political conditions which inspired conservative thought disappeared long ago, conservatism is often dismissed by its critics as a **reactionary** creed. But 'reaction' is one of those political insults which, on closer examination, proves to be meaningless. If it denotes a desire to restore the conditions of the past, anyone can become a 'reactionary' under certain circumstances. Today, the term could be used to fit a Fascist in Germany and a Communist in Russia, both of whom hope to 'turn back the clock'. In Britain, believers in large-scale nationalisation would have to share the 'reactionary' label with people who think that the state should do nothing beyond keeping the peace at home and maintaining armies for possible action abroad – the first wants to return to the conditions which prevailed until the 1980s, while the second idealises mid-Victorian Britain. A more relevant charge is that conservatives have rarely attempted a systematic exposition of their beliefs, except at times when they feel that their view of the world is under threat. But this is an integral aspect of conservative belief. When they are happy with things as they are, consistent conservatives simply see no reason to write at length on behalf of what they regard as a common-sense view of the world. Unlike representatives of the other main ideologies, they see no purpose in working to improve human nature so that people can realise their true potential. In their view, human beings are and will always remain a very mixed bunch.

A third point is that conservatism seems to support the Marxist view that ideology is a reflection of class interest (see above). In this case, the class in

---

Paternalism

the belief that people in power should act in the interests of other people (often the poorest in society) and thereby limit the free choice of those people.

Reactionary

a term used to denote an individual who rejects key elements of contemporary political/social practices and hopes to restore the situation which prevailed in the past.

question is obviously the aristocracy. Burkean conservatives would argue that aristocratic rule is in everyone's interest. If aristocrats are best equipped to govern, they have a duty to do so whether they like it or not; after all, if they leave the task to others who lack the necessary training, the result is likely to be bad government and social upheaval in which aristocrats will have the most to lose. This is highly characteristic of Burkean conservatism, which is a theory of *responsibilities* rather than *rights* (see Chapter 9). Yet there is a logical flaw in this argument. If human nature is as irrational as conservatives think, there is no reason to feel confident that more than a handful of aristocrats will live up to their responsibilities. In theory, conservatism is more than simply a justification for the interests of a particular class. In practice, though, it was often used to defend people who evaded their responsibilities and took full advantage of their privileged social status.

Finally – perhaps most importantly – we must avoid the common mistake of assuming that any statement of principle put out by the Conservative *Party* is inevitably a product of conservative *ideology*. To do so is to assert some kind of continuity between the thinking of Edmund Burke and the underlying beliefs of a group of people who (at the time of writing) have a parliamentary majority in the United Kingdom, more than two centuries after Burke's death. We have already noted the affinity between Burkean conservatism and an aristocratic socio-economic order that barely survived him (although, of course, landed gentlemen continued to dominate politics for many years after 1800). We can also appreciate that particular party labels might persist for a variety of reasons, even if the original principles have been abandoned. So, before we can say that any members of the Conservative Party today are distinctively *conservative*, we should examine their ideas in relation to other ideological traditions, to see whether any of them provides a better fit. The fact that Burke himself was a member of the Whig Party – the distant forerunner of today's

Analysis 16.2

Neo-conservatism

The controversy over the 2003 war on Iraq brought to wider notice a group of politicians who were close associates of the US President, George W. Bush. Happy to be labelled as 'neo'-conservatives, they had actively promoted the conflict and harboured even more ambitious designs for the reshaping of the Middle East. In domestic affairs, their overall aim was the reaffirmation of traditional institutions, notably the family. They were also strong believers in the virtues of the free market.

Neo-conservatism is not exclusively a US phenomenon; the label was also applied to some New Right supporters of Margaret Thatcher, who upheld traditional moral values and also laid special emphasis on the family. However, the ideas are particularly suited to the United States, where cultural norms and social institutions originally developed in a context of resolute individualism and suspicion (if not outright hostility) towards the state. Thus the 'neo-cons' (and the 'alt-right' which emerged in the United States after 2010) can pose with some plausibility as the guardians of a long-established American way of life. In the United Kingdom, by contrast, institutions evolved in a very different context, and in recent decades they have been undermined rather than strengthened by the market forces which neo-conservatives support. Thus the neo-conservative label is a source of confusion in the British context; people who associate themselves with this American tradition of thought have far more in common with doctrinaire Victorian *liberals* than with Edmund Burke.

Liberal Democrats – should be a sufficient warning against the automatic association of party labels with political belief systems.

Socialism

Capitalism

an economic, political and social system based upon the private ownership of property and the creation of wealth.

Egalitarianism

a political programme that aims to increase equality, based on the belief that people should be treated equally.

Bourgeoisie

in Marxism, the dominant class made up of owners of the means of production, which exploits the proletariat.

Proletariat

in Marxism, a class of manual workers who need to sell their labour to earn money.

While conservatism reflects an aristocratic, largely rural society, modern socialism is a product of the Industrial Revolution. Robert Owen (1771–1858), whose *A New View of Society* is generally regarded as an early socialist tract, was actually a mill-owner who believed that the working class was being dehumanised by industrial capitalism. Karl Marx, whose study of that system led him to believe that he had discovered 'scientific' laws of historical development leading to an inevitable socialist revolution, was given financial and intellectual support by Friedrich Engels (1820–95), whose family fortune also came from manufacturing and who was himself a successful entrepreneur.

Although socialism has many variants, its core idea is that the character of human beings is 'environmentally' determined. That is, people are decisively shaped by the circumstances in which they find themselves. The key to realising human potential is thus to create the right environment to enable them to flourish. Socialists believe that human beings can only fulfil their true potential in a context which fosters cooperation. On this view, **capitalism** is unnatural because it forces workers and employers alike into a competitive, confrontational environment. Instead of labouring together for the common good, workers spend their lives creating profit for their masters. They can take no pleasure from the productive process; in the terminology favoured by Marxists, they are 'alienated' from the results of their own labour. This would be the case even if profits were being derived from products which were socially useful. In practice, modern capitalism is biased towards the production of unnecessary luxury items for the minority who can afford them.

Another key principle for socialists is **egalitarianism**. Economic inequality, they believe, prevents harmonious living. In particular, advanced capitalist society divides people into two classes: the owners of the 'means of production' (the **bourgeoisie**), and the working class (the **proletariat**). Under capitalism, the apparent interests of these two groups are diametrically opposed. The bourgeoisie owes its livelihood to the exploitation of the workers. Socialism implies that if the owners of the means of production understood their real interests they would give up their economic power, because only then could they escape from the degrading struggle for wealth which brings no spiritual satisfaction. Indeed, in some ways, life is even more unsatisfactory for them, because the economic hardship of the workers creates a sense of human solidarity which their bosses can never experience since their fellow-capitalists are also imprisoned within a competitive environment. Unfortunately, their thinking is conditioned by a system which makes them believe that competition is 'natural'.

Thus socialists believe that human potential can only be fulfilled after the abolition of classes, and the destruction of private ownership of the means of production. But how is this to be achieved? This has been a divisive issue among people who nevertheless shared the distinctive socialist view of human nature. Marx and his followers believed that capitalism would have to be overthrown in a violent revolution. Although they recognised that capitalism had greatly increased the productive capacity of mankind, the system was doomed because of its internal contradictions. Over time competition for new markets becomes increasingly frantic, and profits decline. Inefficient firms are forced out of business, thus swelling the ranks of a proletariat which faces ever harsher working conditions. This new level of exploitation stimulates class consciousness among the workers: at last they realise where their true interest lies, they have the numbers on their side to confront the bickering band of capitalists, and above all they are united. Once the revolution has been won, they will seize control of the state and use its power to abolish all productive private property. Production could then be geared to genuine need, and everyone will be glad to contribute their labour according to their abilities. Character traits which capitalists believe to be natural to human beings, such as selfishness, will disappear. Contrary to the charge of Marx's ideological opponents, the logic of his thinking implies a future without any kind of coercive state apparatus; even the production of goods could be organised on a purely voluntary basis.

Although Marx's revolutionary doctrine won a small dedicated following in Britain, it represents only one strand of socialist thought. Earlier writers like Owen had thought that society could be transformed by peaceful means. In the year after Marx's death (1883), a group of middle-class activists founded the Fabian Society, which preached a philosophy of gradual reform on socialist lines. The Fabians were tireless propagandists and statistical compilers, at a time when governments were badly informed. They believed that they could persuade influential people in central and local government to implement their policies without the necessity for violence.

Social democracy

The main point of dispute between the socialist revolutionaries and the 'gradualists' concerned the nature of class conflict. Marx and his followers believed that the bourgeoisie was incapable of making meaningful concessions, even to save itself. But the Fabians could point to peaceful reforms in the second half of the nineteenth century (notably under the premiership of the Conservative Benjamin Disraeli) which enlisted the state in the quest to improve working conditions. The parliamentary road to socialism was given added support in 1899, when the German politician Eduard Bernstein (1850–1932) published *The Preconditions of Socialism*. This book can be seen as the founding document of social democracy, or 'revisionism'.

Bernstein argued that, contrary to Marxist theory, capitalism was showing itself to be highly adaptable. Far from stumbling from one crisis to the next, by the end of the nineteenth century it seemed as healthy as ever. Furthermore, bourgeois parliaments really had made meaningful concessions, for example, extending the right to vote to members of the working class. Not only did Bernstein conclude that revolution was unnecessary; he even accepted that capitalism could be compatible with social justice. Provided that they were subjected to state regulation, private enterprises could be allowed to stay in business.

Revisionism of one kind or another was always more popular than revolutionary Marxism within the British Labour Party (which, according to the party's general secretary Morgan Phillips (1902–63), 'owed more to Methodism that to Marxism'). The last piece of the UK's social democratic jigsaw was supplied after the Second World War by the economist and Labour MP Anthony Crosland (1918–77). His book *The Future of Socialism* (1956) argued that the clash between the owners of capital and the workers had been superseded by a technological revolution. Economic power was no longer a matter of ownership; it depended on expertise. Only skilled managers knew how to run modern factories. Their chief interest lay in the efficient working of their factories, so they could be trusted to improve conditions of employment and to avoid friction with the rest of the labour force. In these conditions, economic inequality became a less important or relevant consideration than the establishment of 'equality of opportunity', which would ensure that individuals of high status would owe their positions to personal abilities rather than unmerited environmental advantages. Crosland was a vocal advocate of comprehensive education, which (he hoped) would provide every child with an equal chance to join the professional managers who would hold the balance of power in a future society, thus implementing the peaceful social revolution which Marxists deemed to be impossible.

British social democrats continued to call themselves 'socialists'. But to Marxists, they were nothing less than traitors to the working class. If we look again at the characteristic socialist view of human nature, we can appreciate the force of this point. Socialists believe that work in a capitalist economy is dehumanising, whether or not it is regulated by the state. Economic exploitation might be reduced by regulation, but it will continue to exist because capitalists cannot survive unless they pay their workers less than the full value of their labour (hence, in the eyes of socialists, policies like New Labour's minimum wage are typical 'bourgeois' tricks which cannot disguise the inhumanity and injustice of the capitalist system). And even under the control of professional managers, firms will tend to produce goods which yield the highest profits, whether or not they satisfy any 'genuine' social need. At best, then, the capitalist system might give people a roughly equal chance of living equally degrading lives. More likely, economic inequalities will continue to ensure that the children of the rich take an unjustified share of the material spoils. Thus, from the Marxist perspective, Crosland's managerial class would at best be the well-fed dupes of their shareholders.

Ironically, it can be argued that the Marxists who supported the 1917 Bolshevik Revolution in Russia were equally untrue to socialist doctrine. Marx argued that the prospects for socialism depended upon the emergence of working-class consciousness, and this could only happen in a fully-fledged capitalist society. By contrast, capitalism had barely developed in the Russia of 1917. Although it took many years for the full horror of the Soviet Revolution to register among Western socialists, the initial bloodshed provided a welcome propaganda coup to the opponents of socialism in Britain and elsewhere. In turn, this made the peaceful, revisionist alternative much more attractive for people who hoped to build more equal and harmonious societies with the ballot box, their ideas and their eloquence as their only weapons.

One intriguing point arising from this discussion is the ambivalent relationship between conservative thought and socialism. Conventionally, we assume that these ideologies are completely antagonistic, but this view is derived from an equation of *ideological* conservatism with the outlook of the post-war Conservative *Party*, which as we have seen is not necessarily appropriate. Leaving aside the polarised politics of post-war Labour and Conservative politicians who claim to act in their name, socialism and conservatism have at least one common feature of considerable importance. They both assert that the well-being of society as a whole should override the interests of any individual. During the nineteenth century, traditional conservatives could join socialists in deploring the corrosive social effects of industrial capitalism. As a result, Victorian thinkers like John Ruskin (1819–1900) have been honoured by socialists and conservatives alike.

Liberalism

While socialism developed in reaction to the social impact of the Industrial Revolution, the origins of liberalism are more controversial. Marxists see it as an attempt to justify the rise to power and subsequent dominance of the bourgeoisie, which replaced the aristocracy as the ruling class as a result of the Industrial Revolution. But it can also be associated with the emergence of the Protestant religion (although for many Marxists this is just another way of making the same point, because they interpret Protestantism as a manifestation of bourgeois ideology).

Certainly liberal thought predates systematic socialist thinking. One of the classic texts, John Locke's *Two Treatises of Government*, was published as long ago as 1690. Locke clearly belongs in the liberal tradition because of his emphasis on natural rights, which he believed were a gift to individuals from God. Government, Locke argued, was only legitimate if it arose from the **consent** of the individual. On the basis of this contractual theory, Locke built a justification for the removal of any government which failed to protect the rights of its citizens. Although it would be wrong to see Locke himself as an early advocate of universal adult suffrage, many later democratic theorists enlisted his work in support of their ideas.

At the core of liberal thinking is the concept of the free, rational individual. Government is only legitimate if it is based on consent, reflecting the wishes of rational citizens. Crucially, such a government should be *limited* in the scope of its activity, because rational individuals can be trusted to look after their own affairs for the most part. But there must be a framework of law to protect life and property from individuals who fail to understand the rational advantages of peaceful, profitable co-existence. Governments may levy taxation, but only with the free consent of their citizens. In the eighteenth century, these liberal ideas were used by the American colonists to provide a principled basis for their rebellion against the British crown.

As a dissenter from the established Anglican church, John Locke argued passionately for religious toleration (at least for fellow Protestants). This element of liberal thought was given its finest expression by the Victorian philosopher (and briefly Liberal MP) John Stuart Mill (1806–73), in his tract *On Liberty* (1859). Mill believed that an individual should only be subject to interference when he or she caused harm to others. The obvious difficulty here is that 'harm' is an ambiguous concept. For example, the very existence of non-believers in the world causes moral offence to fanatical followers of many religions, equating in their eyes to serious 'harm'. But Mill, like most secular-minded liberals, believed that his 'harm principle' would provide a guarantee of freedom of thought and speech to all 'rational' people like himself, and that through free discussion human beings were bound to acquire more accurate knowledge. This aspect of his thought is best characterised as an early example of **pluralism** – a belief, common to many liberals, that the expression of diverse opinions is the only way to promote the cause of truth.

However, as befitted a near-contemporary of Marx, Mill was troubled by the impact of the Industrial Revolution. In later life, indeed, he flirted with socialist economic ideas. This was an early symptom of the serious rift which opened up in the liberal ranks towards the end of the nineteenth century. Broadly speaking, after this time, liberals could be divided into two distinct camps:

1. '*laissez-faire*', or its most recent manifestation, neo-*liberalism*. Laissez-faire liberalism is based on the idea that individuals are free so long as they are not subject to *deliberate* interference from anyone else. For laissez-faire liberals, the state exists merely to protect individuals from such interference, either to their lives or their property. If it goes beyond this role, the state itself becomes the main enemy to freedom. Laissez-faire liberals are particularly suspicious of any

Consent

agreement or permission, although it can in practice be merely acquiescence (or 'tacit' consent).

Pluralism

the belief that a diversity of people and values is beneficial.

suggestion that the scope of state action should be expanded in the interests of society. In their view, 'society' does not exist: there are only individuals and their families, who should be left to pursue their own interests in their own way, provided that their actions do not prevent anyone else doing the same.

In the second half of the twentieth century, laissez-faire ideas were revived, not just because of the perceived threat to the West emanating from totalitarian regimes like the Soviet Union but also because democratic governments were themselves taking a more active part in economic management. *In The Road to Serfdom* (1944), the Austrian-born economist Friedrich von Hayek (1899–1992) argued that this process would lead to the extinction of freedom if left unchecked, and that the threat existed in supposedly 'liberal' countries like the United Kingdom and the United States, as well as fascist Germany and the Communist Soviet Union. Hayek's ideas had a profound influence on Margaret Thatcher, among others. To reflect the fact that laissez-faire ideas had been revised and updated in the modern context, Hayek and those who shared his views were described as 'neo-liberals'.

2. *new liberalism.* Not to be confused with the advocates of neo-liberalism, new liberals envisage a far more positive role for the state. Their position arose in response to the poverty experienced by the majority of the British population during the Industrial Revolution, which became an influential political factor as more working people won the right to vote. New liberals had no objection to economic inequality. But they thought that people should at least be protected against the effects of unemployment which was no fault of their own, and of ill health or old age. They also argued that the state should provide at least a rudimentary education for all children, to give them a reasonable chance of developing into rational adult individuals.

Equality of opportunity

equal access to the procedure by which an office or benefit is allocated.

New liberalism was not so far removed from the social democratic ideas of Anthony Crosland, examined earlier. Like him, the new liberals were arguing for something like **equality of opportunity** rather than a guaranteed equality of economic outcomes. There was, though, a theoretical difference underlying this broad agreement on practical policies. The new liberals believed that equality of opportunity would guarantee that every individual had a realistic chance of fulfilling his or her potential through competition in a capitalist economy. That is, they were still committed to core liberal ideas concerning human nature. The social democrats, by contrast, retained a preference for the harmonious, cooperative society which had fuelled the original socialist vision. In other words, new liberals and social democrats could support the tentative beginnings of what became Britain's welfare state (see Chapter 3), without necessarily sharing the same hopes for the *ultimate outcome* of these policies (Table 16.1).

Ideology and British political parties

This brief survey of the 'traditional' British ideologies provides a basis for an assessment of the principles of the main parties. When studying the impact of ideology on the political parties, we have to remember that these organisations

TABLE 16.1 Typical attitudes of the main ideologies on key issues

Issue	Laissez-faire liberalism/neo-liberalism	Social democracy/new liberalism	Socialism	Conservatism
Economic competition	Natural to human beings and productive of prosperity and progress	Acceptable within limits	Destructive of human harmony and happiness	Natural to some, but likely to disturb social stability
Inequality of income	Morally acceptable; provides incentives to excel	Gap between rich and poor must not be too wide	Morally repugnant	Inevitable in any human society, but damaging if allowed to grow too wide
Welfare state	Acceptable as a 'safety net' for the poor; if too generous creates 'dependency culture' and destroys incentives	Relatively generous provision essential in a civilised society	Merely a prop for corrupt capitalist system	Necessary to prevent social discontent; reflects duty of rich to the poor
Law and order	Harsh punishment for those whose actions interfere with the peaceful operations of the free market	Punishment must include an attempt to reform criminals	Capitalist laws are merely devised to defend the existing economic order	All humans are potentially evil. Punishment should fit the criminal as well as the crime
Globalisation	A welcome development; people should have the opportunity of buying and selling in every market without restriction	In theory trade should be spread as widely as possible, but it should not result in exploitation at home or abroad	Closer links between the peoples of all nations are essential, but the profit motive can only divide human beings	We find it hard enough to understand our neighbours. Links of any kind with the wider world are likely to be unsettling

are broad coalitions (otherwise, they would not have been so successful over the years). However, it is possible to make generalisations about the most influential ideas within each party at different times and to trace the key developments.

The Conservative Party and conservatism

Party labels are adopted in specific historical circumstances, and subsequent developments can make them misleading, for reasons which must be explored. This is particularly true of the Conservative Party. When the Tory Party began to use the 'Conservative' label in the early 1830s, its supporters were trying to resist constitutional changes which they regarded as unacceptably radical. Their opponents, the Whigs, were arguing for a (limited) extension of the electoral franchise, and attacking the privileged position of the Anglican Church. Resistance to these changes was based on the 'Burkean' conservative argument that existing institutional arrangements worked

Controversy 16.1

Meritocracy and education

A useful illustration of the way ideologies are constrained by the context in which they operate is provided by the idea of 'meritocracy', particularly in relation to schooling.

All three of Britain's main political parties claim to embrace 'equality of opportunity' – the idea that people should prosper according to individual merit, rather than the circumstances of their upbringing.

In practice, though, the concept gives rise to considerable difficulties for members of all the main ideological 'families'. Since socialists believe that economic inequality causes social friction, their own understanding of equal opportunities relates to the chances of living a worthwhile life in a harmonious, egalitarian society. Comprehensive education, in which children are taught in mixed-ability classes, thus has obvious attractions to socialists. But from the socialist point of view, there remains a major difficulty in today's society arising from parental influence, which can give certain children crucial advantages and leave them with the complacent feeling that competition is better than cooperation.

Things are no easier for liberals or social democrats. Laissez-faire or neo-liberalism argues that equality of opportunity is guaranteed when there are no deliberately imposed barriers to individual advancement. Books like *Self-Help* (1859), by the journalist Samuel Smiles, proved that it was possible for some individuals to rise through their own efforts in the Victorian period, long before the introduction of the modern welfare state. Yet many successful entrepreneurs, in Victorian times and more recently, have owed their prosperity to luck. Laissez-faire liberals might reply that individuals 'make their own luck'. But it is still the case that some individuals find it easier than others to be 'lucky', particularly if they have wealthy parents and attend public school alongside others with similar advantages.

Social democrats and new liberals have paid the most serious attention to this problem since equality of opportunity is arguably their most important ideal. But they have fared no better than their ideological rivals. Even the Attlee government judged it politically impossible to abolish public schools – Attlee himself was the product of one (Haileybury) – and the operations of the free market in housing are now reinforcing a 'two-tier' system even within state-run institutions, because wealthy parents can relocate to areas which will ensure that their children can attend the best state schools. Arguably, the recruitment of children into the best schools because of the location of their parental home is even more difficult to justify than the previous system of selection by ability at the age of 11, and thus even more distant from any meaningful idea of 'meritocracy'. Where such selective schools still exist, the children of the affluent have obvious advantages in the competition for places.

The undeniable inequalities in educational opportunity in Britain which have persisted despite the idealism of reformers since 1945 cast serious doubts on the rhetoric of all the main parties, however sincere they might be in their efforts to raise standards across the board. In effect, they are now trying to devise policies which will convince a bare majority of the electorate that their children can enjoy something which would satisfy a very loose definition of the term 'equality of opportunity', while hoping that no one will look too closely at the true implications of that phrase. Whatever their academic merits, the 'academies' and 'free schools' championed to the point of obsession by Tony Blair, David Cameron and others seem unlikely to bring genuine 'equality of opportunity' any closer. The idea that 'rational' parents should be provided information about the academic outcomes in various schools seems impeccably 'liberal'. Yet to the extent that this has generated a 'competition' between schools which results in the lowering of morale among teachers and pupils in those which are judged to be 'failing' seems to make it unfit for any principled purpose.

adequately, and radical reform based on abstract principle was sure to make things worse. This argument proved less persuasive at the time than the Whig case for change. However, the Whigs were themselves anxious to keep reform within limits and after their most notable victory, the Great Reform Act (1832) which extended the vote to comfortable middle-class property owners, they claimed that the constitution was now 'perfect'. But they had made it far more difficult to argue against further electoral reforms. These duly arrived, in 1867 (inspired by the Conservative, Disraeli), then in 1885, 1918 and 1928, by which time almost all adults over 21 could vote.

From our earlier discussion, we can appreciate why these developments were deeply disturbing to traditional conservatives. At every step, the extension of the franchise took Britain further away from the ideal of benevolent rule by an aristocratic elite, and put the choice of governors in the hands of people who (according to conservative assumptions) were unfitted directly to participate in politics. There were further blows to the conservative world view in the constitutional crisis of 1910–11, which resulted in drastic reductions in the power of the House of Lords (see Chapter 8), and the First World War, which suggested that conservatives had good reason to distrust human nature but also left them struggling to provide any constructive visions for the future. In addition, the carnage of 1914–18 fell with particular severity on the children of aristocratic families, thinning the ranks of promising individuals who might otherwise have lived up to Burkean ideals.

As we have seen, ideology is action-orientated. Taken together, the developments of 1832–1918 deprived Burkean conservatives of a positive rationale for political action in Britain. Remaining adherents were far more likely to withdraw from public life – or to revise their thinking in order to accommodate new realities. Traditional conservatives who remained in politics were most likely to gravitate towards new liberalism, which at least offered the chance of relative social stability and could be squared with Disraelian state paternalism. But the Liberal Party, which had carried through an ambitious programme of social reform in the years before the First World War, was still the obvious home for new liberals. The Conservative Party itself looked doomed to extinction.

As it turned out, the Conservatives were able to take advantage of disastrous splits within the Liberal Party. They had already benefited from earlier Liberal divisions over home rule for Ireland. But the quarrel between the Liberal leaders, Asquith and Lloyd George, over the conduct of the First World War put an end to that party's prospects of forming a government on its own. Ambitious young people who would otherwise have been happy to join the Liberals now regarded the Conservative Party as the obvious outlet for their talents, and as the main focus of opposition to the Labour Party. The trend was not restricted to the young; Winston Churchill, who had defected from the Conservatives to the Liberals in 1904, decided to rejoin his old party 20 years later.

'Built to Last' and 'the Big Society': the ideology of David Cameron

In 2006, Conservative Party members overwhelmingly endorsed a statement of principle entitled 'Built to Last'. Although it was the product of wide consultation, the document clearly reflected the thinking of the newly elected party leader, David Cameron. The main points were:

- The Conservative Party should encourage economic enterprise in a way which improves living standards for all.
- The party should fight social injustice and help the disadvantaged, through voluntary action, as well as through the state.
- It should take action to preserve the environment, since 'there is more to life than money'.
- It should work to improve public services like health, education and housing.
- Conservatives should take the lead in trying to end global poverty.
- The party should be resolute in maintaining national security.
- There should be greater devolution of power to local communities, and opposition to 'any proposed European Constitution that foreshadowed the emergence of a single European superstate'.
- Conservatives should embrace the diversity of Britain and represent this by encouraging a wider variety of parliamentary candidates.

All this was in marked contrast to a statement of personal beliefs issued in January 2004 by the then Conservative leader Michael Howard. Howard's list of principles ('I Believe') was dominated by suspicion of the central state. This attitude was not entirely absent from 'Built to Last', which stressed the importance of handing back power to local communities, the need to encourage the voluntary sector and the dangers of an identity card system (which Michael Howard had strongly recommended when he was Home Secretary under John Major). Yet 'Built to Last' also included a declaration of belief in 'the role of central government as a force for good'. Though barely noticed by commentators, this was actually a highly significant shift from Conservative Party rhetoric since Margaret Thatcher took the leadership in 1975.

There were other notable departures from Thatcherism. The opening declaration of 'Built to Last' included the assertion that 'there is such a thing as society'. This was a clear reference to one of Mrs Thatcher's most notorious expressions of individualism, but some of Thatcher's successors (notably Iain Duncan Smith) had already affirmed their belief in the existence of society. It was more significant that Cameron's document admitted that there was more to life than material prosperity, especially since this was linked to a concern for the environment and for the reduction of global poverty.

Some aspects of 'Built to Last' could easily have appeared in a 'New' Labour document. This was particularly true of its stress on individual responsibility (which had been a favourite theme for Tony Blair) and its advocacy of an open, meritocratic society which was free from discrimination on irrelevant grounds such as gender or race. It would be too much to say that the document marked a return of the party to its pre-Thatcherite, One Nation tradition. Even so, 'Built to Last' could be presented as an effective answer to critics who depicted the Conservatives as 'the nasty party'.

In the build-up to the 2010 general election, Cameron used the phrase 'the Big Society' to explain a key aspect of his thinking. Many commentators were puzzled by this slogan, and even some Conservative candidates expressed doubts about its electoral potency. However, Cameron clearly believed that it was entirely compatible with 'Built to Last'. From this perspective, it was best understood as an attempt to chart a 'third way' between the ideological poles of state control and excessive individualism; the state should continue to guarantee a 'safety net' for those unable to help themselves, but many services currently provided by the public sector could just as easily (and even more effectively) be provided through voluntary effort.

The problem with 'the Big Society' was not its clarity or logic, but rather its *practicability*. Cameron seemed to be assuming that the voluntary urge was alive and well in the United Kingdom, and that if only the state would get out of the way there would be an inexhaustible supply of active citizens ready to work for their communities without significant material reward. At a time when even people who were willing to volunteer were often unable to do so because of their busy daily routines, this seemed naïve at best. At worst, the Big Society could be seen as a cunning ploy which would result in profit-making private companies, rather than well-meaning individual citizens, filling the vacuum left by the retreating state. Thus an idea which was supposed to mark a distinctively 'conservative' alternative to Thatcherism could inadvertently work to the advantage of people who denied Cameron's proposition that 'there was more to life than material prosperity' (Photo 16.1).

PHOTO 16.1 David Cameron – the face of 'caring Conservatism'? (© Rupert Hartley/David Hartley/Shutterstock).

Thus the Conservative Party survived as an institution, thanks partly to its adaptability but mainly to luck. However, its name was now a source of confusion rather than an accurate indication of its ideological character. From 1918 (if not before), the majority of prominent Conservatives were, in fact, best regarded as *liberals* of various kinds. By this time, the party included many individuals who had been prominent in the Liberal Party itself and saw no reason to change their beliefs just because they had switched partisan allegiance for tactical reasons; other Conservatives saw the advantages of seizing fertile ideological ground from the remaining, faltering Liberals.

If the Conservative Party was no longer 'conservative' in a distinctive ideological sense, we have seen that liberalism had divided into two broad camps by the early twentieth century; so the party's new course was certainly not predetermined. In the fight against Labour, the Conservatives might have been expected to embrace the laissez-faire strand of liberalism. After all, a creed which denied the very existence of 'society' presented a stark contrast with the full-blooded 'socialism' which Labour allegedly espoused. Many of the grass-roots activists in the Conservative Party did indeed adopt this position, and managed to convince themselves that their version of liberalism represented authentic *conservatism*. But up until the mid-1970s, the leading members of the parliamentary party (like the ex-Prime Minister Edward Heath) were new liberals, who still accepted Disraeli's positive view of the state even if they had relinquished his vision of a hierarchical social order. To satisfy their more radical constituency supporters, the leaders often included laissez-faire tropes in their rhetoric. Thus, for example, the party campaigned in 1950 on a platform of freedom from government interference. But when it returned to office in 1951, it retained almost all of the welfare institutions established by the post-war Attlee government, and made little effort to reverse its programme of nationalisation. The leadership, at least, saw no reason to depart from the broad framework of the post-war 'consensus' (see Analysis 16.3).

In 1970, Heath came to office on much the same platform. His rhetoric had suggested a significant reduction in the role of the state, but he hoped to cut what he regarded as wasteful expenditure and counter-productive government activities rather than wishing to curb the role of the state as an ideological priority in itself. When his government foundered under the impact of high inflation and industrial disorder, the laissez-faire liberals within the party seized their belated opportunity to argue that successive leaders had 'betrayed' true 'conservatism' since 1945, if not before. Thatcher's victory in the 1975 leadership election triggered a prolonged debate between her supporters and those who remained loyal to Heath. Although this was strictly a dispute among liberals of different kinds, both sides claimed to represent the 'true' British conservative tradition!

Thatcherism and the new right

The strength of Thatcher's convictions is reflected in the fact that, unusually among British politicians, her name is used as a shorthand ideological term. As we have seen, she was strongly influenced by the neo-liberal economist Friedrich von Hayek. She once declared that there was 'no such thing as society', a much-debated phrase by which she meant that individuals should take responsibility for themselves rather than blaming their misfortunes on their circumstances. Yet she also supported a strong line on law and order and personal morality, urging a restoration of 'Victorian values' in place of the 'permissive' attitude to social matters which she and her supporters traced back to the 1960s.

It is often argued that these beliefs made Thatcherism an unstable – if not self-contradictory – ideological compound, advocating the widest possible freedom in some spheres of conduct and heavy restraint in others. The impression of incoherence is increased by differences within the British 'new right' which supported Thatcher. Some believed that economic freedom was much more important than social stability, while others (the so-called neo-conservatives (see Analysis 16.3)) reversed these priorities. These diverse groups coalesced in the Thatcher years and supported the Conservative Party because of their shared antipathy towards various elements of the

Analysis 16.3

Ideology and the post-war 'consensus'

The framework of policies established by the Attlee government is often identified as the basis of a post-war 'consensus' which embraced all three of the major parties. Usually this is characterised as a 'social democratic' consensus. This chapter suggests a slightly different interpretation. We can accept that the impulse behind the policies arose *mainly* from revisionist or social democratic principles, reflecting the beliefs of most senior Labour Party figures at the time. But Labour's programme of nationalisation, and the welfare state, could be endorsed from a variety of ideological perspectives. Parliamentary socialists could see these developments as first steps towards the ultimate goal of a cooperative society, in which the means of production would no longer be in private hands.

For their part, new liberals welcomed the advances towards real equality of opportunity. They certainly harboured reservations about the extent of nationalisation, but they could acquiesce given the fact that the nationalised industries were essential economic assets which had been struggling in the private sector. Social democrats, of course, felt no such qualms about the encroachments of the state. Burkean conservatives – the few that featured in the parliaments of 1945–51 – could welcome the element of paternalism and the implicit desire for a more stable society, while remaining deeply sceptical that agents of the state (or indeed anyone else) could run giant monopolistic enterprises in the public interest.

In other words, the post-war consensus can be regarded as a broad policy framework which was acceptable to all except revolutionary socialists and laissez-faire liberals. In turn, it is no surprise that those ideologies, which had proved impossible to reconcile with the trend of policy under successive governments since 1945, suddenly seemed much more attractive when the general assumptions underlying the 'consensus' came under intolerable strain due to the economic difficulties of the 1970s (see Chapter 3).

post-war consensus, which Thatcher herself openly attacked on the grounds that it was based on 'socialist' thinking (although as we have seen, it is far more congruent with new liberal/ social democratic ideas).

Whatever the coherence of new right ideas, Thatcher's diverse disciples are best understood within the context of laissez-faire liberalism. Even so-called neo-conservatives, who take much of their inspiration from the United States, make the rational individual the focus of their thinking, and believe that the state should minimise its interference with the free market. And if the nature of Thatcherism is to be taken from the ideas of the Prime Minister herself, its place within the laissez-faire tradition is unmistakable. 'Economics are the method', she declared in 1981; 'the object is to change the soul'. If the state stepped back from economic interference, she believed, individuals would be freed to take their destinies in their own hands. As the earlier quotation suggests, Mrs Thatcher assumed that this new sense of personal liberation would in itself transform the moral outlook of most Britons, restoring something like the values which had made Victorian Britain so prosperous. However, there were bound to be people who continued to reject Victorian values to the extent of breaking the law; and the punishment of law-breakers was a proper role for the state. In this sense, Mrs Thatcher saw no contradiction in her support for what Andrew Gamble dubbed 'the free economy and the strong state'; like the laissez-faire liberals of the nineteenth century, she thought that the state should crack down on activities which were incompatible with the efficient operation of the free market. The armed forces should also be provided with generous funds from the taxpayer, to defend Britain against the Communist Soviet Union. Mrs Thatcher regarded defence against non-Communist states as a lower priority. By a supreme irony, Thatcher-inspired defence cuts encouraged the Argentine regime to invade the Falklands Islands, resulting in the 1982 conflict, whose successful outcome greatly increased her government's popularity.

In office (1979–90), Thatcher was forced to compromise on numerous occasions, contrary to the image of the 'Iron Lady' who urged her supporters to 'think the unthinkable'. For example, in 1984 she was forced to abandon plans to charge university tuition fees after protests from party supporters; it was left to Tony Blair's Labour Party to make this very controversial idea seem viable. However, Thatcher's pragmatic streak reflected her awareness of ideological adversaries within her own party who were looking for an opportunity to bring her down, and (to a much lesser extent) a recognition that her ideas were never accepted by a majority of voters. Thus, for example, while Thatcherite thinking pointed to the scrapping of the welfare state, there was never any chance that institutions like the National Health Service (NHS) could have been abolished without stimulating widespread opposition. As it was, Mrs Thatcher overreached herself by introducing the poll tax, a way of raising revenue for local government which was designed to fall on individuals regardless of their financial resources (see Chapter 3). This provoked a campaign of civil disobedience, a mass rally in London which turned into a riot, and a significant swing in the opinion polls towards the Labour Party. Although disagreements about Europe helped to inspire the party revolt which ejected Thatcher from office in November 1990, the poll tax was a strong contributory factor to the background of discontent. For Thatcher, it was an ideological step too far, enraging even people who otherwise agreed with her individualistic attack on the state.

The Labour Party and socialism

We have seen that after the First World War, the Conservative Party was regarded as the main focus of opposition to socialism in Britain. But was there really any socialism to oppose? Judging by Clause IV of the party's constitution, adopted in 1918, the Labour Party was indeed committed to socialist goals. The clause pledged:

> To secure for the workers by hand or by brain the full fruits of their industry and the most equitable distribution thereof that may be possible, upon the basis of the common ownership of the means of production, distribution and exchange.

Yet this striking declaration of socialist aims had only been accepted as part of a deal to keep the party's intellectuals within the party fold. After the formation of the Labour Representation Committee (LRC) in 1900, real power lay with the trade union movement, whose primary aim was to secure the election of working men to parliament. In the party's early years, most Labour MPs owed their seats to cooperation with the (reformist, but hardly revolutionary) Liberal Party. When the Labour Party formed its first (minority) government in 1923, far from storming Buckingham Palace, the new ministers conformed to all the usual proprieties. During the General Strike of 1926, when a revolutionary situation really could have developed, the party's leaders hoped for a reasonable settlement as quickly as possible. And when capitalism seemed to be entering a final crisis after the Wall Street Crash of 1929, the second Labour government collapsed because it could offer no constructive alternative to orthodox capitalist economic management.

The post-war government (1945–51) of Clement Attlee presented the Labour Party with its first real chance to prove that socialism could be achieved by parliamentary means. The government was elected by a landslide, swept into office by a widespread feeling that the time had come for a decisive change because the Conservatives had failed between the two world wars. Labour's socialists still look back with nostalgia to these days. Throughout its six years in power after 1945, Attlee's party was faced with crippling economic difficulties. Even so, it took into state ownership gas, coal, iron and steel, the railways and the Bank of England. It also established the NHS, against concerted opposition from the medical profession.

This was indeed a formidable policy programme. But did it really represent an advance towards *socialism?* Most of the government's acts of nationalisation targeted industries which had been struggling badly in the private sector. Even the Conservatives had contemplated nationalising the railways, and had established the British Broadcasting Corporation (BBC) under state control; the traumas of the privately owned coal industry had triggered the General Strike of 1926. If the Attlee government's programme of nationalisation had represented a preliminary shopping list, to be supplemented by profitable concerns in the chemical or light engineering industries, Labour would have proved that it was serious about the commitment enshrined in Clause IV. The party was re-elected in 1950 with a very slender majority but lost an ill-timed general election a year later. Had it secured a second comfortable majority in 1950, it might have proposed further radical action. But its room for manoeuvre would still have been restricted. Britain's post-war economic revival depended crucially on US assistance. A few months before the government's defeat in 1951, the Chancellor of the Exchequer Hugh Gaitskell imposed limited NHS charges to help pay for a massive defence rearmament programme. This was Britain's response to American demands during its war against Communism in Korea. The decision provoked the resignation from the Cabinet of the founder of the NHS, Aneurin Bevan, along with the future Prime Minister Harold Wilson.

After the Labour Party returned to opposition, leaving Britain with a 'mixed' economy and a welfare state which provided a guaranteed income for pensioners and the unemployed, the party was divided over the best way forward. The initiative in this dispute was taken by Hugh Gaitskell's supporters, who took a 'revisionist' or social democratic line. As we have seen, this position received powerful support in these years from Gaitskell's friend Anthony Crosland, who provided plausible practical and theoretical arguments to reinforce a position to which most senior Labour figures already subscribed. When Gaitskell became leader in 1955, he tried to persuade his party to abandon Clause IV, but failed to convince the trade unions which had a vested interest in nationalisation.

By this time, the alignment of ideological forces within the Labour Party had shifted. In the early days, party intellectuals tended to be attracted by socialist theory, and accused the trade unions of supporting the capitalist status quo if it allowed them to improve the standard of living of their members in relation to other workers. The revisionist argument reflected the fact that many of the next generation of Labour intellectuals, like Gaitskell himself, might never have joined the party if the Liberals still enjoyed realistic prospects of forming a government. Gaitskell's successor as leader, Harold Wilson, was another intellectual of this kind, having been a member of the Liberal Party at Oxford University. Wilson had sided with the Bevanite opponents of Gaitskell, but after the latter's death in 1963 he proved that the differences had been more about personality and tactical appreciation than any profound ideological disagreement.

Wilson's two stints as Prime Minister (1964–70 and 1974–76) were marked by struggles against economic difficulties more than the forward march of socialism. Whatever the preferences of Wilson himself, his second period in Downing Street coincided with an economic crisis which undermined the social democratic assumption that growing prosperity would continue to fund a generous welfare state (see Chapter 3).

After the Labour Party lost office in 1979, a bitter post-mortem took place on the party's recent record. The 'revisionists' were in retreat, and indeed four senior figures from that wing of the party left to establish the Social Democratic Party (SDP) in 1981. Under the leadership of Michael Foot (1980–83) – a liberal by heritage and in principle, whose romantic view of the working class fostered a contradictory, uncritical attitude towards the union movement – it looked as if Labour might finally commit itself wholeheartedly to socialism. A campaign to 'democratise' the party, headed by the former Cabinet minister Tony Benn, unseated several MPs for their insufficient commitment to socialist ideals, although the extent of this ideological witch-hunt was exaggerated by sections of the media. Benn himself came within a whisker of winning the party's deputy leadership.

Labour fought the 1983 election on a manifesto which was described as 'the longest suicide note in history'. In fact, it was no more radical than the party's policy platform of February 1974 – when it had defeated the Heath government. Both Tony Blair and Jeremy Corbyn entered parliament on the basis of the alleged 1983 'suicide note'. The main differences were that this time it was widely assumed that if the party won, it really would act on its radical promises; and the Conservative-supporting press, which idolised Margaret Thatcher, was far more active in publicising Labour's 'extremism'. As a result, the 1983 general election was an occasion when the two main parties found that the charade which they had been acting out for so many years had suddenly become a reality. Conservatives had grown accustomed to attacking Labour's 'socialism', while recognising (in private, at least) that the party's leaders presented no serious danger to capitalism. Meanwhile, Labour had been fulminating against the Conservatives as hard-nosed apologists for greed and exploitation, while accepting that most of them were very agreeable and well-meaning parliamentary colleagues. Now, for the first time in post-war British history, the parties engaged in a genuine (and bitter) ideological battle. The conflict, though, was one-sided, not least because the tabloid press was so effective in attacking Labour (see Chapter 5).

After the Labour Party's crushing defeat in 1983, the process of ideological polarisation between the two main parties was brought to an end. Foot's successor Neil Kinnock embarked on the task of making his party 'electable' again. For Kinnock, that meant restoring the dominance in policy terms of the 'revisionist' or social democratic perspective. But although he ensured the defeat of socialist activists – some of whom had organised within the party as members of the Militant Tendency (see Chapter 15) – he failed to convince the public that he was sufficiently 'prime ministerial' and under his leadership the Labour Party lost two further elections. His successor John Smith (1992–94) belonged firmly to the social democratic tradition and the party was far keener to unite behind its leader than it had been in Kinnock's day. But Smith never had the chance to test the popularity of his ideas in a general election.

'New' and 'old' Labour

When Tony Blair was elected leader after Smith's sudden death in 1994 his first priority was to shed the ideological baggage of the past – including the period of Smith's leadership, which had done so much to advance Blair's own career prospects. Within a year, he had succeeded where

Gaitskell had failed, persuading his party to revise Clause IV of the party's constitution. The new clause spoke of a 'common endeavour' to ensure that individuals could realise their 'full potential' in a 'community' where:

> Power, wealth and opportunity are in the hands of the many not the few, where the rights we receive reflect the duties we owe, so that, freed from the tyranny of poverty, ignorance and fear, we may live together in a spirit of solidarity, tolerance and respect.

The new clause described Labour as 'a democratic socialist party'. This was a peculiar form of words. If the new clause proved anything, it was that Blair and his allies were not socialists of *any* kind. As we have seen, socialists believe that 'solidarity, tolerance and respect' are impossible to realise in a society dominated by capitalist ideas because of the divisive nature of the profit motive. Blair's goal, by contrast, was to extend opportunities *within* capitalist society. On paper, this ambition could be squared with the social democratic tradition. However, Blair had gone out of his way to avoid using that label. Instead, he began to talk about a 'third way' – an alternative to socialism and unrestricted capitalism. Yet revisionist social democracy was itself a 'third way' of precisely this kind. Gradually it became clear that Blair's reluctance to associate himself with the social democratic tradition arose from ideological considerations. Blair differed from social democrats in his emphasis on 'wealth creation', rather than the redistribution of wealth to reduce social inequality. Instead, he thought that redistribution should aim at the reduction of *absolute* poverty; once this had been achieved, it was no business of the state to close the gap between the best and worst-off in society. His focus, rather, was on 'success' – however that word might be defined.

Blair also differed from social democrats in his marked preference for the ethos and practices of private enterprise, even in the provision of state services like health and education. Before he became Prime Minister, Blair made it clear that he would not reverse any of the privatisations of the Conservative years. In fact, although the government was forced to take over the functions of Railtrack, the privatised company which maintained Britain's railways, New Labour was keen to explore the possibility of further sales of state assets, and to involve private sector companies in public projects through the Private Finance Initiative (PFI) (see Chapter 10).

After the 2005 general election, when Blair was faced with frequent backbench rebellions as he fought to secure a tangible legacy in domestic policy, he tried to reconnect himself with the social democratic tradition. But by that time, it was clear to most observers that this was a rhetorical device, which could not be reconciled with his policy priorities in the public services. Overall, Blair's ideas can best be understood in the context of the continental European tradition of Christian democracy, which has been particularly influential in Italy, Germany and Norway. In turn, Christian Democratic ideas are very closely related to new liberalism, which also emerged at the end of the nineteenth century. The only significant difference is that Christian democrats – like Blair – laid a stronger emphasis than new liberals on the community (as opposed to the state), stressing individual duties, as well as rights. On the continent of Europe – particularly in Italy and Germany – Christian democracy has provided the basis for powerful and consistent opposition to socialist parties since the Second World War. It is a remarkable irony that (for various reasons, not all related to ideology) Labour chose an overtly *anti-socialist* leader at a time when the perceived threat from Communist states had disappeared. Blair made no secret of his desire to overturn many of his party's most cherished traditions, but even he was prudent enough to be evasive about the true character of his thinking. His approach illustrated the importance of ideological labels, which can matter at least as much as the beliefs themselves.

Despite Blair's election-winning charisma, he did not succeed in converting the bulk of his party. His ideological opponents, given the collective name of 'Old Labour' (emulating

Controversy 16.2

Blair and 'the forces of conservatism'

In his speech to the Labour Party conference in September 1999, Tony Blair launched a savage attack on what he called 'the forces of conservatism'. Part of this was aimed directly at the parliamentary Opposition. Among other things, Blair accused the Conservative Party of having fought against giving the vote to women (in fact, their rejection of female suffrage had been shared by many supposedly progressive Liberal MPs), and he even tried to connect British conservatives with the murderers of Dr Martin Luther King. However, he had a wider target in mind. He was evidently satisfied that the 'forces of conservatism' included anyone who opposed New Labour, including union members who were currently resisting reform of the public services.

The example shows how important it is for serious students of Politics to subject political rhetoric to careful analysis, rather than accepting statements at face value. As so often when politicians attack the ideology of their opponents, Blair's speech told us far more about himself. Labour Party's official thinking had undergone many changes since 1983, but one constant factor was an instinctive, tribal reaction to the word 'conservatism'. Blair's use of the blanket term 'forces of conservatism' was obviously intended to make his 'Old' Labour Party critics think carefully before opposing him, in case they inadvertently assisted people who wanted to turn the clock back to the days of unchecked racism and sexism. Yet, on the account offered in this chapter, there are no significant 'forces of conservatism' left in the United Kingdom, in an ideological sense. It certainly is not very rational to accuse socialists, who continue to hope for radical change and an egalitarian society, of harbouring secretive 'conservative' leanings; but by 1999, Tony Blair evidently thought that his rhetorical powers were so effective that he could persuade a Labour Party conference to applaud anything.

Thatcherite jibes against 'wets' in their own party), were mostly adherents of social democracy. Some party members would still like to see themselves as socialists, and a few (like Jeremy Corbyn) refuse to relinquish the 'Clause IV' vision of industries run for public rather than private gain. However, their main goal is defensive – to obstruct the intrusion of free market principles into the public services, particularly in the fields of health and education, and to resist the encroachment of the state in the field of civil liberties (including trade union rights). Although they could agree with Blair's stated aspiration of extending opportunity, they doubted whether these words could mean very much when economic inequalities were continuing to grow. From the perspective of long-standing Labour loyalists, it may appear that Blair's main achievement was *not* to make his party 'electable' – it would have won in 1997 under any other competent leader – but rather his ability to make people who disagreed so fundamentally with him accept his leadership for so long.

It is commonly assumed that Blair's rivalry with his Chancellor of the Exchequer, Gordon Brown, was based at least in part on ideological differences. In fact, the uneasy relationship between the two provides some fascinating insights into the respective roles of ideology and personality in internal party politics. Many of the Labour MPs and activists who disagreed with Blair's principles looked to Brown as an alternative leader. This meant that the 'Brownites' tended to sympathise with Old Labour ideas, while the 'Blairites' were determined to stick to the New Labour course. Brown himself seemed happy to encourage his supporters to think that there would be a significant shift in government policy if (or rather when) he succeeded Blair as Prime Minister. However, the evidence suggests that Brown was only a 'Brownite' to the extent that, like his supporters, he wanted to remove Blair from Number 10. He insisted on full control of economic policy, but it is doubtful that Blair would have changed many of his domestic decisions, at least until the last couple of years before Brown succeeded him as Prime Minister. Certainly, Blair agreed with Brown's drive to reduce the proportion of children in poverty; but, as we have seen, this did not involve a serious attempt to reduce economic inequality by imposing heavy taxation on the rich. Brown was also a passionate advocate of involving the private sector in state activities like health and education, especially through the controversial PFI. Thus when Brown succeeded Blair he had no desire for a significant change of policy substance; only events beyond his control forced him to take a more interventionist role in the economy, provoking a new debate about Labour's beliefs. By the time Jeremy Corbyn became leader in 2015, it was 'New' Labour which had begun to look 'Old'.

The Liberal Democrats and liberalism

Blair often expressed regret that the close relationship between the Liberals and Labour in the early years of the twentieth century had proved short-lived. He argued that their separation had allowed the Conservatives to dominate the century, and set back the cause of 'progressive' politics. Blair's view said more about his approach to politics than it did about the true relationship between Labour and the Liberals. The main obstacles to a merger – considerations of social class, and the emotional, almost tribal loyalty that parties generate – were political factors which Blair consistently downplayed. But if the two parties had been able to overlook these points and strike a deal before the Labour Party was fully established at the beginning of the twentieth century, they would have imported significant ideological differences into the ranks of the merged organisation.

As we have seen, the ideological history of the two main parties is extremely complicated. By contrast, the Liberals (now the Liberal Democrats) have been much more straightforward. Until quite recently, the party has been dominated by new liberals. The Asquith government (1908–16) introduced several important social reforms, which are often cited as laying the foundations of the welfare state. True to this legacy, during the 2001 general election campaign the party argued for tax increases to fund better public services.

However, in 2004 several prominent Liberal Democrats contributed to a book which reminded the party that liberalism has always been suspicious of the state (its title, *The Orange Book*, was a mischievous echo of *The Yellow Book* (1928), which had promoted more active state intervention to alleviate the worst effects of a global economic downturn). Before the 2005 general election the Liberal Democrats again argued for higher taxes and a modest increase in public spending. But the subsequent deposition of Charles Kennedy as Liberal Democrat leader reflected the growing influence of *The Orange Book* faction, some of whom had become prominent MPs. Ironically, while the contributors to *The Orange Book* imagined that they were being radical, they were actually working to bring their party closer to the new 'consensus' in British politics (see below), and thus making the Liberal Democrats *less* distinctive in ideological terms.

Kennedy's replacement as leader, Sir Menzies Campbell, was seen as the most likely candidate to unite the party membership. This meant that Campbell would have to come to terms with *The Orange Book* faction, and within a few days of becoming leader he had persuaded his party to drop its objections to privatisation of the Royal Mail. Later the party also abandoned its pledge to increase taxes on the better-off. When Campbell stood down in October 2007, his position was contested by Nick Clegg and Chris Huhne, both of whom had contributed to *The Orange Book*. As in the Blair-Brown feud, their perceived ideological differences were less important than their conflicting personal ambitions.

While social democracy and new liberalism have several common characteristics, *The Orange Book* emphasised a crucial difference. It reminded its readers that all liberals take the individual as their primary focus, whereas social democrats concentrate on collective interests. So, although Blair considered it tragic that the Liberal Party and Labour Party did not unite, a merger between the Liberals and the *Conservatives* (while they remained under new liberal leadership, until 1975) would have been no less appropriate. But we have also seen that after the Liberal Party split during the First World War the Conservatives were regarded as providing the best chance of preventing the Labour Party from winning elections. As a result, members and supporters of the Liberal Party who feared the possibility of a truly socialist Labour government tended to defect to the Conservatives, while those who accepted the need for state intervention and recognised that the Labour Party was never a full-blooded socialist party moved in the other direction. Thus, while Churchill rejoined the Conservatives when the Liberals faltered, Richard Haldane, who had been a senior Liberal minister under Asquith, ended up as a Labour Lord Chancellor. It was as if ideological liberals had been transformed into a pool of talent from which their more successful rivals could draw promising recruits; by the same token, those who remained within the Liberal Party produced policy ideas which Labour and the Conservatives were happy to plagiarise.

As Prime Minister (1940–45, 1951–55), Churchill continued to hope that the remaining Liberals would follow his example and join the main anti-socialist party. But the Liberals struggled on, and seemed set to benefit from their perseverance at the beginning of the 1980s, when Labour adopted a more socialist outlook and the Conservatives plumped for Thatcherism. If ideology had been the main political factor, a significant number of Conservative and Labour MPs would have defected to their natural Liberal home at this point. The Liberal/SDP Alliance might even have emerged as the largest parliamentary grouping, reflecting the fact that a majority of the electorate continued to sympathise with new liberal/social democratic ideas about the role of the state throughout the Thatcher period. But institutional ties proved so strong that no more than a handful of Labour MPs, and only a single Conservative, left their parties – and even then they joined the newly founded SDP rather than going straight to the Liberals. Even the founder-members of the SDP were divided in their attitudes towards the Liberals, and this made the eventual merger between the parties (in 1988) a very messy affair, with senior figures like David Owen of the SDP remaining aloof.

Benjamin Disraeli famously advised a colleague to 'Damn your principles! Stick to your party'. For almost all of the last century Liberals and Liberal Democrats have acted as if it were possible to be consistent in both of these respects. Ironically, they have often been accused of electoral opportunism – trying to 'split the difference' between their chief rivals – and on the rare occasions when they have endorsed policies for 'pragmatic' reasons they have been criticised more harshly than their opponents. This tells us more about the British electoral system, which has made it much harder for Liberals to project their distinctive approach, than about the party itself.

A new 'consensus'?

In June 2004, Labour and the Conservatives began to introduce their main campaign themes for the following year's general election. Both Blair and Michael Howard emphasised the importance of choice in public service provision. During the campaign itself, this appeal was directed towards 'hard-working families'. There was a clear assumption shared by the two leading parties that members of such families would have very similar ideas. The Conservatives reinforced this point with the main slogan for their advertising campaign: 'Are you thinking what we're thinking?'

If there had been a significant ideological difference between the two party leaders, we would expect them to have meant different things even when they used the same words, due to contrasting views of human nature. In this case, Blair and Howard certainly found scope to attack each other's ideas. Howard was far more explicit than Blair in urging the direct involvement of private enterprise and the voluntary sector in the delivery of public services. But the practical impact of each programme would be greatly to reduce the direct role of the state.

Both Blair and Howard argued that their policies would ensure that everyone enjoyed the range of choice in services which was currently available only to the well-off. The concept of 'choice' is rightly associated with liberalism, which focuses on the rational individual. One of the intellectual 'gurus' of Thatcherism, Milton Friedman, published an influential book entitled *Free to Choose* in 1980. For all the bickering over policy details, Blair and Howard clearly shared Friedman's (and Thatcher's) core assumptions about human nature, seeing the average Briton as a 'consumer-citizen' (see Chapter 3). Before the 2005 general election, this theme was made explicit in speeches by the Health Secretary, John Reid, and Labour's campaign coordinator Alan Milburn. It was left to Charles Kennedy of the Liberal Democrats to argue that the emphasis in public services should be on *quality* rather than choice.

The debate over choice added weight to the claim that a new consensus had emerged in British politics. Despite three very comfortable election victories, Labour did little to change the broad framework of policy that it inherited from the Conservatives. It also, notoriously, was happy with the regime of self-regulation in the UK's banking sector, whose activities plunged the country into the economic crisis which overshadowed Labour's last years in office. In some respects, it went further than the Conservatives, for example, in its use of the PFI, which guarantees a high rate of return for private companies that invest in public sector projects such as new hospitals and schools.

The emergence of this new elite consensus is best understood against a background of socio-economic change, combined with the influence of democratic institutions. The old terminology of class no longer makes much sense in Britain (see Chapters 4 and 18). At the same time, much greater geographic mobility and insecurity in the job market have combined to generate a more individualistic ethos in Britain as in other Western countries. The advertising industry works on the ('Thatcherite') assumption that individuals are preoccupied with the material status of themselves and their immediate families. When parties call in the advertisers to enhance their appeal to the public, it is no surprise that their broadcasts and slogans echo similar assumptions about human nature. The 2005 theme of 'hard-working families' was repeated in the 2015 general election, despite the fact that such families had derived few discernable benefits from the decisions of successive governments in the intervening decade.

These developments complement institutions which reflect liberal ideas. The principle of 'one person, one vote' is, of course, in itself distinctively liberal, and the main theoretical support for universal franchise has come from liberals like John Stuart Mill. As a pluralist, Mill wanted elections to be free and equal contests between people of divergent views. He argued that principled disagreement is healthy, since even the truth becomes stale when everyone thinks the same way.

Of course, liberal democratic institutions do not guarantee the success of parties which profess liberal principles. The example of Hitler's National Socialists between the wars shows that even parties which detest democracy can win significant support under a system which gives the vote to most adults. Even so, the necessity of playing for power by liberal rules does have a tendency to make the most serious competitors think along liberal lines. For example, political campaigning nowadays is geared towards attracting floating voters in key constituencies (see Chapter 17). Such voters are assumed to exercise 'rational choice' in elections, opting for the party offering policies which will benefit themselves and their families. If the crucial voters in general elections are assumed to be distinctively liberal in their preferences, it is hardly surprising that all the parties with a serious chance of securing parliamentary representation tend to adopt policies (and use rhetoric) of a liberal flavour. As such, by joining Labour and the Conservatives in the 'middle ground' on economic issues, the Liberal Democrats could argue that they had acted in accordance with the work of the political scientist Anthony Downs (see Chapter 2). The problem, from the pluralist perspective, is that if all the parties are seeking the support of the 'median voter', *real* voters might lose interest in the whole process.

Within the broad framework of liberal ideas, laissez-faire is the strand which places most emphasis on individual self-interest. Thus, even if the leaders of the two main parties were not inherently sympathetic to laissez-faire, they would have plenty of good reasons for devising policies which conform to that tradition. Tellingly, the most radical 2005 manifesto commitments from both main parties were those which would have found most favour with laissez-faire liberals (in comparison, the tax increases proposed by the Liberal Democrats were extremely modest, although both Labour and the Conservatives tried to present them as a return to the 'punitive' tax regime of the 1970s). But it would be wrong to suggest that by 2005 British politics had fallen under the domination of a straightforward laissez-faire consensus; after all, even under Thatcher, the Conservatives continued to accept the welfare state, which is highly suspect to any laissez-faire liberal, and under David Cameron continued to insist that the state should help the poorest in society (see Case study 16.1). 'Post-Thatcherite' consensus is probably a more useful (though still contestable) term for a period which, like the previous 'consensus', was effectively brought to an end by an economic crisis.

The end of New Labour?

In November 2008, with the UK economy entering a period of serious recession, the Chancellor of the Exchequer Alistair Darling delivered a Pre-Budget Report which included several controversial measures. The biggest surprise was a declaration of intent to raise the highest rate of income tax from 40 to 45 per cent from the beginning of 2011, should Labour be re-elected.

Several newspapers took this as a sign that New Labour was dead. After all, promises *not* to increase income tax rates had featured heavily in the party's successful election campaigns of 1997, 2001 and 2005. Darling's decision came amid other reminders of 'Old' Labour; the government had recently nationalised more than one private financial institution, and taken sizeable stakes in several others. However, the death of New Labour seemed to be an exaggeration. First, massive state involvement in the banks was an enforced and very reluctant move, like the nationalisation of the bankrupt Rolls-Royce company by the Conservative government of Edward Heath in 1971. Second, while the tax increases did mark a shift from previous promises, they were hardly dramatic; affecting only those who earned more than £150,000 per year, they would leave the rate for the highest earners far below the level it had been for most of Mrs Thatcher's premiership. Indeed, since the measure would raise relatively little revenue for the state, it seemed to be motivated mainly by a desire to cause political embarrassment for the Conservative Party, which would look like the 'rich person's party' if it criticised a move which would have no impact on 'Middle England'.

Even so, reintroducing the unfamiliar idea of higher income tax did promise to enliven political debate between the main UK parties, and left open the possibility that the new higher rate could be increased to 50 per cent in a future budget (this was duly announced, for incomes over £150,000, in April 2009). During the election campaign of 2010, there was talk of clear ideological division between Labour and the Conservatives, but ultimately the parties differed in the *timing* of public spending cuts which almost everyone agreed were necessary. Ironically, the renewed talk of ideological division over economic policy had been generated by changes in the

Case study 16.2

Ideology and Cameron's coalition

In the last months of Gordon Brown's premiership, as it became increasingly clear that the next election would be the closest contest since 1974, speculation about a possible coalition tended to be based on the assumption that the Liberal Democrats would join forces with Labour. In part, this reflected the Liberal Democrat strategy under Paddy Ashdown's leadership (1988–98), when the party had abandoned the idea of 'equidistance' between its two senior rivals and become an obvious partner-in-waiting for Labour. In turn, this approach arose from an assumption that, in ideological terms, the Liberal Democrats were much more compatible with Labour than the Conservatives.

However, by 2010 the basis for such assumptions had been undermined by developments within the Liberal Democrat and Conservative parties. As we have seen, David Cameron was determined to 'move on' from Thatcherism. In particular, he worked to soften the party's image on social questions. This brought him closer to Liberal Democrat territory. At the same time, the Liberal Democrat *Orange Book* faction was attempting to steer their party away from high taxation and public spending, thus coming close to Conservative economic thinking on the subject.

As a result of these moves, although there were still important differences between the Liberal Democrats and the Conservatives (particularly on questions like electoral reform, immigration and European integration), the ideological 'direction of travel' of both parties was converging during the 2005–10 parliament. In this context, the economic problems which faced Gordon Brown's government are strongly relevant. While, as we have seen, Labour did not suddenly rediscover the full-scale economic interventionism of the Attlee or Wilson years, its instinctive preference for 'statist' remedies was not difficult to discern. On this subject, the rekindled Liberal Democrat suspicion of the central state (and a commitment to 'localism' which it shared with Cameron's Conservatives) meant that although the coalition was not an ideological match made in heaven, it was almost certainly a more congenial arrangement than a Labour–Liberal Democrat deal might have proved.

During the coalition, Cameron was able to claim that his 'Conservative' instincts for tax-cuts and a smaller state had to be restrained because of Liberal Democrat opposition. In reality, he probably would have hoped to pursue very similar policies even if his party had secured an overall parliamentary majority in 2010. In May 2015, when he became Prime Minister of an exclusively Conservative government, there was no sign of a radical change in domestic government policy. The challenges to the 'post-Thatcherite consensus' came from other parties and movements.

global economy which were largely outside the government's control – the very factor which is usually cited as the reason why UK parties had come *closer together* since the end of the Cold War and the fall of Thatcher.

In its 2015 general election campaign, under 'Red' Ed Miliband's leadership, Labour reaffirmed its support for a 50 per cent tax rate on incomes over £150,000, while promising to bring back the lower tax rate of 10 per cent which Brown had scrapped. This allowed the Conservatives to score some easy partisan points about Labour's alleged addiction to 'tax and spend'. However, since the rapid reduction of the UK's indebtedness was common ground between the major parties, the most noteworthy aspect of the debate was the coalition's insistence that spending cuts should bear almost the whole brunt of the 'austerity' programme: before 1979, all three main political parties would have opted for a roughly equal mix of spending cuts and tax increases to reduce a structural budget deficit.

After Labour's defeat in 2015, senior party figures, as well as hostile media commentators, agreed that the party had lost at least in part because of its perceived hostility to the private sector. In reality, in 2015 Labour was friendlier to business than it had been at any time before 1992. The change in Labour's outlook was to come after 'Red Ed's' resignation as leader.

The Corbyn 'insurgency' of 2015

When Ed Miliband resigned immediately after the 2015 general election, political observers expected that his successor would emerge from a field of candidates who would either seek to renew Tony Blair's appeal to 'Middle England', or discover a way to reconnect with Labour's disillusioned 'core support' which also managed to attract a proportion of uncommitted voters. However, 'orthodox' candidates of this kind would be faced with a problem which few observers had expected during the 2010–15 parliament – how to recoup some of Labour's losses in Scotland, which had been transformed from a Labour heartland to a wasteland almost overnight. By outflanking Labour in its opposition to economic austerity, the Scottish Nationalist Party (SNP) had established itself as the main party of the 'left' in Scotland, as well as being the authentic voice of nationalism to voters of all political persuasions. None of the mainstream leadership candidates – Andy Burnham, Yvette Cooper and Liz Kendall – were judged to have offered satisfactory answers to the party's various dilemmas.

However, they were not the only candidates on offer in 2015. Jeremy Corbyn, Labour MP for Islington since the 'suicide note' election of 1983, put himself forward; and, open-minded MPs who hoped for a wide-ranging ideological debate within the party added their names to Corbyn's personal supporters, ensuring that he received sufficient nominations from within the Parliamentary Labour Party (PLP) to go forward to a vote of the membership as a whole (see Chapter 15).

Like a human time-capsule planted in 1983, Corbyn seemed to have resisted the apparent logic of events since he first entered parliament. Thus, among other things, he supported the principle of nationalisation, aspired to a restoration of trade union rights, wanted to increase taxation on higher earners, sought a more interventionist role for local government in education and housing, opposed Britain's possession of the nuclear 'deterrent' and wanted the country to withdraw from NATO's military structure. These views were hardly concealed during the 2015 leadership election contest; Corbyn aired them inexhaustibly, in rallies and in broadcast debates. Major New Labour figures, including Tony Blair himself, advised party members to reject Corbyn – but to no avail. Although his chief opponents, Andy Burnham and Yvette Cooper, departed from the New Labour agenda in important respects, both failed sufficiently to distance themselves from the party's recent past; Liz Kendall, who openly embraced it, won less than 5 per cent of the votes.

Unfriendly critics were quick to compare Corbyn with Michael Foot, who had led the party in 1983 when the former was first elected to parliament. However, from an ideological perspective the parallels were superficial. Essentially, Foot was a romantic liberal, whose desire for self-identification with the Labour movement induced him to support some highly illiberal measures during his ministerial career. Corbyn, by contrast, fulfilled the definition of 'socialist' as well as any significant politician since the days of Nye Bevan (who, for all his working-class origins, found it impossible to disregard the spurious attractions of aristocratic life). However, despite his emphatic and unexpected victory Corbyn was still faced with the challenge of reminding Labour of its ideological roots – or rather, of persuading his party that the achievement of socialism, rather than revisionist social democracy, was its historic mission. After that, he would have to embark on the modest task of convincing the British public that it really wanted to elect a truly socialist government for the first time.

For Corbyn and his supporters, the party's 2017 manifesto was a promising first step. It included pledges to re-nationalise the railways, water companies and the Royal Mail. Tuition fees would be abolished, and the Coalition's controversial welfare policies scrapped. However, while these were radical, 'consensus-busting' ideas, in other respects Corbyn was more cautious. Taxes on the rich and on businesses would be raised, but to nowhere near pre-Thatcher levels. The Labour leader had to accept uneasy compromises on NATO and nuclear weapons. Opinion surveys showed considerable support for most of the headline proposals, in sharp contrast to the Conservative manifesto which included proposals on adult social care which were deeply unpopular even among the party's core supporters.

The positive reception of the 2017 Labour manifesto was a further blow to the party's 'Blairite' wing, which had insisted that such ideas were sure to be electoral liabilities. However, Labour's chances of a decisive breakthrough in 2017 were hampered by two significant problems: first, the public estimation of the leader himself, who was considerably less popular with the electorate as a whole than with party members; and the question of Britain's impending withdrawal from the EU, which had caused Theresa May to call the election in the first place and which cut across established partisan loyalties.

Nationalism and 'Brexit'

In Britain, nationalism has traditionally been associated with relatively small Westminster parties – until the introduction of devolution in the late 1990s, since when the SNP has become a major player at Westminster, as well as the governing party in Scotland. Even in the 1970s, these groups could play a crucial role thanks to the decline of the major UK parties, as when the 1974–79 Labour government depended upon nationalist votes to keep it in office. As well as drawing on a deep feeling of identity with their country, SNP policy makers have been able to exploit social democratic sentiment north of the English border, which is no longer satisfied by the Labour Party. Although it has been less successful to date, Plaid Cymru in Wales currently enjoys the same ideological opportunity. In Northern Ireland, it could be argued that strongly Unionist and Republican parties are 'nationalists' – they just have different ideas of the nation to which they should belong.

However, it would be a mistake to confine a discussion of nationalism in UK politics to parties which make it the central focus of their campaigns and policy programmes. By the 1960s Labour had joined the Liberals in supporting devolution, and even the Conservatives adopted the policy (for Scotland) in the early 1970s. The Conservatives, in particular, have been sensitive to possible challenges from parties like the National Front (NF), whose anti-immigration stance was inherited by the British National Party (BNP), and, in more 'respectable' form, by UKIP and the subsequent Brexit Party. In the 1979 general election, NF support dropped considerably, largely due to the hard line on immigration pursued by the Conservatives under Thatcher. In 2010 and 2015, the Conservatives adopted policies on immigration and the EU which were clearly designed to prevent party supporters from defecting either to the BNP (in 2010) or UKIP (in 2015).

The narrow victory for 'Leave' in the 2016 EU referendum is often attributed to nationalism – particularly the English variety, which (on this view) had been unable to express itself amidst the constitutional changes affecting other parties of the United Kingdom and which saw opposition to European integration as an appropriate outlet. This is a highly complex and controversial question, which cannot be answered adequately here. However, some relevant points can be raised.

First does modern nationalism constitute a distinct ideology, on our definition of the term? The problem is that nationalists agree on only one thing: the need for a nation to govern itself. They have different ideas about nationhood. Culture, language, religion and geographical boundaries can all be used by nationalists to define 'their' community. Some deny that newly arrived immigrants can form part of the nation, while others (like Zionists in Israel) welcome all newcomers who share their views. Politicians who assert the right of self-government for their own nation sometimes feel able to deny the same right to others abroad.

We have seen that all ideologues are affected by circumstances. But it would hardly be an exaggeration to say that everyone can become a nationalist under the right circumstances. Nationalism is characteristically found whenever a community (however defined) feels that its identity is under threat. Thus it can arise when a community is denied the right to self-government – or when members of an established nation perceive that they are in danger of losing that right. In modern Britain, the first kind of nationalism is represented by Scottish and Welsh supporters of devolved power within the United Kingdom (or complete independence), and by opponents of the Union in Northern Ireland. The second variety has been increasing over the last few decades, among people throughout the United Kingdom who oppose European integration, and others (not always, but very often, the same people) who are troubled by the consequences of mass immigration.

In the early years of the twenty-first century, all the main parties were painfully conscious of a possible surge in support for the BNP in the wake of large-scale immigration from Eastern Europe and incipient demands from English nationalists who felt that their own national identity was insufficiently recognised. The main response was to associate the BNP with violence and prejudice, rather than to *contest* ideas which tend to be dismissed as 'fascist' without any examination of the possible meaning of that word in the UK context. This approach seems to have been successful with regard to the BNP; but this merely assisted the rise of the 'more respectable' UKIP, which attracted considerable support from nationalists of various kinds who had grown disillusioned with the major parties, particularly in respect of their attitude towards the EU and 'national sovereignty'.

UKIP, indeed, can be seen as a grass-roots movement whose success derived from the tendency of the major parties to adopt an apologetic attitude towards developments which should either be embraced or decisively opposed. Thus, for example, while stressing the economic benefits of immigration, New Labour took steps to reduce the numbers of newcomers from Europe, and tried to impose a model of 'Britishness' on applicants for citizenship (see Chapter 4). For many years, Labour and the Conservatives have appealed to nationalist sentiment in their attitude to asylum seekers, and during the 1990s, they engaged in a long-running battle for 'ownership' of national symbols like the Union flag.

On the EU, the three main parties disagreed profoundly on where the national interest lay, but all of them regularly asserted that they would stand up for it in any European negotiations. The most dramatic example of nationalism cutting across ideological lines came in the 1975 referendum on membership of the European Economic Community (EEC), when the leading figures in the 'no' campaign were the renegade Conservative Enoch Powell, an apostle of laissez-faire in domestic matters, and Tony Benn, who was a figurehead for socialists within the Labour Party. These politicians were united only by their dissatisfaction with the contemporary political scene. Despite the disadvantages it faced under the first-past-the-post electoral system, UKIP attracted more than four million voters in the 2015 general election. More than any other statistic, this illustrated the much greater extent of public dissatisfaction in the run up to the 2016 general election, fuelled at least in part by measures of economic 'austerity' which had been accepted to varying degrees by all three of the main UK parties.

Well-informed individuals could support 'Leave' in the 2016 referendum for a variety of reasons. Socialists could argue that the EU was (and had always been) a 'capitalist club', whose rules restricted the scope for national governments to implement appropriate economic policies and whose relationship with the developing world (in particular) was highly exploitative. 'Thatcherites', by sharp contrast, insisted that the EU was far *too* interventionist, placing unnecessary burdens on business and misguidedly protecting member states from the refreshing challenges of a global free market. 'Remainers' could argue that an institution which was attacked so fiercely from both ideological flanks must, for that very reason, embody a kind of 'common sense' middle-ground position. This argument gained far less traction in 2016 than it had done in 1975, mainly because the context of the second poll lent itself to far more strident appeals to nationalism. The official 'Leave' campaign argued that opponents of the EU of all ideological shades should come together and resist what had become an existential threat to Britain as a sovereign state. It was time for the people (and/or their true representatives) to 'take back control'.

At the time of writing (June 2020) the debate is still raging on and continues to divide people who would otherwise agree on the key ideological question – i.e. what principles should inform the governance of the society to which we belong? The only safe bet is that when the protracted process is over the coalitions which formed over Brexit will break apart as the old questions reassert themselves.

Alternative voices

While the decline of conservatism and socialism leaves liberalism as the dominant ideology in Britain, it does not enjoy an unchallenged monopoly of political thinking. Apart from nationalism, for our present purpose we can identify two 'alternative' perspectives – environmentalism and feminism – although reasons of space mean that we can hardly hope to do them justice.

Environmentalism

We have already seen how the Industrial Revolution affected the three main ideological traditions. Environmentalism, by contrast, can be seen as the ideology of post-industrialism *par excellence*. As evidence mounts of the damage done by more than two centuries of intensive exploitation of the earth's natural resources, the environmental (or 'green') movement has grown from a small fringe grouping to an important force in many Western countries.

The most committed environmentalists (often described as 'dark greens' or 'deep ecologists') believe that human beings are an integral part of nature and not superior to the rest of creation. From this perspective, they argue for a radical change in Western lifestyles. The throwaway, affluent consumer society is utterly short-sighted, they insist. It has made human beings into an endangered species. In order to save themselves from environmental catastrophe, people should start treating the world and all of its inhabitants with proper respect.

While deep ecology is clearly a distinctive ideological position, many people who think of themselves as 'greens' flinch from its full implications. Concern for the environment is compatible with traditional conservatism in several respects; in particular, conservatives who deny that human beings can be fully 'rational' must always suspect the claims of science and technology. By the same token, however, some conservatives doubt the science which 'proves' the culpability of human beings in promoting climate change. Meanwhile, socialists can argue for environmental protection from the same viewpoint which inspires their opposition to the economic exploitation of human beings. But the ideology which has most difficulty in accommodating green thought is liberalism. Typically, the environmentally conscious liberal will buy an electric car, recycle empty wine bottles and think seriously about investing in roof insulation to reduce energy consumption at home. To the deep ecologist, this response to environmental damage is wholly inadequate, but it is only to be predicted given the liberal view of human nature. New liberals can accept limited state intervention, either through regulation or the tax system, to tackle the problem at the margins. But laissez-faire liberals oppose even this, and usually give their backing to any scientist who disputes the evidence for climate change. Perhaps one day this evidence will become too glaring even for laissez-faire liberals to ignore; but if they ever take it seriously enough to change their lifestyles, they will have undergone an ideological conversion and ceased to be laissez-faire liberals.

The coalition government which took office in 2010 promised to be the 'greenest' in history, which in the eyes of environmental campaigners would not be too difficult to achieve. The result, however, fell below even the most modest 'green' expectations. The Liberal Democrats had little discernable effect on policy, and the most noteworthy developments were the government's enthusiasm for the controversial process of fossil-fuel extraction known as 'fracking', along with wrangling over the best way to expand London's airport capacity.

All of the major UK parties would have to go much further to be classified as 'true' greens, and would risk electoral damage if they insisted on a radical retreat from the consumerist ethos. Thus, in 2000, when lorry drivers and farmers protested against high taxes on fuel, hardly any politician chose to defend government policy by referring back to its original rationale, which was to deter inessential motoring. Under the coalition, attempts by councils to enforce recycling on reluctant consumers were relaxed after friction with local residents, and subsidies for sources of renewable energy were scrapped. In November 2013, David Cameron, who had once tried to promote his 'caring' side through association with environmentalism, referred to such measures as 'green crap'.

The inability of 'mainstream' UK parties to accommodate radical environmentalists has fuelled increasing support for the Greens since the 1970s. However, the urgency of the problem, and the perceived inadequacy of orthodox party-based politics as a potential remedy, has led many activists to undertake campaigns of non-violent civil disobedience. In recent years demonstrations of various kinds have been associated with Extinction Rebellion (founded in London in 2018); in 2018 and 2019 'strikes' by schoolchildren, inspired by the youthful Swedish activist Greta Thunberg, attracted support across 150 countries.

Feminism

On a superficial view, feminism was the most successful political movement in Britain during the twentieth century. Indeed, it can be argued that any loss of impetus by feminism today is a direct result of considerable improvements in women's rights, at work and in the home. The significant advances over the last century are symbolised by the election of 102 women Labour MPs in 1997, the introduction of all-women shortlists in winnable constituencies and a record seven female Cabinet ministers appointed in 2001. These developments would have stunned even 'progressive' British politicians at the beginning of the twentieth century, and were superseded in 2015 (when 191 women were elected, and seven women were again appointed to cabinet positions) and 2019 (220 female MPs). Some commentators believe that women already enjoy equal status to men in all important respects, and that we are now in a world of 'post-feminism', in which even official language has been cleansed of gender-biased words (like 'chairman' or 'fireman'). This view is open to serious objections (see Chapter 3), but it is not confined to those men who dislike the results of this social revolution.

However, rather than regarding feminism as a separate ideology, it can be argued that the victories of the feminist movement have almost all accompanied the rise of *liberalism*. That is, reforms, such as votes for women (1918 and 1928) and the Equal Pay Act 1970, could not have been resisted by any consistent liberal, whether male or female. Liberals oppose discrimination on any grounds apart from the merits of the individual; so those Liberal MPs who set their faces against female suffrage in the early twentieth century were untrue to the creed they purported to follow. By contrast, socialist feminists have very little to celebrate today. For them, meaningful women's liberation could only come with an end to the economic exploitation of both sexes. The proportion of women who have entered the workforce on a part-time basis since the 1970s is celebrated by many liberals, on the grounds that it undermines the traditional idea of total economic dependency on a male breadwinner. But consistent socialists can only interpret this development as a backward step for humanity as a whole, since it has provided capitalism with a new pool of labour, often willing to take on low-paid, semi-skilled work.

On this view, feminism is rather like environmentalism and nationalism. In its mainstream forms, it is not an ideology at all, but rather an integral part of other belief systems which give rise to ideas about the best way of living for human beings as a whole. But there are many varieties of feminism, one of which does conform to our interpretation of ideology. This is 'radical' feminism, expressed by writers like Mary Daly (1928–2010), which focuses on the oppression of women by men. On this view, male aggression causes wars, and creates antagonism in the workplace. Far from being a separate, 'private' domain, radical feminists argue that the family is a male-dominated or 'patriarchal' institution which reflects the unequal power relations found in all aspects of life. For some radical feminists, the only solution is strict segregation of the sexes. Indeed, bio-technological developments hold out the prospect that the male of the species could soon be redundant even for reproductive purposes.

Radical feminism has brought several crucial practical gains for women, particularly by drawing attention to the (still) significantly under-reported crimes of rape and violence within marriage. Its insistence that 'the personal is the political' has also enhanced understanding of the political sphere. But like 'deep ecology', it gains limited (and usually hostile) coverage in the mainstream media, precisely because it cannot be assimilated by the dominant ideology, liberalism. The extent to which the popular image of feminism has been infiltrated by liberal assumptions is symbolised by the long-running debate about women 'having it all' – that is, raising a family, as well as enjoying material success in a competitive capitalist environment. Non-liberals could raise the counter-claim that this kind of life entails missing out on a wide range of truly enriching experiences. Ultimately, this debate is concerned with equal rights to free competition in the marketplace – a characteristic liberal argument, like almost every other topic in contemporary British politics which is taken seriously in parliament or the media.

In 2015, a new Women's Equality Party was launched. It had limited initial electoral success, but, despite criticism that it focused unduly on middle-class concerns, after just a year its reported membership was more than 50,000.

Conclusion and summary

This chapter has shown that ideology does play an important role in British politics, but that it needs to be assessed in the context of other influences, notably institutional factors and socio-economic developments. Politicians are well aware of the importance of ideological traditions and tend to use labels to boost their own credibility with party members, or to discredit their opponents. As a result, their statements need to be appraised very carefully rather than being taken at face value.

Ideology is best understood as a set of beliefs ultimately arising from a particular view of human nature. The introduction of democratic institutions in Britain, starting with the Great Reform Act of 1832, has encouraged politicians to address the perceived interests of the 'rational' individual voter. This tendency, combined with significant social change since the nineteenth century, has helped to forge a distinctively liberal 'consensus'. Political apathy in Britain can partly be attributed to the coincidence between the ideas of all three main parties between the early 1990s and the global financial crisis which began in 2007 – a 'post-Thatcherite' or neo-liberal variant of the previous post-war 'consensus' in which new liberal thinking had prevailed, envisaging a leading economic role for a highly interventionist state.

Since the crisis of the late 'noughties' was a direct result of neo-liberal ideas and practices, it was natural for people in the United Kingdom and elsewhere to look around for alternatives. The election of Jeremy Corbyn as Labour leader in 2015 showed that even individuals working within the main parties can attract considerable support if they offer something distinctive. However, Corbyn's leadership coincided with the culmination of years of passionate debate over Britain's membership of the EU. While many socialists (including Corbyn himself) regarded the EU as a product of neo-liberal ideology, during the 2016 referendum campaign the chief campaigners for withdrawal were themselves neo-liberals. Like Donald Trump in the United States, they used nationalistic, populist rhetoric to cut across traditional ideological boundaries. For short-term tactical reasons they were happy to filch policy proposals from various ideological traditions; but in the UK context it was clear that their opposition to the EU arose chiefly from the restrictions it imposed on free market practices, and that their short-term aim was to enact 'neo-liberalism in one country'.

Although the termination of Corbyn's improbable leadership early in 2020 marked an obvious setback for socialists within the Labour Party, most of his policies had proved popular and he had succeeded in reasserting this position as an alternative to neo-liberalism. Shortly after his resignation, the outbreak of the COVID-19 pandemic provided a further challenge to 'post-Thatcherite' assumptions about the proper role of the state, when Conservative ministers were still preoccupied by the European question. Growing environmental concerns, and greater focus on issues like gender and racial equality, created a highly unstable context in which the mainstream ideologies – essentially products of 'modernity', and thus based on assumptions about human existence which looked increasingly questionable – could only survive if their advocates adopted new techniques of persuasion.

Further reading

The literature on ideology is voluminous, but not all of it is relevant to an understanding of British politics. On ideology in general, there are accessible and balanced accounts such as P. Wetherly (ed.), *Political Ideologies* (Oxford: Oxford University Press, 2017); A. Heywood, *Political Ideologies: An Introduction* (London: Red Globe Press, 6th edition, 2017); and A. Vincent, *Modern Political Ideologies* (Chichester: Wiley-Blackwell, 3rd edition, 2009). Far less has been written about the relationship between ideas and practice in Britain. S. Griffiths and K. Hickson (eds.), *British Party Politics and Ideology after New Labour* (Houndmills: Palgrave Macmillan, 2010) is an honourable exception, along with M. Beech, 'The Ideology of the Coalition: More Liberal than Conservative', in M. Beech and S. Lee (eds.), *The Conservative-Liberal Coalition* (Houndmills: Palgrave, 2015), pp. 1–15. For earlier accounts, see M. Garnett, *Principles and Politics in Contemporary Britain* (Exeter: Imprint Academic, 2006) and R. Leach, *Political Ideology in Britain* (London: Palgrave, 2002).

On Labour's political thought see M. Beech, K. Hickson and R. Plant (eds.), *The Struggle for Labour's Soul. Understanding Labour's Political Thought since 1945* (London: Routledge, 2nd edition, 2018) and G. Foote, *The Labour Party's Political Thought: A History* (London: Palgrave, 3rd edition, 1997). The advent of New Labour provoked considerable discussion about 'Blairism'. There is a thoughtful account by S. Driver and L. Martell, *Blair's Britain* (Cambridge: Polity, 2002). Anthony Giddens, a key participant in the debate, defended Blair in a series of books. See in particular his *The Third Way. The Renewal of Social Democracy* (Cambridge: Polity, 1998) for a contrast to the view presented in this chapter. An alternative interpretation is presented by T. Bale and N. Huntington, 'New Labour: New Christian Democracy?', *Political Quarterly*, Vol. 73, No. 1 (2002), pp. 44–50. Another strongly argued account from a different perspective is R. Heffernan, *New Labour and Thatcherism* (London: Palgrave, 2001).

Most writers on conservatism – whether hostile or favourable – tend to equate it with the current beliefs of Conservative Party leaders. With this caution in mind, readers should consult D. Willetts, *Modern Conservatism* (London: Penguin, 1992), and P. Dorey, *British Conservatism: The Politics and Philosophy of Inequality* (London: I. B. Tauris, 2011). K. O'Hara, *Conservatism* (Reaktion Books, 2011) is closer to the argument of this chapter. A hostile account of Thatcherism, I. Gilmour, *Inside Right: Conservatism, Policies and the People* (London: Quartet, 1978) is still relevant today. A. Gamble, *The Free Economy and the Strong State* (London: Macmillan, 2nd edition, 1994) explores the internal contradictions of Thatcherism. M. Garnett, 'The Free Economy and the Schizophrenic State: Ideology and the Conservatives', *Political Quarterly*, Vol. 75, No. 4 (2004), pp. 367–72, assesses the character of 'conservative' ideas under Cameron's predecessors. R. Hayton, *Reconstructing Conservatism? The Conservative Party in opposition, 1997–2010* (Manchester: Manchester University Press, 2012) gives appropriate coverage to ideological questions. Good historical accounts of British conservatism are E.H.H. Green, *Ideologies of Conservatism. Conservative Political Ideas in the Twentieth Century* (Oxford: Oxford University Press, 2004), K. Hickson (ed.), *The Political Thought of the Conservative Party since 1945* (London: Palgrave, 2005), and M. Garnett and K. Hickson, *Conservative Thinkers* (Manchester: Manchester University Press, 2009).

The Liberal Party has been virtually ignored by academic writers on ideology, partly because of the unfounded assumption that it, rather than its main rivals, adopts policies out of opportunism more than conviction. The publication of K. Hickson (ed.), *The Political Thought of the Liberals and Liberal Democrats since 1945* (Manchester: Manchester University Press, 2009) would thus have been welcome enough even if it had not coincided with fascinating developments in Liberal Democrat thinking. A useful but brief account (still relevant after three decades) is R. Behrens, 'The Centre: Social Democracy and Liberalism', in L. Tivey and A. Wright (eds.), *Party Ideology in Britain* (London: Routledge, 1989). See also the *Political Quarterly* special edition, Vol. 78, No. 1 (2007) and D. Laws and P Marshall (eds.), *The Orange Book: Reclaiming Liberalism* (London: Profile Books, 2004). There is an insightful discussion of the ideology in J. Gray, *Liberalism* (Buckingham: Open University Press, 1986).

On environmentalism, a good introduction is A. Dobson, *Green Political Thought* (London: Routledge, 4th edition, 2007). On feminism in Britain, see J. Lovenduski and V. Randall, *Contemporary Feminist Politics. Women and Power in Britain* (Oxford: Oxford University Press, 1993), and the *British Journal of Politics and International Relations* special issue, Vol. 6, No. 1 (2004). For two contrasting views of nationalism in Britain, T. Nairn, *After Britain* (London: Granta, 2000) and S. Heffer, *Nor Shall My Sword: The Reinvention of England* (London: Weidenfeld & Nicolson, 1999). The far right in Britain is examined in N. Copsey, *Contemporary British Fascism. The British National Party and the Quest for Legitimacy* (London: Palgrave, 2008); R. Ford and M. Goodwin, *Revolt on the Right: Explaining Support for the Radical Right in Britain* (London: Routledge, 2014) is the essential text on UKIP.

Websites

Probably the most useful sources on the internet for this chapter are the sites of the parties themselves, where students will find statements of general aims, as well as links to speeches and press releases. See, in particular, www.conservatives.com; www.greenparty.org.uk; www.labour.org.uk; www.libdems. org.uk; https://www.sinnfein.ie/; www.snp.org; www.plaidcymru.org; and www.ukip.org. Those interested in the ideas and legacy of Margaret Thatcher can access a treasure-trove of material (complete with insightful commentary) on the site of the Thatcher Foundation (https://www.margaretthatcher.org/).

By completing an online questionnaire, the Political Compass (www.politicalcompass.org) will place respondents on a left-right axis and an authoritarian-libertarian axis. The site also locates political parties and politicians and includes some interesting commentary on the problems of the left-right dichotomy.

Part 5

Participation

Elections and electoral systems

Introduction

Elections are central to democratic politics, providing a direct link between government and citizens. At a general election, voters reach a verdict on the record of the party in office and the relative merits of the policies offered by rival political parties, express a political preference by voting for their favoured candidate and, thereby, choose representatives to act on their behalf in the decision-making process. In combination, the votes of individual citizens in territorial constituencies determine both the make-up of the legislature and the political colour of the government. Voting remains the primary political activity undertaken by many citizens, but electoral turnout has declined, prompting concerns about the health of democracy in the United Kingdom.

Elections in the United Kingdom

Elections in a liberal democracy should be competitive, free and fair. A competitive election is one contested by a number of parties, presenting voters with a meaningful choice. For an election to be free, citizens must enjoy basic civil liberties such as freedom of speech and association, the right to vote in secret and the right to join a political party and stand as a candidate. In a fair election, the votes of individual citizens should be of equal worth: 'one person, one vote, one value'. High standards are required in the administration of the electoral process: citizens should have easy access to polling places, the counting of votes should be transparent and, if disputes arise, there should be recourse to the courts. Governments should not be able arbitrarily to change electoral law to their own benefit. More exacting criteria include equitable treatment of candidates and parties in terms of resources (e.g. campaign funding) and balanced reporting by the media. More controversially (from the UK perspective), liberal democratic theory supports the contention that the electoral system should also accurately translate votes cast into seats won.

Case study 17.1

Fixed-term elections

It often used to be said that the British Prime Minister enjoyed a significant political advantage because he or she could decide upon the date of the general election. The Prime Minister had to deliver a formal request to the monarch to dissolve parliament, but it was highly unlikely that the monarch would ever withhold consent. The only restriction was that the general election had to be called no later than five years after the date of the previous contest. In many other liberal democracies (e.g. the United States) the dates of legislative and presidential elections are fixed in advance by law. In the United Kingdom, the Scottish Parliament, Welsh Assembly and Northern Ireland Assembly were all established on a fixed four (now five)-year basis.

Being able to call a general election at a time of one's choosing was not necessarily the advantage it might appear. In the autumn of 2007, Gordon Brown allowed speculation to build that he would call a general election that November. Labour was some ten points ahead in the opinion polls and Brown had enjoyed a successful first party conference as Prime Minister. David Cameron later admitted that the Conservatives had gathered at their own annual conference fearing that they would lose a November election, but announcements on tax cuts and a stirring speech from Cameron himself triggered an immediate upturn in the party's poll ratings. Within days, Brown let it be known that no general election would be held in 2007 or 2008. The damage had been done: Brown had dithered and failed to seize the moment. James Callaghan was widely believed to have blundered when deciding not to go to the polls in autumn 1978 – the 'winter of discontent' followed and Labour lost the May 1979 general election. History duly repeated itself when Labour lost office in the election of May 2010.

The 'non-election' of 2007 prompted Liberal Democrat calls for fixed-term parliaments at Westminster. This would create a more level playing field by giving all parties advance notice of the election date. But it would not stop the government from manipulating the economy or introducing short-term populist measures, particularly if they were facing defeat. Fixed-term elections were also very likely to produce still longer election campaigns. The 2007 *Governance of Britain* Green Paper did not support fixed-term elections, but did propose that the Prime Minister should seek the approval of the House of Commons for the dissolution of parliament before formally asking the Queen.

After the election which *did* take place, in May 2010, the new coalition government announced that it would act in line with Liberal Democrat thinking on the subject and a bill was duly introduced in July. It proposed that elections should now take place on the first Thursday in the May of the fifth year after the previous general election (i.e. the next general election would take place on Thursday 7 May 2015). The only ways to evade this procedure would be if a government was defeated in a vote of confidence (and failed to overturn the vote within 14 days), or if two-thirds of the whole House of Commons voted for a motion calling for an early dissolution. Among its implications, the legislation recognised the de facto loss of monarchical prerogative, since the letter of the constitution asserted the monarch's right to decide on the dissolution of parliament. The legislation met opposition from the Lords, who defeated the government more than once over the insertion of a 'sunset clause', meaning that the legislation would automatically lapse after the next election unless parliament chose to renew it. Now back in opposition, Labour decided that it also favoured fixed-term parliaments, but argued that four years was a more suitable interval.

The debate in the Commons was uninspiring, to say the least, since it was embarrassingly obvious that the coalition partners had decided to prioritise this constitutional change (rather than more pressing options, like reform of the House of Lords) for narrow partisan reasons. Most Conservative backbenchers regarded the measure with mixed feelings, and before the first fixed-term parliament ended its career in 2015 an attempt to repeal the relevant Act attracted considerable support. The battle with the Lords had ended in an agreement to review the legislation in 2020. Before then, the 'loopholes' in the Act had been exploited twice. In 2017 Theresa May wanted an early election, and got her way although the result fell far short of her hopes and expectations. In 2019 Boris Johnson (despite his disclaimers) was equally keen to consult the voters, and parliament complied with his wishes. On this occasion the outcome was much more satisfactory for the Prime Minister.

As we have seen in earlier chapters, significant parts of the UK polity are not elected. These include the head of state (the hereditary monarch), the second chamber of the legislature (the House of Lords), and quangos that distribute public funds. In common with many liberal democracies, judges and civil servants are appointed on merit rather than elected.

General elections are the most important electoral contests held in the United Kingdom: all 650 members of the House of Commons are elected in single-member constituencies using the simple plurality system. Since 2011, the timing of general elections has been fixed at five-year intervals, except in unusual circumstances which can still lead to the early dissolution of parliament (see Case study 17.1).

Regional and local bodies are also elected, using a variety of electoral procedures. Devolved institutions in Scotland, Wales and Northern Ireland are now elected at five-year intervals. Local councillors serve four-year terms of office but local authorities have different electoral cycles. In some, all councillors face the electorate at the same time; in others, a third or a half of members are elected at a time. In 2019, 24 local authorities in England and Wales had directly elected mayors with four-year terms of office.

Constituency

a geographical territory in which electors choose one or more representatives to serve in the legislature.

Should a vacancy arise in a contest in which the simple plurality system is used, a by-election is called to choose a new representative (in proportional representation (PR) list systems, the next candidate of the same party from the original party list fills the vacancy.) This is a one-off contest held in the **constituency** where the vacancy has arisen. By-elections to the House of Commons can attract considerable publicity and often produce shock results as electors protest against one or other of the main parties. The incumbent Conservatives failed to win any of the 18 by-elections contested in the 1992–97 Parliament, losing eight seats in the process. The poor showing by the Tories in the September 2003 Brent East by-election persuaded many Conservative MPs to back the vote of no confidence that ended Iain Duncan Smith's tenure as party leader the following month. Labour bucked the trend by not losing a single seat in by-elections held between 1997 and 2003 (when it lost Brent East to the Liberal Democrats in the aftermath of the Iraq war). But under Gordon Brown it suffered a number of heavy defeats, notably in Crewe and Nantwich in 2008 (which was the Conservative Party's first by-election gain since 1982), the 'ultra-safe' seat of Glasgow East in the same year and Norwich North in 2009.

Between 2010 and 2015, there were several noteworthy by-elections, some of which were triggered by the enforced resignation of the incumbent MP. The results were ominous for all three of the main parties. Labour lost Bradford West to their former MP (and now leader of the Respect Party), George Galloway. In the autumn of 2014 Douglas Carswell and Mark Reckless defected to UKIP from the Conservatives and retained their seats under their new party colours. In the South Shields by-election of May 2013, the Liberal Democrats performed the remarkable feat of finishing seventh of nine candidates, with just 1.4 per cent of the vote – its worst by-election performance since 1948. However, in December 2016 the party won Richmond Park, unseating the Conservative Zac Goldsmith who had triggered the contest in protest over government plans to expand Heathrow Airport, and in August 2019 it won Brecon and Radnor after the incumbent Conservative, Chris Davies, had been unseated under the terms of the Recall of MPs Act 2015 (see below). In 2017 the Conservatives took Copeland from Labour – the first gain for a party in government since 1982.

The electoral process

The Ministry of Justice is responsible for the conduct of general elections, as well as local elections in England and Wales. Along with the respective territorial ministries, it coordinates electoral issues concerning the devolved assemblies. Electoral law is not subject to special constitutional procedures and can be changed through normal parliamentary procedures. The Blair government introduced new electoral systems for elections to the European Parliament, devolved assemblies and executive mayors; extended the franchise to the homeless; imposed limits on national campaign spending; and created an independent Electoral Commission to oversee the conduct of elections and run pilot schemes on alternative methods of voting. In July 2010, the coalition government introduced legislation to fix the dates of future general elections, without considering that any special procedure might be needed for this major constitutional innovation (see Case study 17.1). Another change introduced individual voter registration (previously a single member of a household had registered the details of all qualified voters). After a transitional period individuals would now appear on the official register only as the result of positive action on their part (rather than leaving it to someone else).

The Electoral Commission also maintains a register of political parties and scrutinises their funding. The two main parties spend large amounts on general election campaigns. In 1997, the Conservatives spent £28.3 million, Labour £25.7 million and the Liberal Democrats just £3.5 million. Following recommendations made by the Neill Committee on Standards in Public Life, the Political Parties, Elections and Referendum Act 2000 set a ceiling on national campaign expenditure, and these limits are revised on a regular basis. In 2010, there were new rules for the regulation of spending by local parties in constituency campaigns. Apart from spending during the campaign proper (i.e. between the dissolution of parliament and polling day), limits were imposed on the 'long campaign' – a pre-election period of up to a year. In 2019, the limit per candidate during the long campaign was £30,000, plus nine pence per voter in rural constituencies and six pence per voter in urban ones. In the 'short' period, the limit was £8,700 per candidate plus nine pence per elector in rural constituencies and six pence per elector in urban ones.

Challenges to the validity of an election are usually heard in the High Court (see Chapter 9), but proven cases of fraud in general elections are rare. In 1997, the High Court ruled that the contest in Winchester should be re-run because of procedural irregularities (rather than fraud) at the count. At the subsequent by-election, the Liberal Democrats turned their initial majority of two votes into one of almost 22,000. In 2010, there was a dramatic legal challenge to the return of the former Labour minister Phil Woolas for his constituency of Oldham East and Saddleworth. The Liberal Democrat candidate, Elwyn Watkins, alleged that Woolas had made improper reflections on his personal character. A specially convened Election Court found against Woolas, and the High Court subsequently confirmed that his comments had breached the 1983 Representation of the People Act. The result was nullified and Woolas was barred from standing for election for three years. At the subsequent by-election, Watkins (who had lost by just 103 votes in the 2010 election) was defeated by more than 3,500 votes; Labour retained the seat. The case raised serious questions about the future conduct of elections. Where was the line to be drawn between 'robust' campaigning rhetoric and personal slurs which could be subject to legal scrutiny? The 2010 ruling suggested that candidates would have to tread much more carefully – otherwise there was a prospect that UK general elections might start to be decided in the courts, months after the voters had given their democratic verdict. In 2015, the re-election of the Liberal Democrat MP Alistair Carmichael in Orkney and Shetland was challenged by four constituents who had been angered by his leaking of a memo purporting to show that the Scottish National Party (SNP) leader Nicola Sturgeon favoured David Cameron over Ed Miliband as the next Prime Minister. Before the election, Carmichael had denied being the source of the leaked memo, which was an inaccurate report of a private conversation. Carmichael retained his seat – the only Scottish Liberal Democrat MP to survive in 2015 – by a margin of less than a thousand votes over the SNP candidate, whose chances of victory might have been greater if voters had known of the MP's transgression (indeed, Carmichael admitted that the incident would have forced him to resign as a minister). The legal challenge to the election result was boosted by an online 'crowdfunding' campaign, which raised more than £60,000. Eventually Carmichael's victory was confirmed.

Four independent Boundary Commissions, one for each nation of the United Kingdom, determine the boundaries of Westminster constituencies. They review the size of the electorate in each constituency every 8 to 12 years and recommend changes based on population movements. New constituency boundaries for England and Wales came into force at the 2010 general election. Constituencies should be as equal 'as is practicable' in terms of the size of their electorate, but in 2010 more than 50 constituencies had a population 20 per cent higher or lower than the aggregate electoral quota. The Isle of Wight had an electorate of 110,000 while, at the other extreme, Na h-Eileanan an Iar (the Western Isles) had 21,837 voters. The number of Scottish seats was reduced from 72 to 59 in 2005; before then Scottish constituencies had averaged 55,000 voters compared to 69,000 for English constituencies. The Parliamentary Voting System and Constituencies Act of 2011 set the framework for a rationalisation of the system, instructing the Boundary Commission to redefine 600 (rather than the existing 650) constituencies, with electorates which in most cases should be within 5 per cent of 76,641. Among other changes, the anomalous Isle of Wight would now have two MPs. A general feeling among Liberal Democrats that their coalition partners had not acted in accordance with the spirit of their initial agreement provoked the party into opposing these boundary changes, which would have benefited the Conservatives. Accordingly, subsequent legislation postponed the reform until after the 2015 general election. A new review was conducted in 2018, broadly confirming the previous proposals; but in March 2020 the government decided to keep the size of the Commons at 650 after all, claiming that after 'Brexit' MPs would have more work to do.

Voting

Elections are traditionally held on a Thursday, with voting taking place from 7am to 10pm. Schools, village halls and other non-political buildings are transformed into polling stations (Photo 17.1). On entering, the voter identifies him or herself to officials and is given a ballot paper bearing an official stamp. This lists all candidates standing in the constituency in alphabetical order, and includes party names and logos. On general election ballot papers, a cross (✕) is placed in the box next to the name of the chosen candidate. Where PR is used, voters enter one or more numbers on the ballot paper to indicate their preferences. Failure to indicate one's choice clearly may result in a ruling that the ballot paper has been 'spoiled', rendering it invalid.

Citizens who are unable to vote in person can apply for a proxy vote – where another person undertakes the act of voting on their behalf – or a postal vote. Those eligible for a proxy vote include people working away from home (e.g. in the armed forces). Postal votes were available on demand for all citizens from the 2001 general election onwards. Prior to this, people requesting a postal vote had to state a reason and have their application approved by Electoral Registration Officers. In 2017, 8.4 million people (18 per cent of the electorate) requested postal votes, compared to 1.7 million in 2001 and 0.7 million in 1997.

Concerns about falling turnout prompted the government to authorise the Electoral Commission to carry out pilot schemes on alternative methods of voting at local elections. They have tested the practicality and impact on turnout of:

- all-postal ballots;
- touch-screen electronic voting in polling stations;
- remote electronic voting via text message and internet;
- weekend voting and extended voting hours;
- voting in supermarkets.

Trials of all-postal voting have produced the biggest increase in turnout. More than 50 all-postal voting pilots were held at local elections between 2000 and 2004. There were significant increases in turnout in many cases: the 32 areas using all-postal ballots in 2003 had an average turnout of 49 per cent compared to an average elsewhere of 35 per cent. Turnout rose by

PHOTO 17.1 An unusual polling station – or an attempt to increase turnout? (© Justin Tallis/AFP/ Getty Images).

22 percentage points in the four regions that used all-postal ballots in the 2004 European Parliament elections. However, there was also evidence of fraudulent practice in the latter. The Electoral Commission recommended that all-postal ballots should not be held again.

Among the fraudulent practices reported in 2004 were multiple voting, intimidation and vote stealing. Agents of political parties were permitted to handle postal ballot papers. A High Court judge presiding over a case of vote rigging in Birmingham described the all-postal ballot system as 'an open invitation to fraud'. Concerns about the security of postal ballots also surfaced at the 2005 general election. The government responded by requiring that those voting by post must provide both a signature and date of birth on the statement sent with the ballot papers.

Remote electronic voting allows an individual to transmit an encrypted vote using the internet, telephone, mobile phone text message or digital television. E-voting has the potential to increase participation as more people have access to the requisite technology, but the local pilot schemes produced only a small increase in turnout. Ministers had talked of an 'e-enabled' general election in the near future, but concerns about the security and secrecy of e-voting saw the Electoral Commission warn against its usage and these doubts prevail despite continued small-scale experiments. Extended hours, weekend voting and mobile polling at local elections have all been tested, but the impact on turnout has been limited. Opinion polls, however, suggest that most electors welcomed the availability of alternative forms of voting. The 2007 *Governance of Britain* Green Paper (Cm 7170) launched further consultation on moving elections to weekends. The 2008 White Paper *Communities in Control: Real People, Real Power* (Cm 7427) proposed that local authorities should have a new duty to promote democracy and would be able to provide incentives for voting in local elections (e.g. entry into a prize draw). But politicians should not regard such schemes as a panacea: new methods of voting are no substitute for engaging electors in politics.

Functions of elections

Elections serve a number of functions, the relative importance of which is disputed. Standard democratic theories focus on 'bottom-up' functions, concentrating on the opportunity that elections provide for voters to participate in politics, hold decision-makers accountable and influence the political agenda (see Analysis 17.1). Democratic elitists play down the role of ordinary citizens: general elections occur at five-year intervals (or less), voters have a limited choice and political participation for most citizens is restricted to the act of voting. This perspective stresses the 'top-down' function of elections, which are regarded as a means of bolstering the legitimacy of the political system and providing consent for the government.

British elections fall between these two poles, as they provide resources both for voters (e.g. the chance to hold politicians accountable and choose between competing parties) and for the government (e.g. securing a **mandate** to govern). Three key functions of elections – representation, participation and popular control – are now considered in relation to the United Kingdom.

Mandate
an authoritative instruction.

Representation

In a representative democracy, voters choose a small number of people to act on their behalf in the decision-making process. But there are competing views on who or what a Member of Parliament should represent. It is generally accepted that an MP is a representative rather than a **delegate**. Delegates are chosen to act on behalf of others on the basis of clear instructions: they must faithfully relay and obey the views of those they represent. **Representatives**, by contrast, are free to decide how to vote based on their independent judgement. This model of representation originally drew upon the elitist notion that MPs are better informed and more adept in affairs of state than their constituents, but it also recognises the problems an MP would face in ascertaining the considered views of constituents (especially at short notice) and translating their opinions into a single parliamentary vote.

While MPs are theoretically free to reach their own decisions, they are likely to come under pressure to act in the interests of their constituency and their party. MPs represent *all* citizens within their constituency, not just those who voted for them. They act on behalf both of individual constituents and the perceived collective interests of their constituency. All MPs receive numerous requests for help, and may take up those grievances with public bodies. An official request from an MP can remove bureaucratic barriers that remain frustratingly impenetrable to the average citizen. An MP defends the interests of their constituency as a whole by, for example, lobbying for public goods and protesting against decisions which have an adverse effect. Some MPs have particular difficulty in balancing the interests of constituency and party. For example, in the 1980s, when Labour was opposed to nuclear power, Jack Cunningham

---

Delegate

an individual who is authorised to act on behalf of others but who is bound by their instructions.

Representative

(noun) an individual who acts on behalf of a larger group but is permitted to exercise his or her judgement in doing so; (adjective) exhibiting a likeness or being a typical example.

Analysis 17.1

Direct democracy and the right of recall

Direct democracy involves citizens in the decision-making process in their own right: they vote directly on issues rather than electing representatives to act on their behalf. Examples found in Switzerland and the United States include referendums in which electors vote on government proposals, popular initiatives in which a group of citizens get a policy proposal placed on the ballot paper, and the recall of elected officials. In the United Kingdom, referendums have been held on a variety of subjects and local citizens can stage own-initiative ballots.

Supporters of direct democracy argue that representation requires individuals to give up their autonomy (i.e. their capacity to be self-governing). Furthermore, no person can fully appreciate the breadth and depth of another individual's experiences, interests and values. Nor can an MP represent the variety of views held by constituents; aggregating interests leaves minority voices unheard. Direct democracy, its supporters claim, boosts participation and improves political education. It is also argued that new communications would enable citizens to watch a televised political debate before delivering an instant verdict on the issue via telephone, text message, the internet or digital television.

Representative democracy, however, should also mean more than voting in a general election every five years. Citizens can make representative democracy work more effectively by expressing their views through other forms of participation, for example, by contacting their local councillors or MPs, organising petitions or joining pressure groups (see Chapter 19). In recent years, especially since the 2009 expenses scandal (see Chapter 8), interest has centred around the idea of a right to recall representatives. All three main party leaders declared themselves in favour, with varying degrees of enthusiasm; at the 2010 general election, Nick Clegg argued that new elections should be held in constituencies where a minimum of 5 per cent of constituents demanded one.

After the formation of their coalition in 2010, the Conservatives and Liberal Democrats reaffirmed their belief in the idea, pledging themselves to 'early' legislation. However, the trigger for a new election would now be 10 per cent of constituents, and the MP would have to be guilty of 'serious wrongdoing'. These new qualifications suggested cold feet among ministers; without some safeguards of this kind, even MPs with cast-iron integrity could theoretically be subjected to constant challenges (or even unseated) by a small number of 'frivolous' constituents. However, it was difficult to explain such concerns to the voting public, since it implied that ordinary citizens could not really be trusted to exercise the franchise responsibly. Misgivings within the coalition were reinforced when the National Union of Students (NUS) took up the cause, hoping to use the mechanism to 'sack' Liberal Democrat MPs who had 'broken their word' on tuition fees. Such initiatives raised the possibility that Nick Clegg could be removed from parliament by the legislation which he had championed.

In view of such considerations, it was not surprising that there was no 'early' legislation after all. But this powerful genie could not be shoved back into its bottle, and after considerable consultation, the 'right to recall' was affirmed in a statute passed in the weeks before the 2015 election. Critics claimed that its terms basically confirmed the existing situation, in which MPs found guilty of serious offences would be compelled to resign without any input from the voters. In 2018 the DUP's Ian Paisley junior was suspended from the Commons for 30 days after failing to disclose free holidays from the Sri Lankan government; a subsequent petition demanding his 'recall' narrowly failed to reach the 10 per cent threshold. In April 2019 the Labour MP for Peterborough, Fiona Onasanya, became the first MP to be unseated after being jailed for motoring offences; her party retained the seat despite a strong challenge from the newly formed Brexit Party. In June 2019 the Conservative MP for Brecon and Radnorshire, Chris Davies was removed by petition after receiving a community service order for falsifying expense claims. He was re-selected as his party's candidate but lost the ensuing by-election to the Liberal Democrats.

served as the party's MP for Copeland, a Cumbrian constituency with a local economy which depended heavily on the Sellafield nuclear reprocessing plant. Despite the hardening of Labour's opposition to nuclear energy after the 1986 Chernobyl disaster, Cunningham remained a strong supporter. In 2017 Cunningham's successor, Jamie Reed, resigned in order to take up a position at Sellafield; Labour lost the ensuing by-election.

Almost all MPs elected since 1945 have represented a political party. They have owed their positions, to some extent at least, to the parties that selected them and resourced their campaigns.

Analysis 17.2

Positive action

Positive action (also known as 'positive discrimination') refers to schemes which provide special arrangements for social groups that are historically under-represented or politically disadvantaged. These schemes might include all-women shortlists (AWS) or quota systems, under which a percentage of seats is reserved for individuals from a particular section of society. In the United States, positive action has been used to boost the representation of ethnic minority groups in educational institutions. Positive action has also proved effective in bringing about greater gender equality in assemblies in other EU member states.

Proponents argue that only positive action will overcome structural inequalities in the representation of women. Existing selection methods perpetuate under-representation. The Conservatives, with just 17 women out of its 197 MPs in the 2005 Parliament, opposed positive action, preferring to persuade autonomous local associations to adopt women candidates rather than impose them. A 2002 study of Conservative selection procedures by the Fawcett Society – *Experiences of Conservative Party Women in Parliamentary Selections* (London: Fawcett Society, 2002) – found that 'overt discrimination and sexual harassment' were significant factors in the failure of women to get selected in winnable seats. But career choices, and lack of wealth or political connections, also prevented women from seeking political office in the first place.

David Cameron's 'A-list' initiative required that Conservative constituency associations in key target seats must choose from a priority list of candidates, half of whom had to be women. The A-list was dropped in 2006, but constituency associations were required to draw up shortlists on which at least half the candidates were women. These initiatives boosted the number of female Conservative MPs from 18 before the 2010 general election to 68 in 2015; after the 2019 general election the total had climbed to 87. More than half of Labour (104 of 202) and Liberal Democrat (7 of 11) MPs were female, thanks partly to their use of AWS.

Female politicians often see themselves as having a 'feminised' style of politics that is more consensual than the confrontational culture of the House of Commons. The presence of women MPs also seems to have a positive impact on female participation. A 2004 Electoral Commission study – *Gender and Political Participation* (London: Electoral Commission, 2004) – reported that turnout among women in 2001 was 4 per cent higher than among men in seats that had a woman MP. Women were more likely to agree that 'government benefits people like me' in seats with a female MP (49 per cent compared to 38 per cent).

Supporters of positive action believe that women MPs best understand issues such as motherhood, abortion and sexual discrimination. In *New Labour's MPs: Women Representing Women* (London: Routledge, 2004), Sarah Childs examined the parliamentary activities of the 102 women Labour MPs elected in 1997. She found that they were more likely to take up women's issues, but that the House of Commons, as a gendered environment, limited their impact. Opponents of positive action argue that individuals need not to have suffered discrimination themselves to regard it as wrong. It would be a mistake to assume that the values and interests of all women are identical simply because of their shared gender. Finally, critics may argue that positive action runs counter to the principles of equality of opportunity and selection on the sole basis of merit.

In return, party whips demand loyalty in parliamentary votes. Elections provide parties with a channel of elite recruitment. Activists are mobilised, candidates are recruited and successful ones join the party ranks in the House of Commons and possibly the government. A handful of independent MPs have been elected in recent years. The former BBC reporter Martin Bell beat Neil Hamilton, who was tainted by 'cash for questions' allegations, in Tatton in 1997, helped by the absence of Labour and Liberal Democrat candidates. Dr Richard Taylor's campaign against the closure of a local hospital helped him to win Wyre Forest in 2001 and to retain the seat until 2010. Peter Law resigned from the Labour Party after a dispute over the use of an AWS for his Welsh Assembly seat and won Blaenau Gwent in the 2005 general election. An independent candidate, Dai Davies, retained the seat at a by-election in 2006 following Law's death but lost heavily to Labour in the 2010 general election. In 2019, ten sitting MPs who had left their parties for various reasons contested seats as Independents (if one includes three who stood on behalf of the newly formed 'Change UK'), and all were defeated (see Case study 17.2).

To stand for parliament, an individual must be at least 18 years old. Certain groups are disqualified from sitting in the House of Commons, including non-UK citizens, prisoners serving their sentences, bankrupts, members of the House of Lords, judges, police officers and civil servants. Candidates must pay a deposit of £500 which is forfeited if they secure less than 5 per cent of the vote. In 2019, £636,500 was forfeited in this way; lost deposits cost the Green Party £232,500. In 2010, the Liberal Democrats were the only party not to lose a single deposit, but their dismal showing in 2015 meant 341 forfeited deposits, at a cost of £170,500 (a Twitter account was set up especially to chart the disaster). After an equally expensive election in 2017 they recovered sufficiently in 2019 to lose 'only' £68,000.

Case study 17.2

The short and eventful history of Change UK

In February 2019 seven Labour MPs announced that they were leaving the parliamentary party because of disenchantment with Labour's direction under Jeremy Corbyn. Their grievances included Corbyn's failure to devise a clear policy on 'Brexit', but also his alleged inability to take decisive action in the face of numerous accusations of anti-semitism within the party. They were quickly joined by three pro-Remain Conservative MPs, Sarah Wollaston, Anna Soubry and Heidi Allen, who cited their party's hard-line attitude towards Brexit, along with a more general departure from 'One Nation' ideas (see Chapter 16) as their reasons for leaving.

Initially the MPs formed an Independent Group within parliament, but in March this was officially registered as a party – 'Change UK – the Independent Group' – with a view to fielding candidates in May's European Parliamentary elections. In advance of the elections two former Conservative (but now independent) MEPs joined Change UK; intended candidates included the well-known journalist Gavin Estler and Rachel Johnson, the sister of the ex-Foreign Secretary, as well as the former Conservative Cabinet minister Stephen Dorrell and Jacek Rostowski, who had served as Deputy Prime Minister of Poland.

From the outset, media commentators drew comparisons between Change UK and the Social Democratic Party (SDP) of the 1980s. In at least two respects, the comparison augured well for the new party. A major weakness for the SDP was its dominance by ex-Labour politicians; only one Conservative MP had felt sufficiently alienated by Thatcherism to jump ship. Change UK could be expected to appeal to disillusioned supporters of both main parties. Second, the up-coming elections to the European Parliament would be held under PR, as they had been since the 1994 contest. This system, as opposed to simple plurality, would give Change UK a chance to establish a vote-winning reputation at an early stage; even if it failed to attract overwhelming support in any single parliamentary constituency, it could win seats in the European Parliament on the basis of more broadly spread regional appeal (as UKIP and the Greens had done in 2014).

As it turned out, Change UK won just 3.3 per cent of the vote in the European elections, failing to secure a single seat. This effectively marked the end of the party; in June six MPs resigned, including the interim leader Heidi Allen and the charismatic Chuka Umunna. In the 2019 general election only three candidates stood under the Change UK banner; all had been elected for their previous parties in 2017, but they were all defeated this time round.

In some ways, the failure of Change UK was like an accelerated re-run of the history of the SDP. A serious problem for both of these new parties was their relationship with the Liberals/Liberal Democrats. In both cases, if the leading figures had been able to act like tactical voters in elections they would almost certainly have thrown their support behind the longer-established party, with which they agreed on a range of key issues. However, senior politicians are faced with more complex considerations. In 1981, the 'Gang of Four' who created the independent SDP regarded the Liberal Party as a relic from the past – a vehicle for protest votes rather than a serious contender for office. In 2019, by contrast, the Liberal Democrats had recently formed part of a coalition government; and, as a result of that unhappy experience, both Labour and Conservative defectors had reason to regard the Liberal Democrat 'brand' as toxic. The overall result was that, since Change UK felt unable to live with the Liberal Democrats but was equally unable to thrive without them, it did neither one thing nor the other and had to accept the inevitable consequence of spreading confusion among their most likely (former 'Remainer') ranks.

Second, just like the early SDP, Change UK received adequate funding from sources which ranged from very wealthy individuals to thousands of ordinary well-wishers. However, also like the SDP it could not establish a party organisation overnight. More importantly, it was difficult to discern a distinctive socio-economic interest group which Change UK could represent – apart from the pro-EU businesspeople whose natural political home (if any) was the Liberal Democrats.

Thus while Change UK enjoyed theoretical advantages over the SDP in its attempt to 'break the mould' of British politics, some disadvantages were basically unchanged. Indeed, in hindsight the biggest advantage enjoyed by the SDP was denied to Change

UK. When the SDP was founded in 1981, two of the 'Gang of Four' were not MPs, and were thus available as candidates for seats which might fell vacant. Roy Jenkins and Shirley Williams were sufficiently well-known to win parliamentary by-elections (in 1981 and 1982) despite the bias of simple plurality against third-party candidates. The alternative strategy for Change UK MPs was to resign the seats they already occupied and trigger by-elections. Ideally, this would have given voters in their constituencies a chance to take part in a mini-referendum on the way in which the main parties had responded to the 2016 Brexit vote. For whatever reason, the Change UK MPs decided against the only strategy which could have created a bandwagon effect in their favour, at a time of polarisation when many voters had returned to their two-party, 'government versus opposition' mentality. The result was inevitable; in the 2019 general election Change UK barely enjoyed an opportunity to explain the ways in which it proposed to 'change' the UK, as opposed to offering voters a moderated version of the 'post-Thatcherite' policies which had been in place since 1990. By December 2019 it had become a rump of a party, and disappeared completely after its undignified defeat.

When election deposits were introduced, in 1918, candidates were required to stump up £150 – about £8,500 in the values of 2020. This considerable sum meant that candidates either had to be independently wealthy, very popular among people of limited means or confident of securing financial support from well-funded organisations. The raising of the deposit to £500 in 1985 served no useful purpose at all, either for democrats or elitists; at most, it might make highly principled but impecunious independent candidates think twice before standing.

An alternative perspective on representation suggests that parliament should be a microcosm of society. Major social groups should be represented in numbers proportional to their presence in society. The House of Commons still scores poorly: most MPs are white, male and middle class (see Chapter 8). Only 65 MPs elected in 2019 were members of minority ethnic groups – exactly 10 per cent of the House of Commons, compared to 14 per cent of the UK population. It was, at least, a major improvement compared to 2010, when just 27 BAME candidates were elected. A record 220 women MPs were elected in 2019 – a stunning improvement on the 23 women MPs in 1983, but still little more than a third of the House of Commons. The record is better in the devolved assemblies where women constituted 42 per cent of the Welsh assembly and 35 per cent of the Scottish Parliament in 2011. The Sex Discrimination (Election Candidates) Act 2002 permits parties to use positive measures (like AWS) to reduce inequality in the numbers of women and men elected in Britain. This is permissive rather than obligatory: parties are not compelled to adopt positive action (see Analysis 17.2).

For many critics, while recent changes in parliamentary demography are welcome, they only address a part (and arguably a secondary part) of the real problem. If a large proportion of new women and BAME MPs are 'career politicians' who have set their sights on a seat at Westminster from an early age, they might *look* more like the British population, but they will be equally 'out of touch' with normal citizens as their white, middle-aged male counterparts. It is true that long experience of politics is likely to enhance relevant skills, like the ability to conduct negotiations and reach agreements which advance the national interest. Equally, though, the limited life experiences of 'career politicians' are likely to leave them with an overdeveloped sense of politics as a means of self-promotion and slavish devotion to the interests of their parties. A cynic might even say that Westminster took its biggest stride towards true representation during the 2009 expenses scandal, which revealed a level of dishonesty which was a fair approximation to that of the British public as a whole.

Participation

Elections give citizens an opportunity to participate in the political process by voting for the candidate of their favoured party. Competitive elections were a feature of British politics long before the democratic era. But the United Kingdom has only been a mass democracy since 1928, when full adult suffrage was achieved (see Timeline 17.1). The minimum voting age was reduced to 18 in 1969 and there is significant support for a further reduction to 16 (see Controversy 17.1).

To be eligible to vote, an individual must be included on the electoral register. Until the passage of the Electoral Registration and Administration Act (2013), forms were sent to each

TIMELINE 17.1

The development of the electoral system

1832	Great Reform Act. Extends the franchise to middle-class property owners in urban and rural areas, reforms electoral law and redistributes seats. The electorate totals 700,000 people, 5 per cent of the adult population
1867	Parliamentary Reform Act. Extends the franchise to urban householders and redistributes seats. The electorate reaches 2.2 million, 13 per cent of the adult population
1872	Ballot Act. Introduces the secret ballot
1884	Franchise Act. Extends the franchise to rural labourers and redistributes seats. Electorate tops five million, 25 per cent of the adult population
1918	Representation of the People Act. Abolishes the property qualification and extends the franchise to men aged 21 and over. Extends the franchise to women aged 30 and over. Reform of electoral law. Electorate makes up 75 per cent of the adult population
1928	Representation of the People Act. Extends the franchise to all women aged 21 and over. Universal adult suffrage is achieved
1948	Representation of the People Act. Ends plural voting, achieving principle of 'one person, one vote'
1969	Representation of the People Act. Reduces the minimum voting age to 18
1985	Representation of the People Act. Extends the franchise to British citizens living abroad and extends absent voting to people on holiday
2000	Representation of the People Act. Allows those without a permanent residence to join the electoral register. Paves the way for pilot schemes to test alternative methods of voting
2000	Political Parties, Elections and Referendums Act. Establishes an Electoral Commission to oversee the conduct of elections and referendums. Sets a ceiling on spending by political parties during general election campaigns
2011	Change to AV system is rejected
2011	Passage of Fixed-Term Parliaments Act
2013	Passage of Electoral Registration and Administration Act. Replaces registration of voters by household with individual registration

household by local authorities every autumn. Now, qualified voters register themselves, providing proof of identity, at any time during the year. People without a permanent address can register using a declaration of local connection. Rules on registration were tightened in Northern Ireland in 2002. Here, individuals must provide more information when registering and show photographic identification at the polling station. A full version of the electoral register is available for public scrutiny, but since 2002 individuals have been able to choose not to have their names and addresses included in an edited version that marketing companies may purchase.

In 2019 the total UK electorate numbered more than 47.5 million people. Only a small number of people are denied the right to vote in general elections. These include children, members of the House of Lords, people convicted of electoral fraud within the last five years and those judged incapable of reasoned judgement because of mental illness. Prisoners detained at the time of a general election have long been denied the vote. The European Court of Human Rights ruled against this restriction four times between 2004 and 2015, but the government has been reluctant to change the law. Citizens of Commonwealth countries and of the Irish Republic who are resident in the United Kingdom are permitted to vote in general elections. The Maastricht Treaty gave citizens of EU member states resident in the United Kingdom the right to vote in local elections and European Parliament elections but not general elections. UK citizens who have lived abroad for less than 15 years can vote by post in general elections.

Controversy 17.1

Votes at sixteen

A campaign to reduce the voting age from 18 to 16 gathered momentum in 2003 when the Electoral Commission launched a study of the issue and the main political parties debated it at their annual conferences. The 'Votes at 16 Campaign', which included a range of youth organisations within its ranks, pressed for change. Some government ministers expressed support (though Tony Blair was 'undecided') as did the Liberal Democrats. However, in 'Votes at 16?', (*Talking Politics*, Vol. 16, No. 2, 2004, pp. 62–64), David Denver and Philip Cowley present a powerful argument against a reduction in the voting age.

The 'Votes at 16 Campaign' noted that 16-year olds have some rights and duties but not the right to vote. But the rights it highlighted are limited in practice. Sixteen is the minimum school leaving age, but only 5 per cent of 16-year olds were in full-time employment in 2001. People can legally engage in sexual activity at 16, but require parental consent to marry in England and Wales before they reach 18. It is illogical to suggest that the right to have sex or leave school at 16 means that this should be the minimum voting age. Nor can the 'no taxation without representation' argument be reasonably extended to children who pay VAT on goods such as mobile phones and CDs. Eighteen is the minimum voting age in most liberal democracies.

Supporters of a reduction in the voting age claim that 16-year olds are better equipped to engage in political activity than previous generations because of citizenship education in secondary schools in England. We might expect this to improve the political literacy of young people, but people under 25 are still less likely to vote than other age groups. A lowering of the voting age is not a panacea: politicians would be better advised to focus their efforts on engaging young people who are already qualified to vote and addressing their cynicism about party politics. Finally, a survey conducted by ICM found that 78 per cent of voters believed that the minimum voting age should remain at 18, with insufficient life experience and immaturity the main reasons cited. Only 33 per cent of people aged under 25 backed votes at 16.

The Electoral Commission's 2004 report *Age of Electoral Majority* (London: Electoral Commission, 2004) ultimately recommended that the minimum voting age should remain 18 although it did say that people should be able to stand for parliament at 18 rather than 21. The 2006 report *Power to the People* (London: the Power Commission, 2006) supported the vote at 16. The Labour Party's 2008 National Policy Forum recommended that a pledge to reduce the voting age to 16 should be included in its next general election manifesto. It duly appeared, but in a watered-down form; if elected Labour would have allowed a free vote if a proposal had emerged from a further period of consultation.

In the September 2014 referendum on Scottish independence, 16–18-year olds were given the right to vote, and the outcome seemed to contradict the argument about low turnout among this age group. According to some estimates, around three-quarters of these new voters participated in the poll; certainly their alleged reluctance to vote did not have a serious detrimental effect on the overall turnout, which was an astonishing 84.6 per cent. Votes at 16 was duly advanced with renewed confidence in the 2015 general election campaign, by Labour, the Lib Dems, the Greens, Plaid Cymru and (predictably) the SNP. But in fact, the Scottish referendum made no difference to the argument either way. On the one hand, that poll had a uniquely energising effect throughout Scotland; if a majority of 16–18-year olds did decide to participate on that occasion, this said nothing about their probable propensity to vote on a regular basis (indeed, in Scotland the turnout among over-18s in the 2015 general election was 71.1 per cent – very impressive compared to the rest of the United Kingdom, but still nothing like the 2014 figure). On the other hand, those who argued that enfranchising 16-year olds would depress the overall turnout figure were really saying that extending the right to vote in that way would make a very bad rate of participation look even worse, which suggested that the real problem in the United Kingdom was the lack of interest shown by people *already qualified* to vote, rather than the probable attitude of 16–18-year olds (see below). In any event, under individual registration, it could be expected that only the most committed 16–18-year olds would make the necessary effort, so that in terms of overall turnout they would be unlikely to make much difference.

In 2015 the Scottish Elections (Reducing of Voting Age) Act received the royal assent, enfranchising 16–18-year olds for Scottish Parliamentary and local elections. A similar measure (for Senedd elections) has been implemented in Wales.

Turnout

the proportion of eligible members of the electorate who vote in an election.

Declining turnout

Elections since 1992 have been notable for a sharply reduced **turnout** compared to the previous post-war record. At the 2001 general election, turnout fell to just 59.4 per cent, the lowest ever under the full franchise. Five million fewer people voted than in 1997, which itself had seen the lowest turnout since

TABLE 17.1 Estimated turnout at the 2019 general election

Category	Turnout (%)	Change since 2017 (%)
Gender		
Men	63	+2
Women	59	−0
Age		
18–24	47	−7
25–34	55	−0
35–44	54	−2
45–54	63	−3
55–64	66	−5
65+	74	+3
Social class		
AB	68	−1
C1	64	−4
C2	59	−1
DE	53	−0

Source: Ipsos MORI, www.ipsos-mori.com.

1945. In 2005, turnout recovered slightly – to 61.3 per cent – but this was still well below the then post-war average of 78 per cent. In 2010 the turnout was 65.1 per cent, but this was bitterly disappointing since the election was closely fought and had featured the first ever televised debates between the main party leaders (see Table 17.1). Since then the figure has hovered around two-thirds (67.3 per cent in the fiercely contested 2019 election).

'Second-order elections' tend to see an even lower turnout than general elections (see Analysis 17.3). Only 24 per cent voted in the 1999 European Parliament election and 29.6 per cent at the 2000 local elections, but subsequent contests saw an improvement, in part because of all-postal ballots. This is not an exclusively British phenomenon, however: turnout has fallen in many liberal democracies.

A number of explanations have been offered for the decline in turnout:

- rational choice theories;
- the changing relationship between voters and parties;
- sociological accounts focusing on differential turnout among different social groups.

Rational choice theory suggests that voters will abstain if the 'costs' of voting outweigh the potential benefits. When asked why they abstained in the 2001 election, many non-voters cited practical matters such as inconvenience or absence. Trials of all-postal ballots in local and European Parliament elections have produced increases in turnout. Studies confirm that people are more likely to vote when the contest in their constituency is close and their vote is more likely to matter. Turnout has been lower in safe seats than in marginal seats in recent elections.

A second group of explanations focuses on the relationship between parties and voters. Dissatisfaction with Westminster politics and the main political parties has clearly contributed to the low turnouts since 1997. A *Guardian*/ICM survey of 2013 found twice as many non-voters citing negative feelings towards politicians rather than boredom as reasons for their failure to participate. Trust in politicians has declined sharply, and little more than one tenth of the electorate feels a very strong attachment to a party; those who lack a strong attachment are less likely to vote. Non-voters were also more likely to believe that there was little difference between Labour and the Conservatives in 2001 and 2005. Former Labour supporters who abstained were often disillusioned by the position the party had adopted in government and by Tony Blair's leadership. Turnout among working-class voters in Labour heartlands, many of them disillusioned by New Labour's record on public spending, was notably low in 2001 and 2005. The 2001 campaign failed to mobilise voters (only 27 per cent were 'very interested') and those with little interest in it were less likely to vote. Turnout at the 2010 general election might have been better had confidence in politicians not fallen to record lows in the wake of the expenses scandal.

Although close contests and sharper policy divisions became the norm after 2010, there was no corresponding movement in turnout, especially among younger voters. Once the non-voting habit takes hold it is probably difficult to shake off. However, the low turnout since 1997 should not be taken automatically as symptomatic of a general lack of engagement with politics in itself. Rather, surveys show that most people are interested in politics, broadly defined, and see voting as an important civic duty (see Chapter 19).

Case study 17.3

Young people and voting

People aged under 25 are some of the least likely to vote at a general election. Only 35 per cent of young people voted in 2001 compared to 76 per cent of those aged over 65 – and this may be an overestimate because relatively high numbers of young people are not registered to vote. We would expect turnout to be lower in 'second-order elections', but the 15 per cent turnout among people under 35 at the 2003 Welsh Assembly elections is particularly poor. In 2010, turnout among the 18–24s rose more than any other age group (though of course from the lowest base); in 2015, alarmingly, the figure for young males fell by 8 percentage points, a slump which was obscured to some extent by the rise of five points among females aged 18–24. The overall turnout among 18–24-year olds in 2019 was a more respectable 47 per cent, but this still compared badly with the 74 per cent of voters over 65.

Differential turnout in terms of age became a very controversial political topic after the 2016 EU referendum. According to estimates, 18–24-year olds were much more engaged by this single-issue contest than by general elections; turnout among registered voters in this category was around 64 per cent. However, the corresponding figure among 65–74-year olds was 80 per cent. Among the younger group, the Remain/Leave split was estimated at 75-25; in the older cohort, it was 34–66. For disappointed 'Remainers', the obvious argument was that younger people were most likely to be affected by the decision – or, at least, to be affected by it for much longer than pensioners. On the other side, though, people aged 65–74 could be said to have a better-informed view since they had been affected by 'Europe' for most of their adult lives.

A MORI survey carried out for the Electoral Commission after the 2001 general election suggested that young people were the most likely to say that 'no one party stands for me' and that they felt 'powerless' in the electoral process. Young people were more likely than other non-voters to claim that voting was 'unimportant'. Negative attitudes about Westminster politics and the established political parties were prevalent, with politicians viewed as unrepresentative of the wider population.

Much was made of the fact that viewers cast over 15 million votes during Channel 4's Big Brother 2 programme in 2001, more than any of the main parties managed at the general election of that year.

The Electoral Commission reports, *Voter Engagement and Young People* (London: Electoral Commission, 2002 and 2004), found that young people had relatively low levels of interest in politics at Westminster. However, when politics is recognised as meaning far more than the activities of the Westminster Village, young people showed an interest in political issues such as the war in Iraq, the state of the environment and university tuition fees. Young people were reportedly the most likely group to talk with family and friends about political issues during the 2001 campaign.

The MORI survey found that young people who did feel that voting mattered cited participation ('having a say') as more significant than civic duty. This suggests that the onus is on politicians and the media to mobilise young people rather than expecting them to vote out of a sense of obligation. To overcome apathy, political issues must be explained effectively and made relevant to the lives and interests of young people. Greater availability of e-voting may also persuade those who complain about the inconvenience of going to the polling station to vote, although making participation in general elections as easy as voting in a TV talent contest might be seen in some quarters as a retrograde step.

Controversy 17.2

Compulsory voting

A radical suggestion for improving election turnout is to make voting compulsory. Voting would be mandatory for all eligible electors; non-compliance would result in a fine. A number of states (including Australia and Belgium) operate compulsory voting, and turnout is indeed significantly higher there than in the United Kingdom. Advocates argue that voting is not just a right but a civic duty. Nor should it be considered a 'burden', since the costs of voting are low compared to other social activities. Compulsory voting would improve the representation of social groups among whom turnout is currently low. It would also encourage electors to take an interest in politics – and political parties to provide better-quality campaigns. One idea, advanced by the Institute for Public Policy Research (IPPR) think tank, is to reduce the voting age to 16 and make it compulsory for 'first timers' to participate.

Opponents claim that compulsory voting infringes the individual liberties that are the bedrock of liberal democracy. Apathetic citizens would be punished for failing to take part in a process about which they have limited knowledge and no real interest. Those who choose to abstain because they do not want to give a positive endorsement to any of the mainstream parties in a contest with a limited field would have to spoil their ballot paper. Alternatively, the ballot paper might give electors the chance to vote for 'none of the above'. Were 'none of the above' to garner more votes than the other candidates, a new field would be required. Finally, as has been noted about other proposals for boosting turnout, compulsory voting disguises rather than addresses the root cause of the problem, namely disengagement from contemporary party politics.

Sociological accounts concentrate on differential turnout among social groups. Turnout has been highest in constituencies with high proportions of elderly, university-educated and middle-class voters in recent elections. Groups least likely to vote are the working class and young people. Since young people and other minority social groups are reluctant to participate, they are under-represented in the political process.

These interpretations of declining turnout offer different perspectives on how participation might be improved. The rational choice view implies that making the act of voting easier, for example, through postal voting or making it compulsory will improve turnout (see Controversy 17.2). Interpretations which focus on the relationship between parties and voters suggest that politicians must engage people in the political process more effectively. The final interpretation suggests that efforts must be targeted at certain groups, particularly young people.

Popular control

At a general election, voters can hold the government accountable for its record in office. If it has performed poorly, it is likely to lose support on grounds of 'competence' (see Chapter 18). MPs can be held accountable individually for their performance as constituency representatives, though despite recent interest in the 'right to recall' this is usually a minor consideration for electors who increasingly regard elections, and politics as a whole, in national rather than local terms.

Elections offer an opportunity for a two-way exchange between parties and voters. Parties inform voters of their policies and seek to persuade them of their merits. Voters may get the chance to make candidates aware of their policy preferences during a campaign, for example at public meetings or on the doorstep. But the exchange is an unequal one, and the scope for voters to influence policy at election time is limited (although reports of a negative response to Conservative proposals on adult social care in the 2017 contest forced Theresa May into a dramatic policy 'u-turn'). Instances of direct popular control over the political agenda via the electoral process are rare. Electoral defeats may persuade a party to ditch unpopular policies and pitch its appeal at a different group of target voters, as with the emergence of the New Labour project after 1992. Ideally, election campaigns should gauge public opinion through private polls and focus groups prior to an election, adapting their message before the formal campaign begins.

Manifesto

a document in which a political party sets out its policy programme.

The 'mandate'

The doctrine of the mandate holds that the winning party at a general election receives an authoritative instruction from the electorate to implement the programme it put forward during the campaign. Parties issue **manifestos** setting out their main policies should they win office. This amounts to a promise of legislative action, though the governing party determines the order of priority among the manifesto pledges. But the doctrine is extremely problematic. Relatively few voters are aware of the details of party manifestos. Non-party members have no say over a manifesto, nor can they use the ballot box to signal their endorsement (or rejection) of specific proposals. The doctrine of the mandate does, however, imply that governments should not introduce major policy changes that were *not* put before voters at a general election. Thus, for example, in January 2013 David Cameron announced his intention to hold a referendum on EU membership, but only if his party won a majority at the next general election.

In recent elections parties have issued headline pledges which simplify the idea of a mandate and, in theory, made it easier for voters to judge whether they have fulfilled their promises. Labour's pledges included specific commitments, for example, to cut class sizes to 30 for five- to seven-year olds (1997) and to recruit 10,000 extra secondary school teachers (2001). Labour and the Conservatives both issued six key pledges in 2005 and the Liberal Democrats 10. In 2015, Ed Miliband had his six key pledges carved into an eight-foot stone, which, he suggested, would have been placed in the garden of Number 10 Downing Street if he had ever reached that destination. After Labour's defeat, the Ed-stone was discovered in a warehouse in East London.

Post-war governments have a reasonable record in implementing their manifesto commitments. Labour claimed in 2001 and 2005 to have achieved its headline pledges and the majority of its commitments, though the methodology behind these claims has been questioned. Exceptions to the doctrine of the mandate arise regularly. Labour's 2001 manifesto stated that 'we will not introduce "top-up" fees and have legislated against them', but two years later, the government brought forward legislation on differential university tuition fees. Days after the 1997 election, the Blair government gave the Bank of England the authority to set interest rates, but no mention had been made of this in Labour's manifesto. The negotiations leading to the formation of a Conservative-Liberal Democrat coalition in 2010 involved the dropping or modification of manifesto promises on both sides (most notably the Liberal Democrat commitments on university tuition fees). Uniquely, since very few people could be presumed to have voted in 2010 in the hope that the election would result in a coalition between these two parties, the new government issued a document which looked like a *post-election* manifesto. The key pledge – to eliminate the bulk of the structural deficit in governmental finances – had not been fulfilled by 2015. Instead, ironically, the erstwhile coalition partners found themselves boasting that they had lived up to the promise made by *Labour* in 2010 – i.e. to work towards the elimination of the structural deficit over more than one parliament.

The idea of a popular 'mandate' to implement specific proposals is open to obvious objections, particularly in the United Kingdom which operates a disproportional electoral system. For example, supporters of Boris Johnson could claim after the 2019 general election that he had secured an overwhelming mandate to 'Get Brexit Done', as he put it. However, parties which had proposed either to halt the 'Brexit' process or to hold a second referendum won more votes than their 'Leave'-supporting rivals and, in any event, the slogan's implication that the Brexit process could be terminated very quickly if Johnson and the Conservatives won the 2019 election was demonstrably false.

Choice

In 2019, 3,322 candidates stood for election. This was a significant drop from the record figure (4,133 in 2010: an average of 6.3 candidates per seat). Even so, this is an impressive number, which might suggest that voters had a meaningful choice in these elections (including 11 candidates who stood against Boris Johnson in Uxbridge and South Ruislip; Lord Buckethead of the Monster Raving Loony Party finished a respectable sixth). In practice, however, choice is limited. Many constituencies are 'safe seats' in which one party has a substantial lead over its nearest rival that almost guarantees its victory. In such seats, supporters of other parties have little prospect of influencing the outcome. In ideological terms, choice has widened since the 'New Labour' years, but even the advent of Jeremy Corbyn and the combustible issue of 'Brexit' had little effect on participation in elections.

Finally, it is worth noting that in the British parliamentary system, general elections determine the composition of the House of Commons. Control of the executive is decided indirectly, as the party with a majority of seats forms the government and its leader becomes Prime Minister. But when making their choice, most electors think in terms of choosing the government and Prime Minister rather than their local MP, as if Britain really does have a 'presidential' system of government (see Chapter 7).

Election campaigns

Ideally, election campaigns should educate citizens about key issues and the policies of the main parties, enabling electors to make informed decisions. In practice, the information provided by parties and the media is imperfect, and many citizens show limited interest. Parties have two main aims in a campaign: to persuade voters of the merits of their policies and personnel (and/or the dangers of voting for their inadequate opponents), and to ensure that their supporters make the effort to vote. The national campaign is the key vehicle for the former, whereas the latter is undertaken by activists at constituency level. Parties run carefully planned campaigns that exploit new technologies and techniques largely imported from the United States; even social media, which is becoming increasingly important in the United Kingdom, was first exploited systematically by candidates in America. They employ 'spin doctors' and advertising organisations to convey their messages, and use private polls and focus groups to track their impact. Parties must adhere to national and local campaign spending limits, but their attempts to communicate with key voters are not confined to formal campaigns.

Party strategists try to set campaign agendas by promoting issues they regard as vote-winners. Candidates are expected to follow instructions and avoid going 'off-message'. Recent contests have also seen an increase in negative campaigning in which the policies and integrity of rival parties are challenged ruthlessly. Often parties can use (or rely upon) friendly newspapers to do dirty deeds on their behalf. Before the 2015 general election, press attacks on Labour's Ed Miliband included an attempt to denigrate him through his late father, as well as the use of unflattering photographs involving a bacon sandwich. Personal attacks on Jeremy Corbyn seemed ineffectual in 2017, but the Conservative-supporting press learned from its mistakes and did its best to ensure that Corbyn was discredited long before the beginning of the 2019 election campaign.

Careful planning cannot guarantee a successful campaign, nor will a good campaign necessarily bring electoral success. Observers judged Labour to have run the best campaigns in 1987 and 1992, but the Conservatives won both elections. John Major made a public appeal for unity on Europe to rebel Conservative MPs during the 1997 campaign, further exposing the divisions in his party. The dull 2001 campaign sprang to life on 16 May when Labour's manifesto launch was overshadowed by the barracking of Jack Straw at a police conference, the haranguing of Tony Blair by the partner of a patient at a Birmingham hospital and the punch John Prescott landed on an egg-throwing protestor in North Wales. Labour had lost control of its carefully calibrated agenda, but the press response to the day's events was relatively restrained and the incidents had little impact on the polls. Similarly, in the 2010 campaign, Gordon Brown's description of a voter as a 'bigoted woman' probably had no effect on the result, despite excited media speculation at the time. Indeed Labour held on to the Rochdale constituency where the exchange took place. Whenever a party loses a general election the organisation of the campaign invariably attracts critical comment. This was particularly true of the 2017 Conservative campaign. However, the party's effort in 2019 was not much of an improvement; on one occasion Boris Johnson decided to take refuge from reporters in an industrial refrigerator. The fact that the Conservatives secured a clear overall majority made it possible for the Prime Minister's supporters to claim that he had run a competent campaign, but seasoned election observers could not be fooled by the concerted acclamation of 'Boris' by the right-wing press.

Despite the advent of the Internet, television is still the crucial medium for political communications. Most voters derive their political information from television, so parties expend much energy on efforts to secure favourable coverage. This has lessened the direct contact between politicians and voters, with voters treated as spectators rather than participants in the electoral process. Television news tends to simplify complex issues by relaying sound bites and concentrating on party leaders rather than providing incisive analysis. This tendency was reinforced in 2010, since the campaign featured the first ever televised debates between the three main party leaders. The age of 24-hour news has brought over-exposure: viewing figures for television news fell during the generally dull 2001 campaign. Unlike terrestrial TV broadcasters, the print media do not have to adhere to guidelines on equitable coverage of the main parties. Most newspapers endorse a party during a campaign, and this support frequently colours reporting, especially by the tabloids (see Chapter 5).

Parties have traditionally used billboard posters and newspaper advertisements to relay their messages. These have produced some memorable slogans and images – for example, the 1978 Conservative poster showing a long dole queue under the caption 'Labour isn't working' – but their impact on voting behaviour is limited. Television election broadcasts are allocated to parties according to the number of candidates standing in the election. They have the reputation of being dull, though some have employed innovative techniques (e.g. *Chariots of Fire* director Hugh Hudson's 1987 biopic of Labour leader Neil Kinnock) or have courted controversy (e.g. those by the British National Party). A predictable recent trend has been the recruitment of celebrities to appear in such broadcasts (e.g. in 2015, Labour was delighted to call on the services of the *Sherlock* actor, Martin Freeman).

Parties have also embraced new technologies to woo the electorate. Labour and the Conservatives use sophisticated computer programs to identify target voters, particularly those in marginal seats. They then contact them by telephone, email or text message and may even post a campaign DVD. Labour sent text messages to 100,000 young people at 10.45pm on the final Friday of the 2001 election campaign, implying that opening hours for pubs would be extended if the government was re-elected. Direct contact can be crucial in converting voters, but people's dislike of cold calls and spam email means that it can also be counter-productive. The Internet is used by parties to relay information to activists, journalists and voters. The significance of the Internet in 2001 was minimal, as only a third of homes could access it at the time. It figured more prominently in subsequent elections, and has become a highly controversial topic due to the activities of 'data-harvesting' companies like Cambridge Analytica (see Chapter 5). However, it is difficult to judge whether the parties are right to devote so much of their spending to companies like Facebook. Much online political activity takes place within 'echo-chambers', where people who have already made up their minds talk to each other and ignore alternative opinions, however well-argued.

Parties focus their resources on a relatively small number of marginal and target seats, whose results may be crucial in deciding the overall election outcome. The Conservatives and Labour directed much of their campaign efforts at 800,000 voters in crucial marginal seats in 2005. In 2010, the Conservatives (advised and funded by their former Treasurer, Lord Michael Ashcroft) began to commit resources to their target seats well in advance of the election to avoid new legal restrictions on campaign spending. In 2015, the party had narrowed its crucial battleground to 23 seats and 100,000 uncommitted voters. It was particularly successful in mopping up seats in the South-West of England where the incumbent MP was a Liberal Democrat coalition colleague. In 2019 the Conservatives had considerable success in eroding the 'red wall' of Labour seats, mainly in the North of England, where the majority of voters had supported 'Leave' in the 2016 EU referendum. It won 13 of its top 20 target seats.

Voter mobilisation was traditionally the responsibility of constituency parties, but national party headquarters now use computerised records and telephone canvassing to target key seats. Nonetheless, activists still engage in doorstep canvassing to get the vote out. Studies show that strong local campaigns produce an increase in support that can be decisive in close contests.

The significance of the national campaign is less clear. A majority of voters decide how to vote before the campaign gets underway, but opinion polls often register considerable movement as undecided voters make up their minds and waverers switch sides (see Case study 17.4). This was particularly true in 2010, when many voters attracted by the Liberal Democrat campaign nevertheless decided to stick with the two main parties in the last few days. Such 'churning' will not be decisive unless most of those who change allegiance move in the same direction. Labour's lead slipped during the 1997, 2001 and 2005 campaigns, and support for the Liberal Democrats increased, perhaps because of their greater than normal exposure. In 2015, confident expectations of another hung parliament, with Labour and the Conservatives virtually neck-and-neck, proved unfounded; experts debated whether the opinion polls had been misleading or if there had been a late haemorrhaging of support for Labour. In 2017, Theresa May asked parliament to authorise a 'snap' election because the Conservatives looked sure to win easily; over the ensuing campaign the opinion polls narrowed sharply and the election itself produced a 'hung' parliament. An increasingly volatile electorate makes it increasingly difficult to explain election verdicts after the event, let alone to predict them accurately.

Case study 17.4

Opinion polls

Opinion polls are surveys of the views and political behaviour of a sample group of the population at a particular moment in time. They are conducted by professional organisations (e.g. Ipsos MORI or YouGov) on behalf of the media, political parties and other interested organisations and individuals. Polls tend to be based on between 1,000 and 2,000 people who form a 'representative sample' of the electorate. Traditionally, polls were conducted through face-to-face interviews, but most organisations now undertake questioning by telephone or (increasingly) via the internet. When estimating levels of support, opinion polls usually have a margin of error of plus or minus 3 per cent. This means that the actual support for a party on 30 per cent in the polls should be somewhere between 27 and 33 per cent.

During a general election campaign, opinion polls appear frequently and are scrutinised by politicians, strategists and commentators looking for signs of fluctuations in the electorate's mood. Critics are concerned that the media often focus on opinion polls rather than the policies of the main parties. Some would like opinion polls to be banned during the final stages of an election campaign, as happens in France.

Such arguments are commonly heard when the polls give misleading signals. The 1992 general election exposed concerns about the reliability of opinion polls. Virtually all the polls conducted during the campaign failed to predict a Conservative victory: they had systematically underestimated Conservative support. A post-election review conducted by the polling organisations put their inaccuracy down to the reluctance of some Conservative voters to reveal their true intentions. The pollsters subsequently adjusted their calculations to take account of these 'shy Tories'. All polling organisations correctly predicted comfortable Labour victories in 1997 and 2001 but still exaggerated the party's support.

Labour's lead in the final opinion polls conducted in the 2005 election campaign was marginally greater than the actual result. But the MORI/NOP 'exit poll', based on a survey of 20,000 actual voters, correctly predicted a 66-seat Labour majority. More sophisticated techniques had been employed to measure support among different social groups, using a methodology developed by David Firth and John Curtice. In 2010, the poll, involving interviews with 16,500 voters conducted at 130 polling stations, predicted a hung parliament with the Conservatives leading Labour by 307 to 255. The result on the night (the Thirsk and Malton contest was delayed) was 306–258. In 2015, the exit poll caused consternation, since it predicted that the Conservatives would easily be the largest party in the face of persistent pre-election polls which pointed to a virtual dead-heat with Labour. The ex-Liberal Democrat leader Paddy Ashdown proclaimed that he would eat his hat in public if the exit poll was vindicated – it had predicted a disastrous night for his party – and was not the only senior political figure to suffer embarrassment. In 2017 the exit poll predicted a 'hung' parliament, and in 2019 it only slightly exaggerated the likely Conservatives majority. This exemplary record testifies to the skill of the team which compiles the exit polls, while also underlining the difficulties faced by polling organisations which try to gauge public opinion through smaller samples, and when even voters themselves cannot be certain which side they will support when they reach the sanctuary of the polling station.

Electoral systems in the United Kingdom

Electoral systems translate votes cast by citizens into seats for candidates. There are three main types:

1. **Majoritarian systems**, in which the winning candidate is the one who secures the most votes. These are non-proportional systems and produce significant disparities between votes won and seats allotted. Candidates are normally (but not invariably) elected in single-member constituencies.

Majoritarian System

an electoral system in which the candidate with the most votes is elected.

2. **Proportional systems** produce a closer fit between votes cast and seats allocated. Electors rank candidates in order of preference in multi-member constituencies.

3. In **Mixed systems** some representatives are elected using a majoritarian system in single-member constituencies and the remainder are elected by PR in multi-member constituencies. These 'list seats' are allocated to parties on a corrective basis.

Proponents of majoritarian systems believe that the chief function of an electoral system is to produce a decisive result, strong government and a clear relationship between an MP and his or her constituents. Those who favour proportional systems hold that an electoral system should accurately translate votes into seats, ensure that votes are of equal value and provide a real choice for voters.

The simple plurality system

Under the simple plurality system – commonly known as 'first-past-the-post' – the victorious candidate does not need to obtain a majority of the votes cast (i.e. 50 per cent + 1 vote) but only a plurality (i.e. one more vote than the second-placed candidate). In contests involving three or more candidates, the winner may fall a long way short of an overall majority. Simple plurality is used in single-member constituencies for general elections, in local elections in Wales and for many local elections in England. Some English local elections are conducted under a system in which multi-member constituencies are used, and electors have as many votes as there are seats to fill. Votes are not ranked or transferred.

For much of the post-war era, the simple plurality system has offered the main parties the prospect of winning power with comfortable parliamentary majorities. It favours parties with strong nationwide support, but disadvantages parties whose support – even when substantial over the country as a whole – is spread thinly. Simple plurality often gives the party that scores most votes a 'winner's bonus' of additional seats. A small swing can produce a landslide victory. The Conservatives won majorities of over 100 seats on just over 42 per cent of the popular vote in 1983 and 1987. Labour's 43.4 per cent of the vote in 1997 produced a parliamentary majority of 179.

The electoral system was biased in favour of Labour between 1992, when the Conservatives' 41.9 per cent of the popular vote translated into a 51.6 per cent share of seats in the Commons and a parliamentary majority of 21, and 2015. Labour won a 167-seat majority in 2001 on 40.7 per cent of the vote and in 2005 won 55.1 per cent of seats on 35.2 per cent of the vote. The bias towards Labour arose from a number of factors:

- Differences in constituency size. The average electorate in Labour-held seats in 2005 was 67,000 but was 73,000 in Conservative-held seats. In 2010, the gap narrowed, but Conservative-held seats still contained about 4,000 more voters. The difference is explained mainly by population movements from urban to suburban and rural constituencies since the pre-1997 revision of boundaries.
- Turnout is lower in Labour-held seats. The mean turnout in Labour-held seats was 61.1 per cent in 2010 compared to 68.3 per cent in seats won by the Conservatives.
- Labour secured its largest vote swings in constituencies where it mattered most in 1997, winning a series of seats from the Conservatives. It held on to many of these in 2001 when the swing to the Tories in these seats was less than the national average.

- Anti-Conservative tactical voting helped Labour win additional seats in 1997 and 2001 but has been less important in subsequent contests.
- Labour benefited from the over-representation of Scotland and Wales at Westminster in the 1997 and 2001 elections. The number of Scottish constituencies was reduced in 2005, but Labour still benefited in 2010, reducing the scale of its defeat.

In short, Labour's vote was more efficiently distributed: it required fewer votes to win seats. Labour won one MP for every 33,358 votes it secured in 2010, the Conservatives one MP per 34,979 votes and the Liberal Democrats one MP for every 119,944 votes. As a result, if Labour and the Conservatives had polled the same share of the vote in 2010, Labour would have enjoyed a comfortable parliamentary majority.

Not the least dramatic of many developments in 2015 was a radical change in this picture. When experts claimed that, on the basis of the opinion polls, it was quite impossible for the Conservatives to win an overall parliamentary majority, their predictions were underpinned by an assumption of a continuing pro-Labour bias. As it turned out, however, the system was about to spring a major surprise on the pundits, as well as the parties; the Conservatives required just over 34,000 votes to win a seat, while the figure for Labour increased to more than 40,000. Although the Conservative vote was less productive in 2017, the party's candidates still enjoyed an advantage over Labour and that pattern was further accentuated in 2019 (see Table 17.2).

The most remarkable contrast in Table 17.2 does not lie in the improved 'electoral efficiency' of the Conservatives; indeed, that has remained fairly constant since 2015, and only improved because the party gained numerous seats in 2019 on slender majorities. Much more telling is the inability of parties opposed to the main Conservative policy – 'Brexit' – to convert votes into seats. The Greens and the Liberal Democrats both became noticeably less 'efficient' in 2019. The biggest gainer, Sinn Fein, was of little use to 'Remainers' since its elected members stuck to their boycott of the Westminster parliament. The figures do not include the Brexit Party, which accumulated 644,000 votes without winning a single seat; since Nigel Farage's party did not challenge any incumbent Conservatives, these votes were disproportionately damaging to Labour. The SNP, once again, attracted the fewest 'wasted votes'; but even this was helpful to the Conservatives, since any kind of accommodation between the SNP and Labour was regarded by most English voters as more problematic than the dubious deal cobbled together between Theresa May and the DUP after the 2017 election.

Under simple plurality there are no rewards for coming second. The Liberal Democrats have been consistent losers under this system. In 1983, the Liberal/SDP Alliance won 25 per cent of the popular vote, 2 per cent less than Labour, but secured only 23 seats compared to Labour's

TABLE 17.2 Average number of votes required to win a single seat, 2017 and 2019 general elections (thousands)

Party	2017	2019
Conservative	43.0	38.3
Labour	49.2	50.8
Liberal Democrat	197.7	336.0
Scottish Nationalist	27.9	25.9
Democratic Unionist	29.2	30.5
Sinn Fein	34.1	26.0
Plaid Cymru	41.1	38.3
Green	525.7	866.4

186. The Liberal Democrats won fewer seats than their vote merited in 1997, 2001 and 2005 but managed to add to their tally of seats on each occasion (despite their share of the vote falling in 1997). The 62 seats they won in 2005 was the highest third-party total since 1923; for once, their candidates required fewer than 100,000 (96,400) votes to win a seat. The SNP and Plaid Cymru, which have regional strongholds, have always been treated more kindly by the system: in 2015 the SNP's performance was remarkable, but still not quite as good as that of another nationalist party, the Northern Irish DUP, which of course was fishing in a much smaller parliamentary pond.

Parliaments between 1945 and 1970 contained an average of 10 MPs from third or minor parties. For the period 1974–2010, the figure was 54 MPs, with 85 MPs from outside the two main parties in the House of Commons after the 2010 election. The figure in 2015 was 87 MPs – the SNP gain of 50 MPs being virtually cancelled out by the 49 Liberal Democrat losses. In 2017 and 2019 the respective figures were 88 and 82. The evidence of 2017, in particular, suggested strongly that the 'others' would continue to form a significant part of the House of Commons; in that election votes for the two main parties recovered sharply, but this was not reflected by any reduction in the ranks of the 'others'. The trend owed much to tactical voting, disillusion with the main parties and a concentration of resources on target seats, which in combination eroded the inbuilt tendency of first past the post to maintain the *appearance* of two-party competition even though the reality on the ground was becoming increasingly complex.

Advantages and disadvantages of simple plurality

Supporters of the simple plurality system believe that it has a number of advantages. First, and most important, it is easy to understand and operate. Voters are familiar with the system; most view it as legitimate and even before the referendum on electoral reform in 2011 (see below) it was evident that there was no groundswell of opinion in favour of radical change. Single-member constituencies create a clear relationship between an MP and electors. General elections usually produce a clear outcome: the party securing the largest number of votes tends to get a majority of seats in the House of Commons. Simple plurality is thus said to produce strong and responsible government. Governing parties normally have working majorities which allow them to exercise significant control over the legislative process and implement their manifesto commitments. Voters are presented with a clear choice between two main parties and can hold the governing party accountable for its record in office.

Proponents of the simple plurality system depict coalition governments, common in PR systems, as less effective and less accountable – although coalitions in states such as Germany have been stable and successful, and the cliché that 'England does not love coalitions' originated in a partisan remark by the Conservative politician, Benjamin Disraeli, rather than painstaking academic analysis. However, the negotiations that precede coalition formation weaken the relationship between electors and the government as they tend to be confined to a handful of senior figures and may see a party dropping some of its policies. A minority party in a coalition might exercise more influence than its limited popular support merits. In the context of the debate over the UK's electoral systems, these arguments lost some of their force when simple plurality produced a hung parliament and a coalition government in 2010; politicians (especially within the Conservative Party) might have hankered after the return of 'business as usual', and many voters might have lamented the policies pursued by the 2010–15 government, but with one or two exceptions, it would seem unreasonable to attribute the coalition's shortcomings to the fact that it was a government of two parties rather than one. In 2017, having lost her slender parliamentary majority, Theresa May rapidly agreed a 'confidence and supply' arrangement (effectively ensuring her government's survival) with the DUP, which had attracted less than 1 per cent of the UK vote in the election.

In summary, the main advantages of simple plurality are:

- It is easy for electors to understand and use.
- Single-member constituencies mean that MPs are representatives of clearly defined geographical areas.
- By giving the party with a plurality of votes a majority of parliamentary seats, it normally produces strong and stable government.
- It promotes (though does not guarantee) a two-party system in which electors have a clear choice between alternative governments.

A major counter-argument levelled by critics of the simple plurality system is that it does not allocate seats equitably. Rather, it is unashamedly disproportionate: the number of seats won by parties does not accurately reflect their share of the nationwide vote. Parliament is thus very far from being a reflection of political opinion in the country. As noted earlier, simple plurality gives an 'unfair' advantage to the two main parties, an additional bonus to the election 'winner', and often discriminates against small parties. Results under simple plurality have become increasingly disproportional since the post-1970 emergence of a multi-party system. The landslide results of 1983, 1997 and 2001 were particularly disproportional, as were the nail-biting contests of 2010 and 2015.

The party winning most votes in a general election has twice since 1945 been rewarded with fewer seats than its nearest rival. The last time a UK government won an overall majority of the vote at a general election was in 1935 when the Conservative-dominated National Coalition secured 54.5 per cent. No single party has won a majority of the popular vote since 1900. The highest post-war share of the vote is the 48.8 per cent won by Labour in 1951; but on that occasion, the Conservatives (with 48 per cent of the vote) actually won 26 more seats. In February 1974, the Conservatives received more votes (37.9 per cent) than Labour (37.2 per cent) which won four more seats. Labour's 35.2 per cent of the vote in 2005 was the lowest ever recorded by a 'winning' party. Only 21.6 per cent of the electorate (9.6 million people) voted for Labour candidates in that election.

As winning candidates only need to secure a plurality of votes, many MPs are elected on a minority of the popular vote in their constituency. Two-thirds of MPs elected in 2005 (426 MPs) failed to secure an absolute majority of the vote in their constituencies, the highest proportion in UK electoral history until 2010, when in a slightly larger House of Commons 433 out of 650 were elected without an absolute majority. The figure fell sharply in 2015, but still more than half of MPs failed to secure 50 per cent of the votes cast. In 2010, 111 MPs were elected on less than 40 per cent of the vote – more than double the number in 2005. Again, the proportion in this category fell sharply in 2015, but 191 MPs were elected with the support of less than 30 per cent of their constituencies' registered voters. In Belfast South, the Social Democratic and Labour Party (SDLP) candidate Alasdair McDonnell retained his seat in 2015 with just 24.5 per cent of the vote – the lowest winning proportion in UK electoral history.

The simple plurality system does not meet the requirement for 'one person, one vote, one value'. Disparities in constituency size mean that votes are of different value. A substantial number of votes are 'wasted' because they do not help to elect an MP. Wasted votes include those for a losing candidate – 53 per cent of votes cast in the United Kingdom in 2010 – and those cast for the victors over and above a one-vote lead over their nearest rivals. The latter accounted for a further 19 per cent of votes cast in the United Kingdom in 2010, meaning that about 72 per cent of votes were 'wasted' overall. In 2015, there was a smaller proportion of votes for losing candidates; but when 'superfluous' votes for winning candidates were included, the 'wasted' figure was even larger than in 2010 (74.4 per cent). In 2017 and 2019 the wastage rate fell, but in the latter contest 14.5 million people voted for losing candidates while a further 8.1 million merely increased the winning candidate's margin of victory – a grand total of 22.6 million votes which made no difference to the outcome (see The Electoral Reform Society's report on the 2019 contest at https://www.electoral-reform.org.uk/latest-news-and-research/publications/the-2019-general-election-voters-left-voiceless/#sub-section-27).

Parties can be grossly overrepresented in particular regions or counties: for example, in 2005, the Liberal Democrats won all five seats in Cornwall on 44.4 per cent of the vote across the county. The other side of the coin is that parties can also be under-represented; in 2015, the Liberal Democrats won 22 per cent of the vote in Cornwall, but all six of the seats fell to the Conservatives (who won 43 per cent of the vote; in 2005 they had won nearly 32 per cent of the Cornish vote but none of the five seats). Large parts of urban Britain are 'electoral deserts' for the Tories at parliamentary level. They won 24 per cent of the vote in the six English metropolitan counties outside London in 2005 but only five out of 124 seats.

Critics of simple plurality also claim that many voters are denied an effective choice. In most cases, a single official candidate, selected by local party members from a shortlist of names approved by the national party, stands on behalf of each political party (though see Case study 17.5). This process denies voters a choice between different candidates from the same party – though the same applies under the 'closed list' system of PR. The poor prospects for small parties persuade some electors to vote tactically. Here an elector whose first-choice party has little chance of victory votes instead for the candidate best placed to prevent their least-favoured party from winning. This is a tactical decision rather than a positive endorsement. Research conducted at the time of the 2019 general election suggested that more than a quarter of voters were most concerned to prevent the victory of a party they disliked, including a third of 'Remain' supporters (https://lordashcroft-polls.com/2019/12/how-britain-voted-and-why-my-2019-general-election-post-vote-poll/).

Case study 17.5

Open primaries in the United Kingdom

In the 2005 general election, the Conservative Party was represented by two candidates who had been chosen after 'hustings' open to all voters. One of the candidates, Rob Wilson, won the seat of Reading East against expectations. In 2010, the party extended the experiment, holding 'closed primaries' (i.e. allowing all local party members a vote in the selection of candidates) for 116 seats. In Totnes and Gosport (both of which were already Conservative-held), the primaries were 'open' – all local voters, including people who disliked the party, could participate.

The overall outcome was extremely encouraging, since the Conservatives gained 48 of the seats in which primaries were held. However, the initiative was not quite as 'democratic' as it might have looked; the shortlists of candidates in the primaries were drawn up in the usual fashion. The all-postal Totnes ballot cost the party almost £40,000.

After the apparent success of open primaries in 2010, David Cameron announced plans to hold them in 200 constituencies before the next election. In 2014, the

Conservatives held open procedures to select candidates to fight by-elections at Clacton South and Rochester and Strood, against former Tory MPs who had defected to UKIP. Both Conservative candidates were defeated, but in the 2015 general election, Kelly Tolhurst toppled the sitting UKIP MP, Mark Reckless. However, these were contests in which the Conservatives had a special reason to hope for the kind of extra publicity which an open primary provides. Elsewhere, it was evident that Cameron had lost much of his enthusiasm for a procedure which has such obvious potential to produce results which embarrass the national party. This did not deter local parties, 13 of whom held primaries in 2015; the Conservatives gained three of the seats, but the initiative seems to have lost momentum since the end of the coalition and especially since the divisive 2016 referendum. There is less reluctance among the parties when choosing candidates for positions like London's Mayor, since the attendant publicity is almost certain to be helpful (or, at least, if the process produces the 'wrong' result the damage to the national party will be easier to limit).

Finally, the simple plurality system is said to foster division rather than political cooperation. Critics blamed the electoral system for the 'adversarial' politics of the 1960s and 1970s, when small shifts in voting behaviour brought frequent changes of government, dramatic reversals of policy and political instability. Since the 1980s, the simple plurality system has been cited as a key factor in periods of one-party rule in which the Conservatives won four successive general elections and Labour three very comfortable victories without securing more than 44 per cent of the vote. By contrast, in 2010 the system failed to produce an outright winner. Some commentators claimed that the electorate had somehow *intended* this to happen, but that was a dubious rationale of the contest (as was the claim that in 2015 the voters worked together in order to ensure that the Conservatives were pushed over the winning line).

In summary, the main disadvantages of simple plurality are as follows:

- It does not effectively translate votes cast into seats won, producing disproportional outcomes that reward the largest party and disadvantage some small parties.
- Parties and MPs need only secure a plurality of the vote to win.
- Votes are not of equal worth and substantial proportions are 'wasted'.
- Electors have a limited choice of candidates with a realistic chance of winning.

Other electoral systems

Alternative Vote (AV)

an electoral system in which the winning candidate must secure an absolute majority in a single-member constituency. Voters rank their preferences, and votes are redistributed until one candidate secures an absolute majority.

Aside from simple plurality, there are two other main types of majoritarian electoral systems, the **Alternative Vote (AV)** and the **Supplementary Vote (SV)**. In the AV system, the victorious candidate in a single-member constituency has to achieve an overall majority of votes cast. Electors number all candidates in order of preference. If no candidate secures an absolute majority of first preferences, the lowest placed candidate is eliminated and his or her second preferences are transferred to the remaining candidates. This process continues until one candidate secures an absolute majority.

**Supplementary
Vote (SV)**

an electoral
system in which
voters indicate
their first and
second prefer-
ences only. If no
candidate wins
an absolute
majority, all
but the top two
candidates are
eliminated. Sec-
ond preference
votes are added
to their tally and
the candidate
with most votes
is elected.

The main advantages of AV are as follows:

- Winning candidates must secure an absolute majority of votes cast.
- The close link between MPs and their constituencies is retained.

The major disadvantage is:

- AV is not a proportional system. If used in recent general elections, it would have produced even greater discrepancies between votes won and seats allocated than simple plurality. It is possible for a candidate to win almost 50 per cent of first preference votes but still lose the election.

The SV is a variant of AV. Here the elector records only a first and second preference by putting a cross in the first preference column and another in the second preference column on the ballot paper. If no candidate in the single-member constituency wins more than half of the first preference votes, all but the top two candidates are eliminated. The second preference votes from eliminated candidates are examined and any for the remaining two candidates are redistributed. The candidate with the highest total is then declared elected. SV is used to elect mayors in a number of British towns and cities, including London (see Table 17.3), and in November 2014 was the chosen method to elect Police and Crime Commissioners (see Chapter 9).

The main advantages of SV are as follows:

- The winning candidate is likely to have secured wide-ranging support.
- Second preferences of all voters who supported minor parties can be counted (unlike in AV).

The main disadvantages of SV are as follows:

- Winning candidates need not secure an absolute majority of votes cast.
- It is not a proportional system.

Proportional representation systems

The term 'proportional representation' (PR) is a general one which embraces hundreds of different voting systems. These systems tend to produce a closer fit between votes and seats, but the level of proportionality depends on district magnitude (i.e. the size of the multi-member constituencies). Minor parties will win more seats in a contest in which the entire country is treated as a single multi-member constituency than in one based on regions.

TABLE 17.3 Election of Mayor of London, 2016

Candidate	Party	First preference (%)	Second preference (%)	Final vote tally (%)
Sadiq Khan	Labour	44.2	65.5	56.8
Ken Livingstone	Labour	40.3	34.5	43.2
Sian Berry	Green	5.8		
Caroline Pidgeon	Liberal Democrat	4.6		
Peter Whittle	UKIP	3.6		
Sophie Walker	Women's Equality	2.0		

The list system and the Single Transferable Vote (STV) are examples of PR systems used in the United Kingdom. In the **list system**, political parties submit a list of candidates in multi-member constituencies (often known as 'regions'), the size of the list reflecting the number of available seats. Seats are allocated according to the proportion of votes won by each party in the constituency. Electors cast a single vote. In an 'open list' system, electors can vote for any candidate from within a party list or for a non-aligned candidate. In a 'closed list' system, electors can only vote for a pre-determined party 'slate' or for an independent candidate; party managers determine the rank ordering of their candidates within the party list. A closed list system was used for elections to the European Parliament in Great Britain, where 70 of the UK's 73 members were elected in multi-member regions in England, and also in Scotland and Wales.

In the United Kingdom, the d'Hondt system is used to calculate the allocation of seats on a proportional basis (see Case study 17.6). This employs a 'highest average formula': the total votes for each party are divided by the number

List System

a system of proportional representation in which electors choose between party lists. Seats are allocated proportionally according to the share of votes secured by each party.

Case study 17.6

The d'Hondt formula

The d'Hondt formula is a 'highest average' system that uses a divisor method rather than a quota to allocate seats. It was devised by Belgian lawyer and mathematician Victor d'Hondt in 1878. Under d'Hondt, the total votes for each party are divided by the number of seats it already has, plus the next seat to be allocated. The first seat goes to the party with the largest number, the next seat to the next highest number and so on.

The following example is taken from a hypothetical election to the Scottish Parliament in which the d'Hondt formula is used to allocate list seats. The Conservatives, who did not win any constituency seats, win the first two list seats to be allocated. Labour wins the third and the SNP the fourth; the Liberal Democrats are not allocated a list seat.

	Con	SNP	Lib Dem	Lab	Winner
Constituency seats won	0	4	2	2	
List votes	35,000	80,000	30,000	50,000	
First divisor	1	5	3	3	
First seat	**35,000**	16,000	10,000	16,666	**Con**
Second divisor	2	5	3	3	
Second seat	**17,500**	16,000	10,000	16,666	**Con**
Third divisor	3	5	3	3	
Third seat	11,666	16,000	10,000	**16,666**	**Lab**
Fourth divisor	3	5	3	4	
Fourth seat	11,666	**16,000**	10,000	12,500	**SNP**

of seats it already has, plus the next seat to be allocated. Thus, the party totals are divided first by one (0 seats plus one), then by two (one seat plus one), then by three (two seats plus one) and so on. The first seat goes to the party with the largest number, the next seat to the next highest number and so on, until all seats are allocated.

The main advantages of the list system are as follows:

- The high degree of proportionality between votes cast and seats won.
- Each vote has the same value.
- It is relatively easy for electors to understand their role, as they are required to cast just one vote.

Single Transferable Vote (STV)

a system of proportional representation in which voters rank candidates in multi-member constituencies in order of preference. Votes are transferred from lowest placed candidates until the required number of candidates reaches a specified quota.

The main disadvantages of the list system are as follows:

- The d'Hondt formula can favour large parties over smaller ones, albeit to a limited extent.
- Electors have a restricted choice of candidates in closed list systems, where party officials determine the order of candidates and can stifle dissent by placing non-conformists at the bottom of the list.
- Multi-member regions can weaken the bond between elected representatives and their constituents.

In the STV system, electors number their preferences and can vote for as many or few candidates as they like in multi-member constituencies. To be elected, a candidate must achieve a quota. In the United Kingdom, the **'Droop quota'** is used and is calculated as follows: [votes / (seats + 1)] + 1. Any votes in excess of this quota are redistributed on the basis of second preferences. If a candidate reaches the quota on the first count, they are elected and their surplus second preferences redistributed. Otherwise, the lowest placed candidate is eliminated and their second preferences are transferred. This process continues until the required number of seats is filled by candidates meeting the quota.

Droop Quota

an electoral quota used in proportional representation systems that was originally devised by Henry Richmond Droop in 1868.

STV is used to elect the Northern Ireland Assembly, where 90 members are elected from 18 multi-member constituencies which each return five members. In Northern Ireland, STV is also used for local elections; the system has been in place for Scottish local elections since 2007, and is now optional for Welsh councils.

The main advantages of STV are as follows:

- It is broadly proportional and ensures that votes are largely of equal value.
- Electors have a wide choice of candidates, including a choice between candidates of the same party.

The main disadvantages of STV are as follows:

- It is less accurate in translating votes into seats than list systems or some versions of AMS (see below), particularly if multi-member constituencies contain few seats.
- It is possible to win an election without gaining an absolute majority of votes.

- Large multi-member regions weaken the relationship between representatives and their constituencies.
- It is likely to produce coalition governments, which may give disproportional power to minor parties that hold the 'balance of power'.

Mixed systems

Additional Member System (AMS)

a mixed electoral system in which a proportion of representatives are elected by a majoritarian system in single-member constituencies; the remainder are elected by the list system in multi-member constituencies and these list seats allocated to parties to produce a more proportional outcome.

The **Additional Member System (AMS)** is the leading example of a mixed electoral system; it is now often called the Mixed Member Proportional (MMP) system. The elector has two votes, one for a constituency representative and the other for a party list. Constituency MPs make up at least half of the legislative assembly and are elected by the single-member plurality system (or possibly the AV). The remaining members are elected through a party list in multi-member regional constituencies (or from one national list). The list seats are allocated to political parties on a corrective basis, often by the d'Hondt formula, producing a more proportional outcome. Members elected for list seats are known as 'additional members'; list seats are also referred to as 'top-up seats'.

AMS is used in the United Kingdom for elections to the Scottish Parliament, the Welsh Senedd and the Greater London Assembly. The Scottish Parliament has 129 members, 73 of whom (or 57 per cent) are elected in single-member constituencies with the remaining 56 being 'list members' (43 per cent) elected in eight multi-member regions (see Table 17.6). The SNP won a larger share of the constituency vote than Labour in the 2007 Scottish Parliament elections, but 16 fewer of these seats – its 26 regional list seats gave the SNP an overall lead over Labour of just one seat. In 2011, when the SNP secured a comfortable overall majority, it trailed Labour 22 to 16 in regional seats even though it had won 17 per cent more votes; in 2016, when it lost its majority, the SNP suffered heavy losses in regional seats. The Welsh Assembly has 60 members, 40 of whom are elected in single-member constituencies (67 per cent) while 20 are 'list members' (33 per cent) chosen from five multi-member regions (see Chapter 12).

There are 25 members of the London Assembly, 14 of them elected in single-member constituencies (57 per cent) and 11 list members (43 per cent) chosen from a single multi-member area encompassing all of Greater London. The variant of AMS used for the London Assembly is distinctive, as parties must reach a threshold of 5 per cent of the vote to be eligible for seats.

The main advantages of AMS are as follows:

- The results are broadly proportional and votes are less likely to be 'wasted'.
- A proportion of MPs represent single-member constituencies, preserving a link between representatives and their constituents.
- Electors have two votes: the first can be used to support a candidate and the second a political party.

The main disadvantages of AMS are as follows:

- It creates two categories of representative in the legislative assembly, one with constituency duties and one without a distinct base.
- The closed list system restricts voter choice and may give party bosses significant influence over the order of candidates.
- Small parties may be under-represented.

Electoral reform

Campaigners have been pressing for change to the electoral system for over a century. The Proportional Representation Society, a forerunner of today's Electoral Reform Society, was formed in the 1880s. In 1918, a Speaker's Conference recommended that a mixed electoral system should be used for general elections. A bill introducing the AV system was passed by the House of Commons in 1931 but rejected by the House of Lords.

Labour's belief that it must take office in its own right to achieve its objectives has historically led the party to support the simple plurality system. But support for electoral reform gained ground in the Labour movement during its long spell in opposition between 1979 and 1997. Neil Kinnock established a committee chaired by Professor Raymond Plant to examine alternatives to simple plurality. It backed the AMS for elections to a Scottish Parliament, and a regional list system for European parliamentary elections. While the Labour leadership endorsed these proposals, Plant's recommendation that the SV be used for Westminster elections was more contentious. Party leader John Smith did not support it, but committed Labour to holding a referendum on electoral reform.

Tony Blair was unconvinced about electoral reform for Westminster but maintained the referendum pledge. Labour agreed a joint agenda for constitutional reform with the Liberal Democrats that included a commitment to PR for other contests. As Prime Minister, Blair established an Independent Commission on the Voting System chaired by Lord Jenkins. It proposed the hybrid system – 'AV+' (also known as 'AV top up') – for general elections. Most MPs would be elected in single-member constituencies, using the AV system, which (as we have seen) requires the victorious candidate to secure an absolute majority. Some 15–20 per cent of MPs would be list members, elected from open lists in 80 multi-member constituencies and allocated to parties on a corrective basis. This would have produced a hung parliament in 1992 and a comfortable Labour majority in 1997.

The government did not act upon the Jenkins Report, and the impetus for reform dissipated. In its 2001 and 2005 manifestos, Labour promised a review of the operation of the new electoral systems. When it was finally published in 2008, the Review of Voting Systems offered little new in terms of analysis or insight into government thinking. The Brown government continued to support the status quo for Westminster elections until late 2009, when it suddenly decided that a change to AV was a good idea. This conversion was not unrelated to the looming prospect of a 'hung' parliament, in which Liberal Democrat support would be essential. This was in keeping with New Labour's previous approach to reform; political self-interest made reform attractive to Labour MPs when they were in opposition, but enthusiasm waned quickly once the simple plurality system had delivered the landslide victories of 1997 and 2001. For their part, the Conservatives opposed electoral reform even though they had benefited from it in Scotland and Wales. They feared that PR would see Labour–Liberal Democrat coalitions returned at Westminster, and the Tories excluded from power, for the foreseeable future.

The 2011 AV referendum

After the inconclusive 2010 general election it was obvious that the question of electoral reform would be central to any negotiations for a coalition with the Liberal Democrats, who had campaigned (as usual) for the introduction of STV but were ready to compromise with parties who were willing to countenance electoral reform of some kind. Labour was far from being united on the issue, but its position was certainly less hostile than that of the Conservatives. In his discussions with the Liberal Democrats, David Cameron promised that he would at least try to ensure the passage of legislation paving the way for a referendum on AV – far from ideal in Liberal Democrat eyes, but at least preferable to simple plurality. However, even that could hardly be a cast-iron promise given the negative attitude of many Conservative backbenchers; and Liberal Democrats could be sure that many senior Conservatives would campaign hard against AV if the referendum was called. In deciding to go into a coalition with the Conservatives, Nick Clegg evidently decided that helping to form a secure government (which could not have been the case if he had joined forces with Labour) was so important that a deal had to be struck, even if it meant a significant risk that a referendum would reject AV, possibly ensuring the preservation of simple plurality for at least another generation. Ironically, if AV had been used in the 2010 election it would have produced a clear parliamentary majority for a Liberal Democrat-*Labour* coalition.

The legislation was duly introduced in July 2010, and received the Royal Assent in February 2011. Not surprisingly, the Parliamentary Voting System and Constituencies Bill encountered resistance, particularly in the House of Lords where the government was narrowly defeated on an amendment which (as in the 1979 referendums on devolution) stipulated that the support of at least 40 per cent of the electorate would be required for the proposition to be passed. Eventually, the Commons overruled the Lords on this point. The government also revised the wording of the referendum proposition, after consultation with the Electoral Commission. The final version read:

> At present, the UK uses the "first past the post" system to elect MPs to the House of Commons. Should the "alternative vote" system be used instead?

The date for the referendum was fixed for 5 May 2011, to coincide with elections to the devolved institutions and local government. Nick Clegg was criticised for this decision by opponents of reform, although as it turned out the timing was profoundly unhelpful for him and his party.

The obvious precedent for the AV referendum was the 1975 poll on Britain's membership of the EU (then the EC), which was the only previous nationwide referendum (see Chapter 19). As in 1975, Labour and the Conservatives were divided. However, although Labour did not take an official position on the issue, its new leader, Ed Miliband, supported a 'yes' vote. The overwhelming majority of senior Conservatives, including David Cameron, favoured the retention of simple plurality. But whereas the 1975 result had been a (misleading) triumph for 'moderate' politicians, in opposing AV Cameron was siding with some unlikely groups, including the BNP and the Communists. The SNP, Plaid Cymru, Sinn Fein, the SDLP, the Greens and even UKIP supported the case for change, along with a host of celebrities. The 'no' side found it difficult to muster any sporting or show-biz figures with any credibility, which was another big difference from 1975 when almost all the celebrities were recruited to what turned out to be the winning side.

In a further contrast to 1975, the spending of the two sides was quite evenly matched, within an official limit of £5 million. In 1975, the pro-Market campaign had massively outspent its opponents, without any restraints on its funding. In 2011, the 'yes' campaign depended heavily on just two donors – the Electoral Reform Society and the Joseph Rowntree Reform Trust – while the 'no' vote was backed by a large number of wealthy Conservative Party supporters. Opinion within the press was also divided more equally than it had been in 1975 – which was not difficult, since in that year the only unequivocal backer of withdrawal had been the Communist *Morning Star*. However, the balance in terms of newspaper circulation was strongly tilted against AV supporters. *The Guardian, The Independent,* the *Daily Mirror* and the *Financial Times* were in favour; ranged against them were the *Daily Telegraph, The Times,* the *Daily Mail, The Sun* and the *Daily Express* (a line-up broadly similar to that in the 2016 'Brexit' referendum: see Chapter 5).

However, probably the biggest factor in the defeat of the AV campaign *was* a clear echo of 1975. In the EC referendum, the most valuable card in the hands of 'yes' campaigners was that a 'no' vote would have changed the status quo by placing politicians under considerable pressure to pull Britain out of 'Europe' (indeed, since the verdict would have put the voters at odds with most senior UK politicians a 'no' vote might have triggered a major political and constitutional crisis). In the absence of much public urgency (or deep knowledge) on the issue, 'yes' was the default vote for much of the electorate in 1975. In 2011, the 'safe' vote was 'no'. Although voters were clearly disenchanted with the political class in the wake of the expenses scandal (see Chapter 8), it was difficult to explain how and why a change in the voting system would redress this specific grievance.

Since the public in general lacked an incentive to inform itself about the issues, it was no surprise that the overall level of debate on AV itself was generally poor. Nick Clegg's arguments in favour of the change were handicapped by the revelation that, commenting in the context of Labour's tactical manoeuvring before the 2010 general election, he had referred to the AV system as 'a miserable little compromise'. Attempts to rationalise this quotation were unconvincing, not least because the Liberal Democrats so obviously would have preferred a referendum on a proportional voting system like STV. On the 'no' side, the most effective argument concerned the alleged cost of a new system. In the straitened economic circumstances of 2011, it even became a question whether the referendum itself should not be considered a waste of money. However, the scare stories about the cost of AV were spurious, and given the centrality of voting systems to the health of liberal democracies, the overall cost of the referendum itself (somewhere in the region of £100 million) was less exorbitant than the opponents of change made it sound.

Initial opinion polls suggested that the 'yes' campaign would prevail, and it was only in the final few weeks that opinion swung decisively towards the rejection of reform. The outcome of the poll on 5 May was an almost exact replica of the 1975 referendum – just over two-thirds of those who voted opted to support the status quo. The big difference was the turnout – just 42.2 per cent this time, compared to 65 per cent in 1975, despite the Liberal Democrat insistence that the AV poll should coincide with other elections. As it happened, these contests gave many erstwhile Liberal Democrat voters their first chance to issue a decisive rebuke to Clegg for various decisions since the polls closed in the general election of 2010, such as the failure to honour his pledge on university tuition fees. Thus, rather like the 1975 referendum, the 2011 poll can be seen as a verdict on individuals as much as on the substance of policy. David Cameron – who backed the 'no' campaign with too much gusto for the taste of many Liberal Democrats –had always insisted that the outcome of the referendum would make no difference to the continuation of the coalition. Given that a change from simple plurality was supposed to be a cardinal article of faith for the Liberal Democrats, Clegg's reaction to the result was surprisingly muted.

In one respect, the failure of AV made little difference to Clegg and the Liberal Democrats: if it had been introduced they still would have suffered very significant reverses in the 2015 general election. They would have fared far better under STV. Then again, if reform of any kind had been approved in the 2011 referendum Liberal Democrat prestige and morale would have received a considerable fillip, making these alternative scenarios more hypothetical than usual (Table 17.4).

TABLE 17.4 Seats won at the 2015 general election under different voting systems

Party	Simple plurality	Alternative Vote	Single Transferable Vote
Conservative	331	337	276
Labour	232	227	236
Liberal Democrat	8	9	26
Other	79	76	112

Source: The Electoral Reform Society, www.electoral-reform.org.uk.

Impact of the new electoral systems

Despite its relative inaction on electoral reform for Westminster, 'New' Labour introduced multiple electoral systems into the UK polity. The simple plurality system is now used only for general elections in Great Britain, and local elections in England and (for the time being) Wales. The devolved institutions in Scotland and Wales are elected by the AMS, as is the Greater London Assembly. Great Britain's representatives in the European Parliament were elected by the regional list system of PR. The STV is used for elections to the Northern Ireland Assembly, as well as in Scottish local government elections. Elected mayors in English towns and cities are chosen by the SV.

A more complex pattern of voting behaviour has developed under the new electoral systems. The multi-level UK polity clearly has a number of party systems rather than a standardised two-party system (see Chapter 14). Minor parties and independent candidates have performed better in these contests than in Westminster elections. This is to be expected in 'second-order elections' that do not determine the government of the United Kingdom (see Analysis 17.3), but PR has also been a factor in the improved showing of smaller parties. It has produced more proportional results, awarding minor parties seats they would not have won if the simple plurality system were used. The Liberal Democrats were under-represented in the European Parliament until the change to PR in 1999. UKIP, the Brexit Party and the Greens also performed remarkably well in the European Parliament, and won seats in the London Assembly. The Conservatives failed to win any constituency seats in the 1999 Scottish Parliament election, despite scoring 15.5 per cent of the relevant vote, but were allocated 18 'list' seats.

No electoral system can translate votes into seats with complete accuracy. PR systems are much more effective than majoritarian ones. The 'deviation from proportionality' figures in Table 17.5 show the disproportionate effect of simple plurality. The much-improved figure for 2017 was caused by the virtual implosion of UKIP in that year and the corresponding improvement in the performance of the two main parties.

The number of seats in a constituency (the 'district magnitude') is a factor in the proportionality of the alternative systems. Minor parties are often under-represented when the d'Hondt formula or STV is used in small multi-member constituencies. In the 2003 Welsh Assembly elections, a party needed to win 8 per cent of the vote to be sure of a list seat. To be entitled to a seat in the London Assembly, a party must reach an electoral threshold of 5 per cent of the vote. The British National Party narrowly surpassed this threshold in 2008, securing its first seat on the Assembly.

Table 17.5 Deviation from proportionality (DV) in recent UK general elections

Year of election	Deviation from proportionality (%)
2005	20.7
2010	22.7
2015	24.0
2017	9.3
2019	16.7

Note: DV is determined by calculating the difference between each party's percentage vote share and seat share, summing all deviations (ignoring minus signs) and halving the total.

> ## Analysis 17.3
>
> ### Second-order elections
>
> Political scientists classify national parliamentary and presidential elections as 'first-order elections', whereas sub-national and local elections are considered to be 'second-order elections' (as were elections to the European Parliament). The introduction of PR for many second-order elections in the United Kingdom has increased the likelihood that small parties will fare better than in general elections.
>
> The main characteristics of second-order elections can be summarised as follows:
>
> - Turnout is lower than for first-order elections.
> - Support for the governing party at national level is likely to decline, as electors take the chance to register a protest vote against its record in office.
> - Smaller parties perform better.
> - Electors vote on the basis of national issues rather than issues specific to the institution that is being elected.

Electors have realised that their vote is less likely to be wasted under PR. Significant numbers have engaged in 'split ticket' voting at the Scottish Parliament and Welsh Assembly elections, supporting a major party in the constituency vote while giving their list vote to a minor party. The main parties in Scotland tend to poll fewer list votes than constituency votes, although the Conservative bucked this trend in 2016 (see Table 17.6). In the 1998 Northern Ireland Assembly elections, the nationalist SDLP won the most first preference votes but the Ulster Unionist Party took the most seats as its votes were more effectively distributed and it benefited from vote transfers. In turn this had a significant impact on the composition of the Assembly, turning an 'anti-Agreement' majority of first preference votes within the unionist bloc into a 'pro-Agreement' majority among unionists in the Assembly. The Scottish Executive (1997–2007) and Welsh Assembly government (2000–3, 2007–11) gave their citizens a taste of modern coalition rule before the arrangement was extended to the United Kingdom as a whole by the inconclusive 2010 general election.

Electors are becoming more familiar with the new electoral systems and are generally supportive, but there have been some high-profile problems. At the 2007 Scottish Parliament election, 146,000 ballots were rejected because they had not been completed properly. A report by Canadian expert Ron Gould concluded that the decision to ask electors to record their votes for the simple plurality constituency candidates and the regional lists caused confusion. He also criticised the SNP's decision to use the description 'Alex Salmond for First Minister' rather than the party name on the ballot paper. The government backed Gould's recommendations on a return

TABLE 17.6 Elections to the Scottish Parliament, 2016

	Share of constituency vote (%)	Constituency seats won	Share of regional list vote (%)	List seats won	Total seats
SNP	46.5	59	41.7	4	63
Conservative	22.0	7	22.9	22	29
Labour	22.6	3	19.1	21	24
Green	0.6	0	6.6	6	6
Liberal Democrat	7.8	4	5.2	1	5

to separate ballot papers for constituency and regional contests, and that party names should appear first on the regional ballot papers.

The Commission on Boundary Differences and Voting Systems (the Arbuthnott Commission) examined electoral systems in Scotland after 2007. It proposed a move to an open list system (which the government rejected) and supported the use of a single ballot paper. Dual candidacy (the practice of standing for both a constituency and list seat simultaneously) had been banned for the 2007 Welsh Assembly elections, but was backed by Arbuthnott and allowed to continue in Scotland (it was restored in Wales in 2014). The UK government's *Review of Voting Systems* (Cm 7304, 2008) offered little new and did not make concrete recommendations, but it did highlight the following:

- Any move to PR for Westminster would lead to an increase in the number of small parties represented, a greater likelihood of coalition governments and multi-member constituencies.
- It would not guarantee higher turnout or better social representation.
- It could produce unintended consequences. There has been friction between constituency and list members in the Scottish Parliament and Welsh Assembly (now Senedd) over the imbalance in constituency work and on dual candidacy. Problems with ballot design have also been evident.
- There is limited public knowledge of, and interest in, electoral reform. Public support for PR has not increased, and there is concern about the influence of small parties and coalitions on government decision-making.

In the 2011 AV referendum, although reformers continued to hope for change, the cautionary tone of these remarks about the public appetite for alternative voting systems was apparently vindicated.

Conclusion and summary

Elections in the United Kingdom generally meet the 'competitive, free and fair' criteria outlined at the start of this chapter, but some elements of the electoral process are problematic. Electoral law is not enshrined within a written constitution, leaving the government free to change the electoral system or enfranchise new voters without having to depart from normal legislative procedures. Some of the changes introduced by the Blair governments, including the use of the closed list system for European parliamentary elections and the decision to hold all-postal ballots in four regions at the 2004 contest, have been criticised by opposition parties and independent commentators. Spending limits have been introduced for national election campaigns, but Labour and the Conservatives continue to enjoy resources way beyond the reach of other parties. Terrestrial television broadcasters must follow strict guidelines in their coverage of election campaigns, but the press is free to present issues in a partisan way, which makes its idiosyncratic pattern of ownership into a serious problem from the democratic perspective. The UK media might be 'free', after a fashion, but it could hardly be described as 'fair' unless one adopts a convoluted definition of that much-abused word.

No one can dispute that the simple plurality system produces disproportional results. As such, it discriminates against small parties and many votes are wasted. But it has contributed to long periods of stable government by parties that have a respectable record of putting their manifesto commitments into practice – or, at least, of attempting to do so with commendable sincerity. Low turnout is perhaps the most pressing concern, particularly if some social groups or shades of opinion are under-represented. Yet efforts to improve turnout by introducing postal or e-voting themselves raise questions about electoral fraud and the secret ballot. Greater political engagement is the key to improving the health of democracy in Britain, and this depends on a much more positive two-way relationship between political parties and electors.

Further reading

A convenient summary of British electoral history in the era of 'Dealignment' is D. Denver and M. Garnett, *British General Elections since 1964* (Oxford: Oxford University Press, 2014). Every general election since 1945 has been the subject of more detailed analysis in the 'Nuffield series'. The most recent is D. Kavanagh and P. Cowley, *The British General Election of 2017* (London: Palgrave, 2019). J. Tonge, S. Wilks-Heeg and L. Thompson (eds), *Britain Votes: The 2019 General Election* (Oxford: Oxford University Press, 2019), contains numerous lively and well-informed contributions. D. Wring, R. Mortimore and S. Atkinson (eds.), *Political Communication in Britain: Campaigning, Media and Polling in the 2017 General Election* (Houndmills: Palgrave Macmillan, 2018) is also part of an invaluable long-running series.

D. Kavanagh, *Election Campaigning: The New Marketing of Politics* (Oxford: Blackwell, 1995) is a useful but rather dated introduction. More detailed pieces include D. Denver, G. Hands and I. McAllister, 'The Electoral Impact of Constituency Campaigning in Britain, 1992–2001', *Political Studies*, Vol. 52, No. 2 (2004), pp. 289–306. The crisis of voter turnout in the early part of the century is examined by P. Whiteley, H. Clarke, D. Sanders and M. Stewart, 'Turnout', in P. Norris (ed.), *Britain Votes 2001* (Oxford: Oxford University Press, 2001), pp. 211–24, and J. Curtice, 'Turnout: Electors Stay Home – Again', in P. Norris and C. Wlezien (eds.), *Britain Votes 2005* (Oxford: Oxford University Press, 2005), pp. 120–29, and in *Voter Engagement and Young People* (London: Electoral Commission, 2004). Possible solutions are assessed in *May 2003 Pilot Schemes* (London: Electoral Commission, 2003), *Age of Electoral Majority* (London: Electoral Commission, 2004) and K. Faulks, 'Should Voting be Compulsory?', *Politics Review*, Vol. 10, No. 3 (2001), pp. 24–25. On the representation of women, see *Gender and Political Participation* (London: Electoral Commission, 2004) and R. Campbell and J. Lovenduski, 'Winning Women's Votes? The Incremental Track to Equality', in P. Norris and C. Wlezien (eds.), *Britain Votes 2005* (Oxford: Oxford University Press, 2005), pp. 181–97.

The best text on electoral systems is D. Farrell, *Electoral Systems: A Comparative Introduction* (London: Red Globe Press, 2nd edition, 2011). J. Curtice, 'The Electoral System: Biased to Blair?', in P. Norris (ed.), *Britain Votes 2001* (Oxford: Oxford University Press, 2001), pp. 239–50, exposes the bias in Britain's single-member plurality system. *The 2019 General Election: Voters Left Voiceless* is the latest of many critical reports from the Electoral Reform Society (see: https://www.electoral-reform.org.uk/latest-news-and-research/publications/the-2019-general-election-voters-left-voiceless/); the Society continues to produce well-argued reports and articles available on its website www.electoral-reform.org.uk. P. Dunleavy and H. Margetts, 'Comparing UK Electoral Systems', in P. Norris and C. Wlezien (eds.), *Britain Votes 2005* (Oxford: Oxford University Press, 2005), pp. 198–213, examines the systems used in the United Kingdom.

Official reports on electoral reform include Review of Voting Systems: The Experience of New Voting Systems in the United Kingdom since 1997 (Cm 7304, 2008) and the Report of the Independent Commission on the Voting System [the 'Jenkins Report'] (Cm 4090, London: HMSO, 1998). Also worth consulting are Britain's Experience with Electoral Systems (London: Electoral Reform Society, 2007) and Changed Voting Changed Politics: Lessons of Britain's Experience of PR since 1997 (London: Independent Commission on PR, 2004).

Websites

The Electoral Commission's website (www.electoralcommission.org.uk) provides a wealth of information including official results from recent elections and reports on turnout and alternative methods of voting. Background material and assessments of recent developments can be found on the sites for the Constitution Unit (www.ucl.ac.uk/constitution-unit), the Electoral Reform Society (www.electoral-reform.org.uk) and Unlock Democracy (www. unlockdemocracy.org.uk). All include copies of their excellent newsletters.

Richard Kimber's UK Political Info site (http://www.ukpolitical.info/Links.htm) has links to a multitude of sites on elections and electoral systems. UK election results can be found at www.election.demon. co.uk. The opinion poll organisations, Ipsos MORI (www.ipsos-mori.co.uk), Populus (www.populus. co.uk) and YouGov (www. yougov.com), provide data from past and present polls. Two blogs explore opinion poll trends: www.ukpollingreport.co.uk and www.politicalbetting.com. The Fawcett Society (www.fawcettsociety.org.uk) campaigns for increased representation of women, and the Votes at 16 Campaign (www.votesat16.org.uk) for a reduction in the minimum voting age.

Chapter 18

Voting behaviour

Learning outcomes

After reading this chapter you will:

- be able to evaluate the influence of social class on voting behaviour;
- be able to assess the role of short-term factors (e.g. issues, party leaders and perceptions of party 'competence') on the decisions of voters;
- be in a position to judge which theories of voting behaviour provide the most convincing accounts of the outcomes of recent general elections.

Introduction

Two major approaches have dominated the study of voting behaviour in the UK since the end of the Second World War. The first focuses on the social characteristics of voters, particularly occupational class, and their long-term attachments to the Labour and Conservative parties. This perspective was dominant from 1950 (when the first systematic research was conducted) to 1970 – a period in which most electors voted for parties that were believed to represent the interests of their social class. Since 1970, social class has become less effective in predicting how people will vote. Accordingly, political scientists now concentrate on a series of short-term factors, such as issues, party leaders, and voter perceptions of the main parties, which influence an individual's decision on how to vote. This chapter focuses on these approaches and assesses voting behaviour in recent general elections. However, it should be remembered that the simple plurality electoral system does not translate votes into seats in the House of Commons accurately. It must also be noted that turnout fell in general elections during the 1990s and 2000s, although it has recovered slightly since (see Chapter 17).

Social Class
a social group defined by economic and social status.

Class voting and partisanship

The period of 1945–70 was one of relative stability in British voting behaviour. Studies at this time concentrated on the social attributes of voters, identifying a strong relationship between **social class** and voting, often termed 'class alignment'. Peter Pulzer proclaimed in *Political Representation and Elections in Britain* (London: George Allen & Unwin, 1967) that 'class is the basis of British party politics; all else is embellishment and detail'. Social class was determined by occupation: the working class consisted of people in manual occupations, such as builders and scaffolders, train drivers, and factory workers; and the middle class, those in non-manual jobs, such as office workers, managers, and accountants. A majority of people voted for their 'natural class party', that is, the party apparently representing the interests of their social class. Typically in this period, up to two-thirds of the working class voted for the Labour Party, while as much as three-quarters of the middle class voted for the Conservatives, as illustrated by Table 18.1.

Seemingly confirming Pulzer's claim, social class formed the main social and political cleavage in the UK at this time. Labour self-consciously claimed to represent the interests of the working class, while the Conservatives, although purportedly promoting 'One Nation' policies, were most sensitive to the perceived priorities of middle-class property owners and employers. The middle class are sometimes referred to as the salariat because they were paid a monthly salary, rather than a weekly wage. Within British society, class consciousness was previously more pronounced, and class boundaries were more clear and stable than is the case today. Economic and political elites were largely composed of upper-class and middle-class men, many of them educated at public schools such as Charterhouse, Eton, and Harrow, and then at Oxford or Cambridge University (Oxbridge). Social mobility was limited, so few working-class men (and even fewer women) went to university or achieved promotion to higher-paid managerial positions. This also meant that for the vast majority of the working class, earnings remained static throughout their lives; apart from any pay increase awarded, their wages remained broadly similar throughout their working lives. By contrast, not only were salaries of the middle class invariably higher to begin with, they also increased with promotion to more senior posts, or via annual increments to reward experience and loyalty.

Partisanship or 'partisan alignment' was another key feature of UK politics in the early post-war period. As Table 18.2 shows, more than three-quarters of voters reported a positive attachment to a major party, identifying themselves as either Labour or Conservative supporters. Of these, 43 per cent 'very strongly identified' with a party at the time of the 1964 and 1966 general elections, and 40 per cent identified 'very strongly' with the Conservatives or Labour. The two main parties thus had a considerable pool of loyal supporters – their 'core vote',

TABLE 18.1 Social class and party support in 1959, 1964, 1966, and 1970

	1959	*1964*	*1966*	*1970*
Middle-class Conservative	67	62	60	64
Working-class Labour	57	64	69	58
Middle-class Labour	21	22	26	25
Working-class Conservative	30	28	25	33

Source: David Butler and Donald Stokes, *Political Change in Britain* (London: Macmillan, 1969).

TABLE 18.2 Party identification in 1964, 1966, and 1970

	1964	*1966*	*1970*
'Very strong' party identification	43	43	41
'Very strong' Conservative or Labour identification	40	39	40

Source: David Butler and Donald Stokes, *Political Change in Britain* (London: Macmillan, 1969).

which could be relied upon not just to identify with their favoured party but also to turn out in elections. This also meant that the two main parties were compelled to compete for the minority of non-aligned or 'floating voters' at election time, citizens who were assumed to be non-ideological, and therefore mainly located on the 'centre ground'. In other words, this would have encouraged the two main parties to adopt a more 'moderate' stance on most issues, for fear that being viewed as too ideological or radical would alienate this vital section of the electorate.

Class identity and partisanship were fostered during the process of **socialisation** which began in childhood. Political views developed through social learning in the home, at school and university, in the neighbourhood, and at the workplace. An individual brought up in a council-owned property in a northern city, who left school at the minimum age to work in a manual occupation where he or she joined a trade union, would be likely to feel a strong working-class identity and vote Labour. A similar process would engender long-term loyalty to the Conservative Party among more affluent individuals whose parents worked in non-manual occupations, and were home-owners, often in southern England and/or in the suburbs of a town or city.

Socialisation

the process by which individuals acquire values and beliefs in their formative years.

The stability of voting behaviour between 1945 and 1970 underpinned, but also partly reflected, Britain's stable two-party system in which the Conservatives and Labour averaged more than 91 per cent of the vote in the eight general elections in this period (see Table 18.1). At 78 per cent, electoral turnout was relatively high. Between them, the two main parties held almost 98 per cent of seats in the House of Commons. They were well matched: the Conservatives spent 13 years in office and Labour 12, with each party winning four general elections from 1945 to 1970, and each attracting 43–46 per cent of the total vote in every general election during this period. Party support was high, strong, and relatively stable.

Finally, this was an age of 'consensus politics' (see Chapter 13), in which neither Labour nor the Conservatives strayed far from the median voter – that is, the hypothetical centrist 'floating voter' who occupies the electoral centre ground with roughly equivalent numbers of voters to their left and right. The electoral centre ground is not necessarily the same as the *ideological* centre ground. Between 1945 and 1970, the median voter was positioned on the centre-left of the political spectrum and the main parties shared similar commitments to Keynesianism and the welfare state, reflecting the legacy of the period during the Second World War and for some years afterwards, when what might be called 'collectivist' values were widely popular.

Limits of class voting

Although most electors voted along class lines in the period 1945–70, there were significant exceptions. Attention has been focused on two main 'deviant' groups – working-class Conservatives and middle-class socialists. If they had not captured the votes of up to one-third of the then numerically dominant working class, the Conservative Party would not have achieved its three general election victories in the 1950s. Some explanations of working-class

Conservative support focus on the values held by working-class Tories, including 'deferential' attitudes towards the Conservative Party given the social status of its leaders, its authoritarian values (on issues such as law and order, immigration, and welfare 'scroungers'), and its professed patriotism, often manifesting itself in hostility to foreigners and the European Union (EU). Others looked at the social status of working-class Conservatives, suggesting that the rising affluence of skilled workers (the C2s) after 1945 might account for their allegiance, because as they enjoyed improved living standards and a more prosperous lifestyle, they were attracted to the Conservatives, and perhaps ceased to view themselves as working class. Meanwhile, studies of support for Labour among middle-class voters also examined their ideological values (e.g. belief in egalitarianism, human rights, civil liberties, racial and sexual equality) and occupation; many middle-class Socialists are employed in caring or people-orientated professions in the public sector or local government, particularly education, health, and social work. Often, they view their jobs as a means of creating a fairer society, or of helping the 'victims' of Capitalism, and as such, they see themselves as motivated by altruism, rather than a materialistic concern to make lots of money.

One problem with the class and partisan alignment models of voting behaviour is the implication that issues are not particularly important to voters, because they simply vote for 'their' party in each election. However, what was more likely is that voters viewed issues through the stance or ideology of their party: a Conservative voter would almost automatically assume that their party was the best to tackle rising crime, while a Labour voter similarly assumed that their party had the best policies for tackling poverty. In other words, it was not that voters were unconcerned about particular issues, but that their interpretation of those issues was shaped by their existing political values and allegiance.

Dealignment

Since the 1970s, Britain has experienced a process of both **class and partisan dealignment**, and thus greater 'fluidity' and volatility in the way that much of the population votes. **Class dealignment** refers to the weakening of the relationship between social class and support for a particular political party. Since 1970, fewer people have voted for their 'natural class party'. Working-class support for Labour has declined, as has middle-class support for the Conservatives. The Alford Index of relative class voting is one way of measuring the incidence of class voting. It is calculated by subtracting Labour's percentage share of the middle-class vote from its share of the working-class vote. The more supportive the working class is of Labour relative to the middle class, the higher the Alford Index score. In 1964 it stood at 42, but it fell as low as 20 in 1997 before recovering slightly in 2001. In 2010, when for the first time more than half of Labour's vote was composed of middle-class voters, the Index was down to 17, and fell to just 6 in 2015.

Partisan dealignment refers to the decline in the scale and strength of voters' identification with the main political parties. Fewer voters have a strong attachment to either Labour or the Conservatives. In 2001, only 13 per cent of respondents described themselves as 'very strong' supporters of one of the main parties compared to 43 per cent in 1964. This means that their core vote has shrunk, as has party membership: the Conservatives had 2.5 million members in the mid-1950s but about 150,000 in 2019. Meanwhile, Labour Party membership fell from 750,000 in the mid-1950s to about 210,000 in 2014, although it soared to about 600,000 after the 2015 general election, due mainly to Jeremy Corbyn's candidature and subsequent victory in Labour's leadership contest. Dealignment has produced greater electoral volatility, with more people switching support from one party to another in elections; fewer voters feel loyalty to one particular party compared to the 1960s, and so are much more likely to vote for different parties in different elections. A notable recent example was between the 2015 and 2017 elections, when one million voters switched from Conservative to Labour, as did 800,000 people who had voted for the United Kingdom Independence Party UKIP two years earlier. Research conducted by Lord Ashcroft (publishing per centages rather than raw numbers) shows that of people who voted Labour in 2017, 9 per cent switched to the Conservatives in 2019, 7 per cent transferred their support to the Liberal Democrats, and only 1 per cent switched to the Brexit Party. Although the Conservatives won the election very comfortably, they too lost some of their 2017 support: 8 per cent switched to the Liberal Democrats, 5 per cent to Labour, and 2 per cent to the Brexit Party (https:// lordashcroftpolls.com/2019/12/how-britain-voted-and-why-my-2019-general-election-post-vote-poll/).

The dual process of class and partisan dealignment has naturally had an impact on other aspects of British general elections since the early 1970s. The combined share of the vote won by Labour and the Conservatives in the last five decades has decreased overall, although 2017 and 2019 did see an increase again, albeit still not to the same level as prior to 1970. For example, as Table 18.3 illustrates, whereas the two main parties had polled 96.8 per cent of votes cast in the 1951 general election, their combined share fell to 75.1 per cent in February 1974. After recovering slightly to 80.8 per cent in 1979, by the 2010 general election, the two main parties together

TABLE 18.3 Conservative and Labour share of the vote in general elections of 1945, 1950, 1951, 1955, 1959, 1964, 1966, 1970, 1974 (Feb., Oct.), 1979, 1983, 1987, 1992, 1997, 2001, 2005, 2010, 2015, 2017, and 2019

Election year	Conservative vote %	Labour vote %	Combined vote %	Other parties' share %[a]	Turnout %
1945	39.6	48.0	87.6	12.4	72.8
1950	43.4	46.1	89.5	10.5	83.9
1951	48.0	48.8	96.8	3.2	82.6
1955	49.7	46.4	96.1	3.9	76.8
1959	49.4	43.8	93.2	6.8	78.7
1964	43.4	44.1	87.5	12.5	77.1
1966	41.9	48.0	89.9	10.1	75.8
1970	46.4	43.1	89.5	10.5	72.0
1974 Feb.	37.9	37.2	75.1	24.9	78.8
1974 Oct.	35.8	39.2	75.0	25.0	72.8
1979	43.9	36.9	80.8	19.2	76.0
1983	42.4	27.6	70.0	30.0	72.7
1987	42.3	30.8	73.1	26.9	75.3
1992	41.8	34.2	76.0	24.0	77.7
1997	30.7	43.4	74.1	25.9	71.5
2001	31.7	40.7	72.4	27.6	59.4
2005	32.3	35.2	67.5	32.5	61.3
2010	36.1	29.0	65.1	34.9	65.1
2015	36.9	30.4	67.3	32.7	66.1
2017	42.4	40.0	82.4	17.6	68.7
2019	43.6	32.2	75.8	24.2	67.3

[a] Third parties here includes the Brexit Party (in 2019), Green Party, Liberals, Liberal Democrats, Plaid Cymru, SDP, SNP, UKIP, and the Northern Ireland parties.

polled only 65.1 per cent of the UK vote, although there has been a recovery since then, rising to 82.4 per cent in 2017 before falling back to 75.8 per cent in 2019. In other words, while the combined share of the vote of the two main parties has not fallen at every general election, the overall trend has been downwards since 1970.

In tandem with this decline in class and partisan dealignment, and the resultant diminution of support for the two main parties, support for 'third' parties has increased considerably. In the 1945–70 period, the Liberals averaged 7 per cent, whereas between 1974 and 2010, the average share of the vote won by the Liberals and their successors was 19.4 per cent. Nationalist parties in Scotland and Wales made electoral breakthroughs at Westminster in the 1970s, and continued to prosper, with the SNP becoming the largest Party electorally in Scotland in recent elections. Minor parties such as the British National Party (BNP) recorded notable support in the 2000s, winning nearly 4 per cent of votes cast in England in the 2001 election, even though it only fielded 33 candidates. It also attracted enough support in five seats to retain its deposit. Even more notable was UKIP's performance in the 2015 general election, when its four million votes constituted a share of 12.6 per cent cast nationally (and pushed the Liberal Democrats into fourth place), while the Green Party's one million votes in 2015 constituted a share of 3.8 per cent. The Greens had previously won the Brighton Pavilion seat in the 2010 election, with Caroline Lucas elected as the Party's only Member of Parliament (MP), and she was then re-elected in 2015, 2017, and 2019.

Explaining dealignment

Social and economic changes over the last 40 years have eroded traditional class identities and weakened the relationship between class and voting. The proportion of people in manual occupations has declined since the 1960s, with notable falls in industries such as car production, coal mining, steel-making, and ship-building. Employment has risen in service industries (e.g. in retail, catering, and computing) and parts of the public sector (e.g. in social services). From being the largest social class in the early post-war period, the working class is now smaller than the middle class, on any realistic definition of these contested terms. However, although the middle class has greatly expanded since the 1980s, it has also become less secure, as the character of the labour market has undergone profound changes. The prevalence of '9-5' jobs and 'jobs for life' have receded as more people (especially women) work on a part-time basis, are employed on flexible or zero-hour contracts, or are self-employed. Also, in the twenty-first century, increasing numbers of middle-class job are being affected by automation: for example, online banking means that there are fewer high-street banks, and those that remain are replacing staff with machines, so that financial transactions do not involve any interaction with another person. The same trend is apparent with some airport check-ins, with passengers scanning their tickets, and then weighing-in and labelling their suitcases via a machine, rather than queuing at a check-in desk. Of course, while such automation is presented in terms of making services more efficient or quicker for customers, the underlying objective is to save money for the companies concerned; replacing people with machines means that millions of pounds are saved on salaries and occupational pensions, thereby massively increasing profits and shareholders' dividends.

The most popular typology of social class used by social scientists and opinion pollsters features the following categories:

- A – higher managerial, administrative, or professional
- B – intermediate managerial, administrative, or professional
- C1 – supervisory, clerical, and junior white-collar workers
- C2 – skilled manual workers

- D – semi-skilled and unskilled manual workers
- E – casual workers, people reliant on state benefits (e.g. pensioners and the long-term unemployed).

The highest two categories are often merged (as AB), as are the lowest two (DE).

The working class has decreased in size since the 1960s. Although various organisations try to allocate individuals to different classes, from the political perspective *perceptions* could be said to matter the most; objective class is how someone is defined by organisations or social scientists, but subjective class is how an individual defines or perceives himself or herself. Some (objectively) middle-class people with left-wing views will insist that they are working class, just as some affluent or aspirational manual workers will vehemently deny that they are working class. Certainly, greater social mobility, increased affluence (for some), and growing job insecurity among sections of the middle class – the precariat (**prec**arious sal**ariat**) – have blurred the boundaries between the middle class and working class compared to those in the 1950s. More people from working-class backgrounds enter further or higher education (which expanded in the 1960s, and then again in the 1990s), have non-manual occupations, and own their homes. Standards of living for many have improved and the ownership of consumer goods has widened.

Indeed, such changes led some academics to challenge the traditional typology of social class. The psephologists (experts on voting behaviour) Anthony Heath, Roger Jowell, and John Curtice devised an alternative typology in the 1980s (see Analysis 18.1), which challenged claims that there had been a decline in absolute class voting, whereby less of the working class was voting Labour. Instead, they claimed that much of Labour's declining electoral support during the 1980s and 1990s was due to: (a) an inadequate definition of working class, and (b) the shrinking of the industrial, manual, working class. With regard to the former critique, they suggested that hitherto all manual workers had been simply (and simplistically) classified as 'working class', but this overlooked the extent to which some of these workers either occupied supervisory positions (factory foreman), were self-employed (a painter and decorator, for example), or ran their own small business (e.g. a plumbing firm employing three people). For all of these categories, it was argued, the workers involved enjoyed somewhat more authority, status, or independence (and perhaps slightly higher remuneration or incomes) than other manual workers, and as such, they shared some characteristics with, or proximity to, the lower middle class – including a greater inclination to vote Conservative (see Analysis 18.1).

With regard to the shrinking of the traditional working class, Heath, Jowell, and Curtice suggested that this was the major reason for Labour's declining electoral support; it was not that Labour was attracting significantly fewer votes from the industrial working class itself, but that this working class had shrunk due to changes in Britain's economic structure and associated patterns of employment. Many manual workers continued to vote Labour – but there were simply fewer of them – while the Conservative-voting voting middle class had expanded. Meanwhile, some political scientists, such as Ivor Crewe, identified a 'new working class' in the 1980s, which was employed in 'cleaner' industries, such as light engineering, chemicals, and electronics, often employed in factories on 'business parks' or industrial estates just outside towns, often in southern England along the 'M4 corridor'. These accounted for many of the new jobs and businesses created in the 1980s, and for many of the workers employed in these newer or expanding industries, the wages and status were often higher, which meant that they were less inclined to identify with the old 'proletariat', and were therefore less inclined to vote Labour. This debate over the decline in Labour's working-class support exercised psephologists into the 1990s, but the academic consensus now holds that both accounts are valid; they are not either/or – the working class has become smaller demographically, due to changes in the economy and the labour market, and the proportion of the remaining working class which regularly votes Labour has also declined.

Analysis 18.1

Social class

In studies of voting behaviour, social class is defined in terms of occupation. This approach is considerably narrower than concepts of class used by Marxist theories of conflict between the owners of the means of production (the bourgeoisie or capitalist class) and those forced to sell their own labour (the proletariat or working class). Social scientists engaged in empirical work have constructed various typologies of social class to distinguish between occupations and income levels. The most important has been the ABC1 classification which has been used by opinion pollsters and most social scientists.

Election analysts Anthony Heath, Roger Jowell, and John Curtice argued in *How Britain Votes* (London: Pergamon, 1985) that the ABC1 typology failed to take account of social and economic change. They devised their own categories in which the working class formed a smaller proportion of the electorate:

- Salariat (managers, administrators, professionals, semi-professionals)
- Routine non-manual (clerks, secretaries, sales workers)
- Petty bourgeoisie (small proprietors, self-employed manual workers, farmers)
- Foremen and technicians (blue-collar workers with supervisory functions)
- Working class (rank-and-file manual workers in industry and agriculture).

The limitations of the ABC1 typology have also been recognised by government statisticians who have constructed a new typology:

- Higher managerial and professional occupations (e.g. company directors, doctors, and lawyers)
- Lower managerial and professional occupations (e.g. nurses, journalists, and junior police officers)
- Intermediate occupations (e.g. secretaries)
- Small employers (e.g. farmers)
- Lower supervisory occupations (e.g. train drivers)
- Semi-routine occupations (e.g. shop assistants)
- Routine occupations (e.g. waiters, refuse collectors)
- Long-term unemployed.

Political parties increasingly identify specific groups of voters whose support is believed to be crucial to their prospects of electoral success. Some of the informal categories they use have entered political folklore. In the 1980s, the Conservatives targeted aspiring skilled and semi-skilled working-class voters in southern England – a group labelled as 'Essex man'. A decade later, Conservative attention had shifted to 'Worcester woman', middle-class women in provincial cities. These groups were identified alliteratively on the basis of either electoral geography or their assumed shared characteristic/lifestyle. Tony Blair coined the term 'Mondeo man' for the 30-something middle-class home-owner whose support New Labour needed if it was to win the 1997 election, while William Hague, as leader of the Conservative opposition, spoke of 'pebbledash people', an allusion to middle-income home-owners whose homes, often semi-detached houses in the suburbs, had a 'pebbledash' coating on the outside walls; a style which had once been fashionable. Rather more recently, Theresa May alluded to the Conservatives' need to appeal to the growing number of voters who were 'just about managing' (the JAMS) as their earnings barely kept pace with the increased cost of living in an era of austerity. Her successor, Boris Johnson, pitched much of his appeal, in 2019, to 'the left behind', voters often living in impoverished northern towns which had not benefitted from economic modernisation, the expansion of higher education, new technologies, or globalisation, and who had allegedly been abandoned by Labour; the latter allegedly more concerned with 'identity politics' and appealing to 'oppressed' minorities (other than the working class).

Although most of the academic debate concerning class dealignment focused on changes concerning the working class, and the reasons for Labour's declining electoral support among this section of British society, parallel changes have occurred among the middle class since the 1980s. It is widely accepted that the middle class or salariat has expanded, as the number of white-collar or professional jobs (many of which now require a university degree) has increased, but this highlights a seeming paradox: if the middle class has traditionally voted Conservative, and the middle class has significantly expanded, then surely the Conservatives should have performed much better electorally between 1997 and 2017? The answer to this apparent puzzle is that dealigment has occurred among the middle class too, resulting in lower support for the Conservative Party, and that the expansion of the middle class has also been accompanied by fragmentation and differentiation within it. The middle class is not a unified, homogenous, bloc sharing the same economic interests, social values, or political outlook. Instead, as with the working class, there are important differences within the middle class, and these have become more important, and had a greater political impact, since the 1990s. There are four main aspects to this change. First, alongside more traditional middle-class careers, occupations, and professions such as accountancy, banking, and law, there has emerged a new range of white-collar jobs in 'creative industries', IT and media. The latter are probably rather less inclined to vote Conservative than the former. Second, many of these new middle-class jobs have been undertaken by university or art-school graduates – reflecting the expansion of higher education since the 1990 – and various surveys have shown that people who have attended full-time education beyond the age of 18 tend to have more liberal or 'progressive' views and values, and are therefore much more likely to vote for Labour, the Liberal Democrats, the Greens, or, in Scotland, the SNP. For example, in the 2019 election, Labour attracted more support from university graduates than from people who had left school at the earliest opportunity, perhaps with few, if any, qualifications – although Conservatives would probably cite this as 'evidence' of students being indoctrinated by left-wing lecturers! Similarly, university graduates were among the main supporters of Remain (in the EU) in the 2016 Referendum, whereas Leave was strongly supported by voters who did not have post-16 qualifications.

The third reason why the expansion of the middle class has not significantly benefitted the Conservative Party is that much of the salariat is employed in the public sector, in careers such as nursing, probation, teaching, and social work. At the risk of generalisation, people who work in these 'caring' or people-orientated professions tend, overall, to have more 'liberal' or progressive values, and perhaps view their choice of career as their small contribution to creating a better society or working with the socially disadvantaged. For these reasons, many public sector workers are more inclined to vote for left-leaning, liberal, or 'progressive' political parties, rather than vote Conservative. Of course, there might also be an element of self-interest behind their apparent altruism, namely a calculation that Labour, the Liberal Democrats, the Greens, or the SNP are all likely to spend more on the public sector, and perhaps do more to protect (or increase) jobs and improve pay. This links to an argument advanced in the 1980s by Patrick Dunleavy, who identified a new public sector, private sector, cleavage among the electorate. This division had two dimensions: between people employed in the public sector and those working in the private sector; and between people who relied on the public provision of goods (e.g. housing and transport) and those using private suppliers. According to Dunleavy, those who were employed in the public sector, or used public sector services, were more inclined to vote Labour, regardless of their class category, while those who worked in the private sector, or used private sector services, were more likely to vote Conservative, even if they were working class. As such, Dunleavy suggested, these 'sectoral cleavages' transcended traditional class-based patterns of voting and Party loyalties.

The fourth change concerning the middle class in recent years, and which is also likely to weaken its support for the Conservatives, is the increasingly precarious character of many white-collar jobs and careers. We have already noted the term 'precariat' – used to refer to the increasingly insecure or temporary (fixed-term contracts) nature of some middle-class jobs – yet until relatively recently, many of them were viewed as secure jobs for life. For example, working in a high-street bank was, until a couple of decades ago, often viewed as a rock-solid and respectable career, but now automation, online banking, and relentless cost-cutting and branch closures means that thousands of bank clerks and cashiers have been made redundant. The same trend is apparent at many airports, where customers are increasingly expected to check-in their luggage and print off their boarding passes, rather than go to a check-in desk where a member of an airline's staff would carry out these tasks. Similarly, customers scanning their purchases at self-service tills in supermarkets means that far fewer check-out staff need to be employed. Advances in technology, artificial intelligence, and the rise of 'smart robots' will mean even more once safe middle-class jobs disappearing in the years ahead, with no guarantee that (enough) new jobs will be created to provide work for those white-collar workers made redundant by technological advances and corporate cost-cutting. At least some middle-class workers affected by, or fearful of, these changes might consequently decide to vote for a political party promising to protect (or create) jobs, and strengthen employment rights, rather than one which insists that those workers must embrace change and competition, become more flexible, lower their expectations, and accept that governments cannot prevent the operation of 'the market' or resist globalisation.

Class dealignment had a knock-on effect on party identification, because people who lack strong class identities were then less likely to feel a strong attachment to their 'natural class party'. Better education and a less deferential style of political reporting in the media were also cited as factors in partisan dealignment. Yet political parties themselves bore some responsibility for the weakening of party identification. In the

1970s, Conservative and Labour governments failed to deliver on policy commitments (or voters believed that they had not 'delivered') or arrest the UK's economic decline. Opinion polls registered declining levels of satisfaction with the performance of the main parties and their leaders. Furthermore, gaps emerged between the ideological positions of the main parties and their supporters. Labour moved to the left in the late 1970s, while the Conservatives shifted to the right after Margaret Thatcher became party leader in 1975. Many voters committed to the post-war consensus defected to the Liberals or the Social Democratic Party (SDP), which was formed in 1981 by disillusioned Labour moderates. The Liberal/SDP Alliance won 25 per cent of the vote in 1983 but was denied a breakthrough at Westminster by the simple plurality electoral system (see Chapter 17). A new centre party also briefly appeared in 2019, when some Labour moderates, disillusioned with the state of the party under Jeremy Corbyn's leadership (or lack of!), left to form an 'Independent Group' – which then became Change UK – joined by three senior pro-European Conservatives similarly disaffected with their party under Theresa May (see Chapter 14).

Consequences of dealignment

Class and partisan dealignment posed particular problems for the Labour Party. The decline in the size of the working class, and divisions within what remained of it, meant that Labour's core vote was shrinking. Between 1979 and 1992, Labour lost four general elections, averaging just 32 per cent of the vote. Its share of the skilled working-class (C2) vote fell from the 49 per cent it achieved when winning the October 1974 election to 32 per cent in 1983 (see Table 18.4). This seemed a damning refutation of those on the Left who repeatedly argued that Labour's declining working class support was due to the Party's failure to offer 'true' Socialist policies.

The Conservatives and Labour (belatedly) reacted to dealignment by adapting their ideology and targeting groups of voters beyond their core support. From the late 1970s, Thatcher's populist brand of capitalism attracted support from the new working class, with policies such as lower income taxes and the sale of council houses which matched its aspirations. Support for the Conservatives among skilled working-class voters rose from 25 per cent in October 1974 to an average of 40 per cent between 1979 and 1992. In the 1990s, New Labour strategists recognised that the party had to extend its appeal to skilled workers and middle-class voters in southern England. Middle-class (ABC1) support for Labour increased from just 16 per cent in 1983 to 34 per cent in 1997. In the early 1990s, Labour won support from middle-class voters who worked in the public sector and regarded Thatcherism as hostile to the National Health Service (NHS), local government, and state education. Under Tony Blair, it also attracted support from middle-class voters who worked in the private sector and felt that New Labour could be trusted to manage the economy.

Recent elections have provided further confirmation of class and partisan dealignment. Support for Labour increased across all social groups in 1997, but its most significant gains were among middle-class voters where it enjoyed a 12-point increase in support. Labour maintained its cross-class appeal in 2001 and 2005, though its working-class vote declined by ten points. The Conservatives made gains among working-class voters (C2 support was up 7 per cent between 1997 and 2005) but continued to lose ground among professional and managerial voters (down a further 3 per cent between 1997 and 2005). The 2001 and 2005 elections thus produced a pattern that ran counter to the post-war norm: the Conservatives made gains among working-class voters but lost further middle-class support, while Labour experienced sharper falls in its working-class

TABLE 18.4 Class voting since 1974

Party	Middle class (ABC1)	Skilled working class (C2)	Unskilled working class (DE)
Conservative			
1974 (Oct.)	56	26	22
1979	59	41	34
1983	55	40	33
1987	54	40	30
1992	54	39	31
1997	39	27	21
2001	38	29	24
2005	37	33	25
2010	39	37	31
2015	41	32	27
2017	46	45	38
2019	43	49	47
Labour			
1974 (Oct.)	19	49	57
1979	24	41	49
1983	16	32	41
1987	18	36	48
1992	22	40	49
1997	34	50	59
2001	34	49	55
2005	31	40	48
2010	27	29	40
2015	28	32	40
2017	38	41	47
2019	33	31	34

Source: Ipsos MORI, www.ipsos-mori.com; ABC1 figures for 2015 compiled from a reweighted aggregate of YouGov polls (our thanks to Professor Denver for providing these data); data for 2017 and 2019 from Ipsos MORI, www.ipsos-mori.com.

vote than its middle-class vote. In 2010, despite Labour's attack on the privileged social background of David Cameron and many of his senior colleagues, the trend continued; the Conservative improvement was most marked among working-class voters; while Labour's support held up reasonably well in the middle-class categories, its working-class vote took a further plunge. The most interesting feature of the 2015 general election was an increasing class polarisation among women: in the highest social categories (AB), Conservative support rose by 10 percentage points (largely, it seems, at the expense of the Liberal Democrats), while among those in the C2 category a fall of 7 percentage points in Conservative support was mirrored by a Labour rise of 8 points.

Meanwhile, in the 2017 general election – which Labour contested on a notably left-wing manifesto (redolent of 1983) – Labour's support among the ABC1s rose by 10 points, from 28 per cent in 2015 to 38 per cent, while the Conservatives' support among the C2/DEs in 2017 was 12 points higher than that in 2015. In the 2019 general election, Labour's ABC1 support fell by five points, while the Conservatives' support among the C2/DEs further increased, from 42 per cent to 48 per cent: by 2019, almost half of the British working class was voting

Conservative. Also, after decades of growing support for 'third' parties (see next paragraph), the 2017 election was notably for the renewed strength of the Labour and Conservative Parties, who won a combined total of 82.4 per cent of votes cast, although the SNP remained the largest Party in Scotland, winning 35 out of the 59 Scottish seats.

Another major consequence of dealignment since the 1970s has been the increased electoral support enjoyed by 'third' parties (see Chapter 14), with the SDP/Liberal Alliance winning seven million votes in the 1983 general election (just one million fewer than the Labour Party), while in 2010 the Liberal Democrats won almost seven million votes. Then in the 2015 general election, the United Kingdom Independence Party (UKIP) won almost four million votes, while the Green Party was supported by just over a million voters. However, a major problem encountered by 'third' parties in general elections is that Britain's First-Past-The-Post electoral system means that the number of votes won in general elections has not been matched by the number of seats won in the House of Commons. For example, seven million votes won by Liberal Democrats in 2010 represented 23 per cent of votes cast, yet they only won 57 seats out of 650 in the House of Commons, which constituted just under 9 per cent. Meanwhile, the four million votes won by UKIP in 2015 represented 12.6 per cent of votes cast nationally, yet they only had one MP elected.

A further consequence of dealignment has been increased electoral volatility: as voters are less attached to a particular political party, so they are more willing to 'switch' their votes – voting for Party A in one election, Party B in the next. This increased volatility has actually had two specific consequences. First, it has meant that the 'swing' between the main parties from one election to the next has often become larger than in the 1950s and 1960s (when alignment meant that far fewer people 'switched' their support in each election). For example, in the 1950s, the maximum 'swing' between Labour and the Conservatives was 1.7 per cent; in 1979, the Conservatives won with a swing of 5.4 per cent from Labour; and in 1997, New Labour won with a swing of 10 per cent from the Conservatives since 1992. However, as Britain has moved away from a two-party system, so the 'swing' has often been less marked, because voters have often 'switched' from Labour or Conservative to a 'third' party, rather than simply between the two largest parties.

The second consequence of increased electoral volatility has been that for many voters, the decision about which party to support has been made during the election campaign itself. Clearly, when the vast majority of voters were 'aligned' to a particular political party in the 1950s and 1960s, most of them knew how they were going to vote long before the campaign began; there was little or no decision to reach. Since then, however, increasing numbers of voters have made their minds up during the campaign itself. This is clearly illustrated in Table 18.5 (based on

TABLE 18.5 When voters decided which party to vote for in the 2017 and 2019 general elections (%)

	2017	2019
On polling day itself	15	16
In the last few days	10	10
In the last week	8	8
In the last month	19	24
Since beginning of the year	9	9
More than a year ago	8	7
Always knew	30	28

Source: For 2017, http://lordashcroftpolls.com/wp-content/uploads/2017/06/GE-post-vote-poll-Full-tables.pdf, page 11, Table 4; for 2019, https://lordashcroftpolls.com/2019/12/how-britain-voted-and-why-my-2019-general-election-post-vote-poll/.

in-depth post-election surveys conducted by Lord Ashcroft), which shows at which stage of the campaign voters made their decision about how to vote in the 2017 and 2019 general elections.

Not only do these figures illustrate the scale and significance of dealignment in recent general elections, but they also illustrate how important the campaigns themselves have become, as many voters make their decision on the basis of how the parties or their leaders perform in the weeks leading up to polling day, and how credible their policy pledges are judged to be. For the parties themselves, this means that the election campaigns have become more important, and this is reinforced by 24/7 news coverage and social media.

One other consequence of dealignment has been an overall decline in electoral turnout in recent decades, although there has been a modest recovery in the most recent elections. Back in 1950, turnout had been (a never to be repeated) 83.9 per cent, but by 2001 it had fallen to just 59 per cent. It subsequently increased somewhat thereafter, such that in the last four general elections (2010, 2015, 2017, and 2019), turnout has been in the 65–69 per cent range. It is often assumed that lower electoral turnout, compared to 60 years ago, is a sign of increasing apathy and political disengagement. For some non-voters, this is certainly true, but it is important to recognise that **not** voting in a general election might be a conscious and rational decision. The non-voter might reason that their vote will not make any difference, or they might claim that they do not like the candidates, parties, or policies on offer: 'they're all the same' or 'they're as bad as each other'. It is also the case that for some citizens in recent decades, political engagement has taken different forms, other than simply voting for a party: involvement in social movements and direct action have increased – Occupy [London], anti-fracking protests, demonstrations against climate change, #MeToo, anti-Brexit marches and rallies, etc. (see Chapter 19). These are all 'political', but go far beyond the narrow definition of party politics associated with five-yearly general elections, and as such, they are often viewed as more meaningful or worthwhile by those involved, although obviously they might also vote in elections too.

Other social factors

Several other social factors are also relevant to voting behaviour. There are, for example, important regional variations in voting in Britain (as noted in Chapter 4). No party can convincingly claim to be strong across the whole country. A 'north-south' divide in electoral geography has become more pronounced in the last 40 years, as Conservative support has become concentrated in the south of England, the suburbs and rural areas, whereas the Conservatives' share of the vote in northern England and the Midlands fell by more than 10 per cent in the 1997 general election, when the Party also ended up with no seats in Scotland or Wales. The Conservatives have recovered somewhat in these areas since, winning 11 seats in Wales in 2015, and 14 in 2019, while in Scotland, the 2017 election saw the Conservatives win 13 seats – almost twice as many as Labour. The one exception to recent Conservative dominance (hegemony) in the southern half of England has been London: in 2015, for example, Labour won 45 seats in the capital compared to the Conservatives' 27, although the Conservatives did win the elections for the London Mayor in 2008 and 2012 (when Boris Johnson was the Party's successful candidate).

Beyond parts of London, Labour's traditional electoral strongholds were Scotland, Wales, and northern England, in large urban or inner-city areas, and council estates. For example, in the 2001 election, Labour won 32 (out of 36) seats in northern England, 60 (out of 70) in the north-west, and 47 (out of 56) in Yorkshire and Humberside. Labour also won 56 seats in Scotland (compared to the Conservatives' one), and 34 of Wales' 40 parliamentary seats. However, since

2010, these erstwhile Labour strongholds have succumbed to strong challenges from other parties. In 2015, for example, an enormous surge in support for the SNP saw the Party win 56 seats, while Labour lost 40, ending up with just one MP north of the border. Meanwhile, although Labour still won a majority of seats in the northern districts of England, it did so less emphatically, as the Conservatives made inroads in some of these seats. For example, in Yorkshire and Humberside, Labour saw its number of seats fall to 33 while the Conservatives won 19, and in the north-west, the respective tallies were 51 and 22; the red tide of 1997 and 2001 was ebbing, and an increasing number of blue islands were being revealed. However, it was in 2019 that Labour's northern 'red wall' collapsed most spectacularly, when many working-class voters, impatient to 'get Brexit done' and unimpressed (to put it mildly) with Jeremy Corbyn as Labour leader, switched to the Conservatives. As a consequence, many of Labour's formerly 'safe' northern seats returned a Conservative MP, such as Blyth Valley, Burnley, Darlington, Dewsbury, Keighley, Redcar, Scunthorpe, Wakefield, and Workington.

Regional patterns of support are sometimes a result of variations at constituency level. Different types of people, neighbourhoods, and constituencies are concentrated in different parts of the country. The Conservatives perform best in rural or predominantly white-collar constituencies, and those with relatively high numbers of home-owners and pensioners. Many of the most prestigious or highly paid jobs are in southern England, particularly in London itself, with many of those employed in such jobs commuting from the adjacent 'home counties' – such as Berkshire, Hertfordshire, and Surrey – where property prices are often especially high. Not surprisingly, these are staunchly Conservative areas. Similarly, there is a relatively high elderly population in many 'retirement towns' on the Essex or south (English Channel) coast, such as Bexhill, Bognor Regis, Budleigh Salterton, Clacton, Frinton-on-Sea, Poole, and Worthing, and these have generally been rock-solid safe Conservative seats for decades. By contrast, Labour has traditionally been most successful in constituencies which have high levels of socio-economic deprivation, many of which are found in inner cities or former 'mill towns' in northern England, or in ex-mining towns in South Wales. Differences within regions can also be pronounced: Greater London contains some of the poorest, as well as the richest parts of the UK. Local campaigns may also be important, as in south-west England where the Liberal Democrats were effective in local and parliamentary elections, at least until the party decided to join the Conservatives in coalition in 2010.

There has also often been a political division based on gender, as the Conservatives have generally attracted more support than Labour among women voters. In the mid-twentieth century this gender gap was said to reflect social attitudes of the time (e.g. support for the family unit, Labour's 'macho' image and rhetoric as the Party of men working in heavy industry) and the low numbers of women in the workforce. However, the Conservatives' lead among women voters disappeared in the 1990s and early 2000s, when Labour led the Conservatives by 44-32 and 42-33 respectively (see Table 18.6). This lead proved temporary, though, because from 2010 onwards, the Conservatives regained their lead over Labour among women voters, although in 2017, this was only by one point, but then it increased to nine points in 2019. It should be noted, though that in all general elections since 2010, more men than women voted Conservative; while the Conservatives have regained their lead among women voters over Labour, their lead over Labour among men is considerably higher – in 2019, it was 15 points.

Meanwhile, older voters have been more likely to support the Conservatives, while younger voters are more likely to vote Labour. This demographic or age-cohort pattern was especially evident in 2019, as illustrated by Table 18.7. Whereas 62 per cent of people in the age group of 18–24 voted Labour, only 17 per cent of those aged 65+ did so, yielding a Labour lead of 43 among those in the 18–24 cohort. Conversely, whereas only 19 per cent of those aged 18–24

TABLE 18.6 Gender and voting since 1974

	Men	Women
Conservative		
1974 (Oct.)	32	39
1979	43	47
1983	42	46
1987	43	43
1992	41	44
1997	31	32
2001	32	33
2005	34	32
2010	38	36
2015	38	37
2017	44	43
2019	46	44
Labour		
1974 (Oct.)	43	38
1979	40	35
1983	30	26
1987	32	32
1992	37	44
1997	45	44
2001	42	42
2005	34	38
2010	28	31
2015	30	33
2017	40	42
2019	31	35

Source: Ipsos MORI, www.ipsos-mori.com; You, Gov https://yougov.co.uk/topics/politics/articles-reports/2019/12/17/how-britain-voted-2019-general-election.

TABLE 18.7 Voting by age cohort in the 2019 general election

Age group	Conservative	Labour	Lib Dem	Other	Cons lead over Labour
18–24	19	62	9	10	–43
25–34	27	51	11	11	–24
35–44	36	39	13	12	–3
45–54	46	28	14	12	+18
55–64	49	27	11	13	+22
65+	64	17	11	8	+47

Source: Ipsos MORI, *How Britain voted in the 2019 election*, 20 December 2020 https://www.ipsos.com/ipsos-mori/en-uk/how-britain-voted-2019-election.

voted Conservative, 64 per cent of those aged 65+ supported the Conservatives, thereby giving the Conservatives a lead of 47. It is commonly assumed that the Conservative lead among older voters is due to life-cycle changes, whereby people lose their youthful idealism and desire to change the world as they take on more responsibilities at home and in work, and perhaps acquire a material stake in society (mortgage, investments, savings) which they are afraid of losing in their sunset years. However, this popular or 'common sense' view has been challenged by the notion of 'generational cohorts', which argues that the main reason why older people tend to vote Conservative is that they were brought up by parents who themselves voted Conservative due to the absence of a viable Labour Party in the early twentieth century (the first proper Labour government not being until 1945). As such, it might be that many of today's Conservative-voting pensioners have not become Conservative with age, but have always been Conservative, because that is how they were raised. If true, this theory implies that in the next couple of decades, the Conservatives' inbuilt support among older voters will decline, as today's middle-aged voters reach old age, having perhaps voted Labour or Liberal Democrat all their adult lives.

A further possible factor might be that political events in an individual's younger years then shape their long-term political attitudes. For example, older voters might fondly recall Britain as it was before it joined the European Economic Community, or before it became a multicultural society, or before the liberalisation or legalisation of abortion, divorce, and same-sex relationships (until 1967, sexual activity between men was unlawful, and those caught could be sent to prison), or before the abolition of the death penalty and conscription (compulsory military service for young people, to teach discipline). Many older voters hold strict or 'conservative' moral views, and thus disapprove of these changes; indeed, they might well blame them for many of the social problem Britain faces in the twenty-first century, and hence want to turn the clock back to an apparent Golden Age when, they believe, things were much better than they are today.

One other important aspect of the electoral age divide is turnout, because traditionally a much larger proportion of older people have actually turned out to vote. Political parties are increasingly targeting those approaching and above pensionable age. For example, in 2019, turnout among 18–24-year-olds was 47 per cent, while the figure for those over 65 was 74 per. Moreover, due to the post-war (1945) 'baby boom', and also people living longer due to better healthcare and lifestyles, there are more older voters anyway (they outnumber the 18–24 age cohort, for sure), and the fact that pensioners are much more likely to vote in elections has, in effect, given the Conservatives a double advantage.

Religion formed an important political and social cleavage in the UK until the mid-twentieth century. Anglicans were more likely to support the Conservative Party, originally in part, because of its opposition to Home Rule for Ireland (favoured by Irish Catholics), whereas the Liberals were favoured by non-conformists. The Conservatives were able to win industrial seats in the west of Scotland into the 1960s, thanks to the support of working-class Protestants. Since then the decline of religion in public life has weakened (though certainly not eradicated) the relationship between religious denomination and voting. According to YouGov, in the 2017 election (the relevant data for 2019 were not available at the time of writing), 58 per cent of Church of England/Anglicans voted Conservative, compared with 28 per cent voting Labour – although this might have been because Anglicanism has traditionally been more prevalent among the middle class (i.e. was it social class or religion which underpinned this party allegiance?) – whereas 42 per cent of Catholics supported Labour, compared with 40 per cent voting Conservative. Labour enjoyed a much more extensive lead in 2017 among Muslims, with 85 per cent reporting a vote for Labour, compared to 11 per cent voting Conservative. However, the Conservatives were much more popular among Jewish voters, enjoying a lead of 63/26 over Labour – a lead almost certainly boosted by the anti-semitism allegations which the Labour Party was increasingly subject to from 2016 onwards. Indeed, it is reasonable to assume that the Conservative Party's support among Jews will have increased further in 2019, and Labour's correspondingly diminished. As we saw in Chapter 12, religion remains extremely important in Northern Ireland, where most Protestants vote for Unionist parties and most Roman Catholics for nationalist parties.

According to the latest census, the UK's non-white population constitutes about 13 per cent of the population, and so political parties have boosted their efforts to attract ethnic minority voters in recent years, although the effectiveness of these campaigns is open to question. In *Race and British Electoral Politics* (London: Routledge, 1997), Shamit Saggar noted that ethnic minority electors tend to vote on class lines (many were in low-paid occupations) rather than on the basis of 'race' issues. In 2019, Ipsos MORI report that among BAME voters, Labour led the Conservatives by 64 per cent to 20 per cent, while 12 per cent of these voters supported the Liberal Democrats, although it is very important to emphasise that ethnic minority voters should not be viewed as a single, homogeneous, social group.

Rational choice approaches

Thus a range of social factors continued to influence voting behaviour in recent general elections, whereas class, age, gender, religion, and ethnicity tend to be *long-term* factors. Models of voting behaviour that focus on the social characteristics of voters downplay the significance of short-term political factors. They assume that voters have stable partisan loyalties and tend to vote for the same party throughout their lives. This approach is also *deterministic*, because it rather implies that voting behaviour is determined by an individual's upbringing, background, and position within society. Yet as we have already noted, to some extent, sociological and demographic approaches to voting behaviour have been rendered far less persuasive by class and partisan dealignment.

Rational Choice Theory

a theory that interprets political behaviour on the basis that individuals act rationally and explore the costs and benefits of their actions before reaching decisions.

Alternative approaches to voting behaviour, drawing upon **rational choice theory**, put the individual voter at the heart of their analysis. They focus on the processes whereby voters decide which party to support in each general election. Individuals are assumed to make informed political choices by examining the relative merits of the main parties and their policies, and/or judging which party will make them materially better-off. Understanding voting behaviour in this way means considering several short-term factors, most notably:

- issues
- party leaders
- the economy
- governing competence.

The most convincing explanations of recent election outcomes focus on voters' perceptions of the key issues facing them, their families, or/and the country generally, the competence of the main parties, and the extent to which their leaders are judged to be competent, reliable, trustworthy, or 'Prime Ministerial'. This is a diluted variant of the rational choice approach, based on the view that voters draw on such perceptions, rather than a deeply considered appraisal of manifestos, for example, when making judgements about issues and election campaigns.

Issues

The notion of issue voting means that many people now decide how to vote by comparing the policies put forward by political parties on key issues, particularly as many voters have become 'dealigned' from a particular party. To have a significant impact on the outcome of an election, issue voting involves a number of factors or processes: a significant number of voters identify a particular issue as being important; they recognise differences in the policies put forward by the main parties on the issue; they identify one of the parties as having the best or most credible (feasible or realistic) policy on that issue and vote for it accordingly. Prior to 2017, most voters ranked 'the economy' or 'economic management' as the most important issue, usually followed by the NHS, and education. Between 1979 and 1992, the Conservative Party enjoyed a strong lead over Labour as the party which had the best policies/policies for managing the economy, and therefore of delivering the economic growth and prosperity on which employment and higher living standards depended, and, in turn, a higher volume of tax revenues with which to fund public services and pensions. However, economic problems in the early 1990s, Britain's enforced withdrawal from the European Exchange Rate Mechanism (ERM) in September 1992, and Tony Blair's 'modernisation' of the Labour Party from 1994 onwards meant that in 1997, 2001, and 2005, the Conservatives were less trusted than New Labour on the key issue of economic trust or competence. However, following the global financial crash in 2008, 'normal service' was resumed, with the Conservatives once again more trusted than Labour on the issue of 'economic competence' in the 2010, 2015, 2017, and 2019 general elections. The Conservatives have also been much more trusted than Labour on issues such as defence, immigration (strictly controlling), and law and order (a tough stance on crime and punishment), whereas Labour has usually enjoyed a strong lead over the Conservatives on issues such as education and (defending) the NHS.

There are, however, a number of problems with the issue voting model. First, general elections are rarely decided on the basis of a single issue. It is also likely that voters will favour some of a party's policies, but dislike others (e.g. many Labour voters never really agreed with the Party's pre-1994 or post-2015 commitment to extending public ownership/nationalisation of industries). Many voters will not even be aware of detailed policy commitments, particularly because very few people actually read the parties' manifestos.

Analysis 18.2

Valence issues

Following the above discussion about 'issue voting' we turn to the closely related concept of 'valence voting', which was originally developed by Donald Stokes (see, e.g., 'Spatial Models of Party Competition', *American Political Science Review*, Vol. 57, No. 2 (1963), pp. 368–77). This approach differs from the issue voting model (or the spatial model) which focuses on issues whereby the main political parties offer *rival* programmes, and instead considers voters' perceptions or judgements about the *competence* of parties to deliver the desired policy goal(s). Voters form judgements about the likelihood of political parties delivering low inflation, higher employment, low levels of crime, wider home-ownership, quality healthcare, better (or better-funded) education, national security, and so on. To enhance their prospects of election success, political parties concentrate on those valence issues on which they are viewed by the public as being the party most likely to achieve policy success: the Conservatives have often given prominence to economic issues, while Labour has highlighted social issues, most notably education and the NHS.

The valence model has been employed convincingly in studies of several recent British general elections, notably by the British Election Study team, H. Clarke, D. Sanders, M. Stewart, and P. Whiteley, in *Political Choice in Britain* (Oxford: Oxford University Press, 2004), and more recently *Affluence, Austerity and Electoral Change in Britain* (Oxford: Oxford University Press, 2013). In 2001 and 2005, Labour and the Conservatives put forward similar policies on the economy and public services, but more voters judged Labour to be the Party most likely to deliver a strong and stable economy and better public services. In 2010, there was greater divergence between the party programmes, especially on the economy where the Conservatives put forward a radical plan for budget deficit reduction. Five years later, ironically, it could be argued that in practice the Conservatives had implemented Labour's more gradual approach to deficit reduction; but, for a variety of reasons, David Cameron and George Osborne were credited by the voters with more economic 'competence' than Labour's Ed Miliband and Ed Balls.

However, in 2017, there was a stark departure from the 'valence voting' of recent general elections, as Conservative and Labour voters clearly prioritised different issues, as illustrated in Table 18.8.

Clearly, for almost half of Conservative voters, the most important or 'salient' issue in the 2017 election was Brexit, followed by who would be the best prime minister. Austerity/public spending cuts, poverty/inequality, and education (including student fees) simply weren't considered important, or acknowledged as a problem. By contrast, a third of Labour voters cited the NHS/hospitals as the most important issue, followed by austerity and cuts in public spending. For Labour voters, Brexit was the third most important issue, closely followed by poverty and inequality.

In the 2019 general election, Brexit – 'getting Brexit done' – was again cited as the most important issue by Conservatives, but this time their number had risen to 72 per cent, although this time 41 per cent of Conservatives cited the NHS as an important issue, followed by economic competence, best political leadership, and (curbing) immigration. Among Labour's 2019 voters, 74 per cent prioritised the NHS, while the second most important issue (cited by 28 per cent)

TABLE 18.8 Ranking of issues, in terms of their importance, by Labour and Conservative voters in the 2017 election (% citing as most important)

Issues	Labour	Conservative
NHS/hospitals	33	3
Austerity/cuts in public expenditure	11	0
Brexit	8	48
Poverty/inequality/homelessness	7	0
Economy/jobs/employment/growth	6	11
Education/schools/universities/HE fees	6	0
Welfare benefits/tax credits	4	1
Political leadership/best prime minister	4	13
Pensions/social care	4	1
Terrorism/national security	3	7
Immigration/migrants/asylum seekers	3	9

Source: Ashcroft. *How did this result happen? My post-vote survey*, 2017, available at: //lordashcroftpolls.com/2017/06/result-happen-post-vote-survey/.

was 'stopping Brexit', followed by poverty/inequality, public spending cuts, and climate change (see Lord Ashcroft's post-election polling, available at https://lordashcroftpolls.com/2019/12/how-britain-voted-and-why-my-2019-general-election-post-vote-poll/). That a significant proportion of Labour voters cited issues such as poverty and inequality, and climate change was indicative of the emergence – or increased importance – of new issues in the twenty-first century, and how these were impacting upon party support.

New issue cleavages?

As the class cleavage that underpinned the post-war party system faded due to class and partisan dealignment, new issue cleavages structured around identity politics have emerged. Identity politics is crucial to an understanding of the rise of the Scottish National Party and Plaid Cymru, while also helping to explain the decline of, first, the Scottish Conservative Party and then, more recently, the Labour Party, both parties failing to persuade voters that they were adequately representing Scottish interests and identity. Identity issues are also critical to the party system in Northern Ireland (see Chapter 12). Overall, though, despite impacting on party competition significantly in some regions of the UK, identity politics has not opened up an overall political cleavage equivalent to the class cleavage of the early post-war period, or (as yet, despite the SNP surge of 2015) brought about a fundamental realignment in the UK party system. However, some critics have argued that one of the reasons for Labour's poor performance in 2019 was that the Party's predominantly middle-class left-wing mass membership, especially its activists, had recently prioritised identity politics in terms of campaigning against racism, sexism, homophobia, and transphobia, and that this protection or promotion of the rights of 'oppressed' or discriminated-against racial and sexual minorities had alienated some of Labour's former working-class supporters, who felt that the Party had ceased to defend or represent them.

Immigration and European integration have featured prominently in recent general elections, with the former having risen up the political agenda periodically, in the 1970s and again since the late 2000s, although in these two periods, the origins of the immigrants were different: in the late 1970s, there was concern about the scale of immigration from parts of the Caribbean, India, and Pakistan, whereas more recently the main concern has been migrants from parts of Eastern Europe, most notably Poland and Romania, following the expansion of the EU in 2004 and 2007. In the 1970s, the political beneficiary of such concern was the National Front (subsequently superseded by the BNP) before the Conservatives, in 1979, stole their thunder by promising tough curbs on immigration (whereupon electoral support for the National Front crumbled), whereas the more recent 'moral panic' about immigration has benefitted UKIP and then the Brexit Party. The Conservatives have always been ready to satisfy popular concerns by adopting authoritarian or hard-line positions on immigration and asylum seekers – while accusing Labour of being 'a soft touch' – varying only in the degree of subtlety or strength of rhetoric which they have used. Immigration was the issue on which the Conservatives enjoyed their biggest lead (41 points) over Labour in 2005, although on this occasion, it did not persuade significant numbers of voters to switch directly from Labour to the Conservatives, partly because the issue itself did not rank highly enough compared to more 'salient' issues, and perhaps, also, because New Labour responded with its own tough measures and populist rhetoric (in 2009, Gordon Brown publicly pledged to 'create British jobs for British workers').

The issue of Britain's relationship with the EU was seen as a potential vote winner by the Conservatives before the 1997 and 2001 elections. Conservative policy on membership of the European single currency – one of flat rejection – was more popular than Labour's 'maybe, if the conditions are right' approach. Yet the Conservatives did not reap significant electoral rewards; indeed, Conservative divisions on the issue seriously damaged the party in 1997. A 'save the pound' message featured prominently in the 2001 Tory election campaign, but Europe was ranked only tenth among voter concerns in that election. The Conservatives did gain some ground among elderly and working-class voters, but the Eurosceptic position – and William Hague's portrayal of Britain becoming 'a foreign land' under Labour – also reinforced perceptions, among many other voters, that the Conservatives were extreme and 'out of touch'. Europe barely figured in the 2005 general election campaign, in part because Labour had promised a referendum on the EU Constitutional (Lisbon) Treaty. In 2009, David Cameron carried out his threat to withdraw his MEPs from the pro-EU European People's Party in the European Parliament, but before the end of the year he had to renege on his promise to hold a referendum on the Lisbon Treaty, which had already been ratified by all the member states. In the 2010 election campaign, he argued that the Conservatives could 'repatriate' (return) some of the powers which had passed to the EU since 1973, although informed observers understood that his efforts were highly unlikely to succeed. By 2015, Cameron had been induced to promise an 'in-out' referendum if re-elected; despite considerable media pressure, Labour Ed Miliband resisted a similar pledge. That the EU had become a major issue for some voters in 2015 was evident from the fact that UKIP won four million votes.

Controversy 18.1

Who supported UKIP?

UKIP is in many respects a very interesting phenomenon in recent British politics. Founded in 1992, as the Anti-Federalist League, it fielded 17 candidates in that year's general election and attracted 0.01 per cent of the overall UK vote (around 0.5 per cent per candidate). In 1997, it ran in nearly 200 constituencies, recording an average vote of just over 1 per cent. By 2005, it was able to contest 496 seats, but although its average performance had continued to improve, it still only won an average of 2.16 per cent of the vote in each seat. Its results in by-elections were equally uninspiring – until the contest at Hartlepool in September 2004, when it topped 10 per cent of the vote. In that year, UKIP achieved much greater national prominence through a third placing in the European Parliamentary elections. Five years later, in the same elections it finished runner-up behind the Conservatives in terms of vote share, matching Labour's tally of MEPs (13). The 2014 EP election turned out to be a three-cornered contest (despite the usual low turnout), and UKIP narrowly beat both the Conservatives and Labour (with 27.5 per cent of the UK vote).

In by-elections held in October and November of 2014, UKIP won two of the three seats, finishing a close second in the other one (the supposedly 'safe' Labour constituency of Heywood and Middleton). The party had briefly been represented at Westminster in 2008 by the Conservative defector Bob Spink. The successful candidates of 2014 (Douglas Carswell and Mark Reckless) were also former Conservative MPs, and their victories caused considerable unease within their former party. It was also ominous for the Conservatives that at a time when their own party membership was falling, UKIP was proving adept at attracting new recruits.

The rise of UKIP had not passed unnoticed among political scientists. Before the European elections of 2014, Robert Ford and Matthew Goodwin had published a detailed study (*Revolt on the Right – Explaining Support for the Radical Right in Britain:* London, Routledge, 2014). The authors argued that UKIP was an electoral threat to Labour, as well as the Conservatives, since it appealed to traditional working-class voters who felt increasingly alienated by Labour, and the Left's apparent obsession with 'identity politics' (the rights of racial and sexual minorities and oppressed). Their research coincided with other findings, which indicated that the typical UKIP supporter would be male, middle-aged or older, white, and with lower educational qualifications than the average Briton. UKIP was attractive to some of the relatively affluent AB social category, but drew significant support from the skilled working class (the C2s which had rallied behind Margaret Thatcher); a large proportion were home-owners (although this was not surprising given the age profile of UKIP supporters). UKIP's electoral appeal was enhanced further by its charismatic and 'populist' leader, Nigel Farage, who cultivated the image of an anti-politician politician and anti-EU patriot who was 'out there' with ordinary people against the allegedly corrupt or self-serving liberal elites who looked down with disdain at the voters from inside their Westminster bubble – even though Farage himself was a public school-educated, commodities trader in 'the City'.

Despite winning just one seat in 2015 – Douglas Carswell's Clacton South – UKIP won four million votes (a share of almost 13 per cent nationally), and came second in 120 constituencies, faring particularly well in the North East (14 per cent of the overall vote), Yorkshire and Humberside, and Eastern England (outside London, where the party's appeal was limited). Whatever the precise impact of UKIP on Labour's electoral fortunes, its performance clearly verified pre-election warnings that its rise would hurt that party as badly as the Conservatives; indeed, there was evidence that UKIP's ability to attract disillusioned Conservatives had 'peaked' at the time of the 2014 European elections, whereas it had obvious potential to eat still further into Labour's support base. After the 2015 election, UKIP certainly had established itself as something like the ultimate party of protest against the 'career politicians' who inhabited the 'Westminster bubble'; apart from attracting support from the Conservatives and Labour, it was 'respectable' enough to draw in protest voters who previously supported the Liberal Democrats, while being sufficiently radical in its anti-immigrant rhetoric to satisfy voters who had been left without a natural home since the virtual extinction of the BNP.

Following the Leave victory in the 2016 EU referendum (see Chapter 13), Farage resigned as UKIP leader, although he re-appeared as leader of the new Brexit Party in 2019, to provide a political voice for those who were frustrated that the Conservative Party had failed to deliver Brexit three years after the referendum. In the meantime, UKIP continued, but as a much weaker political entity without Farage's leadership and 'media savvy' skills, and prone to bitter leadership clashes and infighting.

Party leaders

During the era of alignment, political scientists and psephologists paid little attention to the role of party leadership in influencing how people voted, because it was widely accepted that social class and partisan identification or loyalty were the main influences. In recent years, however, with the increase in dealignment, and alongside the rise in issue and valence voting, voter perceptions of party leaders have been recognised as highly significant factors in shaping electoral choice. Voters

TABLE 18.9 Party leadership ratings in elections since
1992 (leader of winning party in bold)

1992	
John Major	**38**
Neil Kinnock	27
Paddy Ashdown	20
1997	
Tony Blair	**40**
John Major	23
Paddy Ashdown	15
2001	
Tony Blair	**51**
William Hague	14
Charles Kennedy	14
2005	
Tony Blair	**40**
Michael Howard	21
Charles Kennedy	16
2010	
David Cameron[a]	**33**
Gordon Brown	29
Nick Clegg	19
2015	
David Cameron	**42**
Ed Miliband	27
Nick Clegg	6
2017	
Theresa May[b]	**50**
Jeremy Corbyn	35
Tim Farron	N/A
2019	
Boris Johnson	**37**
Jeremy Corbyn	19
Jo Swinson	14

[a] Strictly speaking, David Cameron's Conservatives did not actually win the 2010 election, because they failed to achieve an overall parliamentary majority, but the Party won the most seats, and formed a coalition government with the Liberal Democrats, whereupon Cameron did become a prime minister.

[b] May did not win outright in 2017, but the Conservative were the largest party, and she remained the prime minister.

Source: Ipsos MORI, www.ipsos-mori.com.

have become increasingly influenced by the perceived character, communication skills, credibility, empathy, and integrity of party leaders, coupled with the extent to which they can be viewed as 'Prime Ministerial' – can voters imagine a party leader as an occupant of 10 Downing Street who is capable of providing Britain with strong and effective political leadership. The increased importance attached to party leadership has been reinforced by the 24/7 media, which often focuses on what the main party leaders are doing and saying. As such, some voters use the perceived personal qualities of party leaders as a mental shortcut to help them decide which party to vote for. Table 18.9 shows how the leaders of the three main parties have been rated since 1992.

John Major was viewed as a more capable prime minister than Neil Kinnock in 1992 (38 per cent to 27 per cent) and, in a close contest, this was probably a key factor. However, by 1997, the leader of what had become New Labour, Tony Blair clearly outscored the seemingly hapless Major (40 per cent to 23 per cent), and fared even better against William Hague in 2001 (51 per cent to 14 per cent) and Michael Howard in 2005 (40 per cent to 21 per cent). When Gordon Brown finally became leader at the end of June 2007, his initial popularity was high, but by July 2008, his net satisfaction rating (those satisfied with his performance against those who were dissatisfied) had plunged to –51 per cent, according to Ipsos MORI. In April 2010, when he announced the beginning of the general election campaign, Ipsos MORI's opinion survey showed that Brown had recovered to an extent, but his rating was still only 29 per cent compared to David Cameron's rating of 33 per cent. Cameron's personal popularity increased by the time of the 2015 general election, in spite of the austerity measures imposed by the coalition government, rising to 42 per cent, while Nick Clegg's plummeted to just 6 per cent. In 2017, Jeremy Corbyn was never able to match Theresa May's overall approval rating, in spite of her poor campaign, and again in 2019, Corbyn heavily trailed Boris Johnson, in spite of strong criticism of Johnson's character and integrity by some of his former journalistic and Conservative political colleagues. Yet however unsuitable some commentators judged Johnson to be as a prime minister, Corbyn was deemed even less credible, competent or likeable. Indeed, many of Corbyn's critics in the Labour Party itself held him personally responsible for the Party's defeat (e.g. it was often claimed his name 'came up on doorsteps' when voters told Labour canvassers and campaigners why they would not be voting for the Party this time), the clear implication being that if Labour had been led by someone – almost anyone – else, it might have won, or at the very least, deprived the Conservatives of an overall majority and thus produced another Hung Parliament and coalition government.

Economic factors

Economic voting models point to a correlation between the recent performance and imminent prospects of the economy and voting behaviour. If the economy is performing well, voters are more likely to support the governing party at a general election. But it is not just objective factors such as the levels of inflation, interest rates, and employment that are important. Personal economic expectations – 'will you be better or worse off under the governing party in the next year?' – are significant. An economic voting model developed by David Sanders used various economic data (e.g. interest rates, inflation, and unemployment) and perceptions to predict election outcomes. His economic voting model predicted accurately the outcome of the 1992 general election when, despite a recession, the Conservatives convinced enough people that they were the party most likely to provide future economic prosperity, whereas many voters feared that Labour would make things worse, by taxing and spending too much, and so stalling the apparent recovery.

The economy was in better shape in 1997, but the Conservatives were still defeated heavily. Crucially, economic recovery had not been accompanied by a widespread 'feel-good factor'. Though inflation and interest rates were low, many voters were worried about their personal economic prospects, given increasing job insecurity and problems in the housing market. Nor did the Conservatives get the credit for the economic upturn. Instead, the Major government was associated with tax rises, high interest rates, and, most importantly, sterling's exit from the ERM in 1992. This collapse of their economic policy on what quickly became known as 'Black Wednesday' was a defining moment in the demise of the Conservative Party: its opinion poll ratings dropped dramatically shortly after and took over a decade to recover. More than half of voters identified the Conservatives as the best party to manage the economy at the 1992 election; by 1997 Labour was narrowly ahead.

Having persuaded voters that they could be trusted to run the economy, the Blair governments then benefited from their economic record in office. Inflation, interest rates, and unemployment levels were all lower in 2001 and 2005 than they had been in 1992 and 1997. On the issue of economic management, Labour enjoyed a 34 point lead over the Conservatives in 2001 and a 20 point lead in 2005. More voters felt that the economy would improve or stay the same than those who thought it would get worse. During these campaigns, Labour also ensured that memories of economic problems under the Conservatives remained fresh in the minds of voters.

In 2010, the economy was clearly the most important issue; although all three main parties accepted the need for a drastic reduction of the budget deficit, and thus cuts in public spending, the Conservatives proposed immediate radical action while Labour and the Liberal Democrats urged a more gradual approach. According to Ipsos MORI, 29 per cent of voters believed that the Conservatives had the best policy on economic management, a three-point lead over Labour; of course, Labour had been in government when the 2008 financial crash occurred, and so found it more difficult to retain voters' trust on the issue of economic competence in the 2010 election.

In the 2015 general election, in spite of five years of austerity and stagnant wages or standards of living for millions of ordinary voters, the Conservatives still enjoyed a lead over Labour of as much as 18 percentage points (the precise figures varied between polling companies, mainly due to slightly different survey techniques) on the issue of economic competence or trust. Much of the Conservative message in the 2015 campaign was that the 2008 financial crash had been caused by the 'reckless' public spending of the 1997–2010 Labour governments, in which Gordon Brown had been Chancellor for ten years. Regardless of the fact that the crash had originated in the US banking system, and then spread across the Atlantic, the coalition government's repeated allusions to 'clearing up Labour's mess', and claims that as chancellor, Gordon Brown had 'maxed out on the nation's credit card', persuaded many voters that electing a Labour government would result in a repeat of the 'excessive' borrowing and spending that had allegedly 'tanked' the economy in 2008: 'You don't hand the keys straight back to the driver who crashed the car', Conservatives insisted. Many voters did not particularly like the Conservatives, but they were scared of Labour, and as such, in Hilaire Beloc's words, they 'clung to nurse, for fear of something worse'.

By 2017, though, public support for austerity had declined considerably, to the extent that Labour's explicit anti-austerity economic programme, entailing higher taxes on the better-off, and some borrowing, to boost public services, infrastructure projects, and job-creation schemes, was much less of an electoral handicap than its critics (including those in the Party associated with New Labour) had anticipated. Far from the electoral annihilation that many polls and pundits predicted, the Corbyn-led Labour Party rose from 30 per cent of the vote in 2015 to 40 per cent, which was enough to deprive Theresa May's Conservatives of an overall parliamentary majority. However, in the 2019 general election, although Brexit was the main issue, Labour suffered, partly not only because of Corbyn's lack of popularity, but also because the Party's many multi-billion pound spending pledges were not viewed as credible or affordable by many voters.

It should be borne in mind that when voters prioritise economic competence, they might not view it as an alternative to improved public services or social provision, but as a perquisite of it. Rather than treating it as an either/or choice, many voters might reason that until or unless a party has secured economic stability or growth, and, in turn, higher tax revenues, it will not be able to fund increased spending on education, the NHS, or pensions. This is often one of the messages transmitted by the Conservatives; that only they have the economic competence to manage the economy successfully, and thus generate the necessary wealth and revenues to spend on public services and pensions. Hence the vital importance of proven or anticipated economic competence in shaping many voters' choice of political party from one election to the next.

Governing competence

Along with perceptions of economic competence, many voters will make a more general (retrospective) judgement about the *overall* performance of the incumbent government when deciding how to vote, and a *prospective* evaluation of the likely competence of the main opposition party; does it look and sound like a credible government-in-waiting, and would it be likely to perform better than the current administration? In *Elections and Voters in Britain* (London: Palgrave, 2nd edition, 2007), David Denver refers to this as 'judgemental voting'. If the governing party is widely perceived to have performed well in office, it will be well placed to win the next general election. Although competence in specific areas (most notably the economy, as just noted) can be very important, voter judgements on governing competence are based on many factors, including policy success, the performance of the prime minister, and party unity. Voters who lack strong partisan loyalties will respond positively to a governing party that has implemented popular policies, has presided over a healthy economy, has an effective leader, and offers a coherent vision.

Conversely, governments that are judged to have failed to achieve or display a modicum of governing competence can expect to be punished at the polls. Policy failures, weak leadership, a lack of direction, and obvious disunity will undermine a governing party's chances of securing another term in office. In a general election, voters are presented with a choice between possible alternative governments. As well as considering the government's record, voters also judge whether the main opposition party would be likely to perform better if it were in power. Consciously or not, they compare the relative merits of the parties, including their ideology, policies, leaders, and general fitness to run the country.

Case study 18.1

Tactical voting

Tactical voting occurs when voters decide to transfer their support from a favoured party to the one which is best placed to defeat the political party they like least. This was especially evident in the 1997 general election when some Labour supporters in Conservative-held constituencies where Labour came third in 1992 switched their support to the second-placed Liberal Democrats, since they had the best chance of defeating the incumbent Conservative MP. Pippa Norris estimated that tactical voting cost the Conservatives 48 seats in 1997. About one in eight electors voted tactically in 2001. Anti-Conservative tactical voting undoubtedly helped Labour and the Liberal Democrats hold on to many of the seats they won four years earlier.

The ideological proximity of Labour and the Liberal Democrats (at that time: but see Chapter 16) meant that their supporters were more willing to vote for their second-choice party in the hope of defeating the Conservatives. Effective local campaigning and media publicity also made voters more knowledgeable about the likely impact of tactical voting.

Anti-Conservative tactical voting appeared to be in decline at the 2005 general election. First, the Liberal Democrats did not make significant inroads in Conservative-held constituencies in southern England, because few Labour voters switched to them. Second, the Conservative vote increased in seats they already held, suggesting that anti-Tory tactical voting was declining. The Liberal Democrats may, however, have benefited from small-scale anti-Labour tactical voting in constituencies where they were Labour's closest challenger. In 2010, it has been argued that some Labour supporters voted Liberal Democrat in marginal constituencies which had been targeted by the Conservatives, in the hope that this would prevent David Cameron's party from securing an overall majority. If so, tactical voting succeeded, but only up to a point; rather than resulting in a Labour-led coalition, the arithmetic of the 2010 general election forced the Conservatives to seek a deal with the Liberal Democrats who had benefited from Labour's tactical voters.

In 2015, there was obvious potential for tactical voting to have a decisive effect, since another close contest was anticipated. Several newspapers and numerous websites encouraged 'vote swapping' for a variety of reasons, in a manner which suggested that voting for one's second favourite party (or, rather, voting to defeat the party one likes *least*) had become perfectly respectable in an era when few voters felt overwhelming enthusiasm for any of the options. However, the impact of tactical voting seems to have been limited. For example, while the SNP's opponents were urged to rally behind the best-placed pro-Union candidate in Scottish seats, the initiative was unsuccessful and might even have rebounded against its instigators due to the complexity of party competition in Scotland. Thus, for example, in the border constituency of Berwickshire, Roxburgh, and Selkirk, the Liberal Democrat cabinet minister Michael Moore saw his vote share fall by more than a quarter compared to 2010, and Labour also lost support. It seemed that pro-Unionist voters were rallying around the Conservatives, whose candidate had come second in 2010; but, if so, they rallied in vain, because the SNP vote share soared by 27.4 points and they took the seat by just over 300 votes. UKIP, which never had the remotest chance of winning the seat and whose candidate had won less than 600 votes in 2010, doubled its vote share to 2.4 per cent; if it had decided not to field a candidate in 2015, it is reasonable to suppose that the SNP would have lost.

In Sheffield Hallam, the constituency held by Nick Clegg, there was considerable speculation that Conservatives would vote tactically to ensure that the coalition's deputy prime minister would retain his seat. In this instance, tactical voting probably proved effective. In neighbouring Sheffield Central, the Liberal Democrat candidate almost won in 2010, with more than 40 per cent of the vote; in 2015 the party finished fourth, with less than 10 per cent. More than any local factors, this was a verdict against Nick Clegg personally, and his decision to take his party into coalition with the Conservatives; Clegg's vote in Sheffield Hallam itself fell only by 13.4 percentage points, while the Conservatives who had held second place in 2010 dropped to a very distant third. If Conservative supporters really did switch sides in a (successful) attempt to keep Clegg in parliament, their tactical decision proved pointless for two reasons: their favoured party secured an overall majority, and thus had no further need for Lib Dem support; and the overall outcome in 2015 was so bad for Clegg and his party that he immediately resigned as leader.

The press and party support

One other aspect of voting behaviour to consider in the context of dealignment is the role of the press in shaping voters' views and choice of party. After all, if traditional sources of party identity and loyalty have declined, then the press might have acquired a greater influence or importance in shaping people's political views and values, and thus their voting patterns. The overwhelming majority of Britain's national daily newspapers are (and almost always have been) strongly supportive of the Conservatives, and thus regularly publish news items, opinion pieces, and editorials which are strongly critical of the Labour Party and its leaders, a political bias which becomes even more blatant during a general election campaign. Yet, for a number of reasons, we need to be careful not to exaggerate the influence of the press on their readers' voting behaviour or political views. After all, while up to 75 per cent of Britain's national newspapers openly support the Conservatives, the Party has never won more than 44 per cent of the votes cast in general elections since 1945, not even in its mid-1980s Thatcherite heyday. Clearly, some readers of pro-Conservative newspapers do not vote in accordance with their paper's politics. This can be seen in Table 18.10, which highlights the apparent relationship between newspaper readership and party support in the 2017 general election. We say *apparent* relationship because establishing a direct or causal relationship between the newspaper some-one reads and the political party they vote for has always been problematic, partly because their political views and values can be acquired from a variety of sources and experiences, and partly because it is often difficult to determine whether someone's political allegiance derives from their newspaper, or whether their choice of newspaper is based on their political beliefs; does someone vote Conservative because they read the *Daily Mail*, or do they read the *Daily Mail* because they vote Conservative?

Certainly, as we would expect, there was a strong correlation between readership of pro-Conservative newspapers and actually voting Conservative in the 2017 general election (this has always been the case). For example, 74 per cent of *Daily Mail* readers voted Conserva-tive, while 79 per cent of *Telegraph* readers did so. Meanwhile, the vast majority of *Daily Mirror* readers (68 per cent) voted Labour, as did 73 per cent of *Guardian* readers. However, what was most notable was the sometimes sizeable minority of newspaper readers who did not vote how their paper exhorted them to do. It can be seen that in spite of the *Mail's* dire warnings of the disastrous consequences of a Corbyn-led Labour government, 17 per cent of the paper's readers still voted Labour, as did 24 per cent of *Times* readers (with a further 14 per cent backing the Liberal Democrats) and 30 per cent of *Sun* readers. Conversely, 19 per cent of *Mirror* readers sup-ported the Conservatives, as did 8 per cent of *Guardian* readers. Clearly, some readers ignored the recommendation of their newspaper about which party to vote for, perhaps because they recognised its partisan bias and 'screened' it out, or because they acquired their political views from other sources, and these proved to be more influential than what their newspaper was telling them. Moreover, some people read a particular newspaper in spite of the paper's political stance, not because of it.

TABLE 18.10 Newspaper readership and voting in 2017

	Daily Express	Daily Mail	Mirror	The Sun	Daily Telegraph	Financial Times	Guardian	Independent	Times
Labour	15	17	68	30	12	39	73	66	24
Conservative	77	74	19	59	79	40	8	15	58
UKIP	3	3	2	3	1	2	0	1	1
Lib Dem	2	3	6	3	6	14	12	12	14
Greens	2	1	1	1	1	3	3	2	2

Source: YouGov, How Britain voted at the 2017 general election, 13 June 2017, https://d25d2506sfb94s.cloudfront.net/cumulus_uploads/document/smo1w49ph1/InternalResults_170613_2017Election_Demographics_W.pdf.

Realignment or dealignment?

The elections of 1997, 2001, and 2005 were highly significant in post-war British history. For the first time, Labour won three successive victories, and on each occasion it secured sizeable parliamentary majorities. The 1997 general election was the Conservatives' worst performance in a century, and was followed by their second and fourth worst performances. The Liberal Democrats made steady progress, securing the highest number of third-party MPs for more than 70 years in 2005.

The significance of New Labour's 1997 landslide victory can be assessed by applying a typology of general elections used by electoral analysts such as Pippa Norris. It identifies three categories of election outcomes:

1. *Maintaining elections:* traditional left-right issues dominate the campaign and existing patterns of support remain largely intact.
2. *Deviating elections:* there is a temporary downturn in the normal share of the vote for the majority party, which was caused primarily by short-term issues or personalities.
3. *Critical elections:* significant and durable realignments occur in the electorate, leading to major consequences for the party system. Realignment is evident in three areas: the social basis of party support, the partisan loyalty of voters, and the ideological basis of party competition.

Critical elections are unusual occurrences, Labour's 1945 victory being the only clear post-war case in the UK. It produced Labour's first majority government, marked the rebirth of a two-party system, and paved the way for 30 years of ideological 'consensus'. The 1979 contest was certainly significant, since it marked the beginning of a new polarisation in political debate as Labour adopted more radical policies in opposition to the more abrasive ideological leadership of Margaret Thatcher. However, despite a significant challenge from the Liberal/SDP Alliance, two-party competition survived. The 1997 general election also brought important changes:

1. The social basis of party support has been markedly different since the mid-1990s. New Labour was a catch-all party with a broad appeal rather than a narrow, class-based one. It made significant gains from middle-class voters in 1997 and maintained much of this support in 2001, 2005, and 2010. Middle-class support for the Conservatives fell in each of the three contests, but they made small gains among working-class voters in 2001, 2005, and 2010.
2. The partisan loyalties of voters have declined. This phenomenon is easily detectable in opinion polls, but also in terms of 'real' votes in recent elections. An unusually large number of voters (around one million) switched directly from the Conservatives to Labour in 1997. Declining loyalties are also apparent in the low turnouts since 1997, and in the willingness of voters to support different parties at different elections. This has been evident in elections to the European Parliament (where UKIP came top of the poll in 2014) and to the Scottish Parliament, at least until the 2015 general election which apparently saw the end of widespread 'split-ticket' voting (favouring Labour in elections to the Westminster parliament, and the SNP in Scottish Parliamentary contests).
3. The ideological basis of party competition was transformed by the emergence of New Labour. It achieved this by positioning itself in the electoral centre ground – the location of the 'median voter' – and persuading voters that it could be trusted to manage the economy. By accepting the market economy and promising not to raise income tax, New Labour won over voters who were dissatisfied with the Conservatives' performance in office in the 1990s. The ideological gap between the two main parties had narrowed. Only one in five voters detected a great deal of difference between Labour and the Conservatives in 2001 and 2005. In the 1997, 2001, and 2005 elections, New Labour was positioned in the electoral centre ground with the Liberal Democrats to their left and the Conservatives placed on the right of centre.

Even before the 2010 general election, it was doubtful whether these developments represented the significant and durable realignment necessary for the 1997 contest to be labelled a 'critical election'. The trends outlined above are better viewed as further evidence of electoral *dealignment* rather than realignment. The explanatory value of class voting has continued to fall, but recent elections mark a continuation of a trend, not its beginning nor its end. New Labour's cross-class appeal and the big drop in the Conservative vote marked a sharp change from the 1979 to 1992 period in which the Tories won four successive general elections. The Conservatives' standing in the opinion polls barely moved between 1997 and 2005, hovering around the mark of 30–33 per cent. The narrowing of the gap between the two main parties after 2001 resulted mainly from a fall in support for Labour, rather than an increase in Tory support. But relatively few New Labour voters felt a strong sense of attachment to the party, as low turnout and the decline in working-class support for Labour confirmed. The proportion of people voting for the two main parties also fell in 1997, 2001, and 2005; it barely exceeded 65 per cent in 2010, and only edged up slightly in 2015 due mainly to the demise of the Liberal Democrats. In 2017, though, two-partyism seemed to have returned, as the Conservatives and Labour attracted a combined total of 82 per cent of votes cast, and although this declined again in 2019, due to a slump in Labour's support, the two parties still attracted the overwhelming majority of votes, while the Liberal Democrats made only a slow recovery from their 2015 collapse. We should be wary of drawing longer-term conclusions or extrapolating trends from the 2019 election, though, because it was a unique election, dominated by Brexit, and the unpopularity (for many voters, especially erstwhile Labour supporters) of Jeremy Corbyn.

Conclusion and summary

The 2005 general election showed the limits of Labour's electoral 'hegemony', and the result of the 2010 contest consigned the party to opposition after 13 years in office. Labour's electoral coalition of middle-class and working-class voters held together in 2001 and, to a lesser extent, 2005, but this was due to a combination of short-term factors – a healthy economy, Labour leads on key issues and the unpopularity of the Conservatives – rather than an enduring shift in partisan allegiances. The decline of Labour since 2005 has fostered a Conservative resurgence, but despite the apparent regularity in the fluctuation of party fortunes, the underlying theme has been one of electoral volatility affecting UK politics as a whole.

As we saw above, voter perceptions about the leaders of the main parties and their perceived competence, particularly in respect of their ability to manage the economy, have been crucial to the outcome of recent general elections. This factor, which had given Labour such a formidable advantage while Gordon Brown remained as chancellor, turned into a vote loser for the party almost as soon as he moved into Number 10, fuelled by his indecision on an autumn 2007 election. Valence politics – voter perceptions of government competence, and the relative merits of the party leaders – were once again set to play a decisive role. David Cameron's Conservatives racked up substantial poll leads without having to spell out their policies in great detail. As it turned out, the Conservatives did not convince enough voters to give them an overall parliamentary majority, but, as an opposition, they proved convincing enough to deny Labour a historic fourth term. As the major force in coalition with the Liberal Democrats between 2010 and 2015, they proved persuasive enough to win an overall majority in 2015 – but only just.

Voting behaviour in the UK is infinitely less predictable than was the case some 50 years ago. In the early 1960s, Labour and the Conservatives had large core constituencies composed of individuals with strong and enduring class and party loyalties. Since the 1970s, class and partisan dealignment have brought about much greater electoral volatility. Voters often make up their minds on the basis of their perceptions of governing competence. Judgements about which political party would provide a sound economy and effective public services have been critical factors in recent general elections; failing this level of political knowledge, voters take a 'short cut' by basing their decision on their perception of the rival party leaders. The three general election victories won by New Labour with its cross-class appeal suggested to some observers that there had been a 'sea-change' in voting behaviour. However, detailed analysis confirmed that the UK still has a dealigned electorate with few strong ties to the main political parties. From that perspective, the indecisive 2010 result was far less surprising than the fact that the Conservatives were able to secure a narrow overall majority in 2015. The role and scale of dealignment was further evident in the 2017 and 2019 elections, with Labour attracting a notable increase in support from those in social categories AB/C1 in 2017, while the Conservatives, in both elections, saw their share of working-class (C2/DE) support increase significantly, particularly in 2019. Moreover, in the 2017 and 2019 elections, Conservative and Labour voters generally prioritised different issues, with Brexit and immigration much more important to the former than to the latter.

Further reading

The best introductions to voting behaviour in post-war Britain are D. Denver, C. Carman, and R. Johns, *Elections and Voters in Britain* (London: Palgrave, 3rd edition, 2012) and P. Norris, *Electoral Change since 1945* (London: Blackwell, 1997). D. Denver's 'The Results: How Britain Voted', in A. Geddes and J. Tonge (eds.), *Britain Votes 2015* (Oxford: Oxford University Press, 2015) is an excellent and accessible analysis of the 2015 result. H. Clarke, D. Sanders, M. Stewart, and P. Whiteley, *Political Choice in Britain* (Oxford: Oxford University Press, 2004) is the definitive study of voting behaviour since the 1960s, but the statistical analysis is accessible only to specialists in the field. More recently, the same authors have produced *Affluence, Austerity and Electoral Change in Britain* (Oxford: Oxford University Press, 2013) which combines detailed expert analysis with accessible commentary. D. Denver and G. Hands (eds.), *Issues and Controversies in Voting Behaviour* (London: Prentice Hall, 1992) is a collection of articles which can still be consulted with profit.

For a general survey of general elections in the era of 'dealignment' designed for the general reader as well as specialists, see D. Denver and M. Garnett, *British General Elections since 1964* (Oxford: Oxford University Press, 2014). Each general election since 1945 has been the subject of a detailed study in the 'Nuffield series'. On the 2015 election, see D. Kavanagh and P. Cowley, *The British General Election of 2015* (London: Palgrave, 2015), which is very readable and contains useful statistics. A. Geddes and J. Tonge (eds.), *Britain Votes 2015* (Oxford: Oxford University Press, 2015) contains valuable insights into voting behaviour. For an examination of the 2017 election, see J. Tonge, C. Leston-Bandeira, and S. Wilks-Heeg (eds.) *Britain Votes 2017* (Oxford: Oxford University Press, 2018). For the 2019 election, see J. Bartle and N.J. Allen, *Breaking the Deadlock: Britain at the Polls, 2019* (Manchester: Manchester University Press, 2020).

For the long-running (but now apparently settled) debate on class dealignment, see A. Heath, R. Jowell, and J. Curtice, *How Britain Votes* (London: Pergamon, 1985) and the review in I. Crewe, 'On the Death and Resurrection of Class Voting', *Political Studies*, Vol. 35 (1986), pp. 620–38. The impact of social change is explored in P. Dunleavy, 'The Political Implications of Sectoral Cleavages and the Growth of State Employment', *Political Studies*, Vol. 28 (1980), pp. 364–83 and 527–49. Partisan dealignment is examined in I. Crewe and K. Thomson, 'Party Loyalties: Dealignment or Realignment', in G. Evans and P. Norris (eds.), *Critical Elections* (London: SAGE, 1999), pp. 64–86.

The economic model of voting is set out in D. Sanders et al., 'The Economy and Voting', in P. Norris (ed.), *Britain Votes 2001* (Oxford: Oxford University Press, 2001), pp. 225–38. On party leaders, see

D. Denver and M. Garnett, 'The Popularity of British Prime Ministers', *British Journal of Politics and International Relations*, Vol. 14, No. 1 (February 2012), pp. 57–73, and G. Evans and R. Andersen, 'The Impact of Party Leaders: How Blair Cost Labour Votes', in P. Norris and C. Wlezien (eds.), *Britain Votes 2005* (Oxford: Oxford University Press, 2005), pp. 162–80. On issues, see P. Whiteley et al., 'The Issue Agenda and Voting in 2005' in the same volume (pp. 146–61). The rise of valence politics is examined in J. Green, 'When Voters and Parties Agree: Valence Issues and Party Competition', *Political Studies*, Vol. 55 (2007), pp. 629–55, and R. Johnson and C. Pattie, 'Where Did Labour's Votes Go? Valence Politics and Campaign Effects at the 2010 British General Election', *British Journal of Politics and International Relations*, Vol. 13, No. 3, (August 2011), pp. 283–303.

S. Saggar (ed.), *Race and British Electoral Politics* (London: Routledge, 1997) is a detailed study of ethnicity and voting behaviour. On women and voting, see R. Campbell and J. Lovenduski, 'Winning Women's Votes. The Incremental Track to Equality', in P. Norris and C. Wlezien (eds.), *Britain Votes 2005* (Oxford: Oxford University Press, 2005), pp. 181–97.

Websites

General election results are available on a number of sites. The Electoral Commission (www.electoralcommission.org.uk) publishes detailed breakdowns of the results, while the BBC has results at www.bbc.co.uk/news/election/2015/results. Richard Kimber's online archive (www.politicsresources.net/area/uk.htm) provides links to hundreds of election-related sites. The website of Harvard academic Pippa Norris (www.pippanorris.com) includes both commentary and data.

Extensive data and analysis of the 2015 general election can be found on the British Election Study 2010 website (www.britishelectionstudy.com). Data on past elections are at www. data-archive.ac.uk/findingData/besTitles.asp. Most opinion poll organisations post their poll findings online. The best site is that of MORI (www.ipsos-mori.com), as it includes detailed information and expert commentary. YouGov's site (www.yougov.com) includes commentary from political analyst Peter Kellner. Other polling organisations include Populus (www. populuslimited.com) and ICM (www.icmresearch.co.uk). The Electoral Calculus site (www. electoralcalculus.co.uk) predicts the results of UK general elections.

Campaign organisations include Operation Black Vote (www.obv.org.uk), and the Fawcett Society (www. fawcettsociety.org.uk), which promote participation by ethnic minorities and women, respectively.

Chapter 19

Participation beyond elections

Learning outcomes

After reading this chapter, you will:

- be able to outline the major forms of non-electoral participation in the UK;
- appreciate the chequered history of referendums in UK politics;
- understand the complex relationship between pressure groups and liberal democracy in the UK.
- be able to explain the rise of new 'social movements'.

Introduction

The Swiss-born philosopher Jean-Jacques Rousseau (1712–78) once suggested that the English people are only 'free' during elections. He meant that these were the only occasions when members of the public could behave like true citizens, and take a meaningful part in shaping the laws by which they were governed. Even at election time, during the eighteenth century this citizenship was a privilege enjoyed by a few rather than a right extended to all British adults. Women were not allowed to vote, and most men were excluded from the franchise by a haphazard range of qualifications applied in different constituencies, but usually linked to property ownership, which meant that in a typical constituency, only a few wealthy men could vote. If the average Briton really was 'free', in Rousseau's sense, it was because they could (and often did) make their feelings felt by cheering or jeering rival candidates.

Despite the very different context of today, Rousseau's remark is still suggestive of a major dilemma for all representative democracies. Elections give citizens regular opportunities to dismiss unsatisfactory representatives, and some theorists of liberal democracy argue that because governments know they might be voted out at the next election, this will encourage more responsible conduct and sensible policies during their term of office. This, though, is rather naïve, as some governments which have been in power for a long time seem to become arrogant or reckless, and convinced that they are politically immortal. Certainly, the electorate's judgement can only be delivered at the end of a term of office (notwithstanding numerous opinion polls and occasional by-elections between elections), by which time many unpopular or damaging decisions could have been made, and much misery endured by some sections of the electorate. In the UK, instead of submitting themselves to the voters as soon as they lose public confidence, governments have either called elections when their popularity is high (for what might be temporary reasons), or hung-on for as long as possible in the hope that their prospects will improve. There are, though, numerous ways in which citizens can register their feelings between elections. In this chapter, we will look at referendums, pressure groups (also known as 'organised interests'), and other forms of participation in the UK, most notably the relatively recent growth of social movements, in order to assess whether or not they meet Rousseau's challenge.

Referendums

Referendum

a mechanism allowing voters to choose between different options in a particular policy area.

Referendums are ballots in which citizens are asked to give their views on specific policies. As such, they can be seen as a return to the kind of direct democracy which was practised in Athens and elsewhere in the ancient world, and which inspired Rousseau (see Chapter 1). Usually, a referendum offers voters a binary choice, asking them to choose between two options: Yes/No, For/Against, etc.

Ostensibly, the history in case study 19.1 suggests that after a slow start, the British have become very keen on the referendum, following the long-established practice of many other European countries and the USA. However, this impression should be qualified, because after the European Economic Community (EEC) poll in 1975, it took another 36 years for the whole population of the UK (as opposed to citizens of north-east England, Scotland, Wales and Northern Ireland) to be asked to pronounce formally on an issue – in spite of repeated demands for further nationwide referendums in the interim. The main general principles concerning the suitability of referendums are:

- They can be appropriate ways of deciding constitutional issues of overriding importance (thus the Blair government initially promised a referendum on a European Union [EU] constitution, then rejected the idea on the grounds that the terms of the ensuing Lisbon Treaty would not have an impact comparable to the original proposals).
- Although in principle their verdicts can be brushed aside (they are often 'advisory'), in practice they have more 'entrenched' status than Acts of Parliament.
- They can be called when an important proposal affects a specific section of British society. In these instances, on the mainland of Britain, the vote has so far been restricted to the people who are directly affected, usually on a regional basis.

Referendums: for and against

The relatively recent increase in the use of referendums within the UK gives rise to interesting possibilities at a time of technological change. The Internet and other modes of instant electronic communication have been exploited by the media to conduct polls on a wide range of issues, and provide an immediate snapshot of public opinion (although a cynic might suggest that some newspapers will only publish polls whose 'verdict' reflects the political stance of the editor or owner on a specific issue). Could these innovations be used by governments – or even make traditional understandings of government redundant? The old ideas of direct democracy envisaged 'face-to-face' societies where citizens could discuss topical issues in person, without having to appoint an elected intermediary. In a large society, such direct or mass discussions are not feasible or practicable – quite apart from concerns over 'social distancing' – but might we be able to achieve the same effect, instead, via virtual reality?

Case study 19.1

Referendums in the UK

1973. The 'border poll' in Northern Ireland

Voters in Northern Ireland were asked if they wanted to remain within the UK. There was an overwhelming 'yes' vote, but this proved very little since opponents of the Union organised an effective boycott. Critics claimed that the referendum was nothing more than a way of confirming what everyone knew already – i.e. that the majority in Northern Ireland was Protestant and favoured a continuation of the link with the rest of Britain. In their eyes, the real problem was the status of the Catholic minority, which had suffered discrimination for decades (see Chapter 12).

1975. Continued UK membership of the European Economic Community

The first UK-wide referendum was held on 5 June 1975, over Britain's membership of what was then the EEC. The Labour Prime Minister, Harold Wilson, resorted to the vote chiefly because his party was seriously divided. A 'yes' vote, he hoped, would give him the authority to override the objections of colleagues who wanted the UK to withdraw. On a high turnout (nearly two-thirds), the 'yes' campaign secured what could be presented as a conclusive result. Virtually every region of the UK voted in favour of membership. In England, there was a 'yes' vote of 69 per cent. But critics could argue that the poll had been held too late. On a question of such importance, voters should have been asked whether they wanted to join in the first place. By 1975, the 'no' camp was fighting an uphill battle, asking people to overturn a decision which had already been taken. Furthermore, the 'yes' campaign was much better funded and enjoyed almost unanimous media support.

1979. Devolution for Scotland and Wales

Voters in Scotland and Wales were asked if they wanted devolved assemblies, with limited powers (see Chapter 12). In Scotland, the 'yes' campaign secured a very narrow victory – by less than 100,000 votes – on a turnout of less than two-thirds. In practice, this meant that the case for a Scottish Assembly had been rejected, because the required level of support had been set by law at 40 per cent of qualified voters. The eventual figure was less than 33 per cent. The Welsh had been offered an assembly without independent law-making powers. The measure was opposed even by some government Member of Parliaments (MPs), like the future Labour leader Neil Kinnock. Only about 20 per cent of those who voted endorsed the proposal, on a turnout of less than 60 per cent. In neither of these abortive attempts to secure popular approval for devolution were English voters asked for their opinions. The failure of the project led directly to the downfall of James Callaghan's Labour government, which was deserted by MPs from the nationalist parties and defeated on a House of Commons vote of confidence in March 1979 – less than a month after the ill-fated referendums.

1997. Devolution for Scotland and Wales

Eighteen years after the 1979 polls, a New Labour government made another attempt to secure approval for devolution. In Scotland and Wales, the turnout was even lower than it had been first time round. This was somewhat surprising since opinion was still sharply divided. In Scotland, the 'yes' campaign fared better, winning 63.5 per cent of the votes on 11 September 1997. But the Welsh poll, held a week later, was a cliff-hanger; only 50.3 per cent of those who voted gave their approval. This partly reflected the fact that the powers conferred on the Welsh assembly would be severely limited, whereas the Scottish people were given a parliament with the authority to make laws and raise additional taxes (see Chapter 12); it also showed that some sections of the Welsh electorate remained opposed to devolution in *any* form.

1998. Devolution for Northern Ireland

Northern Ireland held its second referendum on 22 May 1998, after the Belfast (or 'Good Friday') Agreement of the previous month. The deal was accepted by more than 70 per cent of those voting (and turnout was exceptionally high, at almost 90 per cent). A resounding 'yes' was also delivered in a similar poll conducted in the Irish Republic. The vote paved the way for a new devolved assembly, which embarked on a somewhat chequered history (see Chapter 12).

2004. Regional assembly for the North East

New Labour hoped to extend its devolution project to the English regions, proposing that assemblies should be established with limited powers and budgets. Initially there was strong support for the idea; in five regions (the North East, North West, the West and East Midlands, and Yorkshire and Humberside) a 2002 BBC poll found that almost three-quarters of respondents were in favour. However, by 2004 government confidence in positive outcomes had been sapped. Ultimately, only one poll was held in the North East in November 2004. In an all-postal ballot, nearly 50 per cent cast a vote. The result was almost a mirror image of the 2002 BBC poll; 78 per cent of voters were *against* the plan. Voters had begun to feel that a North East assembly on the proposed lines would be a 'white elephant' – a talking shop which increased local taxes without taking any useful action.

March 2011. Referendum on extending the law-making powers of the Welsh Assembly

On 3 March 2011, Welsh voters were asked to decide whether the law-making powers of their National Assembly should be extended. The 2006 Government of Wales Act had stipulated that a further referendum would be needed before the Assembly took on legislative competence over the 20 devolved (domestic) subject areas, which currently required Westminster's assent. The Assembly unanimously agreed to hold the referendum in 2009 after an All Wales Convention had reported that the chances of a 'yes' vote were good. All four main parties in Wales supported the 'yes' vote; the 'no' campaign was headed by the 'True Wales' group, which depicted itself as a grassroots body representing a wide range of interests. On paper it looked like a mismatch, but while the final result was decisive, it showed that the people of Wales were lukewarm rather than effusive. Turnout was just 35.2 per cent, and, of those who voted, more than a third opposed the extension of powers. Nevertheless, the outcome was a sufficient basis for the law-making powers to be granted (see Chapter 12).

May 2011. Referendum on the Alternative Vote (AV)

When the 2010 general election resulted in a 'hung' parliament, the Liberal Democrats made a referendum on electoral reform a precondition of any coalition deal with either of the two main parties. Although most Conservatives were opposed to change, the party leadership was willing to support the passage of legislation to trigger a referendum; Labour sounded more enthusiastic about change, but lacked enough parliamentary strength to form a stable coalition. In accordance with the Conservative-Liberal Democrat coalition agreement, the Parliamentary Reform Bill became law in February 2011 and the referendum was set for 5 May (to coincide with local and devolved assembly elections). The campaign was dominated by arguments about the alleged costs of the proposed AV system – and by the unpopularity of the Liberal Democrats, thanks to controversial decisions taken by the coalition government. Many members of the public apparently found it difficult to master the different systems, or to enkindle much enthusiasm for the issue. The new Labour leader Ed Miliband supported change, but many senior figures within his party took a different line. As a result, a conclusive defeat for the 'yes' campaign was not surprising. Turnout was just 42.2 per cent, and 67.9 per cent of these voted 'no'. Although the public debate had been unsatisfactory in many ways, it seemed to have ended the prospects for electoral reform in the near future (see Chapter 17).

September 2014. Referendum on Scottish independence

After its remarkable overall victory in the 2011 Scottish Parliamentary election, the Scottish National Party (SNP) could not be denied its long-cherished dream of holding a referendum on independence from the UK. Following negotiations with the coalition government at Westminster, the necessary legislation was passed in November 2013. The fact that the vote would be held in the year that marked the 800th anniversary of the Scottish victory over the English at the Battle of Bannockburn seemed to underline the romantic, even Quixotic, nature of the SNP's initiative. For many months, opinion polls suggested that the referendum would result in an emphatic 'no', but the gap began to narrow in late 2013 after the SNP government released a White Paper advertising the benefits of independence. The final polls before the referendum itself (18 September 2014) were close enough to suggest that the verdict could go either way.

Ultimately Scotland voted 'no', by 55.3 per cent to 44.7 per cent, on a turnout of 84.6 per cent that was all the more remarkable because the electorate included 16- to 18-year-olds who were confidently expected (by the opponents of independence) to be reluctant participants. The final margin was sufficiently wide for supporters of the union to claim that the matter was closed for the indefinite future. But in the last days of the campaign, various senior pro-Union politicians had made promises of extensive new powers for the Scottish government, even if the 'Better Together' campaign prevailed. These last-ditch offers may or may not have made the difference; but if not fulfilled to the letter, they could easily be used by the SNP as a pretext to call another poll in the near future.

2016. Referendum on whether the UK should Remain in or Leave the European Union (EU)

The Conservative Party had become increasingly Eurosceptic since the 1990s (see Chapter 13), but whereas some of its MPs wanted to renegotiate the terms and conditions of the UK's membership as the basis of remaining a member of the EU ('soft' Eurosceptics), others ('hard' Eurosceptics) wanted the UK to withdraw from the EU altogether. David Cameron naturally found this a difficult intra-party division to manage, but this problem was compounded by the growing electoral support which the United Kingdom Independence Party (UKIP), led by the charismatic Nigel Farage, was attracting, much of it from disillusioned right-wing/anti-EU Conservative voters. Cameron therefore promised, in 2013, that he would hold a referendum on the UK's continued membership if the Conservatives won the next general election, due in 2015; a clever ruse to ensure that Eurosceptics of both types had a motive to return a Conservative government, although this still did not prevent UKIP from winning four million votes in 2015. In the meantime, Cameron held a series of meeting with other EU leaders, in the hope of negotiating better terms and conditions for the UK's membership, which he could then 'sell' to soft Eurosceptics – which opinion polls had suggested was also the stance of much of the British public – in order to secure a 'remain' vote in the Referendum. However, few were persuaded that Cameron had secured tangible improvements for the UK during his negotiations, and so when the Referendum was finally held on 23 June 2016, 52 per cent of voters opted to Leave the EU, while 48 per cent chose to Remain, a result which supporters of Brexit (the portmanteau word soon widely used to refer to the *Br*itain's *exit* from the EU) joyfully insisted represented 'the will of the people', in spite of the narrowness of Leave's victory. Cameron resigned within hours of the result being announced, but it was not until January 2020 that the UK finally left the EU, due to years of arguments, both inside the Conservative Party and beyond, about what sort of relationship the UK would have with the EU after leaving: what sort of trade deals would the UK be able to negotiate with the EU? What rights (if any) would EU nationals living in the UK continue to enjoy and what rights would Britons living in EU member states continue to enjoy (would they all – well over one million of them – have to return home to the UK)? How much 'divorce settlement' would the UK have to pay the EU for unilaterally terminating the membership? How would trade be conducted between Northern Ireland and the Irish Republic (would a 'hard border' have to be re-established, and if so, how would this impact on the relative peace and stability secured by the 1998 Good Friday Agreement)?

Since 1998. Elected mayors

On 7 May 1998, London voters agreed in a referendum to hold elections for a directly elected mayor and a Greater London Authority. Although the 'yes' campaign secured more than two-thirds of the votes, turnout was miserable at 34 per cent. Other towns and cities have held referendums on the subject of an elected mayor; they can be called either after a majority vote among local councillors, or if a petition is signed by 5 per cent of residents. But by the summer of 2014, only 16 referendums (out of 51 which had been held) had resulted in an affirmative answer. Even Tony Blair's constituents in Sedgefield spurned the suggestion, and in October 2008, the voters of Stoke-on-Trent decided to abolish the mayoralty they had agreed to establish just six years previously (Hartlepool followed suit in 2013). The turnout in the referendums has usually been low (Ealing managed less than 10 per cent when rejecting the proposition in 2002). This has not deterred successive governments from seeking new ways to 'encourage' local voters to adopt the mayoral model. Polls were held in ten major cities in May 2012; in only one instance (Bristol) did the electorate reach the desired conclusion (and that was on a turnout of less than a quarter). On the same day, the voters of Doncaster decided to retain the existing elected mayor.

Even this rude rebuff could not derail the deeply laid schemes of central government. Returned to office with a slender majority in 2015, the Conservatives offered additional powers as a sweetener to cities which surrendered to the orders from above. An 'interim' mayor for Manchester was appointed in order to accustom recalcitrant voters to the institution which they had rejected just three years earlier.

Local referendums

Councils sometimes hold local referendums on issues like the level of spending or development projects. As early as 1981, a referendum was held in Coventry on the issue of local taxation. In February 2005, Edinburgh voted against its council's proposed congestion charging scheme to restrict city traffic. Under the terms of the Local Government Act 1972, voters working through their parish councils are allowed to call local referendums on their own initiative. Only a small number of supporters are necessary. These 'do-it-yourself' referendums are not binding, but councillors would be unwise to ignore clear results on sizeable turnouts. One reason why central governments might be wary of local referendums is that they can also be used as ways of generating publicity on controversial *national* issues – for example, anti-euro campaigners have forced referendums to stop their councils preparing for UK adoption of the single currency. Yet the Brown government conceded that the public demand for participation at local level (partly inspired by the example of countries like Switzerland and the USA) had to be satisfied. The 2007 Green Paper, *The Governance of Britain* (Cm 7170), referred to the need for greater consultation of local residents, but this initiative was not followed up. After the 2010 general election, the Conservative and Liberal Democrat coalition partners were committed in principle to decentralisation, whereupon the 2011 Localism Act removed remaining restrictions on the right of local citizens to demand referendums.

The subject of e-voting is discussed elsewhere (see Chapter 17). At present, there is no prospect of routine government decision-making being entrusted to voters in this way. More likely, innovations like all-postal ballots, which encourage voter participation, might foster the use of a referendum whenever a reasonable case can be made for one, rather than reserving it for situations which clearly fall into the categories listed above. However, such ballots have already come under suspicion because of allegations of fraud, and in a bitter and closely fought referendum, the dangers of abuse are obvious. Internet voting would be liable to similar objections. Despite these problems, there is much to be said in favour of more frequent referendums. Some issues are clearly too important to be decided exclusively by politicians who may not invariably reflect the views of their constituents, and it can be argued that local residents are the best people to judge proposals which crucially affect their interests. More generally, participation in referendums can enhance the level of public interest in political issues.

However, referendums are still viewed with suspicion in some quarters, which is when the term 'plebiscite' is likely to be adopted to express disapproval, or cast doubt on the legitimacy or validity of the result. Professional politicians might regard them as a challenge to parliamentary sovereignty on the grounds that parliament is (or should be) the highest political authority in the country, with democratically elected governments making decisions on behalf of 'the people', whereas a referendum (even though often designated as advisory) is effectively saying 'let the people, rather than parliament decide'. However, this is a difficult case to argue in a democracy, where the legislature is supposed to reflect the views of the public and MPs often refer to themselves as 'servants of the people'. A more serious point was advanced by Margaret Thatcher (then leader of the opposition), when she spoke against the bill which paved the way for the 1975 referendum on EEC membership, arguing that the use of the referendums was often associated with dictatorships in which tyrannical leaders want to 'prove' that they have the support of 'the people'. This so-called support, though, is often attained through fear, intimidation, or somehow 'rigging' the referendum to ensure the desired result. However, in the context of intimidation, violence, and vote rigging, *any* supposedly democratic device can be manipulated by an unscrupulous government; the referendum is not really any more susceptible to these abuses than elections.

In a liberal democracy like the UK, some of the obvious sources of manipulation can be avoided. For example, the independent Electoral Commission must inspect the wording of the questions put to voters, to ensure that the referendum options are presented as objectively as possible. Thus, the Electoral Commission objected to the proposed wording for the Scottish independence referendum – 'Do you agree that Scotland should be an independent country?' – which was duly replaced with the more neutral 'Should Scotland be an independent country?'. In 2015, the proposed question for an in-out referendum on EU membership – 'Should the United Kingdom remain a member of the European Union?' – was revised on the advice of the Commission to read 'Should the United Kingdom remain a member of the European Union or leave the European Union?', which was regarded as a more neutral wording.

Plebiscite

an often derogatory or disapproving term for a referendum, implying that it has been held as a populist tool to boost the authority of the government or leader, rather than genuinely gauge the views or preferences of 'the people'.

A further problem with referendum questions is that they, almost unavoidably, over-simplify issues by presenting people with an either/or choice, because asking them to choose between two stark alternatives is almost certain to deliver a majority in favour of one of them – although this raises the issue of whether any majority, however small, should be deemed adequate, or whether a specified majority (65/35, for example) should be required for the result to be deemed conclusive. One of the reasons why the result of the 2016 referendum on whether the UK should leave or remain in the EU subsequently proved controversial was that the margin of the Leave victory was rather narrow, 52-48, and the former UKIP leader, Nigel Farage, had previously suggested that he would not accept a 52-48 vote in favour of Remain as the clear and settled will of the people. However, leaving aside this important issue, the other problem with the framing of referendum questions is that if they were to offer more than two simple choices, in order to reflect the complexity of wider range of options on a specific issue, it is likely that no single option would attain majority support: asking voters to choose from four options might, in theory, yield 25 per cent in favour of each.

A further problem with some referendums are the motives of the political leaders who decide to hold them. We have already noted that in dictatorships, some tyrannical leaders hold referendums to 'prove' that they have the support of their cowed or brainwashed people, but even in liberal democracies like Britain, prime ministers might decide to a referendum for somewhat cynical or self-interested reasons. Back in 1975, critics argued that the referendum on continued membership of the EEC was a cynical exercise on the part of Harold Wilson, who claimed that the UK terms had been significantly improved, although in truth negotiations by his government had left them broadly unchanged. However, Wilson's main motive in calling the referendum was really to appease 'anti-marketeers' within his own party, and as such, his decision to call a referendum was an exercise in internal party management: 'My party can't agree on this important issue, so we'll let you, the people, decide instead'. Wilson also suspended the constitutional convention of collective responsibility so that cabinet colleagues could campaign for a 'yes' or a 'no' vote, but given the balance of forces on either side, he was confident that his own preferred 'yes' option would prevail; if he had been less confident, he probably would not have called the referendum in the first place. The 2011 referendum on extending the powers of the Welsh Assembly was called *after* surveys had revealed a satisfactory level of support for the 'yes' campaign; the SNP has made no secret of its intention to call another independence poll *only* when the answer looks likely to be 'yes'.

The 2011 referendum on electoral reform also arose from unusual circumstances. It was the main price demanded by the Liberal Democrats before they would join a coalition government with either Labour or the Conservatives after the inconclusive 2010 general election. Historically, the Conservatives had always resisted a change from simple plurality (first-past-the-post), so on this occasion it could be said that David Cameron and his colleagues agreed to consult the people because they had no alternative, and on the assumption that they could campaign against a 'yes' vote with every hope of denying their Liberal Democrat allies their main objective in politics (see Chapter 17). Besides, the only other option that people were being presented with, alongside the existing first-past-the-post electoral system, was the AV, but this is not a 'proportional' system. As such, although there was clear vote in favour of retaining Britain's existing electoral system, it is not true to claim that 'the people' decisively rejected proportional representation; they were not offered such a choice. This again shows how political leaders can often secure the result they want either by 'framing' the referendum question in a specific way, or by the type of options or alternatives they ask voters to choose between – offering some but excluding others.

As we noted in Case study 19.1, David Cameron subsequently decided to hold a referendum on whether the UK should remain a member of the EU, yet in so doing, he was not motivated by a genuine desire to enhance democracy and 'people power', but by a concern to manage an increasingly divided Conservative Party – just as Wilson had held the 1975 referendum as a tool of intra-party management – and prevent a further loss of electoral support to UKIP. Cameron was also confident that he would win the promised EU referendum, partly because he had enormous self-confidence in his own perceived charm and powers of persuasion, and partly because he was confident that he could, before holding the referendum, negotiate improved terms and conditions for the UK, whereon he could recommend a Remain vote on the basis of having secured a better deal for Britain (see Chapter 13). It proved to be a serious miscalculation by Cameron, and precipitated the premature end of his political career.

Equally questionable or controversial, though, have been more recent decisions *not* to hold referendums. The Blair and Brown governments resisted polls on the two European issues of a single currency and a constitution, at least in part because of a fear that the public would defy their wishes. Also, having planned to hold referendums on devolution in four English regions, Labour eventually calling only one – in the North East, where the opinion polls had indicated that this area provided the best chance of securing a 'yes' vote; when the government actually lost, it scrapped plans to hold the other three; see Case study 19.1.

Another difficulty with referendums is the question of turnout. Should there be a minimum level which has to be exceeded before the results are considered to be binding? Against the wishes of the then Labour government, in 1978 provisions of this kind were included in the legislation for referendums on devolution for Scotland and Wales. In the case of Scotland, the 'yes' campaign narrowly prevailed when the vote was held in 1979, but it did not secure the necessary level of support from the electorate as a whole. It could also be argued that on issues of far-reaching constitutional significance something more than a simple majority of votes would have to be registered; for example, the proposal might require the support of two-thirds of voters. A more mundane consideration is that referendums are expensive, regardless of whatever the method of voting; the 2011 AV referendum cost approximately £100 million. Against these practical problems, however, is the unquestionable popularity of the referendum among a UK public which has come to see itself as more trustworthy than its elected representatives. Refusal to hold a referendum, against concerted public demands, can be more politically damaging than letting the poll go ahead and ending up on the losing side. In 2007, when the EU's Lisbon Treaty was signed, David Cameron offered the public a 'cast-iron guarantee' of a referendum on any changes which might result. Two years later, when the Treaty had been ratified by all EU states, Cameron was forced to renege on his 'guarantee', leaving him vulnerable to ridicule from opponents on his own backbenches, as well as the prime minister, Gordon Brown.

The referendum is not the only way of allowing citizens a direct role in decision-taking. The last Labour government introduced a facility whereby individuals and groups can use the Number 10 website to exercise their traditional right of petitioning on specific subjects, but initially the results were mixed at best. The coalition government strengthened the system, promising that e-petitions would trigger parliamentary debates on specific subjects if they attracted more than 100,000 signatures (perhaps even leading to the introduction of bills). This system was introduced in August 2011, amid speculation that the restoration of the death penalty would be an early focus of campaigning (see http://epetitions.direct.gov.uk). Thus, from the outset, the initiative seemed to be faced with its obvious pitfall. If the Commons debated capital punishment or EU membership (another predictable early favourite among e-petitioners), many MPs would feel pressurised to speak and vote against their private consciences, and thus act as *delegates* rather than *representatives* (see Chapter 8). If, however, they opposed the clear wishes of the e-petitioners – as a majority of MPs did after the debate on EU membership in October 2011 – they could be accused of treating the electorate with contempt, thus further fuelling the growing resentment against allegedly out-of-touch or self-serving politicians. Thus, the MPs were left hoping that petitioners would be satisfied that their favourite ideas had been debated at all, regardless of whether actual legislation ensued. As such, the initiative resembled the right to 'recall' sitting MPs and force by-elections. Evidently, the coalition government felt that this was even more perilous to parliamentary sovereignty; even though all three main parties had espoused the idea in the 2010 general election, progress was painfully slow. It was clear that the right to recall was never going to be granted merely because constituents had decided that they disliked their current representative, and that clear evidence of misconduct would be required. But aggrieved voters were unlikely to be satisfied with this condition if, for example, their MP consistently voted against their expressed wishes on controversial topics (like capital punishment). When legislation finally emerged in the last weeks of the coalition government, it restricted the 'right to recall' to cases where the offending MP would almost certainly have resigned anyway (or been sent to prison).

Pressure groups

Referendums and e-petitions do allow members of the public to have some say in policy decisions between elections, but in most of these instances, the decision to consult 'the people' rests with the politicians. In that sense, for advocates of direct democracy, referendums merely underline the limitations of public influence over the policy process.

By contrast, pressure groups often communicate their opinions when politicians would prefer to be left in peace. There is a wide variety of such groups in the UK, and in recent decades, their popularity has been growing (see Table 19.1). Increasing activity of this kind need not be a source of unease; on the contrary, it could be taken as a sign that **civil society** in Britain is healthy, with a highly motivated citizen body, ready to exploit any opportunity to participate in public debate. However, when party membership and voter turnout are declining, the simultaneous rise of pressure groups (and other forms of practical political expression) suggests that people are increasingly dissatisfied with the orthodox political process and are searching for alternative and less formal channels of influence.

The most recent 'Audit of Engagement' (published in 2019) asked people which political activities they had engaged in during the previous 12 months, and also which they would be willing to pursue. Table 19.1 shows the results. In terms of political activity undertaken in the previous 12 months, all had either remained the same, or declined, with the exception of boycotting products for ethical, environmental, or political reason, yet even here, the increase was minimal. Perhaps most striking was the increase in the proportion of respondents who had undertaken none of the activities, up from 25 per cent to 39 per cent. Meanwhile, there was also a general decline in the number of people who said that they would be willing to engage in any of these activities, with only three of them maintaining the same number as the previous year. Overall, the number of people who said that they would not be willing to participate in any of these political activities rose from 12 per cent to 22 per cent.

Civil Society

the sphere of voluntary activity, where associations can be formed independently of the state. Such organisations (sometimes referred to as 'intermediate institutions') include clubs, pressure groups, political parties, and religious organisations. A strong civil society is regarded as an essential element in any liberal democracy.

TABLE 19.1 Number of people who had done, in last 12 months, or would be willing to (previous year's figure in brackets) (%)

Activity	Had done	Would be willing to
Contact a local councillor or MP/MSP/WAM	12 (12)	37 (43)
Created or signed an e-petition	22 (24)	34 (38)
Created or signed a paper petition	8 (10)	29 (37)
Boycotted specific products for ethical, environmental, or political reasons	11 (10)	23 (27)
Participated in a public consultation	5 (6)	22 (25)
Donated money to a charity or campaign group	17 (23)	20 (26)
Taken an active part in a campaign	5 (5)	18 (18)
Participated in a demonstration or march	4 (4)	18 (19)
Attended political meetings	3 (3)	17 (17)
Contributed to an online or social media discussion or campaign	10 (10)	16 (21)
Contacted the media	3 (4)	15 (19)
Donated money/paid membership fee to a political party	5 (5)	11 (11)
None of these	39 (25)	22 (12)

Source: Hansard Society, *Audit of Political Engagement* 16 (2019).

TABLE 19.2 Confidence in the following to act in the national interest (%)

	Total/fair amount of confidence	No/not very much confidence
The military/armed forces	74	25
The Judiciary	62	37
Civil servants	49	49
TV companies	47	52
Trade unions	43	54
Banks	36	63
MPs	34	66
The government	33	66
Peers (House of Lords)	33	65
Political parties	29	70
Newspapers	29	70
Big business	26	72

Source: Hansard Society, *Audit of Political Engagement* 16 (2019).

An optimist might argued that these figures were *not* a cause for concern for democrats, because they could reflect people's general contentment or even happiness with the way that their council, region, or the country was being governed; they had felt no need to become politically involved, not were likely to, because politicians and other public officials were taking the correct or most effective decisions already, and could be trusted to continue doing so. If this was the case, what would really be a cause for it concern would be a sharp increase in political engagement, because that would suggest a sudden or widespread dissatisfaction with political decisions, or even the system itself. Back in 1954, in an article called 'In defence of apathy' in the academic journal *Political Studies*, W.H. Morris-Jones had argued this. However, this is not the reason for the current degree of political apathy of disengagement in Britain. On the contrary, as Table 19.2 illustrates many people now have little faith in the political system or politicians, and instead often believe that other individuals or bodies are more reliable or have more integrity, and can thus be better trusted to act in the national interest.

Only a third of British people retain confidence that MPs and governments will act in the national interest, whereas significantly higher numbers of people have faith in civil servants, banks, judges, the military, and trade unions to serve the national interest. If two-thirds of people do not trust politicians, then it is understandable that a growing number of people will decide that political participation is pointless; they will not be listened to. Indeed, this 'audit of political engagement' found that only 31 per cent of British people believe that political involvement can change the way that the country is governed, and only 15 per cent believed that they had any influence over national decisions; 83 per cent felt that they had little or no influence over such decisions.

The nature of pressure groups

Pressure groups are voluntary organisations which resemble political parties in some important respects. Their growth need not be at the expense of the parties; people can be members of both kinds of organisation. The key differences between parties and pressure groups are:

- One of the main functions of political parties is to contest elections. Pressure groups do not normally put up candidates; if they do so, they are usually aiming to win publicity rather than form a government (or even to win a single seat).
- The goal of pressure groups is to exert influence over office holders. Political parties seek to hold office themselves.
- Parties develop policies over a wide range of issues. Pressure groups tend to focus on one specific area of policy (although subjects like the environment generate proposals which seriously affect numerous policy areas).

Insiders and outsiders

Political scientists also distinguish between different kinds of pressure groups. For example, an important distinction is often drawn between *insider* and *outsider* groups (see Analysis 19.1). Insider groups work in close cooperation with their target audience (politicians and officials at the most appropriate level). They are accepted as members of **policy networks** (or **policy communities**), and are usually consulted during the preparation of any legislation which might affect them. The outsiders, by contrast, are only consulted by governments if and when this has become unavoidable. While they are excluded from the corridors of power, they tend to favour tactics which will win them widespread media coverage in order to bring pressure from outside the policy-making arena to bear on key decision-makers.

Prolonged contact between outsider groups and their target organisations can result in a change in their status and behaviour. Over time, they may be accepted as new insider groups, and begin to place less emphasis on public campaigning since they now enjoy private access. The same development is likely to push some former insider groups into the cold. In turn, they can be expected

---

Policy Networks

made up of ministers, officials, and pressure groups sharing an interest in a specific policy area. Non-governmental members of a policy network can expect to be consulted by ministers on a fairly regular basis, and such groups have 'insider' status.

Policy Communities

some groups or organisations (e.g. financial institutions in the City of London) are always consulted by governments when their interests are affected. Their relationship with government is so close that they are said to participate in a tightly knit policy community, making it difficult for any other groups to have a meaningful influence.

to adopt more vigorous tactics in order to attract publicity and win back their former influence over policy (see Case study 19.2).

The debate on hunting with dogs is a good example of this process at work. Under the Conservative governments of Margaret Thatcher and John Major (1979–97), opposition to hunting was a guarantee of outsider status. Parts of the 1994 Criminal Justice Act were seen as attempts to criminalise even peaceful demonstrations in rural areas. In general, media coverage was unsympathetic to hunt saboteurs. But with the election of the Blair government in 1997, the hunters became the hunted. The previously self-assured hunting lobby felt threatened, and formed the Countryside Alliance to uphold what it saw as a key human right. Mass demonstrations in favour of hunting were held in London in 1999, 2002, and 2004. On the latter occasion, a group of activists managed to get inside the chamber of the House of Commons before being apprehended. After the government invoked the Parliament Act (1949) to push the ban on hunting with dogs through the House of Lords in November 2004, the Home Secretary David Blunkett announced that the police would not be given extra resources to keep track of illegal hunting – they could now use the money previously allocated to a crackdown on hunt saboteurs!

Ironically, although evidence had been produced which indicated that hunted animals suffer acute stress, the dramatic reversal of roles in this dispute owed little to new arguments or scientific findings. A party with a long history of opposition to hunting – some of it undoubtedly inspired by class considerations, as well as real concern for animal welfare – had won a landslide electoral victory and felt that hunting was one controversial issue on which it could take radical action. Not every supporter of the ban was a Labour MP, and the party included a few passionate opponents of the measure; but the anti-hunting case always enjoyed an overwhelming majority

Analysis 19.1

Insider and outsider groups

Wyn Grant, a leading academic commentator on pressure groups, has identified sub-groups within the broad categories of insiders and outsiders – see his *Pressure Groups and British Politics* (London: Palgrave, 2000).

Among the insiders, Grant lists the following:

- high-profile groups, which enjoy close contacts with the government but are also willing and able to reinforce their position by using the media;
- low-profile groups, which work behind the scenes and try not to advertise their influence;
- 'prisoner' groups, which can sometimes be taken for granted by governments because they are dependent upon ministerial sympathy.

Grant's 'outsider' sub-categories are:

- potential insiders, dedicated to winning close contact with the government;
- outsiders by necessity, excluded from the corridors of power because they lack the necessary importance or skills;
- ideological outsiders, whose principles cannot be accommodated within the existing political system.

Case study 19.2

Pressure group tactics

The tactics adopted by pressure groups depend heavily on circumstances. An **insider** group, which is recognised as a member of a policy community, can operate quietly behind the scenes, sending representatives to official or informal meetings with officials and ministers. It will be kept informed of all relevant departmental decisions, and will be given the chance to influence legislation before it is introduced in parliament (or even before the proposal has taken shape). Often such groups will employ professional lobbyists, whose sole business is to monitor and influence the thinking of top decision-makers. **Insider** groups are granted access to (and by) policy makers because: (a) they have resources which politicians or civil servants need (such as specialist or technical knowledge) or they occupy an important/powerful position in society (such as big business); (b) their policy goals are viewed as 'legitimate'; (c) their conduct and tactics are deemed to be moderate and responsible.

Outsider groups, by contrast, must try to bring pressure to bear on ministers through activities such as demonstrations and boycotts, or by organising petitions. The recent tendency of groups to perform attention-grabbing stunts shows the perceived power of the media to influence public opinion and thus, indirectly, politicians. However, it will also tend to alienate important decision-makers still further, particularly as politicians will not want to be seen responding favourably to 'mob rule'. Thus, although groups can still move from 'outsider' to 'insider' status, there is a tendency for their initial position to be self-reinforcing. Outsiders will often feel compelled to behave in ways which make it difficult for politicians to speak to them even if they wanted to, while insiders will get to know the key people, thus consolidating their place in the policy network. Usually, a pressure group will be initially ascribed **outsider** status because it is either promoting a policy which governments do not consider important or desirable (CND's advocacy of nuclear disarmament, for example), or it does not possess any specialist knowledge that policy makers wish to obtain (for example, a group representing lone parents or the unemployed). Also, outsider groups do not occupy a position of power in society or the economy, and so governments will often feel able to ignore them.

in the Commons as a whole. In all, the MPs passed bills outlawing hunting with dogs on ten separate occasions (the Lords rejected the measure every time; see Chapter 8). Parliamentary time of nearly 300 hours was absorbed by these debates, but mostly this was occupied by arguments which had been heard many times before. The outcome reflected a changed parliamentary situation, which itself owed little or nothing to the issue of hunting.

Thus, the fluctuating fortunes of pressure groups can often be influenced by circumstances beyond their control. In relation to hunting with hounds, the fluctuations did not stop with the passage of the 2004 Act. The 2015 Conservative Party manifesto included a pledge to allow a free parliamentary vote on the issue, and David Cameron himself argued that Labour's legislation had done nothing for the cause of animal welfare. Other well-placed opponents included the Prince of Wales. However, in July 2015 Cameron's government abandoned a vote on the issue, after the SNP announced that its MPs would oppose it even though any subsequent legislation would only affect England and Wales. Thus, the moral issues for and against fox-hunting looked set to become a test case for the 'West Lothian Question' – i.e. whether MPs sitting at Westminster for seats outside England should be allowed to vote on issues affecting that country, while English MPs cannot affect decisions made on matters which have been devolved to institutions in Scotland, Wales, and Northern Ireland (see Chapter 6).

'Sectional' and 'cause' groups

Another helpful distinction can be made between groups which coalesce around some economic interest, and those that campaign for a principle which has little or no relevance to their material situation. The first of these are usually designated 'sectional' groups, although this label gives the misleading impression that such bodies invariably have a divisive effect on society. Most 'cause' groups consist of well-meaning activists who just want to make the world a better place, but some are quite capable of polarising opinion. The difference is that unlike the sectional groups, they are not normally motivated by selfish considerations (although this view is contested by the New Right; see Analysis 19.2 and Chapter 16).

Since sectional groups are generally perceived to fight for their own material interests, wherever possible, they try to convince the public that important principles are involved in their struggle. For example, the British Medical Association (BMA) might seek to persuade the public that if the government does not recruit more doctors, or increase their salaries, then the NHS will suffer (further) staff shortages, which will mean longer waiting lists and times for patients needing surgery. This makes the task of analysis more complicated in practice than the sectional/cause distinction might suggest on paper. It is difficult to categorise an organisation like the Countryside Alliance, whose members support the freedom to hunt in principle, as well as defending the direct and indirect economic interests of many people living in rural areas. But the Alliance has many unusual features; it is one group which can probably expect more public support from its 'sectional' arguments (e.g. avoiding rural unemployment, protecting livestock from foxes) than its moral 'cause' (upholding the freedom to do whatever one likes so long as no other human being suffers physical harm). However, critics often point out that many successful 'cause' groups, like charities, have developed into 'sectional' interests, with their top personnel commanding high salaries and seeking to extend their activities for the purposes of self-promotion. This view has been fostered by the tendency of pressure groups – even 'outsiders' like the Countryside Alliance – to employ people with grandiose business-style titles, like 'Chief Executive'. Equally, while many activists have opposed the construction of new roads, wind turbines, or airport developments as a matter of principle, others have betrayed the so-called 'NIMBY' (Not In My Back Yard) syndrome, feeling far less strongly about similar proposals which would affect other parts of the UK (and thus would have no impact on the value of the properties). These qualifications mean that students of pressure group politics need to treat the distinction between 'cause' and 'sectional' groups with some caution, and make informed judgements on the *primary* purpose of the organisations under review.

One important difference between 'sectional' and 'cause' groups is that the former usually have a specific catchment area from which they can hope to draw support. In other words, they will be able to target their recruitment efforts at people who share the same economic interest (e.g. trade unions can appeal to workers who do similar jobs). The membership of cause groups, by contrast, is usually subject to no such limits. This means that these groups will normally have to devote considerable energy to the task of tracking down potential sympathisers (although the Internet has overcome this difficulty to some extent). However, certain sectional groups have the chance of exerting very serious pressure on governments by virtue of their role in society. For example, in January

Analysis 19.2

Pressure groups and the New Right

According to representatives of the New Right, who were prominent among the supporters of Margaret Thatcher, all human activity is self-interested. Thus, there can be no distinction between 'sectional' and 'cause' groups. Even if they are not conscious of their real motivation, people who campaign for a moral cause are doing so because they derive some benefit from their activity, even if it is the psychological benefit of being recognised as a 'do-gooder', or virtue-signaling.

Many representatives of the New Right have also deplored the practical effect of pressure groups. They argue that campaigning activity distracts government from the pursuit of the general interest, leading to misguided policy decisions and, all too often, the misuse of taxpayers' money. Certainly, the New Right believed that by the 1970s, successive governments were unable to take tough but necessary decisions because of (potential) opposition for various pressure groups, and that both the number and range of such groups had increased to such an extent that the autonomy and political authority of politicians had been compromised and constrained. This was deemed particularly true with regard to the alleged power of trade unions, who were deemed to enjoy 'beer and sandwiches' via their regular access to 10 Downing Street. Thus, did the New Right believe that British governments needed to extricate themselves from their apparent reliance on pressure groups, and thereby reverse the apparent 'overload of government'? Of course, the close and often cosy relationships between successive post-war governments and many pressure groups were itself integral to the era of 'consensus politics', which Margaret Thatcher rejected in favour of 'conviction politics'. Besides the New Right reasoned, how could Conservatives radically reform education, the NHS, or the police if ministers were simultaneously obsessed with maintaining cordial relations with the teaching unions, health unions, or the Police Federation? Hence the New Right transformed many former *insiders* into *outsiders* (Photo 19.1).

PHOTO 19.1 Lovers of democracy, enemies of the fox. The Countryside Alliance speaks out in defence of rural life (© Ian Waldie/Getty Images).

Case study 19.3

Pressure groups, the EU, and devolution

The establishment of devolved institutions in Scotland, Wales, and Northern Ireland has provided pressure groups with important new opportunities. Despite the limitations on their powers, they still have the scope to satisfy many pressure group demands within those territories. In themselves, victories in these forums are heartening for pressure groups, but they can also set precedents for action elsewhere. Thus, for example, the Scottish Parliament took action against hunting and smoking before the UK parliament had done so; almost certainly the moves had some influence on the subsequent decision-making process at Westminster and Whitehall. In 2009, the Scottish Parliament passed the Disabled Person's Parking Places (Scotland) Act, after a campaign by a pressure group which drew attention to the abuse of such facilities by able-bodied motorists. Moves in Scotland to introduce minimum pricing in the sale of alcohol were e challenged in the courts but have already attracted considerable interest at Westminster.

One advantage of the devolved institutions is that, since they are relatively new, they provide opportunities for groups which have been crowded out in London by longer-established 'insider' groups. The employment of lobbyists at Edinburgh and Cardiff is therefore a shrewd investment for new groups. Also, post-devolution Scotland and Wales have adopted a much more inclusive consultative policy style, with relevant pressure groups and professional bodies (such as the BMA and teaching unions) granted a clear input into the policies which affect them and their members – the opposite of what happened in London during the 1980s and 1990s.

UK pressure groups have also been active at Brussels and Strasbourg for many years. This is not just because of the importance of EU law, but because the European Commission actively encouraged pressure groups, even providing financial support to many campaigning organisations. Indeed, during the Thatcher-Major premierships, when many pressure groups found themselves excluded from the corridors of power in Whitehall, many of them opened full-time offices in Brussels, to foster close and regular contacts with EU officials, who often proved much more approachable and receptive than policy makers in London.

2008, more than 20,000 police officers marched through Central London in support of a pay claim. Although the government made no immediate concessions, they had to treat this demonstration with far more respect than they would have accorded to a much larger gathering of people who were marching in support of a moral cause. At the same time, complaints from the armed forces about inadequate equipment and medical care arising from the 'war on terror' met with rapid and positive responses from government. During Gordon Brown's premiership, the use of the media by senior representatives of the armed forces (whether serving or recently retired) was sometimes characteristic of an 'outsider' pressure group – with the crucial difference that the armed forces could take for granted a formidable body of support regardless of the quality of their arguments.

Despite their disadvantages, some cause groups are very successful recruiters and fundraisers. The Royal Society for the Protection of Birds (RSPB) has more than a million members, and in 2018–19, it had an income of £144.6 million, while the Royal Society for the Prevention of Cruelty to Animals (RSPCA, founded in 1824) enjoyed an income of £142 million in 2018. However, in sectional groups, there is sometimes the problem of the 'free rider' – someone who expects to derive material advantage from a policy change, but abstains from any activity on the assumption that others will make the necessary effort. Indeed, in the case of trade unions, non-members will often benefit from the improvements to pay or working conditions negotiated by a union, even though they have not made any financial or practical contribution.

Other distinctions can be drawn in the increasingly crowded cast of pressure groups. Some, like the environmental groups Greenpeace (founded in 1971) and Friends of the Earth (1969), are truly transnational in the scope of their activities, while others are strictly local, like the groups that are formed to protest against the construction of a new road, or the closure of hospitals and post offices. However, new forms of communication, especially social media, make it easy for such small organisations to liaise with larger, more experienced campaigning groups with similar objectives. The Internet is an obvious channel of communication, and has played an important role in the worldwide protests against the war against Iraq in 2003; its potential for affecting events was demonstrated even more dramatically by its part in mobilising opposition to several regimes in North Africa and the Middle East in 2010–11. But cheap air travel also makes it possible even for groups with limited resources to share information face-to-face. For example, in September 1998, environmental campaigners from Sweden, Poland, France, and Germany attended a training camp in Staffordshire to learn such skills as tunnelling and tree-house building. The UK animal rights movement is respected by similar groups across the world, and is very happy to give advice to advance the worldwide cause.

'Peak' organisations and neo-corporatism

Corporatism

a system in which representatives of employers and trade unions are formally incorporated within the policy-making process.

Neo-Corporatism

a system in which the government regularly seeks to facilitate agreements between trade unions and employers.

Sectional groups in the UK were particularly prominent in the two decades after 1960. During that period, both Conservative and Labour governments consulted closely with representatives from both sides of industry – the employers, chiefly organised in the Confederation of British Industry (CBI, formerly known as the Federation of British Industry), and employees whose trade unions are affiliated to the Trade Union Congress (TUC). Such bodies are described as 'peak' (or 'umbrella') organisations because they represent a number of 'affiliated' groups linked by similar interests.

This close cooperation between governments and key peak organisations is a variety of **corporatism** (see Chapter 3). In its pure form, corporatism is a method of decision-making which overrides democratic institutions, and is associated in particular with the Italian fascist regime of Benito Mussolini. In the UK, the system was far more benign than the fascist version, and is probably best described as 'liberal corporatism' or **neo-corporatism**. Under this arrangement, the elected government's role is to act as an 'honest broker' in the national interest, facilitating agreements between trade unions and employers. The key assumption is that decisions are most likely to be accepted by both sides of industry if they are taken in consultation with senior representatives of the most prominent 'peak' organisations. Unlike in Mussolini's Italy, parties were free to compete in elections to decide which one would be most effective in presiding over this arrangement.

The key landmark in the history of British corporatism was the formation of the National Economic Development Council (NEDC, or 'NEDDY') by the Conservative government of Harold Macmillan in July 1961. The NEDC provided a forum for regular discussions between the government, the FBI (later the CBI), and the TUC. However, the arrangement never lived up to original hopes and had broken down by the early 1970s, even though NEDDY survived for two more decades. The usual explanation for the failure of neo-corporatism in the UK is that the trade unions became too powerful. After repeated and unsuccessful attempts at reform, successive governments felt compelled to appease the unions, with the result that the British economy came close to collapse in 1974–76. Another explanation is that the 'peak' organisations on both sides were unable to deliver on formal agreements, because they could not exert control over their members. Thus, while the TUC as a whole was usually ready to compromise, individual trade unions continued to prioritise the economic interests of their members even when these obviously conflicted with national goals. Equally, while larger companies within the CBI usually avoided confrontation with the unions for the sake of an easy life, smaller businesses proved more willing to break off negotiations and take the risk of provoking disruptive strike action.

The end of corporatism

By the mid-1970s, many commentators were arguing that the UK was becoming 'ungovernable' (see Chapter 3), largely because of the demands of various sectional groups which were powerful or persuasive enough to force concessions from the government. When Margaret Thatcher came to office in 1979, she was determined to free her government from this predicament. She did not abolish the NEDC – that decision was left for her successor, John Major, in 1993 – but in opposition, she showed no inclination to negotiate with the TUC, and before the end of her first term in Downing Street she had provoked a public clash with the CBI, which was deeply concerned at the damaging impact her government's economic policy was having on manufacturing industry.

In fact, the CBI found itself increasingly being ignored, alongside the trade unions, as Thatcher was much more sympathetic to the ideologically aligned, pro-free market, anti-trade union, Institute of Directors. Thatcher was also on close and cordial terms with many influential business figures and was determined above all to curb the power of the trade unions. When major industrial disputes occurred in the 1980s, the Thatcher governments did not usually adopt a stance of formal neutrality as previous governments had usually done, but unequivocally sided with the employers, often urging them to 'stand firm' against trade union 'bullies'. Almost every other year of her premiership featured a new piece of restrictive legislation. However, a more potent weapon was the government's economic policy, which accelerated the decline of heavily unionised manufacturing industries. In 1979, there were more than 13 million workers affiliated to the TUC; by the time of Thatcher's departure, the figure was down to about 8.5 million, but by the 1990s, there was no prospect that trade unionists would recover the influence they had enjoyed in their heyday, when their leaders seemed to be at least as powerful as elected politicians. Indeed, a defining feature of Tony Blair's New Labour was that the trade unions would not enjoy any restoration of their former power or influence, but would instead be treated with 'fairness, but not favours', alongside other pressure groups. After all, the major decline in trade union membership during the 1980s and early 1990s – due to de-industrialisation, privatisation, and a general sense among many workers that, as they had lost their influence or power, there is little point becoming a member – meant that by 1997, their members constituted barely a third of British workers, and as such, New Labour focused on appealing electorally to the majority of workers and voters who did not belong to a trade union, and might not vote for (New) Labour if it was seen to be 'too close' the trade unions. While the unions were understandably disappointed at Blair's lukewarm attitude towards them, by the mid-1990s, they were so glad to see the back of the openly hostile Conservatives that New Labour's stance was actually a relief.

While Thatcher's critics claim that her attitude towards the trade unions was vindictive and driven by partisan considerations – employers who awarded themselves huge salary increases were never castigated by her for being greedy or selfish, warned that they would 'price themselves out of work', or told to be grateful they had a job in the first place – she proved more than willing to pick squabbles with 'establishment' bodies like the BMA and the Bar Council (which managed to repel most of her proposed reforms of the legal profession: see Chapter 9). Even the Police Federation – previously regarded as an archetypal 'insider group' – was occasionally unhappy, despite the allegation by left-wing activists that the police had become no more than 'Maggie Thatcher's boot-boys' in return for their favourable treatment in wage negotiations, and their zealous policing of industrial disputes and associated picket lines. Since this trend continued under Thatcher's successors, it was not surprising that by 2008 the police had begun to accept the necessity of industrial action of some kind, and in January of that year more than 20,000 officers demonstrated in London for better pay and conditions.

New social movements

Whatever the fate of the neo-corporatist bodies which formerly wielded so much influence, it can be argued that Thatcher provided a wholly unintended boost to some pressure groups and other extra-parliamentary campaigns. Many existing bodies were reactivated by the perceived need to oppose her reforms directly, since the electoral process was unable to dislodge her, and others owed their formation to the impetus of Thatcherite policies. For example, Stonewall (named after the 1969 riots in New York's Greenwich Village following a police raid on the Stonewall Inn frequented by the local LGBT community) was set up to campaign for gay and lesbian rights in the wake of the controversial Clause 28 of the Local Government Act 1988, and the Anti-Poll Tax Federation was prompted by the community charge, which became law in 1989–90. The apparent or relative success of these movements helped to inspire others. But even before Thatcher's attack on long-established organisations, particularly trade unions and other professional representative bodies, it was possible to identify a change in the character of pressure groups and their style of campaigning. Commentators now refer to 'new social movements', which can be distinguished from traditional pressure groups because of the following:

- Their membership tends to be diverse, cutting across old class boundaries.
- They have broad ideological objectives rather than focusing on specific issues.
- Their immediate aim is to win publicity and to bring pressure to bear on decision-makers through the media or by mobilising public awareness or opinion, rather than engaging in discreet lobbying of ministers and senior civil servants.
- They pursue *ad hoc* or tactical coalitions of different groups with broadly similar objectives, often coming together for single campaigns, then diverging without establishing a settled hierarchical structure, or even a formal system of membership.

The first new social movement in the UK is usually taken to be the Campaign for Nuclear Disarmament (CND, founded in 1958). CND tended to attract young, middle-class supporters, who marched every year from the nuclear weapons research facility at Aldermaston, Berkshire, to rallies in London's Trafalgar Square. At that time, CND was widely portrayed as a 'subversive' organisation whose activities threatened to leave the West defenceless against the Soviet Union. But in 1960, the Labour Party conference passed a motion endorsing CND's aims, against the fierce opposition of the party leadership. This decision was subsequently reversed, but a similar motion was passed in 1981 and Labour fought the next two elections on an anti-nuclear defence policy.

CND's concern for the future of the planet and its varied inhabitants (threatened by nuclear annihilation) was shared by members of environmental groups, such as Friends of the Earth, Greenpeace, and the Animal Liberation Front (1976), which mushroomed in the 1970s. These organisations were far more radical – preferring (or reluctantly acknowledging their almost unavoidable) 'outsider' status and pursuit of direct action – than older groups concerned for the environment, such as the National Trust (1895), the Campaign for the Protection of Rural England (1926), and the League Against Cruel Sports (1924). However, over time the older bodies were themselves influenced to some extent by the new climate of activism; the National Trust, for example, had a long-running and bitter debate in the 1990s about allowing hunting on its land, and despite the fact that the RSPCA still enjoys monarchical patronage, in 2013 concerns about its activities led the Archbishop of Canterbury to depart from recent tradition and refuse to take an honorary role within the organisation. By contrast, Friends of the Earth eventually decided to become a more 'responsible' or 'respectable' environmental campaign group by turning away from direct action and public 'stunts', in favour of lobbying and evidence-based submissions to such bodies as parliamentary select committees.

Other new social movements were inspired by the American civil rights movement of the 1960s, and in the second half of that decade, the UK's Labour government implemented a series of measures designed to curb discrimination against women, homosexuals, and ethnic minorities. The success of these campaigns owed much to the sympathetic stance of Roy Jenkins (Home Secretary 1965–67). The 1970s saw further legislation like the Equal Pay Act 1970 and Sex Discrimination Act 1975, which improved working conditions for women, and the Race Relations Act 1976, which tightened previous legislation on racial discrimination. Other groups were founded to campaign on behalf of the poor and the disabled.

Case study 19.4

Black Lives Matter

Black Lives Matter, often cited on social media as #BlackLivesMatter, was established in July 2013, following a trial in which the man who shot black teenager Trayvon Martin, in Florida on 26 February 2012, was acquitted; he had successfully pleaded that the shooting was in self-defence following an altercation between the two men, although Martin was unarmed. The verdict, and indeed the conduct of the trial itself, caused considerable controversy, with the then US President Barak Obama, publicly commenting that 'Trayvon Martin could have been me, 35 years ago', due to the manner in which young black men were often assumed to be engaged in (or more likely to engage in) unlawful or criminal activity or anti-social behaviour, merely because of the colour of their skin and racial background. Martin's murder recalled other high-profile attacks on unarmed black men, most notably that on Rodney King, who had been violently assaulted by police officers in Los Angles in March 1991. Although the assault had been secretly filmed and the images then publicly released, the police officers were subsequently acquitted, a verdict which prompted riots in several major US cities.

When Trayvon Martin's killer was acquitted in 2013, Black Lives Matter was created, both to campaign against violence and discrimination against people of colour, and to raise public awareness of the continued prevalence of racism. Although it originated in the USA, Black Lives Matter, like most social movements, is transnational in its organisation and activities, the latter mostly consisting of peaceful demonstrations, and other public campaigns, many of them via social media (such as online petitions and videos), to highlight both racism in general and various cases in particular, the latter often involving the (unpunished) murders of black people, often by police officers or 'vigilantes'. Also like many other social movements, Black Lives Matter is a decentralised, non-hierarchical, 'organisation', which eschews the notion of leaders in favour of localism and community-based activities. In the USA, local Black Lives Matter groups are known as 'chapters'.

Black Lives Matter was prominent in the international protests which followed the murder of George Floyd, in May 2020, after a police officer had knelt on his neck for nine minutes during an arrest and ignored Floyd's claim that 'I can't breathe'. The incident was filmed, and the film then went viral, whereupon the incident attracted criticism from church leaders, political leaders, and governments around the world, as well as international bodies like the United Nations. In Britain, June 2020 saw several Black Lives Matter demonstrations, marches, and rallies, and although the murder of George Floyd was the original impetus for such protests, they soon began to highlight aspects of racism in Britain, and also the country's racism legacy via colonialism and the slave trade. With regard to the latter, prominent (mainstream and social) media attention was focused on events in Bristol on Sunday 7 June, when a statute of Edward Colston, a local merchant who became involved in, and profited from, the African slave trade in the late seventeenth century, was toppled from its plinth in the city centre and then dumped in the local harbour. This prompted anti-racist campaigns in other British towns and cities to demand the removal of statues commemorating former local dignitaries who had profited from the slave trade; for example, in Oxford, there were renewed demands to remove a statue of Cecil Rhodes. Indeed, some councils decided themselves that they would remove such statues, even without being lobbied to do so, while some also announced that some road names would be changed. Meanwhile, back in Bristol, Colston Girls' School announced that it would be changing its name (Photo 19.2).

PHOTO 19.2 Black Lives Matter demonstrations in the UK, June 2020 (© Oli Scarff/AFP/ Getty Images).

Case study 19.5

Extinction Rebellion

Extinction Rebellion is a social movement campaigning to tackle climate change by highlighting humanity's continued destruction of the environment through its materialistic lifestyles based on the endless acquisition and consumption of material goods and products, and the associated political obsession with pursuing economic growth and increased profits or shareholder value, regardless of the negative impact on many people's (mental and physical) well-being and work-life balance, and the destruction of the natural world. Extinction Rebellion insists that we can no longer continue with this economic model and lifestyle; if we do, the damage to the environment will be so severe that many life forms and creatures will become extinct, with the human race itself at ever-increasing risk from extreme weather and rising temperatures, more forest fires (some of them spreading to urban districts and destroying homes, as has happened in California, and parts of Australia, recently), droughts and floods, crop failures and food shortages, rising sea levels and coastal towns/cities disappearing under water, and loss of essential biological diversity as various insects and animals die out.

Formed in London in October 2018, at a peaceful protest in Parliament Square, Extinction Rebellion has since expanded to become an international social movement with groups in many other countries around the world. Like many other social movements, there is a strong emphasis on avoiding a strong national leadership, and instead being decentralised and participatory. At the same time, there is a strong willingness to co-operate and collaborate with other environmental campaigners on specific issues, thereby reflecting Extinction Rebellion's commitment to being open and inclusive, and thus developing a new way of conducting politics. Extinction Rebellion is politically non-aligned, and relies primarily on non-violent direct action, rallies and civil disobedience (such as sit-ins or mass sit-downs in public spaces, and temporarily blocking roads), as well as campaigns, and information dissemination via social media. It believes that traditional parliamentary methods of pursuing political change, such as writing to MPs, have mostly proved ineffective; many politicians have either ignored environmentalists, insisted on the need for further research (a classic delaying tactic to get an issue of the political agenda, and thus avoid taking action which might upset vested interests), or enacted inadequate or half-hearted measures, often in response to lobbying from big business and other corporate concerns. Extinction Rebellion also believes that existing structures of political power – like those in the economy – are themselves part of the problem, for they entail concentration and centralisation in the hands of a minority (an overemphasis on strong leaders who others passively obey or defer to), and are thus the antithesis of mass participation, decentralisation, and meaningful democracy.

In recent years, pressure groups and social movements have continued to proliferate and to form alliances of varying duration. In 1991, 250 groups opposing the government's road-building programme were brought together under a loose umbrella organisation, Alarm UK. A similar coalition – 'Plane Stupid' – coalesced to oppose the expansion of Britain's airports, alongside bodies with more specific objectives like No Third Runway Action Group (NoTRAG) which has campaigned to prevent expansion at Heathrow. UK groups participated in anti-globalisation demonstrations, notably at Quebec and Seattle in 1999, and before the G8 meeting at Gleneagles, Scotland, in 2005. A demonstration against a G20 meeting in London in April 2009 was marked by serious clashes between protestors and police; there were almost 200 injuries and one man (not involved in the protest) died in controversial circumstances. Although these campaigners do target politicians, they acknowledge that governments are increasingly powerless to restrain vast multinational firms, and so they also direct their activities against giant companies like McDonald's, Esso, and Coca-Cola. As well as demonstrating, they try to mobilise the power of sympathetic consumers through boycotts – as we noted in Table 19.1, almost a quarter of respondents said that they would be willing to participate in a boycott of a product for environmental, ethical, or political reasons. The role of financial institutions in the global economic crisis which began in 2007 provoked worldwide attempts to 'occupy' parts of key financial centres, including the City of London.

Until quite recently, it was possible to advance persuasive general explanations for the emergence of new social movements. Increasing affluence has often been identified as a factor. The prominence of middle-class activists in the ranks of environmental campaigners, for example, suggests the rise of a 'post-materialist' consciousness among people whose basic material needs are now met (via employment or welfare), and who enjoy the necessary leisure time for political activism. Such campaigners are likely to be well-educated, and be both aware of and angry about the persistence of continued discrimination against women, ethnic minorities, and the LGBT community. Meanwhile, people who give up eating meat on principle can now choose from a wide range of vegetable-based products to provide a nutritious diet, while campaigning against industrialised farming methods, the rearing of cattle solely for human consumption, and the battery farming of chickens for egg production. At the same time, environmental and wildlife campaigners might highlight the damaging impact, on Britain's wild birds, of agricultural pesticides designed to kill insects which would otherwise damage crops, or of the removal of hedges (which birds use both for nesting, and eating insects or berries) to free-up more farmland for crop growing or cattle rearing (Photo 19.3).

On this view, prosperity has generated many of its own critics who are concerned with quality-of-life or social justice issues, and who are sufficiently well-motivated and resourceful or 'savvy' enough to use the mass media, and more recently social media. These activists are sometimes difficult to categorise according to traditional ideological 'families', although many could

PHOTO 19.3 Extinction Rebellion protests in the UK, January 2020 (© Wiktor Szymanowicz/Barcroft Media/Getty Images).

probably be considered left-leaning, libertarian, progressive, or 'green' (while sceptical or scornful of traditional political parties and electoral politics) – or they might insist that in the 'post-modern' era, ideological labels and definition are themselves outdated and obsolete. Certainly, their prominence in pressure groups and social movements suggests a degree of disillusionment with mainstream party politics, to the extent that they have decided that 'single issue' direct-action campaigns are more meaningful or motivational than traditional modes of political activity and lobbying.

Pressure groups and democracy

Positive assessments of pressure group activity usually arise from a pluralist perspective (see Chapter 1). That is, it is assumed that an extensive array of such groups, covering a wide variety of subjects, is a sign of a healthy liberal democracy with an active citizen body. Free competition among such groups is likely to promote good government because campaigners on all sides of a question can be expected to assemble the most persuasive evidence in support of their favourite causes. With guaranteed access to a free press, they have reason to hope that the most rational case will win the argument and be reflected in government decisions. Some groups are even set up explicitly to demand a greater role in decision-making for the public as a whole; for example, the 'I Want A Referendum' campaign was established in an attempt to force the government to consult the people on further European integration.

From the pluralist viewpoint, the recent decline of the old sectional pressure groups is a welcome development. While pluralists acknowledge that unions and businesses are important interests in British society, in their heyday they tended to monopolise government attention, and the voice of the consumer was often neglected in the 1960s and 1970s. The relative decline of these powerful organisations has left space for other groups (like the Consumers' Association, which struggled to make headway when it was founded in 1957, but now commands widespread respect through its magazine *Which?*).

However, a more pessimistic view of recent developments is also possible. From the perspective of the New Right (see Analysis 19.2), any increase in pressure group activity is deplorable in itself. Even those who reject the ideological view that pressure group activity only results in increased demands on public expenditure can question the benefits of competition between interested organisations. In its most familiar form, the pluralist case assumes that there will be something like a level playing field for the competing groups, which ensures that rational decision-makers will tend to accept the most compelling argument. However, during the 1990s a series of scandals revealed the extent to which privileged access to politicians could be bought, regardless of the quality of the case they were hired to present, or the extent to which it enjoyed public support. Apart from rare cases of direct bribery, well-financed organisations could hire the most skilful and eloquent lobbyists, some of whom obviously gave a higher priority to pleasing their clients than to the cause of good government. This approach would come naturally to 'sectional' groups, which are themselves primarily concerned with the material interests of their members. However, the lasting legacy of lobbying activity in this period was greater public disillusionment with the political system, despite the conclusions of the Nolan Committee (see Chapter 8), and other bodies which promised tighter regulation of the links between decision-makers and extra-parliamentary organisations.

For pluralists, it can only be an additional cause for concern that the recent growth in pressure group activity has coincided with a fall in more orthodox forms of democratic participation. In their view, government has a crucial part to play in mediating between the different groups, and, ideally, the government at any time should represent a large proportion (if not an overall majority) of the public. However, with electoral turnout currently lower than in previous decades, political parties can win decisive parliamentary majorities with the support of a relatively modest proportion of the UK electorate. It would be highly dangerous to assume that the relatively low turnout in recent general elections reflects widespread contentment among the public as a whole. The continued popularity of new social movements suggests an increasing number of people who hold beliefs which cannot be accommodated by the main political parties. The marked tendency for movements to spring up in determined opposition to government policies is an indication that discontent is spreading far beyond the usual suspects or 'trouble-makers'. Equally, a feeling that politicians no longer stand up for the interests of ordinary people has helped to spawn far-right 'direct action' or street-politics groups like the English Defence League (EDL), which since 2009 has been involved in numerous clashes with Muslim groups and anti-racist protestors, and which thrives on confrontation and provocation.

The main worry about the rise of pressure groups is that relatively small, highly motivated, but 'unrepresentative' organisations can exercise an influence on government decisions far in excess of their public support. Indeed, in recent years the most popular organised movements (like the groups which opposed the Iraq war) have tended to fare badly compared to relatively small, often informal alliances which enjoy elite and/or celebrity support. The most influential individuals in Britain today, it can plausibly be argued, are people who, far from being elected to authoritative positions, do not even have to coordinate their efforts with others in something like an organised pressure group – rather, they are business leaders who can merely pick up their mobile telephones and arrange conversations with key political figures at a moment's notice, to Tweet their dissatisfaction with ministers over a particular issue or policy, and thereby prompt their many 'followers' to do the same. The financial sector, whose ill-advised dealings precipitated the 2007–08 global economic crisis, did not need any formal organisation to press its claims on government; when the problems began, it was immediately apparent to policy makers around the world that the banking system should be supported, because it was 'too big to be allowed to fail'. By stark contrast, the 'Occupy' movement, which involved demonstrations in almost 100 cities worldwide, quickly became the target of tough state action against so-called mob-rule and 'anarchy'.

Whatever the limits to the power of organised pressure groups, it is also pertinent to ask whether their own internal procedures satisfy democratic criteria. In the 1980s, Conservative governments criticised trade unions because their leaders were not truly accountable to members; for example, officials like Arthur Scargill, the controversial left-wing President of the National Union of Mineworkers (NUM), were elected for life. Legislation was introduced to rectify this situation, and also to force unions to ballot their members before they made financial contributions to the Labour Party. However, the Conservatives seemed less troubled by the extent to which quite secretive business organisations, like Aims of Industry, channelled funds into their own party, and workers rarely, if ever, have any 'voice' when their company or organisation appoints a new leader. Similarly, while trade unions are required, by law, to hold a ballot of members before pursuing industrial action, employers are under no comparable obligation to gauge the views or support of their employees before taking key decisions which will have a major impact on the company's workers, in terms of relocation, worse employment conditions, or major redundancies.

Questions about the democratic credentials of pressure groups extend beyond the most familiar sectional groups. Some organisations, like CND, have actively encouraged the autonomy of local groups rather than trying to coordinate their campaigning from the centre. However, the 'iron law of oligarchy' (see Chapter 15) suggests that there is a tendency for all organisations to fall under the direction of an 'elite' leadership group as they grow larger. This problem is accentuated in the contemporary context, as media outlets try to identify specific individuals who have the authority to speak on behalf of organised groups. Equally, the need to avoid negative publicity provides an incentive to impose discipline on the membership, to the extent of expelling activists who do not toe the 'official' line.

Conclusion and summary

The increase in pressure group activity, the growing demand for referendums on a variety of subjects and at different government levels, and the rise of new social movements which often engage in forms of 'direct action' constitute a serious challenge to representative democracy as it has been understood in the UK; it is certainly not compatible with the traditional 'Westminster model' of decision-making and parliamentary politics. Recent developments draw attention to the fact that the current system of representation is a means to an end, not an end in itself. No political system can provide satisfactory outcomes for everyone; but unless representative democracy satisfies a significant majority of the people most of the time, its legitimacy will be called into question, and a growing number of dissatisfied citizens will either become apathetic, or politically active.

However, those looking for alternative methods of political engagement or influence via referendums and/or pressure groups are confronted with obvious difficulties. Despite recent technological advances, the referendum is still at best a very cumbersome device. We argued in the previous edition of this book (2012) that it was possible to envisage circumstances in which, far from providing authoritative decisions on emotive issues, closely fought referendums could actually reinforce and inflame existing divisions within society. At the time, it seemed unlikely that the 2014 Scottish referendum on independence would reinforce this point, but, regrettably, this was a poll which left a legacy of considerable bitterness on both sides. The same is even more true of the 2016 'Brexit' referendum, which unwittingly exacerbated and entrenched divisions in British society – not only between Leavers and Remainders, but between the different sections of society that these two political positions or preferences often derived from and reflected: older vs younger, social conservatives vs social liberals, nationalists vs internationalists, uneducated vs educated, provincial vs cosmopolitan, small-town residents vs city dwellers, the insecure vs the self-confident, left-behind vs go-getters. Pluralists argue that government can act as an impartial arbiter between competing pressure groups, but this idea is more persuasive as a theory than as a guide to, or reflection of, actual practice; no government can be wholly impartial. But this does not mean that things would improve if the existing system of representative democracy was replaced by a parliament of pressure groups. The ideas of such groups often conflict in a way which leaves no room for compromise. Furthermore, pressure groups themselves are not invariably democratic organisations which guarantee their members a realistic chance of meaningful participation. In any case, while it is no surprise that political scientists should undertake detailed study of pressure groups – given their interest in organisations whose structure is (usually) open to analysis – the student of British politics should never overlook the extent to which influence over elected politicians can be wielded by individuals whose positions within key private sector enterprises ensure that they can expect a decisive policy input without having to join forces with anyone else, and any pretence to democratic legitimacy.

Meanwhile, dissatisfaction or disillusionment both with traditional electoral/parliamentary politics and orthodox pressure group activity has manifested itself in the emergence of new social movements, often campaigning on broader issues pertaining to the environment, ethnicity and race, human rights, and gender/sexuality – what are often termed 'identity politics'. For the participants in such social movements, traditional modes of politics are generally unattractive or futile, because they are often dominated by older, white, men (thus reflecting and perpetuating institutional racism and patriarchy, even if unwittingly), or/and 'corrupted' by the prevalence of corporate interests. From this perspective, the decline both in membership of political parties and voting in general elections – which alarms many democrats – does not mean that people are becoming less interested in politics *per se*, but that they are turning away from politics as it has previously been pursued, and instead pursuing alternative means of campaigning and new or more innovative ways of highlighting injustices and inequalities: consciousness-raising. It is still politics, but not as we previously knew it.

Further reading

A useful brief introduction to referendums is E. Magee and D. Outhwaite, 'Referendums and Initiatives', *Politics Review*, Vol. 10, No. 3 (2001), pp. 26–28. I. Horrocks and D. Wring raise questions about technology and participation in 'The Myth of E-thenian Democracy', *Politics Review*, Vol. 10, No. 4 (2001), pp. 31–32. It is still worth consulting D. Butler and U. Kitzinger, *The 1975 Referendum* (London: Macmillan, 1976), which provides a comprehensive and incisive account of the issues involved in the first UK-wide referendum. M. Qvortrup, *A Comparative Study of Referendums: Government by the People* (Manchester: Manchester University Press, 2nd edition, 2005) compares the UK experience with that of other liberal democracies. An account of how the UK's 2016 'Brexit' Referendum was conducted is provided in the Electoral Commission's *Report: 23 June 2016 referendum on the UK's membership of the European Union* (https://www.electoralcommission.org.uk/who-we-are-and-what-we-do/ elections-and-referendums/past-elections-and-referendums/eu-referendum/report-23-june-2016-referendum-uks-membership-european-union). For a series of blogs on UK referendums, see the Institute of Government's 'Never mind the ballots: referendums in the UK' (https://www.instituteforgovernment.org.uk/blog/never-mind-ballots-referendums-uk).

On pressure groups, see W. Grant, *Pressure Groups and British Politics* (London: Palgrave, 2000), and the same author's 'Pressure Politics: The Challenges for Democracy', *Parliamentary Affairs*, Vol. 56, No. 2 (2003), pp. 297–308. B. Coxall's *Pressure Groups in British Politics* (Harlow: Pearson, 2001) is concise and accessible. Although its findings are slightly dated, R. Baggott's *Pressure Groups Today* (Manchester: Manchester University Press, 1995) is still well worth reading. On new social movements, see P. Byrne, *Social Movements in Britain* (London: Routledge, 1997), and on environmentalism, R. Garner, *Environmental Politics* (London: Palgrave, 2nd edition, 2000). Two special issues of the journal *Parliamentary Affairs* are highly recommended: Vol. 56, No. 4 (2003) focuses on participation and includes articles on pressure groups and protest politics; Vol. 51, No. 3 (1998) looks at new social movements. For a rather more recent overview, see M. Grasso, 'Political Participation', in R. Heffernan, C. Hay, M. Russell, and P. Cowley (eds.), *Developments in British Politics 10* (Basingstoke: Palgrave Macmillan, 2016), P. Whiteley, *Political Participation in Britain* (Basingstoke: Palgrave Macmillan: 2011), and Houses of Parliament, *Trends in Political Participation* (2015). The Hansard Society has issued a number of detailed reports on political participation in Britain, which until 2007 were overseen by the Electoral Commission. See www.auditofpoliticalengagement.org.

Websites

On referendums, see the Electoral Commission website (www.electoralcommission.org.uk). There is a wealth of pressure group material on the Internet. This is only a sample list:

Black Lives Matter: www.blacklivesmatter.com
British Medical Association: www.bma.org.uk

Campaign for Nuclear Disarmament: www.cnduk.org
Child Poverty Action Group: www.cpag.org.uk
Confederation of British Industry: www.cbi.org.uk
Countryside Alliance: www.countryside-alliance.org
Extinction Rebellion: www.rebellion.earth
Fathers4Justice: www.fathers-4-justice.org
Friends of the Earth: www.foe.co.uk
Greenpeace: www.greenpeace.org
League Against Cruel Sports: - www.league.org.uk
MeToo: www.metoomvmt.org
National Trust: www.nationaltrust.org.uk
No Third Runway at Heathrow Airport: www.no3rdrunwaycoalition.co.uk/
Royal Society for the Prevention of Cruelty to Animals: www.rspca.org.uk
Royal Society for the Protection of Birds: www.rspb.org.uk
Stonewall: www.stonewall.org.uk
Stop HS2: www.stophs2.org/

Part 6

Conclusions

Chapter 20

Governance and democracy in the UK

Learning outcomes

After reading this chapter, you will:

- be aware of key areas of continuity and change in British politics;
- be able to evaluate the current health of democracy in Britain.

Introduction

This concluding chapter reviews the two main themes of the book: the transition from government to governance and the changing nature of British democracy. It examines the major changes which these developments have wrought in British politics, while identifying significant areas of continuity.

The old order changes

The standard view of British politics in the twentieth century depicted the UK as a highly centralised state in which decision-making authority was concentrated at the centre. The British constitution encouraged this centralisation of power. The doctrine of parliamentary sovereignty – the cornerstone of the traditional constitution – established the legislative supremacy of parliament, which could make law on any matter of its choosing. No other body had the authority to overturn Acts of Parliament. Unlike most other liberal democracies, Britain had an uncodified constitution which did not establish a clear separation of powers between the legislative, executive, and judicial branches of the state. The legislature and executive were in practice *fused*. The largest party in the House of Commons formed the government, and could use its parliamentary position to enact a legislative programme largely unchecked. The simple plurality electoral system and two-party competition added to the executive's institutional advantages by translating a plurality of votes garnered in general elections into working parliamentary majorities. Beyond Westminster, local government was weak and there was no other tier of elected sub-national government in Great Britain.

As we have seen in this book, many of these defining features of the Westminster model of British politics have come under strain in recent years (see Table 20.1). The shift from government to governance, and the constitutional reforms introduced since 1997, have been important drivers of change in British government and politics. In several key aspects the landscape which students of British politics explored before 1997 has been transformed. Previous editions of this book were written when New Labour was seen as the main driver of change, but since 2016 there have been times when it seemed that political developments in Britain were no longer being directed by any individual or organisation – that, to misquote Ralph Waldo Emerson, 'Events are in the saddle, and ride mankind'.

Government to governance

Government involves decision-making through formal institutions and rules; it is hierarchical, with clear lines of control and accountability. 'Governance' refers to the intimate involvement of multiple non-state actors and networks in decision-making, based on bargaining and co-operation. It is characterised by fragmentation rather than centralisation, interdependence rather than hierarchy, regulation rather than command, steering rather than rowing.

Adherents of the Westminster model held that decision-making power in the executive resided either with the cabinet or, as was increasingly the case in the twentieth century, the prime minister. The latter thus sat at the apex of a hierarchical system of government. A more sophisticated approach is offered by the core executive model, which views the core executive as fragmented, and the relationships between its key actors as characterised by dependence rather than command.

Organisational change within the civil service has added to the complexity of central government. The post-1988 'Next Steps' reforms separated the policy-making and policy-implementation roles of government departments, the latter being transferred to executive agencies which enjoy significant autonomy. The private sector's role in delivering public goods has been extended through market testing and the Private Finance Initiative (PFI). This dispersal of functions away from the core executive makes it more difficult for the centre to control the policy process. The Blair governments tried to address this by embracing the concept of 'joined-up government' and strengthening Downing Street's capacity to coordinate policy implementation – but with limited success in terms of rational decision-making.

The state's socio-economic role has diminished since the early years of the post-war period when it controlled nationalised industries (e.g. coal and electricity), used economic policy instruments to maximise employment, and expanded the welfare state (e.g. creating the National Health Service [NHS]). The Conservative governments of Margaret Thatcher and John Major (1979–97) reduced the state's role in economic management and the provision of public goods, by privatising nationalised industries and extending the role of market forces in the welfare state. These trends continued under subsequent governments. The post-war interventionist state was replaced by an enabling or regulatory state, which set the framework through which public goods were provided by specialised agencies or the private sector. The impact of the global financial crisis which began in 2007 forced the government of Gordon Brown to revert to earlier practices – including the effective 'nationalisation' of several banks. It was clear that this was intended as a temporary measure, which was undertaken in the hope and expectation that the new 'normality' would be restored within a few years. However, the effects of government 'austerity' were still being felt when the basis of UK politics was shaken by the Brexit referendum, and in turn the disruptive process of leaving the EU was incomplete when the state was subjected to the

TABLE 20.1 The Westminster model under strain

Features of the Westminster model	Challenges to the Westminster model
Uncodified constitution	De facto 'higher law' (e.g. Scotland Act 1998) brings constitution closer to codification
	Human Rights Act 1998 attempts to give a clearer definition of the relationship between citizens and the state
Parliamentary sovereignty	Primacy of EU law (until 2020)
	Devolution of competences to Scotland, Wales, and Northern Ireland
	Courts can declare legislation to be incompatible with the Human Rights Act 1998
	Referendums held to be binding even without parliamentary sanction; official encouragement of citizens' initiatives through e-petitions, etc.
Prime ministerial government	'Sofa government' and bilateral policy making undermines collective government under Blair
	Growing strength of Downing Street machine and influence of unelected 'special advisers'
	Lack of clarity on ministerial accountability, in the wake of agencification and marketisation
	Doctrine of collective ministerial responsibility diluted under coalition government
Civil service	'Next steps' reforms separate policy-making and policy-implementation roles
	Marketisation and new public management
	Special advisers given authority over civil servants
Unitary state	Devolution of power to Scotland, Wales, and Northern Ireland
	SNP government in Scotland after 2007
	Scottish referendum (2014) produces a much higher vote in favour of independence than expected
	'English Question' is addressed but anomalies remain
	Greater autonomy for major cities; elected Mayors emerge as potential challengers to the central state which often imposed them against local wishes
	Coronavirus pandemic underlines and accentuates the fragmented nature of the UK state
Judiciary	Increase in judicial review and willingness to challenge politicians
	Creation of Supreme Court
Simple plurality electoral system	New electoral systems beyond Westminster
	Decline in turnout
	'No' vote in 2011 (Alternative Vote) AV referendum leaves demands for change unsatisfied
Two-party system	Decline in support for Labour and Conservatives; rise of 'others' (UKIP, SNP, etc.)
	2010 general election inconclusive – formation of first coalition government since 1945
	2015 general election sees major challenges to remaining Conservative and Labour 'core vote', from UKIP and the SNP
	2017 election sees partial restoration of two-party competition but leaves minority Conservative government dependent on parliamentary support from DUP
	Multi-party politics beyond Westminster
	Brexit referendum cuts across party divisions
	Party funding concerns

additional shock of the coronavirus pandemic. In March 2020 a government which was elected on the promise that it would 'take back control' on behalf of Britons introduced a lockdown which prevented people from visiting family members, but still allowed visitors from abroad to arrive in the UK relatively free from restrictions. The absurd contradictions between these policy positions can only be explained by an underlying hope that they would facilitate the quickest possible resumption of post-Thatcherite 'normality'.

Before these momentous happenings, the shift from government to governance was also evident at local level, where service provision functions had been transferred from elected local authorities to quangos, private companies, and voluntary bodies thanks to policy initiatives begun during the Thatcher years. Local authorities used to be the predominant actors in the delivery of services such as education and housing but, under pressure from the centre, they have had to reinvent themselves as policy facilitators and service coordinators within their communities. Their role in education was undermined by various initiatives – academies and free schools, league tables, etc. – which were justified in the name of 'parental choice' but which had the intended effect of diluting political accountability. Even their supervisory role over policing was reduced by the introduction of directly elected Police and Crime Commissioners in 2012. The coronavirus pandemic made local authorities even more dependent on financial support from the centre.

Multi-level governance

The UK is now a multi-level polity. Central government does not monopolise decision-making authority, having transferred legislative competence to sub-national tiers of government. Until Britain's official withdrawal in 2020, the European Union (EU) had sole authority in some policy areas (e.g. trade and agriculture), and shared competences with its member states in others (e.g. the single market), where national governments did not exercise veto powers. EU law was directly applicable in the UK and overrode domestic law should conflict arise. Membership of the EU had significant implications for British government, requiring Whitehall departments, local authorities, and the courts to adapt their practices to conform to those of the EU. British government and politics was, to some extent, 'Europeanised' before the 2016 referendum, and despite the narrow 'Leave' victory it was difficult to be sure that old habits would die as quickly as those who wished to 'take back control' presumably wanted.

Whatever the UK's future relationship with the EU, Westminster has delegated legislative authority, covering a wide and increasing range of policy areas, to devolved bodies in Scotland, Wales, and Northern Ireland. Parliament remains sovereign, but does not have full supremacy over policy across the UK, accepting a position of non-intervention in devolved matters. Devolution has had significant implications not only for politics in these parts of the UK but for the UK political system as a whole. In health and education, devolved bodies have pursued policies different from those implemented in England by the UK government. New machinery for managing intergovernmental relations has also been put in place. Initially the UK government expected meetings of Joint Ministerial Committees to be fairly humdrum affairs, but thanks to Brexit they have become extremely contentious.

Constitutional reform

The post-devolution UK no longer satisfies the typology of a unitary state – one in which all component parts of the state are governed in the same way from a strong centre – which was a key feature of the Westminster model. Rather, the UK state is quasi-federal in character with a formal division of legislative authority between different tiers of government, and institutional arrangements to handle intergovernmental relations.

However, the developing process of devolution is just one of the significant elements of the programme of constitutional reform initiated by New Labour after 1997. Few major institutions have been untouched. The House of Lords now consists primarily of appointed members and Conservative dominance has ended; a predominantly (if not wholly) elected second chamber is now very likely in the long term, even though the major parties have been working hard since 1997 to hold up the process. Significant reforms to the judiciary, notably the creation of a Supreme Court, were intended to create a clearer demarcation between the executive, legislature, and judiciary. The Human Rights Act 1998 provided a framework of reference for the courts on cases concerning the relationship between the individual and the state. Along with the Scotland Act (also passed in 1998) it introduced an element of codification into the constitution, since such legislation can be viewed as de facto 'fundamental law'. Such laws could be amended (or even, as many Conservative politicians would like in the case of the Human Rights Act, revised *and* renamed as a 'British Bill of Rights'). However, an attempt to repeal them outright would encounter such serious opposition within and outside Westminster that in practice they can be regarded as 'entrenched' – permanent fixtures in the constitutional fabric.

The more things change...

Constitutional reform and the trend towards governance have brought about significant changes in British politics. But the story of the development of the UK polity in recent years would be incomplete without mentioning some elements of continuity. Although sometimes genuinely radical, changes to the constitution since 1997 did not in themselves bring about a wholesale transformation of the UK polity. Key features of the Westminster model persist. Change has often been incremental rather than fundamental; evolutionary, not revolutionary, on an optimistic view, but often panic-stricken adaptations to developments outside anyone's control. Political actors have also tried to respond in a pragmatic fashion to the challenges they face, adapting existing practices rather than ditching them completely.

Labour's reforms did not provide the UK with a codified constitution. The sovereignty of Westminster, in constitutional theory at least, was preserved. The Scotland Act 1998 states that the Westminster parliament remains sovereign and retains the power to make laws for Scotland. The Human Rights Act 1998 also sought to preserve the sovereignty of parliament, as did relevant clauses in the coalition's European Act 2011. If the courts find legislation incompatible with the 1998 Act, that legislation is not automatically struck down: it is for parliament to decide on amendments. Nor is the new Supreme Court able to overturn legislation. The rule of law is still susceptible to the authoritarian whims of central government, particularly with respect to national security, counter-terrorism, and surveillance of the activities of citizens through electronic media.

Liberal and radical critics always questioned the coherence and comprehensiveness of New Labour's reforms. They argued that the Blair and Brown governments opted for limited change to the House of Lords, territorial politics, electoral reform, and citizens' rights. A more radical approach would have seen an elected upper house, greater powers for the devolved assemblies, proportional representation (PR) for Westminster elections, and a UK Bill of Rights. The Conservative-Liberal Democrat coalition initially suggested a far-reaching programme of constitutional development, but by its very nature it was more likely to pick and choose from its own menu, implementing the measures which would best suited its short-term interests.

The introduction of fixed-term parliaments was an obvious example of self-interested reform, on the part of both coalition partners. It was implemented in a way which suggested that, over their decades of principled opposition to the Westminster model, the Liberal Democrats had unconsciously absorbed some elements of its ethos. If fixed-term parliaments had really been vital to Britain's constitutional well-being, as the coalition claimed, a question of such magnitude should have been submitted to the people's verdict through a referendum. Instead, it was forced through parliament as quickly as decency allowed. The 2011 referendum on electoral reform did give the public a direct say, but only on the AV system, which is not proportional; the status quo was preserved, thanks at least in part to the prime minister's intervention and some highly misleading commentary in Conservative-supporting newspapers. After his defeat in the 2016 EU referendum, David Cameron decided to make up the constitution on the spot, talking in his resignation statement as if Britain had suddenly become a direct rather than a representative democracy, in the hope that his Conservative Party would somehow find a way to benefit from the mess that he, as its leader, had made.

A strong centre

The 'core executive' model notes that many actors within the core executive possess significant resources, and that no single individual monopolises decision-making. But prime ministers – even within coalition governments – have significant advantages, as they enjoy access to resources that are not available to other actors. They still have considerable patronage powers, can set the strategic direction of the government, and can intervene in specific policy areas of their choosing. Margaret Thatcher was not the first prime minister to delegate crucial decisions to cabinet committees dominated by her supporters, or to rely on unelected personal advisers, but she took full advantage of these devices in order to avoid protracted arguments in the full cabinet. The decision-making role of cabinet continued to decline, as Tony Blair developed a 'sofa government' in which decisions were taken in informal meetings with ministers and advisers.

PHOTO 20.1 Ancient rituals have survived the modernisation of the constitution (© Suzanne Plunkett/WPA Pool/Getty Images).

A concentration of resources at the centre has further increased the potential for prime ministerial predominance. Although between 2010 and 2015 David Cameron did not lead a single-party government, in many respects his conduct remained consistent with patterns set by his immediate predecessors. Both Theresa May and Boris Johnson had to be restrained by the courts from effectively excluding parliament from the 'Brexit' process. The Prime Minister's Office and the Cabinet Office have been bolstered in recent years, and, whatever the instincts of individual prime ministers, it is difficult to envisage a significant reduction in the drive to coordinate policy making and set targets for policy delivery. The reach of the Treasury was also extended during Gordon Brown's period as chancellor through the Comprehensive Spending Review process and the development of public service agreements. If anything, Treasury oversight over the policy process was greater under Osborne (in an era of 'austerity') than it ever was under Brown; the main difference was that, unlike Blair, David Cameron seemed relaxed about the Treasury's dominant role. Friction between the Downing Street neighbours resumed under May (with Philip Hammond) and Johnson (with Sajid Javid); after the 2019 general election Johnson felt strong enough to confront the Chancellor and force his resignation, but this is a long-running institutional battle which might not yet be finally settled.

Outwardly, at least the central institutions of the British state remain strong (Photo 20.1). A 'Whitehall ethos' which values centralised decision-making and policy coordination remains largely intact. Downing Street and the Foreign Office ensure that governmental departments and devolved administrations adhere broadly to a policy line developed at the centre. Actors in the core executive have much greater access to important resources compared to other tiers of government. Government departments are the most powerful actors in policy networks because they have the greatest resources. Under the devolution settlement, the UK government is still responsible for the crucial areas of economic, constitutional, and foreign policy. The UK government is the dominant actor in intergovernmental institutions, such as the Joint Ministerial Council. Since the 1970s, the centre has also been able to restructure English local government and curtail its powers, even over its (already limited) revenue-raising capacity.

The enabling state is less active in the economy and society than was the case during the post-war Keynesian welfare state consensus. But government maintains a critical macroeconomic policy role. Under New Labour, it intervened to promote competitiveness, training, and social justice; the Conservative-dominated governments since 2010 retained some of these roles and added others (e.g. an attempt to promote 'green' technological development). The nationalisation of Northern Rock and the £850 billion bail-out of other banks in 2008–09 confirmed the state's continued capacity for economic intervention; the government response to the coronavirus pandemic in 2020 extended to virtually every sector of the economy. In other respects, the interventionist role of the state has been increasing over recent decades. Libertarians bemoan the development of a 'nanny state' which has regulated people's lifestyles by criminalising smoking in public places and fox-hunting. The 9/11 terrorist attacks in the USA led to a greater emphasis on national security in most liberal democracies. In the UK, funding for the security services has increased, terrorist suspects have been detained without trial, and thanks to various means of electronic surveillance, it is difficult to identify any aspect of life in which 'privacy' is guaranteed even for ordinary, docile British civilians. During the 'lockdown' of Britain which began in March 2020 during the coronavirus pandemic, some defenders of traditional British liberties were concerned about the long-term implications: in their eyes, the public seemed to accept all too readily that the state had the right to curtail their activities.

The condition of British democracy

The UK's status among liberal democracies cannot seriously be challenged, but it remains an idiosyncratic example, retaining many of the features of a majoritarian rather than a consensual democracy. It is one of only a small number not to have a codified constitution. Other features which have marked the UK out as different from other liberal democracies in Western Europe include the concentration of power at the centre, the weakness of local and regional government, an unelected second chamber of parliament, a relatively weak rights culture, the simple plurality electoral system, and a legacy of two-party dominance which remains potent in media coverage even if the voters themselves now exhibit much weaker and more varied preferences. Claims from liberal and radical critics that the UK was insufficiently democratic were influential in the Labour Party during the 1990s. New Labour's programme of constitutional reform improved the health of British democracy in some respects, but has also created new problems and left others untouched. The following section offers a brief examination of the condition of British democracy by assessing shortcomings in four areas central to New Labour's reforms: modernisation of the constitution, improved accountability, stronger rights for citizens, and higher levels of political participation.

Modernisation

The buildings which house the Scottish Parliament and Welsh Senedd symbolise the new face of UK politics. But the most familiar images of the UK state are still the Westminster Parliament, 10 Downing Street, and Whitehall. Ancient parliamentary traditions have also survived constitutional modernisation unscathed. While many of these hangovers from a pre-democratic *ancien regime* are trivial (like the ceremonies surrounding the annual opening of parliament), others are of political significance. For example, despite the removal of most hereditary peers from the House of Lords, this important legislative body remains unelected despite various pledges from the major parties since Labour's 1997 manifesto commitment to democratisation.

Gordon Brown's *The Governance of Britain* Green Paper (Cm 7170, July 2007) and the Draft Constitutional Renewal Bill 2008 (Cm 7342) briefly revived hopes that New Labour would produce a coherent constitutional settlement. Among the proposed reforms were changes to the role of the Attorney General, enshrining the core values of the civil service in legislation, and a greater role for parliament in the prerogative powers exercised by ministers on behalf of the Crown. They covered some of the most important functions of the state, notably the deployment of the armed forces and declarations of war. The Draft Constitutional Renewal Bill proposed that the executive's powers to deploy the armed forces in a conflict situation should be limited, and subject to parliamentary scrutiny. In 2010, legislation emerged from this process with the more modest title of 'Constitutional Reform and Governance Act'; it bore out fears which radical reformers had expressed at an early stage, showing that whatever their original intentions, UK governments retained the habit of trying to get away with piecemeal reform even when their own arguments pointed to the necessity of radical change. Since 2010 the most important innovation – the 2011 Fixed-Term Parliaments Act – was a tactical device rather than a serious constitutional reform, and its shortcomings were exposed by the early dissolutions of 2017 and 2019.

The devolution project remains unfinished. The powers of the Welsh institutions increased incrementally, as competences were transferred from Westminster on a case-by-case basis: a referendum on primary legislative power won majority support in 2011. Further devolution has followed, in the wake of developments in Scotland. Even before the 2014 referendum on independence, the powers of the Scottish Parliament and government were scheduled to be extended, following the report of the Calman Commission. Although the supporters of an independent Scotland were defeated in 2014, the latter stages of the campaign caused consternation among pro-union politicians, who were forced to promise significant new powers (particularly over the raising of revenue) even if Scottish voters decided to keep their country within the UK. With the demise of plans for elected assemblies in the English regions and controversy over the voting rights of Scottish Members of Parliament (MPs) at Westminster, the 'English Question' emerged as a potent political issue and although parliamentary procedures have been adjusted the 2016 referendum suggested that many English voters wanted more radical ways of 'taking back control'.

Accountability

The countervailing trends of centralisation and fragmentation in the core executive have prompted concerns about the accountability of central government. Tony Blair's preference was for a 'sofa government', in which decisions were made in small, informal meetings of advisers and ministers. A greater reliance on special advisers undermined the traditional policy advice function of the civil service. The neglect of formal mechanisms for collective decision-making resulting from sofa government was criticised in the Butler Report, which emphasised the absence of checks and balances in the cabinet system in the run-up to the war in Iraq; the findings were confirmed by the subsequent Chilcot Inquiry. The increased incidence of policy disasters such as the poll tax, the Millennium Dome, the Child Support Agency, and (arguably) the coalition government's health reforms also indicate that for many years policy proposals have not been scrutinised sufficiently within the core executive or in parliament.

But claims of 'elective dictatorship' are not a new feature of British politics – Lord Hailsham used that form of words in the mid-1970s, and fear of the thing itself has a much longer pedigree. The fusion of the executive and legislative branches allows the government to force legislation through parliament without effective scrutiny. Despite recent reforms which relinquish some influence to MPs who are not members of the executive, government still controls the essential elements of the parliamentary timetable and utilises the whip system to make it difficult for backbenchers to amend government bills. The 2009 expenses scandal further reduced the public standing of Britain's elected representatives. Nevertheless, although the Commons contains more 'career politicians' than ever before, some MPs are now more willing to assert their independence by rebellion or threatening to withhold their votes, and concessions were extracted even from the Blair and Brown governments, despite their comfortable majorities. Given David Cameron's parliamentary vulnerability, it is not surprising that this trend persisted under his premiership. Although MPs voted for key measures during the 'Brexit' process – triggering Article 50 of the Lisbon Treaty, authorising 'snap' general elections in 2017 and 2019, etc. – they insisted on an active role against the obvious wishes of the executive. The House of Lords continues to inflict numerous defeats on the government, notably on civil liberty issues. Parliament has more opportunities for pre-legislative scrutiny, and select committees carry out important investigations into the work of government departments and agencies; the autonomy of these committees has been boosted since 2010, after considerable government resistance. Unfortunately, parliament continues to produce badly framed acts, and is ill-equipped to scrutinise secondary legislation.

The publication of the *Ministerial Code* since 1992 has clarified ministerial accountability to parliament. Even so, the circumstances in which ministers should resign have become more, rather than less, debatable since 1979. Political pressure exerted by the prime minister and/or the media appears more significant than the constitutional convention that ministers should resign when they or their departments are found to be guilty of serious political or administrative errors. Reform of the civil service has blurred the lines of accountability still further. The distinction between policy strategy (for which ministers are responsible) and operational decisions (made by agency chief executives) sheds only limited light on the issue.

Local government is, in some respects, in a healthier position than it was 30 years ago. The Blair government gave greater discretionary powers to local authorities which are deemed to be delivering high-quality services, and encouraged them to play a more active community leadership role. But local authorities have only limited powers, must meet centrally determined targets, and have little financial autonomy. The local quango state also expanded, with the creation of bodies such as regional development agencies (RDAs) and registered social landlords. The coalition announced the abolition of RDAs in 2010; in part their functions were taken over by local enterprise partnerships (LEPs), but these bodies received no central government funding. Initiatives like the 'Northern Powerhouse', involving elected politicians (notably Mayors) and local businesses, seemed promising on paper but it was unclear whether leading figures would truly be accountable to local voters and thus have the political clout to wring concessions from the centre.

Concerns about the accountability of policy makers played a key role in the decision to leave the EU in 2016. The 'democratic deficit' in the EU was resented by many British voters because policy competences were transferred from national governments, which are (theoretically) accountable to their legislatures and electorates, to the EU where the main executive body (the European Commission) is not directly elected. Thanks to the general weakness of legislative institutions (including Westminster), there was limited scrutiny of decisions made by the Council of Ministers. The European Parliament was given greater legislative and scrutiny powers in an attempt to close the democratic deficit, but it did not enjoy the levels of legitimacy of national parliaments and few British voters felt they could influence their 'own' MEPs, let alone a majority within the Parliament. In theory the decision to withdraw from the EU should lead to greater accountability within the British system, but this remains to be seen.

Rights

Supporters of the Human Rights Act 1998 argued that it strengthened the rule of law by giving legislative recognition to basic civil liberties. The Freedom of Information Act 2000 gave citizens a statutory right of access to information held by public bodies. However, the Blair government ensured that there were significant exemptions within its own legislation, and (for example) full access to MPs' expenses was blocked until they were leaked to the *Daily Telegraph* in 2009. Meanwhile, civil liberties were curtailed by a plethora of anti-terrorism legislation introduced after the 9/11 attacks in the USA and the July 2005 London bombings. The House of Lords and the judiciary have been resolute in their approach to these and other rights issues, but their independent power is limited. The legality of the 2003 invasion of Iraq under international law was also questioned, and despite the defeat of the coalition government over intervention in Syria (2013) limited military operations continue to be conducted without parliamentary approval.

The record of the Blair and Brown governments on non terror–related domestic matters was also criticised by civil liberties campaigners. Legislation introduced under Blair allowed complex fraud cases, and cases where jury nobbling is suspected, to be heard by judges alone, thereby restricting the right to trial by jury. The double jeopardy principle – namely, that individuals acquitted of a serious crime should not be tried again for the same offence – was overturned by the Criminal Justice Act

2003, after eight centuries. This legislation also enabled judges to allow juries to hear details of defendants' previous offences, and made it easier for future governments to erode other long-established rights; for example, the 2010–15 coalition curtailed the circumstances in which legal aid would be granted in certain cases. Controversial proposals for the introduction of identity cards seemed to be abandoned in July 2009 but in one form or another the issue was likely to recur.

Participation

Low turnout has been a depressing feature of recent elections in the UK. Fewer than six out of ten registered electors voted in the 2001 general election, a figure that has only improved marginally since then, despite closely fought contests. On polling day over-excited media commentators habitually report queues outside polling stations, but these are usually caused by administrative inadequacies rather than excessive demand for ballot papers. In 2015 some media outlets acclaimed an overall figure of less than two-thirds as a great success, and attributed it to the good weather on 7th May! Participation is even lower in local and European Parliament elections, and approached the level of farce in November 2012 when Police and Crime Commissioners were elected for the first time. The Scottish Referendum of 2014 was an one-off exception to a well-established trend; given the level of feeling generated by the issue, the 2016 referendum turnout (just over 72 per cent) was mediocre at best. Even on a subject with obvious implications for Britain's long-term future, younger voters were far less likely to participate than pensioners.

Dismal levels of voter participation undermine the legitimacy of the British political system and bring into question the representative function of elected bodies or individuals. Parties which win elections invariably claim a 'mandate' to govern, even when (as usual) they have failed to win support from a majority of those eligible to vote. The 'mandate' claim was even advanced on behalf of the Conservative-Liberal Democrat coalition, although hardly any individual who voted for either party can have hoped in advance that the 2010 election would result in a coalition between them. In 2015, the Conservatives won a lower proportion of the vote than their party had attracted in the supposedly disastrous election of February 1974; yet because the media had expected another hung parliament and a coalition government, this relatively poor outcome was presented as a resounding 'mandate' for continued 'austerity'. The idea of a 'mandate' became even more questionable in 2017 and 2019, since the key issue of 'Brexit' cut across traditional partisan loyalties.

As we have seen (Chapter 18), the views of social groups that exhibit low levels of turnout (e.g. those aged under 35) are under-represented in the political process, and despite recent improvements the proportion of women and representatives of the ethnic minorities in parliament still does not come close to matching the profile of the population as a whole. Although a recognisable demographic relationship between parliamentary representatives and the people who elect them is a reasonable expectation, in the UK a more serious problem is the prominence of 'career politicians' in parliament – or, rather, the paucity of MPs who have won their seats after prolonged exposure to workplace experiences which would be familiar to their constituents. This problem seems particularly acute when individuals have used careers such as journalism or public relations as a preparation for politics.

The low levels of turnout also pose questions about the efficacy of political parties, election campaigns, and the electoral system. Partisan dealignment has seen a loosening of the bonds between parties and voters. Those without a strong partisan attachment, unsurprisingly, are less likely to vote. Party membership has also slumped in comparison to the mass organisations of the 1950s, which have been replaced by 'electoral professional' parties. The main parties target a relatively small number of voters, continually pestering those in marginal seats with the full range of artillery available to campaigners (personalised letters, social media advertising, doorstep canvassing, etc.) while ignoring individuals in constituencies where the result seems inevitable.

Election campaigns, and a partisan press that focuses on 'spin' rather than substance, have alienated many citizens. Non-voters are more likely to feel that the two main parties offer the same sort of policies, and for good reasons. Between 1997 and the financial crisis which broke out in 2007, broad agreement between New Labour and the Conservatives on the primacy of the free market brought greater political stability than was the case in the adversarial politics of the 1970s, when parties in power sought to unravel the policies introduced by their predecessors. But it also entailed that electors were presented with a limited choice, and radical perspectives were rarely aired. Judgemental ('valence') voting, based on short-term perceptions, had already largely replaced a range of long-term (mainly sociological) explanations for voting behaviour in the UK. The re-emergence of ideological divisions, especially after the election in 2015 of Jeremy Corbyn as Labour leader, did little to revive electoral turnout; after 2016 traditional bones of contention, like nationalisation, were over-shadowed by the over-riding issue of 'Brexit'. Many voters were now inspired to participate not because of enthusiasm for 'their' party, but by a desire to help keep the other side out of office.

A classic two-party system was a central feature of the Westminster model. The period since 1970, however, saw the development of multi-party systems in local, sub-national, national, and European electoral arenas. There is genuine multi-party competition in elections to the devolved assemblies. At Westminster, the two-party system has been eroded but far from eradicated: Labour and the Conservatives still hold a clear majority of seats, despite a prolonged and painful decline in support. Competition between three or more parties is the norm in general elections, but the simple plurality electoral system means that this is not translated accurately into multi-party politics in the House of Commons. The Conservatives (1979–97) and Labour (1997–2010) held office alone for considerable periods, giving the UK some of the features of a dominant party system. The 2010 general election outcome was very different; but even before the resounding rejection of electoral reform in the 2011 referendum, speculation about a new era in which coalitions would be the rule rather than the exception seemed premature. The loss of many Labour seats in the North of England in 2019 was hailed by many Conservatives as the harbinger of a new period of electoral 'hegemony', but the volatility of the British electorate precludes even short-term predictions.

Evidence from other liberal democracies suggests that PR has a positive effect on turnout, as electors are less likely to feel that their votes are wasted. The Blair government introduced PR for elections to the devolved assemblies, the European Parliament, and executive mayors – contests in which turnout tends to be lower than for general elections. However, the rejection of the non-proportional AV system in the 2011 referendum banished the idea of PR for Westminster into the diminishing distance. Trials of new voting methods such as all-postal ballots and e-voting produced higher turnout but also raised predictable concerns about the security of the ballot.

Election turnout is lowest among young people. In 2005, for example, only 37 per cent of 18- to 24-year-olds voted. Although things have improved somewhat, a marked discrepancy remained, and this is a particular cause for concern as it suggests that political parties are failing to engage young adults in the political process. Again, though, non-voting is not the whole story: young people may be reluctant voters, but many have been mobilised by intensely political issues such as university tuition fees, climate change, and racism. The number of students enrolled on Politics courses at school, college, and university has also increased. However, all too often the passion of young people who understand the relevance of political knowledge is fuelled by a reaction against the attitudes of their contemporaries, many of whom have little or no interest in the forces which have already begun to shape their lives. With so much information literally at their finger-tips, serious students of British politics are more knowledge-rich than ever; regrettably, though, the Internet has widened the distance between people who are eager for information and those who utilise the same technology for very different purposes. It has also encouraged campaigning practices which are dubious at best, and fostered the development of 'echo chambers' in which people of similar views encourage each other to think that their opponents are either stupid, unpatriotic, or both.

Low turnout is often said to be a symptom of a wider malaise in British democracy. Opinion poll evidence has revealed significant levels of dissatisfaction with traditional party politics and a lack of trust in politicians; these negative feelings increased sharply after the 2009 expenses scandal and again in the wake of 'Brexit' (see Table 20.2). But just as non-voting among the young should not be taken as evidence of apathy, disillusion with politics at Westminster does not necessarily equate to a lack of interest in politics. Surveys suggest that most people are interested in politics (broadly defined), and participation in political activities such as demonstrations and consumer boycotts has increased. New pressure groups have emerged, many of which focus on civil liberties and lifestyle issues (see Chapter 19); they might not be easily to accommodate within the existing party system, but this is a reflection on the parties rather than the level of public engagement with serious political debates. Despite concern from politicians and the media about a decline of respect and community, Britain has also retained its strong tradition of civic activism. This is evidenced in the large number of people who belong to voluntary organisations, or serve on community bodies such as school boards. Although David Cameron's idea of a 'Big Society' engendered perplexity and even ridicule in some quarters, before the 2010 general election its message made complete sense to many active citizens who must have been disappointed by the practical results of the initiative.

In *Why We Hate Politics* (London: Polity Press, 2007), Colin Hay argues that disillusion with politics should be understood not simply in terms of the 'demand side', but as a 'supply side' problem. Whereas the former position implies that a disengaged public 'get the politicians they deserve', the latter pins some of the blame for the decline in traditional forms of participation on politicians. For Hay, 'depoliticisation' is a crucial factor: by handing over decision-making powers to non-elected agencies or to private bodies through market testing, politicians have created a climate in which citizens do not believe that government and politics can make things better. The influence on politicians of rational choice theory, with its focus on individual self-interest, and public choice theory, with its focus on the efficiency of markets, has fuelled mistrust in government among voters. This tendency has been enhanced by the prevailing discourse on globalisation, which suggests, for example, that governments can do little to protect people from the harsh realities of global markets. Another well-argued book by a political scientist, Gerry

TABLE 20.2 Rating the system of governing Britain

	1973	*1995*	*2010*	*2019*
Question: Which of these statements best describe your opinion on the present system of governing Britain?				
Works extremely well and could not be improved	5	3	1	2
Could be improved in small ways but mainly works well	43	19	30	23
Could be improved quite a lot	35	40	39	35
Needs a great deal of improvement	14	35	25	37

Source: Hansard Society/Ipsos MORI, Audit of Political Engagement, hansardsociety.org.uk.

Stoker's *Why Politics Matters* (London: Palgrave, 2006), suggests that the electorate has become individualised and dangerously naive. Voters think like consumers, expecting governments to be able to meet their personal demands without appreciating the complexities of political life, in a democratic system which has to provide collective solutions for society's ills and reconcile conflicting interests. Yet, as Stoker's title suggests, he has not given up on political participation; rather, he envisages new opportunities through direct democracy and civic engagement. Unfortunately, both Stoker and Hay were writing *before* the expenses scandal which seemed to confirm all of the more simplistic assaults on the formal democratic system in Britain, and the economic crisis which emphasised the tendency of developments in global markets to dictate the direction of policy in the UK.

From Blair/Brown to Cameron/Clegg

Tony Blair left 10 Downing Street on 27 June 2007, having made history as the only Labour leader to win three successive general elections. However, his political legacy is less certain, as suggested by the fact that despite his remarkable election-winning record he featured no higher than sixth in a 2004 league table of prime ministerial performance based upon the assessments of political scientists and historians.

Clement Attlee (1945–51) and Margaret Thatcher (1979–90) are the only genuine agenda-setting prime ministers of post-war British history. Both brought about significant changes to the British state and society. As we have seen, Attlee presided over the reconstruction of the British economy after the Second World War, the creation of the welfare state, the nationalisation of key industries, the establishment of Britain's nuclear deterrent, and the beginning of the end of the British Empire. Thatcher's premiership saw a restructuring of the British economy that helped arrest Britain's long-term relative economic decline, privatised underperforming nationalised industries, introduced market mechanisms into the welfare state, and generally reasserted the authority of central government. These are legacies with which Blair's record could not be compared, even by the most devoted adherent.

Assessments of Blair's record are complicated by the fact that so much seemed to go wrong for his party (and the country) almost from the day that he stood down. This confronts us with questions about the relative importance of individuals, compared to other factors such as institutions and global developments, in affecting a country's fortunes. Pro-Blair 'revisionists' of the future will no doubt try to build an argument on Gordon Brown's indisputable limitations as a political leader; it can certainly be conceded that, had the global economic downturn begun seriously to affect Britain *before* Blair's departure, the situation would have been explained (or 'spun') to the British public more effectively. However, no one can claim seriously that the economic implications for Britain would have been less onerous had Blair continued in office. Even if one tries to exonerate Blair by pointing out that Chancellor Brown insisted on complete control of the economy between 1997 and 2007, the fact remains that Blair did not sack him. Therefore, Blair must be regarded as guilty either of agreeing to policies which helped to bring about the economic crisis (a lax regime of financial regulation and a programme of excessive public spending), or of failing to curb a colleague whose policies were far removed from the economic 'prudence' of which he had once boasted. Overall, then, the story of New Labour should not be seen as a case of 'what might have been', and as such it seems fair to judge the 1997–2010 record in one piece rather than creating an unjustified distinction between 1997–2007 and 2007–10.

From this perspective, despite the obvious differences between New Labour's record and that of the Conservatives between 1979 and 1997, there remain some striking parallels. Both parties held office for protracted periods, arguably giving them ample opportunity to address the problems they had identified at the outset. However, the dominant figures in each period (Thatcher and Blair) were both removed, by opposition within their own parties rather than by the electorate, while they still believed that they had plenty of unfinished business. They were succeeded by colleagues who never had the chance to fulfil their own agendas, due to difficulties which (arguably) both had helped to foster in their respective spells as Chancellor of the Exchequer (John Major had been the Chancellor who took Britain into the European Exchange Rate Mechanism, while Gordon Brown was accused of 'imprudence' in the level of public spending and of failing to regulate the financial sector).

Instead of speculating too much about the relative qualities of individuals – 'Were Major and Brown really big enough to fill the shoes of their predecessors?' – it is more profitable to look at underlying changes in the nature of UK government between 1945, when Attlee won his landslide, and 1990, when Major took over from Thatcher. In 1945, Britain undoubtedly had a 'government'. Ministers, advised by highly skilled and public-spirited civil servants, were in charge. Nye Bevan, the founder of the NHS, once remarked that he wanted to be informed whenever a bed-pan was dropped in a British hospital. This was not meant to be taken literally, but it was a vivid evocation of British government under the 'Westminster model', which meant that ministers had to take their responsibilities very seriously. In return, they had every reason to expect that their decisions would result in corresponding actions all the way down the chain of command.

Although Attlee and Thatcher were political 'game changers' of equivalent impact, they worked in opposite directions. Attlee was happy to exercise control over an interventionist government machine which had just carried Britain through a devastating war; Thatcher felt that because of excessive state interference under Attlee and his successors, Britain had 'lost the peace'. Although Thatcher was a firm believer in the power and dignity of the state, her insistence that it should withdraw from many of its functions ultimately had the effect of weakening it as an agent of national unity, and her period in office coincided with developments within the global economy which would in any case have fostered latent divisions within the UK body politic (between 'north' and 'south', as well as between rich and poor). To her admirers, this makes Thatcher's seizure of the Conservative leadership in 1975, and her election victory in 1979, very timely occurrences; she anticipated the economic tide, and whether or not she really understood its likely effects, her decisions helped to remove the obstacles in its path. However, these decisions also greatly assisted the transition from government to governance in the UK and made life much more complicated for any successor who wanted to make a comparable difference to the way in which the country was governed.

In short, in 1979 Thatcher took over what was still in essence Attlee's state – one in which it was conceivable for ministers and civil servants to issue directives and expect action to follow – and in 1990 bequeathed a state which was becoming far more dependent on negotiation if it wanted to achieve anything like its original objectives. When he became prime minister in 1997, Tony Blair had never held government office and (by his own admission) was not exactly sure how to proceed. However, he found it impossible to conceal his admiration for Margaret Thatcher, and he clearly followed her lead in asserting that the comparative weakness of John Major had been a temporary 'blip' in the story of British government, attributable to Major's personal shortcomings, as well as the defects of his party which, by implication, Blair thought unworthy of its former leader. Ironically, despite his longer experience of the political process, Gordon Brown seemed equally star-struck in Thatcher's presence, suggesting that he also regarded her as an example that any aspiring prime minister should try to follow.

However, Thatcher's example was dangerously misleading because her incessant attacks on key elements of the post-war state had been all too successful. For a variety of reasons, the British public was no longer as obedient as it had been in 1945, or even in 1979. Those who agreed with Thatcher absorbed her message and refused to accept that 'the Man in Whitehall' always knew best. Her opponents responded to government instructions in the same negative fashion, so long as she and her ministers were telling them what to do. This phenomenon was most clearly demonstrated in Scotland, which was thoroughly alienated from Westminster and Whitehall long before 1997; but arguably other parts of the UK were disenchanted to a dangerous degree. This mood – at best, one of reluctant compliance with 'Thatcherism' and its practical effects – found its most vivid expression a decade after her departure in the fuel crisis of 2000, which briefly made the country as 'ungovernable' as it had been for much of the 1970s.

Although the British tax regime helped to provoke this barely remembered national crisis, ultimately the unrest of 2000 was caused by movements in the global economy which Blair could not control. In response, he switched his attention to matters in which his interference could be more effective, including the habits of his fellow citizens (notably smoking). But a British prime minister, like a US president, has the greatest chance of making a difference by opening hostilities with somebody. In the USA, the legislature technically has the right to declare war, but presidents have been able to evade this constitutional provision by making war without an official declaration, or by other technical devices. In the UK, although the situation is a little more complicated, prime ministers have inherited the Royal prerogative power to commit troops to action without a parliamentary vote; and if such a vote takes place in advance of action, they can usually be sure of the outcome, either by relying on their inbuilt majority among MPs or by hinting that they possess secret information about the intentions and/or capability of the chosen enemy.

Tony Blair's conduct in the build-up to the war in Iraq will always be controversial. For our present purpose, all that needs to be noted is that Blair's experience of foreign affairs had been theoretical at best before he became the prime minister, and that the itch for activism in any British prime minister since 1990 is most likely to be satisfied by overseas adventures, not least because the scope for effective domestic interventions is now so limited. When Gordon Brown succeeded Blair in 2007, it was generally thought that he had been waiting for the chance to pursue a distinctive policy agenda but had been thwarted by Blair's refusal to step down. In truth, Brown had used his power base in the Treasury to deny Blair a referendum on the euro and followed the same basic approach as Blair so far as the public services were concerned – that is, they both persuaded themselves that the future funding of the welfare state was entirely dependent on the operations of the 'free' market. If anything, Brown was even more impressed than Blair by the idea that the private sector always knew best. The inevitable result was that, having sensed and resented 'New' Labour's preference, the *public* sector proved equally resistant to the reforming ideas of Brown and Blair. If even less progress towards 'reform' was made under Brown, that was because his premiership was dominated by economic problems largely caused by global events outside his control.

Against this background, David Cameron's political career before 2010 looks like a rehearsal for a play which has already been served with a notice of closure. Initially, an ardent follower of Mrs Thatcher's ideology, he admired Blair's vote-winning prowess to such an extent that he pronounced himself to be Blair's, rather than Thatcher's, heir. However, being 'heir to Blair' entailed taking on the task of public sector reform, which had proved too tricky for the master himself. To make matters worse for Cameron, after the 2010 general election it meant inheriting an economic crisis without the backing of an overwhelming parliamentary majority. In the context of the current analysis, it was significant that Cameron, in coalition with the Liberal Democrats, proposed to address the crisis by cutting spending further and faster than Labour would have done. In tandem with Cameron's attempt to revive the voluntary sector through his 'Big Society' initiative, this looked like a relatively coherent plan to 'shrink the state'. If the strategy succeeded, it would reduce still further the explanatory power of the Westminster model – and make it more difficult in future for historians and political scientists to judge the performance of prime ministers whose ability to influence the domestic policy agenda can no longer be compared to the situation in the days of Attlee or Thatcher – or even Blair/Brown.

The backlash from the Blair years also had a serious effect on Cameron's room for manoeuvre in foreign policy. In August 2013, his government was defeated on a House of Commons motion designed to pave the way for military strikes against the Assad regime in Syria. There was still nothing like a UK version of the US War Powers Resolution (1973) – whose terms have in any case been evaded by more than one President – and the response of some government ministers claimed that parliament had been guilty of an act of presumption. However, the vote suggested that, even if the House of Commons was not trying to prise the former Royal Prerogative over matters relating to war and peace out of the executive's hands, in future major issues of foreign policy would have to be conducted on the basis of full co-operation between the branches of government. Thus, as so often, the constitutional legacy of the Cameron coalition might be very different from the one which its Conservative and Liberal Democrat protagonists envisaged back in 2010 (when the idea of a closely fought referendum on Scottish independence was no less improbable than the prospect of a parliamentary defeat on a major foreign policy initiative).

'Brexit' and after

In the 2015 general election campaign, the Conservatives concentrated on the economic record of the 2010–15 coalition, hoping that voters would reward them for steering the economy through difficult times and forget that average living standards had remained stagnant since 2010. The fact that the party was able to secure a narrow overall parliamentary majority suggests that many voters were prepared to give it the benefit of the doubt on this key isssue. Cameron himself could be forgiven for hailing the result as a personal vindication. However, he had indicated that he would stand down as prime minister before the next election, presumably in an attempt to douse speculation about his position until that time.

Whatever his critics might allege, Cameron had proved to be a successful leader of the coalition government, not least because his 'tribal' instincts lay with the Conservative Party, even though his more rational faculties inclined him to the Liberal Democratic side on many issues. Temperamentally, he seemed to prefer delegation to domination; as such, his style of government seemed to verify the core executive model, in which ministerial resources are exchanged in a continuous process of bargaining and negotiation. However, as the leading figure in a single party government after the 2015 general election, Cameron faced more complex challenges than the ones which had forced John Major to trigger a Conservative leadership election in 1995.

The previous edition of this book (2016) closed with the thought that 'In the run-up to the referendum on EU membership, the task of exploring British politics has rarely been more fascinating – or complicated'. The course of events in 2016–17 is best summed up by the titles of two excellent books by the journalist Tim Shipman – *All Out War* (2016), on the referendum campaign, and *Fall Out* (2017), on the 2017 general election. Since 2016, among numerous developments, the House of Commons has voted that the government held it in contempt, and the Supreme Court has effectively ruled that a prime minister (Boris Johnson) misled the monarch when asking her to prorogue parliament. In the 2019 general election, seats which looked destined to remain in Labour's hands forever were seized by the Conservatives, who in the month before the election had been engulfed by divisions which led to the removal of the party whip from 21 MPs (many of them very senior figures). After almost a decade of governing without a secure majority, the Conservatives were restored to a commanding parliamentary position in December 2019. But the issue of Brexit was still not resolved when, in March 2020, the impact of the global coronavirus pandemic forced the government to impose unprecedented restrictions on individual freedoms. Coming on top of an ongoing political and constitutional crisis in which the future of the UK itself was increasingly open to question, this was easily the most series challenge to the British system of government since 1940, when the nation looked in danger of defeat by Nazi Germany.

It would be comforting to think that the extreme turbulence which has affected British politics since the global financial crisis of the late 'noughties' would soon be replaced by a return to relative calm. Given the multiple sources of instability and the very uncertain economic outlook at the time of writing (June 2020), such hopes seem unduly optimistic. Perhaps on this occasion the most appropriate conclusion would be that the explorer of British politics is unlikely to be short of thought-provoking materials in the coming years.

Conclusion and summary

Political scientists have been more perceptive when they explain the recent past than in their predictions of the near future. For example, few observers in 2005 could have anticipated that the 2010 general election would result in the formation of a coalition government comprising the Conservatives and the Liberal Democrats, who had seemed to be implacable enemies until David Cameron won the Conservative leadership. The end of the coalition in 2015 was much more predictable, given the decline in Liberal Democrat fortunes; but the small overall Conservative majority was a major surprise. Even after the polls closed on the day of the 2016 referendum, leading 'Leave' campaigners thought they had lost; the result triggered chaos within a government machine which had deliberately refused to make contingency plans for withdrawal. When Theresa May asked parliament to authorise a 'snap' general election in 2017, the only question seemed to relate to the likely size of her party's victory. When the country was asked to vote again in December 2019 Mrs May had returned to the backbenches and the prime minister was Boris Johnson, whose chances of leading the Conservative Party seemed to have been ended when he withdrew from the 2016 contest to succeed David Cameron. This is just a sample of the surprising developments since the previous edition of *Exploring British Politics* was published; a comprehensive list of unexpected happenings would fill a substantial chapter on its own.

Despite the understandable preoccupation with 'Brexit' and the coronavirus pandemic, many of the underlying issues reviewed in this concluding chapter will remain on the political agenda. The process of constitutional reform is set to continue, with further changes in the 'quasi-federal' relationship between the constituent countries of the UK. Brexit has increased the institutional friction between Britain's branches of government, but there were already problems which needed to be addressed, such as the future of the House of Lords. On leaving the EU, the population of the UK is more diverse than ever, and its voters are increasingly volatile, demanding, and disillusioned.

Further reading

For a vivid account of the 2016 referendum and its aftermath, see T. Shipman, *All Out War: The Full Story of Brexit* (London: Collins, 2016) and *Fall Out: A Year of Political Mayhem* (London: Collins, 2017). Further instalments from the same author will follow. The academic journals *Parliamentary Affairs*, *Political Quarterly*, *British Journal of Politics and International Relations*, and *British Politics* include articles on recent developments in British politics and in British political science. Biographies of individual prime ministers offer valuable insights, particularly those written by Anthony Seldon and his collaborators (e.g. A. Seldon with R. Newell, *May at 10* (London: Biteback, 2019). As always, political memoirs are more suspect, but still worth reading if only for comparison with other sources (e.g. D. Cameron, *For the Record* (London: Collins, 2019)). Among many widely discussed studies of factors which led to Brexit, see D. Goodhart, *The Road to Somewhere: The New Tribes Shaping British Politics* (London: Penguin, 2017). The ensuing state of British democracy is examined in P. Dunleavy, A. Park, and R. Taylor, *The UK's Changing Democracy: The 2018 Democratic Audit* (London: London School of Economics, 2018).

Given the succession of challenges faced by British politicians since 2007, it is fascinating to re-examine the situation before the era of 'austerity'. Even then, academic commentators were deeply concerned about the state of British democracy. See, for example, S. Weir and D. Beetham, *Political Power and Democratic Control in Britain: The Democratic Audit of the United Kingdom* (London: Routledge, 2002) and D. Beetham et al., *Democracy under Blair* (London: Politico's, 2003). Gerry Stoker, *Why Politics Matters* (London: Palgrave, 2006); Colin Hay, *Why We Hate Politics* (London: Polity Press, 2007); and M. Garnett, *From Anger to Apathy* (London: Vintage, 2008) offer readable accounts of the malaise in British democracy.

Websites

The Democratic Audit site (www.democraticaudit.com) includes briefings on the health of British democracy, as does the Hansard Society/Ipsos-Mori Audits of Democratic Engagement (https://www.hansardsociety.org.uk/projects/audit-of-political-engagement). The Constitution Unit (www.ucl.ac.uk/constitution-unit) has regular updates on constitutional reform. The BBC News website (http://news.bbc. co.uk) is an unmatched source of information on developments in British politics, whatever its critics might allege; Politicshome (www.politicshome.com) is also recommended. New blogs on British politics are emerging on a weekly basis, although the quality varies greatly. Among the most informative and entertaining are www.politicalbetting.com, www.ukpollingreport.co.uk/blog/index.php, and www.conservativehome.blogs.com.

Index

Note: **Bold** page numbers refer to tables; *italic* page numbers refer to figures.

accountability **5**, 15, 17, 20–2, 24, 31, 43, 149, 162, 165, 173, 184, 189, 196, 199, 201, 210, 226, 236–8, 245, 266, 271, 276, 279, 284, 289, 292, 294, 304, 305, 313, 316, 324, 325, 329, 352, 387, 628–30, 634–6

Adams, Gerry 363, 365

Additional Member System (AMS) 311, 342, 348, 351, 353, 355, 421, 430, 431, 553, 554

agencification 284–5

Alford Index 565

Alliance Party (NI) 363, **369**, 435, 437

alternative vote (AV) 6, 159, 161, 549–50, **555**; referendum on 599

Amsterdam Treaty (1997) 382, 385, 390, 391

Anglo-Irish agreement (1985) **188**, 364

armed forces 14, 16, 49, 150, 157, 375, 498, 524, **606**, 612, 634

Ashcroft, Lord 41, 541, 548, 566, 574, 575, 582

Ashdown, Paddy 151, 154, 427, **443**, 464, 507, 543, **585**

asymmetric power model 23, 28, 31

Attlee, Clement (and 1945–51 government) 46, 48, 50, 53, 66, 149, 171, 249, 295, 388, **443**, 451, 459, 492, 496, 497, 499, 507, 640, 641, 643

Bagehot, Walter 25, 146, 168

Bank of England 19, 46, 65, 154, 160, 200, 242, 279, 280, 296, 300, 344, 499, 539

Barnett formula 337, 342, 347, 348, 357, 360–2, 376

Benn, Tony 120, 189, 198, 227, 410, 455, 500, 511

Beveridge Report 46, 47 219–21

biography, political 41

Blair, Tony: *vs.* Cameron's conservatives 445–6; and constitution 151–60, 168–70, 172; devolution 341, 351, 355, 358–60; electoral system 522, 533, 539, 540, 554, 559; ideology of 479, 493, 494, 498, 500–5, 508, 509; and Iraq war 114–18; and media 111–14; Mondeo man 569–70; party leadership ratings **585**; party organisation 455–7, 459, 461–3, 470–3; political legacy 640–3; as Prime Minister (and Labour government 1997-2007) 8, 15, 33,

45, 46, 51, 55, 66, 74, 114, 154, 170, 243, 281, 295, 300, 327, 353, 359, 391, 393, 400, 413, 443, 464, 504, 587, 608, 614–15, 628, 631, 632, 635, 636, 638; referendums 596, 601, 604, 608, 615; sofa government 632–3

Blunkett, David 113, 177, **190**, 192, 259, 265, 608

Boundary Commission 523

bourgeoisie 486

British Bill of Rights 20, 253–4, 631

British Broadcasting Corporation (BBC) 46, 101, 105, 114–19, 122, 124, 125, 128, 129, 171, 198, 234, 258, 290, 292, 345, 359, 499, 529, 598

British Election Study (BES) 39, 581

British Empire 50, 51, 83, 145, 200, 413, 640

British National Party (BNP) 76, 82, 312, 432, 510, 541, 557, 567, 582, 584

Britishness 92–3

Brown, Gordon: and Britishness 92–3; as Chancellor of the Exchequer (1997-2007) 32; constitutional reform 156–8; and 2010 general election 118–19; and local authorities 311; as Prime Minister (and labour government 2007-10) 66, **152**, **153**, 178–9, 391–4; rivalry with Blair 502–3

BSE crisis (1996) 63, 73, 191, 300, 324, 391

Burke, Edmund 212, 482, 484, 485, 491, 493, 497

Butler Report (2004) 199, 635

cabinet: collective responsibility **5**, 24, 140, 141, 167, 171, 184–9, 603; and ministerial responsibility 5, 25, 140, 189–92, 198, 214, **629**

cabinet office 168, 174, 182–3, 185, **190**, 196, 199, 235, 281, 282, 290, 292, 293, 406, 633

Cable, Vince 127, 189, 467

Callaghan, James (and Labour government 1976–9) 56, 57, 60, 170, 172, 188, 189, 191, 303, 340, 443, 452, 453, 464, 520, 598

Calman Report (2009) 160, 345–6

Cameron, David: and Big Society 93, 199, 281, 321, 322, 494–5, 639, 643; and conservative modernisation 445–8; and 2010 general election 118–19; as opposition leader (2005-10) 592–3; as Prime Minister 109, 116, 118–19, 121, 122, 126–9,

159–63, 173, 174, 178–81, 186, 188, 189, 197, 199, 200, 209, 213, 253, 281, 283, 286, 311, 321, 340, 346, 356, 370, 376, 390, 394–6, 399, 402, 406, 407, 409, 410, 411, 413, 414, 428, 443, 445–50, 453, 461, 465, 470, 474, 493–5, 506–7, 512, 520, 523, 528, 539, 549, 555, 556, 573, 581, 583, **585**, 586, 589, 592, 600, 603, 604, 609, 632, 633, 635, 639–44; *see also* Conservative-Liberal Democrat coalition (2010-15)
Campaign for Nuclear Disarmament (CND) 615, 621, 624
Campbell, Alastair 40, 112, 113–15, 158, 196, 459, 462
Campbell, Sir Menzies 107, **443**, 465, 474, 503
career politicians 168, 236, 245, 458, 531, 584, 635, 637
Carrington, Lord 140, 150, 184, **190**, 191
cash for honours scandal (2006) 471–3
Child Support Agency 20, 30, 80, 284, 635
Churchill, Sir Winston 46, 49, 50, 51, 109, 139, 170, 171, **443**, 493, 504
Citizen's Charter 93, 181, 278–9
citizenship 10, 91–4, 192, 210, 344, 510, 533, 595
civil liberties 25, 27, 32, 65, 149, 151, 156, 159, 214, 250, 502, 519, 565, 635, 636, 639
civil service **5**, 24, 32, 37, 47, 149, 157, 158, 174, 178, 182, 183, 194–200, **215**, **235**, **241**, 275, 276, 278, 280–4, 286, 288, 289, 319, 354, 430, 628, **629**, 634–6
Clarke, Kenneth 255, 262, 408, 446, 448, 476, 483
Clegg, Nick: and coalition government; 158-59, 196, 555, 556. and 2010 general election; 118, 121, 139, 427, **443** (bold), 466; as Liberal Democrat leader; 107, 465, 504, **585** (bold), 589
Cold War 13, 49–50, 67, 365, 380, 508
collective responsibility, doctrine of 140–1, 171, **629** (bold)
common law 138–9
Commonwealth 6, 49, 51–2, 64, 68, 77, 83, 150, 335, 389–90, 403, 406
Compulsory Competitive Tendering (CCT) 293, 309, 319
consensus, post-Thatcherite 64, 504–6
consensus, Post-War 46–55, 56, 66–7, 496, 497, 572
conservatism 482–6, **491**, 491–6, 502, 511, 512
Conservative-Liberal Democrat coalition (2010-15) 30, 64, 65, 138, 169, 221, 238, 244, 248, 249, 262, 280, 288, 289, 292, 294, 296, 300, 311, 313–14, 317, 318, 320, 321, 323, 330, 331, 350, 355, 356, 358, 359, 361, 370, 427, 539, 599, 631, 637; and constitution 158–61
Conservative Party: funding of 469–77; and ideology 482–6; leadership 443–8; membership **450**, 450–1; organisation of 461–7; origins of 420–3; sources of support 562–5
consociationalism (NI) 367, 368
constitution: conventions 139–41; definition of 135; and devolution 146, 334–76; and European Union 141; and fusion of powers 25, 237; and judiciary 247–71; and prerogative powers 138, 142, 170, 634, 642; principles of 141–8; sources of 136–41; uncodified 136
consumerism 94, 279

Cook, Robin 39, 115, 140, 187, **188**, 192, 214
Corbyn, Jeremy 97, 124, 125, 169, 228, 298, 302, 400, 401, 409, 410, 411, 428, 443, 452– 454, 456, 457–63, 474, 476–8, 500, 502, 503, 509–9, 514, 529, 540, 565, 572, 576, 585–7, 592, 638
core executive 4, **5**, 28, 29, 31, 32, 38, 167–200, **276**, 280, 300, 301, 304, 324, 628, 632, 633, 635, 643
corporatism (and neo-corporatism) 26, 54–5, 613–15
Coulson, Andy 125, 126, 129
Council of Europe 51, 137, 379
council tax 18, 61, 309, 317, 318, 321–7, 331
Countryside Alliance 74, 225, 251, 608, 610, *611*
credit crunch 31, 33, 65, 98, 279, 296, 448
Crewe, Ivor 110, 324, 568
Crosland, Anthony 327, 487, 488, 490, 499
Crossman, Richard 40, 148, 168, 189
Crown Prosecution Service (CPS) **232**, **260**, 267, 471

Dahl, Robert 13
delegates 7, 163, 212, 213, 307, 464, 526, 604,
Delors, Jacques 380
Democratic Unionist Party (DUP) 24, 140, 170, 203, 213, 241, 362, 363, 365–7, 369–71, 373, 427, 429, 434–5, **436**, 545, 547, **629**
Denver, David 533, **573**, 588
devolution 4, 8, 25, 27–9, 37, 64, 65, 72, 146, 151–3, 155, 156, 160, 162, 165, 193, 217, 258, 264, 276, 280, 300, 305, 309, 311, 314, 317, 321, 322, 330, 334–76; policy divergence 347, 351, 354–5, 357, 376, 431
d'Hondt formula 368, 551–3, 557
differentiated polity model 23, 28, 38
Douglas-Home, Sir Alec 139, 171, 242, **443**, 444, 450
Downs, Anthony 34, 35, 506
Droop quota 552
Duncan Smith, Iain 83, **188**, 192, **443**, 446–8, 450, 453, 457, 465, 474, 494, 522
Dunleavy, Patrick 36, 170, 571

early day motions (EDMs) 207
Ecclestone, Bernie 470
Eden, Sir Anthony 51–3, 171, **443**
education 46, 64, 65, 78, 85, 91, 159, 181, 184, **185**, 190–4, 198, 204, 213–17, **229**, 231–4, 241, 252, 256, 278, 280–2, **285**, **291**, 293, 294, 300, 308–10, 316, 317, 320, 322, 330, 331, 335, 337, 342, 343, 349, 353, 354, 359, 360, 367, 374, **384**, **397**, 398, 431, 433, 434, 442, 471, 482, 488, 490, 492–4, 501–3, 526, 528, 533, 565, 568, 570–2, 580, 581, 584, 587, 611, 630
egalitarianism 486
elected mayors 152, **153**, 269, 309, 311–15, 321, 322, 331
Electoral Commission 161, 162, 226, 292, 346, 468, 469, 478, 522, 524, 525, 528, 532, 533, 534, 536–7, 555, 560, 602
electoral turnout, decline of 17, 20, 21, 91, 94, 97, 203, 237, 564, 575, 621, 638

elitism 14, 399, 482

enabling state 38, **276**, 278, 633

England: Bank of England 19, 46, 279; council tax revaluation 327; crimes in 265; devolution 355–7; economic inequality 86; ethnicity 2011 census 77; judicial system 248–9; national and regional divisions 71–3; national identity **375**; referendum result 2016 396–9; religious affiliation **82**; Westminster model abroad 6

English Defence League 76, 82, 621

e-petitions 604, 605, **606, 629**

environmentalism 511–13

euro (single currency) 9, 39, 381, 382, 393, 394, 406, 410, 411, 601, 642

European Commission 329, 387, 407, 612.

European Convention on Human Rights 65, 138, 143, **153**, 154, 156, 251, 252, 253, 254, 271, 368

European Council 379, 382–4, 388, 391, 394, 406

European Council of Ministers (now council of the European Union) 193, 382, 406, 415

European Court of Human Rights (ECHR) 137, 155, 251–4, 258, 533

European Court of Justice (ECJ) 254, 380, 381, 394, 405

European Economic Community (EEC) 25, **303**, 511, 578, 596, 597

European Exchange Rate Mechanism (ERM: and 'Black Wednesday,' 1992) 27, 324, 580, 641

European Free Trade Association (EFTA) 52, 389

European Parliament (EP: and elections to) **153**, 379, 380, 387, 428, 437, 467, 468, 522, 525, 529, 530, 533, 535, 551, 554, 557, 558, 559, 583, 591, 636–8

European Union (EU) 8, 19, 29, 51, 73, 74, 77, 138, 141, 147, 148, 162, 178, 181, 182, 184, 188, 193, 200, 253, 276, 303, 317, 378–414, 565, 596, 600–3, 623, 630

Europeanisation of UK governance 405–7

euroscepticism 384–8, 408–10, 443

e-voting 525, 537, 559, 602, 638

executive agencies *see* Next Steps agencies

expenses scandal (2009) 116, 118, 125, 159, 163, **190**, 203, 225–6, 238, 446, 462, 527, 531, 536, 556, 635, 639, 640

Factortame case (1990-1) 254, 405

Falconer, Lord 155, 260, 261

Falklands War 59, 64, 114, 140, 150, 181, **190**, 191, 222, 256, 498

Farron, Tim **443**, 466, 467, **585**

Fathers4Justice 81

feminism 81, 511, 513–14

financial sector (and City of London) 9, 25, 68, 75, 78, 80, 90, 97, 179, 181, 226, 234, 249, 277, 279, 280, 286, 288, 295, 300, 344, 382, 385, 392, 393, 621, 641

first-past-the-post (or simple plurality) 6, 63, 96, 148, 155, 210, 218, 243, 411, 421, 424, 426, 429, 432, 434, 435, 437, 457, 511, 544, 574, 603

fixed-term parliaments 6, 7, 138, 139, 146, 159, 235, 472, 476, 520, 521, 532, 632, 634

focus groups 8, 42, 463, 538, 540

Foley, Michael 168, 183

Foot, Michael **443**, 500, 509,

fracking 512, 575

free-riders 34

Freedom of Information Act (FOIA) 20, 32, 39, 151, **153**, 154, 195, 226, **354**, 636

fuel blockades/protests (2000) 74, 180

gender 78–81, 85, 94, 96, 144, 150, **224, 231, 232**, 237, 255, 446, 450, 458, 494, 513, 514, 528, 529, **535**, 576, **577**, 579, 622,

globalisation 27, 29, 38, 73, 173, 200, 216, 275, 301–4, 397, 404, 409, **491**, 570, 571, 618, 639

Good Friday Agreement (1998) 27, 181, 268, 358, 362, 363, 365–72, 401, 434, 435, 598, 601

Green Paper 221

Heath, Edward (and 1970–4 government) 40, 56–8, 61, 170, 172, 338, 362, 389, 390, 408, 424, 425, 443, 444, 450, 496, 500, 506,

House of Commons: accountability 236–8; backbenches 205–6; debates in 222–7; government formation 203–4; legislative process 217–21; opposition party 204–5; parliamentary weapons 207–8; party whips in 206–9; passage of a bill 219–22; question time 227–35; representation 210–17; speaker role 209–10

House of Lords: composition 240–2; reform of 242–4

Human Rights Act (HRA, 1998) 8, 20, 27, 28, 65, 91, 138, 143, 151, 153– 157, 225, 250–4, 629, 631, 636

Hutton Inquiry (2003-4) 114–18

ideology: British political parties 490–8; conservatism 482–6; liberalism 488–90; social democracy 487–8; socialism 486–7

immigration 27, 35, 51, 74, 76–8, 84, 90, 95, 97, 119, 190, 192, 195, 231, 249, 250, 251, 263, 283, 285, 295, 303, 372, 391, 396, 398, 411, 432, 483, 507, 510, 565, 580, 581, 582, 584, 593

inequality 71, 85, 86–90, 95–8, 484, 486, 488, 490–2, 501, 503, 515, 531, 581, 582

institutionalism 33, 36–8

International Monetary Fund (IMF) 57, 71, **303**, 385

internet 100–2, 116–17, 125, 127, 129, 297, 524, 525, 527, 541, 542, 596, 602, 610, 613, 639

Iraq War (2003) 15, 50, 114, 115, 117, 158, 227, 254, 427, 522, 621

Irish Republican Army (IRA) 120, 362, 363, 365, 366, 370, 371, 435

Islam 81–2

Jenkins, Roy 153–5, 222, 424, 531, 554, 616

Johnson, Boris 20, 25, 27, 33, 70, 84, 86, 97, 122, 124, 125, 129, 130, 139, 150, 159, 162, 163, 165, 169, 170, 173–6, 178, 180–2, 185–8, 196, 197, 206, 212, 228, 263, 264, 269, 283, 311, 319, 373, 390, 402,

410, 411, 413, 427, 443, 444, 447, 448, 521, 530, 539, 541, 570, 575, 585, 586, 633, 643, 644
judicial review 249–51, **629**
judiciary 5, 8, 25–7, 137, 144, 153, 155, 174, 243, 247–71, **606**, **629**, 631, 636

Kelly, Dr David 114, 117, 195, 258,
Kennedy, Charles 107, 389, **443**, 460, 465, 466, 474, 503, 505, **585**
Keynes, John Maynard (and Keynesianism) 47, 48, 53, 54, 56, 60, 66, 315, 364
Kinnock, Neil 110, 120, 125, 338, 409, 425, 429, **443**, 445, 454, 455, 461, 462, 478, 500, 541, 554, **585**, 586, 598

Law Lords 156, 251, 255, 258, 259–62
leader debates, televised: 2010 118–19; 2015 119–25
Leveson Inquiry 127–9, 174, 300
liberal democracy 11–17, 20, 21, 23–5, 48, 67, 78, 88, 91, 94, 100, 101, 105, 125, 128, 137, 145, 146, 163, 202, 237, 243, 270, 419, 440, 519, 537, 595, 602, 605, 620
Liberal Democrats: and coalition government (2010-15) 19, 140–1, 192–4, 198, 204, 213, 221, 262–4, 270, 281, 285, 289, 290, 292, 293, 296, 299, 300, 321–3, 326, 327, 332, 346, 350, 351, 398, 420, 426, 427, 430, 448, 454, 472, 483, 512, 520, 522, 530, 546, 553, 559, 585, 603–5
Lisbon Treaty 160, 163, 263, 303, 380, 382–7, 390, 393, 394, 405, 409, 410, 413, 583, 596, 604, 635
local government 4, **5**, 18, 24, 27, 29, 31, 61, 62, 65, 142, 149, 151, 181, 191, 193, **215**, **229**, **231**, **232**, 266, 275, **276**, 280, 281, 290, **291**, 293, 295, 307–32, 335, 337, 338, **343**, 351, 355, 356, 358, 359, 407, 437, 487, 498, 508, 555, 557, 565, 572, 601, 615, 627, 633, 636
localism 321–2

Maastricht Treaty 63, 222, 250, 380, 381, 386, 389, 390, 391, 408–10, 449, 533
McGuinness, Martin 366, 367, 370, 371, 435
Macmillan, Harold (and Conservative government, 1957-63) 51, 52, 54, 55, 171, 176, 242, 389, 425, **443**, 444, 614
Macpherson Report (1999) 76, 258, 268, 269
Major, John: and media 109–18; as Prime Minister (and Conservative government 1990-7) 15, 40, 61, 62, 64, 67, 85, 93, 106, 109, 111, 120, 140, 152, 154, 169, 170, 172, 174, 177, 179, 186, 189, 191, 226, 258, 264, 277, 288, 325, 365, 391, 392, 409, 413, 425, 429, 443, 446, 449, 453, 494, 540, 585, 586, 608, 614, 628, 641, 643; and Europe 61–3, 140–1, 378, 391, 392, 402, 409, 410, 411, 413
Mandelson, Peter 111, 113, 114, 174, 177, **190**, 192, 453, 459, 462
manufacturing industry 9, 75, 80, 152, 278, 318, 338, 340, 614
market-testing 277, 284, 286
Marshall Plan 49
Martin, Michael 225, 226

Marx, Karl (and Marxism) 71, 83, 84, 95, 480, 486, 487–9
media: and democracy 108–9; influence of 104–9; and phone-hacking scandal 125–9, 247, 269, 270, 300; and politicians 108, 110–18; theories of 104–8; varieties of 101–4
Mellor, David 109, 177, **190**
Members of Parliament (MPs): career politicians 168, 236, 245, 458, 531, 584, 635, 637; and expenses scandal 116, 118, 125, 159, 163, **190**, 203, 225–6, 238, 446, 462, 527, 531, 536, 556, 635, 639, 640; as representatives 25, 36, 39, 42, 52, 54, 66, 146–8, 163, 202, 211, 212, 214–17, 221, 237, 238, 252, 255, 331, 350, 363–5; right of recall 526–7; social background of 214–17
meritocracy 79, 85, 87, 194, 492–3
Michels, Robert (and 'Iron Law of Oligarchy') 14, 452, 474
Miliband, Ed 121, 180, **443**, 453, 456, 461, 508, 523, 539, 540, 555, 581, 583, **585**, 599
Militant Tendency 454, 500
Mill, John Stuart 13, 489, 505
miners' strike (1984-5) 60, 149, 257, 266
Ministerial Code 185–6, 188–9, 192, 635–6
monarchy 5, 6, 25, 91, 135, 138, 146–8, 150, 157, 217, 336, 344, 375, 420
monetarism 58, 60, 62
multi-level governance 4, 460, 630
Murdoch, Rupert 101–3, 105–7, 120–1, 125–9, 150, 257, 445

National Front 76, 82, 510, 582
National Health Service (NHS) 30, 46, 50, 52, 95, 97, 198, 221, **223**, 234, 277, 280, 283, 286–8, 290, **291**, 293, 294, 299, 316, 329, 355, 375, 398, 412, 498, 499, 572, 580, 581, 587, 610, 611, 628, 641
National Security Council (NSC) 178, **187**
nationalisation 32, 46, 53, 281, 295, 296, 298, 304, 316, 400, 413, 424, 429, 452, 453, 484, 496, 497, 499, 506, 508, 580, 628, 633, 638, 640
nationalism 95–6, 508–11, 513
neo-liberalism 489–92, 514
new institutionalism 36–7, 152, 341
New Labour: and constitutional reform 151–5, 259–62; creation of 18, 33; end of 506–8; ideology of 64–6, 591; organisation 462–3; and state 280–1
New Right 38, 57, 172, 277, 278, 283, 309, 384, 485, 496–8, 611, 620
News Corp 102, 106, 125–8
newspapers, circulation of 102, 123, 555
Next Steps agencies 191, 194, 195, 199, 284, 289
Nice Treaty (2000) 382–3, 393
Nolan Committee on Standards in Public Life 292, 620
North Atlantic Treaty Organisation (NATO) 49, **231**, 302, 303, 345, 393, 403, 509
North Sea oil 59, 60, 338, 345
North-South divide 72, 575
Northern Ireland: communal tensions 362–3; devolution 337, 341, 342, 354; direct rule and

devolution 363–4; Good Friday Agreement 366–71; government to governance 19; local government structure 308; national and regional divisions 71–3; peace strategies 364–5; police service 268; policy divergence **354**; timeline 365–6; and Westminster model 25–8

Northern Ireland Assembly 27, **152**, 268, **343**, 359, 366, 367, **369**, **407**, 434, 435, 520, 552, 557

Northern Rock bank 33, 296

Norton, Philip 206

nuclear weapons 75, 213, 345, 452, 509, 615

Office for Budget Responsibility (OBR) 19, 65, 160, 200, 291–3

Office for Standards in Education (OFSTED) 293, 317

Ombudsman 249, **291**

opinion polls 8, 10, 91, 100, 104, 107, 110, 115, 119, 121, 159, 161, 163, 169, 172, 175, 179, 180, 205, 346, 348, 353, 359, 369, 392, 425, 428, 444, 453, 457, 464, 466, 472, 475, 498, 520, 525, 542–3, 545, 556, 567, 569, 572, 586, 591, 592, 595, 599, 600, 604, 639

Osborne, George 67, 160, 181, 193, 234, 277, 279, 286, 288, 356, 581, 633

Owen, Dr David 424, 464, 504

Paisley, Dr Ian 362, 366, 367, 370, 371, 435, 527

Parliament: accountability 236–8; decline of 27; parliamentary sovereignty **5**, 17, 24, 27, 28, 32, 42, 138, 142–3, 147–9, 156, 161, 163, 263, 276, 302, 304, 335, 374, 386, 396, 403, 405, 411, 602, 605, 627, **629**, 631

party leaders, electoral importance of 584–6

party systems 4, 5, **5**, **26**, 312; classification of 421; European Parliament 411; local government 312; Northern Ireland 434–7; Scotland 430–4; Wales 430–4

paternalism 484

path dependency 37

payroll vote 214

pensions 82–3

Pimlott, Ben 48

Pinochet, Augusto 257, 303

Plaid Cymru 72, 122, 152, 241, 338, 339, 341, 349–52, 354, 431, 434, 509, 534, 545, 546, 555, **566**, 582

plebiscite 602

pluralism 12–13, 104, 489

police 264–70; and media 125–7

Police Service of Northern Ireland (PSNI) 268, 366, 367, 370

policy divergence 354–5

policy networks 29–31, 301, 328, 607, 609, 633

political parties: decline of 216, 424–6, 431, 474, 509, 588, 614; functions of 441–2; funding of 469–73; and ideology 461–3; organisation of 463–8; typology of 475

politics, definition of 8–11

poll tax 18, 27, 61, 152, 181, 221, 309, 324, 325, 333, 339, 340, 429, 449, 451, 498, 615, 635

Ponting, Clive 195, 256

poverty 72, 76, 79, 84, 86–91, 95, 97, 98, 291, 304, 338, 422, 469, 484, 490, 494, 501, 503, 565, 581–2

Powell, Enoch 51, 227, 409, 511

Prescott, John 126, 174, 192, 193, 214, 358, 540

pressure groups: and democracy 620–2; insider and outsider groups 607–8; nature of 607; new social movements 615–20; sectional and cause groups 610–13

primary elections 458, 474

Prime Minister, powers of 4, 5, 32, 38, 66, 148, 157, 168–81

Prime Minister's Office 181–82

Prime Minister's Question Time 227–35

Private Finance Initiative (PFI) 234, 280, 286–9, 293, 295, 326, 470, 501, 503, 505, 628

private members' bills 221–2, **223**

privatisation 16, 17, 29, 58, 60–2, 65, 150, 176, 181, 221, 278, 281, 294–9, 429, 455, 465, 501, 503, 614

proletariat 486

proportional representation 6, 26, 96, 155, 210, 244, 342, 348, 349, 367, 368, 420, 426, 521, 544, 550–4, 603, 631

qualified majority voting (QMV) 382–4

quangos 18, 29, 31, 149, 150, 275, 277, 278, 289–93; and local government 293–4, 330

race relations 76, 77, 82, 616

rational choice theory 23, 33–6, 535, 579–89

Redwood, John 63, 152, 179, 188, 409, 448, 449

referendums: on alternative vote system (2011) 554–6, 599; on devolution (1979) 597–8; on devolution (1997/8) 598; on elected mayors 601; enhanced powers for Welsh Assembly (2011) 598–9; on EU membership 123–4, 162–4, 396–9; on future of Northern Ireland (1973) 597; local 601; on regional government (2004) 598; on Scottish Independence (2014) 160–1, 599; on UK membership of EEC (1975) 597

Regional Development Agencies (RDA) 152, 292, 330, 355, 356, 636

regulatory state 18, 276, 278, 280, 295, **297**, 304, 628

religion 71, 72, 81–2, 94, 96, 252, 268, 335, 488, 489, 578, 579

research methods 23, 38–42

Respect Party 312, 522

Rhodes, Rod 28, 29, 31, 38, 55, 200, 328, 617

Right of Recall 159, 526–7

Robinson, Peter 362, 366, 367, 371

rule of law 143–4

Salmond, Alex 339, 340, 346, 351, 353, 431, 468, 558

Scargill, Arthur 60, 621

Scarman, Lord 267, 268, 269

Schengen Agreement (1985) 382, 385, 412

Schuman Plan (1950) 51, 379

Schumpeter, Joseph 14

Scotland 3, 8, 19, 25, 27, 37, 64, 71, 72, 97, 121, 122, 123, 138, 144, 145, 146, 148, 151–3, 155, 156,

160–1, 164, 185, 193, 218, 225, 242, 263, 264, 280, 281, 301, 305, 308–10, 312, 319, 325, 330, 334, 335–55, 358–61, 367, 371–5, 396, 419, 420, 426, 430–4, 460, 468, 508–10, 521, 534, 545, 551, 554, 557, 559, 567, 570, 574, 575, 578, 589, 596–8, 600, 602, 604, 610, 612, 619, 629, 630, 631, 635, 642

Scottish National Party (SNP) 97, 121, 122, 152, 160, 161, 162, 164, 207, 215, 217, 225, 338, 339, 340–2, 344–8, 350–3, 357, 359, 360, 371, 373, 376, 407, 430, 431, 434, 437, 460, 468, 477, 478, 508, 509, 523, 534, 545, 546, 551, 553, 555, 558, 566, 567, 570, 571, 574, 576, 582, 589, 591, 599, 600, 603, 609, 629

Scottish Office 5, 276, 337, 339, 341

Scottish Parliament (and government) 19, 138, 143, 152, 156, 161, 193, 199, 276, 330, 339–49, 351–3, 359–61, 367, 403, 407, 430, 431, 433, 438, 460, 520, 531, 534, 551, 553, 554, 557, 558, 559, 591, 599, 612, 634, 635

Senedd: see Welsh Parliament (and government)

Short, Clare 115, 140, 187, 188, 189, 459

Single European Act (SEA, 1985; and Single Market) 61, 380, 389

single transferable vote (STV) 27, 153, 244, 312, 330, 349, 354, 367, 368, 421, 434, 435, 465, 551, 552, 554, 556, 558

Sinn Fein 268, 362, 363, 365–7, 369, 370, 371, 434, 435, 438, 467, 545, 555

sleaze (under Major government) 27, 150, 192, 225–6, 246, 430, 473

Smith, John 28, 110, 121, 341, 410, 443, 455, 457, 500, 554

social class 36, 42, 52, 84, 118, 120, 434, 535, 562, 563, 567, 568–72, 578, 584

Social Democratic and Labour Party (SDLP) 363, 365, 367–71, 434–6, 547, 555, 558

Social Democratic Party (SDP) 14, 34, 409, 410, 424, 425, 432, 437, 459, 462, 464, 466, 476, 500, 504, 530, 531, 545, 572, 574, 591

soundbite 109

special advisors 190, 195–97

spin doctors 65, 100, 103, 111, 112, 114, 196, 459, 470, 475, 476, 540

statute law 138

Steel, David 443, 464

sterling 40, 48, 53–5, 57, 62, 63, 161, 191, 198, 303, 344, 391, 392, 586

Sturgeon, Nicol 122, 225, 340, 346, 352, 356, 360, 468, 523

Suez Crisis 52–4, 64, 171, 389

supplementary vote (SV) 266, 314, 549, 550

Supreme Court 8, 27, 137, 153, 156, 248, 249, 251, 253–6, 260, 261, 263, 264, 270, 358, 629, 631, 643–4

tactical voting 426, 427, 530, 545, 546, 588–9

Tebbit, Norman 64, 78, 181, 450

terrorism (and 'War on Terror') 49, 262, 612

Thatcherism 38, 45, 57–64, 88, 110, 148–51, 173, 277, 278, 321, 340, 409, 425, 426, 481, 494–8, 504, 505, 507, 530, 572, 642

Thatcher, Margaret (and Conservative governments 1979–90) 58–64, 172, 391, 481, 498, 628, 640; Bruges speech (1988) 62, 389, 391, 408; fall from power (1990) 61–3, 169, 391

Tisdall, Sarah 195, 256, 262

trade unions 12, 25, 26, 34, 54, 58, 62, 65, 75, 84, 102, 105, 149, 172, 176, 181, 215, 216, 241, 256, 257, 302, 305, 319, 340, 351, 356, 392, 407, 424, 425, 433, 453, 454, 457, 461, 469, 473, 498, 499, 502, 508, 564, 606, 607, 610, 611, 613–15, 621

Treasury 18, 19, 32, 33, 37, 40, 65, 168, 169, 176, 184, 185, 187–90, 192, 193, 198, 199, 204, 229, 231, 234, 239, 242, 279, 280, 285, 291, 292, 295, 296, 300, 324, 326, 342, 344, 348, 361, 392–4, 406, 407, 633, 642

Trimble, David 365–7, 369

two-party system 5, 6, 25, 26, 28, 34, 42, 312, 419–27, 429, 547, 564, 574, 629, 634, 638

Ulster Unionist Party (UUP) 249, 362, 363, 365–9, 371, 421, 434, 435, 436, 439, 558

unemployment 33, 47, 53, 56–60, 76, 78, 88, 95, 278, 338, 348, 363, 393, 395, 398, 424, 490, 586, 587, 610

unitary state 144–6

United Kingdom: citizenship 91–5; economic divisions 83–6; ethnicity 74–8; formation of 71–4; gender 78–81; nationalism 95–6; post-devolution 373–5; religion 81–4

United Kingdom Independence Party (UKIP) 25, 78, 97, 110, 122, 160, 266, 312, 329, 352, 373, 386, 395, 397, 404, 410, 411, 414, 428, 431, 432, 437, 445, 467, 468, 470, 510, 511, 522, 530, 549, 555, 557, 566, 574, 582–4, 589–91, 600, 603, 604, 629

United Nations (UN) 19, 49, 53, 114, 261, 262, 302, 303, 378, 617

United States of America (USA): constitution of 137, 142, 147, 154, 194, 520, 526; 'special relationship' with UK 49–50, 64

Unlock Democracy 151

voting behaviour: class alignment 562–3; dealignment 565–75; economic voting models 586–7; election outcomes 591–2; ethnicity 579; gender 576, 577; influence of age 577, 578; partisan alignment 563–4; public/private sector 571–2; rational choice 579; regional factors 575–6; religion 578; tactical voting 588–9; valence voting 580–1

Wales 8, 19, 20, 25, 37, 63, 64, 71, 72, 77, 82, 86, 144–6, 148, 150–5, 160, 185, 188, 190, 193, 218, 225, 231, 232, 234, 248, 249, 255, 259, 260, 261, 263, 265, 266, 268, 270, 280, 284, 293, 299, 301, 305, 308, 309, 310, 314, 318, 319, 325, 327, 330, 331, 334–55, 358–61, 367, 372–6, 396–7, 401, 419, 420, 424, 426, 430–4, 438, 460, 463, 468, 509, 521–3, 533–4, 540, 544, 545, 551, 554, 557, 559, 567, 575–6, 596–9, 604, 609, 610, 612, 629, 630

welfare state 46, 52, 93, 171, 249, 276–8, 280, 292,
    293, 336, 483, 490–2, 497–500, 503, 506, 564, 628,
    633, 640
Welsh Assembly (now Senedd) 152, 156, 199, **276**,
    299, 339–41, 348–50, 352–4, 358, 407, 431, 438,
    520, 529, 531, 536, 553, 557, 558, 559, 598–9, 603
Welsh Office **5**, 276, 337, 339
Westland affair 188, 190, 222
West Lothian question 160, 225, 359–61, 374,
    376, 610

Westminster Model 4–11, 15, 17, 19, 23–8, 29, 31,
    36, 38, 42, 275, **276**, 429, 622, 628, **629**, 631, 632,
    638, 641, 643
White Paper 221
Whitelaw, Viscount 242
Wilson, Harold (and Labour governments 1964–70
    & 1974–6) 55–7, 140, 141, 164, 170, 171, 188,
    189, 283, 338, 389–91, 408, 410, 424, **443**, 453,
    499, 500, 507, 597, 603, 604
World Trade Organisation (WTO) 302, 303, 412